The New York Times
20th Century in Review

THE RISE OF
THE GLOBAL ECONOMY

Other Titles in
The New York Times 20th Century in Review

The Balkans
The Cold War
The Gay Rights Movement
Political Censorship
The Vietnam War

The New York Times
20th Century in Review

THE RISE OF
THE GLOBAL ECONOMY

Editor
Michael Veseth

Introduction by Louis Uchitelle

Series Editor
David Morrow

FITZROY DEARBORN PUBLISHERS
CHICAGO   LONDON

For information write to:

FITZROY DEARBORN PUBLISHERS
919 North Michigan Avenue, Suite 760
Chicago IL 60611
USA

or

FITZROY DEARBORN PUBLISHERS
310 Regent Street
London W1B 3AX
England

British Library and Library of Congress Cataloging in Publication Data are available.

ISBN 1-57958-369-5

First published in the USA and UK 2002

Interior Design and Typeset by Print Means, Inc., New York, New York

Printed by Edwards Brothers, Ann Arbor, Michigan

Cover Design by Peter Aristedes, Chicago Advertising and Design, Chicago, Illinois

CONTENTS

Preface by Michael Veseth... vii

Introduction by Louis Uchitelle.. xi

Part I   Globalization in Context... 1
    What Is Globalization?..2
    The Many Faces of Globalization 24
    Globalization 1900 51
    The Collapse of the Global Economy 69

Part II   The Post-War Political Foundations 93
    The Bretton Woods System..94
    Critical Moment: The Uruguay Round 114
    Economic Nationalism 132
    Critical Moment: The NAFTA Debate 153
    The Rise of Regionalism 170
    Critical Moment: The Maastricht Treaty...192

Part III Business Goes Global... 205
    The Evolution of the Multinational Corporation...................................206
    A Global Division of Labor..237
    Global Finance 256
    A World Wide Web 282
    Critical Moment: The OPEC Oil Embargo 297

Part IV The Human Faces of Globalization 313
    One World, One Market, One Culture?..314
    Thinking Global, Acting Local 339
    Critical Moment: The Nike Sweatshop Debate......................................368

Part V   The Financial Crises 391
    The Collapse of the Bretton Woods System...392
    The European Monetary Crisis 416
    The Peso Crisis...438
    The Asian Financial Crisis 462

Part VI Resistance to Globalization 505
    Backlash 506
    North-South Tensions...521
    Critical Moment: The Battle in Seattle 544

General Index.. 565

Byline Index 585

PREFACE

This book tells the story of the rise of the global economy in the 20th century as seen through the eyes of *The New York Times*. In telling this story, we learn both how the world changed in the century just past and how *The Times* changed, too, in providing its readers with the information that they needed.

The story of globalization might seem like a pretty simple one to tell. How hard can it be to report the unrelenting march of multinational corporations and the remorseless incursion of global (mainly American) brands into foreign markets? Coca-Cola. Disney. McDonald's. Nike. That's the story of globalization, right?

In fact, globalization offers a much richer and more complex story, a story that has challenged several generations of writers and editors from nearly every one of the newspaper's sections from economics and business to domestic and international politics, to sports, religion and more. It is a big story, so big that even a substantial volume like this really only sketches the main outline.

Why is this story so complex? Because globalization is not simply a result—Big Macs and CNN wherever you go in the world. Rather, it is a process. The globalization process is about economics, but it is actually as much political as it is economic and as much social as it is technological. (Actually, globalization is more social than it is technological.) The story of globalization in *The New York Times* spans the paper's coverage because the causes and effects of globalization reach into every corner of the lives of *Times* readers. *The Times* has commented upon and reported this process in exceptional depth and detail. There is probably no better way to tell the complicated true story of the rise of the global economy than to read the pages of *The New York Times*.

Globalization As Reported by *The Times*

Globalization is both very new and surprisingly old. At the start of the 20th century, *The New York Times* told its readers of a world that was surprisingly similar to today's integrated global economy. There is a sharp sense of déjà vu in reading articles from this era, some of which are included in this book. Most of the issues that we associate with the contemporary globalization debate were explained and debated in the pages of *The Times* in the first years of the 20th century. *The Times* also covered the collapse of the global economy that had reemerged after World War I. These stories from the 1920s and 1930s contain enough parallels to today's front page news to make any reader anxious.

While globalization is not a brand new thing, the realization that we live in a global economy is relatively new. It wasn't until the collapse of communism and the end of the cold war that the idea of a global economy took hold and the vocabulary needed to describe and understand it came into common use. The table below tracks the use of the term *globalization* in *The New York Times* over the period 1980–2000 (the full text of *The Times* is available in a computer-searchable format starting in 1980).

Time Period	Globalization References
1980–84	2
1985–89	164
1990–94	213
1995–2000	1309

Clyde H. Farnsworth may have been the first to use the term *globalization* in *The Times* on February 8, 1981 in an article on the Tokyo Round GATT trade negotiations. Farnsworth noted that the United States was in an awkward position in these meetings, pushing for open markets abroad even as it considered new protective barriers at home.

> Such *globalization* of economic issues has both increased their complexity and presented new challenges for the United States. Third world countries, for example, which have been the fastest growing market for American exports, are now rapidly developing their own industrial base and are competing increasingly in the traditional manufacturing sectors such as steel, automotive equipment, metalworking, rubber, apparel and footwear (italics added).

Although the evolution of the postwar global economy began even before the guns of World War II were silenced, our collective focus on the cold war's divisions prevented us from fully appreciating the extent to which global networks had formed. Even after the collapse of communism, frequent use of the term *globalization* did not begin until late in the 1990s, as the following table shows.

Year	*Globalization* References
1990	47
1991	49
1992	43
1993	37
1994	37
1995	58
1996	87
1997	205
1998	189
1999	265
2000	505

The widespread recognition of the idea of a global economy really owes its existence to the Asian financial crisis of 1997 and the protests at the Seattle meetings of the World Trade Organization, two events that highlight, respectively, the instability of global finance and the backlash against multinational corporations and the new global division of labor. We arrived at an understanding of the existence of globalization more by confronting the problems associated with it (which were news) than by an understanding of its gradual actual development (which, taking place a little at a time in thousands of locations, was inherently less newsworthy). It is not surprising, therefore, that a large proportion of *The Times* articles that address directly the issues of globalization come from the 1990s and especially the last years of the 1990s.

The Times's Coverage of Globalization

There are several particular features of *The Times's* coverage of globalization that should be noted here. *Times* readers have enjoyed an especially rich educational experience because *The Times* has consistently resisted the temptation to over-simplify the story or to make it one-dimensional. In his book *The Lexus and the Olive Tree, Times* columnist Thomas L. Friedman defined globalization as everything and its opposite. *The Times's* coverage of the globalization story certainly reflects this view of globalization as a complex, dynamic and multidimensional experience.

Although *The Times* reports the news from many different angles, it cannot be said that all sides always get equal treatment. Newspapers, obviously, report news, so changes, especially sudden ones, necessarily get extra attention. Thus we learn the most about the globalization of financial markets when these markets experience a crisis, such as the Asian crisis of 1997, not when they operate smoothly. And free trade is more likely to appear on the front page when it is associated with human suffering (as in the stories of sweatshop labor) than when it quietly creates opportunities and satisfies consumer needs. *The Times* does tell both sides of these stories (or all sides, really), as the articles collected here show, but it is inevitable that some aspects are given more attention than others.

The particular strengths of *The Times* coverage of globalization evolved throughout the 20th century. In the first decade, for example, *The Times* featured broad coverage of international news, but its strength was really the depth of domestic issues and effects, especially political issues. Gradually *The Times* developed deep expertise on international economics, technology and culture to match its strengths in other areas. The result is that, by the 1990s, the staff of *The Times* was capable of producing on short order clusters of articles that, taken together, supplied remarkably deep and multi-dimensional analysis of the critical moments in the news.

The breadth, depth and evolution of *The Times's* analysis are especially apparent in the newspaper's coverage of the several financial crises associated with globalization's shaky development during the 20th century (collected in Part V of this book). When the Bretton Woods monetary system collapsed in 1971, the reports stressed the domestic economics and international politics. By the time of the Asian financial crisis in 1997, however, both the expertise of *The Times* staff and the interests of their readers had expanded to reach from the grass roots of Thai villages to the boardrooms of global hedge funds. *The Times's* ability to mobilize this sort of deep reporting and analysis on a wide range of international and global issues is an amazing accomplishment.

Organization of This Book

The story of globalization is told here in six parts. Within each part are several thematic sections that contain articles and images arranged chronologically.

Part I, Globalization in Context, offers an introduction to the issues and themes that are developed in greater depth throughout the book. These ideas are introduced in four ways: in stories and articles about globalization (the process or outcome), in stories about people who are affected by globalization, in a brief portrait of the first era of globalization, and in a sketch of some of the economic and political forces (especially financial instability and economic nationalism) that caused that global world to collapse.

Globalization may be primarily an economic edifice, but it rests upon a political foundation. Part II, Post-War Political Foundations, examines the Bretton Woods system, a post-war plan to establish international political institutions to support an expanding international economy. The rising interdependence that the Bretton Woods system made possible produced both a resurgence of economic nationalism and the rise of regional economic agreements, often viewed as a way to achieve the benefits of economic globalization with fewer political costs. Three critical moments in the political development of globalization are highlighted here. The Uruguay Round of the GATT tested the strength of the political consensus for global trade liberalization. The NAFTA debates in the U.S. and Mexico tested the strength of the forces of economic nationalism that opposed this trade initiative. And finally the Maastricht treaty tested the commitment of European Union members to further deepening of their regional economic and political union.

Part III, Business Goes Global, tells the story of the globalization of business and finance. The rise of multinational corporations is told along with the bigger story—the creation of a new global division of labor. Special attention is given to the globalization of finance, since financial markets are the most global markets of all. The role of science and technology is acknowledged as a "world wide web" of information, ideas and people. Finally, the critical moment of the OPEC oil embargoes of the 1970s is recounted. In many respects, this oil crisis and its political and economic consequences ended the first stage in the rise of the post-war global economy and opened the door to an era of faster, deeper economic international integration.

The Times is famous for reporting all the news that's fit to print. All the news, when it comes to globalization, includes articles about the tension between new and old, modern and traditional, home-grown and foreign. Part IV, The Human Faces of Globalization, collects articles that report both the tendency of global markets to homogenize culture and to strengthen the local traditions. The critical moment of the debate over sweatshop-like production of Nike products brings the many dimensions of this process into focus.

Financial crises are one of the distinguishing features of the global economy. Part V, Financial Crises, follows the evolving pattern of financial crises and the search for a solution by tracing the collapse of the Bretton Woods system and the financial crises in Europe, Mexico and Asia. Other significant financial crises, including the Latin American debt crisis of the 1980s and the Russian financial crisis of the 1990s, are omitted simply for lack of space.

The rise of the global economy in the 20th century ended with a backlash, seen most clearly in the street protests of the 1999 Seattle World Trade Organization meetings. This book ends therefore with Part VI, Resistance to Globalization, a collection of articles that illustrate the two faces of globalization—the attractive face that entices and the repulsive face that produces the backlash.

Acknowledgements

I have enjoyed the challenge this book has presented: to organize articles drawn from a century of *The New York Times* so that they can tell the globalization story in their own words with a minimum of commentary and synthesis. There are a number of persons who deserve thanks for helping me with this project. My thanks to Commissioning Editor David Morrow for asking me to take on this book and for his help and encouragement.

I want to acknowledge the direct and indirect contributions of Leonard S. Silk to this volume. As Economics Editor of *The Times* for many years, Mr. Silk wrote a number of the stories collected here (his contribution is especially important in the sections on the OPEC oil embargo and the collapse of the Bretton Woods system). Mr. Silk edited a previous volume of collected articles, *The United States and the World Economy* (New York Times/Arno Press, 1979), that form the foundation on which this book was built.

I'd also like to thank Maxine Cram for her creativity and efficiency as my research assistant. It was a pleasure to work with her. Thanks go out to my colleagues at the University of Puget Sound for their support and especially to my wife, Sue Trbovich Veseth. Finally, I would like to thank the editors, columnists, and reporters of *The Times* for providing me with such a rich vein to mine.

Michael Veseth is Professor of Economics and Director of the International Political Economy Program at the University of Puget Sound in Tacoma, Washington. He is author, co-author or editor of more than a dozen books including "Introduction to International Political Economy," "Mountains of Debt: Crisis and Change in Renaissance Florence, Victorian Britain, and Postwar America" and "Selling Globalization: The Myth of the Global Economy." He is married to Sue Trbovich Veseth.

INTRODUCTION
By Louis Uchitelle

The global economy has always existed. Going back centuries, the advanced nations of the day rarely restricted commerce to within their borders. Prosperity demanded expansion. That has certainly been the case since the late 19th century, when globalization flourished, except in the years between the two world wars.

What keeps changing is the nature of the global economy, as the articles in this volume illustrate. That nature is much different today than when I first encountered the global economy as a young foreign correspondent in Argentina in the late 1960's. Then the United States dominated trade and foreign investment in the non-communist world. "The American Challenge," a much-cited best seller by French journalist Jean-Jacques Servan-Schreiber, warned in 1968 that American industry would overrun Western Europe with its initiative, energy, managerial skill and financial muscle.

"It is enough to watch American investment skim gently across the earth like the fabled swallow and watch what it takes away, how 'it thrusts, twists, enfolds, tears away, carries off, breaks open, and attacks,' " Mr. Servan-Schrieber wrote, paraphrasing Andre Malraux. No one imagined that 15 years later Japan and West Germany, particularly Japan, would be the fabled swallows.

Such was the awe in which America was held. Hoping to barricade themselves against American intrusion, most nations, including Argentina, erected high tariffs. The goal was to nurture native-owned industries. But the protected markets only encouraged inefficiency and price-gouging, particularly in the less developed countries, and it did not stop the United States anyway. Because of high tariffs, a General Motors could not export a car to Argentina and sell it at a price that Argentines could afford. So G.M. leaped the tariff wall and built cars in Argentina.

By the late 1960's, American companies were a huge presence not only in motor vehicles but in every major Argentine industry, with Britain, France, Germany and Italy also moving in. The Argentines limited the profits that foreign companies could send home, the hope being that the companies would reinvest and expand in Argentina, bringing their technology in the process. But a General Motors or a Ford had other ways of channeling revenue back to America while keeping technology and high value-added work at home.

Their Argentine subsidiaries, for example, paid in dollars for high-tech parts made in America and exported to Argentina for assembly in cars. The subsidiaries paid royalties for design, although the new models that appeared in Argentina were often the same models that had appeared on American streets several years earlier. The finished steel also came from America, and when an Argentine consortium tried to get financing abroad for a local steel mill, it met with considerable opposition from the American embassy and from the U.S. Steel Corporation, whose local representative made his case with journalists like myself. The Argentines could not match U.S. Steel's technological prowess, the representative argued, or the cost savings that came from the economies of scale embedded in America's mass production economy.

The Associated Press and United Press International participated in globalization, 1960's style. As A.P.'s chief of bureau in Buenos Aires, I not only reported on Argentina for American and European media, but headed a staff of more than two-dozen journalists who covered Argentina for Argentine dailies and radio stations. A.P.'s competition was U.P.I, not an Argentine news service. We charged in dollars, not pesos, and sent some of the money home to cover A.P.'s worldwide costs, always describing the remittances as payments for services rendered, not profit.

How distant those days seem. How drastically the global economy has changed in only a generation, as the opening sections of this collection of *New York Times* articles help to explain. America's mesmerizing influence soon gave way, a casualty in part of the Vietnam setback. When Juan Domingo Peron came back to power in the early 1970's, one of his first acts was to close down A.P.'s and U.P.I.'s national services. A news service owned by Argentine newspapers took its place, at first less efficiently but in time quite effectively.

State-of-the art steel mills also came to the less developed world, including Argentina. As tariffs and other barriers to free trade and the free movement of capital fell—not only in Argentina but in many countries across the globe—globalization shifted in character. Instead of a top-down system, modern factories and the latest technologies began to appear in many countries, and corporate behavior changed. Instead of assembling cars separately in Argentina or Brazil or Chile, General Motors, Ford, Fiat and Volkswagen began to produce for several Southern Cone countries, intertwining production to do so. Much of the final assembly took place in Brazil, the most populous country, while Argentina specialized in making parts and Chile delivered the necessary copper wire.

A borderless global system came gradually into being. Gillette, for example, now assembles its latest-model razors in several countries from parts made by Gillette or by subcontractors inside and outside the United States. American telephone companies have put call centers in Mexico City as well as in American cities, so that an Hispanic in New York, dialing "411" to get the telephone number of a friend in Pittsburgh and preferring to speak in Spanish, could be shunted to the Mexican operator. The Mexican operators earned a fraction of the wage paid to their counterparts in, say, Scranton, Pa., but they had at their fingertips the same computerized database as the English-speaking Scranton operators. And Ford, phasing out auto assembly in Mexico for the Mexican market, nevertheless put a state-of-the art engine plant in Chihuahua instead of in Michigan or Ohio. The motors go north to be incorporated in cars that roll off a Ford assembly line in Wichita, Kan.

Not only did borders disappear, but mass production went global, as these examples illustrate, and the American home market was not exempt. Japanese and West German companies were the first to breach the control that American corporations had on the mass market in the United States and on the economies of scale made possible by mass output. As tariffs gradually fell after World War II, modern transportation and communication gave the Japanese and West Germans the opportunity to sell their products competitively in the United States. Finally, they had an outlet for the excess production that their home markets were not large enough to absorb. The quality of this exported merchandise, particularly Japanese autos, was often an improvement on American quality and every bit as high tech. That was true of Japanese electronics, Korean and Brazilian steel, Chinese textiles and apparel, to name just a few.

The competition decimated American companies at first. The Rust Belt became a measure of the decimation. But Corporate America gradually responded. One response was to shift production abroad, where labor was far less expensive than in the United States, but increasingly as skilled. Any number of companies called on computer nerds in India or Ireland or Taiwan to write computer software, for example, and computer technology increasingly made its way to the less developed countries, particularly in southeast Asia, often carried home by these nations' young people who had been educated in the United States. By the late 20th century, the global economy had bloomed in its new borderless format. Its chief characteristics were intertwined corporations, intricate supply networks and mass production emanating at last from more than a few nations.

For all the intertwining, the industrial nations still had the advantage, taking the lead in setting the new rules and garnering much of the income because their multinational companies were so ubiquitous. And the past intruded; the crises that endangered the new global system were not unlike the crises that brought down a global system that had flourished and then disappeared early in the 20th century. Excess capacity became a crippling problem as the 20th century ended, just as it had been in that earlier era. By 2001, the new global system had the capacity to produce much more than people wanted to purchase or could afford to purchase. That discouraged investment and expansion, drove down prices and profits and pushed many workers out of jobs.

The other danger was financial. In that earlier period, not only goods and services but capital moved easily across borders, as it does today. And the capital flows at the end of the century got out of hand, just as they did in the 1920's and 1930's. With restrictions lifted, investors everywhere, and particularly in America, began to chase high returns by speculating in the 1990's in foreign stock markets, in foreign exchange and in risky overseas loans, mainly loans in less developed countries. The payoff was handsome until the financial markets in New York, London, Europe and Tokyo realized that the speculation would not pay off as promised, and the money might even be lost.

That happened in Asia and Russia in 1997 and 1998 and in Mexico in 1994. The disruption was enormous, as borrowers defaulted and speculators pulled their money or refused to make new investments and loans. The United States Government and the International Monetary Fund—founded at Bretton Woods in 1944 to prop up currencies in a less turbulent world—furnished billions of dollars in bailout loans. But they exacted a promise from the governments of the nations in crisis. In exchange for the bailout money, these governments were required to impose painful austerity measures that shrunk public spending and worker benefits. The cure drew stiff criticism as a cruel and unfair aspect of the global economy in its new format.

The Asian Tigers and Russia did bounce back, but they were still repairing the damage in 2001 when a new crisis appeared. Falling demand and excess capacity brought recession and fresh strain on the global system, just as they had in the global system that came apart in the Great Depression and World War II. Many of the dispatches in this book document that earlier globalization and its undoing.

The global economy that arose in the late 19th and early 20th centuries never was described as borderless or global. Not until the 1990's did the word "globalization" become widely used, in *The New York Times* and elsewhere, as a description of the emerging system. In contrast, nation-states never lost their identity in that earlier era. Boundaries played a defining role, particularly for the dominant industrial nations, and so did their clearly defined colonial holdings and their equally defined spheres of influence among less developed countries. These colonies and lesser countries furnished the industrial nations with the inexpensive raw materials that were so important to manufacturing.

Manufacturing, the great source of rising income, stayed in the industrial nations, which exported their excess production, often to the less developed world in exchange for raw materials and food. Breakthroughs in transportation and communication—the steamship, continental railroads, refrigerated transports, the ocean-crossing underwater cable—facilitated the growing trade. Tariffs were even lower then than they are today and capital flowed freely, particularly from Europe to America, which became an industrial powerhouse in this period, using the foreign capital to help achieve that goal.

Mass immigration in an age of no quotas swelled America's population, supplying the necessary horde of consumers for the world's first mass market. In response, the giant corporation first appeared between 1880 and 1920. And this American invention became the forerunner of today's multinational.

Overexpansion, excess capacity and reckless speculation in the 1920's, followed by the Great Depression and World War II, finally destroyed that global system. "Although it is often said today that globalization is irreversible, it proved very reversible early in this century," Nicholas D. Kristof, a *Times* correspondent, wrote in a 1999 article included in this volume.

Reversal could happen again. Public opposition to globalization became suddenly rather formidable in late November of 1999, when protests and rioting disrupted a meeting of the World Trade Organization in Seattle. Ministers from many nations had gathered to discuss a new round of reductions in tariffs and other trade barriers. Globalization contributed considerably to the prosperity that lifted many economies in the late 1990's. But the distribution of that prosperity was starkly unequal, and the protesters blamed the rapidly developing global system. They have continued to do so in a drumbeat of protests ever since.

The protests go beyond the usual opposition to sweatshops, environmental damage and outsourcing to low-wage countries. Many of the protesters come from the less developed countries where they are members of non-government organizations, the so-called NGO's. They object to the reigning view that tariffs and other barriers to free trade and capital flows should be dismantled as quickly as possible.

Mainstream economic theory holds that free trade increases every participant's prosperity. That is true if the participants are on an equal footing economically, exporting the goods and services that each produces most efficiently and importing what others are best at making. The problem is that the industrial countries are better than the less developed nations at nearly everything. So when the United States gains the right to ship, tariff free, lumber and paper to Mexico or packaged food to India, less efficient production in these countries is destroyed. These are industries that provide necessary employment and income and that tariffs should protect until the industries can flourish in an open, global economy, the protesters argue.

Even today, the United States uses quotas and anti-dumping suits to protect its steel industry and the industry's high-wage jobs from lower-cost, high quality imports from Asia, Latin America and Europe. Hardly free trade.

The less developed nations have an antidote in the new global production networks and the foreign investment that makes them possible. But it is only a partial antidote, one that relegates these nations to making parts and not final products—in sum, without sufficient control over how the foreign capital is allocated. In the early days of American industrialization, the nation's entrepreneurs, with support from government, allocated foreign capital and protected their infant industries from foreign competition until they could stand on their own.

Gradual globalization in this fashion is in fact the correct model, some economists argue, among them Dani Rodrik at Harvard University's Kennedy School of Government. If you are a Brazil or Mexico or India or Indonesia, he argues, you are too large to rely on trade or foreign investment as the engine of growth. "Historically, economic development has always been a fine balance between being open to globalization and protecting your infant domestic industries. A developing country grows rich by cajoling, subsidizing and otherwise coercing domestic investors. The United States had such a strategy. The tragedy is that all the evidence from America's own economic history is being neglected in the current rush to globalize."

The protesters agree, of course. The developing struggle, and *The Times*'s coverage of it, is well represented in this collection. Hopefully there will be a companion volume, a few years from now, chronicling how the struggle was resolved in the endless saga of the global economy.

Louis Uchitelle has covered economics for The New York Times since 1987. He has also served as an editor at The Times and as a foreign correspondent, writer and editor at The Associated Press. He has written on a wide range of economic issues, with emphasis on national trends, business and labor, technology and productivity, and Federal Reserve policy. In the early 1990's, he spent more than 20 weeks in Russia and the Ukraine, reporting on the former Soviet Union's plunge into capitalism.

PART I

GLOBALIZATION IN CONTEXT

The rise of the global economy in the 20th century is a big story, with many characters, motives, plots and subplots that together span several human generations. It is a story that is too big to be told all at once. You need to approach it a little at a time, like a television mini-series or like Richard Wagner's four-part opera cycle of "The Ring" (which George Bernard Shaw famously interpreted as the story of the rise and fall of global capitalism).

Part I of this book uses articles drawn from a full century of The New York Times to set the stage. The articles collected here provide historical context for the story of the rise of the global economy and introduce briefly many of the most important themes that are developed more fully throughout this book. This first set of articles is therefore useful both as historical documents and as a guide to how the various elements of the complete story come together. Look briefly, for example, at the first three articles collected here.

James Reston's column, "In Pursuit of Happiness," written on the Fourth of July 1981, begins the story in dramatic fashion. Americans like to celebrate Independence Day, Reston writes, but real national independence is impossible in our interconnected and interdependent world. Instead of Independence, maybe we should celebrate cooperation day, since that is what we really need if we are to avoid confrontation and dependence. Reston's theme—the tension between the desire for autonomy and the reality of inter-dependence—is one that runs throughout this book.

The economist Lester Thurow follows with a piece called "Economics First" that points out a fundamental asymmetry between economics and politics in a global age. Markets, everyone knows, disrespect borderlines. Goods, services, people, money, ideas and cultural artifacts move naturally within local, national and especially global markets that bear no resemblance to the lines on a map. Politics, however, is still fundamentally based on national borders. The governance of global markets therefore is beyond the boundaries of any individual nation-state—it requires international political cooperation. Global economics happens first, Thurow says here. When will international political institutions evolve to match it? The tendency of economic systems to outgrow their political foundations is another consistent theme of globalization. Many of the articles in this collection report on attempts to build a solid political foundation for the emerging global economy.

Finally, Jon Bowermaster's fine article "Calhoun County Goes Global" describes the many human tensions, problems and opportunities that globalization creates as Local (in this case Alabama) confronts Global. This article highlights the fact that globalization is not just about money and cars, it is about people. Globalization causes people with different backgrounds and interests to come into contact with each other in a variety of ways and circumstances. This human interaction can be simultaneously uncomfortable and rewarding. The two human faces of globalization is another recurrent theme of this book.

These articles convey the sense that globalization is a human phenomenon, not just an abstract concept. This, of course, is one of the strengths of approaching globalization through the coverage of The New York Times. We are necessarily exposed to the ways that real people think about global economics, how they act upon those thoughts and how they are acted upon by the forces thus unleashed.

It is a common misconception that globalization is new and that it is inevitable or unstoppable. Articles drawn from the first half of the 20th century indicate that globalization is both older than we might think and more fragile, too. In "Globalization 1900" we

1

encounter articles that describe an interconnected world not so very different from today. Although the names and faces have changed in 100 years, the economic motives and the political and social reactions to globalization are not fundamentally changed.

The fact that we have experienced globalization before, however, does not necessarily mean that we understand it better now than we did then. In "The Collapse of the Global Economy" we learn how the reconstructed global market of the 1920's was destroyed by the forces of economic nationalism and social unrest, both magnified by the global financial crisis. The articles presented here on protectionism and financial crisis in the 1930's clearly foreshadow The Time's coverage of the global economy in the 1990's.

Because there is room for only a few articles in each of these sections, they necessarily provide images that are more like impressionist paintings than high-definition photographs. This is especially true of the sections on the rise and decline of the global economy in the period 1900–1939, where just a few articles must stretch to cover many ideas and several decades. The purpose of this section, however, is to provide context and to raise themes to be developed more fully later, and these articles accomplish that purpose admirably.

WHAT IS GLOBALIZATION?

July 5, 1981

IN PURSUIT OF HAPPINESS

By JAMES RESTON

MARTHA'S VINEYARD, Mass., July 4—The Declaration of Independence has proved to be so popular over the last 205 years that declaring independence in pursuit of happiness has become a fad and even a danger.

Almost everybody seems to be doing it these days. The baseball players, who are not among the "truly needy," have declared their independence of the baseball owners, and vice versa, so there is no baseball on this glorious Fourth.

The airline traffic managers are declaring their independence from the airline owners; the Sunbelt states from the Frostbelt states; the government workers from the governors and mayors; even husbands from wives, and children from parents. The evidence is clear in every morning's headlines: in the divorce and crime rates, and the tragic accounts of wayward and abandoned children.

The noble words of "independence" in Jefferson's time, and of "self-determination" in Woodrow Wilson's time, now have a different meaning. They have been corrupted into meaning not only "independence" and "self-determination" for the nation, but independence and self-determination for the region, for races, industrial managers or unions, and ultimately for the individual—or self-determination for "self" in this Me-First Generation.

There is obviously something to the notion that progress is made by conflict, but in many ways it is not now working. The Japanese, who are the most spectacular successes of the modern industrial world, have done rather well by rejecting the principle of "confrontation," and insisting that the future lies in "cooperation" between government and business, labor and management, research and development.

As a result, we are now sitting around in our Toyotas, listening on our Sonys, to the tragedy of Detroit, where managers and the unions are still arguing about how to avoid bankruptcy, still insisting on the prospect of progress by confrontation rather than cooperation.

It is the same tragic story all over the world. The Soviets think they can defend their borders against another Napoleonic or Hitlerian attack by building a modern nuclear arsenal, with missiles aimed at every capital in Europe and even every major city in the United States. President Reagan thinks he can match them with the largest peacetime defense budget in history—at the expense of the social programs for the relief of the poor and the education of the middle class.

In Israel, India, Pakistan, Ireland, Iran, we see "religious wars," which are not even waged by "believers." They have even forgotten the principles of compassion and forgiveness which their religions had in common.

On July 4, 1776, the "thirteen United States of America" unanimously declared that, in Mr. Jefferson's words, "When in the course of human events it becomes necessary for one people to dissolve the political bands which have connected them with one another . . . a decent respect to the opinions of mankind requires that they should declare the causes which impel them to the separation."

Mr. Jefferson argued for national independence for America, but not for the independence of the several states to do what they liked, or for institutions, let along individuals, to "proclaim liberty" for themselves. He would have thought that that would be anarchy, and he would probably be surprised today to see his fellow countrymen claiming independence for themselves and their institutions or regions—the independence he intended for the nation alone.

It is not a popular thought, but maybe the idea of "independence" has gone too far. For the first time in history, we have a world economy in which what happens in Saudi Arabia affects the price of fuel for every gas pump and farm in Sycamore, Ill., and the corn crop in Sycamore affects the relations between the United States and the Soviet Union.

If Ohio burns soft coal instead of expensive oil, it poisons the atmosphere and kills the lakes of Canada. If we do not control the spread of nuclear fuel, even terrorists can hold not just a few hostages but whole nations to ransom.

So declarations of independence are a dime a dozen these days. Over a hundred nations have copied Mr. Jefferson, and proclaimed that, at last, they are on their own. They are going so far as to shake their fists at their adversaries.

But even the most powerful of the independent nations are not on their own. Moscow cannot dictate to Poland, and Washington cannot dictate to Europe about putting missiles in Holland and Germany.

So maybe what we need, between our Declaration of Independence on the Fourth of July and the French Declaration of Independence on Bastille Day—the 14th of July—is a declaration of interdependence, stating that, alone and separate in confrontation, we can probably do very little, but that through cooperation, it might even be possible to create a safer and a more decent world.

* * *

November 15, 1982

ECONOMICS FIRST

By LESTER THUROW

CAMBRIDGE, Mass—Over the last three decades, the economies of the world's industrial countries have gradually grown more integrated, but their economic policies have not. Sooner or later, the inconsistencies of such a system had to be tested.

Growth has stopped here and around the world, protection has started everywhere, whole countries are going broke. But no one country alone can break out of the economic quicksand in which we are all stuck.

The French, denied their requests at the Ottawa and Versailles summit meetings for coordinated economic expansion, have seen their attempts to go it alone defeated. Monetary and fiscal stimulus succeeded in increasing consumption 4 percent from mid-1981 to mid-1982, but production rose only 2 percent. The result was a flood of imports and a plunge in the value of the French franc. The stimulus of French imports slowed the economic contractions in other countries but could not start vigorous economic growth at home.

Then, as the French stimulation slowed, the West German contraction intensified. Industrial production fell 4 percent between the second and third quarters of 1982. With the West German economy in a state of free fall, economies in the rest of Europe can only sag. And with sagging European economies, the American economy can get only worse.

The third world is broke. Mexico's crisis is the first of many crises to come. There are no solutions for third-world countries. They can only meet their debts if they are allowed to export more of their production to the industrial world, but that is economically and politically impossible with stagnant industrial economies.

The French are now retreating to economic austerity and a "go it alone" assault on the international trading system. The American Government just organized a world steel cartel to keep foreign steel out of our economy. The end of this process is worldwide economic disintegration.

We already know that President Reagan's present course is a failure. He promised real growth rates of 4 to 5 percent per year starting in the fall of 1981 if his program was adopted. It was adopted, but one year later those growth rates are not to be seen.

To "stay the course" when we have only to look at the United Kingdom to see what a similar program brings three and a half years after it is adopted is a form of economic masochism. British unemployment is 14 percent and rising. Vigorous growth is nowhere to be seen.

The French were right and President Reagan wrong at the summit conferences. The world needs to coordinate monetary policies to dramatically lower interest rates, and it needs to prevent the wide swings in currency values that make economic investment and planning impossible. No one can run successful economies if there are going to be 40 percent swings in the value of major currencies in the matter of a few months. No one knows the best place to invest or the cheapest source of supplies.

The American economy is still so big and the dollar so important, however, that it is not possible to reflate the world economy or control currency fluctuations without American cooperation. President Reagan must be forced to alter his policies.

To do this, a new and different summit should be quickly organized. It should be a summit meeting composed of those governments and political parties that believe in the necessity for economic stimulation. Instead of a meeting between Francois Mitterrand and Ronald Reagan, it should, for example, be a meeting between President Mitterrand and the Congressional leaders of the Democratic Party—both of whom already agree on the need for economic stimulation.

The first item on the agenda should be agreement on the specific monetary policies and foreign exchange policies that would permit coordinated expansion of our economies. The second item on the agenda should be plans for bringing about coordinated external and internal political pressures on the Reagan Administration to adopt those policies.

Diplomatic protocol simply has to bend with the current reality of economic integration. Such a meeting has to take place since it is no longer possible to set domestic policies domestically. Without American cooperation, the French Government cannot adopt the domestic economic policies it wishes to adopt. Without French cooperation, the Democratic Party cannot get the economic stimulation it wants for America. And even if it could get a different policy, the policy would not work in the face of European contraction.

In an integrated world economy, domestic economic politics have to extend across national borders. To get what they want, the Democrats will also need to form alliances with members of the opposition party and foreign countries.

Lester Thurow, professor of economics and management at the Massachusetts Institute of Technology, is author of the forthcoming book "Dangerous Currents: The State of Economics."

*   *   *

December 2, 1990

CALHOUN COUNTY GOES GLOBAL

By JON BOWERMASTER

From his third-floor office, Mike Clayborne looks out over the verdant hills of Calhoun County, Ala., through the haze of a steamy spring afternoon. While the view is distinctly Southern, the conversation is purely global. Now in his second year as president of the local Chamber of Commerce, in Anniston, Clayborne is describing how his community is participating in the world marketplace: competing for branch plants from Southeast Asia, marketing a variety of services across Europe and Asia, selling Alabama-made goods to markets from Norway to Saudi Arabia.

On the credenza behind him sits a small black flag holder, with miniatures of the Stars and Stripes and the Alabama state flag protruding at angles from each side. Between them is the flag of South Korea. While Clayborne holds forth about the county's latest trade mission (to Japan) and the Memphis public relations firm that was recently hired to help promote Calhoun County worldwide, I ask if that little Korean flag is aimed at a particularly ripe prospect. He smiles and reaches into his desk drawer and comes out with a fistful of miniature flags—from Great Britain, Japan, Finland, Hungary, Yugoslavia, Taiwan and a couple of countries he can't identify. "These are key economic development weapons today," he says, brandishing the flags that he picked up for a dollar apiece at a variety store in Gatlinburg, Tenn.

"We feel the world's economy is a two-way street," Clayborne says with a determined grimace, "and that there's plenty of room for all of us. If these little flags help one iota, the symbolism is worth every penny."

It is hardly a secret that the world economy has become one big, evolving, complex international bazaar. Chopsticks are made in Minnesota for export to Japan. Schwinn bicycles are made in Hungary; so are G.E. light bulbs and Levi's jeans. Silos made in North Dakota are cut in half and shipped to Norway as warehouses. Chicken feet—once the refuse of Virginia poultry fanciers—are sent to Hong Kong, to be made into soup. In Japan, Mazda manufactures the Ford Probe, partly owned by Ford. It's sold as an American car. "There is no longer such a thing as an 'American economy,' " insists Robert B. Reich, an economist and Harvard professor.

As a result of all this global economic shrinking and booming, industrial development has taken on new twists in places like Calhoun County, Ala. Until recently a slick economic development presentation consisted of sending out a couple of officials with a slide projector to show pictures of vacant industrial land. Today those officials are as likely to be courting new businesses in Cairo as in Chicago.

It used to be that to woo new business to town, Calhoun's leaders would gather prospective investors over tables full of barbecued pork, char-grilled catfish, fried chicken, corn on the cob, coleslaw, fries and an array of spicy sauces at Betty's Bar-B-Q or the Goal Post. They would boast about the county's cheap wages and lack of unions. Today those pitches are more likely to take place over kimchi at one of several local Oriental restaurants.

Yet Calhoun County, Ala., couldn't be more red, white and blue. Giant American flags decorate the water towers across the county; three more hang, hugely, from the rafters of the Quintard Mall. Most offices and front porches boast the Stars and Stripes, and not just on holidays.

The 158-year-old county is wedged into a narrow sluice cut through the foothills of the Appalachians in eastern Alabama; Atlanta lies 90 miles to the east, Birmingham 60 to the west. Between are long stretches of blacktop lined by little but scrub pine, sandy soil and smaller, quieter towns. The biggest employer in the county is the Federal Government: the Army's Fort McClellan pumps more than $300 million a year into the local community, the Anniston Army Depot an additional $260 million. The county's economy has been steeped in small manufacturing since the 1870's: pig iron, textiles and cast-iron pipe have been its backbone. Bass fishing is the biggest participant sport, football and stock-car racing the activities most favored by spectators. There are no liquor sales on Sunday, no parking meters on the wide cement streets of Anniston, the county seat (population 35,000). This is no new-age suburb—no "penturbia" nor "micropolitan"—but small-town America in the deep South.

Despite the pervasive aura of Americana—from the strip malls to the Stars and Bars—around every corner in this rural county lie hints of an encroaching world. Five of its bigger manufacturing plants—employing 10 percent of its work force—are foreign-owned. Of the top 25 businesses in the county, 20 face stiff foreign competition. Three hundred jobs at Magic Chef are threatened by South Korea's entry into the microwave-oven market. Nearly a third of the local Monsanto plant's output was shut down after the financial instability that ensued from Tiananmen Square. A yellow, red and blue billboard on Highway 21 advertises "Full Gospel Korean Church." The local daily paper has recently hired its own foreign correspondent. At a Hardee's one early recent morning, conversation among several retirees revolved around the best way to pick huckleberries (seated, with a constant eye out for rattlesnakes) and the recent economic turmoil in Georgia. Soviet Georgia.

You might expect the long tentacles of the international economy to have infiltrated New York, Los Angeles and

Miami. Yet there may be no better place to illustrate just how drastically the world economy has shrunk in recent years than in rural Alabama. In fact, virtually every town and county in the nation has stepped—some boldly, some with hesitance—into this changing marketplace. Many say just in time. From 1984 through March 1989, Japan invested $72 billion in the United States. Between 1987 and 1989, United States imports to Mexico increased by 70 percent, to $24.9 billion. In 1989 the United States sent $79 billion worth of goods to Canada. In Europe, 12 countries are working to create the world's largest common market, with 325 million consumers and a combined gross national product of nearly $5 trillion. Like everybody else, folks in Calhoun County want a piece of the action.

Competing in this new world mart is arduous, especially in Alabama. Most foreign investors know all about California and New York. Many think Atlanta is a state. But when it comes to Alabama, they generally think first of George Wallace, not exactly a selling point. The state ranks near the bottom in many categories deemed necessary to lure investment—safe environment, good education, sound economy. Yet despite such apparent roadblocks to economic growth, Alabama has more than 190 foreign-based manufacturing investments from 22 nations, and finances three overseas development offices, in Tokyo, Seoul, and Eschborn, Germany.

Beyond the borders of Calhoun County there is a feeling that it may soon be too late for some American industries to jump into the increasingly crowded global marketplace. As a result, some experts insist, American industry—and government—must make this new game a priority. Yet the question persists in many quarters: Is this a good thing? The answer is: It is unavoidable and inevitable.

"New technologies of worldwide communication and transportation have redrawn the playing field," Robert Reich says. "American industries no longer compete against Japanese or European industries. Rather, a company with headquarters in the United States, production facilities in Taiwan, and a marketing force spread across many nations competes with another, similarly ecumenical company."

Reich says places like Calhoun County are ripe for inclusion in this marketplace if they act now. "The new economy operates on a smaller scale and is far better suited to rural environments," he insists, but cautions that rural America must shift its dependence from productions of low-value, high-volume products like grain and simple manufactured goods to high-tech manufacturing services.

Others believe that sending local chamber representatives out after foreign investment is a boondoggle that brings little improvement to local economies. Carol Conway, deputy director of the Southern Growth Policies Board, says Calhoun's leaders should leave such tasks up to people with more experience: there are now a multitude of state and Federal agencies that specialize in working with foreign investors. "Even if they do get face to face with a potential foreign client, are they up on global policy enough to not insult their audience?" Conway wonders. "Do they understand foreign protocol? Not even a lot

of state international development offices are as knowledgeable as they should be."

There are also pros and cons to the methods used to attract foreign investment, whether it be the sale of an existing business or a new branch operation. "The pros are—especially with the Japanese—you are bound to have fresh investment, not just mergers and acquisitions," Conway says. "It also gives an international flavor to the community, which we desperately need. The cons are dependent upon how you attract them, what you're promising them. If you're promising tax breaks that last for years and years, that's hardly the best use of public funds."

Reich says: "The mistake often made by local chambers of commerce and state governors when drumming up business is that they focus only on the number of jobs, not the quality of jobs. Attracting Volkswagen or Honda to set up a facility nearby employing 5,000 routine assembly-line jobs at a cost of $5 million in tax abatements may not be a great accomplishment.

"Ultimately for a British, Dutch or Japanese company to come into town isn't necessarily better or worse than a California or Massachusetts company. If they bring good jobs, build up the ability of the work force, this type of 'foreign' investment is probably a big plus. But if jobs are unskilled or routine, and fail to add new skills, the investment may ultimately cause small towns to suffer in the long run." Another generation of assembly-line workers is not what we need.

Not everyone in Alabama thinks jumping into the global marketplace is a good idea. June Collier, president and chairman of National Industries, a $124-million-a-year auto parts company based in the state capital, Montgomery, is a loud critic of United States companies who allow themselves to be bought by foreigners: "The first thing I would advise these 'leaders' is that they are derelict in their duty if they don't realize they are selling out our country." Once foreign companies have bought American businesses, Collier insists, they'll start using economic leverage to control politics and government. She would like to see a law that aims at shutting down foreign investment in the United States. "If you're not a citizen of this country," she says, "you should not be able to buy anything you can't take home with you."

Harvard's Reich maintains that Collier is out of step: "Whether she realizes it or not, we are all part of a global economy. Money is now international. It can be passed by a flick of a button from nation to nation. To try to put barriers across borders is as foolish as it fruitless."

Blue Mountain (population 250) sits smack in the heart of Calhoun County. Its frame houses are crumbling and peeling; their predominantly black residents are old, veterans of decades of factory and field work.

The focal point of the tiny village is Blue Mountain Industries, a 93-year-old manufacturer of yarn, twine, rope and other textiles. Its sprawling red-brick plant has tin roofs and metal awnings. The whir of machinery drifts from inside the plant, through large windows open to the spring breeze. Behind, in an overgrown field, are two horseshoe pitches, a long-abandoned backstop and rickety bleachers. In front, an American flag waves against a bright blue sky.

The absentee owner of Blue Mountain Industries is Hanson Trust Ltd., a $12.5 billion British conglomerate that bought the mill in 1975 (the company's third foreign owner). Hanson owns many businesses in many countries—Blue Mountain is just one in its portfolio. But according to Blue Mountain's president, Al Rothwell, who has been with the company since the 1950's, it makes little difference to Calhoun County who owns the company, as long as it stays profitable. The pluses of foreign ownership? "You never have a cash crunch; there are plenty of dollars in hard times," he told The Anniston Star, the local newspaper. The downside? "When you're with a conglomerate, everything's for sale."

Blue Mountain Industries is just one of five foreign-owned manufacturers in Calhoun County. Defense Research Inc., a small-weapons-component maker, was sold to a West German defense contractor in May 1989. Jenkins Manufacturing Company, which sells wood and steel doors, has been owned by a British hardware manufacturer since 1987. Three Southern Ready-Mix plants are owned by a leading Finnish construction-materials maker. Southern Tool Inc., employer of 410, is owned by a $350-million-a-year British-based company, Triplex Lloyd.

County leaders expect that more home-grown manufacturers will sell out to foreign companies in the next few years, keeping pace with a national trend: the Bureau of Economic Analysis in Washington reports that in 1988, 24,460 non-bank companies in the United States were partly owned by foreign investors. The reasons for selling are varied but simple: sales bring expansion capital, openings to new markets and provide a base for further investment.

H. M. (Mack) Burt Jr. is chairman and chief executive officer of Southern Tool. A native of nearby Talladega, he has been with the company since 1968, and rose through the ranks until he was made a group vice president in 1979, charged with overseeing the Calhoun County factory, three plants in Atlanta and one in Scotland. In 1983 he put together a leveraged buyout of the precision castings maker. A year ago he closed the deal that sold the company to the British. Today a Union Jack flies briskly in the breeze in front of his factory.

Why did he sell and run the risk of raising local ire from businessmen who would prefer to see industry in town remain home-grown? "In late 1987 I could see that we were reaching the end of our ability to finance our own growth," says Burt, relaxing in a leather chair in his company's Oxford, Ala., headquarters. "Receivables and inventory were both up and cash had disappeared. But I could see there was still room to grow. We had to either borrow more money—which venture capitalists are against—or find another investor. And this one was not to be a financial play, but a strategic one."

With the help of a regional brokerage firm, Burt began looking for a buyer. "We had been approached by companies, most from the United States, but the chemistry just wasn't there. Then Triplex Lloyd surfaced. They wanted to establish a presence in the U.S., and they wanted a base company to build from." Burt checked them out, while they pored over his books. The deal was signed in July 1989. They have already assigned him the task of searching out more American businesses to buy, while the sale has opened doors for Southern Tool across Europe and given Burt $2 million or $3 million to invest in expansion.

Burt and Southern Tool are emblematic of one kind of cross-border investment—selling existing businesses—that has become prevalent across the United States. But many local governments are still making efforts to entice foreign investors to build new plants and branch operations in their town. Perhaps the most inventive—some would say outlandish—tool Calhoun County leaders are using to attract such investment is a planned Japanese school. Spearheading that effort is A. W. Bolt, a lawyer who attended Jacksonville State and has practiced in town since 1977.

Silver-haired and patrician, Bolt gets red-faced with frustration when talking about the forces that have compelled the town to go to such economic-development lengths. "We're just trying to play the game according to the rules that others have made," Bolt says. "If American industry continues to have the philosophy of 'Let's don't make it, let's just sell it,' and continues to try to make the easy buck on the sell—if foreign countries are the only people who've got the guts and the know-how and the capital to manufacture, then they may be our ultimate saviors. So far we've found foreign investors to be right good citizens and we're glad they're here."

The Japanese school had its origins in one of the Chamber of Commerce missions to the Far East. "We found," Bolt says, "that one concern of Japanese businesses was that the executives they would send to America would bring their families, and their children's education would suffer by comparison to their peers back home. They were concerned they would be out of sync with language, math and the discipline the Japanese use in their educational system."

Based on those concerns, other communities in the United States have started "Saturday schools"—classes intended to keep young Japanese students on a par with their competition back home. As an enticement to potential Japanese investors, a group of Calhoun County leaders raised $20,000, secured space at Jacksonville State, purchased textbooks and lined up a teacher. Now all they need are students. Clayborne, the chamber president, insists a Japanese company is one of his most desired goals—nearly 6,000 Alabamians already work for Japanese-owned businesses, but none yet in his backyard.

While attempts to attract foreign investment get a lot of attention, many of Calhoun County's businesses have already plunged deeply into the changing marketplace. Ribbon, pool tables, twine, ball bearings, pumps, auto carpets, lumber, jet engine components, lamps, children's clothing—all are made in Calhoun County and sold overseas from Scotland to Saudi Arabia. Steve Lopiano at Samson Cordage Works sells braided rope in Japan. Jim Ulrey at Southern Metal Processing licenses his company's technology across Europe. Roy Hathorn, chairman of R & J Machinery in

Anniston, has sold his foundry equipment in 16 different countries since 1961, and is in the process of importing Chinese-made tractors for sale in the United States and elsewhere. "International sales could easily be 100 percent of our business one day," he says.

Trying to educate the local community about the changing world around it is the responsibility in part of The Anniston Star, published and edited by H. Brandt Ayers. His grandfather was an early publisher of the county's first paper, The Daily Hot Blast, which was founded in 1883; the paper's motto was: "Three essentials of a good home—1. Pure Air; 2. Good water; 3. A salubrious climate." Ayers knows that if his hometown is to prosper, that motto must be stretched to include "international understanding."

Ayers has been involved in foreign affairs all his life. His grandfather sold the paper to become the first Southern Baptist missionary to China. When his father, Col. Harry Ayers, returned to Anniston and bought the paper back, his own worldly philosophy was wrapped up in the warning he gave his two children over the nightly dinner table: "He who fails to take heed of problems far away will soon find trouble near at hand."

As a result of that early indoctrination, The Star includes an abundance of foreign coverage. Recently, Ayers hired a reporter to work half time covering local business, and the other half traveling the world reporting economic and social stories from a Calhoun County perspective. "It's a world that's gotten very, very small," he says, "and if we're going to try and deal with it, we've got to know the competition. What they're thinking, what their lives are like. What we want our guy to send back are Ernie Pyle-like stories. I want him to go to Korea, to a microwave plant, and ask them if they give a damn about Magic Chef in Anniston. I want him to give us a glimpse of that worker's life, so that we can better understand the competition. We can't wait to get that news from other news organizations, it'll be too late."

Calhoun county recently had good economic news—namely, that Defense Secretary Dick Cheney's proposal to shut down 35 military bases (one of which was Fort McClellan) has been shelved. People are also less concerned about the possibility of layoffs at the county's biggest employer, the Anniston Army Depot. The future of the nation's only Army base for rebuilding tanks has brightened considerably since troops and tanks were sent to Saudi Arabia.

Yet, if in years to come, defense budgets are slashed, the price of peace could still cost Calhoun County jobs. Elmer Wheatley, economic development guru of the Anniston Chamber, insists that now is the time to diversify the local economy by whatever means necessary. He is convinced that foreign investment is the county's ultimate economic savior, and that ultimately what is good for the businessman's pocket will prove good for the community at large. Wheatley points out his window where a pair of window washers dangle three stories above the sidewalk. "See these guys? They don't care who owns the businesses, as long as they get their paycheck every week, can stop at the Quik Mart on their way home and

get a six-pack and watch the Atlanta Braves win a couple times a week on the tube."

For all the fast-coming economic changes, Calhoun County's leaders insist they are optimistic about the future. "There are only two basic human tendencies, fight or flight," A. W. Bolt says. "I think communities are much the same way. Most people in this community love it here. They're going to stay and fight."

And if in the next decade 50 percent or more of the local populace is employed by companies with foreign flags flying proudly in front of their Alabama plants, will Calhoun County have won the fight? "Probably," Bolt says with a frown. "Probably."

Jon Bowermaster is the co-author, with Will Steger, of "Saving the Earth: A Citizen's Guide to Environmental Action."

*   *   *

February 9, 1997

A QUICK GUIDE TO BIG IDEAS, IF YOU DIDN'T GET TO DAVOS

By JUDITH H. DOBRZYNSKI

DAVOS, Switzerland—Davos, the shorthand by which the World Economic Forum's annual jamboree in this ski resort is known, is over for this year. Nelson Mandela, Yasir Arafat, Bill Gates and Jack Welch, among others, spoke. And while they were not talking—in fact, even while they were up there on the podium—the business elite used their view from these Alpine peaks to ponder and discuss where the world is and where it may be going, in forums large and small.

So your company declined to pay the $20,000 entry fee, plus expenses, to send you to Davos? Do not despair. If Tom Peters, the consultant, can offer "Business School in a Box," surely what goes on in Davos can be summarized in, say, 1,200 words. Here's the skinny you need to make it look like you were here.

Think of Davos as a kind of global Renaissance weekend, only bigger, longer (six days) and more serious. With as many as nine panels happening at once—and many more, somewhat lighter topics (like Chinese medicine and the future of movies and television) programmed for discussion over daily lunches and dinners—Davos is a pot-au-feu of conversation starters and conversation stoppers.

Except for the plenary session speeches, Davos conversation is considered to be off the record. Here, lacking attributions to protect both the innocent and the guilty, are some of the more thought-provoking tidbits.

Globalization

This year's focus may have been "Building the Network Society," but the Globalization Question reigned in the way that the German Question once dominated European politics. No one doubted the inevitability of globalization, which is a product of the triumph of capitalism. But many fear it, for many reasons.

Some see globalization as the villain behind increased poverty, unemployment and inequality. They believe it threatens the sovereignty of nations, especially small ones that feel obliged to court international capital no matter the impact on their social and development agendas. Direct foreign investment, someone pointed out, is growing faster than international trade.

Globalization may be harmful, too, because it homogenizes the world's cultures. National cultural differences are being sacrificed on the mega-brand altar of companies like Disney and MTV, which thrive by peddling the same products everywhere.

Paradoxically, some experts say quick and nimble small companies may well end up being more powerful than huge corporate titans that fall behind in technology. One man even predicted the demise of America's largest corporations.

The Information Age

In contrast to globalization, the arrival at last of the Information Revolution won many more plaudits than raspberries. In the political sphere, for example, information technology is seen as undermining repressive governments.

Government

One drawback to the information age is that it exposes and demystifies all governments, exacerbating the loss of confidence in them. In some areas, governments are struggling to make themselves relevant.

Yet governments themselves contribute mightily to that loss of faith. They tend to do things that succeed in the short term but fail in the long term. For example, the social welfare systems that European nations erected after World War II to protect people are now hurting them, as they steer away jobs and wealth. Unemployment is rampant.

Plutocrats know that these social systems must be dismantled—after all, not a single net new job has been created in Europe since 1970—but they have done nothing to create a constituency for change.

Banks

The very existence of banks is in doubt. Some experts believe that new forms of commerce, like the use of cyber-money, will make them obsolete. Others predict that they will thrive in the information age because they are the only institutions trustworthy enough to make electronic commerce work.

Crime

Like everything else, crime is going global. Experts expect organized crime—drug trafficking, money laundering, financial fraud and corruption—to increase. They worry about increases in digital terrorism, with hackers wreaking havoc on information networks. And they fear the emergence of black markets in nuclear material that the Soviet republics never tracked after their empire broke up.

Health

Nearly half of United States cancer patients are now surviving at least five years—and the challenge to health care providers is to make that percentage, at the least, hold for the rest of the world.

Scientists are scrambling to discover genetic secrets, but one avenue of exploration—testing for genetic susceptibility to various diseases—carries its own risk: nearly everyone will be at risk for some disorder. How genetic profiles will be used—including by insurance companies—and who will have access to them remains a huge question. True confidentiality is unlikely.

And what will happen if courts accept the idea that some criminal behavior has a genetic basis?

The Environment

Energy is still being used—and wasted—in vast amounts, degrading the environment. Some experts say the only answer is to reduce energy consumption, to make people live more frugally. But others say information technologies can help countries and consumers cut back by eliminating the waste. For example, better traffic management could slash the gasoline wasted in traffic jams.

Learning

Education must reach more people—and it must go to them rather than forcing individuals to go to schools to learn. People may then see education as a lifelong activity, rather than something that takes place when they are young.

It's also not too late to join the information age—worldwide, fewer than 5 percent of people use computers, although the proportion in the United States is upward of 30 percent.

Population

By 2000, half the world's population will be under 20, with profound consequences. The vast majority will live in poor nations, many in the streets of mega-cities that cannot provide jobs.

Worriers are certain that these leaps in population will test the world's ability to feed everyone. Still, recent surveys in China show that the amount of arable land there is greater than previously thought, and some scientists see biotechnology as the savior that will increase food production. No matter what happens, food may well cost everyone a lot more.

The Frenzy

Are you tired? Just wait. The pace of life in the developed world will only get faster, leading some to suggest that some people will opt out of post-industrial life altogether and others to predict a big business in building sanctuaries for the harried. Alienation is a huge risk.

Considering that a huge part of Davos is the talk that goes on in the corridors, attendees had a good Davos if they covered anywhere close to the ground outlined here. If it all sounds squishy, however, remember that Davos functions best when it provides questions, not answers. After all, Elie

Wiesel said at one meeting, "Questions unite people, and answers divide them."

*   *   *

February 13, 1997

WE ARE NOT THE WORLD

By PAUL KRUGMAN

CAMBRIDGE, Mass.—It is a truth universally acknowledged that the growing international mobility of goods, capital and technology has completely changed the economic game. Nations, conventional wisdom tells us, no longer have the power to control their own destinies; governments are at the mercy of international markets.

Some celebrate this development, saying that both rich and poor nations benefit. At the same time, a growing number of journalists, union leaders, politicians of both parties and even businessmen deplore it, blaming globalization for instability, unemployment and declining wages.

But both sides have it wrong. They take the omnipotence of global markets for granted—not realizing that reports of the death of national autonomy are greatly exaggerated.

A certain fascination with the march of globalization is understandable. For half a century, world trade has grown faster than world output, and international capital now moves more quickly than ever before. The rapidly expanding exports of newly industrializing economies have put pressure on less-skilled workers in advanced countries even as they offer unprecedented opportunities to tens of millions in the third world. (The wages of those workers are shockingly low but nonetheless represent a vast improvement on their previous, less visible rural poverty.)

But while global economic integration is increasing, its growth has been far outpaced by that of "global economy" rhetoric. Two recent books by economic journalists, William Greider's "One World, Ready or Not" and Robert Kuttner's "Everything for Sale," are jeremiads about the evils of unfettered economic globalism. Politicians like Patrick J. Buchanan and Ross Perot have made careers out of assailing open markets. Even the financier George Soros warns, in the current issue of The Atlantic Monthly, that global capitalism is now a greater threat than totalitarianism to "open society."

Such oratory has become so pervasive that many observers seem determined to blame global markets for a host of economic and social ills in their countries, even when the facts point unmistakably to mainly domestic—and usually political—causes.

For example, critics of globalization often cite France, whose Government has taken no serious action to reduce its double-digit unemployment rate, as the perfect example of how states have become powerless in the face of impersonal world markets. France cannot act, according to a recent New York Times article, because of the demands of "European economic integration—itself partly a response to the competitive demands of the global marketplace."

French policy is indeed paralyzed—not, however, by impersonal market forces but by the determination of its prestige-conscious politicians not to let the franc decline against the German mark. Britain, which has been willing to let the pound sink relative to the mark, has steadily reduced its unemployment rate with no visible adverse consequences.

The cause of France's paralysis, in other words, is political rather than economic. True, the country must meet the conditions laid down by the Maastricht treaty of 1991, which is supposed to lead to a unified European currency. But creating this currency is more a political than an economic project. Its main purpose is to serve as a symbol of European unity, and many economists think that the costs of the common currency will exceed its benefits. It would actually be more accurate to say that French politics has battered markets rather than the other way around.

And what about the United States, where the continuing power of the Government—or at any rate that of the Federal Reserve—to push the economy around can hardly be questioned? Critics of the global economy invariably reply that America may be creating lots of jobs but that they are tenuous because of the prevalence of downsizing, which is a reaction to international competition (a line of reasoning that also provides a good excuse for companies undertaking layoffs).

Come again? Newsweek ran a story last year, titled "The Hit Men," about executives responsible for massive layoffs. The chief executives of AT&T, Nynex, Sears, Philip Morris and Delta Air Lines were high on the list. Of course, international competition plays a role in some downsizings, but as Newsweek's list makes clear, it is hardly the most important cause of the phenomenon. To my knowledge there are no Japanese keiretsu competing to carry my long-distance calls or South Korean conglomerates offering me local service. Nor have many Americans started buying their home appliances at Mexican stores or smoking French cigarettes. I cannot fly Cathay Pacific from Boston to New York.

What explains this propensity to overstate the importance of global markets? In part, it sounds sophisticated. Pontificating about globalization is an easy way to get attention at events like the World Economic Forum in Davos, Switzerland, and Renaissance Weekends in Hilton Head, S.C.

But there is also a deeper cause—an odd sort of tacit agreement between the left and the right to pretend that exotic global forces are at work even when the real action is prosaically domestic.

Many on the left dislike the global marketplace because it epitomizes what they dislike about markets in general: the fact that nobody is in charge. The truth is that the invisible hand rules most domestic markets, too, a reality that most Americans seem to accept as a fact of life. But those who would like to see us revert to a more managed society in all ways hope that popular unease over the economic influence of people who live in far-off places and have funny-sounding names can be used as the thin end of an ideological wedge.

Meanwhile, many on the right use the rhetoric of globalization to argue that business can no longer be expected to meet any social obligations. For example, it has become standard for opponents of environmental regulations to raise the banner of "competitiveness" and to warn that anything that raises costs for American businesses will price our goods out of world markets.

But even if the global economy matters less than the sweeping assertions would have us believe, does this "globaloney," as the cognoscenti call it, do any real harm? Yes, in part because the public, misguided into believing that international trade is the source of all our problems, might turn protectionist—undermining the real good that globalization has done for most people here and abroad.

But the overheated oratory poses a more subtle risk. It encourages fatalism, a sense that we cannot come to grips with our problems because they are bigger than we are. Such fatalism is already well advanced in Western Europe, where the public speaks vaguely of the "economic horror" inflicted by world markets instead of turning a critical eye on the domestic leaders whose policies have failed.

None of the important constraints on American economic and social policy come from abroad. We have the resources to take far better care of our poor and unlucky than we do; if our policies have become increasingly mean-spirited, that is a political choice, not something imposed on us by anonymous forces. We cannot evade responsibility for our actions by claiming that global markets made us do it.

Paul Krugman, a professor of economics at the Massachusetts Institute of Technology, is the author of "Peddling Prosperity" and "Pop Internationalism."

* * *

June 18, 1997

THAT WAS THEN AND THIS IS THE 90'S

Today Looks a Bit Like the Golden Postwar Years Until You Look More Closely

By LOUIS UCHITELLE

With the war barely over, Life magazine laid out, in a 1946 photo essay, a "roseate and wondrous" American dream. A single-story stone-and-clapboard home appeared in the centerfold photo. And spread over the front lawn were the gadgets of the envisioned prosperity: a convertible, a three-burner electric stove, a small television screen embedded in a bulky wooden cabinet, a children's slide, flimsy aluminum lawn chairs, a plastic garden hose, a gasoline lawn mower.

In hindsight, Life's vision was surprisingly modest. The next quarter-century turned out to be a golden age, and as living standards rose, the furnishings of Life's American dream became commonplace, even in the homes of many working poor.

Then came 1973, one of the great turning points of the post-World War II era. It was the year in which the dollar came off the gold standard; the oil embargo struck; worldwide grain shortages developed. The widespread rise in prosperity came to a halt. Inflation, stagnant wages, shrinking unions, growing income inequality, spreading poverty and outdated factories all left scars. An economy that had been so plentiful for so many for so long suddenly followed a different path, leaving big portions of the population behind.

Now the United States appears to be at another turning point. Some of the hallmarks of the 1946–73 era are reappearing. Perhaps 1997 will turn out to be as much a landmark in American economic history as 1973. But the new age, if it materializes, is not likely to re-create the postwar sense of bounty. Instead, people are carrying into the future the residue of the stagnant years, and their compromised expectations. Rather than counting on rising prosperity, Americans are betting that by working ever harder, they may manage to cling to leadership in the world economy.

"We are not in any sense back," said Robert M. Solow of the Massachusetts Institute of Technology, a Nobel laureate in economics. "There may be some economic measures that are equal to or even better than the pre-1973 years. But not the level of well-being."

Three statistics from the old days have reappeared: a low inflation rate, an unemployment rate of less than 5 percent and a return of corporate profits, as a share of the overall economy, close to the hefty levels of the 1960's. Not since the pre-1973 era have such hallmarks of a vibrant economy coexisted so persistently.

Naturally enough, these parallels with the golden era are generating considerable optimism. At McKinsey & Company, the consulting firm, William Lewis, director of its Global Institute, declares that America's competitive laissez-faire economy should be the model for all nations.

Wired, the monthly bible of the digerati, proclaims that the global economy, led by the United States, is entering a "long boom," driven by powerful new technologies and the spread of capitalism to nearly every region of the world. And Fortune magazine, in a long article this month, states flatly of America: "These are the good old days."

But for most Americans, it is not like the good old days. Holding onto a job now takes precedence over upward mobility, or getting decent annual raises. Just prolonging an expansion has become more important than generating the robust economic growth that made the pre-1973 period golden. Corporate success in global competition has become an overriding goal, even at the price of greater wage inequality or leaving some groups behind.

Longer hours on the job have displaced the pre-1973 goal of more leisure time to use the lawn furniture in Life's "family utopia." And job insecurity—"cowed labor," in the phrasing of the economist Paul Samuelson—has become an accepted means of prolonging the economic cycle, mainly by suppressing wage increases and inflation.

"Before 1973," said Richard T. Curtin, director of the University of Michigan's consumer confidence surveys, "there was this deep belief in personal financial progress. In that sense, it is very different today. We don't expect a recession. But we no longer have much faith that our incomes will rise."

While many Americans have clearly acquired more possessions, prosperity itself has a different meaning. The pre-1973 economy often expanded in a given quarter at a 9 percent annual rate, or more. Since 1973, that has never happened. But when growth reached 3.8 percent in the fourth quarter of 1996 and a rare 5.6 percent in this year's first quarter, it was hailed with glee. "What people once called inadequate growth they are more likely to judge quite positively today," Mr. Curtin said.

Looking back, 1973 has taken on the watershed status in American economic history of years like 1870, which ushered in the Gilded Age, and 1929, the start of the Depression.

In 1973, the year the last American ground troops left Vietnam, the post-World War II generation was suddenly confronted with events that brought home just how much the global economy could alter their lives. Weak world grain harvests and the oil embargo introduced shortages, which fed inflation. So did President Richard M. Nixon's decision to take the dollar off the gold standard, allowing the currency to fall quickly in value. That made American food products more affordable abroad and they were snapped up, particularly by the Soviet Union, in a frenzy of deals that sent domestic prices soaring.

The oil and food price shocks diluted the effectiveness of the wage and price controls imposed by the Nixon Administration in 1970 to counter the costs of the war. By 1973, inflation had become the No. 1 economic issue; the inflation rate doubled that year. And partly as a result, the nation's policy makers, along with many economists, did an about-face in their view of the economy's productive capacity. The national output, once viewed as boundless, now seemed quite constrained.

Until 1973, the big economic issue had been how to generate enough demand to keep the economy growing strongly. The standard measures included tax cuts, public works projects, jobs programs, a higher minimum wage. Supply was taken for granted. The prevailing view was that companies could always jack up production without much strain. "We overestimated how much capacity could grow," said Herbert Stein, who was President Nixon's chief economic adviser in 1973.

That complacency changed by 1973. Economists and policy makers came to attribute the supply shortages, and the rapid price increases, to limited capacity. Supply could not rise to match demand after all, the new view declared, because the nation lacked the necessary productive capacity. And soon attention focused on data that increasingly suggested built-in ceilings on the output of goods and services. "When belief shifted, reality did, too," said David Collander, an economic historian at Middlebury College.

Capacity is three things. It is enough workers to make or provide all that Americans seek to buy. It is enough factories, offices, warehouses and stores, and enough machinery, computers and other equipment to produce all the goods and services that Americans want. Finally, there is productivity, or the amount that workers, using the buildings and equipment, can produce in a given time period. If productivity does not grow fast enough, supply cannot either. Demand can outstrip supply.

From 1946 to 1973, productivity rose, on average, nearly 3 percent a year. But after 1973, the annual advances averaged only 1 percent, well below the long-term trend of more than 2 percent a year in the century after the Civil War.

So, starting in 1973, the nation's policy makers increasingly dealt with the perceived ceiling on supply by restricting demand. The restraint came from the Federal Reserve, whose principal tool for regulating the economy was interest rates. If unemployment got too low, that meant not enough labor capacity, and the Fed, rather than risk wage pressures and shortages, raised interest rates to discourage spending and reduce demand. By the end of the 1970's, with inflation and unemployment rising in tandem, the Fed chose to fight inflation with higher rates, paying much less attention to unemployment.

In this atmosphere, labor's bargaining power came unglued. Corporate profits weakened along with demand. The nation's capital stock per worker—the machinery and equipment available for each worker to get the job done—has grown more slowly in each decade since 1973, despite huge investments in computers. And, starting in 1973, the United States entered what is arguably its longest period of slow economic growth since the Civil War.

The official statistics say that economic growth is still modest. But the simultaneous arrival of low inflation, low unemployment and strong profits has some economists—and many corporate executives—convinced that the official statistics must be wrong. Solve the mismeasurement, they say, and the nation's economic growth rate in recent years, supported by rising productivity, will come out looking a lot more like the pre-1973 years.

"We are not putting enough resources into getting the right data," said Lawrence Klein of the University of Pennsylvania, a Nobel laureate in economics.

The new view is this: After much painful revamping and downsizing, American companies have regained their old efficiency, particularly in manufacturing. New technology and computers have played a big role in all this. So has deregulation, giving the companies flexibility to respond quickly to changing circumstances.

But there is a different, less sanguine, way to explain the reappearance of the symptoms of the 1960's. Productivity has not risen, according to this view. The new technologies, flashy as they are, do not begin to raise output and income as did those of the past—the railroad, the electric motor, the assembly line, the telephone, the gasoline engine, the jet airliner.

"There are hints every so often," Mr. Solow of M.I.T. said, "that the productivity pace may be picking up, but they are mere hints."

Instead, the new capacity is coming largely from overseas in the form of new factories and skilled, low-wage foreign labor that is quickly at the service of American consumers in an increasingly energetic global economy.

"If a Chinese manufacturer makes something that Wal-Mart then decides it wants," Mr. Lewis of McKinsey & Company said, "it buys in China and distributes massively in the United States."

The second source of more capacity is the American worker himself. In the 1950's and 1960's, most families relied on one earner. Rising productivity pushed up incomes, making that possible. Today two or more people work in most households, and some studies say the typical American is working a greater number of hours, as well.

"People say to themselves, 'There is a possibility a year or two down the line I'll be without a job, but now the economy is booming, and if the boss offers more hours I'll take them,' " said Barry Bluestone, a University of Massachusetts economist and the co-author of one such study. "They have to, to keep up consumption."

Of such trends are turning points made—not back to the pre-1973 era or some other prosperous period, but to harder days of uncertainty. "It is impossible for anyone to say we have not entered into a new period," said Jeffrey Garten, dean of the Yale School of Management, "but too soon to say that we have."

*   *   *

February 8, 1998

GATHER THE NATIONS TO PROMOTE GLOBALIZATION

By PETER D. SUTHERLAND and JOHN W. SEWELL

It is time for a serious rethinking of how international institutions and world leaders cope with the stresses and strains of globalization. The Asian economic crisis shows that ad hoc actions by the International Monetary Fund and the World Bank are just that—temporary measures, often necessary, often effective.

At the Overseas Development Council, however, we believe that only a carefully designed summit conference on globalization can point the way to longer-term measures to prevent and anticipate future crises.

The world is starting to feel the full impact of globalization—the whirlwind of trade, investment and technological change that can build up an economy overnight and bring it low just as quickly.

Over all, the effects of globalization have been good. Prompted by unprecedented liberalization, world trade continues to expand faster than global economic output, unleashing a wave of productivity and efficiency that has created millions of jobs. Even more impressive is the stunning increase in international investment that builds roads, airports and factories in poorer countries. In the 1990's alone, foreign investors have poured $1 trillion into developing economies.

Although globalization raises living standards for many, it also increases countries' vulnerability to volatile capital markets, makes life more difficult for those dislocated by change and threatens to leave part of the world behind. It is no coincidence that the disappointing economic performance of most of the sub-Saharan region comes while trade and investment there lag behind the rest of the world.

Globalization offers four main challenges:

• To insure that its fruits extend to all. Most forecasts say economic growth in the developed world will continue to slow and that expanding markets in developing countries are needed to insure that living standards keep rising. Four billion people exist on less than $1,500 a year. Globalization can lift them from poverty and turn them into customers.

• To calm the fear that growth is destabilizing. The Asian crisis, threatening some of the most formidable economic competitors in the world, amplifies this fear of globalization. Still, the cost of being left behind by globalization is usually much greater than the potential for instability.

• To assure wealthier nations that international competition will not start a race to the bottom. Polls show that more and more people blame global trade and investment for economic upheaval in established economies. Indeed, there is ample evidence that globalization is helping most economies across the board and that stagnant wages in the United States and unemployment in Europe have other causes.

• To address the problems that are complicated by expanded trade, investment, technology and communication. The ability to confront problems like environmental degradation, disease, crime and terrorism—will depend on increasing global cooperation.

Undoubtedly, globalization of trade and investment has weakened the independence of governments and made life less predictable for many people. But those who would build barriers to trade and investment to recapture an earlier era of independence are confusing the cause and effect of globalization. In pursuit of higher living standards, we have created a new world of global markets and instant communication, delivering gains in efficiency and competition that are beyond the powers of governments. The goal is not to disenfranchise the individual but to give individuals more power to control their destinies by lowering costs, broadening choices, delivering more capital and opening more markets.

As an important first step in addressing the challenges of globalization, the O.D.C. proposes a meeting of a group of world leaders from the old industrial countries, emerging economic powers and those countries facing marginalization.

Existing international groupings are inadequate. The Group of Seven, for the leading industrial nations, is too narrow in membership; the World Bank and I.M.F. are too focused on finance.

We know that many people view summit conferences as a waste of time. Much of this sentiment comes from the annual G-7 conference, a process that started losing its sense of purpose a decade ago. But other conferences have been successful when designed around specific themes. The 1994 meeting of Pacific Rim leaders, for example, kicked off free-trade negotiations.

The Globalization Summit conference that we propose would be a one-time event, and we hope it could take place before the end of 1999. Such a conference would not be expected to produce sweeping accords on specific issues and would not supersede any other forum.

Unlike the G-7, this meeting should include countries representing all regions and levels of development. A group of about two dozen leaders would be big enough to allow broad participation, but small enough for all to have a say.

Participating governments would decide the agenda. But we propose that a committee of wise men and women chosen by those governments suggest an agenda covering the challenges of globalization.

These challenges are among the most difficult facing our world and strain the abilities of governments to confront them independently. A meeting may not solve all these problems, but collective action can be a crucial first step in generating the confidence needed to do so.

Peter D. Sutherland is chairman of the Overseas Development Council, an international policy research institute based in Washington, and chairman of Goldman Sachs International. John W. Sewell is president of the Overseas Development Council.

*　　*　　*

May 23, 1999

A BETTER SYSTEM IN THE 19TH CENTURY?

At This Rate, We'll Be Global in Another Hundred Years

By NICHOLAS D. KRISTOF

If anything seems obvious today, it is that globalization is a new and powerful force that is erasing national borders and linking the world in an unprecedented web of trade and investments. As one tycoon put it: "The world is a city."

But that was Baron Carl Meyer von Rothschild, in 1875, reacting as stock markets tumbled all around the world, in unison, feeding off each other.

Perhaps the greatest myth about globalization is that it is new. By some measures, its peak occurred a century ago, making the 20th century memorable in economic history mostly for its retreat from globalization. In some respects, only now is the world economy becoming roughly as interlinked as it was more than a century ago.

"We're still not back to where we were 100 years ago," said Charles W. Calomiris, a professor of finance and economics at the Columbia University's Graduate School of Business.

Labor is less mobile than it was in the last century. In those days, passports were unnecessary and people could travel freely from one country to the next, to visit or to work.

That mobility led 60 million Europeans to move to the Americas or Australia or elsewhere, and it helped fill up the United States. In 1900, according to the census, 14 percent of the American population was foreign born, compared to 8 percent today.

It's not just labor. The 1860's and 1870's were a golden era for free trade, and goods moved easily across borders. As late as 1879 an astonishing 95 percent of Germany's imports were still free of duty. Low trade barriers led to an explosion of trade, so that American exports soared to 7 percent of the gross national product in the late 1900's; it is 8 percent today.

Even capital seems to be less mobile now than in the 19th century. A "capital mobility index" prepared by the International Monetary Fund for a report in 1997 suggests that capital movements as a proportion of economic output are still well below the levels of the 1880's.

How can this be? A century ago, England and France invested hugely in developing countries—places like the United States, Australia and Canada. England invested a larger share of its wealth abroad at that time than it does now.

Foreign capital financed one-third of domestic investment in New Zealand and Canada in the late 19th century, and one-quarter in Sweden. In contrast, foreign capital accounted for only about 10 percent of domestic investment in emerging markets in the 1990's, according to the I.M.F.

"To me as an economic historian, it was really the 19th century that represented the birth of the global economy," said Alan M. Taylor, an economist at Northwestern University. "These days, it's just getting back to where it was 100 years ago."

Mr. Taylor suggested that 19th-century investors might well have had a larger share of their stock portfolios invested abroad than investors do today. He noted that Americans often have living rooms full of goods from all over the world, but their portfolios still tend to be focused in the United States. That discrepancy, he said, may be an anachronism related to financial markets' being less globalized than markets for goods (at least until recently).

In some respects, globalization predates the 19th century. Chinese demand for silver in the 16th through 18th centuries played a role in financing the Spanish empire and the slave trade. China absorbed perhaps half of the global production of silver, and that bolstered prices and created wealth for mining magnates in the Americas—who traded their silver for slaves. After passing through several hands, the silver was used to purchase Chinese porcelain and silk.

Although it is often said today that globalization is irreversible, it proved very reversible early in this century. After economic integration reached a peak in the late 19th century, there was an astonishing retreat after World War I and especially after the Great Depression. Since World War II, trade and international investment rose again, and they have soared in the last couple of decades.

"After the first world war, we had a massive interruption and reversal of the long-term trend," said Jagdish Bhagwati, an international economist at Columbia University. "One

Immigrants arriving at Ellis Island in an earlier version of globalization. Labor is less mobile than it was a century ago.

interpretation is that now we're just climbing back on that trend."

Still, today's globalization is new in some important ways, and arguably it touches many more people than the earlier kind.

Professor Bhagwati noted that trade in the 19th century consisted mostly of commodities. Now it is mainly manufactured goods with parts from so many countries that it is difficult to describe the finished products as made in any one nation.

Capital flows are also different, says David Hale, chief global economist of the Zurich Group, a financial services company. In the 19th century, capital movements represented the savings of a relatively small group of prosperous families in England and France who were investing for the long term. Today investments are far more broadly based, he said, and much more likely to be leveraged and short term, more flighty and speculative.

One result is that capital rushes around the globe much more quickly than ever before, and is more prone to sweep into countries and then out. Technology has created an electronic herd but as yet no electronic cowboys to control the herd.

Indeed, for a world without telephones or computers, the 19th century had its economic advantages. Output shot up and down like a roller coaster, but mostly up. Professor Calomiris has recorded 90 major banking crises over the last 20 years, and he notes that they often led to runs on national currencies. In contrast, in the period from 1870 to 1913, he can find only five major banking crises, and just one of those led to an exchange rate crisis. In many ways, he argues, 19th-century globalization worked better than today's.

"It's very hard to recapture the successes of the earlier period," Professor Calomiris said, but he thinks it is worth a try. It may seem heretical to tinker with the 21st-century process by looking over one's shoulder for models a hundred years past, but it is a reminder that globalization may well be older than nationalization.

* * *

July 13, 1999

GLOBALIZATION WIDENS RICH-POOR GAP, U.N. REPORT SAYS

By JUDITH MILLER

UNITED NATIONS, July 13—Globalization is compounding the gap between rich and poor nations and intensifying American dominance of the world's economic and cultural markets, according to the latest human development report published today by the United Nations Development Program.

The 262-page report, the 10th the program has issued, is the first to focus on the spread of the Internet and computer technology as well as the impact of globalization. It concludes that the so-called "rules of globalization" should be rewritten to save the 60 countries that are worse off than they were in 1980 from falling even further behind.

While short on specific proposals for making international markets work "for people rather than profits," the report recommends, as have previous versions, faster debt relief, redirection of aid to the poorest countries and a task force to review "global governance." It also endorses a tax of one American cent on lengthy E-mails to raise $70 billion a year that could be used to connect the world's Internetless.

The report warns that the glaring, growing inequalities in the distribution of wealth pose a "dangerous polarization" between rich and poor countries.

As in previous reports, it says little about what role the poorest nations themselves play in their predicament. It says little about the corruption and mismanagement of resources in many of the poorest countries that have discouraged foreign investment and squandered millions of dollars in foreign aid.

The report highlights the dominant role of the United States, and as a result, of English—the language of choice for 80 percent of web sites—in the new global telecommunications marketplace. It notes that 26 percent of Americans use the World Wide Web—as opposed to 3 percent of Russians, 4 one-hundredths of 1 percent of the population of South Asia and 2-10ths of 1 percent for Arab states. And it says that the United States has more computers than the rest of the world combined.

It also notes that the annual sales of General Motors are larger than the gross domestic products of Thailand or Norway, and that Ford generates more income than Saudi Arabia. America and the other rich, industrialized nations hold 97 percent of all worldwide patents, it says.

Moreover, the report says, the gap between globally well-connected and unconnected peoples is likely to grow even faster given the technology explosion. The number of Internet users today, 150 million, is expected to grow to 700 million by 2001. An American needs to save a month's salary to buy a computer; a Bangladeshi must save all his wages for eight years to do so.

Richard Jolly, a British economist and the report's main author, said the report is neither anti-American nor anti-free market. "The report specifically endorses markets as the best guarantee of efficiency," Mr. Jolly said, "but not necessary of equity."

America, he said, was among the first to appreciate the dangers of monopoly and, as such, to pass antitrust laws to dilute concentrations of economic power. The international community, he said, has yet to figure out how to deal with such global market concentrations.

*   *   *

August 28, 1999

RAYMOND VERNON, A SHAPER OF GLOBAL TRADE, DIES AT 85

By STEVE LOHR

Raymond Vernon, who helped shape the postwar system of international trade as a Government official and influenced thinking about the global economy as a scholar, died on Thursday at his home in Cambridge, Mass. He was 85.

The cause was cancer, said his daughter, Heidi Vernon.

Mr. Vernon was a member of the Marshall Plan team that guided the economic revival of Europe after World War II, and worked on the development of the International Monetary Fund and the General Agreement on Tariffs and Trade. After serving in the Government in the Securities and Exchange Commission and the State Department for nearly two decades, he went to Harvard University in 1956 and never left.

At Harvard, Mr. Vernon first led an ambitious three-year research project on the New York metropolitan region that was regarded as a pioneering work in urban studies—the work was supported by the Ford Foundation and the Rockefeller Brothers Fund. Afterward, at the Harvard Business School and later at the John F. Kennedy School of Government at Harvard, Mr. Vernon focused for decades on the study of the international economy—especially the increasing role played by multinational corporations and the limits to governmental power.

"Ray Vernon was the father of globalization long before people used that term," said Daniel Yergin, an author and business consultant. "His work has had a phenomenal effect on several generations of thinking about how the global economy works."

Mr. Vernon's books on these subjects—including "Sovereignty at Bay" in 1973, "Storm Over the Multinationals" in 1977, and "Beyond Globalism" in 1989—were influential and often far-sighted.

In "The Commanding Heights," a 1998 best seller by Mr. Yergin and Joseph Stanislaw, the authors, recognizing the scholarly foundation laid by Mr. Vernon in the study of relations between Government and the global marketplace, wrote, "It is impossible to write about these issues without acknowledging the profound intellectual impact that Prof. Raymond Vernon has had on them over the half-century."

Kim B. Clark, dean of the Harvard Business School, called Mr. Vernon "one of the most influential scholars of his generation, a true pioneer in the study of multinational corporations and the international economy."

Born on Sept. 1, 1913, in New York City, Mr. Vernon was one of four children in a family of Jewish immigrants from Russia.

His father, Hyman, drove a truck delivering seltzer water to restaurants and bars in the Bronx, and Mr. Vernon and his two brothers helped their father heft the crates of seltzer on and off the truck.

Their family name was Visotsky, but the children changed it to Vernon, beginning with Raymond's older brother, Sidney. Recalling her uncle's explanation, Heidi Vernon said he changed his name to improve his chances of being accepted into medical school. All four of the siblings—Sidney, Leo, Raymond and Corrine—earned doctoral degrees.

Mr. Vernon received a bachelor's degree from the City College of New York in 1933, and earned a Ph.D. in economics from Columbia University in 1941.

At the S.E.C., where he worked from 1935 to 1946, Mr. Vernon handled various assignments from studying the behavior of floor traders and specialists on the New York Stock Exchange to planning securities enforcement programs.

While at the State Department, he was one of the negotiators who brought Japan into the GATT trade system and helped secure nondiscriminatory treatment for Japanese exports.

In the early 1950's, as acting director of the Office of Economic Defense and Trade Policy, he oversaw trade with the Soviet-bloc nations and encouraged their trade with non-Communist countries.

Mr. Vernon's economic perspective, according to Mr. Yergin, who knew him for many years, was shaped by having grown up in the Depression and by his years at the S.E.C. "He believed in markets, but he also saw the weaknesses— where they can go wrong," Mr. Yergin said.

In 1956, Mr. Vernon went to Harvard to head the three-year study of the New York metropolitan region. His urban studies project concluded with a measured though prescient projection—continued growth and prosperity for the three-state region, but decline for broad swathes of the region's inner cities.

Mr. Vernon began his research into multinational corporations in 1965. His early work anticipated that multinationals—as efficiency-seeking enterprises—would transfer labor-intensive work on standardized products to developing nations. In "Storm Over the Multinationals" he analyzed how the pragmatic decisions of increasingly global companies held a growing sway over economic forces once controlled by governments, like trade flows and levels of investment.

Later, when European nations tried to combat the power of American multinationals by fostering the creation of state-owned "national champion" corporations, Mr. Vernon predicted early on that the tactic would prove to be poor policy.

"His view was that state-owned enterprises could not compete with the investor-owned multinationals, which are more flexible," said Robert Stobaugh, a professor emeritus at the Harvard Business School. "His research became part of the foundation for the privatization push of the 1980's."

Short and wiry, Mr. Vernon was an athlete until cancer slowed him down last year. An avid oarsman, he could be seen daily at dawn on the Charles River in his single scull. He competed for decades in the annual Head of the Charles crewing competition. Icy winters did not cool his competitive zeal. In his 80's, in fact, he set a world record for his age group in one class of "indoor sprints," rowing machines with odometers attached. He was a member of the Cambridge Boat Club for 40 years.

"One of the great sadnesses of his life," said his daughter, Heidi, "was that he was not able to be on the river these last months."

Mr. Vernon's wife of 60 years, Josephine, died in 1995. Mr. Vernon is survived by his two brothers, Sidney and Leo, and his sister, Corinne; and by his two daughters, Heidi Vernon of Newton, Mass., and Susan Vernon Gerstenfeld, also of Newton, Mass., four grandchildren and seven great-grandchildren.

Mr. Vernon, the renowned student of multinationals, was once employed by a multinational-in-the-making. In 1954 he went to work for Forrest Mars Sr., who built the Mars candy empire. Mr. Vernon was placed in charge of planning, finance and new products. He oversaw the development effort that led to chocolate-covered peanut M & M's.

The new peanut variety was a success, and, in the candy industry, Mr. Vernon was called "the man who put the crunch in M & M's."

Mr. Vernon's foray into the private sector was short-lived, since he went to Harvard after less than two years in the candy business. But he would always talk of his M & M exploits at family gatherings, impressing the younger members of the Vernon clan, recalled his daughter, Heidi. "He told the grandchildren that he was the person who figured out how to get the letter M on each and every piece of candy," she said, "and they'd all believe him."

* * *

November 28, 1999

THE NEXT BIG DIALECTIC

By KURT ANDERSEN

I've always been skeptical of people who predict the future professionally, of the Alvin Tofflers and John Naisbitts as well as the Jeane Dixons and Pat Robertsons. For one thing, it's pretty much impossible to make confident predictions without sounding portentous and creepy. And purporting to describe the warp and woof of life 100 years from now is an extreme folly. On the other hand, the time frame insures that no one will be able to tell me I was wrong if, in 2100, it turns out I was wrong.

At this end of this century, as we bask happily and stupidly in the glow of our absolute capitalist triumph, no long-range historical forecasters are considered more insanely wrong-headed than Karl Marx and Friedrich

Engels. Yet the death of Communism makes this moment a fine one to consider the emergence of Marxism 150 years ago as a historical phenomenon, economically determined, rather than as the social and moral debacle it became. In fact, looking back, Marx and Engels seem prescient about the capitalist transformation of life and work. Writing about globalization in "Principles of Communism" in 1847, Engels sounds very 1999.

"A new machine invented in England deprives millions of Chinese workers of their livelihood within a year's time," he wrote. "In this way, big industry has brought all the people of the earth into contact with each other, has merged all local markets into one world market, has spread civilization and progress everywhere and has thus ensured that whatever happens in civilized countries will have repercussions in all other countries."

He failed only to mention Euro-denominated McDonald's menus and MTV.

In "Das Kapital," Marx also foretold the present cyber-age, in which computers design toasters and skyscrapers, and software is designed by other software: "Modern industry had therefore itself to take in hand the machine, its characteristic instrument of production, and to construct machines by machines. . . . Machinery, simultaneously with the increasing use of it . . . appropriated, by degrees, the fabrication of machines proper."

Marx and Engels were right in the middle of the transformation. Just before their births, during the final years of the 18th century, a handful of machinists and tinkerers—John Wilkinson, Richard Arkwright, Eli Whitney, a few others—had ignited the Industrial Revolution with their amazing devices to cut screws, pump water, spin wool and gin cotton. Those machines, hitched to James Watt's steam engine, begat factories and steamships and railroads, which begat industrial capitalism on a frenzied new global scale, which, just a half century after the first revolutionary mechanical marvels, begat Marx.

Now, during the final years of the 20th century, a handful of scientists and tinkerers—William Shockley, Jack Kilby, Robert Noyce, Jim Clark, Tim Berners-Lee, a few others—have ignited the current technological revolution with their amazing new devices: the transistor, the integrated circuit, the microcomputer, the World Wide Web. The PC and the Internet begat a new fluidity of capital and information, which is begetting postindustrial capitalism on a frenzied new global scale, which will surely beget some radical and infectious critique of this radically new order.

In other words, the 21st century will have its Marx. This next great challenger of the governing ideological paradigm, this hypothetical cyber-Marx, is one of our children or grandchildren or great-grandchildren, and he or she could appear in Shandong Province or Cairo or San Bernardino County. By 2100, give or take a couple of decades, it's a good bet that free-market, private-property capitalism will be under siege once again, shaken as in 1848 and 1917 and the 1930's by the tremors that the magnificent and ferocious system itself

unleashes. History does not always repeat itself, but as Mark Twain may have said, it rhymes.

What will this next great "ism" look like?

The ascendant revolutionary ideology of 2100 won't be Luddite. Theodore Kaczynski was the Ned Lud of this cycle, an angry, violent lunatic of no real historical significance. Marx, for his part, was not opposed to the new technology of the Industrial Revolution—it was the steam-powered weaving machines and railroads and all the rest that were going to allow his collectivist utopia to emerge.

In "Das Kapital," he wrote that "improved communications" had been the key to increased productivity and prosperity, that the "last 50 years have brought about a revolution in this field . . . the entire globe is being girdled by telegraph wires . . . the time of circulation of a shipment of commodities to East Asia, at least 12 months in 1847, has now been reduced to almost as many weeks . . . and the efficacy of the capital involved in it has been more than doubled or trebled." It seems improbable that the next great world-historical agitator will demonize technology qua technology.

The poor are always with us. The unequal distribution, among nations and classes, of digital resources—hardware, software, communications bandwidth—will help shape the early versions of the revolutionary ideology. Today's self-justifying optimists in Redmond and Silicon Valley claim that the price of computers and telecommunications will continue to fall to the point that everyone on earth, rich and poor, will share in the millennial bounty. Maybe. Eventually. But for the next couple of decades it's going to be ugly as the computer-rich get much richer and the computer-poor even poorer.

The present money moment won't last. As the digital age finally has its first and second (and third and fourth and fifth) financial busts over the next half-century, the particular magic spell of circa-2000 laissez-faire hyper-capitalism will be broken. The computer revolution won't be turned back, but the financial giddiness will subside.

On this classic economic idea, late-20th-century Wall Street bears and 19th-century communist pioneers agree. "Ever since the beginning of this century," Engels wrote, "the condition of industry has constantly fluctuated between periods of prosperity and periods of crisis; nearly every five to seven years, a fresh crisis has intervened, always with the greatest hardship for workers." After a few periods of serious 21st-century hardship, with I.R.A.'s and 401(k)'s reduced in value by half overnight, alternative social and economic arrangements might not seem so preposterous.

The great new philosophical and political schism of the 21st century will concern computers and their status as creatures rather than machines. In my lifetime, the sentimental regard for computers' apparent intelligence—their dignity—will resemble that now accorded gorillas and chimps. And it will not stop there. In his book, "The Age of Spiritual Machines: When Computers Exceed Human Intelligence," Ray Kurzweil, the computer scientist, quite convincingly predicts that around 2030 computers will begin to seem sentient—that they will "claim to be conscious." And by the end of the century, he writes, there will no longer be "any clear distinction between humans and computers."

I find his scenario altogether plausible. And as it unfolds, I am certain that this astonishing new circumstance—machines that think, machines that feel—will provoke political and religious struggles at least as profound and ferocious as the earlier wars over Christianity, human rights and abortion. A machine-liberationist movement will arise. And by 2100, the 21st century will have its Gandhi, too.

Kurt Andersen is the author of "Turn of the Century," a novel.

* * *

December 20, 1999

GLOBAL ECONOMY DANCES TO POLITICAL TUNE

By DAVID E. SANGER

WASHINGTON—A decade ago, it would have been hard to imagine that at the end of the century the world economy would mix unparalleled American ascendancy with such pervasive global anxiety, or that free-marketeers would be celebrating the triumph of market capitalism while so many around the globe questioned the cost of its victory.

After all, as 1989 came to a close it looked like the end of this century and most of the next would belong to Japan and its neighbors. Instead, the 1990's proved to be Japan's lost decade, and a buoyant Asia's rude awakening about the laws of economic gravity.

In 1989, the Berlin Wall had just fallen, and the wrenching economic and political adjustments to freer markets that would follow were just beginning. In retrospect, the predictions about the contours of those adjustments missed the mark: Nations like Poland made the shift much faster than expected, but the early enthusiasm about the speed of Russia's move to a market economy proved wildly optimistic. Instead, 10 years later, the West's billions of aid dollars intended to bolster capitalism in its own image seem to have been largely wasted, though it is unclear that a different strategy would have worked any better.

And who a decade ago could have anticipated the stresses of globalization? How it would tear up the insides of the Nissan worker who told a Japanese newspaper recently that for most of his life he had naively believed that "lifetime employment meant you had a job for life?" Or how a small-town American investor whose closest encounter with Thailand before 1997 had been seeing the film "The King and I" could find her life roiled by a previously unknown relationship between the health of her pension fund and the inability of Thailand's finance ministry to monitor its banks' lending portfolios?

Finally, who would have imagined that in the last weeks of the fading millennium, with American unemployment at record lows and prosperity at record highs, the brewing anxieties of a decade of global change could spill out into a wild scene on the streets of Seattle? Or that seemingly everyone with a grievance about capitalism's worst excesses would seize the opportunity to vent anger at the World Trade Organization, a group most Americans were only vaguely aware existed before the first week of December?

Of course, none of this has evoked much humility in the millennial forecasting business. In the past few months, it seems as if prognosticators worldwide have been turning out impressive-looking charts plotting the life expectancy of the American expansion, or the speed of the Asian recovery, or the future of the euro. (Each such forecaster might find useful a copy of the Congressional Budget Office's 1996 projections for what the budget deficit would look like today, which only missed by about $305 billion.)

The lesson of the 1990's, at home and abroad, is that global politics and global economic fortunes are not only inseparable, but each makes the other almost impossible to predict.

Global economic tensions, however, are easier to scope out than global economic outcomes. And tensions abound, all set to play out over the next few years. Here are a few:

Seattle was just the start. Over the next five years, the backlash against globalization will worsen.

Sure, the protestors who helped derail the world trade talks in late November and early December could not agree among themselves whether to order a latte or a cappuccino. And it is highly unlikely that the extremists in Seattle, those who think the trade organization's officials thunder around in black helicopters, will move to the forefront of the debate. But the mainstream groups that made themselves heard—the labor unions and the environmentalists, the Ralph Nader followers and those fearful of a loss of national sovereignty—are starting to articulate their worries far more effectively than ever before. And they have a lot of allies around the world.

Almost any place one lands these days—Tokyo or Bombay or Brussels—the complaint is the same: the United States is trying to rig the global trading system to benefit its own, and its own want to own the world. Of course, the Clinton administration wants the Internet to be tariff-free because the biggest beneficiaries will be Microsoft and America Online and the American merchants who are kings of the Web. Of course, there is nothing new in such complaints: Europe has been fretting about American multinationals since the 1960's. But America's emergence as the world's unchallenged military and economic power, and its role as the largest exporter of popular culture, have ignited a new level of passion.

"The question we get from the developing world is, 'What's in this for us?' " Charlene Barshefsky, the United States trade representative, said as she nursed the wounds of Seattle. "They want to reopen many of the market liberalizations of the past decade, and get more time or a better deal. We hear it every week."

Moreover, the political impetus to use trade to solve the world's other ills seems likely to accelerate. Already the

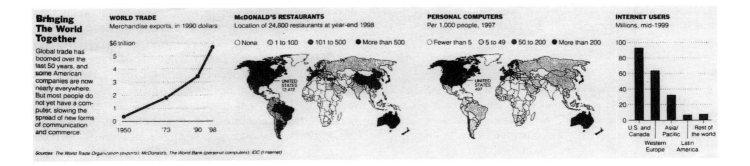

Bringing The World Together

Global trade has boomed over the last 50 years, and some American companies are now nearly everywhere. But most people do not yet have a computer, slowing the spread of new forms of communication and commerce.

WORLD TRADE Merchandise exports, in 1990 dollars

McDONALD'S RESTAURANTS Location of 24,800 restaurants at year-end 1998
○ None ◐ 1 to 100 ◑ 101 to 500 ● More than 500

PERSONAL COMPUTERS Per 1,000 people, 1997
○ Fewer than 5 ◐ 5 to 49 ◑ 50 to 200 ● More than 200

INTERNET USERS Millions, mid-1999

Sources: The World Trade Organization (exports); McDonald's; The World Bank (personal computers); IDC (Internet)

same international community that insisted in 1998 the world would end if Russia were not bailed out is pressing to cut off the I.M.F.'s lending to Moscow to protest Russian tactics in Chechnya. Such choices—between our moral and political imperatives and our economic sensibilities—are getting harder every year, around the world. And the drive to link core labor standards and environmental standards to trade agreements will heighten the tension, pitting industrial democracies against developing nations that feel certain the system is being rigged to make it harder for them to get on the road to prosperity by raising exports.

Maybe none of this will ultimately affect global trade, which has risen fifteenfold since 1950. But it could well make international economics the new battlefield.

The digital divide around the world will get a lot worse before it gets any better.

The past five years have seen a sharp three-way split among the players in the global economy. The United States leads the way in the overconnected sweepstakes: Its penetration of personal computers, cell phones and Internet access is at or near the top of the charts, fueling the new economy, if one exists. Europe follows closely, with Japan belatedly kicking into e-gear.

But many countries in the world are still struggling with getting hard-wired phones into houses. They have pockets of high-technology skills, but no infrastructure.

And then comes James D. Wolfensohn, the president of the World Bank, with the uncomfortable reminder that half the world's six billion people today live on less than $2 a day. Building digital networks is not likely to be their first priority.

On the one hand, this is an enormous economic opportunity; as e-commerce spreads it can insert the poorest nations into the global economy at a faster pace than ever before. But it seems just as likely that the new economy will speed the concentration of wealth in the hands of the richest nations, leaving others farther behind. And even within the wealthiest nations, the access of minorities and the poor to computers and the Internet is lagging greatly, suggesting that the global divide may become increasingly visible at home, too.

Japan is coming back, and China is speeding its transition to a market economy. But scratch beneath the surface and you discover nasty, unresolved battles that will continue for years.

Japan and China are the big bets of the next five years, and the riskiest.

No question there is good news at last from Japan. Foreign investors are finally snapping up Japanese assets and taking the lead (and the blame) in paring down bloated companies and getting rid of excess workers. Consumers are gradually spending again. The world's second-largest economy may soon start acting like it wants to hold on to that standing.

But as always in Japan, just as the news gets better, the political will begins to falter. Prime Minister Keizo Obuchi, facing re-election, is suddenly pulling back from the toughest economic reforms. "Basically, I do support restructuring," he told the Far Eastern Economic Review recently, "but not the kind of drastic restructuring common in the U.S. and Europe." Translation: No more layoffs on my watch. Still, Japanese cognoscenti whisper reassuringly that the prime minister should be ignored: Japan Inc. is now taking its marching orders from the global marketplace, even though politicians cannot admit that the old Japanese model is dead.

That is hard to believe. The next 5 or 10 years will be a constant battle between market reformers and government interventionists. If the market reformers win, it will be largely because the government has run out of cash to keep priming the pump. But the rest of the world is watching, because if Japan can resist American-style capitalism, there is hope they can, too.

China is an even more complex case. Its agreement to make vast openings in its market in return for entry into the World Trade Organization is the start of a battle, not the end of one. It will pit entrenched industries that want to fight the opening against government officials, led by Prime Minister Zhu Rongji, who contend that only competition will whip China's most inefficient industries into shape. But it will also pit the government against itself. Mr. Zhu is betting that the Communist party can open the economy without losing control over the political system. After all, Singapore did. But Singapore is a very, very small place.

The United States Treasury Secretary, Lawrence H. Summers, told the Trilateral Commission early in the year that the fate of the world economy depended on the fate of the American economy, that the fate of the American economy depended on the fate of the stock market and that the fate of the American stock market depended on a small handful of stocks that are trading at remarkable premiums.

He was just being flip, right?

Mr. Summers said soon after his comments were reported that he had been speaking off the record; that his view, as conveyed by people at the meeting, was greatly oversimplified, and that, as treasury secretary, he did not speculate about markets.

Even if Mr. Summers's view was oversimplified, he is clearly worried that some market segments have outpaced the strong United States economic fundamentals, like low unemployment, high productivity and continued growth, that he is always talking about. But listen to him carefully, and it seems as if the new big risk to the global economy may actually be close to home.

* * *

January 1, 2000

ECONOMIC THINKING FINDS A FREE MARKET

By FLOYD NORRIS

Will the forces of globalism continue to push the world toward American-style capitalism?

As the 21st century begins, advocates of the free market have no doubt that they have won the economic argument. Socialism is dead. Moreover, as a means of creating wealth and material progress, American capitalism seems to be clearly superior to the Asian variety, with its greater level of government planning, or the European version, with its emphasis on social welfare and protection of workers from losing their jobs.

The proponents see the coming era as a period of global transformation: prosperity will rise around the world as technological change and global integration spread along with democracy. "This new boom has the potential to pull the whole world into it, allowing literally billions of people to move into middle-class lifestyles," Peter Schwartz, Peter Leyden and Joel Hyatt write in their 1999 book, "The Long Boom: A Vision for the Coming Age of Prosperity."

Certainly capitalism has extended to areas where it was previously unfamiliar. From Ghana to Mongolia, stock markets have sprung up, even as the world's largest—the New York Stock Exchange—scrambles to hold on to its position as technology opens up new ways to trade. Private enterprise is the dominant economic force, and it is hard to see that changing soon.

Moreover, the technological revolution brought on by computers is tying the world together as never before. Peter F. Drucker, the business historian and management thinker, compares the effect of the Internet to that of the railroad. By lowering transportation costs, the railroad made national businesses possible. Now, with information available instantly, the Internet allows even small businesses to have global ambitions, and it places pressure on nations to relax regulations and cut taxes that make it more difficult for their businesses to compete.

That pressure is to follow the American path. By making it relatively easy to start companies—and to hire and fire workers—the American way has produced innovation. Microsoft, the company that investors think is worth more than any other, did not exist a quarter-century ago. Without such flexibility, the computer revolution might not have been so dominated by American companies.

But the forces of globalism and American capitalism face resistance. The Asian economic collapse in 1997 brought home the risk to countries of dealing with huge, uncontrolled capital flows. Free trade may bring overall benefits, but there are losers whose political influence may be substantial. The protests at the World Trade Organization meeting in Seattle last month united those who fear world government with those who want stricter standards on the environment and the treatment of workers.

The suspicion has grown, even among Americans, that globalism is really a means of helping big business. In a poll of Americans by the Program on International Policy Attitudes at the University of Maryland, 54 percent said that Washington trade officials gave "too much" consideration to the views of multinational corporations; 73 percent believed "too little" attention was paid to the views of "people like you."

That viewpoint has little support among major political leaders, but it could yet resonate. Jude Wanniski of Polyconomics, a conservative research organization, complains that multinational corporations want "an international trade bureaucracy that serves their interest all the time."

"This means," he said, "having more international government under their control, beyond the reach of ordinary Americans who do not understand the imperatives of this new bang-bang world of cyberspace and megadeals."

That such resentment has appeared now—with the American economy booming and the current period of growth soon to become the longest in its history—may indicate just how vigorous the debate could become, if and when the economy stumbles.

It may be worth recalling that a century ago there was also a trend toward globalization. Improved transport and instantaneous transmission of information—remember the telephone and telegraph?—were hailed as being certain to bring the world together. Trade barriers fell—until World War I. Charlene Barshefsky, the United States trade representative, says that much of what has been accomplished in trade talks over the last couple of decades has simply removed roadblocks that were erected between the two World Wars. Had people acted in an economically rational way, the gains in free trade made a century ago might not have been lost. But they did not.

The economy a millennium ago was far different from ours, but it may hold a lesson as a new millennium begins. In their book, "The Year 1000," Robert Lacey and Danny Danziger write that honey was the principal source of sweetness. "People paid taxes with it, and it was a lucky day when a swarm of bees settled in your thatch," they write. Not only was honey valuable, but beeswax provided the best candles, and thus the most reliable lighting system.

"Thus," observed Marc Faber, a Hong Kong-based money manager, in a review of that book he sent to clients, "it is probable that honey and beeswax were as precious a commodity in medieval times as the Microsoft operating system is today."

When sugar arrived in Europe, the value of honey collapsed. Mr. Faber thinks something similar will happen to the value of Microsoft one day.

That change is not on the immediate horizon. For now, the information economy is king, and its effects include pressures on other countries to come closer to American-style capitalism. The extent to which opposition to global capitalism slows or even reverses that trend may be the most important economic story of the next few decades.

*   *   *

January 2, 2000

ONCE AND AGAIN

By PAUL KRUGMAN

CAMBRIDGE, Mass.—Beginnings are always difficult: even the most tough-minded writer finds it hard to avoid portentousness. And since this is a quadruple beginning (new year, new century, new millennium, and, for me, new column), I won't even try. What follows are some broad opening-night thoughts about the world economy.

I deliberately say world economy, not American economy. Whatever else they may have been, the 90's were the decade of globalization. Both the bad news (it was a banner decade for financial crises) and the good (living standards in much of the world continued to rise, in some cases—China—spectacularly) were closely tied to the ever-increasing integration of national economies with each other, to the seemingly unstoppable logic of growing trade and investment.

Or is it unstoppable? You see, we've been here before.

Historians sometimes call it the First Global Economy: the era from the mid-19th century onward in which new technologies of transportation and communication made large-scale international trade and investment possible for the first time. In their quest to create that global economy, to abolish the traditional constraints of geography, engineers accomplished miracles—laying telegraph cables beneath the Atlantic, digging tunnels through the Alps and building paths between the seas. The Panama Canal, whose construction required breakthroughs not only in earth-moving technology but in medical science, was the high-water mark of the age (literally: the locks raise ships 85 feet above sea level).

And just as the canal reached completion, the global economy fell apart.

To some extent, the First Global Economy was a casualty of war. The Panama Canal and the Western Front both went into action in August 1914. The war and its indirect consequences—hyperinflation and political instability in Germany, isolationism in the United States, and so on—partly explain why the forces of globalization went into a retreat that by 1945 left the world economy thoroughly Balkanized. But the truth is that even before 1914, though the volume of trade and investment continued to expand, the globalist idea was on the defensive. Intelligent men might explain that wars were no longer worth fighting and borders obsolete; a sophisticated, cosmopolitan elite—like the U.S.-educated technocrats who ran Mexico until they were overthrown in 1911—might move freely between continents; but the political foundations for a global economy were never properly laid, and at the first serious shock the structure collapsed.

We are now living in the era of the Second Global Economy—a world economy reconstructed, largely under American leadership, over the past half century. It took a long time to put Humpty Dumpty back together again: the share of world output entering into trade didn't reach its pre-1914 levels until the 1970's, and large-scale investment in "emerging markets"—that is, places that are to today's world economy what America was to our great-grandfathers'—has revived only in the last decade. But this time the economic achievement is built on stronger foundations—isn't it?

Well, yes—but maybe not strong enough. True, we have gotten better at making the distinction between commerce and conquest—trade no longer follows the flag and blatant imperialism is out of style. (We handed the Panama Canal back last month.) And Western nations seem to have more or less grown out of the saber-rattling nationalism that led to catastrophe back in 1914. But now as then the global idea is very much a minority persuasion, all too easily portrayed as an ideology of and for a rootless cosmopolitan elite that is out of touch with ordinary people.

For that, surely, is the lesson of the trashing of the World Trade Organization meeting in Seattle last November. Not that the protesters were right: it is a sad irony that the cause that has finally awakened the long-dormant American left is that of—yes!—denying opportunity to third-world workers. But though the facts may be on the side of the free traders, though global trade really ought to have mass public support, one can hardly deny that the opponents are winning the propaganda war. For the moment, as long as it seems to deliver the goods and services, globalization is tolerated; but it is not loved.

The big economic question for the next century, in other words, is really political: can the Second Global Economy build a constituency that reaches beyond the sort of people who congregate at Davos? If not, it will eventually go the way of the first.

*   *   *

May 7, 2000

GLOBALIZATION: UNSPEAKABLE, YES, BUT IS IT REALLY EVIL?

By JOSEPH KAHN

The media coverage has faded. The tripartite enforcers of global capitalism—the World Bank, the International Monetary Fund and the World Trade Organization—still make loans and settle trade disputes. But the protesters who rang the alarm about global economics in Seattle and in Washington left a distinct legacy: they made globalization a naughty word.

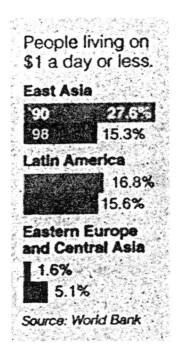

People living on $1 a day or less.

East Asia

'90 — 27.6%
'98 — 15.3%

Latin America

16.8%
15.6%

Eastern Europe and Central Asia

1.6%
5.1%

Source: World Bank

Stanley Fischer, the No. 2 official at the International Monetary Fund, says world leaders will have to come up with another way of describing economic integration if the idea is ever to become popular again. Lawrence H. Summers, the Treasury secretary, delivered a long address on world development policies recently without so much as mentioning the term.

Among both mainstream economists and their left-leaning critics, it has become axiomatic that globalization leaves too many poor people behind. At best, it is described as a blunt instrument for growth that inflicts collateral damage on people who do not have the education or resources to defend themselves. At worst, it actually increases poverty, worsens social divisions and shifts power from people and governments to multinational corporations.

Mark Weisbrot, an economist at the Center for Economic and Policy Research in Washington whose writings are part of the protesters' intellectual canon, argues that globalization, as defined by the American government and the Washington-based lending institutions, has systematically failed to help poor countries grow wealthy.

"No nation has ever pulled itself out of poverty under the conditions that Washington currently imposes on underdeveloped countries," he says.

That assertion is disputed, of course, but less vigorously than might be expected. The idea that globalization has done more to help the haves than the have-nots has become economically correct—a litmus test for progressive internationalists.

A growing body of evidence does suggest that 1990's-style global integration did far less to relieve poverty and inequality than its early supporters predicted. But the record also shows that the process is probably less economically harmful than some critics maintain.

The World Bank recently released one of the few comprehensive attempts to assess the impact of globalization. The bank, a leading target of some protesters, has also been flagellating itself recently, pledging to become a more effective poverty fighter. And its report, "Assessing Globalization," is less than cheery.

The report found that progress on poverty reduction has been glacial. The number of people in extreme poverty—surviving on $1 a day or less—fell only slightly from 1990 to 1998, from 1.3 billion to 1.2 billion. The population in developing countries increased during that period, so the change in percentage terms was somewhat greater, from 29 percent to 24 percent.

The only region of the world where poverty declined much was East Asia—from 27.6 percent to 15.3 percent. It barely budged in sub-Saharan Africa and actually increased in the former Soviet bloc.

The report also found that many nations that opened their doors widest to foreign trade saw income accrue mostly to the rich. China, the United States and Latin America all had bigger gaps between rich and poor by the end of the decade.

The figures help explain why few people these days talk about globalization as if it were a new Enlightenment. But if the era of globalization has hardly been one of universal prosperity, it is probably too early to conclude that economic integration is actually to blame for stubborn poverty.

The report finds plenty of support for the premise that economic growth is the best antidote to poverty, and that the most open nations are usually, though not always, the fastest growers, whether wealthy or poor.

It also finds some nations where the gap between rich and poor narrowed, rather than widened, as reliance on trade grew. That suggests, at a minimum, that the correlation between economic integration and social inequality is inexact. Other factors—effective government policies, strong labor laws—are also at work.

In fact, the only safe conclusion about globalization's impact may be that no sweeping conclusion is possible. East Asia and the former Soviet bloc, for example, both globalized extensively in the 1990's, to diametrically opposed economic results.

Or consider another example. Incomes in both African and Latin American nations were growing faster before globalization took hold than they have lately. But it's hard to say globalization is to blame, since Latin America has opened wide to trade and investment recently, but Africa has by some measures become less open.

The protesters were right—globalization is no panacea. But neither does it seem to be the disease some critics claim.

*   *   *

December 31, 2000

GLOBALIZATION GROWS UP AND GETS POLITICAL

By FAREED ZAKARIA

George W. Bush's appointments of Colin Powell, Condoleezza Rice and Donald Rumsfeld as secretary of state, national security adviser and defense secretary, respectively, have been met with general acclaim. But some commentators have wondered how this new team, which is better versed in political and military affairs than in economics (though Mr. Rumsfeld has an impressive background in business) will be able to manage American foreign policy in the age of globalization.

You know the argument: The world has been utterly transformed in recent years, globalization is sweeping old models aside, technology is bringing us together faster and more furiously than ever before, markets rule and governments follow. And did I mention the Internet changes everything?

Actually, there's a great deal of truth to these ideas, though they are often expressed with irrational exuberance. Globalization is a revolutionary force, and it is here to stay. But the globalization of the next 10 years is going to be different from that of the last 10. American foreign policy will have to focus less on the economics of globalization than on the politics.

In the 1990's, in the first phase of globalization, economics reigned supreme. After decades of flirtation with statism, countries around the world dismantled economic controls, deregulated industries and liberalized their economies. As capital markets flexed their muscles, governments began to think that they had little power over their own destinies. They were forced into a golden straitjacket, limiting their policy options to propitiate the long bond.

But as we enter the second decade of globalization, countries have come to realize that the constraints of capitalism are not nearly as tight or as predictable as many had believed. In Europe, governments are reforming their economies but have retained their cherished welfare states. And they are doing well, none more than Sweden, where the government spends over 60 percent of the gross domestic product. Several European countries—Sweden, Britain and Denmark among them—chose to defy the conventional wisdom and have not adopted the single European currency. Markets have not punished them; indeed, they have been rewarded.

Meanwhile, in negotiations over everything from genetically modified food to cultural affairs, economics is taking a back seat to politics. Europeans have decided that they are willing to pay a price in inefficiency for their political values (no matter how strange those values might seem on this side of the Atlantic).

Ignoring the political dimensions of globalization has already had its costs. Nowhere was this made clearer than in the East Asian economic crisis of the late 90's—particularly in Indonesia. In the wake of that crisis, the International Monetary Fund and Washington helped topple President Suharto's regime, hoping that radical economic and political reform would follow. Instead, the entire country has been unhinged. Over the last two years, the Indonesian economy has contracted almost 50 percent, wiping out 20 years of economic growth, throwing tens of millions of people below the poverty line and embroiling the country in ethnic violence.

If there is an image that reflects the diplomacy of the 1990's, it is that famous picture of Michael Camdessus, the I.M.F. chief, arms folded, glowering over President Suharto while the old man signed on the dotted line, agreeing to the fund's terms for a bailout. There will be no more such photo-ops.

Consider the contrasting fate of Malaysia, which has recovered from the East Asian crisis as fast as any of his neighbors despite the recalcitrance of its strongman, Mahathir Mohammed. As one Indonesian scholar commented sadly: "Many in my country wish that Suharto had done what Mahathir did—defied the I.M.F., moved at our own pace—and we would be better off today."

Or consider trade. Talks over the expansion of global trade are stalled—and not because of a few hundred latte-sipping protesters dancing outside World Bank meetings, though they are also part of the new politics of globalization. Third-world countries believe that without some concessions from the West, these talks have become a one-way street in which they alone open their markets. But Western countries are not about to get rid of domestic subsidies that have powerful constituencies, like European and American farmers, no matter how they distort global markets. Globalization goes only so far.

And then there is the Middle East, where the seductions of globalization have not fared well. President Clinton, Shimon Peres and others painted a picture of a new Middle East, based on cooperation, economic interdependence and growth. But Yasir Arafat understands that in such a world the Palestinian Authority—and he personally—would not prosper. Countries like Ireland and Israel benefit greatly from their access to the global economy—and so they take political risks. But most of the world is governed by political elites who dare not liberalize because to do so would unsettle their own power—think of Africa, Central Asia and South Asia. To them, globalization is not an opportunity but a threat. If there's no gold to be had, why put on the straitjacket?

Globalization is the dominant force in the world today and a profoundly progressive one. But when Washington advocates economic liberalization, it should bear in mind the political context in which particular countries, and regimes, exist. When it tries to expand free trade, it must broker political compromises to move negotiations forward. In dealing with Europe, for example, it will have to use political persuasion to modify the European Union's views on agriculture, not to mention those on sanctions against Iraq.

Finally there is the underside of globalization. The bloody crossroads of the next decade will be where globalization meets terrorism. All the wondrous developments of the new economy—falling costs, fewer borders, easy communications—help international terrorists and criminals as much as they do businessmen. And only well-exercised power—military, economic and political—can meet this new threat.

So the challenge faced by the new Bush administration is not the challenge of the 1990's. Recall that the last era of globalization, in the late 19th century, was also fast and furious. It also saw the birth of fantastic new technologies, like electricity, that changed the world. It also raised millions out of poverty. And it was undone not by bad economics but by bad politics—nationalist rivalries that led to World War I. Today, the economics of globalization are in good shape. The politics are not.

Fareed Zakaria has been appointed editor of Newsweek International.

THE MANY FACES OF GLOBALIZATION

February 28, 1993

CAPITALIST DIASPORAS

TRIBES: How Race, Religion, and Identity Determine Success in the New Global Economy
By Joel Kotkin
343 pp. New York: Random House. $24.

By GARY Y. OKIHIRO

As Joel Kotkin describes Edmond de Rothschild, he "sits nervously, pondering his far-flung concerns." The chairman of over a dozen financial companies around the globe, from the West Indies to Tel Aviv, and the head of his family's Paris-based Compagnie Financiere, Edmond de Rothschild does not rest easy on his vast wealth but occupies himself in trying to multiply the family fortune. "We are different for a simple reason," he tells Mr. Kotkin, the author of "Tribes: How Race, Religion and Identity Determine Success in the New Global Economy." "Many families disappear in one generation because they don't realize that . . . you must have discipline and that you have to work whether you like it or not."

Like Edmond de Rothschild, Vinny Gupta, an Asian-American entrepreneur in Canton, Ohio, reflects on his success and on the declining work ethic. "The fundamental thing is that by and large people in America have forgotten what the next world can be," Mr. Gupta says. "They think luxury is a birthright." Mr. Gupta tells Mr. Kotkin that he arrived in America in the early 1970's, intent on getting a degree in industrial technology and returning to his family's small steel business in India. Instead he worked as a metallurgist in several American foundries and studied the business with an intensity that surpassed his American counterparts. "I'd get to spend 10 minutes talking business and they'd spend two and a half hours eating lunch. . . . talking about scuba diving and what they'd do on their vacations," Mr. Gupta recalls. Eventually he bought a crumbling plant, invested in new machinery and pushed the company's sales from less than $2 million to about $10 million over a seven-year period.

Although these two stories might have been taken from a book about the virtues of hard work, Mr. Kotkin, the co-author, with Yoriko Kishimoto, of "The Third Century," uses them to show why various ethnic groups—the Jews, Japanese, British, Chinese and Asian Indians—have managed to become economic successes.

As he sees it, the modern world is a vast network crisscrossed by labor and capital, markets and ideas, goods and services. This network, which connects the farthest reaches of the globe into a unified system, makes a shambles of state borders and national identities. And the people who best negotiate this complicated web, he believes, are the ethnic groups that are dispersed around the world. These "global tribes," as Mr. Kotkin calls them, are able to work the economic currents. "As the conventional barriers of nation-states and regions become less meaningful under the weight of global economic forces," he predicts, "it is likely such dispersed peoples—and their worldwide business and cultural networks—will increasingly shape the economic destiny of mankind."

The end of the cold war did not bring an end to history, Mr. Kotkin argues. Rather, new forces came into play, reconfiguring history's face. Communism's collapse, he believes, boosted the prospects for global tribes, and positioned ethnicity as "a defining factor in the evolution of the global economy."

Although Mr. Kotkin's global tribes—the Jews, the British, the Japanese, the Chinese and the Asian Indians—occupy different corners of the world and have very different histories, all hold in common a strong sense of ethnic identity and solidarity, a belief in scientific progress and "historically conditioned values" that help them succeed economically. "In the post-cold-war era, where ideology has faded and peoples seek definition from the collective past," Mr. Kotkin writes, "dispersed groups such as global tribes seem particularly well adapted to succeed within today's progressively more integrated worldwide economic system."

The paradox of global tribes, he notes, is that though they conjure up images of anachronistic, chauvinistic, insular and regressive social tendencies, the members of global tribes are quite the opposite—quintessential cosmopolitans, scientists and capitalists whose values of self-sufficiency, hard work, thrift, education and family solidarity enable them to succeed economically. Their values set the global tribes apart from others; they aspire to achieve a universal world order based on technological determinism. And that, Mr. Kotkin says, is "the road that can lead, ultimately, toward a workable cosmopolis."

Despite the apparent common-sense appeal of this analysis, it is seriously flawed. His reasoning about how global tribes form is as follows: If there is a culture that holds to the Protestant work ethic (or some version thereof) and its members migrate seeking economic opportunity throughout the world, they will create a commercial diaspora, and their work ethic and group solidarity will enable them to dominate local finance, production and trade. The centers of capital accumulation that they set up will then become linked to form "a seamless global network . . . united by a common ethnic identity."

But in what sense do the Jews, British, Japanese, Chinese and Asian Indians constitute tribes, kinship groups with a common ancestor? Each of Mr. Kotkin's global tribes features a huge range of national, ethnic and racial differences. And those who share the cultural values that supposedly enable prosperity are not only the very rich but also the laborers. Members of global tribes, in other words, are not uniformly affluent, and this indicates that culture alone does not determine economic success. Unless one can demonstrate the unity of the economic activities of each ethnic group, one cannot credit the financial achievements of individuals like Vinny Gupta and families like the Rothschilds to their ethnic affiliation. Besides, even if one supposes that these so-called tribal economies do exist, they would not be the exclusive entities that Mr. Kotkin imagines. Chinese capital flows as easily through British as Chinese hands.

Perhaps the most disturbing aspect of Mr. Kotkin's analysis is his tendency to gloss over or omit complex historical and social realities. Some of the population dispersions that led to the formation of these so-called tribes were voluntary migrations, part of grand imperial designs, but others were forced migrations brought about, for instance, by the slave and coolie trades. The lives of people who planted themselves in strange soil are not simple economic success stories or parts of business expansions; they are a complicated mix of continuities and changes, some good and some bad, involving the migrant and indigenous populations alike.

It seems to me that Mr. Kotkin's search for "definition from the collective past" arises from his concern over the apparent lack of definition from the collective present. Along the "tribal frontier," where cultural diversity abounds—for instance, in some of America's major cities—he writes, there are conflicts between different immigrant groups and between the newer and older communities. As the immigrants adapt to prevailing Anglo-American standards, to an ethic of hard work, thrift, self-sufficiency and family values, he predicts, the confusion and chaos will die down, and America's downward slide will be arrested.

The historical lesson he draws from the Jews, Japanese, Chinese, British and Asian Indians is that their ascendancy is built upon "Anglo-Saxon standards of business, science and political economy." Insofar as they subscribe to Anglo-Saxon morality and values, they have become cultures of plenty. (Asians, accordingly, are called the "new Calvinists.") Conversely, those who have failed to conform to Anglo-Saxon standards have become cultures of poverty that must be pacified and "tamed." "The only alternative" to taming those who do not hold to such standards, Mr. Kotkin dramatically writes, "is chaos, the total breakdown of civilized society." History, I believe, offers other lessons.

Gary Y. Okihiro is an associate professor of history at Cornell University and the author of the forthcoming book "Margins and Mainstreams: Asians in American History and Culture."

* * *

March 17, 1994

FOR A FURNITURE MAKER, A TASTE OF A GLOBAL FUTURE

By EDWARD A. GARGAN
Special to The New York Times

COLUMBUS, Miss.—It was August, when this part of the country sags under a slathering of humidity and heat. T. Scott Berry was up the road from here at a dealers show in Tupelo, displaying some of the furniture he makes. He was in the back of a warehouse, not doing much of anything, when he got a call from the desk. A man was there to see him.

"So I go out and there's this guy standing there," Mr. Berry recalled. "I almost threw him out, but I said, O.K., I'll talk to him."

Three months later, at the invitation of the Chinese man who came to call, Mr. Berry, a descendant of Arkansas mule traders and Mississippi furniture makers, was in Beijing trying to figure out how to work China into plans for his family company, the Johnston Tombigbee Furniture Manufacturing Company. He returned with a deal to have the Chinese make chairs for him; the first shipment will arrive next month.

Entering the Global Market

"I was trying to move as fast as possible," said Mr. Berry, 40, a tousle-haired redhead who charges like a halfback through his vast factories, clambering over conveyor belts, scrutinizing racks of rough wood bedposts and calling out to many of his 1,000 employees by name. "It could be the future."

Here in Columbus, a town of 23,800 people, of white-columned antebellum mansions and a main street languorous in its pedestrian traffic, the global economy seems to intrude in a scattering of Japanese cars, a handful of Chinese restaurants and not much else. But for Johnston Tombigbee, the future probably lies as much in China—in cities like Dalian, in what used to be Manchuria—as it does in America's Southern heartland.

China, with Asia's fastest-growing economy, has aggressively sought out international markets for its growing industries, including furniture. Chinese business officials are diligently trolling the waters of trade shows, scrutinizing merchandise, buttonholing manufacturers, looking for deals. And furniture makers like Mr. Berry are often obliging in an effort to lower manufacturing costs and increase profitability.

Mr. Berry's new Chinese partner, a man named Yang Yijian, who he said preferred to be called James, quoted Johnston Tombigbee prices for the chairs that were two-thirds lower than what Mr. Berry pays in countries like Brazil.

"I said to myself, where is cheap labor and massive amounts of raw material?" Mr. Berry said. "I thought it was Brazil, but now it looks like it's China."

Although Taiwan has exported furniture to the United States for several years, China has made a big push only in the last year, according to Bruce Plantz, the executive editor of FDM Furniture Design and Manufacturing, a trade publication.

For the first nine months of 1993, furniture imports from China were worth $225 million, up 56 percent over the corresponding period of 1992. And combined imports from China, Malaysia, Indonesia, Singapore and the Philippines were up 52 percent from 1992, to $687 million. During 1993, the value of the United States wholesale residential furniture market was about $18 billion, according to Mr. Plantz.

For Johnston Tombigbee, the cheap labor and materials in China are the backbone of an expansion strategy. With reported sales of $40 million last year, Johnston Tombigbee ranks 139th among the top 300 makers of furniture in America, according to FDM. But Mr. Berry says he intended to move up the ladder by expanding into higher-end furniture, which he has started to make in Honduras and the Philippines, and by reducing the number of parts in other finished products to make them easier to produce in China.

"I see my furniture being made mostly of foreign-made parts," Mr. Berry said. "I would say that foreign countries like China will play a big part of it. With all the growing Government intervention in manufacturing, whether it's the E.P.A., OSHA, workers' comp, we'll get to the point where we'll be an assembler and packager. That's what will happen."

A Company's Revival

Seven years ago, Johnston Tombigbee had all but collapsed, largely the result of family warfare and not a small bit of neglect and weak management, Mr. Berry said. He had quit the family business—"I had all I could stand," he recalled—and was wandering around Brazil, looking for someone to make some furniture he could sell in the United States. Then his wife called.

"I told him the company was going to be sold," Ruth Berry said, "and I told him to get home and fix it. It was worse than moribund."

Mr. Berry hurried back to Columbus and the shards of the family business.

The factories, including the original brick factory, were silent. There were no orders, no piles of lumber, not a piece of furniture. And 1,000 people were out of work. "It was pretty scary," Mr. Berry said, "but when you're 34, 35, you're bold." Boldness, in this case, meant three plans for the business, ranging from liquidation of remaining assets, to a partial restart of the factories coupled with some importing of furniture, to a complete start-up of all the factories.

"We did a full-blown massive restart," he said, "and that's where we are now."

Johnston Tombigbee is among the small, specialized furniture makers battling for the great American middle-class home market. The company, in its modest prime, specialized in wooden beds, dressers and side tables—what is known in the trade as "promotional bedroom furniture."

While the company still produces wood furniture cheaply, China holds the promise of even lower costs. That is why Mr. Berry agreed to give the Chinese an opportunity to make what is known as a sled chair, about the simplest and cheapest wood chair made. It sells for about $50. With a padded fabric-covered seat and back held together by two square-shaped wooden frames, the bottoms of the squares mimic runners on a sled.

Mr. Berry recalled telling Yang Yijian during his visit to Tupelo that "when you get back, I'll fax you a print of the chair and send you a sample so you can make it."

"He quoted me an outstanding price on it, an unbelievable price," Mr. Berry said. "This chair costs me $12.50 from Brazil. James gave me a quote of $4.50."

Mr. Yang told Mr. Berry that he represented the Guangming Furniture Company in Dalian in northeast China. Within a month, the company had shipped some samples of a sled chair frame to Mr. Berry in Columbus. He sent back some of his bedposts and bought a ticket to Beijing.

"When I showed up at the Grand Hotel, they had these bedposts all made for me," Mr. Berry said. "It was pretty clear that they could absolutely do what I needed done."

While a good proportion of the furniture sold in the United States is made abroad, none of the sort of nine-piece ensembles that grace the bedrooms of middle America are manufactured there. "There are too many parts," Mr. Berry said. "So far it doesn't make any sense."

But with the prices Guangming is offering, Mr. Berry is redesigning his furniture to reduce the number of parts for pieces like dressers, and to make the parts interchangeable.

Mr. Berry still finds his relationship with Mr. Yang somewhat enigmatic. "I'm not sure who I'm dealing with James Yang to a certain extent," he confessed. "But it was obvious to me that James was the kind of guy I could make a relationship with and the kind of guy I could do business with."

Next month, Mr. Yang will come here with a vice president from the Guangdong Development Bank, one of China's new lending institutions that is looking for investment deals with American companies. Mr. Berry said that while sled chairs and bedposts are a start, a deal with a Chinese bank to build a furniture factory in China is now a growing possibility.

Mr. Berry said he did not yet know the long-term implications of foreign manufacturing on his business or on the size of his work force. "We can't meet all our orders as is," he said.

Yet he is proceeding with caution. "I just put my toe in it with the sled chair," he said. "But now, I'm up to my knees, but cautiously, to see if any sharks are out there. But if this works, it's a gold mine."

* * *

January 7, 1995

SPOON-TO-SPOON COMBAT OVERSEAS

By JOHN TAGLIABUE
Special to The New York Times

MORGES, Switzerland—The great American breakfast cereal wars have gone global.

For decades, the Kellogg Company has been introducing American-style cereals in countries where people traditionally break the nighttime fast with little more than coffee and a newspaper.

Building on a base created before World War II, Kellogg now operates 20 factories worldwide to make products like Rice Krispies and Corn Flakes. Over the last year, Kellogg seized the opportunity afforded by the collapse of Communism to open plants in Latvia, Belarus and Russia. And the company is charging into Asia with a new factory near Bombay, India, and another under construction in Guangzhou, China.

But now, General Mills Inc., the rival American cereal giant, has entered the fray with products ranging from Cheerios to Count Chocula. Five years ago, General Mills and Nestle, the Switzerland-based food giant, formed a joint venture called Cereal Partners Worldwide in this town near Geneva. The intent was to challenge Kellogg's virtual monopoly outside North America.

For both Kellogg and General Mills, the overseas growth comes as a respite from headaches in a saturated market at home. United States cereal manufacturers recently fought a war of promotions, with coupons and other offers cutting into cereal prices that some American consumers were criticizing as too high. Kellogg reported that in the first nine months of 1994, its sole bright spot was continued double-digit growth abroad.

Cereal Partners expected sales totaling $450 million in 1994, well on its way to reaching a goal of $1 billion by the end of the century. The joint venture, which had moved into most West European countries and Mexico by 1992, marched last year into Chile and Southeast Asian countries including Thailand and the Philippines. Last month, it acquired Poland's biggest corn flakes manufacturer as a bridgehead to Eastern Europe, bringing to 18 the number of countries where it sells its products.

"Our mission is to become a clear, strong No. 2, behind Kellogg," said Stephen R. Demeritt, the president and chief executive of the venture.

For its part, Kellogg is trying to put the best face on the rise of new competition. "To put it in perspective, what you are seeing is ready-to-eat cereals becoming a global growth category," said Anthony T. Hebron, a spokesman for Kellogg in Battle Creek, Mich.

Still, the scrimmaging has been rough. As Cereal Partners prepared to introduce Cheerios to Europe, Kellogg did an end run by shipping its Cheerios taste-alike, Honey Nut Loops, to European stores. Kellogg has also responded with a wave of new products around the world, like Basmati Flakes from the new Bombay plant.

Over the last decade, Kellogg has used aggressive marketing, gradual shifts in European eating habits and what had been a near absence of competition to develop markets in countries as diverse as Sweden and Spain.

Kellogg has long had a presence overseas. It built factories in Sydney, Australia, in 1924, and in Manchester, England, in 1938. But not until 1956 did the company begin shipping Corn Flakes from the factory in Manchester to the Continent.

In its expansion, the company has faced many obstacles, including Europe's general north-to-south falloff in matters of breakfast. The Irish, for example, consumed 17 pounds of cereal per person in 1993, the highest rate in the world. But for most people in France, Italy or Greece, breakfast continues to be little more than a cup of coffee and, maybe, a croissant.

Moreover, eating cereal means drinking cold milk in the morning, which is anathema to people in Italy, where cold liquid on an empty stomach is considered unhealthy, or in Poland, where milk is often scalded before serving for sterilization.

High prices for all prepared breakfast cereals have been another deterrent. Italian homemakers spend the equivalent of $4 for a 13-ounce box of Rice Krispies, partly because of higher European labor costs, but also because of expensive television advertising and higher prices under the European farm system for the durum wheats and flint corn that go into the products.

Competition was sparse when Kellogg began its big overseas expansion after World War II. In England, the major competitors were companies like Quaker Oats or private labels carried by supermarket chains. On the Continent, manufacturers of muesli held a thin market share.

Kellogg's steady growth abroad was a welcome breeze for the American parent company, whose earnings had flattened as it saturated the domestic market. By 1994, the overseas share of Kellogg's revenues had risen to 40 percent from 34 percent in 1987.

"The reason investors buy Kellogg's in the first place is because of the potential for overseas growth," said Steve Galbraith, who follows cereal companies at Sanford C. Bernstein & Company in New York.

In 1994, overseas sales accounted for roughly 36 percent of Kellogg's estimated pretax earnings of $1.1 billion, compared with 21 percent in 1987.

In the 1980's, the prospect of grabbing a slice of this rich market lured Nestle, the world's largest food company, into a tentative effort to sell breakfast cereals. The company began selling several varieties in Europe, including a chocolate-flavored product called Chockells. In 1989, Nestle decided to join forces with General Mills and added its own cereals to the joint venture.

"General Mills said, 'We've got the cereal technology, and we're a strong No. 2,' " said Mr. Demeritt, who headed General Mills' operations in Canada before joining Cereal Partners. For its part, Nestle brought in a formidable global sales force and manufacturing base.

Analysts call the venture a marriage made in heaven. "Mills wanted a built-in sales infrastructure," said William Maguire, who follows cereals at Merrill Lynch in New York. "Nestle sells, but didn't produce well. Mills had the technology and products."

Building on Nestle's earlier markets, Cereal Partners began in Britain, France, Spain and Portugal. The partners quickly added the cereals division of Ranks Hovis McDougall P.L.C., the British food company, thus acquiring the rights to sell two prized brands, Shredded Wheat and Shreddies, outside North America.

With market shares in European countries ranging from about 10 percent to 20 percent, Cereal Partners still trails Kellogg, which controls half of Europe's ready-to-eat cereal market and almost 43 percent of the global market.

Start-up costs for Cereal Partners have been high. Though neither General Mills nor Nestle would confirm the figures, Mr. Galbraith estimated that the partners had sunk as much as a half-billion dollars into the joint venture, and would probably spend $1 billion by 2000.

But in 1994, Mr. Demeritt said, Cereal Partners turned a pretax profit in its four original European markets for the first time. Some analysts, including Mr. Galbraith, say Cereal Partners can break even on its entire operation by 1998.

For Kellogg, the arrival of General Mills may have been a blessing in disguise. Or at least that is what Cereal Partners says.

"Everybody profits from a rising tide," Mr. Demeritt said. "And that is what we've got."

*   *   *

February 19, 1995

FROM CATASTROPHE TO LANDSLIDE

THE AGE OF EXTREMES: A History of the World, 1914–1991
By Eric Hobsbawm
Illustrated. 627 pp. New York: Pantheon Books. $30.

By STANLEY HOFFMANN

Having written a three-volume history of the "long 19th century" (1789–1914), the great British historian Eric Hobsbawm has now turned to the "short 20th century" (1914–91). Mr. Hobsbawm explains at the outset that he is not a specialist of the 20th century and that his purpose is not to "tell the story" of this period but to "understand and explain why things turned out the way they did, and how they hang together." This he has done, and the resulting book, "The Age of Extremes," is powerful and thought-provoking, demonstrating once again that when it comes to interpretation, the best works of history are those in which the author's own special perspective is given free play.

Mr. Hobsbawm's perspective is shaped by Marxism. He is far more interested in the "infrastructure" of modern societies—the forces of production and the relations among classes—than he is in the political "superstructure." The reader of "The Age of Extremes" will, for instance, find almost nothing about the politics of the Nazi Reich or of the New Deal, or about the ups and downs of politics in Western Europe after World War II.

Similarly, the confrontations and crises of the cold war are given short shrift and the wars in the Middle East are disposed of in half a page. There are many references to nationalism and ethnic conflicts, but little systematic attention to the importance of these issues; the civil war in Sri Lanka is discussed without any mention of ethnicity. The chapters on the arts are a bit perfunctory, except for Mr. Hobsbawm's acerbic remarks on post-modernism and on the disappearance of the barriers that used to exist between art and life—barriers that allowed one to write the history of jazz in terms "quite similar to those applicable to classical music," but that no longer enable one to distinguish individual rock musicians from "the huge flood of sound" with which we are inundated.

This does not mean that Mr. Hobsbawm plays down the importance of political leaders and movements, or of the modern state. But what concerns him is their connection with the great economic and social forces that constitute, for him, the warp and woof of history. His focus is on capitalism and socialism, and on the battle that ended with the victory of the former.

He divides the century, and his book, into three parts. The first is "The Age of Catastrophe," which includes the two world wars and the Great Depression. He says very little about the wars themselves; it is their social and economic consequences that interest him, and particularly the difference between the effects of the first war, which "solved nothing," and those of the second, which "actually produced solutions, at least for decades."

The book's second part is devoted to "The Golden Age" of economic growth and social transformation, from 1945 to the early 1970's. The third is called "The Landslide," and it covers the vicissitudes of capitalism in the 70's, 80's and 90's, the collapse of the Soviet system and the turmoil in an increasingly fragmented third world.

Mr. Hobsbawm's perspective leads him to insist several times that liberal and Communist states had much in common: they were both heirs of the Enlightenment, "equally committed to equal rights for all races and both sexes. . . . More to the point, after 1945 they were virtually all states which . . . rejected the supremacy of the market and believed in the active management and planning of the economy by the state." It was this range of agreement that had made a common front against fascism possible. Indeed, Mr. Hobsbawm has shrewd things to say about how fascist activism mobilized the "strong but often inert" traditional forces of conservatism and counterrevolution, and he dismisses the leftist cliché about fascism being the expression of "monopoly capitalism." As he puts it, big business "can come to terms with any regime that does not actually expropriate it, and any regime must come to terms with it."

In his account of the Soviet system, Mr. Hobsbawm takes the position that Marx has been vindicated in his expectation that Communism could prevail only where there was advanced capitalism: a revolution in a country as backward as Russia, unless it succeeded in spreading to the capitalist world, was bound ultimately to fail. Paradoxically, without the military assistance of the Soviet Union, he insists, Western liberal capitalism would not have survived the Nazi onslaught. But the over centralized and inflexible Soviet economy was brought low both by its slowing down in the 70's and 80's ("an increasingly tired ox," "its dynamism contained the mechanism of its own exhaustion") and by its interaction with the capitalist world economy, which allowed the Kremlin leaders to stop "trying to do anything serious about a visibly declining economy" and to rely instead on imports of consumer goods and on exports of energy to pay for them.

Again, paradoxically, Mr. Hobsbawm regards the Soviet system as the victim of the capitalist crisis of the 1970's—one that left the stronger capitalist world standing. His account of the final crisis of the Soviet Union, and of the contradiction between the glasnost of Mikhail S. Gorbachev, which undermined authority, and his perestroika, which could only be carried out from above, is brilliant: "The alternative to party authority was not the constitutional and democratic authority, but, in the short run, no authority."

Mr. Hobsbawm contrasts the bureaucratic, conservative elements of the Communist system with the restless, turbulent essence of capitalism. He shows how, in the Golden Age, thanks to technological innovation, the world was fundamentally transformed, old familial solidarities were destroyed, the countryside was emptied, cities and insecurity grew. A global economy emerged, with transnational corporations, a new international division of labor and the rise of offshore finance ("The most convenient world for multinational giants is one populated by dwarf states or no states at all"). The tremendous economic expansion of the Golden Age he finds beyond any "really satisfactory explanations." But he emphasizes that it came from a capitalism that was not purely laissez-faire: "a substantial restructuring and reform of capitalism" had produced the mixed economy, and that "democratized the market," reduced inequality, eased unemployment and gave governments a major role in the management of the economy.

In the early 70's, Mr. Hobsbawm says, the global economy heated up and the old social-democratic remedies proved themselves no longer workable—because globalization had deprived states of effective controls and "the interests of various parts of the traditional social-democratic

constituency" had begun to diverge. The result was a number of regressive social and political phenomena: the rise of xenophobia, "an increasingly separate and segregated 'underclass' " and the emergence of identity groups, each with its own brand of exclusiveness. At the same time, the ideology of the free market, which sees the state as the enemy, came back in apparent triumph. Believers in the free market or in the notion that liberal democracy and capitalism are twins will not enjoy this volume. Neither will economists, whom Mr. Hobsbawm dismisses several times.

A sharp critic of unfettered capitalism, Mr. Hobsbawm also finds almost nothing good to say about the United States. He writes that the apocalyptic tone of the cold war was largely the result of the country's electoral politics and of its own ideological definition of the nation ("Americanism"). He is highly critical of American interventions in the third world, and he blames America for serious environmental problems.

Nor does he find much to look forward to at the end of this century. It is his view that the international system has no clear structure or group of great powers, that interstate and internal wars have merged and are multiplying, that the means of destruction and terror are being "privatized" and that all political programs appear to have failed. The world is facing formidable population and environmental crises, he says, and global capitalism does not seem able to provide an adequate number of jobs. Instead, it tends to replace human labor with machines, and to drive production into low-wage areas.

The nation-state, Mr. Hobsbawm maintains, is being eroded from above and from below. But with the irresistible spread of the global economy, and in the absence of a global threat, capitalism is unlikely to reform itself. Mr. Hobsbawm also points out that many intellectuals are increasingly uneasy about a science without practical and moral limits; "chaos theory" (concerned with the unpredictable effects of minute causes) and "catastrophe theory" (concerned with sudden ruptures provoked by gradual changes) now flourish.

Mr. Hobsbawm is convinced that questions of economic distribution will dominate future politics, issues like the inequity of incomes in the developed countries and the gap between the industrialized nations and the rest of the world, particularly the countries of sub-Saharan Africa that appear to have been abandoned by the international capitalist economy. But he ends on a note of gloom about how democratic those politics will be. He thinks that public opinion, in this century of the common people, is an unavoidable force, but that many of the decisions that will need to be made may be highly unpopular.

"The structures of human societies themselves, including even some of the social foundations of the capitalist economy, are on the point of being destroyed by the erosion of what we have inherited from the human past," he argues. Our world must change, but "we do not know where we are going. . . . And the price of failure, that is to say, the alternative to a changed society, is darkness." This conclusion is made gloomier still by his all-too-convincing account of the flaws and failures of the different blueprints for change, particularly the revolutionary faith of Communism, that have already been tried out in the "age of extremes."

Despite all that it leaves out, and despite some repetitions (the student revolution of 1968 and the Chinese Communist takeover of 1949 are covered twice), "The Age of Extremes" is a bracing and magisterial work from a rich and acerbic mind. It proves the vitality and importance of an approach to history—common to Marxists and to the French Annales school until the 1970's—that emphasizes long-range trends and the dynamics of economic and social systems. There are other approaches. But it would be a serious loss if the sophisticated Marxist one that Mr. Hobsbawm practices were to disappear.

Stanley Hoffmann is the Douglas Dillon Professor of the Civilization of France and the chairman of the Center for European Studies at Harvard University.

* * *

May 23, 1996

ECONOMICS LESSON IN A BORDER TOWN

Why That Asian TV Has A 'Made in Mexico' Label

By ANTHONY DePALMA

TIJUANA, Mexico—The towering blue sign that lights up the night at Samsung Group's sprawling new industrial complex seems out of place in this gray and grubby border town.

But in the months since it was erected, the 70-foot steel structure has become an unofficial landmark, at once a beacon for poor and restless Mexicans looking for work and a symbol of the free-trade forces that are siphoning manufacturing jobs from the United States.

When Kwang Ho Kim, the president of the South Korean conglomerate, pushed a button to activate the assembly lines at the $212 million plant on March 29, Tijuana, with a population of about one million, quietly nudged a step closer to matching the entire United States in the number of workers involved in making television sets and parts.

In all, 24,600 people are employed here by Samsung; by Japanese companies like the Sony Corporation, Hitachi Ltd. and the JVC unit of the Matsushita Electric Industrial Company, and by other electronics manufacturers. Together, the Mexican Government says, they assemble more than nine million television sets a year. In the United States, where more than 90 companies once built TV sets, television-manufacturing jobs—mostly production of picture tubes, receivers and cabinets—have fallen to 30,000 nationwide, according to the Electronics Industry Association.

"Tijuana's got first-world equipment with third-world labor," said Harley Shaiken, a professor at the University of California at Berkeley who specializes in labor issues and the global economy. "They now have the ability there to handle a

surprising level of complexity and some very sophisticated processes."

Mexico has always had cheap labor and thus has been a magnet for American manufacturers of low-technology consumer goods like clothing and hand tools that can be mass-produced here at a fraction of the cost in the United States. But with trade barriers falling, it has become easier for multinational corporations to make high-tech products in border towns like Tijuana and ship them worldwide.

For the old factory towns and aging industrial parks of the United States, however, Samsung's new tower looms more like a warning flare than a beckoning light. "We invented the television in the United States, and they're going to take it completely out of the country," said Nelson Silva, a forklift operator who was shop steward at a JVC assembly plant in Elmwood Park, N.J., before it shut down in March and moved to Tijuana. "I'm bitter that we lost these people, lost these jobs, not just at JVC but all over America," Mr. Silva said in a phone interview.

The big manufacturing companies say the competitive pressures of the global economy leave them no choice but to abandon workers like Mr. Silva and flee to cheap-labor countries. According to them, an Asian company churning out televisions in a Mexican town for export to American consumers is the wave of the future.

It was the 1994 North American Free Trade Agreement that sealed Mexico's status as a manufacturing center for the entire continent. In years past, Samsung operated on the principle that the best way to penetrate a market was to make the product in the same country where it was sold, said Young M. Kwon, president of Samsung Electro-Mechanics America Inc. in Tijuana.

Indeed, after being declared dead in the 1970's, the victim of low-cost foreign competition, the television manufacturing business in the United States was revived in the 80's. Foreign—mostly Asian—producers, spurred by political pressures and business efficiencies, opened American plants to supply the United States market.

But with the free-trade agreement guaranteeing a vast free-market zone of nearly 400 million people, Mr. Kwon said, the necessity of building TV's in the United States evaporated. "We consider this place, or America, or Canada, or in the future Latin America, one block in the market," he explained. Indeed, almost 90 percent of the 1.5 million color TV sets that Samsung will produce in Tijuana this year will be sold in the United States.

While Samsung moved its manufacturing operations here from Ridgefield Park, N.J., in 1991, it waited until the trade agreement took effect three years later to begin a big expansion. It now plans to spend $581 million over four years to double TV production to three million sets a year, as well as to turn out more picture tubes and produce more complicated items like microwave ovens. The total Samsung work force, now at 2,300, could quadruple to 9,300.

At the company's plant here, the global economy is less an economic concept than a lesson in cultural accommodation.

In the entrance lobby, a sign that begins in Spanish and ends in English instructs visitors to remove their shoes and put on slippers before entering the plant.

The popularity of Tijuana among Japanese electronics companies has driven real estate prices so high that newcomers are looking at other border sites, setting off interstate bidding wars within Mexico. In April, the Daewoo Corporation of South Korea announced that it would open a $250 million picture-tube plant in the Baja California city of Mexicali because the state had offered a better deal than had neighboring Sonora.

But as production surges on the Mexican side of the border, it is drying up to the north. Nearly 200 people lost their jobs when JVC closed the plant in Elmwood Park. "Imagine it, nine lost years I spent working there," said Angela Nasareo, a 39-year-old assembly line worker from nearby Paterson who was let go in March. In a phone interview, she said she was offended that the young women in Tijuana who now have the jobs she and her colleagues lost make about $50 a week, compared with the $9 an hour she had earned. "There the company wants more quantity than quality, that's all," she said.

The United States Labor Department says the North American Free Trade Agreement has so far resulted in the destruction of 66,600 American jobs. Nevertheless, Labor Secretary Robert B. Reich said the trade accord's overall effect on the American labor market had been benign.

"The premise of Nafta is that trade is not a zero-sum game," Mr. Reich said in an interview in Mexico City, where he met with the Mexican and Canadian labor ministers. Since the accord was signed, he said, increased American exports have created hundreds of thousands of American jobs that pay more than the old manufacturing jobs they replace. "There is no evidence that Nafta has been bad for American workers," he said.

It has certainly been good for Mexican workers. The trade accord eliminated tariffs on most of the electronics products entering the United States from Mexico, causing an estimated 50 percent increase in exports in the first two years. The freer access sweetened the deal for Asian companies that had already made Tijuana their first stop in North America because of its proximity to Silicon Valley and the port of Long Beach in California.

In the recent Mexican recession, the border plants known as maquiladoras, which assemble products from imported parts, were a singular bright spot. Employment grew by more than 13 percent to over 151,000 and maquiladora exports rose more than 10 percent.

Now, the television manufacturers are showing that their plants can offer the local economy more than just the low-paying assembly jobs of the maquiladoras. To meet local-content standards imposed by the trade agreement, the Asian companies have invited some of their traditional providers to join them in Tijuana. Already, at least half a dozen South Korean and Japanese concerns have started producing parts in the city.

Samsung and Daewoo are building factories to produce picture tubes, which are considered the most complex part of the television production line and which until recently were made mostly in the United States. Samsung thinks that by 2000, about 90 percent of the parts it needs will be produced locally, providing higher paying jobs and contributing more to the local economy.

Samsung also plans to open a research and development headquarters, but in San Diego instead of Tijuana. Despite their disappointment at that choice, Mexican officials are upbeat about Mexico's increasing standing as a maker of big-ticket durable goods. Increasingly, they point out, the big automobile companies are switching output to Mexico. The city of Matamoros has already become one of the largest producers of automobile parts in North America, for example, turning out wiring assemblies for car factories in the United States and Canada as well as those in Mexico.

As more factories manufacture finished goods from scratch rather than just assembling parts shipped from the United States, they offer workers an opportunity for advancement to more skilled positions with higher pay. For all that, though, Tijuana's greatest advantage remains cheap labor. Seventy percent of Samsung's workers are young women who dropped out of school before completing the sixth grade. The starting salary for a 45-hour week is 345 pesos, or about $50.

Still, for 17-year-old Mariana Delgado Caballero, it is enough. She is working her first job after having migrated with her father from the central state of Guanajuato in 1995. She says they had no intention when they arrived here of sneaking across the border into the United States, as so many millions of Mexicans before them have done, but the shy way she says it suggests that such an escape is very much on her mind.

And while attaching tiny brass pieces to a tuning board for eight hours a day at Samsung is not her idea of a magical route to a better future, she is glad to be making money at all. "I'll do it," Miss Delgado said, "till I have the chance to better myself."

*   *   *

July 12, 1996

JORDAN'S BUNKER VIEW ON SNEAKER FACTORIES

By IRA BERKOW

Michael Jordan, pancake cap turned backward on his head, was seen yesterday on a television film clip blasting a golf ball out of a bunker in Fresno, Calif. Jordan is on vacation, for about three months, obviously enjoying a much-deserved rest after leading his team to another National Basketball Association championship. It is a much greater rest than that enjoyed by many of the people who, at bottom, help make him one of America's richer people.

That is, the male and female workers in the virtual feudal system of sneaker factories in Indonesia. And the child laborers in soccer ball-manufacturing factories under the aegis of the Nike "Swoosh." It is Nike, that swelling international octopus, and its commercials that have helped elevate Air Jordan into one of the world's most recognizable figures. For his good name and charming smile, Nike pays Jordan a $20 million a year endorsement fee, about half of Jordan's annual income.

Meanwhile, the laborers in Asian countries who produce the Nike products sweat under the minimum wage, or at a minimum wage that is under the poverty level. They are people who may work 60 or 70 hours a week under sometimes brutal conditions, including forced overtime. Workers have been known to be beaten, and when strikes are threatened, the instigators are fired.

In a human rights report by the State Department to Congress a few years ago, a special point was made about the "horrors" in exploitation of workers in the sneaker-making factories in Indonesia.

Nike has retorted that it subcontracts its work and has little say in how the workers are handled. Nike has said it has tried to improve conditions. But Jeff Balinger, the head of Press for Change, an organization that has monitored conditions in factories in Indonesia since 1989, said, "The abuses continue."

When asked about this last month, Jordan did not distinguish himself. "I think that's Nike's decision to do what they can to make sure everything is correctly done," he said. "I don't know the complete situation. Why should I? I'm trying to do my job. Hopefully, Nike will do the right thing, whatever that might be."

Why should Jordan not know what abuses are taking place. Not only is he a citizen of the world, but one also profiting hugely from the Nike undertaking. As for "not knowing the complete situation," why not look into it. Or pay someone responsible to investigate or go there. Indonesia has golf courses.

The plight does not involve only Nike and Jordan. Other prominent sneaker and sports-gear manufacturers such as Reebok and Adidas have also consigned their work to areas of cheap labor around the world. And those who promote the products in America include virtually every widely known athlete who has made a dent in our consciousness.

But Jordan, as World Sports Hero No. 1, is the most visible—and respected—of the athletes, and Nike, a multibillion-dollar company, and its owner and founder, Phil Knight, whose stock in the organization is reportedly worth $4.5 billion, are the industry leaders.

Some sports stars in this century have courageously gone beyond the arena to make an impact on society. There were, among others, Muhammad Ali and his stand against American participation in the Vietnam War; the Olympic athletes who backed President Carter's decision not to participate in the Moscow Games after the Soviet Union invaded neighboring Afghanistan; the vigor of Arthur Ashe's protest of South African apartheid and John McEnroe, who turned down $1 million to play there; to be sure, Jackie Robinson, and his white teammate, Pee Wee Reese; Hank Greenberg setting a

standard for baseball stars to join the military after Pearl Harbor; Billie Jean King, fighting for women's rights; Martina Navratilova seeking greater understanding for gays and lesbians; Jim Brown's activism in the inner cities.

Michael Jordan has been a wondrous basketball player; he has been a good, hard-working, law-abiding citizen, and one who has entertained us mightily.

But the Michael Jordans of the world—from Charles Barkley to Andre Agassi to Frank Thomas—can do more. Not on every issue, of course. But at least on those that have a direct link to them. Pure self-interest ought to have its limits.

Even a gifted athlete has an obligation at times to poke his head from the bunker.

*   *   *

April 6, 1997

FAT CAT SPAT: LOOK WHO'S CARPING MOST ABOUT CAPITALISM

By DAVID E. SANGER

WASHINGTON—It wasn't long ago that the most astringent critiques of capitalism came from the left. Armed Zapatista guerrillas in the Mexican jungles and the fast-disappearing Socialists of Japan complained that leaving the world to the ruthless efficiency of the market not only made fat cats fatter and the impoverished poorer, but it also undercut human dignity and skewed national values.

They lost the argument. Save for odd corners of the world like Cuba and North Korea, the ideology of the market economy reigns supreme. Political leaders vying for investments from overseas cut their budget deficits and privatize industry to satisfy the most feared figure on the international scene: the bond-rater from Standard & Poor's, whose thumbs-down in the global coliseum signals the world's biggest investors to take their billions elsewhere.

Now the inevitable backlash to market-worship is well under way. But to really hear the excesses of capitalism denounced, listen to some of the world's confirmed capitalists. Perhaps fearful that the side effects of economic globalization are more severe than anyone thought, or that they could spin out of control, prominent members of the monied classes and their conservative allies are questioning whether markets have become too unfettered. The only hitch is that they can't agree on the nature of problem, to say nothing of what to do about it.

Evidence of this rethinking is everywhere. The latest meeting of the World Economic Forum in Davos, Switzerland—which views itself as the world-class assemblage of the free-market elite—was devoted to ways of ameliorating the worst consequences of economic competitiveness. George Soros, the man who broke the British pound and assembled a $2.5 billion fortune, seized the cover of The Atlantic Monthly recently with a rambling account titled "The Capitalist Threat."

The "uninhibited pursuit" of laissez-faire ideology, a perplexed-sounding Mr. Soros reported, results in a loss of equilibrium. Education and other features of civilized society that don't promise a quick return on investment get short shrift, and nations become "preoccupied with their competitiveness and unwilling to make any sacrifices for the common good." Mr. Soros does not advocate the bar-the-door approach to free trade that other billionaires—Ross Perot or Sir James Goldsmith, for example—have urged. But he takes the view that governments have to reclaim their power from the markets.

The new critics have their conservative cheerleaders, though some of those bring a different agenda. There is William Bennett, the conservative's minder of values, who worries less about disequilibrium than about the erosion of national decorum.

Hollywood's production line of sex and violence has been Mr. Bennett's easiest target, but now the debate has moved on to regulating the Internet—and made odd bedfellows. In defending the Communications Decency Act before the Supreme Court last month, the Clinton Administration found itself allied with the Christian Coalition and Senator Jesse Helms in support of the regulatory state. And it was fighting not only the American Civil Liberties Union but the United States Chamber of Commerce, which warned in a friend-of-the-court brief that the United States would put itself at a competitive disadvantage if it began regulating the ultimate expression of global free enterprise.

Echoes From the Past

None of these arguments is new; there are echoes of Tory conservative thought and the Progessive Era tame-the-oligarchs movement in all of them. What's surprising is that many of the new concerns come from the oligarchs themselves, who see that globalization is causing instability that could unmake the market revolution. And some come from conservatives whose rallying call in the 80's—shrink the government and save the markets—has turned into gospel. Even Bill Clinton says the era of big government is over.

But victory left the victors divided. Libertarians persist in defending the untrammeled markets. Patrick J. Buchanan and Ross Perot struck a different chord with arguments that economic integration, starting with the North American Free Trade Agreement, impoverishes working Americans and impinges on American sovereignty by letting "faceless foreign judges" review American laws challenged by our trading partners. Meanwhile, those who worry about income inequality, job insecurity and pornography on the Net talk about getting the Government to intervene.

The same divisions, and odd alliances, can be found wherever politicians, labor unions and business executives believe they have lost their ability to control market forces. Not surprisingly, political leaders find it hard to give up the power that comes from running, and interfering with, a national economy.

In Europe, it is no longer just labor leaders who argue that global competition threatens the Continent's social safety net. Now the chief executives of some of Europe's biggest industrial enterprises are voicing nervousness about the European Monetary Union, the world's most ambitious attempt to erase national boundaries. In Germany, some industrialists are protesting the strict budget-cutting requirements that are part of the deal for countries that want to enter the monetary union. They talk about inflation and unemployment, but their real fear is that Europe's common currency, the Euro, will prove far more unstable than the German mark—meaning that Germany will be dragged down by lesser economies.

Then there are the South Koreans, who waxed enthusiastic about the wonders of global competitiveness in the 70's and 80's, as American companies moved production there. Now the same forces that brought suburban manses and sports cars to the industrial tangle of Seoul are moving to China and India, scared off by wages that shot up during the democracy movement. When South Korean companies rammed a bill through the Parliament that would allow them to move operations out of the country just as the Americans were doing, the protests grew so ugly that President Kim Young Sam had to go on television to apologize. The law is being amended.

"What we're seeing in the backlash overseas is a reaction to the American style of quick downsizing to become instantly more competitive," said Clyde Prestowitz, who heads the Economic Strategy Institute here. "For decades executives in Europe and Japan have been inculcated with the thought that they have a responsibility to maintain employment and social stability, and now they find this in direct contradiction to the global imperative."

So how much of this backlash is warranted, and how much is driven by the torrent of globaloney about economic integration? The answer is a little of both. Paul Krugman, the M.I.T. economist, says the importance of global markets is overstated because "pontificating about globalization is an easy way to get attention" at conferences like Davos. And politicians, of course, have good reason to throw up their hands and blame mysterious global forces for their national economic woes. France springs to mind.

But it is also clear that globalization's effects have been understated by many economists because they are maddeningly hard to measure. Laura D'Andrea Tyson, President Clinton's chief economic adviser until a few months ago, agrees with estimates that 20 to 25 percent of the growth in wage inequality in America comes from the global market, in which even a complex job can be done half a world away—say, having software written by an Indian engineer. Such nervousness could explain why Vice President Al Gore, back-pedaling on the wonders of globalization, has fallen silent about the need to extend free trade agreements.

No One to Make the Rules

Ultimately, taming the excesses of a global free market is going to be next to impossible because no one can agree on who should do the taming. Who would mandate a minimum wage and create a Social Security system for the world? Who would tell India that it can't build car factories because there are already too many sport utility vehicles polluting the world? Who would rule that Washington should be allowed to regulate what children can see on the Internet, but that China should not be allowed to regulate what dissidents can say on it? These are the "disequilibriums" dividing fans of capitalism around the world. They aren't going to get any easier.

* * *

July 24, 1997

THE GLOBALUTIONARIES

By THOMAS L. FRIEDMAN

JAKARTA, Indonesia—There is a fascinating revolution going on in Indonesia. It's not always visible, but if it succeeds it could save this country from the dead hand of the Suharto regime, which after 30 years in power is a spent force, without energy or ideas.

Wimar Witoelar, a popular Jakarta talk-show host, described the Indonesian revolutionaries to me as those 20- and 30-year-olds, most of them educated and working in the private sector, "who want to get rich without having to be corrupt and who want to have democracy but don't want to go out in the streets and get killed for it."

What's interesting is their strategy. The Suharto regime allows no space for a democratic opposition to emerge. So what the pro-democracy, pro-clean-government forces are relying on is not a revolution from below, not a revolution from above, but a revolution from beyond.

Their strategy is to do everything they can to integrate Indonesia into the global economy on the conviction that the more Indonesia is tied into the global system, the more its government will be exposed to the rules, standards, laws, pressures, scrutiny and regulations of global institutions, and the less arbitrary, corrupt and autocratic it will be able to be. Their strategy, in short, is to Gulliverize the Suharto regime by globalizing Indonesian society. As a military analyst, Juwono Sudarsono, put it: "The global market will force upon us business practices and disciplines that we cannot generate internally." Or as another reformer here remarked to me: "My son and I get our revenge on Suharto every day by eating at McDonald's."

Indonesia's "globalutionaries" include business school grads who want Indonesia in the World Trade Organization (W.T.O.) and APEC and Asean; young entrepreneurs who welcome foreign investment here so that any move the Suharto regime makes with the domestic economy, and any shenanigans it might try, will have international implications; and human rights activists who use the Internet to get their stories out and whose hackers occasionally break into—and alter—government web sites. The Indonesian press can't directly rebuke the Suharto regime for its rampant nepotism. So instead it reports with great relish on how the U.S. and Japan are taking Indonesia before a W.T.O. court to protest the fact that Indonesia's national car factory—controlled by the President's son—is being protected by all sorts of tariffs out of line with W.T.O. norms.

Many, of course, have made a similar argument about China—that the more it is integrated into the global economy, the more open and pluralistic it will inevitably become. But what is interesting about Indonesia is that it isn't outsiders making this argument to justify their business dealings here. It is Indonesian reformers making the argument as a self-conscious political strategy.

So globalization has many dark sides, from environmental degradation to widening the gap between rich and poor, but what you see in Indonesia is its most important upside—the ability to generate pressure on autocratic regimes when no domestic space is available.

While everyone is focusing on the question of whom President Suharto will appoint as his next vice president and likely successor, I would argue that it almost doesn't matter. The really interesting succession in Indonesia is already happening, and it is the one being mounted in the private sector by the globalutionaries. They are plugging Indonesia into the world in ways that will, over time, redefine both politics here and the limits of what's possible—no matter who succeeds Mr. Suharto.

In the meantime, if the U.S. wants to promote this process of opening up and democratizing politics in Southeast Asia it needs a multifaceted strategy. It has to work with military officers who want to professionalize their ranks, give protection to the nongovernmental human rights organizations when they come under attack for reasonable activities and find every way possible to encourage countries like Indonesia to integrate with the global economy and institutions, rather than cutting them off, which is idiotic.

It would be nice if every democracy movement could be led by a hero like Andrei Sakharov. But you have to work with what you've got, and around here the biggest agents of change are the globalutionaries.

* * *

November 12, 1997

BUONA NOTTE, GUTEN TAG: EUROPE'S NEW WORKDAYS

With Unemployment High, the Continent Experiments With the Time Clock

By JOHN TAGLIABUE

BOLOGNA, Italy—For 20 years, Amadeo Nassetti's routine had been as immovable as the huge machines he works on at a factory here owned by Bonfiglioli Group. He put in the same eight hours a day, starting at 8 A.M., five days a week.

But last year, his 21st at Bonfiglioli, a world leader in the manufacture of gearboxes and electrical motors, Mr. Nassetti suddenly needed a dance card to keep track of his schedule. Instead of 40 hours a week, he found himself working fewer than 32, and in rotating shifts starting as far apart as 6 A.M. and 10 P.M. Some weeks he worked four days, others five; some weeks he worked Saturdays, in others he had four-day weekends. This fall, the 57-year-old Mr. Nassetti has a

34-hour week, with most Saturdays and Sundays off. The only thing that has remained the same is his salary.

Mr. Nassetti's shorter but far less predictable schedule is corporate Europe's answer to an bitter debate now sweeping the Continent about jobs. As politicians, labor leaders and employers argue over the age-old vision of cutting working hours, some bigger companies, like Bonfiglioli, have already taken out the ax. But they are doing it to enhance their competitiveness, particularly internationally, and not to help cut unemployment, as some are urging, by letting those without work take up the slack.

"It was not really an issue of reducing hours but of gaining flexibility," said Sonia Bonfiglioli, the company's chief executive.

Adding jobs has been the goal of left-wing politicians and union leaders searching for ways to slice Europe's persistently high unemployment, double the level in the United States. If the Continent cannot increase the size of its economic pie, they argue, then workers should make do with a smaller slice—though no less pay—so that more people can come to the table.

The idea has caught on in Italy, where the Government recently pledged to trim the maximum legal workweek to 35 hours, from 40, by the year 2001. The French have made a similar vow.

But those moves have isolated Paris and Rome from the rest of the 15-member European Union, which rejects the idea as ineffective. And they have splintered labor into angry camps.

Some in labor's mainstream say a rigid system of shorter hours, by itself, could actually cost jobs by adding expense to European companies that already have trouble competing effectively in the global market. Shorter hours should be negotiated on a company-by-company basis, the mainstream says, with cuts in pay, if necessary, and above all with an eye to increasing a company's productivity.

But those on the left say governments must require employers to redistribute work, after shortening hours, to create new jobs. Otherwise, they argue, the exercise only serves to cement the privileges of existing employees. France and Italy, however, are tending toward a system that would not require new hiring. Instead, the Government would merely provide incentives to add workers, through tax breaks, perhaps, or subsidies toward the social security and health costs of any new employees.

As the debate rages on, more and more companies, like Bonfiglioli, say they cannot wait for a resolution. Growing into the role of multinational players, they have an immediate need to deal with surges and declines in the global economy, and one way is to be flexible with hours.

In short, the goal for these companies is not social engineering, but corporate re-engineering. Mr. Nassetti is working less but arguably harder, given the wear and tear of an ever-changing schedule. And while Bonfiglioli did some hiring, that was only because there was more demand for its products.

In arguing against legislation to force lower hours on a company without allowing other changes in work rules, Ms. Bonfiglioli said, "Reducing hours only makes sense under conditions of greater flexibility."

The twists and turns of the debate are all on display at Bonfiglioli. Since it negotiated a deal with its unions to cut the hours of Mr. Nassetti and his colleagues, its payroll has grown to 930 from 863.

Such results make proponents of shorter hours exult. Nerio Nesi, the economic spokesman of the Communist Refoundation Party, which demanded and got the pledge of a national law mandating a 35-hour week, cites his party's slogan, "Work for everyone, by working less." Companies can pay for the extra employees, he said, by dipping into profits.

But Ms. Bonfiglioli begs to differ.

In 1995, her company found itself with a sudden surge in demand for its sophisticated gearboxes and motors, as economies around the world emerged from recession and sales of the automobiles, farm tractors and other machinery that contain gearboxes jumped. Last year, the company, which was founded in 1956 by Ms. Bonfiglioli's father, Clementino, had sales of $207 million, compared with $98 million five years ago.

The sharp rise in orders presented the company with some difficult decisions, however. More overtime, the classic recipe for bolstering production, was prohibitively expensive, with metal workers in the company's seven factories pocketing 25 percent bonuses for overtime on Saturdays and 50 percent on Sundays. Moreover, the construction of a new factory was risky: if demand fizzled, Bonfiglioli would be stuck with a surplus plant and staff.

But by winning the right to move Mr. Nassetti and others around to night and weekend shifts as production needs dictated—and without having to pay them at overtime rates for the privilege—the company was able to greatly increase output with a minimum of additional employees. And because it could use the existing factories more efficiently, by keeping the machines running virtually around the clock, there was no need to build an extra plant.

Changes like these largely reflect the new realities of doing business on a global stage. Faced with the vagaries of international markets, many European companies are trying to find ways to be responsive without incurring excessive fixed costs. The goal is to create so-called breathing factories, in which production expands and contracts with demand, like a living organism.

Companies in the United States, of course, went through similar adjustments in recent years as they cut millions of jobs, switching instead to contract workers and outsourcing to remain competitive. But in Europe, with rigid social structures, strong labor unions and far higher unemployment, the pressure to achieve flexibility is even greater.

And indeed, Ms. Bonfiglioli acknowledges she was only copying a model for cutting working hours that was created in Germany several years earlier by Volkswagen, Europe's largest auto maker. At that time, VW faced the possibility of having to lay off about a third of its work force in Germany, or about 30,000 people, as an aging product line and the European recession combined to hollow out demand.

To avoid the huge layoffs, Volkswagen negotiated a complex package in 1993 with the powerful metal workers' union to cut the average workweek to less than 29 hours—from 36 hours—distributed over four days. In return, the union agreed to have wages reduced by up to 15 percent.

VW saved 20,000 of the 30,000 jobs, but in exchange it got the right to increase the workweek to as many as 35 hours, without paying overtime. Now, revived European economies and a renewed product line have caused demand to soar.

Peter Hartz, Volkswagen's chief of personnel and architect of the plan, says his goal is to extend the program to all 280,000 employees around the world.

And Volkswagen's model has found emulators elsewhere in Germany. In Munich, BMW operates its factories on similar principles, based roughly on a four-day week. Siemens, the electrical and electronics conglomerate, was able to save 5,000 jobs at one factory with a similar deal.

What animates the left's drive for shorter hours, say experts like Aris Accornero, a professor of industrial sociology at Rome University, is the conviction dating back to Karl Marx and other classical leftist theoreticians that "life, in effect, begins after work." Historically, however, the proposal has been "the daughter of desperation, not of hope," Professor Accornero said.

In the Great Depression, the Geneva-based International Labor Organization broached the idea of shorter hours, and in France, the leftist Government of Prime Minister Leon Blum put it into effect, slashing the week's hours to 40, from 48, the professor said. In the United States, socially innovative companies like Kellogg, the cereal maker, experimented with a 36-hour week.

Yet rarely do shorter hours serve to create more jobs, Professor Accornero said. Indeed, to regain productivity lost by shorter hours at equal pay, companies usually respond with better organization of work, which often means more stress for the remaining employees and more automation, which further reduces jobs. And the experience at Volkswagen bears this out.

"We got jobs, at the price of more intensive work," said Hans-Jürgen Uhl, the secretary general of the worker council at VW's main German plant, in Wolfsburg. "There is a subjective feeling of increased performance, and the work force will continue to drop." Where once two secretaries toiled, now there is one, he said, and while workers once took an extended coffee break to celebrate a colleague's birthday, they now do it after hours. Meanwhile, the drive to greater productivity continues, translating into fewer jobs.

Thanks to new manufacturing technology, said Hans-Peter Blechinger, a Volkswagen spokesman, VW's new Golf compact takes 20 hours to build, against 30 to 33 hours for the outgoing model. "In the medium term, we foresee a drop in employment because of productivity improvements," he said.

To get more productivity out of workers, VW is even trying to squeeze out the old notion of life beginning only after work. The goal of Mr. Hartz, the personnel head, is to turn each VW worker into an "entrepreneur on the factory floor, who acts decisively without orders from above to achieve the company's goals." Volkswagen and the unions hammer the message again and again at the work force. To induce workers to identify further with the company's goals, VW initiated a stock purchase program.

But such efforts to bind workers to their company's life only serve to accelerate what Kurt Vogler-Ludwig, a labor market specialist at the IFO Institute for Economic Research in Munich, describes as a widening split among European union leaders. Those who believe that embracing such a philosophy is the only road to preserving existing industrial jobs are increasingly at odds with more radical leaders, he says, who accuse the mainstream unions of essentially selling out to management to preserve the perks of those who are still employed.

"Now the unions represent more and more the interests of those with jobs," Mr. Vogler-Ludwig said.

For their part, the mainstream unions were angered by the demand in Italy for a 35-hour week. A nationwide law would shackle negotiating flexibility, their leaders said, and ultimately destroy jobs.

"We should have a reduced number of hours," said Sergio D'Antoni, head of the CISL union. "But we also have to reduce the cost of work."

*   *   *

April 12, 1998

SURPRISES IN THE GLOBAL TOURISM BOOM

By BARBARA CROSSETTE

UNITED NATIONS—If those spring holiday airport crowds seem worse than ever this year, think of that suitcase on your foot as merely a harbinger of even bigger things to come. Travel—yearround and around the world—is taking off on a phenomenal upward trajectory, with the numbers of tourists growing faster, proportionately, than the population of the countries they come from, or go to visit. Trips closer to home are also on the increase almost everywhere. Spending on travel is expected to grow fivefold in the next two decades.

An industry that moves so many people from place to place—on as many as six billion trips a year—and accounts for 10 percent of the world's annual economic growth is bound to have more than just economic effects. Decades ago package tours began laying waste to Spain's Costa Brava, Caribbean islands and some priceless Himalayan valleys. In the hamlet of Lukla, the jumping-off point for Mount Everest, they started serving muesli and french toast for breakfast and selling nice, soft toilet paper for trails with no toilets. Borneo's jungles got video. Want a picture of a stately African Masai hunter or an Igorot villager in Luzon? Pay up. You take their privacy, and maybe their souls. They take your money.

But mass travel has another side. More people are meeting people than at any time in history. In a country like China, where millions are beginning to travel, this exposure could

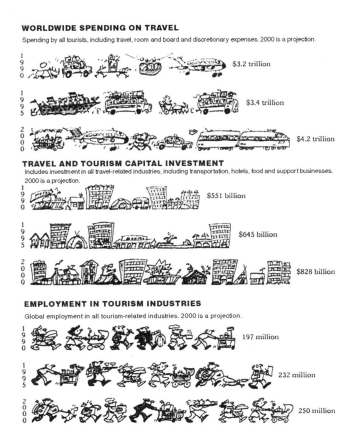

WORLDWIDE SPENDING ON TRAVEL
Spending by all tourists, including travel, room and board and discretionary expenses. 2000 is a projection.

1990 $3.2 trillion
1995 $3.4 trillion
2000 $4.2 trillion

TRAVEL AND TOURISM CAPITAL INVESTMENT
Includes investment in all travel-related industries, including transportation, hotels, food and support businesses.
2000 is a projection.

1990 $551 billion
1995 $645 billion
2000 $828 billion

EMPLOYMENT IN TOURISM INDUSTRIES
Global employment in all tourism-related industries. 2000 is a projection.

1990   197 million
1995   232 million
2000   250 million

either bind the country or further fragment it as people decide how much alike or different they are. Imagine the earful tour groups from Beijing or Shanghai might get traveling in Tibet or Hong Kong some day. Travel creates jobs and earns hard currency in scores of countries, including the United States, where it is a major export and services industry. Its very destructiveness has sounded alarms, and not just a few countries have awakened in time to save their land and heritage, learning in the process how precious their culture is.

Travel, even group tourism, has been around for centuries. People have long teamed up on pilgrimages, as we know from Chaucer's "Canterbury Tales." Thomas Cook, the father of modern tourism, got his start in the British Midlands taking groups to temperance rallies (tea and sandwiches included). The difference now is scale. Wide-bodied aircraft, deregulation and competition mean more routes and lower fares. With the almost complete collapse of Communism, many barriers have fallen or been torn down, releasing pent-up demand for travel in both directions: visitors out, visitors in. Rudimentary English has become the industry's international language.

Even Americans, still laggards at crossing borders when compared with many Europeans and Asians, picked up a record number of passports—six million—in the last year, the State Department says, and there are now more than 45 million American passports in circulation.

In an age of global economics, business travel has pushed up passport applications, not only for the traveling executive.

Family members are now nearly three times as likely to be included on business trips than in 1990. Robert Kaplan, who poked around the far corners for his book, "The Ends of the Earth" (Random House) said business travelers are now probably the most savvy tourists. "Look at Forbes, Fortune—what business people read," he said. "They are filled with articles about the outside world."

Paradoxically, the electronic connections enjoyed by businesses and home computer owners may be encouraging, not discouraging, travel. The Travel Industry Association of America found that six million Americans booked trips online this year, often after browsing through electronic encyclopedias, atlases and the home pages of state or foreign tourism authorities. The association predicts that by the end of 1998 bookings via the Internet may rise to 18 million.

Voyages to Granny

Cyberspace can never beat the heat, the smells, the sounds, the sense of Foreign. For Mr. Kaplan, the experience of arrival may be the tipoff to a place.

"Look closely at airports and you can see how a country is doing," he said. "Is the airport safe? Do you have to pay bribes? Airports are quasi-governmental places." Closer to home, he added, "you don't have to leave Penn Station to know that New York is getting better."

As more immigrants become United States citizens, getting to grandmother's house is no longer just a jaunt over the river and through the woods, but more likely a voyage over continents and seas. Immigrant families, fewer of whom have had to renounce all ties to their homelands because of political dangers, are traveling back to keep their children in close touch. Americans with deeper roots here go to take a look at where their neighbors came from.

When Catherine O'Neill, an expert on refugees, and her husband, Richard Reeves, the political writer, went globetrotting with their joint extended family a year ago, she handed out questionnaires at each stop. "I really felt that they are going to live in a global world, and that to understand it only from the perspective of the U.S. and Europe is not really seeing it," said Ms. O'Neill, the author with her husband of "Family Travels: Around the World in 30 (or So) Days" (Andrews and McMeel). "I asked them: In this country do they have jobs that we don't have in the United States? What kind of movies are being advertised? How do people get around the streets? In your life, will this country be important?"

Twenty years ago, when the world's population was 4.4 billion, 287 million people took international trips, according to the World Tourism Organization. By 1996, when global population stood at about 5.7 billion, 595 million international tourists were on the move. In 2020, the tourism organization's experts predict, 1.6 billion of the world's 7.8 billion people will take a foreign trip.

Internal Travel

Billions more will take their first, modest vacations closer to home. For example, a man in Beijing named Wang and his

Round and Round They Go. And Where They Stop and Shop.

THE TOP DESTINATIONS
International tourist arrivals
(excluding same-day visitors)

RANK 1996 (1985)	ARRIVALS Millions
1. France (1)	62.4
2. United States (4)	46.3
3. Spain (2)	41.3
4. Italy (3)	32.9
5. Britain (6)	25.3
6. China (13)	22.8
7. Mexico (9)	21.4
8. Hungary (11)	20.7
9. Poland (22)	19.4
10. Canada (7)	17.3
11. Austria (5)	17.1
12. Czech Rep. (16)	17.0
13. Germany (8)	15.2
14. Russia † (18)	14.6
15. Hong Kong (19)	11.7
16. Switzerland (10)	10.6
17. Portugal (15)	9.7
18. Greece (14)	9.0
19. Turkey (27)	8.0
20. Thailand (25)	7.2
21. Malaysia (21)	7.1
22. Singapore (23)	6.6
23. Netherlands (20)	6.6
24. Belgium (17)	5.8
25. Ireland (24)	5.3

WHO EARNS THE MOST
International tourism receipts
(excluding transportation).

RANK 1996 (1985)	RECEIPTS $ billions
1. United States (1)	$64.4
2. Italy (2)	28.7
3. France (4)	28.4
4. Spain (3)	27.4
5. Britain (5)	19.3
6. Germany (7)	16.5
7. Austria (6)	14.0
8. Hong Kong (12)	10.8
9. China (21)	10.2
10. Switzerland (8)	8.9
11. Canada (9)	8.9
12. Australia (27)	8.7
13. Thailand (23)	8.7
14. Poland (77)	8.4
15. Singapore (15)	7.9
16. Mexico (10)	6.9
17. Netherlands (14)	6.3
18. Indonesia (43)	6.1
19. Turkey (18)	6.0
20. Belgium (13)	5.9
21. Russia (16)	5.5
22. South Korea (35)	5.4
23. Argentina (29)	4.6
24. Portugal (24-tied)	4.3
25. Japan (24-tied)	4.1

WHO SPENDS THE MOST
International tourist spending
(excluding transportation).

RANK 1996 (1985)	SPENDING $ billions
1. Americans (1)	$52.6
2. Germans (2)	49.8
3. Japanese (4)	37.0
4. British (3)	25.4
5. French (5)	17.8
6. Italians (10)	15.5
7. Austrians (8)	11.8
8. Dutch (7)	11.4
9. Canadians (6)	11.1
10. Russians (–)	10.6
11. Belgians (12)	9.9
12. Swiss (9)	7.5
13. South Koreans (25)	7.0
14. Brazilians (19)	6.8
15. Taiwanese (17)	6.5
16. Swedes (14)	6.3
17. Poles (50)	6.2
18. Singaporese (24)	6.1
19. Australians (15)	5.3
20. Spanish (21)	4.9
21. Norwegians (16)	4.5
22. Thais (43)	4.2
23. Danes (18)	4.1
24. Chinese (40)	4.0
25. Mexicans (11)	3.4

WHERE THE TOP SPENDERS GO
The number of tourists arriving in each nation in 1996 from the nations that spend the most on international tourism, in millions.

AMERICAN TOURISTS		GERMAN TOURISTS		JAPANESE TOURISTS	
Mexico	20.3	France	13.4	U.S.	5.0
Canada	13.0	Spain	10.6	Hong Kong	2.4
Britain	3.3	Austria	10.2	Italy	1.7
France	2.6	Italy	6.8	China	1.6
Italy	2.4	Poland	6.7	S. Korea	1.5
Puerto Rico	2.2	Hungary	3.3	Singapore	1.2
Germany	1.6	Britain	3.0	Guam	1.0
Bahamas	1.3	Netherlands	2.3	Thailand	0.9
Spain	1.0	Switzerland	2.0	Taiwan	0.9
Jamaica	0.8	U.S.	2.0	Australia	0.8

BRITISH TOURISTS		FRENCH TOURISTS		ITALIAN TOURISTS	
France	9.9	Britain	3.8	France	5.3
Spain	8.7	Spain	3.4	Spain	2.2
Ireland	3.2	Italy	2.4	Britain	0.9
U.S.	3.1	U.S.	1.0	Germany	0.8
Greece	1.6	Germany	0.8	Austria	0.8
Italy	1.6	Belgium	0.8	U.S.	0.6
Germay	1.4	Portugal	0.6	Greece	0.5
Portugal	1.3	Turkey	0.6	Croatia	0.5
Netherlands	1.0	Austria	0.6	Switzerland	0.4
Belgium	0.8	Tunisia	0.5	Egypt	0.4

Sources: World Travel and Tourism Council; World Tourism Organization

Illustrations by Sue Truesdell for The New York Times

small family recently boarded No. 1 Special Tourism Bus in the Chinese capital for their first trip to the Great Wall, about 60 miles away. Xinhua, the Chinese news agency, which told their story, said that Mr. Wang was one of nearly 77 million people who visited tourist sites in or around Beijing last year. They spent, on average, about $10 a family.

In India, the world's second-most-populous country, whole villages charter buses and occasionally trains to take people with very little expendable income to places that were out of the reach of earlier generations. Tour operators everywhere are finding that standards of living need to rise only marginally for people to get an itch to hit the road. Perhaps even because of hard times—like the economic stress Asia is now experiencing—the popularity of short trips continues to rise.

Not every place is automatically threatened by an invasion, said Mr. Kaplan. "Are we messing up the world?" he asked. "I see that more in the Caribbean than anywhere else, where the islands are so small. But the Hyatts and Marriotts in a place like Cairo kind of disappear among the 14 million people."

The widely held view among environmentalists—who don't know whether to weep or cheer at the news that ecotourism is now one of the fastest-growing travel sectors—has been that mass international tourism has been the most damaging to natural settings. But as numbers of domestic travelers grow, that assumption cracks. In the case of India, with nearly a billion people, foreign travelers are still very small in number—not even one-sixth of the 17 million tourists who go to Thailand annually, for example. Indian beaches and mountain resorts, monuments and historical sites are taking a trouncing from short-haul Indian visitors. Similarly, Southeast Asia is experiencing a boom in

the construction of clubs and golf courses for the local business class, and it has forever altered rural landscapes.

Countries can respond to environmental and cultural problems imaginatively. The Himalayan kingdom of Bhutan raised prices and limited the number of tourist visas issued; it also developed with the World Bank a trust fund for protecting one of the last pristine mountain environments in Asia. The World Bank and the United Nations Educational, Scientific and Cultural Organization, have both helped the Mexican state of Oaxaca excavate, preserve and display Meso-American archeological ruins—saving sites but also making them accessible to tourists in a controlled way.

"Oaxaca is the best example of how you can have cultural tourism enhance the value of a historical site by having a local population very committed not only to conservation but to helping new generations create a new heritage of living cultures," said Lourdes Arizpe, a Unesco cultural official and a Mexican anthropologist. "Otherwise, we turn the world into a museum."

For both tourists and hosts, fortifying cultures as well as buildings is important, said Deborah Luhrman of the World Tourism Organization. "Tourism provides the money to restore local sites and monuments," she said. "It also helps the people who live there to understand the value of what they have."

"Travel is one of the basic human rights now," Ms. Luhrman said. "It is part of what makes the quality of life better. For some people, the right to travel has become part of political freedom."

*   *   *

March 28, 1999

A MANIFESTO FOR THE FAST WORLD

By THOMAS L. FRIEDMAN

In the winter of 1996, I accompanied Madeleine K. Albright, then the United States Ambassador to the United Nations, on a trip to the war zones of Africa. During the last stop, in Rwanda, she asked her staff to pose for a picture outside her Air Force 737. The group included a Greek-American, a Czech-American, Jewish Americans, black Americans and white Americans. There were Air Force crewmen from small towns and diplomats from Ivy League colleges, and they were all standing there shoulder to shoulder.

As I watched the Rwandan ground crew curiously watching the picture-taking, I couldn't help wondering what they were making of this scene, which represented America at its best: the spirit of community, the melting pot, the willingness to help faraway strangers in need and, most important, a concept of citizenship based on allegiance to an idea rather than to a tribe. As a picture, it represented everything that Rwanda was not.

And as I stood there, I started to get mad—not just about the tragedy in Africa but also about a budget debate that was then going on in Congress. We have something tremendously special in America, I thought, but if we want to preserve it, we have to pay for it and nurture it. Yet, when I listened to the infamous 1994 class of freshman Republicans—and when I hear echoes today, with the likes of the House majority leader, Dick Armey, boasting that he has traveled abroad only once—I heard mean-spirited voices, voices for whom the American Government was some kind of evil enemy. I heard men and women who insisted that the market alone should rule. And I heard lawmakers who seemed to believe that America had no special responsibility for maintaining global institutions and stabilizing an international system that benefits us more than any other country. And as I thought about all this on the tarmac of Kigali airport, I said to myself: "Well, my freshman Republican friends, come to Africa. It's a freshman Republican's paradise." Yes sir, nobody in Liberia pays taxes. There's no gun control in Angola. There's no welfare as we know it in Burundi and no big government to interfere with the market in Rwanda.

But a lot of their people sure wish there were. Like the desk clerk in Luanda, Angola, who looked at me as if I were nuts when I asked her if it was safe to take a walk three blocks from the hotel, down the main street of the capital in the middle of the day. "No, no, no," she shook her head—not safe." I'll bet she wouldn't mind paying some taxes for 100,000 more police officers.

And then there was the Liberian radio reporter who demanded to know why the Marines came to Liberia after the civil war broke out in 1989, evacuated only the United States citizens and then left. "We all thought, 'The Marines are coming, we will be saved,' " he said. "How could they leave?" Poor guy, his country has no marines to rescue him. I'll bet he wouldn't mind paying some taxes for a few good men.

Employers don't have to fret about those pesky worker-safety rules in Angola, let alone services for the handicapped. The 70,000 Angolans who have had limbs blown off by land mines get by just fine on their own. You can see them limping around the streets of Luanda in Fellini-esque contortions, hustling for food and using tree limbs as a substitute for the human variety. And in Rwanda and Burundi, no one is asked to pay for Head Start, Medicaid, national service or student-loan programs. Instead they just have a Darwinian competition for scarce land, energy and water, with Tutsi and Hutu tribesmen taking turns downsizing one another to grab more resources for themselves.

Many in Congress are reluctant to go on trips abroad. They think it looks bad to their constituents. Too bad. They want all the respect and benefits that come with being an American in today's world, but without any of the sacrifices and obligations that go with it. They should come to war-torn Africa and get a real taste of what happens to countries where there is no sense of community, no sense that people owe their government anything, no sense that anyone is responsible for anyone else, and where the rich have to live behind high walls and tinted windows, while the poor are left to the tender mercies of the marketplace.

I don't want to live in such a country, or such a world. It is not only wrong, it will become increasingly dangerous. Designing ways to avoid that should be at the heart of American domestic and foreign policy. Unfortunately, neither the Democrats nor the Republicans are thinking in those terms. They behave as if the world is now safe for us to be both insular and mindlessly partisan. To the extent that there is serious discussion about a shared national interest, it is about whether we can define a new common threat—Iraq, China, Russia—and not a new common mission. The "big enemy" is still the organizing principle of American internationalism, not the "big opportunity"—let alone "the big responsibility."

America does have a bipartisan national interest to pursue, and it has an enormous role to play. But we won't begin to fully grasp that until we understand that we are in a new international system. For the last 10 years we've been talking about "the post-cold-war world." We've described the world by what it isn't—it's not the cold war—because we don't know what it is. Well, what it is is a new international system called globalization. Globalization is not just a trend, not just a phenomenon, not just an economic fad. It is the international system that has replaced the cold-war system. And like the cold-war system, globalization has its own rules, logic, structures and characteristics.

Unlike the cold-war system, which was largely static, globalization involves the integration of free markets, nation-states and information technologies to a degree never before witnessed, in a way that is enabling individuals, corporations and countries to reach around the world farther, faster, deeper and cheaper than ever. It is also producing a powerful backlash from those brutalized or left behind.

If all the threats and opportunities of the cold-war system grew out of "division," all the threats and opportunities of the globalization system grow out of "integration." The symbol of the cold-war system was a wall, which divided everyone. The symbol of the globalization system is the World Wide Web, which unites everyone. In the cold war we reached for the hot line between the White House and the Kremlin—a symbol that we were all divided but at least someone, the two superpowers, were in charge. In the era of globalization we reach for the Internet—a symbol that we are all connected but nobody is in charge.

If the cold war had been a sport, it would have been sumo wrestling, says Michael Mandelbaum, a foreign affairs expert at Johns Hopkins University. "It would be two big fat guys in a ring, with all sorts of posturing and rituals and stomping of feet, but actually very little contact until the end of the match, when there is a brief moment of shoving and the loser gets pushed out of the ring, but nobody gets killed."

If globalization were a sport, it would be the 100-yard dash, over and over and over. And no matter how many times you win, you have to race again the next day. And if you lose by just a hundredth of a second it can be as if you lost by an hour.

The driving idea behind globalization is free-market capitalism. The more you let market forces rule and the more you open your economy to free trade and competition, the more efficient and flourishing your economy will be. Globalization means the spread of free-market capitalism to virtually every country in the world.

The defining document of the cold-war system was the Treaty. The defining document of the globalization system is the Deal. While the defining measurement of the cold war was weight, the defining measurement of the globalization system is speed—in commerce, travel, communication and innovation. The cold war was about Einstein's mass-energy equation, $E=mc2$. Globalization is about Moore's Law, which states that the computing power of silicon chips will double every 18 months.

The cold-war system was built around nation-states, and it was balanced by two superpowers: the United States and the Soviet Union. The globalization system is built around three balances that overlap and affect one another. One is the traditional balance between states and states. The next is the balance between states and "supermarkets"—the huge global stock and bond markets. (The United States can destroy you by dropping bombs, and the supermarkets can destroy you by downgrading your bonds.)

The last is the balance between states and "super-empowered individuals." Because globalization has brought down the walls that limited the movement and reach of people, and because it has simultaneously wired the world into networks, it gives more power to individuals than ever before to directly influence markets and nation-states. For instance, Osama bin Laden, the Saudi millionaire with his own global network (Jihad Online), declared war on America, and the Air Force had to launch cruise missiles at him. We launched cruise missiles at an individual—as though he were another nation-state.

As the country that benefits most from global economic integration, we have the responsibility of making sure that this new system is sustainable. This is particularly important at a time when the world has been—and will continue to be—rocked by economic crises that can spread rapidly from one continent to another. America has had 200 years to invent, regenerate and calibrate the balances that keep markets free without their becoming monsters. We have the tools to make a difference. We have an interest in making a difference. And we have the responsibility to make a difference.

Sustaining globalization is our overarching national interest. The political party that understands that first, the one that comes up with the most coherent, credible and imaginative platform for pursuing it, is the party that will own the real bridge to the future.

Designing a strategy to promote sustainable globalization at home and abroad is no easy task. And it is made even more complicated by the effects of globalization, which have intensified the world's long-running love-hate relationship with America. For the moment, America has many of the most sought-after goods, services and innovations in the global market. What people thought was American decline in the 1980's was actually America adjusting to the new system before anyone else. We're already around the second turn before some others have laced up their shoes. Globalization-is-U.S.

Because we are the biggest beneficiaries and drivers of globalization, we are unwittingly putting enormous pressure on the rest of the world. Americans may think their self-portrait is Grant Wood's "American Gothic," the strait-laced couple, pitchfork in hand, standing stoically outside the barn. But to the rest of the world, Americans actually look like some wild, multicolored Andy Warhol print.

To the rest of the world, American Gothic is actually two 20-something software engineers who come into your country wearing beads and sandals, with rings in their noses and paint on their toes. They kick down your front door, overturn everything in the house, stick a Big Mac in your mouth, fill your kids with ideas you never had or can't understand, slam a cable box onto your television, lock in the channel to MTV, plug an Internet connection into your computer and tell you, "Download or die."

We Americans are the apostles of the Fast World, the prophets of the free market and the high priests of high tech. We want "enlargement" of both our values and our Pizza Huts. We want the world to follow our lead and become democratic and capitalistic, with a Web site in every pot, a Pepsi on every lip, Microsoft Windows in every computer and with everyone, everywhere, pumping their own gas.

No wonder, therefore, that resentment of America is on the rise globally. In 1996 I visited Teheran and stayed in the Homa Hotel. The first thing I noticed was that above the front door in the lobby were the words "Down With U.S.A." It wasn't a banner. It wasn't graffiti. It was tiled into the wall. A short time later, I noticed that Iran's mullahs had begun calling America something other than the "Great Satan." They had begun calling it "the capital of global arrogance."

The Iranian leadership had grasped the important distinction between "global arrogance" and old-fashioned notions of imperialism, when one country physically occupies another. Global arrogance is when your culture and economic clout are so powerful and widely diffused that you don't need to occupy other people to influence their lives. Well, guess what? The Iranians aren't the only ones talking about America as "the capital of global arrogance." The French, Germans, Japanese, Indonesians, Indians and Russians also call us that now.

In most countries, people can no longer distinguish between American power, American exports, American cultural assaults, American cultural exports and plain old globalization.

Martin Indyk likes to tell the story of when, as Ambassador to Israel, he was called upon to open the first McDonald's in Jerusalem. McDonald's gave him a colorful baseball hat to wear, with the golden arches on it, so he would be properly attired as he ate the ceremonial first Big Mac in Jerusalem— with Israel Television filming every bite for the evening news. At that moment, an Israeli teen-ager walked up to him, carrying his own McDonald's hat, which he handed to Ambassador Indyk with a pen and asked: "Are you the Ambassador? Can I have your autograph?" Somewhat sheepishly, Ambassador Indyk replied: "Sure. I've never been asked for my autograph before."

As the Ambassador prepared to sign his name, the Israeli teen-ager said to him, "Wow, what's it like to be the ambassador from McDonald's, going around the world opening McDonald's restaurants everywhere?"

Ambassador Indyk looked at the Israeli youth and said, "No, no. I'm the American Ambassador—not the ambassador from McDonald's!" Ambassador Indyk described what happened next: "I said to him, 'Does this mean you don't want my autograph?' And the kid said, 'No, I don't want your autograph,' and he took his hat back and walked away."

Oh, well. The trick for America is to lead without being too overbearing, to be generous without overextending ourselves and to be tough without engendering too much resentment. But how?

First, forget about the political labels from the cold-war system. Democrats and Republicans, liberals and conservatives; these terms are meaningless today. Instead, to locate yourself and your opponents in the new era, consider the accompanying chart of globalization identities.

The line across the middle from left to right describes how you feel about globalization. At the far right end of this line are the "Integrationists." These are the people who really welcome globalization because they think it is either good or inevitable and want to see it promoted through more free trade, more Internet commerce, more networking of schools, communities and businesses, so that we can have global integration across 24 time zones and into cyberspace.

At the far left end of the globalization line are the "Separatists." These are people who believe that free trade and technological integration are neither good nor inevitable, because they widen income gaps, lead to jobs being sent abroad, homogenize cultures into global mush and lead to life being controlled by distant, faceless market forces. They want to cut off and kill globalization now.

So the first thing you have to do is locate yourself somewhere on this line. Are you a Separatist? An Integrationist? Or something in between?

Now look at the line running from top to bottom of the matrix. This is the distribution axis. It represents what sort of policies you believe governments should adopt to go along with globalization. At the lower end of this line are the "Social-Safety-Netters." These are people who believe that globalization will be sustainable only if it is democratized, in both the economic and the political sense.

Obviously, not everyone agrees with this approach. That's why at the other extreme from the Social-Safety-Netters are the "Let-Them-Eat-Cakers." These are people who believe that globalization is essentially winner-take-all, loser-take-care-of-yourself. They want to shrink government, taxes and safety nets, and let people reap the fruits of their own labor or pay the price of their own ineptitude.

So next you have to locate yourself on this distribution axis. Are you a Social Safety-Netter? Are you a Let-Them-Eat-Caker? Or something in between?

Bill Clinton is an Integrationist Social-Safety-Netter. Newt Gingrich, the former Speaker of the House, was an Integrationist Let-Them-Eat-Caker. That's why Clinton and Gingrich were always allies on free trade but opponents on Social Security-welfare spending. The House minority leader, Dick Gephardt, is a Separatist Social-Safety-Netter, while Ross Perot is a Separatist Let-Them-Eat-Caker. That's why Gephardt and Perot were allies in their opposition to Nafta but enemies on Social Security and welfare.

Al Gore and George W. Bush are interesting hybrids. Gore is an Integrationist Social-Safety-Netter, but not on the extreme end of either. He has certain Gephardtist leanings when it comes to free-trade issues that might alienate his labor-union base. Bush is an Integrationist Let-Them-Eat-Caker, but also not on the extreme end of either. He has certain Clintonite leanings on education, training and social spending that should appeal to centrist voters.

I'm an extreme Integrationist Social-Safety-Netter. I believe you dare not be a globalizer without being a safety-netter and social democrat, because if you don't equip the have-nots, know-nots and turtles to survive in the new system, they will eventually produce a backlash that will choke off your country from the world. And I believe you dare not be a safety-netter or social democrat without being a globalizer, because without ever-increasing integration, you will never generate the incomes and absorb the technologies needed to keep standards of living rising.

But what does it mean to be an Integrationist Social-Safety-Netter? I think it means articulating a politics, geo-economics and geopolitics of sustainable globalization.

Politics

The first thing a politics of sustainable globalization must include is a picture of the world, because no policy is sustainable without a public that understands why it's necessary. This is particularly true with globalization, because the people who are hurt by it know exactly who they are, but the people who benefit from it tend not to understand that at all. After World War II, successive Presidents instructed Americans about the One Big Thing in the world that would be at the center of American politics—containing Communism. Today, globalization and rapid technological change are that Big Thing. And that means virtually every aspect of national policy—health care, welfare, education, job training, the environment, market regulation, Social Security, free-trade expansion and military strategy needs to be adjusted so that we get the most out of the globalization system and cushion its worst aspects.

For instance, a politics of sustainable globalization would have to include a strategy for giving as many people as possible a financial stake in the Fast World. Whenever I think about this, I always recall a story that a Russian journalist, Aleksei Pushkov, told me back in April 1995 about one of his neighbors in Moscow. "He was this poor driver who lived in the apartment off the entryway. Every Friday night he would get drunk and sing along—over and over in a very loud voice—with two English songs: 'Happy Nation' and 'All She Wants Is Another Baby.' He had no idea what the words meant. When he got really drunk, he'd start beating his wife and she would start screaming. He was driving us crazy. I wanted to throw a grenade at him.

"Anyway," Pushkov continued, "about eight months ago, I don't know how, he got a share in a small car-repair shop. Since then, no more 'Happy Nation,' no more singing all night, no more beating his wife. He leaves every morning at 8:30 for work and he is satisfied. He knows he has some prospects in life now. My wife said to me the other day, 'Hey, look at Happy Nation'—that's what we call him—he's an owner now.' "

Integrationist Social-Safety-Netters feel that there are a lot of things we can do to democratize globalization economically, promote social stability and prevent our own society from drifting even further into high walls and tinted windows. These measures need not be all that expensive, nor do they have to involve radical income redistribution—or lavish welfare programs that violate the basic, neoliberal free-market rules of the system.

To that end, I believe that each Administration should offer an annual piece of legislation that I would call the Rapid Change Opportunity Act. It would accompany whatever integrationist policy the White House is pursuing that year—whether it be Nafta expansion or most-favored-nation status for China. The act would vary each year, but its goal would be to create both the reality and perception that the Government understands that globalization spreads its blessings unevenly, and therefore the Government is constantly going to be adjusting its safety nets and trampolines to get as many people as possible up to speed for the Fast World.

Last year, my Rapid Change Opportunity Act would have included pilot projects for public employment of temporarily displaced workers; tax breaks for severance pay for displaced workers; free government-provided resume consultation for anyone who loses a job, a further extension of the Kassebaum-Kennedy act, so that laid-off workers could keep their health insurance polices longer, and a national advertising campaign for one of the best, but most under-reported, bipartisan achievements of the Clinton era: the Workforce Investment Act.

Signed in August 1998, the act brought together and energized all the Government's job-training programs, including individual training accounts that workers can use for any training they believe will most advance their job opportunities, one-stop career centers for every job-training program and an increase in youth training programs by $1.2 billion over five years.

I would also include, in the Rapid Change Opportunity Act, increased lending to Asian, African and Latin American development banks to promote training of women, micro-lending to women and environmental cleanup. I'd also like to see an increase in financing for the International Labor Organization's new initiative for creating alternatives to child labor in countries where children are most abused. It's true: a hand-up really is better than a handout.

Even if we waste some money on these hand-up programs, the Rapid Change Opportunity Act would be a tiny price to pay for maintaining the social cohesion and political consensus for integration and free trade. Our motto should be: "Protection, Not Protectionism. Cushions, Not Walls. Floors, Not Ceilings."

Geo-Economics

I once wrote a fantasy about global investing that went something like this: I brushed up on my German and bought some German corporate bonds. I studied a little Japanese and picked up a few stocks on the Nikkei. I got a tip from a waiter at my local "House of Hunan" and bought a few shares on the Shanghai Stock Exchange. My broker tried to sell me some Lebanese bonds, but I told him that I already had wallpaper. I even did my thing for Russian reform by brushing up on the Cyrillic alphabet and buying a few Russian T-bills.

But after all this, I discovered that I had forgotten two little English words, "Alan Greenspan." Because when the Fed Chairman suddenly raised United States interest rates in the mid-1990's—making the extra interest investors were getting on foreign bonds less attractive—everyone started dumping securities in these foreign markets and bringing their money home. I got creamed. I was a bad lender, chasing higher rates of return without regard to risk.

Over the years I got a little smarter and became a better lender. I started doing my global investing through a mutual fund. A short time after Russia's economy went into a tailspin, in August 1998, I got a letter from that fund—Tweedy, Browne Global Value—reporting that its profits were down a bit because of the turmoil in international markets triggered by Russia's default. However, the fund was not down as much as many others because it had stayed away from Russia. The letter said of Russia that Tweedy "cannot understand investing in countries with little political stability, no laws protecting investors and a currency that may be put to better use as Kleenex." Yes, the Tweedy letter added, in the prior two or three years the Russian market increased fivefold, and then overnight lost 80 percent of its value—a complete round trip." Russia, it turns out, was a bad borrower.

I tell these two stories because they capture in microcosm the two biggest threats to today's global financial system— crises triggered by "bad lenders" and crises triggered by "bad borrowers." Just as there are drug users and drug pushers, in global economics there are bad borrowers, like Russia, and bad lenders, like myself. We need to address both.

Let's start with bad borrowers. I believe globalization did us all a favor by melting down the economies of Thailand, Korea, Malaysia, Indonesia, Mexico, Russia and Brazil in the 1990's, because it laid bare a lot of rotten practices in countries that had prematurely globalized. People keep referring to what happened in countries like Indonesia as an economic "crisis." Well, excuse me, but I don't consider the downfall of the most corrupt, venal, greedy, ruling family in the world— the Suhartos—a crisis. People talk about Indonesia or Russia or Thailand as if they had these charming, efficient and equitable financial systems before big bad globalization came along. Hogwash! Globalization simply exposed a bunch of flimflam regimes and crony-capitalist systems that were not up to the demands of the global system. The real crisis in these countries is not economic, it's political.

The tragedy is that globalization flattened not only the crony capitalists but also a lot of little folks who were just working hard and playing by the local rules (however flawed). In the new geo-economics, we now have an opportunity to assist the innocent victims by helping their countries get up to speed. The only lasting way to do it, though, is to encourage them to become not just emerging markets but also "emerging societies" (like Poland, Hungary and Taiwan), with real regulatory and democratic institutions. That way, as they plug into the global system they can handle its inevitable surges and excesses. The real crisis will come if we don't take advantage of this moment.

All sorts of would-be geo-architects want to set up some new global institutions to slow down capital flows. This is both wrong and futile. We want to keep global capital flows as free as possible—and even if we didn't, there's no way to restrict them anymore. The answer for countries is local, not global.

I like to compare countries to computers. Today, for the first time in history, we all have the same basic piece of hardware—free markets. The question is, which countries will get the economic operating systems (neoliberal macroeconomics) and software (regulatory institutions and laws) to get the most out of those free markets and cushion them from the worst surges coming from the "electronic herd" of global investors.

Russia is the egregious example of a country that plugged into the herd with no operating system and no software, with predictably horrendous results. Thailand, South Korea and Indonesia plugged into the herd, but with a slow operating system: what I call "DOScapital 2.0" (crony capitalism). It

was great for getting these countries from an average income of $500 per capita to $5,000. But when they wanted to move from $5,000 to $15,000, and the speed of the electronic herd moved from a 286 chip to a Pentium III, and they were still using DOScapital 2.0, a message came up on their screens: "You Have Performed a Series of Irrational Investments. Cannot Save Items. Delete Memory of All Inefficient Banks and Firms, and Download New Software and Operating System."

Thomas L. Friedman is the foreign affairs columnist for The New York Times. This article is adapted from his book, "The Lexus and the Olive Tree: Understanding Globalization," to be published in April by Farrar, Straus & Giroux.

* * *

April 14, 1999

CAN THIS BE PARIS?

The French Learn to Speak Fusion

By WILLIAM GRIMES

PARIS—There is a dessert in Paris called the wonton kumquat Nutella. It cannot be found in Escoffier, or anywhere else, for that matter.

Served at a new Right Bank restaurant called Cafe Mosaic, the kumquat surprise comes in a bamboo steamer that holds a very undessert-like display of three soft wonton envelopes, each containing a whole kumquat and a small puddle of molten Nutella, the commercial chocolate and hazelnut spread. The thing is awful. But in Paris, it may be the wave of the future.

In this city of bistros, brasseries and three-star shrines, a new type of restaurant seems to be taking hold: ultradesigned, up to the minute and emphatically un-French in style and culinary point of view. The spaces tend to be large and, by French standards, quite noisy. The waiters and waitresses, who are very young, ply their trade with an almost American casualness. The food is strange.

Fusion has come to France, and it feels funny. Influences from Asia, America and—heaven help us—even England have been creeping into one of the world's most rigidly codified cuisines. Like steam opening a mussel, the cultural pressures of the new global economy, and the internationalizing of taste, have forced the inward-looking French to look outward on a peculiar new world. Classically minded chefs are trying to assimilate concepts like Afro-Thai cuisine and to accept the idea that patrons care as much about the setting as they do about the food on the plate. The result is a new culinary moment in France, one that Gault-Millau magazine is calling "the new disorder."

All this and the euro, too—it's a lot to swallow. But Paris seems titillated by the strange new dances that its chefs are trying out, and the theatrical spaces in which they perform them. They have mobbed the new Lo Sushi, designed by Andree

Putman, where patrons pick up their sushi plates from a conveyer belt, and Man Ray, a hip-to-the-hilt Pacific Rim restaurant whose owners include Johnny Depp and Sean Penn. The new restaurant wave has attracted a group that Patrick Derderian, the owner of Zebra Square and Bermuda Onion, recently called "the happy few"—about 5,000 young and restless diners who move from address to address, their ranks swelled by well-to-do young professionals who, like the scene makers, want more than food from a restaurant.

"It appears that the era of the brasserie is over," said Miguel Cancio, a restaurateur and the consultant behind Man Ray, Barfly and Buddha Bar. "People want more—they want to be transported somewhere else, and to be entertained."

Asian, barely three weeks old, could stand as an archetype for the new fussy French fusion restaurant. It is enormous, a 400-seat, two-level affair that occupies about 16,000 square feet of prime real estate on the swank Avenue George V. The decor is high-tech teahouse, with an emphasis on dark, exotic woods that contrast sharply with the polished concrete floor and a Zen garden of dazzling white sand and bleached rocks that sends out vibrations conducive to spiritual peace. The sound system broadcasts a third-world mix of weird animal noises, rain-forest drips and tribal grunts and chants.

The menu makes more stops than a German tour bus. The dim-sum cart rolls by, followed by mixed plates of Japanese sushi, Vietnamese spring rolls and a green salad with sesame dressing. Dishes bear names like Ming beef, chicken Chitchat, Paradise Lost salad, and the intriguingly named "Delta Brochette Pff, Pff," which turns out to be chunks of chicken thigh on a stick.

It's a menu to read as much as to eat. Each dish is a statement, a little like the macaroni and cheese at Spoon, Alain Ducasse's new restaurant with the cheeky American accent. The dish itself is not as important as the fact that it's on the menu, like the fish and chips at Alcazar, Terence Conran's shiny new Left Bank brasserie on the Rue Mazarine.

Alcazar is nothing if not shrewd. Under the direction of Guillaume Lutard, formerly the senior sous-chef at Taillevent, the kitchen turns out a carefully calibrated mix of brasserie standards, seafood platters, pan-Mediterranean fare and the occasional English dish, like bread and butter pudding, or fish and chips. It's world food for young diners who move easily from Los Angeles to New York to Paris to London and who feel most comfortable in casual, sleekly designed restaurants that buzz and hum.

Alcazar's design is crisp and clean to the point of being antiseptic. The large open kitchen, with its gleaming white tiles and shiny stainless steel fixtures, is so pristine it could serve as a hospital operating theater, which is, in fact, what it looks like. On the blond-wood tables, the salt and the pepper, arranged in neat piles, come in a precision-tooled rectangular steel ashtray (available for about $15 on the way out), and the American-style selection of four rolls (plain sourdough, rye sourdough, black-olive and walnut) is served in what seems to be an oval Shaker box but on closer inspection turns out to be the lid to a container of cheese.

Alcazar is cute that way. Every touch has been thought through with one aim in mind: to make diners feel that they are the actors in a first-class production, with all the right props in place.

It's a set-design approach to dining that was perfected at Buddha Bar. Some of the heat has cooled at this first of the mega-restaurants, but when it opened in late 1996, it created a sensation. It was the Parisian equivalent of Balthazar or Asia de Cuba in Manhattan, a highly wrought stage set that allowed chic young Parisians to put on a show for themselves.

The scene has since shifted, but the decor remains. Buddha Bar is a fever dream of tropical elegance, its dense, opium-inspired interior rich with exotic woods, betasseled chandeliers and lush fabrics. Upstairs is a mile-long bar in the form of a dragon ship. Downstairs, there's the unignorable Buddha, a serene mass of beatitude seated on a square pedestal large enough to support a Cadillac. Rising nearly 60 feet to the ceiling, he has the air of a customer waiting patiently for a very big meal.

When it comes, he will want more spice. The lurid sensibility that went into the decor evaporated mysteriously at the kitchen door. The menu, a pan-Asian and French smorgasbord, skips blithely from Vietnamese spring rolls to Korean-style grilled steak to miso-glazed turbot, an Asian package tour for the timid. When it comes to the desserts, the exotic mask drops entirely. Except for a blancmange with coconut milk, the line-up is as French as a cancan. There's nothing wrong with any of the food, exactly, and the restaurant's excellent hot sauce, served on the side, works wonders on just about everything except the blancmange, but on the plate, Asia seems as remote as Buddha's smile.

In the United States, chefs have embraced the new ingredients and spices of Asia, Latin America and the Caribbean with a sometimes unseemly passion. They may not always love wisely, but shyness has not been a problem. In Paris, however, fusion resolutely refuses to fuse. When it comes to visual style, and atmosphere, the French cannot be beat. They seem to have no trouble with the theatrical elements of dining, or the international design idiom that goes with flashy fusion cuisine from Sydney to Miami. There are not many New York restaurants, for example, to equal the drop-dead elegant Telegraphe, recently redone in a blend of Viennese Secession and Art Nouveau by the design team behind the three-star Ambroisie.

But the intercultural mingling that energizes American chefs tends to stump the French, for reasons that are not that hard to figure out. A cooking tradition as ancient and deeply ingrained as France's presents every chef with a hundred reasons not to try anything funny. America, by contrast, has always been a "why not?" culture, and the national tendency toward experimentation has been powerfully reinforced by an unending influx of new immigrant groups and new cuisines.

The example of Jean-Georges Vongerichten shows that a French sensibility and Asian ingredients can produce spectacular results, but his brethren here in the old country appear to be struggling a bit with their spring rolls and their sesame vinaigrettes. They either pussyfoot or, like a teetotaler who falls off the wagon, go wild and shoot up the town.

Cafe Mosaic, the Mad Max of Paris restaurants, falls into the second category. Deceptively, the interior is cool and understated, with dark wood blinds covering the windows facing the busy Avenue George V, and a suave semicircular bar, decorated with a vase of white orchids, off to one side of the room. All the more shocking, then, to witness the parade of oddities streaming out of the kitchen. Anise-steamed crayfish whiz by in a mason jar. The "salade verte" turns out to be a half-head of iceberg lettuce, sitting on the plate like a stooge. Then come the kumquat wontons a la Nutella, or even better, the "orange a l'orange," a glistening orb of citrus fruit, preciously situated in a large gray bowl, that oozes an orange cream when pierced with a fork.

Some of this is thrilling, like the smoky roast pepper, with a sauce of anchovies, chickpeas and soy, or the ruby-colored pigeon breast mired in a gooey plum-peanut sauce and surrounded by kumquats. All of it is cartoonish. At table after table, French diners, after a scandalized intake of breath, were laughing as the plates arrived, and who could blame them? In retrospect, the two mini-baguettes placed on the table at the beginning of the meal seem like the last word in irony.

It's the kind of small gesture that conceals a big fact: French cuisine has entered the postmodern era.

* * *

April 17, 2000

AN UNLIKELY CHAMPION OF A NEW TRADE PACT WITH CHINA

By ERIC SCHMITT

WASHINGTON—Sander M. Levin hardly fits the classic free-trade profile. He is a liberal Democratic congressman from the Detroit suburbs who proudly owns a 94 percent career voting record with organized labor.

Yet with thousands of protesters in town to demonstrate against the World Bank, the International Monetary Fund and what they view as the evils of globalization, Representative Levin will be lucky if he isn't hanged in effigy.

The 68-year-old legislator is fine-tuning a plan that could give wavering House Democrats the political cover they want to vote yes on the biggest trade deal in years, an accord with China. If Mr. Levin succeeds, Congress will help hand Beijing a diplomatic coup while opening new markets for American goods but will still keep leverage over China's behavior on human rights, religious tolerance and the environment.

"Members are searching for a way to both keep the heat on China and get the benefits of what we negotiated," Mr. Levin said in his Capitol Hill office, where photographs of Thomas P. O'Neill and Robert F. Kennedy adorn the wall. "We have to strive to combine active engagement with constructive confrontation."

For 20 years Congress has gone through the motions of an annual debate and vote to grant China the same trading privileges that Washington gives almost every other country. Congress has never refused to provide this plum.

But now China is on the verge of joining the World Trade Organization, and as part of a deal negotiated last fall, President Clinton promised to try to lift the annual review and grant Beijing permanent trading status.

The House will vote just before Memorial Day, but the outcome is too close to call. The fate of the agreement rests with about two dozen uncommitted Democrats. Passage in the pro-business Senate is considered certain.

Enter Mr. Levin, a senior member of the House Ways and Means Committee, who is one of the fence-sitters and has long wrestled with trade issues. He voted against the North American Free Trade Agreement in 1993 and opposed giving President Clinton fast-track authority to negotiate trade pacts. He has voted both for and against granting China normal trading status.

"I'm an activist internationalist who's worked on both sides: expanded trade and expanded issues of trade," said Mr. Levin, who banged on Japan's doors in the 1980's to pry open its market to American automobiles.

Mr. Levin came away from a 10-day trip to China in January convinced that this trade agreement would influence the future of U.S.-China relations for years to come.

"I came back feeling that changes in China are irreversible, but that the direction is not inevitable," said Mr. Levin, who talked to students, artists and intellectuals about how free trade could open up China's repressive society. "You have to shape globalization."

Mr. Levin sees himself as an organizer and a problem solver, and set out to steer all sides to a middle ground. He has drawn up a plan to monitor China once it joins the W.T.O., and to react swiftly to any violations. The proposal sets up a Congressional-executive branch commission to monitor China's behavior on human rights and trade—the biggest concern of opponents to giving up the yearly review—and arms it with a quiver of rewards and penalties.

The plan would also write into law promises China made to the United States to avoid surges of Chinese exports into the American market.

At first, no one on Capitol Hill paid much attention to Mr. Levin's plan. But by the time lawmakers headed home last week for a recess and the administration anxiously sought to nail down undecided votes, the idea was catching on. Backers say Mr. Levin's plan could swing 10 to 15 votes.

Mr. Levin is not flashy, nor is the low-key, details approach he has used in shopping his plan to about 40 undecided Democrats and Republicans. A Democratic colleague once described him as "a pit bull with manners."

"What Sandy is doing is extremely helpful because he's trying to get some accountability over time," said Representative Tom Allen, a Maine Democrat whose vote is up for grabs.

The China trade wars have catapulted Mr. Levin into the limelight somewhat to the chagrin of his party's leaders.

Representative Richard A. Gephardt of Missouri, the House Democratic leader who is strategically neutral on the vote, has been dismissive of Mr. Levin's efforts, choosing to broker his own third way with the White House.

The No. 2 Democrat in the House, David E. Bonior of Michigan, is leading the charge against the deal, and has called Mr. Levin's plan toothless.

In a rare flash of pique, Mr. Levin bristles at that criticism: "It has a lot of teeth in it, and I hope they're sharp and will bite when they need to."

Sander Martin Levin, the grandson of Russian and Polish Jews, was born and raised in Detroit. After earning degrees from the University of Chicago, Columbia University and Harvard Law School, he threw himself into the political arena.

Mr. Levin served in the Michigan State Senate for five years, but after two failed attempts to become governor in the 1970's, he thought he was washed up in politics. He was assistant administrator of the Agency for International Development during the Carter administration.

But in 1982, Michigan's 12th Congressional District opened up, and Mr. Levin has occupied it ever since, forming the lesser-known half of the Levin brother act in Congress. (Mr. Levin's younger brother, Carl, is the senior senator from Michigan and ranking Democrat on the Armed Services Committee.) Mr. Levin and his wife, Vicki, have four grown children.

For Mr. Levin, who worked one summer at a Dodge auto assembly plant, the China pact brings his trade career full circle: "My feeling on trade is that it's more than the humdrum of tariffs. A key part of economic life is rolling up your sleeves on a daily basis to work it out and to avoid the extremes."

* * *

May 5, 2000

SPRECHEN SIE TECHNOLOGY?

Europeans Try to Relax Borders for Skilled Workers

By JOHN TAGLIABUE

PARIS, May 4—Eric Perbos-Brinck gave up a promising management career last year at Promodes, the big French retailer, to start an Internet company called Bravonestor.com. He began in November with just 2 people, but already has 10 employees, with plans to hire 5 more in the next few weeks. To fill the jobs, Mr. Perbos-Brinck, 31, casts his net wide. One of his programmers is Moroccan. The designer of search engines is Senegalese. Both were studying in France as exchange students when Mr. Perbos-Brinck found them in a desperate search.

"It's difficult and it's an issue," he said. "One of my American investors said, 'This is war, so get anyone you can, anywhere.' "

Mr. Perbos-Brinck's polyglot staff would not draw a second glance in the United States, where the technology industry's ravenous demand for skilled workers has created a multinational, multicultural work force that includes many foreigners. But in Europe, his effort to find qualified help has collided with one of Europe's most divisive issues: immigration.

The historic European antipathy toward immigrants has only sharpened in recent years. But with the European economy on the rebound, unemployment dropping from the extremely high levels of the mid-1990's and leaders clamoring to catch up with the United States in high technology, business faces a serious problem.

Although job creation is gradually reducing overall unemployment rates, Europe finds itself in the curious situation of facing much higher unemployment than in the United States yet simultaneously suffering a critical shortage of skilled high-technology workers that is expected to worsen.

The shortfall is particularly acute in Internet and Web-related businesses because European countries have not trained enough workers of their own with high-technology skills, a problem they are just beginning to address.

As a result, even as overall opposition to immigration remains deeply entrenched, European governments are under pressure to find ways around these obstacles for at least some high-technology workers.

In Britain, Gordon Brown, the chancellor of the exchequer, proposed in March to relax rules on hiring skilled foreigners.

In Germany, the chancellor, Gerhard Schröder, set off a stormy debate with a proposal to lift visa restrictions so that software experts from India and elsewhere could work in Germany. Even though the plan has not been approved, it has already attracted about 1,800 applications or requests for information.

Pre-empting a final decision, cities like Frankfurt have begun to make exceptions to the rule that keeps foreign computer experts out.

For Ernesto Schmitt, such openings in Europe's immigration net cannot come too soon. Mr. Schmitt, 28, set up Peoplesound.com, a London company that sells music over the Internet, and he uses all the tricks common to start-ups in the United States to find and keep talent, including the use of aggressive international headhunters and the promise of equity stakes in his company. Yet recently, when he discovered talented potential employees in South Africa, he decided he could not hire them. "We did not want the pain of waiting six months for them to get visas," he said.

The new economy is not waiting for governments to act on the shortage, which is leading to brawls for talented people. At big corporations, once the safe domain of career-oriented young Europeans, the best talent is being lured away by headhunters; other gifted young executives are leaving of their own accord, willingly forfeiting the security of the old economy for the rough-and-tumble risk of the new.

Mr. Schmitt, who grew up in Belgium, the son of a Uruguayan mother and German father, is perhaps typical of the new brand of European Web business leader. A self-styled frustrated disc jockey, he took the idea for his company from American models like MP3.com but rejiggered it for the European market. After attracting investors including Bernard Arnault, the wealthy chairman of the LVMH Moet Hennessy Louis Vuitton luxury goods group, he gave up the comfort of a secure job at the Boston Consulting Group to plunge into the new economy.

Olivier Gravelle, 29, operating in sparsely furnished offices in Paris, recently set up the French unit of Wideyes.com, an online job search company much like Monster.com in the United States. Wideyes, founded in Sweden about a year ago, now employs 70 people there and in Britain, France and Spain. By the end of the year, after moving into Germany and Italy, it expects to have about 230 employees.

"There is a war for talent," said Mr. Gravelle, who is French. Aggravating a basic shortage of skilled workers, upstart companies are acquiring established businesses—he cites the successful hostile bid by the British wireless company Vodafone AirTouch for the German phone giant Mannesmann—and needing new-style managers who are suited to the speed and complexity of electronic business.

"People who come to us looking for jobs want mobility; they want to change jobs and to change geographically," Mr. Gravelle said. Young Europeans, he added, "understand their duty to manage their skills and their careers."

Mr. Gravelle himself left a secure job at the consultants Booz Allen & Hamilton in November to join Wideyes. He had met the Swedish founders of Wideyes earlier, while working in Scandinavia for the French bank Credit Lyonnais, before joining Booz Allen.

Five years ago, that kind of mobility was the preserve of a small elite. Today it is so common that European companies are having to learn how to hold on to talented people, often employing means, like stock options, that not long ago were considered symptoms of very un-European greediness. Last month, for example, when Societe Generale in France announced the sale of shares in its online banking unit, Fimatex, it did so not least to enable it to retain talent by offering stock options, after the executive who started Fimatex was lured by stock options to a competitor.

Consulting companies are among the main beneficiaries of the growth, as demand soars from corporations that are in need of skilled help.

Marc A. Enjolras, a partner at Andersen Consulting in Paris, says Andersen will hire 250 people in France this year, increasing its staff to 2,750.

To avoid losing people to Internet start-ups, Andersen France is introducing a number of retention measures already in use in the United States. Starting this year, Andersen's French employees will receive "e-units," or shares in a $1 billion venture capital fund that the firm established in December. In France, as elsewhere, Andersen is also shortening the path to full partner by eliminating the rank of associate partner.

Hugues Bertrand, director of the Center for the Study of Employment and Qualification in Marseille, a port city plagued by high unemployment and urban decay, said that in large measure "companies that are successful are those that are creative and active in finding people." Much European job growth is coming not in technical professions, he added, but in traditional fields like education, career training and health and fitness services. "Preparation need not be so much technical as social—dealing with people, running an organization," he said.

Many business leaders argue that the shortage of technology workers is real and that failure to address it will stunt Europe's revived growth.

Bernard Vergnes, the 54-year-old chairman of Microsoft Europe, points to a study commissioned by Microsoft and published in March by the International Data Corporation that suggests that European demand for skilled professionals in telecommunications and computers will outstrip supply by as much as 13 percent over the next three years.

Microsoft recently joined a group of Europe-based technology companies, including British Telecommunications, Nokia of Finland and Siemens of Germany, as well as IBM Europe, to urge greater cooperation between industry and governments in training skilled technology workers.

Hardest hit by the shortages, according to the International Data study, will be Germany, which has the largest European economy and is the heart of European Internet business. Demand for talent in Germany is expected to exceed supply by as much as 15 percent, or more than 400,000 jobs.

Touring a computer fair in March, Mr. Schröder, the German chancellor, responded to industry's demands for help by taking a chapter from United States policy and promising to offer temporary work permits—a kind of German green card—to as many as 20,000 skilled foreigners, notably from India and Eastern Europe. In return, German industry leaders promised to step up the training of domestic computer experts.

The plan quickly drew fire from labor unions and opposition parties, who cited Germany's 4 million unemployed and 7.3 million foreigners, the highest number of immigrants in any European country. It also faced criticism from Mr. Schröder's own labor ministry. Gerd Andres, the ministry's No. 2 official, said the plan would only "bring cheap labor into the country."

German cities have jumped the gun on this issue. In Frankfurt, the German financial capital and a major computer center, the local investment promotion agency, with the approval of local immigration officials, has persuaded six software companies from India to establish affiliates in the city.

The agency's director, Hartmut Schwesinger, said recently that six more Indian companies were about to follow and that he was in discussions with 30 more.

Still, given the Continent's distaste for foreigners, not everyone is convinced that foreign workers will come even if the German proposal is repeated across Europe.

Andrew Milroy, who oversaw the shortages study for International Data, recalled talking with Sri Lankan and Indian software experts who said they would not be inclined to accept a European invitation.

Mr. Milroy recalled their saying, "Europe is just not a welcoming place to live."

*   *   *

September 24, 2000

MOVEMENT

Growing Up and Getting Practical Since Seattle

By ROGER COHEN

PRAGUE—With her Danish mother, her Syrian father, her French passport and her Oxford education, Annie-Christine Habbard, 31, seems every inch the global citizen equipped to succeed in a shrinking world. Yet here she is, chic in black, articulate in several tongues, at the annual meeting of the World Bank and the International Monetary Fund, protesting the state of the globe. What she wants is more social justice, respect for human rights, a "counterpower" to high finance and, for good measure, a more equitable distribution of the spoils from a new Chad-Cameroon oil pipeline.

Say "anti-globalization" and stormy images come to mind: ransackers of McDonald's restaurants in France, smashers of Seattle storefront windows. The police on every corner here, and the shuttered shops, confirm the power of such specters, and indeed some protesters say they want a repeat of Seattle. But the specter of violence can deceive. The deeper reality is more significant: that of an increasingly sophisticated, intellectually robust protest movement, mixing idealism with pragmatism, that is fast playing catch-up with the forces of multinational capital.

It is time to change icons: replace the angry visage of Jose Bove, the French farmer recently imprisoned for storming a McDonald's, with the cool features and articulate aplomb of Ms. Habbard.

"Ours is a new planetary citizenship, reflecting the fact that decisions have migrated from state level," Ms. Habbard, the deputy secretary general of the Paris-based International Federation of Human Rights, said. "Voting for national representatives, an old expression of citizenship, achieves nothing, because they have scant power. We have to be here to fight the political battles that will ensure globalization does not continue to accentuate inequities."

She is not alone. More than 350 citizens' organizations are here—debt-reliefers, save-the-Earthers, human-dignity-firsters, and everything in between, representing lands from Mauritius to Mexico. Forget right and left and the stale duels of national politics: the battle of universal principles against universal capital now unfurls.

It might be argued that the lines are being drawn in the wrong place. The $1.2 trillion traded daily on world money markets equals the entire lending of the World Bank over its 55 years of existence. But all that fast-moving money has no identifiable face. By contrast, the altar of market liberalization, privatization and public spending cuts is identifi-able, and the protesters are sure such orthodoxy has run its course.

Ms. Habbard is determined to change the world through international human-rights law where her predecessors deployed Marxist revolution or flower power. She is intensely pragmatic. She has lawyers behind her, ready to use the body of international law to compel the World Bank to avoid loans to any projects that might compromise human rights. Multinational corporations are more difficult to control, she concedes, but they are the next target. The Internet links her to other groups like Greenpeace or Friends of the Earth, with their own batteries of lawyers. Nothing dreamy here: this fight to shape globalization has all the romance of a corporate takeover battle.

Organizations like Attac in France, whose membership has increased in two years to 26,000, including more than 20 members of Parliament, argue for taxes on international capital flows, codes of conduct obliging multinationals to respect human rights and restraints on the activities of United States pension funds that pursue returns in Europe in ways that cut back jobs. For Bruno Jetin, a French economist, such measures are essential to "put equality and human beings back at the center of economic debate."

Such ideas have a particular resonance in France, where equality is a founding principle of the republic and rapid Americanization in recent years has stirred uneasiness. But everywhere in Europe, where the state's heavy role in balancing the excesses of the market had been widely accepted, the triumph of the private sector causes some unease. One challenge before these Europeans—and all the anti-globalists—is to make the case that their concern for equity will not hobble growth in the developing world, as it sometimes has done on this continent. On the other hand, the intellectual ammunition of the anti-globalists has also been reinforced by the spread of poverty in places that include Eastern Europe—a trend that has led James D. Wolfensohn, the World Bank president, to use some very strong language here.

"Today you have 20 percent of the world controlling 80 percent of the gross domestic product," he said. "You've got a $30 trillion economy and $24 trillion of it in developed countries. The income of the top 20 is 37 times the income of the bottom 20, and it has doubled in the last decade. These inequities cannot exist. So if you are looking for systemic breakdown, I believe you have to think today in terms of social breakdown."

Dramatic words. But another side to the story clearly exists. Open markets and free trade have slashed poverty in East Asia, and a few countries in Africa have also begun to respond to this recipe of economic opening. As Daniel Bachman, chief economist at The Globalist.com, an online magazine, pointed out: "Globalization can also improve conditions by forcing a race to the top." In states like Argentina, the dismantling of local oligarchies caused by open markets has had a tremendous liberating effect. In a place like Haiti, subsistence wages may be undignified, but they are better than starvation.

Globalization can also be a very fertile process. Much has been made of the Americanization of the world, but cultural currents are more mixed than that, and the United States has also been Europeanized, from its coffee to its eating habits. In some areas, such as data privacy, stricter European standards seem likely to prevail, to Americans' benefit.

Yet the president of the World Bank warns of a social breakdown because of the very global economic system he is deemed to personify. So there is clearly a problem, and a growing one. Its nature is economic and political. Some basic statistics are not encouraging—about 1.2 billion people still living on less than $1 a day, another 1.3 billion people on $2—and the diverse protests stirred by such numbers are now so vigorous that dialogue and compromise have become essential.

"If we do not succeed in making clear to citizens that globalization is to their benefit, we run a big political risk," said Caio Koch-Weser, a senior German economic official. "There's a feeling in the population that nobody's in charge. People are afraid of losing jobs to the whims of multinationals. We need to bring Wall Street to Main Street."

This sharpening of official concern reflects the fact that a decade of globalization has allowed a keener dissection of its characteristics. The wild denunciations of the inhuman scourge of rampaging global capital in the French author Viviane Forrestier's immensely popular "The Economic Horror" (one million copies sold worldwide, but unpublished in the United States), have given way to subtler analysis. Often this has concentrated on the way a global economy can prompt a "race to the bottom," as the cheapest labor and lowest taxes are relentlessly sought out. The net effect has been described by the German sociologist Ernest Beck as "the Brazilianization of the West"—the progressive recourse to uninsured, temporary workers—and the slow dismantlement of the welfare state.

John D. Clark, a development specialist on leave from the World Bank, has argued that globalization was always a highly selective thing. Advocates of free trade really wanted only an unrestrained market for capital. The result has been to maximize returns on capital, while minimizing returns to labor. "The world over, gaps between rich and poor have widened as richer populations and countries raced ahead of poorer," Mr. Clark wrote recently.

Many economists dispute that view. But officials seem convinced that beyond debt relief, an enormous effort must now be made to give more people the basic tools to benefit from a global economy: education, lifetime training, access to technology, encouragement for the stock ownership that alone will spread America's brand of popular capitalism, in which even blue-collar workers benefit from investing. Without such measures, the distorting effects of the wild premium placed by modern markets on talent and technology seem likely to grow, miring a third of humanity in abject poverty.

The other new priority seems to be dialogue. Mr. Wolfensohn spent time Friday with non-governmental organizations including the Bolivian Episcopal Conference, the Coalition for Democracy and Civil Society of the Kyrgyz

Republic, and a representative of something called World Vision from Uganda. Questions ranged from corruption to control of multinationals to that Chad-Cameroon oil pipeline. The meeting, in such a setting, amounted to a first. But the evolution is natural enough: world politics, however cumbersome, for a global economy.

*   *   *

September 26, 2000

INTERNATIONAL LENDERS' NEW IMAGE: A HUMAN FACE

By JOSEPH KAHN

PRAGUE, Sept. 25—Deepa Narayan, a Indian woman with a steely gaze who spends much of her time in the poorest villages on earth, speaks of power, voice and equality as the keys to ending poverty. Keeping men from beating women does far more to raise living standards than any dam project ever did, she argues.

She would make a fine spokeswoman for protesters who plan to blockade World Bank and International Monetary Fund officials in their hotels here on Tuesday, when they hope to send a message that global lending agencies hurt the poor.

But Ms. Narayan, 48, works for the World Bank, and seems to like it there. And therein lies one of the messages emerging from the meetings here: the World Bank and the International Monetary Fund are successfully repelling the attacks.

Like those who disrupted the World Trade Organization's meeting in Seattle last year and the bank and the fund's meeting in Washington last spring, the protesters here view the World Bank and the monetary fund as retrograde institutions that carry water for multinational corporations. But increasingly the protesters are aiming at moving targets. The bank and the fund are, by the standards of huge bureaucracies, changing quickly, largely because of outside pressure.

In fact, Ms. Narayan just completed a two-year, two-volume survey of 20,000 people who live on less than $1 a day. She and others at the bank say the study is one of several revolutionizing who gets the bank's $30 billion in loans each year.

"I think some of the protests have been helpful in bringing about changes," Ms. Narayan said on the sidelines of the bank's annual meetings here today. "But they are also worrying. You can destroy overnight what has taken so long to build."

Ms. Narayan's study, called "Voices of the Poor," is one example of how James D. Wolfensohn, an American who is the World Bank's president, has tried to reinvent poverty programs. But equally telling is how he and Horst Kohler, the German who is managing director of the I.M.F., have cast themselves as allies of governments and charity groups in poor countries, sometimes taking stands against the rich nations that provide most of their financing.

The Prague meetings may be remembered among globalization experts as the time when the two institutions, so much under attack, managed to gain some footing. Their tormentors on the streets, always at a disadvantage because of their small budgets and mixed messages, seem to be taking the blows.

"Wolfensohn and Kohler have become extremely important allies for us," said Trevor A. Manuel, South Africa's finance minister and the chairman of the Prague meetings. "Our real problem is the U.S., Britain and France. The protesters seem not to understand these things."

He was referring to the reluctance of lawmakers in the rich nations, especially in the United States Congress, to provide more money to the bank and the fund that could be used to relieve the old debts of developing countries.

Mr. Manuel also criticized the reluctance of industrial countries to share power at the two lending agencies. Mr. Wolfensohn and Mr. Kohler have quietly pushed ministers of wealthy nations, especially Europeans, to give up some voting power.

Many critics are actually spending more time inside the Congress Center in Prague than on the streets this year. Mr. Kohler and Mr. Wolfensohn gave entry passes to some 300 charity and watchdog groups so that they could attend the annual meetings, and the outreach seems to be working. Many protesters now call the two lending agencies potential friends or, at worst, ciphers.

"They are civil servants," Ann Pettifor, organizer of the Jubilee 2000 coalition of debt-relief groups, said of Mr. Wolfensohn and Mr. Kohler. "We know who the bad guys are. It's the G-7," referring to the Group of 7, the organization of seven leading economic powers.

To some outside protesters, a mix of anarchists, Marxists, student activists and environmentalists, hers is a distinction without a difference. But their lack of discrimination is a handicap.

Their main protest event is scheduled for Tuesday, when the bank and the fund hold their formal meeting ceremonies. The Group of 7 ministers, including Treasury Secretary Lawrence H. Summers, attended sessions on Saturday at the German Embassy here unhindered. Some ministers have already left.

The bank and the fund, along with the World Trade Organization, make appealing protest targets as symbols of globalization. Their leaders are hand-picked, not elected, and they have historically been secretive. They make tens of billions of dollars of loans each year.

But they are accountable to nations who are members, rich ones most of all, but also poor ones. And, like any bureaucracy, they are scrambling to survive in a new era, making themselves imperfect proxies for multinational corporations or other presumed forces of evil.

Take Mr. Kohler, the new managing director at the fund. He took over the reins of the Washington-based monetary fund at perhaps the low point of its reputation last spring, when it was under attack for mismanaging bailouts in Asia and Russia in recent years.

He quickly departed on what he called a listening tour of 16 developing countries and when he returned he began talking about changes in how the fund makes loans. He says he will streamline the much criticized conditions its attaches to its money.

For instance, when the fund provided $40 billion in emergency financing to Jakarta during the Asian crisis, it attached a list of more than 100 conditions. It required, for example, that the government disband its clove monopoly and eliminate price subsidies on basic foodstuffs, seen as ways of using the lending as leverage toward a free market.

Mr. Kohler said the conditions went too far, alienating Indonesians. "I will not have another Indonesia," he said.

He also agreed to eliminate a requirement the fund had imposed on Mozambique. There, fund officials had told the government to eliminate import tariffs on sugar, which the government had imposed to help the troubled industry. Mr. Kohler now says he will no longer force developing nations to adopt trade liberalization that rich countries like the United States or those in Europe have not yet undertaken.

At the World Bank, Mr. Wolfensohn routinely points out that almost half the world's population lives on less than $2 a day. He readily admits that many of the bank's traditional clients have not done much to improve the lives of the poor.

Although Mr. Wolfensohn is a former investment banker, he is proving hard to outflank on the left. He gave Ms. Narayan's team of economists latitude to write what the bank calls its World Development Report, a flagship document that—after much internal debate—threw stones at the orthodox temple of development economics by challenging the notion that all loans should aim to stimulate growth. Freeing trade, privatizing government companies and limiting government spending were once seen as main ingredients.

The latest report does not attack those ideas. Instead it focuses on "empowering" poor people, addressing dysfunctional family structures, and cutting government middlemen out of aid distribution. It reads like something written by people Mr. Wolfensohn himself once described as the "Berkeley Mafia."

Bank officials promise that their loan portfolio will look radically different in five years, reflecting the report's new priorities. But it already looks quite different than it did when Mr. Wolfensohn took power five years ago when the bank spent one in five of its aid dollars on electrical infrastructure projects. Today that ratio is 1 in 50.

This year the bank is spending hundreds of millions of dollars to fight AIDS and malaria. It has begun a $500 million pilot program in Indonesia examining how to channel aid directly to villages where poor people live, rather than entrusting authorities to do that for them.

All this talk raises pressure on the bank and the fund to make far more progress in fighting poverty in the next decade than they did during the last, when living conditions for the poor in Africa, the former Soviet Union and much of Latin American actually deteriorated.

But now, at least, the protesters have worthy challengers in the battle for public opinion.

GLOBALIZATION 1900

January 1, 1900

TRADE CONDITIONS THROUGHOUT THE WORLD

What the Past Year has Evolved and the Prospects for 1900 as London Sees Them

By A. J. WILSON

LONDON, Dec. 31—The year 1899 has been one of industrial progress and development in all parts of the world. Every European nation of any importance has taken a step forward, and the increased competition between them has only served to develop their business. Germany continues to make strenuous efforts to conquer English markets in foreign countries, and is especially seeking to compete with her for a more important share in the carrying trade of the world. France likewise, although more feebly, struggles with determination at least to retain her old markets, and has this year made some small progress in enlarging her foreign trade. Her mercantile marine, however, stagnates, and, in spite of £400,000 per annum in subsidies from the State, can barely hold its own against the non-subsidized Nord Deutsche Lloyd, now the largest commercial shipping company in the world, let alone against England. Even Spain is waking up a little, and finds herself richer in the means for internal development now that the resources and workers are no longer drained away by her colonies. Italy, too, moves, and Russia, but Austria-Hungary and the principalities of the lower Danube have had the promising outlook of the earlier part of the year almost destroyed by the partial, in Roumania almost complete, failure of the harvest. Southern Russia is affected by the same scourge, which seems indeed to have injured mankind almost from Rangoon westward to Budapest, if not to Land's End. Our own trade has been increasingly expansive since the Spring, less so in bulk than in prices, but still expansive, in spite of famines, wars, and the set-back caused by successive years of drought in Australia as well as by the increase in local and United States competition in the Far East. Out of the Australian and other droughts, indeed, a certain compensation has arisen for us in the higher prices of wool and the increased business done by Argentine, so that the buying power of these countries has not been diminished.

Genesis Of Expansion Periods

Misfortunes often commence periods of expansion provided the losses are only partial. The poor crops of western Europe in 1897 started the present business revival in the United States, and from there it spread to Europe until it now combines every country influenced by and emulous of Teutonic and Anglo-Saxon industrial development. No better measure of the motives governing nations hitherto laggard can be had than that afforded by the remarkable prosperity of our textile machinery manufacturers. Japan appears at the present to have nearly completed her orders for such, but Russia, China, India, Turkey, Italy, and in a small way, Spain, are all active buyers. Even the United States is coming for some of the tools with which to furnish the new cotton mills of the South, and the fact is ominous of strenuous competition to come. In other machinery our trade is also good, and it may be noted as a fact interesting to you that our export sales of British-made sewing machines alone will this year exceed £1,250,000.

But in one important field the United States and the Continent are altogether beating England. She was the pioneer of railways worked by steam, she is last—and a long way last—in the adaptation of electricity as a motive power for any purpose. Electric lighting has come into use here slowly, but is as yet by no means well developed in many parts of the country, and the best of the machinery by means of which light is generated comes from the United States. It is the same with electric railway plant and appliances, and the use of these with us is yet in its infancy. On the Continent it is altogether different, and one chief cause of the financial tight place most European money markets find themselves in lies in the speed with which they have locked capital up in enterprises of every description designed to utilize electricity as a motive and light giving force.

Mention of money brings us to the darker side of the picture, but that will be best dealt with in an estimate of prospects for the coming year.

The Outlook For 1900—In Money

All through the latter half of 1899 rates of interest have been mounting or stationary at an oppressively high level on European money markets, until the position of some of them has become dangerous. It is not that any one market appears poorer on the surface. They are in appearance all either stronger or very little weaker than they were a year ago. In the matter of gold the Bank of England is as well supplied now as at the end of 1898 and the Bank of France is nearly £3,000,000 richer. The banks of Austro-Hungary and Spain have also increased their stocks of this metal, and the Imperial Bank of Russia alone shows an important loss, officially accounted for by the larger quantity of coins in circulation or in the hands of other banks. Including the New York Associated Banks as among the losers and deducting the gains shown by the banks of Austria, France, and Spain, it may be approximately stated that the world's money market as a whole is poorer in gold by about £15,000,000 than it was a year ago. It is this in spite of the fact that new supplies considerably exceeding £50,000,000 have been furnished to it by the mines in the past twelve months, but this is merely the usual consequence of enlarged commercial and industrial activity. Raw materials rise in price and in many places food and clothing, wages advance, and larger numbers earn them.

Coin or its substitute, notes, therefore, pass more extensively into circulation, and the poverty of the money market becomes the riches of the industrial classes.

The Gold Movement In India

There is consequently nothing to be alarmed about in this aspect of the money markets taken by itself. Nor is the added fact that India is endeavoring to establish a State note circulation on a gold basis of much importance. Its Government can only go a little way in that business, because pulled up by two difficulties, the difficulty of borrowing and the impossibility of getting more than a certain amount of paper money into circulation. It has forced out 265,000,000 rupees now and holds 57,000,000 rupees in gold, 30,000,000 of it in London. Its disturbing power is, therefore, nearly over.

Where Has The Gold Gone?

Yet all the world wants more gold by reason of excessive capital commitments in every market. These commitments strain credit, and should they also induce a breakdown at any point the demand for gold to fill the gap may be so intensified as to cause a check and prostration, perhaps, at many points. Nowadays, thanks to electricity, one market can come to another's assistance with a promptitude that has prevented dangerous panics on several occasions; but if all markets are nearly alike strained rapidity of intercommunication might aggravate instead of lessen the pressure upon all. The puzzle is, where has all the gold gone? In the five years ended with 1899 the world has received at least £275,000,000 of new gold, and of that less than £50,000,000 has been added to the visible stock upon which the world's credit operations rest. The Bank of England is nearly £20,000,000 poorer than in June, 1897. All the balance cannot have disappeared in the arts, nor half of it. Where, then, has it gone? Into circulation and into private hoards, whence no power known to man can draw it out again. Hence, the vital importance of the Transvaal supply, which had risen at the time the mines were stopped to fully one-fourth of the world's output. In a little time the value of this African gold would have been £2,000,000 a month had peace been maintained, for it latterly exceeded £1,000,000 per month, and all this has been temporarily lost. Increased output elsewhere is too slow to make good the deficiency thus caused, and therefore I look for distressed money markets and possibly collapse in places in the near future. Your market bears daily witness to the unpleasant effects of excessive capitalization, and ours is not a whit behind. We have launched out recklessly in all directions and speculated to excess so that our position is now most dangerous. Beyond question 1900 is going to be a year of financial stress and trouble on more than one great centre of banking credit.

Your excess of energy in new company production, in industrial expansion of all kinds, generally too liberally capitalized, was started by the splendid opportunity your abundant crops and Europe's scarcity gave you in 1897, ours by the money released through our sales to you of your securities heretofore held here, and by the progressive increase in our South African and Australian gold supplies. The harvest of excess in both countries may have to be reaped in 1900. But so much turns upon the course of the South African war that confident prediction is unusually difficult, and I rather fear serious trouble.

*   *   *

April 4, 1900

AN EXPERT ON OUR EUROPEAN TRADE

Mr. Robert P. Porter gives in the current number of The North American Review a valuable article on "Our European Trade." It is practically a well-reasoned and well-fortified argument in favor of such reciprocal arrangements with Germany and France as will enable us to retain and extend our trade in food products, raw materials, and especially in manufactures, with these countries, which, with Great Britain, contribute four-fifths of all our trade with Europe.

Mr. Porter still wears the uniform of a protectionist. He recounts with much satisfaction how he helped to keep Samuel Randall in the protectionist camp, and he gleefully attributes the present command of a large part of the markets of the world by American products to the fact that "both Judge Kelley and Mr. Randall, and later Major, now President, McKinley, builded better than they knew." It is a fair case of "post ergo propter." It is nothing more. If Mr. Porter could point us to another country, with the same advantages of situation, climate, population, resources, institutions, and the same enormous field of absolute internal free trade, and if he could show that such a country with a tariff for revenue only had been out-stripped by the United States with its high protective tariff, he would make a fair case for attributing our advance to the tariff. Of course, he can do nothing of the sort. His argument in this matter is, however, purely academic. We are not disposed to quarrel with it since it does not prevent his advocacy of a policy of constantly freer trade with our chief customers and sustaining that policy by reasons extremely cogent.

With Great Britain over half of our export trade is done, but we need not worry ourselves as to its future progress being impeded by unfavorable legislation. There is no immediate prospect, and practically there is no prospect at all, that under any circumstances that country will seek to hamper our commerce directly or indirectly. The case is different with Germany and with France, especially the former. German trade is subject to an influence that we have not seen elsewhere so clearly traced as by Mr. Porter—the influence of Russia. That power is seeking in every direction to advance the demand for her exports, some of the chief of which come into competition in German markets with our own. She has secured already one treaty that will prevent any increase in the duty on her grain sent into Germany, though our own grain is liable to such increase in the present state of our treaty relations. There is in Germany a powerful party constantly agitating for protection against American food products, precisely as the Tory landlords of England fought for the taxes on English imports of food. Against these, as in England, are arrayed the manufacturers, steadily growing in strength, wealth, and influence, and the operatives, also a rapidly increasing class. The only way in which we can strengthen our interest in Germany, as Mr. Porter clearly shows, is by commercial treaty. "The main object of this treaty," he says, "should be similar to the main object of the other treaties, (negotiated with other countries by Caprivi) to secure for Germany cheaply, as imports, the necessaries of life and the raw materials of industries, in return for which Germany might secure certain reciprocal reductions in duty on her exported industrial products."

During the last five years the average imports from Germany have remained practically the same, at about $88,000,000. In the same five years our exports to Germany have advanced from $92,000,000 to $156,000,000. Of course, it cannot be safely inferred that any such rapid and marked change in the two branches of our German trade will continue. But that it should have taken place at all is a fact of the greatest significance. It is a part of the great mass of evidence that we are becoming in commerce literally a world power, and that our policy must change with our progress. The French have a happy phrase for the ideas of statesmanship based on narrow experience and limited knowledge. They call them "politique de cloche," or parish statesmanship. That is the sort we have been practicing in our tariff legislation, while the Nation has steadily and rapidly outgrown the petty conditions assumed by that legislation. If we are to hold our own in the immensely broader field on which we have forced an entrance, we must in every way seek the utmost freedom for our energies.

*   *   *

April 13, 1900

THE FUTURE OF OUR TRADE WITH CHINA

We infer from a careful reading of the very interesting article in the current number of McClure's by Mr. William Barclay Parsons on "The American Invasion of China," that he believes that we have a chance for a tremendous development in that direction if we will comply with certain conditions, which are not impracticable, but are extremely difficult.

The two points of greatest importance on which Mr. Parsons dwells are, first, that China is not, as generally supposed, overcrowded, but, on the contrary, is in many parts relatively thinly populated, and, second, that the Chinese are ready to buy foreign goods, if the goods suit them, and will buy more and more of them as their purchasing power is increased by the development of their resources and their increased power to sell. Both these points are of the greatest significance. The rest of the world has been used to look on China as outworn, a land of teeming millions with fixed and unchanging habits, with whom trade might be of large volume but would necessarily be of very limited variety and subject to little change except in

amount. Mr. Parsons, after traversing the empire for 1,100 miles, in part through the most thickly populated portion and also through the portion hitherto the most rigidly guarded from the incursion of foreigners, reports that China is a country of trade opportunities as varied as they are vast, and that in the development of its resources and of the wants of its people it may be accepted as a growing country.

With reference to the possible expansion of commerce with America and with the rest of the world, there are certain facts that exist nowhere else on the globe. The people are numerous, but not too numerous for the resources at their present disposal, and not nearly numerous enough to secure the proper use of the great resources known to exist. They are as a class industrious and law-abiding, their very patience under bad government being a security for their progress under better conditions. They are more honest than any other Oriental people and apparently quite as honest as the best of the Occidentals. They have a natural aptitude for trade and industry. They have provided an organization for the financial operations of trade that is extensive, trustworthy, and, within its limits of action, skillful. Though very conservative in many of their ideas and customs they have shown in the last quarter of a century that they can feel new needs and supply them from foreign sources. Within that time they have practically taken to new kinds of food, of light, and of clothing. Where else in the world is there a people of one-fourth their number that promises to the trade of the United States so many chances of a great and rapidly enlarging field for selling and for buying?

This brings up the consideration of what appears to us the most interesting and valuable lesson enforced by Mr. Parsons's article. He does not formulate it definitely, but it is inevitable from his facts. It is that our trade with China will grow in proportion as we can make and keep it equal and free. The Chinese will buy of us in direct proportion to their increased ability to sell to us and to others. A purely one-sided business will not prosper, and in the ratio that the business is made one-sided it will stagnate or dwindle. Something has lately been accomplished toward freedom and equality of trade with China in the informal agreement secured by the United States with European powers as to the "open door" in those parts of China where these powers may secure control or controlling influence. But it is to be recalled that none of those powers, except Great Britain, is honestly devoted to the emancipation of trade, and that we are ourselves in theory and in practice opposed to it. While the agreement is now preferred by them to that practical exclusion of all which has heretofore prevailed, neither they nor we are really in earnest in wishing that trade shall be unfettered. Neither they nor we are at all hesitant as to excluding each other from the markets any of us happen to control. At heart, judging them and us by our action in our own markets, we are one and all anti-traders, wedded to the theory that profit is to be got only from selling and not from buying as well. This theory we must abandon if we are to gather the full harvest awaiting us in China.

*   *   *

September 3, 1905

JAPAN AND CHINA FIND A READY MARKET HERE

New York Offers a Profitable Field for Their Exports

GOOD PRICES ARE OBTAINED

Japanese Silks and Curios in Particularly Brisk Demand—
The Tale as Told by Statistics

Although the fact is not generally known, Japan and China find New York one of the most profitable foreign markets for their goods, and while this city may not be the largest buyer of the products of the two great nations of the Far East, the merchants of Nippon and the Celestial Kingdom have no reason to complain of the prices obtained here.

During the fiscal year ended June 30 last, Japan exported to this country from Yokohama merchandise valued at $44,527,259, the bulk of which was composed of raw silk and silk goods, the value of the former being $31,974,945 and the latter $6,076,933. Tea was also received in the United States from the Mikado's kingdom to the extent of $3,867,940; curios, $1,005,326; provisions, $426,650; chip and straw braids, $356,469, and cotton goods, $290,491.

While statistics as to the proportion of Chinese and Japanese goods coming to New York are difficult to obtain, Custom House officials yesterday ventured the opinion that fully 50 per cent. of all imports from the two Eastern empires find their way to this city. This is particularly true of Japanese silks and curios, for both of which New York is the chief market in the New World.

A representative of one of the leading firms of Japanese importers in this city spoke yesterday in enthusiastic terms of American appreciation of his country's products.

"Until a short time ago," the importer said, "there was, comparatively speaking, little interest in the United States in things Japanese. With the growth of wealth and culture, however, the change is very marked. I need not, of course, refer to the steady and increasing demand for our silks. Every American woman knows the esteem in which Japanese silk goods are held in this country. They are more popular each succeeding year.

"It is in the Japanese lacquered ware and curios that we now find the most profitable market. Naturally, New York is the best American centre of distribution in this country for Oriental fine art productions. In the first place, there is more wealth here than in any other city, while another important factor is the out-of-town visitor. All prosperous Americans visit New York and leave their good money. They are looking for objects of art to embellish their homes, and just now there is decided interest in the products of Japan."

Chief among the articles sent by Japan to this country may be enumerated silks, silk fans, silk embroidered underclothing, wooden eggs, dolls, brass vases, brass censers, silk embroidered handkerchiefs, paper cutters, cotton toys, bric-à-brac, teapots, porcelain cups and saucers, queer fish in cans, paper napkins, embroidered panels, bronzes, straw mattings, baskets, lily bulbs, &c.

Many of the curios find their way into the private collections of wealthy Americans. The Japanese population on the Pacific Coast consumes the more ordinary line of imports, such as foodstuffs and sake, the National beverage of Nippon. All the high-priced articles, however, are reserved for sale to Americans.

Last year China exported approximately $30,000,000 worth of merchandise to this country. About one-third of the exports found their way to New York. While some of the Chinese products are in demand among the American people, it is probable that the larger proportion is distributed among the Chinese population. That this is so is evident from a perusal of the importations, which include preserved ginger, table covers, pickled lemon and other fruits, joss tables, incense sticks, opium, felt sole silk shoes, dried frogs and lizards, nuts, mushrooms, canned carambola, canned lichee, pressed fruit, dried birds' nests, flower bulbs, opium bowls and pipes, dried salt beans, and bamboo shoots.

Customs officials said yesterday that many of the Chinese entries were of such an unusual character that the Treasury representatives were at a loss to know how to classify the merchandise under the terms of the Dingley tariff law. Neither the Chinese nor the Japanese exporters show a disposition to invoice their goods at correct foreign market values, and as a result the Government appraisers at New York frequently are under the necessity of advancing prices and levying penalties on the merchandise.

In addition to the high-class Oriental stores to be found along Broadway and Fifth Avenue, there are several hundred Japanese and Chinese shops on the east side. An inspection of the stocks along Mott, Pell, and adjacent streets will reveal to the average American a multitude of articles absolutely unknown to the people of this country.

* * *

January 7, 1906

INFLUENCE OF POLITICS ON INTERNATIONAL EXCHANGES

Commercial Supremacy of a Nation Gauged by Its Foreign Trade, Asserts John Gardin, Manager of Foreign Exchange Department, National City Bank.

While the occurrences in the political world are not the prime factors in the movement of the exchanges, they nevertheless cannot be considered as secondary in importance. Money or its equivalent is supposed to move from one country to another to meet the demands of commercial exigencies, but these demands are oftentimes accelerated or retarded by happenings in the realm of politics. Not alone the disturbances in the comity of nations have an unexpected effect, but those of a local nature very frequently exert an influence that is sometimes far reaching. The natural query always is, why trade and industrial relations should in any way be mixed up in matters that are supposed to concern the diplomat alone, but it must be borne in mind that the present day statesmanship has for its object the welfare of the commercial community of its respective country more than perhaps the territorial aggrandizement of the country itself, on the natural grounds that the former being accomplished the latter will follow as a matter of course, with the added satisfaction that the desired result has been attained by peaceful means rather than by a resort to arms, which always, no matter how glorious the carryout, entails sacrifice of a most revolting nature.

The commercial supremacy of a nation nowadays is gauged by its foreign trade, and every effort is made to encourage relations with foreign countries, in order to afford an outlet for surplus products. Commercial treaties are considered of more importance than defensive and offensive alliance, and whereas at one time only the inhabitants of the tight little isle were reproachfully commented upon as a nation of shopkeepers, the whole civilized world falls under this category at the present time.

The commercial traveler of to-day is the pioneer of civilization; into the remotest corners of the earth does he penetrate in order to dispose of his wares, and woe betide the unfortunate inhabitant if harm befalls him. The agencies of the entire commonwealth, military and civil, are set in motion to right even a supposed injury, and it is this absolute confidence in the protection of his home Government that fosters the venturesome spirit that builds up new empires on the basis of a commercial fabric. In the acquisition of new territory the question of strategical importance is a matter of minor consideration alongside the all-absorbing one of trade relations—the latter are given the most careful study, and Governments are the first to lend assistance toward the exploitation of any new field of enterprise.

It thus becomes apparent that commercial rivalry is oftentimes the cause of international dispute, and when these misunderstandings assume dangerous aspects the markets the world over show the effects in a most unmistakable manner. Undoubtedly the most sensitive of all markets is the money market, which in reality can be likened to the pulse of the body politic. So sensitive are the financial centres that the slightest rumor of friction between any two nations causes a decline in all securities on every Stock Exchange in the world, regardless of where they are located. No one likes to fish in troubled waters, and it is the fear of what might happen that influences values.

Certain causes produce certain effects, and this can be demonstrated mathematically, but the money markets have a method of reasoning peculiarly their own, and it is this uncertainty of effect following a given cause that upsets all calculations in monetary matters. Equally surprising is the effect of an occurrence that has been expected for a long time—certain results should follow when it actually happens, but to the amazement of all, the exact opposite takes place—the laws of cause and effect are set at naught and the speculator who has done the least thinking is frequently the one who reaps the harvest. All this is evidence that as values are more or less matters of sentiment, they are governed by laws absolutely psychic in their nature.

The principal financial centres of the world are of course the capitals of the four nations that play a leading role in the affairs of nations. They are the planets around which the lesser constellations revolve, but it quite frequently happens that occurrences in the satellites set the ball rolling that has far-reaching results. London, in this respect, plays the foremost part, but at times the pivotal point is transferred across the Channel, but that occurs only under exceptional circumstances.

The banking system in vogue in London has reached a development that is the envy of the rest of the world—it is absolutely scientific, governed by laws that are as infallible as the laws of nature, and this need not be surprising, as they are the outcome of long experience and are based upon that most natural law—common sense. Money, or, rather, the value of that commodity, rises and falls absolutely with the exigencies of supply and demand—certain currents set in at certain times of the year that deplete or replenish the vaults of the great basks, and the value of money is gauged according to the course that these currents take. London is also the principal clearing house of the world, and this feature in no small degree has given that metropolis its financial supremacy.

In Germany the conditions are still in a more or less primitive state, and this is why that country is so sensitive to political occurrences—actual money is still the means of settlement in most transactions, as the check system is known in practice only to the larger commercial institutions. It is then not surprising that a strain is easily brought about. Much, however, is being done along the proper lines and the country is being gradually educated to the value of utilizing the existing banking facilities.

In France conditions are somewhat similar, only the distribution of wealth is greater than it is in Germany. The citizen, or rather, as he likes to be called, the "bourgeois," be he small or large, is a capitalist; and the height of his ambition is to retire from active business and live upon the revenue derived from his investments. As a class, the Frenchman is thrifty to an extent that puts any other nation to shame; and it is this very condition that gives the financial institutions in France their enormous strength.

Upon investigation it will be found that, while the deposits in the various banks are something enormous, the depositors are widely distributed throughout the country, which makes absolutely for the safety of the concerns interested. Furthermore, the French capitalist, small as well as large, has implicit confidence in his banker, and his dictum is the law as far as the investor is concerned. This argues for a peaceful condition in monetary matters, and it has never been so successfully demonstrated as during the troubles in connection with the Russo-Japanese war. France is loaded up with Russian securities, to the extent that the rest of the world has been alarmed; but France itself has been wonderfully quiet under the strain. And this condition is due simply to the circumstance that the French banker is cognizant of his power over his clientele.

The Far Eastern War

The world has been on the tenterhooks during the whole year as to what the result of the Japanese victory would be. The calamity howlers predicted financial ruin, not alone to Russia, but to Germany and France as well, but the least of all concerned, apparently, was the French investor, and it is really marvelous to consider the power that has been exerted by the French financial institutions to hold any possible fears of their clientele in check over the outcome of this, for Russia, disastrous war.

As an example, let us take the last Russian loan that was issued in Paris at about 97 per cent to the public. These bonds to-day are quoted at 480f., equal to 96—a loss of only 1 per cent! Such a condition of affairs could not be possible in any other country, and the French banker certainly deserves the highest encomiums for the masterful manner in which he has maintained control over conditions. Occasionally, during the darkest periods of present Russian history, the value of Russian securities held in France has declined to a considerable extent; but it is claimed, how true, of course. It is impossible to determine; that this was due mainly to machinations on the part of a certain coterie of disappointed financiers, who resorted to this method to gain private revenge. Of course, this is rumor; but be that as it may, the world is to be congratulated that their efforts were in vain.

International welfare is so closely knitted together at the present day that an injury to one country is an injury to all and this was never so clearly demonstrated as during the panicky year of 1898, but then the panicky conditions were infectious rather than contagious. The trouble was inherent throughout the world, and only needed an excessive ebullition in one spot to produce a general eruption. It started then in Australia, leaped to England, thence to America, and then followed a period of depression that held away in every country, Germany, for instance, has not yet entirely recovered from it, although other countries have long forgotten the spell, and are now in a period of prosperity which particularly finds its climax in the United States. It is claimed by many that we are now approaching the apex, but whether this is so or not need not worry us at the present time. Suffice it to say that contentment is the spirit that governs the destinies of our country at the moment.

To revert to European affairs, it is a great satisfaction to the world at large that, owing to the determined stand that at last has been taken by the Russian Government the internal conditions prevailing there are promissory of a satisfactory solution. A change in government would probably lead to a disturbed condition of affairs as far as Russian governmental liabilities, &c., are concerned, but what really is more important than this is the troubled state of commercial matters. Trade and industry are at a standstill, and it is-generally

feared that the neighboring States will suffer more in proportion than commercial Russia itself will, inasmuch as there the Government, with its all-decreeing powers, through extension of clemency to debtors may be able to tide them over their present difficulties; but these same governmental edicts do not extend to the creditors in Germany, Austria, France, and England, and these are the ones who possibly may have to suffer if the disturbed condition continues for any length of time. So far very little trouble in this respect has become apparent, and it is to be hoped that the clouds will gradually dissolve, and that the new year will bring about the promise of political salvation to a down-trodden proletariat.

That the present troubles can be likened to the boiling of the cauldron by which the dross is thrown to the surface and swept away cannot be denied; and it is to be hoped, when the atmosphere has again cleared, that that country will take its rank among the civilized nations of the earth, although in a moderate degree at present, still with the elements of progress that are inherent there is no doubt that with the established freedom of the people a new empire, and that one of intelligence, will gradually force its way to the front. This would mean a further prosperity to the trading nations of the world; as with education come requirements which, while familiar to other nations, have ever been foreign to Russia.

Taking it all in all, while the world is still upon the anxious seat, and many affairs have still to be settled before the old order of things can be replaced on the broad basis of the fellowship of man, each day that passes is a gain in the right direction, and toward a normal condition of affairs. Speed the day when this has been brought about!

Exchange conditions in the United States of America have been abnormal the year around. The year started in with exchanges against us, and this is an argument of prosperity—in fact, a truer one than official returns, &c. It means the increasing importation of luxuries, in the purchase of which people indulge only when times are good. Furthermore, the amount of money spent abroad by American citizens is something enormous.

In the early part of the year, during a brief sojourn in Europe, the writer had occasion to make inquiries of quite a number of bankers who are familiar with such matters, and who have made it their life study, as to what extent it is generally supposed that funds are used abroad for the pleasure of American travelers, and the estimates ranged from three hundred to four hundred millions of dollars. This is a vast amount of money to be taken out of the country, and is equal for the year 1905 to the amount of surplus exports over imports, as shown by the Custom House records.

That this is no insignificant factor in the course of the exchanges goes without saying, and a further cause for the high exchange is the enormous consumptive power of the country under the present prosperous conditions. Very little cotton has been exported, and, while we have had an immense wheat crop, which formerly found its way abroad, to a great extent this year it is all being used up by our own people; in fact, during the forepart of the year considerable quantities were imported. Luxuries continue to pour in through the various ports of the country, and the foreigner has not been slow in taking advantage of the demand to enhance the prices of his wares.

Another argument for the general prosperity of the world is shown in the demonstration of the various methods of arriving at the prices of commodities in England, Germany, France, and this country. Each method evidences a degree high above the normal. For instance: The index figures of The London Economist show an increase in the price of commodities of practically 10 per cent. over and above the prices that prevailed thirty or forty years ago, which were then established as the normal ratio.

What wonder, then, is it that this country takes the lead in this respect? Where other countries are prosperous, this United States, with its enormous natural resources, the energy of its people, and their adaptability to circumstances, with their labor-saving machinery, occupies the foremost rank, and it would not be surprising if this condition, now that we are on the upward grade, were continued for a goodly time.

JOHN GARDIN

*   *   *

January 7, 1906

REMARKABLE YEAR IN COFFEE

Retrospect of 1905 by Louis Seligsberg, Secretary of the New York Coffee Exchange

The year under review has for many reasons been one of remarkable occurences in the history of the coffee trade and of coffee speculation. While the statistical position of the article has been steadily improving every month since the crop year began, showing less coffee in sight than at the corresponding period of the preceding year, the price of coffee has followed a downward course from the opening quotations of the year. Prices have undergone smaller fluctuations during 1905 than in any year since 1808 while speculation and business on the Exchange and in the distributing markets reached almost as large a volume as in the banner year of 1904. The sales on the New York Coffee Exchange alone aggregated over 21,000,000 bags. The difference between the highest and lowest quotations for the current month at the beginning of each month was only 1½ cents per pound, while in former years the range of prices represented variations of 2½, 3, and 4 cents per pound between the extreme prices of a given year.

The anomaly of a large business on all the three leading Exchanges of the world (New York, Havre, and Hamburg in the order of importance), and narrow fluctuations indicates the absence of wild speculation and the prudence of operators, but may also demonstrate the existence of factors of grave import and far-reaching influence entirely outside the channels of supply and demand or growth and decline of production.

The magnitude of the Brazilian crops, 73 per cent. of the production of the world, necessarily places that country in the foreground, and, in an annual retrospect of the business, we need only consider the other coffee-growing countries in passing and as they affect the general situation. Brazil practically dictates the course of events for Central American and the West Indies. Thus it will appear to the statistician that, while the year began with the price of January coffee at 7.65 cents and ended with the value of the same option at 6.35 cents, a decline of 17 per cent., the price in Brazil on Jan. 1, 1905, was 5$700 per 10 kilos (5,700 reis per 22 pounds), while on the last day of the year the same quality of coffee was quoted at 4$050 per 10 kilos (4,050 reis per 22 pounds) a decline of 28 per cent. Translated into plain English, this means that Brazil has suffered more from the decline of its chief product than prices in consuming countries indicate.

It is true that owing to the rise in sterling exchange—from 137/8d. sterling per 1,000 reis at the beginning of the year, to 167/8d. sterling per 1,000 reis on Dec. 29, the purchasing power of Brazilian currency has apparently increased, but, unfortunately for the planters, the scale of wages paid by them and the principal expanses of cultivation, picking, and preparation have hardly undergone a perceptible change during the year, if reports from primary sources are to be credited. It is this state of affairs that has given rise to all kinds of schemes looking to the amelioration of the planting interests. The most visionary plans proposed seem to have been abandoned: the Governments of the three coffee-growing States of São Paulo, Rio, and Minas have recently united on what may still be considered a tentative scheme of imparting steadiness to coffee values. The movement is known as the "Valorisaçao Movement," and has for its object the raising by a foreign load of the sum £12,000,000 to be employed under the direction of foreign bankers in (1) limiting the expert from Brazil to a maximum of 10,000,000 bags per annum, the extent of the most recent crops, (2) in determining at what price it will be necessary to purchase coffee in order to protect the planters from actual loss, it being assumed that the prices now ruling in Brazil and which have practically been current (with the exception of 1904) for three years do not cover the actual cost of production and maintenance of farms.

The Federal Government of Brazil does not appear to look with disfavor upon this "amelioration" plan, being rather disposed to aid the coffee planters by some protective measures, and even to stand sponsor for the interest and redemption of the loan if public policy dictates the imperative need of coming to the rescue of the planters, who represent a large and powerful element in the Brazilian population.

It will depend upon the wisdom of the Brazilian economists whether a measure for the improvement of the conditions that now prevail among the planters, and which conditions are characterized as deplorable, will bear the much-needed golden fruits. Discussion of these movements in Brazil and (beginning last Summer) of the probability of an import duty being placed on coffee in this country, either as a revenue measure or in retaliation for Brazilian discrimination against American products, has from time to time given unusual impetus to transactions and caused new interests to enter the market, which, added to the large arbitrage trading between Europe and New York, helped to swell the aggregate of the sales for this year. That the study of all questions pertaining to coffee has been carefully undertaken by our own Government is well illustrated by the comprehensive monograph on coffee issued in Washington last September.

Formerly New York was known to carry a small stock of coffee in proportion to the business done here. The facilities for handling, financing, and distributing this important staple have of late years so extensively increased that a visible supply of 5,000,000 bags, which ten years ago might have been considered a stupendous burden for the owners, is to-day no burden at all. American and foreign bankers are only too anxious to avail themselves of the opportunities offered through the New York Coffee Exchange for investing their funds in loans secured by an article whose intrinsic value does not deteriorate by age, but frequently improves.

The world's possible supply of coffee on Jan. 1, 1906, was fully 1,200,000 bags smaller than at the same date in 1903—12,700,000 bags, against 13,900,000.

If the claims of well-informed observers are correct that the consumption of coffee is steadily increasing, owing to growth of population and on account of almost complete abandonment of adulterants (superinduced by the low price of the article), the annual deliveries of coffee from the seaboard markets to consumers, which for over three years have remained stationary (at about 10,000,000 bags per annum), may indicate a material decrease of reserve stocks in the hands of inland dealers, both here and in Europe.

Assuming the world's consumption of coffee at over 16,000,000 bags and this year's production of Brazil coffee as a little larger than last year's (the receipts from July 1 to date are about 70,000 bags in excess of the same period in the preceding crop year) there would remain more than 6,000,000 bags to be gotten from all other coffee-growing countries, i.e., Mexico, Venezuela, and Colombia, Central America, and East and West Indies. This quantity does not appear to have been or to be forthcoming; merchants are agreed upon that point. Whether this crop year, ending June 30, 1906, will show that production has again fallen behind the requirements of consumption to the extent of 1,000,000 bags as it did during 1904, or of a much larger quantity, will not be definitely known until the annual statistics are completed.

The price of No. 7 spot coffee during the year ranged between the two extremes of $8^7/8$c and $7^1/2$c, and is now on Dec. 29, 8 cents per pound. The closing price of Nos. 4 and 3 spot coffee, the qualities at present delivered on exchange contracts is $8^3/4$c and 9c respectively, which prices correspond approximately with the value of January coffee at 6.40, taking into consideration the different terms of payment and settlement for spot coffee and the premiums some spot coffees command.

Concerning the prospects for the new year, without entering the field of prediction it may be proper to state the known facts and to indicate the probabilities likely to ensue. In 1902 the São Paulo Government passed a law prohibiting the planting of coffee trees except where replanting was necessary to replace exhausted plantations. This law is still in force, and production has been kept within established limits in the entire Santos district. Unfavorable weather during 1903 and 1904 reduced the yield in the Rio, Minas, and Santos sections for 1904–1906 crops; during the past six months atmospheric conditions have been, to say the least, irregular, and views as to the next crop, beginning July 1, 1906, vary considerably. That the low prices realized by Brazilian planters during the past four years have brought about neglect of plantations is no longer doubted, nor is it denied that neglect is a serious obstacle to large crops.

At this season of the year when Brazilian planters must make financial arrangements for the requirements of growing crops, large estimates are the rule, and it may be the part of prudence not to lay too much stress on such predictions.

What 1906 must demonstrate will be whether the present price of coffee, which is supposed to be below the cost of production, will not, of itself, be a sufficiently potent argument in favor of an advance, which advance would, of course, become by such extraneous influences as have been alluded to in the earlier part of this article.

LOUIS SELIGSBERG

* * *

January 7, 1906

THE NATIONS OF SOUTH AMERICA

Story of Their Prosperity and Progress Becomes More and More Interesting

WASHINGTON, Dec. 30—The story of South America, its progress and its prosperity, grows more and more interesting. Among all the nations of South America none has done more to make its resources known and available than Argentina. It has long been playing a leading part in the great southern continent. In 1903 its imports aggregated $131,206,600, and its exports $220,984,524. Of the imports Germany furnished $17,009,322 and received $26,812,873. Of the exports the United States supplied $16,684,954 and received $8,126,346. Belgium supplied $5,448,572 and took $20,143,012. Brazil furnished $5,350,976 to the tables of imports and $8,545,127 to those of exports. France sent $12,708,238 and took $34,294,945. Italy sold $14,702,193 and bought $4,358,554. The United Kingdom sold $44,826,749 and bought $35,600,922. It is a long, interesting story that is told by our Consuls, Ministers, and special agents.

Over the pampas of Argentina roam innumerable cattle, and the breeding efforts recorded are as remarkable as any in the world. Next to Australia, Argentina is one of the world's great sources for the supply of wool. Meat stored in refrigerator ships is finding its way in huge quantities to all parts of the world, particularly to Europe.

The population of Argentina increased from 1,375,481 in 1860 to 4,860,324 in 1903; the imports from $22,441,120 to $131,206,600; the exports from $14,322,589 to $220,984,524. It is doubtful whether any country, even our own, can show a greater increase.

There is nothing that is possible to Europe or the United States that is not possible to the people of South America. They have mines of gold, silver, copper, iron, coal, &c., a splendid climate, fertile soil, and numerous rivers. As capital pours in, as railroad facilities increase, as harbors are deepened, as quays and docks are constructed, as canals are cut, and factories are established, South America will emulate Europe and the United States. As the Germans and Italians pour in, the possibilities will become realities.

What has been said of Argentina may be said of Brazil. This vast country, lying partly in the tropics and partly, in the south temperate zone, is larger in its area than the United States, Brazil having 3,218,130 square miles, the United States 2,976,479 square miles. The country is enormously rich in minerals, chief among which are diamonds, for which Brazil has long been famous. Indeed, up to the discovery of diamonds in South Africa, Brazil was the world's chief source of supply.

Its soil is rich, coffee and tobacco growing in great abundance. Its forests are full of the world's hardest and richest woods, among them mahoganies and the rubber trees. In the campus cattle abound, Brazil is growing more and more important as a source of supply for the raw materials of trade and as a market in which to sell the products of the great outside industrial world.

Conditions are said to be favorable to the United States, though the figures furnished, if carefully analyzed, can hardly be said to support this claim. For example, the United States supplied Brazil in the years 1894–8 with $68,800,000 of its imports, Germany $68,500,000. In 1899–1903 the figures were: United States, $56,100,000; Germany, $50,200,000. Of manufactured goods the United States supplied in the first period $39,306,000, and $35,329,000 in the second period, while Germany supplied $65,469,000 and $50,214,000 in the two periods, respectively. In 1903 the United States took 41.21 per cent. of Brazil's exports; in 1904, 50.31; Great Britain, 19.33 and 16.17; Germany, 14.83 and 13.93; France, 9.45 and 5.07; Austria, 2.71 and 2.79; Belgium, 1.90 and 1.61 per cent. in the corresponding years.

It is hard to think that a trade is entirely satisfactory that is as one-sided as that between Brazil and the United States. Brazil sells as the major part of her products—coffee, rubber, woods, &c.—and buys the better part of all she needs from our commercial rivals. If she got better goods at equal prices, or even somewhat interior goods at cheaper prices; there would be no ground for finding fault; but it is a notorious fact that many of the goods that go to Brazil from Germany, at least, could be supplied by the United States superior in qual-

ity and at the same or even lower prices. The lesson being taught by Brazil is one that is being forced upon us in other parts of South America. An effort should be made to secure a readjustment or realignment of our commercial relations with those parts. Any effort, intelligently and energetically carried out, must result in greater general trade and a better and more equitable balancing on both sides.

*　　*　　*

January 7, 1906

OUR GOODS IN CHINESE MARKETS

Showing of San Francisco Leads American Export Trade

During the year just closed the commercial relations of the United States with the countries of the Orient made a grand step forward, the total exports of those much-sought markets being the largest in both volume and valuation for any year since trade relations were established. Comparatively few people realize the great future or even the present value of the markets of China and Japan to the United States and the ease with which a large portion of it may be secured for this country. The total value of merchandise exported from the United States to China in the ten months ended with October, 1905, was $50,104,767, while for the corresponding ten months of the previous year the total was $20,557,184. No other branch of America's export trade can show such a phenomenal development.

Last year's total to China was the greatest in history up to that time, and now, one year later, that high mark is not merely increased, but multiplied two and one-half times. Surely a market showing such results is worth looking after and cultivating carefully. The exports to Japan have grown almost as rapidly, the figures being nearly the same as to China. The greatest increase to Japan was in raw cotton. The United States shipped 324,668 bales of raw cotton to Japan in the first eight months of 1905, while the total for the corresponding months of 1904 was 47,295 bales. The valuation of this cotton in 1904 was $2,930,198, while the valuation for the same months of 1905 is $17,434,047. For the calendar year 1905 the total will exceed 500,000 bales and the valuation will be over $25,000,000. This shows how quickly the Japanese mills resumed operations after hostilities ceased.

Japan now has thirty ports open to foreign trade. At four of these in 1902 Japanese vessels registering 19,609,745 tons and foreign ships registering 12,092,615 tons were cleared. Osaka, sometimes called the Liverpool of Japan, as Japan is called the England of the East, is a beehive of human industry. Day and night there is a constant whirl of machinery—a ceaseless murmur of the turning wheels. It has more than a million people. About eight years ago $11,250,000 was appropriated to build docks and supply the harbor with facilities commensurate with the requirements anticipated when the Panama Canal is completed. Some $9,000,000 has been expended, but the plans of the engineers call for further expenditures of about

$20,000,000 before the city has what is deemed requisite. Everywhere in all the large Japanese parts the people are busy. They are building not alone for to-day, but for the coming decades. Breakwaters, dikes, piers, wharves, dry docks, and warehouses are being built, equal to those of Liverpool, London, Hamburg, or any other great world port.

Twenty years ago the imports of Japan were valued at $25,000,000, of which the United States supplied $2,000,000 and Great Britain $11,000,000. In 1904 Japan bought merchandise abroad to the value of $185,660,000, of which the United States supplied about $29,000,000 and Great Britain $37,000,000. The principal commodities imported were as follows:

```
Mineral oils ............................. $5,500,000
Flour ..................................... 4,600,000
Raw cotton ................................ 4,500,000
Machinery ................................. 2,000,000
From and steel goods ...................... 1,900,000
Cotton manufactures ....................... 1,100,000
Leather ................................... 1,700,000
```

Japan's exports during 1904 aggregated $159,000,000, the principal countries purchasing the supplies being as follows:

```
United States .......................... $50,432,000
China ................................... 33,857,000
France .................................. 18,087,000
Hongkong ................................ 14,024,000
Korea ................................... 10,154,000
Great Britain ............................ 8,787,000
Italy .................................... 6,011,000
```

A similar tabulation might be made for China, but the above is sufficient to demonstrate how the trade of the United States is developing in the Orient and also to show what extensive preparations have been and are now being made in those countries for the accommodation of the vast commerce of the future, which those people recognize as a certainty.

These statistics are given to show in concise form the character of the market and the facilities being prepared for the convenience of commerce. The question at once comes to mind: What are the American merchants doing to maintain the advantages already gained. All firms which have business relations with the Orient should seek to enlarge their field of operations, and all merchants who contemplate selling goods there should begin at once. The utmost diligence should be used, for there are the waiting markets, and the sellers of Germany and other European nations are already on the ground and will not be slow in pressing the merits of their products. The prediction has been freely made that this coming year will determine whether America loses or retains its prestige and share in the trade of China.

The Chinese boycott has been pronounced by our Consuls to be a sort of culmination of years of remonstrance at what the Chinese believe is unjust discrimination on the part of this country toward their countrymen. The Chinese are a primitive people in many respects, and they are adopting modern ideas very rapidly. The alarm that was created among our shipping interests by the threat of boycott has disclosed to that people that they have a means of retaliation which would prove strikingly effective. China is now in the process of awakening to a sense of her latest power, and she is coming to a realization of the true value of her markets. China as a Government can have no cause to feel any resentment toward this Government, but the people of the higher classes over there cannot understand why they should be treated differently from corresponding classes of other nations.

In his recent message President Roosevelt answered this whole question when he said: "To obtain justice from others we must be just ourselves." That China has not taken advantage, as has Japan, in the world's political development must not be construed to mean that the country does not exist. The predictions of recent years are many that the time is not far distant when China will startle the world with her onward movement.

The crying need in the development of trade with China is the increase of her purchasing capacity. China's foreign trade amounts now to a trifle less than $1 per capita. Japan's trade is $7 per capita, although twenty-five years ago it was no greater than is China's now. If China's trade can be developed to $2.50 per capita it would mean a trade of $1,000,000,000 per annum. To prepare a way for the United States to obtain a share of such a market is certainly worth the strongest and best efforts of American merchants.

In a general way the character of the exports to China and Japan was about the same as for the two or three previous years. The inhabitants over there are slow to indulge in new products or commodities, but substantial progress has been made. They are taking a greater variety of our food supplies than ever before, they are buying more cotton and more machinery, while the demand for small household appurtenances is rapidly growing greater. In this Oriental trade San Francisco, and incidentally the entire Pacific Coast, has just closed the greatest year in her existence. The exports of merchandise from San Francisco for the first eleven months were as follows:

1905	China	Japan
January	$242,607	$1,218,224
February	906,371	1,078,986
March	1,152,178	3,416,223
April	1,089,809	2,043,126
May	894,156	2,414,585
June	720,573	1,933,977
July	1,529,468	1,126,829
August	1,336,364	1,061,361
September	889,201	1,031,227
October	526,127	866,772
November	943,764	1,432,226
Total	$10,230,678	$17,623,536

Both of these totals represent an increase of over 100 per cent., as compared with the same months of 1904. These figures give some idea as to the volume of San Francisco's trade in the Orient. During 1905 the total exports from San Francisco by sea were: $65,000,000, and it will be noticed that the shipments to China and Japan aggregated $27,854,214 for eleven months. It is also safe to say that when the record is computed for the twelve months and the shipments to Korea and other Oriental ports are added, the total will be just about one-half of San Francisco's entire sea commerce. During 1905 there were eight cargoes cleared from San Francisco for Oriental ports valued at more than $1,000,000 each, exclusive of treasure. The largest cargo was on the steamship Mongolia, which sailed on March 18, 1905, for China and Japan with a merchandise cargo invoiced at $1,947,917, and the smallest of the eight was considerably over the million-dollar mark.

The imports from China and Japan at San Francisco show a handsome increase for the first eleven months of the year, as compared with the total for the corresponding months of 1964.

1905	China	Japan
January	$1,020,954	$1,855,725
February	332,779	1,385,507
March	604,231	1,140,478
April	291,117	1,421,074
May	801,782	1,551,946
June	433,392	1,314,139
July	378,669	563,035
August	478,218	1,695,926
September	685,819	979,328
October	587,631	1,292,482
November	618,836	956,902
Total	$6,233,428	$14,156,542

In the case of San Francisco these imports compare exactly with the exports. The city's total imports for 1905 were $45,000,060 and with the totals to China and Japan combined for eleven months, amounting to $20,389,970, it is evident the total for the year will equal one-half of the imports. San Francisco's entire ocean trade, both exports and imports, is about evenly divided, one-half with the Orient and the other half with the balance of the world.

W. B. THOMPSON

* * *

January 7, 1906

TACOMA VIEW OF JAPAN'S YEAR

Food Problem of the Island Empire and Our Milling Trade

TACOMA, Dec. 30—Twelve and fifteen years ago, following the establishment of the first steamship lines between Vancouver and Tacoma and the Orient, steamships brought from Oriental ports full cargoes and returned westward almost light. During the intervening years the situation has been reversed to such an extent that the bulk of cargo from the Orient is now only 20 to 25 per cent. of that of the immense cargoes of American products shipped to the Orient. Under the pressure of immense shipments of war materials, the value of exports from the United States to Japan amounted to $46,647,001 during the ten months ended Oct. 31, 1905, as compared with $21,085,585 and $16,264,757 for the corresponding periods of 1904 and 1903. Imports into the United States from Japan during the ten months ending Oct. 30, 1905, amounted to $42,000,000, as compared with $41,000,000 and $38,000,000 for the corresponding periods of 1904 and 1903.

The war materials shipped in such quantities to Japan during the first half of this year comprised steel rails, locomotives, railroad cars, and other railroad equipment, together with flour, meats, and other army food supplies.

Following the war the Japanese people are practicing rigid economy, which makes them conservative in ordering even necessities. This policy of conservatism has been emphasized by Japan's failure to secure an indemnity from Russia, which was expected by the masses of her people. This policy will probably continue while her finances are being rearranged and until the inauguration of great public works, including the building of railways in Korea and Manchuria, putting large amounts of public money into circulation.

Japan's Food Problem

The food question is rapidly becoming as important in Japan as in England. An estimate of this year's rice crop, issued Oct. 24 by the Department of Agriculture and Commerce, shows a diminution of 25.7 per cent. compared with last year, and of 13.9 per cent., compared with a normal year. The rice yield for this year aggregated 38,000,000 koku, as compared with 51,000,000 in 1904 and 46,000,000 in 1903. Experience proves the yield of rice to be subject to much fluctuation according to weather conditions. This subject is one of the greatest interest to the United States, and especially the Pacific Coast, since Japan's future food supply will naturally come largely from this country. The food situation in Japan is thus described in the Nov. 3 issue of the Japan Chronicle:

"It is not unnatural, therefore, that the Japanese should gradually turn their attention from agricultural to manufacturing industries, which, if fully developed, may enable Japan, like England, to depend upon foreign countries for her food supply. Even now Japan obtains a considerable amount of food from abroad. Last year's rice crop in this country was exceptionally good, the yield amounting to 51,430,000 koku. But the supply was evidently inadequate to feed the population, judging from the large amount of food supplies Japan imported from abroad during the same year. The importation of foreign rice in 1904 amounted to close upon 60,000,000 yen in value, not to mention flour to the value of nearly 10,000,000 yen imported during the year. It is true that during the same period Japanese rice to the value of 4,724,000 yen was exported, but the amount is trifling in comparison with the import, and when deducted the balance remaining constitutes the amount which Japan spends in buying rice to fill the inadequacy of the domestic supply.

When these figures are considered together with the fact that the population of Japan is increasing at the rate of more than 400,000 per year, it is not surprising that the question of food supply should engage the serious attention of her public men. Efforts are being made to increase the yield of rice by extension of the area of cultivation, and by the introduction of agricultural improvements, but it is evident that the increased production by these means can hardly be at a rate to keep pace with the rapidly increasing pressure that is put on Japan's food resources.

It may be interesting in this connection to give the value of flour and rice imported into Japan and also of Japan's rice exported during the last five years:

Year.	Import of Flour-Yen.	Import of Rice-Yen.	Export of Rice-Yen.
1900	3,882,000	9,021,000	3,576,000
1901	2,873,000	11,878,000	6,908,000
1902	3,278,000	17,750,000	6,679,000
1903	10,324,000	51,960,000	4,959,000
1904	9,624,000	50,792,000	4,724,000

It will be seen that while these figures exhibit considerable fluctuations, there is a general tendency to an increase of imports and decrease of exports, which is more noticeable when it is taken into consideration that for some years past the harvests have been good. Japan is gradually developing into a manufacturing country, and will in the future come to be dependent in large part on foreign countries for her food supply.

Pacific Coast millers say that if Japan shall gradually, as is expected, increase her flour imports, with a corresponding decrease in rice imports, it will not be long before all the exportable wheat and flour grown on the Pacific Coast will be needed to supply the Japanese demand.

A year ago flour was being sold to the Japanese at an average cost of $3.60 per barrel, free on board coast ports. Present prices average $3.20 per barrel, present lower prices corresponding to the average lower wheat prices. Puget Sound millers are just now investigating to ascertain whether Japan is importing any flour from Australia, as are some of the Southern Chinese cities, due to the anti-American boycott. The Australian flour costs more and is not likely to be purchased in quantities by Japan. Preceding the recent war, the increase in Japan's consumption of flour was phenomenal. The outlook for 1996 is indefinite and uncertain, owing to the economical turn just now prevailing.

The rice imported from Rangoon and Siam comprises chiefly a cheap brown variety, which will not stand competition with American flour, when the Japanese people have the money with which to purchase the latter.

Several flour mills have been built in Japan during the last two years. A number of cargoes or partial cargoes of wheat have been shipped from coast ports to these mills. Their number will undoubtedly increase with the expansion of the new Japanese policy of importing raw products and exporting finished products.

Shipments of raw cotton from Pacific Coast ports to Japan were especially heavy during the early part of this year. They have subsequently fallen off somewhat, apparently due to the general policy of retrenchment. It is expected that gradually Japan will increase the number of her cotton mills, and increased quantities of American cotton will be mixed with cheaper grades from India to keep them running.

In the same manner it is practically certain that within a few years Japan will use her own coal in transforming the iron ores of Korea and Manchuria into rails and other products of iron and steel, thereby supplying to a large extent her own demand.

There is a continued and steady demand for American petroleum, which is shipped chiefly from Atlantic coast ports. Other manufactured products bought from the United States comprise bar iron, oil cake, woolen goods, sheetings, dyes, alcohol, tobaccos, machinery and tools of all kinds, electric machinery, wire, and other copper products.

Dried fruits in increasing quantity are being shipped to Japan from Pacific Coast States. Annual shipments of salmon and other fish from the Pacific Coast will average about 10,000 tons. These are chiefly the lower grade of fish, including the dog salmon, which Americans do not eat. Last Summer a Tacoma firm salted three cargoes of dog salmon in Alaskan waters, making shipment to Yokohama in three Japanese sailing vessels. Of American lumber Japan buys only large timbers for special purposes, her northern islands supplying ordinary grades at a minimum cost.

Japan's Market Here

The United States continues to be the largest market for Japanese teas. Practically the entire crop enters through Pacific Coast ports, while a large part of the China teas used in the United States come via Suez.

The United States is a steady buyer of the largest part of the Japanese silk crop. Though smallest in bulk, this constitutes in value one of our chief imports from the Mikado's kingdom. The silk is brought by the fastest steamers crossing the Pacific, and shipped to the silk mills about New York by express trains.

The American consumption of Japanese mattings is growing from year to year. The bulk of the mattings come through Puget Sound, owing to exceptional facilities and the erection at Tacoma of a large bonded warehouse, which usually contains mattings to the value of $300,000 to $500,000.

Year by year the fleet of steamships plying between Pacific Coast and Japanese ports has grown to large proportions. The steamship lines started from Tacoma in 1892 and from Vancouver. B. C., in 1888 comprised vessels which carried not to exceed two or three thousand tons of cargo. The Pacific Mail steamers out of San Francisco were of similar size. These smaller vessels have now been replaced by the big Minnesota and Dakota, sailing from Puget Sound, the Mongolia and Manchuria, plying from San Francisco, and many other steamships of nearly the same size. There are now thirteen to fifteen regular sailings each month of vessels of this class from Puget Sound, San Francisco, Portland, and Vancouver. Westward cargo offerings have been so heavy that during the last year fifteen large special cargoes have been shipped from Puget Sound to the Orient, and a number from each of the other ports.

The Japan Mail Steamship Company is the fifth maritime enterprise in the world in point of tonnage. It now comprises 73 steamers with an aggregate displacement: of 250.905 tons. The company is building 9 steamships, together with 39 tugs and launches, which will raise the displacements to 273,068 tons. During the half-year ended Sept. 30 the gross profits of the company amounted to over 4,000,000 yen. A regular dividend was declared at the rate of 10 per cent., together with 2 per cent, as a special dividend, making 12 per cent, in dividends paid by the company during the year ended Sept. 30.

Under the pressure of military necessity the Japanese have built a number of narrow gauge railroads in Manchuria besides other standard gauge lines in Korea. These, and especially the lines in Manchuria, are to be rebuilt and extended, creating a splendid system of railroads under Japanese ownership and operation. All this work involves a heavy outlay, and the materials, as heretofore, including rails, locomotives, and other equipment, will come from the United States.

Three of the largest brewing companies in Japan have just combined for the formation of one strong company. The value of beer exports from Japan has risen from 520,000 yen in 1902 to 750,000 yen in 1904, and 1,200,000 yen during the first ten months of 1905. The new brewing combination intends to introduce economies, which will result in increased beer exports, especially to China and Korea. The result may be to affect the increasing demand for American beers in China and the Philippines.

EDWARD MILLER

* * *

January 7, 1906

INDIA'S COMMERCIAL EVOLUTION

Cheap, Trashy German Goods Have Made Bazaar Dealers Suspicious

Consul General Wilbur of Singapore, Straits Settlements, has furnished the Department of Labor and Commerce with a long and valuable letter from Mr. Hugo J. M. Ellis of the firm of Ellis & Co., an American firm doing business in that section. Many of the conditions which he describes as appertaining to his territory, which extends to Ceylon, Burma, Java, and Siam, are equally applicable to British India. He states that his trade is not with savages or confiding Indians, but with some of the shrewdest and craftiest traders in the world, who were traders when our ancestors were savages. Not only are they good traders, but they are extremely conservative. When they once prove the worth of a particular brand they stick to it with tenacity, and in some cases where a "chop" or brand is concerned price is no object.

Methods of doing business vary considerably in all parts of this firm's territory. In no two are they alike. A style or shape of shoe that may be popular in Burma may not sell for half price in Singapore. Our manufacturers cannot realize that each of these countries contains an entirely different race of people. While the Chinaman is the principal trader in nearly all of these ports, he has to buy what suits his customers. Naturally a native or Chinese dealer is not going to give a very large order for the first time on an American product changed to suit his particular style until he is satisfied that the American concern can do as well as the English or German, and that it is to his advantage to change.

Mr. J. H. Scholes, an American who has been in India for several years engaged in business, also contributes information that will be valuable to persons engaged in Oriental trade. He states that the general reputation of American goods in India is high, but it is almost impossible to sell anything without samples. Pictures of machinery, &c., in catalogues are of little or no use among these people, who have never seen or heard of most kinds of American machines. One peculiarity of the Oriental races is that nearly every individual is naturally suspicious, and, believing every other man to be likewise, he invariably wants to see samples of what he buys or orders. He will take no man's word without proof. Germany has flooded the country with cheap, trashy goods, which have made the bazaar dealers more suspicious. Many private purchasers will not buy German goods now, and this fact would assist materially in increasing consumption of American goods.

There are almost no goods of American origin sold in Burma. Importers of goods from other countries invariably speak disparagingly of American goods, especially of machinery. An order for an American sawmill was about to be closed recently by Mr. Scholes in Burma, when some engineers told the prospective purchaser that American sawmills were not adapted for sawing the hard timber of that country, and consequently the order was not placed. Mr. Scholes further states his confidence that nearly all lines of American goods would find ready sale if properly pushed on American business plans. Many bazaar merchants wish to handle American textile goods and wares of different kinds, and there are many novelties which would become popular if made known.

Consul Fee of Bombay transmits a review on the progress made in the tea industry in that country. The area under tea in India at the end of the year 1904 extended over 524,517 acres, about 64 per cent. of the whole being in the valleys of the Brahmaputra and Surma, in Assam, and about 26 per cent. in Bengal, and the other tenth is divided between northern and southern India. Since 1903 a reduction in the area cultivated is noticeable the more so as for nineteen years previously an annual increase had been recorded. The annual output of tea, however, is steadily, increasing, which fact warrants the assumption that by more scientific methods the land itself is far more productive than formerly.

The total tea productions for 1904 are nearly 25,000,000 pounds, more than for the year 1900. The total production of tea for all India for the year 1904 is given as 222,203,661 pounds, this amount being greater than was produced in any previous year and just double the production of fifteen years ago. According to the returns of the registrars of Indian joint-stock companies and the published accounts of the companies registered in London, the capital engaged in the production of tea amounts to about $60,778,000.

It is asserted that 81 per cent. of this capital belongs to shareholders in companies whose head offices are in London. This gives a general average capital of $115 per acre. But the true capital value must be slightly larger since the amount of private capital engaged in the industry is unknown, while the area under tea represents the private property as well as the companies gardens. The number of persons employed in the industry in the year 1904 is returned as 475,266 permanently and 76,009 temporarily, or altogether 551,275 persons, which works out to about one person on the average to the acre.

The taste for India and Ceylon tea has gone on increasing for many years. Great Britain in very fond of it; Germany is growing so, Eastern people are taking kindly to it. Push, enterprise, and science have helped to put this tea in a favorable position. In many out of the way places, in far-off Africa, the islands of the sea, Ceylon's and India's agents have been making markets for this tea.

The output of coal for India has increased every year for the last nineteen years. From 1,294,221 tons in 1885, it has increased to 8,216,706 tons in 1904. The exports from Calcutta in 1904-5 amounted to 2,375,977 tons, about three-fourths of this being loaded into coasting vessels including 770,589 tons of bunker coal shipped for use on steamers engaged in the foreign and coasting trades; 3,146,566 tons left the port, or nearly 45 per cent. of the output of Bengal collieries in 1904.

It was reported from Bombay that at the close of 1904 India had 212,964 acres of land under coffee. This indicates a reduction in acreage of 13,078 acres as compared with 1903. It is noticeable that in spite of the falling off in the amount of land planted, the amount of coffee exported has constantly increased. England takes more than 20,000,000 pounds a year. France took 11,000,000 pounds in 1904. The export prices per hundredweight (112 pounds) ranged from $15.25 and $16.87 during the last five years, the highest price being paid in 1904-5.

The commerce of India is constantly growing. From German sources it is stated that the imports by sea for the last fiscal year aggregated $322,288,305 in gold.

* * *

January 21, 1906

FOREIGN TRADE RECORD

Exports and Imports in 1905 Exceed All Previous Years

TRADE BALANCE OFFSETS

Imports Increasing More Rapidly Than Exports—$1,000,000,000 Added to Total Yearly Trade Since 1896

The foreign commerce of the United States last year exceeded all previous records, having reached the enormous total of $2,996,767,518, including the imports and exports of specie. The balance of trade in our favor which was the net result of this great volume of foreign business amounted to $447,603,497. In 1900 our total commerce was smaller by $450,000,000 than it was last year, but the balance in our favor in 1900 was $200,000,000 greater than it was in 1995.

The bearing of this balance of trade on the relations between this and foreign money markets is particularly interesting at this time, when so recently as ten days ago international bankers were expressing the opinion that our indebtedness to Europe was so large that gold exports would probably be necessary in order to pay off such part of this debt as was immediately falling due. Had we actually a credit balance abroad of $447,000,000 as a result of our last year's trade with foreign countries we would be extending accommodation to European markets in place of their extending monetary assistance to us. Since 1900, when the record trade balance in our favor of $648,786,399 was recorded, we have exported all told $2,977,420,113 more merchandise than we have imported. It is safe to say, however, that in no one of the six years during the course of which these exports occurred was the net balance much if at all in our favor. This, of course, is due to the fact that the unreported items are more than enough to effect the actual excess of exports over imports.

What this adverse balance due to unreported factors amounts to it is very difficult to estimate with any accuracy. The amount has been variously stated all the way from $250,000,000 to $750,000,000. While the latter figure seems excessive, the smaller amount is probably much below the actual figure.

This adverse balance is due to a number of factors. Among the most important of these are the expenses of American tourists abroad, the sums paid to foreigners by way of ocean freights and for insurance, and the dividends and interest paid to foreign holders of American securities. Some of these items, of course, are offset to some extent by similar items in our favor. Thus, from the last-named item must be

"JOHN BULL AND HIS ISLAND"

deducted the amount due to this country on foreign securities which have been placed in this market. Among these are the Japanese bond issues of last year, and several issues of Mexican bonds and other securities of companies operating in Mexico from which Americans derive income. So, too, a certain amount of money is spent here by travelers from abroad. In each item, however, the balance will be a debit one for this country.

Another item that is by no means negligible is the money earned in this country by immigrants and by them sent to foreign countries. In this connection it is interesting to note that the foreign money orders issued at the New York Post Office last year amounted to no less than $46,181,432, while the amount received on money orders from abroad was only $6,554,936. Much of this doubtless represents money sent to relatives abroad by foreigners residing in this country.

The money spent by American tourists in foreign countries has by some bankers been estimated as high as $400,000,000/a year. Half of this sum is more generally recognized as the probable amount of such expenditures. The country's expenses for freight and insurance charges are estimated at $250,000,000, and the net payments on account of foreign investments in this country can hardly amount to less than $50,000,000. This makes, counting the $40,000,000 sent by money order, a total of $540,000,000. The average excess of exports of merchandise over imports for the past six years has been about $496,000,000, which is $44,000,000 a year less than the yearly debit balance on the unreported items.

Our total foreign commerce has increased year by year for many years past, with the single exception of 1902, when our total foreign commerce was about $60,000,000 smaller than it had been in 1901. Since 1896 we have added over $1,000,000,000 to our annual foreign trade. Our exports of merchandise during this period increased over 60 per cent. and our imports over 72 per cent. The average yearly increase in exports since 1896 has been about 7 per cent. and the average increase in imports about 8 per cent. Thus our imports have steadily increased at a more rapid rate than our exports. Somewhat curiously, although the increase in both imports and exports was greater last year than the average for recent years, there was still about 1 per cent. difference in the increase of the two items, exports having increased 12 per cent. and imports 13 per cent.

* * *

January 6, 1907

NEW YORK'S POSITION AS A WORLD CENTRE OF FINANCE

George Paish, Editor of The Statist, Believes the Future of New York to be National Rather Than International

LONDON, Dec. 19—In discussing the position of New York as a world's centre of finance and in endeavoring to form an opinion of its future standing in the international monetary system, it is desirable to separate the material and important from the immaterial and unimportant. New York has been a great money market for a very long period; but it has been an international money market for less than a decade. The reason for this is obvious. Prior to 1897 the United States was a debtor country not merely because of the very large amount of foreign capital that had been imported, but also in consequence of its growing indebtedness to other lands. Since 1897 the United States has been a debtor country only because of the great amount of capital imported up to the early nineties; and it has become a creditor country from the point of view that it has had surplus capital to invest abroad.

But a great international money market depends for its existence on its ability to continue to find capital for those that need it, both at home and abroad. Prior to 1897 the United States needed the whole of its own growing capital and a great deal more besides for the development of its resources and had no capital available for developing the resources of other countries. On the other hand, England, France, and Germany have for many years had more than sufficient capital for their own use and have had large amounts for foreign investments. Hence London, Paris, and Berlin have been great international money markets for a much longer period than New York.

From 1897 to 1904 the United States had a large amount of capital that it did not need for its own development and was willing to employ its surplus wealth, first, in redeeming a portion of its own indebtedness to other countries, and, secondly, in supplying capital to Canada, to Mexico, to Cuba, to the Philippines, to Japan, to South America, to South Africa, and to Europe. There has also been a disposition to place American capital in China and in Russia. The amounts of American capital exported and invested in other countries in 1898, 1899, 1900, and 1901 reached large figures, and five or six years ago many persons both in the United States and in Europe assumed that New York would become the premier international money market, because at that time any foreign country offering attractive securities could raise capital in New York. The trend of events since 1901 has, however, not favored this view, and year after year there has been less American capital available for investment abroad than in the previous year.

Now we have reached a period in which America is no longer employing a portion of its capital abroad; indeed, apparently it is again importing foreign capital for the development of its industries. Indeed, all the signs are favorable to the importation of a large amount of capital into the United States in the next few years. In fact I regard American experience of the last ten years as absolutely exceptional and unlikely to recur for many years.

Of course the importation in place of the exportation of capital does not prejudice the real standing of New York as a money market, although it affects its position as an international monetary centre. There is no special advantage in a money market possessing what is termed an international instead of a national character. England, France, and Germany employ a portion of their capital in other countries because they cannot find advantageous use for it at home. Up to the early nineties the United States imported capital because it could find profitable employment not merely for the whole of its rapidly growing wealth, but also for a great deal of additional wealth. And that country is the most happily situated which can find reproductive employment within its own boundaries for the largest amount of capital.

To appreciate the reason that New York was able to supply capital for international purposes in recent years, it is essential to glance over the events of the last twenty or twenty-five years. In the eighties peace prevailed and the European creditor nations had a very large amount of capital available for investment in any part of the world where it could be profitably employed. The United States offered one of the most promising fields for the investment of this capital and a vast quantity of European capital was consequently sent to America for the construction of an unprecedented length of railway. In the eighties no less than 73,000 miles of railway were constructed in the United States.

The effect of this vast construction of new railway was twofold. First, the United States was fully supplied with transportation facilities and did not need to build any appreciable additional amount in the nineties, and, secondly, the necessity and scope for foreign investment in the country were restricted.

In the early nineties the Sherman Silver act created grave distrust and ultimately caused the 1893 panic with all its consequences. The depression into which the United States fell in consequence of its currency troubles had several important results. It stopped the importation of capital from abroad, it forced American people to become more economical than they have been for many years, and it drew out all the inventive and organizing faculties of the Nation by which much greater efficiency was secured.

The result of this combination of conditions was that previous capital expenditures became much more fruitful, that the additions to the appliances needed to swell the production of the Nation were very small and that in consequence of economy and of increased efficiency the surplus wealth grew in a very rapid manner.

In other words, America produced a vastly increased amount of wealth and provided all the capital needed rapidly to develop its own industries and to invest a large sum in other countries. The economy practiced in the United States in the nineties is still fresh in the memory of us all. Every one remembers that house construction was practically at a standstill, that the expenditures of even reputed wealthy families were reduced to relatively low figures, and that every one strained to produce a large amount of commodities and produce for sale in the foreign markets.

It should be noted that one of the fruits of the depression from 1893 to 1896 was the great progress in the economical and scientific operation of railways by which the people of the United States have been saved hundreds of millions of dollars and by which they have been able to use a very large amount of capital for the development of other industries which otherwise would have been required for constructing additional railway accommodation. It is unnecessary to give statistical data in proof of this statement. Confirmation may be had in the surprise which has been expressed at the large amount of capital which American railways have been required to raise in the last two years. The American people had become so accustomed to railways needing practically no capital for the development of their business that now the limits of economy have been nearly reached and additional railway facilities upon a large scale have to be provided out of capital in order to deal with the growing traffic, they express their amazement.

In brief, the ability of the American people to find capital in the last seven or eight years, not merely for the development of their own natural resources, but also for employment in other countries, was the direct result of the economies they practiced and the increased efficiency they attained from 1893 to 1900 or 1901. And the international character of the New York money market from 1897 up to the present time has resulted from the American people having produced a surplus supply of wealth which they sent to other countries for employment and for which they received payment in securities.

But the position to-day is entirely different to that of ten years ago, or even of five years ago. Where distrust then existed there is now confidence. Where economies were practiced there are now liberal expenditures. The house building trade which in the nineties was abnormally depressed is now exceedingly active, and vast amounts of capital are being spent both to house America's rapidly growing population and to provide for what we may term the less economical house expenditure of a Nation whose wealth has grown and is growing in such a remarkable manner. To indicate the amount of capital needed to provide for the house requirements would take me into figures which I wish to avoid. But I may say that the capital expenditures on house and building construction in the United States in 1907 will be several times greater than the amount of capital that was spent upon house construction in 1897, which was about the time that New York began to figure as an important international money market.

Again, the vast growth of traffic which the railways have to transport and the very great density to which the traffic has attained are necessitating immense capital expenditures upon new lines, upon widenings, upon rolling stock, and upon plant. Hence a portion of the margin of capital which America recently had available for investment in other countries is disappearing in consequence of the urgent need for additional railway facilities.

Thus, instead of remaining an international money market in which foreign countries can obtain capital, New York is rapidly becoming, if it has not already become, a national money market where builders of houses, railway companies, manufacturers, farmers, merchants, miners, and others will obtain the capital for developing the natural resources of the home country. And if there is not enough of home capital available to meet all the requirements New York must import capital from abroad.

The change from an international to a national money market will not be to the disadvantage of New York. Only the character of the business will alter, not the amount.

Thus I anticipate that the United States will have no capital for employment in other countries for many years to come and will on the contrary resume the importation of capital for the development of its railway system, its industries, and its great agricultural and mineral natural wealth.

GEORGE PAISH

*   *   *

January 6, 1907

REASONS FOR THE FINANCIAL SUPREMACY OF LONDON

Its Predominance Not Menaced by New York, Writes Sir J. Herbert Fritton, Director of Barclay & Co. and Chairman of the Indo-European Telegraph Company

LONDON, Dec. 10—The growth of the United States of America, decade by decade, in population, in trade external and internal, and in accumulated wealth, is a continual marvel to us as we look across the ocean; while it compels the acknowledgment that it is destined to be continuously greater in the future. No wonder then that the question arises: Is New York now or will it ever be the financial centre of the world? The question is not one which is of academic interest only, nor is it one which is asked in New York alone. On the European coasts of the Atlantic and on the American coasts of the Pacific the interest in this question is keen to-day, and likely to be keener in the future.

Let it not be supposed, however, that sensible people look with jealousy or astonishment at the growth, which gives rise to the question, albeit, it is the growth of a rival. That it is inevitable for a nation like the United States, whose increase of population in the ten years 1895–1905 is from 68,934,000 to 83,143,000—or more than a third of the whole population of the United Kingdom, with its boundless resources of mineral and agricultural wealth, and its intellectual vigor, to outstrip us is certain; while, all rivalries not withstanding, we recognize the fact that we shall find in her an increasingly good customer as her requirements increase pari passu with her powers of purchase.

London knows well enough that the daily New York clearing bankers' settlements are in excess of hers, but this does not disturb her. What would disturb her equanimity would be to find that in the great marts of the world a bill of exchange drawn in dollars and payable in New York was more in demand than one drawn in British sterling payable in London, but she sees as yet no sign of this.

There can be no doubt that London has been the financial centre of the world since Venice and later Amsterdam successively lost that proud position, and that she holds it rather by force of circumstances than by either good fortune or good management.

Her supremacy does not, to my mind, seem as yet seriously threatened, though Paris, Berlin, and New York have each made great strides of late years in the international race.

I postulate the following reasons for her position, and I predict that when they are found united in any one other centre, whether in the Old World or in the New, London will have to bow and confess herself beaten:

1. To be a financial centre of the world it is necessary that a city should be the unquestioned financial centre of its own country.

2. That its own country should sell to all nations, should lend to all nations, and should buy from all nations.

3. That it should have large accumulated resources seeking world-wide outlets.

4. That it should have a mercantile marine as large as, or larger than, the aggregate of any other two or three countries combined.

5. That its sons should be able to hive off to distant shores retaining their citizenship, and be proud to administer and govern dependencies and colonies, not as separate units, but as parts of a great whole.

6. That cost of production and consequent power to export not be enhanced by unnecessary legislation.

7. Last, but not least, that a well grounded confidence exist throughout the world that her coin of the realm—that in which values are computed—her money of accounts, be a definite and unchanging weight of gold, and that there be a certainty that all holders of documents whereby is assigned to them at a given date such and such a value expressed in that money of account, shall be able, without let or hindrance, to obtain, if they desire, the equivalent weight in gold of the prescribed fineness at the moment when they are entitled to claim it.

A treatise might be written on each of these propositions, but it suffices now to inquire how far in the case of New York these conditions are fulfilled.

1. It may be presumptuous in one who has not recently visited the United States to ask whether New York is really the financial centre of the country. Apart from stock exchange transactions, I am under the impression that Chicago might put in a claim, but I readily admit that I do not believe it could be substantiated.

2. The United States is, from its geographical range and climatic conditions, so self-contained, and its magnificent resources demand such a vast capital for their development that the incentive to foreign trade is not nearly so strong with her as with us.

3. If we except from the mercantile marine tonnage of the United States that employed on the rivers and the Great Lakes, her sea-going tonnage is, save in the North Atlantic trade, quite insignificant. The example of France is not encouraging to the advocates of bounties either in tonnage or mileage.

Great Britain and her dependencies own more than half the aggregate world's tonnage.

4. The colonial policy of the citizens of the United States has not yet had much chance of asserting itself; it seems still to be of an experimental order.

5. The fiscal system of the United States, which has admirers on this side, and not only admirers, but advocates strenuous and persistent, is admittedly a factor in keeping up the cost of production. For fifty years this country has gone on opposite principles, and has no reason, judging from the returns of exports and imports, to regret the free admission of the greater part of the latter.

6. But it is in the last of my propositions that I find the chief reason for the predominance of London as the financial centre of the world.

A banker of many years standing, I look back with pride and satisfaction to the part played by the City of London during the raging of the bimetallic controversy, when, as it is generally acknowledged, "one square mile" stood apparently "contra mundum" and conquered. The adhesion to our gold standard thus assured, other nations, notably the United States and Germany, fell into line, but France, as a member of the Latin Union, still holds to a "limping standard," while India has actually adopted one of the same nature.

France may claim that in times of great demand for gold she can prevent its export by imposing a premium thereon and thus keep her rate of discount steady, but this practice effectually shuts her out from attaining that financial standing among the nations to which she would otherwise be entitled. In Germany a different method is understood to be used to prevent or delay the free export of gold, viz., the disfavor. I had almost used a stronger word, meted out by the highest financial authorities to any who at an inconvenient time would dare to require gold for export.

In the United States the intervention of the Treasury (via Mr. Secretary Shaw's report submitted to Congress on Dec. 5th last,) or the non-intervention according to the views held by that Minister at any given time, so materially affects the price of exchange by securing indirectly that which the Bank of France goes directly—viz., the establishment of a premium on gold, that New York is, without question, like Paris, unfavorably situated, and rendered thereby less able to take its proper place among the nations.

In London, on the other hand, the only place of which this can be said, the influx and efflux of gold is absolutely free.

Here gold accommodates itself to the movement of the exchanges undeterred by the frowns of the mighty and unhindered by artifices or regulations.

We have our own disputes, it is true, as to this gold question, but these turn on how to facilitate at the least cost to the nation the movements of bullion, not how to hamper or to reverse their natural course.

I have expressed myself freely and frankly, as I understand the representative of your great newspaper invited me to do.

The more clearly the true conditions affecting the trade of the world—that exchange of goods against goods perpetually in progress—are understood, the better for international trade.

It is possible that we may see a sort of duality established between New York and London, each keeping a central stock of gold subject to the issue of gold certificates against it current on either side, and thus the actual transmission of bullion across the Atlantic and back again may be minimized. In this way New York would undoubtedly make a great stride toward financial supremacy.

I feel tempted to add the conviction of an old free-trader held for many years, that when, if ever, the United States adopts external free trade, though the shock to her internal trade would at first be great, while the benefit at first to this country would be as great, in the long run she would so effectually undersell Great Britain that our supremacy would be wrenched away from us in spite of other and unfavorable conditions. Absit omen!

J. Herbert Tritton

*   *   *

October 18, 1907

WIRELESS JOINS TWO WORLDS

Marconi Transatlantic Service Opened with a Dispatch to The New York Times

MESSAGES FROM EMINENT MEN

Prime Minister Clemenceau, the Duke of Argyll, Lord Avebury and Others Send Greetings

10,000 WORDS THE FIRST DAY

Marconi in Personal Supervision at Glace Bay and Greatly Pleased with the Results

SIR HIRAM MAXIM'S TRIBUTE.

His Message to Peter Cooper Hewitt in New York, Who is Trying to Pick Up the Oversea Messages

By Marconi Transatlantic Wireless Telegraph to The New York Times

LONDON, Oct. 17—This message marks the opening of the transatlantic wireless service. It is handed to the Marconi Company here for transmission to Ireland, and thence to Cape Breton, Nova Scotia, and New York. As it is limited to fifty words, I can send at present only one of the many messages received for transmission to The New York Times to signalize the event. This message, from Privy Councillor Lord Avebury, formerly Sir John Lubbock, follows:

"I trust that the introduction of the wireless will more closely unite the people of the United States and Great Britain, who seem to form one nation, though under two Governments, and whose interests are really identical. AVEBURY."

The Collapse Of The Global Economy

October 30, 1929

STOCKS COLLAPSE IN 16,410,030-SHARE DAY, BUT RALLY AT CLOSE CHEERS BROKERS; BANKERS OPTIMISTIC, TO CONTINUE AID

CLOSING RALLY VIGOROUS

Leading Issues Regain From 4 to 14 Points in 15 Minutes

INVESTMENT TRUSTS BUY

Large Blocks Thrown on Market at Opening Start Third Break of Week

BIG TRADERS HARDEST HIT

Bankers Believe Liquidation Now Has Run Its Course and Advise Purchases

Stock prices virtually collapsed yesterday, swept downward with gigantic losses in the most disastrous trading day in the stock market's history. Billions of dollars in open market values were wiped out as prices crumbled under the pressure of liquidation of securities which had to be sold at any price.

There was an impressive rally just at the close, which brought many leading stocks back from 4 to 14 points from their lowest points of the day.

Trading on the New York Stock Exchange aggregated 16,410,030 shares; on the Curb, 7,096,300 shares were dealt in. Both totals far exceeded any previous day's dealings.

From every point of view, in the extent of losses sustained, in total turnover, in the number of speculators wiped out, the day was the most disastrous in Wall Street's history. Hysteria swept the country and stocks went overboard for just what they would bring at forced sale.

Efforts to estimate yesterday's market losses in dollars are futile because of the vast number of securities quoted over the counter and on out-of-town exchanges on which no calculations are possible. However, it was estimated that 880 issues, on the New York Stock Exchange, lost between $8,000,000,000 and $9,000,000,000 yesterday. Added to that loss is to be reckoned the depreciation on issues on the Curb Market, in the over the counter market and on other exchanges.

Two Extra Dividends Declared

There were two cheerful notes, however, which sounded through the pall of gloom which overhung the financial centres of the country. One was the brisk rally of stocks at the close on tremendous buying by those who believe that prices have sunk too low. The other was that the liquidation has been so violent, as well as widespread, that many bankers, brokers and industrial leaders expressed the belief last night that it now has run its course.

A further note of optimism in the soundness of fundamentals was sounded by the directors of the United States Steel Corporation and the American Can Company, each of which declared an extra dividend of $1 a share at their late afternoon meetings.

Banking support, which would have been impressive and successful under ordinary circumstances, was swept violently aside, as block after block of stock, tremendous in proportions, deluged the market. Bid prices placed by bankers, industrial leaders and brokers trying to halt the decline were crashed through violently, their orders were filled, and quotations plunged downward in a day of disorganization, confusion and financial impotence.

Change Is Expected Today

That there will be a change today seemed likely from statements made last night by financial and business leaders. Organized support will be accorded to the market from the start, it is believed; but those who are staking their all on the country's leading securities are placing a great deal of confidence, too, in the expectation that there will be an overnight change in sentiment; that the counsel of cool heads will prevail and that the mob psychology which has been so largely responsible for the market's debacle will be broken.

The fact that the leading stocks were able to rally in the final fifteen minutes of trading yesterday was considered a good omen, especially as the weakest period of the day had developed just prior to that time and the minimum prices for the day had then been established. It was a quick run-up which followed the announcement that the American Can directors had declared an extra dividend of $1. The advances in leading stocks in this last fifteen minutes represented a measurable snap-back from the lows. American Can gained 10; United States Steel common, 7½; General Electric, 12; New York Central, 14½; Anaconda Copper, 9½; Chrysler Motors, 5¼; Montgomery Ward, 4¼; and Johns Manville, 8. Even with these recoveries the losses of these particular stocks, and practically all others, were staggering.

Yesterday's market crash was one which largely affected rich men, institutions, investment trusts and others who participate in the stock market on a broad and intelligent scale. It was not the margin traders who were caught in the rush to sell, but the rich men of the country who are able to swing blocks of 5,000, 10,000 up to 100,000 shares of high-priced stocks. They went overboard with no more consideration than the little trader who was swept out on the first day of the market's upheaval, whose prices, even at their lowest of last Thursday, now look high in comparison.

The market on the rampage is no respecter of persons. It washed fortune after fortune away yesterday and financially crippled thousands of individuals in all parts of the world. It was not until after the market had closed that the financial district began to realize that a good-sized rally had taken place and that there was a stopping place on the downgrade for good stocks.

Third Day of Collapse

The market has now passed through three days of collapse, and so violent has it been that most authorities believe that the end is not far away. It started last Thursday, when 12,800,000 shares were dealt in on the Exchange, and holders of stocks commenced to learn just what a decline in the market means. This was followed by a moderate rally on Friday and entirely normal conditions on Saturday, with fluctuations on a comparatively narrow scale and with the efforts of the leading bankers to stabilize the market evidently successful. But the storm broke anew on Monday, with prices slaughtered in every direction, to be followed by yesterday's tremendous trading of 16,410,030 shares.

Sentiment had been generally unsettled since the first of September. Market prices had then reached peak levels, and, try as they would, pool operators and other friends of the market could not get them higher. It was a gradual downward sag, gaining momentum as it went on, then to break out into an open market smash in which the good, the bad and indifferent stocks went down alike. Thousands of traders were able to weather the first storm and answered their margin calls; thousands fell by the wayside Monday and again yesterday, unable to meet the demands of their brokers that their accounts be protected.

There was no quibbling at all between customer and broker yesterday. In any case where margin became thin a peremptory call went out. If there was no immediate answer the stock was sold out "at the market" for just what it would bring. Thousands, sold out on the decline and amid the confusion, found themselves in debt to their brokers last night.

Three Factors in Market

Three factors stood out most prominently last night after the market's close. They were:

Wall Street has been able to weather the storm with but a single Curb failure, small in size, and no member of the New York Stock Exchange has announced himself unable to meet commitments.

The smashing decline has brought stocks down to a level where, in the opinion of leading bankers and industrialists, they are a buy on their merits and prospects, and brokers have so advised their customers.

The very violence of the liquidation, which has cleaned up many hundreds of sore spots which honeycombed the market, and the expected ability of the market to right itself, since millions of shares of stock have passed to strong hands from weak ones.

Bids Provided Where Needed

One of the factors which Wall Street failed to take into consideration throughout the entire debacle was that the banking consortium has no idea of putting stocks up or to save any individuals from loss, but that its sole purpose was to alleviate the wave of financial hysteria sweeping the country and provide bids, at some price, where needed. It was pointed out in many quarters that no broad liquidating movement in the stock market has ever been stopped by so-called good buying. This is helpful of course, but it never stops an avalanche of liquidation, as was this one.

There is only one factor, it was pointed out, which can and always does stop a down swing—that is, the actual cessation of forced liquidation. It is usually the case, too, that when the last of the forced selling has been completed the stock market always faces a wide-open gap in which there are practically no offerings of securities at all. When that point is reached, buying springs up from everywhere and always accounts for a sharp, almost perpendicular recovery in the best stocks. The opinion was widely expressed in Wall Street last night that that point has been reached, or at least very nearly reached.

Huge Blocks Offered at Opening

The opening bell on the Stock Exchange released such a flood of selling as has never before been witnessed in this country. The failure of the market to rally consistently on the previous day, the tremendous shrinkage of open market values and the wave of hysteria which appeared to sweep the country brought an avalanche of stock to the market to be sold at whatever price it would bring.

From the very first quotation until thirty minutes after 10 o'clock it was evident that the day's market would be an unprecedented one. In that first thirty minutes of trading stocks were poured out in 5,000, 10,000, 20,000 and 50,000 share blocks at tremendous sacrifices as compared with the previous closing. The declines ranged from a point or so to as much as 29½ points, and the reports of opening prices brought selling into the market in confused volume that has never before been equaled.

In this first half hour of trading on the Stock Exchange a total of 3,259,800 shares were dealt in. The volume of the first twenty-six blocks of stock dealt in at the opening totaled more than 630,000 shares.

There was simply no near-by demand for even the country's leading industrial and railroad shares, and many millions of dollars in values were lost in the first quotations tapped out. All considerations other than to get rid of the stock at any price were brushed aside.

Brokerage Offices Crowded

Wall Street was a street of vanished hopes, of curiously silent apprehension and of a sort of paralyzed hypnosis yes-

terday. Men and women crowded the brokerage offices, even those who have been long since wiped out, and followed the figures on the tape. Little groups gathered here and there to discuss the fall in prices in hushed and awed tones. They were participating in the making of financial history. It was the consensus of bankers and brokers alike that no such scenes ever again will be witnessed by this generation. To most of those who have been in the market it is all the more awe-inspiring because their financial history is limited to bull markets.

The machinery of the New York Stock Exchange and the Curb market were unable to handle the tremendous volume of trading which went over them. Early in the day they kept up well, because most of the trading was in big blocks, but as the day progressed the tickers fell further and further behind, and as on the previous big days of this week and last it was only by printing late quotations of stocks on the bond tickers and by the 10-minute flashes on stock prices put out by Dow, Jones & Co. and the Wall Street News Bureau that the financial district could get any idea of what was happening in the wild mob of brokers on the Exchange and the Curb.

* * *

January 6, 1930

CHINA FACES CRISIS AS CURRENCY FALLS

Banks in Difficulties With Mexican Dollars at 38 Cents Gold and Dropping

SHANGHAI, Jan. 5 (AP)—The Nanking Government today was confronted with an acute financial problem in the form of depreciated currency as a result of the steady decline in the value of the Chinese silver dollar (commonly called Mexican), in addition to the grave political uncertainties with which China has been struggling. That dollar is now worth only 38 cents gold, as compared with 49 cents a year ago. Bankers and financial experts predict that its value will slump as far as 30 cents, possibly further.

As a result of this currency decline, which is unprecedented in the last quarter century, merchants, especially importers, both foreign and Chinese, have felt much hardship due to their commitments being payable in gold. Numerous importers are refusing to accept shipments. This refusal has placed many Chinese banks in a difficult position and failures are predicted.

A dispatch from Peking said five Chinese banks there had failed and that ten others were tottering.

The decline in the value of the silver dollar also has resulted in a sharp upward movement of general prices. Sellers are seeking to recoup losses, which are mounting as the dollar declines.

The situation has placed the Nationalist Government in a difficult position in meeting foreign loan obligations. Payments of these require a huge portion of the funds originally allotted to domestic uses in order to offset the unfavorable exchange.

T. V. Soong, Minister of Finance, admitted that the currency situation was "very serious." He expressed the belief, however, that the crisis would be surmounted, adding:

"If China can enjoy peace, allowing trade to flourish, the dollar crisis will disappear. But if more wars arise the financial future is obscure."

It is generally considered that the only lasting solution of this crisis will be for China to establish gold as the currency standard. This is considered impossible at present.

* * *

March 25, 1930

SENATE PASSES TARIFF BILL, 53 TO 31, AFTER OPPONENTS ASSAIL RATE BOOSTS; HOUSE TO ACT ON CONFERENCE IN WEEK

FEW INSURGENTS OPPOSE

Only Five Join With 26 Democrats Against the Measure

FARM TARIFF PLAN BEATEN

La Follette, Harrison, Blaine and Blease Assail "Grundy" Bill as Proponents Await Poll

BORAH FIRM ON DEBENTURE

Smoot Pledges Senators Will Hold Out for It, as House Chiefs Plan Conference Fight

Special to The New York Times

WASHINGTON, March 24—After nearly ten months of labor, the Senate passed the tariff bill late this afternoon by a vote of 53 to 31. The measure was approved in the upper chamber amid scenes marked by sharp conflict and intense excitement. Washington had been waiting for this moment for months, but many were apprehensive that something might happen to impel the Senate again to postpone action and start another verbal marathon.

Forty-six Republicans and seven Democrats voted for the proposed tariff act, while five Republicans and twenty-six Democrats were against it. Included among the Republicans who stood by the bill on final passage were eight members of the Democratic-insurgent coalition, which lost control of the measure a few weeks ago through a new combination effected by the Old Guard leadership.

These eight were Senators Borah, Brookhart, Frazier, Howell, Nye, Pine, Schall and Cutting.

The seven Democrats who deserted the main body of their party to vote for the bill were Senators Bratton, Broussard, Copeland, Kendrick, Pittman, Ransdell and Trammell.

The Vote on the Bill

Here is the roll-call on the bill's passage:

FOR THE BILL—53
Republicans—46

Allen	Hastings	Pine
Baird	Hatfield	Robinson (Ind.)
Bingham	Hebert	
Borah	Howell	Robsion
Brookhart	Johnson	Schall
Capper	Jones	Shortridge
Couzens	Kean	Smoot
Dale	Keyes	Steiwer
Fess	McCulloch	Sullivan
Frazier	McNary	Thomas (Idaho)
Gillett	Metcalf	
Glenn	Moses	Townsend
Goff	Nye	Vandenberg
Goldsborough	Oddie	Walcott
Greene	Patterson	Waterman
Hale	Phipps	Watson

Democrats—7

Bratton	Copeland	Ransdell
Broussard	Kendrick	Trammell
	Pittman	

AGAINST THE BILL—31
Republicans—5

Blaine	McMaster	Norris
LaFollette	Norbeck	

Democrats—26

Ashurst	Harris	Steck
Barkley	Harrison	Swanson
Black	Hawes	Thomas (Okla.)
Blease	Hayden	
Caraway	Heflin	Tydings
Connally	McKellar	Wagner
Dill	Sheppard	Walsh (Mass.)
George	Simmons	Walsh (Mont.)
Glass	Smith	Wheeler

Pairs.

For the bill—Cutting, Deneen, Grundy, Reed, Gould, Republicans; Fletcher, Democrat.

Against the bill—Brock, Overman, Stephenson, Robinson of Arkansas, King, Democrats; Shipstead, Farmer-Labor.

Recommittal Motion Defeated

Just before the bill was passed Senator Thomas, Democrat, of Oklahoma, moved that it be recommitted to the Finance Committee with instructions to redraft it by limiting the revision to the increased rates contained in the farm schedule and the amendments to the administrative provisions. This was beaten by a vote of 70 to 9.

Those who voted for the Thomas motion were Senators Blease, Caraway, Smith, Thomas of Oklahoma, Walsh of

Montana, and Wheeler, Democrats, and McMaster, Nye and Pine, Republicans.

The bill now goes back to the House, where it originated in Ways and Means Committee hearings beginning in January, 1929. If the Longworth-Tilson-Snell organization has its way—and it generally does—the House will send the bill to conference without delay and with instructions to its managers to disagree to all Senate amendments.

Representative Hawley, chairman of the Ways and Means Committee, said tonight that, while no time had been set for taking up of the tariff bill in the House, it was probable that it would not come up before Monday. The House desires to get some of the pending legislation out of the way before it considers the bill and asks for a conference with the Senate.

A farm bloc coalition has been forming in the House for some weeks, designed to hamstring the House conferees by directing them to accept the upward rates in the agricultural schedule voted by the Senate. But Speaker Longworth and his Steering Committee profess confidence in their ability to defeat any move that may be engineered by this bloc.

Opinions vary among leaders in Congress as to how long the tariff bill is likely to remain in conference. Chairman Hawley of the Ways and Means Committee believes the conference committee will be able to conclude its labors in little more than three weeks. Chairman Smoot of the Senate Finance Committee is of the same opinion.

Senate Opposition More Vocal

The closing scenes attending the passage of the bill were full of animation and color. The galleries were packed, and there was little or no trouble in maintaining a quorum on the floor. The principal speeches were made by critics of the bill, its supporters being confident of the action and wishing to curtail the debate as a means of accelerating the decision.

Rumblings of trouble in conference over the Senate's debenture and flexible tariff amendments, both of which have been disapproved by President Hoover, were heard as the debate progressed.

Senator Borah of Idaho indicated that he would vote for the bill, but he admitted that he had misgivings over the fate of the two amendments mentioned and the Norris antimonopoly provisions. If the conference scrapped these clauses, Mr. Borah emphasized, practically all of the insurgent Republicans would vote against its report.

On a demand from the floor, Senator Smoot pledged that the chamber's conferees would abide by the Senate's decision on these amendments up to the point of deadlock and would then report back to give the Senate another opportunity to vote on the provisions.

Senator La Follette of Wisconsin denounced the measure as "the worst tariff bill in the nation's history." He said that it should be known hereafter as "Grundy's billion-dollar tariff bill."

Senator Harrison of Mississippi injected a little humor into the proceedings when he announced that his colleague, Senator Stephens, was paired with Senator Grundy of Pennsylvania.

"If my colleague were present he would vote 'no,' " said Mr. Harrison. "I understand that if Senator Grundy were present he would vote 'aye.' "

Senator Robsion, Republican, of Kentucky, spoke of the bill in terms of praise, while Senators Nye, Republican insurgent, of North Dakota, and Connally, Democrat, of Texas, assailed it. Senator Walsh, Democrat, of Massachusetts, assailed the rate structure, asserting that it would prove extremely burdensome to the great mass of consumers and react on the party responsible for it.

Calls for Vote Interrupt Caraway

Senator Caraway, Democrat, of Arkansas, chairman of the lobby investigation committee, closed the debate. As he criticized the bill sharply, there were cries of "Vote, vote!" from the Democratic side of the chamber.

"Just wait a minute," said Mr. Caraway; "your time will come."

Concluding with a statement that the bill was a bad one from the consumers' standpoint and that it should be beaten, Mr. Caraway announced his intention to vote against the measure.

Bad feeling was shown frequently throughout the debate. Senators were tired and weary and tempers exploded from time to time. Mr. Harrison, who probably will be one of the Senate conferees, wanted to, print a table showing equivalent ad valorem duties, in connection with one prepared by Chairman Smoot. Mr. Smoot objected in vigorous terms.

The Senate will be represented on the conference committee by Messrs Smoot, Watson and Shortridge, Republicans, and Simmons and Harrison, Democrats. The House conferees will be Representatives Hawley of Oregon, Treadway of Massachusetts and Bacharach of New Jersey, Republicans, and Garner of Texas and Collier of Mississippi, Democrats.

The bill was received by the Senate from the House on May 29, 1929. The Finance Committee began hearings on June 13 and ended them on July 18. The bill as redrafted by the Republican committeemen was reported to the Senate on Sept. 4. Debate began Sept. 12 and continued until Nov. 22, when the extra session, called to act on farm relief and the tariff, ended. The tariff debate was resumed at the beginning of the regular session called on Dec. 2 and has continued since, except for other business admitted to consideration by unanimous consent. In the time consumed the Senate established a record for tariff measures.

La Follette Prominent in Debate

Senator La Follette, one of the most vigorous in the debate, asserted that the measure was "free from the pretense" of protecting "infant industries" and that no one had made the claim that it was based upon the Republican principle of "equalizing costs of protection at home and abroad."

"The Grundy billion-dollar tariff bill," he said, "eclipses the 'tariff of abominations' of 1828 in its impositions upon the public and by comparison dwarfs the injustice and iniquity of the Payne-Aldrich act of 1909, which wrecked the party in 1912."

Mr. La Follette said the bill represented "a series of deals conceived in secret but executed in public with a brazen effrontery that is without parallel in the annals of the Senate." The rate structure, he declared, was "the product of a combination of lobbyists, who pooled their interests to secure the rewriting of this piece of legislation during the final weeks of its consideration."

As the youthful Mr. La Follette hammered the Republican bill in the same biting invective that his late father employed in previous years in the same forum, the "elder statesmen" sat up and took notice.

He realized, Mr. La Follette went on, that some Senators regarded the Congressional flexible provision, the farm debenture plan and the Norris amendment, which he described as a "device whereby duties may be removed when domestic price-fixing or monopoly is proved," as constructive achievements which justified voting for the bill. He continued:

"In my judgment, however, indefensible duties, estimated to increase the consumers' burden by $1,000,000,000 a year, constitute too great a price for people to pay for constructive legislation, which it is the duty of Congress to enact without imposing this enormous tax on the great body of citizens.

Would Not Condone "Vote Trading"

"Furthermore, it seems to me that a vote for the bill condones the votetrading deals by which some of the most unjustifiable rates in the bill were obtained. For the first time in the history of the Senate, avowed lobbyists testified under oath regarding the deals by which they proposed to secure the duties they wanted. Votes were changed overnight, not by argument, nor by new evidence.

"The farmer has been betrayed and many new burdens of industrial tariffs have been placed upon his back for every alleged benefit which he may secure from this bill. The farmer's back has been the springboard from which the industrial lobbyists have leaped to new and higher tariff rates for the benefit of the special industrial interests they represent.

"Not only the farmers and wage-earners, but the mass of the consumers of the country are by this bill delivered over to the trusts and combinations to be exploited to the limit, without hope of relief from competition, either at home or abroad. It is now clear that the bill has sown seeds of international ill-will which the United States is already reaping in the form of retaliatory measures."

Here Mr. La Follette read a part of the cable dispatch printed in yesterday's New York Times setting forth that France contemplated reprisals in the form of higher rates on American automotive products in retaliation for the increased duties on laces in the Senate bill.

"This tariff bill is driving the nations of Europe into a movement to create a customs union whose barriers will be built primarily to exclude our products," he resumed. "It has levied virtual embargoes upon the products of those nations whose friendship we should be anxious to preserve. It has struck a blow at our foreign trade, through the expansion of which we should now be seeking to relieve the existing unemployment situation created by the decline in our own purchasing power.

Setback for Merchant Marine

"This iniquitous measure will thwart the efforts to build up a national merchant marine, no matter how many hundreds of millions of taxpayers' money may be poured out in subsidies. We cannot hope to maintain a merchant marine without cargoes for our ships, and foreign trade cannot be preserved by excluding the products of our best customers.

"This bill as it stands today will, I believe, do more to create sectional ill-feeling than any measure that has been before the Senate within the memory of its oldest member. It places burdens on the entire people for the benefit of special groups and local interests, which they are bound to resent and which they will eventually repudiate.

"By levying heavy duties upon all kinds of commodities, from raw materials not produced in the country to the most highly finished products, it will tend to force a readjustment on the entire price structure of American industry and check purchases and consumption at the very time when an expansion of trade is vitally needed for the restoration of prosperity.

"The Grundy tariff bill is an absolute violation of the President's message urging a limited revision of the tariff for relief of agriculture and for the protection of those industries in which there has been, to quote the President's exact language, 'a substantial slackening of activity and a consequent decrease in employment due to insurmountable competition in the products of that industry.'

"For this general upward revision, obtained after the coalition of Progressives and Democrats had worked for months to prevent it, the leaders of the President's own party in both houses of Congress are responsible. This is the result which they sought from the beginning, and which they achieved in the end with the assistance of a few tariff-hungry members of the opposition party who exalted sectional interests above the common good.

"As I see it, a vote for the Grundy bill, either as it passes the Senate or when it comes back from conference, is a vote to turn the Senate into a market-place where legislation is written by bargaining and where the lobby with the largest number of votes to trade dictates the terms of legislation."

Borah Holds to the Amendments

Speaking with great earnestness, Senator Borah emphasized his interest in the debenture, flexible tariff and Norris anti-monopoly amendments. He indicated his purpose to vote for the bill on the ground that he wanted particularly to stress his advocacy of the debenture plan, which, he said, amounted to the payment of a bounty to the farmers.

"I cannot help but believe," he said, "that the debenture, or the bounty, is an indispensable part of the protective system so far as the protective system is concerned. Many of the rates on agricultural products designed to help the farmer will prove ineffective. On the other hand, most of the rates imposed on the products that he buys will prove effective.

"In the original conception of the protective system, payment of a bounty to take care of agriculture was advocated. That was regarded as essential because the farmer sells in an open market and buys in a protected market."

Mr. Borah said there had been suggestions that when the bill emerged from conference it would be minus the debenture plan.

"I have some suspicions myself about it," he remarked, "but I have to accompany the principle to its grave, and I want to be there in the procession when it takes place. If we take debenture out of this bill and leave the farmer without the protection which that would give him, what will we have done for agriculture at this session of Congress? We will go away from here without any substantial, permanent benefit to the cause for which we were called here."

Referring to the Farm Board's activities, Mr. Borah said:

"Assuming that the Farm Board is not more successful in the future that it has been in the past, we must look elsewhere for relief for the farmer. If we had raised the agricultural rates as originally proposed and let the industrial rates stand as in the present law, the farmer would have derived benefits from the tariff. But as things have been ordered the only alternative left for those who advocated relief for the farmer is the payment of bounties as proposed by the debenture amendment."

Senator Borah said that unless the flexible tariff provisions were modified as proposed by the Senate, Congress would once more signify its approval of the delegation to the President of power to levy taxes.

"I am not willing," he said, "to place myself in a position where I seem to have surrendered to the present law with respect to the flexible tariff."

Senator Borah concluded with a regret that there would be no friend of the debenture plan on the conference committee.

"If debenture goes out of this bill in conference and stays out, that does not mean that the fight for the principle is over," he said. "It means that the fight will have just begun."

Conferees Are Pledged

Senator Connally suggested that Mr. Borah should not nurse the delusion that the bill to be reported by the conference would contain either of the amendments relating to debenture and the flexible tariff, or the Norris amendment.

"The men who will serve as conferees on behalf of the House and the Senate are opposed to debenture," the Texan said, "and over in the White House sits and Executive who is opposed to all of them."

Senator Simmons of North Carolina, Democratic spokesman on the bill, called upon Senators Smoot, Watson and Shortridge to tell what their attitude would be in conference on the controverted amendments. Each in turn gave assurances that he would stand by the Senate Mandate until it was certain that an agreement could not be reached, and then come back to the Senate for instructions. Senator Simmons expressed himself as satisfied.

"It is needless to say," exclaimed Mr. Simmons, "that the Democratic conferees will never yield on any of the propositions we are discussing."

Senator Blease, Democrat, of South Carolina, charged that, in the making of the tariff bill, "the consumer had been sand-bagged and left by the side of the road." He urged his fellow-Democrats not to prolong the agony, but to let the bill be acted on as speedily as possible.

Walsh Attacks Rate Structure

In this attack on the rate structure of the bill, senator Walsh of Massachusetts insisted that in many instances duties on raw products had been increased without extending compensatory benefits to finished manufactures. This was notably true, he said, in textiles, candy and leather.

"Fourteen materials that enter into the tanning of leather have been increased.

"If President Hoover listens to the voice of industry, he will veto this bill," Mr. Walsh said.

The effect of the bill, he charged, would be to increase food prices, building costs and rents, and generally to lay an additional burden on the consumers that would run into the hundreds of millions of dollars.

"The bill," Mr. Walsh concluded, "means injury to the American people and to American industries of every class and kind. Mr. Hoover has the opportunity no American statesman ever had before. I believe he will take advantage of it.

"I believe he will veto this bill and endear himself to the hearts of the people. I believe he will renounce and condemn and repudiate a bill made in such an unscientific, slip-shod, log-rolling and trading manner as this, without purpose, without aim, without benefit and filled with burdens of unmeasured proportions to our people."

Blain Reads of "Boycott" Threat

Senator Blaine submitted some evidence that, he said, indicated a disposition in some quarters to influence the judgment of the Wisconsin Senators on the tariff bill. He said that Friday he received a copy of a telegram from Mrs. H. E. Thomas, Republican National Committeewoman for his State, reading:

OKMULGEE, Okla., March 12—Mrs. H. E. Thomas, Republican Committeewoman, Sheboygan, Wis.

There appears to be a spontaneous boycott against Wisconsin products starting in the mid-continent oil field, because of Senator Blaine's attack on oil organization. The boycott seems to be growing, although apparently sponsored by no organization. Will you wire us any information you may have that will help us stop boycott. R. D. PINE.

"If Mr. Pine states the truth in that telegram," Mr. Blaine said, "the same oil interests who are organizing this boycott against the products of my State were engaged in an unlawful undertaking. To enter into an organization for the purpose of boycotting products in interstate commerce is denounced by the statutes of the country as a criminal act."

Mr. Blaine said that R. D. Pine was "a business partner" of Senator Pine of Oklahoma. He charged that Mr. Pine's request for information "as to how to stop the boycott was a merely subtle design.

"The whole principle of the telegram was to interest the Republican National Committeewoman to bring such influence, as Mr. Pine might imagine she might have, to control the action and the votes of the Senators from Wisconsin on the question of oil."

As to the existence of a boycott Mr. Blaine said he was convinced that "this telegram does not tell the truth."

Franklin Issues Denial

OKLAHOMA CITY, March 24 (AP)—Wirt Franklin, president of the Independent Petroleum Association of America, denied today that his organization has any connection with a reported boycott on Wisconsin products, which Senator Blaine of Wisconsin said he had been informed was instituted in Oklahoma in retaliation for his opposition to a tariff on petroleum products.

"The Independent Petroleum Association would not stoop to the low tactics of the Senator from Wisconsin," Mr. Franklin said.

*   *   *

April 8, 1930

HIGHER TARIFF WINS FAVOR IN AUSTRALIA

Opposition Lessens as Move to Avert Profiteering Is Made by the Government

MORE PRODUCTION SEEN

Manufacturers Also Predict Lower Prices—Earlier Borrowings Assailed by Economists

Special Cable to The New York Times
MELBOURNE, Australia, April 7—Measures considered adequate to combat profiteering under the new prohibitive Australian tariff have been taken during the week-end and opposition to the government's drastic action to restore the balance of trade appears to have died down.

The Conservative newspaper Argus, however, declares that the tariff must aggravate the burden of the high cost of production by causing further inflation and delaying the internal economic adjustment essential for the restoration of credit abroad.

Economists blame earlier Commonwealth and State governments for extravagant borrowing, both in London and New York. Australian manufacturers welcome the tariff changes, predicting largely increased production in the secondary industries and a reduction in prices.

The opposition in the commercial community and in Parliament has been less than anticipated because the view is taken that a drastic situation demands drastic remedies. Never before have financial stringency, both in Australia and in overseas markets, and an enormous reduction in the value

and volume of Australia's exportable primary products existed at the same period.

SYDNEY, Australia, April 7 (AP)—The Commonwealth Government is keenly concerned in the reaction of other countries to the recent drastic increase in tariffs and the prohibition of importation of a number of articles, taken as a temporary measure to alleviate Australia's economic ills.

E. G. Theodore, Commonwealth Treasurer, today declared there would be no justification for any retaliatory measures against Australia, because the tariff changes were not directed at any particular country but were forced upon the Commonwealth by economic circumstances.

Prime Minister James Scullin expressed gratification that influential newspapers of Great Britain, judging by cables reaching Australia, were taking the correct view of the government's action. He added that the result of the South Australian State elections on Saturday, which showed a definite swing toward the Labor party, might be taken as the first expression of Australian public opinion of the government's policy.

*   *   *

May 5, 1930

1,028 ECONOMISTS ASK HOOVER TO VETO PENDING TARIFF BILL

Professors in 179 Colleges and Other Leaders Assail Rise in Rates as Harmful to Country and Sure to Bring Reprisals

Special to The New York Times
WASHINGTON, May 4—Vigorous opposition to passage of the Hawley-Smoot tariff bill is voiced by 1,028 economists, members of the American Economic Association, in a statement presented to President Hoover, Senator Smoot and Representative Hawley by Dr. Claire Wilcox, associate professor of economics at Swarthmore College, and made public here today. They urge the President to veto the measure if Congress passes it.

Economists from forty-six States and 179 colleges, among them Irving Fisher of Yale, Frank W. Taussig of Harvard, Frank A. Fetter of Princeton, Wesley C. Mitchell of Columbia, J. Laurence Laughlin of the University of Chicago and Willford I. King of New York University join in the statement.

Arguing against increased tariff rates they declare that the pending bill will raise the cost of living and injure the "majority of our citizens," that under it the vast majority of farmers would lose and that American export trade in general would suffer.

Asserting that America now faces the problem of unemployment, the economists challenge the contention of high tariff proponents that higher rates will give work to the idle. Employment, they state, cannot be increased by restricting trade, and American industry, in "the present crisis, might be spared the burden of adjusting itself to higher schedules of duties."

They urge the administration to give regard to that "bitterness which a policy of higher tariffs would inevitably inject into our international relations."

The text of the statement is:

"The undersigned American economists and teachers of economics strongly urge that any measure which provides for a general upward revision of tariff rates be denied passage by Congress, or if passed, be vetoed by the President.

"We are convinced that increased restrictive duties would be a mistake. They would operate, in general, to increase the prices which domestic consumers would have to pay. By raising prices they would encourage concerns with higher costs to undertake production, thus compelling the consumer to subsidize waste and inefficiency in industry.

"At the same time they would force him to pay higher rates of profit to established firms which enjoyed lower production costs. A higher level of duties, such as is contemplated by the Smoot-Hawley bill, would therefore raise the cost of living and injure the great majority of our citizens.

"Few people could hope to gain from such a change. Miners, construction, transportation and public utility workers, professional people and those employed in banks, hotels, newspaper offices, in the wholesale and retail trades and scores of other occupations would clearly lose, since they produce no products which could be specially favored by tariff barriers.

"The vast majority of farmers also would lose. Their cotton, pork, lard and wheat are export crops and are sold in the world market. They have no important competition in the home market. They cannot benefit, therefore, from any tariff which is imposed upon the basic commodities which they produce.

Predict a Double Loss

"They would lose through the increased duties on manufactured goods, however, and in a double fashion. First, as consumers they would have to pay still higher prices for the products, made of textiles, chemicals, iron and steel, which they buy. Second, as producers their ability to sell their products would be further restricted by the barriers placed in the way of foreigners who wished to sell manufactured goods to us.

"Our export trade, in general, would suffer. Countries cannot permanently buy from us unless they are permitted to sell to us, and the more we restrict the importation of goods from them by means ever higher tariffs, the more we reduce the possibility of our exporting to them.

"This applies to such exporting industries as copper, automobiles, agricultural machinery, typewriters and the like fully as much as it does to farming. The difficulties of these industries are likely to be increased still further if we pass a higher tariff.

"There are already many evidences that such action would inevitably provoke other countries to pay us back in kind by levying retaliatory duties against our goods. There are few more ironical spectacles than that of the American Government as it seeks, on the one hand, to promote exports through the activity of the Bureau of Foreign and Domestic Commerce, while, on the other hand, by increasing tariffs it makes exportation ever more difficult.

"We do not believe that American manufacturers, in general, need higher tariffs. The report of the President's Committee on Recent Economic Changes has shown that industrial efficiency has increased, that costs have fallen, that profits have grown with amazing rapidity since the end of the World War. Already our factories supply our people with over 96 per cent of the manufactured goods which they consume, and our producers look to foreign markets to absorb the increasing output of their machines.

"Further barriers to trade will serve them not well, but ill.

Affect on Investments Abroad

"Many of our citizens have invested their money in foreign enterprises. The Department of Commerce has estimated that such investments, entirely aside from the war debts, amounted to between $12,555,000,000 and $14,555,000,000 on Jan. 1, 1929. These investors, too, would suffer if restrictive duties were to be increased, since such action would make it still more difficult for their foreign debtors to pay them the interest due them.

"America is now facing the problem of unemployment. The proponents of higher tariffs claim that an increase in rates will give work to the idle. This is not true. We cannot increase employment by restricting trade. American industry, in the present crisis, might well be spared the burden of adjusting itself to higher schedules of duties.

"Finally, we would urge our government to consider the bitterness which a policy of higher tariffs would inevitably inject into our international relations. The United States was ably represented at the world economic conference which was held under the auspices of the League of Nations in 1927. This conference adopted a resolution announcing that 'the time has come to put an end to the increase in tariffs and to move in the opposite direction.'

"The higher duties proposed in our pending legislation violate the spirit of this agreement and plainly invite other nations to compete with us in raising further barriers to trade. A tariff war does not furnish good soil for the growth of world peace."

The signers include many economists connected with banks, public utilities, manufacturing industries, merchandising concerns and other business establishments.

The number signing from leading universities are: Columbia 28, New York University 22, Cornell 18, Harvard 25, Yale 14, Princeton 17, Dartmouth 24, Chicago 26, Wisconsin 23, Pennsylvania 13, California 11, Stanford 7, Illinois 14, Northwestern 9, Minnesota 15, Missouri 15.

ORIGINATORS AND FIRST SIGNERS

PAUL H. DOUGLAS, Professor of Economics, University of Chicago.

IRVING FISHER, Professor of Economics, Yale University.

FRANK D. GRAHAM, Professor of Economics, Princeton University.

ERNEST M. PATTERSON, Professor of Economics, University of Pennsylvania.

HENRY R. SEAGER, Professor of Economics, Columbia University.

FRANK W. TAUSSIG, Professor of Economics, Harvard University.

CLAIR WILCOX, Associate Professor of Economics, Swarthmore College.

* * *

May 10, 1930

EUROPE AGAIN HINTS AT A TARIFF WAR

Economic Writers Revive Idea of Conference to Decide on Combative Measures

HOOVER CALLED ONLY HOPE

He Is Seen as the Sole Big Man in America With Understanding of Continental Problems

By CARLISLE MacDONALD
Special Cable to The New York Times

PARIS, May 9—As the moment approaches for the final adoption of the Hawley-Smooth tariff bill in the United States, European business opinion is concerning itself more and more with the effect of the new duties upon exports and the means which the Continent should take to "defend itself" against the menace of American protectionism.

In France, where agitation against the American tariff builders has been almost continuous from the day the new measure was introduced in Congress, economic writers in the daily press again are openly discussing the probability of a bitter tariff war between the Old World and the New. The idea of a European tariff conference to consider ways and means of combating American protection has been revived, and the response to the suggestion has been especially enthusiastic in those countries which feel they will be hard hit by the new American rates.

Belgium, Holland, Switzerland, France and half a dozen other countries appear to welcome consultation on the question of defensive action and it will be very surprising if such a meeting does not materialize after the new duties become law.

In the minds of some commentators, President Hoover stands forth as "the sole hope" of Europe, since in the Chief Executive they see one big man in American public life who is sufficiently acquainted with the European mentality to anticipate the dangers which the new tariff holds for American trade abroad.

La Journée Industrielle, leading organ of French business, comments today on "the apathy" of Congress in the face of European protests. Its members, the paper observes, do not seem afraid of reprisals, which are sure to follow, especially in the case of American automobiles, but on the contrary seem to feel that the menace is added reason for standing firm for the new tariff. Those who are responsible for the new rates must come up for re-election in November, the newspaper goes on to say, and they are convinced the electors will be more favorably disposed if they do not weaken before European criticism.

"Members of Congress know well that the masses of American workmen, reinforced by the troops of disappointed speculators, are strongly in favor of protectionism," concludes the paper, "Decidedly, Mr. Hoover is the only hope of Europe."

In a leading editorial in Le Quotidien, entitled, "Can Mr. Hoover Limit the Catastrophe which the American Protectionists are Preparing?" the writer concludes with this warning:

"If the Yankees, abusing their strength and present wealth, apply integrally their program of protectionism, there will be nothing for us to do but resort to reprisals, and that would mean war."

* * *

May 18, 1930

OUR TARIFF STIRS UP A SWARM OF REPRISALS

Heavy American Exports of Manufactured Goods Give Other Countries a Chance to Make Their Resentment Felt

By HENRY KITTREDGE NORTON

When 1,028 economists and professors of economics sent their joint warning to President Hoover on the ill effects upon this country which might follow the passage of the present tariff bill, we may assume that it was read—or at least glanced over—by most of the members of Congress. Yet there is little likelihood that a single vote in either the Senate or the House will be changed from "Yea" to "Nay" out of deference to this mass manifesto from the halls of learning.

The making of tariffs in this country has always been much more a matter of politics than of economic science. The effective political forces of the country ever since the first protective tariff of 1816 have generally been in a position to demand and obtain an ever-rising schedule of rates. And during all this time economists have insisted that a protective tariff was economically fallacious. The political representatives of the American people have seldom, if ever, heeded their counsel.

There was one item in the memorial to Mr. Hoover, however, which is worthy of special examination. The economists pointed out that the adoption of the tariff bill now pending would provoke foreign reprisals. This is not in itself a new factor in the situation. The purpose of a protective tariff is to divert to Americans business that might otherwise go to foreigners.

We should hardly be surprised if the foreigners affected do not welcome an increase of rates. They have protested regularly and vigorously against all of our tariff increases in the last thirty years. There is, however, no known case in which a single schedule has been lowered in response to foreign protest. Reciprocity, yes. We have on occasion lowered our rates in return for a corresponding favor from some other country. But we got—or thought we got—value received.

Nevertheless the economists' warning of foreign reprisals cannot be lightly dismissed as a mere repetition of an outworn and discredited argument. We have been able to ignore foreign resentment and protest in the past because of the nature of our foreign trade. As long as the great bulk of our exports consisted of food-stuffs and raw materials we were selling something the foreigner had to buy. The older and more crowded countries of Europe had to feed their millions and to obtain the raw materials to keep their factories working. They might, in an access of asininity, raise a tariff against our exports, but they would go right on buying them. The only effect of such a tariff would be to increase the prices they themselves had to pay.

Up to the end of the last century, however, manufacturing for export was incidental to the main industrial interests of this country. There were a number of articles which we could produce under especially favorable conditions for foreign consumption. But the great field for most of our industries was the large and rapidly expanding home market. If occasionally our manufacturers overestimated the home demand, they could dump the surplus abroad, and they would condescend to fill foreign orders when they were importuned by buyers from overseas. But, generally speaking, the export of manufactured goods was hardly more than an incident in our industrial life.

With the turn of the century our industries had begun to overtake the home demand. The possibilities of foreign markets were more carefully investigated and the more readily salable of our products began to go abroad in an increasing volume. By 1913 we were exporting manufactured products nearly equal in value to our exports of foodstuffs and raw materials.

Exports and the War

Then came the great war with its unprecedented demand for all kinds of products from this country. There was plenty of demand for food and materials, and even more for manufactured articles. In the midst of the struggle the latter constituted as much as 65 per cent of the goods we sold abroad. For two years after the war the disorganization in Europe served to keep alive the demand for both classes of exports.

The last decade has given us new things to think about. Europe no longer offers an easy market for anything we desire to sell. The production of the war-stricken Continent—agricultural, mineral and industrial—has more than recovered its pre-war volume. Not only that, but in its rehabilitation Europe has adopted many of the methods and processes which have given power to American industry. The manufacturing nations of Western Europe are challenging the American manufacturer, both in their home markets and in those markets which are open to both on equal terms.

There is false consolation in the thought that even if Europe recovers her old share of world trade, America will be no worse off than she was before the war. But we cannot go back. In the last fifteen years American industry has been organized on a basis which demands a foreign outlet for a share of its product. Even though this share is no more than 10 per cent, it may easily constitute the difference between profit and loss—between prosperity and depression. The export trade is no longer an incident in American industrial life. It has become a necessity.

It is this new factor which gives significance to the economists' warning against foreign tariff reprisals. Such reprisals are no longer an idle threat. The enormous development of our productive power, of which in our materialistic moments we are apt to boast a bit, has undermined our industrial independence. We have the industrial machine, but it is an incubus unless we can keep open foreign markets which will absorb its surplus products. Over those markets the foreigner has the same measure of control that we have always enjoyed over our own. He is at last in a position to retaliate against American tariff policy, and he will be no less eager to do so because he has so long been impotent against it.

Retaliation an Actuality

Foreign retaliation is not merely a possibility of the future. It is not even dependent on the passage of the present tariff bill. It is a present actuality. It finds expression not only in high tariff walls which increase the difficulty of American competition with foreign manufacturers, but it takes the form of contingent quotas, specific limitation of American sales, and various other restrictions which materially reduce the sales of American manufacturers abroad.

France has been particularly active in this direction. The chief object of her attack has been the American motor industry. Her protective tariff on motor cars has been raised to the point where it is extremely difficult, if not impossible, for American cars to compete. When Mr. Ford tried to evade this tariff by erecting an assembling plant in France, the tariff on imported parts was promptly boosted to a point which made his French assembled car cost as much as an imported one. About the only road left open for American profit in the French motor market is for Americans to buy and operate French factories, as General Motors is reported to have done. That may bring a profit to the investors, but the benefit to American industry and labor is only indirect and incidental.

France is not the only country which is applying to American imports restrictions analogous to those which our tariff works upon their exports. Poland limits the import of motor cars from any one country to 1,000 tons a year. Czechoslovakia will receive only 800 cars from any one country. Austria sets the figure at 300. The regulations are universal in their application. There is no open discrimination against the United States. But the joker is in the fact that America is the only country which would sell up to the quota in any case. And if America had a free hand she could sell two or three times the quota allowance.

Italy has taken no official action against American motor cars. But the Italian Automobile Club conducts a relentless campaign against their importation and has proposed to brand all owners of foreign cars as "bad Italians."

Lesser American industries have also felt the pinch. American canned goods entering France must carry an indication in French of the country of origin in raised or sunken letters. This means that the American manufacturer must decide what part of his goods he will send to France before they are packed. The effect has been practically to close the French market to American canned salmon and materially to reduce the import of other canned goods from this country.

Statement as to Origin

British officials in India and Ceylon play a variation of this same tune. There it is provided that any product so marked as to suggest that it is of British origin must, if it comes from some other country, bear an equally conspicuous statement of its actual origin. The use of the English language on labels is construed to be a suggestion of British origin. American manufacturers have been put to considerable trouble to meet the British requirements in this regard.

And now comes Canada, our nearest neighbor and our best customer, to add the weight of her rebuke to our tariff proceedings. And a weighty rebuke it is. We have been selling to Canada about $800,000,000 worth of goods a year. In other words, about two-thirds of Canada's imports have come from this country. In return we have bought from her less than $500,000,000 worth a year. In the effort to enable our farmers to share in the hypothetical benefits of protection, Congress has inserted in the pending tariff bill a number of increases, such as those on live stock and meat, which will be most seriously felt by our northern neighbors. They have protested and come to the conclusion that their protest was futile. On May 1 the government announced in the Canadian Parliament that, beginning at 9 o'clock the following morning, the Canadian tariff would be fixed at new high levels. The new rates will not become permanent until Parliament formally approves them. Meanwhile, American exporters will have to accept them.

According to the analysis of our own Department of Commerce, the new rates will affect adversely more than 25 per cent of our exports to Canada. Great Britain enjoys a tariff preference in the Canadian market paying duties which usually run about half those paid by American producers. We have been able to meet this competition under the present rates, but when Canada raises her tariff she increases the British preference proportionately. It other words, Canada is deliberately and at some expense to herself turning over to British manufacturers a large share of her trade, which even under our present tariff she is willing to allow to remain with us.

The Favored Nation Clause

One reliable weapon by which we have thus far defended ourselves against the full effects of tariff retaliation has been the most favored nation clause in our commercial treaties. This clause in a treaty with any country assures our exporters the same treatment in the markets of that country as that accorded their competitors from other lands.

But this weapon is about to be stricken from our hands. We have no commercial treaty with Canada, and negotiations for such treaties with a number of other countries have been halted by the rates proposed in the tariff bill. The German Minister of Economy has officially stated to the Budget Committee of the Reichstag that the present treaty with the United States will not be renewed upon its expiration in 1935. The reason he gives for this is that Germany must have freedom of action in her commercial policies.

Such a move, if concurred in by other European countries, would open the door to unity of action in Europe against the American tariff. It would be possible for Austria or Czechoslovakia or Poland, for example, to place a prohibitive duty on American motor cars while admitting competitive products from other countries upon the payment of a small duty or none at all. Germany, France, Britain and the rest could adjust their tariffs as between themselves according to the accepted European practice of diplomatic bargaining. At the same time all of them could unite in excluding American products.

Europe would then buy from us only what she could not get elsewhere. We could be excluded from every competitive market on the Continent. In that case we should have an opportunity to measure in terms of dollars and cents the net value of a high protective tariff to an exporting country. If the economists are right, that value may have to be written in red ink.

* * *

May 25, 1930

NORTHWEST STIRRED BY THE TARIFF BILL

Farmers, at the End of the Long Debate,
Complain of Broken Promises

By HERBERT LEFKOVITZ
Editorial Correspondence, The New York Times
ST. PAUL, May 19—With the exception of the McNary-Haugen bill, it would be necessary to go back to free silver days to find an economic question that has occupied these Northwestern States in such long and strenuous debate as the Hawley-Smoot tariff bill has done. The Northwest does not like the results of the tariff revision. Such praise as the bill receives is apologetic and without enthusiasm. The condemnation, on the other hand, is whole-hearted and downright.

The bill, of course, has its defenders, but the key to the dominant opinion is probably furnished by Governor Christianson, who has declared that had he been in the United States Senate he would have voted against the bill. He made this statement in the speech with which he opened his campaign the other day to take the Republican Senatorial nomination away from Senator Schall, who voted for the bill last March. It is worthy of notice as a straw in the wind that, although Governor Christianson has been classified in the past as a regular Republican, his speech was that of an insurgent.

Now the farmers themselves apparently are turning thumbs down on the bill. The Farmer of St. Paul is taking a poll of its readers on the new tariff. Only the first returns are being received but they seem conclusive. Out of 100 votes, 93 were against the tariff, only 7 for it. These votes are well scattered through Minnesota, North and South Dakota. The editors of The Farmer are satisfied that the verdict against the tariff will be overwhelming.

Basis of the Hostility

This hostility to the tariff revision has nothing to do with doctrinaire considerations of free trade against protection. This tariff, however, has had to contend with certain reservations of faith which are novel in the history of agricultural protection, and this just at a time when more was being demanded and expected of the tariff than ever before.

The tariff thinking of farmers has been deeply affected by the long controversy over the McNary-Haugen bill. The central thesis of that measure has found lodgment in the mind of agriculture. It is that the major crops move into export, are largely unaffected by tariffs and that before protection can work with efficiency for the farmer there must be some device to segregate the surplus from the portion of the crop that is consumed at home.

This doctrine rules out wheat, cotton, tobacco, hogs, cattle and corn in greater or less degree from the inner circle of protection. The export debenture was an expression of the new skepticism of agriculture toward the tariff. This reasoning of course is not new, but it required the long schooling of McNary-Haugenism to give it vitality.

At the same time, the farmers as a class unquestionably are convinced that they have much to gain from protection, especially on their many crops which are consumed entirely at home, and that one of the important elements in their difficult situation is the fact that their rates are lower than the general level of the Fordney-McCumber tariff.

"Grundyism" the Enemy

What the farmer expected, and understood as having been promised, was a tariff limited pretty much to revision upward of the agricultural schedule. It is not denied that the increases are in general satisfactory, so far as that schedule by itself is concerned. There is complaint about the starches and oils, but this would be no serious obstacle. The cause of the hostility is summed up in the convenient name of Senator Grundy, who has come to symbolize all the evils of the revision. The bill has been identified with Grundyism, and Grundyism is a hateful shibboleth.

The Hawley-Smoot bill is therefore being condemned as dishonest promise-keeping. The farmers believe that the bill they are getting is not the one they were led to expect. To accept it by acquiescence would be to take partial payment as satisfaction in full, and the prevailing thought seems to be that it would be better to go back to the Fordney-McCumber rates, which are acknowledged to be unfair, and make a fresh, clean start with this kind of farm relief.

And certainly, if the bill becomes law, it may be taken for granted that the Hawley-Smoot tariff will have a heavy load of responsibility to carry, for it will be blamed for whatever misfortune may come along in the next few years.

*   *   *

June 22, 1930

ARGENTINE FARMERS PROPOSE REPRISALS

Ask Government to Adopt a Defensive Tariff Unless Washington Cuts Rates

FAVOR A STUDY OF COSTS

On Such a Survey They Would Base a Plea to Us—La Nacion Sees Our Duties Rooted in Prejudice

Special Cable to The New York Times

BUENOS AIRES, June 21—The president and secretary of the Argentine Rural Society conferred today with the Minister of Agriculture on behalf of their organization and urged the government to undertake an investigation of the cost of production of Argentine agricultural products affected by the new American tariff with a view to making a formal diplomatic protest to Washington in an effort to have the duties reduced. They suggested the advisability of adopting defensive tariff measures in the meantime against American imports.

The Minister promised to give their suggestions careful attention and arranged for another conference with the Rural Society officers.

La Nacion, discussing editorially the new American tariff, says it is impossible for the American legislators to determine the production costs of agricultural products coming from such widely differing zones as the Illinois plains, the North Dakota wilds and the Argentine Mesopotamia district."

Arguing that the cost of production has less weight in fixing American duties than partiality and prejudices, La Nacion points out that the Tariff Commission studied the Argentine costs of producing flax-seed and found them 51 cents a bushel under the American costs and that President Hoover raised the duty to 56 cents, giving the American producers 5 cents' margin. But they were not satisfied even with this, the editorial points out, and the Hawley-Smoot bill raised the duty to 65 cents.

La Nacion says that recent years have seen a universal movement toward a new ideal of civilization, the economic cooperation of all humanity. It points to the Dawes and Young plans as efforts toward this ideal by setting up machinery for the payment of reparations without impoverishing the debtor nations, it being recognized that the financial ruin of one nation means the ruin of others.

"Yet now, says La Nacion, "we are confronted with a curious and interesting episode in the world's march toward its future organization. Precisely when science and industry are using prodigious developments to unite humanity, we find that a nation as fantastically rich as is the United States determines to shut itself up within its own castle behind a prohibitive tariff wall based not on the principle of capacity or competition, but on the principle of refusing to buy abroad anything that can possibly be produced at home."

The tariff is no longer a question of protecting agriculture or industry or of leveling living costs between city and country, says La Nacion, but of a determination to reserve the home market exclusively for home products.

* * *

June 22, 1930

EUROPE WEIGHS MEANS TO FIGHT OUR TARIFF

Resentment Appears in Many Proposals for Retaliation, While Those Who Had Hoped for More Liberal Trade Relations Now View the Future Doubtfully

By P. J. PHILIP
Wireless to The New York Times

The Hawley-Smoot Tariff law, which went into effect last week, has brought the nations of Europe to a consideration of retaliatory measures. France is the first country to formulate a policy; there the Committee on Customs has proposed to the Chamber a withdrawal of the most-favored-nation treatment for the United States in case no relief from the high rates on French exports to the United States can be obtained. While the French Government is expected to move slowly, the temper of the country is reflected in the favorable reception given the proposal by the Deputies. In the article which follows the general reaction of European countries to the American law is discussed by the Paris correspondent of The New York Times.

Paris—It was with a kind of shiver that Europe learned last week-end that the Hawley-Smoot bill had been passed by the Senate and House and that it was likely to receive Presidential approval. It was not a shiver of fear. It was the kind of shiver every one has experienced when, in the middle of a pleasant party, some one has said the wrong thing or done something which brings a sudden tense feeling of self-consciousness.

That was what Europe felt at the end of last week. Just in the middle of the pleasant conversations which were going on here about the possibilities of European federation and the reduction of customs barriers, the American Congress dropped a brick. For one whole day everybody was silent, gasping, trying to get breath, or to change the conversation, just as some one always says, "What lovely weather!" when some one else has made some terrible faux pas.

Europe's Opinions

Then the French press in a tone of pained resignation asks what the United States will do next. The British papers express sorrow in Olympian periods and the German press sounds a kind of "look out" note of warning. In their various ways they declare the tariff victory in the Senate and House was a disastrous defeat for thinking America and a greater injury to the world at large than anything that has been done about the war debts.

The press of all other countries has joined in, and it may safely be said that nothing the United States Congress has done in its history has been so universally unpopular in Europe as passing the Hawley-Smoot bill.

On the whole, comment which has been made has been restrained and even a little ponderous. Those newspaper editors who are not economists took their cues from those who were, or read up some of the reports of the various customs

EUROPE GOES INTO A HUDDLE TO MEET THE TARIFF THREAT.

commissions which have sat in Europe ever since President Wilson recommended the lowering of barriers as the best guarantee of peace, and they have all unanimously concluded that the only safety for the world, economically and financially, lay in greater freedom of trade. Benjamin Franklin had come to the same conclusion a century and a half ago and in a letter to Vergennes stated plainly and bluntly, as was his wont, that the freer trade was the better it would be for every nation and every person.

So the editors had ample material on which to found their argument that this time the United States was wrong. Senator Watson has been their special mark. His prophecy that within thirty days of the passing of the bill the whole economic and financial situation of the United States would be changed was at once seized on as a target at which to shoot. Thirty days is a short time in which to place the fulfillment of any prophecy. Every one is going to watch during the next thirty days for that wonderful recovery which the Senator believes will come. If he is right, then undoubtedly these European editors who have laughed at him will make ample apology. They will also discard all their old textbooks and reports of commissions on tariffs and will begin clamoring for their own countries to "Watsonize" their customs barriers. For Europe is always willing to learn from America even when, as in this case, it believes Congress has less to teach than Owen D. Young and those others who in their own country have protested against passing this act.

Ever since the bill was first propounded France has been foremost in Europe's protest against it. It undoubtedly has been argued by supporters of this bill that these protests were selfish or at least interested. Of course they were. That is just why they were made. France is legitimately interested in France. She has to pay her debts to the United States, and how else, she argues, is she to pay the debts except by exporting her manufactures in those special lines which she believes she can produce better than they can be produced anywhere in America? French goods have a market in the United States of long standing and there will still be a market despite the Hawley-Smoot tariff. But it is a French business axiom that to get one must give. There must be exchange. So in this effort to impose an even heavier penalty on those Americans who like French perfumes, dresses, olive oil or anything else of French origin—that is to say, on France's customers in the United States—French merchants naturally feel an injustice is being done. They are perfectly confident that within a short time the situation will readjust itself to the new prices and that there will be just as much French merchandise sold in the United States as before. Even prohibition has not reduced the export of French wines to the United States by 100 per cent or anything like it.

Fear of "Dumping"

There is, however, another angle which is regarded more seriously. All over Europe there is a definite fear that this effort by the United States to protect its own markets will coincide with a serious effort to dump surplus goods of American manufacture in Europe. No one has any objection to buying American products if they are good. The American automobile is sought after by all those who can afford to pay for it, with its existing duty and gas consumption. American watches, American canned goods, American radiators, American agricultural implements have a normal and natural market in every country of the old continent. That market grew steadily in the first years after the war. It grew just as long as Europe had the money to pay for these imports. A good deal of that money, it is true, was borrowed in America, but the man who lends money to a safe borrower on condition that he will trade with his shop gets two-fold interest, and that was what the United States was doing.

Now things look somewhat different. France has got back on her feet financially. Per head of population she has a larger gold reserve than the United States. She is not likely to have to borrow any more. She is not even likely to have to ask American concurrence in any further Young plan loans. She can absorb them herself.

Germany is breaking out into a new effort with the probability of cheaper production costs than any other country. England is in the throes of an agitation for free trade within the empire and protection against either German or American dumping. The small countries are all lined up and ready to follow the lead of their bigger neighbors.

In such a situation there is every element, in the opinion of all those Europeans competent to judge, of a first-class commercial war which may be less bloody but will not be less costly to culture and progress than one with shells, tanks and airplanes.

Hopes of Leniency

Here it should be said at once that even though the bill has been passed it is hoped and believed that its application will be less stringent than some of its makers would like.

There are two ways in which Europe can retaliate. Either she can close her markets tighter against American exports by raising customs barriers, or she can form cartels and combines within her own union. Except tobacco and potatoes, America has given to Europe very little new raw material, if any, that was not known or findable before Columbus sailed. And tobacco and potatoes are no longer uniquely American products.

There is talk of the formation of a non-ferrous metal combine among the European nations to assure their own supply and "free Europe from American domination." There is a revival of the European automobile cartel. There is new interest in all possible sources of supply of gasoline, cotton, wheat—anything which normally and naturally comes from America but may now be brought from elsewhere.

A World Problem

Those responsible for the passage of the new tariff law have been prodigal of warnings that retaliations will not pay. Perhaps they won't. That is not really the point at issue. What is at issue is whether Europe, America and the whole world are to try to solve the question of production, supply, sale, wages and scale of living together or whether one continent is to struggle with another for special rights and privileges.

Here in Europe an effort was being made quietly, reasonably and with wide vision, to try to bring about a new order of international relations and intercourse. Goodness knows how much Europe needs it. Jules Sauerwein, foreign editor of the Matin, who has just been making a tour of Eastern and Central Europe, writes to his paper: "I have not needed to make inquiries in any high quarters about the situation in these countries. It has been only too easy to see for myself how all the symptoms of a serious crisis are developing. Each country is struggling by itself to try to save itself and struggling against such terrible obstacles as closed markets, closed credit, closed minds. To them all this extra turn of the screw applied to the closing of the American market has come as a kind of final blow to their hopes. It has, however, served one purpose. They are thinking more seriously of Briand's proposals for federation, for the admission by governments of the principle of which all economists have approved—the interdependence of countries and the mutual extension of markets. Perhaps some good will come out of the action of the American Senate."

These countries which in the last two years and again now have raised their protests against the new American tariff are not, perhaps, themselves guiltless. They have raised barriers everywhere against their neighbors, seeking to stimulate artificially manufactures in a way which too often has brought immediate retaliation at the expense of their natural productivity. Along those five thousand miles of new frontiers which the Versailles treaty established there is an absolutely strangling cordon of tariffs. In an effort to protect its home markets every Continental country went tariff mad at the end of the war. Even that ancient citadel of free trade. Great Britain, put on "safeguarding duties."

That was ten years ago, and Europe has found that it has not paid. It is difficult to alter the system. As in disarmament, the question is, who is to begin first. Interests of every kind, fear, all those crippling weaknesses of mankind, stand in the road. Cautiously Briand has put his foot forward on the new path, the path of cooperation and freedom. And now, unexpectedly, from that country to which Europe has been taught in these last years to look for leadership and inspiration, has come this recrudescence of the old evil of narrow protectionism with its falsification of all values.

A Backward Step

That, at least, is how those who had begun to hope for greater liberalism in the world, for saner trade, for expansion instead of intenseness of artificial competition, regard the Hawley-Smoot law. Perhaps they may be pessimistic, even wrong in their outlook. Neither the new tariff nor the example it has set may prove as bad as they fear. Senator Watson may triumphantly appear among the prophets. But Europe as a whole and France in particular does not share his confidence. They believe the United States has taken a step backward in a not too forward world.

There has come over those who were hoping for better things a kind of depression which finds expression in many ways. It has even roused a certain element of fear. For those who know how easily a hungry crowd can be stirred and how responsible is the task not only of those who govern, but those who control the world's wealth, have begun to wonder what the effect will be of this new demonstration of ineptness by those who hold the keys of the capitalistic system. They see in what has been done an encouragement for the fomenters of revolution.

"Is the capitalistic system doomed to die through excess of production, that is to say, through excess of wealth?" the editor of the Nationalist Liberte wrote the other evening. "Is it to die simply because those who direct it are incapable of organizing it aright?"

There are leaders of capital in the United States who will have sympathy with this opinion, and this should be made clear, that in condemning the majority in Congress for what it has done, Europe still differentiates that majority from America.

*   *   *

June 29, 1930

MORGENTHAU SEES TARIFF REPRISALS

Former Ambassador, Back From Europe, Declares Hostility to the Measure is Keen

GOLD STAR MOTHERS HOME

139 Return on the America—Rev. F. P. Duffy Tells of Plans for 69th Regiment Reunion

Henry Morgenthau, former Ambassador to Turkey, returned yesterday on the United States liner America from an observation tour of Europe, and issued a statement attacking the tariff and declaring that foreign countries were preparing to retaliate.

Mr. Morgenthau was in Vienna, Paris, Berlin, London and other leading European cities. He said his observations indicated that foreign business greatly resented the high American tariff and felt that it was an unfair action, especially in the light of post-war depression abroad.

"Practically all foreign countries are suffering yet in the readjustment following the war," Mr. Morgenthau said. "The United States became a creditor nation after the war, and has failed to assume full responsibility as a world power. The Europeans are in deep distress and are looking for the cause. Unfortunately they ascribe a large portion of the blame to us."

Mr. Morgenthau said Europeans pointed out that they had helped us in 1866 after our war, and "put us on our feet again." They think now that the United States should take the same supporting stand in Europe's time of need, he said.

"Europeans are resenting our conduct and are planning to retaliate," Mr. Morgenthau continued. "They have learned the strength of the boycott and are organizing to apply it against our productions. It will benefit the United States very little if a few manufacturers sell more goods through the exclusion of Europe's goods if it results in Europe's refusing to purchase our productions.

"Europe did not abandon the League of Nations when we failed to join it. Neither will she go into bankruptcy because we have adopted and are pursuing so short-sighted a policy. Europe will suffer a while, and so will we. The question who will suffer the most no one can answer at present."

Also on the America were 139 Gold Star Mothers, the majority from California and North Dakota. One of them, Mrs. Margaret Price, 68 years old, was carried off in a stretcher in Hoboken yesterday, having made the long trip to France without seeing the grave of her son. Mrs. Price collapsed before her ship reached Cherbourg and, after examination by French physicians, was placed in a hospital. Another, Mrs. Fanny Price, arrived yesterday convalescing from pneumonia. She is 55.

The Rev. Francis P. Duffy, wartime chaplain of the "Fighting Sixty-ninth," returned on the America after making arrangements for the reunion of men of the regiment in France in July. He said the veterans would sail July 16, on the United States liner President Roosevelt, and would be guests at a big reception at Chalons-sur-Marne. They will visit battlefronts and cemeteries for two weeks.

On the America also were Alfred Kahn and James N. Whitaker of the Radio Corporation of America, who tested the new photo-radio device on the ship. Reception was not very good until the America left Queenstown, officers said. After that the ship received many newspaper columns and a message from President Hoover.

* * *

December 28, 1930

KLEIN SEES DANGER IN EUROPEAN SLUMP

He Predicts Political Instability Unless Ranks of Idle Decline in Immediate Future

SOBER LEADERSHIP NEEDED

Assistant Commerce Secretary, After Study Abroad, Stresses Our Interest in Foreign Situation

Special to The New York Times
WASHINGTON, Dec. 27—Asserting that the political front of the principal European countries will be determined largely by the economic developments of the immediate future, Dr. Julius Klein, Assistant Secretary of Commerce, declared in a statement today that unless there is some decline in the ranks of unemployed, which may well exceed 7,500,000 in Europe by February, "we may expect recurrences of political instability."

In his statement Dr. Klein described observations made during his two months' trip through Central and Western Europe, the Balkans, Syria, Turkey and Upper Egypt, studying the prevailing economic conditions as they influence the sale of American goods.

"The opening weeks of 1931 will bring economic Europe to one of the major cross-roads of the long, arduous journey out of the abyss of the 1921 collapse," Dr. Klein said. "The intervening decade has been prodigious in accomplishments, many of them with abundant American capital, in the greatest task of reconstruction ever confronting Western civilization

"But the remaining months of this Winter will require more grave, crucial decisions in economic affairs than any similar period since the post-armistice crisis. There will be a need for the utmost of sober, farsighted leadership and a minimum of flamboyant oratory and parliamentary gymnastics."

Warns of Superiority Complex

The European aspects of the world depression, he said, have a direct bearing on our own situation.

"With Europe still the market for half our exports and responsible, through her imports from South America and the Far East, for a good deal of the demand for the rest of our oversea trade, it should be obvious that the gravity of the economic situation in the Old World scarcely warrants an exuberant superiority complex on our part."

Dr. Klein said in this connection that many Europeans are beginning to realize that their satisfaction during the early stages of our depression was a bit premature. Recent statements of executives abroad, he said, indicate their realization that the restoration of American buying power is essential in leading the business world out of its slump.

Pointing to the "continuous barrage" on war debts, reparations, tariffs and other major issues, Dr. Klein observed that "the grim spectre of dire economic necessity, lurking behind the spectacular political foreground, is all too frequently the real determinant of events."

He said that this did not indicate the total lack of sincerity in these recurrent protest, but that "obviously domestic political uncertainties, due in many cases to the multitude of parties in the various Continental parliaments, averaging well over twelve or fourteen in most countries, account largely for the frequent outbursts on the part of political leaders in their struggles toward coalitions and compromises.

Assails European Trade Barriers

"Such pronouncements," he continued, "often seem to have economic implications of the utmost gravity, causing considerable alarm to our business interests; but closer scrutiny reveals the political expediency which dictated them. The general situation, both internal in one country after another, as well as the international position, imperatively requires the utmost of sobriety and penetrative factual analysis.

"Intra-European trade barriers still continue to present a major obstacle to general European recovery. From a quarter to three-quarters of the commerce of each Old World nation is with its immediate neighbors. This accounts for the evident disappointment among trade leaders everywhere over the failure to make much headway of late toward simplification of import quota restrictions, of customs procedure or anything approaching a tariff truce.

"There is indeed a distinct indication that European business leaders have become thoroughly wearied of the jockeying of pseudo-economic ententes and alliances for obviously political purposes.

"There is almost universal concern throughout Europe regarding Russian dumping, not so much on account of the volume, as the apparent irresponsibility with which the given traffic has been carried on.

American Share of Trade Holds Up

"Several of the leading countries are, of course, heavy consumers of Russian raw materials, so that except for the traders involved there is little concern over any price cuts incidental to the Russian operations.

"There is, however, a fear that the evident irregularities and excesses of the present raw material dumping might be a foreboding of similar operations with industrial wares if the Soviet program of large scale industrial expansion is ever materialized.

"One striking feature of the trade situation from our point of view is the constancy of the American share in European commerce. In almost every single case the percentage which we enjoy of the trade of the Old World nations in both directions has held steadily in spite of bitter agitation regarding tariffs, immigration, war debts and other issues.

"In other words, figures as to declining values in our commerce by no means tell the complete story, since such declines are almost universal. It is the indicator of our relative status in the whole picture of the trade of any given nation, and therein we have emphatically not suffered to any substantial degree, and have, on the contrary, improved our position in many instances."

* * *

September 21, 1931

GREAT BRITAIN SUSPENDS GOLD PAYMENTS TODAY; CLOSES STOCK EXCHANGE, DISCOUNT RATE UP TO 6%; GERMAN BOERSES SHUT, STOCK MARKET HERE OPEN

PARLIAMENT TO BACK MOVE

Cabinet Is Unanimous in Decision to End the Drain on Gold

KING TO SIGN BILL TONIGHT

London Hopes Drastic Measure Will Not Be Necessary More Than Six Months

MACDONALD EXPLAINS STEP

Government Says Withdrawals of Funds Since July Forced Its Action

By CHARLES A. SELDEN
Special Cable to The New York Times

LONDON, Sept. 20—Great Britain will go off the gold standard tomorrow. Legislation amending the existing financial laws to that effect will be rushed through Parliament in the course of the day and will receive the King's royal assent tomorrow night.

To accomplish this, the new National Government, which is responsible for this drastic step, is assured of the necessary majority in the House of Commons to pass the measure through all its Parliamentary stages in one sitting. The House of Lords, which ordinarily does not sit on Mondays, has been summoned for an emergency session to take the required concurrent action.

Bank of England Approves

A unanimous decision to abandon the gold standard was reached at an emergency session of Premier MacDonald's Cabinet today after consultation with the Bank of England, which agreed it was the only thing to do.

The Bank of England tomorrow will raise the discount rate to 6 per cent from 4½ per cent.

The London Stock Exchange and all provincial exchanges will be closed for the day.

Although there is no suggestion in the government statement as to how long this state of affairs will continue the official announcement implies it will be only temporary by saying the suspension is "for the time being."

The expectation, or at least the hope, is that it will last only six months if within that period the country manages to balance its international trade as well as its budget.

It was hoped this shock to British government finance would be averted by the change in government a month ago with the subsequent achievement of balancing the budget and cutting down government expenses, but it is evident now that the change was too long delayed.

Blow Was Long Impending

The present blow has been impending a long time. Now that it has fallen, the situation is explained as due both to international and domestic causes. The foreign factors involved, according to the British appraisal of the situation, have been the hoarding of gold by the United States and France and the recent drain on sterling because of the financial difficulties of other countries.

Diminished foreign confidence in the stability of the pound was another vital factor which had gone too far to be entirely corrected by the recent change in government and by the effect of big loans from New York and Paris. The recent "pay cut mutiny" in the British navy also was one of the various causes of the cumulative effect, which is today's decision to abandon the gold standard.

Also England put a terrific strain on herself six years ago by returning to the gold standard as part of her post-war financial policy and by her whole attitude toward the payment of her war debts. Of all countries on this side of the Atlantic which participated in the war, England is the only one which has not cut the value of its currency. Great Britain alone returned to the prewar gold parity of its currency while France divided the franc by five.

Plus all this international strain, England has been attempting to carry on at the same time a most expensive experiment in socialism, which, with its enormous cost of unemployment insurance, caused the downfall of the Labor Government just a month ago.

Although the British public does not know tonight what is going to happen tomorrow because newspapers, informed only in the strictest terms of confidence, reveal nothing this evening, there is a tremendously tense feeling everywhere, with the realization that something ominous is in store. Downing Street was filled with an excited, anxious crowd, as it was four weeks ago when the Labor Government fell.

The hurried visit of the Prince of Wales to see Premier Mac-Donald at Chequers and the coming of Mr. MacDonald to London on a Sunday to meet his hastily summoned Cabinet let the public know the country had run into another crisis.

David Lloyd George, Liberal chief, whose illness has kept him from participating in politics since the beginning of the events which led up to the budget crisis, issued his first public statement tonight as follows:

"If the nation remains steady and united, we shall pull through all right. Our resources are quite adequate to meet the situation but a factional fight among ourselves at this juncture would be unpatriotic lunacy.

"A mere threat has precipitated this second and graver crisis. British common sense, if given a chance, will find a way out."

London Times Blames Us

The financial editor of The London Times, in reviewing the situation, is severely critical of the United States for what he calls its violation of the rules of the gold standard game. He will say tomorrow:

"It is necessary to emphasize the fact that the international economic crisis has played a large part in the temporary abandonment of the gold standard. The responsibility for this belongs to the countries which have hoarded gold on unprecedented scales. Creditor countries which insist on payment in gold are asking for the impossible.

"Prohibitive tariffs keep out goods, and unless the creditor nations relend the credits due to them the debtor nations must pay gold to the extent of their resources and then default.

"The gold standard game can only be played according to its well-proven rules. It cannot be played on the new rules practised since the war by France and the United States.

"The grave situation in the United States is due to her gold inflation which temporarily lifted her prices well above the war level. This boom collapsed in 1929, and she was faced with the necessity of deflating those prices to the level which her own actions have helped bring about. In the course of that deflation her gold stocks will gradually be redistributed and the world will be able to return to the gold standard but only if the rules of that standard are properly observed.

"The gold standard has served the world well in the past but the world cannot continue to have its affairs devastated by the improper handling of the gold standard.

"The real crux of the present crisis is the unprecedented fall in prices which has driven most countries off the gold standard and left them in a position in which a default upon their contractual obligations in gold is unavoidable."

The Government, no doubt, will have the support of the Labor Opposition in Commons for its emergency legislation tomorrow because the Socialists have always denounced the country's return to the gold standard under Stanley Baldwin's Conservative administration as premature.

* * *

September 21, 1931

NEW YORK BANKERS CONFER

See No Need for Drastic Action—Investments in London Moderate

RECENT LOANS PROTECTED

Federal Reserve Can Demand Gold— Morgan Credit Payable in Dollars

EFFECT ON PRICES FEARED

Britain's Action Also Expected to Have Repercussions on World Credit Situation

American security markets will not follow the lead of the London Stock Exchange, but will be open for business as usual today. No emergency has developed here to warrant any action similar to that in the foreign countries, it was stated authoritatively last night.

New York bankers held informal conferences here yesterday, at which the new London crisis was discussed, but no concerted action seemed to them to be called for, it was said. The bankers were in communication with British banking authorities by transatlantic telephone.

According to a competent authority, the short-term balances of American banks in London do not exceed $50,000,000, while Great Britain's external obligations in this country, exclusive of the $125,000,000 credit recently granted by the Federal Reserve banks to the Bank of England and the $200,000,000 private banking credit to the British Treasury, do not exceed $500,000,000.

No further supporting measures will be taken to defend the pound sterling at this time, it was stated. The private banking credit which was opened on Aug. 28 last, while not yet actually used up, will be exhausted shortly with the taking up of forward commitments made by the British banking authorities in their recent attempts to bolster the pound.

Banker Sums Up Situation

The British financial difficulties, as they are understood here, were summed up last night by an important international banker as follows:

The emergency measures taken by the British Government to check the heavy outflow of gold from London will undoubtedly occasion widespread surprise here, although the steps to be taken are by no means unprecedented. During the early days of the Great War, it will be recalled, Great Britain suspended the Bank Act temporarily, and in 1920 sterling went as low as an exchange value of $3.20 as against parity of about $4.86¼. It was not until 1925 that the country returned officially to a gold basis.

The terms of the announcement by the British authorities make it clear that the suspension of gold payments by the Bank of England is a temporary measure and in no way affects the obligation of the British Government to meet in gold such obligations as it may have outstanding in foreign currencies. Undoubtedly the government had a design in making clear this last point.

The dollar obligations of the British Treasury in this country are in the form of both long-term bonds and short-term credits, the latter secured by treasury bills payable in gold dollars of the present standard of weight and fineness. The phrase that the official announcement uses undoubtedly has reference to such obligations as these, payable in the United States of American and France.

Heavy Pressure on Sterling

London dispatches in the last few days have made it clear that the sterling exchange was being subjected to enormous pressure. The starting point of this pressure dates back to Germany's difficulties in early July, last. These difficulties caused repercussions in many other Continental centres which had heavy funds outstanding on loan account in Germany. These centres, in order to protect their own positions, began gradually to draw on their balances in London. The drain began to make itself felt especially from Holland, Switzerland and Sweden. Chili, Brazil and other South American countries such as were having their political difficulties drew out their London funds for immediate use at home.

Even so, however, London financial dispatches indicated confidence that with support from abroad, Great Britain would be able to sustain the pound at parity. This feeling was reinforced by the $250,000,000 credit which the Bank of England arranged about Aug. 1 with the Banque de France and the Federal Reserve Bank of New York.

Further cooperation was secured as recently as Aug. 28, last, through aggregate credits of $400,000,000 from the French market and from an American banking group, arranged by J. P. Morgan & Co. These credits have undoubtedly been utilized, but not with sufficient effect as to offset the continued drain from London, which since Wednesday last, has been on an enormous scale.

Shares Dumped on London

London's ordinary strength as a financial centre has in this instance been a weakness by reason of the fact that London is the only international market where the securities of almost every country on the globe are listed and find a ready market. Such securities from every part of the world have been recently dumped on the London markets and the proceeds withdrawn, thus greatly accelerating the outflow of funds. While, therefore, the step now announced by the British authorities is unexpected, the reasons for it as made clear by the Treasury statement are not difficult to understand.

Just what effect Great Britain's procedure will, in the long run, have upon the American situation, it is difficult to forecast. The British Government's outstanding obligations in this and other foreign markets are comparatively limited and, inasmuch as in America they are payable in gold dollars, the British declaration as to purpose will have reassuring effect. In 1920, with sterling far below par, there were no direct effects that were apparent upon the American market, except an increasing tendency for foreign countries to look upon New York as the world's centre. The gold holdings of the Bank of England still remain at about $650,000,000.

Chief Effects on Britain

The effects of the new move in England itself will be much more marked than anywhere else. With the certain degree of inflation that is likely to ensue, even though limited in extent, the tendency of prices will be to rise. This may result in a temporary increase of business activity there, although wages will probably be held down. In fact one school of financial philosophy, led by John Maynard Keynes, has for months past been urging the partial devaluation of the pound and a certain degree of inflation.

The effect of today's developments may also well be to increase the clamor in England for a protective tariff so as to cut down the import of commodities and reduce the balance of payments for foreign goods. It will be of interest to observe the debate in Parliament tomorrow and the criticism to which the new National Government will undoubtedly be subjected because of its now confessed inability to protect sterling at parity.

War Loans Chief Holdings

The principal holdings of the American public in British Government bonds are in the United Kingdom of Great Britain and Ireland external 5½ per cent loan of Feb. 1, 1917, issued during the war to finance the purchase of war supplies here. This loan is outstanding in the amount of $143,584,000, all of which, presumably, is held in this country. The loan is payable in gold dollars and is therefore not affected by the fluctuations of sterling.

In addition, Great Britain owes a principal amount of $4,600,000,000 to the United States Government on account of the war loans, all of which is payable in dollars. Sterling obligations in the hands of the American public, which may be affected by yesterday's action, include about $10,000,000 of the 4 per cent funding loan of 1919, which was marketed here in 1928 by the Guaranty Company, and an unknown but probably small amount of the 5 per cent War Loan of 1917. Both of these issues are traded in on the New York Stock Exchange and have recently experienced marked declines.

The credit of $250,000,000 extended jointly in equal parts by the Federal Reserve banks and the Bank of France on Aug. 1 last calls for the purchase of sterling bills and, as a result of its operation, the Federal Reserve System has recently acquired $125,000,000 of prime commercial paper, payable in sterling. Provision was made in the credit contract, however, whereby there was guaranteed to the Federal Reserve banks the repayment of the loan in gold if they required it. As a result of this provision the Federal Reserve does not stand to lose anything by the fall in sterling.

Morgan Credit Due in Dollars

In the case of the private banking credit to the British Treasury, of which $200,000,000 was supplied by bankers here, payment is due in dollars, since the proceeds of the credit have been supplied to the British Government in the form of dollar balances.

American financial affairs, in the opinion of prominent bankers, are apt to be more seriously affected by the British crisis through its repercussions on world security and commodity markets than through any loans made by them to Great Britain, since most of the world's commodity terial markets are in London and since most of the world's commodity financing is done in London, the difficulties of sterling may lead to further recessions in the commodity price level, bankers fear.

With the London Stock Exchange closed today, some disturbance in the American markets is to be looked for, bankers said last night. They pointed out, however, that our stock market had already undergone an unprecedented degree of deflation and that, to some extent, at least, the severe declines of last week had discounted British news.

One important aspect of the British position which was emphasized by bankers last night is the tremendous foreign wealth of the country. Great Britain is estimated to hold about $20,000,000,000 of investments abroad of which possibly $3,000,000,000 to $4,000,000,000 is held in this country. This enormous reserve of foreign investments which Great Britain can draw on in her need even exceeds the foreign holdings of the United States, which are variously estimated at from $15,000,000,000 to $17,000,000,000.

Dollar's Ascendency Likely

The removal of sterling from the gold standard will add further to the ascendency of the dollar in the international money markets. The faltering behavior of sterling for some time past has detracted from the position of London as a centre for the financing of world trade, driving an increasing amount of such business to New York. This movement, it is expected, will be accelerated by the suspension of the gold redemption clause.

The decision of the British authorities to remove sterling from the gold standard, implying as it does that no further efforts will be made in the immediate future to support the pound, was foreshadowed by the extraordinary weakness of the exchange on Saturday.

On light offerings sterling plunged to $4.84½ for cable transfers, an extreme drop of 1 5–6 cents, and rallied only moderately to close at $4.84½, a net drop of 15–16 cent on the day. Bankers here ascribed the fall of sterling in New York to a reflection of the disturbed financial markets in London rather than to any new developments in the attitude of this market.

Actually bankers here were making fresh efforts at the close of last week to defend sterling by refusing to accept orders for speculative sales of the exchange.

*   *   *

September 21, 1931

THE BRITISH GOVERNMENT'S STATEMENT

Special Cable to The New York Times

LONDON, Sept. 20—*This is the statement issued by the government tonight, announcing suspension of the law requiring that the Bank of England sell gold at a fixed price:*

His Majesty's Government have decided after consultation with the Bank of England that it has become necessary to suspend for the time being the operation of Subsection 2, Section 1, of the gold standard act of 1925, which requires the Bank to sell gold at a fixed price.

A bill for this purpose will be introduced immediately, and it is the intention of His Majesty's Government to ask Parliament to pass it through all stages Monday, the 21st of September. In the meantime, the Bank of England has been authorized to proceed accordingly in anticipation of the action of Parliament.

The reasons which led to this decision are as follows:

Since the middle of July, funds amounting to more than £200,000,000 (about $1,000,000,00) have been withdrawn from the London market. The withdrawals have been met partly from gold and foreign currency held by the Bank of

England, partly from proceeds of a credit of £50,000,000 (about $250,000,000), which shortly matures, secured by the Bank of England from New York and Paris and partly from proceeds of French and American credits amounting to £80,000,000 (about $400,000,000) recently obtained by the government.

During the last few days withdrawals of foreign balances have accelerated so sharply that His Majesty's Government felt that they were bound to take the above decision.

This decision will, of course, not affect the obligations of His Majesty's Government or of the Bank of England which are payable in foreign currencies.

Gold holdings of the Bank of England amount to some £130,000,000 (about $650,000,000) and, having regard to contingencies which may have to be met, it is inadvisable to allow this reserve to be further reduced.

There will be no interruption of ordinary banking business. Banks will be opened as usual for the convenience of their customers, and there is no reason why sterling transactions should be affected in any way.

It has been arranged that the Stock Exchange shall not be opened on Monday, the day on which Parliament is passing the necessary legislation. This will not, however, interfere with the business of current settlement on the Stock Exchange, which will be carried through as usual.

His Majesty's Government have no reason to believe that the present difficulties are due to any substantial extent to the export of capital by British nationals. Undoubtedly the bulk of withdrawals has been for foreign accounts.

They desire, however, to repeat emphatically the warning given by the Chancellor of the Exchequer that any British citizen who increases the strain on exchanges by purchasing foreign securities himself, or is assisting others to do so, is deliberately adding to the country's difficulties.

The banks have undertaken to cooperate in restricting purchases by British citizens of foreign exchange except those required for the actual needs of trade or for meeting contracts, and should further measures prove to be advisable his Majesty's Government will not hesitate to take them.

His Majesty's Government have arrived at their decision with the greatest reluctance. But during the last few days international financial markets have become demoralized and have been liquidating their sterling assets regardless of their intrinsic worth. In the circumstances there was no alternative but to protect the financial position of this country by the only means at our disposal.

His Majesty's Government are securing a balanced budget and the internal position of the country is sound. This position must be maintained. It is one thing to go off the gold standard with an unbalanced budget and uncontrolled inflation. It is quite another thing to take this measure not because of internal financial difficulties but because of excessive withdrawals of borrowed capital.

The ultimate resources of this country are enormous and there is no doubt that the present exchange difficulties will prove only temporary.

Gold Standard Subsection to Be Suspended

Subsection 2 of the British Gold Standard act of 1925, which is to be suspended, reads as follows:

The Bank of England shall be bound to sell to any person who makes demand in that behalf at the head office of the Bank during office hours of the Bank, and pay the purchase price in any legal tender, gold bullion at the price of £3 17s 10½d per ounce troy of gold of the standard of fineness prescribed for gold coin by the coinage act of 1870, but only in the form of bars containing approximately 400 ounces troy of fine gold.

* * *

September 22, 1931

MORGAN HOLDS GOLD DECISION A 'HOPEFUL EVENT'; CALLS STEP A STAGE TOWARD REVIVAL OF TRADE

Copyright, 1931, by The Associated Press

LONDON, Sept. 21—J. P. Morgan broke his almost iron-clad rule against talking for publication today to say that England's latest move to solve her financial difficulties seemed to him to be not a discouraging but a hopeful event.

While most of the world was excited upon learning that overnight Great Britain had decided temporarily to suspend her gold standard, the financier received a correspondent in his private office in the London headquarters of Morgan, Grenfell & Co., near the Bank of England, and expressed his optimism.

"This step seems to me to be the second necessary stage in the work of the National Government, the first being the balancing of the budget," Mr. Morgan said.

"The completion of the government's work will be the restoration of trade in this country.

"This being the case, it seems to me to be a hopeful and not a discouraging event, and one which brings the great work of the government much nearer to accomplishment."

The statement was solicited from the banker and was not volunteered by him. He discussed the financial situation for upward of an hour and the correspondent left with an impression that while Mr. Morgan did not discount the seriousness of Great Britain's predicament, he was convinced that she would win through.

Although it is not permitted to quote all Mr. Morgan said, he did not express any pessimism, and he added a word of tribute for the character and stability of the English people.

Other financial commentators requested that their names be withheld, but here are some of the points made by several American bankers, all of whom are widely known:

"Suspension of the gold standard by Great Britain not only was not unexpected but was a logical and foregone conclusion."

"From the standpoint of the financial expert, it was the correct move."

"The only criticism offered is that it should have been done before."

"Far from being disconcerting, this move has cleared the atmosphere."

As one banker put it: "We had on our hands a patient who had to undergo an operation to save his life. We were anxious. But now the operation is over and we are feeling relieved."

Britain, experts said, was not going to let herself get caught as Germany was, just after the war, when the mark crumbled to practically nothing because Germany's reserves had been wiped out.

* * *

March 6, 1933

ROOSEVELT ORDERS 4-DAY BANK HOLIDAY, PUTS EMBARGO ON GOLD, CALLS CONGRESS

The President's Bank Proclamation

Special to The New York Times

WASHINGTON, March 5—*The text of President Roosevelt's proclamation on the banking situation, issued at the White House at 11 o'clock tonight, was as follows:*

BY THE PRESIDENT OF THE UNITED STATES OF AMERICA

A Proclamation

WHEREAS there have been heavy and unwarranted withdrawals of gold and currency from our banking institutions for the purpose of hoarding; and

WHEREAS continuous and increasingly extensive speculative activity abroad in foreign exchange has resulted in severe drains on the nation's stocks of gold; and

WHEREAS these conditions have created a national emergency; and

WHEREAS it is in the best interests of all bank depositors that a period of respite be provided with a view to preventing further hoarding of coin, bullion or currency or speculation in foreign exchange and permitting the application of appropriate measures to protect the interests of our people; and

WHEREAS it is provided in Section 5 (b) of the act of October 6, 1917 (40 stat. L. 411) as amended, "that the President may investigate, regulate or prohibit, under such rules and regulations as he may prescribe, by means of licenses or otherwise, any transactions in foreign exchange and the export, hoarding, melting or earmarkings of gold or silver coin or bullion or currency . . .";

WHEREAS it is provided in Section 16 of the said act "that whoever shall wilfully violate any of the provisions of this act or of any license, rule or regulation issued thereunder, and whoever shall wilfully violate, neglect or refuse to comply with any order of the President issued in compliance with the provisions of this act, shall, upon conviction, be fined not

more than $10,000 or, if a natural person, imprisoned for not more than ten years or both . . .";

NOW, THEREFORE, I, FRANKLIN D. ROOSEVELT, PRESIDENT OF THE UNITED STATES OF AMERICA, IN VIEW OF SUCH NATIONAL EMERGENCY AND BY VIRTUE of the authority vested in me by said act and in order to prevent the export, hoarding or earmarking of gold or silver coin or bullion or currency, do hereby proclaim, order, direct and declare that from Monday, the sixth day of March, to Thursday, the ninth day of March, nineteen hundred and thirty-three, both dates inclusive, there shall be maintained and observed by all banking institutions and all branches thereof located in the United States of America, including the Territories and Insular Possessions, a bank holiday, and that during said period all banking transactions shall be suspended.

During such holiday, excepting as hereinafter provided, no such banking institution or branch shall pay out, export, earmark or permit the withdrawal or transfer in any manner or by any device whatsoever of any gold or silver coin or bullion or currency or take any other action which might facilitate the hoarding thereof; nor shall any such banking institution or branch pay out deposits, make loans or discounts, deal in foreign exchange, transfer credits from the United States to any place abroad, or transact any other banking business whatsoever.

During such holiday, the Secretary of the Treasury, with the approval of the President and under such regulations as he may prescribe, is authorized and empowered (a) to permit any or all of such banking institutions to perform any or all of the usual banking functions, (b) to direct, require or permit the issuance of clearing house certificates, or other evidences of claims of assets of banking institutions, and (c) to authorize and direct the creation in such banking institutions of special trust accounts for the receipt of new deposits which shall be subject to withdrawal on demand without any restriction or limitation and shall be kept separately in cash or on deposit in Federal Reserve Banks or invested in obligations of the United States.

As used in this order the term "banking institutions" shall include all Federal Reserve Banks, national banking associations, banks, trust companies, savings banks, building and loan associations, credit unions, or other corporations, partnerships, associations or persons, engaged in the business of receiving deposits, making loans, discounting business paper, or transacting any other form of banking business.

IN WITNESS WHEREOF I have hereunto set my hand and caused the seal of the United States to be affixed.

Done in the City of Washington this 6th day of March, 1 A. M., in the year of Our Lord One Thousand Nine Hundred and Thirty-three, and of the Independence of the United States the one hundred and fifty-seventh.

(SEAL) FRANKLIN D. ROOSEVELT

By the President:
CORDELL HULL,
Secretary of State

PART II

THE POST-WAR POLITICAL FOUNDATIONS

A dynamic global economy cannot long survive without a stable political foundation to support it. The collapse of the global economy in the 1930's was due both to the instability of global financial markets and to the implosion of its political supports. The reemergence of the political forces of protectionism and economic nationalism contributed as much to the collapse of that global economy as the stock market crash of 1929.

As the post-war world began to unfold, the need for sturdy new political institutions to underpin the international economy was very clear. Even as World War II raged, Allied leaders began to lay the groundwork for an international political system that could withstand the pressures of a new global economy. The articles collected in Part II report on post-war political events and trends, highlighting three "critical moments" in the political development of the global economy.

We begin with an impressionistic account of the rise of the Bretton Woods system. Allied leaders, meeting in Bretton Woods, New Hampshire in 1944, drew up a blueprint for post-war international political and economic institutions. Three main organizations eventually emerged to provide political governance to the emerging international economy: the International Monetary Fund (IMF), the International Bank for Reconstruction and Development (the World Bank) and the General Agreement on Tariffs and Trade (the GATT). The first section, "The Bretton Woods System," covers the emergence and consolidation of these institutions into a relatively durable international political system.

The Bretton Woods system was not immune to political tensions (indeed, as we will see in Part V, the monetary system collapsed in 1973). A critical moment in the politics of the Bretton Wood system took place during the GATT's Uruguay Round of negotiations. Having reached agreement on the least divisive issues surrounding international trade, could GATT members move on to solve the more difficult and contentious problems that remained? We draw upon The Times's exceptional coverage of this moment in history to look at the continuing search for the limits of international political consensus.

The forces of "Economic Nationalism" did not disappear under the Bretton Woods system, as reported in the articles collected here. As economic interdependence increased, the tension between autonomy and interdependence became more intense, as did the battle for jobs in a world of increasing economic competition. These tensions are examined in detail through The Times's coverage of the critical moment of the North American Free Trade Agreement (NAFTA) debates. The political issue of whether NAFTA should be expanded to include Mexico (along with the U.S. and Canada) distilled the forces of economic nationalism in all three nations. The articles collected here explore many dimensions of these issues, with special emphasis on the views in Mexico and in the U.S.

Regionalism is often presented as a desirable compromise between autonomy and interdependence. Regional political and economy alliances, it is said, are ways to get the most important gains from international markets while making the fewest political compromises. Regional political agreements are sometimes easier to negotiate, too. The rise of the global economy at the end of the 20th century was also "The Rise of Regionalism." NAFTA, the European Union and Mercosur are just three examples of a powerful ongoing political trend towards regional economic and political alliances.

What are the limits of regional cooperation? This question is explored in the critical moment of the negotiation of the Maastricht Treaty. At Maastricht in the Netherlands, the member states of the European Union tried to find consensus on both economic and monetary union (and the creation of the single currency, the euro) and also on a plan for a deeper political union. The outcome was in doubt until the last moment, making this a critical moment indeed.

As these articles make clear, economic cooperation seems to be easier to achieve than political cooperation. Regionalism therefore may not be the way that a political foundation is created to match the dimensions of the global market.

THE BRETTON WOODS SYSTEM

July 4, 1944

WORLD BANK URGED BY KEYNES AS VITAL

By RUSSELL PORTER
Special to The New York Times

BRETTON WOODS, N. H., July 3—Lord Keynes, chairman of the British delegation to the United Nations Monetary and Financial Conference, described for the first time today the broad outlines of the plan for setting up of a $10,000,000,000 international bank for reconstruction and development to "guarantee" international loans somewhat after the fashion of the Reconstruction Finance Corporation in domestic loans.

Speaking at an afternoon meeting of the bank commission, which will draw up proposals for approval by the conference as a whole, Lord Keynes, who is economic adviser to the British Treasury, said that the plan originated in the United States Treasury.

He called it a sound, fundamental contribution to the post-war task of rebuilding the world for a new age of peace and progress and declared that it would promote "expansion" and not "inflation."

The World Bank program is entirely separate from the currency stabilization goals of the proposals for an international monetary fund, also being considered here, but both plans are closely related, not only to one another, but also to the whole broad United Nations program of international cooperation to lay the economic foundation for the post-war world. The bank and the fund are intended to be permanent institutions.

Lord Keynes urged the delegates and their technical advisers, who had not given as much attention to the bank as to the fund, since they have considered the fund to be the more urgent problem, to speed their consideration of the bank proposals.

He asserted that the bank should be ready by the end of the war, so that the liberated countries would know immediately what credit resources they could rely on and thus proceed with their reconstruction programs, get back into production and resume their role in world trade as quickly as possible. Any time lag, he warned, would prevent the establishment of good government and good order and might postpone return of Allied soldiers to their homelands.

He said that the "novelty" of the bank proposals lay in their guarantee feature, which points up the "international character" of the proposed institution. Under this plan, he

CORBIS/UPI

M. S. Stepanov, head of the U.S.S.R. delegation, with John Maynard Keynes at Bretton Woods.

added, post-war foreign loans would come mainly from the United States, the world's largest creditor nation, but the risks would not fall exclusively on the Government or investors of this country, being spread rather over all the bank's member countries in proportion to their capacity.

Guarantees would be "joint and several," he stated, up to the limit of any member's subscription and the guaranteed bonds to be issued would be of the first order, because they would be backed by the full resources of the bank in gold or free exchange, would be safeguarded against waste and extravagance, and would have the guarantee of the borrowing country.

There would be a guarantee for the annual servicing of interest and amortization, he added, so that the debt would not fall due suddenly as a lump sum obligation. A 1 per cent annual commission would be paid by the borrower on long-term loans, a provision which he characterized as a mutual pool of credit insurance.

Lord Keynes' statement was regarded as designed largely to counteract criticism from orthodox American banking circles, which have expressed skepticism of his post-war ideas because of his longtime advocacy of deficit financing, and from others who have declared both the fund and bank proposals to be of British origin cleverly designed to entrap the United States into playing the "Santa Claus" role after this war, although in a form other than after the last war.

His emphasis on the soundness of the bank plan, its American origin and its safeguards for American investors was viewed as an appeal to American sentiment, as was his linking of prompt acceptance of the plan to quick return of the troops.

Although reconstruction would mainly occupy the bank in its early days, he declared, it would later have another primary duty—"to develop the resources and productive capacity of the world, with special attention to the less developed countries, to raise the standard of life and the conditions of labor everywhere, to make the resources of the world more fully available to all mankind and so to order its operations as to promote and maintain equilibrium in the international balance of payments of all member countries."

* * *

July 23, 1944

ANALYSIS BY MORGENTHAU OF MONETARY AGREEMENTS

Special to The New York Times

BRETTON WOODS, N. H., July 22—*The text of Secretary Morgenthau's radio broadcast tonight marking the completion of the international conference was as follows:*

I am gratified to announce that the conference at Bretton Woods has completed successfully the task before it.

It was, as we knew when we began, a difficult task, involving complicated technical problems. We came here to work out methods which would do away with the economic evils—the competitive currency devaluation and destructive impediments to trade—which preceded the present war. We have succeeded in that effort.

The actual details of a financial and monetary agreement may seem mysterious to the general public. Yet at the heart of it lie the most elementary bread and butter realities of daily life. What we have done here in Bretton Woods is to devise machinery by which men and women everywhere can exchange freely, on a fair and stable basis, the goods which they produced through their labor. And we have taken the initial step through which the nations of the world will be able to help one another in economic development to their mutual advantage and for the enrichment of all.

'Faced Differences Frankly'

The representatives of the forty-four nations faced differences of opinion frankly, and reached an agreement which is rooted in genuine understanding. None of the nations represented here has had altogether its own way. We have had to yield to one another not in respect to principles or essentials but in respect to methods and procedural details. The fact that

we have done so, and that we have done it in a spirit of good-will and mutual trust, is, I believe, one of the hopeful and heartening portents of our time.

Here is a sign blazoned upon the horizon, written large upon the threshold of the future—a sign for men in battle, for men at work in mines, and mills, and in the fields, and a sign for women whose hearts have been burdened and anxious lest the cancer of war assail yet another generation—a sign that the peoples of the earth are learning how to join hands and work in unity.

There is a curious notion that the protection of national interest and the development of international cooperation are conflicting philosophies—that somehow or other men of different nations cannot work together without sacrificing the interests of their particular nation. There has been talk of this sort—and from people who ought to know better—concerning the international cooperative nature of the undertaking just completed at Bretton Woods.

National Interests Cited

I am perfectly certain that no delegation to this conference has lost sight for a moment of the particular national interest it was sent here to represent. The American delegation, which I have the honor of leading, has been, at all times, conscious of its primary obligation—the protection of American interests. And the other representatives have been no less loyal or devoted to the welfare of their own people.

Yet none of us has found any incompatibility between devotion to our own country and joint action. Indeed, we have found on the contrary that the only genuine safeguard for our national interests lies in international cooperation. We have come to recognize that the wisest and most effective way to protect our national interests is through international cooperation—that is to say, through united effort for the attainment of common goals.

This has been the great lesson taught by the war, and is, I think, the great lesson of contemporary life—that the peoples of the earth are inseparably linked to one another by a deep, underlying community of purpose. This community of purpose is no less real and vital in peace than in war, and cooperation is no less essential to its fulfillment.

World Accord Called Vital

To seek the achievement of our aims separately through the planless, senseless rivalry that divided us in the past, or through the outright economic aggression which turned neighbors into enemies would be to invite ruin again upon us all. Worse, it would be once more to start our steps irretraceably down the steep, disastrous road to war.

That sort of extreme nationalism belongs to an era that is dead. Today the only enlightened form of national self-interest lies in international accord. At Bretton Woods we have taken practical steps toward putting this lesson into practice in monetary and economic fields.

I take it as an axiom that after this war is ended no people—and therefore no government of the people—will again tolerate prolonged or widespread unemployment. A revival of international trade is indispensable if full employment is to be achieved in a peaceful world and with standards of living which will permit the realization of man's reasonable hopes.

What are the fundamental conditions under which the commerce among the nations can once more flourish?

First, there must be a reasonably stable standard of international exchange to which all countries can adhere without sacrificing the freedom of action necessary to meet their internal economic problems.

This is the alternative to the desperate tactics of the past— competitive currency depreciation, excessive tariff barriers, uneconomic barter deals, multiple currency practices and unnecessary exchange restrictions—by which governments vainly sought to maintain employment and uphold living standards. In the final analysis, these tactics only succeeded in contributing to world-wide depression and even war. The International Fund agreed upon at Bretton Woods will help remedy this situation.

Long-Term Aid Championed

Second, long-term financial aid must be made available at reasonable rates to those countries whose industry and agriculture have been destroyed by the ruthless torch of an invader or by the heroic scorched-earth policy of their defenders.

Long-term funds must be made available also to promote sound industry and increase industrial and agricultural production in nations whose economic potentialities have not yet been developed. It is essential to us all that these nations play their full part in the exchange of goods throughout the world.

They must be enabled to produce and sell if they are to be able to purchase and consume. The Bank for International Reconstruction and Development is designed to meet this need.

Objections to this bank have been raised by some bankers and a few economists. The institution proposed by the Bretton Woods conference would indeed limit the control which certain private bankers have in the past exercised over international finance. It would by no means restrict the investment sphere in which bankers could engage. On the contrary, it would expand greatly this sphere by enlarging the volume of international investment and would act as an enormously effective stabilizer and guarantor of loans which they might make.

Private-Loan Guarantee Sought

The chief purpose of the Bank for International Reconstruction and Development is to guarantee private loans made through the usual investment channels. It would make loans only when these could not be floated at the normal channels at reasonable rates. The effect would be to provide capital for those who need it at lower interest rates than in the past, and to drive only the usurious money lenders from the temple of international finance. For my own part, I cannot look upon the outcome with any sense of dismay. Capital, like any other commodity, should be free from monopoly control and available upon reasonable terms to those who would put it to use for the general welfare.

The delegates and technical staff at Bretton Woods have completed their portion of the job. They have sat down together and talked as friends, and have perfected plans to cope with the international monetary and financial problems which all their countries face in common. These proposals now must be submitted to the Legislatures and the peoples of the participating nations. They will pass upon what has been accomplished here.

Looks to World of Future

The result will be of vital importance to everyone in every country. In the last analysis it will help determine whether or not people will have jobs and the amount of money they are to find in their weekly pay envelopes. More important still, it concerns the kind of world in which our children are to grow to maturity. It concerns the opportunities which our children are to grow to maturity. It concerns the opportunities which will await millions of young men when at last they can take off their uniforms and can come home to civilian jobs.

This monetary agreement is but one step, of course, in the broad program of international action necessary for the shaping of a free future. But it is an indispensable step in the vital test of our intentions. We are at a cross-road, and we must go one way or the other. The conference at Bretton Woods has erected a signpost—a signpost pointing down a highway broad enough for all men to walk in step and side by side. If they will set out together, there is nothing on earth that need stop them.

* * *

July 20, 1945

SENATE VOTES 61-16
TO ADOPT BRETTON ACT

U. S. FIRST TO DO SO

Bill Returns to House, but Acceptance of Minor Changes Is Assured

MAJOR AMENDMENTS FAIL

Taft Proposal to Ban Nations With Currency Curbs Is Defeated After Long Debate

By JOHN H. CRIDER
Special to The New York Times

WASHINGTON, July 19—The Senate passed the Bretton Woods bill by a vote of 61 to 16 this afternoon assuring United States membership in the first international institution in history designed to maintain stable currency exchanges and provide cooperative long-term credits for reconstruction and development.

All that remained for this country to put its final stamp of approval on the agreements reached a year ago at Bretton Woods, by representatives of forty-four nations, was acceptance by the House tomorrow of several Senate amendments and the signature of President Truman, both of which were foregone conclusions.

Thus, after four days of Senate debate and a year of public discussion on the complicated proposals, which involve ultimate investment by this country of $5,925,000,000 in an International Monetary Fund to stabilize exchanges and remove restrictions on currency transactions and a Bank for Reconstruction and Development, the Senate passed the bill by more than a two-thirds majority of those voting, which would have been required had the bill been presented as a treaty.

Barkley Congratulates Taft

Passed by the House on June 7 by a vote of 345 to 18, the bill had been expected to pass the Senate, but its most ardent supporters had not looked for such an overwhelming majority, particularly in view of the battle against the bill waged for four days by Senator Taft, Republican, of Ohio, for which he was congratulated on the floor today by his principal opponent, Senator Barkley.

Nineteen Republicans and one Progressive voted for the bill, and only two Democrats, Senators Wheeler of Montana and O'Daniel of Texas, opposed it.

Among the Republicans supporting the measure were Senators White of Maine, the minority leader, and Vandenberg of Michigan, a leading Republican supporter of the United Nations charter which comes up for debate Monday.

Before the Bretton Woods agreements can be regarded as effectively ratified, nations having 65 per cent of the quotas of the $8,800,000,000 fund and subscriptions to the $10,000,000,000 bank must accept the agreements and deposit the initially required parts of their quotas and subscriptions by Dec. 31. Original capital of the bank will be $9,100,000,000, but $10,000,000,000 is its contemplated eventual capitalization.

United States Is First to Ratify

This country was the first of the participating nations to ratify the agreements. Administration leaders have said that once the United States acted the others would rapidly follow suit.

There appeared to be no doubt that the prerequisite ratification would be obtained by the end of the year, but experts predicted that it would take from six to eighteen months for the two institutions to begin functioning.

Most of the debating period from 11:15 A. M. until passage of the bill at 5:13 P. M. was used in discussing a proposal by Senator Taft, providing that no member shall be entitled to use the fund's resources until it had removed all exchange restrictions on current transactions listed in Sections 2, 3 and 4 of Article VIII of the Fund Agreement.

Mr. Taft asserted that his amendment would make certain that the fund actually was used for the purpose of removing exchange controls, which was one of its stated objectives.

"It would destroy the whole purpose of the plan," Senator Barkley replied. "No man who has been very ill is expected to get up and walk right away. These countries which have been the principal victims of the war are not out of bed yet. They are not even convalescent."

The Kentuckian then explained that the "sterling area," which Mr. Taft had said would be used by the British for restrictive purposes, was similar to the "dollar area," in that countries in the "sterling area" did their principal trading with Britain and kept balances in London, just as countries in the "dollar area" did most of their trading with this country and kept balances in American banks.

"There was no aspect of the prewar sterling area arrangement which was contrary to the purposes of this fund," Mr. Barkley added.

When Senator Aiken, Republican, of Vermont, asked why there was so much criticism of the British and Russians, Mr. Taft said that the United States did most of her trading with the British, and that the United Kingdom and Russia had the next largest quotas in the fund to this country.

Senator Tobey, Republican, of New Hampshire, said that the Taft amendment would "hamstring" the whole arrangement, adding that the Ohioan had not read all of the section of the fund agreement relating to exchange controls but only that part permitting them to be retained during a five-year transitional period under constant surveillance of fund officials.

What he omitted to read, Mr. Tobey continued, was that the agreement required all members to end wartime exchange controls as soon as possible and put the fund officials under obligation to see that this was done.

"I would not impugn the good faith of Great Britain," Senator Tobey asserted.

"I am not questioning their good faith," Mr. Taft replied. "I am merely saying that under the agreement they are permitted to do these things."

Senator Barkley said that the exchange controls were put on when "Britain was all that stood between the rest of the world and Hitler."

Barkley Urges Flexibility

There must be flexibility in the Fund plan, he added, to enable Great Britain to work her own way out from under these controls.

The amendment would, in effect "serve notice on Great Britain that she couldn't belong to the Fund," Mr. Barkley asserted. Moreover, he added, it would require a reconvening of the forty-four nations to adopt the proposed amendment to the articles of agreement.

Senator Tunnell, Democrat, of Delaware, accused Senator Taft of making an "untrue statement" when he denied the amendment would keep Great Britain out of the Fund, and the Ohioan insisted that what Mr. Tunnell said was untrue.

Mr. Taft described the agreements as anything but final, pointing to a number of "reservations" taken to them by some of the Bretton Woods delegates. He frequently referred to Great Britain as "our greatest customer" who has "become practically an economic isolationist."

Senator Barkley replied that the "reservations" were nothing more than statements of what some of the nations represented at Bretton Woods "wanted but didn't get."

The amendment was defeated 53 to 23, with ten Republicans voting with the Democrats.

Senator Ball, Republican, of Minnesota, offered an amendment requiring that the American representative on the fund ask its board to impose restrictions on any member which after three years had not removed exchange restrictions.

He said that the proposal would require no acceptance by the other forty-three nations and would not even assure that the board would accept the American's recommendation, but Mr. Barkley opposed the amendment primarily on the grounds of the "parliamentary situation," which finds the House without a quorum so that if objection should be made in the House, the whole legislative process would have to be repeated. The House, he added, would only accept the minor amendments of the Senate Banking Committee.

Vandenberg Supports Ball

Senator Vandenberg supported the amendment, stating that he could not see how it could possibly interfere with "the launching of this great adventure."

The amendment was rejected 46 to 29.

Other amendments voted down were as follows:

Two by Senator Millikin, Republican, of Colorado, one to prohibit the "scare currency" section of the fund agreement from being used as an excuse for violating international obligations and another to strike out entirely "the "scarce currency" section which gives the fund authority to "ration" currencies which become in excessive demand.

Another Taft amendment to refer the bill back to committee with instructions to report it back without provision for the bank, on the grounds that the latter duplicates the Export-Import Bank.

One by Senator Langer, Republican, of North Dakota, to prevent the resources of the fund or bank from being used for making armaments.

* * *

December 28, 1945

28 NATIONS SET UP
THE BRETTON WOODS BANK

FUND ESTABLISHED

$8,800,000,000 Will Be Employed to Stabilize World Exchanges

BANK HAS 9 BILLION

Plans Rebuilding Loans—Russia Absent but May Sign Later

By JOHN H. CRIDER
Special to The New York Times

WASHINGTON, Dec. 27—The International Monetary Fund and the Bank for Reconstruction and Development came into being this afternoon when representatives of twenty-eight nations signed documents confirming that their Governments had ratified the Bretton Woods Agreements and deposited the nominal initial payment toward expenses of the organizations.

Although representatives of the Soviet Union signed the first documents at Bretton Woods in July, 1944, Russia was not among the twenty-eight signers today. There was no official indication of what Soviet action would be, but most officials expected that the U.S.S.R. would qualify and sign by the Dec. 31 deadline.

The International Monetary Fund is a new kind of world currency pool to maintain stable conditions of exchange as an essential prerequisite for a high level of international trade.

The Bank is a medium for international sharing of risks in the making of loans for world reconstruction and development. The Fund will have $8,800,000,000 in gold and currencies at the start, and the Bank initial subscriptions of $9,100,000,000.

The agreements provide that the seat of the institutions shall be in the country having the largest quotas and subscriptions (the United States) and it is confidently expected that the two institutions will be situated in or near New York City, now generally recognized as the financial capital of the world, unless the United Nations Assembly decides to place them at some other point, together with all other UNO organizations.

Fred M. Vinson, Secretary of the Treasury, who was vice chairman of the United States delegation to the Bretton Woods conference, signed the two documents in behalf of the United States at ceremonies in a "conference room" of the State Department that formerly served as the Navy Department Library.

Hailed as Mission in Peace

"We can be thankful," he said, "that the history we are now writing is not another chapter in the almost endless chronicle of war and strife."

He added that, on the contrary, it was "a mission of peace" for which the plenipotentiaries had gathered and, he said, "not just lip service to the ideals of peace—but action, concrete action, designed to establish the economic foundations of peace on the bedrock of genuine international cooperation."

The two documents were signed by the Ambassadors or Ministers of the twenty-eight countries, including France, which only ratified the agreements last night. Four other countries were ready to sign but unable for various reasons to do so.

These were Mexico, whose Ambassador had been grounded by weather on a flight to Washington; Czechoslovakia, whose Ambassador was ill and planned to sign the documents later at his embassy; and Peru, whose Ambassador was not sure at the last minute whether the action of his home government constituted complete ratification.

The signing nations were as follows:

Belgium, Bolivia, Brazil, Canada, China, Colombia, Costa Rica, Ecuador, Egypt, Ethiopia, France, Greece, Guatemala, Honduras, Iceland, India, Iraq, Luxembourg, Netherlands, Norway, Paraguay, Philippine Commonwealth, Poland, Union of South Africa, United Kingdom, United States of America, Uruguay and Yugoslavia.

Denmark to Sign Later

Henrik de Kauffmann, the Danish Minister, answered to the call for Denmark and handed Acting Secretary of State Dean Acheson a note informing him of the intention of Denmark to adhere to the two institutions, which Denmark was permitted to do by action of the Bretton Woods conference. Denmark will sign and become a member of the Bank and Fund after a quota in the Fund and a subscription to the Bank have been assigned to her.

The nations signing today represented not only more than the 65 per cent of the quotas of the Fund, but constituted more than a majority of the forty-four nations attending the Bretton Woods Conference. The Fund agreement provided that countries having 65 per cent of the Fund quotas must ratify the agreements before Dec. 31, 1945, if this institution was to be created.

The nations signing today represented holders of about 80 per cent of the Fund quotas totaling $8,800,000,000. The bank subscriptions, although not exactly the same as the Fund quotas, were nearly so.

Ceremony Is Impressive

The ceremony in the old Navy library room was impressive, if not even solemn, so much so that cameramen's flash bulbs went off faster than ever at the novelty of a smile on the lips of the Agent General for India, Sir Girja Shankar Bajpai, as he wrote his name on the documents.

During most of the period of the signing, Secretary Vinson chatted with the Earl of Halifax, the British Ambassador, who sat on his left.

Mr. Acheson, who presided, said he hoped the ceremonies would "not be regarded in any narrow way," since "the significance of what we do reaches far beyond the creation of these institutions" and was "symbolic of the ever-increasing cooperation between the nations of the world to bring about peace and a better life for all men."

When the signing had been completed he announced:

"I am pleased to announce that the agreements are now in full force and effect."

He introduced several persons who, he said, had played a major part in bringing the institutions into being. The first was Harry White, Assistant Secretary of the Treasury. Mr. Acheson said of him that "no one had done more." Mr. White is generally regarded as the principal author of the Fund agreement and is expected to be named American representative on the Fund board.

Mr. Acheson introduced former Secretary of the Treasury Henry Morgenthau Jr., who, he said, had been in charge of all of the preliminary work on the Bretton Woods institutions.

Mr. Morgenthau, who was head of the United States delegation to Bretton Woods and chairman of the conference, likened the institutions to "another tree planted by the late President Roosevelt, which will grow throughout the years."

Officials said they did not believe that the institutions could be organized and put on an operating basis in less than six months.

* * *

April 19, 1947

NEW BANK PUTS AID ON SELF-HELP BASIS

McCloy Explains International Reconstruction Unit Seeks an Expanding World Economy

PRIVATE FUNDS RELIED ON

Agricultural, Sociological and Labor Aims Also Discussed Before Life Underwriters

The International Bank for Reconstruction and Development is prepared to extend its facilities to those peoples who are willing to aid their own recovery through cooperative effort and thus create an expanding world economy, John Jay McCloy, president of that institution, declared yesterday in his first public statement on its program.

With other leaders in various phases of the nation's economy including agriculture, labor and sociology, he addressed the seventh annual forum on current economic and social trends conducted by the New York chapter, American Society of Chartered Life Underwriters, held in Town Hall, 123 West Forty-third Street.

After stressing the need for the investment of capital on an international scale for productive purposes to achieve "stability, prosperity and progress" as a means to peace, Mr. McCloy announced that branches would be opened soon in foreign centers convenient to those nations that have applied for loans.

Bank's Functions Explained

He explained that "the size of the bank will be limited only by the confidence of the investor" in the prime investment market, and that operations would be subject to the limitations imposed in this country by the Securities and Exchange Commission. France. Poland, Czechoslovakia, the Netherlands, Luxembourg, Denmark and Chile were listed as nations that have applied for loans.

"The financing of the world's needs is not only an opportunity; it is the satisfaction of a desperate need," Mr. McCloy declared in his prepared address. "The United States today is in a position to contribute to a prosperous and expanding world economy by assuming leadership in international investment which its dominant productive position makes inevitable. The International Bank is the mechanism by which economic rehabilitation may be accomplished in the great part of the world where the economic community has been destroyed or demoralized."

Describing this international banking institution as essentially an activity of private capital rather than a governmental operation, the new president explained that the funds that would be required to repair the ravages of war might not be available in the private market without some form of international guarantee as that afforded by the International Bank.

Private Investment Stressed

"In the long run, however," he continued, "international investment of capital is primarily the function of the private market, not of public agencies. The founders of the bank recognized this when they wrote into the charter of the bank that one of its fundamental purposes is to promote private foreign investment, and that, to this end, no loan may be made by the bank when the loan is otherwise available to the borrower in the market on reasonable terms."

Although several of the executive directors of the institution "represent potential borrowers," according to Mr. McCloy, he explained that the charter of the bank forbids making any loan that is disapproved by a loan committee of officers of the institution.

The outlook in other phases of the nation's economy was presented by Dr. Herrell DeGraff, associate Professor of Land Economics at Cornell University; Walter W. Cenerazzo, organizer and president of the independent Watch Workers Union. and Dr. James H. S. Bossard, Professor of Sociology and director of the William T. Carter Foundation at the University of Pennsylvania. Stanley High, who acted as moderator of the forum, summarized the public's point of view.

* * *

May 10, 1947

WORLD BANK LENDS FRANCE $250,000,000

LOAN FOR 30 YEARS

Interest Is 3 ¼% With No Repayment Needed During First 5 Years

NEW REQUEST NOT BARRED

Funds Are for Aid in Economic Revival—French See Need for $600,000,000 More

---

By CHARLES HURD
Special to The New York Times

WASHINGTON, May 9—The World Bank began operations today by lending $250,000,000 to France to assist that country in its reconstruction and development of post-war economy. This was the first loan made by the $8,000,000,000 institution set up under the Bretton Woods Charter as an adjunct of the United Nations.

The loan papers were signed shortly after 5 P. M., at the bank's offices here by three persons. John J. McCloy, president of the bank, signed for the institution; Henri Bonnet, French Ambassador, signed for the French Government as guarantor of repayment, and Wilfrid Baumgartner, president of the French Credit National, signed on behalf of that Government corporation, to which the loan technically was made.

The loan runs for a term of thirty years, with no repayment expected in the first five. It bears interest at the rate of 3 ¼ per cent, plus an additional 1 per cent a year on unrepaid balances. This premium payment for the building up of a special reserve, was specified for all loans made by the bank in its Articles of Agreement.

The loan to France was made in the name of forty-four nations that are subscribers to the bank, and the money was lent against capital assets technically estimated to total more than $8,000,000,000.

Since, however, the only money that may be used at this time for loans by the bank consists of slightly more than $700,000,000 in United States dollars held by the bank, the loan actually is a credit in dollars advanced by the bank, with all subscribers to the bank bound to stand as surety in case of default.

The loan was notable also for the fact that, if the funds are claimed by France immediately, they will be taken from the working capital of the bank. In the near future, according to plans already being prepared, the bank plans to cover its loans by means of debentures to be sold in the open market.

The loan papers were signed within a few hours after the twelve executive directors of the bank approved the final details of the long negotiations that have preceded the culmination. France requested a loan of $500,000,000 last October, or twice the sum that was granted. However, the bank announced that it would consider, without present commitment, another application by France "later this year."

"Although the bank is not now prepared to make any commitments with regard to a further loan," an announcement said, "it will be willing to consider an additional application from France later this year. Any new application will be considered in the light of the funds which the bank will then have available for lending and of the progress made in carrying out the French economic and recovery program."

This announcement was taken by informed observers to mean that the bank, rather than desiring to limit France, wished first to learn the extent and terms of the money it could borrow in the United States market. Many other applications for loans are pending. A study is now being made on the basis of a questionnaire sent to financial institutions to test the reaction of investment circles to the bank's operations.

An official description of the French loan summarized its basis as follows:

"The loan is being made to assist France in the reconstruction of its war-torn economy and to finance the import of specific goods and equipment necessary to its economic rehabilitation. A portion of the proceeds will be devoted to the modernization of the steel industry, including a modern strip mill.

"The transportation system is to be improved by the purchase of locomotives and freight cars, cargo ships and canal barges, and commercial airplanes. Coal and oil, essential to industry and transport, figure largely among the prospective purchases, as do industrial raw materials, including semi-finished steel products and non-ferrous metals.

"Under the loan agreement, the bank will obtain full information concerning the goods to be purchased with the proceeds of the loan, and their utilization. France will be free to purchase in whatever markets are most advantageous."

Deferment for five years of any repayment was ascribed to the fact that "the French national recovery program calls for heavy imports during the next five years."

The loan was based, the bank stated, on France's evident need, plus "the recovery prospects of France," as well as a realization of the position of France in relation to the European picture as a whole.

A summary of the French economic position gave a reassuring picture. It stated that by the end of 1946 production had been restored to 90 per cent of the 1938 level and exports to 75 per cent of that year's rate.

This recovery was achieved, however, at the cost of heavy imports that reduced France's gold and "hard currency" holdings from $2,614,000,000 at the date of liberation to about $1,000,000,000, and had caused other borrowings abroad equivalent to $2,600,000,000.

At the same time, the expectation was voiced that France would achieve, in 1950, the restoration of equilibrium in the franc area. The crucial "gap" would occur between now and 1949, and the prospectus stated that it was "a serious one."

France was said to expect to balance her governmental budget this year. In the meantime, the summary added, it was expected that French industry would reach the 1938 level of production and achieve, by 1950, a production level 30 per cent greater than that of 1938.

* * *

October 31, 1947

23 COUNTRIES SIGN NEW TRADE PACTS

---

6 Nations, Including U.S., Agree to Put Geneva Agreements Into Effect on Jan. 1

EASTERN BLOC STILL SPLIT

Soviet Union and 7 Others Refuse Bids to Conference at Havana to Form ITO

By MICHAEL L. HOFFMAN
Special to The New York Times

GENEVA, Oct. 30—Twenty-three nations signed the final act of the Geneva Trade Conference in the Council Room of the United Nations Palace in Geneva at 10 A.M. today.

In a ceremony lasting one hour and a half, plenipotentiaries of countries representing three-quarters of the world trade solemnized the end of the longest economic conference in history with markedly little oratory or fanfare. It was the 203d day of the conference.

Six countries, Belgium, Canada, Luxembourg, the Netherlands, the United States and the United Kingdom also signed a protocol binding their governments to put the new tariff schedules attached to the general agreement on tariffs and trade into effect Jan. 1.

This protocol will become binding when France and Australia sign. France will sign probably in New York within ten days while approval of the tariff schedules by the Australian Cabinet the day before yesterday assures that country's signature in time to meet the Nov. 15 deadline.

Brazil Encounters Difficulty

It was learned today that Czechoslovakia also would sign the protocol shortly but that Brazil, which had intended to become the "key" country by signing in Geneva, had found last-minute constitutional difficulties about signing without parliamentary ratification.

Winthrop G. Brown of the United States State Department, who literally snatched the Anglo-American tariff accord and thus the whole conference back from what seemed like certain failure twice, signed for the United States.

Though many delegates had already hurried home to prepare for the Havana meeting Nov. 21, the gorgeous black and gold council chamber was comfortably full for the ceremony. There was a ripple of laughter when the much-discussed document was brought in by the secretariat at Chairman Max Suetens' request.

The document stands about eighteen inches high and weighs nearly forty pounds. It contains 2,040 pages bound under one cover and nineteen complete tariff schedules covering more than 10,000 items.

Chairman Suetens' address reviewed the long history of the meeting and contrasted its success with the failures of former tariff conferences.

"The signing of the final act today," he said, "marks the completion of the most comprehensive, the most significant and the most far-reaching negotiations ever undertaken in the history of world trade."

The chairman also announced the names of thirty-two countries that had accepted invitations to the Havana Conference, and eight countries that had refused. The latter list perhaps is most interesting. It includes the Soviet Union, the Ukraine, White Russia, Yugoslavia, Bulgaria, Saudi Arabia, Ethiopia and Siam.

Eastern Split Continues

Czechoslovakia has accepted and Poland is still expected to accept, the Eastern bloc seems destined to continue its split on the vital question of trade cooperation with the rest of the world.

In addition to signing the general agreement and the protocol several nations exchanged notes confirming adjustments in previously existing treaties or agreements necessitated by the completion of the multilateral accord. The United States had to sign supplementary agreements with seven countries with which trade agreements are now in force.

Canada, Britain and South Africa also exchanged notes today releasing each other from obligations to maintain imperial preference margins in any future negotiations with non-empire countries. These notes were exchanged secretly, however, and not as part of the general signing ceremony.

Though twenty-three countries signed the final acts they represented only nineteen customs areas. Belgium, the Netherlands and Luxembourg, members of the Benelux customs union, signed separately, as did Syria and Lebanon and Pakistan.

As the delegates dispersed to reassemble in three weeks in Havana, the dominant mood was one of confidence in the ability of this group to lead the United Nations successfully through the final stages of the formation of the International Trade Organization. Chairman Suetens said today's signature was irrefutable proof that the basic idea of the trade organization was right and that it could work.

* * *

November 18, 1947

TARIFF CUTS AFFECT 60% OF U. S. TRADE IN 23-NATION PACTS

Geneva Accords Yield Gains to America Affecting About $1,500,000,000 of Sales

OUR DUTIES GO TO '13 BASIS

British Imperial Preferences Reduced—New Scale Seen as a Long-Term Help

Tariff reductions ranging up to 50 per cent of present rates on major imports, and affecting 60 per cent of United States trade, were disclosed yesterday by State Department sources in a conference at 2 Park Avenue.

An analysis by these sources of the general trade and tariff agreements signed in Geneva by twenty-three nations shows that foreign countries concerned were making concessions or "bindings" to maintain present duties that would affect about one and a half billion dollars of United States exports.

The American reductions, estimated as bringing the general level of United States tariff schedules to the lowest point in thirty-four years, cover some 45,000 items listed in 1,350 pages. The pacts are designed to give long-range stimulus to international trade through the removal of artificial trade barriers. The signatory countries conduct from 65 to 70 per cent of the world's trade.

Revisions Effective Jan. 1

The United States tariff revisions will become effective Jan. 1. It was indicated that a Presidential proclamation would be issued early in December, setting forth the items on which tariff cuts would be made effective. Simultaneous reductions in tariffs and trade concessions will be made

effective then by the United Kingdom, Canada, Australia, France and the countries composing the Benelux customs union—Belgium, the Netherlands and Luxembourg.

The text of the general agreement on tariffs and trade provides that the countries signing the protocol, or provisional application, will, so far as their laws permit, put the new duties into effect in January.

To date the United States, Britain, France, Australia, Canada, Belgium, the Netherlands and Luxembourg have signed the protocol. For these countries not only the new tariffs but also the rules of international commercial conduct embodied in the draft charter of the International Trade Organization go into provisional effect at that time. Substantive parts of the agreement are subject to change, according to the outcome of the Havana Conference, opening tomorrow.

The nations making the chief concessions are Canada, the United Kingdom, France and the Benelux countries.

Additional nations will make the pacts effective in accord with the specific legislative and constitutional requirements of their own countries not later than June 30, 1948. Their action will be followed by additional Presidential proclamations adding to the items coming within the scope of the pacts.

Wool Tariff Cut 25 Per Cent

Among the outstanding reductions in the United States tariff from present levels are:

Wool, 25 per cent, or from 34 cents a pound to 25 ½ cents; Scotch and Canadian whisky, 40 per cent, or from $2.50 to $1.50 a gallon; beef and veal, 50 per cent; butter, 50 per cent, depending upon quota; sugar, 33 $1/3$ per cent; rayon and staple fiber, 20 per cent, and copper 50 per cent.

Rubber and newsprint are held to their present "free" basis. Woolens and worsteds are reduced to 25 per cent from 35 to 45 per cent, with the right to increase them reserved if imports rise to 5 per cent of United States production. Cattle has been maintained at present duty levels, but the import quota has been increased.

Other products showing major tariff cuts included all softwood lumber, portland cement, wheat and wheat flour, bauxite, quicklime, high-quality furs, jute, burlap, manganese ore, textile machinery, photograph film, steel products and electrical items.

The over-all tariff reductions, according to State Department sources, will affect $500,000,000 in United States imports. The concessions granted by the fifteen nations with whom the United States has direct signatory pacts will affect also $500,000,000 in exports from the United States, as measured in 1939, the last pre-war year. The "bindings," or maintenance of present tariff rates in the pacts will cover an additional $900,000,000 in trade, it was added.

In estimating that the United States tariff level on Jan. 1 will be the lowest in thirty-four years, analysts said it would bring the new basis to that of the Underwood Tariff of 1913. This tariff had a general level of about 16 per cent of the value of imports subject to duty, which was estimated to be about the same as that to be established under the Geneva pact. No comment on this phase was made at the conference yesterday.

British Empire preferences were reduced substantially. The agreement also calls for a ban on import quotas by foreign countries, except under certain specified conditions. State Department officials indicated, however, that while the agreement was viewed as the longest step in history toward the removal of trade obstacles, the short-range outlook for international trade was affected by dollar shortages and the continuance of import regulation in many countries for the sake of stabilizing their economies.

Concessions Granted to U. S.

Among the major concessions granted on United States exports were:

Reductions on American automobiles in almost every one of the twenty-three countries. There were widespread reductions on United States electrical appliances, radios, refrigerators, and office and agricultural machinery.

England bound to the free list United States wheat, raw cotton and a total of 77,000,000 pounds of ham a year. France reduced the duty on United States wheat by two-thirds, on lard by 59 per cent, on canned fruit by 50 per cent, and on automobiles by nearly half. The United Kingdom duty and Empire preference on canned salmon was cut 50 per cent. Canada, England, Australia and New Zealand allowed tariff or preference cuts on American tobacco. Concessions were made on aircraft by Canada, France, Australia, Czechoslovakia and other nations.

Major concessions also were obtained on trucks, motorcycles and parts. Concessions were granted on American apples, oranges, grapefruit and dried fruits.

A number of British Empire preferences were wiped out entirely, while others were reduced substantially, thus placing the United States exporter on a more competitive status in the markets of the various British Commonwealth nations.

Reciprocal Tariffs Supplanted

The Geneva agreement, which runs three years, replaces the reciprocal trade pacts between the United States and seven other countries, the latter consisting of Canada, England, The Netherlands, Cuba, Belgium, Luxembourg and France.

Under the agreement, the "most-favored nations" clause is accepted by all the participating nations.

Trygve Lie, General Secretary of the United Nations, last night hailed the General Agreement on Tariffs and Trade "as a substantial step on the part of the United Nations toward the establishment of economic well-being and prosperity, which are among the cardinal aims of the United Nations."

Declaring that the signatory countries represent a substantial majority of world trade, and that the reductions they have granted cover the greater share of their imports and exports, he added:

"It can, therefore, be safely said that an initial successful attack has been carried out in a key sector of international trade.

"Under the future international organization, the establishment of which is to be one of the principal purposes of the forthcoming Havana Conference, it is intended that this work on the reduction of trade barriers will be carried on so that it may include an ever-enlarging percentage of the trade of nations."

Foreign traders here hailed the General Agreement on Tariffs and Trade as a major step toward the reduction and elimination of trade barriers, although they expressed the belief that its chief benefits would be of long rather than of a short-range character.

The National Foreign Trade Council said:

"We welcome the announcement of the general agreement on trade and tariffs negotiated at Geneva, Switzerland, as a major advance toward the lowering of barriers to American export and import trade, taken despite admittedly difficult economic conditions throughout most of the world.

"The full benefits of the agreement cannot be expected to become immediately effective, but as recovery and stabilization programs are put into operation, the improvement of commerce due to the reduction of trade barriers should be widely felt. The agreement serves substantially to stem the tide of restrictive devices, resorted to during the post-war economic emergency. An exhaustive analysis of the agreement is to be carried out by the Council and a formal statement issued at a later date."

Speaking for importers here, Morris S. Rosenthal, president of the National Council of American Importers, praised the Geneva trade pacts "as the most significant step taken since 1930 in eliminating trade barriers in the form of excessive duty rates."

Importers' Duties Stressed

"The composite effect of the modification in duty rates," he said, "provides a new tariff structure. American importers must assume a heavy responsibility to give full effect to the objectives of the tariff reductions by taking all necessary steps to speed up the volume of imports of desirable materials and consumer goods as rapidly as greater supplies become available at more reasonable prices.

"In those cases where high tariffs have long burdened the American consumer with no compensatory benefit to any efficiently operated domestic industry, the reduced duties ultimately will be passed on by importers, to the advantage of the consuming public."

The general provisions of the agreement are divided into three parts. Part I gives legal effect to the tariff concessions set out in the schedules of the agreement and, in addition, lays down the basic rule of non-discrimination in tariff and customs matters generally.

Part II deals with barriers to trade other than tariffs, such as quotas, protective excise taxes and restrictive customs formalities. These provisions are intended to prevent the value of the tariff concessions from being impaired by the use of other devices, and also to bring about the general relaxation of non-tariff trade barriers, thus assuring a further quid-pro-quo for the action taken with respect to tariffs.

Part III covers procedural matters and other questions relevant to the agreement as a whole. Included in Part III are provisions setting out the relationship between the agreement and the proposed charter for an International Trade Organization, to be acted on in Havana beginning Friday.

Six Months' Work Fruitful

Special to The New York Times

GENEVA, Nov. 17—The extensive changes in tariffs are designed to ease greatly the existing unbalance in world trade.

This most extensive and deepest slash in world trade barriers is the result of six and a half months of bargaining in the Geneva Trade Conference.

In the case of the United States alone, more than three-quarters of more than 1,800 items in the tariff, many of which have as many as fifteen subclassifications, have been either reduced or bound. Some countries, notably France, have produced entirely new tariffs, which by their terms are not comparable with previous import regulations.

Among the benefits for United States farmers obtained by the American team were removal of the 20 per cent Canadian duty on most types of fresh fruits, the complete removal of British preferences on dried fruits—apples being bound on the British free list—and a flat 10 per cent duty without quotas (after the transition period) on all dried fruits in France.

*   *   *

September 14, 1949

MONETARY FUND BIDS NATIONS DEVALUE IF OTHER STEPS FAIL; TRUMAN URGES FREER TRADE

HINT TO CRIPPS SEEN

Pound Is Not Mentioned, but Experts Feel Aim Is to Prod Britain

48 COUNTRIES AT PARLEY

President Calls on Delegates to Remove the 'Obstacles' That Handicap Commerce

By H. WALTON CLOKE

Special to The New York Times

WASHINGTON, Sept. 13—Devaluation of currencies was recommended by the International Monetary Fund today as remedial action for any of its forty-eight member countries that are unable to solve their dollar deficiency problems by other methods.

The Fund's recommendation was contained in its annual report made public today at the opening session of the institution's fourth annual meeting. Financial leaders of the member countries are attending. The report did not specifically mention the British pound sterling, but there was little doubt in the minds of experienced observers that it was focused on Britain's dollar crisis.

Associated Press Wirephoto

Mr. Truman receives from Maurice Petsche, French Finance Minister, a gavel made from a tree at Bretton Woods, N.H., where international agreements were reached in 1944 to found the World Bank and the Monetary Fund.

Although the report referred only to "deficit nations" in general, it was considered by a great many persons here to be added gentle pressure for sterling devaluation.

Financial leaders of the United States, Britain and Canada concluded discussions here yesterday of the British economic problems. There was no mention, however, of a sterling devaluation. In fact, Sir Stafford Cripps, Britain's Chancellor of the Exchequer, had previously rejected proposals along this line.

Truman Pleads for Stability

President Truman, attending a joint meeting of Fund delegates with those representing the International Bank for Reconstruction and Development, said a stable international economy would be the greatest boon to world peace. He also urged dropping the "obstacles" to world trade.

He expressed hope that the representatives of the forty-eight member countries would go home thinking in terms of "cooperation on a world basis for the welfare of the world as a whole."

The President's remarks gave emphasis to the principal theme of this meeting—international cooperation and how it could help the economic recovery of dollar-deficient countries.

Before President Truman left the platform Maurice Petsche, France's Finance Minister, gave him a gavel made from a tree at Bretton Woods, N. H., where the Bank and Fund were conceived in 1944. President Truman smilingly assured the Finance Minister that he would use the gavel on any future occasion where he might be called upon to preside.

Fund's Report Significant

The Fund's report assumes added importance when considered in the light of the program, aimed at solving the British financial problems, that resulted from the three-power conference. Some United States officials believe that pound devaluation eventually must be adopted.

Devaluation of the pound, now valued officially at $4.03, would mean in terms of foreign trade a lowering of the price of British-made products. This, in turn, would be expected to increase exports and result in more dollars for Britain.

The subject of the pound's devaluation is expected to come before the Board of Governors of the Fund at their closed sessions, but it will be part of a discussion of the desirability of a general revaluation by debtor countries to increase their exports and encourage trade.

The International Bank for Reconstruction and Development, sister institution of the Fund, also is holding its annual meeting. The Bank emphasized in its annual report, filed with its Board of Governors this morning, that it could not provide the answers "to all or even a major part of the world's financial ills" through its lending powers.

Eugene R. Black, president of the Bank, stressed that it was "beyond both the purpose and the power of the Bank, for example, to cure the 'dollar shortage.' "

The articles of agreement of both the Bank and the Fund were drawn up by the United Nations Monetary and Financial Conference at Bretton Woods, N. H., in July, 1944.

It is the purpose of the Bank to act as a lending agency to its member countries by making or underwriting loans for reconstruction and industrial development. The primary purposes of the Fund are to facilitate the growth of international trade and to eliminate foreign exchange restrictions that hamper such trade.

Camille Gutt, managing director of the Fund, presented the institution's report to its Board of Governors. He stressed in a speech to the board that no nation alone could solve the financial ills of the world. "A large international effort will be necessary to arrive at a real settlement," he said.

"Further measures of restriction and discrimination offer no permanently satisfactory solution to [trade] payments difficulties," the Fund declared in its report. "A constructive solution to the payments problem requires the deficit countries to do all they can to make more of their output available for export, and to offer these exports at prices which will call forth greater demand in dollar markets."

The Fund also stressed that prolonged dependence on restrictions and discrimination would be likely to divide the world economy into economic blocs, each with its own price structure and each tending increasingly to insulate itself from the rest of the world. Such insulation would be required to protect the bloc's own inconvertible system by trade restrictions and exchange controls.

"The task of increasing dollar exports cannot be delayed in the hope that it can be quickly completed by some extraordinary effort at the eleventh hour," the Fund said. "The magnitude of the dollar payments problem requires that every constructive means should be used to meet it," the report added.

"For the creditor countries, this means maintaining high levels of national income, reducing the barriers to trade, and facilitating the flow of international capital. For the deficit countries, it means the reduction of their export prices to a competitive level, in order to meet as much as possible of their payments problem through the expansion of trade on a multilateral basis."

The Fund emphasized that the deficit countries "cannot afford to forego any suitable instrument, including any necessary exchange adjustment that could expand their dollar exports."

Where a very large price reduction in a country's goods is necessary to expand exports, "it would in many cases seem possible only through an adjustment in the exchange rate," the Fund added.

The Fund warned, in an apparent reference to Britain's efforts to balance trade accounts by her austerity program and import restrictions:

"It may be preferable for a country to change an unsuitable exchange rate through the machinery of Fund consultation rather than to subject its economy to the risks of serious deflation and unemployment or to impose restrictions that keep imports so low as to endanger its well-being and efficiency."

The Bank's annual report did not command the attention of that of the Fund because of the topical content of the latter's 122-page message. Mr. Black stated that the Bank now had the resources to help finance "all of the sound, productive projects in its member countries that will be ready for financing in the next few years, that can appropriately be financed through repayable foreign loans, and that cannot attract private capital."

The Bank' report emphasized the role the institution might play in building up the world's under-developed areas, as set forth in President Truman's Point Four program announced in his inaugural address.

Mr. Black stressed that foreign development financing preferably "should be derived mainly from private sources." He also was severely critical of proposals for "fuzzy," long-term, low interest loans which, he contended, were nothing more than international subsidies of "a disguised grant to the borrower."

The Bank's report described the salient features of eight loans that it had made during the past year, aggregating $191,600,000. Thus far, the Bank has made loans totaling $716,600,000 in France, the Netherlands, Belgium, Denmark, Luxembourg, Chile, Mexico, Brazil, Finland, India and Colombia. Twenty more reconstruction and development projects are now under consideration.

One of these is a loan of "moderate size" requested by Yugoslavia. The final loan is expected to be less than the $250,000,000 suggested. Last week the Export-Import Bank granted a $20,000,000 loan to Yugoslavia.

* * *

October 10, 1949

31 NATIONS PUBLISH DUTY CUTS AIMED AT SPURRING TRADE

80% of Global Sellers Take Part in Common Revisions Downward of Customs

ANNECY SUCCESS HAILED

U. S. Gets, Gives Concessions—Signing of Protocol Begins Today at Lake Success

---

By MICHAEL L. HOFFMAN
Special to The New York Times

GENEVA, Oct. 9—Thirty-one countries representing twenty-eight customs areas released new customs tariff schedules today incorporating the results of the summer-long trade conference held at Annecy, France.

The protocol, the signature of which will start in motion the process of putting new, lower duties into effect on some 7 per cent of total world trade, becomes open for signature at Lake Success tomorrow.

For the second time in two years the United States will make a significant reduction in import duties, in furtherance of its policy of attacking trade barriers in all forms throughout the world. This would have been a significant event in any case, although less trade is affected than by the basic multilateral accord signed at Geneva in 1947.

The United States action is doubly significant because of the Washington financial talks of last month when attention was concentrated on the necessity for the United States, as the world's principal creditor nation, to move away from its traditional policy of high import barriers.

[The State Department, hailing the Annecy accords, said that the United States had obtained concessions on a segment of United States exports that in 1947 amounted to more than $500,000,000. In return, the United States granted to other countries concessions on a segment of United States imports that in 1948 amounted to more than $143,000,000.]

Trade System Broadened

The general significance of the completion at Annecy of the "second round" of trade negotiations is that they broaden and strengthen the trading system established by the free nations of the world, incorporated in the General Agreement on Tariffs and Trade.

The agreements have confirmed the success of an entirely new technique of negotiating tariff reductions. This technique and the framework of the principles of commercial policy within which the member nations agree to operate emerge from the Annecy meetings as a proved method of international cooperation on a practical economic level, the like of which has never been seen before.

Twenty-three nations adhering to the agreement, together with ten that will shortly join, form a kind of club, the price of admission to which is demonstrated willingness to carry out in good faith a reduction of trade barriers and adherence to common rules of conduct in international trade matters.

Member Nations Listed

Together, these thirty-three countries account for more than 80 per cent of world trade. The twenty-three original members are Australia, Belgium, Brazil, Burma, Canada, Ceylon, Chile, China, Cuba, Czechoslovakia, France, India, Lebanon, Luxembourg, the Netherlands, New Zealand, Norway, Pakistan, South Africa, Southern Rhodesia, Syria, the United Kingdom and the United States.

The ten new members, all of whom have completed negotiations with each other and with some or all of the old members, are Denmark, the Dominican Republic, Finland, Greece, Haiti, Italy, Liberia, Nicaragua, Sweden and Uruguay.

Admission to the "club" is by no means automatic. Colombia, which negotiated at Annecy, failed to complete negotiations with enough countries to warrant applying for membership. If Colombia had applied, there is reason to believe that the necessary two-thirds approval of the old members could not have been obtained.

The schedules of duties of the participating countries, lowered or bound under the Annecy protocol, fill more than 200 pages of small type. The United States has granted reductions or bindings on a wide variety of items, although a relatively small part of its total imports is affected. These include steel cutlery, forgings, plywood, bacon, hams, butter, cheese, macaroni, several fruits, cocoa and chocolate, rum, aquavit, vermouth, matches, silver, jewelry, works of art and umbrellas.

The most controversial items in the new United States schedules, judging from the record of negotiations in Annecy, are the concessions on butter and lemons.

In negotiations with Denmark, the United States agreed to permit the entry of 10,000,000 pounds of butter at seven cents a pound duty during the summer months. Previously, a rate of fourteen cents a pound had applied during those months, with the quota for the period Nov. 1 to March 31 permitting entry at a seven-cent rate.

The ability to sell luxury quality butter in the United States market was regarded by Denmark as essential to her entire recovery program.

In negotiations with Italy, the duty on lemons was lowered from two and one-half to one and one-quarter cents a pound, with the reservation that if imports exceeded 5 per cent of the total United States production during any one year, the duty would be doubled on all excess over that quantity.

The widest world interest will be in the Italian tariff, which is entirely new, having been changed from the old pre-war basis of specific duties to a tariff expressed almost entirely in ad valorem terms. It is unquestionably a "high tariff" judged by the average rates of duty. Most manufactured products must pay from 25 to 40 per cent duty. Duties are high both on raw materials and finished products.

Even so, traders will welcome the simplification and clarification of the tariff of this important trading country so that they will know where they stand.

The third series of negotiations for Sept. 1950 is already being planned, Eric Syndham-White, executive secretary of the Interim Commission for the International Trade Organization, said here today. Means for incorporating Western Germany into the trade system is the most important single problem to be settled in advance.

* * *

October 28, 1957

GATT, AT AGE OF 10, HAS BIG PROBLEM

Trade Pact Nations Ponder Whether Europe Pool Will Violate Obligations

1957 MEETING GOING ON

Organization Marks Tenth Anniversary This Week— 37 Members Now

Special to The New York Times

GENEVA, Oct. 27—In a cluttered cosmos of international organizations, the General Agreement on Tariffs and Trade shines faintly. Yet it influences commercial tides in thirty-seven of the world's largest trading nations.

Strictly speaking the GATT, which is ten years old this week, is not an organization at all. It is rather a code of conduct, a contract pledging thirty-seven nations to the belief that tariffs and discriminatory trade policies obstruct economic progress.

Reducing tariff barriers is the agreement's first order of business, but not its only one. Rules and precepts also are laid down on import and export restrictions, taxation and trade regulations, and balance-of-payment problems.

At annual meetings like the one now in session, member nations negotiate reciprocal trade concessions and examine complaints. Almost any subject bearing on international trade is liable to come up at the private sessions.

The agreement was never meant to be an independent entity. Ten years ago it was conceived as an adjunct to the proposed United Nations International Trade Organization. But the organization never materialized, mainly for lack of United States participation. This left the general agreement to do what it could about stabilizing and freezing tariff levels before the advent of a post-war boom.

Cats Achieved

Concerted attacks on tariffs were opened by the GATT nations in 1947 and 1949 and considerable reductions were

achieved. In the winter of 1954–55, when it became clear that ambitious projects for international trade cooperation through the United Nations were unavailing, the GATT nations drafted an Organization for Trade Cooperation to administer their agreement and give it a permanent legal existence.

Again the United States demurred, although it had worked long and effectively within the agreement to promote liberal, multilateral trade. Congressional opponents claimed that the O. T. C., by making recommendations on international trade, would collide with the United States freedom to determine its own policies. To date the organization has not been ratified by Congress.

"This failure to ratify the agreement has signified the abdication of leadership by the United States in the field of commercial policy on the international plans," Canada's delegate L. D. Wilgress, said today.

A lack of vigorous enforcement powers has limited the achievement of the agreement. Fifteen of the thirty-seven nations refuse to grant full non-discriminatory treatment to one of the members, Japan. Some nations have turned from tariffs to quantitative restrictions for protection (the United States among them, in an effort to cope with mounting agricultural surpluses.) The GATT has recently intensified its campaign against this device.

Trade ministers from the GATT nations are in Geneva this week to discuss the consequences of six European nations' decision to form a common market in association with their overseas territories. This presents the GATT with its newest and thorniest problem: will the six, all members of the agreement, create a new preferential area in violation of their individual obligations to other members?

The trade ministers do not wish to interfere with the political unity that may grow out of the common-market scheme. Their overmastering concern is to assure that the common market will be "outward-looking," with liberalism prevailing over protectionism. And that, by common consent, is the GATT's goal.

* * *

October 5, 1958

AIMS VINDICATED BY FUND AND BANK

Former, Especially, Was Viewed Dubiously Once— Both Fulfill Big Roles

By PAUL HEFFERNAN

The hunger for more capital, experienced by nations big and small, rich and poor, capitalist and socialist ever since the end of World War II, is knocking at the door of the twin institutions set up at Bretton Woods.

The International Bank for Reconstruction and Development and the International Monetary Fund are by no means running out of money. But almost overnight, it seems, the major problems surrounding the functioning of these institutions have undergone dramatic change.

Only ten years ago the question was seriously raised whether the World Bank, as a long-term lender of capital, could perform any significant service in the post-war world under the rules adopted at Bretton Woods. And the opinion was widely expressed that the function of tiding nations over temporary shortages of foreign exchange, assigned to the Monetary Fund, had no place at all in the postwar world.

It Was Dispensable

It was even proposed in responsible financial circles that the fund be liquidated, or, at most, be continued as a subsidiary activity of the World Bank.

Today there is no question about the functions being fulfilled by the Bretton Woods twins. Both are leaving their stamp on history in a big and probably a lasting way.

Since 1946, membership in the bank and fund has doubled. The member nations then numbered thirty-four; today they number sixty-eight. Russia and Communist China are the only large nations that are outside.

Of the European non-members, most are the Russian satellites—Czechoslovakia, Poland, Hungary, Rumania, Bulgaria and Albania. Switzerland and Portugal are the only sizable non-Communist European nations that do not belong. Outside of some principalities and sheikhdoms, the other non-members are New Zealand, Nepal, Cambodia, Laos, Yemen and Bhutan.

By June 30 of this year, the bank had made 204 loans totaling $2,828,700,000 in forty nations. The fund over the same period had permitted thirty-five nations to draw a total of $3,100,000,000 to cope with exchange crises. Twenty-eight nations have used the fund's resources more than once.

More Capital on Way

The first formal steps probably will be taken at the New Delhi meetings this week to increase the capital resources of both lending agencies. The bank's subscribed capital is now $9,510,400,000, of which $3,175,000,000 represents the subscription of the United States. The capital subscriptions to the fund total $9,193,000,000, of which the United States share is $2,750,000,000.

While both the bank and the fund now see a need for adding to subscribed capital, the need varies with the function. For the bank a substantial increment in capital would serve largely as a guarantee against enlarged lending. Like most of the present subscribed capital of the bank, the new subscriptions might not be required in cash for years if ever. The reason is that the bank raises its lending money by selling bond issues in the public market. Most of the capital subscription is a stand-by security fund to meet the bank's

obligations only if borrowers should default. Adding to the capital of the bank, then, need impose no financial strain on any member nation.

With the fund the problem is different. The fund gets its money only from capital subscriptions. For years these were virtually untouched. Suddenly in 1955, demands on the fund became substantial and frequent. As a consequence, the fund's uncommitted holdings of gold and convertible currencies shrank by July this year to $1,400,000,000.

Per Jacobsson, managing director of the fund, fears that this working balance is not enough if the fund is to fulfill its function under present international economic conditions. Here is how Mr. Jacobsson viewed the problem in a recent study:

Fund Held Inadequate

"The physical volume of world exports fell by 7 per cent from 1937 to 1947, but in the next ten years increased by 90 per cent, a rate of expansion almost unknown in the past. The prices of goods moving in international trade increased by 140 per cent between 1937 and 1957. Fluctuations in the balance of payments which may require use of the fund's resources are therefore potentially much larger now than when the fund quotas were established.

"If any lack of confidence were to set in, the potential movements of funds connected with the shifts in the financing of trade would likewise be larger. The fund's ability to provide assurance to its members and to act quickly on a massive scale if emergencies arise depends upon its having adequate resources, which have been made available in advance of any specific emergency. It is doubtful whether, with world trade greatly expanded in volume and value, the fund's resources are sufficient to enable it fully to perform its duties under the Articles of Agreement."

The Monetary Fund may thus be said to have at last come into the function for which it was created at Bretton Woods. With the Bank, however, a significant modification from the original blueprint has taken place.

At Bretton Woods, the Bank was viewed largely as a clearing house for public financial transactions. Loans could be made only to government bodies or to borrowers having the backing of a government guarantee. But with the passing of the years, the accent on World Bank lending is passing to undertakings—public or private—where the payoff of the loan can be related realistically to the productivity of the project financed. More and more, the loans are being made not to central governments, but to government-backed agencies charged with the burden of earning the debt redemption money.

* * *

January 8, 1962

PRESIDENT IS TOLD TARIFF BARRIERS ENDANGER WEST

Long-Secret Report Warns of Economic Disintegration Without 50% Reduction

By FELIX BELAIR Jr.

Special to The New York Times

WASHINGTON, Jan. 7—A long-secret report has warned President Kennedy that "disintegration of the Free World economy into separate trading systems" may result unless Congress authorizes 50 per cent cuts across the board in tariff rates.

The report, compiled by a task force studying foreign economic policy, said the failure of the United States to liberalize trade would have "political consequences of a most serious order."

These, it said, would be in addition to "a formidable competitive disadvantage" to American exporters implicit in the growing European Common Market.

The report also proposed a virtual scrapping of the existing embargo on exports of strategic materials to nations of the Communist bloc. It favored a new policy that would acknowledge the mutual advantages of expanding East-West trade and that would invite the Soviet Union to join in a code of fair practices for international trade.

Basis of Program

Although it was submitted to Mr. Kennedy as President-elect just before his inauguration, the report remains the basic rationale for the liberalized trade program he plans to ask Congress to approve at this session. The program would replace the expiring Trade Agreements Act.

The present trade agreements legislation requires that the President obtain concessions equal in value to the concessions the United States makes in the area covered by negotiations. It takes no account of concessions with respect to non-tariff trade barriers that this country might seek.

The new program would give the President authority for the first time to negotiatate whole categories of tariff rates with a view to their reduction. It would also enable him to seek trade concessions in return for commitments not restricted to the trade field.

The task force was headed by George W. Ball, who later became Under Secretary of State. Other members of the group included college professors and private consultants, many now holding high Administration posts.

Apparently reluctant to risk rejection of the new trade program during the first Congressional session of his Administration, the President did nothing, except in the field of foreign aid, about the report's many urgent and sweeping recommendations. Most of the aid proposals have since been carried out, but without adoption of the scope of expenditures proposed.

Britain's decision to seek membership in the European Common Market, a continuation of the United States'

balance-of-payments deficit last year, and the expiration of the trade agreements legislation next June, decided the President on an immediate course of action on the new program. The balance of payments is the measure of payments into and out of the country by individuals, business and governments.

The task force proposed Presidential authority to negotiate mutual trade concessions by cutting present tariff rates as much as 50 per cent. The cuts would be made in annual steps through 1966. The task force also proposed these further legislative authorizations:

- "Assistance to labor and industry in adjusting to tariff reductions to replace the 'no serious injury' principle.
- "Revision of the existing peril point provision so that it (A) is a device for determining what individual tariff rate adjustments should be made within a given category, and (B) goes into operation only after negotiations are completed on average reductions for each category." A peril point, determined by the Tariff Commission, is the level below which the tariffs cannot be cut without causing serious injury to domestic industry.
- "Revision of escape clause standards [under the Reciprocal Trade Agreements Act] so that the clause applies only when (A) injury occurs to an industry as a whole, and (B) adjustment to the increased imports cannot readily be made.
- "Trade adjustment assistance that would come into effect after a finding by the Tariff Commission of injury under the escape clause.
- "Authority for the President to reduce or remove duties, import taxes and quotas on articles produced principally by the less developed countries.
- "Authority to make or receive types of reciprocal concessions other than tariff reductions in trade negotiations.
- "Revision of the national security provisions of trade agreements legislation to permit reduction of duties and an increase in quotas: use of measures other than tariffs to protect national security interests: relaxation of import restrictions, in concert with other members of the Organization for Economic Cooperation and Development, to accommodate trade with a country under Soviet economic pressure.
- "Amendment of the Battle Act to safeguard normal trade against the disruptive practices of the Communist bloc.
- "Authority for the President to suspend the embargo on furs and to suspend discriminatory tariff treatment for Soviet bloc imports."

Because of the operation of a modified concept of existing "peril point" and "escape clause" provisions, the report found that it would be possible to make uniform 50 per cent cuts in all negotiable categories of tariff rates.

For that reason it proposed that "the new legislation should provide authority to make greater than 50 per cent reductions on certain items on which there is now a high level of tariff protection."

At the time the report was submitted, its authors considered it unlikely that Britain and the six other countries in the Free Trade Association would seek membership in the European Common Market. Britain's decision to do so presumably underscores the arguments for broad Presidential tariff powers.

"This tariff-cutting authority is necessary," said the report, "if we are to match the reductions to be made in the internal tariffs of the European Common Market and the Free Trade Association. In that way we could receive the benefits of the generalization of these reductions on a most-favored-nation basis." All nations having most-favored-nation provisions in agreements with the United States get and receive concessions on a basis of equality with any other nation.

"Since those two trading groups will have reduced their tariffs by 50 per cent across the board by 1966," the report said "The United States, armed with the authority we propose, would be able to prevent divisions of the industrial countries of the Free World by wide-spread trade discrimination."

As explained in the report, "the peril point mechanism serves as a limitation on the tariff-cutting authority of American negotiators in trade agreement negotiations." Under the Trade Agreements Act the President must explain to Congress any cuts below a peril point.

The escape clause mechanism, on the other hand, comes into play after tariffs have been reduced if the Tariff Commission determines that increased imports following a reduction cause "serious injury."

"The task force is of the strong opinion that the 'no serious injury' doctrine should be substantially abandoned," said the report. "The United States should recognize frankly that the liberalization of trade essential to a prosperous Free World will require that tariffs be reduced to the point where it will be necessary to accept some temporary and local injury to certain American firms, industries and communities."

To mitigate such possible hardships, the group proposed the inclusion of "trade adjustment provisions" in any authorizing legislation. But it suggested that this relief take the form of higher tariff rates only in extreme cases, such as when producers and workers in an industry are being displaced by competitive imports faster than the workers can be absorbed into alternative employment.

Such tariff relief could be applied by the President even where displaced workers were already receiving relief compensation, but it was recommended that such relief be of "limited duration" and progressively reduced.

Federal Loans Backed

A trade adjustment program should rely in the main on Federal loans to finance industry relocation, accelerated tax write-offs, and related procedures, the report said.

These would include retraining of workers, additional unemployment compensation, early retirement benefits and the like. Such benefits would be available "without regard to whether or not the affected industries or workers are located in areas of substantial labor surplus."

The study group suggested that unilateral tariff concessions to under-developed areas be conditioned on parallel concessions to such areas by other industrialized countries. Such concessions could take the form of reduction or removal of consumption taxes or other restrictions on imports of tropical products, raw materials or materials in the early stages or processing and "certain light manufactures."

Such concessions would not only promote export earnings of under-developed areas, according to the report, but would tend to remove discriminations implicit in preferential trading systems maintained by Britain and the Common Market countries for their former overseas possessions.

To further the purpose of trade liberalization, the report urged abolition of the following provisions of the Tariff Act of 1930:
- "The provision relating to cost-of-production criteria in fixing and raising of duties.
- "The provision requiring the use of American, selling price in fixing the valuation of certain products.
- "The provision directing customs officers to apply the highest rate of duty when alternatives exist."

Commodity Plan Suggested

Without committing itself to any particular method of approach, the task force said the time had come for the United States to consider ways of stabilizing the export income of under-developed areas producing a single raw material. Commodity stabilization agreements as well as loans to offset income fluctuation were suggested as worthy of exploration.

The report warned in this connection against "commodity agreement techniques that support prices at artificially high levels." It went on:

"The task force feels that much greater consideration should be given to the possibilities of using the resources of the International Monetary Fund for short-term loans to cushion income fluctuations resulting from cyclical variations in production conditions or on the terms of trade of raw material producing countries."

A complete alteration of United States policy on trade with Soviet bloc countries was recommended by the task force. It held this to be imperative not only because the present policy was outmoded and negative but also because it had begun to affect our relations with other industrialized countries as well as with the under-developed areas.

The problem will not go away because Americans consider trade with Communist countries to be "immoral, dangerous and of doubtful economic benefit," said the group. It said such trade would become vastly more important in this decade than in the last because other Western countries had found such trade to be advantageous.

"As a result," said the report, "our Allies have refused to follow docilely the tariff discriminations and export limitations on Communist trade imposed by United States law."

European Trade Cited

Meanwhile, because the United States has refused to face the issue, trade between the Soviet bloc and Western Europe has been developing largely on Soviet terms, the group said. It said the time had come for the United States to give direction to this inevitable development.

It called for "a positive response to Khrushchev's high-sounding trade overtures" and said "the Soviet should be invited to trade with Free World countries on the basis of a code of fair practices designed to remove the distortions and disruptions arising from monopolistic state commerce."

"The code should serve as a model for industrialized and under-developed countries in the negotiation of bilateral treaties or multilateral trade arrangements with the bloc," said the report.

"For example, detailed ground rules, coupled with an effective complaints procedure, would seek to regulate disruptive price undercutting and dumping by reference to comparative world price and cost criteria, rather than to the totally unrelated and unascertainable conditions prevalent in the Communist home market: to provide meaningful reciprocity in conditions governing access to Communist markets; to obtain Soviet commitments to purchase specified quotas of goods in lieu of an otherwise futile most-favored-nation treatment undertaking; to end the wholesale pirating of Western patents, know-how, and technology; and, in general, to ensure that trade and competition are conducted on the basis of commercial considerations."

The report reasoned that "failing East-West agreement, the United States and its industrialized Allies would still possess the economic advantage needed to secure observance of the rules, assuming that a uniform and coordinated policy toward Soviet bloc trade is established through consultation with O. E. C. D. and the G. A. T. T. [General Agreement on Tariffs and Trade]."

On the general question of East-West trade the report continued:

"To blunt the dangers and exploit the opportunities inherent in the bloc's expanding economic commitments, we must persuade other free enterprise countries to take constructive and coordinated action.

"What is needed first of all is some measure of conviction on their part that we are genuinely prepared to recognize the potential economic advantages of expanded East-West trade.

"Only then will we be in a position to assert positive leadership in the formulation and enforcement of safeguards necessary for the protection of the common interest in stable world trade."

*   *   *

KENNEDY ROUND SUCCEEDS; 50 NATIONS TO CUT TARIFFS, LIBERALIZING WORLD TRADE

DUTIES DOWN 33%

Program of Food Aid for Hungry Lands Also Provided

By CLYDE H. FARNSWORTH
Special to The New York Times

GENEVA, May 15—The major trading nations reached agreement tonight in the Kennedy round of tariff negotiations, paving the way for the most ambitious attempt ever made to achieve the liberalization of international trade.

After more than four years of negotiations, nearly 50 countries, accounting for about 80 per cent of world trade, agreed to an average one-third cut in their tariffs, liberalization of trade in agriculture and a program of food aid for the hungry nations.

The agreement probably will lead to a sharp increase in world trade. It also could mean, over the five-year staging of the tariff cuts, somewhat lower prices for much imported merchandise.

An American who goes to buy a new Volkswagen five years from now will pay about $30 less for the car—assuming the dealer passes along the entire amount of the tariff cut. This is about 2 per cent of the retail price and could be offset by other factors, such as auto safety standards, that may drive prices up by then. The United States tariff on Volkswagens, under the Kennedy round terms, is to be cut in half by 1972—to 3 ¼ per cent from 6 ½ per cent.

$40-Billion of Trade

Trade in the products on which concessions have been agreed amounts to some $40-billion. This is about eight times more than the previous round of world tariff cutting negotiated in 1960–61.

The agreement was announced at midnight tonight at the Italian-style Villa le Bocage, overlooking Lake Geneva, which is the headquarters for the organization that supervises the General Agreement on Tariffs and Trade. The GATT organization acted as the host to the trade talks.

Negotiators, who only a few hours earlier had been haggling over the amount of traffic reductions in chemicals, tobacco and canned peaches, congratulated each other and the GATT director-general, Eric Wyndham White. His package of compromises, submitted this morning, served as the general framework for the agreement.

The precise terms of settlement were not known. According to the United States chief negotiator, William M. Roth, they will not be made known until President Johnson signs the agreement some time in June.

Tribute to Kennedy

The Kennedy round is so called because legislation authorizing American participation in the talks was passed by Congress in 1962, during the Administration of President Kennedy.

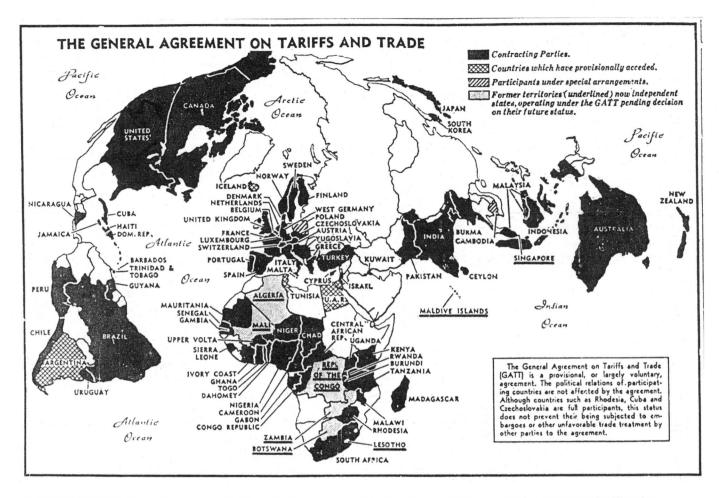

SPANS THE WORLD: General Agreement on Tariffs and Trade encompasses 86 nations, but about 50 took part in Kennedy Round of tariff-cutting.

Mr. Wyndham White told newsmen tonight that the results are a "fitting memory to a great President who was lost to the world too soon."

Mr. Roth said the United States had given or received concessions on products involving $16-billion of American trade. The United States won concessions on agricultural products accounting for $2-billion of American exports of which $650-million was in grains.

Total American exports last year were $27-billion, and American imports were $19-billion.

Winning the agricultural concessions, mainly from Europe's Common Market, which was the great antagonist of the United States in the trade talks, had been one of the major difficulties throughout the long, drawn-out negotiations.

Though the Kennedy round should theoretically lead to lower prices—because it means the slashing of tariffs by the major trading nations—inflation in the United States and Western Europe may hide the effects. Also, there is a question of how much the middleman will pass on to consumers.

Weary Delegates Nap

Mr. Roth said he was finally convinced there would be agreement tonight at 9:25 P.M. when Jean Rey, the chief negotiator for the Common Market, telephoned to make an appointment with him at the Hotel Richemond. Both Mr. Roth and his second in command, W. Michael Blumenthal, were taking naps at the time after all-night negotiations yesterday and talks throughout most of the early part of the day.

It was at this appointment that Mr. Rey, a member of the Common Market's commission and the man considered likely to be the next commission president, said he accepted the Wyndham White compromise proposals with certain alterations that proved satisfactory to Mr. Roth.

After their talks a 650-word communiqué was drawn up. The whole Kennedy round had hinged on agreement by the two giants of international trade.

Mr. Roth estimated the size of the tariff cuts at 33 to 35 per cent. Mr. Rey said he guessed they were somewhere between 35 and 40 per cent.

The Common Market commissioner described the results in the industrial sector as excellent and those in agriculture as "more modest."

The precise date for the first tariff cuts to take effect has not yet been fixed. Most likely it will be either next Jan. 1 or July 1, 1968.

Farm and Chemical Issues

The major issues between the United States and the European Economic Community (as the Common Market calls itself) involved both the agricultural concessions the United States demanded from the community and the community's demands that the United States Congress get rid of the American Selling Price system of computing highly protective duties on chemical imports.

Neither side got all it wanted. The Americans won only modest concessions in agriculture, while the Common Market got no assurance, that the A.S.P. system would be repealed.

The Common Market originally had conditioned all its tariff cuts in chemicals on repeal of the American Selling Price. This was totally unacceptable to the United States, which offered to cut most of its chemical tariffs by 50 per cent.

It is believed that the compromise worked out left the Common Market making three-fifths of its chemical tariff cuts of 50 per cent conditional on repeal of the A.S.P. system and two-fifths automatic.

The world food aid program, representing the biggest multilateral commitment yet under-taken to feed hungry nations, also presented problems to the very end of the negotiations.

The industrial countries agreed to set aside or buy in world markets annually four and one-half million tons of wheat or other grains worth about $350-million to give to the hungry nations.

The United States pressed for the program both to get other nations to share the food-aid burden and to remove grains from commercial markets so that American farmers could self more.

The European nations and Japan objected at first to the idea, but then they slowly swung around. However, Japan held out until the last 24 hours of the negotiations, when she agreed in principle to participate but with certain conditions. The final sealing of Japanese participation in the program has been left for further negotiation.

Japan's contribution would be about 5 per cent. The United States would contribute 42 per cent; the Common Market's six members (France, West Germany, Italy, Belgium, the Netherlands and Luxembourg), 23 per cent; Britain 5 per cent; the four Nordic countries of Sweden, Norway, Denmark and Finland about 3 per cent; Switzerland 0.7 per cent, and Argentina 0.5 per cent. The percentage contributions of other countries are not yet known.

The developing countries did not fare too well in the negotiations, though they certainly got more out of the Kennedy round than in any previous efforts to liberalize trade.

The communiqué issued tonight by Mr. Wyndham White said that for many tropical products it was "not possible to reach agreement at this stage on the elimination or reduction of tariffs because of the existence of preferential arrangements."

Former Colonies a Factor

This referred to the fact that the Common Market could not make concessions because it would disrupt the preference system worked out with former African colonies of Belgium and France.

The United States had conditioned offers it made in tropical products on action by the Common Market.

The communiqué said the developed countries had declared their willingness to try to improve access for other products exported by developing countries such as handicrafts and hand-loomed fabrics.

Tonight's agreement was one of principle in which many of the details remain to be worked out. The results have to be codified and embodied in legal instruments. This could take weeks.

But there is no doubt now that the agreement will be ready for signature by President Johnson before June 30, the expiration date of the special White House negotiating powers under the Trade Expansion Act of 1962.

Nuisance duties—tariffs of 5 per cent or less—have been lopped off by the United States during the Kennedy round on many products traded with Canada. To a large extent this makes the United States and Canada one big free trade area.

Drivers carrying loads of Portland cement between Windsor, Ont., and Detroit now have to stop at the border, fill in all sorts of customs forms and pay a duty of 3 per cent. When the Kennedy round takes effect, this duty will vanish.

The Kennedy round could also smooth the transition if Britain successfully negotiates entry into the Common Market. It also could make Britain's negotiating task easier. If she is unsuccessful, she would still have the greater access to the community's markets provided by the tariff cutting. It was for all these reasons that the British had been among the strongest supporters of the Kennedy round.

One major aim of President Kennedy had been to put solid economic foundation under the Atlantic alliance. The Administration feared that the formation of trading blocs in Europe would slow down trade growth with the United States and, in the long run, damage political relations.

Throughout the tremendously complicated negotiations, Washington badly wanted agreement because of these political considerations. At the same time, however, the American negotiators had to strike what they considered a fair commercial bargain.

The major confrontation came with the Common Market, negotiating as a powerful economic unit. It was a confrontation of equals. In international trade, in fact, the Common Market ranks even higher than the United States.

There were some doubts in the earlier stages of the negotiations whether the Common Market would even be able to participate.

Before negotiating agricultural concessions, the Common Market had to come up with its own farm rules. This brought on a serious crisis, resolved after the Germans agreed to finance the bulk of the community's farm program, provided the French supported the Kennedy round.

* * *

CRITICAL MOMENT: THE URUGUAY ROUND

September 13, 1986

WARNINGS PRECEDE START OF WORLD TRADE TALKS

By CLYDE H. FARNSWORTH
Special to the New York Times

WASHINGTON, Sept. 12—The largest meeting of trade ministers in history will open in Uruguay on Monday to try to initiate the eighth major effort to liberalize trade since World War II.

The conference next week is intended to set the agenda in such fields as agriculture and services for the new trade round, which could take a half-dozen years or longer.

With the global trading stakes higher than ever before and the issues more bitterly divisive, participants are already warning, however, that the session may collapse.

France is resisting an American effort to eliminate all farm subsidies by the year 2000, and is already talking about what to do next year to pick up the pieces from any failure next week. Today, the French warned that, if they were not granted concessions by the big farming nations, the meeting could fail. The Reagan Administration, while maintaining that a failure will put crushing strains on the world trading system, is still threatening to walk out if it does not win approval of its priorities.

The Administration wants to show protectionist forces in Congress that the United States will gain more by opening foreign markets than closing American markets. But to convince Congress, the Administration has to show real opportunities for trade expansion. This is the reason for the push it is making to extend fair-trade rules to services, which employ 75 percent of all Americans and make up 57 percent of the gross national product.

Developing countries, struggling with debt payments and declining prices for the commodities they export, are deeply suspicious about any accommodations they might have to make. They are resisting American demands for international rules covering trade in services, such as banking, insurance and telecommunications, government investment policies that sometimes distort trade flows and counterfeiting and copyright piracy.

The weeklong meeting will bring together the 92 governments, or contracting parties, that are signatories to the General Agreement on Tariffs and Trade, a pact worked out 38 years ago to establish rules for world trade.

The governments, whose ministers will converge upon a vacated hotel gambling casino at Uruguay's beach resort of Punta del Este, sell each other four-fifths of the $2 trillion of annual global exchanges of goods and services.

After seven previous rounds, all within a GATT framework, world trade has grown eightfold. But it is now 13 years since the last effort was started. Called the Tokyo Round, it cut tariffs and made a stab at limiting nontariff barriers, such as government procurement codes, customs valuations, testing guidelines and rules covering subsidies. These are today's biggest restraints to trade growth.

The latest initiative comes as the world economy has been battered by the precipitous rise and fall of oil prices, the foreign debt crisis in Latin America and other developing countries, severe trade imbalances in the industrialized countries and, in recent months, the greatest threat of protectionism in the United States in the postwar era.

Dependent on Global Market

At the same time the United States is more dependent on the global market than at any time in its history. Last year imports and exports represented one-fifth of the nation's output of goods and services. A quarter century earlier they amounted to a tenth.

Reagan Administration officials call the new round a cornerstone of their international economic policy. Global trade expansion is seen as the key to renewed growth and resolution of both the debt crisis and the huge American trade deficit.

By failing to deal with services and such other sectors as investment and intellectual property, "GATT does not address many of the realities of modern trade," said Clayton K. Yeutter, the United States trade representative, who will head the large American delegation to the talks. But developing countries, led by Brazil and India, see the services initiative as a means of pushing American banks and insurance companies into their economies.

Yet the same third world countries are calling for a standstill on protectionist measures in the United States and other developed countries and a commitment to roll back existing protection. Henry R. Nau, formerly on President Reagan's National Security Council and now a professor at George Washington University, said standstill and rollback commitments might lead to the phasing out of American textile, steel and other restrictions.

The European Community and Japan, both of which favor extension of the negotiations to services, might make similar commitments.

Compromises Discussed

Even before the delegates begin to gather at Punta del Este, some compromises have been discussed. One is to swap a freeze by the United States on filing unfair trade cases for a date for completion of negotiations on services. The United States has initiated cases in recent months against Brazil, South Korea and other countries under Section 301 of the Trade Act of 1974. Under threats of import curbs both South Korea and Taiwan recently agreed to permit more American insurance companies to operate in their markets.

Senator Max Baucus, Democrat of Montana and an influential member of the Senate Finance Committee, said:

"There have to be trade-offs. I think we've got to be willing to discuss everything."

In agriculture, Mr. Yeutter has already indicated American willingness to put all its subsidies on the negotiating table. The United States and the European Community each spend $25 billion a year to support farm production. France, the biggest agricultural producer in the European Community, is willing to discuss agriculture but unwilling to commit to any phaseout of subsidies.

The aim of the GATT conference this week is to write a document that would serve as the guidelines for a new trade round. Forty-eight of the participants at a meeting last July in Geneva agreed on one draft, maintaining reservations on some of the language. But 10 developing countries—India, Brazil, Yugoslavia, Nigeria, Tanzania, Cuba, Nicaragua, Peru, Argentina and Egypt—wrote their own draft, which made no mention of services and other areas the United States was interested in.

No Mandate Seen

Those countries, which have become known as the Group of 10, argue that GATT has no mandate for negotiation in the new areas and that industrial countries should live up to their existing anti-protectionist commitments on trade before moving into new fields. Mr. Yeutter was referring to these countries when he said recently that a "small group of nations continues to hold the interests of the majority hostage to their objectives, which seem to me contrary to their own self-interest."

Although GATT is a relatively weak agency, with no enforcement powers or other sanctions, the United States has used it as the centerpiece of its trade policy for nearly four decades. To meet complaints by American companies about unfair foreign trade practices, another American goal in the talks is to strengthen GATT's machinery, especially its dispute settlement procedures.

Ironically, Congress, reluctant to cede authority over American trade policy, rejected a strong world trade organization when the issue was first taken up by the international community in 1947. GATT was not intended to be a trade organization, but only a specific trade agreement.

*   *   *

September 14, 1986

TALKS ON WORLD TRADE TO FOCUS ON PROTECTIONISM

By PETER T. KILBORN
Special to the New York Times

WASHINGTON, Sept. 13—A 92-nation trade conference that starts Monday in Uruguay will deal only with a symptom of the weak world economy—growing world protectionism—and not with the strains of economic disorder that have caused it, international economists say.

Economists say countries with ailing economies are using protectionism as a politically expedient adjustment to the slowest growth in two decades, to the large trade surpluses of Japan and West Germany, to the record United States budget deficit, to the heavy indebtedness of Latin American nations and to the collapse of many commodity prices.

Meeting Is Termed a Sideshow

The United States and other leading nations are trying to tackle these problems by other means and in other forums, with only modest success so far, and the meeting in Uruguay, which will bring together the 92 signers of the General Agreement on Tariffs and Trade, is a sideshow to those efforts, the economists say.

"Whatever legislation eventually results from this conference won't be concluded for six years—if you're lucky," said Robert Z. Lawrence, an economist at the Brookings Institution here.

But Douglas McMinn, Assistant Secretary for Economic Affairs at the State Department and a member of the American delegation in Punta del Este, says, "This is an important meeting. It comes at a critical moment for the world trading system and for the future of long-term world economic growth. But it's not going to solve our trade deficit."

Protectionism—the tariffs, quotas and more subtle practices that countries use to insulate workers and industries from foreign competition—is a political phenomenon that is widely blamed for producing the Great Depression of the 1930's. And Clayton K. Yeutter, the President's special trade representative and leader of the United States delegation to Punta del Este, warns that the recent growth of protectionism is pushing the world economy down that course again.

Behind the laggard growth, economists most often cite not protectionism but the persistent American budget deficits— the product of the Government's large 1981 tax cuts, President Reagan's refusal to raise taxes and Congress's refusal to cut spending.

Congress and the Administration have sought a solution in the Gramm-Rudman-Hollings law, which is intended to balance the budget by 1991, but the law has yet to reduce the deficits. "Our trade deficit," said a senior Administration economic official, "really resides in our budget deficit."

Many economists once saw some virtues in the budget deficits. They say they sparked the burst of economic growth in 1983 because the huge tax cuts left consumers and businesses with more money to spend. The spending spread overseas, helping foreign economies grow on the tide of their exports to the United States.

But as the deficits have persisted, economists now say they are keeping world interest rates higher than desirable, choking spending and investment everywhere and leaving debtor nations with less to spend on goods they import.

Other factors, too, have slowed the world economy and brought on the rise of protectionism. Economists point to volatile oil prices and the reluctance of West Germany and Japan to adopt policies to increase their imports.

They could do so, the United States argues, by following the American lead in cutting interest rates. But for months they have steadfastly refused, out of fear, the Germans say, of reviving inflation.

'Bad Economic Policies'

"All these problems started when the United States put bad economic policies into place and then persisted in continuing those policies," said Sven W. Arndt, an international economist at the American Enterprise Institute, a research organization here.

"One set of bad policies, those that led to the budget deficits, have led to other sets of bad policies, including protectionism," Mr. Arndt said. "Now in Punta del Este, we're sitting with mud on our face, in a glass house, telling other countries how to run their economic policies."

Protectionism is an indisputable evil in strict economic terms, if not always in social and political terms. By preventing foreign competition in their domestic markets, economists say, countries inhibit the virtues of competition—notably, keeping prices down and allowing a nation's industries to grow far beyond the limits imposed by their own domestic marketplace. A world economy of free trade invariably grows faster than one with restricted trade.

Many Trade Restraints Removed

GATT has proved an effective vehicle in reducing protectionism and stimulating economic growth through freer trade. Through seven "rounds" of trade negotiations, GATT has orchestrated the removal of many trade restraints, in particular the tariffs that countries impose on imports. Edward Hudgins, an economist at the Heritage Foundation, calculates that the United States has chopped to about 6 percent tariffs that often exceeded 50 percent of the value of imports in the 1930's.

But the extraordinary world economic growth that the GATT-led agreements produced in the 1960's has given way to a slow erosion of growth that has accompanied the adoption by many nations of non-tariff barriers to trade: subsidies to export industries, preferences to industries in procuring goods and services, licenses and design standards on imported goods and quotas on imports.

Countries also violate GATT's policy requiring that any restraints on imports be imposed on all countries. There has been a proliferation of cartel-like bilateral trade agreements favoring commerce between two nations to the exclusion of others.

The World Bank reports that partly as a result of new protectionist policies, the growth in world exports, which averaged 9.3 percent a year from 1965 to 1970, slowed to 2.6 percent from then on.

Protectionist Moves in U.S.

The United States, long one of the least protectionist countries, has lately resorted to a spate of measures, such as the decisions this summer to curb the imports of Japanese semiconductors and to subsidize exports of American grain to the Soviet Union.

It has taken such steps to cope with the political consequences of a huge trade deficit, which is expected to be $170 billion or more this year, and the associated depression in American agriculture and unemployment in manufacturing.

Economists say the Punta del Este conference could serve a useful, even vital, purpose if it fulfills its stated objective—preparing an agenda for countries to try to negotiate away the new trade restraints and to reduce protectionism in such sectors as agriculture and services, which have not been treated in previous rounds.

'A Pessimistic Picture'

But agreement on an agenda is itself in doubt. "There's a lot of truth to the general view of a pessimistic picture in Punta," said Alan Woods, a deputy to Mr. Yeutter, whose delegation also includes Commerce Secretary Malcolm Baldrige and Agriculture Secretary Richard E. Lyng.

Mr. Yeutter has said he would "walk away" from any agenda that excluded the topics he considers most essential to a new round of trade talks—the subsidies that all countries allow their farmers and the restraints that developing countries in particular impose on such service industries as banking. Even with an agenda, however, the negotiations to reduce protectionism will be long and hard. And the ensuing battles with national legislators to put the agreements to work are expected to last through the end of the decade and perhaps beyond.

* * *

September 15, 1986

3D WORLD STAKE AT TRADE TALKS

By ALAN RIDING
Special to the New York Times

RIO DE JANEIRO, Sept. 13—Disenchanted with past trade agreements and struggling with their own troubled economies, leading-third world countries seem determined to make their voices heard at the 92-nation trade conference that opens Monday in Punta del Este, a beach resort in Uruguay.

Although different stages of advancement and economic interests prevent the developing countries from acting as a single bloc, and they still account for a relatively small share of world trade, experts expect them to play an important role in the two issues that are threatening to divide the members of the General Agreement on Tariffs and Trade.

One group of 10 developing countries, led by Brazil and India, is adamantly opposed to American demands that trade in services be included in the next global round of trade talks. And on the subject of protectionism, Argentina and Uruguay are among the nations pressing a reluctant European Community to eliminate farm subsidies.

Decisions Usually by Consensus

Because meetings of GATT, which is based in Geneva, have traditionally made decisions by consensus rather than voting, continuing disagreement on these issues could paralyze the next trade round. On the other hand, the United States, France and several other countries have threatened to withdraw from GATT rather than yield on major points.

GATT, which was worked out 38 years ago to establish rules for world trade, has long been dominated by the problems and interests of the United States, Western Europe and Japan. But for the past several years, the changing nature of world commerce has increased the difficulty of reaching accords satisfactory to both industrialized and developing nations.

During a visit to Washington last week by Brazil's President Jose Sarney, for example, it was clear that Brazil's huge trade surplus with the United States, combined with its aggressive export strategy and its protection in its own domestic markets, were the main sources of tension between the two countries.

Nowhere have self-interests appeared so incompatible than over Washington's demand that "new issues," such as services, intellectual property and investment, be treated as forms of trade in the next global round of negotiations.

U.S. Competitive Advantage

With most of its work force now in the service sector, the United States wants to liberalize international trade in services in which it holds a competitive advantage. But the so-called Group of 10 developing countries believes a GATT agreement permitting the free flow of services would make it impossible for its members to develop their own capability in these areas.

They have also complained that, while a final draft document prepared by Colombia and Switzerland for the Punta del Este conference and endorsed by some 40 nations anticipates negotiation of "new issues" in the next trade round, it fails to define what falls into the category of services.

"All right, we're talking about banking and insurance, but do we mean just trade credits and export insurance or all banking and all insurance?" one Brazilian official asked. "And we've heard mention of engineering, consulting, telecommunications, publicity, auditing, tourism, architecture, medical services and more. I ask you, what have they in common?"

Nonetheless, the Group of 10, which is made up of Argentina, Nigeria, Yugoslavia, Tanzania, Cuba, Nicaragua, Peru and Egypt as well as Brazil and India, has in recent weeks moved away from its own alternative conference document, which omitted any reference to new issues and merely called for a new round of trade negotiations similar to the Tokyo Round of the 1970's.

Progress Toward Compromise

Instead, this Brazilian official said, since a preparatory meeting in Geneva in late July, progress has been made toward a compromise under which services and other new issues would be discussed simultaneously with a global trade round but in a parallel and clearly separate forum.

"All we're saying is that services should not be thrown a priori into GATT," the official added. "We're willing to be flexible. We've demonstrated that already. There are two small groups of countries with strong feelings at opposite poles. Since 1982, we've made lots of concessions. But the other side has made none."

Significantly, though, even on this issue, there is no unanimity among developing countries. American officials argue that a bloc of 26 nations has been gradually whittled down to the "hard-line" Group of 10. And at least 20 developing countries have accepted the document drawn up by Colombia and Switzerland, among them such important trading nations as Singapore and South Korea.

'Technical Minority'

The Group of 10, though, believes it is only in a "technical minority" and that a marginally different set of proposals could make what one official of a developing country described as the "silent majority" of nations abandon its apparent support for the United States.

The other issue that divides GATT, European Community agricultural subsidies, has placed the United States in the same camp as a number of developing countries such as Argentina and Uruguay, which are important exporters of wool, wheat and meat and therefore in competition with Europe.

Developing countries argue that current international trading rules and practices hurt them indiscriminately, as in the case of services. But they are not acting in concert on the issue of agricultural subsidies because countries that must import meat and grains—and do so from Europe—are happy to benefit from lower prices.

In recent weeks, part of Washington's strategy has been to argue that there is no automatic division between the industrialized and developing nations in GATT. American officials stress that broad agreement exists between the two groups on the need for action in such areas as safeguards, dispute settlement and tropical products.

Nonetheless, both the numerical strength of developing nations, and their new readiness to defend their interests, should insure that they will not go unnoticed this week.

* * *

March 29, 1988

NEW SUPPORT FOR STRONGER GATT

By PAUL LEWIS
Special to the New York Times

GENEVA, March 28—An international consensus is emerging in favor of strengthening the General Agreement on Tariffs and Trade, giving the organization that regulates world trade new authority to review national trade policies.

The proposed changes would give GATT status equivalent to that of the World Bank and the International Monetary Fund in economic policymaking, diplomats here said.

Moves to strengthen GATT are expected to form a central part of an interim package of liberalization measures on which the 80 or so countries hope to agree when they meet in

Montreal in December to review progress at the halfway point in what is known as the Uruguay Round of talks, these officials said.

Support in Europe

Plans to give GATT more power and a higher political profile received an important lift earlier this month at an informal meeting of some 30 trade ministers in West Germany, when the European Community countries came out strongly in favor of the ideas. The proposals have already won broad support from the United States, Canada, Japan and most other industrial and developing countries.

In the past, the United States has frequently pressed for greater GATT power to resolve trade disputes, but countries in Europe and elsewhere have generally been opposed.

The European Community's Commissioner for External Affairs, Willy de Clercq, told the meeting in West Germany that GATT would need greater political weight and prestige if it were to deal successfully with tensions in the international trading system and defeat protectionist tendencies.

Diplomats here think all GATT's members are interested in strengthening the free-trade system because they recognize that GATT is not succeeding in its mission of preventing protectionism and that additional trade restrictions could push the world back into recession.

The Origins of GATT

When the victorious Allied nations set up the I.M.F. and the World Bank to oversee the postwar economic order in 1944, they also planned to create an International Trade Organization with far-reaching powers to regulate commerce, investment and commodities.

But the United States Congress refused to join and the I.T.O. collapsed. Its replacement was the far less ambitious GATT, which in essence is only an agreement among some 96 countries to trade on the most favorable terms available.

While details remain to be negotiated, the Uruguay Round participants are broadly agreed that GATT should conduct regular examinations of member countries' trade policies to insure that these satisfy their free-trade obligations. When they do not, GATT would assess the countries the cost of their protectionist measures.

In addition, GATT plans to hold a big meeting of world trade ministers, probably every two years, to review the international trading situation. Governments hope these meetings will become as prestigious and well publicized as the annual meetings of finance ministers organized by the I.M.F. and the World Bank.

Proposal to Open Meetings

The European Community has suggested that GATT invite leading business people and farmers with an interest in freer world trade to these ministerial meetings as observers, in the same way that top bankers and development experts attend the annual ministerial meetings of the I.M.F. and the World Bank.

This, Mr. de Clercq argued at the West Germany meeting, would help GATT build a private-sector constituency in favor of free trade inside its member countries.

Finally, there are plans to create a new, smaller group of trade ministers from about 18 countries that would meet twice a year to review issues, resolve crises and give greater prominence and credibility to GATT.

The plan for GATT to examine members' trade policies on a regular basis parallels the annual reviews the I.M.F. makes of member countries' economic performance. The review panel would have no power to force changes on a country, but it would highlight international concern and publicize the cost of protectionist action, officials said.

Schedule for Reviews

The biggest traders—the United States, the European Community, Canada and Japan—would probably have their trade policies examined every two years. The next-most-important trading countries would be examined every four years and smaller GATT members would be checked every six years.

The 30 trade ministers who met in West Germany last week plan to reconvene in Pakistan this fall to prepare the package of interim measures they hope to adopt in Montreal in December, diplomats said.

* * *

December 12, 1988

FREER TRADE: NOT YET, MAYBE LATER

By CLYDE H. FARNSWORTH
Special to the New York Times

MONTREAL, Dec. 11—Although everyone went home empty-handed from a weeklong conference here to promote freer trade, global bargaining has begun that could mean more open markets in future years.

Each of the 96 participating governments, signatories of the General Agreement on Tariffs and Trade, sought more concessions than it would cede in the Uruguay Round negotiations to cut barriers in agricultural trade and in banking, construction and other services over the next two years—and generally to revamp the trading system.

But that is not unusual midway into a major trade liberalization effort. This one began at a Uruguayan beach resort in 1986.

Judging from the history of the seven earlier postwar "rounds," like the Kennedy Round of the 1960's and the Tokyo Round of the 1970's, the bargaining dynamic itself pushes nations to make additional concessions as the clock ticks. Otherwise, the whole effort collapses, and no one gets anything.

Should a Uruguay Round compact emerge, participating nations would gain economically through export-led growth of output and productivity. Experience from the past rounds shows that everyone gets a bigger piece of a bigger global pie.

Yet losses—employment and financial—arise in sectors hurt by the greater competition, perhaps steel or textiles in the United States, agriculture in Europe, investment services in Brazil.

The tradeoffs thus involve hard political choices within as well as among nations. Domestic winners and losers are sized up.

"Few countries will be able to liberalize, whether under bilateral or multilateral pressures, unless political leaders are supported by strong domestic interests that gain from such liberalization," said Henry R. Nau, a George Washington University political scientist, in "Domestic Trade Politics and the Uruguay Round," a new book.

For the United States, the European Community and Japan, tradeoffs could pit beleaguered clothing and steel industries, seeking further restrictions on imports from the third world, against robust banking, insurance and airline industries, pushing for third-world market openings.

Third World's Perspective

Mexico, India and South Korea could agree to stiffer codes for the protection of patents and other so-called intellectual property in return for greater mobility of labor-intensive services, including construction teams that wander around the world building bridges and dams.

To reassure third-world countries that they have something to gain from the round, developed countries offered to cut tariffs and other barriers on imports of tropical products, from bananas to jute. But the cuts are modest and, if carried out, unlikely to lead to any surges in exports. The European Community, for example, refused to cut a 20 percent duty on bananas, against zero duty by the United States. Cocoa tariffs would drop from 16 percent to 12 percent in the community and from five-tenths of 1 percent to four-tenths of 1 percent in the United States.

While exploring possible tradeoffs, governments are still chiefly engaged in a feeling-out process, testing each other on the big issues, like agriculture and patent protection, to see how much of each position is muscle and how much is flab.

Yet there were major risks. In the case of the United States and the European Community, the feeling-out now threatens to become a roughing-up as the two largest trading powers go at each other over American demands, unmitigated at Montreal, that all export subsidies and import barriers—politely called T.D.M.'s, for trade-distorting measures—be phased out early in the next century.

Brussels flatly refused to make any such commitment, fearing it would doom its Common Agriculture Policy, which has served as the glue of European integration.

It could be a cold winter on the Atlantic. Washington said that because Brussels seemed unwilling to reform agriculture, the United States had little choice but to step up warfare against community export subsidies.

"American farmers should not be asked to bear the burden of unfair competition, so I will work toward an export-oriented farm bill in 1990 unless the negotiations bring clear results

soon," said Patrick J. Leahy, chairman of the Senate Agriculture Committee and a Vermont Democrat, who participated in the Montreal ministerial meeting.

A Rigid Stand on U.S. Goods

Adding to the chill was word from Brussels representatives Friday that their ban on imports of hormone-treated meat from the United States would go into effect Jan. 1 as scheduled, meaning lost sales of $169 million a year for American exporters.

Washington is prepared to retaliate against such products from Europe as boneless beef, hams, canned tomatoes, instant coffee, fruit juice, pet food and sausage casings. Undeterred, Brussels has counter-retaliation plans against American honey, walnuts, hybrid corn seed, beet pulp and dried fruit.

The deadlock over agriculture sparked fury in other delegations, chiefly the Latin Americans', who had made concessions in services expecting to be rewarded in agriculture.

Led by Argentina and Brazil, the Latin Americans said that none of the agreements reached in Montreal would go into effect until the farm question was settled. So it went: no farm trade, no services, no nothing.

Summing up the linkages involved in these global talks, Bernardo Grinspun, Argentina's special representative for international economic negotiations, said, "We don't like to pay and have nothing to receive."

*   *   *

September 28, 1990

BANKERS CALL FOR RESCUE OF WORLD TRADE TALKS

By CLYDE H. FARNSWORTH
Special to The New York Times

WASHINGTON, Sept. 27—A conference of more than 150 nations closed here today with a call to rescue the Uruguay Round, the floundering multinational effort to break through global trade barriers.

Echoing comments by President Bush that the round is not just a trade issue but a global growth issue as well, the heads of the International Monetary Fund and the World Bank insisted that it must not be allowed to fail.

Scores of finance ministers and central bank governors, speaking at the 45th joint annual meeting of the organizations, both of which have sweeping responsibilities for the world economic system, made similar comments during the weeklong gathering.

Conable Backs More Aid

There was consensus that a failed Uruguay Round—like economic fallout from the Persian Gulf turmoil—represented a threat to general stability.

The gulf turmoil's repercussions were also debated today. Barber B. Conable Jr., the World Bank president, told reporters that should the crisis continue into the new year he would ask industrial countries and oil-producing states to support a significant new lending operation. It would work with a steering group of donor countries to get even more support to the countries hardest hit by the crisis.

President Bush announced to the gathering on Tuesday the formation of the Gulf Crisis Financial Coordination Group to coordinate the flow of billions of dollars of aid that has already been pledged.

Moscow Would Be Welcome

The conference also signaled to the Soviet Union that once it had embarked on its new plan for market-oriented reforms, Moscow would be welcome to the economic club. Soviet representatives here said their government would apply for membership shortly.

On world trade, there was general agreement that the international system was at a critical juncture with its future hinging on the outcome of the Uruguay Round negotiations, begun four years ago at a windy Uruguayan beach resort and scheduled to end at a Brussels conference in mid-December.

But the gap is still so wide on so many key issues that many fear the effort will fail. Committees representing the more than 100 participating nations are bargaining over tariff reductions, liberalization of trade in agriculture, a code of conduct for trade in financial, construction, tourism and other services, improved copyright and patent protection, better ways for settling trade disputes, rules covering trade-related investment practices and other trade issues.

Broadest of Trade Rounds

It is the broadest of a series of postwar negotiating rounds that have succeeded in expanding commerce among nations, their economic output and their living standards over the past 45 years.

Washington is hoping for concessions in agriculture, services and intellectual property protection, like patents and copyrights, which could help American farmers and industry improve exports by billions of dollars.

Yet as part of any bargain Washington will have to offer greater access by foreigners to the American market, probably in such politically sensitive sectors as textiles, dairy, sugar and shipping.

Yet the negotiations are touching sensitive political chords in all countries. The most serious current conflict is between Washington and the European Community and relates to liberalization of farm trade.

The Brussels-based community, with a farm population much larger than the United States, is deeply divided over how far to go to meet the Bush Administration's demands that farm protection, including export subsidies and internal price supports, be virtually ended by the year 2000.

Member nations with politically robust farm constituencies, like Ireland, France and Germany, are resisting market-opening concessions.

Little progress has been made on services either. Arthur Dunkel, director general of the General Agreement on Tariffs and Trade, said there was not even a framework for multilateral rules in services and warned that time is growing "dramatically short."

His Geneva-based organization oversees the trading system and serves as the negotiating forum.

Mr. Conable, the World Bank president, said today that "failure in the negotiations would considerably increase the difficulties we all face, not the least reducing poverty. I call again on the GATT participants to bury their differences for the global good."

A coalition of more than 100 American companies also came out today in strong support of the round, calling on American negotiators to press the so-called zero tariff option. This is an approach under which the United States would eliminate its already low tariffs in a number of sectors in which it is highly competitive, if other countries do the same.

The Zero Tariff Coalition includes American producers of aluminum, beer, construction equipment, copper, diesel engines, furniture, gas turbine engines, lead, lift trucks, paper, semiconductors, toys, wood products and zinc.

*   *   *

November 16, 1990

HOW TO SAVE THE TRADE TALKS

There is new hope that the Uruguay Round of international trade talks, currently stalled by protectionist bickering, will finally pick up speed toward resolution. The White House announced this week that President Bush and his European counterparts had agreed to take charge of the negotiations. The elements of a deal are clear. All that's missing is leadership.

The talks are scheduled to end early next month. Yet there is no agreement in view, primarily because of shortsighted decisions by the industrialized countries.

At the core of the impasse is the attempt by Western leaders to protect the economic privileges of politically powerful domestic industries at the expense of the vast majority of their own citizens. The European Community persists in protecting a few million family farmers, the U.S. proposes to exempt telecommunications, aviation and shipping; Japan won't agree to import a grain of rice. And the industrialized powers have yet to make major concessions on protectionist textile policies.

The key stalemate is over European farm policy. To protect its farmers, the Community keeps food prices high, generating tremendous surpluses that it then dumps on foreign markets at subsidized prices. The policy costs European taxpayers $100 billion a year, and devastates competing farmers in food-exporting countries.

Third-world food exporters are demanding that Europe open up its markets to imports of food and textiles before they agree to rules governing trade in services and intellectual property.

Last week the Europeans offered to cut farm supports by about 15 percent from current levels. That wouldn't provide much help, especially combined with other provisions that would allow Europe to preserve its export subsidies and even raise tariffs on selected products.

The U.S. has also been obstinate. It insists on exempting some key industries from trade talks even though there is nothing to lose by keeping them on the negotiating table. The negotiators are discussing a set of basic principles—such as the obligation for each country to treat domestic and foreign service companies alike—that the U.S. fully supports. Deciding how to apply these principles to individual sectors won't be negotiated until later, and the U.S. will be able to veto any rule it doesn't like.

Liberalized trade could add trillions to economies around the globe over the next 10 years, more than $1 trillion in the U.S. alone. But it won't happen unless Mr. Bush and European leaders make it happen.

Europe must agree to lower export subsidies and forsake raising any other trade barriers. The U.S. must withdraw its proposal to exempt specific service sectors. And the industrialized nations must agree to phase out protectionist textile agreements.

*   *   *

November 30, 1990

CLASH OF FREE TRADE AND NATIONAL INTEREST

By CLYDE H. FARNSWORTH
Special to The New York Times

WASHINGTON, Nov. 29—Free trade is wonderful, most nations agree—except for those instances where it impinges on some powerful national interest.

The Japanese bar rice imports, for instance, to protect the politically influential rice farmers. The United States politely insisted that the Japanese voluntarily limit the number of cars they ship to the American market. The Europeans erect walls against Japanese cars, American semiconductors and American pork and beef.

Now, as ministers from more than 100 governments gather in Brussels next week for trade talks, such exceptions are seen to be strangling the rule of free trade.

And in recent years, some of the 105 nations that belong to the General Agreement on Tariffs and Trade, the world body that oversees trade, have increasingly been using safeguards, escape clauses and anti-dumping measures in GATT rules to create barriers to free trade.

Negotiators at the talks next week—known as the Uruguay Round because the talks began in Uruguay four years ago—will try to write rules that set clear, objective procedures to prevent countries from building such barriers.

The backbone of GATT, which was drafted in 1947, is unconditional most-favored-nation treatment. That means that any reduction of tariffs or other trade concession made by one government to another is automatically extended on a nondiscriminatory basis to all governments belonging to GATT.

In earlier rounds of negotiations during the post World War II era, GATT nations have managed to reduce tariffs by 75 percent, greatly increasing world trade. But the surge of imports has brought joblessness in some areas and other domestic problems. The protectionist exceptions to the rules were intended to provide nations with a means to address such problems—in the short term.

One such step that has become widely used is anti-dumping measures—duties that a government imposes when it finds that an imported product is sold for less abroad than in the nation where it is produced. This is regarded as unfair pricing, a way of building market share in foreign markets.

The biggest cases in the United States have involved steel from Europe and textiles from the Far East. In Europe, dumping charges have been levied chiefly against Japanese consumer electronics.

'Protectionist Measure of Choice'

The U.S. Council for International Business, the American affiliate of the International Chamber of Commerce, has found that in the last decade, the United States, the European Community, Canada and Australia have brought 800 dumping cases, more than half of which have led to the imposition of penalty duties.

"There is no question in my view," said Robert J. Morris, the council's senior vice president, "that anti-dumping actions have become the protectionist measure of choice."

As part of the process of forging a single European market by 1992, the European Community wants to apply restraints selectively against imports of Japanese cars and other consumer products.

But the United States and many third-world nations argue that such selective restraints open the door for collusion.

On the issue of dumping, however, the United States and the European Community are on the same side. Under pressure from domestic industries, they have submitted proposals that would make it easier to win dumping penalties.

Japan and other Asian exporters and most third-world countries, oppose such steps.

Used Against West

But some Asian nations, including South Korea, are pressing their own anti-dumping actions against Western companies.

Earlier this year, E. I. du Pont de Nemours & Company and the Hoechst Celanese Corporation complained to the International Trade Commission, a Federal agency that investigates trade petitions, that South Korean chemical companies were dumping polyethylene terephthalate, a resin used to manufacture soda bottles, at prices below "fair value" in the United States market.

Now the South Korean Government has begun an investigation of Du Pont and Hoechst Celanese to determine whether they are selling below "fair value" the chemical substance polyacetal, used to make plastic goods, in the South Korean market. The South Koreans are also investigating a Japanese company, Asahi Chemicals, on the same grounds.

* * *

April 26, 1991

TRADE BLOC WAR? CONCERN GROWS

By LEONARD SILK

Is the world economy headed for a split into three warring trade blocs—Europe, North America and East Asia?

"Not if we succeed in the Uruguay Round," said Jacques Delors, president of the European Commission, during a discussion in New York this week. Named for the country where the current trade negotiations under the General Agreement on Tariffs and Trade began in 1986, the Uruguay Round broke down in December over Europe's refusal to yield to American demands for drastic cuts in farm subsidies.

Efforts to get the trade talks back on track are going on. But the most formidable obstacle to their success—European resistance to lower subsidies—has not been removed.

Mr. Delors seeks to blame the United States for this. He said he had told President Bush that if the United States continued its "negative" approach, in an attempt to paint the European Community as "the bad guy of the world," the talks would fail. "Bush understands that," Mr. Delors said. "We cannot negotiate under these circumstances."

The Bush Administration regards this as evasion. It denies that it has taken an antagonistic line toward Europe on trade. The United States trade representative, Carla A. Hills, "has said nothing mean," said her spokesman, Timothy O'Leary. He said Mr. Delors was "trying to divert attention from the real issue—outrageously high European agricultural subsidies."

Do the American negotiators see any sign that the Europeans are willing to change their position? "There's nothing yet," Mr. O'Leary said. And what about the future? "It will depend on the mood," he said.

But Mr. Delors said he thought there was "a better mood" ahead for discussing agriculture. "I share the fears of many economists and politicians about a world divided into many blocs," he said.

This view represents a growing awareness that the United States is moving to establish its own regional trade bloc and is prepared to take unilateral action against countries that it deems to be discriminating against American exports.

Following the free-trade agreement with Canada, the Bush Administration is moving aggressively to negotiate a wide-ranging free-trade agreement with Mexico. The Administration faces opposition from labor and environmental groups but is being strongly supported by a coalition of business interests favoring the pact and supporting the Administration's request for "fast track" negotiating authority, which requires that trade agreements be voted up or down by Congress without amendment.

Two motions are now before Congress to end that fast-track authority. But President Bush intends to submit a plan to Congress within the next week to protect workers' rights and the environment to safeguard the Mexican agreement and fast-track bargaining authority. The Administration thinks it has too much at stake to let the Mexican agreement fail.

It believes that the deal is the key to stronger economic growth on both sides of the border. And if the Mexican deal goes through, the Administration means to negotiate a similar free-trade arrangement with Chile and later with other Latin American countries.

Skeptics wonder whether the effort to build an American regional bloc makes sense. Prof. Jagdish Bhagwati of Columbia University calls American regionalism "an empty threat" to the European Community.

In a forthcoming article in Foreign Affairs, he declares: "It is not credible that the United States would shoot itself in the foot, and indeed higher up, by sidetracking her energies and her trade to a region whose fragile democracies, inflations, debts and slow growth rates offer a far less attractive market than the burgeoning Far East and the European Community, both of which are even now more substantial markets for American exports. If the United States turns foolishly away from the world to her own backyard, the European Community's likely reaction would be: fine, get buried in it."

That may be an overstatement. There is full awareness, both here and abroad, how vital to the economic growth of every country expanding world trade has been, and what a threat to future growth would be posed by a splitting off of the United States, Europe and East Asia into hostile regional trading blocs.

If the Uruguay Round fails, the largest German bank, the Deutsche Bank, states in its Bulletin, "the current trend toward inward-looking trading blocs will probably accelerate, and trade conflicts will multiply."

No country wants that outcome, knowing that it could breed recession or depression. Regionalism, based on internal free-trade principles, can contribute to the welfare of the Americas, Europe and East Asia, but only if each region is open to other regions and nations.

* * *

November 12, 1992

A HOPEFUL OUTLOOK ON GATT

Special to The New York Times

GENEVA, Nov. 11—After a series of disappointments, including two occasions this year on which he was told a deal had been made only to find it had not, Arthur Dunkel, the man overseeing crucial world trade talks, says he believes an accord can be reached within the next month.

"We have reached rock bottom, and now there is a chance to bring the Uruguay Round back at full speed in the next few weeks," Mr. Dunkel, the Secretary General of the General

Agreement on Tariffs and Trade, said today. "Everyone knows that if we do not succeed in a very short time, it will be a very long time before we have another opportunity."

The Uruguay Round is the name given to the long-stalled six-year-old GATT trade talks involving 108 nations. A successful resolution could stir the world economy from its long downturn and eventually add about $100 billion to output. The negotiations have been blocked mainly by a festering dispute between the United States and France over agricultural subsidies.

France Signals Moderation

Mr. Dunkel, a mild-mannered 60-year-old Swiss diplomat, indicated that his optimism stemmed from a conviction that Germany was determined to secure an accord by the end of the year and from signs that France was moderating its previously rigid stand.

Mr. Dunkel and officials close to him disclosed that the German Government had wanted a trade accord at the Munich world economic summit meeting in July. But Chancellor Helmut Kohl was sensitive to French concerns, repeatedly expressed in Munich, that a GATT agreement angering the country's large farming sector might tilt the French referendum in September on European unity to a vote of rejection. In fact, France voted narrowly in favor of European integration.

Thus, an understanding emerged in Munich that after the French referendum on Sept. 18, a world trade agreement would be urgently sought, and the final communiqué spoke of a year-end deadline.

"I know personally that Mr. Kohl does not want his summit added to those which failed to come through on their commitments in this respect," Mr. Dunkel said. Previous world economic summit meetings have set deadlines for the trade talks that have not been met.

Because of its close alliance with France, Germany is the one country in Europe with the power to influence the French Government. Mr. Dunkel noted that the French President, Francois Mitterrand, had spoken this week of the "paramount importance" of a world trade agreement—apparently indicating a shift in tone.

Mr. Dunkel spoke in his wood-paneled office at GATT headquarters here, the day after he received a mandate from ambassadors to the trade organization to visit Brussels and Washington in a bid to encourage an accord.

His talks will begin on Thursday in Brussels, where he will meet with the European Community's Agriculture Commissioner, Ray MacSharry, and its External Relations Commissioner, Frans Andriessen, the European Community announced today. Mr. Dunkel will meet on Monday in Washington with Carla A. Hills, the United States trade representative, and Edward R. Madigan, the Agriculture Secretary.

Hard to Get Figures

Illustrating the complexity of the trade talks, Mr. Dunkel said it was much harder to get clear figures on agriculture than in other areas of diplomacy like arms negotiations.

For example, on the dispute over European subsidies for oilseeds, which led Washington this month to threaten to impose 200 percent tariffs on some European goods on Dec. 5, the European Community has offered to take 15 percent of the land producing the seeds out of cultivation next year and said this should reduce production to about 9.5 million tons from last year's 11 million.

"But," Mr. Dunkel said, "then you can get a U.S. agricultural expert saying that with fertilizers and pesticides, you can actually increase oilseed production even as you take land out of cultivation." The dispute, he said, then switches to means of verifying and enforcing a reduction.

U.S. Wants Enforceable Pact

"The Europeans say, 'If there's a problem, we'll sort it out,' " Mr. Dunkel said. "But the Americans say: 'No way. We know it takes at least three years to sort anything out with you. We need an enforceable agreement.' "

Such is the difficulty of the discussions, one GATT official said, that on two occasions this year, Mr. Dunkel was told by negotiators that an agreement had been reached in the world trade talks, which are separate from but linked to the oilseed dispute. But when the proposed deal went to government leaders, it collapsed.

Despite these difficulties, Mr. Dunkel said, a combination of the worsening world economic situation, the growing importance of trade and increasing political impatience could now bring a solution.

"The end of the cold war means that economics are the ground on which international competition and cooperation take place," he said. "That's why opening the world's trading system and avoiding conflict is vital."

*   *   *

February 4, 1993

HEAD OFF A TRADE WAR

By LEONARD SILK

Fears are spreading that the Clinton Administration is moving toward a trade policy so aggressive as to unleash protectionism and a trade war among the major industrial countries. During the campaign, Mr. Clinton was ambiguous about what trade policy he would pursue. On one side, he proclaimed support for an open world economy based on free-trade principles; on the other, he courted business and labor by promising a highly aggressive campaign against foreign countries and companies accused of wiping out American jobs.

Mr. Clinton and his aides now seem to have come down on the aggressive side. The Administration has threatened to block sales to the Government of European telecommunications and power-generation equipment and a wide array of services, charging that the European Community has run a buy-Europe policy against American products. His Trade Representative, Mickey Kantor, declared that the U.S. might withdraw from the government-procurement code of the General Agreement on Tariffs and Trade.

Has Mr. Clinton crossed the Rubicon—or is this just a get-tough threat to get the Europeans and Japanese back to serious bargaining on measures to open markets? Some economists who advised him during the campaign say they are not sure if he is bluffing. But Mr. Clinton's advisers, including those in the Administration, are split into two camps: one urging essentially free trade, the other managed trade, aimed at opening markets abroad with threats of retaliation if foreign governments will not yield. The core of managed trade would be commitments by nations to accept certain proportions of imports in their domestic markets.

Laura D'Andrea Tyson, new chairman of the Council of Economic Advisers, contends that managed trade, not free trade, is the only viable alternative in the real world to protectionism.

But while Mr. Clinton stays remarkably silent on the trade issue, many American industries are seizing what they see as an opportunity to push on an open door for Federal protection or trade relief. Pressures are rising from producers of steel, autos, oil, semiconductors, weapons, movies, textiles and apparel.

Mr. Clinton is running out of time to make up his mind. Producers' demands will drive him to protectionism, which will spread as foreign countries retaliate, as they have already started to do. If he intends to hold to his general endorsement of an open world trade policy, he must act now to block protectionist demands.

How can he do so? By declaring that he will press to bring the Uruguay Round talks of GATT to a successful end, and then moving to strengthen GATT as an instrument for freer trade and investment for all nations.

Protectionism feeds on world recession, sluggish growth and unemployment. Mr. Clinton must go for growth, abroad as well as at home. This means acting immediately to gain the cooperation, not the hostility that will stem from a beggar-my-neighbor trade policy, of U.S. trading partners, including Japan, Germany, Britain, France, Italy, Canada and Mexico.

Expansion by the industrial countries is crucial to nourish growth in the rest of the world—and provide markets and resources to prevent the economic and political disasters threatening the third world and ex-Soviet empire. Flirting with protectionism is flirting with a world catastrophe.

The U.S. should take the lead in building a more open global economic system. The next and more difficult stage will require that other nations address the internal regulations, monopolistic practices and structural differences that are now the principal impediments to the expansion of trade and investment.

But if others, Japan and Germany most of all, do not lend greater support to a U.S. effort to strengthen the world trading system, protectionist pressures will intensify and the only alternative may be a highly inefficient form of managed trade, in which national power rather than economic choice will determine, and distort, trade—to the harm of consumers and producers everywhere.

Leonard Silk is a former economics columnist of The New York Times.

*   *   *

December 3, 1993

WHAT'S WHAT IN THE WORLD TRADE TALKS

By KEITH BRADSHER

The Overview

The United States is negotiating with 115 other nations to broadly rewrite the free trade rules of the General Agreement on Tariffs and Trade, which have governed most international trade for 45 years. GATT was created in 1948 with the aim of expanding economic activity by eliminating tariffs and other protectionist barriers. Trade ministers have successfully completed seven previous rounds of talks to broaden the original agreement.

The current negotiations began seven years ago in Punta del Este, Uruguay, leading negotiators and commentators to call it the Uruguay Round. Its main goal is to broaden the rules to cover trade in agriculture and in services like tourism, insurance and telecommunications. Negotiators are also trying to reduce or eliminate many tariffs.

After years of obstacles, there is a growing sense that the trade talks may finally be headed for a conclusion. They have dragged on so long mainly because of disputes between the United States and Europeans over agricultural subsidies. This summer, Congress gave President Clinton special negotiating authority to clinch a deal by Dec. 15. If agreement cannot be reached by then, the Administration will have to seek Congressional permission for another extension, which could prove politically ticklish because of the recent fight over the North American Free Trade Agreement.

In July, Peter Sutherland of Ireland took over as GATT's Director General. In a few months, he has succeeded in getting the world's governments to regard Dec. 15 as a true, pressing deadline. And Mr. Sutherland has warned that if the talks failed again, national leaders must face the blame for harming the global economy.

What Is At Stake

The Organization for Economic Cooperation and Development, a Paris-based consortium of 24 of the more prosperous nations, estimates that a successful completion of the trade talks would mean about $270 billion more in annual trade by the year 2002. The extra economic output would come from the more efficient use of labor, capital and other resources.

Some American economists, industry groups and labor unions say that the draft version of an accord now being negotiated will channel most of the benefits to other countries, at least in the short run, and some economists question whether the overall gains have been overstated.

But most economists believe that over the course of years, free trade allows each country to specialize in products that it can make most efficiently, trading them for products made more efficiently elsewhere.

The Basics

TARIFFS

These are taxes that Governments collect on imports from other countries. The overall goal of the Uruguay Round is to reduce average tariffs by at least one-third. Previous GATT negotiations have cut average tariffs on manufactured goods to 5 percent from 40 percent in the late 1940's. While other nations' tariffs can be quite high, the average American tariff on manufactured imports is 4 percent. Japan, Canada, the United States and the European Community agreed in Tokyo in July to eliminate tariffs entirely on pharmaceuticals, construction equipment, medical equipment, some furniture, and whisky and beer. In addition, it is proposed that agricultural tariffs be reduced by 36 percent in industrial nations and 24 percent in developing nations. Agricultural tariffs vary widely because they are often charged by the penny per kilogram or liter, rather than as a percentage of the product's value.

QUOTAS

These are limits on the quantity of imports, like American limits on the number of tons of imported peanuts. Previous talks have eliminated most manufacturing quotas except for textiles and finished apparel. The Uruguay Round would eliminate this exception and also require countries to replace their extensive quotas or bans on farm imports with tariffs that provide comparable protection. Quotas are pervasive in international farm trade, and the United States imposes them on dairy products, peanuts and sugar. Some of the new tariffs could start as high as several hundred percent, and would be gradually reduced.

INTELLECTUAL PROPERTY

The agreement, as it now stands, requires that all countries protect patents, copyrights, trade secrets and trademarks, including developing countries, where pirated computer programs, record albums, videocassettes and prescription drugs have been commonly available for years. But Western pharmaceutical manufacturers are angry that the proposed protections will come too slowly to benefit many companies doing business now. Indeed, some drugs will not receive full patent protection in developing countries for 20 years.

A NEW TRADE ORGANIZATION

The current text would create an institution in Geneva to enforce GATT's free trade rules. The new institution would be much more powerful than the GATT Secretariat is now, having the power to assess trade penalties against countries by a vote of two-thirds or three-quarters of the nations, whereas the Secretariat can act only when the members unan-

imously vote to do so—something that is rare. The Clinton Administration and many Rust Belt industries like steel oppose this new organization because it could prevent American companies from seeking Commerce Department penalties on foreign industries that sell their goods in the United States with subsidies, or at unfairly low prices.

INVESTMENT

The proposed text would ban the widespread practice of requiring high local content in some products like cars and of requiring factories to export as much as they import. The aim of that practice is to preserve local jobs and discourage imports. The proposed agreement would limit the ability of countries to favor domestically owned factories at the expense of foreign-owned ones.

TAXATION

The agreement would bar countries from imposing higher tax rates on foreign companies than on domestic ones. The United States is objecting to this rule, which would break a long American practice of individual tax agreements with more than 50 nations. These two-country deals also bar tax discrimination against foreign companies and individuals. But other countries are worried that American efforts to crack down on tax evasion by foreign companies may prove discriminatory, and they are pushing for GATT protection.

MAJOR INDUSTRIES AFFECTED BY THE TALKS

Agriculture. The big dispute holding up the talks for the last three years has been a quarrel between the United States and the European Community over farm subsidies. Last year, the United States and the Europeans agreed to reduce the tonnage of subsidized grain exports by 21 percent, and to limit other farm subsidies. But France, Europe's biggest agricultural exporter, wants the subsidy deal renegotiated. Yesterday, in negotiations in Brussels, the United States tentatively agreed to allow the Europeans to subsidize more grain exports over the next six years than previously planned. In exchange, the Europeans tentatively agreed to convert some of their quotas on farm imports into low tariffs, as Washington demands.

Automobiles. Over the years, the United States and the European Community have each forced Japan to accept limits on its auto exports. The current agreement text would virtually ban these restrictions. Each country would only be allowed one such export limit on any industry, and Detroit car makers worry that they might not get the exemption. The Big Three also worry about clauses in the text that would make it harder to prove that foreign cars were being sold at unfairly low prices in the United States.

Financial services companies. In theory, commercial and investment banks, insurance companies and issuers of travelers checks would all be allowed to do business around the world, subject only to restrictions aimed at protecting depositors and insurance-policy holders. But few developing countries have actually committed themselves to opening their markets, angering American financial-services companies.

The Clinton Administration has antagonized some countries by saying that it will not guarantee the continued openness of the American market except in the cases of countries that considerably open their own markets.

Movies, TV programs and music recordings. The European Community now allows its 12 members to restrict the distribution of foreign films, television programs and recordings in an effort to protect the national culture of each country. Several European countries, notably France, have imposed quotas on these imports. Hollywood wants the quotas eliminated. European Community officials are pushing a compromise that would maintain existing quotas at current levels and not allow new ones.

Steel. Some European government subsidies to uncompetitive steelmakers would be banned. But no agreement has been reached yet on whether to ban many other subsidies, and whether to allow penalties like steeper tariffs on countries that continue banned subsidies.

Textiles and apparel. The current text would phase out textile and apparel quotas over 10 years, but the Clinton Administration is trying to extend this to 15 years. The quotas would then be replaced by less-restrictive tariffs.

*　*　*

December 15, 1993

HOW FREE TRADE PROMPTS GROWTH: A PRIMER

By PETER PASSELL

Free trade means growth. Free trade means growth. Free trade means growth. Just say it 50 more times and all doubts will melt away.

Those who dutifully followed the debate over the North American Free Trade Agreement and are now struggling to figure out what the General Agreement on Tariffs and Trade has to do with the price of peas in Peoria may be excused for a dash of skepticism about a link that is more often asserted than explained. It is, in fact, one of the most widely held yet most difficult to prove ideas in economics.

In the end, the nearly universal conviction that open trade drives global prosperity rests more on observation than on well-developed theory: "We all noticed that the countries doing well were exporting like crazy," said Stanley Fischer, the World Bank's former chief economist.

College instructors love to illustrate the British economist David Ricardo's insight about the gains from free trade with a story about Woodrow Wilson. President Wilson, they say, could type faster than his secretary. But it made sense to leave the White House correspondence to others so he could concentrate on making the world safe for democracy and other higher-productivity endeavors.

A Victorian Example

By this same rule of "comparative advantage," it made economic sense for Victorian England to break the political influence of its cosseted farmers by opening its borders to wheat from central Europe and North America. That allowed entrepreneurs to focus more capital and labor on manufacturing, where it could (and did) make Britain the richest country on earth.

These gains from economic specialization are still nothing to sneeze at. The World Bank estimates that in 1985 free trade in dairy foods would have lowered average prices by two-thirds and doubled global output. All told, free trade in grain, meat, milk and sugar would have added $40 billion to world income—mostly by shifting production away from Western Europe and toward lower cost producers.

And the Organization for Economic Cooperation and Development calculates that the combination of reduced tariffs and more generous import quotas penciled into the new GATT accord would increase world income by $270 billion annually by the turn of the century.

Big as these numbers are, though, they are modest compared with the total world output, which will probably exceed $30 trillion a decade hence. And even if one imagined free trade nirvana in which shirts sewn in Jakarta could be sold as freely in Seattle as shirts made on Seventh Avenue, the direct impact of the resulting global specialization of production would not be overwhelming.

Gary Hufbauer and Tim Elliott of the Institute for International Economics in Washington estimate that free trade would add about 1 percent to the average American's income.

Why, then, is Sebastian Edwards, a development specialist at the University of California at Los Angeles, convinced that "free trade is the cornerstone to modern economic systems?" Because it does not take an econometrician to tell which way the winds of prosperity have been blowing.

In the 1890's, Argentina had roughly the same income per person as the United States and seemed as well endowed with resources, both human and physical. A century of protectionism, though, left Argentina with hundreds of inefficient industries serving only local markets and a living standard roughly a third as high as that of the colossus to the north.

Asian Comparisons

Or compare the economies of Asia that stumbled into the 1960's in more or less wretched condition. Those that focused on the expansion of trade (Hong Kong, Taiwan, Singapore, South Korea, Thailand, Malaysia) have done very well. Those that tried to develop by pushing for self-sufficiency (India, Vietnam, Myanmar, North Korea) have done very badly. And those that came late to the open trade game but are now big players (Indonesia, China) seem to be on their way to a chicken in every wok.

In the end such comparisons may be the only hard evidence that economists have. But it has not stopped them from speculation about the inner workings of the machinery translating trade into growth.

The puckish explanation, suggests Paul Krugman of the Massachusetts Institute of Technology, is that the relationship is, in fact, specious, that cause has been confused with effect.

Countries ready to grow may be more inclined to gravitate toward open trade. More specifically, the cultural values that seem to underpin growth—thrift, rule of law, respect for property rights, fiscal discipline—may also create political systems that are better at defending the interests of efficient, export-minded producers against those of groups demanding a free economic ride.

Certainly the view of the overwhelming majority of economists, though, is that trade kindles growth. "Trade is a vehicle for technology transfer," Mr. Fischer points out, flashing what many see as the free traders' trump card. The successful Asian economies that protect local producers of consumer goods, he notes, have been careful to permit easy access to modern foreign equipment and materials.

What's more, openness to imports generally pays greater dividends than access to faster computers and tougher plastics. It also offers the chance to "learn by looking," suggests Mr. Edwards—"to be exposed to foreign ideas on a massive basis."

Trade is also a source of competition for would-be local monopolists, keeping prices down and disciplining the locals to reduce waste. And it can have a critical impact on competition out in less obvious ways. "Without the Japanese to lead the way on quality control and fit and finish," argues Robert Crandall of the Brookings Institution, it is hard to imagine Detroit would have pulled up its socks.

The 'British Disease'

Mancur Olson, the director of the Center on Institutional Reform and the Informal Sector at the University of Maryland, offers another connection between trade and competition-spurred growth. In every economy special interests are organizing to slow change, he suggests, creating sinecures for themselves and generally preventing boat-rocking innovation. This, he believes, goes a long way toward explaining the failure of many poor countries to grow and the tendency of industrialized countries to catch what has come to be known as "the British disease."

But economic systems can be made more resistant to the infection by increasing the number of actors—companies, unions, property owners—who must be organized and kept in line in order to stifle competition. "The smaller the economy," Mr. Mancur reasons, "the greater the likelihood of successful collusion."

Thus, he explains, expanding the economic borders of economies helps, as in the case of the European Community or the North American Free Trade Agreement, "But global free trade helps even more."

* * *

December 15, 1993

TRADE ACCORD DRAWS A MIX OF REVIEWS

By THOMAS J. LUECK

The trade agreement between the United States and the European Community drew mixed reviews from some big companies yesterday.

Such companies have said throughout the negotiations for a worldwide trade accord that the provisions to protect intellectual property and eliminate barriers on foreign investment could be more beneficial to them than reduced tariffs.

But at least one of the provisions for intellectual property was still under negotiation yesterday, as countries outside the United States and Europe prepared to vote on a worldwide General Agreement on Tariffs and Trade.

At the International Business Machines Corporation, which had lobbied for passage of the GATT treaty, "the most important thing is the extension of the treaty beyond tariffs," said Mark A. Holcomb, a spokesman for the company in Washington.

He said intellectual property rights, like patents and copyright protection for American goods overseas, were crucial for I.B.M. because the company had been losing $1 billion a year to the piracy of its computer software in foreign countries.

Protection Guarantees

Under the agreement, all signatories to the treaty would agree to guarantee the protection of software rights for 50 years after the software was first marketed within their borders, in much the same way that copyright laws protect literature.

Mr. Holcomb also said he supported the elimination of the strict rules on investment by foreign countries. In some of the countries in the treaty, "the restrictions on investment are now so onerous that they represent de facto trade barriers," he said.

Pharmaceutical manufacturers, however, said they were disappointed with the agreement. "Our reaction is mixed at best," said Lou Clemente, senior vice president for corporate affairs at Pfizer Inc.

The chief complaint of drug makers is a provision in the treaty that would give foreign governments 10 years to enact patent protection for pharmaceuticals. In Brazil, Argentina and other developing countries, already big markets for American drugs, the 10-year lag "is going to be a severe disincentive for further investment," he said.

* * *

December 16, 1993

GATT TALKS END IN JOY AND RELIEF

By ROGER COHEN
Special to The New York Times

GENEVA, Dec. 15—A small wooden gavel came down on a table here today, signaling, with a sharp tap, the

About 40 Belgian farmers yesterday protested the accord reached under the General Agreement on Tariffs and Trade, which they fear will threaten their livelihoods. The farmers set fire to a tractor during the demonstration outside the headquarters of the European Community in Brussels.

completion of the long-contested world trade agreement intended to provide the basis for global economic growth and cohesion into the 21st century.

As he lowered his hammer like an auctioneer completing a sale, Peter Sutherland, the Irish lawyer who oversaw the last phase of the seven-year trade negotiations as GATT's Director General, declared, "I gavel the Uruguay Round as concluded."

Representatives from the 117 member nations of the General Agreement on Tariffs and Trade leaped to their feet in the brown-carpeted, granite-walled conference hall here— applauding, cheering, even succumbing to bear hugs.

The Worst Is Past

Their sense of relief was palpable: A deal had finally been done and the worst averted, after a negotiation that at times seemed more likely to reveal the irreconcilable trade rivalries of the post-cold-war world than its determination to pursue a quest for freer trade, lower tariffs and greater economic cooperation.

"There are those, not without reason, who find the post-cold-war world full of new risks and tensions," Mr. Sutherland said. "Today, the world has chosen openness and cooperation instead of uncertainty and conflict. This is a success that will reinforce economic growth."

In fact, as several delegates remarked here today, the 400-page Final Act of the negotiations ended as an incomplete compromise, much better than nothing, but far less than once hoped.

"To conclude this is, in itself, a major achievement," said Luiz Felipe Palmeira Lampreia, Brazil's representative here, "even if we are left with mixed feelings."

Close Call for Clinton

The agreement came after a first, formal deadline in December 1990 was missed and later target dates produced nothing. In the end, Mr. Sutherland announced the conclusion just 10 hours before the cutoff of President Clinton's "fast track" authority, allowing him to send the GATT accord to Congress to be voted on without amendments.

Within an hour of agreement, President Clinton said he would submit the pact to Congress. "This agreement did not accomplish everything we wanted, but today's GATT accord does meet the test of a good agreement," he said in Washington.

After approval by Congress last month of the North American Free Trade Agreement—and the intense battle the President waged to gain that approval—the new accord underscored the Administration's once-doubted commitment to free trade. It also indicated the belief of Mr. Clinton and his advisers that

GATT: The Effect on Industry

It took seven years for 117 countries to agree on a pact that would modify world trade for the first time since 1979. But in expanding rules that would cut some tariffs and eliminate others as a way to stimulate business and investment, negotiators have not satisfied every industry in the United States, despite some estimates the agreement could generate as much as $200 billion in new business. President Clinton notified Congress yesterday that the United States intended to sign the agreement on April 15. Here is a closer look at the industries that won, lost or came away with a draw under GATT.

Agriculture   DRAW

Some groups, like the National Farmers Organization, say freer trade under GATT is bad for agriculture everywhere because it increases efficiency to a point where less efficient farmers are driven out of business and some rural communities threatened with extinction. But most American grain farmers expect to benefit from reduction in worldwide export subsidies under GATT. Fruit, vegetable and rice growers expect better access to foreign markets. Domestic crops protected by strict quotas, like sugar, cotton and peanuts, will see slight increases in import competition over time.

Banking   DRAW

The stakes for the banking industry were small, and the results were inconclusive. The agreement neither opened new markets for American banks nor restricted the ability of the United States to retaliate against countries that maintain barriers. "We did not get stuck with the doors locked open," said Christopher Rieck, a spokesman for the American Bankers Association. Since banks already have access to markets in Europe and Japan, the industry's only concern, which is subject to future negotiations, is gaining the right to open branches in developing countries. This mainly affects Citibank, which is the only American bank interested in running retail branches overseas.

Brokerage Firms   DRAW

The failure of GATT negotiators to agree on a plan for foreign countries to drop barriers to American securities firms was disappointing, said David G. Strongin, director of international finance at the Securities Industry Association. Securities dealers were pleased, however, that the agreement leaves the United States Government the right to negotiate with individual countries about their barriers, rather than requiring use of GATT's formal dispute settlement system.

Insurance   DRAW

"We were disappointed that we did not get an agreement for foreign countries to remove barriers protecting their insurance industry, but the mere fact that, for the first time, financial services such as insurance were on the GATT agenda was important progress," said George Henry, vice president of the American Insurance Association. The GATT talks did produce an agreement to give foreign countries an extra six months beyond the start of GATT on July 1, 1995 to remove barriers protecting their insurance industry. After that, the United States is free to impose trade sanctions against those countries.

Capital Goods   WINNER

The gradual elimination of tariffs should help American makers of capital goods by stimulating world economies and thus demand for manufactured products. American capital goods industries have some of the world's lowest-cost producers, who are well positioned to compete on price and will not miss losing the protection of dumping suits at home. It was "certainly not all we wanted, but our bottom line was this was one heck of a good agreement," said Timothy Elder, a spokesman for Caterpillar, a heavy-equipment maker.

Forest Products   DRAW

The trade pact is expected to be more welcome to the paper industry than to lumber. The United States exports only limited amounts of lumber, and prices of American lumber have been less competitive as logging has become more expensive. American paper makers have more to gain. Until now, they have had to contend with 6 percent tariffs on any liner board, their principal export to the European Community and 9 percent tariffs on bleached board.

Medical Equipment   WINNER

Medical device and equipment makers said smaller companies would be the main winners as tariffs fall by $500 million a year and exports grow by $200 million to $300 million, creating about 3,000 jobs. Even larger companies with overseas plants were pleased. "Lowering trade barriers and eliminating tariffs through GATT is very good news for us," said Raymond V. Gilmartin, chairman of Becton, Dickinson & Company.

Pharmaceuticals   LOSER

The pharmaceutical industry, which lobbied hard for the GATT agreement, was set back by a provision that gives developing countries like India and Brazil 10 years before they will be required to honor foreign patent claims. Trade negotiators said American drug makers lose $4.8 billion in annual sales. Noting that other types of patents must be respected after a five-year transition, Merck & Company, the world's largest drug maker, complained that pharmaceutical patents had been made the objects of discrimination. But the industry also won on some points, including 20-year patent protection from the filing date.

Retail   WINNER

Retailers have been urging an end to quotas and tariffs on imported apparel and fabrics, which they say increase the cost of their merchandise to consumers. Myron E. Ullman 3d, chairman and chief executive of R. H. Macy & Company, which makes much of its private-label apparel abroad, says consumers pay $46 million a year extra. The GATT accord will phase out the tariff and quota system and give retailers the chance to lower prices.

Semiconductors   WINNER

American manufacturers retained the right not to license foreign competitors who would make their products. They also kept the ability to file dumping complaints like those used to fight Japanese competition in the 1980's. There was also a modest gain on European tariffs, which will fall from 14 percent to 7 percent on imported memory products after five years.

Textiles   LOSER

The textile industry will, over 10 years, lose the system of quotas that has served as a barrier to increased imports of fabrics manufactured abroad. "I consider this to be just a complete sellout of this industry," said William Farley, chairman and chief executive of Fruit of the Loom. Manufacturers had pushed for a 15-year phase-out, which imposes tariffs and quotas on imported fabrics and apparel. And they wanted a reduction of tariffs and quotas to be dependent upon other countries like India and Pakistan opening their markets. Neither of the proposals made it into the final package.

Toys   WINNER

"We look at this as a win-win situation for us," said David A. Miller, president of the Toy Manufacturers of America, a trade association that represents more than 200 companies. Lower tariffs will benefit the toy industry because two-thirds of the toys, games and dolls sold in the world are made by American companies. Mr. Miller said some groups of companies would save as much as $150 million.

jobs, growth and national security are, in the end, better served by an open world trading system than protectionism or recourse to regional trading blocs.

In Paris, Prime Minister Edouard Balladur, who repeatedly clashed with the President over issues ranging from agriculture to access for American films to European markets, declared in Parliament that the accord was in France's interest.

"The cultural identity of Europe is protected, the future of French agriculture assured," he said, before winning a vote of confidence by 466 to 90 in the lower house.

Under the agreement, to be signed in Morocco in April and due to come into effect in 1995, worldwide tariffs were cut by an average of one-third, encouraging the freer movement of goods, and industries like agriculture were brought under GATT rules for the first time, implying the gradual elimination of subsidies that are costly to taxpayers.

Little Gain on Many Services

But accords on the world's trillion-dollar annual trade in services like banking and the movie and entertainment industries proved elusive, leaving some of the fastest-developing parts of the world's economy encumbered by national or regional protectionism of the sort that discourages foreign investment.

The agreement, before coming into effect, faces potentially contentious legislative battles in the United States and elsewhere.

Today, South Korean students, angered by the lifting of the country's ban on rice imports, rioted and shouted "Yankee go home." And some Indian legislators denounced what they depicted as the sale of the country to American imperialists after it was announced that the Government had accepted the accord and an eventual lowering of tariffs on textiles.

The agreement came after a series of last-minute flurries. The American trade representative, Mickey Kantor, won an 11th-hour change of name for the new international trade organization that is to be established in 1995 to police the accord and settle trade disputes.

Instead of the Multilateral Trade Organization, it will be called the World Trade Organization.

"It just sounds a lot less bureaucratic and has more gravitas," Mr. Kantor said.

The United States, concerned for some time that the organization could compromise the effectiveness of national trade legislation, withheld final approval of the new body until today.

The European Community bickered among itself to the last.

At the End, Portuguese Textiles

At a meeting in Brussels, European foreign ministers had to allocate more than $450 million to Portugal to compensate it for the GATT accord's effect on the country's textile industry before Portugal would accept it. The Portuguese had argued that the community's gradual lowering of barriers to textile imports was not sufficiently compensated by openings in the textile markets in the United States and in big Asian countries.

The European ministers also approved a speeded-up procedure for taking trade action against countries selling products below cost in the European market before France would announce its approval.

The French Foreign Minister, Alain Juppe, emerging from the meeting, remarked, "I never want to hear the word GATT again."

*   *   *

April 16, 1994

109 NATIONS SIGN TRADE AGREEMENT

By ALAN RIDING
Special to The New York Times

MARRAKESH, Morocco, April 15—Culminating more than seven years of arduous and often bitter bargaining, ministers from 109 countries signed a far-reaching trade liberalization agreement today aimed at stimulating exports and slashing tariffs around the world.

The agreement is the eighth to be concluded since World War II but is easily the most ambitious, reducing import tariffs by an average of 40 percent and embracing for the first time such areas as agriculture, textiles and financial services.

The accord signed today was reached in the Uruguay Round of trade negotiations, the latest set of talks held under the General Agreement on Tariffs and Trade, or GATT. The agreement remains subject to ratification by many governments.

Costs Stymie Congress

In the United States, the trade-liberalization measures will go to the House of Representatives and the treaty itself to the Senate for ratification. But the timing of American action is unclear because Congress cannot decide how to cover an estimated $13.9 billion decline in tariff revenue that will result.

Vice President Al Gore described the impact of the agreement as "truly momentous" and said the Clinton Administration would seek ratification this year. Mr. Gore flew here Thursday to address the meeting and underline the United States' support for the package, which is expected to stimulate American exports.

But Mr. Gore, when he addressed a meeting of ministers here on Thursday, alarmed some developing nations by announcing that Washington would seek in future negotiations to discuss the relationship between trade and both environmental protection and workers' rights.

Major exporting nations in Asia and Latin America fear that the United States, France and some other industrial countries want to link trade to the environment and labor as a means of creating nontariff barriers to reduce the competitive advantage of poor low-wage economies.

Another unresolved problem is whether China, which never joined GATT, can achieve its goal of becoming a founding member of GATT's successor, the World Trade Organization, which was created by the accord signed today. The United States and some other countries contend that China must take further measures to open up its domestic economy before becoming eligible for membership.

Something to Celebrate

While potential conflicts emerged in many speeches here this week, today's final ceremony in this sunny Moroccan desert resort was intended as a celebration of an agreement that more than once seemed out of reach.

In a joint declaration today, ministers from participating governments said the Uruguay Round "will strengthen the world's economy and lead to more trade, investment, employment and income growth throughout the world" and should augur a "progressively more open world trading environment."

GATT has estimated that the accord will increase global income by $235 billion a year. Experts also hope it will stimulate an economic recovery in industrial nations.

The World Trade Organization, in replacing the 47-year-old GATT, will join the International Monetary Fund and the World Bank as the main watchdogs of the global economy. The new body will have far greater authority than GATT to bring order to world commerce.

Perilous Course

On many occasions, the negotiations that began in the Uruguayan resort of Punta del Este in 1986 seemed headed for failure. They collapsed in 1990, and were almost torpedoed again last year by disputes between the United States and the European Union over farm and audio-visual goods. An agreement was finally thrashed out in Geneva in December, three years behind schedule.

Peter Sutherland, the Irish lawyer who heads GATT, was visibly delighted and relieved today that all the squabbling was over. "I'm tempted to do an Irish jig on this table to show what I think," Mr. Sutherland told reporters. "No one got everything they wanted, but that is the nature of these sorts of negotiations."

After a daylong ritual of signing the 22,000-page, 385-pound agreement, ministers pledged in their joint declaration "to resist protectionist pressures of all kinds." They also promised to take no trade measure that could harm the Uruguay Round before the World Trade Organization comes into being, probably next year.

Although 109 countries signed the agreement today, GATT has 125 members, so more are expected to add their endorsements.

The principal beneficiaries of the agreement are expected to be the industrialized democracies and leading third-world exporters like India, Brazil, Malaysia, Pakistan, Singapore, Indonesia, South Korea and, eventually, China. Because of their different interests, these countries often formed different alliances at various stages of the negotiations.

In pressing the European Union to reduce subsidies and other protection of its farm products, for example, the United States had the backing of the so-called Cairns Group of agricultural exporters, including Australia, Canada, Brazil and Argentina.

The accord deals with a new area, services, in an effort to liberalize trade in banking, insurance and tourism. Audio-visual products, like television and movies, as well as shipping and airlines were excluded, largely because of continuing disagreement between the United States and the 12-nation European Union.

Two Crucial Areas

Rules were tightened to prevent "dumping" of goods—selling them at less than their production cost—and to protect intellectual property, a term that covers everything from patents, copyrights and trademarks to the rights of performers and producers of sound recordings.

Developed countries also agreed to a 10-year phasing out of the 1974 Multi-Fiber Arrangement, which was intended to protect the textile industries of the United States, Japan and several European countries from competition from low-wage exporters, principally in Asia.

The backbone of the accord signed today is market access, the opening up of economies to more foreign products, in this case by cutting tariffs on industrial and farm goods by an average of 40 percent. The logic is that more imports mean more exports, which in turn mean more jobs and greater prosperity.

Although Mr. Sutherland, the Director General of GATT, has insisted that "there are no losers" in this accord, some development experts say that many African and Caribbean nations belonging to the "poorest of the poor" category may suffer.

Fears for the Poor

In a study circulated here, Christian Aid, a London-based development group, said these poorest countries "will face higher costs to feed their people as the price of cereals increases in world markets."

For the dominant economies of the world, though, the agreement is considered good news. Mr. Gore said the gross domestic product, or value of goods and services, of developed countries should gain an additional 3.5 percent over a decade as a result of the Uruguay Round accord. "That's an extra year's worth of output for free," Mr. Gore said.

ECONOMIC NATIONALISM

March 7, 1947

ECONOMIC WAR DUE IF TRADE BARS STAY, TRUMAN WARNS U.S.

World Looks to This Country for Leadership in Cutting Barriers, President Asserts

CHOICE IS CALLED OURS

In Talk at Baylor University He Backs the ITO as Device for Preventing Conflict

By FELIX BELAIR Jr.
Special to The New York Times

WACO, Texas, March 6—President Truman asserted today that the United States must take the lead in reducing international trade barriers, or plunge the world into economic war and pave the way for future armed conflicts.

In an address at Baylor University here after receiving an honorary degree, the President, who arrived at 9:30 A. M. after a predawn flight from Mexico City, declared:

"We are the giant of the economic world. Whether we like it or not, the future pattern of economic relations depends upon us. The world is waiting and watching to see what we shall do. The choice is ours. We can lead the nations to economic peace or we can plunge them into economic war."

He said that while the leaders of both political parties were agreed on the indivisibility of the political and economic in American foreign relations, there were some who frowned on bipartisan support of foreign economic cooperation.

World Called at Turning Point

Now, as in 1920, the world has reached a turning point in its history, the President stressed. National economies have been disrupted by war; economic policies are in a state of flux, and in this atmosphere of doubt and hesitation, he warned, the decisive factor will be the type of leadership the United States gives the world.

The President recalled that negotiations would begin in April at Geneva for reduction of tariffs here and abroad, the elimination of other restrictive trade measures and the abandonment of discrimination in international commerce.

The success of these negotiations is essential, he said, to the establishment of the international trade organization, to the effective operation of the International Bank and the Monetary Fund and to the strength of the whole United Nations structure of cooperation in economic and political affairs.

"The negotiations at Geneva must not fail," Mr. Truman asserted.

"Isolationists" Are Warned

Congratulating the leaders of both political parties for having removed, for the time being at least, the subject of foreign economic policy from the political arena, the President said that he would welcome a continuation of bi-partisan support.

The chief executive then struck out against "those among us who would seek to undermine this policy for partisan advantage and go back to the period of high tariffs and economic isolation." To this group, he addressed the following warning:

"Take care, times have changed. Our position in the world has changed. The slogans of 1930 or of 1896 are sadly out of date. Isolationism after two world wars is a confession of mental and moral bankruptcy."

The President said that there was one thing that Americans valued even more than peace, and that was freedom—freedom of worship, freedom of speech and freedom of enterprise.

There is a definite connection between the first two of these freedoms and the third, he added, and throughout history, freedom of worship and freedom of speech have most frequently flourished where a considerable measure of freedom was accorded individual enterprise.

In the United States, the devotion to freedom of enterprise has deeper roots than a desire to protect the profits of ownership; it is part and parcel of what we call American, he asserted.

Recalling the "battles" in the economic war of the 'Thirties, the President said that from the Hawley-Smoot tariff policy in this country, the world went on to the British system of imperial preferences, and from there to the detailed restrictions adopted by Nazi Germany.

The world over, countries strangled normal trade and discriminated against their neighbors. Mr. Truman said that he would not argue that economic conflict was the sole cause of the depression of 1929, but he insisted it was a major cause.

The President stressed that unless this country led the way toward lower tariffs and abandonment of discriminatory practices, governments would be brought increasingly into international trade because of demands for more and stricter controls in retaliation for the curtailing or cutting off of foreign markets.

"The pattern of trade that is least conducive to freedom of enterprise is one in which decisions are made by governments," he asserted.

Under such a system, Mr. Truman warned, it was left for public officials to dictate the quantity of purchases and sales, the sources of imports and the destination of exports. This was the system of the seventeenth and eighteenth centuries, and the President said that "unless we act, and act decisively, it will be the pattern of the next century."

The nations of the world are being driven by post-war economic pressures in the direction of more rather than less regimentation, he said.

Countries seeking to reconstruct their industries are trying to control imports, he added, so as not to exceed exports, and those seeking to build new industries are trying to foster them through the same device.

Lack of available exchange he called still another cause for nations to curtail imports from countries whose currencies they did not possess. All manner and form of controls are being used, he said, including quotas, licenses and other practices that have for their purpose the limiting of imports in conformity with a central plan.

If this plan is not reversed, Mr. Truman predicted, the United States Government would be under pressure, sooner or later, to use these same devices in the fight for markets and for raw materials.

If the Government yielded to this pressure, he said, it would soon be telling every trader what he could buy and sell, and how much, and when and where.

The charter of the International Trade Organization was offered as an alternative to this course, Mr. Truman said. It would limit the freedom of governments to impose detailed administrative regulations on their foreign trade. It would require members to confine such controls to exceptional cases and to abandon them as soon as possible.

The President forecast a larger foreign trade, both imports and exports, under the new organization.

Business is poorer when markets are small, he said, and good when markets are big.

He asserted that there was no thought that the Geneva meeting would attempt to eliminate tariffs or to establish free trade. All that was contemplated was a lowering of tariffs, removal of discriminations and the promotion of freer trade.

Tariffs would not be cut "across the board," the President said. The action would be selective, some rates being cut substantially, some moderately and some not at all. Concessions would be demanded for concessions granted, he added, and there was no thought of sacrificing one economic group for the benefit of another.

The Chief Executive was introduced to his university audience by Pat Neff, president of Baylor, as "just a plain, common everyday citizen with a soul and a heart and a liver just like the rest of us."

Earlier, Mr. Neff stood at the head of a welcoming committee in a pelting rain as the President's plane circled the field and taxied down the runway. Others on hand to greet Mr. Truman were Gov. Beauford Jester of Texas, Attorney General Tom Clark, Senator Tom Connally and Jesse H. Jones, former Secretary of Commerce.

* * *

October 23, 1958

NATIONALISM SEEN AS BAR TO CAPITAL

Chauvinism Must End if U. S. Industry Is to Invest Abroad, Expert Says

An authority on Latin America said yesterday that the trend toward exaggerated nationalism, antagonistic to foreign capital, must be reversed if American enterprise was to continue to venture abroad.

The speaker was Spruille Braden, former United States Ambassador to Argentina and to Cuba, and a former Assistant Secretary of State for Latin American Affairs. He spoke at a luncheon and panel discussion of "United States-Latin American Relationships in Transition," held at the Astor Hotel. About 300 business men attended the event, part of the regular monthly meeting of the international section of the New York Board of Trade, Inc.

Mr. Braden said there must be no confiscation and expropriation by foreign countries without adequate, prompt and effective compensation. He suggested that there must be equitable treatment of foreign enterprises, and no discrimination in matters such as the use of American managerial and technical employes.

Mr. Braden said that foreign governments should remember that the surest way to paralyze existing industries and frighten away potential investors was by excessive or discriminating imposts, waste and corruption.

Gains Held Exaggerated

He said ". . . a misconception prevails that mining and oil companies make exorbitant gains."

"Actually," he continued, "the investigation, equipment and operation of a large mineral deposit, require millions of dollars, plus other millions which must be expended on unfruitful explorations and dry holes. It is absurd to expect such ventures to accept the low return of a triple A bond. Profits must be commensurate with risk."

Another speaker, James H. Stebbins, executive vice president of W. R. Grace & Co., said that his company had found that it paid to identify its interests with the interests of the country in which it operates.

"We believe in selecting businesses which serve and improve the local economy . . . in the development of local management talent and in working in partnership with local capital . . . in requiring our American employes to identify themselves with the South American community, and in staying out of politics."

Henry F. Holland, a former Assistant Secretary of State for Inter-American Affairs, told the group that never before had the foundation of this country's relations with the other American republics been so sound, realistic and constructive as today.

He listed this country's basic foreign policy objectives in this hemisphere as follows:

- To guarantee the peace and safety of the community against all attack or violence.
- To create a policy of non-intervention in the affairs of our neighbors.
- To contribute effectively to the establishment of strong, self-reliant economies in the other American republics.

* * *

March 19, 1961

DEBATE ON JAPAN TRADE

Rising Imports Stir Fears in U. S. Industries and Raise Difficult Foreign Policy Issues

By RICHARD E. MOONEY
Special to The New York Times

WASHINGTON, March 18—Baseball gloves, transistors, plastic raincoats, Diesel locomotives, men's suits, zori sandals. Those, are the things that touchy trade relations are made of.

Each of those items, currently or in the recent past, has been imported to the United States from Japan in such quantities as to set off yells from competing American industry.

The matter is alive right now because two labor unions have joined their industries in protest, threatening to have their members boycott the offending products. One of the boycotts—against transistors—was postponed this week. The other—indirectly against suits—may be called off soon. But the issue remains.

Japan is the United States' second-ranking trade partner. We buy more from Japan than from any other country and sell more to Japan than to any other country, save Canada in both respects. Last year, Japan bought $1,300,000,000 worth of American goods and the United States bought $1,100,000,000 of Japanese.

Textile Sales

The things Japan buys here are primarily basic materials—cotton, scrap iron and such—and the machinery with which to make them into finished products. The things she sells here are the finished products and fish.

The biggest single category of Japanese sales to the United States is textiles and clothing—$252,000,000 last year. Next comes a category called "electrical machinery"—$102,000,000 last year. It ranges from a flood of button-sized transistors to a few pieces of heavy equipment. Another big item last year was $77,000,000 of rubber shoes, mostly those things held on by a thong between the toes.

President Kennedy made the point at a news conference ten days ago that sometimes a protested import amounts to only a tiny fraction of the competing product in this country.

That is true in the case of men's suits. The United States imported about 40,000 from Japan last year while American suit makers turned out 20,000,000. It was true of cotton shirts just a few years ago, but last year's imports from Japan came

to 1,200,000 dozen, against domestic production of 12,000,000 dozen, or 10 per cent—and there were imports from Hong Kong and elsewhere on top of that.

Japan's natural advantage is her huge labor supply and relatively lower standard of living. Japanese labor costs are lower than American, though generous fringe benefits in Japan make this advantage smaller than appears in a straight comparison of hourly wage rates. Japanese skills and productivity, while rising, are nonetheless lower than this country's, and that cuts her advantage, too.

The Arguments

The arguments for limiting the entry of foreign goods are as follows:

(1) Every imported competing product is one less bought from an American factory, which means fewer jobs for Americans, less vitality for American business and less readiness to meet the production demands of a war if one should come. We are sowing the seeds of our own destruction, economic if not political.

(2) The Government has contributed to the import problem, so the least it can do is help to relieve it. The "contributions" include the liberalization that has occurred these last twenty-five years, the post-war foreign aid that built and is still building modern foreign factories and the more recent subsidy on sales of American cotton to foreign manufacturers.

(3) Foreign countries have been far less liberal than the United States. If they will not open up to American goods, the United States must tighten up on theirs.

On the other side, arguing for greater American liberalism, are these points:

(1) Foreigners must sell here to earn dollars so they can buy here, and they buy much more than they sell—a near-record of $5,000,000,000 more last year.

(2) The United States is and wants to be the leader of the free world. The world's economic viability depends on expanding international trade. We are the richest member. We cannot afford allies in distress. We must take a generous position.

(3) When it comes to particular industry appeals for protection, imports are often more blamed than blameable. In the case of transistors, for instance, rising imports may be less to blame for unemployment among electronic workers than the slackness in demand for television sets that has existed for several years.

Administration's Position

The Kennedy Administration's stated position on trade is liberal. The President's balance of payments message to Congress said flatly that "protectionism is not a solution." But his policy has yet to face a major test, and some advocates of liberalism are a little uneasy.

Finally, the liberals are disappointed that the Administration has not accepted their preferred legislative remedy from import problems—a depressed areas type of program that would earmark Federal aid specifically to redevelop or redirect industries and workers who really are suffering because of imports.

The Administration's liberalism lies in its broader policies. Its most important assault on import competition is its effort to nip the price problem in the bud, by restraints on inflation and by incentives to more productive mechanization of industry here.

Relevant to the present question, the United States has two major points to make: That other countries' domestic wage and working standards are too low, and that their barriers to foreign trade—from here, but particularly from Japan—are too high.

* * *

January 5, 1972

THE NEW BIG 5

Nixon Stresses Developing Relations with Emerging Economic Superpowers

By LEONARD SILK

Shortly before the turn of the year, William L. Safire, Special Assistant to President Nixon, told a New York Law Journal Forum that the first of the great changes he foresaw for 1972 would be "a growing awareness of the economic root of international power. Our eyes will become accustomed to the new Big Five in world affairs—the United States, the Soviet Union, the Common Market, mainland China and Japan." What do these portentous words mean? Are they simply inflated rhetoric or do they signify a coming development in United States foreign economic policy whose importance has not yet been appreciated?

The Safire statement repeats a theme that the President himself voiced in Kansas City, Mo., last July 6. Mr. Nixon then declared that there were "five great economic superpowers"—the same named by Mr. Safire—that would "determine the economic future and, because economic power will be the key to other kinds of power, the future of the world in other ways in the last third of this century."

"We now face a situation," said Mr. Nixon, "where the four other powers have the ability to challenge us on every front, and this brings us back home for a hard look at what we have to do."

Domestic and foreign policies were so intertwined, he said, that they could not be separated. Mr. Nixon warned that the United States was reaching the period of "decadence" that had brought down Greece and Rome.

In the past, he said, decadence had resulted from growing national wealth. This had caused earlier great civilizations to lose "their will to live, to improve." But he thought the United States had the strength and courage to meet all challenges.

In that Kansas City speech, delivered only five weeks before the President launched his new economic policy, he linked national health and strength to the free-enterprise system. He delivered a strong indictment of wage and price con-

trols, declaring that such steps were alien to the American system of free enterprise.

On Aug. 15, Mr. Nixon froze wages and prices and subsequently adopted Phase Two controls.

But at the recent American Economic Association convention in New Orleans, Prof. Paul A. Samuelson, America's first Nobel Prize winner in economics, predicted that the Administration would end wage and price controls before the November, 1972, election.

And Assistant Secretary of the Treasury Edgar R. Fiedler said that the best time to get rid of wage-price controls would be before the economy gets back to full employment.

Since Administration economists apparently now regard a rate of unemployment of 5 per cent as tantamount to full employment, rather than 4 per cent as was customary in the past, this could mean suspending controls almost any time in the coming year, assuming even a modest decline in unemployment from the recent 6 per cent rate.

President Nixon himself, in a television interview last Sunday, said that the Johnson Administration's low unemployment rate had been achieved "at a cost of 300 casualties a week" in Vietnam; but he would continue to wind the war down.

Statement Challenged

Declaring that his system of wage-price controls was intended "to break the inflationary psychology," Mr. Nixon also took issue with a statement of Paul W. McCracken, former chairman of his Council of Economic Advisers, that wage-price controls might be needed for years to come.

The restatement of the "five great powers" theme may foreshadow a return by the President to the true free-enterprise creed in 1972. But this need not mean a diminution in White House support for aids to business, especially in the international arena.

In his recently released foreign trade study, Peter G. Peterson, assistant to the President for International Economic Affairs, suggested a number of additional Government aids to business, including help on research and development outlays and exemption from the antitrust laws if needed to spur exports.

The foreign economic policy implications of the "five great powers" concept do not all go in the same direction.

Toward the Common Market and Japan, the concept appears to mean the sort of tough and highly competitive attitude expressed frequently by John B. Connally, Secretary of the Treasury, and by Mr. Peterson.

But toward the Soviet Union and mainland China—foes though these countries may be in the Communist world—Mr. Nixon has adopted a friendly view and has stressed his hopes for growing trade.

United States-Soviet relations, he said in his Kansas City speech last July, have moved from confrontation to negotiation. And he added that he had moved to end the isolation of Communist China because that country had become "creative and productive."

In straight economic terms, it is difficult to see United States trade with Communist China amounting to a great deal for years to come. Despite its enormous population of between 750-million and 850-million, China's gross national product is estimated by Western experts at only about $80-billion—about 7 per cent of this country's. China's exports are chiefly textiles, agricultural materials and foodstuffs.

Peking has signaled its interest in trading with the United States, although it can get most of what the United States could offer elsewhere—for instance in Japan or Western Europe. Nevertheless, China would doubtless like to get certain American products because of their superior quality.

The significance of Mr. Nixon's interest in developing trade with China is certainly more political than economic.

Although the Soviet Union is a far greater industrial power than China, the same logic holds: Mr. Nixon intends to use economic means for political ends. Toward both great Communist states, he is seeking to normalize relations.

Thus, the "five great powers" concept implies that Mr. Nixon is heading into a year of important economic maneuvering among the other four great powers.

The curious paradox is that this champion of the free-enterprise creed will be working for closer economic relations with Communist China and the Soviet Union as he toughens his response toward the growth of economic power in Western Europe and Japan.

*   *   *

January 24, 1973

NATIONS' ECONOMIC MIGHT: NEW CONCEPT IS EMERGING

By LEONARD SILK

Historical eras are marked off by changes in concepts. The period of colonial expansion of the great European powers was a quest for "wealth"—defined as gold and treasure. The end of that era was marked in 1776 by Adam Smith's "Wealth of Nations," in which he defined wealth not as precious metals but as the ability of the people of a nation to produce useful goods and services.

Today, with the initialing of the agreement to end the war in Vietnam, the world appears to be passing from a period of confrontation between the Communist and capitalist powers into what President Nixon, in his second inaugural address, foresaw as "a structure of peace that can last, not merely for our time, but for generations to come."

The new era, if it is to come, is unlikely to result from some outburst of national morality or from a new willingness of sovereign nations to subordinate their interests to those of others. Rather, it will depend on the deployment of power in some form to insure world stability.

Dramatically—and tragically—the old bipolar, cold-war era, and its concept of power, foundered on the inability of the United States, one of the world's two superpowers, to pre-

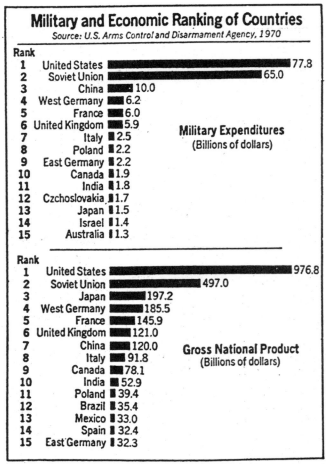

Military and Economic Ranking of Countries
Source: U.S. Arms Control and Disarmament Agency, 1970

Military Expenditures (Billions of dollars)

Rank	Country	
1	United States	77.8
2	Soviet Union	65.0
3	China	10.0
4	West Germany	6.2
5	France	6.0
6	United Kingdom	5.9
7	Italy	2.5
8	Poland	2.2
9	East Germany	2.2
10	Canada	1.9
11	India	1.8
12	Czchoslovakia	1.7
13	Japan	1.5
14	Israel	1.4
15	Australia	1.3

Gross National Product (Billions of dollars)

Rank	Country	
1	United States	976.8
2	Soviet Union	497.0
3	Japan	197.2
4	West Germany	185.5
5	France	145.9
6	United Kingdom	121.0
7	China	120.0
8	Italy	91.8
9	Canada	78.1
10	India	52.9
11	Poland	39.4
12	Brazil	35.4
13	Mexico	33.0
14	Spain	32.4
15	East Germany	32.3

The New York Times/Jan. 24, 1973

vail over North Vietnam, which stood near the bottom of the cellar in the rankings.

The traditional concept of national power had two basic elements:

- The resources a nation could pour into military goods and manpower, as measured by its total defense expenditures.
- The economic capability of the nation to produce goods and services, as measured by its gross national product.

In the prenuclear age, a capability was considered an even better measure of its power than current defense outlays—since in a long war it could shift resources from civilian to military use and thereby mount and sustain a bigger military force than its rivals.

This was the secret of the successful American effort in World War II. Indeed, this formula for power was first demonstrated by the way the North crushed the South in the American Civil War.

The nuclear age seemingly downgraded the significance of a nation's underlying economic capabilities:

What would count in wars that were expected to last a few days (or perhaps only minutes) were forces in being—nuclear weapons immune from attack and ready for instantaneous response to any threat.

Vietnam—"America's longest and most difficult war," as President Nixon called it last week—altered the concept of national power by its incredible length and by its inconclusive outcome. It demonstrated the constraints and limitations upon the use by a superpower of its full military and economic capabilities. Obviously, those constraints were not physical but political and social, both at home and abroad.

3 Trends Interact

The constraints are linked to three interacting trends in the world. Seyom Brown, a Senior Fellow at the Brookings Institution in Washington, describes these trends in the current issue of Foreign Affairs. He says that:

The cold-war coalitions have started to disintegrate. The smaller powers strike postures of independence while the superpowers find the fidelity of their allies questionable and reduce their own commitments. At his second inauguration, President Nixon said: "The time has passed when America will make every other nation's conflict our own or make every other nation's future our responsibility or presume to tell the people of other nations how to manage their own affairs."

Nonsecurity issues—primarily economic—have risen to the top of the diplomatic agenda. To be sure, security issues remain important, but the ability of the United States on one side or the Soviet Union on the other to prevail over allies by threatening to withdraw military protection is decreasing. Europe unites, expands its sphere and forms coalitions with nonaligned countries and the Soviet bloc. So doth the United States. Even the Warsaw Pact countries, though still in the Soviet grip, form new coalitions to reduce the dominance of their superpower.

Friendships and adversary relations have grown more complex and ambiguous. At the height of the cold war each of the two superpowers, while competing for allies around the globe, made sharp distinction between friends and enemies. Nonaligned countries—especially India, Egypt and Indonesia—played the field, but theirs was considered an untenable policy over the long run.

In the new multipolar era, precisely that posture of nonaligned flexibility, says Dr. Brown, "seems to be serving as the model for ealistic diplomacy."

Flexibility Found

President Nixon has put forth his own doctrine of flexibility in his concept of "the five great powers." These are the United States, the Soviet Union, the People's Republic of China, Japan and the European Economic Community.

The President voiced this concept for the first time on July 6, 1971, in Kansas City when he declared that the five great powers would "determine the economic future and, because economic power will be the key to other kinds of power, the future of the world in other ways in the last third of this century."

Critics of the President feel that his five-great-powers concept is too narrow—and that it underrates the significance of the role that many other nations will play as the century wears on.

The President's list does not include Canada, India, Brazil, Spain or Mexico.

Role of Countries

The Nixon concept is also held by his critics to underrate the importance of the underdeveloped countries of Latin America, Africa and Asia to the future stability of the world.

Walter Salant of Brookings feels that the President has overstressed the power of nation states and has neglected the power of "transnational" institutions—especially multinational corporations but also various types of labor, environmental, technological, scientific, religious and cultural communities that are creating their own global networks and which either support or tug against national policies.

In such a world of multiple and cross-cutting coalitions, Dr. Brown contends that the essence of power itself is changing from the direct use or threat of military force to gain national ends to various other kinds of promises or threats.

The basic promises are offers of economic exchange, trade, investment or technical cooperation. The basic threats are to withdraw such support or cooperation.

Pattern of Future

In the new era, Dr. Brown suggests, nations with the most influence are likely to be those that are "major constructive participants in the widest variety of coalitions and partnerships." Such countries would have the largest supply of usable political currency—in effect, promissory notes that say: "We will support you on this issue, if you support us on that issue." Nations will be driven to work together to get scarce energy resources—or valuable technology.

To be sure, the old system—the threat or use of military power—will still be there and will be of decisive importance if issues over aggression or national survival again develop.

But it is the diminished fear of such threats that is forcing scholars—and Presidents, generals and businessmen—to rethink the concept of the power of nations in the post-cold war, post-Vietnam era. This rethinking leads to the conclusion that economic weight and flexibility are becoming the dominant elements of national power.

*   *   *

September 27, 1973

HOUSE PANEL TIES SOVIET EMIGRATION TO TRADE BENEFITS

Requires Moscow First to Relax Minority Curbs— Administration Setback

By MARJORIE HUNTER
Special to The New York Times

WASHINGTON, Sept. 26—The House Ways and Means Committee voted today to deny any new trade privileges to the Soviet Union until it eases its emigration policies for Jews and other minorities.

The committee's action was a major setback to the Nixon Administration and to the American business community. The restriction, adopted by voice vote, was attached to a major foreign-trade bill that is now under consideration by the committee.

Kissinger Plea Undercut

The committee acted about an hour after Secretary of State Kissinger, at a news conference in New York, repeated the Administration's contention that over the long run more could be accomplished to ameliorate the lot of Soviet Jews and others by quiet diplomacy.

[In Nairobi, Kenya, Secretary of the Treasury George P. Shultz said that expanding trade with the Soviet Union would be set back if Congress denied tariff cuts, The Associated Press reported.]

Curb on Nixon's Power

The amendment would deny President Nixon the right to grant "most-favored-nation" status to the Soviet Union or any other Communist country until he certified to Congress that the country involved did not restrict emigration.

While the restriction would apply to all Communist countries, including China, it was principally directed at emigration policies of the Soviet Union.

The amendment was cosponsored by Representative Wilbur D. Mills, Democrat of Arkansas, the committee chairman, and Representative Charles A. Vanik, Democrat of Ohio. It was similar to one proposed in the Senate by Henry M. Jackson, Democrat of Washington.

The dispute over Soviet emigration policies intensified in the late summer of 1972, when Moscow imposed heavy exit taxes, ranging into the tens of thousands of dollars, on Jews seeking to leave the country for Israel.

Russians Shelve Tax

The Soviet Union has now shelved the taxes and is allowing Jews to leave at the rate of about 30,000 a year. However, there is a large backlog of would-be emigrants.

While the easing of the exit tax last spring appeared for a time to dampen the chances for Congressional approval of the proposals by Representatives Mills and Vanik and by

Senator Jackson, the highly emotional issued flared again in recent months, with evidence of renewed Soviet repression against such dissenting intellectuals as Andrei D. Sakharov, the physicist, and Aleksandr I. Solzehenitsyn, the novelist.

As recommended today, the House amendment would prohibit the President from giving most-favored-nation tariff treatment—the allowing of any favorable agreements that were extended to any other country—to a nation that denied Jews or other citizens the opportunity to emigrate, that imposed more than nominal emigration fees, or that imposed fees strictly on the basis of the country to which a person wanted to emigrate, such as Israel.

Certification Required

Under the amendment, the President would be required to certify to Congress every six months that the countries receiving most favored-nation treatment maintained a policy of free emigration.

President Nixon had strenuously opposed the restriction, arguing that it could jeopardize efforts to establish better relations with the Soviet Union.

But while defeated today on the issue of trade restrictions, the Administration won a partial victory when the committee struck from the House amendment a provision that would have also denied trade credits or credit guarantees to the Soviet Union or other Communist countries that restricted emigration.

The move to strike the provision on credits was offered by Representative Herman T. Schneebeli, Republican of Pennsylvania, on the ground that the Ways and Means Committee had no jurisdiction over trade credits.

At present, the President has unlimited authority to grant trade credits.

Annual Veto Power Voted

WASHINGTON, Sept. 26 (AP)—The House Ways and Means Committee also approved an amendment by Representative James C. Corman, Democrat of California, giving Congress annual veto power against trade concessions.

The amendment would require the President to determine each year that the Russians and other Communist countries were meeting nondiscriminatory emigration requirements, and would permit Congress to veto any continued trade concessions.

Shultz Fears Trade Curbs

NAIROBI, Kenya, Sept. 26 (AP)—Secretary of the Treasury George P. Shultz said today that expanding trade with the Soviet Union would be set back if Congress, protesting the treatment of Jews and intellectuals, denied tariff cuts to the Russians.

Mr. Shultz, who will leave for Moscow Friday, said that the issue of Soviet dissidents was a matter "that has no direct connection with arrangements to buy or sell something."

"It's essentially a matter of the internal affairs of the Soviet Union," he added.

Mr. Shultz said that he did not mean to imply the Administration did not care about the plight of the Soviet Jews and intellectuals. But he noted that the two Governments had signed a trade deal, agreeing to lower tariffs. The Secretary is here for the annual meeting of the International Monetary Fund and the World Bank.

* * *

June 27, 1982

RISING TRADE BARRIERS STIR MEMORIES OF US DEPRESSSION

By CLYDE H. FARNSWORTH

WASHINGTON—A surge of aggressive economic nationalism, as strong as any in the last half century, threatens to overwhelm the free-trade policies that have underwritten the postwar prosperity of industrialized nations.

Despite the mutual assurances at the recent Versailles summit meeting, leaders of the most powerful economies in the world are resorting to restrictions on trade as a quick fix to meet objectives abroad and to deal with high unemployment and deteriorating industries at home.

The resignation last week of Secretary of State Alexander M. Haig Jr. was triggered in part by a dispute over stern Reagan Administration measures restricting the sale of equipment and technology to American trading partners dealing with the Soviet Union, trade officials asserted.

The United States has long followed economic policies aimed at lowering trade barriers and avoiding the kind of protectionist battles that exacerbated the world Depression in the 1930's. Today, almost 20 percent of the goods produced in the United States are exported, up 10 percent from a decade ago. One acre out of three of United States farmland is planted for export. Profits and jobs in the United States are inextricably linked to an open world trading system.

Now global recession has forced massive readjustments in traditional industries on both sides of the Atlantic. In the United States the steel industry, operating at only 43 percent of capacity, and auto manufacturers are hard pressed both by foreign competition and shrinking export markets. All industrialized countries are under pressure from powerful domestic interests to adopt protectionist measures.

"Of course such measures trigger countermeasures as countries lose export markets and are pressured to retaliate by their own domestic interests," observed Canada's Ambassador to Washington, Allan E. Gotlieb. "Once this cycle is started it becomes very difficult to stop."

That cycle may have already begun. The Reagan Administration's ban on the sale of American equipment for the natural gas pipeline from the Soviet Union to Western Europe angered Europeans, who were counting on the 3,700-mile project to generate jobs in their depressed industries.

Washington's sanctions, designed to cause the delay if not the collapse of the pipeline in retaliation for continued Soviet repression in Poland, hit less than a month after the Administration set stiff penalties on steel imports from Western Europe. The Commerce Department found that some European nations were illegally subsidizing their steel shipments, and imposed countervailing duties that could price European steel out of the United States market. Last week, in response to the measures, European Economic Community steel makers were told to cut back production.

While the two Administration actions were unrelated, their net effect was to weaken steel industries and add to unemployment in nations that are Washington's closest and most powerful allies. The Western Europeans are likely to retaliate against United States exports of food and textiles.

The United States, which enjoys a trading surplus with Western Europe almost as large as the $18.1 billion American deficit last year with Japan, appeared to be telling the Europeans that they could not sell the output of one of their basic industries either in the United States or in the Soviet Union.

West German Chancellor Helmut Schmidt said President Reagan gave the Europeans no hint at Versailles of the coming pipeline sanctions, although American officials said the measures should have come as no surprise in light of the President's position on Poland. Negotiations to resolve the steel subsidy dispute also broke down the week after the summit, when Europeans refused to accept voluntary export quotas.

A sharpening conflict over farm trade is another thorn in Atlantic relations. The Europeans angrily reject United States charges that they are subsidizing their farm exports, taking away American markets for poultry, grain and other products chiefly in the Middle East.

Trade frictions are becoming equally dramatic with Japan. Criminal charges that two Japanese companies, Mitsubishi Electric and Hitachi, conspired to steal secrets from International Business Machines sparked fresh concern that they were unfair traders.

The Japanese have been pressured in recent years to open up their own capital markets to make them comparable to those they enjoy here and in Europe.

American officials fret privately that the trade deficit with Japan will rise to unacceptable levels, prompting a protectionist-minded Congress to take punitive action. A bill that would cripple Japanese auto sales by requiring up to 90 percent domestic content in all cars sold in the United States already has more than 200 cosponsors in the House.

"The situation on the Hill is the most dangerous since 1930," said David Rohr, staff director at the House trade subcommittee, referring to the year of the Smoot-Hawley tariffs, which some say triggered the Great Depression.

"We need some efforts to hold at bay the pressures for trade restraint until we can get a generalized economic recovery under way," said Bruce K. MacLaury, president of the Brookings Institution.

But as that recovery seems farther and farther off, many experts believe protectionist sentiment will grow and economic nationalism will cast a heavy cloud over any attempts to liberalize trade.

* * *

October 8, 1984

BRAZIL CURBS COMPUTER COMPETITION

By ALAN RIDING

RIO DE JANEIRO, Oct. 7—The Brazilian Congress has overwhelmingly approved a bill excluding foreign companies from participation in much of the country's fast-growing computer and data-processing industry.

The action follows a year-long debate that pitted free-market arguments against nationalist passions.

The bill, which awaits the signature of President Joao Baptista Figueiredo, in essence endorses the military regime's existing strategy of stimulating the growth of a domestic "informatics" industry by protecting it from foreign competition.

Multinational corporations that already make mainframe computers here, including the International Business Machines Corporation and the Hewlett-Packard Company, will be allowed to continue operating. But new foreign investment must be aimed exclusively at export markets, while the lucrative domestic market for minicomputers and microcomputers will be reserved for Brazilian companies for at least eight years.

The Opposition Viewpoint

Critics of the bill have argued that Brazil is isolating itself from the "informatics" revolution since it lacks the resources to develop a technology of its own.

Nevertheless, the bill swept through Congress on a wave of nationalism. The one broad argument heard repeatedly was that, for economic and strategic reasons, Brazil should not depend on high technology developed by the industrial giants. The only way to achieve such independence, the bill's proponents said, was to assure the Brazilian industry of a captive domestic market.

Not surprisingly, Brazilian companies involved in data processing have welcomed the bill. Thanks to existing protectionism, they have grown in number from 2 to 140 in seven years and their sales this year should be close to $1 billion.

"This is not an action that can be described as xenophobic or dictatorial," said Edson Fregni, the president of Scopus, a leading producer, and also president of the Brazilian Association of Computer Industries. "It is a sovereign action."

One Senator Dissents

The bill was passed in a joint session of Congress last Wednesday after party leaders reached a consensus. Only Senator Roberto Campos, a former Planning Minister, who had presented his own bill to remove all Government interference in the industry, spoke out against the new law.

"Brazil has stepped off the racetrack of high technology," Mr. Campos said. "Limiting itself to a domestic market, it will always have more expensive products made with obsolete technology."

He was not without some political support. Even though the new law is an amended version of a Government bill, the official party's candidate for next January's presidential elections, Paulo Salim Maluf, himself a wealthy former businessman, argued that "a competitive entrepreneur needs no law to defend him because the laws of economics will protect him."

But the opposition candidate favored to become Brazil's next president, Tancredo Neves, strongly supported the bill. "Without democratic and national control," he said last month, "the development of informatics technology will permit domination of society without any prospect of liberation."

A National Security Issue

From the time of Brazil's first moves into the computer field in the mid-1970's, the issue has been linked more to questions of national security than to economic logic. For example, the earliest Brazilian-made computers were ordered by the Brazilian Navy for use in its frigates and destroyers. The industry has been governed by decrees issued by the military regime, and the Special Informatics Secretariat formed part of the National Security Council.

With a civilian administration scheduled to take office next March, however, Congress was anxious to remove the Armed Forces from direct control over the industry. One amendment to the Government bill therefore converted the Secretariat into the executive arm of a new National Informatics and Automation Council, which will be answerable directly to the President.

The 18-man council will include eight non-Government members, including representatives of business, and its three-year plans must be approved by Congress. With the Government authorized to channel up to eight-tenths of 1 percent of its tax revenue to a Special Informatics and Automation Fund, the public sector will continue to play a key role in the industry.

The most critical question is whether Brazil can develop its own technology in a field that is changing at dizzying speed with billions of dollars being spent worldwide on research. Most other "newly industrialized countries"—not only South Korea, Singapore and Taiwan, but also Mexico, Argentina and Spain—have opted for a more open policy, welcoming foreign companies as a way of gaining access to their technology.

Supporters of Brazil's approach have argued that, without its so-called market reserve policy, the country would not now have an "informatics" industry that already employs about 18,000 people and has encouraged many young engineers and entrepreneurs to turn their talents to sophisticated technology.

The counterargument is that, so far, Brazil has done little more than "pirate" foreign-made computers, such as the I.B.M. PC and the Apple II, facsimiles of which are currently being produced here by several companies and being sold at prices up to 100 percent higher than their American equivalents. Much of the software for these computers has also been copied without payment of royalties.

* * *

January 31, 1988

WHEN THE WORLD LACKS A LEADER

By LOUIS UCHITELLE

Japan's growing economic strength is gradually dislodging the United States as the dominant economic power of the non-Communist world. But despite its gains, Japan remains unwilling—and probably unable—to shoulder many of the responsibilities that have traditionally gone with global leadership, according to many economists and historians.

The Japanese, in fact, are clinging to partnership with the United States—junior partnership—insisting, as Prime Minister Noboru Takeshita did on his first official visit to Washington this month, that "the very foundation of Japan's prosperity" depends on being America's partner.

The Japanese reluctance to upstage the United States, combined with the American economic decline, means that the Western industrial world is entering one of its rare periods without a dominant leader. With no nation today setting the course charted in the 19th century by Britain and later by the United States, the possible consequences are daunting:

- The dollar and other major currencies would go on fluctuating dramatically in value, perhaps into the 21st century, because none of the industrial nations can agree on fair exchange rates and the United States lacks the clout to impose standards, as it once did.
- Trade disputes would persist, with neither the United States nor Japan able to dominate each other or their various trading partners. As a result, the free trade system that the United States imposed after World War II could founder, with the world breaking up into competing trading blocs.
- Overcapacity in manufacturing, already a problem, could worsen as each trading bloc or major industrial nation—operating without international restraint—tried to develop a full set of industries. The total output would be much more than the world's consumers could possibly buy. Recession and unemployment might result.
- The loss of economic power may also cause United States military and political influence to decline in such strategic areas as the Middle East and Latin America. That has happened to other dominant nations, says Paul Kennedy, a Yale historian, in a new book, "The Rise and Fall of the Great Powers," that speculates on America's fate.

The West, in sum, would fall into the fractiousness and prolonged economic distress that plagued the 1920's and 30's, the last period in which the world lacked a "hegemonic" power. In those years, Britain was losing its dominance and the United States had not yet emerged as the global leader.

Less powerful countries have often been critical of the way Britain and the United States used their power, accusing them of exploitation. Nevertheless, the dominant power has performed a number of vital functions in the world economy, said Charles Kindleberger, an economic historian at the Massachusetts Institute of Technology. These have included providing stability and economic stimulus, by opening its borders to nations that had no other marketplace.

The United States did this for a desperate Europe and Japan after World War II. The United States kept on buying their products when they thrived once again, in the 1970's and early 1980's. But no nation is flinging open its borders to unlimited imports today, although the non-Communist world is living through a period of too much production and not enough buyers. Similarly, no nation fulfilled the role of marketplace of last resort during the 1930's, when world trade was drying up.

In addition, the world's economic leader should serve as the lender of last resort, Mr. Kindleberger said, a role that went unfilled in the case of troubled and inflation-ridden Germany in the 1920's. In the coming decade, some nation might have to do this job for third-world nations unable to keep up with debt payments.

"There has to be a hegemonic force and I come to that conclusion reluctantly," Mr. Kindleberger said.

But many believe that it might not be possible for Japan or any other nation to achieve the hegemonic power that came to Britain in the days of Queen Victoria and Edward VII and to the United States in the Truman and Eisenhower years. For one thing, while Japan is coming to control more of the world's wealth than the United States, the United States economy, measured by the total value of the goods and services that Americans produce, is still the largest in the world—three times the size of Japan's, which is second.

In addition, the United States has military strength and political clout—two other components of global leadership—that far surpass any other non-Communist nation, and Japan has shown no inclination to assume greater military or even political responsibilities.

Superpower status has always required a sense of mission that the Japanese lack, says Prof. Edwin O. Reischauer, a Japan scholar at Harvard and the American Ambassador to Tokyo in the 1960's. "We speak of making the world safe for democracy and we apply our ideas to everyone," he said. "The Japanese have none of this sense of empire. They have trouble even joining a United Nations peacekeeping force."

If no single nation can dominate, economists say, one of two alternatives is likely to develop. One would have the United States and Japan share leadership, with Japan supplying the economic muscle and the United States the political and military strength. That is the solution sought by Mr. Takeshita. "The Japanese are pushing hegemony away," Mr. Reischauer said. "They want to move toward a system of greater interdependence."

In the other scenario, trading blocs would emerge, around West Germany in Europe, the United States in the Western

Hemisphere and Japan in Asia. Each would be a world within itself, trading with the other blocs. The European Common Market, of course, is already operating in this way, with Germany the strongest force. And some experts view the bilateral agreements recently negotiated by the United States with Mexico and Canada, in which a number of trade barriers were removed, as the start of a Western Hemisphere bloc.

The transition from American postwar dominance to some new alignment is drawing considerable attention to the issue of global leadership. Indeed, hegemony, a word seldom heard in the postwar years, is showing up frequently today, not only in journals devoted to foreign policy and economics, but also in newspaper and magazine articles about Western leadership, and in newly published histories, such as Mr. Kennedy's.

Japanese Prowess

The issue is coming to a head because of Japan's spectacular success over the past 18 months in adjusting to an overvalued yen, and the failure of the United States to get enough mileage out of a weak dollar. The yen's strength should have reduced Japan's wealth by making its exports too expensive. But Japan's manufacturing and marketing prowess has allowed it to revamp its business practices without giving up the huge sums that have flowed in from abroad since 1981.

That is in sharp contrast to the American experience in the early 1980's. When the dollar was very strong and the yen was weak, American business went through the same adjustment as the Japanese, but the result was a huge deficit, not a surplus—a deficit that continues to grow, despite the advantages of a weak dollar.

Japan, in effect, is demonstrating a skill that the United States and Britain had in their heydays: the ability to accumulate great wealth whatever the value of its currency.

The reinvestment of this wealth around the world will make other nations more dependent on Japan, says Robert E. Cole, a Japan expert at the University of Michigan.

One way in which Japan is offsetting the handicap of a strong yen is by becoming a nation of enthusiastic consumers instead of exporters heavily dependent on the United States market. While its total exports shrink, Japan's domestic consumption is rising at an annual rate of 10 percent and its economy is growing strongly. Second, Japan is beginning to rely on a new source of wealth. As a big supplement to earnings from exports, the Japanese are beginning to harvest profits and interest from the huge sums that continue to be invested abroad, in factories, real estate, stocks and bonds.

Indeed, the transformation of Japan into a nation of consumers and coupon clippers is occurring much more rapidly than most Americans realize, said Martin S. Feldstein, president of the National Bureau of Economic Research and a former chairman of President Reagan's Council of Economic Advisers.

In addition, the insular Japanese, who until the 1980's manufactured little outside their homeland, are moving production abroad, mainly to factories in the United States, but also to other countries with weak currencies and therefore

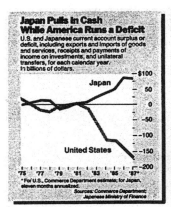 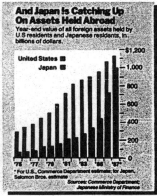

The New York Times/Jan. 31, 1988

lower costs. They are thus forming an international network similar to the one developed by American companies in the postwar years, albeit a smaller one.

The income flowing into Japan from all this overseas activity and from exports rose to more than $80 billion last year from about $50 billion in 1985, when the yen began its rise. In the heyday of its power after World War II, the United States, despite its much greater size, never managed to collect so much wealth from the rest of the world, even when adjustments are made for inflation.

Power of the Purse

As the Japanese spend their riches, they are making decisions that will force on them the mantle of world economic leadership, experts say, no matter how much they might like to defer to the United States.

To take an example, Japan is becoming the chief source of new funds for the World Bank and the International Monetary Fund, which until now have depended on the United States and have been controlled by Americans. And the Japanese are becoming major lenders and investors in Latin America, roles that carry the power to insist that the Latins buy Japanese goods.

Using similar leverage until recent years, the United States made Latin America a big purchaser of American products. The United States is trying to revive this relationship, through its political assertiveness and military presence. But the financing power is passing to Japan.

With economic dominance also comes the power to set the rules for trade. Both Britain and America used their power to enforce a free trade system, because it worked to their benefit. But the advantage lasted only as long as their products and technology were considered the best in the world and were eagerly sought by other nations.

Now that Japanese goods are the favored imports, free trade is beginning to lose its American sponsorship. The decline of free trade as a guiding principle leaves a policy vacuum. Some Japanese argue that their nation should be taking the lead by replacing the free trade concept with a Japanese vision of how the world's economies should behave; as yet, however, no such view exists, the Japanese themselves acknowledge.

Meanwhile, the Commerce Department acts in its relations with Japan as if the United States were still the hegemonic power. That was evident at a recent conference in New York, when Louis F. Laun, the assistant secretary for international economic policy, lectured a group of prominent Japanese executives and economists.

The Japanese Government, he said, should phase out measures that protect troubled industries from foreign competition and should stimulate consumer spending even more than it already does, by helping people to buy larger homes. "The Japanese should have fun, loosen up, and buy," he said. Such paternalistic guidance increasingly draws an angry reaction in Japan, even among Japanese with strong ties to the United States.

"We get this sort of talk every day," said Kenichi Ohmae, managing director in Japan for McKinsey & Company, the American management consulting firm. "Everyone in the U.S. Government talks like a General MacArthur," he said, referring to Douglas MacArthur, who headed the American administration of Japan after World War II.

Divergent Paths

The rise of Japan as an economic giant while the United States retains military and political power generates tensions that could eventually separate the two nations and drive them along divergent paths.

The United States naval force in the Persian Gulf, for example, is protecting oil shipments that benefit Japan as much as any country. Japan has been criticized in Congress for failing to participate in the military action and, more generally, for spending only 1 percent of its gross national product on defense while the United States spends 6 percent.

The Toshiba Corporation stopped selling high-tech equipment to the Soviet Union after the United states protested that the equipment benefitted the Russian military. The Japanese Government even apologized, but some Japanese businessmen were angry that Japan had backed down. They argued that Japan needs the Communist-bloc as a marketplace for its abundance of manufactured goods.

But a policy that would incorporate such activities over the protests of the United States or other nations requires a sense of national mission and conviction that the Japanese prefer to avoid. Their reluctance stems from Japan's disastrous experience with militarism in the 1930's and 1940's and the strong Japanese sense of being apart from the rest of the world—a characteristic reinforced by the language barrier and by centuries of island isolation.

"Japan's success in this respect will require a grand design involving not only economic but also political and military matters," said Masahiko Ishizuka, a columnist for the Japan Economic Journal, which is widely read in the West.

Shared Leadership

Japan not only shuns political assertiveness and military power; it also worries that America's economic decline might also erode its political and military power. That would "put an unwanted burden on Japan," writes Ronald Morse of the Woodrow Wilson International Center for Scholars in the current issue of Foreign Policy magazine. "The Japanese believe they need the United States to get safely into the 21st century."

This unusual division of labor prompts C. Fred Bergsten, director of the Institute for International Economics, a public policy research organization, to argue for the revival of trilateralism, a strategy in which the United States, Japan and Germany would share the leadership of the non-Communist world. Trilateralism was first proposed in the 1970's by Henry Kissinger, David Rockefeller and others when Japanese economic power was becoming evident. It found support in the Carter Administration, which Mr. Bergsten served as a Treasury official, but has not generally been embraced by Reagan officials.

"There is only one way out: a pluralistic management," said Mr. Bergsten, who would extend a Japanese-American partnership to include Germany, which is the world's fourth largest economy, after the United States, Japan and the Soviet Union.

Partnership or trilateralism draws some of its appeal from Japan's failure to generate the take-charge imperial approach once shown by the United States and Britain.

The common Japanese view was expressed recently by Yutaka Kosai, president of the Japan Economic Research Center in Tokyo.

"I have mixed feelings about being a dominant economic power," he said, recalling his boyhood during World War II. "We hope the United States can recover and Japan will be the second fiddle. Being No. 2 is really quite pleasant."

* * *

August 28, 1988

BUSINESS FORUM: THE 'SELLING OF AMERICA'

The U.S. Needs Foreign Investors

By MORTON EGOL

Economic nationalism is on the rise and foreign investment in America is increasingly a target. A recent survey showed that 78 percent of the public would favor limiting foreign investment in this country and 40 percent would like to halt it altogether. Politicians are pandering to the public's fears and advocating restrictions on foreign investments. Instead, they should be explaining the dangers of limiting this kind of investment.

Most informed members of the American business and financial community recognize that foreign investment in the United States is not inherently a problem, but instead a partial solution to deep-seated problems of our own making. They recognize, for example, that Americans' low rate of savings and investment has made our industries less competitive in the world marketplace, forcing us to rely on foreign capital to rebuild our productive capacity.

In the face of increasing "Japan-bashing" and other xenophobic currents, business must take the lead and make rational, straightforward arguments about the importance of maintaining a free marketplace and preventing unwarranted restrictions on foreign investment—arguments like these:

- Restrictions on foreign investment would actually cause higher unemployment. New and improved industrial facilities are one consequence of foreign investment. If foreign money is invested elsewhere, the new and improved factories it helps pay for would compete against American companies, resulting in a loss of business and jobs.

- Restricting foreign investment in United States stocks and real estate would also reduce the flow of capital to the United States, which would drive up interest rates for the remaining capital. If the flow of foreign funds were to dry up, the probability of having a recession would be extremely high.

In addition, changes in the rules for foreign investment in American stocks could sour foreigners on holding any form of American securities, including United States Government debt. Since foreign investors already hold $400 billion in Federal debt—about 20 percent of the total—such a development would create the potential for widespread economic disruption.

One reason foreign companies establish operations in the United States is that they understand that increasing their American market share through exports would increase protectionist pressures. Restrictions on these companies' investment in America would simply force them to increase their production elsewhere, costing Americans jobs.

An economically interdependent world increases understanding among peoples and helps to deter war. Protectionist legislation helped to bring on the Great Depression, which encouraged the disruptive influences that led directly to World War II.

For most of its history, America's development was heavily financed by foreign investors, without giving foreigners any undue influence over Government policy. In most of the recent publicized cases where foreign investors have lobbied against new taxes or other measures, they have made common cause with mainstream American business people as well. And we already have laws governing foreign corporations' and agents' involvement in the political process, which have worked very effectively.

The argument has been made that American skills are being exported to foreign countries along with ownership. The reality is that foreign companies do not need to buy entire companies to obtain American technology. And when they do make an acquisition, they pay fair value for it, thus rewarding and encouraging American technological innovation.

Leading American business people, who confront the realities of the marketplace daily, are in a unique position to help others understand this issue. To better deflect protectionism, American business people need to address it forcefully, in their own home towns and cities, before it inflames the national psyche. We must counter those who would use foreign investors as a scapegoat for our own competitive failings.

Opinion leaders, including the media, also need to take on a stronger educational role. This begins with probing more deeply into the root causes of America's fiscal and economic problems.

The general public, in turn, must make its voice heard in this election year. Americans must demand leadership and genuine cures from our political leaders, rather than parrot-like populism.

Maintaining even-handed treatment of foreign investment will not be easy. The time to speak out is now, if we are to create a climate that encourages our traditional core values of greater personal savings and global competitiveness.

Morton Egol is managing director of Arthur Andersen & Company's worldwide government practice.

* * *

June 21, 1989

ON GLASS HOUSES AND JAPAN-BASHING

By RAYMOND VERNON

CAMBRIDGE, Mass—It is a cardinal principle of love and war that you don't start anything you can't finish. By naming Japan as one of three countries that the Administration regards as unfair in its trade policies, the U.S. Government has blatantly violated that basic tenet. More's the pity since there are better ways of resolving trade disputes.

The Japanese and U.S. economies have become deeply intertwined over the past decade. Indeed, with hundred of billions of dollars of Japan's assets in the U.S., each country has a hand on the other's throat. Threatening Japan in the press makes no more sense than threatening a first strike in nuclear politics.

When President Bush placed Japan on a list of countries accused of unfair practices, he was simply fulfilling the requirements of the 1988 Trade Act. But his public action was offensive in terms of international norms and unacceptable to any self-respecting sovereign state.

The heroic efforts of Carla Hills, the U.S. Trade Representative, to take the sting out of the labeling of Japan deserves this year's Nobel Peace prize. But it cannot be expected to succeed.

Apart from the style of its rebuff, the U.S. enters the dispute with dirty fingernails and soiled hands, a fact of which Japanese officials are acutely aware. U.S. breaches of its own trade commitments to Japan began in 1957, when it cowed Japan into applying a so-called voluntary restraint on the country's exports of textiles. Since then, the U.S. has engaged in a steady trickle of such violations, including the restraints it has obliged Japan to impose on the export of automobiles and steel to the U.S.

The history of Japan's trading practices is nothing for that country to brag about, as scores of U.S. studies have pointed out. But the flow of stories in the U.S. media painting a picture of a wily and unreliable adversary has left a grossly distorted image of who has done what to whom.

No matter. The next steps in this exchange are easy to picture. Already Administration officials have been taken aback by the angry public reaction in Japan—a reaction they ought to have expected. Sensing the risks of a downward spiral of destructive actions and responses, they will now try to take the sting out of their announcement in order to repair relations.

They will remind themselves and the rest of the world that Japan's official trade restrictions are among the lowest in the world. They will admit that the remaining problems of penetrating the Japanese market are no longer governmental restrictions but are more subtle and structural—problems beyond the easy reach of governments. In the end, the two countries will cover up the spat.

But the long-term loss will be substantial. The two countries will find it harder to work together to solve many of the problems in which they have a shared interest—improving conditions for the sale of services in world markets, keeping the European market open to outsiders and maintaining an adequate defense presence in Asia.

Could this sorry episode, with its unfortunate outcome, have been avoided? What is missing in the U.S. relationship with Japan is a mechanism for addressing disputes over economic issues in a less abrasive and more effective way. Japan is attempting to use complaint procedures of the General Agreement on Tariffs and Trade to counter U.S. actions, but the findings of GATT panels cuts little ice with the Congress.

Perhaps the bilateral trade agreement recently concluded with Canada offers a better way. In this treaty, Congress agreed to some remarkable and unprecedented changes in the handling of trade disputes.

Compulsory arbitration is to be used on a wide range of disagreements. And in some cases, binational courts are to be allowed to decide whether the two governments are carrying out their respective laws. These courts will consist of two judges appointed by the U.S., two by Canada and one chosen by the other four. They will have all the powers of an appeals court in their respective countries.

The time is ripe to consider thinking of extending this approach for the settlement of disputes with Japan as well.

Raymond Vernon is professor emeritus at the Kennedy School of Government at Harvard.

*   *   *

July 22, 1990

JAPAN ISN'T PLAYING BY DIFFERENT RULES

By MICHAEL E. PORTER

Slowly and almost imperceptibly, over more than a decade, America has been retreating from one of the most fundamental principles that has distinguished our nation from others: our faith in competition. We have been finding excuses to avoid competition and adopting policies to that effect, often, ironically, in the name of competitiveness. The words of the day are collaboration, relaxing antitrust regulations, managing trade, getting tough on dumping and protecting "intellectual property."

It is claimed that the globalization of markets has created a new era in which the old rules of competition must be discarded, and in which domestic rivalry is unimportant. Japan, widely thought to be playing by different rules, is seen as invalidating the principles of free trade. "Japan Inc.'s" conquest of world markets is said to show that a new balance between competition and cooperation, and a new role for government, is now needed. Or does it?

This line of thinking is seductive to both companies and policy makers, but it is fundamentally flawed. It rests on an incorrect view of what creates competitive advantage in today's international markets, and on a wholly mistaken view of Japan's success. Retreating from competition will not make American companies competitive, or make America competitive.

The Need for a New Paradigm

Our retreat from competition is based on an erroneous, outdated and static view of international competition in which it is believed that low capital and labor costs, a cheap currency, and economies of scale are the keys to competitive success. Thus mergers, alliances, and collaboration to gain scale and avoid wasteful duplication are thought desirable, and government intervention to foster such behavior and to reduce corporate risk is justified. We think we are doing what our successful competitors have done.

However, my recent study of 10 leading trading nations found that competitive advantage in the knowledge- and skill-intensive industries that form the backbone of advanced economies—those of Japan, Germany and the United States—is the result not of static efficiencies but of rapid improvement, innovation and upgrading. Nations and industries prosper because they can achieve high and rising levels of productivity. This occurs when companies continuously upgrade by improving quality, adding new features, penetrating new and more sophisticated market segments and applying new technology and skills to produce their products more efficiently.

Innovation and upgrading result not from a comfortable home environment in which risks have been minimized, but from pressure and challenge—from demanding home customers, from capable home-based suppliers and most of all from local rivalry. In my research I found that the most internationally competitive industries in every nation were those where there were a number of able local rivals that pressured one another to advance. Examples are American software and consumer packaged goods, German cars and chemicals, Italian fabrics and packaging machinery, and Swedish heavy trucks.

Domestic rivals engage in active feuds. They compete not only for market share but for people, for technical excellence, and perhaps most important for "bragging rights." Progress comes not from unitary or collective approaches but from diverse efforts at innovation by such a group of jealous rivals. Local rivals push each other to compete globally—a better way to gain scale than dominating the home market.

The presence of fierce local rivalry also benefits the entire national industry by stimulating the formation of specialized educational and research institutions to serve the industry. For example, every university in the south of Germany has a department of automotive engineering. This attracts and supports entry into supplier and related industries, and is a magnet for talented individuals and for investments in specialized infrastructure. The national environment becomes a self-reinforcing system that promotes rapid progress.

Globalization does not supersede the role of nations and of domestic competition but arguably makes them even more important. National differences in values, institutions and culture are integral to innovation.

Indeed, competitive advantage is often highly localized in regions or cities, in which entire clusters of rivals, their suppliers, related industries and sophisticated customers in close proximity create a rapid rate of progress. Japan, contrary to popular perception, demonstrates more clearly than any nation the incredible power of competition to foster dynamism.

Many Americans think Japanese companies have succeeded because of cooperation, cartels, and government intervention. Japan does have many cartels—such as in agriculture, chemicals, construction, paper and metals—but these are in sectors where Japan is not competitive.

In the world-class Japanese industries there are numerous Japanese rivals that have diverse strategies. These companies slug it out daily in the home market. Market shares fluctuate rapidly, as new products and production improvements are introduced at a stunning rate.

Japan's 9 automobile companies, 34 semiconductor producers and some 300 robotics competitors show how local rivals, each holding only a modest share of the home market, can prosper through rapid upgrading and global sales. The lesson to be learned from Japan is that competition works, not that we should limit it.

Benefits of Duplication

Japanese cooperative research projects, far from eliminating "wasteful" duplication, stimulate more of it. Projects sponsored by the Ministry of International Trade and Investment, take place through independent entities to which government and companies contribute personnel and modest amounts of money. However, companies invest much more internally on proprietary research on the same technologies, stimulated by the fact that all their competitors are working on them, too.

Significant joint production ventures involving Japanese rivals, moreover, were not found in any of the internationally competitive industries I studied. In semiconductor memories, where an American joint-production effort called U.S. Memories is widely viewed as necessary, there is not only no Japanese joint production but no fewer than 13 Japanese competitors producing megabyte chips, some with more than one plant. And all the frenetic innovative activity in Japan takes place within a framework of patent and copyright protection that is looser than America's.

The role of government intervention in Japan is also misunderstood. The direct and heavy MITI intervention in specific industries that Americans associate with Japanese success did not take place in many of the competitive Japanese industries like copiers, VCR's, facsimile machines and robots. Much of the direct intervention that did take place occurred in the 1960's, when Japan was a much less advanced nation. But even then, MITI failed repeatedly when it attempted to consolidate industries in areas like steel and automobile production and machine tools.

The notion that Japan is somehow playing by different rules from ours is misguided and nothing more than a smoke screen to justify suspending competition. Import protection, reluctance to buy foreign goods and "copying" foreign technology were characteristic of America and also Germany when they were developing. Japan is behaving just as we did.

Renewing Competition

What is needed today in American industry is not less competition but more. Instead of relaxing antitrust enforcement, we should be tightening it. Mergers and alliances between leading competitors should be prohibited—they are good neither for companies nor for America. Cooperative research and development involving leaders should be sanctioned only when it is through independent entities involving the majority of industry participants and represents a modest proportion of companies' overall research efforts. The Export Trading Company Act should be sharply curtailed to allow only joint sales promotion abroad and information-gathering activity. The proposal to relax antitrust scrutiny of joint production ventures should be quietly and quickly dropped.

Trade policy should focus on opening up competition rather than using comforting though false arguments to restrict it. The vigorous and increasingly effective efforts of Carla Hills, the United States Trade Representative, to reduce trade barriers in Japan and elsewhere should be the principal focus. Limiting domestic competition in response to trade barriers will only make our problems worse. The "Voluntary Restraint Agreement" should be banished from our trade repertoire. Dumping should be claimed only when foreign rivals persist in selling below their cost, not just when American companies are feeling the heat of price competition. Americans should not be influenced or persuaded by Europe's failure to stem the flood of mergers and alliances that threaten to eliminate competition in many European industries. The results of curtailing competition will prove disappointing in Europe as well.

At the root of many of the policy initiatives limiting competition is a loss of self-confidence in American industry, which is reflected in Washington. Instead of looking forward to the next generation of products and processes, too many companies are scrambling to block challenges to their current market positions through mergers, alliances and trips to Washington to secure government help.

A momentum of retreat has been created that is hard to arrest. Once government begins to "help" by allowing companies to reduce their risk or avoid the painful steps it takes to become truly competitive, almost irresistible demands are created for more help. This retreat must stop before it becomes a rout. This is the lesson of company history and of national economic history. When a nation becomes preoccupied with complaining about other nations' "unfair" practices, its days of economic dynamism are numbered.

What is needed instead is re-commitment to one of America's most unique national values, competition. Ironically, it was America that exported competition to Japan and Germany after World War II. The postwar breakup of their cartels and dominant companies played an immeasurable role in their startling economic success. As uncomfortable as competition always is, it remains the only way that American industry will ever truly prosper.

Michael E. Porter, a professor of business administration at the Harvard Business School, is author of "The Competitive Advantage of Nations."

* * *

April 16, 1992

TRADE CURBS: DO THEY DO THE JOB?

By STEVEN GREENHOUSE
Special to The New York Times

WASHINGTON, April 15—In the midst of the recession and election campaign, protectionist pressures have boiled to the surface, but economists say that import restrictions have had glaringly mixed results for the industries they were supposed to help.

For a few industries like motorcycle manufacturers, protection has provided the breathing room they wanted to begin to regain their strength. But several other industries, most notably autos, are worse off. For some industries, like steel and machine tools, the results of protection have been less than desired. And in most cases, economists generally agree, one clear loser is the American consumer.

"Except for motorcycles, I can't think of a case where the benefits that protection gives to producers outweigh the injury suffered by consumers," said Gary Hufbauer, a fellow at the Institute for International Economics in Washington. He figures that in the mid-1980's quotas on Japanese car imports cost American car buyers an average of $500 a car, whether the car was imported or domestically made.

Weighing Costs and Benefits

Several Presidential candidates, including Patrick J. Buchanan, a Republican, and Edmund G. Brown Jr., a Demo-

crat, have backed protection, viewing it as much-needed medicine for the nation's ailing industries. President Bush and Gov. Bill Clinton of Arkansas say they support free but fair trade and have shunned strong protectionist rhetoric.

The protectionist drumbeat, which reached a peak during the Michigan primary, is expected to remain strong in April when the primaries continue in industrial states like Pennsylvania.

Many economists say they are unenthusiastic about protection because, in their view, Washington's trade negotiators have often failed to chose its most effective forms. This has sometimes produced painful results, as when import quotas prompted Japanese car makers to build factories in Detroit's backyard.

"The lesson is that very often protectionist measures can behave in an unanticipated way and can even be counterproductive," said Daniel Roos, director of the International Motor Vehicle Program at the Massachusetts Institute of Technology.

Tariffs are generally more helpful than quotas, because they have a direct effect in making foreign products less competitive. In contrast, quotas, which limit a product's supply, can strengthen foreign competitors by enabling them to raise prices and profits, giving them more money to expand or develop new products.

"Quotas are an extremely blunt instrument," said Robert Z. Lawrence, professor of international trade at the Kennedy School of Government at Harvard University.

One novel form of protection came in 1986 when American semiconductor companies, worried about cutthroat pricing by Japanese competitors, pressed Washington to get the Japanese to sign an agreement setting a floor on computer chip prices.

Industry analysts say the agreement came too late to save many American producers of the main type of basic memory chips, but by subtly helping persuade Japanese chip makers to be less aggressive, the accord helped American companies making some newer types of chips. Nonetheless, many American computer makers complained that the agreement made them less competitive against the Japanese because they had to pay more for their computer chips.

Companies can grow stronger under protection if they use it as an opportunity to invest in equipment, improve product quality and otherwise shape up, economists say, although lazy companies can use protection as a cushion.

"Quotas give you a window of opportunity," said Eli Lustgarten, an industrial analyst at Paine Webber. "If you don't take advantage of that window to solve your problems, then you're going to disappear."

Labor unions are often the biggest fans of quotas and voluntary restraint agreements. "They are designed to provide an industry with time to adjust to specific foreign competition," said Rudy Oswald, chief economist for the A.F.L.-C.I.O. "It's desirable to allow industries to do that because, otherwise, we will put whole industries out of business."

While most economists say protection means higher prices and fewer choices for consumers, Mr. Oswald argues that protection can mean more competition and lower prices in the long run by preventing Japanese cartels from dominating the American market and jacking up prices.

But in the view of many economists, the political debate about protection too often focuses on the needs of industry, while ignoring consumers, many economists say.

"Protection has cost American consumers big bucks," Mr. Hufbauer said. "If people knew how much it was going to cost them, wouldn't they insist that the nation, that the industries involved, get a better payoff from protection?"

AUTOS
For the Big Three, A Policy Misfires

Cars imported from Japan had 20.5 percent of the American market when a voluntary-restraint agreement on such imports took effect in 1981. Last year, Japanese imports and cars built in Japanese factories in the United States grabbed 30.3 percent of the domestic market. What is more, despite a decade of quotas, the Big Three lost a record $7.5 billion last year.

What went wrong?

The quotas helped Japan's auto makers by fattening their profits. As American demand for Hondas and Toyotas outstripped the supply, prices and profit margins rose, giving the auto makers more money to invest in new models and factories.

The quotas also encouraged the Japanese to build ultramodern factories in the United States. While this has hurt Detroit, many economists say the transplant factories are a positive development, asserting that they are creating jobs and a more efficient domestic car industry, although one that is Japanese-owned.

By limiting the number of cars—rather than the total value of Japanese imports—the quotas gave Honda, Toyota and others a big incentive to build larger, more profitable cars. Honda turned its hot-selling Accord into a midsize car, while Toyota with its Acura, Honda with Lexus and Nissan with Infiniti put new entrants in the upper tier.

At the same time, the quotas swelled the profit margins of Detroit's Big Three, reducing the urgency for them to grow more competitive. Instead, the industry bought financial institutions, computer services companies, electronics companies and foreign auto makers, like Jaguar. If that money had gone into building more modern plants, Detroit would not be in such bad shape, many economists say.

"We created an incentive for the foreign producers to become more competitive, and we created an incentive for the domestic producers not to get more competitive," said Michael Borrus, co-director of the Berkeley Roundtable on the International Economy at the University of California. "What's perverse is American consumers paid for all of this."

The Big Three did invest billions of dollars in new plants, equipment and designs, but most industry analysts say that the Big Three still lag behind the Japanese in managing their employees, building quality into the assembly line and developing efficient factories.

"There have been some successes, but they happen to be in a broader context of failure," said Harley Shaiken, a visiting

Two Pictures of Protectionism

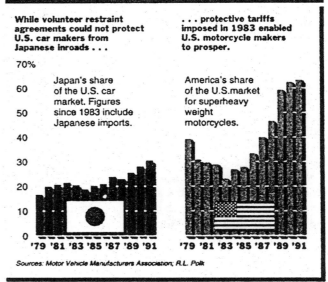

While volunteer restraint agreements could not protect U.S. car makers from Japanese inroads . . .

Japan's share of the U.S. car market. Figures since 1983 include Japanese imports.

. . . protective tariffs imposed in 1983 enabled U.S. motorcycle makers to prosper.

America's share of the U.S. market for superheavy weight motorcycles.

'79 '81 '83 '85 '87 '89 '91   '79 '81 '83 '85 '87 '89 '91

Sources: Motor Vehicle Manufacturers Association; R.L. Polk

The New York Times

scholar at the Institute of Industrial Relations at the University of California at Berkeley.

And Mr. Roos of M.I.T. added: "There is no question that the American product has improved, but you are competing against a moving target. It isn't sufficient to play catch-up baseball."

MOTORCYCLES
Harley-Davidson A Rare Success

After recession and a flood of Japanese imports threatened Harley-Davidson Inc.'s survival in 1982, the Government agreed to impose five years of tariffs on Japanese motorcycles. The tariffs began at 45 percent in 1983 and were scheduled to decline to 10 percent in 1987, before being phased out.

A company known for making the roaring machines Marlon Brando rode in "The Wild Ones," Harley by the early 1980's was known for motorcycles that leaked oil and broke down easily. Under the umbrella of protection, it re-engineered its motorcycles, improved quality, and cut its costs by adopting new inventory methods and laying off layers of management. As a result, its market share has soared to 63 percent in large motorcycles, up from 23 percent in 1983. The plunge of the dollar after 1985 also helped.

"The tariffs gave us time to complete the revitalization that we had undertaken," said Jeffrey Bleustein, executive vice president at Harley-Davidson. "The fact that the tariffs declined told us we better get going as fast as we could."

Harley-Davidson regained its health so quickly that it asked Washington to eliminate the tariffs a year early. In fact, Harley is doing so well it is exporting aggressively to Japan.

"The Harley-Davidson case was exactly the way protection is supposed to work," said Mr. Hufbauer, the economist. "If you had many examples like that, you would be much more enthusiastic about protection."

MACHINE TOOLS
Help for Some, Hurt for Others

The machine tool industry shows how protection can have mixed effects, with some companies saying quotas have rescued them, while others say quotas have nearly drowned them.

In 1986, when imported machine tools were flooding in at bargain prices, the industry asked for protection. The Pentagon lent a sympathetic ear, fearing that the nation's leadership in building weapons would suffer if the industry that made metal-cutting machinery was crippled.

So in 1987, the Government, finding that Japanese and Taiwan competitors had dumped machines on the American market at improperly low prices, got those competitors to accept a voluntary-restraint agreement, called a V.R.A. The quotas sought to keep imports from rising above 50 percent of the market.

Many machine tool manufacturers say the quotas, and the weaker dollar, have stabilized the market and increased their profits, enabling them to spend more on capital investment and developing new products.

Since the quotas took effect, for example, Cincinnati Milacron, a large machine tool producer, has increased its research and development budget by 50 percent, company officials say. It now introduces twice as many new models a year as before the quotas. "The V.R.A.'s have allowed us to rededicate ourselves to turning the machine tool business around," said Christopher C. Cole, vice president for strategy at Milacron.

But some machine tool makers say the quotas have hurt. For example, Brian McLaughlin, chief executive of Hurco, a machine tool company in Indianapolis, said the quotas almost drove his company bankrupt by preventing it from buying parts from Taiwan parts that represented 30 percent of the value of Hurco's machines.

Mr. McLaughlin said Hurco had cut back spending on developing advanced items like electronic controls because the quotas have forced it to invest in low-technology machines to produce basic cast-iron parts once obtained from Taiwan. He said the quotas might push Hurco to move production and 500 jobs overseas.

Choking Off Supplies

"All we want to bring in are a few routine parts from Taiwan, and then incorporate 70 percent U.S. content," he said. "The quotas are telling us, 'You have to take U.S. jobs somewhere else,' because they're forcing up the costs of our production."

While many executives hail the quotas, economists ask why, if the quotas have been so successful, the industry still asked the Bush Administration last year for five more years of protection. In a compromise in December, President Bush extended the quotas for two years.

"We've put a tremendous amount of money into developing new machines over the past few years so we asked for an extension of the V.R.A.'s to give us more time to market these machines so we can make the money back," said John Fedor, president of Masco Machine Inc., a machine tool company in Cleveland.

STEEL
Breathing Spell Spurs A Fragile Comeback

When steel companies and steelworkers lobbied for protection in 1984 and again in 1989, they argued that temporary relief from low-priced imports would allow the industry to regain its strength.

Now, eight years after the quotas began, the nation's major steelmakers have staged a comeback by improving productivity and quality, but they lost more than $2 billion last year because capacity still outstrips demand. The quotas expired March 31, and the Bush Administration has decided not to extend them, preferring to rely on existing trade laws to battle unfairly priced imports.

In the Administration's view, the American industry has been shielded enough from competition and should be able to stand on its own. The industry is certainly a more formidable competitor than before, but many analysts say this transformation was brought about only partly by protection and mostly by the strong dollar and competitive pressures from low-cost, nonunion domestic mini-mills.

History of a Turnaround

Some industry analysts say the big steelmakers did little to increase efficiency in the late 1970's and early 1980's when they were protected by a so-called trigger price mechanism that protected steelmakers against low-priced imports. They say this is a classic example of protection coddling industries into laziness.

The industry's attitude changed radically after 1982, when recession and a strong dollar drove it into crisis. Since then, the big steelmakers have vastly improved quality and productivity, with the number of man-hours required to produce a ton of steel cut in half. Steelmakers have slashed employment from 240,000 in 1984 to 160,000 today, showing that protection is not always friendly to workers. And the industry has spent more than $12 billion on equipment since 1984, although Japanese and Korean companies have helped finance many of these modernizations.

"The V.R.A.'s gave us some breathing room to become more competitive," said Lynn Williams, president of the United Steelworkers of America. For their part, industry officials say the quotas fattened their profits during the late 1980's, giving them cash to invest.

Still, faced with recession and worldwide overcapacity the nation's steelmakers complain that foreign competitors are dumping steel at cut-throat prices. For example, a ton of cold-rolled steel, which is used in automobiles, sells for $440 a ton, compared with $504 a ton in 1980.

All this shows that protection is no panacea. "Just because you've become much more competitive doesn't necessary keep you from losing money," said James Hughes, a spokesman for the American Iron and Steel Institute, the industry trade group.

Correction

An article in Business Day on April 16 about import barriers misidentified the motorcycle that Marlon Brando rode in the movie "The Wild One." It was a Triumph.

* * *

December 19, 1993

THE NATIONALIST ROADBLOCK IN EUROPE

By RICHARD W. STEVENSON

LONDON—The collapse of the merger between Volvo of Sweden and Renault of France reflected many factors, but among them was one particularly worrisome in Europe: rising economic nationalism.

The proposed Volvo-Renault merger fell apart this month against a backdrop of cross-border strains involving many of Europe's large corporations and industries. Volkswagen of Germany, struggling to restore its financial equilibrium, has provoked harsh criticism in Spain with its plan to close its aged Zona Franca car plant in Barcelona operated by its money-losing subsidiary, SEAT, at a time when Spain has one of Europe's highest unemployment rates. At the same time, Volkswagen is squabbling with the Czech Government over its investment plans in Skoda, the car maker.

Airbus Industrie, the four-country aircraft-building consortium based in France, has found it difficult to proceed with proposals to reorganize itself along more efficient lines because each member wants to protect jobs in its own country.

Executives at C.S.A., the Czech national airline, have been feuding with their counterparts at Air France, which owns a stake in the carrier. Four European airlines—S.A.S., KLM Royal Dutch Airlines, Swissair and Austrian Airlines—nearly overcame a host of hurdles, including national economic interests, to agree to a merger this fall. But the talks collapsed when the airlines failed to agree on which American carrier would be their partner. Since then, Austrian Airlines, Lufthansa and Swissair have begun talking about some kind of cooperation, and S.A.S. and Austrian are holding talks with Swissair about a modest alliance.

"There's no question that nationalism is a major problem for a lot of European companies who need to merge or take each other over in an effort to consolidate their industries," said Constantinos Markides, an assistant professor of strategic management at the London Business School.

In the case of Volvo and Renault, it is too early to say whether Volvo's abandonment of the deal will leave it badly wounded, as Pehr Gyllenhammar, the chairman of Volvo, architect of the deal and ardent supporter of Swedish integration into the European Community, said recently. Most of the top managers at Volvo backed the view that its fortunes were turning for the better and there was no need to rush into a full-blown merger with Renault.

The shareholders and managers of Volvo criticized several key aspects of the deal, including the vagueness of the French Government's plan to privatize Renault and the difficulty of putting a precise value on Volvo's share of the merged car-making enterprise. In the end, the merger seemed doomed by a general feeling that Volvo, a symbol of Sweden's industrial prowess, was being bargained away too cheaply to a foreign partner that could not be entrusted with the fate of Swedish jobs.

"The critics of our merger turn their backs on Europe and the world," Mr. Gyllenhammar said with undisguised bitterness. He resigned from Volvo after its decision to scuttle the deal.

To a degree, the spread of nationalism into the affairs of corporations is an extension of the nationalistic sentiments that have played a prominent role in stalling the European Community's attempts to widen and deepen the single market through mechanisms like a single currency.

The trend in some cases, including that of Volvo, is accelerated when one or more of the potential partners—in this case, Renault—is state owned. The French Government, in particular, is viewed throughout Europe as highly susceptible to pressure from workers to take steps to protect their own jobs, even when other, broader economic interests may be at stake.

And the rise of corporate nationalism is perhaps not surprising given the deep recession plaguing most of Europe and the double-digit unemployment rates in most countries.

"These nationalistic problems, looking at them over the long run, are becoming less of a factor over all, but they always become more of a problem during times of economic difficulty," Professor Markides said.

Because nearly all the barriers to trade within the European Community have been eliminated, companies are seeking efficiencies that come with scale, to aid them in competition.

In many industries—especially large employers like the automobile and steel businesses—companies are being pushed toward consolidation by overcapacity and the need to cut costs substantially.

"I would not say that the Volvo situation is in any way, shape or form a sign that cross-border mergers in Europe are dead," said Jim Wadia, a partner at Arthur Andersen & Company, the consulting firm, in London.

Mr. Wadia said, however, that in certain cases bringing companies together had become more difficult, not just when large numbers of jobs might be at stake, but when countries perceived that control of key technologies, or leadership in those technologies, might be at stake.

* * *

April 30, 1998

GLOBAL TUG, NATIONAL TETHER

_____

As Companies Look Overseas, Governments Hold the Strings

_____

By LOUIS UCHITELLE

For nearly three years, Caterpillar Inc. has been banging its head against the Clinton Administration door, trying to get Government-sponsored loans for the sale of its big earthmov-

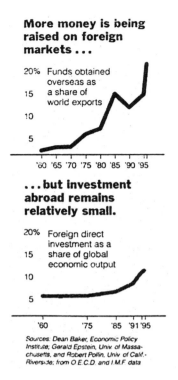

More money is being raised on foreign markets . . .

20%   Funds obtained
15   overseas as
          a share of
10   world exports
5

'60 '65 '70 '75 '80 '85 '90 '95

. . . but investment abroad remains relatively small.

20%   Foreign direct
15   investment as a
          share of global
10   economic output
5

'60   '75   '85 '91 '95

Sources: Dean Baker, Economic Policy
Institute; Gerald Epstein, Univ. of Massa-
chusetts, and Robert Pollin, Univ. of Calif.-
Riverside; from O.E.C.D. and I.M.F. data

ers to China. Beijing is buying them by the dozens to build the giant Three Gorges Dam, which the Administration considers damaging to the environment.

So the Chinese have turned to suppliers in Japan and Europe, where governments are less concerned about the environment and more forthcoming with credit. "We've only managed to sell the Chinese a few off-highway trucks," a Caterpillar official said.

That is hardly the description of a giant multinational ranging unfettered across the world. For all the talk of economic globalization, the process is still in an early stage.

A few multinationals, such as I.B.M., Royal Dutch/Shell or Imperial Chemical Industries, are ahead of the pack in spreading their revenues, research, financing, stockholders and management over many countries. But the majority are more like Caterpillar in America, the Mitsubishi Corporation in Japan or Volkswagen in Germany. For all their involvement in overseas sales and investment, nationality still binds them to home.

"What we have is United States, European and Japanese corporations trying to dress in global clothing," said William W. Keller, executive director of the Center for International Studies at the Massachusetts Institute of Technology. "But if you conceive of globalization as being the rootlessness of corporations, that is a paradox. You don't have corporations without states attached to them. When they need help, you find out who they really belong to."

Many corporations have invoked the competitive pressures of an increasingly borderless global economy as the reason for moving operations and jobs abroad and to press for other concessions.

But a proliferation of treaty negotiations in recent months, aimed at setting rules for the global economy—most of them

favorable so far to business—has raised a fresh question: just how untethered are these companies and who, therefore, should have a voice in the rule-making?

"We have to keep separate that the mobility of corporations has increased from the notion that we are living in a completely seamless integrated world market that gives national government no bargaining power to set standards," said Dani Rodrik, an economist at Harvard. "The latter has not happened."

Some want to stop the process of globalization. But others, including a re-energized American labor movement, are more interested in setting international rules of the road. Indeed, 12 different rule-making negotiations are currently under way.

Most are inspired by the North American Free Trade Agreement and the treaty that set up the World Trade Organization, in which the United States and 116 other nations agreed essentially to recognize W.T.O. rulings as having the power of national law. Several of the agreements now being discussed would require Senate ratification and would be similarly binding. That would push the setting of global rules beyond the voluntary guidelines that have characterized most such agreements since World War II.

"Thus far, the corporations, more than any other group, are shaping the new global regulations," said Raymond Vernon, an economist at Harvard's Kennedy School of Government. "It is not that they are abandoning their countries for a global identity. They are simply pushing abroad and arguing that if the obstacles are cleared away, they will produce enough for everyone and raise all boats."

The recent surge in rule-making brings out strange bedfellows. Corporate America and the A.F.L.-C.I.O. find themselves on one side, favoring an international stage, while the most visible advocates of those who want the rules made in America include Patrick J. Buchanan, the conservative commentator and politician, and Ralph Nader, the liberal consumer advocate.

"Rather than international negotiations, the rules should be written through Congress, where you can have discussion and debate," Mr. Nader said. As an example, he argued, Congress can no longer effectively ban imports of products made with child labor. Because the W.T.O. does not specifically prohibit such trade, such a law could be challenged before the organization, which could then fine the United States.

American corporate executives see in the new wave of rule-making not only the elimination of remaining trade barriers but also the removal of restrictions on investment abroad and greater freedom to purchase foreign companies. For Mr. Nader and Mr. Buchanan, however, these are hidden tools to make the shifting of jobs abroad that much easier. Mr. Buchanan advocates protective tariffs to keep companies at home, while Mr. Nader would discourage job-shifting by canceling tax breaks, imposing a "social tariff" and prohibiting Export-Import Bank loans for exports that contain too many foreign parts.

The bank once financed only those exports manufactured entirely in the United States. But it has relaxed that rule in recent years and now, for example, provides credits to customers of the Boeing Company to purchase aircraft that have as much as 15 percent "foreign content," and sometimes more.

Bucking such trends is futile, says John J. Sweeney, president of the A.F.L.-C.I.O. He calls the Nader-Buchanan approach simplistic. "It is a very good feeling to tell the workers we are going to bring all the jobs back," he said, "but it is not realistic."

With that in mind, the American labor movement has joined corporate America in embracing global rule-making. Instead of waging a losing battle to keep jobs at home, the A.F.L.-C.I.O. is demanding a seat at the rule-making table, with only limited success so far. The intention is to preserve labor standards at home by raising them abroad.

That would be done by writing into every agreement a ban against child and prison labor, as well as guarantees that foreign workers can assemble freely and engage in collective bargaining. "If you can get rid of repression, workers can negotiate their own conditions," Mr. Sweeney said. The Administration included the A.F.L.-C.I.O. prescription in a bill now before Congress asking for $18 billion in new American financing for the International Monetary Fund. The language has survived so far in the House and Senate.

The treaty talks draw little public attention. They range from negotiations to eliminate tariffs on products such as cellular phones and computers to high-level talks between European and American business executives to develop common product standards that would then be incorporated into binding treaties.

The World Trade Organization, born in the tariff-cutting Uruguay Round agreement, plays a big role in this process, setting new standards, reducing more tariffs and eliminating other barriers to trade and investment.

"This is about international commerce," said Diane Sullivan, director of international trade at the National Association of Manufacturers. "Labor and the environment are not excluded, but they are not at the center of the W.T.O's concerns."

These outsiders are clamoring to make their views known in the negotiations for a treaty that is to be called the Multilateral Agreement on Investment.

The agreement is being negotiated under the umbrella of the 29-nation Organization for Economic Cooperation and Development. Government negotiators, most representing major industrial powers, have met periodically at the organization's headquarters in Paris. The last session took place in mid-April. The group's main goal is to produce a binding treaty that would give foreign corporations a legal status equal to that of domestic companies, establish rules for prompt and sufficient payment in cases of expropriation and give foreign companies equal bidding rights in privatizations of state enterprises.

The United States already has a number of similar, bilateral agreements, but this would be the first multilateral treaty. And it is drawing fire from Mr. Nader and others, including labor, which is pressing for a greater say in the talks. As a result, the early May target date for completing an agreement has been postponed at least six months to allow for "consultation and assessment," the organization said this week.

Acknowledging the pressure, Alan Larson, Assistant Secretary of State for Economic and Business Affairs, who represents the United States in the negotiations, said: "There is strong support for measures in the treaty that would advance this country's environmental goals and our agenda on international labor standards. This treaty will not interfere with the ability of the United States to regulate in a normal and nondiscriminatory fashion to protect the environment or worker safety or health."

Faced with such regulation, Mr. Rodrik of Harvard argues, corporations will not decamp. "We exaggerate how effectively corporations can evade national rules," he said.

Indeed, many top executives of United States multinationals see their companies as essentially American in identity. That was evident in interviews with a half-dozen of them, and in the replies of others to a letter from Mr. Nader, who has been campaigning for companies to recite the Pledge of Allegiance, in the company's name, at each annual meeting of shareholders. The pledge would be a gesture of corporate loyalty to the United States in return for the tax breaks and other advantages that companies receive.

None of the 45 corporations that replied to Mr. Nader have agreed to such a proposal. Many argue that it would interfere with efforts to be good corporate citizens elsewhere in the world. Yet most spoke of their companies as essentially American in their management, headquarters, ownership and workers.

"It would be difficult to disassociate ourselves from America, even if we wanted to do so," Steve Burrow, president of the Anheuser-Busch Companies' international operation, said in an interview. "Our packaging is even red, white and blue, and the American eagle is part of our image. But our obligation is to our shareholders, and our international operation is an important part of increasing share value."

All these themes run through Caterpillar's effort to get low-interest credit. The company has moved about 25 percent of its production abroad; the rest is concentrated in the Midwest, where management and research are also centered. But overseas sales are rising rapidly, and the corporate goal is to have 75 percent of sales from abroad by 2010, up from 50 percent today.

The Export-Import Bank plays a significant role in this strategy, already providing low-interest credits for $300 million of Caterpillar's $19 billion in annual revenue. If sales for the Three Gorges project on the Yangtze River in China were to be similarly financed, the total would be $350 million or more.

Capital, of course, now flows relatively easily around the world, making loans available practically everywhere. But when Caterpillar is competing to sell diesel engines to Zambia, gold mining equipment to Russia and earthmovers to China, the global lenders are not so quick to offer low-interest loans.

So Caterpillar and other multinationals continue to turn to their home governments. "In really tough, high-risk, high-opportunity markets, a government will always have greater leverage for repayment than a bank," said William C. Lane, a Caterpillar executive in Washington. "You really have to have someone in your corner."

CRITICAL MOMENT: THE NAFTA DEBATE

March 29, 1990

FREE-TRADE TALKS WITH U.S. SET OFF DEBATE IN MEXICO

By LARRY ROHTER
Special to The New York Times

MEXICO CITY, March 28—In a break with the policy of economic nationalism that has prevailed here since the Mexican Revolution of 1910, President Carlos Salinas de Gortari has agreed to consider negotiations for a free-trade agreement with the United States.

The move represents a huge political gamble and has prompted a spirited public debate.

The Bush Administration said Tuesday that the two Governments had begun "preliminary discussions" that could lead to a pact similar to one that last year eliminated major trade barriers between the United States and Canada.

But such an agreement, which could pave the way for a North American common market, is extremely controversial here and would also force other Latin American governments to rethink their place in the world.

Elimination of Barriers

Free-trade agreements are intended to eliminate barriers to the flow of goods between the countries involved. These restrictions include quotas limiting the import of goods and services or duties on product shipments. For example, the United States-Canadian free-trade agreement, which went into effect on Jan. 1, 1989, calls for duties to be reduced or eliminated on 8,000 categories of products over the next 10 years. The pact also makes it easier for Americans and Canadians to work in each other's markets.

Since coming to power in 1929, the Institutional Revolutionary Party has emphasized development of the Mexican economy by keeping foreign competition out and subsidizing domestic producers. That model was developed in large part to prevent Mexico and its economy from being swallowed by United States interests, whose extensive acquisition of mines, railroads, oil companies and ranches helped detonate the revolution that the party still claims to defend.

Suspicion Still a Force

Over the last decade, a period of crisis marked by stagnation and inflation, Mexico has given up some of its traditional economic isolation by moves like joining the General Agreement on Tariffs and Trade in 1986. But suspicion of American intentions remains a potent force in Mexican politics, and no candidate for office ever gives a speech without promising to protect the country's "sovereignty" and "independence."

There is no timetable for talks about formal economic integration between the two countries, Mexican and American officials said, and the obstacles that must be overcome are likely to be formidable. Among the most politically sensitive issues are the immigration of Mexican labor to the United States and American ownership and exploitation of natural resources in Mexico.

In a statement issued Tuesday, the Mexican Embassy in Washington said "it cannot be confirmed that a free-trade agreement will be established between both countries." Nevertheless, the mere fact that such a possibility is now under consideration has generated immediate alarm and concern here.

"Our way of life is at stake," a political analyst, Lorenzo Meyer, wrote this morning in Excelsior, Mexico's leading newspaper. "We should take decisions knowing, as much as is possible, what we will gain and lose by integrating ourselves with the economy of a great power, one from which we previously considered it our historic and patriotic duty to protect and separate ourselves."

Political parties on both the left, which emerged as the country's second-largest political force in the 1988 elections, and the right have already accused the Salinas administration of rushing too eagerly into Washington's economic embrace and said the North American common market would be a major issue in next year's midterm elections. A columnist, Gaston Garcia Cantu, a fervent nationalist who generally supports Mr. Salinas, recently suggested that what was really at stake was not economic integration but an "annexation" similar to that of Texas in 1836 and a betrayal of the rest of Latin America.

'Tied to Latin America'

Most Latin American countries appear to believe that the destiny of Mexico lies to its north, not to its south, and that the willingness of Mr. Salinas to consider a free-trade agreement with the United States and Canada left them out in the cold.

"Mexico has always talked about the economic integration of Latin America," a South American diplomat here said, "but they are at the gate of the largest market in the world, and whether they like it or not, economic logic dictates that they associate themselves more closely with that market. It appears they have now reached the same conclusion."

Like his predecessors, Mr. Salinas, a 41-year-old Harvard-educated economist, initially shunned too close an economic relationship with the United States and sought trade and investment links elsewhere. In an interview in January 1988 after being named the presidential candidate of the Institutional Revolutionary Party, he said that "I am not in favor" of any free-trade or common market plan because "there is such a different economic level between the United States and Mexico."

But Mexican officials and foreign diplomats here said that since taking office in December 1988, Mr. Salinas had come to question whether Mexico could realistically hope to use Western Europe and Japan as an economic counterbalance to the United States. They say he has been profoundly influenced by recent events in Europe, especially the collapse of Communism in Eastern Europe and the decision of the European Community to eliminate all trade barriers in 1992.

European 'Fascination' Cited

In late January, Mr. Salinas visited Europe and complained that Western Europe's "fascination" with events in the Eastern bloc was resulting in "a relative lack of attention to other parts of the world." A Mexican official said Mr. Salinas was particularly sobered by his meetings with Prime Ministers Helmut Kohl of West Germany and Margaret Thatcher of Britain and his discussions with business executives in both countries.

Mexican officials and foreign diplomats said Mr. Salinas emerged from those contacts with the belief that Mexico could not hope for large flows of European investment during the next few years.

Late in February, the Minister of Commerce and Industry, Jaime Serra, and Mr. Salinas's chief economic adviser, Jose Cordoba, agreed to discuss a unified North American market further while in Washington for talks on other matters.

Bank Debt Converted

Approximately $44 billion of Mexico's commercial bank debt was converted into bonds yesterday, the Mexican Government and Citibank announced. William R. Rhodes, Citibank's senior executive-international, said the transaction was the largest long-term bond issue ever.

Also yesterday, Mexico received $370 million in its first drawdown of some $1.1 billion in new money provided by the agreement.

The 30-year bonds were issued as part of an agreement Mexico worked out with its bank lenders last year and signed earlier this year.

The agreement covered virtually all of the $48.5 billion in medium- and long-term debt that Mexico owes to 470 banks worldwide. Under the plan, the banks chose between making new loans to Mexico or exchanging their debt for bonds on terms that reduce Mexico's debt burden by 35 percent.

*   *   *

April 1, 1990

FOR MEXICO,
FREEDOM BEFORE FREE TRADE

By CUAUHTEMOC CARDENAS

Cuauhtemoc Cardenas was a candidate for the Mexican presidency in 1988. The following is excerpted from an article in the quarterly Foreign Policy.

MEXICO CITY—The decision by Mexico's President, Carlos Salinas de Gortari, to consider a free-trade agreement with the U.S. should not divert attention from the salient problem facing Mexico: the status of the Institutional Revolutionary Party as one of the last remaining authoritarian political systems in the world.

The present regime believes that the key to modernizing Mexico is almost exclusively through the economy. The Government appears convinced that free-market policies, trade and investment openings—and low wages to increase Mexico's competitiveness—will alone bring Mexico into the 21st century.

Eliminating the archaic features of the Mexican political system are definitely not on the current regime's agenda. Those features include paternalism, presidential centralism, populist demagogy, electoral fraud, the captivity of the union movement and of peasant organizations, control of much of the mass media, and corruption and repression. Those elements are crucial to suppressing dissent and preserving the incestuous and undemocratic relationship that the ruling party, known as P.R.I., enjoys with the Mexican state.

The Government hopes to manage the dilemma of separating political and economic reform by relying on U.S. financing and on Washington's political support. The regime is gambling that it can buy off the country's middle classes and neutralize popular discontent with the help of American resources, thus containing demands for democratization that are only skin-deep.

But the economic modernization that Mexico needs cannot be carried out without a thorough democratization of the country's politics and society. This link is not rhetorical. To select and implement the economic changes that the country needs will require broad support from the majority of the Mexican people. This can be obtained only through a true political opening. Otherwise, the necessary economic reforms will not take root.

The issue is not whether the country should be modernized and opened up, nor whether many of the costlier chapters of the Mexican welfare state should be made more efficient and cost effective. Nor is the point whether parts of the state-owned sector of the economy should be made more productive and remain public, be privatized, or simply be shut down. The real issue is how deeply, at what speed and under what conditions the changes should be undertaken.

The true debate lies in who should pay the unavoidable costs of restructuring. To date, the Mexican workers—through sharply lower real wages and dramatic cuts in education, health and housing expenditures—have carried a disproportionate share of the burden.

The only way to place adequate and fair restraints on a reform program like the one Mexico needs is through democratic debate and accountable officials and institutions. Now, economic management is conducted away from public scrutiny. Those arbitrary measures and secret deals have not renewed Mexico's confidence in its economic future nor induced open competition. As has happened with prior economic strategies, business interests and a few politicians have profited immensely.

Americans should be aware of one essential fact: The new Mexican administration offers the U.S. an implicit deal, of which the free-trade agreement is the latest step. Mexico will indiscriminately put in place the type of economic reforms that the U.S. always wanted for Mexico, but the U.S. will accept and protect the existing political system.

This trade-off is highly damaging to the genuine interests of Mexicans. It comes at the expense of Mexico's pride, dignity and sovereignty. The Mexican people want a friendly and balanced relationship with the U.S., but not at the cost of bailing out Mexico's authoritarian government.

This is not to say that Mexican democratization is a quest in which the U.S. should be actively involved. Mexican voters can and will conquer pluralism and will ultimately bury the one-party system that suffocates our society. Both Panama's brand of democratization, imposed under the boots of American infantry, and Mexico's so-called modernization, anti-democratic and dependent on United States financing, offer no bases for a mutually respectful relationship.

* * *

April 22, 1990

WHY MEXICO NEEDS A FREE TRADE PACT

By SIDNEY WEINTRAUB

During the 1980's, Mexico embarked upon what can properly be called its second revolution. This revolution, which relies upon exports for economic growth, recognizes that the majority of Mexico's trade is with the United States and that this trade is in what are called intermediate goods—the engine and not necessarily the automobile, semi-conductors and not always computers. This trade takes place largely within the same industry, even within the same company, between a parent and an affiliate. Partly because of this trade, Mexico has relaxed restrictions on foreign direct investment. The two countries are thus suppliers to each other's production facilities, with around 90 percent of Mexico's exports of manufactured goods going to the United States.

The question arises of whether this mutual industrial reliance is healthy, particularly for Mexico. It makes Mexico vulnerable to an American economic downturn or to American protectionism. With respect to the latter, Mexico has one assurance against widespread American import restrictions: the close alliances that now exist between large companies operating in both countries. Mexican concerns over excessive reliance on the United States market can be dissipated only as Mexican industry increases its competitiveness.

The logical next question is whether this integration is best secured by a more formal agreement between the two countries. Mexican leaders have decided that it is and they have suggested starting the process for free-trade negotiations. Canada also made the decision to enter into a free-trade agreement with the United States to more thoroughly secure access to the American market. By allocating production for a vastly larger combined market, Canada is able to increase its industrial productivity and, thereby, its global competitive position.

The decision to enter into a free-trade agreement with the United States was controversial in Canada out of concern for its national political and cultural identity. It will be sensitive in Mexico as well, out of fear of the loss of national sovereignty. However, if Mexico is to become a developed country, it will have to compete on first-world terms. Mexico cannot do that based on the size of its domestic market alone. That is the logic behind Mexico's suggestion that negotiations for a free-trade agreement begin.

Sidney Weintraub, distinguished visiting scholar at the Center for Strategic and International Studies in Washington, is author of "A Marriage of Convenience: Relations Between Mexico and the United States."

* * *

June 12, 1990

U.S. AND MEXICANS CAUTIOUSLY BACK FREE-TRADE IDEA

By LARRY ROHTER
Special to The New York Times

WASHINGTON, June 11—The United States and Mexico agreed in principle today to move toward negotiating a "comprehensive free-trade agreement" but, in an acknowledgment that substantial economic and political hurdles remained, the two nations stopped short of announcing the start of formal talks.

Officials of both nations said any agreement to dismantle barriers to the free flow of goods, money and labor was likely to face significant opposition in the United States.

Labor, business, political and immigration groups fear a huge influx of Mexican labor and of wages in Mexico that are only a fraction of the American level. With those concerns in mind, President Carlos Salinas de Gortari, who is in Washington on a three-day visit, immediately began lobbying here on behalf of the move.

Calls Were Resisted by Mexico

Until this spring, when Mr. Salinas decided that quicker integration of the two economies was the only way to compete with emerging trading blocs in Europe and East Asia, Mexico had resisted a decade of calls by Republican administrations in the United States for a single market "from the Yukon to the Yucatan." Having made the commitment, however, he now finds Washington hesitant about the timing and extent of an agreement.

In a joint statement issued this morning, President Bush and President Salinas said such an accord would be "a powerful engine for economic development, creating new jobs and opening new markets" on both sides of the border. But a separate American statement also noted that while "the announcement endorses the concept" of a free-trade pact, it "does not initiate negotiations toward that goal."

Officials of both countries said that preliminary "consultations and prepatory work," with Carla A. Hills, the United States trade representative, representing Washington and the

supervisor at the Ford plant, he manages a team that both operates and repairs the computerized equipment that machines engine blocks and crankshafts. Before joining Ford in 1982, he considered emigrating to the United States. Now he earns $1,000 a month, a wage handsome enough in Chihuahua that his wife does not have to work. The couple have three daughters.

"I knew nothing about factories when I came here," Mr. Llanas said. "I spent two months in Michigan for training and people came from there to teach us." Today, he and his colleagues train the newcomers, who always start as assemblers, and work their way up, through a series of in-house training sessions and exams, to technician and supervisor.

Now the Mexico-United States free-trade agreement, just entering the negotiation stage, is likely to accelerate the industrialization of northern Mexico. Without tariff barriers, manufacturing companies, foreign and Mexican, would concentrate on high-volume production. Each plant would be dedicated to a single product, to supply markets in both countries. Factories that for years served only the protected Mexican market would probably be forced out of business as too costly, or upgraded to high-volume production.

But free trade and open borders are still years in the future. For the moment, the foreign companies come for two main reasons: the pool of low-cost, skilled labor and the need to meet a Government requirement that foreign companies generate exports as a quid-pro-quo for the right to serve the Mexican market.

The Chihuahua plant, in fact, was a gamble on Ford's part to try to fulfill this requirement and compete more effectively against Japan by staffing a factory with low-cost labor sufficiently skilled to produce a world-class engine. Major Mexican companies have adopted the same strategy.

Joint Ventures

Whirlpool, for example, is installing a washing machine factory in Monterrey, in a joint venture with Vitro Inc., a Mexican conglomerate that manufactures glass products. Whirlpool pursues lower labor costs while Vitro seeks the technology to manufacture appliances on its own for export to the United States.

"We know that the Mexican labor advantage won't last forever; maybe 5 or 10 years more," said Tomas Gonzalez Sada, president of Vitro Household Products, the joint venture subsidiary. "Once wages rise and the advantage is gone, and Whirlpool perhaps departs, we want to have the technology to continue on our own."

Vitro's strategy will undoubtedly work, economists say. But Mexico has only about 10 manufacturing conglomerates, and they cannot by themselves sustain northern Mexico as an industrial power.

Foreign corporations are indispensable, businessmen and government officials say. But whether they stay, once Mexican wages have risen, depends on whether these companies find themselves hooked on Mexico. Probably the biggest hook is the development of a nearby network of reliable parts suppliers.

Decision Due in November

That, at least, is a major issue in Ford's thinking. The four-cylinder engine made here is soon to be phased out, and by November, Ford will decide whether to retool the plant, a process that could require tens of millions of dollars for new machinery to manufacture a new engine. Ford could also decide to move the factory to another country, the main candidate being the United States.

"The decision will probably be determined by Ford's overall global strategy," Mr. Raymond said. "But a major consideration is ties with local suppliers."

Those ties have come slowly, mostly because Mexican suppliers have had difficulty meeting quality standards. When the engine plant opened seven years ago, 65 percent of the parts were brought by truck or rail from the United States. Now this has been whittled to 50 percent.

Fuel injectors, some valves, the flywheel, the electrical harness and other items are still imported. But Mexican companies now supply the engine block, the intake manifold, clutch plates, piston rods, gaskets and, soon, the oil pan.

Seeking Suppliers

Above all, Ford wanted a Mexican supplier for the engine block, a heavy item that is expensive to ship from a Ford plant in Cleveland. The company finally found Cifunsa, a manufacturer in Saltillo that had been making the blocks for years, but only to the standards required for cars made and sold within Mexico.

Cifunsa was forced into a major upgrade, including a $150 million investment in a new plant. Although Ford did not underwrite the upgrade, it insisted that Cifunsa acquire engine block technology from Fiat and for months Italian technicians worked at the Saltillo factory, helping to train its employees and transferring the technology. "We started with 27 Italians and we still have three here," said Ernesto Garza Martinez, Cifunsa's general director.

Ford experts also spent months at the company, supervising quality. To achieve the cost reductions that come with high volume, Cifunsa was encouraged to also supply engine blocks to General Motors, Chrysler and Volkswagen as well.

Now those engine blocks are less expensive than any available in the United States, Mr. Garza Martinez says, in part because Cifunsa's 2,000 employees are paid much less than their American counterparts.

"We aren't able to make breakthroughs in engine block technology," Mr. Garza Martinez said. "But when others introduce improvements, we are now in a position to apply them quickly to our operation. And we now have in our hands the Fiat process."

*   *   *

July 25, 1993

DEMYTHOLOGIZING THE TRADE PACT

Debate over the North American Free Trade Agreement has been overheated. Critics proclaim the pact—which would eliminate most tariffs and trade barriers with Mexico and Canada over the next 15 years—a national catastrophe, threatening jobs, wages and the environment. Proponents claim Nafta will boost employment and that its environmental provisions are a lovely shade of green.

The truth is more mundane. Nafta would have a modest economic impact in Mexico but a trivial impact on the U.S. economy. Mexico is too small to threaten U.S. firms, and U.S. tariffs are already so low that elimination couldn't possibly lead to a flood of Mexican imports. Nafta spells neither economic salvation nor ruin.

Will jobs disappear? Ross Perot warns that Nafta will take jobs away from up to six million Americans—based on the absurd calculation that the agreement threatens every worker in industries that use a lot of labor. The Administration says that Nafta will boost employment. Neither is correct.

Trade pacts affect where people work, not how many people work. Under Nafta, more Americans would find work in service industries (like insurance) and high-tech manufacturing (computers) for export to Mexico; fewer Americans would work in glass-blowing and apparel industries that would lose out to Mexican imports. But overall employment would not change. With or without Nafta, the U.S. unemployment rate will again hover around 6 percent once the economy recovers.

Unfortunately, the workers displaced by Mexican imports won't be the ones who find the extra work in export industries. Fortunately, the number of displaced workers would be small. The Congressional Budget Office estimates that, over 10 years, Nafta would add fewer than 500,000 to the 20 million workers who'll be displaced for other reasons.

Will wages shrink? Mr. Perot warns that U.S. firms will flee to Mexico to hire low-paid workers; employers who stay will drive down wages to Mexican levels. Some employers will relocate, but Mr. Perot's numbers are cockamamie. Most studies predict foreign investment in Mexico, an economy only one-twentieth the size of the U.S., would rise by no more than about $15 billion a year—a tiny fraction of the $500 billion investment in plant and equipment that takes place every year in the U.S.

Besides, low wages primarily reflect low productivity, giving companies little reason to relocate—otherwise Haiti would rule the corporate world. And because Nafta is expected to increase U.S. exports, it is as likely to raise U.S. wages as lower them—though in neither case by very much.

Will the environment suffer? Critics charge that Nafta will encourage U.S. firms to relocate to take advantage of Mexico's notoriously lax enforcement of environmental laws. The threat is real but small. Few firms face compliance costs larger than 1 percent of total costs, which is too small to warrant the journey.

There are legitimate questions about Nafta's environmental impact: Does Nafta adequately protect U.S. health and safety standards; will it protect the environment along the border? And critics have rightly pointed to the agreement's weak environmental dispute resolution and enforcement mechanisms. But there's still time to make Nafta better when the Clinton Administration negotiates a supplemental accord on the environment.

Regional trade accords like Nafta raise troubling questions because they break with the honorable U.S. tradition of treating all trade partners alike. But Canada and Mexico are special cases because they are neighbors. And Nafta would help Mexico lock in recent market reforms that the U.S. supports. Nafta isn't an economic magic bullet, but it does some good and no great harm.

* * *

August 17, 1993

THE TRADE PACT IS OUR BEST DEAL

By CARLA A. HILLS

WASHINGTON—Now that the U.S., Mexico and Canada have reached supplemental accords to the North American Free Trade Agreement, it is time for President Clinton to come out fighting for Congressional approval.

The supplemental agreements deal with environmental and labor concerns raised by Mr. Clinton, and do so without undermining the market-opening provisions of Nafta.

Legislation should be on every Congressional desk by Sept. 8, when members return. Congress must be pressed to pass the bill by the end of October, so that the accord will enter into force on Jan. 1, 1994, as the parties agreed.

A broad coalition of farmers, manufacturers and service industries that have followed the talks closely believe the U.S. will be far better off with the trade accord than without it. Now, environmentalists should support the package as well. It is the "greenest" trade agreement ever negotiated, one of our best opportunities to insure that trade liberalization and environmental protection proceed hand in hand, rather than fist to fist.

The public, fed so much misinformation, is understandably confused. The President, so articulate and persuasive, can demolish the critics.

Critics assert that Nafta throws our door open to a flood of Mexican goods. Nonsense. Our door is open now. Mexican exporters face an average U.S. tariff of only 4 percent; half their goods come into our country tariff-free. In contrast, our entrepreneurs are locked out of the Mexican market by high tariffs, licensing requirements, buy-Mexican provisions and bans on foreigners selling services.

Some falsely contend that our companies cannot compete with low-priced imports produced by low-paid Mexican workers. But we are competing very effectively. We sold almost $41 billion in goods to Mexico last year, nearly $6 million more than we bought from Mexico. Despite Mexico's low wages and high tariffs, on a per person basis Mexicans last year bought three and one-half times more from us ($477) than we did from them ($137).

Critics also falsely claim that Nafta will cause wholesale relocation of our industry to Mexico. If anything, the accord will help American companies stay home. Today, Mexican incentives and requirements encourage American companies to invest in Mexico, buy Mexican parts and sell more of their Mexican production overseas than they sell in that country. But Nafta changes all that. G.M., for example, will be able to ship cars from Detroit to Monterrey, Mexico, just as it now ships them to Monterey, Calif.

Eliminating Mexico's trade barriers is even more critical for small and mid-sized companies, which create 80 percent of the new jobs in the U.S. These firms usually cannot afford to build facilities in a foreign country. With Nafta, they don't need to move to Mexico to sell to Mexicans.

The alternative to the trade pact is not a new and improved agreement. The alternative is no agreement at all.

Without Nafta:

- Domestic car manufacturers will continue to be forced to build plants in Mexico and export approximately two cars from Mexico for every one they import from the U.S.
- Mexico can continue to close its borders to our apples, corn and grapes at a moment's notice.
- There will be no North American Commissions on Environmental Cooperation and Labor Cooperation, thus ending the successful first steps at collaborative North American action on these issues.
- There will be no new way to channel billions of dollars to the environmental cleanup of the Mexican border.

The accord gives President Clinton the opportunity to lead Congress to a bipartisan victory. This is a battle he can win. Polls show that half of Americans do not understand the trade accord and have not made up their minds; the other half is evenly split between supporters and opponents.

This is a fight that neither the President nor the U.S. can afford to lose. The victory that is within his grasp can be a turning point in his Presidency.

Carla A. Hills, United States Trade Representative from 1989 to 1993, is chairman of a consulting firm that advises American clients.

* * *

August 22, 1993

IN MEXICO, NAFTA ISN'T JUST ABOUT TRADE

By TIM GOLDEN

MEXICO CITY—If any more evidence were needed of his huge stake in the North American Free Trade Agreement, President Carlos Salinas de Gortari offered it generously as negotiations finally came to an end.

After insisting that they would never accept trade sanctions to enforce their environmental and labor laws, Mexican officials agreed to American demands for such penalties in the supplemental accords announced Aug. 13. When that wasn't enough for some congressmen in Washington, Mr. Salinas promised to give millions of Mexican workers a pay raise by linking the minimum wage to productivity.

No one ever said the trade agreement—which has been approved by the Canadian Parliament and is expected to be approved in Mexico soon—would be a partnership of equals. But as the prospects have seemed to darken for its approval in the United States Congress this fall, some supporters of the pact have begun to argue its importance for Mexico in almost apocalyptic terms: The future of a stable, responsible, pro-American government here now hangs in the balance, they say.

As it became evident that the side accords had failed to win over skeptical House Democrats, Mexico's trade envoy in Washington suggested bluntly that the United States might as well choose between the agreement and political uncertainty in Mexico. The official, Hermann von Bertrab, said that after 64 years of uninterrupted rule by Mr. Salinas's Institutional Revolutionary Party, so much as a delay in the trade pact could spell defeat for his chosen successor (Mexican presidents cannot be re-elected).

Gov. Ann Richards of Texas was less coy. A rejection of the agreement would so enrage Mexicans, she said, that "some very serious disturbances" could be expected in Mexico and along the border.

Few people in Mexico dispute that a defeat on Capitol Hill this fall would bring Mr. Salinas's most important initiative crashing down at a singularly bad time. Yet the strength and scope of the expected anti-American backlash are hard to predict.

No Turning Back

To some analysts here, the same economic and political forces that have moved Mexico toward the trade pact make serious upheaval almost unthinkable. Chances of an abrupt reversal of the economic course Mr. Salinas has followed since taking office in 1988 are considered equally remote. Even if his party loses the election, the analysts say, it seems unlikely that its leftist or rightist opposition could re-nationalize the state companies that have been privatized, resume the wild, deficit spending of the past, or turn sharply away from the United States.

"The end of his presidency would be a failure—that's the essential problem," said Federico Estevez, a political scientist at the Autonomous Technological Institute of Mexico. "But I'm not sure that you can push back the reforms regardless of who comes to power next year." Mr. Estevez, a supporter of the agreement, added: "I would like to argue that we'll fall apart, but we won't fall apart."

The trade agreement began as a great gamble for Mr. Salinas in a country of legendary nationalism, and he has raised his bet considerably over the last year. Though his aides have sometimes sought to downplay the pact's importance, calling it just one of many steps in Mexico's transformation, Mr. Salinas has sold it assiduously to wary countrymen, promis-

Joe Cavaretta/Associated Press

"Yes to Free Trade Agreement," headlines in Mexican newspapers read earlier this month as NAFTA supplemental accords were announced.

ing that only more jobs and better pay can come of it. He has endured the humiliation of a series of policy reversals that have followed fast on criticism from the United States. And to a Mexican audience that understands little about separation of powers, rogue legislators or other ways of Washington, he has explained little, insisting that the agreement's passage is inevitable.

The starkest risk, though, remains economic. Last year, in trying to overhaul its oil-centered export base and opening its borders to a flood of foreign goods at the same time, Mexico ran up a deficit of $22.8 billion in its current account, the broadest measure of trade. Even with the Government budget running a surplus, the country counts heavily on foreign investment to cover the shortfall; it counts on the promise of a trade pact to draw and hold the investment.

The consequences of the agreement's failure would depend on how it failed. But whether the pact was flatly rejected by Congress or merely delayed beyond Jan. 1, when it is supposed to take effect, many economists say the disruption could spook foreign investors, especially those with relatively liquid assets like stocks and treasury bills. Because imports cannot be stanched as quickly as those funds can flow back abroad, the current-account deficit would probably rise. Most economists think the Mexican peso is overvalued already. A more serious trade imbalance would raise the pressure for a politically costly devaluation in order to make Mexican exports cheaper and foreign imports more expensive.

"I think the failure of Nafta would lead to a devaluation," said Sidney Weintraub, a political economist at the University of Texas. "But that wouldn't have an immediate effect in containing imports." He and others expect the Salinas Administration would therefore have to restrict imports as well in order to hold down the trade imbalance.

Given the likelihood that some Mexicans would demand retaliation if American legislators rejected the agreement, imports from the United States would be an obvious target. But several Mexican officials said a more serious reversal in the country's relationship with the partner that accounts for more than two-thirds of its trade would be disastrous. Without an agreement, Mexico would need foreign investors more than ever, they noted, and would probably have to open the economy further to attract them.

Aides to Mr. Salinas say that with Mexicans still divided over the trade accord, he is anxious that the Presidential election not turn into a referendum on the issue. Some analysts say the agreement's failure could also shape his crucial decision on which of the quietly rivalrous aides he will nominate to succeed him. And although no governing party candidate has ever lost, the moment has traditionally been one of gathering political tensions, one when presidencies that once seemed glorious begin to grow lame and collapse.

In theory, an opposition candidate like Cuauhtemoc Cardenas, the leftist who nearly beat Mr. Salinas in 1988, might seize such a moment. In practice, however, Mr. Cardenas's party has lost so much support that many political analysts doubt that even a failed trade agreement could lift it to the threshold of power again. Then there is another point militating against the sort of disaster that supporters of the trade agreement have begun to foresee: Privately, at least, aides to Mr. Cardenas say he has no interest in becoming the new champion of anti-Americanism, or even necessarily the new slayer of free trade.

BASICS OF THE ACCORD
What's in It

The Nafta agreement, initiated by President Bush last year and blessed by the Clinton Administration last week, would bring Mexico into a free-trade area with the United States and Canada.

Mexican tariffs against American products currently average about 13 percent, while American tariffs against Mexican goods average 6 percent. But they are complemented by a host of non-tariff restrictions on everything from blue jeans to frozen orange juice concentrate.

Not all barriers would fall on Jan. 1, 1994. Some of the most sensitive—for example, Mexico's restrictions on imported auto parts—would be phased out over a decade. And "import surge" protocols would allow breathing spells for domestic industries devastated by foreign competition. But according to the Administration, half of all American exports would have open access to Mexico on Day One.

Winner and Losers

The rapidly modernizing Mexican economy is a big importer of machines and commodities—what Americans produce best. Since Mexico is already relatively open to these goods, the agreement itself would probably only have a modest impact on American sales. But locking into place President Carlos Salinas de Gortari's commitment to free markets, internal and external, would assure a long-term boost to American industries ranging from aircraft to grain to telephone equipment. And by keeping Mexico's growth on track, it would probably serve many other American industries that would be slaking Mexican consumers' thirst for the material life.

The pact is striking because it marries economies with vastly different levels of wages and productivity. Jobs and profits would undoubtedly be lost in labor-intensive, low-wage American industries including apparel, shoes and household glassware. But Ross Perot's "giant sucking sound" of jobs and investments flowing south is likely to be muffled because the Mexican economy is tiny compared to the U.S. one. Even in the most optimistic scenarios for Mexican growth, it will remain a minor player in most American markets for decades.

In any case, Mexican industry already has relatively easy access to American consumers, as do producers in low-wage countries from Thailand to Turkey. So, for that matter, do illegal Mexican immigrants, who by consensus constitute greater competition for low-wage American jobs than do legal Mexican imports.

Gary Hufbauer, an economist at the Institute for International Economics, estimates that the job growth in American high-wage industries will initially exceed job losses in low-wage industries because exports to Mexico are growing so rapidly. And if the past is a good measure, there will be little or no net impact on jobs as markets redeploy redundant workers to more competitive American industries.

Other Sticking Points

Environmentalists worry that Mexican industrial pollution will poison the American side of the border, as well as fouling Mexico's air and water. American unions have jumped on the regulatory bandwagon, pointing to Mexico's malign neglect of working conditions.

It is not clear, though, why the accord would undermine the environment or labor standards; indeed, trade and investment liberalization would probably reduce cross-border pollution since it would end the artificial concentration of industry in free-trade border zones. Still, the Clinton Administration has worked to defuse the issues, writing side agreements providing for watchdog groups to monitor compliance with national laws.

Another challenge—one with no political teeth—comes from economists who are troubled by the rise of regional trade blocs. They fear that an open border with Mexico would divert more cost-reducing trade with Asia and Eastern Europe. And they wonder whether the North American economic alliance will spur Japan to form a competing bloc on the other side of the Pacific.

The Bumpy Road to Approval

Canada's Parliament has already approved the treaty and Mexico's soon will. Current betting is that Nafta will have a relatively easy time in the United States Senate but will face sharp elbows in the House.

Ross Perot is rallying the opposition, tarring the treaty as a symbol of Washington's indifference to Joe Sixpack. Some environmental groups also remain opposed to it. And the House majority leader, Richard Gephardt, has expressed dissatisfaction with the final package. The contest may turn on the ability of the White House to limit defections among Democrats who have ties to organized labor or to business constituents threatened by Mexican competition.

But the White House's promised lobbying blitz could still be stalled before it has a chance to be tested. A Federal judge ruled last month that treaty approval required an environmental impact statement. If the Justice Department loses the appeal, movement on Nafta could be frozen for months or years.

* * *

November 7, 1993

MEXICO'S HUNGER FOR U.S. GOODS IS HELPING TO SELL THE TRADE PACT

By ANTHONY DePALMA

MEXICO CITY—Pitchmen for the North American Free Trade Agreement always focus on the consumer paradise

Mexico's Urge to Splurge

What People Have

Percentage of households with each item, from in-person surveys
conducted by Roper Starch Worldwide and INRA (Americas)

Mexico
Urban
residents

Color
television
83%

Phone
50%

VCR
63%

Car
53%

Compact
disc
player
24%

Cable
television

Auto
insurance
26%

From a survey
of 5,410 people in 42
Mexican cities conducted
in December. Margin of
sampling error is plus or minus
2 percentage points

**United
States**

Color
television
93%

Phone
92%

Car
88%

Cable
television
62%

VCR
62%

Auto
insurance
79%

Compact
disc
player
30%

From a survey
of 1,985 people
nationwide conducted
in September. Margin of
sampling error is plus or minus
3 percentage points.

Canada

Color
television
98%

Phone
100%

Car
89%

Cable
television
86%

VCR
77%

Auto
insurance
86%

Compact
disc
player
42%

From a survey of
427 people nationwide
in both English and French
Canada conducted in September.
Margin of sampling error is plus or
minus 6 percentage points

Source
"Roper Reports Americas"

Anne Cronin/The New York Times

presented by Mexico's young and growing population: 85 million people, more than half of them under 25 years old, with slowly rising wages but a seemingly insatiable appetite for things made in the U.S.A.

In fact, trade with Mexico already is big business. Mexico imports more than $42 billion in goods and services from the United States, more than three times what it was in 1986, when the Government began lowering tariffs on imports so that some American goods could compete with their less desirable Mexican imitations. Treasury Secretary Lloyd Bentsen, an old Mexico hand, says that with Nafta, trade with Mexico will grow by another $10 billion in three years.

No doubt the argument that Mexico offers vast trade opportunities will be made Tuesday night as Vice President Al Gore presents the Clinton Administration's case for the accord in a televised debate with Ross Perot, Nafta's chief critic. President Clinton, who last week escalated his campaign for approval of the agreement in the face of its discouraging prospects in a scheduled vote in the House a week from Wednesday, is working hard to convince Congress that rising trade with Mexico will more than make up for the American jobs that could be lost because of lower wages south of the border.

For those already involved in the Mexican market, the demand for American products is obvious. Mexicans spent $450 per capita on American goods in 1992, more than consumers in Japan or European countries. The Marlboro man still gallops headlong across television screens here. Wal-Mart recently opened a megacenter in a working-class neighborhood in Mexico City, and J.C. Penney and Kmart will be here soon too. Compact disks can now be bought at Tower Records, mufflers can be replaced at Midas and, at select supermarkets, shoppers can take advantage of promo-

tions offering a stack of fresh corn tortillas free with the purchase of Hostess hamburger rolls.

But although more than 70 percent of everything Mexico imports comes from the United States, not everything American sells. And there is evidence that Mexican consumers could turn fickle once the novelty of widely available American goods wears off. More problematic for American exporters, traditional market research has rarely been able to crack the intricacies of Mexico, where much income is unreported and households routinely cover several generations.

"Even the best statistician would have the hardest time here," said Juan Suberville, general director of two Kmart stores set to open on Mexico City's outskirts next spring. "Mostly, you work on gut feelings."

Taco Bell found out the hard way. Intent on grabbing a niche in Mexico, the Pepsico subsidiary conducted market research that suggested that its fast-food expertise and consistent product could overcome the coals-to-Newcastle disadvantages of trying to sell American tacos here. It opened a stand in a Mexico City parking lot last year and planned 25 more in a year.

Opening the Doors

But only three others ever opened, and none is a runaway success. Company officials say their mistake was to focus too much on Mexican manners, changing their menu and style to be more authentically Mexican. It turned out that what Mexicans wanted was authentically American tacos served in a clean restaurant away from traffic fumes.

The Taco Bell experience is one of many indicators that what Mexicans want most is what they couldn't buy before. When the country's economy was closed to most American goods, Mexicans couldn't buy the Raisinettes or Frosted

Flakes they saw on imported television programs and in movies—only weak imitations.

Under President Carlos Salinas de Gortari, Mexico has been intent on dismantling its import-substitution economy and opening its markets. The doors were cracked ajar in the mid-1980's by lowered tariffs on imported goods. Nafta, which would end tariffs and other trade barriers among the United States, Canada and Mexico over 15 years, would complete the opening of Mexico's economy to the north.

Tariffs act as taxes, artificially pushing up prices. Reduce them, as happened in the 1980's, and suddenly imports start showing up on store shelves. At first, Mexicans couldn't get their fill of imported products like Coca-Cola in cans, which until then had been unavailable. But when the novelty died down, people realized they were paying two and three times what it cost for a Mexican-made Coke, and the American-made version didn't even taste as good. North of the border Coca-Cola is made with corn syrup, while Mexican Coke uses sugar, and Mexicans say they can taste the difference.

"Mexicans are willing to try something new," said Francisco Sanchez-Loaeza, president of Panamerican Beverages, the largest Coca-Cola bottler outside the United States. "But they are becoming more and more demanding."

Coca-Cola was one of a limited number of American products available even when the Mexican economy was closed. Mexicans drink more soda than any other people except those in the United States, in part because drinking water here is so risky. Coca-Cola controls 55 percent of the market and, with Government restrictions lifted, is flooding the market with previously unavailable flavors and bottle sizes, including non-returnable two-liter monsters.

Changing Habits

A big question is how much and how quickly Mexicans will change their shopping habits. Most Mexicans still shop at small stores and street stands—not surprising in a country where street vending has been well established since Aztec times. They go to the store on average eight times a week, while shoppers in the United States go twice. Tortillas, the Mexican staple, are a big factor, because fresh tortillas, made without preservatives, are considered inedible after a day.

But habits are changing. Enrique Legoretta, commercial director in Mexico City for the A.C. Nielsen market-research concern, said that once Mexican consumers glimpse the new consumer world, small stores just don't hold their attention any more. In some ways, Mexicans have shown themselves willing to change their whole concept of shopping. The Price Club has opened two successful stores in Mexico City that are about as different from the street-corner mom-and-pop as can be. The stores are warehouses, selling institutional-size cans of peaches and rolls of toilet paper by the dozen. A typical trip requires at least $100 and a car to haul the booty home. With an average income of anywhere from $3,000 to $43,000 a year, and many families without cars, Mexico seems an unlikely fit for the Price Club.

But Robert Price, the chairman of the company, said he has done well by targeting the top 10 to 15 percent of Mexicans, those with cars and salaries above $43,000 a year. "We've found that Mexicans at that level are more committed to consumerism than Americans," he said. He said if the trade accord passes, fully a quarter of all Mexicans will wind up in the high-income bracket.

Retailers and free trade supporters are also betting on a similar increase in buying power. They know by experience that the sheen of American products could wear off, but say a trade accord ending tariffs, and therefore lowering consumer prices, would mean that they could successfully compete with domestic products.

For now, imports are still getting a boost from the curiosity built up over so many years of living right alongside the biggest marketplace in the world without being able to fully participate in it.

That was what brought Alicia and Esperanza Rendon Huerta to the new Wal-Mart in Mexico City a recent afternoon. The sisters, both in their 60's, spent more than 500 pesos, almost $200, on many things they admitted they didn't really need, including cookies, napkins and several two-liter bottles of Coke.

"We wanted to see what it was like," they said.

No one really knows whether Nafta would make Mexican wages rise or change what Mexicans buy. But it seems certain that markets on both sides of the Rio Grande are coming together. The new Wal-Mart sells tequila glasses made in the United States and Superman pajamas made in Mexico. At last count, salsa was outselling catsup in the United States. And Wonder Bread is baking "authentic" soft tortillas.

* * *

November 15, 1993

MORE EXPERTS, MORE JOBS

By GARY HUFBAUER

WASHINGTON—In an odd alliance with Ross Perot and Pat Buchanan, organized labor, led by the A.F.L.-C.I.O., is waging a scorched-earth battle to destroy the North American Free Trade Agreement. For Mr. Perot and Mr. Buchanan it makes political sense: they both want to be President and are using the issue to draw voters from the Democrat and Republican mainstreams. But for working Americans, whom the A.F.L.-C.I.O. claims to represent, the campaign is a huge mistake. If Congress votes to refuse the pact on Wednesday, a great opportunity to spur U.S. job growth will have been lost.

Organized labor asserts that Nafta will steal U.S. jobs and slash wages. This reflects a grave misunderstanding of how businesses operate. Their task is to make profits. One way to do this is to increase production at locations where costs are low and shrink production where costs are high. But it is a colossal mistake to suppose that these decisions always favor low-wage locations. If that were true, Mississippi and

Missouri would have stripped California and Connecticut of jobs long ago.

Businesses look at the balance between wages and worker productivity. High wages don't necessarily scare businesses away if they are matched by high productivity.

In 1992, the hourly compensation for manufacturing workers in Mexico averaged about one-seventh the U.S. level ($2.35 versus $16.17). But in Mexico, the average yearly manufacturing output per worker was valued at about $9,500 for industries competing in the U.S. market. In contrast, American manufacturing output per worker averages $75,000.

Only union leaders and Ross Perot would be surprised to hear that the productivity ratio between U.S. and Mexican workers (7.9 times higher in favor of the U.S.) is higher than the ratio of hourly compensation (compensation in the U.S. is 6.9 times greater than the Mexican average). These ratios indicate is that in 1992 the balance between productivity and wages modestly favored the U.S. workers, not Mexicans.

For some companies (heavy trucks, telecommunications equipment), the productivity-compensation balance will favor expansion in the U.S.; for others (men's undershirts, automobile bumpers), the balance will clearly favor expansion in Mexico. Both countries will gain by specializing in the goods and services they produce best.

Still, union leaders raise the unlikely concern that Mexico will become a better place to produce everything—that productivity will grow at double-digit rates, with Mexican wages remaining stuck at present levels. Even if this happens, the peso's exchange rate can easily be adjusted so that it would rise sharply against the dollar. Peso appreciation would amount, in effect, to higher paychecks for Mexican workers, and Mexico's across-the-border trade advantage would be quickly lost. (This has happened with several Asian currencies over the past 20 years.)

In evaluating Nafta, however, U.S. workers should look at probabilities, not implausibilities. Members of Congress and workers should remind themselves that the goal of Nafta is to cut Mexican trade barriers, which average 11 percent on imports: they are far higher than U.S. barriers, which average 4 percent. Opening the Mexican market can only help our exports.

The A.F.L.-C.I.O. claims that Nafta will take about 500,000 jobs from American workers. This would require the U.S. to incur a $25 billion trade deficit with Mexico. That is a huge and implausible number, considering that two-way trade between the countries totals only about $100 billion. This year, the U.S. will enjoy a trade surplus of about $4 billion with Mexico, a big improvement over the 1990 deficit of $2 billion. If Nafta is ratified, the U.S. trade surplus with Mexico will likely average about $7 billion annually in the late 1990's. This would probably mean a net gain of about 170,000 U.S. jobs.

The average Mexican buys about $560 of goods and services annually from the United States—much more than the average Japanese or European. Mexico buys about 80 percent of its total imports of goods and services from the U.S. Mexi-

can prosperity automatically translates into more demand for U.S. products and more jobs for U.S. workers.

It is foolish for union leaders to fret about too much investment in Mexico. The more Nafta boosts capital spending in Mexico, the more steel, machinery, heavy trucks and earth- moving equipment U.S. companies will sell. As more Mexican workers are hired at better wages, they will become better customers for U.S.-made clothing, packaged goods, household appliances and autos.

To be sure, Nafta will cause job losses in some U.S. industries such as apparel manufacturing and light electronics. Dislocated workers should be fully and fairly assisted with job retraining. If the A.F.L.-C.I.O. had directed its political energies to shaping the Nafta side agreements on labor, model programs might have been designed. Instead, the unions wasted a golden opportunity by adhering to a take-no-prisoners strategy.

Organized labor cannot achieve its goals of preserving jobs and defending wages just by defeating Nafta. Its strategy inevitably points to erecting new barriers against trade with Mexico and all other countries that fall short of U.S. wage levels. No political agenda would better insure U.S. isolation from the booming markets of Latin America and Asia and ultimately depress U.S. job opportunities and wages.

Many things are wrong with our economy. Public and private savings need to be boosted, the Federal Reserve should give greater emphasis to job growth in setting monetary policy, widespread fears over health and pension security must be allayed. These are worthy goals for the A.F.L.-C.I.O. Defeating Nafta and crippling the Clinton Presidency are not.

Gary Hufbauer, a senior fellow at the Institute for International Economics, is co-author of "Nafta: An Assessment."

* * *

November 15, 1993

A LOW-WAGE GAME PLAN

By SAMUEL BOWLES and MEHRENE LARUDEE
AMHERST, Mass.—Americans justifiably worry that the North American Free Trade Agreement may provoke a flight of jobs to Mexico. But what's wrong with Nafta goes beyond lost jobs. In Mexico, Canada and the United States, even those seemingly unaffected by the agreement will be worse off if it is carried out. Nafta is Victorian economics and will foster Dickensian conditions.

Its proponents say that Nafta would open new markets for U.S. consumer goods. But more important, it would make it far easier for companies to move south and far more difficult for governments to enact coherent development policies.

The agreement would bind all three countries in the straitjacket of 19th-century free market economics, jeopardizing governmental efforts to promote long-term growth of productivity and better living standards throughout the continent.

And it would favor footloose corporations as they bargain with employees over wages and working conditions, with communities over taxes and environmental issues and with local suppliers over prices.

In October, when President Clinton sought pledges from major corporations not to move jobs to Mexico, not a single one signed up. Asked by the Roper polling firm in 1992 if their companies would "shift some production to Mexico . . . if Nafta is ratified," 40 percent of the top executives of U.S. manufacturing corporations answered that this was "very" or "somewhat" likely. For large companies, the figure was 55 percent.

Why do these companies need Nafta? Many have already moved to Mexico. But the agreement would greatly lower their risks, since it would lock the Mexican Government into business-friendly policies for the foreseeable future.

Supporters of Nafta say that few U.S. companies would actually make the move, preferring the vastly more productive American work force. But while average productivity in existing Mexican companies is relatively low, productivity and quality at new U.S.-owned companies there approaches that of those north of the border. Ford's plant in the town of Hermosillo has won quality awards for the Tracers and Escorts it exports to California.

For the boardroom, Mexico spells "workers," not "consumers": for every middle-class Mexican itching to buy a new U.S.-built car, there are dozens of low-wage or unemployed workers lining up for work at a sixth of U.S. wages. Mexico's labor force is larger than the entire labor force in Michigan, Illinois, Ohio, Indiana and Pennsylvania combined. By contrast, the Mexican market, as measured by its gross domestic product, is smaller than New Jersey's.

No one knows how many U.S. jobs will be lost if Nafta is approved. No major studies of Nafta have estimated the number; following textbook assumptions, the models simply ignore the possibility that companies will move.

But the impact would be substantial even if, as seems unlikely, the flight of jobs were minor. What counts is not how many jobs actually leave but the fact that so many could leave. In the same Roper poll, 24 percent of business leaders candidly said that it was either very likely or somewhat likely that "Nafta will be used by [their] company as a bargaining chip to keep wages down in the U.S."

In Mexico, the battering ram that will keep wages down is not the threat to move but a flood of prairie-grown corn. It will bankrupt high-cost farmers, driving them to the cities in search of work and worsening an already severe labor surplus. Even if half a million new jobs open up in Mexico as U.S. companies move south, the number of displaced farmers will mount to twice and perhaps three times this number over a decade.

That would mean intensified competition for jobs and significant downward pressure on wages. Among the rosy projections offered by the pro-Nafta side, the assurance that Mexican wages will soar deserves the Pollyanna prize. Even Nafta supporters concede that the flow of grain south into

Mexico will be matched by an increased northward flow of illegal immigrants in search of work. The Mexican labor surplus thus becomes a North American labor surplus.

But even Mexico cannot beat Sri Lanka or China at the low-wage game. None of the signatories to Nafta should try. The alternative—a high-wage, high-productivity strategy—requires the active involvement of governments at all levels. What boosts productivity is neither governments nor markets alone but a combination of market competition with effective intervention by a development-oriented government. The East Asian economic miracles should have pounded this lesson home.

Nafta would label many of the necessary governmental initiatives "barriers to trade" and could force their retraction. When in 1990 Ontario's provincial government proposed a universal public car-insurance system, U.S. insurance companies invoked the Canada-U.S. Free Trade Agreement and demanded $2 billion compensation. Ontario backed down. Any state in the U.S. that decided to convert to a single-payer health insurance program or to subsidize solar energy or recycling might suffer a similar fate.

Closer economic ties with the rest of the hemisphere are an essential part of any sound U.S. economic strategy. And protection of inefficient industries is no way to promote productivity in the long term.

But Nafta is a giant step down the wrong road. Its "let the chips fall where they may" low-wage game plan promises the continent not three nations but just two: the rich and the poor.

Samuel Bowles is professor of economics at the University of Massachusetts. Mehrene Larudee is staff economist at the Center for Popular Economics in Amherst.

* * *

November 19, 1993

ANGER, FEAR BUT ALSO HOPE ON THE ASSEMBLY LINE

By JAMES BENNET
Special to The New York Times

FLINT, Mich., Nov. 18—As the first shift poured out of the mammoth Buick assembly plant here this afternoon, Bill Ferguson, an Igloo cooler and newspaper in hand, gave his version of the resignation that many auto workers felt about the passage of the North American Free Trade Agreement.

"That sucking sound was there before Nafta," said the 53-year-year-old Mr. Ferguson, alluding to Ross Perot's prediction during last year's Presidential campaign. "I think our jobs—they're gone."

With the pact making it even easier for companies to move their plants, he said, the agreement was also sure to strengthen management's hand in bargaining with his union, the United Automobile Workers. "It's just another chip to use to hold over our heads," he said.

Feeling Let Down

Workers interviewed in this frayed factory town dominated by several huge General Motors plants said they remained suspicious of the trade agreement and its well-heeled corporate sponsors. Even if it did not hurt, they said, the pact would not help preserve jobs like theirs, which pay about $17 per hour with full benefits. And with President Clinton's complaints about big labor's tactics and his own expensive last-minute arm-twisting, they said, he badly let them down.

But many workers also said that with the agreement apparently headed for ratification in the Senate they hoped it would bring some of the benefits that its backers claimed.

"I voted for President Clinton, but I didn't vote for him to do this," said Ed Millington, who has spent 28 of his 46 years in the plants. Still, "I'm a fair person. I'll see how this works."

Some Benefits

Indeed, some said they were optimistic about the agreement's possibilities for the United States, if not for auto workers. "I think it'll be good for the nation," said Ples McDuffie, polishing off a double cheeseburger in Angelo's restaurant and before going back to making steel slugs for spark plugs.

A bigger trade bloc will make the United States more competitive globally, said Mr. McDuffie, and will also break down suspicions among nations. "You look at Europe and everyone else—seems like everyone is going with that structure," he said.

But what benefits the country as a whole may not benefit auto-parts workers like himself, said Mr. McDuffie, who was working a 2 A.M.-to-2 P.M. shift to fill in for colleagues who vanished with the start of deer-hunting season. Mr. McDuffie fears that he and his co-workers could lose their jobs. "I'm against it," he said of the pact. "I don't like seeing our jobs shipped out."

In some cases, workers' resignation about the accord seemed to be a product of despair. "I don't know," said Jim Gardella, when asked if jobs would vanish to Mexico. "Are there any left?" Given the drubbing the local economy has taken, he said, he hoped that in the long run the pact would help promote growth. "I'll wait and see," said Mr. Gardella, who has worked in G.M.'s Buick City complex here for 31 years. In that time, he said, he has seen the work force at the complex shrink from 28,000 to 11,000.

A North American Union

Dave Yettaw, the president of Local 599 here and the leader of a small dissident U.A.W. faction favoring a more aggressive stance toward management, said American labor unions should reach out aggressively to Mexican workers. "We need to have a labor union of North America," capable of calling general strikes, he said. "In the European economic community, that's what they do."

But like many of his union colleagues, Mr. Yettaw said that the first thing that labor needed was a more credible and effective spokesman. "It's a sad state of affairs when Ross Perot stands as the spokesman for organized labor and working people," he said.

Workers who took a longer view of the union's struggles and the American economy said the agreement would not matter much. "I don't think it's a good deal," said Al Federico, 85, a retiree who helped organize the Flint plants in the 1930's, when American auto workers were paid less than what the pact's opponents say Mexican ones are paid now. "But America is too strong, and it will survive this."

* * *

November 21, 1993

NAFTA: THE WHYS AND WHEREFORES

By DAVID ROSENBAUM

It was one of the most emotional sessions in Congress in years. Partisan loyalties and personal friendships went by the boards. After 13 hours of debate and more than 250 speeches, the House of Representatives voted Wednesday, 234 to 200, to put the North American Free Trade Agreement into effect beginning Jan. 1. David Rosenbaum pulls together a sampler of what was said:

"Bill Johnson owns the largest Caterpillar distributorship in the West. There is currently a 20 percent tariff on his products sold in Mexico. Caterpillar has 50 percent of the market. The other half is dominated by Komatsu Company of Japan. Bill says, 'Imagine what will happen when the 20 percent tariff comes off our tractors and it remains on the ones from Japan.' "

—Jerry Lewis, Republican of California
For the agreement

"The Maine footwear industry, the largest in the nation, has lost over 9,000 jobs to countries like Mexico, whose work forces are dominated by low-wage jobs. Similar horror stories can be told about textiles, fisheries and our lumber industry."

—Olympia J. Snowe, Republican of Maine
Against

"Some people may say that I have a democracy fetish. I do not believe that I have one. I think it is irresponsible to enter into a single market with something other than a representative democracy."

—Lincoln Diaz-Balart, Republican of Florida
Against

"I share blood with the Mexican people. And the xenophobic, anti-Mexico slurs that have made the rounds here, including from some Members of the House, I resent that. I resent that very much. . . . We cannot expect to Americanize the world."

—E. (Kika) de la Garza, Democrat of Texas
For

"Hattie Smith worked for U.S. Auto Radiator for 12 years, earning $7.60 an hour. As her last duty before she was fired, Hattie was sent to Mexico to train her 65-cents-an-hour

The final tally.

replacements—13-year-old girls working without protective gear."

—William D. Ford, Democrat of Michigan
Against

"It is not possible for this nation to be politically international and at the same time economically isolationist. It is like asking one Siamese twin to do a high dive while the other plays the piano."

—Amo Houghton, Republican of New York
For

"After seeing decades of deprivation and adversity in our society, I have come to the conclusion that we need some new solutions to the age-old problems of unemployment and the lack of economic opportunity."

—Carrie Meek, Democrat of Florida
For

"We need entry-level jobs in this country."

—Bruce F. Vento, Democrat of Minnesota
Against

*   *   *

June 6, 1994

U.S.-MEXICO TRADE ADVANCES SHARPLY UNDER NEW ACCORD

By ALLEN R. MYERSON
Special to The New York Times

DALLAS, June 5—In the first three months after a new trade agreement took effect, trade between Mexico and the United States rose sharply to record levels.

Imports from Mexico grew much more rapidly than United States exports, cutting the American trade surplus with Mexico for the first quarter nearly in half. The numbers are the first to measure the impact of the North American Free Trade Agreement since it took effect Jan. 1.

The trade imbalance between the two countries has sharpened antagonism between organized labor, which opposed the trade agreement because it feared the loss of American jobs, and leaders in business and Government, who said the pact would create jobs by making Mexico a huge market for American goods.

United States exports to Mexico rose 15.7 percent, to a record $11.85 billion, seasonally adjusted, in the first quarter compared with the comparable quarter a year earlier, according to the Commerce Department. Imports from Mexico rose 22.5 percent, to a record $11.29 billion. That narrowed the nation's quarterly trade surplus with Mexico by 45.1 percent, to $560 million.

Both sides agree that a single quarter is not enough time to determine a long-term trend and that it is difficult to distinguish the effects of the trade pact from other causes of steadily increasing commerce between the two nations. Indeed, many shipments in the first quarter reflected plans made before the trade agreement was approved in November.

Nevertheless, Mickey Kantor, the United States trade representative, said in an interview on Friday that the agreement was already fulfilling the Administration's promises to create jobs. "Nafta has increased trade substantially," he said. "The balance of trade is not as important as the content of trade and the increase in exports. That's what raises our standard of living."

Some economists and trade experts had expected goods to flow more strongly toward Mexico than toward the United States because trade barriers, which have been much higher in Mexico, were falling rapidly. A strong peso also favored Mexican purchasers because it made goods imported from the United States more affordable.

But United States exports have been hurt by the persistent recession in Mexico even as the United States economy has grown strongly. Another drag on trade, according to economists, is the complexity of the new pact. Some manufacturers are still figuring out how it applies to their products.

Labor leaders, although cautious about reaching conclusions so soon, saw evidence that the trade pact was increasing Mexican exports more than imports, at the potential cost of jobs in the United States.

"Mickey Kantor always used to say that Nafta will create 200,000 new jobs by 1995," said Mark A. Anderson, director of the A.F.L.-C.I.O.'s task force on trade. "But that was based on an increasing U.S. trade surplus, and our surplus has declined." Mexico, he said, remained a minor market for United States goods but a major source of cheap labor for United States companies.

Mr. Kantor said he saw no relation between the trade balance and jobs, adding that an improving Mexican economy and growing middle class would increase demand for United States products.

In the first quarter, the largest increase in imports came in motor vehicles, up 48.3 percent, to $728 million, from the first quarter of 1993. Among the largest increases in United States exports were electrical and mechanical equipment for industry, raw materials and motor vehicle parts.

Much of the increased trade appeared to reflect closer teamwork between factories across a fading border, with the United States often sending parts and materials to Mexico for final assembly.

Imports From Mexico Surge

United States trade officials say that imports from Mexico are growing twice as fast as imports from the rest of the world, and American exports to Mexico three times as fast.

"We've really seen the difference with Nafta," said Regina K. Vargo, director of the Commerce Department's Mexico office. "Especially given the relatively flat economy in Mexico."

Quick judgments about the flow of jobs, however, are difficult. Many economists say both nations are likely to gain jobs from increased trade, which would benefit consumers as well.

"The jobs hurt by trade are found in other industries that are expanded through trade," said David M. Gould, a senior economist at the Federal Reserve Bank of Dallas.

Checks with several corporations that campaigned for the passage of the trade agreement in November brought some reports of increased exports and added jobs. Allied Signal Inc., whose chief executive, Lawrence A. Bossidy, led USA Nafta, a business lobbying group, said shipments of Autolite spark plugs to Mexico would reach 20 million this year, up from 12 million last year.

For the company's plant in Fostoria, Ohio, "that's a whole month's production," helping to make the 1,000 jobs there more stable, if not adding to them, said Paul A. Boudreau, Allied Signal's director of government relations.

Lower Tariffs

Under the trade pact, Mexico reduced its tariff on spark plugs to 12 percent this year from 15 percent as the first step toward elimination of the tariff by 1998. The company, however, said stronger marketing and a contract to supply the Mexican operations of the Ford Motor Company had also contributed to its substantial gains.

Texas Instruments Inc. said it was selling three times as many computer printers in Mexico after the removal of a 20 percent tariff, and 10 times as many laptop computers, after a tariff was reduced to 16 percent from 20 percent. But Robert L. Price, a company spokesman, said a stronger sales effort in Mexico had likewise contributed to these advances.

USA Nafta recently published a 15-page list of current and potential export gains, including examples from all three auto makers. General Motors, the report said, had moved enough Chevrolet Cavalier production to Lansing, Mich., from Mexico to create 800 to 1,000 jobs.

G.M. and industry analysts said that the company's quarterly exports to Mexico had risen to more than 11,000 cars and trucks in just the first quarter of 1994 from 1,700 last year. About 8,500 of the cars sent to Mexico, however, were made in Spain, with 1,906 cars and 605 trucks from Canada and the United States.

John F. Smith Jr., the chief executive of G.M., said earlier this year that he expected exports from the United States and Canada to Mexico to reach 15,000 cars and trucks this year.

The auto industry's sharp cutbacks in the United States and heavy imports from Mexico placed it at the center of last year's trade debate. Last year, G.M. sent 89,000 vehicles from Mexico to the United States.

But Mr. Smith noted that most of the G.M. cars built in Mexico, including those for the domestic market, consist largely of parts from the United States. "As sales increase in Mexico, production in Mexico will support more jobs in the U.S.," he said.

Some labor leaders, however, say the failure of exports to rise as rapidly as imports is all the more striking because Mexico has been much more protective. "The reduction of barriers all of a sudden produced a market there," said Arthur Gundersheim, director in international affairs at the Amalgamated Clothing and Textile Workers Union. "Our markets were already open." As far as the trade agreement's effect on United States exports is concerned, he said, "The story is that it hasn't done more."

THE RISE OF REGIONALISM

November 1, 1947

HOFFMAN DEMANDS ACTION BY EUROPE ON ECONOMIC UNITY

Tells Council of O. E. E. C. in Paris Integration Is Not an Ideal but a Necessity

INSISTS ON MORE TRADE

Would Eventually Sweep Away All Tariffs— U. S. Warns Aid May Be Halted

By HAROLD CALLENDER
Special to The New York Times

PARIS, Oct. 31—Paul G. Hoffman, Economic Cooperation Administrator, called upon the Europeans today to demonstrate by early next year that they intend to move toward "an integration of the Western European economy."

He made this appeal in a speech to the European Marshall Plan Council, which was composed on this occasion of the Foreign or Finance Ministers of the European countries receiving dollar aid.

Mr. Hoffman insisted that the "integration" he urged was "not just an ideal" but "a practical necessity." He defined this integration as the formation in Europe of a single market within which quantitative restrictions on movements of goods and moneys "and eventually all tariffs" should be "permanently swept away."

Thus there would be created "a permanent freely trading area comprising 270,000,000 consumers in Western Europe," Mr. Hoffman said.

[Congress will not be asked for a third Marshall Plan appropriation by the Truman Administration unless the Western European governments can agree by January on a plan to integrate their economies, it was stated in Washington on high authority.]

Mr. Hoffman, urging "a far-reaching program to build in Western Europe a more dynamic expanding economy," said the first task was to overcome the dollar shortage. He urged greater incentives for private exporters simultaneously with efforts to prevent inflation. But he insisted that balancing of Europe's dollar trade must be linked with expansion and liberation of European economies.

Mr. Hoffman then urged, as a first step toward "integration," the coordination of national fiscal and monetary policies to prevent too divergent prices and costs.

Mr. Hoffman made it clear he approved steps toward freer trade taken by groups of countries—as proposed by the French, Italians and Belgians—if they did not result in raising new barriers against others. He again pleased the French by denouncing higher foreign than domestic prices for "fuel and basic materials." The French have protested against such double prices for German coal.

It was clear that his hearers thought that transformation of Western Europe into a free trade area was a large order even though the element of surprise was lacking.

The speech was regarded as urging a revolution in the economic organization of Europe, though not as an immediate goal or within any fixed period.

French officials professed to be pleased by the speech which, as Maurice Petsche, French Finance Minister, pointed out, coincided with much that M. Petsche had advocated. For this reason the conclusion was drawn that Mr. Hoffman implicitly had given his approval to the economically liberal bloc of the Continental nations—France, Italy and Belgium— that had found itself on the opposite side of the fence from Britain in recent disputes.

British officials made little comment. But in the British bloc of the planned economy states some contended Mr. Hoffman's proposals ran counter to their programs of restricted imports and consumption as a means of concentration on productive investments. They saw a basic conflict between their socialistic controls of economic life, including trade, and the free-trade Europe that Mr. Hoffman said should be the aim of current recovery measures.

Mr. Hoffman used the word "integration" fifteen times, or almost once to every hundred words of his speech. It is a word that rarely if ever has been used by European statesmen having to do with the Marshall Plan to describe what should happen to Europe's economies.

It was remarked that no such term or goal was included in the commitments that the European nations gave in agreeing to the Marshall Plan.

Consequently it appeared to the Europeans that "integration" was an American doctrine that had been superimposed upon the mutual engagements made when the Marshall Plan began—a doctrine that seems logical to Americans and to many Europeans but that European officials consider remote from the immediate practical issues.

What might be considered the first response to Mr. Hoffman's speech, even though prepared in anticipation of it, was given tonight when the Steering Committee of the Council decided to recommend that quantitative restrictions on one-half the imports in private trade of Marshall Plan countries be removed by Dec. 15.

It was characteristic of the hesitations and difficulties connected with even this partial liberation of trade that the committee reached agreement only by introducing an escape clause. It provided that countries unable to remove quotas to that extent by the deadline set should explain to the council their reasons for failing to do so.

Behind this ostensible agreement lies a half-concealed clash between the British and the French, the latter contending that the proposal by Sir Stafford Cripps, British Chancellor of the Exchequer, for such removal of quotas was disingenuous and one-sided, since the British Government controlled one-third of Britain's imports and Britain had excluded Switzerland, Belgium and Western Germany from the benefits of her own removal of quotas.

The French contended the reason Britain had excluded these three was that their manufactures competed most with the British. The French argued they would benefit less from the proposed measures because the foodstuffs they export were controlled imports in most Marshall Plan states. The French, therefore, were understood to have accepted today's tentative agreement with large reservations, which they expected to define tomorrow.

It was believed tonight the council would adopt recommendations to the member nations that would embrace some points in the Hoffman speech. Sir Stafford's proposal and the proposals of M. Petsche and Sean MacBride, Irish Minister of External Affairs, who urged a world economic conference to discuss surplus production.

M. Petsche advocates periodical meetings of the Finance and Foreign Ministers of the Marshall Plan countries and of the governors of their central banks; a monetary stabilization fund, a special European bank to coordinate investments, regional freer trade blocs and a link between the Marshall Plan council and Council of Europe.

M. Petsche insists the dropping of quotas is useful only if there is also internal financial and price stabilization and if, consequently, there is "equality of European competition." He was pleased that Mr. Hoffman supported him on this point and on the need for monetary consultation.

* * *

March 26, 1957

EUROPEANS UNITE IN CUSTOMS UNION AND ATOM AGENCY

Signing of 2 Pacts in Rome Paves Way for Forming 6-Nation Federation

By ARNALDO CORTESI
Special to The New York Times

ROME, March 25—Statesmen of six West European nations signed today the birth certificate of a European federation of states. The signing took place in the Hall of the Horatii and Curiatii on Rome's Capitol Hill.

The six countries are France, West Germany, Italy, Belgium, the Netherlands and Luxembourg.

The documents attesting to the birth of a new grouping of six European countries were two international treaties and several annexes. One treaty provides for the creation of a European common market, in which goods and persons will ultimately move unrestricted by tariffs or other barriers.

A second creates a European atomic pool for the development and exploitation of nuclear energy.

Machinery Is Established

Accompanying these provisions, which are largely economic, are some political stipulations. The two treaties establish the international machinery that will develop in due course into the organs of a central European government.

This machinery is due to include a Court of Justice, a rudimentary Parliament and the embryo of a future European Cabinet. In other words, the two treaties resume the task of building a united Europe at the point where it was halted with the defeat of the European Defense Community project.

The treaties crown the efforts made by the six West European countries to find a substitute for the European Defense Community project. That plan was defeated by a voting technicality in the French National Assembly Aug. 30, 1954.

Unity Will Be Gradual

The six nations seeking unity met in Messina, Sicily, in June 1955 and decided that the ideal of united Europe was not to be abandoned. For the next twenty months they sought to establish the two organizations covered by the treaties signed today.

The new treaties do not go as far as the European Defense Community project. This was largely military in scope and was aimed at creating an integrated European army.

The treaties signed here aim rather at bringing the six European nations together, first of all economically by incorporating them all in a single market and making them all dependent on the same sources of nuclear energy. Then the organs of a central European government created by the treaties will come into play, gradually, drawing the nations still closer together.

The Assembly and Court of Justice established under the two new treaties will apply to the European coal and steel community established in 1953 by the same six signatory nations. To attain this end a special convention amends the treaty that established the coal and steel community.

The transition will be made slowly and gradually. Even the process of eliminating tariffs almost certainly will not be completed before 1970.

Even greater is the importance that some diplomats attach to getting the French and West German economies integrated in the same economic unit. These diplomats believe it will make a war between France and Germany as impossible as a war between Paris and Marseilles.

The principal signers of the two fundamental treaties and annexes were Dr. Konrad Adenauer, Chancellor of West Germany; Christian Pineau, French Foreign Minister; Paul-Henri Spaak, Belgian Foreign Minister; Dr. Joseph M. A. H. Luns, Netherlands Foreign Minister; Joseph Bech, Premier and Foreign Minister of Luxembourg, and Antonio Segni, Premier of Italy.

A second delegate also signed for each country. In Italy's case the second delegate was Dr. Gaetano Martino, the Foreign Minister.

The six signatory states have a combined population of 160,000,000. They represent, therefore, considerably more than one-half of free, or non-Soviet, Europe.

Rome Mayor Hails Accord

Senator Umberto Tupini, Mayor of Rome, started the signatory proceedings with a speech welcoming the delegates and underlining the importance of what they were about to do. He said they were preparing for Europe "a century of union in peace, freedom and prosperity."

He was answered first by Dr. Martino, then by Dr. Adenauer and then in turn by the heads of all other delegations.

All who spoke underlined that, though European unity had been born, much remained to be done if it was to be kept alive. Dr. Adenauer added that "it is painful for us Germans not to be able to participate in a united Europe as a united Germany, but we have not yet given up hope."

Mr. Spaak said he could hardly contain his enthusiasm and optimism that European unity had taken its initial step.

M. Pineau said he felt certain arrangements could be worked out whereby Britain would associate herself with the common market, or European Economic Community, as it is officially called. Then he added:

"We have created not a small isolated Europe but a great Europe. Our union and our strength will inspire respect in anyone who might be tempted to disturb our peace."

Mr. Bech said the idea of European unity no longer belonged to a few lofty spirits but was shared by the peoples of all European countries. Dr. Luns said that growing prosperity and progress would come to Europe as a result of the treaties.

Almost all speakers had warm words of praise for the part played by M. Spaak in making European union possible.

When the speeches were finished the actual ceremony of signing began. The treaty for the common market or European Economic Community as it is officially called, was placed in front of M. Spaak, who sat at one end of the table. He signed it, quickly followed by the second Belgian delegate.

Then the treaty for the atomic pool, or the European Atomic Energy Community as it is officially called, was placed before M. Spaak, while the common market treaty continued to move from delegate to delegate. So the two treaties moved from the Belgians to the French, to the Germans and to Signor Segni who was sitting at the center of the table.

Then they continued to Dr. Martino, who was sitting at Premier Segni's left and to the Dutch and the Luxembourg delegations.

When all had signed, Mayor Tupini gave each delegate a specially struck gold medal to commemorate the event.

In the evening delegates participated in a reception at Palazzo Venezia where Benito Mussolini once had his office.

Earlier in the day all delegates were present at the final burial of Dr. Alcide De Gasperi, former Italian Premier who worked hard to achieve European unity. He is buried in the Basilica of St. Laurence outside the walls where a monument to him also was dedicated. Dr. De Gasperi died Aug. 19, 1954.

Crowd Gathers Outside Hall

Despite a drizzle that fell all day, a sizable crowd gathered on Capitol Hill while the European treaties were being signed.

Some Communists in the crowd tried to create a commotion but they were quickly set upon by the rest of the watchers. Some Communists were manhandled and some were taken into custody by the police.

Completion of the signing ceremony was announced to the crowd by the pealing of two historic old bells in the Capitoline Tower. The ringing of the bells brought cheers from the crowd.

* * *

January 2, 1959

NEW ERA IN TRADE DAWNS IN EUROPE

Six-Nation Common Market Presents Opportunity and Challenge to Members

By HAROLD CALLENDER
Special to The New York Times

PARIS, Jan. 1—The six-nation common market, which began to take economic effect today, offers to its members both an opportunity and a challenge.

The opportunity is that of a great single market where tariffs and other barriers will gradually be eliminated over a transition period of twelve to fifteen years. France, for instance, will be able to sell in the other countries of the common market—West Germany, Italy, Beligum, the Netherlands and Luxembourg—at diminishing tariff rates and finally without any tariffs. French buyers will eventually be as free to buy in the five other nations as in France.

The challenge is that within this great market French producers must compete with those of five other nations, above all with the highly organized economy of West Germany. They must compete not only in the five other countries but in France herself. For West Germans, for example, will have the same access to the French market that French producers have.

When the common market is fully effective, a French textile manufacturer must treat German textile rivals as if they were Frenchmen, a German chemical producer must treat French chemical industries as if they were German. In the field of trade there will no longer be any national distinctions.

Producers in the six nations have long since planned for both the new opportunities that will open up and for the new competition they will face. Modernization, cutting of costs and amalgamations have been contemplated and it is reported that trade plans reach across frontiers in cartel-minded Europe.

A writer in L'Express told of a small manufacturer of metallic products in Paris who was content with his profits but was lured into the West German market by an agent. He found the Germans would buy large quantities of his goods at prices slightly below those he demanded. He was depressed, but an expert showed him how to modernize his family factory and cut costs so he could easily produce at the German prices. This was a new idea to him, but he jumped at it and his factory expanded.

This is typical of what may happen in France and elsewhere when tariffs among the six nations fall and finally disappear. There will be widespread "reconversions" by producers able to face competition. The devaluation of the franc, reducing costs in terms of the currencies of the five other nations, will facilitate French exports if not offset by inflation.

Not all producers will be able to stand the pace, and badly equipped or high-cost concerns will have to reorganize, combine with others or go out of business when deprived of the protection they now enjoy.

To the other nations of the common market West Germany has lately sent about 29 per cent of her exports, France 24 per cent, Italy 23 per cent, Belgium and Luxembourg a total of 45 per cent, the Netherlands 38 per cent. The common market probably will expand this internal trade, yet its member nations will still require foodstuffs, raw materials and fuel from the rest of the world and will need to export beyond the common market.

It is assumed that the greater tariff-free market will develop larger-scale production and greater aggregate output, as in the United States. In that case the six nations might become more formidable competitors in the world market.

Producers in other countries have considered this possibility while calculating the extent to which they will be handicapped in exporting to the six nations.

British Face Problems

The British have been especially troubled by these problems. Britain will no longer compete on equal terms with West Germany in France, Italy or the Low Countries, where British exports must face the common tariff of the common market while German exports will enter free.

Meanwhile West Germany, by virtue of the stimulus of a free market in Europe containing 160,000,000 people, may grow stronger as a competitor with British manufacturers in South America, for example.

In a dispatch yesterday on the common market it was said that the immediate discrimination against outside nations would be in import quotas. There will be some discrimination in tariffs also, but only by Belgium, the Netherlands and Luxembourg, which will not extend to outside nations the 10 per cent tariff cut they will make for the other common market nations.

This is because their tariffs are lower than the prospective common market tariff. Since their tariffs are low, the discrimination will be small. It will be greater when their tariffs rise to the level of the common market tariff when this tariff takes effect. The common market tariff is to be approximately the average of the present tariffs of the six nations.

*　*　*

February 19, 1960

7 LATIN NATIONS SIGN PACT TO FORM COMMON MARKET

By JUAN de ONIS
Special to The New York Times

MONTEVIDEO, Uruguay, Feb. 18—The foreign ministers of seven Latin American countries signed today a treaty for a free trade zone linking their nations' economies.

The countries involved are Argentina, Brazil, Chile, Mexico, Paraguay, Peru and Uruguay.

The treaty provides for the elimination over a twelve-year period of all trade restrictions on at least 75 per cent of the trade within the area. Any Latin American country may join the treaty group.

At the signing ceremony, in the Red Room of Government House, Foreign Minister Horacio Lafer of Brazil said the treaty "opens a new path" in Latin America toward higher production and living standards. Foreign Minister Homero Martinez Montero of Uruguay said the treaty reflected a conviction that Latin-American countries could grow faster economically by cooperation than by isolation.

The negotiations on the treaty started last September and were assisted by the United Nations Economic Commission for Latin America and the Inter-American Economic and Social Council of the Organization of American States. The United States also offered encouragement.

Treaty Is Popular

The idea of a free trade area, or common market, is popular with most Latin Americans and the treaty has been hailed in the hemisphere's press.

The delegates agreed that the United States could contribute to the success of the treaty in the following ways:

- By supporting the treaty when it is submitted for approval to the organization administering the General Agreement on Tariffs and Trade.
- By offering constructive criticism in inter-American conferences on integrating the trade zone into the hemisphere's trade and investment structure.
- By distributing information on the agreement and its implications for investments.
- By providing loans to private Latin American industrialists seeking to expand their enterprises to take advantage of the market of 140,000,000 persons that would be created by the treaty.

Latin American industrialists fear that only foreign corporations will have enough capital to take advantage of the new market unless the area's companies receive loans.

The treaty must be signed by three signatory nations to go into effect. Delegates expect this stage to be reached by early next year.

In the meantime, the treaty establishes a provisional free-trade association of the seven signatories with offices in Montevideo, the eventual seat of the treaty's secretariat.

As soon as the treaty goes into effect the members will hold the first of twelve annual conferences to negotiate reciprocal trade and tariff concessions.

Each country will present a list of goods on which it will reduce tariffs at least 8 per cent and on which it will ease other restrictions for members of the zone.

Each year an additional 8 per cent reduction must be granted, although the goods on the lists may be changed. Every three years a common list of irremovable goods representing 25 per cent of the area's trade must be established.

The treaty exempts agricultural and livestock trade to protect such activities as the subsidized wheat programs in Brazil and Chile from Argentine competition.

* * *

May 4, 1986

HANGING TOGETHER

THE UNITED STATES AND THE REGIONAL ORGANIZATION OF ASIA AND THE PACIFIC, 1965–1985
By W. W. Rostow
Maps. 265 pp. Austin: University of Texas Press. $30.

By STEPHEN KRASNER

In April 1965 Lyndon Johnson made a speech at Johns Hopkins University extolling the virtues of Asian regionalism. W. W. Rostow—his national security adviser from 1966 to 1969 and now a professor of political economy at the University of Texas—uses this initiative as a touchstone for analyzing United States policy in Asia over the last two decades. He begins with an ingenious defense of America's involvement in Vietnam where, he argues, American commitments and American blood bought much needed time. "In the late winter and spring of 1965 there were not," Mr. Rostow says, "many among the Communist as well as non-Communist leaders of the region who did not believe in the domino theory."

By 1975, when North Vietnam took over the South, many East Asian countries had experienced a decade of explosive economic growth and ASEAN (the Association of Southeast Asian Nations), the most successful regional organization, had been firmly established. This "suffused the region with a degree of inner confidence." Moreover, he maintains, had Congress not sabotaged American military guarantees to the South Vietnamese between 1973 and 1975, the agreements that extricated the United States from Indochina might have been honored.

The regional organization of Asia has, for Mr. Rostow, basically political not economic purposes. He notes that regional integration with regard to trade or other economic activities has not been particularly impressive. The most forceful economic rationale for regional organization is the need for additional investment, especially in raw materials and agriculture. Why such investment should be mounted through a regional organization, rather than bilaterally, is never made clear.

But Mr. Rostow has more important matters in mind than economic development in his endorsement of regional organization, for he sees such arrangements as a way to promote international stability and American interests. The outlandish power the United States exercised at the conclusion of World War II is declining. The Russians remain patient and persistent in their attempts to cement a great arc of domination stretching from Djibouti to Vladivostok. The American public is prone to isolationist impulses.

In Mr. Rostow's view, regional organizations can contribute to a solution for these problems for both Asia and America. They give the smaller states of the area greater leverage in their dealings with both the United States and Japan. They can assure their independence and neutrality and, in doing so, guarantee the freedom of the China Sea and the Pacific. Regionalism can also prevent a single power from dominating Indochina and Thailand, a development that would threaten the "vital interests of India, Japan, the United States, Indonesia, and Australia."

This is all very heady stuff, geopolitical conceptualizing of the highest order. But the pieces of this story are familiar. The Russians are implacable and expansionist. The United States remains the only power capable of preventing the Russians from consolidating control over the whole southern rim of the Eurasian land mass. Local nationalism and the fissures within the world Communist movement are overshadowed by the bipolar conflict. America's vital interests still, for Mr. Rostow, remain tied to Indochina and other parts of the Asian mainland because these areas touch the Pacific, and control of the Pacific is vital for the United States and its allies.

There is none of George F. Kennan's measured judgment of what is critical and what is not. A watery skein links Los Angeles and Bangkok, Thailand. There is little assessment of the potential for conflict between the United States and its present allies over either economic matters in the short term or political and strategic factors in the long term. Despite Vietnam, minimal attention is paid to the domestic requirements for an effective foreign policy in a democratic state.

The author recognizes that American capabilities are declining, but he cannot bring himself to the conclusion that America's ability to control events is eroding as well. Other countries have interests, the United States has responsibilities. It is not necessary to listen very hard to hear the dominoes still falling in Walt Rostow's mind.

Stephen Krasner is a professor of political science at Stanford University.

* * *

September 4, 1988

AS EUROPE UNITES, OUTSIDERS LINE UP TO JOIN THE CLUB

By STEVEN GREENHOUSE

PARIS—As the European Community pushes to form a barrier-free market by the end of 1992, other countries are crowding to join the 12-nation organization lest they miss out on the economic benefits.

The Europe of the 12, as the community is often called, might become a Europe of the 14 by 1995, and some see a Europe of the 18 by early next century. If that happens, the community will become a giant of 400 million people and an even more formidable entity for the United States and the Soviet Union to contend with.

For the next few years the community nations will be too preoccupied with the transition to a single market to undertake the arduous process of admitting new members. But when the community is ready to proceed it is expected to have a number of applications on the table.

Turkey applied to join the community last year. Austria will apply next year, many Vienna officials say, and Norway is expected to seek membership in the early 1990's. Some European Community officials even predict that Sweden, Switzerland and Finland, despite their neutrality, might seek to join, subtly aligning themselves more closely with the West.

In Austria and Norway, among other nations, business executives are leading the campaign for membership. "A lot of people want to be part of the integration of Europe, to be part of a united European economic space," said Sverre Linvedt, director of the Norwegian Export Council. Many executives fear that sweeping away the internal barriers will make it harder for companies from the outside to sell goods to the community. Although American and Japanese executives also worry about a protectionist Europe, such a monolith could especially hurt countries such as Switzerland and Austria, which send two-thirds of their exports to the community.

Many European officials predict that Austria will be the next to join. Austria's conservative People's Party supports membership while the Socialist Party has asked for a study of the issue. With polls showing that most Austrians favor joining, the Government says it will soon decide whether to apply. But many Austrians are hesitant. "Neutrality is a pillar of our foreign policy," an Austrian official said. "We don't think we should give that up to join."

Advocates of membership say Austria can join without becoming aligned with the Western alliance. They point to Ireland as an example of a community member that remains neutral. Opponents argue that it would be better if they could manage to maintain close economic links with the 12 member countries, while remaining separate. Brussels officials look favorably on Austria's applying, but a few say that because the community often takes pro-Western positions, it might be unrealistic for the country to join while expecting to remain neutral.

Neutrality is not an issue with Norway, which is already a member of NATO. In the early 1970's, Brussels approved Norway's application, but it never joined because 53 percent of Norwegians later voted against membership in a referendum. Now the idea of joining is growing more popular, but Oslo refuses to tip its hand. "The major political parties are in favor of joining, but they would like to postpone a decision until after elections in 1989 because it remains a delicate issue," a Norwegian official said.

Scandinavian Neutrality

Sweden is more hesitant about joining because of its long-standing neutrality. But even the Swedes might want in if their powerful private sector becomes convinced that it is missing the benefits. Because of its border with the Soviet Union, Finland is perhaps more concerned about maintaining neutrality. If Norway and Sweden join, however, European officials say there is a good chance that Finland will too. Iceland, a NATO member, may also follow the lead of Norway and Sweden. The officials predict that Cyprus and Malta might also join someday.

Even though Switzerland is surrounded by community nations, it is in no rush to join. Swiss corporate giants like Nestle and Ciba-Geigy are already well entrenched in West Germany, France, Britain and other community nations. Treasuring their neutral role, the Swiss recently voted against joining the United Nations, and any referendum on European Community membership is expected to meet the same fate. Still, some Swiss officials say there could be a change of heart if the Swiss feel handicapped as outsiders.

While all these Western European nations are nudging closer to the community, Eastern Europe has also warmed toward Brussels. Last month, the community and Comecon, the Eastern bloc's trading association, granted each other recognition. Hungary, Poland and Czechoslovakia have also granted diplomatic recognition to the community, and in July Brussels signed a trade pact with Hungary, in part to reward it for its economic changes. Several other Communist nations are seeking similar agreements.

Perhaps the stickiest candidacy would be that of Turkey, which is larger geographically than any of the 12 member nations and whose population is comparable to Britain's. Some Brussels officials say they fear that if Turkey is admitted, its low wages might give its industries an edge over Western Europe's, while millions of the country's unemployed flooded freely across the continent. Some officials also contend that Turkey is not Westernized enough. Another obstacle is Greece's antagonism toward Turkey. In the view of some diplomats, the chief reason Turkey has sought to reconcile itself with Greece, which joined the community in 1981, is to improve its chances of membership.

"There is a fear that this is too large a bit to swallow," said Heinz Kramer, an expert on Turkey with the German Research Institute for International Affairs outside Munich. "They will probably try to avoid a clear-cut answer as long as they can. They recognize Turkey is a very strategic ally, so it is almost impossible to reject them bluntly."

* * *

October 23, 1988

THE MENACE OF TRADE BLOCS

By FLORA LEWIS

PARIS—A watershed in world trade lies not far ahead. Decisions during the next Administration can determine long-term health of the U.S. and world economies, affecting politics and defense.

For the moment, many are giving lip service to the principle of more trade freedom, global cooperation and so on. But a December meeting in Montreal will be a hard-fought prelude to the big trade battle looming. The U.S. chief negotiator, Clayton Yeutter, has warned of a "full-scale confrontation" if the Europeans aren't willing to plan an end to agricultural subsidies.

While they talk free trade, major players are gearing up for a titanic battle of blocs, with undertones of George Orwell's "1984" vision of a world divided among three powers permanently at war.

On one side is Europe with its 1992 target for setting up a true Common Market. The U.S. has warned against the Community surrounding itself with barriers that would make a "Fortress Europe," and Community officials say that isn't their intention. But they continue to insist on an ill-defined notion of "reciprocity," bargaining off concessions with other countries one by one, the opposite of multilateral free trade.

There is also pressure within the Community for a "domestic content" rule, ostensibly to prevent Japanese firms from leapfrogging the wall by setting up European finishing plants for Japanese-made goods. That would be another form of protectionism.

Washington is getting alarmed about the impact on the U.S. At least one Republican senator has argued that in reprisal the U.S. should set up a "Fortress America" trading zone, including Mexico as well as Canada. That would more or less inevitably draw in most of Latin America. The Presidential campaign has shown how much and how broadly protectionist sentiment is growing in the U.S.

Meanwhile, some senior Western officials are seriously concerned at how far the Japanese have gone toward preparing a bloc of their own. It would embrace not only the "four tigers"—Taiwan, South Korea, Hong Kong and Singapore—but also the less developed Asian countries.

That is a hedge. The Japanese would certainly prefer to continue spewing their products around the world and buying where they get the best deals. But they are already thinking of an alternative if that should be prevented by protectionism in other regions. Then, so much for American dreams of a great Pacific-rim economy.

It would be, with a vengeance, the "Greater East Asia Co-Prosperity Sphere" that the Japanese tried to establish by conquest in World War II. The use of force brought Japan's own destruction. In just two generations, the use of trade and productivity has brought the old vision within reach. There is also a lesson in this for Americans who want to entrust the nation's fate primarily to military power.

These are not precisely the three warring blocs Orwell envisaged: Oceania, Eurasia and Eastasia. But the similarity is too close for comfort, including the possibility of a European-Soviet bloc partnership. Orwell was thinking in politico-military terms with Soviet dominance, and that hasn't happened. The West won, largely because it proved able to deliver the goods and prosper with expanding trade.

Now, it is a flourishing Western Europe that is attracting the isolated East. After opposing the Common Market for years, the Soviet Union and its allies are courting it for help in finance and expertise. Comecon, the East bloc's cumbersome and ineffective counterpart, has signed a cooperation agreement with the European Community. One by one, starting with Hungary, Eastern European countries are also signing up individually.

In the last two weeks, West European banks have made deals providing for $9 billion worth of credit to the Soviets, mostly for consumer goods industries that Mikhail Gorbachev needs to give perestroika a chance. Prime Minister Ciriaco De Mita of Italy started a current parade of European leaders to Moscow last week, and will be followed by West Germany's Helmut Kohl and France's Francois Mitterrand.

When he returned, Mr. De Mita spoke publicly of the need for "something like a Marshall Plan" for the Soviet Union, arguing that it can provide "unimaginable commercial advantages." Germany, Britain and France have similar ideas.

The fork in the road to world trade or rival blocs is coming up soon. The U.S. can't make the decision alone, but it has great influence. It needs to be perfectly clear what the choice implies.

* * *

November 20, 1988

THE FREE-TRADE PACT

Will It Make Canada the 51st State?

By JOHN F. BURNS

When Canadians vote in a general election tomorrow, they will be deciding the fate of the free-trade agreement between Canada and the United States. The agreement, already approved by Congress and signed by President Reagan, would, over a 10-year period, eliminate all remaining tariffs on $150 billion in annual trade between the two countries. It would also eliminate or lower non-tariff barriers in areas ranging from agriculture to energy to investment and other services.

Ratification of the agreement depends on victory at the polls for the Progressive Conservatives, who form the present

Government. The two opposition parties, the Liberals and the New Democrats, have called the agreement a formula for turning the country into a "51st state."

To understand the debate, John F. Burns, The New York Times's correspondent in Canada, spoke with John Crispo, a professor in the faculty of management at the University of Toronto, who has been an outspoken advocate of the agreement, and Melville H. Watkins, a professor in the university's department of economics, who has actively opposed it.

Question: Proponents of the agreement see it as a guarantor of Canada's future prosperity, its critics as the road to impoverishment and national disintegration. Which is it?

Mr. Crispo: Already, 80 percent of our goods go into the United States tariff free, but 20 percent don't. A lot of that 20 percent is in resources for which the United States has a tariff schedule rigged against the further processing of these resources in Canada. That 20 percent is very important to us. Furthermore, tariffs are not the issue anymore in international trade. It's non-tariff issues that are restricting international free trade. It's quotas, it's countervail, it's dumping, it's all the phony standards that are used to restrict the flow of goods between our two countries.

We've seldom had a fair break in dispute settlements over trade. One of the most important features of this free-trade agreement from Canada's point of view is the new binding binational dispute settlement tribunal, which is the final court of appeal on the most critical trade disputes between our two countries.

Previously, we have had to go into the final court of appeals as a supplicant before the United States Supreme Court, where we had a voice but no vote and were often there four or five years to get a decision that cost us tens of millions of dollars. Now under the free-trade agreement in these critical disputes we go before a binding binational tribunal where we are equal partners with equal voice and vote and where a decision has to be rendered within 312 days.

Mr. Watkins: Canada and the United States are very close and we're going to remain very close and are going to remain the two countries that have the largest volume of trade of any two countries in the world. But we've always understood that we had to keep a certain arms-length relationship with the United States. The fear is that we are in fact going to alter the rules of the game in such a way as to very much increase the links. I think most Canadians say: "We've learned to live with the United States, we know the benefits of that, we know the costs. We're really not prepared to take a step that involves the risk of a radical alteration in those arrangements."

Q. Professor Crispo, what do you see as the principal benefits of the agreement to Canada when it is fully implemented in 10 years?

Mr. Crispo: The benefits are staggering, even more for Canada than for the United States. Consumers will benefit by more choice and lower prices. Workers over time benefit; I stress over time. We get a chance to move workers out of our low-wage protected, subsidized industries, which include apparel, textiles, furniture, shoes and leather.

Then you have to look at Canada's winning industries. They are all high-paying, many high-tech and high value-added and outward looking. I would include auto, aviation, chemicals, steel, telecommunications, urban transit, resources and most of the service sector.

What is not recognized by all Canadians, is that this agreement is the envy of the world because the world now recognizes that Canada has a hedge. It is plugged into the American market under this deal. If there are trade wars, at least we are protected in terms of our access to the American market.

Mr. Watkins: Eight economic studies have been done in Canada in just the past year on what this agreement will do to the Canadian economy. What they show is that the benefits that will result turn out to be very small. They run at around a 2 to 2.5 percent increase in the standard of living of Canadians from now until the end of time. Should we take all these risks and turn the country upside down in order to get five or six months of economic growth?

Mr. Crispo: Mel is getting away with the usual argument that the real choice is between free trade and the status quo, and that the status quo is all right so why rock the boat? That is not the real choice. The real choice is between free trade and growing American protectionism.

Just three weeks ago, Ronald Reagan vetoed the most vicious protectionist textile bill that has come out of that Congress. He was only sustained in an attempt to override the veto by nine votes.

Now we have a new United States President without the commitment for free trade, without the prestige Reagan had, and we've got a more protectionist Congress. That's why it's so important for us to preserve our existing access.

Mr. Watkins: There is no question that there has existed for some time and still exists in the United States a protectionist mood. But what I am struck by is that the protectionist mood is not the dominant mood in the United States. It is less now than it was five years ago. Mr. Bush beat Mr. Dukakis in the election and Richard Gephardt, who was a protectionist, got badly clobbered in the primaries.

Mr. Crispo: You say that we haven't been hit by that much protectionism? My God, soft-wood lumber, potash, uranium, specialty steel, lobsters, raspberries, Christmas trees, potatoes. You just don't know where they are going to come from next.

Mr. Watkins: You can tell me how many cases the United States has brought against us. But how do you square that with the fact that in the past four years the rate of growth of the Canadian economy has, I think, been second only to the Japanese economy among the advanced industrialized countries. The free-trade agreement is a solution to a non-existent problem.

Q. Since the end of World War II, the Canadian economy has become very much integrated with the United States economy. Yet opponents of the free-trade deal are saying that any further integration of the two economies will destroy Canada as a nation.

Mr. Watkins: If you go back through history, you'll find that travelers who came to Canada, whether it was Alexandre de Toqueville or Friedrick Engels, always said that Canada is quite different. So that the argument that somehow we've become more distinctive just in the past 40 years or so won't hold up. I think what we can say is that Canada has certainly not disappeared.

We've held our own. I think we should understand, though, that part of the way we've done that is by very active Government intervention. What is very much a concern about this particular free-trade agreement is that in a variety of ways it does constrain Government. Culturally, it is a recipe for disaster.

Mr. Crispo: Never in the history of what is essentially a trade agreement has there been so much deliberate dishonest distortion of the non-trade implications of the agreement. Canadians have been told they are going to lose everything. I think the cruelest hoax of all is to have had people who oppose this deal going into old-folks homes, leaving pamphlets and telling the elderly and infirm that this deal is going to cost them their medical and pension plans.

Mr. Watkins: We have a problem which is that every cultural group in Canada disagrees with John. He says culture is protected. How come he can't convince the spokespersons for a single cultural group?

Mr. Crispo: They are against free trade for ideological, philosophical, and political reasons. You have a Social Democratic agenda. You have an agenda calling for more state intervention. You're worried about the free-trade agreement because you say it's going to make it more difficult to socialize Canada, to rationalize things and to regulate things.

Mr. Watkins: You're going to make it sound as though the only people who oppose this deal are New Democrats and socialists. The polls show very clearly that for a long time public opinion was split exactly down the middle on this question. Now majorities in virtually every province and region are opposed. It is a majority Canadian position.

Q. Two aspects of the agreement that are argued as being the most attractive to the United States are the provisions for free trade in service industries, and the provisions for a continental market in energy. Is there anything troubling in this?

Mr. Watkins: In the service area, the United States has got Canada to make the most sweeping concessions that any country has made. I'm struck by the fact that the coalition supporting this deal in the United States is headed by the president of American Express. The United States already has a surplus in services with Canada.

On the energy side, we have one clause in the energy agreement that Canada can't put export taxes on resources or energy. That means whatever price we sell in Canada we must charge the same price to the United States. That means that if OPEC charges go up as they might, for example, in the 1990's, and we want to do what we did in the 1970's—charge America a different price than we charge at home—we can't. To me that's a serious compromising of sovereignty.

The same chapter on energy also has another clause. The parties agree that they can continue to give incentives for oil and gas exploration. That to me is just stunning. Canadians as taxpayers are going to be allowed to pay money in large sums to find and develop oil and gas that we then can't recover. We as Canadian taxpayers—not American taxpayers—have paid for that but can't recover it.

Mr. Crispo: We, on my side, are accused of fear-mongering when we say we're worried about what happens if this deal isn't signed. We've already seen jitters in the international market and in the Canadian stock market. The gnomes of Zurich and London and Wall Street have said, "What are these Canadians going to do, are they going to turn this deal down?"

I think there will be a fairly massive outflow of capital from Canada, part of it speculative but part of it long term. Who is going to put a manufacturing plant in Canada without free trade? Our market is too small. I see real trouble.

I kind of plead with Americans, bear with us. We've got these parochial, provincial nationalists who for ideological reasons are trying to undermine the agreement and everything it stands for because they want to socialize this confounded place. Bear with us while we rally the forces to make the Canadian people understand that we didn't give away the country with this agreement.

*   *   *

November 23, 1988

U.S.-CANADA PACT IMPLIES BIG CHANGE FOR WORLD TRADE

By CLYDE H. FARNSWORTH
Special to the New York Times

WASHINGTON, Nov. 22—The free-trade agreement between the United States and Canada, which is expected to take effect Jan. 1, is likely to lead to significant changes in the world trading system.

Prime Minister Brian Mulroney said in Quebec today that he would use the parliamentary majority he won in Monday's election to seek approval of the trade pact as soon as Parliament convenes the week of Dec. 12. And the opposition Liberal Party, which had used its majority in the appointed Senate to block the agreement, said today that it would allow the measure to go ahead. The pact was approved by the United States Congress in September.

With the accord, the United States and Canada would formalize what is already the largest trading relationship between two countries. The agreement is expected to reduce both countries' cost of doing business, increasing their productivity and competitiveness.

Duties to Be Phased Out

About 70 percent of the $150 billion a year in trade between the United States and Canada is already duty-free. The new pact will eliminate most remaining barriers over 10 years.

Canada will get increased access to a market 10 times its size. In return it will make the bigger tariff cuts because its tariffs are three to four times higher than those of the United States.

The consensus of economists is that in 10 years, with the agreement fully in force, Canada's economy will expand 5 percent faster than it would have otherwise. The American economy is expected to grow 1 percent faster.

One result is likely to be hundreds of thousands of additional jobs on both sides of the border.

"The free-trade agreement will bring prosperity to both nations for years to come," declared Clayton K. Yeutter, the United States trade representative.

Trade Rivalries Overseas

The accord is expected to help both countries meet intensified competition from eastern Asia and Europe, where the 12 nations of the European Community plan to drop all internal trade barriers by the end of 1992.

At the same time, the American-Canadian agreement sends a strong message to the trade ministers of 96 nations who will gather in Montreal in two weeks to discuss a liberalization of global commerce. Those negotiations would have been seriously undercut if Canada had rejected the agreement.

The Montreal agenda includes proposals to reduce barriers to trade in agriculture and in banking, accounting, aviation, tourism and other services. Other proposals would stiffen protection for patents, copyrights and other intellectual property.

The talks are conducted by the General Agreement on Tariffs and Trade, the body that oversees world trade. The talks are known as the Uruguay Round because they began in Uruguay.

Washington and Ottawa share the same objectives for the Montreal talks. In fact their free-trade agreement, which both governments signed earlier this year after two years of negotiations, incorporates many proposals to be discussed in the GATT talks.

The trade alliance of the United States and Canada is expected to give them important leverage in the Montreal talks. Early in the Reagan Administration, James A. Baker 3d, then the Treasury Secretary, and William E. Brock, then the trade representative, served notice that Washington was prepared to form a "club of like-minded nations" to seek freer trade if global liberalization did not materialize.

A Bilateral Threat

Now the United States could go ahead with other bilateral agreements based on its pact with Canada, should the Montreal meeting fall short of its goals. Among the nations that have expressed interest in such agreements are Australia, New Zealand, Taiwan, and Malaysia.

"The bilateral threat remains credible," C. Michael Aho, a foreign trade expert with the Council on Foreign Relations, said of the American options. "This is an insurance policy for both countries, which we can use to prod the multilateral process."

Even if the Uruguay Round does move toward a successful conclusion by the end of 1990, when it is scheduled to end, several officials and private analysts believe that the Bush Administration will seek to reduce barriers that impede trade with Mexico.

Eventually this move could lead to a North American Common Market from the Arctic to Yucatan, embracing nearly 350 million people.

Focus Shifts to Mexico

The agreement with Canada will move American-Mexican trade relations "up front," Commerce Secretary C. William Verity Jr. said in an interview today.

"I think what it will do is push what the Mexicans want and really what the United States wants, which is for a similar type agreement with Mexico," he said. Mr. Verity said an accord with Mexico would "take a little longer because Mexico is not as far along in some respects in trade."

To a considerable degree, Mexico—one of the most heavily indebted countries and yet the most important trading partner for the United States after Canada and Japan—still protects its industries because they are not yet ready to meet outside competition.

Changes for Companies

The free-trade agreement with Ottawa is also expected to have a major effect on multinational corporate strategy. A company that has production and distribution in both the United States and Canada now has to pay duties when its goods cross the border.

Such duties hinder what otherwise would be unencumbered access to labor, raw materials and other economic resources.

The decision to seek a United States-Canada trade agreement came at the so-called Shamrock summit meeting of Mr. Mulroney and President Reagan on St. Patrick's Day in 1985.

The idea was a Canadian initiative. At that time there was great concern that Congress, trying to cope with America's progressively larger trade deficits, would write protectionist legislation that would cut Canada out of its biggest foreign market. Eighty percent of Canada's exports go to the United States.

*   *   *

May 31, 1990

SELLING IN EUROPE: BORDERS FADE

By STEVEN PROKESCH
Special to The New York Times
LONDON, May 30—The single market of 325 million consumers that the 12 nations of the European Community are trying to create is at least two and a half years away, but consumer-products companies are acting as if it were already here.

Scores of companies are creating "Eurobrands," giving products a single brand name throughout most or all of Europe. Many are supporting their products with

"Euro-ads"—advertisements that except for the language, are similar in message and often identical or nearly identical in execution.

For instance, in Britain and France, Mars Inc., the United States candy maker, has already changed the name of its Treets candies to M & M's, the name it uses in the United States.

Over the next five years, Nestle S.A., the giant Swiss foods company, plans to replace several national brands it uses to sell Camembert cheese in Europe with the Nestle brand name.

And the Colgate-Palmolive Company, the big United States consumer products maker, has reduced the number of Palmolive soaps it sells in Europe to only three fragrances, down from at least 10 just a short time ago, said James G.B. Williams, director of planning and research at Young & Rubicam Europe, the London-based European arm of the American ad agency.

"The assumption now at many companies is that everything will be the same unless someone can prove why not," he said.

Worried that presenting different advertisements in different countries might confuse consumers, Philips and Whirlpool Major Domestic Appliances, the European joint venture between Philips N.V., the Dutch company, and America's Whirlpool Corporation, has come up with a single ad concept, executed with minor variations for each country, to establish recognition of its brand throughout the Continent.

Until recently, marketers tended to focus on the things that distinguished Europeans from one another. One big exception has been the American companies that have tried to sell products like Levi's jeans, Coca-Cola and Marlboro cigarettes as a part of American culture. And companies have long sold products to the rich and the young, groups that often have traits in common with their peers around the world.

But the changes sweeping Europe are transforming the way products are marketed, forcing many companies to think Pan-European. While no one believes that the 1992 market unification will instantly homogenize Europeans, most agree that it will make it easier to compete throughout the Continent by eliminating trade barriers and harmonizing national regulations regarding both advertising and product standards.

Deregulation of Broadcasting

Companies are also trying to take advantage of the deregulation of the broadcast industry, which is expected to increase the amount of air time available for advertising.

And they are also trying to capitalize on the convergence in consumer tastes that has resulted from the growing middle class. Europe has enjoyed robust economic growth in recent years—prosperity that is expected to continue because of the single market. Smaller families with two wage earners, single-family housing and the means to travel have become hallmarks of the middle class throughout Europe just as they are in America.

"The specter of 1992 is causing multinational companies to think about whether they are doing the right things," said Neil Kennedy, executive vice president of Backer Spielvogel Bates Europe, the European arm of the ad agency owned by the Saatchi & Saatchi Company.

While a unified Europe means opportunities, it also means competition. To cope, companies are frantically creating and buying Pan-European brands or those that have the potential to be, helping to fuel the acquisition boom in Europe. Nestle, for example, has bought Buitoni, the Italian pasta concern, and Rowntree, the English confectioner.

Companies are also trying to strengthen the brands they have by winnowing their portfolios, making it easier and more cost-effective to manufacture, distribute and advertise their products in Europe.

A handful of daring companies are even abandoning strong national brands in a bid to create Pan-European or global brands. In addition to establishing M & M's as a brand in Europe, Mars is now changing the name of its popular Marathon candy bar in Britain to Snickers, even though some marketing experts warn that the move is risky, given the closeness of the name to nickers, the British term for women's underwear.

Even companies that do not tamper with established national or regional brands are more closely coordinating the way those items are advertised and packaged. Henkel K.G.A.A., the West Germany chemicals concern, uses the same packaging and the same television ad for a detergent that sells under several different names on the Continent.

Market researchers have discovered that there are more similarities in living styles and values among Europeans than they had previously recognized—similarities that seem to grow with incomes and education levels.

Jane L. Hourigan, director of the two-year-old Single Market Unit at D'Arcy Masius Benton & Bowles, advises her Pan-European clients to look for regions in Europe with social or economic similarities. She said marketers of luxury products might therefore want to focus on "the golden circle," the 250 miles around Cologne, West Germany, that takes in almost all of the wealthiest areas of the Continent.

Euro-ads provide marketers with several benefits. For one, creative teams are more likely to end up with an effective advertising campaign by focusing their resources on the development of a single advertisement.

And at a cost of $180,000 to $250,000 apiece, making one or two original commercials rather than a dozen or more means a larger amount can be spent on quality or print space.

Growth in Ad Spending

Vast changes sweeping the communications industry are giving advertisers more opportunities to do just that. They also explain why ad agencies expect the rate of ad expenditures in Europe to grow faster than in the United States.

Most television and many radio stations in Western Europe have traditionally been state-owned. But the deregulation of the broadcasting industry is significantly increasing the number of private stations, including satellite and cable systems. That is making a lot more advertising time available.

J. Walter Thompson estimates that the number of television channels in Western Europe will increase to 91 in 1993, up from 69 in 1987, while the amount of programming will jump to 784,020 hours from 282,755 hours. Ad agencies estimate that as much as one-third of the homes in Western Europe will be receiving satellite channels in 1992.

The standardization of advertising regulations by the European Community should also make life easier for advertisers, although agencies worry that the community directive on advertising, now under development, will be too restrictive. It is possible that all advertising of tobacco products will be banned in the European Community.

Pan-European publications, some in English and others in multiple languages, and the expanding reach of international communications companies, many with both broadcast and print interests, are also growing. These include the empires of Rupert Murdoch, Robert Maxwell and Silvio Berlusconi, and companies like Hachette S.A. of France and Bertelsmann A.G. of West Germany. Mr. Maxwell started publishing a weekly newspaper earlier this month called The European.

Help With Media-Buying

In the meantime, big, centralized media-buying organizations are spreading throughout Europe to help advertisers make sense of the dizzying array of choices and to help them get better prices.

But increasingly, advertisers are having to worry about Europeans being hit with conflicting messages about their products. That is because media from one country are spilling over into another and people are traveling more.

"People are daily exposed to a multiple of messages about Opel," the General Motors Corporation's car brand on the Continent, said Thomas R. Mason, a vice president at Zurich-based G.M. Europe. "It's important that those messages be consistent and complement and reinforce each other rather than portray our products in different lights."

That is one main reason G.M. uses varieties of the same basic "Look at Opel Now" print and television ads in 16 European countries.

* * *

September 28, 1991

ANOTHER END TO EUROPHORIA

By FLORA LEWIS

PARIS—Success is threatening to undermine the European Community. Even before the establishment of a single market, the community has proved an irresistible magnet, playing an important role in the breakdown of the Soviet Eastern European empire. It provided the contrast showing how badly Communism failed.

But now, old suspicions simmer between France and Germany. An interlude of "Europhoria," which replaced the fear of "Eurosclerosis" of the mid-1980's, has given way to another bout of rival jousting.

The long argument over "widening" (admitting more members) versus "deepening" (building stronger institutions) has been superceded. Events moved too fast in the East.

It is now generally accepted that Western applicants can't be excluded much longer, and that Easterners have to be given solid hope for admission when their economies are up to the challenge. President Francois Mitterrand's comment that this would take "decades and decades" boomeranged and was considered an intolerable rejection of the East's appeal for a European embrace.

So the new issue is how fast and far the 12 existing members are willing to go to establish a core firm enough not to be diluted by many newcomers, perhaps as many as another dozen, including ex-Soviet republics. The deadline is December, when two new treaties are to be signed.

The one on economic and monetary union is almost over the hump after a harsh struggle. A compromise provides for a single treaty on a common currency and a central bank, but leaves each country the choice of starting operations by the end of 1996 or joining later. It's a typical E.C. compromise; the laggards, almost surely including Britain, can be left behind without being left out.

Even so, voices in France are complaining that the French economy can't take so much dependence on Bonn, although Paris wants rapid consolidation to tie the Germans westward. High interest rates dictated by the mark, they say, are prolonging recession.

The other treaty, on political and security union, is more decisive on whether there ever will be a united Europe, and in much more trouble. Britain adamantly opposes including even a mention of federation as the ultimate target.

The quarrels over institutional powers come down to whether the nation-state remains the bedrock of the European system, just when nationalism is flourishing again in the East. The division of Europe helped drive the West to pool some sovereignty, the impressive results broke down the wall, and this triumph is sapping the compulsion to unite.

True, tough fights and last-minute agreement are typical of the E.C. There is a momentous push to acknowledge the benefits of integration, which has made war among community members unthinkable. It can again counter the shove of irrepressible national egotism if politicians take a deep breath.

Yugoslavia has become the new bogyman, proof of what can happen when emotion and pressure for rival advantage overwhelm the common interest. Countries like Czechoslovakia fear a contagious example. The West remembers the Balkan powder keg and how it could blow up Europe.

Yugoslavia demonstrates E.C. impotence and divergence on foreign policy. Mr. Mitterrand warned against reverting to the disastrous "game of alliances," when Europeans pursued separate interests and stumbled into war. This persuaded Helmut Kohl to hold off recognizing Croatia.

The U.S. has been of two minds on European unity, supportive yet wary of losing influence. Now is a time for clear support. There won't be much chance for any world order if Europe fritters away its hope to develop capacity for common action. Historical opportunity can end with a whimper as well as a bang.

Flora Lewis is Senior Columnist of The New York Times.

* * *

August 23, 1992

AS GLOBAL TALKS STALL, REGIONAL TRADE PACTS MULTIPLY

By KEITH BRADSHER

WASHINGTON—Colombian roses will be more available in Venezuela, Israeli shoes will be more common in Central Europe and Mexican watermelons will be cheaper in the United States. The reason: a striking proliferation of regional free-trade deals.

Countries around the world have signed and ratified more such agreements in the last five years than in the preceding decade. And an even larger batch of regional deals, including the North American Free Trade Agreement that was formally announced by the United States, Mexico and Canada 11 days ago, have been recently struck by negotiators and are at various stages of approval.

With the end of the cold war and the stagnation of negotiations aimed at simultaneously lowering trade barriers globally, these regional pacts are emerging as the trade side of what has been widely called the New World Order. The success or failure of these arrangements will help determine economic growth and consumer prices around the world, affecting people in ways from the jobs they hold to the price of vegetables at the local supermarket.

Whether the regional trade agreements are a good thing is a matter of some debate. Many economists worry that they may lead to an undermining of global free-trade negotiations under the General Agreement on Tariffs and Trade, the 103-nation pact that has set the world's free-trade rules since 1947. They also fear a rise in protectionism as countries use regional agreements to steer business toward their allies, instead of buying goods from whatever country produces them most cheaply.

"My judgment is that the revival of regionalism is unfortunate," wrote Jagdish Bhagwati, an economics professor at Columbia University and special adviser to the GATT, in a paper presented at a recent World Bank conference. "But, given its political appeal and its likely spread, I believe that it is important to contain and shape it" through GATT rules barring protectionist clauses in the agreements.

But the Bush Administration and some academic economists say that the agreements are not a problem, at least in principle, and a book by an M.I.T. scholar, published last week, suggests that regional free-trade deals are better than no free trade at all, and that they help countries force other countries to open their markets.

"I've never heard anyone in the Administration suggesting that regional agreements are a substitute for multilateral agreements—they can and should be complementary," said Michael J. Boskin, chairman of the Council of Economic Advisers.

The strongest views in favor of regional free-trade pacts come from business groups that see them as a way for the United States to demand deep concessions from its trading partners, while threatening loss of access to the American market if these demands are not met. American officials have been reluctant to pursue this strategy in the GATT, where the American market counts for less.

"Everybody gets caught up with principles instead of threatening retaliation; with some of these countries in the GATT, you can't deal with them civilly," said Harvey E. Bale Jr., the pharmaceutical industry's chief lobbyist on trade issues and a former Reagan Administration trade negotiator.

Whatever the consequences, the rapid spread of free-trade pacts is remarkable. During the past year in the Western hemisphere, five Andean nations have agreed to form a free-trade area, Chile has struck deals with Argentina and Mexico and is negotiating with Venezuela and Costa Rica, and Canada and the United States have agreed to add Mexico to their free-trade area.

Nor is the trend limited to the Americas. The countries of Southeast Asia set up a free-trade area last January, while 11 countries around the Black Sea are moving in that direction. Czechoslovakia, Hungary and Poland have announced plans to negotiate a free-trade area. The seven-nation European Free Trade Association, or E.F.T.A., has inked separate deals with Israel, Turkey, Czechoslovakia, Poland and Hungary.

Even the granddaddy of all free-trade areas, the European Community, is joining the tide. It struck a deal last October to eliminate trade barriers with the E.F.T.A.

Little economic research has been done on why the explosion in free-trade pacts should happen now. Yet five basic reasons appear to explain the new profusion:

- The end of the cold war has shattered the economic ties of former Communist countries and left them to form new alliances which tend to be free-trade deals with neighbors and Western countries.
- Latin American countries have been lowering their trade barriers unilaterally to encourage imports of cheap foreign equipment and other goods that make their own industries more efficient and internationally competitive. Once the barriers have been lowered considerably, free-trade pacts require little additional effort.
- Nations in existing regional agreements are bringing in their neighbors to offer larger markets to companies within their borders. The European Community once meant free trade among six northern European countries, but now includes 12 countries extending the length and breadth of Western Europe, and will involve 19 countries when the pact with the E.F.T.A. is concluded.
- Trade agreements mimic cross-border investment patterns, said Karl P. Sauvant, a senior United Nations economist.

Trade Agreements Are Popping Up All Over

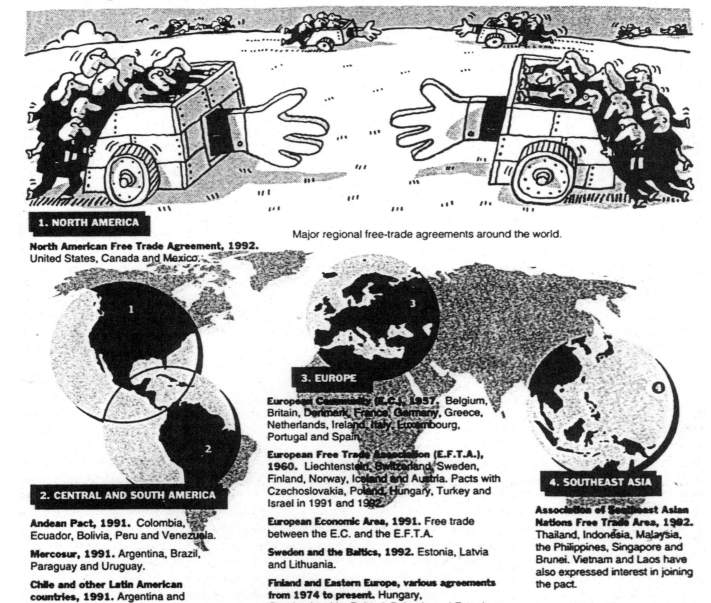

Major regional free-trade agreements around the world.

1. NORTH AMERICA

North American Free Trade Agreement, 1992.
United States, Canada and Mexico.

2. CENTRAL AND SOUTH AMERICA

Andean Pact, 1991. Colombia, Ecuador, Bolivia, Peru and Venezuela.

Mercosur, 1991. Argentina, Brazil, Paraguay and Uruguay.

Chile and other Latin American countries, 1991. Argentina and Mexico.

3. EUROPE

European Community (E.C.), 1957. Belgium, Britain, Denmark, France, Germany, Greece, Netherlands, Ireland, Italy, Luxembourg, Portugal and Spain.

European Free Trade Association (E.F.T.A.), 1960. Liechtenstein, Switzerland, Sweden, Finland, Norway, Iceland and Austria. Pacts with Czechoslovakia, Poland, Hungary, Turkey and Israel in 1991 and 1992.

European Economic Area, 1991. Free trade between the E.C. and the E.F.T.A.

Sweden and the Baltics, 1992. Estonia, Latvia and Lithuania.

Finland and Eastern Europe, various agreements from 1974 to present. Hungary, Czechoslovakia, Poland, Bulgaria and Estonia.

4. SOUTHEAST ASIA

Association of Southeast Asian Nations Free Trade Area, 1992. Thailand, Indonesia, Malaysia, the Philippines, Singapore and Brunei. Vietnam and Laos have also expressed interest in joining the pact.

The New York Times, Illustration by Niculae Asciu

Big companies increasingly assemble manufactured goods in many countries from parts made in many countries. These corporations are demanding that their international production patterns be protected by trade pacts insuring that restrictions are not imposed on shipments of vital parts and finished goods.

- After years of viewing agreements overseas as plots to exclude American exports, the United States is beginning to forge its own agreements and take a benevolent view at least toward similar deals in Latin America. President Bush has set forth a vision of a free-trade area extending from the Arctic to Tierra del Fuego.

But what the Administration may welcome in principle and at home in the Western Hemisphere, it does not always greet abroad. Secretary of State James A. Baker 3d, who today becomes White House chief of staff, recently delivered a stiff warning against trade deals in Southeast Asia that might keep American goods out of one of the world's fastest-growing economic regions.

Mr. Baker's concern over Southeast Asia reflects the concern many academic economists have about creating regional agreements to steer business toward allies instead of the cheapest producer. Since the publication of a famous book, "The Customs Unions Issue," by Jacob Viner, in 1950, economists have generally agreed that free-trade pacts are bad if they divert more existing trade to neighbors than they create in new trade.

Creating trade is good because it allows each country to specialize in those products it makes most efficiently, thereby increasing world economic output. Diverting trade to regional allies is bad, economists agree, because the allies may make goods that could be produced more efficiently elsewhere.

Yet fears of regional agreements may be overblown. After many years of alarms that the European Community may systematically exclude American goods, the fact remains that American exports to the community have more than doubled in the last six years, while imports from the community have risen only 27.3 percent. As a result, the United States has gone from an $18.65 billion trade deficit with these countries in 1985 to a surplus of $16.73 billion last year.

Part of the improvement may reflect the precipitous fall in the value of the United States dollar since 1985. But economic studies of the European Community have consistently shown that, with the conspicuous exception of farm products, the community has created more international trade than it has diverted.

Many of the same worries about protectionism are being raised about the North American Free Trade Agreement by some conservative analysts. Attention has focused on rules that limit eligibility for lower tariffs to goods produced mainly in North America.

Negotiators in Geneva have been stalled for two years in trying to produce a global free-trade accord. A strong argument in favor of pursuing regional accords while waiting for progress in Geneva is set forth in a just-published book by Kenneth A. Oye, director of the Center for International Studies at the Massachusetts Institute of Technology. In the book, "Economic Discrimination and Political Exchange: World Political Economy in the 1930's and 1980's" (Princeton University Press), Mr. Oye criticizes the popular notion that regional trading blocs worsened the Great Depression.

Mr. Oye notes the Smoot-Hawley Tariff Act of 1930 raised tariffs on all imports. Other countries were more selective, keeping tariffs low for neighbors or former colonial possessions so as to hold on to those markets. The result was a plunge in the American share of world exports to 10.3 percent in 1933 from 15.6 percent in 1929.

American exporters responded by lobbying successfully for the Regional Trade Agreement Act of 1934, under which the Roosevelt Administration negotiated deals with France and 10 Latin American countries. The expansion of regional trade then was better than no trade, Mr. Oye contends, adding that this argument applies today.

"The stagnation at the level of the GATT quite naturally leads to bilateral and regional bargaining, and I'm saying that's not bad, insofar as the second-best approach can and does lead to increased openness," he said in an interview.

But other economists, led by Mr. Bhagwati, contend that this view underestimates the enormous reductions in world-wide tariffs on manufactured goods that the GATT has already engineered.

Playing By The Rules Of Origin

Largely unnoticed in the debate over regional free-trade agreements is that almost every one has some rules, known as rules of origin, that require that goods be produced within the participating nations to qualify for lower tariffs.

The rules are intended to prevent nations outside the agreement from taking advantage of the lower tariffs. Mexico, for example, has a 10 percent tax on imported asparagus while the United States has a 25 percent tax. The North American accord will eliminate these taxes over 15 years only for asparagus grown in North America. But the taxes had to stay in place for imports from Peru and other countries, so those countries could not circumvent the higher American tariffs by shipping their asparagus to the United States by way of Mexico.

The preference given to Mexican asparagus could cost Peru some sales; indeed, Latin American, Asian and Caribbean nations worry that the North American trade agreement will cost them exports even if they are more efficient producers.

Some European countries have used rules of origin more restrictive than the North American agreement's. For example, the North American accord requires that at least 50 percent of the value of a car be produced in North America for it to qualify for duty-free treatment, and that percentage will rise to 62.5 percent over eight years.

The Ford Motor Company, which wanted a higher standard, complains that when Nissan recently set up a factory in England, France required that at least 80 percent of the cars' value be produced within the borders of European Community countries. To be sure, the French rules for counting local content then were less restrictive than the North American agreement's, but not enough to outweigh a difference of 17.5 percentage points.

* * *

November 29, 1992

AS IT COMES TOGETHER, IT'S PULLING APART

By R. W. APPLE Jr.

WASHINGTON—In these waning days of the Bush Administration, with the Clinton regime still unborn, two competing forces are at work in the world, one pushing nations closer together and the other ripping them apart.

The clash between the two forces was clearly in evidence last week as the United States and Europe reached a compromise in their incipient trade war—and farmers, politicians and others in France reacted furiously to the deal. Both accord and discord aptly illustrated how, at the same moment, nationalistic political impulses and pressures for economic integration are increasing dramatically. The resulting conflict threatens world stability and presents President-elect Bill Clinton with potentially severe problems.

The end of the cold war and the collapse of the Soviet empire in Eastern Europe are partly responsible. How many times from 1945 to 1990, a senior ambassador in Washington asks, was a fight over trade or politics or weaponry defused with the comment, "We can't afford this, because it might affect the East-West balance?"

No one need doubt the intensity of the feelings—ethnic, religious, national —that push peoples apart. Even as Europe has moved closer together in recent decades, with an economic locomotive pulling a political train, the Catholics and the Protestants have fought an undeclared war in Northern Ireland, and Basque separatists have done something similar in Spain.

Now, as European integration approaches, there are other difficulties; France's unwillingness to accept the deal reducing Government subsidies to farmers is only the most recent, dramatized by attacks on McDonald's and Coca-Cola installations and by troops in Parisian streets. Britain refuses to accept the European Community's passport plan, fearing an influx of undesirables, and Denmark's voters, rebuffing its politicians, have voted down the whole integration plan as an intrusion on nationalism. Germany hesitates to lower interest rates, its own bitter memories of Weimar-era inflation outweighing its pan-European instincts.

In central and eastern Europe, the Parliament of Czechoslovakia on Wednesday approved the division of that country into two republics on Dec. 31. What used to be Yugoslavia and what used to be the Soviet Union continue their process of disintegration into warring or squabbling states and factions.

In Asia, the Japanese worry about their rice farmers, like the French worry about their oil-seed farmers, and opt for measures to protect them at the same time they chide the Europeans and the Americans for giving in to "regionalism"—trading blocs that might exclude the Japanese.

In North America, Canadian voters have rejected, despite warnings of economic difficulties ahead, a hard-won agreement on national unity, and there is opposition in the United States to the North American Free Trade Accord with Mexico and Canada. Even Mr. Clinton finds fault with it, though he wants to modify it rather than scrap it.

'Long Run' May Be Too Long

All of this divisiveness takes place in the face of the conviction of most economists and political leaders, first, that smaller national and regional units usually mean lower standards of living for their citizens, and second, that free trade really does accrue to the benefit of all in the long term. President Bush has stood resolutely for free trade, and so do Mr. Clinton and his advisers, but there are protectionist elements in the Democratic Party (remember the campaign ad with Senator Bob Kerrey as a hockey goalie, blocking the best shots of "unfair foreign competition"?) and on Capitol Hill.

It may be that the lengthy negotiations intended to codify this widespread belief in free interchange in a new General Agreement on Tariffs and Trade—known as the Uruguay Round—will reach a successful conclusion while Mr. Bush remains in office. Few diplomats believe that the French really will pull down that whole temple in wrath over the compromise in the European dispute with the United States, no matter how bellicose the words of French politicians.

But the diplomats may be wrong, and even if they are right, Mr. Clinton will face long-term problems in keeping free trade high on the world's agenda.

The problem that will vex him is the same one vexing Helmut Kohl of Germany, John Major of Britain and dozens of other leaders. Giving up farm subsidies makes farmers angry, and angry farmers vote against governments. Free trade by a rich nation with a neighbor that pays lower wages may suck jobs out of the richer nation, and jobless workers there will vote against the government. Politicians do not like to alienate voters, no matter how lofty the goals.

To put the matter another way, it is difficult enough to persuade the electorate of any nation to yield even a scrap of sovereignty (which is why President Bush was insisting late last week that any American troops sent to Somalia serve under American command). Only the awful memories of World War II prompted the western Europeans to begin doing so over the last 50 years.

Leading the World

It is even more difficult to persuade the voters to do so when some are being asked to yield their present livelihoods in the expectation that, down the road, perhaps in their children's or grandchildren's time, more and better jobs will be created in many countries by liberalized trade rules. Yet that is what Mr. Clinton will try to do, not only as the American President but as the de facto leader of the world's industrialized nations.

Mr. Clinton speaks of an Economic Security Council, by which he means to symbolize the importance he attaches to creating jobs and rebuilding the infrastructure at home as an indispensable first step to strengthen the role of the United States in the world. That mission seems a sensible one to most Western leaders, who have complained that American economic weakness made it hard for this country to play its world role.

But those same leaders are troubled by the very title of the President-elect's new council. To them it has a protectionist ring. It seems to some to signify a combative approach, along with his pledge to focus "like a laser beam" on the domestic economy first.

In fact, Mr. Clinton will have to focus on the problems of the world economy at the same time he focuses on his own. The two cannot in any meaningful way be disentangled. If Mr. Bush failed to assign a high enough priority to turning things around in the United States, he also took a less than commanding approach in meetings of the Group of Seven industrialized nations—among the major forums for coordinating economic policies.

Much will happen before then, but next summer in Tokyo, Mr. Clinton will have his best chance to take charge on the world's struggling economy, and to persuade the Japanese, the Germans and the French to try much harder to put aside their differences for the larger, common good.

Nine years ago this month, Europe was struggling with the question of where American cruise missiles should be based. There were big anti-American demonstrations in the Netherlands, Britain and Italy. This year, the struggle involves trade, not weapons—a nice metaphor for both the blessings bestowed by the end of the cold war and the uncertainties that followed.

*   *   *

December 26, 1992

A WORLD FROM SCRATCH

By G. JOHN IKENBERRY

WASHINGTON—Will the new era be dominated by regional alliances and economic pacts or by a renewal of global and multilateral institutions? The 1990's are shaping up as a struggle between these rival international orders. So far, regional relationships—in Europe, North America and elsewhere—have the upper hand. The emerging world order looks like an old house: new rooms, windows and doors have been added, but the foundation, plumbing and wiring remain in dangerous disrepair.

There is a need to make regional economic experiments complement, not compete, with multilateralism. This requires agreement among the major nations about a blueprint of a new world order.

Most creative foreign policy in recent years has been directed at regional economic integration, particularly in Europe, North America and Asia. These efforts need not compete with the larger global order. Most studies of European and North American integration conclude that it will create more trade than it diverts. Nor are regional agreements necessarily incompatible with the global regime of GATT: Pulling down internal walls without raising external ones is good for the world economy.

The real danger of regionalism lies elsewhere. Regionalism is difficult to shield from domestic and transnational political pressures and disputes. The European Community's hard line against Japanese imports suggests how regionalism deepens fault lines. European and North American regionalism also diverts attention from GATT and other multilateral institutions. The "promise" of European unity and the North American free-trade agreement has reduced the political costs should the current round of multilateral trade negotiations fail. In this real sense, regional and global institutions compete.

The task is to fold regional experiments into global institutional reform. Key will be the relationship among the industrial democracies—the Group of Seven. Some suggest a Group of Seven declaration on the limits and responsibilities of "good regionalism." This would ease fears in Asia and elsewhere about the ultimate aims of recent regional agree-

ments. It would also push the Group of Seven countries to use their next summit to discuss the basic structure of world order. Helmut Kohl and John Major are not Bismarck and Palmerston, and President-elect Bill Clinton certainly has none of the pretensions of Woodrow Wilson, but these leaders must be strongly encouraged to be global architects.

The Group of Seven should also focus on its own inadequate process. The annual summit meetings of heads of state are overly formal, scripted events that produce little more than bland official communiqués. Experts—nicknamed "sherpas"—do the real work in the months leading up to the meetings. Coordination must be strengthened by turning the summits into informal discussions, while formalizing meetings of ministers and experts.

Global institutional reform must also extend to traditional multilateral organizations—the United Nations, International Monetary Fund and World Bank. Without a new mission, they look increasingly like relics. Security Council seats for Japan and Germany are inevitable. Negotiations over this issue should be broadened into an effort to make the U.N. more relevant in international disputes. The 50th anniversary of the International Monetary Fund and World Bank in 1994 and of the U.N. in 1995 will be moments of symbolic opportunity. American officials need to articulate a vision of how these global institutions serve our interests and strategy for shaping the emerging order.

Recession and election-year politics have inevitably obscured the big issues of foreign policy. After World War II, Americans were more worried about the economy than in building a new international order. Stalin provided the jolt to the West for united action. Today there is no such stimulus. Leadership and vision will have to make the difference if we are to put our global house in order.

G. John Ikenberry, a senior associate at the Carnegie Endowment for International Peace, is author of the forthcoming book, "Moments of Creation: The Rebuilding of International Order, 1815, 1919, 1945 and 1990."

*   *   *

December 19, 1993

REGIONAL TRADE MAKES GLOBAL DEALS GO ROUND

By PETER PASSELL

Assorted presidents, prime ministers and political poo-bahs rushed to congratulate themselves last week on the initialing of the new General Agreement on Tariffs and Trade, which ended seven years of bargaining only hours before a self-imposed deadline. Alain Carignon, France's Minister of Communications, called it "a great and beautiful victory for Europe and for French culture." Striking a more statesmanlike pose, Peter Sutherland, GATT's Director General, celebrated the choice of "openness and cooperation instead of uncertainty and conflict."

The first shipment of California-grown rice for Japan under new trade agreement being loaded at the Port of Sacramento last week.

But all that gush raises an awkward question: If global agreement is, in fact, the holy grail of trade liberalization, why have the last three American Presidents campaigned so fiercely for a separate regional trade agreement for North America, and why is Bill Clinton beating the drums for a separate pact linking the Asian economies to the Americas?

The answer in part is that regional deals often accomplish what GATT doesn't, and in part because they are a necessary catalyst to global agreement.

The Bush Administration dismissed the conflict between regionalism and globalism as more apparent than real, insisting that trade negotiators could walk on two (one regional, one global) legs. That is certainly the party line in the Clinton White House, too. However, not all economists—make that political economists—are so sure.

Most do agree that the classic complaint against regional free trade, namely that encouraging commerce within the region diverts trade from low-cost producers outside the region, no longer carries much weight. Worries that "customs unions" would divert more trade than they create stem from the 1950's, when Europe was dismantling internal barriers while maintaining high tariffs that discriminated against non-European imports. But "in today's world of low tariffs, I'd be surprised if there was much trade diversion," says Gary Saxonhouse of the University of Michigan.

Besides, Fred Bergsten, director of the Institute for International Economics, points out that the basic GATT accord already "makes the world safe for regionalism" by binding all 117 member-nations to a code limiting just how inward-looking they may be. Specifically, regional free trade deals cannot pass muster if they create new tariff barriers or raise existing ones against the rest of the world.

Why, then, the concern? Layering the grand global design for open trade with regional side deals could still have unintended consequences.

"When you walk on two legs," warns Jagdish Bhagwati, a trade specialist at Columbia University who has been a senior adviser to the GATT bureaucracy, "you sometimes end up on all fours."

In the best of circumstances, notes Robert Hormats of Goldman-Sachs International, regional accords can set the pace for global liberalization by setting precedents for the more awkward process of GATT-wide negotiation.

The United States' original free trade pact with Canada, for example, created a super-national mechanism for arbitrating disputes. And by no coincidence, argues Mr. Hormats, the World Trade Organization (the new, improved successor to the GATT that was created last week) will have considerably more authority to lay down the international law.

Regional pacts—or the prospect of writing new ones—can also be used to drive the parties back to the global bargaining table. In October, wise heads were all but reading the last rites for the GATT negotiations, as French politicians from both the left and right were tripping over each other to denounce limits on farm subsidies earlier agreed to by the European Community negotiators. Then Congress approved the North American Free Trade Agreement and sent President Clinton off in triumph to Seattle for a tete-a-tete on trade with his Asian counterparts.

Nothing happened at the Pacific summit meeting that directly threatened the mutually vital trade links between America and the European Community. And nothing is likely to happen anytime soon. A dozen formidable obstacles, everything from Japan's clubby business practices to China's lack of enthusiasm for free speech, block Nafta-style economic integration with Asia.

"But without the Seattle meeting," wonders Mr. Saxonhouse, "would Europe have been ready to compromise on GATT?"

Carry a Big Market

That, however, is not the only way to read the tortuous route to compromise in Geneva. Mr. Saxonhouse also wonders whether the imperative to peddle Nafta to Congress like a patent medicine cure for lumbago did not distract—and thereby weaken—America's negotiators at the global talks. "Might we have gotten a better GATT agreement if Clinton hadn't spent so much time on Nafta?" he muses.

For his part, Mr. Bhagwati points to a problematic aspect of what is generally viewed as a virtuous global precedent in Nafta. To undercut opposition in Washington, long-xenophobic Mexico bowed to remarkably intrusive side agreements dictated by the United States, including a promise to clean up purely domestic pollution and one to raise the minimum wage. There are no parallels in the new global accord, but only because the United States had bigger fish to fry. And American environmental groups are vowing to raise the issue in any and every trade negotiation in the future, complicating the prospects for further trade liberalization.

Almost everyone agrees that regional negotiation is an effective tactic for expanding American influence on trade issues. Bilateral deals generally give America the bargaining edge because access to the American market is so much more important to smaller trading partners than access to their markets is to us. If, for example, Chile, Venezuela or Argentina is admitted to Nafta, it will be on terms decreed by Washington. And the more countries that sign on to American terms, the more likely they will serve as precedents for global agreements.

But Mr. Bhagwati fears that what America wants will not necessarily be what is best for the world economy—or even, on balance, for Americans.

Momentum

Certainly the Clinton Administration's willingness to "manage" trade by carving up international product markets by quota and its enthusiasm for playing the tough guy on

anti-dumping disputes has made economists wonder whether Washington is a suitable role model for the young and impressionable.

Others—probably the majority of trade analysts—see more virtue than vice in the dual global-regional tracks.

"A lot of things fell off the GATT table" in those last frantic hours of negotiation in Geneva, reminds Mr. Bergsten. Among the subjects on which everyone agreed to disagree: financial services, telecommunications, French film quotas. "You have to keep the bicycle of liberalization moving forward," he insists, and only regional bargaining can preserve the momentum.

* * *

December 29, 1993

WITH A VIEW OF ONE HEMISPHERE, LATIN AMERICA IS FREEING ITS OWN TRADE

By JAMES BROOKE
Special to The New York Times

RIO DE JANEIRO, Dec. 28—The North American Free Trade Agreement takes effect on Jan. 1, and that event is being seen in many Latin American countries as a first step toward the day when the pact expands south from Mexico, creating a free-trade hemisphere.

Overshadowed by the debate in the United States over job gains and losses from the North American accord, the economies of Latin America, a region long gripped by protectionism, have experienced a free-trade transformation of their own.

Taking North America's free-trade gospel to heart, Latin American nations are bulldozing tariff barriers with such energy that economists in the region predict that most trade within Latin America will be duty-free by the end of the decade.

Mexico is to join a second free trade pact next month. On Jan. 23, the presidents of Colombia, Mexico and Venezuela are to sign an agreement that phases out tariffs over a decade, creating a duty-free market of 150 million people.

Many Latin American leaders, recalling President George Bush's conception of a trade zone stretching from Alaska to Argentina, say that today's free market-directed policies are preparing their economies for a day when the North American trade zone expands south.

With approval of the North American Free Trade Agreement, leaders of virtually every major Latin American nation except Brazil said their country should be next in line to join the North American trade bloc.

President Clinton has encouraged such hopes, saying, "I'll reach out to the other market-oriented democracies of Latin America to ask them to join in this great American pact."

Preparing for free trade with the United States, the average tariff charged by Latin American nations to outsiders has dropped to 15 percent, from 56 percent in 1985. This opening has made Latin America the world's fastest-growing market for goods made in the United States.

Some Specific Expectations

With lower tariffs, United States exports to Latin America rose 27 percent in 1992. Latin America and Europe were the only two regions of the world where the United States had trade surpluses last year.

Half of Latin trade now is with the United States. A continental free trade pact would send duty-free American cars and computers to South America and would let United States consumers buy duty-free Colombian flowers, Chilean grapes and Argentine beef.

Of all the Latin American applicants to the North American group, Chile has the best prospects.

"President Clinton is committed to achieving a free-trade accord with Chile," said Alexander F. Watson, Assistant Secretary of State for Inter-American Affairs, in a recent speech to business people in Rio de Janeiro.

Chile would make an easy addition to the pact. Following a free market, export-driven model, it emerged from the dictatorship of the 1970's and 80's as Latin America's most robust economy. With expansion at an average rate of 8 percent a year since 1990, economists predict that Chile will reach the living standards of Spain in the next 10 years.

Earlier this year, Chilean officials began preliminary talks with the Clinton Administration. And since 1990, Chile has signed free-trade pacts with Argentina, Bolivia, Colombia, Venezuela and Mexico.

United States officials are increasingly telling South Americans that the North American Free Trade Agreement is just the beginning.

"Most of it could happen before the end of the century," Secretary of Commerce Ronald H. Brown recently said in Mexico with regard to a Western Hemisphere free-trade zone. "Venezuela, Chile and Argentina should be in the first wave of countries to be considered."

In the meantime, the regional building blocks of a hemispheric trade zone are taking shape.

Customs union, a dream since the end of Spanish and Portuguese colonial rule in the early 1800's, are integrating major geographic areas: Central America, the Caribbean, the Andean nations and the Southern Cone, which includes Argentina, Brazil, Paraguay and Uruguay.

Idea Already a Success

Thus unfettered, intra-Latin commerce has surged. Trade among Latin America's 11 largest economies jumped 28 percent in 1992, reaching $19.4 billion. In the same year, Latin American exports to the rest of the world stagnated.

"The free-trade agreements have developed beyond all expectations," said Noemi Sanin, Foreign Minister of Colombia, a nation that is negotiating trade accords with 22 other Latin American countries. "Before the end of the century, we aspire to achieve the planet's most important trading bloc—the American bloc."

This is no casual forecast. Timetables for tariff reduction indicate that most trade within Latin America will be tariff-free by the end of the 1990's, according to a study released in October by the Latin American Economic System, an inter-government organization based here.

Again and again, Latin America has proved that cutting tariffs and red tape results in surging trade.

In 1993, trade between Colombia and Venezuela reached $2 billion—four times the level of 1991, the year before a duty-free customs union was established. Rules on product origin have been adopted to prevent the duty-free transshipment of Colombian and Venezuelan goods into the United States by way of Mexico.

After Colombia signed another customs union pact in 1992, its trade with Ecuador jumped by 50 percent in 1993, reaching $350 million.

Within the Andean region, trade increased 20 percent in 1992—the year Venezuela, Colombia, Ecuador and Bolivia cut almost all regional tariffs to zero. In 1993, Andean trade surged 30 percent more, to $3 billion.

In the Southern Cone Common Market—which has become known as Mercosur, shorthand for Southern Common Market—regional trade grew more than 25 percent in 1993, reaching $9 billion. Trade was one-third that level in 1990, the year before Argentina, Brazil, Paraguay and Uruguay signed their agreement.

"Isolated countries have no destiny, no future," President Carlos Saul Menem of Argentina told a regional financial group this month.

With regional tariffs scheduled to vanish in a year, Mercosur has proved so successful that Argentina is now Brazil's second-largest trading partner, after the United States. The share of Brazilian exports to other bloc countries rose from 4 percent in 1990 to 12 percent this year.

Argentine Labor Opposition

Mercosur, which is Latin America's largest regional trade pact, faces high hurdles involving its largest nations, Brazil and Argentina.

The Argentine industrial union warned recently in a letter to President Menem that "if no safeguards are taken, Argentina's productive activity will be totally substituted by imports of Brazilian products." It asked a two-year delay in full tariff integration with Brazil.

To protect its industries, Argentina this year adopted a series of temporary measures against Brazilian imports. To reduce a trade surplus, Brazil increased oil imports from its southern neighbor, making Argentina its second-largest source of imported oil, after Saudi Arabia.

With Argentine officials saying their country could join the North American Free Trade Agreement in 1995, Brazil may be forced to adopt a more flexible negotiating position to preserve Mercosur.

"Brazilian products are invading Argentina," said Luiz Gonzaga Belluzzo, foreign affairs adviser to the governor of São Paulo state. "Menem wants to join Nafta because he wants to avoid being smashed by Brazil."

Of the South Americans, Brazil shows the least interest in joining the North American bloc. In September, at a regional heads of state meeting, President Itamar Franco blocked approval of a nonbinding motion of support for the accord. Instead, he offered a plan for "Merconorte," or Northern Common Market, a free trade pact for Brazil and its Amazon neighbors—Guyana, Suriname, Venezuela, Colombia, Ecuador, Peru and Bolivia.

Brazilians fear that under the North American accord, the United States will import duty-free from Mexico goods that are taxed when imported from Brazil—orange juice, shoes, steel and automobile parts.

"More important than trade diversion, there will be investment diversion," said Carlos Langoni, who is the international studies director of the Getulio Vargas Foundation here. "For the next few years, Mexico will be the most interesting Latin American market for investors."

But the North American accord, Mr. Langoni said, gives powerful support for consolidating free-trade policies in Brazil, which, too, is emerging from decades of protectionism.

"In Brazil, there are still many businessmen asking for quotas, for protective tariffs," he said. "Nafta's approval will make it more difficult for Brazil to move away from trade liberalization."

*   *   *

December 7, 1994

EUROPE SEEKS LATIN FREE-TRADE TIES

By NATHANIEL C. NASH
Special to The New York Times

BRUSSELS, Dec. 1—The European Union is taking steps toward creating its first significant free-trade links with Latin America, in an effort to prevent the erosion of its markets there and to parry efforts by the United States to form a huge free-trade zone in the Americas.

During the last two months, officials from the European Union have negotiated with the four countries of Mercosur, a trading bloc made up of Brazil, Argentina, Uruguay and Paraguay, for the creation of a free-trade zone, first in industrial goods and services, and later in agricultural products.

The European Union has also stepped up its negotiations with Mexico to reduce tariffs, with the aim of not only expanding its Mexican trade but also gaining more access to American markets through Mexico's participation in the North American Free Trade Agreement.

"Europe stands to lose a significant share of its market in that area if we don't act," said Manuel Marin, a Spanish member of the European Commission, the union's executive body.

Late last month, foreign ministers of the Mercosur countries met with European officials here and announced plans to work toward a free-trade zone. Though no strict timetable has been set, the officials expect negotiations on short-term trade liberalization to begin next year, with formal links to be established by 2001. Such a plan is likely to be approved at a meeting of European member countries on Friday and Saturday in Essen, Germany.

The timing is hardly accidental. Many European officials believe that initiatives in Washington to expand free-trade pacts in Latin America beyond Mexico were seriously weakened by last month's Republican victories in Congressional elections.

Europe has been the largest trading partner of the Mercosur countries, accounting for 27 percent of their exports and imports between 1985 and 1992, compared with about 20 percent for the United States. Mexico is Europe's largest single market in Latin America, importing about $7.6 billion of European goods in 1993. But Mexican officials complain that the European Union maintains higher tariff barriers on Mexican imports.

Mexico's participation in Nafta and the economic growth in many South American countries since 1990 have created lucrative markets at a time when purchasing power in Europe is nearly stagnant and expansion in European markets is expected to be modest.

The extent to which the European Union can focus on Latin markets is questionable. It is preoccupied with expanding its own membership, with the proposed creation of a monetary union by the end of the decade and with its own problems of high unemployment, high labor costs, inefficiencies and lack of competitiveness.

Yet Europe is encountering more and more competition for its overseas markets, like those in Latin America and Asia. Studies here have found, for example, that if Europe does not establish strong free-trade links with the Mercosur countries its prominence as a trade partner with the region will be quickly eroded.

Next month the Mercosur countries will institute a system of so-called harmonized tariffs, with future plans for broad integration of fiscal, monetary, industrial and agricultural policies. With almost 200 million inhabitants, the Mercosur region has enormous commercial potential, and imports have more than doubled in recent years.

Other Latin countries, including Chile, Bolivia and Ecuador, are seeking to become members of Mercosur, which some economists predict could eventually form a common market in South America.

Though European officials say it will take some years for a free-trade relationship to develop with Latin America, they hope to take advantage of growing doubts in Latin countries that Washington will expand Nafta to include other countries in the region.

*   *   *

February 4, 1997

TRADE PACTS BY REGIONS: NOT THE ELIXIR AS ADVERTISED

By PETER PASSELL

When efforts to liberalize world trade stalled in the early 1980's, Washington turned its attention to opening trade on a regional basis as the second-best choice. That produced the North American Free Trade Agreement and a dozen similar pacts among other nations. And most economists, who hold that free trade is close to heaven on earth, widely applauded. The regional agreements, they argued, would not just prod reluctant nations like Japan and France to drop their opposition to open markets to global trade, but they would also help developing countries lock in free market initiatives and improve the climate for foreign investment.

But this pragmatic consensus is fraying as the Clinton Administration's drive to create preferential trade areas reaching across the Pacific and Atlantic, as well as throughout the Americas, takes on a life of its own. Some economists are no longer convinced that all roads to open markets really do lead toward the economic Valhalla of a world without trading barriers.

"It's time to raise the warning flag," said Claude Barfield, an economist at the American Enterprise Institute in Washington.

The latest evidence that regional trade pacts like Nafta can have harmful effects on those excluded from the zone comes from the Caribbean Basin, where a World Bank study recently warned that Mexico could grab as much as one-third of the Caribbean's $12.5 billion in exports to the United States.

But the impact could be considerably broader. An unpublished study by a senior economist at the World Bank suggests that Mercosur, the preferential trade agreement intended to eliminate national barriers at the southern end of South America, has diverted substantial trade from more efficient producers outside the region.

The result of preferential trade areas, said Jagdish Bhagwati, a Columbia University economist, has been a "spaghetti bowl of tangled, inconsistent trade standards that just can't be good for efficiency."

It's a safe bet that the doubters will not remain on the sidelines much longer. For while much-ballyhooed trans-Atlantic and trans-Pacific trade initiatives have met considerable resistance both overseas and in Congress, President Clinton is asking lawmakers for the right to pursue "fast track" negotiations toward a preferential trade area for all the Americas, starting with Chile. Moreover, some Administration officials still hope to extend Nafta to the Pacific, admitting, say, South Korea, in hope of putting pressure on the rest of Asia to join.

Every college text on international trade offers grounds to be skeptical of regional trade agreements. If, for example, Mexico trades freely with the United States but maintains barriers against imports from Japan and Europe, it may lose more from the loss of access to Toyotas and Fiats than it gains from easier access to Fords and Chryslers.

But most economists put aside such worries almost four decades ago to celebrate the creation of the European Economic Community, now the European Union. "Economic integration was seen as a bulwark against Communism," Mr. Bhagwati recalled. And while the rationale has changed, economists continued to defer to political strategists on issues of economic regionalism.

When Nafta was being negotiated, policy strategists for President George Bush and Mr. Clinton were never very serious about the argument that a regional pact with Mexico was needed to foster exports of American corn and computers. But they agreed that the pact would commit future Mexican governments to economic modernization that would reinforce the political stability of the continent. And history, they say, has proved them right: "The Mexican currency crisis in 1995 would have had catastrophic consequences" if Mexico had not been treaty-bound to keep its borders open to trade and investment, said Lawrence H. Summers, Deputy Secretary of the Treasury.

C. Fred Bergsten, the head of the Institute for International Economics, argues that the Administration still sees regional zones as advancing world trade: "The idea has always been global liberalization initiated by regional agreement."

Why, then, have many other economists grown skeptical? For one thing, they worry that President Clinton's casual but often repeated equation of trade and warfare is tilting American policy toward economic nationalism—a kinder, gentler version of what Pat Buchanan and Ross Perot have advocated, to be sure, but still a subtle form of mercantilism that threatens to undermine efforts to knit the global economy together.

The new mantra of opening foreign markets while defending our own, they suggest, points toward a "hub and spoke" trading order in which the United States dominates numerous regional preferential trade areas, rather than a worldwide system in which the American economy is merely first among equals. Within Nafta, for example, Washington can muscle preferences for Florida tomato growers that would never pass muster with the more independent bureaucrats at the World Trade Organization.

"People have begun to wake up to the U.S. policy of pressing regional arrangements as an end in themselves," said Gary Saxonhouse, an economist at the University of Michigan.

The skeptics are also influenced by new research examining the risk that productivity-sapping trade diversion will outweigh productivity-enhancing trade creation. In the study that the World Bank has thus far refused to release, Alexander Yeats, principal economist of the organization's International Trade Division, draws disturbing conclusions about Mercosur, the preferential trade pact linking Argentina, Brazil, Chile and Uruguay. The most-traded products within Mercosur "generally are highly capital-intensive goods which members have not been able to export competitively to outside markets," he wrote.

Arvind Panagariya, co-director of the University of Maryland's Center for International Economics, voices related concerns about the proposed Free Trade Area of the Americas. Even if it would help other Latin American countries and Caribbean islands avoid excessive losses to Mexico, virtually all the gains would go to the United States, he concluded. And South American countries with high barriers against imports would risk serious losses from reduced trade with Europe.

Mr. Summers dismisses such doubts, suggesting that the Administration's aggressive pro-regionalism is a kind of policy maker's jujitsu—one that redirects dangerous protectionist impulses into benign market-opening initiatives. "Regionalism is not just good mercantilism, it's good economics," he said.

Trouble is, Mr. Barfield of the American Enterprise Institute said, is that the argument is no longer so convincing to economists themselves.

CRITICAL MOMENT: THE MAASTRICHT TREATY

December 8, 1991

BIRTH OF A MULTINATION, MAYBE

By HELMUT SCHMIDT

HAMBURG, Germany—The number of meetings during the past 24 months at which European leaders and foreign ministers have contemplated the future of Europe is almost uncountable. The labels were different, but the persons have remained more or less the same—and so has the oratory. Many of them ought to be reminded of Shakespeare: "I wasted time, and now doth time waste me." [Tomorrow] they meet again at Maastricht [in the Netherlands]. Will they once more waste time and effort, or will they make urgent and necessary decisions?

The British have a choice to make between the European currency unit (Ecu) and the Deutsche mark. If they opt for European monetary union (Emu) and for a single currency within the common market, they will have a very good chance to develop the City of London as one of the world's most important financial centers. They would also be able to draw on the vast future pool of German capital in the European currency unit.

If on the other hand they opt to say "to hell with the absurd idea of replacing sterling by the Ecu" and maintain their monetary sovereignty, they may at first feel happy about bravely resisting Franco-German pressure. But then, in a decade the British will wake up to the fact that any importance of sterling will have evaporated. This will be either because the Ecu will have become, in its global importance, equal to the dollar (and ahead of the yen); or, even worse for the British, because the Deutsche mark will have become by far the dominant currency in Europe, leaving little room for financial business in other European currencies or for autonomous monetary policies elsewhere in the European Community. Even more than it does today, the Bundesbank will then direct monetary policy purely on the basis of German interests.

The French, Dutch, Italians, Poles, Hungarians and all the rest are faced with a clear choice. On the one hand, they can opt for progress in European political integration—where the latest accord on a Franco-German army corps is a step in the right direction. On the other they can choose to hesitate—and find that Germany, in 10 years, is too powerful a neighbor to handle. If the latter happens, it will prove a development almost impossible to correct.

The Germans, as well, have a choice to make. It is over the nature of European political union. The political class in Germany is aware of the qualms of all our neighbors.

To allay the concerns of our neighbors, German leaders want to have their own country closely integrated into the European Community. But in calling for a fully fledged political union, the Germans are asking for more than the French—and much more than the British—are prepared to agree to. It is understandable that Chancellor Helmut Kohl has tried to stipulate a positive decision on political union as a conditio sine qua non for his agreeing to monetary union. But if he sticks to that condition, he will wreck the ship of Emu and Ecu.

So in Maastricht, Mr. Kohl will have to make his choice. The Chancellor's statement in the Bundestag preparing the parliament for a relatively modest treaty on political union indicates that he is moving in the right direction.

The flood of events in Europe over the last two years has perplexed and confused West European leaders who, understandably, had not been prepared to deal with fundamental changes of this kind. The time has now come for them to face the facts—and confront possible dangers ahead. The political and economic collapse of the Soviet Union is endangering the three Baltic republics, Poland, Czechoslovakia, Hungary and others. They need shelter and support.

The European Community will have to accept them as future member states. It is therefore desirable to associate them with the community and unilaterally to open our markets for their produce, to allow their manufacturing industries to adapt to open competition in quality and prices.

Long before full membership of these new sovereign democracies, the community will have to accept the full membership of Austria, Sweden and Finland (as well, probably, as Norway and Iceland). Within 15 years or so the community will probably consist of 24 member states.

We have to decide now whether we prefer widening the community before deepening its institutions, or whether we should intensify the community before this goal becomes impossible. We should plainly choose the latter. I am not talking of additional regulations for flowers and corks; I am talking of a move to a single currency. A so-called common market with 11 currencies would be a very uncommon market in the world's economic history. It would mean wasting the chance to create proper economies of scale, and would result in the community remaining inferior to North America and even to Japan.

The Dutch Government's proposal for monetary union is not well suited to move us along this path. Most of its more than 80 pages contain superfluous complications and compromises for the sake of national prestige. The worst of it is the lack of a fixed date for the ultimate introduction of the European currency unit as the only European legal tender, and the invalidating clause under which any country may opt out before reaching the ultimate phase. Such a phony agreement is not worthy of ratification. It is necessary that those countries which are willing to commit themselves firmly at Maastricht should introduce the single currency by Jan. 1, 1997.

In the area of defense, the disappearance of the threat of armed conflict between an imperialist Soviet Union and the West has opened up the field for smaller conflicts inside the former Soviet territories and in the Balkans. They may spill over into other European countries. On top of such dangers, it is unlikely that the gulf war marks the end of a chain of six major wars in the Middle East since 1945.

All these risks make it necessary that the Atlantic alliance retain some military muscle. But the U.S. is likely to concentrate much more than in the recent past on its neglected domestic needs. More than in the past, the European democracies will therefore have to prepare their own defenses. The Western European Union during the 1990's will have to be combined with the European Community, of course within the Atlantic alliance; the Franco-German corps may become the nucleus of this future European force.

It is possible that the great statesmen at Maastricht will indeed take the right decisions to shape our common future. It cannot, however, be excluded that they will simply haggle and squabble, exploiting the usual summit TV opportunities and end up approving agreements committing themselves to nothing. Then we will have to regard them not as statesmen but purely as mediocre politicians. If they want a motto for Maastricht, they must turn to Shakespeare: "We must take the current when it serves, or lose our ventures."

Helmut Schmidt was Chancellor of West Germany from 1974 to 1982. This article appeared in The Financial Times on Wednesday.

*   *   *

December 9, 1991

WEST EUROPEANS GATHER TO SEEK A TIGHTER UNION

By ALAN RIDING
Special to The New York Times

MAASTRICHT, the Netherlands, Dec. 8—In an atmosphere of great expectation tinged with no small apprehension, European Community leaders gathered here tonight for a crucial two-day summit meeting that should determine the region's place in the world well into the 21st century.

Their aim is to prepare the 12-nation community to compete with regional economic groups led by the United States and Japan and to exercise greater political influence in international affairs. To achieve this, they hope to speed up Europe's 34-year-old march toward political and economic integration.

They will therefore be taking up proposals to establish a single currency and a regional central bank, to move toward

The New York Times

common foreign and security policies, to give more power to the European Parliament and to harmonize their approaches to social and environmental questions.

Nowhere Near Full Union

The measures fall far short of creating anything resembling a United States of Europe. While some politicians like to evoke the centuries-old dream of full union, it is at least decades away.

Yet if approved, the changes will significantly bolster the community's existing plan to form a single regional market of 340 million consumers on Jan. 1, 1993, eventually turning what is already the world's largest trading bloc into the world's dominant financial power.

Adoption of the Maastricht agenda is far from assured. Britain, long the community's most resistant member, fears an excessive loss of sovereignty. Changes to the 1957 Treaty of Rome, which created the community, require the unanimous assent of its members, and a plan acceptable to Britain has still to be thrashed out.

Specifically, Britain remains at loggerheads with the others over how the community should manage its common foreign and security policy, over whether the 12 should move toward building an independent military capability and over when the community can dictate domestic policies.

Everything hangs on four negotiating sessions over the next two days, with the fate of the summit meeting probably unknown until late Tuesday or, as one European official put it, "the last five minutes." The meeting may even be extended to Wednesday if an accord seems within reach.

'Train Is About to Leave'

"The train to European union is standing at the platform," Foreign Minister Hans-Dietrich Genscher of Germany wrote this weekend, seemingly addressing Britain. "It is about to leave. Anyone who does not climb on board will not stop it from going. They will be left standing alone."

Yet, despite the real risk of an 11-to-1 deadlock, the mood was fairly upbeat as community leaders arrived in this ancient Dutch city tonight, with optimism bolstered by progress made in several disputed areas during a flurry of ministerial talks last week.

For instance, the 12 informally agreed to accommodate Britain's refusal to commit itself to a single currency by 1999. An annex to the planned treaty on monetary union should allow Britain to "opt out" if the British Parliament later blocks disappearance of the pound sterling.

Britain has also strongly objected to a passage in the draft treaty to be voted on this week that the community has a "federal" vocation, but that should no longer be an obstacle to agreement. Other governments now seem willing to change the wording to an endorsement of "ever closer union"—if Britain makes concessions in other areas.

Britain to 'Give and Take'

While wrestling with an anti-Europe group in his Conservative Party, Britain's Prime Minister, John Major, insists that he is ready to "give and take" to reach an "acceptable" agreement.

President Francois Mitterrand of France and Chancellor Helmut Kohl of Germany, who have been the driving force behind this new stage of integration, have signaled that they too will show flexibility. "Britain is complicating the game," a senior French official said, "but we have never wanted Britain's exclusion."

Certainly, the two sides were much further apart when separate inter-governmental conferences on economic and monetary union and on political union began last December. Then, many governments were focusing more on the goal of union than how to achieve it. Now, under British pressure, a step-by-step approach has been adopted.

For instance, on monetary union, rather than rushing toward a single currency, community countries now accept the need for gradual "convergence" of their economies through a leveling of inflation rates and budget deficits. Similarly, before a regional central bank comes into existence, a less formal body to be known as the European Monetary Institute will be charged with coordinating the region's monetary policies.

Events outside Western Europe have underlined the community's limited ability to speak with a single, forceful voice. During the Persian Gulf war, while Britain and France sent troops to the front, the community as such lacked authority to act. More recently, the 12 have been embarrassed by their failure to settle the Yugoslav conflict.

Britain Wants a Veto

Nonetheless, on the eve of the Maastricht meeting, major obstacles still stand in the way of broad agreement on foreign policy and security matters, most of them reflecting British reluctance. While agreeing that the community must act as a bloc if it is to have real power on foreign-policy questions, Britain is insisting that community positions be adopted unanimously, thus enabling it to retain a veto and avoid the risk of being outvoted.

On the sensitive question of regional defense, Britain favors strengthening a nine-nation military pact known as the Western European Union, but argues that French and German demands that it be integrated into the community could undermine the North Atlantic Treaty Organization.

Britain is most prickly about not allowing the community to "interfere" in its domestic affairs—specifically on police, immigration and judicial matters as well as on a broad array of social and environmental questions. Here again, it objects to community rulings through majority vote.

While Mr. Mitterrand and Mr. Kohl have much to gain politically from an agreement, both have warned that they will only go so far to appease Mr. Major. The French leader likes to remind London that he too has a veto right.

Mr. Kohl in turn believes that a stronger Europe must be a more democratic Europe, and to this end, he is demanding that new powers of "co-decision" be given to the 518-member European Parliament, which at present can discuss—but cannot propose or block—community laws.

Mitterrand Backs Kohl

Mr. Mitterrand, who used to say the community's political authority should be exercised by governments rather than legislators or bureaucrats, has now agreed to back Mr. Kohl. Mr. Major may also accept the principle of "co-decision" with Parliament, but only in limited areas.

If the British, French and German leaders can work out their differences, most other problems will fade into insignificance. Jacques Delors, who as President of the European Commission will be the 13th person at the summit table, has complained loudly that his executive body will acquire little additional power, but he has neither vote nor veto.

Working in favor of an accord is fear of the consequences of failure. Any country considered responsible for a breakdown will inevitably face isolation and recrimination. Confidence in European currencies may slump. And the community as a whole could suffer a crisis of identity with long-term negative effects.

Born as a six-nation common market in 1957, the community has known many ups and downs over the years, including squabbles over British entry in the 1960's and economic stagnation in the 1970's. But since 1985, when it agreed to build a single market by the end of 1992, new momentum toward economic integration has also given it a stronger political voice.

The collapse of Communism and, above all, the unification of Germany abruptly changed the European scene in 1989 and 1990, but France was able to persuade its partners—including

Germany—that the moment required the community to establish even more ambitious goals of unity.

Economic Union More Likely

Many experts believe that the community will continue to advance more quickly toward economic union than political integration. Goods, services, capital and people should move freely in the region after 1992, while the prospect of a single currency and regional central bank before the end of the century will accelerate harmonization of economic policies.

With the United States, Canada and Mexico talking about a North American free trade area and Japan working hard to strengthen its trade ties in the Far East, European businessmen are strong advocates of economic union, convinced that otherwise they will be unable to compete. Already, many European companies are engaged in their own "union" through mergers.

Politically, though, community governments seem to have less of a mandate. Polls show that outside Britain, most Europeans have no clear understanding of what is at stake in Maastricht. They also suggest that ordinary citizens are far less enthusiastic than their leaders about ceding sovereignty to "foreigners."

Nonetheless, governments and businessmen agree that Europe's immediate future will be charted at Maastricht. It may be that no one emerges fully satisfied with the result—going too far for some, not far enough for others. But, as one French official put it, "this is a process, and what isn't done now can be done later." In any event, the 12 plan to review any Maastricht treaty in 1996.

*   *   *

December 11, 1991

EUROPEANS AGREE ON A PACT FORGING NEW POLITICAL TIES AND INTEGRATING ECONOMIES

By ALAN RIDING
Special to The New York Times

MAASTRICHT, the Netherlands, Wednesday, Dec. 11— European Community leaders agreed early today on a treaty that sets the 12-nation bloc along a path toward closer political and economic unity including the establishment of common foreign and defense policies and a single currency by the end of this decade.

The two-day summit meeting on regional unity almost broke down during its final hours over Britain's refusal to allow the community to define domestic social policies. But at the last moment a formula was found enabling Britain to decide which community measures it will adopt, thereby accommodating Britain's concerns about loss of sovereignty.

While France, Germany and other governments complained bitterly about Britain's inflexibility, they struggled to find a compromise in order to safeguard their earlier decision to create a single currency and regional central bank no later than 1999.

Associated Press

President François Mitterrand with Jacques Delors, right, President of the European Community, at meeting in Maastricht, the Netherlands.

Britain Gets an Out

That decision, thrashed out by finance ministers Monday and approved by community leaders Tuesday, is already considered the principal achievement of the summit. But it was an integral part of a draft treaty on European union that included numerous contentious political questions.

Britain also refused to commit itself to a single currency and central bank and was allowed to "opt out" of monetary union under the accord worked out here. Mr. Major has long insisted that only the British Parliament could make a decision to abandon the once-mighty pound sterling.

"The history of our Europe teaches us that even if one or two states lag behind, in the end they will follow," said the Dutch Prime Minister, Ruud Lubbers, who presided over the summit. "The process of going to monetary union with one currency is now a fact of life."

'A Significant Step'

The British Prime Minister was nonetheless visibly cheered at having achieved many of his objectives at the meeting. "I am very happy with the outcome," he told reporters early today. "It was a success for Britain and a success for Europe. It marks a significant step forward for the community."

Earlier Tuesday, after Mr. Major spelled out his opposition to community involvement in social questions, President François Mitterrand of France suggested that the "opt-out" formula used by Britain on monetary union would be used to exclude Britain from some social commitments.

Reportedly anxious not to be seen isolated twice in one summit, however, Mr. Major resisted this solution, winning

Chancellor Helmut Kohl of Germany, right, and his Foreign Minister, Hans-Dietrich Genscher, as they awaited the start of the second day of the European Community meeting in Maastricht, the Netherlands.

further concessions from other leaders that seemingly reflected their determination to move forward—with or without Britain—toward closer political integration.

British officials said the eventual compromise involved agreement to drop the so-called social chapter entirely from the draft union treaty. Rather than abandoning their social program, though, the 11 other governments—Belgium, Denmark, France, Germany, Greece, Ireland, Italy, Luxembourg, the Netherlands, Spain and Portugal—decided to sign a separate treaty dealing with this aspect of political unity.

Asked early today whether Britain had become the slow train in a two-speed Europe, Mr. Major said that on the social issue, he was unwilling to risk job creation and investment in Britain. On monetary union, he said Britain could join when it wanted. "We have surrendered nothing," he added, "and we have lost nothing."

Mitterrand Hails Meeting

President Mitterrand, in contrast, hailed the summit as a broad success, stressing not only the watershed decision to create a single currency and regional central bank before the end of the century, but also the community's decision to work for the first time towards a common defense policy.

He also emphasized that Britain had been unable to prevent other community governments from breaking new ground in many new political areas, including the decision to create a regional police security body to be known as Europol. But he added that there was "no divorce" with Britain.

Working in tandem with Chancellor Helmut Kohl of Germany, Mr. Mitterrand has been pressing over the last 20 months for a community commitment to "political unity" aimed at strengthening the community's political profile in international affairs and harmonizing many of its domestic policies.

These were considered important to consolidate the community's existing plan to form a single regional market of 340 million consumers on Jan. 1, 1993, with goods, services, capital and people moving freely within what will become the world's largest trading bloc.

One key objective was to create mechanisms that should enable the community to develop common foreign and security policies. Agreement on this was achieved early today, albeit with Britain successfully insisting that key decisions be taken by governments through unanimity.

More controversial, though, was the idea of establishing a common community defense policy and, eventually, an independent defense capability. Britain—though not alone in this case—fought strongly to insure that this would not weaken NATO, to which 11 of the 12 also belong.

The outcome appears to have pleased both Britain and France, with all community leaders agreeing to build up a nine-nation military pact known as the Western European Union into the community's informal defense arm at the same time as retaining its ties to the North Atlantic Treaty Organization.

Even before the summit, though, many experts anticipated that differences between Britain and its partners over social policy would bring the biggest headaches, not least because Mr. Major has frequently warned against community "meddling" in such areas as working conditions, vacations, maternal leave and other labor-related issues.

Mr. Major's twin arguments were that such interference in the workplace would weaken the competitiveness of the European economies and that, even in cases where unanimity was required, the community's Brussels-based executive commission would use new laws to extend its influence.

"We know we have a body out there that is trying to work around the edges and extend the power of the community," one senior British official said Tuesday, reflecting London's suspicion of the European Commission headed by Jacques Delors. "In this case, we're talking about measures that will increase unemployment."

Mr. Kohl's principal goal at the summit, though, was to increase the power of the 518-member European Parliament as a way of bolstering democracy at a time of growing unification. And here Mr. Major made the concession of accepting the idea of "co-decision" between community governments and the Parliament in some limited areas.

Before coming to this southern Dutch city Sunday night, though, Mr. Major also indicated that he would sign no treaty that included a planned reference to the community's "federal" vocation, a concept viewed in London as a step toward creation of a European government.

Aware that the word "federal" had become an explosive political issue in Britain, other community leaders agreed to drop it. Instead, the new treaty is characterized as "a new stage in the process creating an ever closer union among the peoples of Europe, where decisions will be taken as closely as possible to the citizens."

Aid for Poorer Members

Another issue that emerged in recent days as a threat to the summit was resolved today when the community accepted the demand of its four poorest members—Spain, Portugal, Greece and Ireland—for increased economic assistance to permit them to catch up with their richer partners.

Led by Prime Minister Felipe Gonzalez of Spain, the four won agreement on a legally binding protocol to be attached to the final treaty committing the community to increase the resources of a so-called structural fund and to create a new cohesion fund to help improve the environment and transportation.

Discussion of the community's post-1993 budget will only begin next year, but Spain was anxious to obtain this pledge before the community begins negotiating entry of new members. Today, community leaders indicated they would be ready to take up the applications from Austria and Sweden as soon as next year.

*   *   *

December 15, 1991

SEEN AGAIN AT MAASTRICHT: ADAM SMITH'S INVISIBLE HAND

By CRAIG R. WHITNEY

MAASTRICHT, The Netherlands—As they struggled to put at least some of the pieces of what used to be the Soviet Union back together again last week, Boris N. Yeltsin and the other leaders of his new Commonwealth of Independent States would have done well to keep one eye on the leaders of the European Community.

Europe is steadily pulling itself together, but for the last 46 years it has been a lot easier to do that economically than politically. Last week's European summit meeting at Maastricht was no exception. The 12 leaders who gathered here agreed relatively quickly on a single currency to go with the single, barrier-free market they will have by the end of next year, but they could not advance as far as some had hoped down the road to political union.

Still, when the talks were over it was a lot easier to see what the European Community would look like by the end of the century than it was to see what would become of the Soviet Union. By the year 2000, it is now clear, the European market will be far bigger than that of the United States or Japan, with close to 350 million people and a single currency, at least among the countries on the Continent with the strongest economies; this new currency should be a powerful stimulus to trade, commerce and investment.

An Expanding Club

The new Europe will stretch from the Atlantic to at least the Russian border, if Finland, Sweden, Austria and perhaps Norway have joined by then, as expected. Austria and Sweden have already applied and could be accepted as early as 1995. Poland, Czechoslovakia and Hungary also want in, but for them, as well as for Ukraine if it decides to try, more time will be needed to build market economies.

Economic necessity gave birth to the European Economic Community in 1957. Even Britain, which at first was frozen out of the fledgling Common Market by France and later became fastidious about whether the club was really good enough for it to join, has no serious questions any more about the economic benefits of membership. Prime Minister John Major does not really have any about the benefits of a single currency, but to satisfy the doubters at home who have gathered under the banner of his predecessor, Margaret Thatcher, he had to get his 11 partners to agree that Britain could remain outside the monetary union agreement until its Parliament made the final decision on whether to join.

There is no real doubt that Britain will finally do so, according to politicians of all the major parties there. And that time will come by 1997 if a majority of the European countries qualify as economically ready then or, at the latest, by 1999, under the treaty.

Britain's consistent skepticism about rushing into things is based on an acute awareness that when countries agree to a common currency, they in effect surrender some of their most basic sovereign rights, pooling their sovereignty in monetary affairs. The threat to the pound sterling has been vigorously debated in Britain for months and months. The threat to the mark seems to have caught the German public unaware, according to German diplomats and journalists here who said that only last week did it dawn on Germans that the mark would soon be replaced by something else—the European Currency Unit, or more felicitously, ecu, the same name taken by a royal French coinage in the 17th and 18th centuries.

But in Europe, E pluribus is definitely not yet unum—far from it, as shown by Britain's insistence on staying out of a European-wide program of improvements in working hours, minimum wages and conditions of employment. The leaders of the 11 other community countries argued about this with Mr. Major most of Tuesday before finally throwing up their hands and exempting Britain altogether while they pledged to go ahead on their own. O.K., Mr. Major and his officials joked, if the others want to encourage the Japanese and the Americans to build all their plants in Britain, that's all right with us. The 11 others hope for a British change of heart later on.

'Harmonization'

Continentals often do think in more Cartesian ways than Anglo-Saxons, and the European Community's Executive Commission in Brussels has been pushing for "harmonization" of everything from working hours to value-added taxes on a Continent where no two countries have exactly the same electric plugs, telephone connections or even languages, let alone cultures or historical traditions.

Words mean different things, as well. To Germans, "federal" has come to connote a comfortable decentralization with local control; the structure of Germany's federal republic lets the states decide their own educational and cultural policies. To Britain, whose central Parliament can do or undo systems of local government all over the sceptered isles on the whim of whatever majority is in power in London, talk of a "federal" Europe connotes only an unwanted loss of sovereignty to Brussels.

Differences far smaller than these led to the American Civil War only 78 years after the more perfect union described in the preamble to the United States Constitution. In the preamble to the political union treaty signed in the wee hours Wednesday, Mr. Major made the others take out a reference to a federal vocation for the European Community and settle instead for an "ever closer union among the peoples of Europe," who all now also enjoy citizenship in what the treaty calls the European Union.

It is easy to wonder what exactly that is. Political union remains a vague goal, even though the leaders agreed last week to implement joint foreign policy decisions by majority vote in four areas—arms control, disarmament, nuclear proliferation and economic aspects of security. They also decided to awaken the long-slumbering nine-nation Western European Union and direct it to strengthen Europe's contribution to NATO and build the framework for an independent European defense.

But first the Europeans have to show that they have joint policies, something they haven't demonstrated in relation to the Yugoslav civil war at their eastern doorstep, or even for what has been the Soviet Union. But for all the vagueness and talk about national sovereignty, the outlines of a new Europe are slowly becoming clear. It is something that will give not only Russians but Americans a lot to think about in the years to come.

* * *

April 19, 1992

EUROPE IS GETTING JITTERY ABOUT ARRANGED UNION

By ALAN RIDING
Special to The New York Times

PARIS, April 17—Just four months after the European Community signed a landmark treaty on economic and political unity, the organization is suddenly being shaken by challenges to the agreement and new uncertainty over the region's future.

Although agreement on the Treaty on European Union was the result of tough bargaining before it was approved last December at a meeting of European leaders in Maastricht, the Netherlands, ratification by the community's 12 member nations was taken for granted.

Yet almost immediately, there were signs that many Europeans were less enthusiastic over the treaty than their leaders and, with misgivings now turning into resistance, officials at the community headquarters in Brussels are for the first time acknowledging that the agreement is threatened.

Under the treaty, which can only go into effect after ratification by all 12 members, the community will seek to establish common foreign and defense policies and will create a single currency and a regional central bank by 1999.

Grumbles Are Growing

But complaints are growing louder that this will require too great a surrender of sovereignty are now being heard in France and Germany, whose governments were the driving force behind the treaty. In Denmark and Ireland, there are fears the treaty may be rejected in upcoming referendums.

Adding to the community's glum mood, less than nine months before it is transformed into the world's largest trading bloc, its cohesion is also being tested by disagreements over aid to its so-called "poor four" members and when and how to add new members.

In part, its troubles are a reflection of the general mood of uncertainty gripping Western Europe, brought on as much by economic recession as by the pace of political change. Further, in the last month, governing parties in France, Germany and Italy have all been rebuffed at the polls.

But the Maastricht treaty is also only now being challenged because, in its year-long negotiation, no country except Britain debated its contents. Today, ratification by the British Parliament looks straightforward, but the debate about European union is only just beginning elsewhere.

No Referendum in France

In France, it began last Sunday when President Francois Mitterrand announced he would seek ratification of the treaty by a joint session of Parliament rather than through a popular referendum. Since then, attacks on "Maastricht," as the treaty has become known, have increased.

Criticism in France has so far cut across traditional ideological lines, with not only the Communist Party and the extreme rightist National Front joining together in outright opposition, but also sectors of the main conservative coalition and even the governing Socialist Party rejecting it.

What unites such disparate political groups is simply the view that the treaty surrenders control over French destiny. "No diplomatic instrument has ever had such an irreversible impact on our national sovereignty," said Alain Peyrefitte, the conservative writer. "We are not yet defeated."

Some critics object to certain articles in the treaty, including one allowing foreign residents to vote in local elections. But the problem is that the choice is "take it or leave it" because, once signed in Maastricht, the treaty cannot be amended.

Jacques Chirac, who heads the Gaullist Rally for the Republic, has not yet addressed the substance of the treaty, but he has described it as "abstruse, badly drafted, long, complex and ambiguous." He also said that, since the treaty will require amendments to the French Constitution, these changes should be approved by referendum.

France's other leading opposition figure, Valery Giscard d'Estaing, a former President who leads the Union for French Democracy, has backed the treaty and endorsed Mr. Mitterrand's view that the entire ratification procedure be handled through Parliament.

Criticism in Germany

In Germany, criticism of the treaty began immediately after the Maastricht meeting, as if Germans had not been told that creation of a single currency would mean the disappearance of the mark. Concern that Germany might "import" economic instability through the single currency is now the principal reservation about the treaty.

With the accord due to be ratified by the two houses of the German Parliament, the opposition Social Democratic Party has so far withheld its approval, and some members of the upper house—the Bundesrat—are also unhappy.

The first test will come on June 2 when Denmark holds a referendum on the treaty. Most political parties favor ratification, but a recent poll indicated that 36 percent of Danes will vote against the treaty, 32 percent will support it and the rest are still undecided.

In Ireland, the treaty has become embroiled in a debate about abortion rights. Last December, Ireland was allowed to attach a protocol protecting its constitutional ban on abortion. But after the Irish Supreme Court allowed a 14-year-old rape victim to travel abroad for an abortion last month, Ireland asked to amend the protocol.

Fearing that one amendment could open the entire treaty to renegotiation, the community turned down the Irish request. Instead, this week, the community agreed to issue a special declaration taking note of Dublin's changed position, but there is still concern lest Ireland's June 18 referendum on the treaty become a plebiscite on abortion.

Nervousness in Italy and Spain

In other member countries, such as Italy and Spain, the debate is just starting, but already nervousness about ratification is complicating discussions of two crucial pending issues—the plan to increase the community's budget by $25 billion by 1997 and the method of allowing in new members.

The budget increase is intended to speed development in Spain, Portugal, Ireland and Greece so that the "poor four" can join the single currency union in 1999. But with richer members, notably Germany and Britain, opposing a budget increase, the dispute seems certain to dominate the next community summit in June in Lisbon.

The so-called enlargement question is even more disturbing. The first new members are likely to be Austria, Sweden and Finland. But Turkey, Malta and Cyprus have also applied, and Poland, Czechoslovakia, Hungary and the Baltic states plan to do so. Chancellor Kohl has told the republics of the former Soviet Union not to expect membership, but that could still result in a community of 35 members by early in the next century.

Jacques Delors, president of the community's executive commission, has said he will present a report on enlargement to the Lisbon summit that "without doubt will be a political, intellectual and institutional shock to the 12 member states that, in my view, have not reflected sufficiently on what a community of 35 nations would mean."

* * *

May 23, 1992

THE END OF SOVEREIGNTY

By FLORA LEWIS

PARIS—Europe is experiencing severe growing pains. All 12 members of the European Community must ratify the Treaty of Maastricht, agreed upon by government heads in the Netherlands in December, if European unity is to be achieved. The debates are stormier than expected.

Critics in each country have their own sticking points, plus domestic political feuds that complicate the issue. But the storms should have been expected because matters of nation and sovereignty are being broached directly as never before.

Fundamentally, all members have to face the question of whether democracy and the free market economy are compatible. Both are being urged on ex-Communist and developing countries as the essential double helix of successful societies, necessarily intertwined. The paradox is that advanced states are finding it hard to keep them together as they accept the facts of interdependence.

This is true everywhere, including in the U.S., but Europe must be first to tackle it.

Sovereignty is a matter of frontiers, and democracy is anchored in politically defined territory. But, as Britain's former Foreign Secretary, Sir Geoffrey Howe, has said, "Sovereignty isn't like virginity." There are degrees of sovereignty, and the modern world is eroding the notion of absolute and exclusive nation-states.

The market disrespects sovereign borders as much and wherever it can. The global economy has swollen to a fluid mass that no government can regulate on its own, yet it affects the everyday life of ordinary citizens more and more directly. Jobs, interest rates, the value of money are matters each government talks about to its electorate, but the people are touched by decisions beyond their leaders' control.

Instant, 24-hour access to stock markets around the world, vast international banking entanglements that can confound national monitors as the Bank of Credit and Commerce International did, make a mockery of sovereignty. Likewise the real estate giant Olympia and York, whose properties can't be foreclosed to pay debt like those of lesser operators would be because that would drive down real estate values in too many countries and threaten too many banks.

Some Europeans, like Margaret Thatcher, oppose letting European union nibble away at sovereign command within national borders because they consider Brussels likely to reintroduce socialistic tendencies. Some agree with France's former Defense Minister, Jean-Pierre Chevenement, a socialist, who says it would expose his countrymen to the "power of international money" regardless of their votes.

Jacques Attali, the puckish Frenchman who heads the European Bank for Reconstruction and Development, says that the market needs to overcome borders while traditional democracy needs to keep them. So the aim for the future, he argues, must be a "democracy without frontiers," a superior democracy of overlapping units, where everyone can be a member of a variety of democratic entities of various shapes and sizes.

These are difficult, challenging ideas, and the future citizens of the European Union are stumbling into them as they debate the new treaty. The choice is stark: Europe, yes or no. France, a key founder of the Common Market, is raging with doubt, though most people see there is no going back. The democracy dilemma will have to be addressed with new, transnational countervailing forces, growing out of the growing pains.

This is the way the world is going. Yugoslavia shows what the opposite direction means. The European Community has to lead in defining the issues of sovereignty, economy and democracy. Others won't escape it.

Flora Lewis is Senior Columnist of The New York Times.

* * *

June 3, 1992

DANES REJECT EUROPEAN UNION TREATY BY SLIM MARGIN

By CRAIG R. WHITNEY
Special to The New York Times

COPENHAGEN, June 2—Danish voters narrowly rejected the treaty on European union in a referendum today, throwing into confusion the European Community's plans to build political and monetary unity on the foundations of its economic strength as the world's most powerful trading bloc.

Asked to vote a simple "yes" or "no" to the treaty on monetary and political union that European leaders agreed to in Maastricht, the Netherlands, last December, 50.7 percent of the Danish voters cast "no" ballots, and 49.3 percent voted "yes."

Fear of being overwhelmed by stronger neighbors in a federal Europe that would swallow up Danish sovereignty, a longtime concern here, seemed to be the main reason for the rejection.

Technically, the vote had the effect of vetoing the treaty, since it cannot go into effect as planned on Jan. 1 unless all 12 members ratify it. Plans to eliminate most remaining tariff and trade barriers and border controls among the European Community nations and establish a single European market will not be affected, and can go ahead in January despite the Danish vote.

Treaty Could Die

The treaty could now simply die a quiet death, leaving the European Community simply to become the giant free-trade bloc of sovereign states that the member countries had already planned before the Maastricht accord. Or the other members, with or without Denmark, could agree to renegotiate it and try again.

The closeness of the final Danish results—1,652,999 "no" votes to 1,606,730 "yes" votes from an 82.9 percent turnout of Denmark's 3.964 million voters—left the treaty's supporters not knowing quite what to do next about European union.

Prime Minister Poul Schlüter, whose minority coalition Government, along with all Danish newspapers and most labor unions and employers' associations, had urged voters to approve the treaty, said after the vote was counted that he accepted the plan's defeat.

Danish politicians of all parties, most of which had been urging their supporters for weeks to vote "yes," said tonight that they would meet Wednesday to plan their next step. Other European countries will have to make their own decisions on what to do.

Germans' Second Thoughts

But with politicians in Germany already having second thoughts about the treaty's plans to replace the powerful and stable mark with a more amorphous Euro-currency, and constitutional arguments raging there and in France, opposition to the treaty elsewhere could get a powerful boost now that Danes have rejected it.

Opponents of the treaty in Britain, another traditionally skeptical country which was to begin debate on final ratification of it on Wednesday, were said to be jubilant. But Sir Leon Brittan, a British member of the European Executive Commission in Brussels, called the Danish vote "very disappointing" and said that the commission would meet on Wednesday morning to discuss the results.

Danish voters had been hesitating for weeks on the issues of monetary union and greater political cooperation, but the last public opinion polls had forecast a "yes" vote. What effect the rejection would have on other European countries' plans to proceed with ratification votes was not clear.

Carl Bildt, the Prime Minister of Sweden, which along with Finland and Austria has already applied to join the European Community, as Switzerland and perhaps Norway are expected to do shortly, said that Sweden would go ahead with its application nonetheless.

Next Vote in Ireland

The next test was to come in Ireland on June 18, when voters there were to cast ballots in a referendum on the treaty. The Irish referendum was complicated by that country's constitutional ban on abortion.

A clause in the treaty allows the abortion ban to remain in effect in Ireland even after European countries eliminate the legal and trade barriers among them in January. But opposition to the ban on abortion has risen in Ireland since a pregnant Irish teenager who said she had been raped was briefly prevented from traveling to England last winter to get an abortion.

In Denmark, opposition to the treaty centered mostly on fears that the Danish economy would be dominated by Germany and that Danish political decisions would be taken by a French-speaking bureaucracy in Brussels.

"I voted 'no,'" said Kamilla Kristensen, a 21-year-old student at the university here who crossed an "X" on the "No" side of her ballot today in a voting booth in the central court of Copenhagen's vast City Hall. "It's not because I don't want to be a part of Europe," she said. "It's because the administration in Brussels is too big."

Karsten Hougstrup, a 24-year-old hairdresser, said he voted "yes." "Denmark has made a lot of money because it belongs to the community," he said, before riding off on a bicycle.

2 Parties Opposed Pact

Only two of the eight parties in the Danish Parliament—the Socialist People's Party and the Progress Party—took positions against ratification, on the grounds that European political unity had gone far enough as it was and that Denmark's membership in the European Community would not be endangered even if it rejected the treaty on European unity.

Danish supporters of the treaty, led by Foreign Minister Uffe Ellemann-Jensen, warned that rejecting the treaty would mean a loss of Danish influence in the community at a time when its Nordic neighbors were clamoring to get in. "It's going to be very difficult," he said tonight. "Everybody should think very hard about what to do, and not make any rash decisions."

The treaty provided for a common European currency as early as 1997 in countries that meet the fiscal and monetary conditions set for it and want to participate. Denmark had planned another referendum to decide whether to convert to a common European currency when the time came. Britain had negotiated the right for its Parliament to make the final decision on whether to take part in the monetary union.

Other provisions pledge the 12 European Community members to seek a common foreign and security policy. And 11 of the 12—all except Britain—agreed to try to make their social and labor policies on things like working conditions, minimum wages, and working hours more compatible.

* * *

September 20, 1992

AFTER THE GELDKRIEG

By JOSEF JOFFE

MUNICH—Today, the French go to the polls to decide the fate of Europe. But it hardly matters whether they vote "oui" or "non" on the Maastricht agreement, grandiloquently titled "Treaty on European Union." For its key provisions have already been sunk—blown out of the water by the nasty realities of politics among nations.

The U.S. Constitution originally had seven Articles, strewn across a few pages, to underpin "a more perfect Union." The Maastricht treaty fills some 250 pages. But you don't have to wade through hundreds of titles and protocols to get the gist. It is right there on the first two pages, spelled out in the triple pledge to go for a "single currency" and for a common foreign and security policy.

Alas, Europe has already failed the test of unity, and so a "non" would merely pull the plug on the comatose patient while a "oui" would do little more than prolong the agony. The handwriting has been on the wall all year, and on Wednesday the wall collapsed as if somebody had driven a car full of explosives into its base.

On Wednesday, the granddaddy of the monetary union, the European Monetary System, went into shock when Britain and Italy pulled out after a long, hapless attempt to defend the pound and the lira against devaluation. What's wrong with devaluation? you might ask; after all, the U.S. dollar has been on a rollercoaster for years on end.

That is like asking, "What's wrong with a little blasphemy in a revival meeting?" For, in theory at least, devaluation would trespass against the spirit of Europe. The whole idea of the European Monetary System as a trial run for a single currency relies on a straitjacket of fixed exchange rates. But currencies can stay together only if their masters adhere to the same standards of fiscal and monetary probity.

Except that political leaders genuflect before different altars. They look at their unemployment rates—and then at their electoral calendars. Consequently, they will always try to wiggle out of the jacket, going for economic policies that will strain, then break, the monetary bond.

So why did the European monetary mesh stay around for so long? For one thing, until five years ago the dictatorship of virtue was regularly relieved by a brush with sin. There were lots of realignments, and so everybody could stay on the wagon precisely because he could take an intermittent swig from the bottle. But after 1987, currencies turned into Maginot lines—to be defended at all costs and against all comers. Hence, the time bomb began to tick.

The second reason was more profound: German reunification in 1990. That was like putting the junkie in charge of the coke supply. Originally, those stern-faced governors of the Bundesbank were to play the martinets. They would keep their own Government in line and, by yanking the fixed-parity chain, force the spendthrifts elsewhere to shape up or suffer the ultimate humiliation of devaluation.

That was yesterday. The reunification bill now runs at $130 billion a year. But in Bonn, Chancellor Helmut Kohl chose George Bush as a role model: no new taxes. The result was massive deficit spending, massive borrowing and a nasty bout of inflation. So those gentlemen from the Bundesbank stepped in like programmed robots, sending interest rates into the sky and lighting the fuse on the European Monetary System.

John Major and Giuliano Amato, the Prime Ministers of Britain and Italy, had but one choice: jack up interest rates even more and kill all chances for recovery or delink from the tyranny of the German mark. They decided to stop paying—indirectly—for the costs of German reunification, and this is the end of the grand dream of European monetary union for now.

The other two pillars of union—a common foreign and security policy—crumbled earlier this year under the onslaught of a "new European order" that looks suspiciously like the old. Europe's common foreign policy took a hit in Yugoslavia from which it will not soon recover. "We will do it our way," the European Community told the U.S. when Yugoslavia began to disintegrate.

"Our way," though, looked like a replay of World War I when France and Britain implicitly lined up behind their old ally Serbia, and the Germans behind the former Hapsburg possessions of Croatia and Slovenia. The Serbs got the point: every cease-fire signed under the aegis of the community was broken before the pens were uncapped, and so Lord Carrington, the mediator, rightly resigned before he was laughed out of Belgrade.

A common security policy? Here, too, Yugoslavia acted like a flash of lightning that exposed the frailties of Europe's ambitions. Germany will remain the odd man out as long as it hides behind a debatable constitutional interpretation that proscribes military action beyond self-defense. The Britons, Frenchmen and Italians? They are at least willing to contribute token forces for the relief of Sarajevo.

But this is where harmony bowed out. The French want the Western European Union, the "military arm" of the European Community, in charge. The British would rather march under the United Nations flag. London wants to keep NATO alive. Paris, as usual, opts for "splendid aggravation," loath to accept any arrangement that preserves the "hegemony" of the United States.

The moral of the story is a sad one: Europe has all the wherewithal for a superpower but for two elements: a common interest and a common will. Nor should this come as a surprise. For the past 40 years, history was suspended. The cold war acted as a great disciplinarian, and the two superpowers, the U.S. and Soviet Union, always stood ready to crack the whip of bloc discipline.

Moreover, the strongest power in Europe, Germany, is no longer a shackled Gulliver. It has shed its old dependencies without acquiring the habits of benign leadership. The explosion of the European Monetary System is instructive.

What was perfectly logical for the Bundesbank—to fight fiscal irresponsibility with punishing interest rates—was a perfect disaster for everybody else. But leadership requires more than navel-gazing or a policy that sacrifices European to German unity. To lead is to look out for others, too. Hence the pernicious referendum debate in France, where the proponents of Maastricht fell back on arguments that could hardly reassure their German brethren: that union was the only chance of re-shackling Gulliver-on-Rhine.

Where does Europe go from here—"oui" or "non" in France? The diagnosis is all too clear. The disease is renationalization—with a vengeance in the East and on cats' feet in the West. The threat is not war. But the metaphors have become military ones, which is a nice way to stoke the fires of nationalism. During the currency cataclysm, the Italian press was fond of such shibboleths as "Dunkirk" and "Alamo." And the British press wrote as if "Wilhelm" Kohl had just dispatched his dreadnoughts to Albion.

Perhaps the shock of the First Geldkrieg will teach the Europeans a salutary lesson. Don't overreach; aim lower so as to score higher. Europe is not ready for a "more perfect Union." But the Single Market—providing for the untrammeled flow of goods, people and capital—agreed on before Maastricht will become reality on New Year's Day regardless of how the French vote. And the demise of the European Monetary System might actually be a blessing in disguise. For it will provide enough monetary freedom to cushion the shocks of "Big Bang '93," when the single market kicks in.

The Europeans have seen the future this week; let's hope they don't like it. Like Dr. Spielvogel in "Portnoy's

Complaint," they ought to say: "So. Now vee may perhaps to begin. Yes?" With a new and more modest agenda.

Josef Joffe is foreign editor and a columnist of the Süddeutsche Zeitung.

*   *   *

September 22, 1992

FORWARD WITH EUROPE

For Americans, the news from France is close but clear. European unity lives, and that is in the best interests of the United States, the 12 members of the European Community and global trade. France's 51-to-49 percent "yes" vote on the Maastricht treaty does not guarantee ultimate triumph. But it averts what could have become a slide into nationalist discord.

The road ahead is pitted with rocks and craters: the thinness of the margin, monetary tension and skepticism in countries that have yet to vote. Community leaders will have to find ways to make rolling reassessments. Yet for the moment they can keep rolling forward.

France's referendum on the Maastricht treaty started out as a judgment on debatable details of monetary and political union. By the time of the vote on Sunday it had become a test of the viability of the European Community. Now, with Europe's narrow victory, attention quickly turns to the next set of obstacles, and the next.

The most difficult is how to respond to last week's currency crisis. Fixed exchange rates could not forever bridge the gulf of divergent national goals. The system unraveled because Germany refused to compromise its low-inflation policy for the sake of its partners. Unless Europe's governments are now prepared to sacrifice domestic goals for the sake of wider harmony, plans for a single European currency in this decade will have to be scaled back.

Communism's collapse in East Germany helped detonate the monetary crisis. Communism's collapse elsewhere in Europe demands new trade links, coordination on refugees and a workable collective security system. Europe needs to overcome the apathy, appeasement and obsolete imperial rivalries that have doomed its approach to Yugoslavia. And it needs to relieve Germany of its disproportionate refugee burden.

Eight Community members, including Denmark, still have to ratify the treaty before it can go into effect. That will require addressing grass-roots misgivings about, for instance, loss of sovereignty. Undoing Denmark's negative vote will also require some substantive change.

The close call in France highlights the need for wider citizen involvement in shaping a new Europe. People complain about "Brussels bureaucrats." But that's an oversimplification. Without Brussels functionaries to standardize the rules, there could be no Common Market. The problem does not lie with the bureaucrats but with the elected leaders who negotiated the treaty and arrogantly took their constituents for granted.

As the ratification process moves forward, those leaders, now chastened, will have to make midcourse adjustments on the way to a unified Europe, a reassured America and a more prosperous world.

*   *   *

September 26, 1992

EUROPE STUMBLES, FOR NOW

By FLORA LEWIS

PARIS—Jacques Delors, president of the European Commission, said Thursday that if Britain delayed ratifying the treaty of Maastricht, as Prime Minister John Major said he intended, others—led by Germany and France—may move toward monetary union on their own. That would be a "two-speed Europe," separating the strong and the weak.

But "Europe," in the sense of institution-building, isn't dying. Some countries may accelerate and some may drag behind. Yet all the reasons that impelled a sometimes reluctant, stumbling Europe toward integration for the last two generations remain compelling.

The real changes—the unification of Germany and collapse of the Soviet empire leaving Eastern Europe free but adrift—make the consolidation of European power more, not less, necessary. The treaty's detractors made wide use of the alibi that it is selfish for Western Europe to strengthen its ties while the East is left to wait disconsolately at the back door. But it is a deliberate obfuscation. The East desperately wants a robust, decisive community that offers haven and hope, not a ramshackle corral.

As French supporters of "no" to Maastricht used crocodile tears for Easteners to buttress their argument, some advocates of "yes" used the false pretense that "America and Japan would rub their hands in glee" if Europe were stymied. That was meant to exploit fears of supposed American and Japanese plots to divide and conquer, though in fact both powers have an intense interest in a strong and stable Europe.

It was an ugly, distorted debate, as full of cheap shots and imaginary scarecrows as the U.S. election campaign. But it did show that politicians and technocrats can no longer concoct the necessary transformation of the old nation-state system in Europe among themselves and just expect people to swallow it. That was the big revelation of the votes in France and Denmark (which was as narrow as France's, but negative).

The demonstration of public doubt and confusion can have a harmful effect in the interim. All the major European leaders are weak in their own constituencies—shopworn veterans in France, Germany and Spain, fragile, challenged newcomers in Britain and Italy. There may be a strong temptation for each to play to the noisiest domestic grievances at the expense of longer-term statesmanship.

Democracy remains national, territorial and it isn't easy to sound masterful while telling people the unpleasant fact that they can no longer rely on their government alone to control the forces buffeting them. Economies, especially money, have escaped the old borders.

The resistance to Maastricht, however, can revitalize the European movement by forcing leaders to involve the public—just as the treaty was intended to accelerate Europe's capacity to deal with common problems. Governments, as well as the commission in Brussels, will have to be much more sensitive and energetic at informing and explaining.

People are attached to their national identity, culture and tradition, but these are under stress from global economic and technological change. European leaders need to explain more clearly what sovereignty can and cannot do nowadays. It can protect sale of unpasteurized cheese and the hunt for wood pigeons, which Brussels foolishly thought to ban on grounds of standardizing norms, to the outrage of highly vocal French groups.

It isn't enough to assure peace and prosperity in countries of Europe that once dominated the world and proceeded to tear each other apart in murderous rivalry. That is why the European Community was started. It is why it will continue to live and grow. The dynamics have not changed.

Flora Lewis is Senior Columnist of The New York Times

* * *

October 13, 1993

GERMAN COURT REJECTS APPEAL TO HALT EUROPEAN UNION PACT

By CRAIG R. WHITNEY
Special to The New York Times

BONN, Oct. 12—Germany's constitutional court removed the last obstacle to Bonn's ratification of the treaty on European union today, ruling that the pact could never impose a federal-style government or a common currency on individual members against their will.

Germany is the only member that has not formally ratified the treaty, which was negotiated in the Dutch town of Maastricht at the end of 1991 and has been a rallying point for fears that closer unity would submerge separate European national identities.

Rejection by any single country would have scuttled the treaty, which has been going through the perils of Pauline for the past year and a half as various parliaments and electorates threatened to reject it. Now it can finally go into effect on Nov. 1.

Kohl Welcomes Decision

Chancellor Helmut Kohl welcomed the decision today as "an important milestone in the process of European integration and its continuation," but the treaty and the opposition it aroused may really mark the end of the road toward a United States of Europe.

In its ruling, the German court rejected the view that the treaty would set up a European superstate, with a single currency and a powerful central government in Brussels.

"The Union Treaty founds an association of states with the goal of an ever-closer union of European peoples organized as states," said the ruling, which came on an appeal from treaty critics who argued that it would surrender national power in violation of the German Constitution.

"Overall, the concerns of the plaintiffs—that the European Community, because of its ambitious goals, will develop without new parliamentary rights into a political union whose sovereignty rights cannot be foreseen—were unfounded," the decision by eight judges in Karlsruhe said.

European Leaders to Meet

European Community leaders will meet in Brussels on Oct. 29 to mark the end of the ratification process, and Mr. Kohl said today that he would press for a clear timetable then to carry out the treaty's goals, including a common currency, a common foreign and defense policy, and broader democratic powers for elected community institutions like the European Parliament.

Whatever the leaders agree then, much of the treaty seems fated to be a dead letter. Britain never agreed to the treaty's provisions on labor conditions and other social policies, and got an exclusion written into the text. Danish voters rejected the entire treaty in June 1992, then changed their minds last spring, hedging their approval with conditions.

Britain also insisted on special provisions recognizing the right of the House of Commons to make the final decision about whether to submerge the pound sterling into a common European currency, which the treaty said could come as early as 1997.

PART III

BUSINESS GOES GLOBAL

Globalization is many things (it may even be, as *Times* columnist Thomas Friedman says, *every* thing—and its opposite), but it is undeniably an economic process at its core. The rise of the global economy is fundamentally a story about the expansion of global markets and the development of the private enterprises and public institutions of the market. Part III of this book tells the story of the global expansion and evolution of business in the post-war period.

Some people equate economic globalization with the growth of multinational corporations (MNCs), but in many respects this misses the point because it fails to recognize the inherent complexity of both the MNC phenomenon and the global economy. As the articles in "The Evolution of the Multinational Corporation" indicate, MNCs have not only increased in number during the post-war era, they have also evolved or changed in important ways. At first, MNCs were mainly U.S.-based firms doing business abroad—U.S. home, foreign host. Today, however, the distinction between the corporation's home country and its host countries has broken down. Multinational businesses seem to be based everywhere and to do business everywhere. Along the way the terms used to refer to them have evolved, too—*multinational* became *transnational* and then *global*. But the fundamental issue surrounding multinational corporations throughout this period remained accountability. Since their operations by definition transcend national boundaries, they necessarily also transcend the regulatory structures of individual nations.

The rise of the global economy is also about a changing global division of labor—an economic dynamic that is even more powerful (if perhaps less obvious) than the rise of MNCs. Globalization dramatically alters the pattern of who makes what, where, how and for whom. Globalization thus transforms the global web of jobs, incomes, payments, debts and wealth and alters fundamentally the notion of economic security. These shifts affect every element of society in one way or another. The articles in "A Global Division of Labor" provide important examples of this phenomenon.

It is a cliché to say that we live in the age of global markets, but in fact only a few markets are truly global, and these are mainly financial markets. The story of global finance is one of the most important chapters in the rise of the global economy. Financial markets throughout history have been subject to booms and busts, crises and panics. National financial institutions, therefore, are among the most heavily regulated types of business. But who regulates global financial markets? As the articles presented here indicate, the rise of global finance has not been accompanied by the advent of global financial regulation, and this has created a potentially dangerous situation (a topic further explored in Part V of this book).

Most people associate globalization with high technology, which is perhaps why the existence of a "low-tech" global economy 100 years ago is so hard to imagine. "A World Wide Web" examines the role of technological change in the rise of the global economy. Please note that the term used here is *a* world wide web and not *the* world wide web. The technology of globalization includes the internet, but also much more. The growing importance of technology in business and in society means that ideas matter more than hardware or software. Ideas (or intellectual property, as they are often termed) are much harder to regulate and can more easily be transferred or shared worldwide, and they are among the most valuable things on earth. This web of valuable ideas and the people who create and use them is what technological globalization is all about.

Part III ends with another critical moment—the OPEC oil crisis of the 1970s. In many respects, the shifting patterns of trade and finance that the oil crisis produced created contemporary globalization. Certainly this was a critical moment in the development of global finance and in the evolution of MNCs. It was also a notable moment in *The Times*'s coverage of globalization, with Leonard Silk and his colleagues providing detailed reporting and clear analysis of a complex global economic crisis.

THE EVOLUTION OF THE MULTINATIONAL CORPORATION

December 18, 1966

AMERICAN INVESTMENT ABROAD IS AN INVITING TARGET FOR CRITICS

By RICHARD E. MOONEY
Special to The New York Times

PARIS, Dec. 17—"Rather than be judged as a rival, it ought to be considered an auxiliary all the more precious because it alone permits an increased amount of productive labor and useful enterprise to be set to work."

Alexander Hamilton said it, in 1791, about foreign business investment in the United States. Today the issue runs the other way. The statesmen, financiers and business men of the world talk now about the rising tide of U.S. investment abroad, and not all of them are so tolerant as Hamilton.

The most recent case in point is Britain's Prime Minister Harold Wilson, who said in London recently: "Our American friends, because they are friends, will understand when I say that, however much we welcome new American investments here, as in other parts of Europe, there is no one on either side of the Channel who wants to see capital investment in Europe involve domination or, in the last resort, subjugation."

The British, it must be said, are neither so hostile to, nor leery of, U.S. investment as Mr. Wilson implied. The point of his remarks was not to scare Americans away, but to soften up France for Britain's entry to the European Common Market by appealing to the well-known French hostility *and* leeriness about the overseas expansion of American industrial giants.

The United States is, after all, the greatest and most talented industrial power the world has ever known, and it is still growing. Most European big business is small by the American scale. And thus the European tends to be awed if not frightened, respectful if not resentful.

The over-all book value—which greatly understates the actual value—of direct private American investment in business operations overseas at the end of last year was almost $50-billion. It has grown in recent years at an average rate of more than 6 per cent, and last year alone it grew by 11 per cent.

The impact of all this investment is felt in several ways and many places, mostly in the countries where the investment is made but also in the United States. The impact at home is on the balance of international payments, where the strain of this

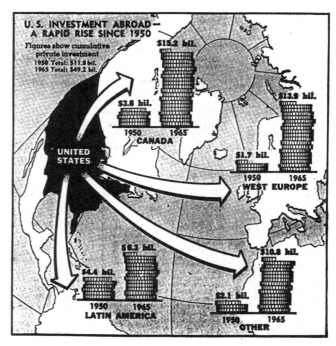

ever increasing wave of outflowing capital caused Washington to tighten controls on it once again this week.

The U. S. business community argues endlessly but futilely that the return on overseas investment eventually brings back into the country much more money than is sent out. The plain fact remains that the Government is concerned with the current outflow and feels it cannot wait for the eventual greater inflow.

This capital flowing out of the United States is, of course, capital flowing into other countries, all of them smaller. It is capable of at least as much impact where it goes as where it comes from. As an inflationary force it can indeed be a problem, but well within the power of the national authorities to dampen. On the other hand, in Hamiltonian terms, the greater effect is the economic benefit of increased "productive labor and useful enterprise."

The big political question, implied by Prime Minister Wilson and asserted by General de Gaulle, is whether this investment leads to "domination" or "subjugation."

To take an extreme but significant example, the United States dominates France's computer industry. To General de Gaulle's distress, this important French industry is almost all

American. Moreover, this domination became subjugation when Washington refused to permit the French Atomic Energy Commission to buy some extra-large computers made in the United States. Recently this ban was lifted, but the French will remember it for a long, long time.

In less extreme circumstances, American subsidiaries are repeatedly under attack for laying off workers, or shifting production, or otherwise disrupting things to suit their world-wide plans, without concern for local conditions.

In general terms, American investment overseas is rarely more than a small fraction of any country's total business activity. In specific businesses in specific countries it can be, and is, much more. But in any case, it is foreign—big, rich foreign. It is an inviting target.

* * *

June 25, 1967

OUTLAYS ABROAD CALLED PERILOUS

Moratorium Urged as Balm to Economic Nationalism

By M. J. ROSSANT

A moratorium on private American investment in foreign countries has been put forward as the first step in a sweeping new program to combat the rising tide of economic nationalism abroad.

The call for a moratorium is the provocative brainchild of Leo Model, head of the Wall Street concern of Model, Roland & Co., Inc., which does a substantial international securities business.

Writing in the current issue of Foreign Affairs, the prestigious quarterly put out by the Council on Foreign Relations, Mr. Model notes that the American stake abroad makes it "the third largest economy in the world" in terms of gross national product.

He reasons that this huge increase in American investment abroad has generated a resurgence of economic "nationalism" that may have very painful consequences for the United States if something is not done to curb it.

A curbing of investment, particularly in Europe, where American companies have almost doubled their stakes in the last five years, is his remedy for removing the threat of American domination and assuring better treatment of American companies.

He also calls on American companies operating abroad to act as good corporate citizens of their host countries. He thinks they should be guided by foreign rather than American practices and suggests that they make more use of foreign nationals in the managements of their subsidiaries, encourage local investors to buy their shares, and deliberately refrain from seeking to control basic industry.

Mr. Model envisions a full-scale effort that goes beyond "nominal" attempts at foreign participation. He insists that American companies abroad must not be subject to the Gov-

ernment's Trading With the Enemy Act, except in emergency, and he suggests that American companies consider setting up holding companies for their European subsidiaries, selling shares wherever the subsidiaries operate.

It is his contention that American business would be served if it took the initiative in reform rather than reacting to foreign demands or depending on the power of the State Department. He said, "The exercise of diplomatic pressure for the benefit of U.S. companies may create serious resentment and merely worsen the investment climate."

Even though Mr. Model wants less Washington influence, the Administration may be more inclined than American industry to welcome a moratorium on private investment. For one thing, a check on dollar outflows would provide immediate help to the nation's ailing balance of payments. For another, it would blunt anti-American attacks, from General de Gaulle and the Arab states, that have grown in virulence.

The plan may gain some support from established American enterprises abroad because Mr. Model puts limits on a moratorium. He does not want to interfere with investments to retain a market position abroad. But he insists that there should be a period of consolidation to prevent expansion into new fields and to buy up existing companies.

Outlook Not Good

A moratorium on new investment would follow the Administration's policy in setting up its voluntary program of restraints for banks and businesses, which hit hardest at companies that were planning to go abroad but had not yet made investments.

But the Administration's program was adopted primarily for balance of payments reasons. Mr. Model is much more concerned about foreign fears and resentment that have arisen from the so-called American "invasion" of their economies.

Since the outlook for the balance of payments is not good and the Arab-Israeli conflict brought new threats of nationalism against American companies, the need for fresh action may gain ground. And in some quarters, at least, the idea of a moratorium seems as attractive as a capital issues committee or other devices to cut down on investment.

In proposing a new program, Mr. Model drew heavily on his personal experience. A native of Germany and a member of the Council on Foreign Relations, he has participated in many foreign ventures in Europe and South America, particularly in Brazil.

He thinks American investment has played a constructive role and can do a great deal more, but he is impressed by the increasing amount of discrimination against American concerns, which could ultimately provoke wholesale discrimination abroad. In his view, Washington's major responsibility is to see to it that wherever discrimination takes place, it is not aimed solely at American companies, and where nationalization is decreed, fair compensation is provided.

It is evident that Mr. Model does not believe his program will eliminate economic or specific anti-American discrimination. With many American companies having resources greater than the entire economy of Belgium and with total American output abroad ranking behind only the United States and the Soviet Union there is bound to be fear and suspicion about the American presence.

But Mr. Model does think that excessive discrimination can be avoided, provided American companies recognize their responsibilities in time. He sums up, "If our companies use their power with consideration for the well-being of other countries, as well as our own, they can be of tremendous help in creating a prosperous world economy . . . Otherwise, their economic power will be a constant irritant in our diplomatic relations with the rest of the world and will ultimately defeat their own interests."

*   *   *

November 5, 1967

OPINIONS VARY ON CAPITAL FLOW ABROAD

By KATHLEEN McLAUGHLIN

Periodically in recent years a hue and cry has been raised against United States investors abroad, with implications of an imminent take-over of one or another nation's economy by alien capital. Protests have been most resounding and most frequent from Canada, but they come by no means exclusively from there.

At a meeting in Brussels a few months ago, Ambassador at Large W. Averell Harriman was irked by a prediction from a Belgian financial adviser that a "confrontation" between Europe and America would develop over increasing United States participation in industry in that region.

If Europeans complained about American investments in their area, retorted Mr. Harriman, why didn't they invest more in the United States, which stood ready to welcome their capital?

Shortly thereafter an executive of an American multinational corporation commented on the growing warmth of the welcome he and his compatriots were getting in Europe, as present and potential investors. Never before, he declared, had they been so ardently wooed.

Divergent Groups

Such conflicting attitudes characterize the divergent groups in most geographical regions, either advocating or opposing entrance of exterior capital. Those opposed to such moves see it as a menace to national sovereignty the advocates hold it to be a boon, essential to maximum development.

Statistically, the record is woefully inadequate, but other evidence is mounting that outward and onward movement of investment funds is increasingly reciprocal, not confined to Americans, and that the tendency to seek profits wherever opportunity offers is common to international-minded business interests at all points of the compass.

Publication in September of the annual report by the Department of Commerce on "International Investments of the United States in 1966" suggests that Americans offer a natural target for attacks by nationalists because of the larger scope of their operations. An equally potent factor undoubtedly is that totals are in the public domain and may be gauged, while those of other countries can only be guessed, for the most part.

Comparable data published over the last 25 years by major industrial nations are no longer available. Those from Britain and Canada, notably, have not been released since 1964.

Sources in this country state that the records are consistently maintained abroad in even more detail, especially by governments exercising close financial controls.

Two reasons are advanced as logical explanations for the cessation of publication elsewhere. One is the complexity of keeping an accurate and up-to-date tally in the face of liquidations in some regions, and delayed notifications of new investments, in others. Another is the risk of unintentional disclosures of identity of some large corporations, through shrewd deduction from changes in an area or country report.

Details Listed

Figures in the latest Department of Commerce summery show that total assets held abroad by United States residents and the Federal Government amounted to $112-billion at the end of 1966, while those held in the United States alone, by foreign residents, were $60-billion.

The tabulated distribution of United States assets abroad last year puts Western Europe in first place, with $32.2-billion; Canada second, with $27.5-billion, and Latin America third, with $19.4-billion.

The same sequence held true for foreign investments in the United States. Western Europe was credited with $35.2-billion, Canada with $8-billion, and Latin America with $5.9-billion.

Until and unless disclosure is made by these and other countries of their assets and investments in addition to those in the United States, the picture of global interchange of investments will remain fragmentary.

Minus the financial aspects, however, the proliferation around the world of crosscurrents of investment capital is readily apparent through hundreds of periodicals and newspapers reporting on international business developments. Their coverage links projects with the names of corporations, large and small, in developing as well as developed lands.

Among emerging countries, those with a growing influx of foreign funds to publicize are usually endowed with commercially valuable natural resources, plus progressive regimes alert to offer a receptive climate for what is often "risk" capital from external sources. In their eagerness, some of these governments have even mortgaged their future revenues too far ahead, by going overboard on the incentives conceded.

Some Keep Barriers

Others, clinging to old resentment and suspicions, have sacrificed years of progress by keeping the barriers high and electing to go it alone, on local initiative.

On the middle ground, both capital-exporting and capital-importing countries at present tend toward the "joint venture" type of partnership, in which technology and backing from abroad are merged with the domestic team's knowledge of their nation's language, traditions and contacts, indispensable in a successful enterprise.

The present tendency of multinational corporations to leapfrog national borders in pursuit of profits could be—and are—impeded by adverse political shifts, or the repercussions of a wave of protectionism, at least temporarily. On the other hand, an impressive number of qualified executives—to whom frontiers loom as irritating frustrations—visualize as inevitable the gradual evolution of the world as an economic whole.

*   *   *

May 12, 1969

MULTINATIONAL VENTURES BACKED

Study by Economist Says Projects Aid Global Economy

By BRENDAN JONES

Multinational corporations, already shaping a new global economy, are ideally equipped to carry out needed world economic development, according to a report made for the International Chamber of Commerce.

The 174-page report, by Dr. Sidney E. Rolfe, economist, was released by the chamber's United States Council at a news conference last week.

In a wide-ranging account of the growth, nature and problems of the multinational, or worldwide, business organization, the study stresses that:

- They are neither a new, nor peculiarly American, phenomenon.
- With investment, technology and organization of world-wide production, they are creating an international economy that is supplanting trade and providing a means for rapid, large-scale development.
- National governments, especially in developing countries, should learn to weigh the benefits obtainable from the big international concerns against the "psychological security" of nationally controlled, but limited, economic growth.

Background Paper

The report will serve as the background paper for the biennial congress of the International Chamber, to be held in Istanbul May 31 to June 7.

The conference will be attended by some 1,500 business leaders from more than 40 countries, including a large group from the United States.

Dr. Rolfe, who is professor of finance at Long Island University, has taught at Princeton and Columbia Universities and has been a consultant to many official and private groups.

His report, entailing about a year of research, contains statistical data and critical comment that make it one of the most comprehensive of recent studies on multinational corporations.

With international oil concerns a prototype, the report notes, modern multinational corporations began developing in the early twentieth century and now number several hundred.

Response to Technology

Dr. Rolfe describes them as "a rational response to modern technology," and as seeking "to produce, finance and market wherever resources can be most efficiently utilized, without respect to national boundaries."

Because American statistics are more detailed and easily obtained, Dr. Rolfe holds, American concerns have appeared to be most prominent in the multinational field.

He offers other data, however, that show there are a substantial number of European, Canadian and Japanese multinational concerns.

Dr. Rolfe cites as the most significant fact about multinational corporations the rapid growth of their production.

That growth by American-based companies, he observes, recently has reached $120-billion a year—more than most countries' gross product—and has grown more rapidly than United States production and export-import trade.

The main object of the study, Dr. Rolfe said at the news conference, was to examine the position of the multinational corporation, its effects on integrating international economies and its challenge to the nation state.

"We are in the midst of change," he remarked, "and not sure where we're going, except we know change is toward a new world economy."

In the report, Dr. Rolfe suggests that developing countries would find multinational corporations the most practical medium for gaining investment, production and technology, management and marketing skills that they could learn to use themselves.

Dr. Rolfe maintains that efforts by developing countries at import substitution have failed because of small markets and high costs.

He notes also that developing countries' insistence on joint ventures limits investment benefits and proposes, instead, stock ownership in parent companies by investors in such countries.

Suggestion on Help

The report suggests, in addition, that multinational companies can help developing countries with industries specializing in export and organize production of components for vehicles and other products by groups of countries.

Most of the fears of multinational corporations, that they would dominate national and social institutions, or callously discharge thousands of workers, have not materialized, the report contends. It adds:

"The economic growth which the international corporation has brought is in fact in the best interests of the nation, which must look to the preservation of economic growth and rising standards of living as one of its most important functions."

* * *

June 15, 1969

FOREIGN SUBSIDIARIES ROCK CURRENCY BOAT

By CLYDE H. FARNSWORTH
Special to The New York Times

PARIS—Sometimes known as the third largest producing unit in the world after the United States and the Soviet Union, the foreign subsidiaries of international companies are complicating problems of the monetary system, and no one really knows what to do about it.

These enterprises—and they are not all American by any means—are behind the massive flows of money that have intensified recent currency crises.

The companies are not out to break the system. In fact, they have perhaps the greatest stake in its stability. But their multinational operations compel them to make "an astute use of their financial sinews," and devise "strategies to offset exchange rate fluctuations," as a background report for the International Chamber of Commerce put it recently.

Corporate treasurers, sensing that all is not well with the British pound or the French franc, draw down their balances in these currencies to absolute minimums. Conversely, they maintain fat accounts in German marks, expecting this currency may be upvalued.

Prudent Management

If they can postpone an order or payment in Britain and France they will do it, and if they can step up purchases in Germany they will do so. This is not speculation as much as it is prudent money management.

"A treasurer would look pretty foolish," one observer said recently, "if he was stuck with a pile of francs on the eve of devaluation."

While the corporate money flows accentuate the problems of central bankers, they may in the long run become an effective device for equalizing wages, rents and interest rates throughout the world.

There are some signs that this may be happening already. The most dramatic example is the upward move in European interest rates reacting through the ratchet effects of the Euro-dollar market to the money squeeze in the United States.

Similar Situations Seen

Prof. Charles P. Kindleberger 2d, an American economist, compares the situation today with those national corporations in the United States after 1890 that spurred the economic integration of the country by borrowing in the cheapest markets and investing where it was most productive in terms of costs and markets.

The international company similarly seeks to produce, finance and market wherever its resources can be most efficiently utilized.

This equalizer effect, however does little to help balance-of-payments adjustments, the key to the functioning of the monetary system.

Some economists contend that the multinational companies may be changing the rules of the game.

Big American companies after their tremendous postwar overseas expansion tend naturally to meet exports orders as much as possible from foreign plants nearer the markets. Though some foreign earnings are repatriated to the parent company, a sizable portion is plowed back into the foreign subsidiary. Meanwhile, additional direct investments may be pumped out by the parent.

All this is a sign of American economic strength. But it does not help the United States get a trade or balance-of-payments surplus.

A Paris-based economist on the staff of the Organization for Economic Cooperation and Development said that surpluses and deficits are becoming anachronisms in the world of multinational companies. Perhaps he puts the case too strongly. But his opinion shows the extent to which some traditional attitudes are changing.

Moves Criticized

The reactions of authorities in Washington and London (where balance-of-payments problems are also acute) have been to restrict private overseas investment with measures that have been criticized by the business communities of the two countries.

The action represents "the temptations of expediency," says economist Sidney E. Rolfe in his background paper for the International Chamber of Commerce.

Why hit investments, he argues, "when all other factors which contribute to adjustment—including the gold price, the level of employment, tourist expenditures, fixed exchange rates, military expenditures and others—are left untouched or actually allowed to work against adjustment?"

The overseas assets of American companies are placed in this study at $60-billion. This is about twice the foreign assets of other countries' corporations.

Dr. Rolfe points out, however, that both the Netherlands and Switzerland invest abroad a greater percentage of their gross national product than does the United States. "France, Germany and Japan probably lag," he reports, "but the latter two promise to catch up quickly."

* * *

June 6, 1971

OVERSEAS EARNINGS BOLSTER U.S. COMPANIES

Gains Help To Offset Domestic Decline

By BRENDAN JONES

"Foreign business made all the difference." . . . "It pulled us out of the hole. . . ."

Such comments by major companies' officials have become fairly common lately in response to the question of how important foreign sales and earnings have been in offsetting the unfavorable effects of the domestic recession.

That overseas operations have given a more-than-usual lift to over-all performance of many of the country's multinational corporations has been evident in the recent run of annual and first-quarter earnings reports.

In many cases the reports have shown gains in foreign business ranging upwards from 15 to 25 per cent acting as a strong counterbalance to the slacker showing on the domestic side of ledgers. And the regularity of the evidence appears to indicate that it is not merely the experience of a few companies. In some industries, foreign business also has offset strike losses.

Clearly, multinational operation has been proving what it is intended to be—the diversification of markets that evens out the ups and downs of recessions in different parts of the world. But it would seem that it has taken a prolonged domestic recession to give special emphasis to this almost axiomatic, reason-for-being aspect of the multinational corporation.

A canvass last week of more than 15 multinational companies disclosed not only the recent profit contribution of foreign business, but also indicated that the surge of expansion abroad of American business is beginning to pay off handsomely.

The canvass, on a random sampling basis, included companies in a variety of fields—automotive, chemical, electronic, metals and a mix of consumer products. In addition to leaders such as General Motors, International Business Machines, Union Carbide and others, the check-out included some medium-sized multinationals.

Along with the statistics, comment was obtained on how corporate officials view foreign business both now and in the future. Among highlights of the findings were the rising percentage of foreign business in total operations of many companies—approaching a rather magic 50 per cent mark—and in a few instances, the emergence of foreign earnings last year as the chief source of profit.

Some of the other findings follow:

For IBM the steady rise of foreign sales through its World Trade Corporation, produced earnings last year that for the first time were more than 50 per cent of the total. Earnings in the United States for 1970—$505-million—were, in fact, some $31-million less than in 1969. But earnings abroad from 108 countries—$512.5-million—were up nearly $115-million, a seesaw reversal of the previous year's performance.

From a peak of $601-million in 1968, IBM's domestic annual earnings have dropped by almost $100-million, but in the same time, international earnings have risen by nearly $242-million.

Against this background, I.B.M.'s chairman, Thomas J. Watson Jr., had good reason to comment at the company's recent annual meeting on the steady growth of foreign operations.

"During the year just closed," he said, "more of I.B.M.'s profit was derived outside the United States than inside—a very exciting turning point in our history."

For companies such as Union Carbide and Minnesota Mining and Manufacturing, which produce and market in all but the Communist countries, foreign business, as against only slight gains in domestic sales, gave a healthy tone to 1970 annual reports.

The big chemical company, which has the largest international sales of any of the American chemical companies, was slightly under its 1969 total for domestic operations, with sales of $2.16-billion. But international sales, at $869.7-million, were up 13 per cent, accounting for 29 per cent of the total, as against 26 per cent in 1969, and this trend has held through the company's first-quarter report.

Maynard H. Patterson, vice president of 3-M's international group, said, "We have been mighty glad to have our foreign business, and our diversification both in products and in markets has proven just the benefit we sought, a way of washing out the bumps of ups and downs in business and also in currency values."

Last year, 3-M's domestic sales, at $1.08-billion, were just $5-million over the 1969 total. But international sales, at $605-million, were up by $70-million, and were close to twice their volume in 1966.

"We are looking ahead," Mr. Patterson commented, "to seeing our international business become the greater part of the total than domestic business. We still haven't attained the penetration of foreign markets we want, but I think that by the early nineteen-eighties, our international sales will have passed the 50 per cent mark."

Despite the growing share of producing countries in oil revenues, the Standard Oil Company (N.J.) saw foreign earnings again become the major part of its total last year. For Standard, foreign earnings had been showing a declining percentage of the total, but in 1970, with domestic earnings at $647-million, they moved ahead to $681-million, or 52 per cent of the total. The gain on the domestic side was $18-million, as against $85-million on the international side.

Commenting on foreign developments, Emilio G. Collado, Standard's executive vice president and a director, said:

"It is particularly clear today that the results of foreign investment are now paying off. Without foreign income, the earnings of many companies would not have fared so well, and without remittances from abroad, our balance-of-payments situation would be much more critical than it already is.

"Direct foreign investment has produced $31.6-billion in profit remittances over the past five years, or $17-billion more than the net capital outflow of $14.6-billion for new investment during the same period."

Commenting on the National Cash Register Company's 1970 showing, in which foreign sales made a seesaw pattern with domestic, Harry R. Wise, the company's vice president for international marketing, said:

"N.C.R.'s strength as a truly multinational company was never better in evidence than in 1970. While economic conditions in the United States were less than good, the International division was able to maintain a fair head of steam with its 25th consecutive record year."

N.C.R., now strong in computer sales, is among the oldest American companies in foreign business, with production and sales in 100 countries. Its domestic earnings last year were $70-million, down from $95.7-million in 1969. But international earnings of $73-million reduced the loss with a gain of $15-million.

Although hard hit in 1970 by the United Auto Workers strike, General Motors found some compensation in a lesser decline in overseas earnings. G.M.'s total earnings last year of $609-million were down sharply from the $1,711,000,000 total of 1969. Overseas earnings—$118-million—also were down, but to a lesser extent, from $160-million in 1969 and accounted for 19 per cent of total earnings, as against 9 per cent the preceding year.

For General Electric, international sales produced a larger percentage of earnings gain than domestic last year. Net international earnings, at $66-million, were up $18-million, or 37 per cent, while the domestic net of $242-million, was up $32-million, or 14 per cent.

Armco Steel Corporation, the leader in its industry in international operations—30 companies in 20 countries and distributors in 70 others—had a 15 per cent rise in foreign sales last year to $218.8-million, while domestic sales, at $1,365,000,000, fell slightly below their 1969 level.

The Dow Chemical company, another leader in international business, has shown a stronger performance abroad than at home through 1970 and the first quarter of this year. Domestic sales last year, at $1,139,000,000, were off from the preceding year, but earnings held even at $144-million. Foreign sales last year, at $771-million, were up $128-million, while foreign earnings rose $20-million to $115-million.

C. B. Branch, Dow president, said that foreign markets obviously would continue to be of great importance and added that "we expect to achieve the 50–50 ratio between the United States and the rest of the world that we have been working toward within the next few years."

Some other companies for which foreign business has been a substantial plus in total returns were Johnson & Johnson, Gillette, Goodyear Tire & Rubber and Cincinnati Milacron.

Johnson & Johnson did well both at home and abroad with net earnings last year of $83.6-million, of which $30-million came from international sales. For Gillette, foreign income of $36-million last year topped domestic by nearly $3-million, a reversal of the 1969 pattern.

* * *

December 5, 1971

LET THE MULTINATIONALS HELP

By JOSE R. BEJARANO

The multinational corporation today is a force that can serve global needs of mankind far better than the medieval concept of nation states.

Such a corporation may be the beginning of a modern supranational form adapted to many worldwide functions. The modern multinational corporation brings together materials, energy, capital and technology, each of which may be concentrated in different parts of this planet, to serve the world market.

Technology transfer, a new area with basic supranational scope, provides an opportunity for pioneer supranational corporate thought and action.

It is impractical, and certainly wasteful, for each country to try to generate its own all-embracing technical knowledge. First, the time spans for developing modern technology of 10, 20 or more years are too long. Second, it would be impossible in many cases. The total cost of technology in such fields as nuclear energy, aerospace and communications far exceeds the gross national product of most nations.

The first step in solving a problem is to recognize it.

Leaders of backward nations must recognize that solutions of technological problems are beyond their means. It is too costly an experiment to find this out by trial and error.

Officials of emerging countries can best foster technological development by enlisting the aid of the transnational business enterprise.

Resources and experience in the modern world of this enterprise are far greater than those of ethnocentric nation states that have been left behind just because of their lack of capacity.

In the pre-industrial era the needs of a society depended upon materials and energy, mostly in the form of human labor. With the advent of the machine, capital became an equal factor with materials and energy. Invisibly, just as pre-industrial labor included craft, capital included technology—how to use the machine.

Even though the industrial revolution found explosive expression through the new legal concept, the corporation, technology remained an implicit factor, more or less accepted as a part of capital when recognized.

Corporations grew, performing miracles beyond imagination and transcending national boundaries. At the same time the nation state, that archaic political form that has survived from the past through a tax partnership with industry, felt the threat of its partner, not only for its domestic prowess but also because the corporation, unlike the state, was not bound by lines on the map.

After recognizing technology as a partner equal in importance to capital, energy and materials, yesterday's governments sought to purchase or steal it in some instances. In others, the creation of technology was stimulated.

Some corporations secreted their technology, some sold it, some traded it. And recognizing its tremendous power, they set about a massive effort to enhance it in a proprietary form.

Some wealthy nations, made rich by industrial enterprise, tried to match or surpass the private corporation through government-sponsored programs. The poorer nations found themselves hopelessly behind, with their sovereignty at risk. For the technology they could buy turned out to be at best today's technology—which tomorrow would be yesterday's technology. Their scant capital driveled into obsolescence. Hopefully, they learned that the problem was greater than they could solve alone.

Before the days of political awakening, developing countries encouraged the multinational corporation to serve national markets and to provide export income. The positive response of multinational corporations in such instances is well known. Many of these same nations, however, under the guise of threatened sovereignty, or to serve political demagoguery, have seriously disrupted the delicate technology transfer network for which they have no alternative.

There are many pressures today to take away from corporations their discretionary practices with regard to technology transfer. There are political pressures that say we are exporting jobs when we are exporting technology. There are nationalists who want to prevent high technology products from being manufactured abroad. And there are pragmatists who want to recoup technological leadership in certain areas where we have been edged out.

Valid arguments can be made for these positions, at least on a short-term basis. Certainly, however, protecting excessive labor costs, declining productivity, obsolescent plants, low product quality or mismanagement are not bases for a valid argument.

The disruptive effects of nationalistic politics are exactly contrary to the alleged concern of some political leaders for the welfare of their people. If the starving and illiterate people of the backward nations are to be fed and educated, they certainly should enlist the aid of those who have learned to do it.

It used to be said that money was a very special thing because it could not be bought with happiness. We are now finding out that technology also is something special, since it cannot be bought with only money.

Many experts believe that the basic cultural patterns of undeveloped nations must change before technology can become a part of their life. Caryl Haskins has pointed out that Asians missed the scientific revolution of the past three centuries because through their history their technology was pragmatic and utilitarian in orientation rather than curious and creative.

Governments are notoriously poor managers. Few nations in the world have the management experience and capability

that we can find in most large corporations. Let us remember that people are poor because of antiquated social structures—not because of business.

Logically, therefore, we should reject the artificial dichotomy between government interest and private interest. There is only one interest, the social interest, and all efforts should be reconciled to serve it. Political abuse is just as censurable as business abuse—Big Brother Government is just as bad as Big Stick Business.

Responsible governments in a cooperative effort with enlightened world corporations can serve efficiently the social interest everywhere.

Nationalism must be recognized as an expensive emotion.

The world corporation to be effective must reach across what essentially are imaginary lines on the map to synergize crude natural resources of undeveloped regions with the capital, technology and markets of the rest of the world.

National technology policies usually are related to certain broad national objectives such as environmental protection, enhancement of international economy, competitiveness in external markets, military capability and intellectual expansion.

An analysis of these objectives leads us to a grouping of technologies into various classes whose distinctiveness is self-evident.

First, there is the Basic Social Group, which would include sanitation, medicine, water treatment, power production, pollution, building, transportation, agriculture and food processing. These are indeed important technologies relating to the elementary fabric of society. As such, each should be readily accessible on a transnational basis, possibly under supranational supervision, but providing for adequate compensation of the developers.

The second group is the Cultural Group. This includes software technology of how to educate, how to govern, how to sell, how to manage, and covers an area of broad human application. This group differs from the first, however, in that it is more closely related to the individual character and mores of the social milieu where it is to be applied.

The third group, the Scientific Group, includes a very advanced field of technology devoted to finding new knowledge. Naturally, this is a highly coveted area, accessible only to highly developed nations who have the necessary trained manpower and financial resources. From this knowledge will grow new technologies.

The fourth array, the Military Group, involves such technologies as how to destroy, or how to make instruments of destruction, or how to manage armies, or how to occupy a territory. This has been in the past an area of very large technology flow between allies while at the same time a most secretly guarded area among potential enemies.

Finally, we have the fifth aggregation, the Industrial Group, which is best known, and in many ways resembles the Military Group because of its commercial warfare aspects—easily transferable among friends, elusive among enemies.

The world business enterprise, sometimes more powerful than nations, has spawned new social structures. Thoughtful persons in all walks of life may well agree with Anthony Jay when he says:

"I find it hard to imagine what harm the international corporation could do that would be comparable to the harm that has been done by nation states."

Remember that the American technological explosion at the beginning of this century was based largely upon European scientific discovery. Charles Kettering wisely put it:

"When you close the door to technology transfer, you close out more than you close in."

Mr. Bejarano is vice president of the Xerox Corporation in charge of its Latin American division. This article is based on remarks he made last month at the National Foreign Trade Convention.

* * *

June 19, 1972

MULTINATIONAL COMPANIES SHIFT COURSE

Survey Finds They Adopt New Methods to Prosper

By BRENDAN JONES

"There is only one way to keep a business going in a foreign country. It must provide benefits for them and for us. You might be able to buy the government for a while, but that kind of arrangement won't last. You'll be out in the end."

This comment by a British executive appears to reflect the working philosophy of most multinational corporations in meeting the growing force of "economic nationalism" in many parts of the world.

It was made in a survey by correspondents of The New York Times on the changing relationships of governments and the big international companies—mainly American—that have burgeoned with the expansion of world trade.

A main finding of the study was that in much of the developing world—notably, the Latin American and the oil-producing countries—the big international companies now are more on the defensive against the power of government than the other way about.

A Sharp Contrast

This role reversal, which has come in only relatively recent years, is in sharp contrast with a past era of "economic imperialism," when international corporate giants such as United Fruit virtually owned many countries.

Some other highlights of The Times correspondents' survey:
- Economic nationalism, broadly, a heightened concern of governments and peoples with control of their resources and economies, is increasing in many forms. These range

from large government ownership of foreign companies to greater regulation of foreign investment.
- Multinational corporations, however, still retain great political influence in the industrial countries—their "native habitat"—but it is exercised with more circumspection than in the past.
- A trend toward partnership of government and business, primarily in the international field. This development is typified by the term, "Japan, Inc.," a reference to the close collaboration of government and industry that has been a dynamic force in Japan's economic upsurge. Trade competition and regional blocs seem to foreshadow also a "U.S.A., Inc.," and a "Europe, Inc."

The Times' study, which covered major world regions, was prompted by the controversy that recently has flared over the impact, politically and economically, of the multinational corporation.

The big world companies, more numerous and more diversified than earlier counterparts, have evolved with the reduction of trade barriers.

In geographical "spread" many clearly range far beyond the bounds of any national or multinational authority.

Some are wealthier than the countries in which they operate and their interests in one part of the world may adversely affect operations in individual countries.

A main spark to controversy has been the charge that the International Telephone and Telegraph Corporation, one of the biggest multinationals, tried to protect its holdings in Chile by plotting to overthrow that country's Marxist President, Salvador Allende Gossens.

Debate over whether the multinational, as such, is good or bad for national economic interest, has been sustained by organized labor's demands for curbs on foreign investments by the big companies. The contention is that these investments in plants abroad are "exporting American jobs."

As a result, major unions are backing the Burke-Hartke Bill to provide Presidential authority to restrict such investment and also limit imports.

From being a major supporter of liberal trade, organized labor has swung to a protectionist stance with the multinationals as their chief target.

Critics of the multinationals see them as shadowy private states putting their own interests ahead of those of any single country. Proponents see them as efficient, profitable instruments for world development.

The Times study indicated that there is as yet little precise evidence to show what effects the multinational corporation—as an institution—may have on national economic policies.

It is evident, however, that the rise of economic nationalism represents a confrontation of governments and multinationals that reflects a considerable uneasiness over the power of the big corporations.

The sheer size of multinationals and the fact that they are largely an enigma to the average person seems to be a main basis for the fears they arouse.

Spread of Concerns Traced

This is aptly expressed by Professor Raymond Vernon in his recent book, "Sovereignty at Bay," on the spread of American multinational companies.

Professor Vernon is an economist and professor of international management at Harvard University's Graduate School of Business Administration. Of the multinationals, he writes:

"They sit uncomfortably in the structure of long-established political and social institutions. They sprawl across national boundaries, linking the assets and activities of different national jurisdictions with an intimacy that seems to threaten the concept of the nation as an integral unit.

"Accordingly, they stir uneasy questions in the minds of men. Is the multinational enterprise undermining the capacity of nations to work for the welfare of their own people? Is the multinational enterprise being used by a dominant power (read 'United States') as a means of penetrating and controlling the economies of other countries?"

Professor Vernon gives no answers to the questions but suggests the creation of a kind of global Justice Department to regulate multinational concerns.

Code Being Drafted

A similar approach has been taken for self-regulation by the International Chamber of Commerce, which presently is drafting what might be called a "code of good behavior" for both governments and multinationals in their treatment of each other.

The sweep of economic nationalism, The Times report indicated, continues in conspicuous forms in the less-developed, ex-colonial countries.

An outstanding example of its effects was the success last year of the 11-nation organization of Petroleum Exporting Countries in winning an increased share of oil countries' earnings from 50 to 75 per cent.

O.P.E.C. members possess about 70 per cent of the world's proven crude oil reserves. And in recent weeks, they have begun, with Iraq's nationalism of the Western-owned Iraq Petroleum Company, a movement for fuller ownership of the big oil companies properties.

The take-over of the once powerful oil companies has followed also the partial or full nationalization of international copper companies in Zambia, Zaire (the former Congo) and Chile. The trend here is with companies involved with natural resources, a sensitive point with economic nationalists.

Sophistication Grows

There is evidence also that governments of developing countries, apart from whether they favor socialistic policies, have also gained a greater sophistication about the earnings of big multinationals and the extend to which they can tolerate government participation.

There is, in effect, a kind of trade-off in that the governments need the revenue, the technology and the sense of control, while private corporations will continue at a smaller share of profits.

Economic nationalism has shown itself also in moves by the Canadian Government—although considered mild—for restriction on foreign investment for the take-over of existing Canadian companies rather than for starting new enterprises. In Australia, which like Canada has been an active promoter of foreign investment, similar regulations are being prepared.

The kind of counter-trend in the more developed countries, where multinationals appear to be maintaining influence, may or may not reflect a deliberate exertion of power by the big companies, the survey indicated.

Rather, the main evidence is that in the industrialized countries, those of Western Europe and also the United States, there is a tendency for governments to be pro-business.

Multinational corporations in countries such as France and Britain are said by observers to have "enormous" political influence, but there is no surface evidence that it is exerted in other than legitimate ways.

As in this country, the survey reports said, big companies practice "conventional lobbying"—a term that takes in all the influence promotion devices—both at home and abroad.

These may include everything from above-board campaigning for or against legislation to the ethically gray areas of lavish entertainment and nepotism.

In a circumspect country such as the Netherlands it is no secret that a company such as Unilever will be assured a sympathetic hearing by government on any matters affecting its prices or earnings.

Top Jobs Assured

Equally, in another circumspect country—Switzerland—the fact that former presidents of the country can be virtually certain of a top job with multinational companies such as Nestle or Brown Bovari raises few eyebrows.

In this country, multinationals seem to be starting a campaign against their critics. The main attack so far has been against the Burke-Hartke Bill in the contention that multinationals have increased domestic employment more than other companies.

There are assertions also that the multinational is the great hope of developing countries and the key to solution of world problems such as poverty and food production.

The growing overlap of the government and business worlds in many countries seems to foreshadow the kind of partnership expressed by the term "Japan, Inc."

For this country, the Nixon economic program has frankly stressed that increased sale of cars is a key economic need, so that, in effect, what will be good for the country will be good for Detroit.

The Administration, in addition to its moves for reshaping world monetary and trade relations, has also taken a lead in making government the means to attaining textile and steel import quota agreements.

And in Europe, the Common Market is a good way along to closer government-business collaboration.

For the multinational and for government, the old byword seems appropriate: "If you can't lick them, join them."

* * *

October 25, 1972

'THE NEW GLOBALISTS'

_____

Multinational Corporations Are Held To Create a Basis for World Peace

_____

By LEONARD SILK

In 1848 Karl Marx and Friedrich Engels put forth the thesis that world peace and a new world order would ultimately be founded upon the common economic interests of working-men in all countries. "Workers of the world, unite!" proclaimed the Communist Manifesto.

Economic Analysis

Now, after a century of global wars, some leading businessmen are offering a counter thesis: that multinational business is creating the basis for peace and a new world order. A spokesman of this doctrine, William I. Spencer, president of the First National City Corporation, recently declared in an address to the American Chamber of Commerce in Frankfurt, West Germany:

"The political boundaries of nation-states are too narrow and constricted to define the scope and sweep of modern business."

Quiet Progress Seen

At a time when politicians have been moving to create regional markets to supersede national markets, he said, businessmen—whom he called "the new globalists"—have been making quiet progress on a much larger scale.

"They see the entire world as a market and as a site for the production of goods and services," said Mr. Spencer. "They understand that ideas can be born anywhere and expressed in any language. They seek profitable opportunity in addressing themselves not to the demands of the privileged few but to the urgent needs of the overwhelming many. Operating with this kind of global vision, they have created that unique economic phenomenon known as the multinational corporation."

Lest this sound like pie in the sky, he noted that his own company had tripled its foreign branches in the last 10 years and now carried on banking operations in 90 countries, with stockholders in 63 countries.

Output Compared

More broadly, he said, multinational corporations now produce an estimated $450-billion in goods and services—15 per cent of the gross world product.

This multinational explosion, said Mr. Spencer, is much more than what Jean-Jacques Servan-Schreiber, the French editor, first named "the American Challenge." The Citicorp

president said that, of the $450-billion total, American multinational companies account for only $200-billion, foreign multinationals based abroad and also operating in the United States account for $100-billion, and what he calls "interproduction abroad" accounts for the remaining $150-billion.

But a leading academic authority on the multinational corporation, Prof. Raymond Vernon of the Harvard Graduate School of Business Administration, warns that resistances to the rapid growth of the multinationals are building up.

Observing the upsurge of nationalism and the squeeze being put on the multinationals in oil, copper and other industries in many parts of Latin America, Africa, the Middle East and Asia and the growth of anti-Americanism in Canada and Western Europe, Professor Vernon asks whether the multinationals may not be approaching the end of an era.

Growth and Decay

He observes that multinational business in particular areas has characteristically undergone "life cycles" of growth and decay. At first, the poorer "host" country eagerly invites the multinational companies in because it needs capital, technological knowledge and access to foreign markets.

But, as time passes, the host country grows less dependent on foreign capital and technology. For a time, it may still fear loss of access to foreign markets. But, as its domestic economy grows and its knowledge of other markets abroad widens, the host country expresses its outrage over the inequity of the terms on which the multinational corporation is operating and exploiting its resources and people. It may eventually expel the foreign element altogether.

That is the scenario unfolding in oil. Professor Vernon thinks the multinational oil companies have played into the hands of the oil-producing countries by—as he sees it—exaggerating the world fuel shortage.

Similar life cycles, he says, can be found in the role of multinational companies in high-technology industries. At first the host countries are worried about technological gaps and capital shortages. When their fear of such gaps and shortages diminishes, they take a less hospitable view toward foreign investors.

At the moment the Europeans are inclined to believe that the technological gap in which they lagged behind the United States—and which alarmed them until the mid-nineteen-sixties—has been closed. They are now more concerned about inflation than capital shortage.

But Professor Vernon thinks the Europeans' complacency may be premature. He foresees a renewal of American technological supremacy in several major areas, such as environmental protection and the development of deep ocean resources.

Indeed, he expects American leads to continue in computers, outer space and aircraft. He says that Europe is littered with the "bleached bones" of failed efforts in those areas.

Certain Advantages

The United States, he believes, has certain enduring advantages in high-technology fields: its high proportion of capital to labor; its very large, high-income domestic market; the heavy demands of the Federal Government; the ample resources in science, technology and higher education, and its national attitudes toward change and competition.

In the diverse and turbulent American economy, says Professor Vernon, "businesses cannot easily negotiate with their environment to stand still." That is, American companies cannot control and moderate change as readily as can companies in Europe or Japan.

Even if American businessmen were willing to enter into such anticompetitive deals, the United States Government stands by with an antitrust pitchfork, which it is fully prepared to jab at giants. So European companies, to increase profits, tend to focus on cost-cutting; Americans are more likely to try to reduce business risks and go after bigger profits through product innovation and diversification.

But Professor Vernon finds no basis for American smugness or euphoria in the likelihood that the United States may re-open technological gaps as the nineteen seventies wear on. He fears new gaps may worsen political tensions if the foreigners' sense of dependence on the United States starts to grow again.

Businessmen—Mr. Spencer's "new globalists"—can't cope with such nationalistic tensions and have not the power to offset national governments, even small ones. "The firm cannot govern," says Professor Vernon, "and government is the problem of the human race."

Yet, within the pattern of "minicycles" that in the past have affected such diverse industries as railroads, life insurance, public utilities, oil, copper and other resources and that may yet arrest the postwar multinational boom in manufacturing and finance, there does appear to be a strong, over-all growth trend.

In 1919 there were only about 180 multinational corporations; today there are some 4,000. The growth trend is likely to slacken, but it still seems far from its limit.

Many factors are working on the side of the business globalists. The speed and availability of communications and transportation are increasing. The international money and capital markets are expanding. There is growing desire in all countries—Communist and capitalist alike—for economic development. And the onrush of new technology promises, on one hand, to satisfy the desire for higher living standards and, on the other hand, intensifies fear of war between the great powers.

Whether the politicians can create the enabling conditions for further progress of the multinational revolution remains the great unknown.

* * *

November 20, 1972

NO U.S. JOB LOSSES FOUND AT MULTINATIONAL CONCERNS

By EDWIN L. DALE Jr.

Special to The New York Times

WASHINGTON, Nov. 19—The most exhaustive survey yet made by the Government of the operations of large multinational companies supports a central conclusion of various private surveys—that domestic employment and exports of these companies have continued to grow relatively rapidly despite their foreign investments.

This and other results of the survey were disclosed last week by government analysts who put the study together. It was released earlier in the week by the Commerce Department in the form of nearly 100 pages of tables, without any interpretive comment.

An earlier and less thorough study of multinational companies by a different division of the Commerce Department came under considerable criticism for its statistical methods.

On the key and controversial issues involved, the one released last week by the highly respected Bureau of Economic Analysis appears to lead to the same basic conclusions, however.

The sensitivity of the data arises from the strongly held position of organized labor that the multinational companies are "exporting jobs." In the case of the newest study, policy-making officials of the Commerce Department apparently decided to let the figures speak for themselves.

The survey provides extensive detail on the operations of 298 United States-based multinational companies with about 5200 foreign affiliates. The years covered are 1966 and 1970.

Highlights of Survey

The following were some highlights derived from the figures by Commerce Department analysts:

- Domestic employment of the 298 companies rose by 2.7 per cent a year during this period, while total private employment in the economy grew by 1.8 per cent a year.
- The same conclusion on employment growth was reached when comparison was made on an industry-by-industry basis.
- Exports of the 298 companies rose from $12.7-billion in 1966 to $29-billion in 1970, a faster rate of growth than for the nation's total exports.
- The companies also showed a growth in imports, but their surplus of exports rose to $7.6-billion in 1970 from $5.3-billion in 1966—a time when the nation's over-all trade surplus was declining from $3.6-billion to $1.9-billion.
- There was a rise from $3.4-billion to $6.2-billion in sales by foreign affiliates to the parent companies, but the great bulk of this was accounted for by "United States-type" automobiles from Canada under the special auto agreement, and petroleum imports.

The survey showed that sales, assets and employment of the overseas affiliates grew much faster in percentage terms in the 1966–70 period than those of the parent companies.

But the parents remained substantially larger than their offspring. For example, total sales of the parent companies in 1970 were $309.2-billion, compared with sales of $114.7-billion by the foreign affiliates.

* * *

September 12, 1973

NADER ACCUSES MULTINATIONALS

Says Concerns Use Secrecy to Perpetrate Abuses

By KATHLEEN TELTSCH
Special to The New York Times

UNITED NATIONS, N.Y., Sept. 12—Ralph Nader, the consumer advocate, charged today that the abuses committed by the giant corporations were concealed by secrecy. He urged a United Nations panel inquiring into the impact of multinational companies to try to get at the "priceless information" now being withheld.

Mr. Nader, testifying at an open hearing here, declared that the success of the consumer movement in the United States has depended on rooting out information. He cited the pressure on the automotive industry to recall vehicles once the defects in their manufacture were disclosed.

"The test of the mettle of the United Nations' inquiry," he declared, is whether it can get corporations to divulge information about their corporate behavior now kept secret."

Mr. Nader, in a wide-ranging attack on the conduct abroad of "world corps," as he called them, charged some companies with dumping products on overseas markets when they were compelled for reasons of safety to remove them from United States sale.

He accused other concerns of selecting overseas sites for pollutant-creating manufacturing. American-based companies permit mining operations in Asia, Africa and Latin America that are virtually "snake pits" and would not be tolerated at home, he added.

These and other abuses continue, Mr. Nader maintained, because "world corps" operate without any controls or regulations on their conduct.

Mr. Nader's attack on the multinationals followed a day of public hearings in which five of the top companies had testified, emphasizing the contributions their operations were making to the economic development of poorer countries.

Ernest Keller, president of the Adela Investment Company, another speaker, told the panel that multinationals increasingly were becoming the "convenient scapegoat" for every mishap.

They are being blamed, he declared, "for the consequence of unseasonable economic and monetary policies, unviable economic concepts, experiments and legislation, that is, for every conceivable mistake and failure for which no one else wants to accept the blame."

* * *

September 12, 1973

MULTINATIONAL COMPANIES DEFEND ROLE BEFORE U.N.

By KATHLEEN TELTSCH
Special to The New York Times

UNITED NATIONS, N.Y., Sept. 11—Leaders of five big corporations went before a United Nations panel today to insist their concerns behave as good guests abroad, contribute to the prosperity of the countries in which they do business and do not meddle in politics.

Almost without exception, they also complained of exaggerated fears that the increasing size and spread of their commercial empires made them an all-powerful group operating beyond the control and regulation of governments.

These were recurrent themes at the opening here of public hearings on the activities of multinational corporations—an inquiry stimulated largely by Chile's charges that the International Telephone and Telegraph Corporation and the Kennecott Copper Corporation tried to subvert the Marxist-oriented regime of Dr. Salvador Allende Gossens. Reports today said the Allende Government had been ousted.

The panel is to take further testimony here and abroad and in the next 12 months make recommendations on the role and activities of some national corporations. One idea already proposed in a United Nations' study is that some form of international monitoring be devised for international corporations.

While the corporation spokesmen today were clearly unwilling to embrace the idea of regulations of their operation, all in varying degrees saw some areas for possible United Nations action, such as in harmonizing tax laws.

There also was sentiment for selective and gradual action that could lead to an agreement covering direct foreign investment.

"No one is in the dark," remarked L. K. Jha, former governor of the Reserve Bank of India and the panel chairman, as the open meetings began in an atmosphere of cordiality. Despite such reassurances, some of the corporation spokesmen tended to sound defensive as they mentioned their concerns' support of such causes as building schools and hospitals or stressed their policies of training foreign nationals for key posts.

Action Areas Discussed

However, some areas for international action did find favor with the corporations:

Irving S. Shapiro, vice chairman of the board of E. I. du Pont de Nemours, Inc., told the panel that serious study should be given to international agreements covering foreign investments that would be similar to those already in existence for trade under the General Agreement on Tariffs and

Trade. Du Pont would like to participate in such a study, Mr. Shapiro declared. Like others, he also cautioned against exaggerating the power of multinationals to unduly influence governments and pointed out that even the smaller states possessed enormous power to control foreign enterprises, "ranging from the subtleties of taxation to expropriation."

Jacques G. Maisonrouge, president of the I.B.M. World Trade Corporation, cautioned the panel against devising institutions for devices that would restrict the useful role that such concerns can play in economic development. Among other measures he had in mind, he said, were demands for divided ownership or local control and he warned: "moves such as these would cripple the effectiveness of many high technology companies, most certainly including "I.B.M."

The I.B.M. executive said a proposal for a code of conduct for multinationals—made in the United Nations study—would be difficult but worth pursuing. It should emphasize greater employment of foreign nationals, especially on directors' boards, he said, adding that this was I.B.M. policy. All the Americans working aboard could be flown back in a single aircraft—providing it was a 747 plane, he said, evoking laughter.

John J. Powers Jr., honorary chairman of the board of Pfizer, Inc., was strongly critical of proposals to create international machinery to control or supervise foreign investment.

"In my view this is an attempt to do too much too soon. For that reason I believe it would fail and we would have lost ground." The most that the United Nations could do at this time, he maintained, was provide a forum for discussion.

Thomas A. Murphy, vice chairman of General Motors, expressed skepticism about attempting to make multinationals accountable to the international community. To add still another layer of regulations to world business would be a step backward, he declared.

Emilio G. Collado, executive vice president of the Exxon Corporation, favored the idea of a voluntary code of conduct, saying it would discourage some corporations from activities that create ill-will. However, he suggested the need for international agreement to reduce the investment risks taken by multinational corporations.

* * *

May 5, 1975

U.S. COMPANY PAYOFFS WAY OF LIFE OVERSEAS

By MICHAEL C. JENSEN

American companies doing business abroad are spending hundreds of millions of dollars each year for agents' fees, commissions and outright payoffs to foreign officials.

The payments range from $5 bribes for customs agents and other minor officials to multimillion-dollar rake-offs on defense contracts. Sometimes even heads of state are involved.

The practice of funneling cash into the hands of government officials or their representatives is long-standing and is defended by many businessmen as the only way they can compete effectively abroad. Indeed, some such payments are officially sanctioned by the United States Government.

Nevertheless, the practice is coming under increased scrutiny in the United States, spurred by disclosures that the United Brands Company, based in New York, paid more than $2-million in bribes to officials in Honduras and Europe.

The Senate Foreign Relations subcommittee on multinational corporations has begun a full inquiry into the United Brands case.

It is also looking into expenditures by the Northrop Corporation, which paid out more than $30-million in agents' fees and commissions, much of it for overseas sales, from 1971 to 1973.

The Gulf Oil Company's disbursements of more than $4-million overseas, most of it reportedly to a single unidentified country, is also being investigated.

Until now, most of the Government attention to corporate bribery has come from the Securities and Exchange Commission, which is responsible for insuring adequate disclosure of corporate activities to shareholders. The current investigations are an outgrowth of the Watergate prosecutions of illegal campaign contributions.

The Internal Revenue Service, which is concerned with the proper handling of foreign transactions for tax purposes, also is looking into some of the foreign situations.

It is apparently not a violation of United States law for an American corporation to bribe foreign officials. Such action may be illegal in the host country, but bribery laws are seldom enforced in many parts of the world.

Few American businessmen will discuss their companies' payoff practices openly, although some agreed to interviews with news reporters with the understanding that they not be identified.

Some of the most blatant cases of bribery have become public, however, and a few have spawned major scandals overseas.

In the United Brands case, for example, Eli M. Black, the chief executive of the company, committed suicide shortly before the company's overseas bribes become known publicly. The ensuing scandal also resulted in the overthrow of the chief of state of Honduras, Gen. Oswaldo Lopez Arellano.

In other cases, there is almost certain to be a growing furor as further details become known. For example, the reported testimony of Bob R. Dorsey, chairman of the Gulf Oil Corporation, about cash "contributions" abroad is being studied by the S.E.C.

Mr. Dorsey and other Gulf officials reportedly told the S.E.C. that foreign politicians had forced them to pay large amounts of cash in order to stay in business.

While some commissions and agents' fees are nothing more than thinly disguised bribes, others are said to be legitimate payments to local representatives overseas, designed to cut through red tape.

The Defense Department authorizes defense contractors to pay "reasonable" agents' fees as part of their "cost of sales" and to pass these costs along to the Pentagon when it acts as the middleman in arms contracts.

In an advisory memorandum issued to several defense contractor associations last summer, the Defense Security Assistance Agency said United States arms manufacturers selling major systems usually limited their standard agents' fees to 4 to 6 per cent of the selling price. It added, however, that on less expensive equipment the percentage sometimes exceeded 25 per cent.

Some Middle Easterners have gotten rich on such fees. Persian Gulf sources say that Adnan M. Khashoggi, a Saudi Arabian businessman who has an international string of industrial and financial ventures, including a bank in California, made his initial capital as the Saudi agent for Raytheon Hawk missiles and Lockheed aircraft bought by Saudi Arabia. Mr. Khashoggi's connection is said to be his friendship with Prince Sultan, the Saudi Defense Minister, and his commissions were said to run to $10-million to $20-million.

American executives say the Middle East is one of the world's most vexing regions as far as doing business is concerned. An illustration of the problems they face there was contained in a limited-circulation Defense Department memorandum entitled "Agents' Fees in the Middle East."

"There is the classic example," the memo said, "of a new vice president of a United States firm who, after reviewing agents' fees, decided that a local Middle East agent's contract could be canceled. All that the company had in the country at that time was a continuous but lucrative servicing contract that had been negotiated many years ago.

"Within 48 hours after the agent had been canceled all local work permits of the company's employes were withdrawn. Needless to say, the agent was reinstated immediately."

Although the most dramatic instances of corruption are those involving millions of dollars, a far more widespread type of bribery takes place at a much lower level. It is variously called baksheesh, la mordita or dash, depending on whether it is offered in the Middle East, Latin America or Africa.

One businessman in Africa said in an interview: "In countries like Nigeria and Zaire, you have to pay small bribes, called 'dash,' to get anything done. It's part of the price of visas, getting customs clearance on materials—even getting your suitcase in the instance of Nigeria."

In other parts of the world, the pressures take a different form. For example, one type of harassment for American companies in the Philippines is the stream of requests for donations for charities from government and military officials or members of their families. Such requests, invariably granted, sometimes run to more than $100,000.

In Italy, on the other hand, requests are more likely to be for contributions to political parties.

An executive of a United States-controlled multinational electronics group, who insisted on anonymity, said: "To do business in Italy, as in other European countries, you have to render all sorts of favors, including outright bribery.

"It's up to your ingenuity to disguise such practices in reports to your board and in financial statements. You send lavish gifts to key people and their wives. You have your own workers install costly appliances in their seaside villas free of charge. You hire their relatives and protégés if you have staff vacancies. Sometimes cool cash changes hands.

"Don't expect company headquarters to give you any instructions on how to handle such situations," he continued. "You are completely on your own—just keep the sales performance going up."

Although many Americans profess astonishment and sometimes disgust at reports of bribery and under-the-table gratuities offered abroad, such practices are also widespread in this country.

Gifts, some of them lavish, often are pressed on officials with purchasing responsibilities in the United States, and a number of corporate contributions to political campaigns were uncovered during the Watergate investigations.

Furthermore, American companies are quick to point out that overseas competitors also employ such methods, making it more difficult to resist the pressures.

For example, the president of a French-based company in international transport won contracts from a foreign ministry official by seeing that he found his way to one of the exclusive and illegal brothels of Paris. He said he clinched the contract by giving the official's wife a high-speed, electric sewing machine from Switzerland.

The importance that American companies attach to employing local representatives was vividly demonstrated by the International Telephone and Telegraph Corporation in mid-1971 after Salvadore Allende Gossens, a Marxist who was opposed by I.T.T., was elected President of Chile.

Confronted with a hostile regime and anxious to protect its telephone properties, I.T.T. moved quickly to foster better relations. In a memo to P.J. Dunleavy, who is now president of I.T.T., J. W. Guilfoyle, another I.T.T. executive, related what had been done to try to improve matters for the company.

He said that two I.T.T. officials were meeting with a Dr. Schaulson, "the consultant I obtained on our last trip," to determine the outcome of Dr. Schaulson's discussions with President Allende. "Schaulson is a lawyer and a former politician," Mr. Guilfoyle wrote, "and is considered friendly with Allende and, as a Christian Democrat, is not committed to the U.P. [Allende's party]."

Later, despite the hiring of Dr. Schaulson, Chile expropriated the telephone company, and I.T.T. was subsequently compensated by a United States Government agency which insures overseas investments.

I.T.T., in response to a query, confirmed that it had hired a Chilean legal consultant but declined to confirm that it was a Dr. Schaulson. The company said it had hired the consultant on the advice of its Chilean outside counsel.

In the Northrop case, a private report written by the accounting firm of Ernst & Ernst disclosed that Northrop made more than $9-million worth of consultants' payments in 1971, then $7.8-million in 1972 and $12.9-million more in 1973. The report pointed out that the big aircraft manufacturer employed 400 to 500 consultants and agents in the 1971–73 period.

The S.E.C. is looking into these overseas disbursements, which it says were made "without adequate records of controls." The commission also says there was no indication whether services provided in exchange for the $30-million were "commensurate with the amounts paid."

"People have said what can we do," said Irving Pollack, an S.E.C. commissioner. "If we don't do it, the customer will go to the Japanese, or the Germans or someone else, and they will pay off.

"The only answer I can see is if the contract goes to the Japanese or the Germans, the Americans should speak up and say, 'You know, we were offered it, but we didn't take it because they wanted us to put $5-million into a Swiss bank account.' "

* * *

October 14, 1980

A CHINESE FACTORY FAILS ITS FOREIGN INVESTORS

By FOX BUTTERFIELD
Special to the New York Times

PEKING, Oct. 13—The first factory in China built under a system in which a foreign company supplies the machinery and raw materials and is paid back with the processed goods has been forced to close down, at least temporarily, because of poor management and inefficient labor, according to the official People's Daily.

The record of the factory, a wool spinning mill, is likely to raise fresh doubts among foreign businessmen about investing in China. It tends to confirm the complaints of some businessmen about the lack of modern, technically competent Chinese factory managers and the low productivity of Chinese workers.

Evidently to try to head off such fears, the People's Daily published an unusually candid account of the troubles in the factory and said the local authorities had moved to reorganize it.

Factory Built in 1978

According to the paper, the plant was built in 1978 at Zhuhai, on the border of the Portuguese colony of Macao, near Hong Kong. Machinery was supplied by two companies owned by overseas Chinese, Novel Enterprises Ltd. of Hong Kong and Macao Textile Ltd. The foreign partners also provided the raw materials and sent a number of technicians and supervisors to the plant.

This arrangement, called compensation trade, was the first form of foreign investment permitted by Peking. Several hundred such factories have been started in the past two years, largely involving textiles and electronics, with companies from Hong Kong, Japan, the United States and Western Europe. Some have proved highly successful.

Unlike true joint ventures, of which Peking has approved only a handful, the foreign partners have no equity in a compensation trade factory. Instead, they are to be paid back in a specified time for their investment by remission of the fees the plant charges for turning out the finished products. In the case of the wool spinning mill at Zhuhai, the guaranteed payback time was five years. The foreign partners normally sell the processed goods abroad.

Nation's Wages Low

The compensation trade formula was worked out to help China take in new technology and expand its industrial base while the foreign companies took advantage of low Chinese wage levels.

But the People's Daily reported that the wool spinning mill's foreign partners ran into a series of problems almost immediately. After a peak of 76,000 pounds last January, production fell in each succeeding month. "What was more serious was that the quality of yarn was not up to a standard acceptable to customers," the paper said. As a result, the two foreign concerns could not sell their product abroad.

"The two companies often put forward positive proposals to the mill and the leading departments concerned with the aim of improving production," the paper added. "However, the departments concerned failed to attach importance to their suggestions."

Skills Found Lacking

A reporter from the People's Daily who went to the factory found that the basic cause of the troubles was that "the management level of the leading members was too low and the workers lacked specialized knowledge and skills." Because of lack of supervision, "packs of raw material which should have been added" in the wool mixing and matching operation were simply forgotten, the reporter wrote. Some machines were "badly damaged due to lack of maintenance and repair and improper handling," the paper charged.

Management was so careless, the reporter said, that 40 percent of the factory's lights did not work, "but for a long time nobody took any notice."

Although workers in compensation trade factories are supposed to be superior in skill, the paper said that in fact the workers sent to the wool spinning mill had been assigned by the local government manpower department without any check of their qualifications. After getting in the factory, they felt assured of a lifetime job, what the Chinese call an "iron rice bowl," and hence some of them became "desultory in work and refused to follow instructions."

The factory's management had no power to discipline or dismiss these people, the paper related.

Management Called 'Complacent'

Despite all these problems, the paper said, the managers remained "complacent" and did not realize the seriousness of the situation until the two foreign partners announced last month that they were terminating their supply of wool.

Since then the Guangdong provincial branch of China's National Textiles Import and Export Corporation and the

Zhuhai city government have sent teams to help reorganize the factory. The paper did not say when the plant might be reopened.

In a separate but related development, a prominent Chinese economist disclosed in Hong Kong last week that Peking might lower the 33 percent income tax on joint ventures that was put into effect in September. Xue Muqiao, an adviser to the State Planning Commission, told a seminar on China's economic development that Peking might consider a system of preferential treatment for some joint ventures.

His statement suggested that China had been having trouble attracting as many foreign investors for joint venture enterprises as it had hoped to have.

* * *

January 18, 1981

JAPAN'S AMAZING AUTO MACHINE

By HENRY SCOTT STOKES

TOKYO—There was a time when Detroit set out to rule the world. American auto makers built up domestic production, started to export and then followed up by moving plants overseas, to make cars and trucks within the markets they served. With this one-two-three punch, Detroit's Big Three became synonymous with American industrial strength, unquestioned leaders in the automotive field.

No more, of course. Chrysler is on its knees and both General Motors and Ford have reported huge losses recently. The new world appears to belong to Japan. In 1980, this nation pulled ahead of the American auto industry for the first time, producing 11 million cars and trucks, up 10 percent, while the United States industry turned out just 7.8 million, down 30 percent. Imports captured more then one-fifth of the American market itself, and 78 percent of them were made in Japan.

Those represent punches one and two, and on both sides of the Pacific their success is unquestioned, the momentum they have built, unchallenged.

"We recognize we've got one competitor," said Henry V. Leonard Jr., vice president and general manager of the General Motors Overseas Corporation's Japan branch.

"We think the Japanese auto makers' competitiveness in world markets will strengthen in the first half of the 1980's," said Ryoji Musha of the Daiwa Securities Company.

The question for the 1980's is whether Japan will follow the Detroit formula—moving the plants themselves abroad. For a combination of reasons—not the least of which are the pressures for stringent import controls in the Western nations whose own industries are suffering from the Japanese onslaught—a lot of people are betting that it will.

Sygma

Assembling a Civic at the Honda plant in Suzuka.

"Whether we want to or not, we'll have to make cars and trucks around the world," said Tadaaki Yukawa, general manager of the international division at Nissan, makers of Datsuns.

The attitudes that are making that assessment more and more common were underlined last week in Washington, with a Congressionally requested report from the Transportation Department. The report said that the severe troubles in Detroit posed a threat to the national security and urged curbs on imports. "Chrysler is just the tip of the iceberg if we don't move on this problem," said Neil E. Goldschmidt, Transportation Secretary.

So far, Japanese direct investment abroad has been concentrated in third-world countries such as Brazil. Now, likely targets include the tough, and expensive, markets in the United States and Europe. In contrast to Detroit, the Japanese both have the cash necessary for such huge investments and lack the home market that could cushion a closing up of the world market. Of the 11 million vehicles made in Japan last year, only half were absorbed by the home market.

As the question of plant-building abroad becomes more urgent, meanwhile, the Japanese have been doing some careful planning on what partners to take in continuing the expansion. According to interviews with experts within the industry and observers, their strategy includes the following:

• Choosing only the strongest Western companies as partners in the belief that in a few years, only a handful of them will survive, while their weaker brethren go to the wall. Experts at the Industrial Bank of Japan said that the only certain independent survivors in a coming "global small-car war" are General Motors, Volkswagen, Toyota and Nissan—and possibly Ford. Thus, while little Honda supplies parts to ailing British Leyland and is discussing a license agreement under which the British company would make Honda models, bigger Mitsubishi Motors is seeking to sever its ties with limping Chrysler, which has depended upon the Japanese company's Colts and other models as continuing best-sellers.

• Targeting, among the potential foreign partners, those ventures in which the Japanese can dominate through financial and marketing strength. Thus, Toyota is holding talks with Ford with an idea to eventual joint production, Nissan has agreed with Volkswagen to manufacture small Audi Passats in Japan and Honda is negotiating with Fiat of Italy and British Leyland about joint production.

• Entering difficult markets in Europe, notably France and Italy, by alliance not with the reluctant leaders of industry but with medium-sized companies that are candidates for outright takeover. Thus, while maverick Honda has approached Italy's Fiat, Nissan is seeking ties with Alfa Romeo in Italy and small truck makers in Spain.

Of the 11 Japanese auto companies Nissan, and its rival Toyota, are clearly dominant, accounting, with their affiliates, for 63 percent of total output. The Big Two also are separated from other companies as not having close ties to other groups. Toyo Kogyo, the Hiroshima-based No. 3 in the industry, which makes Mazda, is part of the Sumitomo Group and

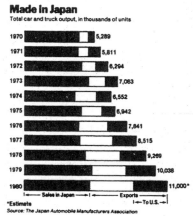

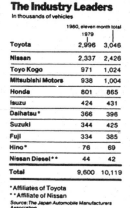

Ford has a 25 percent stake in the company. Mitsubishi Motors belongs to the powerful Mitsubishi Group and is fighting for fourth position in the auto makers' league with Honda. Isuzu, well behind in sixth place, has General Motors as its biggest shareholder with 34 percent of the stock.

Indeed the global industry is a rapidly emerging cats-cradle of increasingly complex cross-ties, including many subsidiary links such as agreement for Nissan to supply Peugeot-Citroen in France with exhaust gas purification technology.

How did the Japanese industry get into its powerful position? "It's not that Japanese cars are so outstanding," said an American here whose company supplies parts to Japanese and American auto makers worldwide. "Renault, for instance, makes cars that are better in some ways and could well cut into Japanese market share after its takeover of American Motors."

As he explained it, the Japanese "are superb copiers. They take Western competitive models, tear them to pieces, learn exactly how to make them and then do better by a mass of minor improvements worked out by design teams. The Japanese advantage is that they produce to a consistent standard, the finish of the cars is good, there are plenty of gimmicks, free extras, and they market well on long-term schedules that don't demand that a manager show an increasing profit quarterly—the Japanese look ahead over a decade or more."

"We are dynamic but not innovators," agreed Ariyoshi Okumura, head of industrial research at the Industrial Bank of Japan. Indeed, Japan appears to have few major surprises down the road in terms of automobile design or engine technology. The companies appear instead to be concentrating on improving what they have, notably on fuel efficiency. Cars here have better fuel economy than in the United States or Europe, all running at better than 30 miles a gallon for small models, and the government set a standard with industry to improve performance another 12.3 percent (from 1978 levels to 1985) in a typically Japanese display of meticulous planning.

The auto makers—particularly Toyota, which is known sardonically to its competitors as "the Toyota bank"—certainly have the financial wherewithal to finance any such advance, and far more. In six of the last 10 years, they have actually reduced the bank loans on which much of Japanese industry borrows. In 1976 and 1977, they were able to finance more than 100 percent of their spending on plant and equipment from internal resources (using the extra to pay back loans) and in 1978 and 1979 were hardly less astonishing, financing well over 90 percent of expenditures with internally generated funds.

Still, there is a reluctance to go head-on with Westerners on their own ground. Some cite the absence of innovation here and the failure of Japan to produce outstanding medium-size prestige cars such as Britain's Jaguar or the German BMW models—both of which sell to discriminating executives in Japan. Others point out worries ranging from a fear that a cut-off of Middle East oil supplies would hurt the industry everywhere, or that a crisis in, say, Poland might hurt international confidence, which appears indispensable to a global drive by Japan. Then there is the attitude that leads to such respectful nods toward the West as occidental manikins in department stores—and Westernized names for the cars sold here.

But there are two other reasons that appear far more important. One is labor. Executives here are appalled by labor conditions in Detroit. "You have this thing called equal opportunity, which means jobs for unqualified minority workers, and then there's the escalating clause in wage contracts to take wages up with the C.P.I.," said an analyst, "and G.M. originated the latter even."

With this in mind, Japanese auto makers say privately that even G.M. may not pose a grave competitive threat, with its planned $40 billion investments in tooling up for production of the new model series. And, they say, they would never be willing to invest in the Northeast. "The South and the Pacific Western rim are far better," said one.

Certainly, the Japanese are wanted in the United States—Toyota has been approached by every state except Alaska and Hawaii in recent years. But it is easier to manufacture at ultra-efficient, robotmanned plants here with Japanese workers and wholly reliable parts suppliers with guaranteed quality control.

The other major problem, one that cuts both ways, concerns import controls. While in the United States, protectionist measures are urged with increasing vigor, the situation in Europe is already tight indeed. Britain allows the Japanese to take a maximum of just 10 percent of its market and France, only 3 percent, while Italy bans imports altogether.

But the Japanese are gaining steadily in confidence and no longer bridle emotionally at import controls or other prohibitions in which some executives here scented a form of racial discrimination. It was a little reminiscent of the notorious Oriental Exclusion Act in the United States in the 1920's that played a big role in turning Japanese public opinion against Americans more than 50 years ago.

In the new emphasis on matter-of-fact business without oversensitivity, Honda is a trend-setter. The only technically innovative auto maker here—its engineer-founder Soichiro Honda, now honorary chairman, supervised development of the fuel-efficient, clean CVCC engine—and lately the biggest seller in the United States, Honda is the first and so far only Japanese company to decide to assemble cars in the United States. That will be at a Marysville, Ohio, plant, which is expected to turn out 10,000 cars a month beginning at the end of 1982.

Its decision to invest in the United States helped to shame its bigger rival, Nissan, to announce plans for a $300 million truck plant in Tennessee. The other industry giant, Toyota, has only a small truck unit at Long Beach, Calif., where it puts flatbeds on the back of otherwise complete small trucks.

One reason is that Japanese lobbyists in Washington and Europe advised that it will be hard to halt the tide toward import controls. "Not that French auto makers insist that harsh action should be taken against Japan," said a member of the French Rothschild banking family here recently. "By hitting Japan hard we might ultimately destabilize the society, which would not be in Europe's interest, I was told," added the cautious banker.

In Washington, the position appears to be hardening, with the choice coming down to either flat import controls by the United States or a tight program of export controls to be imposed in Japan. So the Japanese lobbyists advise, and their words carry weight at home. "These are people who draw basic $200,000 annual retainers, just retainers," said Kinji Kawamura, managing director of Japan's Foreign Press Center here. "The Japanese pay their lobbyists fabulous amounts—and listen to them."

As the incoming administration of Ronald Reagan looks over the balance sheet of trade relations with Japan—Japan's surplus in that trade is expected to soar above current levels of around $10 billion a year—the import question will become more critical.

But will other makers follow the example of Honda and invest in United States production as a way around possible import controls? The Big Two—Toyota and Nissan—seem, by comparison with little Honda, a mixture of shyness and aggression. A reporter who spent three days last year with Toyota long-range planners at company headquarters near Nagoya at the company "castle-town," or Jokamachi, named Toyoda City after founder Sakichi Toyoda, learned little of Toyota's aims in the 1980's. Over lunches on lacquer trays of exquisitely prepared raw fish and bowls of Miso Shiro soup, Toyota staffers instead grilled the visitor on whether the United States planned import controls.

But some Japanese auto experts are indeed appalled by the failure of the Big Two to move into the United States so far. "Really, the Americans are prepared to offer a big and growing slice of their home market to us, and we are looking a gift horse in the mouth," said Ichiro Shioji, a Nissan labor leader who also heads the relatively powerless auto workers union here. As he sees it, the only way for Japan to insure that it keeps a handsome market share in the United States is to invest there extensively. "Volkswagen does it, Renault does it and Michelin does it—but we don't and that's crazy," he said.

* * *

September 20, 1982

CORPORATE POWERS ATTACKED

By PAUL LEWIS

Big multinational corporations are coming under a far-reaching attack by nations that want to see them more strictly regulated. The attack, originating both in the European Common Market and in the Group of 77, the caucus of third-world countries in the United Nations, reflects deepening concern over the wealth, power and global reach of these companies.

The aim of the attack, in each case, is to make large companies more accountable to their employees and to host governments. There are also efforts to force them to do more to advance the industrialization of the third world.

'A Pivotal Year'

"Nineteen eighty-two is shaping up as a pivotal year for international codes regulating multinational corporations," the International Organization Monitoring Service, a Washington group that studies multinational companies, warned in its latest report.

"The important thing is to make sure we don't shackle our business with new rules that will only make the recession worse," said Thomas Spencer, a Briton and a Conservative member of the European Parliament, the deliberative body of the Common Market.

The most immediate threat to the independence of large companies is yesterday's election in Sweden, which returned former Prime Minister Olaf Palme to power. Mr. Palme's Social Democratic Party is committed to forcing Swedish companies—including such well-known multinational concerns as Volvo—to gradually sell controlling shares to the unions representing their employees.

But of more general concern is a controversial plan, debated last week in Strasbourg, France, by the European Parliament, to give unions more of a voice in the European operations of multinational companies.

If adopted in its current form by the 10 Common Market members, the so-called Vredeling plan would require the companies to share confidential, strategic information with their work force. It would also require them to consult their unions on all major decisions.

Another line of attack against the multinational companies will open early next month, in Geneva, when third-world nations will seek control of high-technology patents at a meeting of the United Nations World Intellectual Property Organization. The agency is revising the 1883 Paris Convention, which binds signatory countries to respect one another's patents.

By patenting an invention under the Paris Convention, a company is assured of a manufacturing monopoly in exchange for making the technology available for others to study.

Company representatives argued at a recent meeting in Manila that the Common Market measure, named after its originator, Henk Vredeling of the Netherlands, a former Common Market Commissioner for Social Affairs, would give unions unwarranted powers of interference in business decisions.

" 'Vredeling' as it stands is completely unjustified and will put European companies at a competitive disadvantage," said Heinz Kroger of the Union des Industriels de la Communaute Europeenne. This group, which is based in Brussels, is a European industrialists' organization that is leading the drive to kill the proposal.

Support From Unions

European trade unions, Socialists and quite a number of Christian Democrats generally favor the Vredeling plan, however, arguing that it could help improve productivity and safeguard workers' rights by associating them more closely with management decisions.

In the coming battle over patents in the United Nations property rights organization, the Group of 77 wants to redraft key clauses in the Paris Convention to require multinational companies patenting a new invention to manufacture it in developing countries within 30 months, thus assuring that Western technology is transferred to the third world. If the companies failed to do this, third-world governments would be able to confiscate the patent and award it to another company for use within their own territory.

What the Group of 77 is proposing "is a confiscation system that will encourage companies to keep new technology secret instead of patenting it and risking expropriation," said Philip Johnson, a lawyer with the International Chamber of Commerce in Paris.

The United States, whose corporations probably own about 40 percent of all registered patents, has the most to lose in this battle, and the Reagan Administration has opposed it.

But Australia, New Zealand and Canada, which feel unduly dependent on imported technology, have jumped on the Group of 77's bandwagon and want to be classified as technologically backward countries with the right to take over unused patents.

International respect for patents has been declining in recent years anyway. But many observers fear that the Group of 77's demands for a forced transfer of new technology could lead to a global free-for-all in pirated inventions.

* * *

May 21, 1989

U.S. BUSINESSES LOOSEN LINK TO MOTHER COUNTRY

By LOUIS UCHITELLE

With a new surge of investment abroad, many American companies are shedding the banner of a national identity and proclaiming themselves to be global enterprises whose fortunes are no longer so dependent on the economy of the United States.

Globalization, in fact, is emerging as corporate America's strategy of choice for the 1990's, one heralded in the latest issue of The Harvard Business Review as a main road to industrial prowess. In the name of globalization, American companies' overseas spending on plants and equipment has revived for the first time in a decade, and executives increasingly speak as if the United States were no longer home port.

"The United States does not have an automatic call on our resources," said Cyrill Siewert, chief financial officer at the Colgate-Palmolive Company, which now sells more toothpaste, soaps and other toiletries outside the United States than inside. "There is no mindset that puts this country first."

Goals at Odds With Nation's

Inevitably, such views are putting American companies at odds with widely advocated national goals.

In a growing number of cases, high-paying jobs, including those for engineers and other professionals, are going abroad, instead of being kept at home. Spending by American manufacturers on research, an important source of financing for universities and laboratories, is rising far more quickly overseas than at home, according to the National Science Foundation. And American companies are increasingly supplying foreign markets from their overseas operations, rather than by exporting, a practice that makes this country's trade deficit hard to eliminate.

Perhaps the sharpest test of globalization would come in a recession, when the companies would face public pressure to preserve as many jobs as possible in the United States, thus holding down the unemployment rate. One way to do this would be for them to close overseas operations and pull back production to the United States, exporting from this country to keep their American factories occupied.

No Favoring American Workers

But many executives say the global strategy supersedes preferential treatment for American employees. Motorola Inc., for example, makes telephone pagers in Boynton Beach, Fla., and Kuala Lumpur, Malaysia, with the Malaysian plant now also the design and engineering center for these electronic beepers.

"We'd try to make a balanced decision that took everyone into consideration, Malaysians and Americans," said Robert H. Galvin, Motorola's chairman. "We need our Far Eastern customers, and we cannot alienate the Malaysians. We must treat our employees all over the world equally."

Many global executives also distance themselves from the trade issues that are stirring so much concern in Congress and the Bush Administration. Motorola and the Hewlett-Packard Company, for example, say they will not be directly affected if the United States fails to outdistance other countries in the development of high-definition television, a breakthrough technology that could require every household to buy a new television set.

Going After New Technology

"Whatever the technology that is developed, in whatever country, we'll be going after it for our products," said John

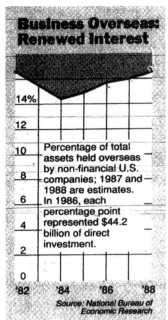

Business Overseas: Renewed Interest

14%
12
10
8
6
4
2
0

Percentage of total assets held overseas by non-financial U.S. companies; 1987 and 1988 are estimates. In 1986, each percentage point represented $44.2 billion of direct investment.

'82   '84   '86   '88

Source: National Bureau of Economic Research

The New York Times/May 21, 1989

Young, chief executive of Hewlett-Packard. These products include semiconductors and electronic measuring instruments made in several countries.

To be sure, American companies still spend much more on plant and equipment in this country than they do abroad: $488 billion last year versus $42 billion overseas. But the outlays have been rising since the mid-1980's.

In addition, companies like International Business Machines, Ford Motor, NCR, Motorola, Colgate-Palmolive and the Stanley Works now collect 30 percent or more of their revenues, and big chunks of their profit, from production outside the country, usually in high-tech factories far more sophisticated than the assembly plant operations that characterized earlier periods of overseas expansion.

THE NEW COMPANY
Corporate America Follows Its Market

Very slowly, corporate America is building up its holdings abroad. Nearly 17 percent of total corporate assets are now overseas, up from 14.4 percent in 1984, according to data compiled by Robert Lipsey of the National Bureau of Economic Research. This amount is greater than that for nearly every other industrial nation and more than three times the percentage of Japan's overseas holdings, although in every developed country the percentages are also rising.

The explanation of this trend is evident in the comments of many American executives, among them John A. M. Grant, executive director of corporate strategy at the Ford Motor Company. "In any country where Ford operates, the value added—the amount of manufacturing done in that country—should be as great as possible," he said.

True to this policy, Ford's auto-making operation in Europe, among the largest on the Continent, now makes or buys 98 percent of its parts, supplies and machinery in

Europe, building up to this level over more than a decade. "The only thing we import from the United States is some machine tools," Mr. Grant said.

Transferring of Wealth

For Ford and many American companies, the big lure of globalization is the promise of Europe and Asia. Sales of many products are growing more rapidly in these two markets than in the United States, and corporate America has decided that they must be served on the spot, not from home. "You cannot really make a penetration with exports," said Ralph Hake, vice president of planning at the Whirlpool Corporation.

But the exodus abroad is raising the possibility that American companies, by expanding foreign production, are transferring too much wealth to other countries. Not only are the factories as sophisticated as those back home, but much of the overseas investment today takes the form of joint production ventures with foreign companies, a rare practice before the 1980's. According to a survey by the Conference Board, a business organization, 40 percent of the overseas investment last year was in such joint ventures, which spread technology quickly across borders.

"There is a decoupling of the corporation from the country; that is what is developing," said Gus Tyler, an official of the International Ladies Garment Workers Union. "The country can be facing economic disaster, and the global corporation can avoid it."

THE REASONS
Success in Past Loses Its Value

Twenty years ago, in a period of overseas expansion that peaked in 1977, the trend was much less of a national problem. For one thing, most American companies insisted on ownership control of their foreign operations, and they kept their best factories, their best jobs and their best technologies at home.

As Richard H. Ayers, chairman of the Stanley Works, put it, the tendency was to equip foreign operations with hand-me-down machinery and technology, used first in this country and then sent abroad, often to make products from parts and materials shipped from the United States.

But in those days, the American multinational company's foreign operations did not have to be as productive and modern as they must be today. For one thing, low-wage foreign labor more than offset the extra cost of using older, less-efficient machinery.

Now, this advantage is gradually being lost as wages rise not only in Europe and Japan, but in South Korea, Taiwan, Singapore, Indonesia and other third-world countries.

"What this means is that there will have to be more investment in high-tech factories around the world," Mr. Ayers said, "because in the long run, you can't escape rising wages."

Rise of Regional Operations

Finally, until the 1970's, many of the overseas operations served only one country's marketplace, a strategy often dictated by tariff barriers. But as these barriers disappear and consumption rises abroad, American companies are closing their one-country factories. In their place, regional operations are emerging that serve a host of countries and draw their parts and materials partly from the United States but increasingly from local suppliers.

The Stanley Works, based in New Britain, Conn., has gone through this conversion process. A factory in Taiwan, originally opened because of the low-wage labor force, has been upgraded to production of quality wrenches, sockets and other tools for auto mechanics. The American market is supplied from this plant.

Most of Stanley's most sophisticated products are still made in the United States. "But if the best markets for any product develop overseas, then I would not hesitate to switch the operation abroad," Mr. Ayers said.

Pursuing this strategy, Stanley's factory in Sheffield, England, has become the company's engineering, design and manufacturing center for wood planes, the metal hand tools used to shave wood. All the world is served from this plant, which was placed in England because Europe has become the biggest market for wood planes and might grow even bigger after 1992, when the 12 members of the European Community plan to remove the last of the barriers that separate their marketplaces.

THE EFFECTS
Jobs and Wealth, Home and Abroad

The leading critics of globalization are union leaders, trying to save American jobs, and some economists and politicians, who assert that any manufacturing operation creates wealth for the host country. The argument is that industry is not only a source of jobs, but also of income for researchers who develop new products, for parts suppliers and for lawyers, accountants and many other service workers.

Realizing this, the Japanese and most European countries find ways to limit globalization and to keep industry at home, said Clyde V. Prestowitz, a trade negotiator in the Reagan Administration and a frequent critic of the Japanese. They do so, he added, through trade barriers, tax breaks and local-content laws that require foreign manufacturers, including Americans, to use locally made supplies.

"My view is that globalization is not really taking place as a worldwide phenomenon," Mr. Prestowitz said. "Only American companies are really doing it."

Whatever the case, American executives defend the practice with growing confidence. Their survival, they say, depends on serving all the world's major markets, and this can be done efficiently in most cases only when production is near each market.

Although globalization might deprive the United States of some factories, Mr. Ayers of the Stanley Works said, "wealth still comes back to the country in the form of dividends to shareholders, who are mostly Americans."

Increase in Foreign Ownership

Americans do indeed hold 93.8 percent of all corporate stock, according to the Securities Industry Association. But foreign ownership is creeping up, from 4.1 percent in 1980 to 6.2 percent through last year's first half.

And foreign ownership of corporate bonds has risen several fold in this decade, to 12.9 percent last year. The interest on these bonds is paid, like stock dividends, from company earnings.

Finally, executives and economists point out that while American companies invested $42 billion in plant and equipment abroad last year, Japanese, European and other foreign companies invested as much here, creating jobs and other benefits for Americans.

"If the argument is that wealth is created where the production is done, then what difference does it make whether the factories are owned by Japanese or Americans, as long as they're here?" said Charles Wolf Jr., director of the Rand Corporation's international economic policy program.

THE POLITICS
Retaliation And Realities

The public debate over trade and other public policy issues has not yet caught up with the changes wrought by globalization, said Jerry Jasinowski, chief economist of the National Association of Manufacturers, an industry trade group.

The Bush Administration, for instance, has threatened to retaliate against a host of barriers to American exports, particularly Japanese and South Korean ones. But this month, the National Association of Manufacturers, out of concern that harsh treatment could harm American investment abroad, refused to endorse such forceful action.

The Goodyear Tire and Rubber Company is among those opposed to retaliation, although in 1984 it had angrily demanded that the Federal Government penalize South Korea for selling tires in the United States below cost. Now, Goodyear is in touchy negotiations with 120 South Korean property owners to buy a huge tract of land for a $110 million tire factory, one that will be big enough to make 10,000 tires a day for the North Pacific rim countries, including Japan. Goodyear already has two other major factories in Asia.

"If companies have the alternative of moving across borders, there is not much point in doing a lot of shouting about trade," said Raymond Vernon, an international economist at Harvard Business School.

Effect on Television Debate

The debate over high-definition television is also being skewed by globalization. Many American companies have expressed interest in helping to develop, with some Federal financing, a system that will make possible the transmission and reception of television images far clearer than what is possible today.

But William F. Schreiber, director of the Advance TV Research Program at the Massachusetts Institute of Technology, said that when it comes time to license companies to produce the new television sets, transmitters and the other spinoff products, "there is no guarantee that the licensees are going to all be American companies."

Even if they are American, they might decide to manufacture abroad, Mr. Schreiber said. So far, the principal contenders to make the new televisions include the Sony Corporation, which is Japanese, and the North American Philips Corporation, which is Dutch-owned. Both make televisions in this country, while the major American contender, the Zenith Electronics Corporation, produces them in Mexico.

Globalization has also raised the concern that American wages will stagnate, growing very slowly while the wages of workers making the same products in countries like Taiwan, South Korea and Singapore catch up.

"The cost disparity between 'old world' and 'new world' labor is narrowing, but it will take years or decades rather than months or days to disappear," said Albert M. Wojnilower, senior economist at the First Boston Corporation. "Eventually, the new labor, its wages rising toward a world scale, competes with the old, not only as workers but as consumers vying to buy a higher standard of living."

*　*　*

October 1, 1989

WORKING WARILY WITH JAPAN

By DAVID E. SANGER

TOKYO—Inside the Austin, Tex., laboratories of Sematech, the research consortium struggling to restore American manufacturing skills in memory chips, the Japanese are distinctly unwelcome. The clean rooms where chips are fabricated are closed to most foreigners. When Sematech needed a Nikon repairman to keep a vital piece of equipment running, he was walled off from the rest of the lab.

"The Japanese burned our industry and buried it," Turner Hasty, a former Texas Instruments executive who is a Sematech top strategist, told a visitor in August. "We are not about to give them a guided tour."

But here in Tokyo, the same American companies that are financing Sematech can no longer afford such a hard-line stance. A few months ago Texas Instruments announced an alliance with Hitachi to design a 16 million-bit memory chip, the next generation. I.B.M. just signed an unusual joint manufacturing deal with Toshiba for making lightweight video screens for laptop computers, a field the Japanese dominate.

These days Japan is by turns America's desperate competitor and its indispensable ally. The ambivalence is hardly limited to high tech. Few question that Sony Corporation's $3.4 billion acquisition last week of Columbia Pictures Entertainment will help both companies in a world where high-definition television, satellite broadcasting and new video technologies are as important to making money in the movies as big-name stars, good plots and romantic tension. But there is a lurking sense that with each deal some critical skills—from making chips to movies—are ultimately improving profits in Tokyo, not at home.

Many economists have long argued that in these days of global markets, it is better to encourage interdependence than to build walls around American companies or, worse, around fundamental technologies. But in Congress at least, fewer and fewer legislators seem to subscribe to that theory.

The Case of the FSX

Earlier this year in the dispute over the FSX fighter jet to be co-developed by the two countries, there were cries that the United States was giving away critical technology that would be used against it. The FSX only became an issue because the agreement required Congressional approval. What Congress has yet to address is whether the same risk applies in private agreements between companies, where the lion's share of technological transfer—in both directions—takes place.

Cracking New Markets

Hardly a week goes by here when some Silicon Valley company does not strike a deal for research-and-development money it cannot raise at home. Often the quid pro quo is a technology that gives Japanese companies a quick entry into markets they could not crack. NEC last week introduced a microprocessor based on a promising design by a midsized Silicon Valley company, MIPS Computer Systems, that will be used for a new generation of work stations.

With increasing frequency, the technology also goes in the other direction. Steve Jobs, the mercurial founder of Apple, obtained an advanced optical disk drive from Canon Inc. for the computer developed by his new company, Next. But Canon got a big stake in the company and marketing rights in Japan.

So far the Government cannot seem to decide when such alliances are good and when they are not. The Bush Administration spent much of the spring talking about a national effort to develop high-definition television without collaborating with the Japanese. But the first image cast on the high-definition screen was the price tag. Japanese industry has already spent nearly a billion dollars on this technology. In recent weeks an Administration nervous about where to get the money has begun warming to the idea of an alliance.

In recent visits to Tokyo, Commerce Secretary Robert A. Mosbacher and Vice President Dan Quayle have done little to clear up the confusion. Both endorsed the idea of Japanese and American companies working side by side. But asked at a forum of American business leaders here whether that meant letting the United States affiliates of Japanese companies into big government projects, Mr. Mosbacher changed the subject. Mr. Quayle toured a satellite plant and talked about the need to cooperate in space. Asked how that squared with the Administration's complaint that Japan is protecting its industry by refusing to buy American satellites, Mr. Quayle said trade "will be dealt with separately." He left his Japanese audience wondering how.

Underlying the seeming contradictions lies a continuing effort to decide which industries are vital to national security. Robert Noyce, the co-inventor of the chip and Sematech's chief, argues that if American inability to compete in mass production of memory chips leads to the demise of the companies that build chip-making equipment, then the country's defense base is threatened. Americans should avoid growing dependent on Japanese technology "even if that means depriving ourselves of Japanese products," he says.

In reality, Mr. Noyce admits, Americans are unlikely to give up their VCR's, stereo systems, video cameras, fax machines and laptop computers in the vague hope of rebuilding American industry. Americans are hooked on Japan. If it is any consolation, Japan is also hooked on the United States. Sony bought Columbia, and promised to keep its hands off it, because American movies are so popular around the world. And it continues to buy American military hardware, even though many argue here that Japan now has the strength to scorn American technology altogether.

For both sides it is probably too late for such thinking. The technological alliances between the two countries are so intertwined that the old labels, "Made in America" and "Made in Japan," are meaningless.

* * *

November 21, 1991

FOR COKE, WORLD IS ITS OYSTER

By ROGER COHEN
Special to The New York Times

ATLANTA—For many companies, globalization proves to be a concept as empty as that other corporate buzzword, synergy. But for the Coca-Cola Company, the process of going global is now so extreme and rapid that its business in the United States has become secondary.

Indeed, because profit margins, sales growth and untapped potential are all much greater overseas than at home—and competition from Pepsico Inc. is milder—the decline in the relative importance of the United States to Coke seems irreversible. Thus, by the end of the decade, the United States may account for no more than 10 percent of the profits of this quintessentially American company, several analysts say.

Coke's top executives—many of whom are not American—appear to have no qualms about this process, although it clearly makes the company more vulnerable to currency fluctuations and international instability.

"Already, 80 percent of our operating income comes from outside the United States, and that proportion is absolutely destined to go higher," said Roberto C. Goizueta, the Cuban-born chief executive who has led Coke through a decade of rapid growth. "Willie Sutton used to say he robbed banks because that is where the money is. Well, we are increasingly global because 95 percent of the world's consumers are outside this country. It's that simple."

Many other companies, however, have not found globalization simple. In contrast to the Japanese, the large domestic market has long lulled American corporations into seeing international expansion as secondary. When companies have gotten around to it, said Ted Levitt of the Harvard Business

School, "the biggest problems have been irresolution in the face of adversity, lack of qualified management and a failure to present a clear, strong message about products."

Coke, however, has displayed not only a long-term commitment to such difficult markets as Latin America and the Philippines, but also tremendous consistency in its marketing and an enthusiasm for bringing foreigners into the top-level management in Atlanta. As the world has become smaller, richer and more homogeneous, this policy has paid off.

Amir Mahini, director of international business research for McKinsey & Company, the big consulting firm, said that in a recent survey of American companies with revenues in the $300 million to $1 billion range, chief executives had identified the choice of management for overseas units as one of the most crucial decisions. "In the best cases, they chose savvy nationals and empowered them," he said.

At Coke's headquarters, the words "domestic" and "foreign" have been banished from the corporate vocabulary to bolster the sense of a single global market. The company is about to begin its first global marketing campaign—six commercials for Coca-Cola that will be broadcast at the same time all over the world. Top executives include two Australians, an Irishman, an Austrian and an Italian. Managers' eyes gleam during discussions of Indonesia but tend to gloss over when talk turns to home.

Speaking in a recent interview, Mr. Goizueta (pronounced Goz-WET-ah), who confessed that he was more at home talking about Coke's Mexican operations than the domestic business, continued:

"We are cranked up to grow, particularly overseas, and we believe that growth will be as fast in the 90's as in the 80's. Back in 1980, our shares traded at $5 and they're now at $65. Is it reasonable to expect that by the end of this decade they'll be worth $700? I answer, why not?"

George Thompson, a beverage-industry analyst at Prudential Securities, said he thought strong foreign sales should enable Coke to sustain its 80's growth in the 90's. But he added that the one conspicuous threat to the company was that its growing reliance on foreign income "makes it very vulnerable to currency fluctuations, particularly a sharp rise in the dollar." With a stronger dollar, foreign earnings would not be worth as much in the United States.

Throughout the world, Coke has used a new flexibility and boldness to expand its international business. It seems that the humiliation of the 1985 experiment in changing the taste of Coke—and the subsequent triumphant reinstatement of the old formula three months later—has taught the corporation the cardinal importance of flexibility, a word its executives use constantly.

Putting Its Drinks In Everyone's Reach

Forsaking its forays during the 1980's into movies, wine and other fields, it has instead chosen to focus relentlessly on establishing an adaptable system that insures that Coca-Cola's soft drinks are everywhere within what its marketing director, Peter S. Sealey, calls "an arm's reach of desire."

While trade barriers, regulations and excessive prudence have defeated or slowed many other corporations in their quest to go global, Coke has used all means available to attack and conquer new markets. In some countries, like Britain and Taiwan, it has used joint ventures with bottlers; in others, like France, it has aggressively established bottling operations that it owns outright. Often Coke is prepared to take a minority stake in a joint project so long as it is satisfied that management meets its standards.

"Our single and relentless focus has been internationalizing this business," said Coke's president, Donald R. Keough. "To do so, we have become the most pragmatic company in the world. We want to do whatever works and we don't want any excuses."

As a result, Coke has raised the international contribution to its profits to 80 percent, from 50 percent in 1985. Meanwhile, over the last five years, the company's earnings have grown at an annual rate of 19 percent, reaching $1.3 billion last year on sales of $10.2 billion. The company's return on equity last year was 39 percent, its highest for 50 years.

Roy D. Burry, an analyst at Kidder, Peabody, predicted that Coke's foreign expansion would continue and "the international share of its income will be at 90 percent very shortly." Mr. Thompson of Prudential Securities added: "Coke is now truly a worldwide business, to a degree no other U.S. corporation I know can match. They can fill a package and put it on a shelf anywhere more efficiently than anyone."

Abroad, Pepsi Is Outgunned

Certainly, Coke's archrival, Pepsi, has been heavily outgunned overseas. Last year, just 16.6 percent of Pepsi's net income came from outside the United States. Where Coke leads the domestic soft drink market by a clear but not overwhelming margin—a 41 percent share compared with Pepsi's 33 percent—the company outsells Pepsi 4 to 1 in international markets.

This clear advantage helps Coke to make much bigger profits in overseas markets.

"They don't have to deal with Pepsi as much so they are able to spend far less on marketing than domestically," said Emanuel Goldman, an analyst at Paine Webber. He estimated that in Japan, where Coke has an 85 percent market share, the company made four times more profit than in the United States on each gallon of concentrate sold. In Europe, it makes three times more.

"Pepsi knows its place," Mr. Goldman contended. "You don't take on an elephant in the jungle, and the world outside America is Coke's jungle."

Pepsi demurs. It is strong in several Eastern European countries and in some others like Venezuela. Moreover, it announced plans this month to invest $1 billion in Spain, where Coke has a typically dominant position with 50 percent of the soft drink market, to Pepsi's 13 percent.

"Throughout the international marketplace, there is plenty of room for both of us to grow," argued Ken Ross, a Pepsi spokesman.

Still, the last decade has seen Coke reinforce its international domination—its overseas market share has grown to 46 percent—and Mr. Goizueta cannot hide a faint but withering scorn for Pepsi. Referring to its planned Spanish investment, the Coke chief executive said:

"They tend to think with their mouths open and they don't always do what they say. That money has not been invested yet, and I'm sure a lot will go on restaurants and snacks. It's wonderful to have a good competitor but I just hope they don't get too distracted with potato chips."

Spots Like Indonesia Put Coke in Heaven

Whatever Pepsi does overseas, Coke sees a lot of factors on its side. Its unit sales overseas are growing at a rate of 8 to 10 percent, compared with just 3.5 percent in the United States, which remains a huge and solid market. This trend, Coke executives argue, should continue because annual per capita consumption of soft drinks made by Coca-Cola overseas remains far below the domestic annual per-capita level of 292 eight-ounce servings.

For example, Indonesians drink 4 servings a year, the French 48, the British 99, the Japanese 112 and Germans 149. Mexicans, the most prolific consumers outside the United States, have reached 263. In the European Community, per-capita consumption is now at the same level as in the United States in 1965; in the Pacific the level is equivalent to the United States in 1939.

"When I think of Indonesia—a country on the Equator with 180 million people, a median age of 18, and a Moslem ban on alcohol—I feel I know what heaven looks like," said Mr. Keough, Coke's president.

It is prospects like this overseas that lead Coke to express no further interest in diversification. "We don't need any other industry in which to move because we have a plateful of opportunities," Mr. Goizueta argued.

Coke rebuts the notion that cultural differences mean there are limits on the growth potential in foreign countries. "I think we can get to U.S. levels throughout the European Community, I really do," said Ralph H. Cooper, president of Coke's European Community group. "Germany will be at U.S. levels within a decade."

Mr. Goldman of Paine Webber declined to predict how fast foreign markets would grow, but said the rate would be fast enough "to mean the U.S. continues to become less important."

To Be Flexible And to Be First

The company now refers to a "multi-local" system—an approach that involves adapting rapidly and very flexibly to local conditions. For example, when the Berlin wall went down, Coke immediately began trucking its drinks into what was East Germany even though it knew it would not immediately get any money out. It later bought all four soft-drink bottling plants in Germany's eastern provinces, investing more than $450 million.

"I had engineers on my back telling me they wanted to do a study, the plants weren't in the right place, they were all beat up and not up to Coke's standards," Mr. Goizueta said. "But I told them we had to move quickly and did not need to put a Coke sign in front of all the plants. It's essential to be flexible and be in first."

Sales in what was East Germany will reach more than 80 million cases this year, up from 21 million last year.

Elsewhere in Eastern Europe, Coke is investing $275 million, convinced that what matters is to be there for the long term and that it can overtake Pepsi in countries like Hungary and the Soviet Union where its rival was dominant before the collapse of Communism.

"We are moving as fast as we can to get the infrastructure into Eastern Europe because we are never going to have opportunities like this again," said John Hunter, an Australian who is head of all Coke's international operations.

Behind Coke's global expansion, Mr. Goizueta sees several key factors, among them that the world is getting younger, more accessible and more uniformly covetous of such brand names as Sony, Gucci and Coke. But this, he argued, is not enough for a company to succeed globally without what he called "a theme or binding mechanism that hold the company, the system, the brands and the consumer together." In the case of Coke, he said, the theme is joy, laughter, sport and music.

One World, One Commercial

This is about to be underlined in Coke's first global marketing campaign, during which ads for Coke, Diet Coke, Sprite and Fanta will be shown around the world at the same time. "The world has now come so close together, we can cut costs and achieve more by doing one promotion globally," said Mr. Sealey, Coke's director of global marketing.

It is in the hope that it can make such promotions more effective that Coke recently hired Michael S. Ovitz, the leading Hollywood agent, to act as a consultant. "The cultural agenda of the globe is set by the U.S. film music and entertainment industry and Mike sits at the apotheosis of that," Mr. Sealey said. "Through him we'll know what the coming trends are and get at least a year's start on our competition."

That may seem a dubious concept in that Mr. Ovitz cannot necessarily predict what will succeed and what will fail. But what is clear is that Coke now has a single-minded dedication to its international agenda.

"They have put together a growth business outside of this country," said Mr. Thompson of Prudential Securities. "Pepsi competes very effectively with them here. But it's really lopsided elsewhere."

* * *

January 1, 1992

U.S. BIOTECH SEEKS FOREIGN BACKERS

By BARNABY J. FEDER

In agricultural biotechnology, the contrast between the American style of creating new businesses and the approach in Europe and Japan is especially stark. The difference has direct bearing on the way biotechnology companies tend to form their foreign alliances, with smaller American players teaming up with bigger overseas companies.

Although some big American corporations like Monsanto have invested heavily in biotechnology, many of the most intriguing developments in the United States have been reported by entrepreneurial start-up concerns like Mycogen, Ecogen, Calgene, Crop Genetics, Biotechnica and DNA Plant Technologies.

Granted, there are highly regarded start-up companies overseas, like Plant Genetic Systems of Belgium, but the research leaders seem to be the giant chemical and pharmaceutical multinationals like ICI of Britain, Rhone-Poulenc of France and Ciba-Geigy of Switzerland.

Part of the difference is the unparalleled access that American entrepreneurs have to venture capital and subsequently, if their companies survive, to the stock market. Sooner or later, though, many start-ups decide they need bigger corporate partners for further financial support, marketing and production skills and other expertise. In agricultural biotechnology those alliances are typically forged with big foreign companies.

The result: a largely one-way flow to foreign countries of research results and technology pioneered in the United States. So far, according to industry analysts, the real cost to American companies has been the surrender of potential foreign markets rather than the creation of potential domestic competitors.

Take Mycogen, a San Diego-based concern that has focused most of its work on biopesticides. These are naturally occurring toxins that Mycogen isolates from microorganisms and mass-produces by genetically engineering bacteria to make them. The toxins are encapsulated so that they will not degrade too rapidly to be useful when sprayed onto fields. These "natural" poisons tend to kill only targeted pests, cause fewer pollution problems, and be harder for insects to develop a tolerance to than synthetic chemicals.

Mycogen has various agreements with the Kubota Corporation of Japan, Japan Tobacco Inc., and a research subsidiary of Royal Dutch/Shell, the British-Dutch petrochemical giant. All of them leave Mycogen with North American marketing rights to the products covered by the agreements, while providing Mycogen with greater marketing resources and expertise.

"We couldn't commercialize this stuff without them," Marie C. Burke, Mycogen's head of investor relations, said of the company's overseas allies.

One result of so much collaborative work is that American agricultural biotechnology is probably closer to the international pack than American medical biotechnology, where

United States companies like Genentech and Amgen are far ahead of the foreign competition. Some observers, like Jim McCamant, editor of the Agbiotech Stock Letter, say the difference is a matter of national policy, not chance. "There's been huge support from the National Institutes of Health for medical biotechnology research," he said.

* * *

July 25, 1994

U.S. CORPORATIONS EXPANDING ABROAD AT A QUICKER PACE

By LOUIS UCHITELLE

American companies are once again rapidly expanding their operations abroad—demonstrating that no matter what the incentives for keeping business in the United States, the urge to spread factories, offices, stores and jobs overseas is irresistible.

The surge in these investments and the jobs they create overseas comes just when exports should be climbing more rapidly than investment abroad. A weak dollar and falling labor costs have made American products increasingly competitive. Yet overseas investment is rising at twice the rate of exports. And for each dollar earned from exports, American companies take in nearly $2 from the sale of what they produce abroad.

"If you are going to be really important in the world market, you are going to grow by producing in many countries, and not by exporting, which has its limits," said Robert E. Lipsey, an expert on overseas investment at the National Bureau of Economic Research. "There are circumstances where this might not be the case, but by and large that is the story."

The issue, of course, is jobs, and who will hold them. American companies employ 5.4 million people abroad, 80 percent of them in manufacturing, and the hot issue in the late 1980's, during a similar surge in overseas investment, was this: Why can't the goods and services that these foreign workers produce be supplied from the United States? Why must companies migrate abroad, shedding some of their national identity and loyalty?

Now that debate is likely to revive, although perhaps with less intensity. American investment overseas remains concentrated in manufacturing, particularly in Europe, Canada and Japan, but manufacturing was an area of more rapid growth in the 1980's than it is today. This time companies like Wal-Mart and Morgan Stanley & Company are leaders—and that tones down the job issue.

Opening a factory in Europe or Mexico or East Asia often suggests that one in the United States may be closed. Wal-Mart's new retail investments in Canada, Brazil and Mexico, on the other hand, or Morgan Stanley's eight offices in East Asia do not suggest cutbacks at home.

"What we are sending abroad, apart from money, is our skill and experience as investment bankers, and you really have to be on site to do this sort of thing," said Stephen S.

Roach, a senior economist at Morgan Stanley, in a telephone interview from Hong Kong, where he was helping his local colleagues advise the Chinese Government on the privatization of an airline.

Morgan Stanley employs 410 people in Hong Kong, and expects to increase that to 500 by year's end, Mr. Roach said. Most of the firm's Asia offices, including two in China, have opened since the late 1980's.

The new surge in investment, in all types of businesses, showed up in recently released Commerce Department data. This investment by American companies in overseas operations rose last year to $716.2 billion, when measured as the cost of replacing the buildings and equipment. The 7.2 percent increase, coming after two years of much less growth, matched some of the better years of the 1980's. In the first quarter of 1994, investment increased even more quickly.

Manufacturing Lags Behind

But while manufacturing still dominates the numbers, representing nearly 40 percent of the total, manufacturing investment rose by only 7 percent last year. Outlays for retail, finance and the like went up by twice that percentage or more.

"It is our belief that, with trade barriers coming down, the world is going to be one great big marketplace, and he who gets there first does the best," said Donald Shinkel, a spokesman at Wal-Mart, which had no stores overseas in the 1980's.

The investment surge, after two years of relatively little growth, coincides with incipient recoveries in Europe and Japan after periods of recession. As business has picked up, sales and profits have risen at American operations abroad, making more money available for investment. These reinvested profits accounted for more than half the outlays last year, the Commerce Department reports.

Booming economies in East Asia, particularly China, Singapore and Hong Kong, also drew investment, and so did nearly every Western Hemisphere country, with Canada, Mexico, Argentina and Bermuda among the leaders—Bermuda being an offshore haven for American banking and insurance companies, while Canada, Mexico and Argentina attracted mainly manufacturing investment.

But the European nations and Japan attracted the biggest share of the manufacturing investment. They almost always do, although they are industrial countries with stronger currencies and higher average labor costs than in the United States.

American manufacturing companies engage in three types of overseas investment, and the one involving the industrial countries is perhaps the most difficult to justify—given that exporting from the United States can be less expensive, said Raymond Vernon, an economist at the Kennedy School of Government at Harvard University.

Still this investment does not draw the greatest criticism, which has been reserved for companies that relocate labor-intensive operations, like auto assembly, or apparel manufacturing, or the assembly of some electronics products, to low-wage countries like Mexico or Thailand. "The United States is simply not the lowest-cost producer in the world, and moving abroad to these countries is inevitable," Mr. Vernon said.

Then there are the Wal-Marts and Morgan Stanleys trying to penetrate new markets in the only way possible, by putting a store or an investment house on site. Since these companies do not hold back operations at home to expand abroad, their tactics are seldom criticized.

Finally there are the situations in which a company can export its product inexpensively enough, particularly when the dollar is weak, but chooses instead to manufacture abroad, mainly for "insurance," as Mr. Vernon puts it. Of course, foreign companies, particularly the Japanese, adopt the same strategy for the United States, establishing many factories here that create jobs for Americans. But they employ 4.9 million Americans, which is 500,000 fewer than the American corporate payroll abroad.

Jobs are also created in the United States when American companies, investing abroad, export parts or machinery to help make their products overseas. But this "American content" makes up only 9 percent, on average, of the merchandise produced, the Commerce Department says. The rest is obtained overseas.

The Gillette Company embraces the strategy of manufacturing abroad rather than exporting, generating jobs overseas rather than in the United States. That has happened most recently in the case of Gillette's new Sensor XL razor blade cartridge.

The cartridge, simple for consumers to use, is difficult to manufacture, involving 10 welds with high-technology laser machines. Production started nearly two years ago at Gillette's main plant, in Boston, but all the output was exported to Europe. "We introduced the product in Europe because razor blade sales there are greater than in the United States," said Thomas Skelly, a Gillette senior vice president.

The new Sensor model is to be sold in the United States starting this year. But rather than expand the Boston operation to handle the additional production—and add jobs, perhaps—Gillette is adding the extra capacity to its Berlin plant, a high-technology factory that will take over the European market.

Currency Issues Discounted

Cost is not the issue; blades are small and not difficult to ship, and the weak dollar gives the United States an advantage—but one that Mr. Skelly, and other corporate executives, dismiss as insignificant. "In the long run, these currency fluctuations, up and down, don't mean a whit in the decision where to manufacture," he said.

Over the years, Gillette has put 62 factories in 28 countries and each tries to operate as if it were a regional company, adjusting as quickly as possible to local competitors. Being close to a market is a priority, promising better returns than exporting from the United States, Mr. Skelly says.

"We are also concerned about having only one place where a product is made," he said. "There could be an explosion, or labor problems." If the Boston workers struck, for example, Gillette would supply the Sensor XL to Europe and the United States from the Berlin plant, and vice versa.

The upshot of this approach is that Gillette employs 2,300 people in the manufacture of razors and blades in the United States and 7,700—more than three times as many—abroad.

Some of those workers are making blades at Gillette plants in Poland, Russia and China, where production costs are less than in the United States. But that is not the case in Germany. "You could ship the blades from here, but you set up there for insurance," Mr. Vernon said. "And the justifications for this approach are not so clear cut."

* * *

September 13, 1995

LUXURIES THEY CAN'T AFFORD

By NATHANIEL C. NASH

FRANKFURT, Sept. 12—The scene at the sprawling Mercedes-Benz factory in Sindelfingen, where the auto maker assembles its popular E-class model, is bedeviled by sloth and confusion, at odds with the popular image of Teutonic efficiency.

The five-story building, built in 1916, is loud and dimly lit, peppered with numerous half-built cars pushed to one side. Many workers stand idle, either with nothing to do or waiting for a car to reach their station. Activity has ground to a halt in large areas, like the dashboard-assembly section, because too much stock has piled up. Unlike modern plants in Japan or the United States, where cars follow a single line after they leave the paint shop, here they are machine-hoisted back and forth as many as 46 times between lines.

Things are better at BMW's 3-series plant in Regensburg in Bavaria, but are still a far cry from the lean and disciplined approach pioneered by the Japanese. Workers pause to knock back beer that they have bought from one of several vending machines on the factory floor. They attach bumpers from a selection of more than 400 styles, install 280 varieties of rear-seat shelves and apply almost any color paint customers can dream up. They also make all the dashboards themselves. The company boasts that all these choices make every model unique, but analysts say the extra costs are a drag on profits.

On top of it all, the workers are among the most pampered in the world, working short hours, earning twice as much as most of their European counterparts and getting 10 weeks of paid holiday every year. Small wonder, then, that the German auto industry is finally saying "Enough."

For a time, Germany's booming economy masked these excesses. But growth has slowed, and now German auto makers are recognizing that they do not know all they should about mass-producing competitively priced cars. As a result, they are taking drastic action to meet the challenge of Japanese and American competition: They are fleeing Germany's high-cost structure and opening new plants abroad, and they

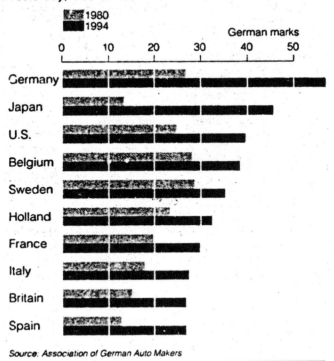

Germany's Cost Disadvantage

Total hourly cost for auto workers, in German marks. Yesterday, a dollar was worth 1.4737 marks.

■ 1980
■ 1994

Germany, Japan, U.S., Belgium, Sweden, Holland, France, Italy, Britain, Spain

Source: Association of German Auto Makers

The New York Times

are re-engineering existing operations at home to make them more efficient.

Nearly every new car that Mercedes, a unit of Daimler-Benz A.G., is developing will be made outside Germany: its mini "Swatch" line in France, its mini-van in Spain and its four-wheel drive sports vehicle in Alabama. BMW opened a plant in Spartanburg, S.C., last year, Volkswagen A.G. is considering building its new Beetle in Mexico and Adam Opel, the West German unit of the General Motors Corporation, is expanding in Belgium, Britain, Poland and Hungary.

In the last four years, the German auto industry has slashed its work force by 160,000 jobs to the current 630,000. And there is more to come: analysts say Volkswagen needs to eliminate 30,000 workers over the next several years.

"I don't see a new auto plant being built in Germany for the foreseeable future," said Kunibert Schmidt, general secretary of the Association of German Auto Makers, the main industry group.

It isn't just the car industry that is moving production to lower-cost countries. Siemens A.G., the industrial-products giant, is building a semiconductor plant in Britain. Bayer A.G. and Hoechst A.G., the drug makers, are building plants in Texas and China, respectively. Other big German multinational corporations have set up operations in Brazil, China and even Japan.

German Industry's New Addresses

The high cost of labor and the growing strength of the German mark have pushed German companies to look outside the country's borders in recent years.

1 Mercedes-Benz   4 Opel   7 Bayer
2 BMW   5 AEG   8 Degussa
3 Volkswagen   6 Siemens   9 Hoechst

The New York Times

But because of its vast size, the auto industry represents the direction of Germany's industrial base. As its exodus continues, more Germans are growing alarmed at the loss of jobs, openly calling for change. And they are getting some.

Most significantly, perhaps, cracks are appearing in labor's hard stand against concessions aimed at raising productivity. Just today, Volkswagen won more flexibility from its workers in a labor agreement that traded pay increases and job guarantees for a change in work rules that would lengthen the workweek to as much as 38.8 hours without incurring overtime costs. In the past, VW workers worked as few as 29 hours a week.

Earlier this month, Opel won similar concessions from the union. And at Regensburg, BMW negotiated an agreement with unions that allows the company to run an entire Saturday shift without paying overtime. The agreement also lets it operate its plant for 99 hours a week, with two shifts of workers, far higher than the typical German workweek.

German auto makers are doing more than just wringing concessions from labor. They are also redesigning cars and adopting Japanese-style production techniques to reduce costs.

BMW, for example, uses a certain amount of just-in-time delivery of parts, like seats, carpeting and engines, to hold inventories down. At Sindelfingen, about 100 miles south of Frankfurt, Mercedes has spent almost $200 million on new stamping equipment. It also takes delivery of its seats from suppliers only hours before they go into the cars, and it is reducing the number of parts it makes for its cars.

Opel recently hired a senior production specialist away from the Toyota Motor Corporation. And Volkswagen is reducing the number of chassis that it produces across its four operating companies—VW, Audi, Skoda in Eastern Europe and SEAT in Spain—from 16 to four.

In addition, German car companies are shopping more aggressively outside their country for cheaper parts, notably in the weak-currency countries of Italy, Spain and France. The trend started at Volkswagen, where Jose Ignacio Lopez de Arriortua, who had been hired away from General Motors and was later accused of stealing G.M.'s secrets, clamped down on the prices Volkswagen paid suppliers.

In essence, Germany is waking up to a problem that it had ignored for too long, experts say: Its high wages, generous benefits and rigid workplace procedures were pricing its products out of world markets, even as the Japanese and the Americans were racing to increase productivity and hold costs down.

German auto workers are the highest paid in the world, typically costing an auto maker $38.50 an hour, almost twice the cost in France, at $20 an hour, and more than twice the cost in Britain, Italy and Spain. German auto wages are more than 40 percent higher than in the United States, and American factories also tend to be much more efficient.

A recent study by the Economist Intelligence Unit of London found that Volkswagen's main plant in Wolfsburg, Germany, produced an average of 23.6 cars an employee a year, while the Ford Motor Company's Wayne, Mich., plant produced 58.8 Ford Escorts. Toyota's Takaoka plant, which makes Corollas, Tercels and Paseos, produces an astonishing 133.6 cars an employee annually.

The turning point began in the early 1990's, when the German economy went into a deep recession and Japan's new luxury cars, particularly Toyota's Lexus and the Nissan Motor Company's Infiniti, hit world markets.

"Lexus was a profound shock," said Daniel T. Jones, a professor at the Cardiff Business School at the University of Wales. "It was just as good as a Mercedes but much lower priced. Mercedes found they were spending more time fixing their cars after they came off the assembly line than Toyota took in making the Lexus."

At that point, Mr. Jones added, "the German honeymoon of being able to make an ever-more sophisticated car without paying attention to price came to an end. They realized how disastrously inefficient they were and it triggered a real movement to learn from these lean techniques."

It was a painful process for a generation of corporate leaders raised on the concept that success would result from manufacturing a finely designed, finely engineered product in Germany and exporting it around the world. Even today, German business leaders get defensive about moving operations to foreign soil. One official at Siemens, for example, insisted that a plan to build a semiconductor plant in Britain was an "extension" of the company's production plans, not a relocation.

The transformation of the auto industry is even more emotional for German workers, since it involves a steady decrease in their numbers and a realization that the perquisites they long took for granted—no Saturday work, few night shifts, six weeks of vacation and nearly a month of holidays, high absenteeism, an ever-shrinking workweek—are coming to an end.

To be sure, Germany still has much going for it. Its work force is highly skilled and its economy remains the powerhouse of Europe. If its unions grant greater concessions, it could sharpen its competitive edge quickly. And it boasts one auto plant that can claim to be a match for the Japanese: the factory Opel built in the former East German town of Eisenach after the fall of Communism.

A so-called green-field plant, Eisenach borrowed many manufacturing techniques practiced by the General Motors joint venture with Toyota in Fremont, Calif. The plant now makes Opel's minicar, the Corsa.

Unlike the BMW and Mercedes plants, Eisenach is remarkably quiet, with no car bodies sitting off to the side. Managers and workers seem busy and wear the same uniform: clean white shirts and dark pants.

Though Eisenach has been rated as the most efficient plant in Europe, with production of 59.3 cars a worker each year, it is likely to be the last auto plant in Germany for a while.

That doesn't mean, of course, that the German auto industry is writing off German workers. Rather, it intends to pursue a two-track production strategy, according to Jens Neumann, a member of VW's management board and the chairman of its North American operations.

"Simple export thinking is not relevant any more," Mr. Neumann said. "It is very tricky keeping the German manufacturing base and at the same time globalizing. You cannot have the one without the other."

* * *

March 5, 1997

THE REAL CHINESE THREAT

By WILLIAM GREIDER

WASHINGTON—China casts such a large shadow over the future that it has become the crux of all debate over the risks and rewards of the globalizing economy.

Prevailing wisdom, promoted by multinational conglomerates and embraced by President Clinton, holds that China's middle-class consumers will lift all boats. The Cassandra school foresees a flood of low-wage exports that will swamp the global system. The argument has taken on greater urgency with the death of Deng Xiaoping and the pending decision on whether China will be allowed to join the World Trade Organization.

The problem with making China the sole focus of the globalization debate is that the inclination to glorify or demonize what Communist leaders call "market socialism with Chinese characteristics" misses the larger point. The real issue should be the flawed nature of the global system itself.

China is best seen as a huge mirror that bluntly magnifies those broader problems. Unfortunately, if it succeeds in becoming a world economic leader, its scale may push the manic logic of global capitalism to predictably dangerous conclusions: increased loss of jobs from higher-paying developed countries to the third world and overproduction of goods relative to demand.

Its Marxist-Leninist dogma notwithstanding, China will do exactly what global capitalism permits and even encourages. Beijing, one might say, is following the Japanese model of developing sophisticated manufacturing but "with Chinese characteristics." It intends to build a world-class industrial base and become a major exporter of technological goods—cars, chemicals, steel, electronics, even commercial aircraft.

To this end, multinationals from Boeing to Volvo, from Airbus to Mitsubishi, are trading elements of production in order to sell aircraft or cars to the Chinese. China, like many others before it, demands jobs and technology as the price of entry. At the huge assembly halls of Xian Aircraft Company, I saw machinists who earn $50 a month assembling Volvo buses and the tail sections of Boeing 737's. The workers are supervised (and sometimes disciplined) by Communist Party cadres. "If you want something done," Boeing's plant manager told me, "you go to the party member and it's done—like that."

Rigid control over the work force has always been part of what economists call the "comparative advantage" of manufacturing in very poor countries. In Indonesia, the ruling ideology is right-wing rather than Marxist, but the suppression of workers' rights is nearly as harsh as in China. Malaysia's burgeoning electronics industry is based on an explicit promise to American semiconductor companies that workers will be prohibited from unionizing. When Malaysia considered lifting this ban, American companies threatened to move to China or Vietnam.

China's industrial strategy is not secret. It publishes blueprints, industry by industry, elaborating how it intends to focus on certain export markets. Party bureaucrats envisage a car industry as large as North America's within 15 years—with a capacity way beyond the potential demand at home. The shoddier cars can be sold domestically; higher-quality models will be exported.

China's vision is not as improbable as many assume. Volvo now ships assembly kits made in Sweden to its Xian plant, but accepts that its buses will soon be made of at least 90 percent Chinese parts. A manager of the Xian Aircraft Company, which is run by the military, boasted that it "already has almost the manufacturing level to produce one whole aircraft at the level of the Boeing 737."

Boeing's strategists do not scoff at this claim. China hopes that with the help of international partners it can launch its own "Asian Airbus," modeled after the government-subsidized aircraft consortium in Europe. Why denounce Beijing for copying Bonn and Paris? Boeing wants a piece of the new venture—a smart strategy for the company, if not for machinists and engineers in Seattle.

The United States is the global system's buyer of last resort. It absorbs China's lopsided trade flows—an astonishing deficit of $40 billion last year—but the rise of low-wage higher-tech industries there now threatens Japan's domination of Asian markets as well. Thus Tokyo is more worried than Washington. "China is a horror story for the rest of the world if it simply grows as an exporting nation," Harou Shimada, a Japanese economist who advises the Government, told me. "If you bring in 1.2 billion workers at those wages, that can destroy the global trading system."

In short, it is China's scale, not its despotism, that threatens the economic system. Even if China were to collapse tomorrow, the threat of lost jobs would not disappear. Low-wage producers from India to Eastern Europe are vying for the same ground.

With this in mind, people should consider the fundamental contradictions of globalization, particularly that the world is generating production much faster than it is creating consum-ers. Economists typically dismiss this analysis, saying that supply and demand will always even out. But consider that the global auto industry will be able to produce 79 million vehicles in 2000, while consumers won't buy more than 58 million. Someone somewhere is going to have to close more car factories—lots of them.

The perverse paradox of globalization is that the very steps companies think they must take to survive fierce new competition actually end up making the worldwide supply problem worse. Moving production to low-wage economies exchanges high-wage workers for very cheap ones. The developing economy enjoys new jobs and rising incomes, but overall consumption power is lost.

As Henry Ford observed in 1913, an industrial system cannot endure if workers cannot buy the things they make. This condition led to 1929, and it is before us again. To save the system, the United States must take real steps to emphasize the condition of workers and wages at home and abroad.

It should, for example, incorporate labor rights into trade negotiations by imposing tariffs on the goods of the most flagrant abusers of workers and giving preferential trade terms to poor nations with more equitable governments. This wouldn't end the pressures on jobs and wages here, but it would boost global consumption.

It should also use the threat of tariffs to keep countries from developing an export advantage through excess capacity. We have the leverage to do this: If not us, who will buy China's $40 billion surplus of goods?

None of this promises to solve the problem of competition from China. But neither will China's growth solve the problems of economic globalization, despite economists' rosy views. Instead of coddling China or depicting it as uniquely evil, the United States should start questioning its own blind faith in the global economy.

William Greider is the author, most recently, of "One World, Ready or Not: The Manic Logic of Global Capitalism."

A GLOBAL DIVISION OF LABOR

November 9, 1980

MADE IN U.S.A.—WITH FOREIGN PARTS

By EDWIN McDOWELL

A Dodge dealer in Mount Kisco, N.Y., offers an unusual optional extra: A bumper sticker that proclaims, "This vehicle built in America by Americans for Americans." On a similar nationalistic note, the United Auto Workers union is advertising in newspapers and on radio for Americans to buy American cars. And at least 12 states have adopted regulations requiring state agencies to do just that.

It is getting harder, however, to buy a car that is not only assembled in America but made entirely with American-made parts. Dodge, despite the bumper sticker, is a strik-ing example. Almost 15 percent of the Dodge Omni and its twin, the Plymouth Horizon, is manufactured abroad. Moreover, only the Chrysler Corporation's ability to buy some 300,000 Volkswagen engines for the cars staved off an even worse financial disaster for the company.

Yet imported parts are showing up in many other American cars as well. The new Ford Escort is being assembled in three countries and the American version contains parts from nine foreign countries. Conversely, the European version of the Escort contains parts manufactured in the United States.

Only a few months ago the talk in the auto industry was about the world or global car, the economical small car of standardized design capable of being assembled with components produced around the world and suitable for American high-

Ford Escort

Nine countries supply parts for Ford's new fuel-efficient Escort.

JAPAN	Manual transaxles
SPAIN	Shock absorber struts
BRAZIL	Rear brake assembly
BRITAIN	Steering gears
ITALY	Engine cylinder heads
FRANCE	Hub and bearing clutch assembly
MEXICO	Door lift assembly
TAIWAN	Wiring
WEST GERMANY	Valve-guide bushing

Source: Ford Motor Company

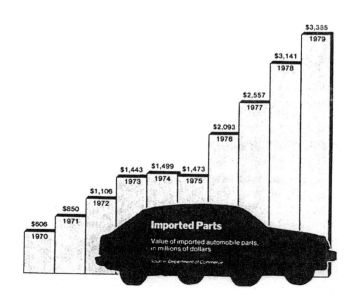

ways, European city streets and African trails. The world car is on its way—the emblem of the new Ford Escort, for example, depicts a globe—but today the most noticeable trend is toward global car parts, in which components from individual countries are going into increasing numbers of cars built by American auto manufacturers and their foreign competitors.

"There's a lot of talk about the world car, but there's an even more general movement toward world components," said Arvid Jouppi, auto analyst for John Muir & Company. Adds Robert McElwaine, president of the American International Automobile Dealers Association, "Imports of components by domestic companies are rising dramatically."

It's all part of a trend in world industry, with the large industrial companies concentrating more and more on high technology, research, design and management, and less developed countries beginning to acquire skills in manufacturing goods, including automobile parts, that they can make cheaper and perhaps even better. South Korea and Taiwan, for example, provide everything from ignition wires to intake valves, while Brazil manufactures entire auto and truck engines. "And the trend is going to continue," said Frank Armbruster, director of interdisciplinary studies at the Hudson Institute. "If you can make an equivalent car for $2,000 or $3,000 less, you do it. And in the current economy, the pressure to do so will remain."

But Mr. Armbruster thinks it may be a mixed blessing. "What does it do to a country's military mobility if, for example, it no longer has people to make engines?" he asked. "During World War II we depended on civilian skills to support us in a conventional war. We shifted people from making sewing machines to making machine guns. What if you no longer have those skills?" Moreover, he said, "What about a small country that specializes in making certain auto parts to supply the U.S. or Japanese market if the bottom drops out of the auto market? It could have a devastating effect on such countries."

Auto parts are big business—an estimated $50 billion a year for the original-equipment market alone. Imported parts and components totaled $6.8 billion last year, according to Mr. McElwaine, while William A. Raftery, president of the Motor and Equipment Manufacturers Association, estimates

that imports of Japanese auto parts soared to more than $2.6 billion last year, from $163 million in 1979.

This is a dramatic turnabout from not too long ago, when almost all the equipment in a car originated in the country of manufacture. A survey earlier this year by Arthur Andersen & Company and the University of Michigan ("U.S. Automotive Industry Trends") indicates that Detroit will import 10 percent of its parts by 1985 and 15 percent by 1990.

Meanwhile, American auto parts makers have begun moving overseas. Borg-Warner, for example, is already established in Japan, Australia and Europe. "In Japan we have a joint venture with Japanese partners, and we deliver about 95 percent of our output to Japanese auto manufacturers, primarily for export," said Thomas Hague, area director for Asia. Its biggest items for the Japanese market are automatic transmissions and seat belts, but elsewhere overseas Borg-Warner manufactures clutches, axles and emission control devices.

The main reason for this international division of labor is economic, the fact that certain countries can perform functions cheaper because of lower labor costs or greater access to raw materials. Workmanship also plays a part. Italy, for example, has proven especially adept at die-casting aluminum, and Fiat helped Ford solve engineering problems with its new British-built Escort engine.

Cars have increasingly been losing their national identity, particularly since the General Motors Chevette went into production in Brazil in 1972 and was soon manufactured in five other nations. The American-built Chevette contains automatic transmissions from France and door hinges from West Germany.

But national politics is involved also. A number of governments require that cars assembled in their countries contain a high proportion of domestically produced components. And the Nissan Motor Company's recent decision to locate a Datsun small-truck assembly plant in Tennessee was reportedly made largely in hopes of staving off quotas demanded by Detroit auto makers and labor unions.

The Cleveland-based Eaton Corporation manufactures hydraulic lifters and intake and exhaust valves at several sites in Europe. It manufactures valves in Spain for autos built in Britain, provides parts for Volkswagen engines built in West Germany that are then shipped to the United States, and it supplies parts from its Saginaw, Mich., facility for the Ford Erika being built in Britain. It is also building a valve plant in Mexico with a Mexican partner.

Carrying the concept of commonality a step further, Ford introduced the Fiesta, designed and developed in Europe, assembled in three countries, and which includes an engine from Britain and Spain, windshield glass from Oklahoma, road wheels from Belgium, a transmission from France, a distributor from Northern Ireland and a fuel tank from West Germany.

Ford's newest world car, the Escort, a front-wheel drive subcompact, is being assembled simultaneously in the United States, Britain and Germany and some of its components are made in Japan (transaxles), Italy (cylinder heads), Brazil (rear brakes), Mexico (door-lift assembly), Taiwan (wire) and Britain (valves). The automatic transmission for the European Escort will be made at Batavia, Ohio, and shipped across the Atlantic. General Motors' "J" car, scheduled for next year, was partly designed in Europe by Opel, G.M.'s West German subsidiary, and will be assembled in the United States, Canada, Australia, Brazil and South Africa.

In what would be a significant step, Japan's Toyota is negotiating with Ford for the possibility of establishing an auto factory in the United States capable of making up to 600,000 cars a year, the investment and output to be shared between Ford and Toyota dealers. If it works out, that will be one step beyond Volkswagen's 1978 decision to begin assembling Rabbits in Pennsylvania. VW, which is considering a second American plant, helped offset high labor costs in Germany by importing entire engines and other major components from Latin America.

Spokesmen for the Big Three generally downplay the significance of foreign parts in their products, even though their affiliates and subsidiaries are the source of many of those parts, because it is a source of some embarrassment that they are increasingly relying on foreign workmanship at the same time some industry officials are seeking quotas on imported cars. A General Motors spokesman, for example, said only about 1 percent of G.M. parts in the United States come from abroad, while Ford says that 94 percent of the value of its product is produced in North America.

But the Isuzu Motor Company, in which General Motors has a 34 percent equity share, will soon be delivering 400,000 transaxles a year to G.M.-affiliated companies outside the United States and will supply G.M. with 100,000 transmission and engine sets annually for small trucks. Isuzu, which also makes Chevrolet's Luv minitruck, will also supply an undetermined amount of diesel engines for the Chevette. Conversely, G.M. supplies transmission systems for Japanese heavy-duty vehicles.

Ford plans to manufacture air-conditioner compressors, alternators, starter motors and car motors in Singapore, and

last year it bought a 25 percent interest in Toyo Kogyo, the fourth largest Japanese auto maker (Mazda cars). Toyo Kogyo not only supplies transaxles for the Escort but also makes the Courier pickup truck sold under the Ford name in the United States. "When Ford put out bids for front-wheel-drive transaxles about 18 months ago the bidding was furious," said Borg-Warner's Mr. Hague. "We got close but the project went to Toyo Kogyo."

Chrysler will receive components from Peugeot in return for helping Europe's largest manufacturer sell its cars in the United States, and it is buying several hundred thousand four-cylinder engines from the Mitsubishi Motors Corporation, of which it owns 15 percent. Mitsubishi engines are available on Chrysler's new front-wheel-drive "K" cars, the Dodge Aries and Plymouth Reliant.

The American Motors Corporation has entered an agreement with Renault, which recently increased its holding in A.M.C. to 46 percent, to build a French-designed medium-sized car in the United States in 1982–83 that will contain about one-half French parts.

It is not just Detroit and its partners whose cars are taking on an increasingly international look. Saab and Lancia are jointly developing cars for the European market for the mid-1980's. Fiat and Peugeot are jointly building light-duty trucks, they will jointly produce a million engines a year and they will jointly make steering systems. Citroen and Fiat are beginning a joint a small utility vehicle manufacturing operation in Italy, and the two of them are engaged in auto research projects with Volkswagen, Volvo, Renault and British Leyland.

Integration is relatively easy in Europe, where the Common Market has encouraged it by reducing trade barriers among member countries. But it is much more difficult elsewhere, because many countries impose high import duties and have laws requiring the use of domestically produced components. Ford do Brasil, for example, used to import most of its supplies, but its cars and trucks now have as much as 98 percent local content.

There are problems in the United States as well, where Federal mileage standards require companies to use 75 percent domestic content in cars counted toward corporate-average fuel economy. As a result, G.M. has stopped selling in the United States the Buick Opel cars made by Isuzu and it plans to phase out imports of Luv trucks. A.M.C., on the other hand, is seeking a temporary waiver of the content requirement for the car it will build with Renault.

Meanwhile, a number of Japanese auto parts manufacturers, prodded by the powerful Ministry of International Trade and Industry, are considering setting up operations in the United States to manufacture everything from radiators to oil seals to cables to springs.

Mr. Jouppi, who was part of a four-member delegation to Japan sponsored by the Commerce Department last summer, said, "We tried to point out that the United States is not only a market to sell autos, you can also manufacture and buy parts in the U.S. Since then a very high level Japanese buying mission came here and in the first two weeks booked $70 million worth of orders. That's not big when you're looking at a multibillion-dollar industry, but it's a start, and an indication of things to come."

* * *

February 8, 1981

THE RETREAT OF AMERICAN EXPATRIATES

By SANDRA SALMANS

In Paris, the French manager of an American-owned bank rebels when the parent company suggests that he curtail his customary five-week vacation. In the Middle East, the German-born manager of an American subsidiary, needing a fleet of cars, instinctively thinks not of General Motors or Ford, but of Mercedes-Benz.

Such problems have become increasingly common for United States multinational corporations as they become more dependent on non-American managers.

High taxes, soaring inflation and a weak dollar have increased the expense of maintaining Americans overseas to the point where United States companies have been hiring more foreigners for managerial and other positions in overseas subsidiaries.

Unless the tax structure for Americans is altered by the new Congress—and some modifications are generally expected—many observers fear that, in the long run, United States interests will be seriously threatened.

"We're getting taxed out of competition," said Peter Giblin, senior vice president-European operations, of Russell Reynolds Associates, an executive recruiting firm.

For many American expatriates, 1980 was the year of homecoming. The number of United States citizens employed overseas, which had begun to decline during 1979, plummeted. In a survey of 306 United States companies, Organization Resources Counselors, a New York-based economic research firm, found that the number of United States expatriates, both blue-and white-collar, fell by 39 percent last year from 1979, to 22,580. In the same period, the number of expatriates from other countries doubled, to 38,091.

As a result, the survey found, United States citizens last year accounted for only 37 percent of total expatriates employed, down from 66 percent in 1979. They are now vastly outnumbered by Britons, other Europeans, Canadians and third-world nationals.

Although the weak dollar is one of several factors that have contributed to the decline of the American expatriate, it is widely agreed that United States tax policy has been the critical factor. The United States is the only major country that taxes its citizens on income earned abroad.

The rationale for this policy, according to Donald Lubick, Assistant Treasury Secretary for tax policy in the Carter Administration, "is that all citizens, no matter where they live, should make a contribution to the cost of running the Government, which is extending protection and benefits in such areas as defense."

In Congress, that view has received its strongest support from Senator William Proxmire, who has periodically inveighed against Americans dwelling in tax-free luxury on the Riviera. "What is there about living abroad that distinguishes them from coal miners in West Virginia or factory workers in Pennsylvania," Howard Shuman, the Senator's administrative assistant, said.

While Senator Proxmire and allies on Capitol Hill believe that the present tax law is generous toward expatriates, industry's view is that it is actually punitive.

In most cases, a United States citizen employed overseas by an American company receives not only a base salary but a handful of allowances to cover extraordinary expenses: incremental cost of living (to maintain a living standard comparable to that at home), housing, schooling for children, and home leave. Often, these allowances equal or even exceed base salary, grossly inflating taxable income.

Until 1978, these allowances were taken into account by permitting Americans working abroad to exclude as much as $25,000 of their income from taxation; income above that amount was taxed in the regular brackets. But in that year, the Foreign Earned Income Act eliminated the across-the-board exclusion, substituting a complex, country-by-country system of deductions.

The change has produced a number of inequities, according to the United States and Overseas Tax Fairness Committee, a Washington lobby group representing some 60 companies. For example, it said, an American employed in Saudi Arabia who earns a base salary of $30,000 could owe the Internal Revenue Service $35,444 when the usual overseas allowances for cost of living and housing differentials are taken into account.

In most cases, the corporation assumes the extra tax burden for its American employee. But as a result, Ben J. Brown, the committee's vice president, said, "that guy becomes an enormous liability for his employer."

If the company absorbs the extra cost, its profits suffer. If it tries to pass on the cost, "it makes it hard to compete with a British employer that is paying tax-free salaries," said Tom Wulf, compensation manager for the Bechtel Group, a San Francisco-based engineering and construction management multinational. "It becomes more economical to hire foreigners."

While political considerations have previously led multinationals to hire and promote more indigenous staff, the rapid and large-scale elimination of Americans from even the top management of subsidiaries is a disturbing development, according to many executives.

"If the procurement people employed by a company are German, they'll tend to buy German," Mr. Wulf said. "As a result, the United States will sell less material and equipment overseas."

In a study commissioned by the Tax Fairness Committee last year, Chase Econometrics, an economic forecasting and consulting subsidiary of the Chase Manhattan Bank, estimated that the replacement of Americans overseas by other

What U.S. Companies Pay for Overseas Employees
The following hypothetical examples are based on a construction supervisor, married and with one child, working in Saudi Arabia. Costs include base salary, overseas premium, overtime, completion bonus and required tax allowances.

American National
Average base salary $25,310
Total cost to U.S. company $74,875
Total cost if earned income tax-exempt $46,702

British National
Average base salary $23,400
Total cost to U.S. company $36,252

Japanese National
Average base salary $26,892
Total cost to U.S. company $39,750

French National
Average base salary $26,800
Total cost to U.S. company $41,800

Source: U.S. and Overseas Tax Fairness Committee

Barbara Maslen

nationalities reduced potential exports from the United States by 5 percent. While the Internal Revenue Service collected an extra $600 million in income taxes from expatriates and their employers, it lost $6.1 billion in potential corporate and personal income tax receipts as a result of the drop in trade, the study contended.

While such figures are disputed by Mr. Lubick and Senator Proxmire, Robert Shriner, Washington director of Chase Econometrics, maintains that they are conservative and that their potential significance is grave. American ventures in the Middle East, Africa and newly industrialized countries such as Indonesia, he noted, have been among the most profoundly affected.

"Those are expanding markets," he said. "We're in a critical period, and we're losing out."

* * *

March 25, 1984

AMERICANS IN BUSINESS IN EL SALVADOR: JUGGLING RISK, FEAR AND RETURNS

By FRED R. BLEAKLEY

SAN SALVADOR—Citibank's retail branch here is now lodged on the second floor of an office building on Boulevard de Los Heroes. Siegfried Guth, general manager, says the bank left its more accessible first-floor office a few years ago after it had been "decorated" twice by terrorist bombs.

Harlow Newton Jr., head of the American Chamber of Commerce of El Salvador, estimates that his own importing business would be at least 30 percent higher if the Salvador central bank would free up more foreign exchange.

And the president of a major American food company plans to expand his joint venture with one of the new agricultural cooperatives to grow cantaloupes, but first he has to teach the Salvadorans the rudiments of good farm management.

Business—as life—goes on in this Central American nation, which has for more than four years been ravaged by social revolution and economic chaos. Where once some 70 manufacturing subsidiaries or sales divisions of American corporations operated, now only about three dozen remain. And the job of managing a multinational corporation has lately taken on a new air of tension, as left-wing terrorists have stepped up their attempts to disrupt the Presidential election, scheduled for today.

Once again, bomb blasts can be heard at dusk and dawn around the capital as rebels dynamite electrical towers and Government forces attempt to dislodge rebel camps from the distant hills. And fears that the city itself will become as unsafe as it was in the early 1980's are returning because of such isolated incidents as the firebombings of three Shell Oil gas stations earlier this month.

Nevertheless, for the foreign companies that have managed to persist during the years of civil strife, operations have continued to be moderately profitable. And, in recent months, despite the recent fireworks, demand for their products seems to have picked up locally and throughout most of Central America. American executives are now saying that the Salvadoran economy has bottomed out, the worst is over—and they seem gingerly optimistic about the future.

"We are here to stay; it's a matter of adjusting to circumstances," said Mr. Guth, Citibank's branch manager. He added that after the elections are over, he plans to open more branches in the capital and possibly in other cities as well.

Indeed, most businessmen expect that the five-year mandate of the new President—who will be the first popularly elected Salvadoran head of state in more than 50 years—will be good for business. The current President, Alvaro Magana, has held only an interim position since his appointment by the Salvadoran constituent assembly in early 1982. And if the transition goes smoothly, the new President could give a new sense of stability to the outside world, said Mr. Newton of the Chamber of Commerce. Still, the personal safety and protection of executives and workers of American multinational corporations operating in El Salvador continues to be a major concern. As one executive put it, "For several years now the left has not bothered us much. But we never know when we might become a target again."

During 1979 and 1980 a number of foreign-owned factories were destroyed and several executives were either kidnapped or held hostage. After that, scores of companies pulled up their Salvadoran stakes. And most of the foreign concerns that did remain called their managers home, replacing them with Salvadorans. The American Chamber of Commerce here estimates that total investment in plants and equipment by American companies has dropped to $50 million from $150 million since the war began. And those companies that stayed, did so because they did not want to abandon their market share and their invested capital.

To minimize risk, American managers and most leading Salvadoran businessmen reside and work behind heavily guarded walls. Often their office complexes do not have any identifying emblem, and they are adamant about not allowing pictures of themselves or their facilities.

Many drive in armored cars. The favorite is the rugged, four-wheel-drive, American Motors Cherokee Jeep Van, locally referred to as a "garkmobile" because of its use by so many of El Salvador's oligarchy. Often the Cherokees are bought in Miami, imported and equipped with up to $50,000 of armor plate and bullet-proof glass in the capital.

Personal safety is only one of the tribulations. Perhaps the most nettlesome business problem for American companies continues to be the scarcity of foreign exchange needed to import foreign machinery or goods. Although some say the situation has improved over the past six months, delays in receiving central bank approval for letters of credit can take months. These letters of financial obligation between a Salvadoran bank and an American bank assure an American supplier of payment for goods it ships to El Salvador even if the Salvadoran importer reneges on the deal. Even parent companies will not ship to their Salvadoran subsidiaries without letters of credit.

Still, American businessmen act as if the worst is truly over. William Boorstein, for instance, a native of Cherry Hill, N.J., left El Salvador in 1979 after escaping from leftist rebels who had held him hostage for 10 days. But last December, at the age of 65, he returned to start up one of the dozens of textile plants that have been lying idle since the nation's internal strife began.

Mr. Boorstein is not alone. American textile manufacturers once again are shipping unfinished goods to the country, to be sewn and sent back. As a result, five factories have been reopened in the past four months.

These are only tentative steps on the road to recovery for an economy that has an unemployment rate of more than 30 percent and still remains the target of left-wing guerrilla attacks. But they buttressed El Salvador's improved balance of payments and gross national product last year and the ability of the country to pay all its foreign debts on time—a feat that was facilitated, of course, by continued American aid.

But some insist that one of Salvador's greatest assets throughout the crisis has been the industriousness of its people, often referred to as the Japanese of Central America. "This is not a mañana country," said Federico Bloch, executive vice president of TACA International Airlines, El Salvador's primary airline. "There's an entrepreneurial spirit here that's like the Orient."

Following are some examples of how managers of some American companies deal with business life in El Salvador:

AVX Ceramic

When it comes to discussing performance of his plant, Roberto Salazar, general manager of AVX Ceramics, says, "I'm not modest." For each of the past three years, he says, his parent company, the AVX Corporation of Great Neck, L.I., judged its El Salvador manufacturing operation, which assembles electronic components for transistors and circuits, to be ahead of its eight other plants (in Israel, Ireland, Japan, Mexico and the United States) in quality and productivity.

Such an achievement is noteworthy, considering that leftist rebels bombed and set fire to 1,200 buses—the basic means of transportation for Mr. Salazar's 1,000 workers—and that bombings of electrical towers can cause the plant to shut down for hours at a stretch. To adjust to a crippled bus system, Mr. Salazar instituted new shifts for his workers. Although it meant shutting the plant down for part of the night and staying open on Sundays, he says he was able to reschedule everyone so that each worker spent the same number of hours on the job per week as before the bombings.

Worker morale has always been high, says Mr. Salazar, because of the strong work ethic of the Salvadoran people. "They'll walk miles or jam into pickup trucks to come to work if the buses are burned," he says. In addition, Mr. Salazar says his company has always paid more in salary and benefits than the law required. Among other things, the plant has a medical clinic for the children of workers and a full-time doctor.

Texas Instruments

Local businessmen say that Texas Instruments, the largest employer of all the American companies here, is by far the most secretive and the most security-conscious. Its executives, who apparently are under order from Dallas headquarters to keep to themselves and maintain a low profile, are rarely seen at Salvadoran business and social events. T.I., in fact, is the only large American company here that is not a member of the local American Chamber of Commerce. The company did not respond to a request for an interview.

With 2,400 employees, all of whom are local women except for supervisors and top management, T.I.'s Salvadoran division assembles components for pocket calculators and digital watches. Those who have seen the factory say it is ultramodern, encompasses several acres of space and is guarded by a highly professional security force, headed by a retired Salvadoran army major. Until last year, T.I. had two manufacturing facilities, but it reportedly consolidated them for security purposes at the present site in Santa Lucia, about six miles outside of downtown San Salvador.

Despite T.I.'s attempts at privacy it was the talk of the business community last year because of what is widely referred to as "the scandal." T.I. will not comment, but according to local business executives and Government officials T.I. dismissed top management from its operation as well as one or two executives in Dallas headquarters because of irregularities in the amount of gold used in the manufacturing process and in the company's foreign exchange account.

In any event, new management is said to be bringing in additional manufacturing equipment and hiring more workers, because of increased worldwide demand for T.I.'s products.

Caess

The elevator to the third-floor office of the president of El Salvador's largest company—Caess—makes its last stop at the second floor. From there a visitor climbs a flight of stairs past a steel door that can be bolted shut in case trouble is reported from the lobby, where several guards with machine guns serve as the first line of defense.

Such precautions are understandable. Twice, Manuel Cano, president and general manager who grew up in Forest Hill, Queens, has been kidnapped. The first time he was taken from his office at gunpoint and company guards rescued him on the street outside. The second time, he was released unharmed after lying on the floor of a car for several hours while his abductors drove around and ordered him to mend his capitalistic ways. About 40 percent of the stock of Caess is owned by 3,500 American stockholders, and another 44 percent is owned by the Baldwin-United Corporation of Cincinnati, which acquired it through a merger with the founding company early this century.

But physical danger is not uppermost on Mr. Cano's mind. Rather, he feels Caess is being "strangled to death" by the Salvadoran Government's refusal to allow the company to increase its rates to consumers so that it will have an adequate rate of return. Earlier this month, for instance, the Government increased the cost of the power it sells to Caess for distribution, but it would not allow Caess to increase its sales to municipalities for electricity used in street lighting or water pumping.

At the same time, Caess has suffered $4.5 million in war-related damage to its equipment, for which it is not reim-

bursed or allowed to make up in rates. And it must shell out $400,000 a year for a private security force, which attempts to protect electrical towers and power lines.

Disrupting electricity is a key part of leftist strategy for damaging the Salvadoran economy. "Last night the rebels knocked out three of our poles," Mr. Cano said in a recent interview as he chain-smoked cigarettes, "How do we continue to finance that? The Government does not appreciate what is happening to us."

Xerox

Like most big companies during the recent recession, the Xerox Corporation stressed the need for greater cost control and sales production. In El Salvador, though, the local Xerox office already had plenty of reason "to run a tighter ship," as its general manager put it. He refused to be identified for security reasons.

Several years ago, the Salvadoran central bank introduced a two-tier rate of foreign currency exchange, which meant that Xerox in El Salvador could once again convert its profits into dollars and send them home to its parent. The catch, however, was that the new rate represented a 60 percent devaluation from the rate at which Xerox had accumulated earlier profits. And because of competitive pressures, the parent Xerox was able to recoup only about two-thirds of that currency conversion loss on its balance sheet.

The rest had to be made up by an austerity program aimed primarily at increasing productivity among the 60-person staff here. Technical service representatives, for instance, increased their workload to 100 machines, rather than the 80 that Xerox representatives are typically responsible for in other countries. And salesmen stepped up their pace so that their level of copier machine sales versus removals was twice as great as it had been three years earlier.

Kimberly-Clark

Giant machines stand idle inside Kimberly-Clark's cavernous tissue-products factory about 20 miles outside San Salvador. But it is not for lack of demand, nor labor strife, nor terrorist actions. The machines are quiet because what was once a simple financial transaction—applying to a local Salvadoran bank for a letter of credit—is now a major, time consuming task. Now, it can take from two to six months, or more, for approval, says Jose Rubio, the company's director of operations.

He has been waiting since last May for approval of a letter of credit that would insure shipment of a $98,000 machine so that the plant can produce a new tissue product. Moreover, because of delays in receiving approval for importation of pulp needed for an already-existing product, Mr. Rubio estimated earlier this month that he was in the midst of a 25-day shutdown of machinery that produces about 40 percent of his factory's $2 million-a-month output.

To cope, Mr. Rubio sometimes submits letters of credit applications to four or five Salvadoran banks. And when possible, he purchases far more than he needs so that he will have an abundance of inventory. As a result, portions of the factory are stacked to the ceilings with bales of crude paper and barrels of dye, but often the machines sit motionless for lack of a spare part.

* * *

September 6, 1987

GARMENT SWEATSHOPS ARE SPREADING

By KENDALL J. WILLS

There will be no backyard barbecues or volleyball games at the beach on Labor Day for the 16 employees of Mr. Wong's garment factory in Manhattan.

Instead, as millions of other workers take tomorrow off to celebrate organized labor's achievements or simply to relax, Mr. Wong's employees, having rested on their one-day weekend, will report to work at 8 A.M. They will log their usual 10 or 11 hours without overtime or holiday compensation. Some will earn less than $3.35 an hour, the legal minimum wage.

"I feel a little guilty," admitted Mr. Wong at his factory one recent Saturday as sewing machines whirred in a monotonous buzz in the background. But he said competitive pressures prevented him from providing the basic standards of pay and working conditions guaranteed by law to workers in this country. His name has been changed in this article to protect his identity.

Situated in the heart of New York City's midtown garment district, Mr. Wong's factory is representative of what government and union officials say is an increasing number of sweatshops, whose workers endure squalid or illegal conditions.

Conditions Can Be Deplorable

"We've found children as young as 12 years old" working in some shops, said Anthony J. Ponturiero, the assistant regional administrator for the wages and hours division of the Labor Department. Besides regular wage and hour violations, he said, agents have found factories with malfunctioning toilets and others where workers were preparing food next to their machines and were eating from plates on the floor.

Such conditions are similar to those that helped fill the ranks of organized labor decades ago.

But today, labor unions are having difficulty drawing these workers into their fold. For many in the apparel manufacturing shops, the wages, though low by American standards, are often higher than what they received in Ecuador, the Dominican Republic, South Korea, Taiwan or other countries where they lived before they arrived in the United States.

What's more, many are aliens who lack proper documentation to work legally. Few speak English.

As a result, the workers often cooperate with the employers in keeping a low profile, and they accept the terms they are offered, according to Labor Department and union officials.

Hard to Organize

"It's hard to organize workers who have few skills or are afraid of being deported," said Jay Mazur, president of the International Ladies Garment Workers Union. "Their employers tell them, 'You talk to the union and I'll turn you in.' "

The apparel business, still the largest manufacturing industry in New York City, is continuing to lose jobs, according to Samuel M. Ehrenhalt, regional commissioner of the Bureau of Labor Statistics. With 105,000 people employed in the industry today, it has lost a quarter of a million jobs in New York alone since its peak in 1948, he said. The industry has also dropped from the second largest employer in the city in 1960 to eighth today.

Coinciding with that decline, membership in the garment workers union in New York City fell about 40 percent in the last decade to about 70,000 members today. Union officials say they hope their efforts to help undocumented aliens gain legal status under the new Federal immigration law will also help to win the workers' trust.

Meanwhile, sweatshops are springing up in New York and elsewhere.

Substandard conditions in garment factories are a "national phenomenon," said Emanuel Tobier, a professor of economics at the School of Public Administration at New York University. But, he added, New York City has a particularly large share of the "preconditions for having sweatshops," including large numbers of immigrants who are willing to take low-paying jobs and aging, deteriorating factory buildings.

Trying to Enforce Standards

Mr. Mazur, of the I.L.G.W.U., criticized the Reagan Administration, saying the Labor Department had reduced its enforcement efforts.

"The Government is really not concerned with enforcing the fair labor standards," he said.

The number of Labor Department compliance agents nationwide has declined by 11 percent since 1980, department officials said. But the number responsible for covering New York City has remained about the same, 29 in 1980, compared with 27 today, they added.

Last year, the agency conducted 146 investigations of possible illegal conditions in all industries in the city, but Mr. Ponturiero said he could not say how many violations were discovered or how many might have been found in the apparel industry.

Intense Pressure on Production

When illegal conditions are discovered, factory owners are issued citations and fined. In cases with numerous violations, lawsuits are brought against the shop owners to recover back wages for the employees.

Despite widespread agreement that sweatshops are increasing, there is little agreement on how to define them or how many there are in the city.

"There are hundreds of sweatshops by almost any definition," said Walter Mankoff, associate director of research at the I.L.G.W.U.

Other union officials say there may be as many as 2,000.

Most labor experts agree that competition in the apparel industry and increasing costs of production in this country have resulted in intense pressure on American manufacturers to produce items ever more quickly and cheaply.

That has caused a realignment in the manufacturing of apparel products. Labor Department officials say Asians in New York City have begun to make inroads into apparel manufacturing, a field previously dominated by people of Hispanic descent and before them, Italians and Jews.

With soaring rents and other production costs largely steady or rising, only labor costs can be adjusted to meet the competition.

Farming the 'Spot Market'

The average wage for apparel manufacturing jobs—$7.16 an hour—is among the lowest of all manufacturing categories, according to Labor Department figures.

Garment manufacturers farm out the cutting, sewing and pressing tasks at the cheapest price to contractors in what is known as the "spot market." Thousands of small contractors, employing cheap labor, compete in that market.

One such contractor is Danny Rhee, an immigrant from South Korea who has been in the business for eight years, often working 12 hours a day, six days a week to keep his business solvent.

Mr. Rhee said the price he receives from the manufacturer to have a blouse sewn—$1.75 to $2.50—is the same as it was eight years ago. Meanwhile, his costs have increased, cutting into profits and making it impossible to increase wages for his employees. The blouse may sell for $30 or more in retail stores.

Mr. Rhee said he had no choice but to accept the price offered by manufacturers. "If I don't accept the deal," he said, "they offer it to someone else."

Some contractors cut corners by employing children, paying less than minimum wages or forgoing overtime compensation. Many employees are paid off the books in cash, so it is difficult for enforcement officials to prove that the law has been broken.

Mr. Rhee said he had invested in advanced-technology sewing machines that save on labor. But if rents continue to climb, he said, he will be forced to move out of his space at 315 West 36th Street within two years. "I see the time coming," he said.

While Mr. Rhee prides himself on keeping a clean and legal shop and helping his employees as best he can, others are unscrupulous, officials say.

"We've walked into places and the news spreads immediately," Mr. Ponturiero said of recent investigations conducted by the Labor Department. "Suddenly we see kids squeeze out the back door and by the time we get to the shop, everybody dummies up."

*   *   *

June 5, 1988

MIXING CULTURES ON THE ASSEMBLY LINE

By JOHN HOLUSHA

FLAT ROCK, Mich—Two distinctly different car models are rolling off the assembly line at a gleaming new automobile plant here, about 15 miles south of Detroit. One bears the block letter badge of Mazda, the other the oval emblem of Ford.

The cars look different but they are, in fact, two versions of the same car, produced by American workers and mostly Japanese managers, using a design developed by Mazda.

More important, however, they are symbols of Detroit's new economics and the complex web of ties that have developed between Japanese car companies and their American rivals. Although there have been alliances of one sort or another between Detroit and the Japanese for years, most recent ones are joint ventures based on a simple economic strategy: Cars are produced for both companies, with a common structure but different appearances. The cars are built in American factories using Japanese management and designs.

These joint ventures, and other alliances ranging from investment in rival companies to the importation of Japanese vehicles for sale under American labels, are helping transform the way the domestic industry operates, changing the nature of competition worldwide and blurring the distinction between American and imported cars. It is a development that is only beginning to leave its mark on the industry's economic landscape.

"I think there will be more alliances and that they will intensify," said Malcolm S. Salter, a professor at the Harvard Business School. "They are less costly than full mergers, give the Japanese access to markets and reduce risks for all."

But the alliances, particularly those with hybrid factories that blend two very distinct cultures, are creating distinct managerial challenges: Management is hard enough in heavily competitive industries, but when culturally different companies are linked—and rival companies, at that—complications are bound to emerge.

Although the joint projects appear to be successful so far, some experts question whether American workers will adapt to the tightly disciplined Japanese system.

"There are two faces to the Japanese system," said Harley Shaiken, a former auto worker who is now a professor of economics at the University of California at San Diego. "One is the increased efficiency, better quality, the consulting with workers. But the other is increased pressure, stress, tightly strung manufacturing. The question is which face will prevail."

Already, some things are clear. "There's no issue that they will adapt some hybrid of the Japanese manufacturing system," said David Cole, director of the University of Michigan's Office for the Study of Automotive Transportation. "That decision has already been made by the competitive environment. It's adapt or get out of the game."

The alliances started to develop several years ago because Japan, faced with import restrictions, wanted greater access to the American automobile market and Detroit needed to tap Japan's skills in small-car making. Detroit so needed the low-cost high-mileage cars that it was willing to cede part of its lucrative domestic market. In doing so, it also ceded part of the culture on which the domestic auto industry was based.

In the Japanese-run ventures, distinctions between workers and their bosses are obscured by the identical uniforms worn by both, quite a shift from Detroit's rigid labor-management structure. Traditional management perks—reserved parking spaces, for example, and executive dining rooms—have been abolished. American workers with Midwest accents lace their conversations with Japanese words and business concepts, words like "kaizen" (continuous improvement) and "wa" (harmony among people), dropped casually into discussions.

At Flat Rock, where the Ford Probe and the Mazda MX-6 are being built, cross-cultural complications were evident from the start.

"Americans have a tendency to plan in more detail in the early stages regarding costs and sales; the Japanese are more vague about these things," said Osamu Nobuto, president of the Mazda Motor Manufacturing (USA) Corporation.

That caused clear frustration for the Ford Motor Company. "For Ford to proceed with a project, we want to know the price and return on investment," said Gary M. Heffernan, a Ford senior executive. "Mazda is run by engineers who didn't have to worry too much about the financial aspects while the yen was weak and they were expanding so rapidly." In the end, Ford decided it needed the new Mazda-designed car badly enough to go ahead with the project.

According to industry experts, dispute resolution is a big obstacle to joint projects, one made more difficult by barriers of language and distance. "You always have internal battles over any new car," Mr. Heffernan said. "Internally, it gets resolved by the boss. With Mazda, we had to try to work those things out at a lower level." This problem appears to have been an important factor in Mazda's decision to build and operate the Flat Rock plant by itself rather than as a joint venture with Ford. "One of the disadvantages of a joint venture is that decision-making is slow," Mr. Nobuto observed.

In other ventures, cultural clashes have emerged over less important matters, but the scars show nonetheless. At Diamond-Star Motors, a joint venture between the Chrysler Corporation and the Mitsubishi Motors Corporation to assemble cars for sale by both companies, one issue was how the office was to be laid out. American executives prefer private offices; the Japanese think having everyone in a big room with no walls promotes better communication.

After much discussion, Diamond-Star officials settled on an open office layout at the plant in Normal, Ill., but with partitions between individuals' work areas. But Yoichi Nakane, the Mitsubishi executive who is Diamond-Star's president and chief executive, is not certain they did the right thing. The partitions, he said, "will create a different way of operating and may cause some problems. A consensus is not always right; it may not get a good result."

There have been other problems. The General Motors Corporation is reportedly unhappy with the sales performance of its imported and domestically made Japanese cars—the Nova, made at a California plant managed by the Toyota Motor Company; the Chevrolet Spectrum imported from Isuzu Motors Ltd., and the Chevy Sprint, imported from the Suzuki Motor Company—and is preparing to shift marketing strategies.

This fall, all three cars will be sold under the Geo brand name, giving no indication that they are related to Chevrolet. The idea, Chevrolet officials have told dealers, is to increase advertising efficiency by promoting one name and to overcome the reluctance of some import buyers to consider a domestic nameplate.

In all the auto alliances, there are limits to cooperation. The Ford-Mazda deal is one example.

"Each company only tells the other what is necessary to explore future opportunities," said Robert R. Reilly, director of strategic planning for Ford. "It would be inappropriate for us to talk about plans for the Lincoln Town Car or Continental," the company's big luxury cars.

Nor is Mazda about to turn over details of its unique rotary engine used in its RX7 sports car. "The rotary engine is a special case," Mr. Nobuto said. "We do not share that with other companies, including Ford."

For every tie established between auto companies, dozens more are discussed and discarded, industry leaders say. The hard part, they say, is to find a project that allows two companies to share costs without cutting into each other's potential sales.

The change in the value of the dollar, particularly with respect to the yen, is bringing a new balance into the relationships between the American auto companies and their partners, allowing the Americans more say in what the new cars—and deals—will look like.

"During the extended period of artificial exchange rates we were forced into the hands of the Japanese to develop new products," said Michael N. Hammes, vice president for international operations at Chrysler.

G.M., according to trade sources, is already planning to supply Isuzu with American-made engines for trucks intended for export to this country. And Mr. Nobotu concedes that when the Probe and MX-6 are updated, they will probably be equipped with Ford rather than Mazda engines and drivetrains.

Mr. Hammes of Chrysler predicted that his company's relationship with the Mitsubishi Motor Company would continue, but on a more equal basis. "It's going to be a two-way street from now on," he said. But such shifting relationships have made the subject of auto joint ventures so sensitive that G.M., which has the most extensive network of alliances, refused to allow its executives to be interviewed for this article.

There is little question, however, that the American industry has learned valuable lessons from its day-to-day contact with Japanese manufacturing managers.

G.M. officials, for example, were shocked to find that the highest-quality car sold by G.M. was produced at the New

United Manufacturing Motor plant in Fremont, Calif., the G.M.-Toyota joint venture known by its acronym, Nummi. And that was the case despite the plant's low level of automation and lack of high technology.

The plant had a reputation as a labor-relations headache when it was operated by G.M., and although it is staffed by the same ex-G.M. workers, Toyota has molded them into an efficient, quality-conscious workforce. G.M. executives with experience at Fremont have been sent by the company to other plants around the country, preaching the gospel of worker involvement.

"Nummi changed the direction of the American automobile industry," said Maryann N. Keller, an analyst with Furman Selz Mage Dietz & Birney. "Nummi proved that it was not machines, it was systems and software that created high quality. At G.M., you never admitted there was a problem. The Japanese look at problems as an opportunity and encouraged open discussion of problems."

Nummi produces models known as the Chevrolet Nova and Toyota Corolla FX16. There was no equity exchange in the deal and relations between the two companies are necessarily distant because of antitrust considerations: G.M., after all, is the world's largest auto maker and Toyota is No. 3.

Nummi is hardly the only alliance in which G.M. has a major role. G.M. owns 41.6 percent of Isuzu, mainly a truck maker, and imports an Isuzu model sold as the Chevrolet Spectrum. It owns 5.3 percent of Suzuki, and imports a car sold as the Chevrolet Sprint.

Chrysler and Ford also have other alliances, but they are less scattershot. Chrysler linked up with Mitsubishi in the early 1970's to import small, fuel-efficient cars when its domestic lineup was large and thirsty; today it owns 24 percent of Mitsubishi stock.

It still sells the Mitsubishi-made Dodge Colt, Premier and Vista models to buyers who prefer imports, but the fuel economy of its domestic cars has improved dramatically. Later, the two companies developed the joint venture called Diamond-Star Motors.

Ford acquired a 25 percent interest in Mazda in 1979. Initially Ford sold Mazda cars under the Ford label in the Asia-Pacific market; now the Mercury Tracers that Ford makes in a plant in Hermosillo, Mexico, are based on Mazda designs. The arrangement at Flat Rock is the most recent arrangement. This wave of alliances surprised the experts. A decade ago most auto executives and industry analysts were predicting a shakeout in the international industry, with just a handful of giant companies surviving into the 1990's. But, experts said, managers in car companies all over the world were unwilling to yield autonomy, which thwarted merger activity.

"It is very difficult to work out the details of mergers because most companies want to keep control of the business," said Ford's Mr. Heffernan. "So we found ways to get the benefits without actually merging."

The greatest benefit, of course, stems from the economics of the deals. In general, the cars produced for both partners

have a common structure but a different look that enables them to be marketed as different vehicles.

The cars made at Flat Rock, for example, the Ford Probe and the Mazda MX-6, share the same basic understructure and engine, but the Probe is a sporty hatchback and the MX-6 a more conservative sedan.

"This is an example of where two interests come together," said Mazda's Mr. Nobuto. "We would not have done it if the cars were competing."

* * *

July 24, 1989

ONLY THE BOSSES ARE AMERICAN

By LOUIS UCHITELLE
Special to The New York Times

BESANCON, France—The Stanley Works is an old-line Yankee manufacturer, but walk through its factory here and nothing other than the name is recognizable as American.

The managers and engineers are French. The hand tools produced here are made from European steel and plastic. The new machines on the assembly line are mostly designed on the premises by Stanley's engineers and built either by them or by subcontractors nearby. Not one screw comes from the United States.

Thus is the Stanley Works, an old New England name associated with hardware and tools, evolving into a global company. And it is a far different animal from the multinationals of the 1950's and 1960's. In that day, American corporations supplied their overseas factories with machinery, technology and materials from home. Today's global companies spread wealth abroad—as Stanley is doing in eastern France.

'No Longer American'

"We are going to wake up soon to the fact that a lot of American companies are no longer American," said Robert B. Reich of Harvard's Kennedy School of Government.

Stanley is far from losing its American identity, but its experience in Besancon is representative of that of many American manufacturing companies. That includes learning manufacturing tricks not widely practiced at home and trying to get used to the idea that foreign managers should be left to run things their way.

These days, Stanley is concentrating European production in Besancon and in Sheffield, England, after closing plants elsewhere in Europe that were marginally profitable. It has spent $16 million on automation in the past two years, nearly 9 percent of the company's capital investment worldwide.

The idea is to put these factories on a par with Stanley's operations in the United States, although the process is slow and leads to some striking contrasts at the factory here. Two women, for example, sit side-by-side, pulling at levers that hand-stamp the Stanley name on saw blades, one at a time. Nearby, a new $500,000 machine with robotic arms and computer controls assembles steel measuring tapes, almost unattended.

Stanley purchased the plant here quite by chance in 1970, from a French entrepreneur, Michel Quenot, who made tape measures and had grown tired of labor troubles and other headaches. But if Richard H. Ayers, Stanley's chairman, had paid a consultant millions to find an ideal site for a global factory, he could not have come up with a better place.

Watchmaking had been Besancon's main industry and chief source of jobs. The collapse of the watch companies here and in Switzerland in the late 1970's—victims of the new digital technology—sapped the work force of its notable militancy. Strikes today are rare, and wage increases for Stanley's factory workers barely keep up with inflation. (Skilled workers seldom earn above $15,000 a year, and most engineers receive under $40,000.)

Modern Factory In a Quaint Setting

The upheaval still changing Besancon is not evident. The city is picturesque, with old stone buildings and busy, cobbled shopping streets in the foothills of the Jura Mountains. Dairy farms, ski slopes and pine forests are close by. Government jobs (Besancon, with a population of more than 150,000, is the capital of a French region, Franche-Comte, and the site of a major Army base) help to keep the city bustling.

Important for Stanley, engineers who once ran the region's watchmaking factories now make electronic devices and intricate factory machines. The operators of these small machine shops are gaining a reputation as experts in an automation technique known as flexible manufacturing. The local engineering school that once trained people for watchmaking now has a research center for flexible manufacturing.

Companies like Stanley help finance that research by paying for projects that aid production. "We give industry 40,000 hours of help a year," said Jean-Louis Vaterkowski, the school's director. Some students at the school serve internships at Stanley, gaining experience as they help to assemble machinery.

Flexible manufacturing is well-suited for producing small quantities of different-model products, and Stanley is installing the computer-controlled "flexible" machinery—even designing some in-house—to manufacture its steel tape measures. The tapes come in various lengths, and the goal is to make the dozen or so different models on the same assembly line. So far, Stanley can produce, say, 10,000 tapes that are 5 meters long and then reprogram the machinery for a run of 8-meter or 10-meter tapes. Other models still require more hand assembly.

In some ways, automation is reducing Stanley's role as a lifeline for Besancon's unemployed, who represent about 7.5 percent of the work force. It has allowed Stanley to reduce its payroll to 520 people, from 750 in 1979. Labor now is less than 10 percent of total production cost, giving workers little leverage to push for wage increases.

Marcel Truche, 40 years old, the intense chief of operations in Besancon, tries to spend an hour each day on the factory floor, greeting workers warmly and listening to complaints and suggestions. He considers this important for efficiency, but he never mentions wages or job security. "I have refused to speak of these subjects," he said. "They know that."

Whatever the impact on labor, the manufacturing expertise building up here is being exported to Stanley engineers in the United States, and such cross-fertilization is considered by economists to be one of the great benefits of globalization—a benefit that helps Stanley capture inexpensive technologies. "We have talked increasingly of bringing engineers from other countries to the United States," Mr. Ayers said.

European Taste For Local Products

But concentrating production in Besancon (besides measuring tapes, saws and carpenter's levels are made here) and in Sheffield (wood planes, screwdrivers, drills and numerous cutting tools) has been an obstacle to sales—one that could endure into the 21st century.

The problem is that West Germans, French, English, Italians and Spanish differ in their tastes for consumer goods, despite all the talk of a unified European marketplace by 1992. They might buy the same model cars, washing machines and vacuum cleaners, says Yves Rouyer, Stanley's vice president for European tool sales. But for most other items, including tools, tastes are provincial.

That became painfully evident when Stanley closed its West German factory, which made tools with German labels. Sales fell sharply in West Germany, where carpenters, plumbers and do-it-yourselfers prefer either national brands or cheap imports from Asia, and they are just beginning to recover, with products made at Sheffield or Besancon.

"Sales would increase at a faster pace if we had a presence in Germany," said Geoffrey L. Baldwin, president of Stanley's European tool division. He has been looking for a West German tool company to buy, but he is running into an obstacle imposed from American headquarters.

Mr. Ayers wants the European operation to return a profit of more than 25 cents a year, on average, for each dollar invested in factories and machinery. That's hard in West Germany, with the highest labor costs in Europe, and Mr. Ayers's belief is that the inability to achieve high returns "may preclude investment in some foreign markets."

Mr. Baldwin accepts the restriction. "I work within an American culture that tends to seek short-term profits," he said. Meantime, he and Mr. Rouyer, the marketing vice president, pursue a somewhat tricky strategy—trying to get all of Europe to buy tools made in Besancon and Sheffield, while giving the impression that Stanley somehow produces these tools in every country.

For Obfuscation

A new distribution center in Rotterdam, the Netherlands, is dedicated to this obfuscation. It receives the tools from Besancon and Sheffield and then sends them in small quantities to local hardware stores and wholesalers in, say, Norway or West Germany.

The computer in Rotterdam even bills the customers in kroner or marks, with instructions in Norwegian or German to mail the checks to local addresses. If a problem arises, a local Norwegian or West German employed by Stanley pays a call.

"The English think Stanley is a British company," Mr. Ayers said. In Besancon, the name on the factory's letterhead is Stanley-Mabo—Mabo being the French company that Stanley bought to obtain the factory. A line of handsaws purchased from Peugeot still carries the Peugeot name, for now.

Even for products that do sell easily across borders, like Stanley's steel measuring tapes, there is an obstacle. One best-seller, a 5-meter steel ruler that unwinds from a yellow and chrome-colored case, is priced at $8 in northern Europe, but $6 in Spain. That increases the danger that hustlers will buy batches of them in Spain for resale at a 25 percent markup in the North, Mr. Rouyer said. "We're trying to harmonize the price," he said.

If the Spanish balk at $8, then Stanley might try another tactic—but it would be one that would undercut production in Besancon. The company might import a less expensive 5-meter ruler from its Taiwan factory—and sell it for $6 or less in Spain, under a different brand name. "We're considering that option," Mr. Baldwin said.

American Bosses Of a Global Concern

Mr. Baldwin, an Englishman, thinks he should have the final say in such matters, as head of the European tool operation, whose $160 million in sales last year accounted for 8 percent of Stanley's total revenue. A truly global company, he says, is composed of largely autonomous divisions in the world's major markets, the United States, Europe and East Asia. In fact, he joined Stanley in 1981, at age 40, because it seemed to offer an opportunity for an experienced engineer to get into the top management of a company beginning to upgrade its European operations.

By Mr. Baldwin's autonomy standard, however, Stanley is only partway along the road to global status. While his proposals are usually approved—including proposals to acquire European companies—he consults almost daily on many topics, even telephoning the home office for permission to release information to a newspaper reporter. What's more, he says he and other foreign managers lack the status accorded Stanley's American-born executives.

Indeed, the best salaries go to Americans and so do the 10 or so highest executive jobs. This tradition will probably change as globalization proceeds, Mr. Ayers said, but for the time being Mr. Baldwin calls attention to the gap. "We have the problem of integrating salaries for non-Americans," he said.

He notes, for example, that with the top Stanley job in Europe, he earns $100,000 a year in base salary, plus $60,000 in bonuses—sums below the incomes of Stanley executives with similar responsibilities in the United States. His base salary is $20,000 below that of Robert E. DePatie, the only American executive in Europe for Stanley. Mr. DePatie works for Mr. Baldwin.

Goal of Autonomy

With all this, Mr. Ayers says autonomy is the goal. "If I were to dictate technology or how to sell in Europe, we would go backward," he said.

Mr. Baldwin, who makes his headquarters near London, applauds such statements and so does Mr. Truche, whose base salary is $80,000—also below the pay of his American counterparts. "We gain essential expertise developing our own technology," said Mr. Truche, who trained as an engineer. "No one can maintain the equipment or make improvements in it as well as we can. Quality manufacturing isn't possible without a great deal of local control."

Somewhat wistfully, Mr. Baldwin notes that if Europeans had the spending power of Americans, "then Stanley might become a European-oriented company." That's still far away, and meanwhile Mr. Baldwin answers to Robert G. Widham, the group vice president for tool sales in the United States and abroad.

Mr. Baldwin likes to describe Mr. Widham's cross-examinations on his periodic visits to Europe. One began on a two-hour drive from the airport in Geneva to Besancon. Using one-page reminders of the points he wanted to discuss, Mr. Widham (who calls such discussions "report cards") kept tossing the sheets of paper on to the back seat as he covered each item—until Mr. Baldwin drove so fast on the winding mountain highway that all discussion stopped.

*   *   *

December 2, 1990

PETER PAN, GARFIELD AND BART— ALL HAVE ASIAN ROOTS

By BARBARA BASLER

HONG KONG—In a gray concrete building on a dusty side street in the southern China town of Shenzhen, a young Chinese woman sits at a metal desk, carefully painting in a sketch of the cheerful Disney character Baloo the Bear. The woman, who speaks no English and has never traveled beyond the bustling border town only 45 minutes by train from Hong Kong, is at work on an episode of the Disney television series "Tale Spin" that will be seen just weeks later, half a world away, by millions of young Americans watching their afternoon cartoon programs.

She is but one of hundreds of such Asian artisans. In response to the growing popularity of animated fare, American producers have been relying more and more on overseas studios to help them turn out high-quality, reasonably priced television and full-length feature cartoons. Today, much of that animation work is being done in Asia. Japan, Taiwan, Korea, the Philippines and now China are all home to studios that are frantically scrambling to satisfy the craving of American audiences for animated cartoons.

In the early 1970's, Hollywood producers, looking for ways to cut rising labor costs, began sending some of their animation work to Mexico, Australia, Canada and Spain. By the early 80's, these producers were turning more and more to the Far East, where the Japanese, with their own flourishing animation industry, had a pool of skilled workers as well as a string of subcontractors—some in Taiwan and Korea—set up to handle the work.

"The primary reason people sent work abroad was to save money," says Milt Vallas, vice president of Pacific Rim Productions Inc. "But by going overseas, by locating cheaper labor sources, they were able to put more into shows, making them more complicated than ever, with more movement, better backgrounds, more special effects."

The lower labor costs mean substantial savings on the total expense of a production: a half-hour cartoon produced in Asia costs from $100,000 to $150,000. If that episode were produced entirely in the United States, the price would roughly double.

The Chinese woman sits at one of 200 desks lined up under a bank of bright fluorescent lights in the painting section of the Pacific Rim studio. The two-year-old facility is spread out over three warehouselike floors, where 450 Chinese and a handful of Westerners are working on projects that include ABC-TV's new Saturday-morning cartoon series "The Wizard of Oz"; "Peter Pan and the Pirates," Fox's new weekday cartoon series, and "An American Tail Part II," a sequel to the 1986 animated movie produced by Steven Spielberg and scheduled for theatrical release next fall.

Although there are similar studios in Ireland, France, Australia and even Poland, Mr. Vallas estimates that more than 60 percent of the animating of America's Saturday-morning cartoon series is done in Asia. Even Fox's phenomenally successful prime-time show "The Simpsons" is produced in Asia, at the Akom Studio in Seoul. The five-year-old outfit, which employs approximately 500 people, is also busy with several other American cartoon shows, including CBS's Saturday-morning series "Muppet Babies."

A top-quality cartoon generally involves hundreds of artists and requires approximately 18,000 separate cels or drawings, each of which must be copied, painted and photographed. For a full-length feature like Disney's 1989 movie "The Little Mermaid," animators turned out close to 100,000 cels.

In the Wang Film Production Company in Taipei, more than 1,000 people are at work on at least half a dozen animated series, including such Saturday-morning staples as CBS's "Garfield" and "Bill and Ted's Excellent Adventures"; Fox's "Bobby's World," produced by Film Roman; NBC's "Rick Moranis in Gravedale High," produced by Hanna-Barbera, and the syndicated weekday show "Tiny Toons," produced by Warner Brothers.

"This is a peak for sure," says Robert A. Marples, a production supervisor for Hanna-Barbera, who has been with the company for 22 years and is in Taipei overseeing two current cartoon productions. "Anyone in animation now is up to their ears in work."

Today, there are about a dozen studios in Asia that can produce an entire cartoon, including the drawing of the char-

acters and the background scenery. Still, virtually all of the pre-production work for Asian projects is done in America or Europe, where the scripts are written, the characters are designed and sample background drawings are made to illustrate the look of the cartoon.

While some Asian studios can produce whole projects, they also work on bits and pieces. Pacific Rim, for example, does all the production work on "Peter Pan and the Pirates" and "The Wizard of Oz," including the animation drawings. But for Disney's "Tale Spin," the animation drawings are done in France and then shipped to Pacific Rim for painting and other follow-up work.

The managers of these overseas operations are reluctant to discuss specific salaries, but one animation executive says that "a rule of thumb is that an Asian makes in a month what an American would make in a week." In Hollywood, an apprentice animator earns roughly $750 a week; an experienced one makes $1,500 to $2,000.

"Some people credit the movie 'Roger Rabbit' with generating a new interest in animation," says Mr. Vallas, who frequently travels between Los Angeles and China. "And after that, Disney's 'Duck Tales' broke new ground by giving us a high-quality animated series for television."

That series, he believes, "bridged the gap between high-quality, full-length feature animation and television animation. Now, there is a huge demand for high-quality animated TV shows." The success of "The Simpsons" is also likely to foster other animated shows in prime time, he adds.

The animation process is tedious, time-consuming and sometimes nerve-wracking. "We are literally working on shows that will be on the air within weeks," says Randall M. Chaffee, a third-generation animator who is the executive producer and manager of Pacific Rim. "If you miss a deadline, there is a huge fine to pay, from $100,000 to $200,000."

All this foreign contracting means that every instruction must be carefully translated. But even meticulous translations can leave room for misunderstandings when the people drawing and coloring the cartoons have minimal knowledge of American humor, culture and slang.

Mr. Chaffee recalls a mix-up that occurred last year when Pacific Rim was working on an episode of the syndicated cartoon "Maxie" that involved a football game.

"The Chinese don't play football," he says, "so they didn't know that at the line of scrimmage the two teams need to have on uniforms of different colors, and all members of a team must consistently wear the same color. Our people had the players wearing blue, red, yellow. In one scene, the quarterback passed the ball to his receiver. But he was wearing a red uniform and the receiver had a blue uniform, so to Americans it looked like an interception."

The football, Mr. Chaffee adds, was not pigskin brown but "a bright Day-Glo orange. They had never seen a football, after all."

Such slip-ups are caught by the Western supervisors, he says, and don't make it onto the air.

Lindy Kerr for The New York Times

Li Yan Gang, an animator in the Chinese town of Shenzhen, paints backgrounds for Fox's new "Peter Pan."

Sometimes, directions come in the form of American slang that gets translated too literally. "There was a cartoon with 'Transformer' characters having this raging laser battle," recalls Mr. Vallas, "and as the bad guys were being routed, the layout artist wrote, 'Enemy is now out to lunch.' The Japanese animator drew the scenes and suddenly, in the middle of this pitched battle, he had all these fighting guys sit down and start to eat."

Still, when they appear on television, series produced in studios scattered around the world look familiar and seamless.

"One day you might see a 'Peter Pan' made in Shenzhen and the next day a 'Peter Pan' made in Manila," says Mr. Vallas.

While labor unions in America are still highly sensitive about the loss of production jobs, several producers contend that the availability of cheaper labor in Asia has helped spur an interest in animated shows that has doubled back to the United States, creating a fresh demand for the skilled writers, animators and layout artists there.

"In the U.S.," says Mr. Vallas, "it's even to the point where people who had left the business or retired are coming back."

Mr. Vallas, who has worked in the technical end of animation, was with the prolific Hanna-Barbera studio for years. Later, he opened his own small Los Angeles company that did subcontracting jobs for the larger studios, "until they

began sending their work to Asia, about five or six years ago. Then all my work dried up."

He and his partners subsequently set up their own studios in Shenzhen and Manila, with an office in Hong Kong to help oversee and coordinate the two.

With costs rising in Japan, Taiwan and Korea, Mr. Vallas predicts that the next studios will be opening in Thailand and Indonesia. And, he adds, "in a few years, even Vietnam could be turning out American cartoons."

Turtles With Brogues?

On two floors of a large office building in the center of Dublin, 120 Irish animators, painters and cameramen are producing one of the most popular TV cartoon series in America: "Teen-Age Mutant Ninja Turtles." The studio, Murakami-Wolf Dublin, is barely two years old; it was started by Jimmy T. Murakami and Fred Wolf, both of whom had had extensive experience in American animation. It was Mr. Wolf who developed the Turtle cartoon from the comic strip, originally producing the episodes in California and subcontracting some work in South Korea.

Although the shows are still developed in Los Angeles, the production details—the animation, painting and camera work—are handled in Dublin. In a recent telephone interview, Mr. Murakami said he was attracted to Ireland because of Government incentives and grants to foreign companies that create jobs.

"There are three animation studios in Dublin now," he added. "But the other two, Emerald City and Sullivan-Bluth, produce mainly feature-length animated films."

Although Mr. Murakami thinks that Dublin is a fine place to locate a studio, citing particularly the number of talented, English-speaking workers, he said he doubted that other studios would open there. "While the people are hard-working and have a good attitude—they are not always asking when their next break will be—their wages are not that much lower than an American's. I think people looking to save money and stay close to Europe will be moving to Eastern Europe soon."

* * *

January 1, 1992

INTERNATIONAL FLIGHTS, INDEED

By JOHN HOLUSHA

Every new airliner is the product of international cooperation. In the new Boeing 777 program, for example, the Boeing Company is manufacturing only the wings, nose structure and engine nacelles. The rest of the wide-body airplane will come from hundreds of subcontractors in North America, Japan and Europe. The main fuselage sections, for example, will be fabricated in Japan; the wing flaps come from Italy.

The McDonnell Douglas Corporation, Boeing's only domestic rival in the airliner business, wants to go even further. It is seeking to sell 40 percent of its civil airliner business to the Taiwan Aerospace Corporation, a newly formed entity that has the backing of the Taiwan Government. Because no military technology is involved, the deal requires no approval from the United States Government.

But the arrangement could have far-reaching policy implications for the $30-billion-a-year airliner industry, in which the United States has long been the world leader, with more than 75 percent of the market.

A Widespread Practice

International cooperation in aircraft development and manufacturing is a fact of life for several reasons.

For one thing, the other guys do it. To preserve their aircraft industries, the Governments of Britain, France, Ger-

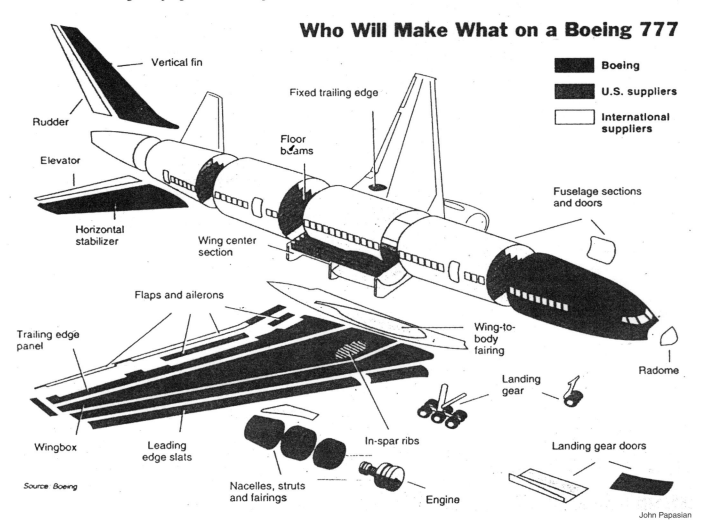

Who Will Make What on a Boeing 777

■ Boeing
▨ U.S. suppliers
□ International suppliers

Vertical fin
Rudder
Elevator
Horizontal stabilizer
Fixed trailing edge
Floor beams
Wing center section
Flaps and ailerons
Trailing edge panel
Wingbox
Leading edge slats
Nacelles, struts and fairings
In-spar ribs
Engine
Wing-to-body fairing
Landing gear
Fuselage sections and doors
Radome
Landing gear doors

Source: Boeing

John Papasian

many and Spain have collectively poured an estimated $25 billion into Airbus Industrie, the Paris-based consortium that has developed into a big force.

Officials of Airbus say they are interested in taking on Japanese companies, like Mitsubishi Heavy Industries, Fuji Heavy Industries and Kawasaki Heavy Industries, as limited partners if the consortium proceeds with plans to build a 600-seat jet transport some airlines say they might need. (A Boeing 747 seats between 385 and 400; the new Boeing 777, which will seat up to 375, is designed for service requiring a twin-engine plane.)

In the case of McDonnell, the aircraft builder needs the capital from a Taiwan deal to stay in the game. McDonnell is hoping to develop an all-new airplane, the MD-12, to challenge the Boeing 747 and Airbus A340 in the long-haul market. The company's current models, the MD-11 and MD-80, are updated versions of older designs, and do not compete directly with the 747 because of size and range limitations.

But even Boeing, which has produced a majority of the world's airliners flying today, cannot go it alone. Aircraft purchases are political as well as economic decisions, particularly in parts of the globe where governments either own or heavily influence the national airlines.

Boeing officials say that to sell in some Asian and European markets, they have to include local manufacturers in aircraft programs. And by subcontracting parts of the planes to low-cost manufacturing areas, the company helps hold down overall expenses.

Boeing executives say they are acutely conscious that jetliners are among the few complex manufactured goods that American companies can still sell to the world, and the company knows that the Japanese Government has repeatedly focused on commercial aviation as an industry to conquer.

The strategy for keeping control of the business, Boeing executives say, is to contract out some parts, but to keep wing manufacturing, final assembly and integration of the electronic, hydraulic and mechanical systems firmly in-house. Uniting several million parts into an airplane that flies reliably and at low cost is not a skill that can be easily learned from the outside, they assert.

But some in the industry fear that McDonnell, which has nowhere near the bulging, $100 billion order book of Boeing, may have to trade key technology for the financing it needs to build the MD-12. That could be the first step toward true Asian competition for the American airliner industry, critics say.

There are other concerns, too. The next generation of airliners may have to be supersonic to shrink the vast distances between North America and the Pacific Rim. Some American aerospace executives say such a project may be too big and risky for even Boeing to tackle alone, especially in a future in which Pentagon spending is unlikely to subsidize aerospace research to the extent it has in the past half-century.

* * *

January 1, 1992

COSTS MAY BE TOO HIGH FOR ALL-AMERICAN CHIPS

By DAVID E. SANGER
Special to The New York Times

TOKYO—When the Reagan Administration first pressed to open Japan's market to American semiconductors in the mid-1980's, the issue seemed as straightforward as an on-off switch: There were American chips, which the Japanese were not buying, and there were Japanese chips, of which the Japanese could not seem to buy enough.

The result was the United States-Japan semiconductor trade agreement. But when the pact came up for renewal this past year, American companies were still complaining that their market share still fell far short. In private conversation, however, many corporate executives acknowledged that the whole idea of an all-American chip was fast becoming a historical artifact. No industry has seen a bigger blitz of international alliances.

Siemens A.G. of Germany and the International Business Machines Corporation in 1991 forged what may become the industry's most dynamic partnership, one likely to reach across a startling range of chip technologies. In December, the companies announced a working prototype of the world's first memory chip capable of holding 64 million bits of information, about the equivalent of the text in six weekday issues of this newspaper.

But just behind them are Texas Instruments Inc. and Hitachi Ltd. of Japan, which recently announced that their researchers, fresh from the joint development of a 16-megabit memory chip, were headed for the 64-megabit generation. Then there is the Motorola-Toshiba team, the A.T& T.-N.E.C. pas de deux and—in what is already proving to be the most politically explosive alliance—I.B.M. and Toshiba, which a few months ago began jointly developing and manufacturing color liquid crystal display screens for laptop computers. (Each screen is essentially a large chip.)

While the specifics of each deal differ, their common point is a pooling of intellectual resources in creating the chip architecture and designing it for easy manufacture. Politically, it still makes a difference whether the circuits are etched on silicon in Kumamoto—one of Japan's biggest chip-making regions—or in California's Silicon Valley.

Manufacturing technology still counts for a lot, though, and it is in this regard that the new alliances may not prove the huge success stories that companies had predicted.

Motorola built a joint-venture plant in Sendai, Japan, and quickly moved to transfer the technology to Britain and to Texas. The transfer was only a partial success. "In Texas, we just could not convince our managers to step aside and let people named Seki or Nishihara run their operations for a year," a Motorola executive said a few months ago.

And there was constant haggling over trading Motorola's microprocessor designs for Toshiba's manufacturing technology. While both sides said the big issues had been worked out, each reportedly harbors suspicion that the other is holding back.

Already, the international alliances are tying American technology policy into knots. Corporate executives concede that it is increasingly difficult to argue in Washington that Fujitsu, Hitachi, N.E.C. and Toshiba are scheming to keep them out of the Japanese market, while at the same time signing new partnership agreements.

But in the end, what is driving the alliances is not politics, but money. Designing an elaborate new chip and building the factory to produce it has become a half-billion-dollar enterprise. No one wants to take that kind of risk alone.

* * *

September 1, 1992

GLOBAL ISSUES WEIGH ON TOWN AS FACTORY HEADS TO MEXICO

By KEITH BRADSHER
Special to The New York Times

CORTLAND, N.Y., Aug. 26—When the red brick buildings on Main Street were new eight decades ago, and the autos were bulky, black and few, a local steel company brought hundreds of low-wage workers here to upstate New York from Italy and the Ukraine rather than pay more to local workers.

Today, the steel company has long since closed and a rainbow of sleeker vehicles cruises Main Street. But once again a big local employer, this time the Smith Corona Corporation, is looking for cheap foreign labor.

Rather than importing foreign workers, however, Smith Corona announced last month that it was moving its typewriter manufacturing operations to Mexico, most likely to Tijuana. Although it plans to keep its much smaller engineering, distribution and customer service divisions here, Smith Corona will lay off 875 of its 1,300 workers in the next 12 months.

'Starting All Over Again'

Smith Corona workers were generally unwilling to discuss the pending layoffs. But one worker who did talk was Barbara E. Miller, who assembles the typewriter mechanism that flicks the correction ribbon into place. "At 50, I'm not really looking forward to starting all over again," she said recently, as she sat on a hay bale near the large gray barn that she rents with her husband. "I have five weeks of vacation; it's back to scratch."

Corporate decisions like the one by Smith Corona have become a centerpiece in the national debate over President Bush's recently announced free trade agreement with Mexico and Canada.

The company's move highlights the continuing loss of high-wage manufacturing jobs to countries where labor costs are significantly lower.

The free trade agreement is "going to be responsible for a lot of these moves, and the least the American people can expect of their Government is some assistance," Ronald T.

Walsh Jr., Cortland's Mayor, and a Democrat, said over bacon and eggs at the Community Restaurant on Main Street.

Free-market economists say that while towns like Cortland may be hurt by the trade pact, the nation will benefit over all as consumers save on everything from cantaloupes to T-shirts. Some factory relocations are good, economists contend, because they show that companies are doing business wherever they are most efficient, thereby increasing North America's overall economic output.

Most economists also contend that technological change is a larger factor than foreign trade in producing blue-collar layoffs. Smith Corona, whose typewriters have been a common graduation gift for several generations of Americans, employed 4,400 people in the mid-1970's. The company halved its work force in the late 1970's and early 1980's when it began building typewriters with fewer mechanical parts and more electronic equipment. The mechanical parts required considerable labor but the electronics can be stamped together cheaply.

Smith Corona's move followed a similar decision in October by the Zenith Electronics Corporation to send most of its remaining American television production to Mexico from Springfield, Mo. These moves were among the reasons for President Bush's announcement this month that, if re-elected, he would budget an extra $2 billion a year in Federal aid for workers who lose jobs because of foreign competition, environmental regulations or post-cold war shrinkage of the United States military.

Unemployment in Cortland County, at 8.3 percent in June, has been below the state average, in part because new industries, producing everything from garbage cans to packaging material, have flourished in this county of 49,000 people.

Staying With Typewriters

As for Smith Corona, some analysts would attribute its problems to its own management, which continued making portable typewriters while the rest of the world moved on to portable computers.

"Their market analysts simply did not seem able to come to grips with the way things were moving," said Raymond G. Thorpe, a Republican and the Town Supervisor of Cortlandville, an area of dairy farms and cornfields that includes Smith Corona's factory and surrounds the much more populous city of Cortland. "They could have diversified into a lot of other areas to keep going, but they didn't do it."

G. Lee Thompson, the chairman and chief executive of Smith Corona, said the company had briefly participated in a joint venture in the personal computer market and found the market unprofitable. Personal computers with basic accessories cost at least $1,000 and are too complicated and expensive to compete with typewriters, which sell for less than $400.

Manual typewriters are no longer made in the United States, and only a few are imported each year from India, Brazil and elsewhere. Smith Corona also makes personal word processors, which basically consist of a computer printer, a computer screen and a keyboard but have very little computer processing power.

Carla A. Hills, the United States trade representative, contends that the United States is better off when companies move to Mexico and keep some operations in the United States—as Smith Corona is doing—rather than move halfway around the world to Southeast Asia.

Mr. Thompson and Jerry K. Pearlman, Zenith's chairman and chief executive, said they had to seek lower labor costs abroad. Moving to Mexico would keep more jobs in the United States than would moving to Asia, they contended in separate telephone interviews, adding that the prospect of a free trade agreement had not affected their decision.

"I believe, short term, there are going to be some displacements," Mr. Thompson said. "I believe long term the United States, Canada and Mexico have to form an alliance."

More and more companies are setting up operations south of the border—nearly 2,000 factories in northern Mexico employ 500,000 workers to make goods for the United States while paying little or no tariffs under a Federal program to help Mexico. The moves reflect the extent to which technology, managerial skills and investment money have become more mobile than workers, turning poor countries into increasingly attractive places to build factories.

John R. McGrath, Smith Corona's senior vice president for operations and engineering, said labor costs accounted for a quarter of the cost of making a typewriter, and that moving to Mexico would allow Smith Corona to cut labor costs by four-fifths. Although moving will cost $15 million, it will save that much money every year after that, he added.

Smith Corona, which is traded on the New York Stock Exchange but is nearly half-owned by Hanson P.L.C. of Britain, pays manufacturing workers $11 an hour. Fringe benefits and factory supervisor compensation push the company's labor costs to $18 an hour. It estimates that labor in Mexico will cost less than $4 an hour.

Competition Overseas

Smith Corona must reduce its costs to compete with low-priced typewriters imported from Japan and Southeast Asia, Mr. Thompson said. Labor costs in Asia are considerably lower than in the United States, though Japan's advantage may be partly a function of more efficient manufacturing processes. Mr. Thompson, however, blames the Bush Administration for not doing more to shield the company from unfairly cheap imports.

Over the last 12 years, the Commerce Department has repeatedly found Smith Corona's archrival, Brother Industries of Japan, guilty of selling its typewriters at unfairly low prices. But Brother has mostly avoided paying punitive Customs duties, by selling typewriters not subject to duties and by opening a typewriter assembly factory in Bartlett, Tenn.

Both Gov. Bill Clinton, the Democratic Presidential candidate, and President Bush have detailed plans for extra Federal spending on job training programs to help unskilled and semiskilled workers like those at Smith Corona. But these programs will not help Smith Corona's workers if the economy does not start growing more quickly.

The New York Department of Labor has "a lot of money ready to spend, but after 18 months of recession here in New York, what can we do?" said Roger A. Evans, a department economist. "The tougher issue is the job market."

Judy K. Davison, Cortland County's employment and training grant administrator, said her office had over the years met virtually all requests for help, although it has sometimes done so by asking local schools and colleges to accept students without collecting any tuition.

Aside from the job impact, city and county leaders played down the overall effect on the community. Smith Corona plans to keep the only large building it owns here while allowing leases on other buildings to expire, so local leaders do not expect an immediate drop in property tax revenues. Local leaders also say that a third of the company's workers commute from neighboring counties and that the company has not been a strong supporter of civic causes.

"They have been a modest citizen-donor type," Mr. Thorpe of Cortlandville said.

City Loses Aid

When reductions in state revenue-sharing last year forced the City of Cortland to cut its budget for parks and youth programs by $143,000, to $492,000, the community responded by raising much of the money through voluntary donations. Cortland Asphalt Products resurfaced a 100-car parking lot in a park for a fraction of the usual price, saving the city $15,000. Smith Corona sponsored a swimming pool party for children that cost less than $300, said Francis N. Tokar, the city's parks and youth programs director.

David P. Verostko, the company's corporate vice president for human resources, said an annual fund-raising drive for the United Way was "the one major activity we do."

Smith Corona's severance pay policies are quite limited. The company, which earned $22.1 million on sales of $371.7 million during its fiscal year that ended on June 30, is offering half a week's pay for each year of service.

To receive the money, which Mr. Thompson describes as a "job continuance package," employees must stay with the company until they are actually laid off.

GLOBAL FINANCE

March 22, 1983

NEW YORK:
THE WORLD FINANCIAL MARKET

By ROBERT A. BENNETT

It was an unusual assortment of people who met in the boardroom of the Bankers Trust Company last fall, and the purpose of the meeting was as exotic as the gathering—to develop gold and diamond deposits in Guinea in West Africa.

Seated around the huge, highly polished teak table were capitalist bankers in their pin stripes, Marxist ministers from Guinea in flowing white robes, London bullion dealers, Swiss commodities traders, Australian oilmen and a number of Wall Street lawyers.

All were there to turn the gold-and-diamond dream into reality. And all that was needed was money. But, in such a complex transaction, involving diverse investors from around the world, putting together a workable financial package took an unusual degree of sophistication. And that is why they had come to New York.

As exotic as it was, the gathering was not that uncommon for the city these days. More than ever before, New York is where the deals are made.

In the last decade, the city has become the capital of world finance. While New York has long been an important financial center, its role has grown rapidly in recent years as more foreign and out-of-state banks have opened offices here.

Today, there are 336 offices of foreign banks in New York City, at least twice as many as 10 years ago. That number does not include local banks that have been taken over by foreign institutions, such as the Marine Midland Bank, the nation's 16th largest, which was acquired by the Hongkong and Shanghai Banking Corporation, and the National Bank of North America, the 41st largest, which was bought by Britain's National Westminister Bank.

Such vitality in the financial sector has been having a profound effect on the city's economy. Over the past five years, according to Samuel M. Ehrenhalt, regional commissioner of the Federal Bureau of Labor Statistics, the city's financial services industry—mainly banks and securities firms—has directly created 200,000 jobs, offsetting a decline of similar size in its manufacturing sector.

Although New York still can boast that it provides more manufacturing jobs—463,000—than any other city in the United States, last year for the first time it had more people employed in finance—488,000—than in manufacturing, Mr. Ehrenhalt said. Moreover, Mr. Ehrenhalt and city officials estimated, the financial industry has indirectly created tens of thousands of additional jobs in other service businesses, ranging from law, public relations and accounting, to hotels and restaurants.

But there are problems, too. The benefits of New York's vibrant financial sector have not been spread evenly. The boom has been almost exclusively in Manhattan—and in a limited area, from the Battery to 59th Street. Few direct benefits, however, have crept into Harlem or the outlying boroughs.

In addition, many New Yorkers who had worked in blue-collar jobs have not been able to find positions in the financial industry. About two-thirds of the jobs created in New York during the last five years have gone to commuters, Mr. Ehrenhalt said. Bankers and city officials say they expect Manhattan's boom to seep eventually into the other boroughs.

Oil Crisis Helped New York

No one, however, denies Manhattan's financial business is surging. The growth began in the mid-1970's, after the oil-producing countries quadrupled the price of petroleum, creating a financial crisis for the rest of the world.

Led by the major New York institutions, the world's commercial banks stepped in to "recycle" hundreds of billions of dollars from the oil producers to the oil consumers.

"Until the oil crisis of the 70's, London was a rival of New York," said David Rockefeller, the retired chairman of the Chase Manhattan Bank and now chairman of the New York Partnership, a nonprofit group whose membership is drawn from city officials and business and labor leaders.

"That's no longer true," Mr. Rockefeller added. "New York now is unquestionably the financial center of the world."

Even Londoners Agree

Even many British bankers agree New York has moved into the lead. "There has been a shift away from London to New York during the last three years," said David F.V. Ashby, chief economist of Grindlays Bank of London, in a recent telephone interview.

Even now, the problems many third-world borrowers are having in paying off their huge loans have been bolstering New York as a financial center, although the city's banks are among those forced to wait for their money.

"When someone has to discuss a $5 billion problem, there is little choice, they must come to New York, not London, Brazil or Washington," said Mr. Rockefeller.

More than money, it is deal making that creates a financial center. And a real financial center attracts people from a rich mixture of economic and political systems, whose needs are as varied as their backgrounds.

Money and Those Who Serve It

A financial center involves the buying and selling of securities, the making of loans, the managing of assets, the manipulating of currencies, all of this served by a financial press, lawyers, accountants and public relations people.

But, according to many people involved in the financial community, it also needs entertainment and cultural activities to make people want to visit the city. Felix G. Rohatyn, a partner in the investment banking firm of Lazard Freres & Company, said: "We use the restaurants, the hotels, the high-priced barber shops and buy a lot of tickets for the New York Rangers, the Jets and the theater. And we support the operas and the museums."

This combination of assets creates what urban economists describe as the "critical mass" it takes to create an international financial center. And once that point is reached, the center begins to feed on itself, as more and more banks and related businesses flock to the city, bringing even more business with them.

"It's the place to be, it's the Rome of the modern era," said Deputy Mayor Kenneth Lipper. Before joining city government at the beginning of the year, Mr. Lipper was a general partner in the investment banking firm of Salomon Brothers.

Contacts Outweigh Computers

Despite the computerization of the financial world, Mr. Lipper said, big-time banking is still a "people business." Making contacts remains a critical element and, thus, the financiers keep the city's hotels and top-quality restaurants busy.

Last Sept. 9, for example, while the Institute for Foreign Bankers was holding a lunch for 150 people in the Basildon Room of the Waldorf Astoria, the Israeli-owned UMB Bank was giving a lunch for 70 people in the hotel's Cole Porter Suite. And in the evening, the Mitsui Bank of Japan held a dinner for 500 on the Starlight Roof.

Foreign and out-of-state banks have been contributing to the boom in office space, some on a grand scale. For example, the Bank of America, based in San Francisco, has 1,500 employees in New York. It has leased the former Biltmore Hotel and is converting it into a 26-story office building. It will be known as the Bank of America Plaza.

The Continental Illinois Corporation of Chicago, which has 370 employees in New York, recently completed a 44-story building on Madison Avenue between 53d and 54th Streets.

'We Have to Be Here'

"New York is a major market in many ways and we have to be here," said Andries H.J. Jansma, vice president and general manager of Continental Bank International, a New York subsidiary of the Chicago bank.

"New York is the center for dollar movements around the world," he continued. "Ultimately every dollar transfer anywhere, whether in Asia, Africa or Europe, ends up as a dollar movement through banks in New York." More than $200 billion in international transactions is cleared through New York banks each day.

"We definitely see New York getting even stronger as an international financial center," said August Belmont 3d, senior vice president of the Security Pacific National Bank of Los Angeles. The bank, which had only three employees in New York a decade ago, has almost 1,000 today. "If you

want to finance a complex project, like building a railroad or building a ship, in New York you can call on a huge variety of services."

Bankers say that New York's role as an international financial center has been greatly enhanced by the creation at the end of 1981 of an international banking zone. The zone allows banks to establish international banking facilities to conduct international transactions free from some domestic banking regulations and some local and state taxes. Already, there are 121 facilities in the city, with total assets of $42 billion.

Back-Office Work in Delaware

With modern technology, the computerized back-office work of the financial industry does not have to be physically close to where the decisions are made. So, while the wheeling-and-dealing aspects of the world of finance now seem to be captive to New York, the remainder of the operations are less tied to the city than ever before.

Citibank, for example, has moved its nationwide credit-card operations from Long Island to South Dakota. Citibank, the Morgan Guaranty Trust Company, the Chase Manhattan Bank, the Manufacturers Hanover Trust Company and Chemical Bank have established subsidiary banks in Delaware, partly to escape higher New York City taxes.

Bankers attribute the exodus to a number of factors. "My worry is that the business climate is deteriorating," said James O. Boisi, vice chairman of the Morgan Guaranty Trust Company. He cited recent increases in taxes on banks and corporations that were imposed to avoid an increase in the subway and bus fare. Mr. Boisi said he was more concerned that the city's banks had not been consulted about the increases than he was about the amount of money involved.

Some bankers also complained about the quality of the city's clerical work force, and some said it is easier outside the city to find people willing to take part-time jobs.

High Rents in Manhattan

Another problem, according to Karen N. Gerard, the city's former Deputy Mayor for Economic Development, is Manhattan's high rents. Mr. Lipper said the city is "negotiating with some insurance companies and brokerage firms about sites in Queens and Brooklyn, where they could get land and space at prices equivalent to those in the suburbs."

Some businesses have been reluctant to move part of their operations to the other boroughs. Mr. Lipper said he thinks much of the problem is psychological. "The trouble is, no company wants to be the first to move to Queens," he said.

City officials and some leaders of the financial community also are seeking to upgrade the educational system to improve the quality of the work force.

Some private companies have been establishing programs aimed at training students for jobs in demand. The American Express Company, for example, has contributed $200,000 to the Board of Education to develop a curriculum for a new high school that would prepare students for jobs in the financial industry. Some of the jobs would be margin clerks, stock traders, commodities traders and specialists in market financial services.

* * *

December 31, 1985

THE EUROBOND MARKET BOOM

By STEVE LOHR
Special to the New York Times

LONDON, Dec. 30—Sports cars, mink coats and ski trips were hot items this year on holiday shopping lists of the well-heeled players in the Eurobond market. With higher salaries and hefty bonuses spread liberally throughout London's version of Wall Street such pricey purchases are just one indication of the boom in the international capital markets.

Countries, companies and banks raised a record $135.5 billion in the Eurobond market in 1985, an increase of 70 percent over 1984, according to Euromoney Bondware, a data service. Eurobonds are debt securities that are sold outside a borrower's country to raise capital in any one of several currencies. Even though London is considered the hub, the market itself is an electronic one that is unregulated and taps big investors in all parts of the world.

"This has been an extraordinary year for the Euromarkets," said Hans-Joerg Rudloff, the deputy chairman of Credit Suisse First Boston Ltd., the leading underwriter of Eurobonds. "It has to level off somewhat, but 1986 should be another big year."

American Involvement

American corporations and banks tapped the Euromarkets as never before, raising nearly $36 billion in the Eurobond market, up 71 percent from 1984. "For much of 1985, the Eurobond market supplied cost-competitive credit to American corporations in unprecedented quantities," noted Steven Kaempfer, a managing director of the Swiss Bank Corporation International.

The list of American concerns that raised funds in the Euromarket included not only regular borrowers such as G.M.A.C., I.B.M., Citicorp and General Electric Credit, but also a bevy of newcomers including Metropolitan Life, Pacific Bell and Emerson Electric.

The lower cost of borrowing in the international debt market was the incentive for these American borrowers. During the year, the rates on Eurodollar bonds ranged from 15 to 35 basis points less than the coupons on American corporate bonds issued in the United States. A basis point is one-hundredth of a percentage point.

Yet to borrowers in the Euromarkets, mainly big corporations, banks and countries, whose debt portfolios often run well into the billions of dollars, fractions of a percentage point add up. For instance, a difference of 10 basis points on $1 billion in debt equals $1 million in interest payments a year.

More Costly

For American borrowers, the Eurobond market became more costly and less attractive in the last quarter of 1985, as investors shunned the dollar after the United States currency weakened appreciably.

In 1986, most Euromarket experts are anticipating increased borrowing in non-dollar currencies, continued expansion of refinancing and financial arbitraging as borrowers and investors stalk the globe for the best terms possible and a jump in the use of new financial instruments, such as Euronotes, which are short-term versions of Eurobonds.

In 1985, the international capital markets witnessed the second consecutive year of enormous growth in the new issues of Eurobonds. The $135.5 billion raised in 1985 was nearly three times the $48 billion of debt issued in 1983.

The surge in Eurobond activity has been fueled by the broader trends that have been transforming the international capital markets. Several countries, including France, West Germany and Japan, opened up their capital markets this year to allow more Eurobond issues. And the United States last year eliminated the interest equalization tax, making it easier for American borrowers to attract foreign investors.

Trim Costs

As the international capital markets have blossomed, borrowers have increasingly moved to trim financing costs by bypassing their traditional lenders, commercial banks, and selling their debt to investors in the marketplace. Moreover, with interest rates generally declining in 1985, some of the new-issue volume was the result of refinancing, as old bonds were called and replaced by a new issue with a lower interest coupon.

Recent innovations have also expanded financing and investment alternatives dramatically. Interest rate swaps are one example. Once regarded as an arcane maneuver, the swap is now commonplace, with an estimated 80 percent of the Eurobonds issued linked to a swap deal. The basic concept of an interest rate swap is straightforward. Two borrowers raise money separately and then agree to make each other's interest payments, one in fixed rates and the other in floating rates. But swap arrangement can be far more complicated, involving several currencies and several counterparties, with a bank acting as the middleman.

Other Innovations

Floating-rate bonds have also grown rapidly. In 1985, $55.7 billion of floating-rate bonds were issued, up from $31.7 billion in 1984. These bonds are an adaptation to the era of volatile interest rates, since the interest rate is refixed regularly, usually every three or six months.

One of the hottest niches of the Euromarkets falls outside the category of Eurobonds. The expansion of the market for short-term financial instruments called Euronotes has been striking, with the amount outstanding today estimated at $13.5 billion, up from $3.8 billion at the end of 1984. A year from now, Merrill Lynch said, the volume of Euronotes outstanding could well reach more than $45 billion. Euronotes are one-month, three-month or six-month negotiable money market notes that resemble American commercial paper. In fact, a portion of the Euronote market is called Euro commercial paper.

"This is the fastest-growing sector that the Euromarkets have ever seen," said Kevin Regan, an executive director of Merrill Lynch International in London. Investors have shown enthusiasm for Euronotes as they have turned away from American bank certificates of deposit, after the highly publicized credit problems of some United States banks in the past year.

'Hopping in Soon'

At present, the 110 active issuers include a handful of nations and a dozen quasi-government institutions, while the remainder are mainly big European corporations, such as Unilever and British Petroleum. Few American companies have tested the Euronote market so far, but Mr. Regan said he expected many of them "to be hopping in soon."

Debt denominated in currencies other than dollars picked up in part because of the worldwide trend toward currency and capital-market liberalization. Moreover, there was less enthusiasm for dollar-denominated issues after the Group of Five meeting in September, when the Governments of the five leading industrialized nations agreed to adopt policies that could cause the dollar to decline in value through most of 1986.

The dollar is by far the dominant currency in the Eurobond market, with just under 70 percent of all issues in 1985 denominated in dollars. That share, however, is down from more than 78 percent in 1984.

The currency that provided the most dramatic example of relaxed government controls, leading to a surge in its use, was the Japanese yen. In 1985, yen-denominated Eurobond issues jumped more than sixfold, to $6.9 billion, up from $1.1 billion in 1984. In December 1984, the Japanese Ministry of Finance dropped certain restrictions on Euroyen issues, including the Government's tight rationing of offerings to one or two every three months. Foreign critics complain about the restrictions that remain.

"But compared to 1984, the Euroyen market is very, very liberalized now," said Hiroshi Toda, an executive director of Nomura International Ltd. in London.

Such major American corporations as I.B.M., Dow Chemical, United Technologies and Allied-Signal have all introduced Euroyen issues, taking advantage of the eased regulations and seeking to diversify the currency mix of their debt portfolios.

*   *   *

April 1, 1986

REDRAWING THE FINANCIAL MAP

By JAMES STERNGOLD

Hardly a day passes now without one of the Wall Street giants opening a new office abroad, raiding top talent to beef up overseas operations or acquiring a foreign securities company.

The announcements are coming like drumbeats, marking the sharply increased pace of competition among investment banks and commercial banks in the burgeoning international arena. To mention but a few: Salomon Brothers recently said it would open a Frankfurt office; Shearson Lehman Brothers and Paine Webber hired top London merger specialists to bolster their European businesses, and Goldman, Sachs & Company said it would grow from 60 to 100 staff members in Tokyo this year.

American firms increasingly look upon New York as but one of three legs, including London and Tokyo, that will form their foundations for the future. Not only are American corporations increasingly raising capital abroad, but foreign governments have also been lowering barriers to the flow of capital in and out of their countries.

U.S. Becoming a Region

"Could the American market someday be just a region for us? That won't happen tomorrow but, yes, you certainly could find that that might be true," said Jerome P. Kenney, chief executive officer of Merrill Lynch Capital Markets, which is spearheading the international expansion of Merrill Lynch & Company, America's largest securities firm.

"When you do a big deal, it isn't from Massachusetts to Illinois, you know," Mr. Kenney said. "It's all the way around the horn, to Tokyo and London." Merrill Lynch, in fact, has hired Michael von Clemm, the recently departed chairman of Credit Suisse First Boston and one of the founding fathers of the Euromarket, which is the borderless capital market centered in London.

"Frankly, I don't think any of us could have believed a few years ago that the growth over there would be like this," said Alvin V. Shoemaker, chairman of the First Boston Corporation, which participates in London mostly through Credit Suisse First Boston, a joint venture that was the Euromarket's leading underwriter last year.

Ungainly terms such as "internationalization" and "globalization" have been securities industry buzzwords for more than a decade, nebulous phrases about a future that many sensed would push the frontiers of Wall Street as far as telephone lines could stretch. The difference today is that such thoughts no longer come from starry-eyed forecasters, but are urgent, nuts-and-bolts issues that are permanently altering the financial map.

Substantial Cost

But all this growth is not coming without a substantial cost. It is sharply intensifying competition in the industry, stretching the capital of the investment banks thinner and thinner, which makes them more vulnerable to unexpected jolts, and it is setting the stage for what could prove a large shakeout down the road.

"The fact is that there is no historical precedent for this—there has never been a truly global business like this is becoming," said Samuel L. Hayes 3d, a professor of investment banking at the Harvard Business School. "The firms are throwing much more money and people at this than they have just about anything before, while there is so much uncertainty. It puts them at much greater risk."

This has put enormous pressures on the resources of nearly every firm.

"We are running up against the limits of our own resources to expand overseas," said Roy C. Smith, the head of international finance at Goldman, Sachs. "That means the limits of people, capital and even space."

Goldman's London office, for instance, has expanded from 180 in mid-1984 to 300 today. Meanwhile, its Tokyo operation has grown from two in 1974 to 60 today, and it plans to build to 100 this year, Mr. Smith said. "We're investing more than we're taking out," he added.

Morgan Stanley & Company, the venerable investment banking house, recently broke with its past by selling shares to the public for the first time, largely to finance its overseas growth.

"We see opportunities to make investments in our business overseas that exceed our ability to retain earnings, frankly," said Richard B. Fisher, Morgan Stanley's president. "We have done a lot of planning, but if anything, we have underestimated the growth of international transactions."

Some Are Cautious

But some firms are holding back. Robert E. Linton, chairman of Drexel Burnham Lambert Inc., said he was cautious, especially in London, where expansion has been frenzied.

"From my point of view, there are clearly a lot more questions than answers on how things will sort out," Mr. Linton remarked. "We are not gearing up to the extent of our competitors" in London. "We like to make money. We want to see what develops, because maybe it will grow the way they expect. And maybe it won't."

The impetus for this revolution is coming from two principal sources: the increasingly slippery nature of capital because of electronic technology, which makes information just as accessible to a trader in Paris, Tokyo or the Bahamas as it is on Wall Street, and financial deregulation, a worldwide trend that is old news in the United States, but which is gaining momentum overseas.

London is well ahead of other foreign centers in liberalizing its markets, but Tokyo is moving ahead, too, though at a cautious, snail's pace.

Another factor that has heated up the competition is the entrance of commercial banks into the Euromarket race. American banks are restricted from underwriting activities in the United States by the Glass-Steagall Act. But abroad they are free to compete head-to-head with the investment banks.

The Morgan Guaranty Trust Company, Citibank and the Bankers Trust Company are among the more active.

Indeed, international transactions are fast becoming a big chunk of Wall Street's business. At Shearson Lehman Brothers, from 5 percent to 30 percent of every initial public stock offering the firm underwrites is sold overseas, and about a quarter of its merger activity involves a foreign party, according to Francois de St. Phalle, manager of the international department. About 40 percent of the mammoth $1.3 offering of securities in Rockefeller Center last year, for instance, went to foreign investors.

Thus, in the Darwinian world of investment banking, expansion into Europe and Asia is no longer just an option. "Our international efforts are not a nice side deal for us," said Francis P. Jenkins, a managing director who heads the international division of First Boston. "We can't survive without them. The global market is a reality."

Little Time to Deliberate

Added Ronald Stuart, a managing director who heads international capital markets and trading at Salomon Brothers: "You can't deliberate for long on whether you'll do it or not. If you want to be a factor, you have to get in the market in the early growth phases."

Previously, the overseas business of the American firms was rather narrow in scope. Many firms had focused on selling American securities to wealthy foreign investors. It was a lucrative, but limited, business. And it gave American corporations an added source of capital.

Today, the Wall Street firms are increasingly doing almost the same mix of business abroad as at home. They are structuring and underwriting securities aimed specifically at foreign investors; they are making markets in foreign and United States securities for overseas investors, and they are providing financial advice, including merger and acquisition counseling, to foreign corporations.

"We had been just selling U.S. securities products overseas for years," said James T. Barton, president of Prudential-Bache Securities. "But a few years ago it dawned on us that we had to grow internationally in a much more meaningful way."

Mr. Jenkins of First Boston commented, "You wouldn't know if you were in Chicago or Tokyo with our firm," even down to the furniture in the Tokyo office, which was ordered from New York.

Setting up shop abroad, however, does not guarantee success. The battle to buy a slice of the international market has been cutthroat. Both American and foreign competitors for underwriting deals are increasingly offering lucrative terms to issuers to win the business. The problem is they sometimes end up selling the securities at prices below what they paid and the thin underwriting commissions they charge are not enough to make up the difference.

The foreign merchant and commercial banks have developed into formidable competitors. During the just-completed quarter, only three American or American-affiliated firms made it into the ranks of the top 10 Euromarket underwriters, as measured by dollar volume. In the first quarter of 1985, by comparison, seven of the top 10 were American or American affiliated, according to IDD Information Services.

'Hara-Kiri' Bonds

For a while, Japanese securities firms trying to break into the Euromarket through underwritings of yen-denominated bonds were putting together deals at such a loss to themselves that the deals became known as "hara-kiri" bonds. Mr. Kenney of Merrill Lynch estimated that one of every three or four financings in the Euromarkets was done at a loss to the lead underwriter.

The result is that a shakeout within the industry is looming, many predict. "The question is not if you can grow, it is a question of whether you can do it fast enough,," Mr. Kenney said. "It's going to be war."

Mr. Shoemaker of First Boston added: "The best are going to survive, but in the long-term there may not even be room for a second tier. You'll have two or three major Japanese firms, two or European firms, and perhaps seven or eight American firms at the top. Getting to that level, though, is where you'll see the real scrambling."

* * *

December 14, 1986

ROLL THE DICE AND CROSS YOUR FINGERS

THE FINANCIAL REVOLUTION
By Adrian Hamilton
268 pp. New York: The Free Press. $19.95.

CASINO CAPITALISM
By Susan Strange
207 pp. New York: Basil Blackwell. $24.95.

BY BENJAMIN M. ROWLAND

Should world financial markets be regulated more? Could they be, even if this was desirable? There is a growing concern, which transcends partisan politics, that the world financial system may be out of control. Regulations are probably less restrictive today than at any previous time in this century. But the verdict is mixed. For many, Adam Smith's benign invisible hand has become an invisible fist clutching a pair of dice. We have all entered the casino.

Two new books, both by British authors, examine the financial and monetary system over the past 15 years from very different vantage points. Their conclusions, however, are disquietingly similar.

"The Financial Revolution" by Adrian Hamilton, currently industrial editor of The London Observer, is a balanced and highly readable tour of the myriad of events, actors, institutions and financial techniques that have given rise to the world financial system in its present state. This book is aimed at a wide audience. It is certainly among the best books of its

kind since Martin Mayer wrote "The Bankers" in 1974 to describe the then radical, but by today's standards almost placid, pace of innovation in the financial marketplace.

The revolution described by Mr. Hamilton has its origins in a familiar chain of events: the rise of United States overseas indebtedness, the growth of a Eurodollar market, the suspension of gold-dollar convertibility and the onset of floating exchange rates—rates fixed neither to a price of gold nor to one another, but allowed to float without any defense against the play of market forces. But neither these events nor the economic dislocations associated with them were sufficient to spark the revolution. The essential catalyst was technology.

Technology has enabled the market to amass, digest and exploit information to an unprecedented degree. Today, Telerate, Quotron and Reuters screens flash information simultaneously to market centers around the world to the point where it would appear that success is determined by reflexes almost as much as intelligence. Governments and their regulatory authorities are sitting ducks in the world of instant information. They sit transfixed as clever market operators broker the interest rates of one against the exchange rates of another. They are unable to protect themselves; to do so only invites attack from another quarter. The author quotes the former Citicorp chairman Walter Wriston:

"The information standard has replaced the gold standard as the basis of world finance. The iron laws of the gold standard and later the gold exchange standard have been replaced by new laws which are just as in-flexible. . . . It's also something that has made control impossible. Kings and princes can no longer hide what they're doing. . . ."

Moreover, as the author points out, the economic, to say nothing of the social, purpose of this heightened financial activity is not always easy to discern: "The major manufacturing industries are contracting. The Third World has been shut off from new funds. The funds within the system are moving in ever faster circles, chasing the marginal profit . . . they can glean from their own movement."

The financial revolution has not been entirely without benefit to the world at large. A more rigid system might well not have survived OPEC or the third-world debt crisis. The revolution has also coincided in many countries with the return of whole sectors of the state-owned economy to private ownership—itself a probably healthy reaction to past excesses of state ambition. But, as Mr. Hamilton points out, finance is unlike other industries because it "so directly affects both the savings and well-being of individuals and confidence in the commercial system as a whole."

Whereas Mr. Hamilton is inclined to attribute the financial revolution to factors by and large beyond the control of any of its participants, Susan Strange, a professor of international relations at the London School of Economics, holds states and statesmen to a higher standard of accountability. "Casino Capitalism" is a polemic in the best sense of the word. Her strong views are well grounded in empirical observation and well tested against widely different schools of thought. The book's central tenet is that every system needs an anchor. For monetary and financial stability to exist, an economic system must be rooted in something. The postwar anchor of that system was the United States until it abandoned the role in 1971 by ceasing to make the dollar convertible into gold at a fixed price. A new mooring has not been found.

That system contained the seeds of its own destruction. The "exorbitant privilege"—to use de Gaulle's phrase—of the gold exchange standard was that it allowed the United States to behave as though it had unlimited credit. The behavior persists; only now, without the formal mechanism of fixed rates, there is little or no delay between the act and its consequences on the value of the dollar. Lifting the anchor—switching from fixed to floating exchange rates—has done nothing to eliminate financial risk or reduce the inherent need for stability. Companies still have to plan and control costs if they are to operate successfully. Under the old system, currencies remained relatively stable. Now if individual institutions want stability they can obtain it, for a price, by creating hedges against future uncertainties. And just as the ending of fixed exchange rates brought turbulence to the currency markets— because one of the few ways to take pressure off of currencies is to change interest rates—the turbulence was passed along to the huge markets for debt securities. Thus the costs of maintaining financial order went "from the public sector to the private and then, in the end, to the consumers."

Free markets are meant to foster creative problem solving. By this measure, at least, the "privatization" of the monetary and financial system has been a huge success. The growth of new financing instruments and techniques (and, of course, the capital required by the companies that offer and trade them) has been truly astonishing. But they are far from being an unalloyed good. No financial instrument was ever invented that could not be used for speculative as well as defensive purposes. As with handguns, whether they're dangerous depends a lot on who owns them.

Moreover, one speculator's risk-avoiding hedge can produce unanticipated and potentially adverse consequences for another, even though no harm was intended. (Remember, risk cannot be removed, it can only be reallocated.) Thus, anyone with several million dollars and a good computer can take substantial and near-riskless profits from the stock markets by selling or buying a representative basket of securities and setting it off against transactions in stock index futures. Meanwhile, as in the record two-day, 128-point decline in the Dow Jones industrial average in September, those unable to protect themselves in like fashion pay the cost.

It is the sheer arbitrariness of the casino, at least for ordinary people, that makes for such grave consequences. As Ms. Strange writes: "For when sheer luck begins to take over and to determine more and more of what happens to people, and skill, effort, initiative, determination and hard work count for less and less, then inevitably faith and confidence in the social and political system quickly fades. Respect for ethical values—on which in the end a free democratic society relies—suffers a dangerous decline."

In the unregulated market of the casino, those who can do so press their advantage to the limit. Not to do so means being displaced by someone more ruthless than yourself. For this reason, in the financial system, as in any system, "there is always an indeterminate trade-off between the two imperatives—between the need to compete and the need to moderate competition for the sake of order."

But how to restore order, and who is to take the main responsibility? By elimination, Ms. Strange concludes that the job can be handled only by the United States. No international organization could perform this role because no state would consent to the necessary transfer of sovereign control over its affairs. Nor—because so high a level of cooperation strains belief—could the job be shared by the stronger economies, such as those of the United States, West Germany and Japan. Although weaker than before, the United States is not, she asserts, as weak as it thinks.

Certain of Ms. Strange's specific recommendations may not stand up to scrutiny. One suggestion, for example, is that the United States could extend "lender-of-last-resort" privileges to any country that agreed to accept its (presumably stringent) conditions for membership. Being voluntary, this would be no more threatening than "allow[ing] U.S. courts to be used by foreigners, if they wish to do so, to sue an aircraft manufacturer, a group of airlines or a chemical company."

Whether the United States chooses formally to don the mantle of financial stabilizer again, it is a role no one will be likely to discharge well until this country gets its own house in order. For the world financial system has become intolerant of apparently unlimited American spending. Washington, too, must make the hard choices among defense and irrigation projects and welfare and aid to the third world, or there will be no stability. Wise leadership was never more needed—or more distant.

Benjamin M. Roland is an international investment banker with Shearson Lehman Brothers

*   *   *

March 23, 1987

AT THE CURRENCY NERVE CENTER

By STEVE LOHR
Special to the New York Times

LONDON, March 22—Above the Barclays Bank's sprawling currency-trading floor in London, the air is filled with cigarette smoke and coded shouts: "What's the cable?"

The foreign exchange dealers, row after row of them, nearly all in their 20's and 30's, are umbilically linked to the market with three video screens and two telephones each. It is an arena of split-second decision-making and emotions spilling over into joyful yells and anguished groans.

This is the rawest nerve of the international financial system, the foreign exchange market, where only seconds after some news announcement—trade figures, housing starts, election results, whatever—an impact is felt in the value of the affected country's most visible asset, its currency.

Enormous Stakes

For the major players—banks, securities houses, multinational corporations and investing institutions—the risks in this huge market can be staggering unless properly hedged and managed. The enormous stakes were underscored by Volkswagen's recent announcement that it might have suffered losses of nearly $260 million in what it said was a case of fraud involving its foreign-exchange operations.

With its staff of 140 people trading more than $9 billion a day, the Barclays dealing room is one of the biggest in London, the world's currency-trading capital. Here, and in a few hundred similar trading floors across the globe, is where the ultimate judgment will be rendered on last month's Paris agreement by the United States and five other major nations to stabilize the dollar.

Yet there is an inherent conflict between the government officials and the currency traders. The governments may want stability, but foreign-exchange dealers desire the opposite. "We want volatility," said Steve Dagleish, a 34-year-old trader at Barclays. "We thrive on it. That's how we make money." An axiom of the business is that any trader complaining of exchange-rate volatility is a trader who lost money that day in the market.

Two Views of Volatility

Two decades ago, Harold Wilson, then the British Prime Minister, blamed the slumping value of the pound on the "gnomes of Zurich"—his colorful image for currency market speculators. And government officials have complained ever since about the perversity, in their view, of sharp exchange-rate movements, an instability they regard as almost an infringement on national sovereignty, hampering efforts to craft monetary and fiscal policies.

Currency market veterans view it differently. "Foreign exchange speculators make convenient scapegoats for the central bankers and finance ministers," said Claude Tygier, a New York foreign-exchange consultant, who was formerly a bank currency dealer. "But speculators only take advantage of trends or expectations in the market. And those market conditions are created not by the speculators but usually by failed government policies and poor economic performance."

Still, there is no denying that exchange rates have become increasingly volatile in recent years, and much of the difference is explained by changes within the market itself. Because of new technology, financial deregulation and huge trade imbalances among major nations, the foreign currency market is mushrooming in size and increasing in importance.

Central Banks' Role Diminished

One policy implication is that the role of central banks in the currency market is greatly diminished. With perhaps $200

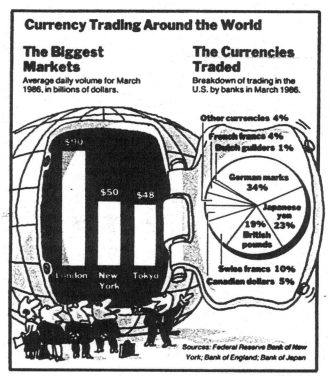

Currency Trading Around the World

The Biggest Markets
Average daily volume for March 1986, in billions of dollars.

$90 $50 $48
London New York Tokyo

The Currencies Traded
Breakdown of trading in the U.S. by banks in March 1986.

Other currencies 4%
French francs 4%
Dutch guilders 1%
German marks 34%
Japanese yen 23%
British pounds 19%
Swiss francs 10%
Canadian dollars 5%

Sources: Federal Reserve Bank of New York; Bank of England; Bank of Japan

Niculae Asciu

billion traded a day in the global foreign exchange market, governments can no longer control rates by dipping into their treasuries to intervene. Their reserves are tiny compared with the size of the market.

Last year, a three-government study of foreign exchange trading in New York, London and Tokyo found that $188 billion in currencies was being traded every day in those three financial centers, about double previous estimates. And the previous survey by the Group of Thirty, a New York-based research group, had been done just two years earlier.

With its international financial tradition and its placement in a time zone between Tokyo and New York, London is the hub of foreign exchange markets. In last year's survey, London accounted for $90 billion a day, while New York had $50 billion and Tokyo $48 billion.

Pact's Value Is Suspect

The size of today's global foreign-currency market means that the value of a pact among the major industrial nations is suspect, unless the governments agree to basic policy shifts. Otherwise, they are high-level cheerleading exercises that, at best, can only lend added weight to existing trends in the market.

For example, the Group of Five meeting at New York's Plaza Hotel in September 1985, often deemed a great success, had little if any effect on rates, according to Brendan Brown, chief international economist at County Natwest Capital Markets Ltd. in London. The decline in the dollar desired at the time had begun the previous February and continued afterward.

"I'm entirely prepared to believe that the dollar, Deutsche mark and yen rates would be exactly the same today if the Plaza meeting never took place," Mr. Brown said.

An Uneasy Calm

In the wake of the Paris meeting, the currency markets have settled a bit. Dealers say some calming of the market was inevitable because most market participants agree that the biggest part of the dollar's decline, nearly 40 percent in the last two years, has run its course for now. They also point out that the dealers themselves wanted a few months of a bit quieter trading. "People are just tired," one trader said. "They're tired of getting all the late-night calls."

How long the uneasy calm will last is uncertain. But everyone agrees that perceptions in the foreign-exchange marketplace, not vague government pronouncements, will be the crucial verdict. The activity in the Barclays dealing room explains the nature of the modern currency trading business and what influence the roughly 10,000 dealers around the world have on exchange rates and national economies.

At 40 years old, Trevor Cass, the chief manager, is walking history by the standards of the foreign exchange business. To be sure, the simplest version of currency trading goes back thousands of years to the money changers of biblical times. But the modern-day industry really began in 1972 when the postwar system of fixed exchange rates was abandoned.

Technological Improvements

Mr. Cass started as a trader in 1965, a few years after the telex replaced cablegrams as the means for handling trans-Atlantic transactions. (The earlier use of cables to transmit rates explains the current dealing-room usage of "cable" to mean the dollar-pound exchange rate.) The telex meant that the time required to complete a transaction went from a few hours to several minutes. By 1970, telephone service replaced the telex as the preferred medium for international dealing.

Then, about four years ago, the Reuters network and video screens, allowing virtually instant access to bank dealing rooms worldwide, became the international standard.

"The technology has changed everything," Mr. Cass said. "And the technology creates volatility."

Most Trading Done by Banks

Today, 90 percent of all turnover in the currency markets is trading among dealers, mostly banks, while only 10 percent is generated by outside investors or corporations buying currencies to finance trade or for investment purposes. Trades are typically done in blocks of several million dollars, with no fees charged.

Banks make money on razor-thin arbitrage profits—for example, selling a currency on slightly more favorable terms to one bank than it acquired that currency from another bank. Most profits, however, come from positioning—correctly anticipating short-term movements in currencies.

Bank traders typically focus on where rates are headed over the course of a few hours. Carrying large inventories of a given currency overnight is a risk the banks usually avoid. Because dealers tend not to carry large positions for long, most currency economists agree that the traders have far less impact on exchange-rate trends than do major investors such as corporations and fund managers. The traders, of course, are speculators. But their speculation would mostly affect currency prices for a few hours, while it is longer-term investors whose decisions can influence rates over the course of weeks or months.

* * *

October 22, 1989

THE REALITIES OF 'FRIDAY THE 13TH'

By LESLIE WAYNE
Thank you, Tokyo.

Had it not been for the Japanese, the recent 190-point drop in the Dow Jones industrial average could have gone from a scary market aberration to a disastrous financial freefall. With global exchanges now linked, as trading closed in New York that Friday, all eyes were on how Tokyo would open the following Monday. But because Japan remained calm, disaster was averted. "If it weren't for Japan holding up, I'd say that internationalization was a disaster," said Barton M. Biggs, a managing director at Morgan Stanley & Co.

But the fact that Japan held firm illustrates the benefits—and the risks—of continued market globalization. Financial theory teaches that there are no returns without risk and greater stock market links give investors the opportunity to make more money in more places. With that, however, comes new risks: of a system that is far more vulnerable to sudden jolts and of individual central banks that are increasingly unable to do anything about it.

"The danger of globalization is that if everyone goes crazy at the same time, you've got a bigger problem than before," said Hans Stoll, director of financial markets research at the Owen Graduate School of Management at Vanderbilt University. Said Richard Levich, a finance professor at New York Unversity's Stern School of Business: "You've got more eyes focused and when news comes out you've got more people running through a small door."

And that rush is what almost took place when the Dow plunged 190 points in the last 45 minutes before the New York Stock Exchange closed on Oct. 13. The Federal Reserve Board took advantage of the weekend, when most markets were closed, to try to calm the markets by promising liquidity.

Financial experts say the event adds several points to the debate about the impact of greater market internationalization:

• The appetite for foreign equities will increase despite such terrifying market plunges because these securities help provide diversification that reduces portfolio risk.

• On any single day, except for times of worldwide panic, most stock exchanges generally act independent of one another. In general, they respond to specific economic, cultural and regulatory environments in their countries—

differences that keep the various equity markets from marching in lock step. A rise in prices in London doesn't automatically spell a rise that day in Tokyo.

- Over time, globalization will reduce the power governments have over their nation's economy. The increased ease with which money can flow across borders means policy makers can no longer assume that their nation's capital is captive. Because of this, some say financial markets will play a larger role in overriding, or even setting, economic policy.

- When a worldwide market panic sets in, globalization can take a bad situation in one market and create an international crisis. This took place during the stock market plunge in October 1987 when "hot money" from investors seeking to liquidate their positions at any price circled the globe.

- Investors have less of a safety net than they once had because there is now no single lender of last resort. In the past, jittery American markets could be calmed by assurances of ample liquidity from the Federal Reserve. While such assurances are still powerful, globalization lessens their impact. This is because central banks all have different national interests and cannot be expected to act as a united front during a crisis.

"It doesn't really matter whether globalization is good or bad," said James Rogers, a finance professor at the Columbia University Business School. "Nothing can be done about it. Electronics and communications are changing the world. There's lots of money sloshing around the world and it's got to go somewhere. Many of the economies are closely linked and that means their markets will be closely linked. Now, everyone has to worry."

Cross-Border Craze

Certainly, nothing appears to be halting the trend toward greater cross-border equity trading. As American firms set up shop overseas and foreign investment houses settle here, it has become increasingly easy for investors to buy the stocks of other nations.

Since 1980, foreign trading in United States securities has increased by 19 percent annually to reach $384 billion at the end of 1988. American purchases of foreign equities have increased by about 30 percent annually, reaching about $151 billion in 1988, according to the Securities Industry Association.

From an investment perspective, globalization provides investors a safe way to get greater portfolio diversification without reducing their expected returns. The notion is that investing in many countries provides safety since as one country's market goes up, another's may go down.

As a result, overseas investments are becoming a standard part of most institutional portfolios. And, increasingly, mutual funds made up of stocks from a single country or geographic region are being bought by retail investors. Since 1985, global equity funds have grown faster than the mutual fund industry in general. With about $20 billion in

assets, they now represent about 10 percent of the total mutual fund market, according to the Investment Company Institute.

Yet their returns can be wiped out in one terrifying moment if investors panic. While long-term investors may be fine, those with short-term focus can be devastated.

"This time we saw the Frankfurt market drop after our market dropped," said John J. Phelan, chairman of the New York Stock Exchange. "But that seemed to be a local condition rather than enormous amounts of hot money running around the world. Hot money makes the markets riskier, more volatile, for short periods of time. What we saw after 1987, is that if you hung on, in most markets in the world you would have been better off than before 1987 occurred."

Ironically, for all the market linkages, studies show that exchanges generally perform independently of one another. "The evidence shows that markets are driven by what happened in local economies," said Gary P. Brinson, president of Chicago-based Brinson Partners, which manages about $12.5 billion.

Of course, there are global economic trends that can affect many markets similarly. For instance, most world markets have rebounded since the 1987 crash, largely due to sustained global economic growth. The tendency of markets to respond to different cues, while still keeping an eye on one another, was also evident in the Dow's recent 190-point plunge. New York fell on Friday and then recovered on Monday. London and Tokyo remained firm on Monday.

Japanese Composure

"When the Japanese market didn't overreact, other markets sensed what was happening and came back into synch," said Joseph R. Hardiman, president of the National Association of Securities Dealers Inc.

The events also reflect the influence that investor psychology has on the markets. For instance, Mr. Brinson said Japanese investors are generally less sensitive to risk considerations and are more likely to ride out a storm. "They have been through an ebullient period of their economy," he said. "Their currency and their markets are strong. It's given the Japanese a great deal of self-confidence about their situation."

Likewise, the unexpectedly steep decline of 13 percent in the Frankfurt exchange reflected unique West German attitudes. "We were flabbergasted that the German market went down as far as it did," Mr. Brinson said. "German investors are almost hyper risk-averse and if any global event takes place, it is amplified within the minds of the German people."

In fact, these differing responses to the 190-point drop in New York has turned some notions about the German and Japanese markets on their heads. Theoretically, the underpriced German market should be considered a less risky investment than the Japanese market, where stocks are considered overpriced. But that theory did not hold in the most recent drop.

"German individuals panicked because of what was happening in the United States," said Mr. Biggs of Morgan Stanley. "After what happened last week, the risk premium for

Germany should go up, and for Japan it should go down. What all professionals agree is that Japan, the most over-priced market in the world, consistently understands panic better than anyone else."

Increased market globalization is also bringing about shifts in power between financial markets and their home governments. "The most significant implication of globalization is that a domestic government cannot really control the economic destiny of a country because the capital will leave," said Michael A. Petrino, president of Matrix Capital Management in Greenwich, Conn. "For instance, if you have a disadvantageous tax policy, the capital will leave, unemployment will go up and you get thrown out of office. This means that markets will determine economic policy to a larger degree than they did when we had highly segmented markets."

And this means a new role for the central banks. Steven Einhorn, chairman of the investment policy committee at Goldman, Sachs, said that increased market links have brought about heightened international economic policy coordination, with the Group of Seven's attempts to stabilize foreign exchange rates one prominent example. After October 1987, virtually all major central banks provided liquidity to their economies. "They acted like our central bank, and going forward, they would continue to do that," Mr. Einhorn said.

But others aren't so sure. "Averting a crisis requires coordination of central banks; and when there are national interests that diverge, you may not be able to assure that," said William L. Silber, a professor of finance at New York University's Stern School of Business. "A crisis in Japan, for instance, may lead the Japanese central bank to do something that may not be in the best interest of all other countries. You do not have the safety net of a single central bank except to the extent that central banks agree to cooperate. That's a safety net, with holes."

Global Limitations

Still, for all these links, barriers remain that prevent the worlds' exchanges from becoming more fully integrated. The limitations are real: back-office operations are often cumbersome and time-consuming, settlements in different currencies can be problematic and regulations vary significantly among countries, as do corporate accounting standards.

"The major barrier to greater globalization is regulation," said Morris Mendelson, a professor of finance at the Wharton School of Business. "America doesn't like Americans being taken for a ride on foreign exchanges. And there are significant clearing and settlement problems. Let's say you want to trade Japanese securities in Tokyo. You've got to ship them off to Tokyo and convert your money to yen. That's a lot of delays." But Steven H. Reynolds, managing director of the investment group at the Bankers Trust Company, noted that many of these barriers are falling. "Ten years ago, the limitations were infinite," he said. "Day by day, they are being broken down. The world is changing rapidly toward a more unified system."

What is more, informal contacts among traders and bankers are solidifying. Mr. Reynolds said that after the October 1987 crash, "there was little cooperation and coordination among market participants." But, this time, "principals in this country contacted people overseas and exchanged knowledge so that investors didn't act irrationally."

* * *

July 23, 1991

IN WORLD MARKETS, LOOSE REGULATION

By DIANA B. HENRIQUES

Seeking lush profits, investors have invaded foreign stock markets with a vengeance, but international regulators and stock-exchange officials have made scant progress toward developing uniform rules and standards to bring order to an expanding global marketplace.

The regulatory lag is ominous given the huge sums that are landing overseas, the increased importance multinational companies place on these markets for raising capital and the higher investor risks that come with loosely regulated markets. Already, some professional money managers have backed away from some stock markets and others are scrutinizing companies to try to avoid greater risks.

A crisis in one market is heard almost instantly around the world as investors and companies react to industry rumors, political scandals and price fluctuations. The New York stock market crash in 1987 caused problems overseas. More recently, when Japan's stock market scandal broke several weeks ago, it was blamed for a dip in New York prices.

Wherever they seek profit, investors confront a patchwork of securities laws and inconsistent enforcement policies that are a sharp contrast to the rules for American securities markets. The differences, which have existed for generations, have come into sharp relief recently as pension and mutual funds and other investors in many nations, including the United States, aggressively seek investment opportunities in these unfamiliar markets.

The pace of this trend is startling: The net purchases of foreign stocks and bonds by American investors tripled from 1988 to 1990, and market researchers expect those sharp gains to continue.

But recent market scandals in Japan and Germany underscore the fact that foreign markets are a long way from Kansas. The controversy in Japan disclosed that it was not unusual for a brokerage firm to reimburse important customers for major trading losses. In Germany, the nation's banks dominate the markets and the country's largest bank, Deutsche Bank, is said to have a nest of insider trading in its midst.

To Americans, these differences are fundamental and often bewildering. Consider the uneven vigilance over insider trading, the trading of stock based on information not yet publicly available, which has been a celebrated focus of regulators and prosecutors in the United States.

In Germany, while insider trading is considered unethical and there are efforts under way to ban it, it is perfectly legal. In France, regulators won the power to assess civil fines against insider traders but they never have. Japan enacted its first insider trading law less than two years ago and has not prosecuted anyone.

Basic information about stocks varies widely, too. Many foreign markets are plagued by chronic manipulation, in which traders or major investors work in concert to produce artificial movements in stock prices. The level and frequency of public disclosure about corporate finances and ownership is uneven from market to market and accounting standards remain a hodgepodge, according to a recent study by Ennis, Knupp & Associates, a research firm in Chicago.

American companies with publicly traded stock disclose revenues and profits quarterly. In Japan and Greece, the reports are scheduled every six months, but in Greece some companies do not comply, and Japan does not punish companies for misleading reports.

Some Markets Are Avoided

"Chaotic—that is the best word to describe the current state of international regulation," said John H. Gillies, vice president of the international unit at the Frank Russell Company, a leading pension fund advisory firm. "In 10 years, the answer might be different. But there has been very little progress so far."

Gary Bergstrom, president of Acadian Asset Management, a global investment firm in Boston, said there were numerous markets around the world that he avoided because of regulatory gaps. "And those are markets that are not necessarily obscure," he said. "Sweden is a good example of a market that has not been very hospitable to foreign investors."

Officials engaged in the difficult task of building a worldwide regulatory framework argue that they have made great strides, given how little time they have had to tackle the task. But it has been slow work.

In the European Community, for example, a campaign to establish uniform securities rules, so-called harmonization, began strongly but recently has bogged down in disputes over how quickly trades should be made public and whether to permit securities to trade away from formal exchanges. The hope, now fading, was that by 1992 brokerage firms that met their home country's standards could do business elsewhere in the community, and investors would find at least a minimum level of protection.

Off to a Slow Start

Beyond the Common Market, the International Organization of Securities Commissions, the linchpin agency working for global consistency, got off to a slow start. It did not take shape as an international body until 1984 and had no executive staff until January 1987. "From 1987 until now, things have moved very, very quickly," said Paul Guy, secretary general of the group, which is based in Montreal. "Everyone would agree that we're still not moving quickly enough—but no work had been done at all before that."

Since it lacks any formal power over its members, the group's first task, Mr. Guy said, is to establish its own credi-

bility with national regulators. It also had to "discover what was out there," he said. "No inventory of what rules were in existence had been done."

The organization agreed last November on a slate of elementary principles to govern their markets—that brokerage firms should deal "honestly and fairly" with their customers, for instance, and should "try to avoid conflicts of interest." The group's 80 members have pledged that they will try to carry out these principles in their home markets, Mr. Guy said.

Privately, some officials complain that one obstacle has been the intransigence of United States regulators. "There is a feeling that they have the best regulations and the best disclosure and the best of everything, and that should be the standard applied worldwide," an official said. "But that's not possible. A lot of people feel the United States standards are too high, too complicated and too expensive."

S.E.C. Chief Reacts

Richard C. Breeden, chairman of the Securities and Exchange Commission and chairman of the international group's technical committee, reacted harshly to that complaint. "It is true that we are unwilling to engage in a race to the bottom," Mr. Breeden said. "But 10 years ago, people said that the only way for us to harmonize worldwide regulation was for us to decriminalize insider trading. And today, insider trading is illegal in all major markets, or soon will be."

He also noted that he had negotiated agreements under which the S.E.C. and its counterparts in eight markets have agreed to cooperate—"and that's up from zero agreements a decade ago."

The Federation de Internationale des Bourses de Valeurs, the Paris-based organization that represents the world's stock exchanges, has also been advocating the development of mutually compatible standards and practices. So far, it has little to show for its effort. But it recently named John J. Phelan Jr., former chairman of the New York Stock Exchange, as its new chairman with an eye to enhancing its presence in the harmonization effort.

Everyone agrees, however, that American investors abroad are unlikely to ever encounter a trading environment the exact equivalent of what they find at home. Markets are a product of their distinctive cultures, a fact that might prompt a detached observer to say, "Vive la difference!" But for those who must grapple daily with the risks and rewards of global investing, the message in all this diversity is clear: "caveat emptor."

*　*　*

July 24, 1994

WHEN MONEY TALKS, GOVERNMENTS LISTEN

By THOMAS L. FRIEDMAN

WASHINGTON—Think about the meaning of these numbers: The global currency markets trade about $1 trillion worth of dollars each day. When the world's 17 largest central banks, led by the Federal Reserve, intervened last month to try to prop up the dollar, they dug deep into their pockets and came up with about $5 billion and change, which they threw into the market in an effort to bid up the value of the American currency. No wonder they had little effect on the dollar. The central banks were like a zoo keeper trying to calm a starved gorilla by offering it a raisin for lunch.

It really wasn't the fault of the governments, though. Raisins, it seems, are all they have sometimes, compared with the assets of the huge capital, currency and bond markets they are trying to influence. Whose world is this anyway? The answer is that it is increasingly Adam Smith's world—a world in which the balance of power between global financial markets and governments is tilting toward markets. When it comes to global markets these days, the motto of governments is: "There they go, I must catch up, for I am their leader."

Twenty-two-year-old bond traders with ice water for blood tyrannize the President, passing judgment on his economic performance by raising or lowering interest rates; the markets devour central bank cash with nary a burp, and the portfolio managers, playing global Monopoly, move cash from country to country, deciding which governments deserve to "Pass Go" and collect $200 billion and which should go directly to jail and be starved of the capital to raise living standards.

This shift in power is driven by a combination of factors. The revolution in telecommunications and data transmission has knit Tokyo, Frankfurt, London and New York in a seamless web of financial interactions that operates at a speed, and in volumes, beyond the grasp of any single government. This technical revolution, though, has been accompanied and fueled by a political revolution. Over the past decade there has been a widening acknowledgment, from Albania to Alabama, that when it comes to allocating resources, markets work better than governments, whether the issue is providing telephone service or investment capital.

"Basically, governments have consented to a regime that allows markets to boss them around," said Stanford University economist Paul Krugman, "because the conventional wisdom, fed by experience, says that to throw up barriers to these market forces is to invite economic stagnation, if not disaster."

From the State of South Carolina to the government of Brazil, leaders believe that a central role of government is serving as a broker—a broker between their constituents and the global markets. As more countries have gone capitalist, there is a huge global competition for cash and investors, so that governments can build the roads, power stations and telephone systems that are the foundation for higher living standards. Governments used to do that with their own cash—as the Marshall Plan rebuilt much of Europe after World War II—but they don't have it anymore.

So the role of governments now is increasingly to entice private investment—to get B.M.W. to build a plant in Mississippi, or to get portfolio managers to invest in the Shanghai

stock market—by assuring stable currencies and sound economic fundamentals.

"During the cold war," said Labor Secretary Robert Reich, "we used the Soviet threat to get the public to accept certain changes and to build certain institutions, from the national highway system to the space program. They were all justified in national security terms. Today, with the Soviet threat gone, governments now use the global markets in the same way. We have to adopt this economic policy, initiate this training program for our work force, build this world-class airport, because if we don't we won't be able to attract global capital and raise our standard of living."

The role these markets have in promoting democracy is ambiguous. Markets demand stability, but they don't discriminate between the Singaporean form or the Jeffersonian form. "There is a brutal Darwinian logic to these markets," said the investment banker Felix Rohatyn. "They are nervous and greedy. They look for stability and transparency, but what they reward is not always our preferred form of democracy."

The struggle between markets and governments is not new. When the invention of the telegraph and the railroads knit the fragmented American economy into a single unit in the 19th century, it took 50 years for the Federal government to catch up and set up institutions like the Securities and Exchange Commission. Now national economies have been knit into a global economy, but so far national governments have not forged many super-national institutions to monitor it, because nations are reluctant to cede any sovereignty to global institutions.

An Enormous Challenge

This creates an enormous challenge for regulators, says Arthur Levitt Jr., chairman of the S.E.C., which is responsible for upholding the standards of an American securities industry that is increasingly operating outside the S.E.C.'s grasp. "Morgan Stanley, dealing with a Tokyo insurance company, can have as big an impact on our system here as Morgan Stanley dealing with General Motors." The problem, though, added Mr. Levitt, is that many of the dealings between Morgan Stanley and a Tokyo insurance company are happening at a speed and in a global marketplace beyond the reach of his regulators.

The big debate in Congress over whether to ratify the new General Agreement on Tariffs and Trade is over how much sovereignty to cede to this super-national trade body. Opponents argue that GATT will give the World Trade Organization in Geneva the power to override certain American environmental laws and safety and health standards, if they violate the principles of free trade. This is often called the "GATTzilla versus Flipper" debate because GATT has ruled against American laws banning the import of tuna caught in nets that also sweep up dolphins.

A similar debate is going on in Asia with its new economic grouping, called APEC for "Asia Pacific Economic Cooperation." But it has no last name. Asia Pacific Economic Cooperation—what? Organization? Institution? The reason

APEC has no last name is because the member states were so worried about ceding sovereignty to it, they would not even call it an organization.

"Those in America who worry about the loss of sovereignty to GATT, or those in England who worry about a loss of sovereignty to the European Union, may seem at times like the King who stood on the beach and tried to stop the tide," said the Harvard University political theorist Michael J. Sandel. "But those who are worried have a point. These global markets are not accountable to any citizens. They don't necessarily reflect decisions that we have made on the basis of our collective values. One of the biggest challenges for democracy in our time is to develop political institutions that will be powerful enough to deal with global markets, but accountable enough to enable citizens to feel that they are still in control."

* * *

February 27, 1995

MARKETS SHAKEN AS A BRITISH BANK TAKES A BIG LOSS

By RICHARD W. STEVENSON
Special to The New York Times

LONDON, Monday, Feb. 27—The abrupt collapse late on Sunday of a venerable British investment bank set off a chain reaction of steep losses in financial markets halfway around the world early today in a stark illustration of the global financial system's interdependency.

The bank, Barings P.L.C., the oldest investment firm in Britain and one of the most illustrious, was left with no choice but to seek bankruptcy protection after a frantic rescue effort by the Bank of England, the nation's central bank, came up short.

The extraordinary and fast-breaking series of events was set off when Barings discovered late on Thursday that a trader in its Singapore office had made and lost, to the tune of at least $750 million, an unauthorized financial gamble on the direction of Japanese stock prices. Barings, which was founded in 1767, helped finance the Louisiana Purchase and served as an investment adviser to Queen Elizabeth II, was in ruins by late Sunday, its legacy a meltdown that unnerved investors worldwide.

The affair raised questions about the adequacy of the oversight of complex financial instruments known as derivatives that allow investment firms to make huge bets without putting up much money in advance. And it made clear the risks of global finance today, with market turbulence spreading across time zones as fast as the rising sun.

"This is a quintessential British bank brought down by Japanese futures traded in Singapore," said Henry Hu, a professor at the University of Texas Law School and a specialist in derivatives. "It highlights the international nature of finance today."

Within hours after dejected Barings employees began trooping out of the firm's headquarters in London's financial district Sunday night and bankruptcy administrators swarmed in, the effects of the firm's collapse were roiling Asia as markets there opened for business.

In Tokyo, nervousness caused by the Barings collapse sent stocks plunging. The Nikkei index of 225 stocks closed down 660.33 points, or nearly 4 percent, at 16,812.61. Most other markets, including Hong Kong, were unsettled as investors pondered how to avoid getting caught in the backwash of the collapse.

While the effects of Barings' failure were felt in many markets in Asia, the sense of crisis was acute in Singapore, where the ill-fated financial bet was made. The Singapore International Monetary Exchange, which trades the futures and options that made up the bet, scrambled to limit the effects of the crisis. In Singapore stock trading today, the Straits Times industrial index fell 1.75 percent.

The Singapore exchange was sure to face questions about why it and the nation's central bank did not detect and raise warning flags about the huge position being taken by Barings in recent weeks. The fact that Barings had made an unusually big bet on Japanese stock prices was well known in Asian markets for weeks.

The Bank of England, in a statement, sought to calm investors, saying the London markets, Europe's largest, would open for business as usual today and that it would provide funds to make sure the banking system continued to function normally.

The central bank said the problems were "unique to Barings and should have no implications for other banks operating in London."

While Barings is not as big as S. G. Warburg, Britain's leading investment house, it has been one of the industry's strongest performers in the last year. The chairman, Peter Baring, one of a number of family members working at the firm, had been expected to announce record profits for 1994 this week.

The privately held company has long been one of the most aggressive investors in emerging markets in Asia, Latin America and Eastern Europe, and also has a presence in the United States through its 40 percent stake in Dillon, Read, the Wall Street investment bank.

Dillon, Read's management, which owns the remaining 60 percent and retains complete operational control, said on Sunday that it wanted to buy back the stake held by Barings. Barings paid $78 million for the stake in 1991.

As the company cracked and then crumbled over the last few days, regulatory officials and Barings executives had to scramble just to piece together what had happened.

Barings executives said the fatal investments appeared to have been a classic attempt by a trader to cover mounting losses by making bigger and bigger bets.

They said that they were trying to locate Nick Leeson, the 28-year-old head of their futures trading operation in Singapore. They said he was believed to have left Singapore, but that they had no further information about where he might be.

As they dug into the firm's records, they discovered that the Singapore office had bought large quantities of futures contracts tied to movements in the Nikkei, as well as options linked to the same index, they said. Most of the contracts expire in March, Bank of England officials said, and have run up large losses.

By the end of the day on Friday, Barings executives calculated to their horror that the losses on the position exceeded the company's net worth. They immediately called in the Bank of England, the primary regulator for both investment houses and commercial banks in Britain.

The Bank of England said the losses stood in excess of $750 million as of Sunday night. The contracts are still open, the central bank said, "exposing Barings to unquantifiable further losses until the contracts expire or are otherwise closed out."

All of the equity in Barings is held by the Baring Trust, a charitable organization. As of last June 30, its total capital, which serves as its cushion against losses, was around $750 million, although not all of that would have been in forms that would be immediately accessible in a financial crisis of the sort it faced this weekend, executives said.

Early this morning the Singapore exchange said it would take over the Barings contracts to manage their orderly liquidation. Ultimately, the administrators of the bankruptcy, the accounting firm of Ernst & Young, will decide how best to sell the rest of the Barings assets to pay creditors.

Starting on Friday night, Bank of England officials began working out options for a solution, including finding a single buyer for Barings who could bring in new capital, selling the company in chunks or putting it into bankruptcy.

The central bank put out the word to banks and investment firms in London that Barings was in trouble. It met over the weekend with both foreign and British concerns, including some American investment banks, officials said.

By Sunday, the Bank of England was concentrating on a plan under which a group of about 14 British institutions, both all the major commercial banks and investment houses, would inject hundreds of millions of capital into Barings to keep it afloat, but only if a way could be found to cap the losses on the futures contracts.

Bank officials said an intense effort was mounted to find buyers for the contracts. But with investors uncertain about how the Tokyo market would respond to the crisis, there was little interest. Matters were not helped by the eight-hour time difference between London and Tokyo.

"The technical considerations defeated everybody," said a Bank of England official. "We tried everything. But we couldn't find a counterparty who was willing to take out the position at an acceptable price."

With the British banking group unwilling to sign on to a plan that exposed them to undetermined but mounting losses, the plan fell apart. There was one remaining option: for the Bank of England itself to step in, inject enough capital to allow Barings to close the positions, and then sell Barings as a whole or on pieces to get some of its money back.

But the central bank, despite the concerns about the stability of international markets, declined to take that step.

"The Bank of England cannot put itself in the position of signing a blank check," the official said.

In the United States, the Treasury Department said that an interagency committee was watching Barings' troubles. "We've been briefed by the appropriate international authorities and we're monitoring the situation through the President's Working Group on Financial Markets," Jon Murchinson, a Treasury spokesman, said late Sunday.

The working group is led by Treasury and also includes the Federal Reserve, the Securities and Exchange Commission and the Commodity Futures Trading Commission.

Federal Reserve officials had no immediate comment on Baring's troubles.

Bank of England officials said they did not regard the problem in this case as one peculiar to derivatives, the financial instruments whose value is derived from an underlying factor such as stock or bond prices. In a case where a trader is taking unauthorized positions, they said, the real question is the strength of an investment house's internal controls and the external monitoring done by exchanges and regulators.

Barings executives offered no immediate explanation of how their internal system could have missed the large position in Singapore, which would have required putting up a substantial sum as a margin payment. They did not say whether the contracts were bought for its own account or for those of customers.

In Singapore today, The Singapore Business Times quoted officials as saying the case would be referred to the Commercial Affairs Department for possible criminal investigation.

Barings, which has assets of more than $9 billion and more than 4,000 employees around the world, is likely to be broken up as Ernst & Young seeks to generate cash to cover its losses, industry executives said.

Likely to go on the block soon is its asset management subsidiary, which manages more than $46 billion and would be attractive to many big investment firms. Barings' investment banking and securities businesses are likely to prove less attractive to potential purchases, industry executives said.

*   *   *

March 21, 1996

PRIVATE CAPITAL IS KING IN THE NEW ORDER OF WORLD INVESTMENT

By PETER PASSELL

Looking for hard evidence that the world economy is becoming more seamless? Look no farther than the World Bank's report, released last week, on capital flows from rich countries to poor. In 1990, net flows were just over $100 billion, with less than half the money coming from private investors. Last year the number reached $230 billion, with 70 percent private.

The crisis in Mexico, despite all the attention it generated, barely created a ripple in the tide. While portfolio investment—purchase of stocks and bonds—was $12 billion lower in 1995 than the previous year, the decline was more than offset by direct investment.

The only bad news in this upbeat report is the implicit acknowledgment that sub-Saharan Africa is being left in the dust, with no means of attracting private capital and little access to government aid. Even here, though, there is a glimmer of hope. "The World Bank and International Monetary Fund are beginning to realize the only way to deal with Africa is to postpone debt payments" as a first step to reopening the door to lending, said Albert Fishlow, an economist at the Council on Foreign Relations.

Six years ago, roughly 10 percent of cross-border direct investment ended up in developing countries. Now the figure is above 35 percent. Meanwhile, the security of lenders has grown, even as debt soared. In 1985, when developing countries owed $1.1 trillion, debt service absorbed 23 percent of their export earnings. In 1995 the debt approached $2.1 trillion, but debt service represented just 16 percent of export revenues.

But the investment has not been evenly distributed. China has absorbed almost a third of the world total over the last three years, while South Korea, Malaysia, Indonesia and Thailand slurped up another third. Indeed, East Asia accounts for two-thirds of the total growth in net capital going to developing countries since 1990. Argentina, Mexico and Brazil account for much of the rest.

The pattern reflects the growing sophistication of investors. Not so long ago, third-world countries were fairly crudely graded according to risk. But in 1994 and 1995, the terms of newly issued private debt varied widely—and rationally. China, Malaysia and Thailand, for example, received loans maturing in a decade or more at interest just one percentage point above United States Treasury securities. At the other end of the risk spectrum, Latvia, Bolivia and Brazil paid four percentage points above the "riskless" rate on loans with maturities of three years or less.

"The capital market is becoming more discriminating," explained Kwang Jun, a senior economist at the World Bank and the principal author of the analysis accompanying the annually published statistics.

That suits Mr. Jun (and most economists), who would much prefer to let markets rather than multilateral institutions like the I.M.F. discipline the economic policies of sovereign states. Indeed, it now appears that the discipline imposed by the global capital market did a pretty good job in inoculating other emerging economies from contagion by the Mexican peso crisis.

For one thing, investors are more accustomed to treating developing countries as individual cases. For another, Mr. Fishlow points out, Brazil, Chile and Argentina recognized the importance of maintaining sufficient foreign currency reserves to buffer their economies against panic.

But there is a downside to this new order in which private capital is king: Countries that don't pass muster are truly isolated. Grants and loans from "official" sources—governments and lenders like the World Bank—have not grown in the last decade. In fact, they would have fallen sharply, if not for the huge loan in 1995 to get Mexico through the devaluation.

The former Soviet empire (with the great exception of eastern Germany) is the most visible victim of the invisible hand. For while there would obviously have been problems in throwing money at these economies in transition, a more generously inclined world would have found ways to provide a better safety net for the old, the young, the sick and the unemployed. Indeed, the failure to protect the weak has dimmed the prospects for rapid reform and given new political life to the old Communist elite.

Measured in sheer misery, though, the biggest loser has been sub-Saharan Africa, where net private capital flows have averaged less than $2 billion annually since 1990 and official development assistance is a drop in a large leaky bucket.

Debt forgiveness alone would not open the door to growth in heavily indebted poor countries with wretched domestic economic policies. But it is a start—and apparently the current inclination of official lenders. Encouraged by the major economic powers at last summer's economic summit meeting in Halifax, Nova Scotia, the World Bank and the I.M.F. are finally planning a fresh approach to development assistance.

* * *

March 16, 1997

FINDING COMMON GROUND FOR GLOBAL MARKETS

By THOMAS A. RUSSO

With trillions of dollars changing hands daily in the global financial arena without a universal gatekeeper, market participants and regulators should consider taking matters into their own hands by creating voluntary guidelines to promote market stability worldwide.

Conflicting regulatory regimes of various nations now govern the global financial markets, placing needless stress on the system and on individual investment firms. Regulation is largely haphazard, depending on the transactions or entities involved and the jurisdiction of a regulator. Cross-border activities can be highly, moderately or minimally regulated and, sometimes, completely unregulated, leading to regulatory arbitrage in which firms seek the jurisdiction of least resistance.

Because there is no omnipresent regulator in the sky (because none has worldwide jurisdiction), there is only one viable solution to firms' flying beneath the regulatory radar: We should develop universally applicable voluntary standards that, in the long run, could apply to most globally traded financial instruments.

Legislative solutions are out of the question when, even within individual nations, modest efforts to harmonize regulation have failed. And despite admirable attempts by American and other regulators, the task of revamping global financial regulation has proved insurmountable for any one regulator in any one country at any one time. One-size-fits-all regulation just can't be done.

On the other hand, experience shows that voluntary action can succeed where laws cannot. The model is the voluntary framework devised in 1995 by the Derivatives Policy Group, made up of the six largest United States investment banks, covering their affiliates' activities in over-the-counter derivatives—those not traded on a regulated exchange. The group, formed at the suggestion of Arthur Levitt Jr., chairman of the Securities and Exchange Commission, and later supported by the Commodity Futures Trading Commission, reflected a vision of cooperation between government and industry in an area where legal jurisdiction was unclear.

The group succeeded by developing a set of guidelines where few if any had formally existed before. So it makes sense, as a second step, to fill the worldwide jurisdictional gap in over-the-counter derivatives by expanding this type of voluntary initiative across national borders. The third and final step would be to use this model as a blueprint for the spectrum of worldwide market activities.

A global derivatives policy group would provide a forum for addressing risk concerns over activities that extend beyond geographical, as well as legal, boundaries. It would help reduce regulatory arbitrage—in which participants can select the jurisdiction of least regulation—and thereby promote competition on a level playing field. More important, it would bring under one umbrella the extensive over-the-counter derivatives market, where the failure of one or more firms could cause a financial meltdown worldwide.

If this model works for derivatives, it could also become the foundation for guidelines in other areas—if it retains the derivatives group's approaches to four main areas:

- Counterparty relationships. Voluntary guidelines should encourage firms to specify the nature of their trading relationships to reduce the uncertainty that exacerbates legal risk, as exemplified in derivatives cases like the dispute between Bankers Trust and Procter & Gamble. In such cases, the companies thought the investment firms were their advisers and the firms thought they were dealing at arm's length. The relationships should be made clear up front, not left to be defined years later by the courts.
- Management controls. Although strong management controls are an integral part of any business, they are not the cornerstone of many regulatory structures, including the securities laws of the United States. A voluntary initiative should have a detailed risk-management structure that addresses the myriad risks facing firms in the financial markets—including legal, credit, documentation, operational and market risks.
- Capital. Capital standards have been developed at different times, in different places and for different reasons. Setting aside enough capital based on the risk taken, however, seems to be the consensus approach

among international regulators; this idea should be adopted in any global voluntary system.

- Reporting to regulators. Regulators need to be advised of key risk elements of a global financial business in order to assess systemic risk. Just as it would be impossible to have a super-regulatory structure, given that there is no regulator with global jurisdiction, it would also be impossible to have a credible global voluntary structure without a connection to an existing regulator that could monitor global risk.

A voluntary structure must also contain audit-verification procedures by independent accounting firms. Without yearly audits, a set of guidelines could easily become an empty promise.

If it is to succeed, of course, this voluntary initiative will need two ingredients that were so important to the derivatives group: the leadership of key regulators and the enthusiastic support of the most senior leaders of the financial services industry.

It's time to acknowledge the reality of a global marketplace through consistent voluntary guidelines that encourage prudence and reduce risk worldwide. In the 21st century, it will make little difference where a financial company or regulator is based. What will matter is the stability and the viability of the system at large.

Thomas A. Russo is a managing director of Lehman Brothers and its chief legal officer.

*   *   *

September 18, 1997

CLINGING TO ITS PAST, EUROPE IS WARILY AWAITING THE EURO

By ROGER COHEN

MOSBURG, Germany—Franz Schmid is old enough to have suffered his share of European upheaval, and now, as the century wanes, he is convinced that the Continent is on the brink of another disaster, one that will wipe out all he has slowly built from the ruins of Hitler's war.

A retired hairdresser with a solid house beside a Bavarian brook, Mr. Schmid experienced the inflationary chaos that gave Hitler his start. He was drafted into the German army and captured on the Russian front. When he put his life together after 1945, rising early, never taking a vacation, it was the rock-solid German mark that measured his passage to a modest affluence.

His conclusion: play with currencies and you play with fire. So, like about 60 percent of his fellow Germans, he is alarmed by a plan to ditch the world's second-largest reserve currency, the mark, and use a new money to change Europe. "The mark is part of us," Mr. Schmid said. "What do we need a worthless new money for?"

But several European governments—including Germany's—appear ready to scrap their national currencies and

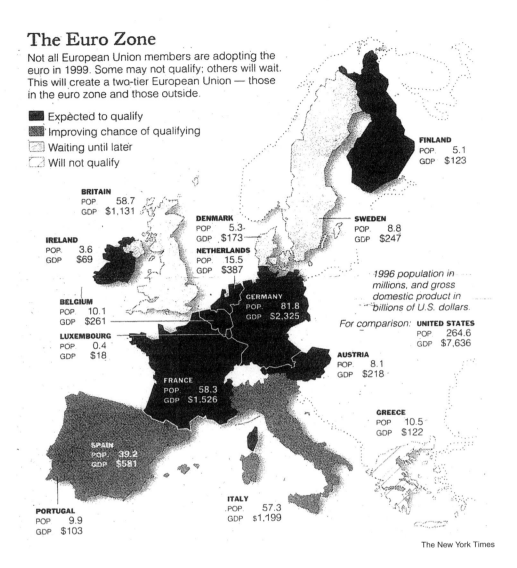

The Euro Zone

Not all European Union members are adopting the euro in 1999. Some may not qualify; others will wait. This will create a two-tier European Union — those in the euro zone and those outside.

■ Expected to qualify
▨ Improving chance of qualifying
▩ Waiting until later
☐ Will not qualify

BRITAIN
POP. 58.7
GDP $1,131

IRELAND
POP. 3.6
GDP $69

DENMARK
POP. 5.3
GDP $173

NETHERLANDS
POP. 15.5
GDP $387

FINLAND
POP. 5.1
GDP $123

SWEDEN
POP. 8.8
GDP $247

BELGIUM
POP. 10.1
GDP $261

GERMANY
POP. 81.8
GDP $2,325

LUXEMBOURG
POP. 0.4
GDP $18

1996 population in millions, and gross domestic product in billions of U.S. dollars.

For comparison: **UNITED STATES**
POP. 264.6
GDP $7,636

AUSTRIA
POP. 8.1
GDP $218

FRANCE
POP. 58.3
GDP $1,526

GREECE
POP. 10.5
GDP $122

SPAIN
POP. 39.2
GDP $581

PORTUGAL
POP. 9.9
GDP $103

ITALY
POP. 57.3
GDP $1,199

The New York Times

replace them with a single money, the euro, by 1999. They are set to impose the currency on restive, sometimes openly hostile, citizens, for whom union has become synonymous with stagnation and sacrifice. The political risk is enormous.

That risk is being taken with a bold aim: to forge greater European unity in an attempt to arrest the continent's relative decline in an American-dominated world. "There is nothing more political than money," said Richard Descoings, director of the French Institute of Political Studies. "Once each person has a euro in his pocket, the money will unite us as Americans are bound by the dollar."

But this has been a lousy decade in Europe. Unemployment is at levels not seen since the 1930's. Over the past five years, growth averaged little more than 1 percent, less than half the American level. The globalization embraced by the United States has struck fear into the European soul; war in Bosnia has shaken the continent.

For some time now, Europe has labored under a dread conviction that Asia is rising, America roaring along, while the old Continent sleeps amid its predatory ghosts.

The euro is potent medicine for this malaise. Each country that joins the common currency will surrender part of its national sovereignty by turning over key economic decisions to a European Central Bank in Frankfurt. This bank will set interest rates and impose a fiscal discipline so strict that a profound reshaping of Europe's costly welfare state appears inevitable.

In the United States, too, there is a broad push to reshape welfare programs. But Europe is a customs union, not a country, and the cuts in spending required by adoption of the euro result from the planning of faceless central bankers rather than an election in which one vision for the future has trumped another.

Skeptics worry that the architects of the euro are inviting disaster by imposing a single economic policy on diverse countries with vastly differing traditions, national identities and economic philosophies. But supporters insist that this surrender of national sovereignty is the only way for Europe to challenge the United States' global economic power, closing the American century with an act of European emancipation.

"The euro has come to be seen as a thing imposed by an elite," said Dominique Strauss-Kahn, the French Finance Minister, "but it is the only way to make Europe strong in the decades to come."

Chancellor Helmut Kohl of Germany, already in the history books as the helmsman of German reunification, thinks he has a vision that will immortalize him a second time: end a bloody century—in which Europe twice ripped itself to shreds and the United States twice came to its rescue—by creating a single money in a market of 372 million people. Which will usher in a united Europe with a united Germany at its heart.

To reassure his fellow Europeans once and for all about his country's intentions, Mr. Kohl stands ready to sacrifice the country's best-loved symbol, the mark. It is an extraordinary political step—akin to suggesting that the surrender of the American flag might somehow be in its people's interest. The euro will rise or fall with Germany, which accounts for 25 percent of the European Union's total output.

The outcome remains very much in doubt. The euro is to become Europe's money on Jan. 1, 1999. Will it bring strength or chaos, unity or renewed outbursts of European nationalism, as a Frankfurt bank becomes the scapegoat for massive unemployment?

Love, Hate and the Euro Feared as Currency, Favored as Strategy

Faces at the European Commission in Brussels tend to light up at the euro's potential to spur Europe's economy. But Mr. Schmid, the retired hairdresser, sees folly where so-called Eurocrats see fortune.

His fears are those of the average German burgher. He has given some of his savings in marks to his son, Toni, to change into dollars. He equates the dollar's 20 percent appreciation against the mark over the past year with the mark's looming demise.

Franz Schmid was 12 years old when, in 1923, inflation reached more than two billion percent. To buy $1, 4.2 trillion marks were needed. In the same year, the young Adolf Hitler was arrested after he tried to lead a march on Berlin.

His family ruined, Franz was sent to work as an apprentice to a barber, only to be drafted into Hitler's army just as he had acquired his first hairdressing salon and was beginning to make his way.

Poland, France, Russia: Mr. Schmid invaded them all, an ordinary German swept along in a tide. Then, in 1944, he was captured by the Red Army and taken to a prison camp in Siberia. On carts in summer, on sleds in winter, he carried corpses out to woods where the wolves ate them. Only his skills in cutting Soviet officers' hair saved him.

A second lesson in the vagaries of money awaited him on his return to a devastated Germany in 1947. His life savings—a bank deposit of 1,500 Reichsmarks—were worthless, devoured by the inflationary financing of the war. Dollars alone, sent by two sisters who had emigrated to New York, bought him food until a new currency, the Deutsche mark, was introduced on June 20, 1948.

"The new currency was hope, the first hope, really," Mr. Schmid said. "I got married eight days later, and the photographer asked for 100 marks, and that seemed a staggering amount. But with time, the mark became part of us. It was stable. Germany without the mark is not Germany! I feel I'm about to lose my money for the third time."

Mr. Schmid is now 86. But almost one-third of Germans are over 55, and even many younger people grew up in homes where old, devalued Reichsmark bills were kept as symbols of money's vulnerability. It is, at the root, fear of chaos that leads 60 percent of Germans to say they oppose the euro project.

"It is amazing how deep the trauma goes," said Hans-Georg Gerstenlauer, the European Commission's representative in Berlin and an enthusiastic supporter of the euro. "I remember my parents talking repeatedly about hyperinflation, and they were infants when it happened."

During an interview, Hans Tietmeyer, president of the Bundesbank, talked repeatedly—almost obsessively—about the "sustainability" of monetary union: that is, the question whether Germany's low inflation and solid currency can be enduringly extended to the European Union. He repeatedly expressed concern that the euro might be blamed for the continent's economic woes. He seemed to be fighting his own doubts.

In the end, Germany fears the euro as money but favors it as strategic salvation. This country is, on some levels, still trying to persuade wary neighbors that its nationalism was buried with the Third Reich.

"We are looking for a different identity because nationalism is really taboo," said Walter Hasselkus, the German chief executive of Rover. "That identity is Europe."

The Case for the Euro: Unshackling Europe To Take On the U.S.

The economic logic behind the plan is simple. "What," asked Jean-Claude Trichet, governor of the French Central Bank, "would the single American market be without a single money in Texas and California?"

In other words, the European Union's single market in goods and services is incomplete without a single currency and will be invigorated by having one. Over 60 percent of the trade of European Union states is with other countries in the union: the euro will simplify and stimulate this trade.

Like many European executives, Horst Teltschik, a member of the executive board of BMW, the German auto maker, sees the case for the new money as self-evident: "We export one-third of our production to other European Union countries, "and we've suffered a lot from exchange rate fluctuation. The euro will eliminate that risk."

For example, since BMW bought the British Rover auto company three years ago, sterling has appreciated more than 10 percent against the mark. As a result, the new Rover dealerships opened by BMW in Germany are having difficulties. "We should raise Rover prices to match the mark's level," Mr. Teltschik said, "but we can't, so for now we take losses."

Of course, companies trading between New York and Phoenix do not face such fluctuations. In this sense, the euro is intended to make Europe more like America. Corporations including Siemens and Unilever have made clear that they believe they will benefit greatly from the change.

Executives say that business will be spurred by easier corporate planning, pricing and billing. European financial markets will be opened up to new competition; inefficient policies will be less sustainable; pressure will rise on countries to make their economies attractive to business. The dollar will at last have a real rival.

The union's economy is roughly the same size as America's; it accounts for 20.9 percent of world trade, more than the United States' 19.6 percent; its population is bigger by about 100 million people, providing the largest single market in the world.

Why, therefore, should the euro not eventually make strong inroads into the dollar's international dominance, expressed in the fact that the dollar is the currency for close to 60 percent of international trade and 80 percent of financial operations?

Imagine oil priced in euros rather than dollars. Imagine the United States no longer able to assume that its deficits are automatically financed because the world wants dollars. Imagine Europe one day showing the same "benign neglect" for the euro that America does for the dollar because the domestic European market will be so big.

Such visions are by no means shared by everyone. "A German racket to take over the whole of Europe," was what Nicholas Ridley, a former British Industry Minister, once called the euro. The remark was revealing of a corner of the British psyche. Abstruse and abstract, but as intimate as the coins in a pocket, the euro beams a spotlight into the diverse recesses of the European heart.

Up to now, Britain, Denmark and Sweden have indicated that they will probably not join the planned "first wave" because of their reservations about the project. To these countries, the economics look too risky and the politics of a formal abandonment of national sovereignty too sensitive. But they may join later.

The United States has its doubts as well, although European integration has been in the American interest for more than 40 years. It has provided a steady opening of markets on which American corporations from I.B.M. to Toys 'R' Us have thrived. It has been a bedrock of America's postwar emergence as a European power.

"Important as monetary union is," said Lawrence H. Summer, Deputy Secretary of the Treasury, "we sometimes have an impression of an introverted Europe, of navel-gazing."

Richard C. Holbrooke, a former Ambassador to Germany and Assistant Secretary of State for Europe, was blunter: "Almost a decade has gone by since the Berlin wall fell and, instead of reaching out to Central Europe, the European Union turned toward a bizarre search for a common currency. So NATO enlargement had to fill the void. Tell me, would you leave your money in German marks if the mark is going to become the lira and you can move to the dollar?"

Italy, however, is eager to dissolve itself and its lira into Europe as soon as possible. "We've always had a healthy inferiority complex here about tall, blond people," said Luigi Spaventa, a former Budget Minister. "For us, it's the euro or Africa." In Portugal and Spain, where a decade of membership in the European Union has been synonymous with the end of dictatorship and the advent of prosperity, the euro is similarly coveted.

France is ambivalent. It cares little for the franc. Moreover, in the heady days of the Cold War's end, it was France that exacted a commitment from Germany to adopt the euro as a condition for reunification. The strategic desire to harness German economic power inalienably to French political ambitions remains. But the cession of sovereignty that the euro entails raises the specter of an end to "La France."

In Britain, the ripples of Mr. Ridley's remark have not entirely faded. Tony Blair's Labor Government has called for a sober look at the euro. But unease persists about loss of sovereignty to a bank in Germany and the less flexible economic model of continental Europe. The Conservative Party has torn itself apart over the issue.

To attempt to marry such diversity by creating a European money may appear the folly of this fin de siecle. "Kohl wants the euro for the history books," said Denis Tillinac, a French writer. "But why must we pay for his obsessions? You can share a home, you can even persuade people to eat together, but you can't force them to make love."

The Case Against the Euro: In Monetary Policy, Can One Size Fit All?

The political theory in Paris and Bonn is that you can. As Norbert Walter, the chief economist at Deutsche Bank in Frankfurt, put it, "Why not try to be great?"

Perhaps the answer is because it can be dangerous. Historically, monetary union has usually followed political union. The Federal Reserve was not established until 1913. Europe has opted to do things the other way around.

There is no European government, and peanuts would be a kind description of Europe's budget. Paltry would be an overgenerous portrayal of Europe's foreign policy. As the Bosnian war illustrated, political Europe is still as feeble as it is fragmented. The projected expansion of the union in the next century to bring in Poland and other Central European countries could cause yet more fragmentation.

By minting a money without making a government, and by surrendering control of monetary policy to a central bank while shunning the creation of other federal institutions, European states are heading into largely uncharted territory.

"This is the first time in history that the creation of a single money on a territory is not being accompanied by political centralization," said Olivier Klein, a French economist. "But money corresponds to a state power. And that is why we will have to move toward a more federal political structure in Europe."

Yet many European voters appear to despise the very federalism that the euro seems to promise. A recent cartoon in the daily Le Monde shows a despondent Frenchman. "Funny," he says, "We seemed to have more fun before Maastricht!"

Herein lies the paradox of the euro, a project sometimes suggestive of a journey begun so long ago that nobody can remember why a certain destination was chosen.

"We are going a new way in Europe," Mr. Tietmeyer, the Bundesbank president, said. "I don't see a readiness for a European superstate with one tax system, one big central budget, one security system. I have to accept that. So the basic question is whether there is enough common ground for monetary union."

The planned European Central Bank will—if the euro is broadly adopted—set a single monetary policy from Rotterdam to Rome, from Berlin to Barcelona. National room for economic maneuver after Jan. 1, 1999, will be limited.

Thus, if Italy hits a recession as the Netherlands booms, Italian authorities will no longer be able to lower interest rates to stimulate activity. They will not be able to devalue the lira.

Italians are unlikely to migrate en masse to Amsterdam for jobs, as Americans might move to a booming Arizona from a depressed Vermont. Europeans, in general, do not like to move.

Nor will a European federal budget transfer resources to Italy, as the United States Federal budget transfers money to depressed areas through Medicare and Social Security payments.

Nor, finally, will there be room for generosity in national budgets, because of the new fiscal discipline: no deficits larger than 3 percent of output. This has been the Bundesbank's draconian condition.

Europe, in other words, had better be a truly convergent economy, more or less responsive to the same economic medicine from Helsinki to Lisbon, or there will be tensions that will find a readily available target in the European Central Bank.

"How will a Europe with the euro deal with regional recessions?" asked Paul Krugman, a professor of economics at M.I.T. "I would put the odds of a collapse at one in four."

It is easy enough to imagine, for example, the invective of a group of newly unemployed French citizens told in mid-1999 that the government is essentially powerless because of decisions made in Frankfurt. Rather than uniting Europe, an unstable euro in a depressed continent might easily spur new nationalisms. Currency speculators would be quick to seize on instability.

"One can certainly imagine potential disasters in the one-size-fits-all approach to monetary policy," Eddie George, governor of the Bank of England, said in an interview. "I am feeling nervous for the whole of Europe."

Germans and the Euro: Reclaiming Berlin, Learning From Bonn

Toni Schmid, the hairdresser's son, works for the Bavarian state government. He is nervous, too. But unlike his father, he may be more willing to accept the euro, however reluctantly. He sees that giving up the mark is the price for a united Europe to which Germany is irrevocably harnessed, a Europe whose economic policy is largely set by a bank in Frankfurt.

A member of the postwar generation, Mr. Schmid sees the euro as shaped less by the direct trauma of Nazism than by the angst of being German in the aftermath of the Holocaust. Born in 1950, he was a member of the first generation of Germans to go abroad after the war. Everywhere, the mark was the finest money. In Western Europe it was admired, in Eastern Europe coveted.

But respect was not the only thing encountered outside Germany. There was the realization, in Mr. Schmid's words, "that you were not normal." Your fathers had started the war and butchered millions of people. You had not chosen those fathers, but there it was. You were different.

On a visit to Ireland, Mr. Schmid recalled befriending a couple. He was French, she British. On parting, the woman said to him, "You know, it's really strange, I never thought I would have a German friend." The remark stuck in his mind.

And there, perhaps, lies the root of Germany's euro dilemma: a strong, much-loved money, the mark, on the one hand; an uncertain identity, a bad history, on the other.

A half-century after the war, the country, whole again, stands squarely at the center of Europe. Its economic domination is clear enough. The German economy is almost a third bigger than France's.

But Germany also has its doubts. And it knows—especially since reunification—that its allies need constant reassurance. Indeed, the euro was given a decisive push by unification. It was the most convincing reassurance, the most sweeping sacrifice, that Mr. Kohl could offer his neighbors.

There is a telling symmetry in the fact that the scheduled readoption of Berlin as German capital—the return to the Reichstag and the Brandenburg Gate—is set to coincide with the adoption of the euro in 1999. The reunification with Germany's past will thus be tied to the abandonment of the mark, the very emblem of German postwar strength. Put another away, Berlin will be reclaimed but with the lessons of Bonn.

"If you give away the mark you give away respect," Toni Schmid said, "and most Germans hate the idea. But Europe has been sacred for 50 years. No political party can say no to it. That is why Germans are not yelling."

Mr. Kohl is gambling that he can win over people like Mr. Schmid to his vision of a Europe where morale and growth can return to France and Germany, and where, perhaps, a new European identity can be born.

It will also be a place where interest policy reflects the interests of all European states.

The Bundesbank's insistence during much of the 1990's on high interest rates to tame the inflationary pressures of German reunification imparted a crippling blow to the economies of other European countries, which had to apply the same interest rates as the continent entered recession. The euro's image was thus battered.

The challenge facing the German Chancellor is therefore enormous, and German history offers a cautionary tale. The last German leader to embark on such far-reaching change was Bismarck, who declared the creation of the German Empire in 1871. His united Germany, bringing together 18 states, grew out of the customs union, or zollverein, between

German states established in 1834, just as the euro seems set to emerge from European customs union.

Within 19 years of German unification, however, Bismarck was ousted. Mr. Kohl, who reunited Germany in 1989, has been in power 15 years. The vote he faces next year will hinge on the politics of the euro. Like Bismarck, Mr. Kohl may yet find that his countrymen's memory is short. "Kohl wants to be a European saint and he is ready to pay with the mark," said Toni Schmid. "But to many of us, the price looks too high."

* * *

November 20, 1997

ONE WORLD, ONE ECONOMY, ONE BIG PROBLEM WITH CURRENCIES

By PETER PASSELL

The global economy is here, and the consequences can be unnerving. Currency after currency has come under pressure in recent months as investors, fearing that their assets would erode in value, converted their holdings into dollars.

This week South Korea reluctantly acknowledged the inevitable and stopped buying back won that were fleeing to safety. For the moment Brazil remains defiant, vowing to defend the exchange value of the real even if it drives the economy into a recession. And Japan suddenly seems vulnerable to the financial storm, with investors withdrawing yen from the shaky banking system and buying dollars with the proceeds.

The sobering reality is that free international money markets and greatly expanded trade have made currency troubles more contagious. "Once currency panics begin, they take on a life of their own," concluded Jeffrey Sachs, director of the Harvard Institute for International Development.

But this latest series of crises, which has laid low almost all the Asian currencies and threatens to spread to Latin America, has prompted soul-searching even among the high priests of free market orthodoxy. A huge speculative infusion of foreign cash into the banks and stock markets of developing countries can strain rudimentary regulatory systems, encourage borrowing for consumption and lead to speculative booms in real estate. "The regulation of domestic banks and stock markets is not up to the challenge of hot money," argued Robert Hormats, co-chairman of Goldman Sachs International.

The sudden withdrawal of that money can cause local currency collapses that leave even the most productive industries with debts they cannot repay. "Sometimes inflows are excessive and sometimes they may be sustained too long," acknowledged Stanley Fischer, a deputy managing director of the International Monetary Fund.

No one is suggesting that Asia or Latin America go back to the bad old days when individuals and corporations needed permission to hold foreign currency. But the governments have other tools that could be used to tame market excess: regulations that favor direct foreign investment in businesses over purchases of stock shares, that inhibit short-term foreign investments and that discourage local businesses from accumulating big debts in foreign currency.

If the currency crisis that engulfed Thailand, Malaysia, Indonesia and the Philippines late in the summer had stopped there, it would have been easy to explain. Foreign investors, eager to cash in on the latest Asian miracle economies, had been happy to support the last decade of explosive growth. But as the currencies appreciated in recent years and exports leveled off, foreigners headed for the exits.

"Currency speculators probably started the process, selling Thai baht once it was absolutely clear the only direction the currency could go was down," said Steven Radelet, an economist at Harvard University. "But domestic banks and corporations piled on," he added, and for understandable reasons: With huge debts in dollars and yen, they couldn't afford to hold their assets in a currency whose exchange value was in jeopardy.

At first Asian governments defended their currencies by using dollar reserves to buy them back on world currency markets. But these reserves were insufficient, and some were forced to let their currencies "float," with the exchange values largely determined by private supply and demand.

The International Monetary Fund is lending additional reserves to these governments in return for their pledges to reduce imports and tighten financial regulation. This is no free lunch, though: belt-tightening will slow growth and delay the day when they join the club of affluent industrial economies.

What surprised almost everyone in the recent turmoil was how easily and quickly the panic spread to rock-solid Singapore, Taiwan and Hong Kong. If the infection from these lean-and-mean Southeast Asian tigers startled Western investors, the fall of the currencies now at risk—the Korean won, the Brazilian real and the Japanese yen—could really shake them.

For years, South Korea's spectacular growth covered a cozy, sometimes corrupt relationship between the Government, the banks and the giant conglomerates that led to overbuilding of industrial capacity. Workplace inefficiencies, compounded by increased competition from other Asian economies that allowed their currencies to depreciate, has recently pushed much of the big business community (and its lenders) to the brink.

Brazil may be next. "Everyone agrees that Brazil's currency is overvalued," said Richard Segal, the head of fixed-income research at Santander Investment Securities in New York. But in the context of the recent 20 to 40 percent depreciation in some Asian currencies, he suggests, it would be extremely difficult for Brazil to manage a modest devaluation of, say, 10 to 15 percent.

With no easy options on the table, Brazil is trying to tough it out. At best that means tight budgets, high interest rates and temporary tariffs to discourage imports of consumer goods. At worst, capital flight could make this sacrifice meaningless: Brazil could be forced to float the real—and then clean up a banking system that has heavy debts in dollars.

Most economists remain cautiously optimistic that developing economies with high savings rates, a strong work ethic and business-friendly governments will weather this crisis. But all bets are off if Japan, with an economy 10 times the size of Korea's, is hit by panic in its huge capital market.

Japanese banks, battered by losses in real estate and stocks, have virtually stopped making loans. While the Government did close one large insolvent bank in orderly fashion this week, the fear now is that depositors will withdraw their money from others before Tokyo musters the political will—and some $500 billion in public money—for a systemwide rescue.

Japan has huge reserves of foreign currency to buy yen and offset the flight of capital to dollars. Whether the Government would do so, though, is a real question, since a decline in the value of the yen would make the recession-prone Japanese economy more competitive in world markets.

Last week, Treasury Secretary Robert E. Rubin warned Tokyo that the United States would look askance at a back-door attempt to bolster Japanese exports at the expense of American companies. "There are echoes of the early 1930's," when moribund economies engaged in competitive currency devaluations in order to jump-start exports, said John Makin, a senior fellow at the America Enterprise Institute's Asian Studies Program.

The lesson here is that the evolution of financial markets in Asia and Latin America has not kept up with the revolution in global capital markets. Foreign banks and mutual funds stand ready to lend vast sums to the favored economy of the month—and just as ready to demand their money back when things turn sour. Yet the financial systems in developing countries are not geared to prevent hot money from ending up in office buildings that no one wants to rent or BMW's that buyers can't afford.

Regulators in these places have actually encouraged borrowing in foreign currency—a habit left over from an era in which foreigners were wary of lending. In the Philippines, for example, interest on foreign currency deposits is exempt from the withholding taxes levied on local currency deposits.

Fiercely defending fixed exchange rates creates similarly perverse incentives, Mr. Sachs argues. In the case of Thailand and Malaysia, the exchange rates were so stable for so long that borrowers assumed their governments would never leave them holding the bag under devaluation pressure.

Indeed, the inability of most developing countries to regulate banks and stock exchanges in ways that encourage productive foreign investment while discouraging speculative bubbles is leading many economists to reconsider certain kinds of restraints on international capital movements. "It's really hard to keep your house in order" when foreign currency is easy to obtain at bargain rates, Mr. Radelet allows.

Some countries have managed modest capital constraints that do not inhibit growth. In Chile, for example, foreigners are permitted to hold easily redeemable bank deposits, but the interest they earn is taxed at a punitive rate. And to prevent a run-up in the currency that would make its exports uncompetitive, Switzerland has at times barred its banks from paying any interest to foreigners.

The idea, some say, is to throw sand in the wheels of a global capital machine that doesn't learn new lessons easily and that forgets the old ones in a flash. "You don't hear any investment bankers talking about systemic market failure after the collapse in Asia," Mr. Sachs said.

For others, though, a modest reduction in capital mobility has become thinkable largely because the alternative is not. "Flat-out capital controls are an invitation to corruption and inefficiency," Mr. Hormats said.

* * *

December 13, 1997

ACCORD IS REACHED TO LOWER BARRIERS IN GLOBAL FINANCE

By EDMUND L. ANDREWS

GENEVA, Saturday, Dec. 13—Under the darkening clouds of Asia's financial crisis, the United States and more than 100 other countries signed a global trade agreement early this morning to open up the world's financial markets.

The agreement, reached after protracted negotiations that ended early this morning, commits countries to dismantling hundreds of barriers and admitting foreign banks, insurance companies and investment firms to their markets.

The new agreement could lead to big changes in countries from India and Indonesia to Brazil and Argentina. At its essence, the nations legally committed themselves to giving foreigners more freedom to own and operate companies in all segments of the financial services industry.

The United States, which already allows unfettered access to its financial markets, conceded nothing in the agreement. Most of the changes will be in Asia and Latin America, where countries retain many restraints on foreign banks, insurers and brokerage firms.

Even so, some economically desperate Asian countries like South Korea and Malaysia refused to commit themselves to expanding foreign access much beyond current limits—despite the meltdown ravaging their currencies and stock markets.

The new pact could also draw sharp criticism in Congress, where some lawmakers are already suspicious of the World Trade Organization, the international body that will oversee and enforce it.

Some in Congress are still angry about a tentative ruling in which the trade organization rejected the Eastman Kodak Company's complaints about restrictions in the Japanese market. But Congress has no power to block the new pact. The Clinton Administration had the authority to negotiate and sign the agreement, which goes into effect immediately.

The new pact is less dramatic than many American companies had hoped it would be. Nonetheless, the fact that it was signed at all was viewed with considerable relief, and proponents said the deal could help reverse the tide of pessimism caused by the Asia crisis. "I don't think it would be good for confidence in the financial markets if this deal failed," said Patrick Low, the W.T.O.'s director of economic research.

Several of America's biggest investment firms immediately praised the pact. "This agreement advances the cause of free and open markets, which will help bring the benefits of a more integrated financial system to people everywhere," David H. Komansky, chief executive of Merrill Lynch & Company, said. Jon Corzine, chairman of Goldman, Sachs & Company, said the pact would be "a powerful engine of prosperity."

A lot is at stake. American banks and investment companies have led a worldwide expansion in financial services, from orchestrating corporate mergers to exporting American-style pension funds. International bond and stock sales have doubled in the last five years, as companies from Daimler-Benz to France Telecom listed their shares on stock exchanges. Institutional investment has ballooned, while international currency trading has swelled to $1.2 trillion daily.

Against this backdrop, it was the Asian financial crisis that overshadowed most of the talks. Though the United States has pushed harder than any other country, executives here said Treasury Secretary Robert E. Rubin and the U.S. trade representative, Charlene Barshefsky, had been worried that walking away from an agreement would aggravate investor uncertainty even more.

In Washington late Friday night, President Clinton welcomed the accord, saying it would insure market access in sectors where the United States led the world. "In the wake of recent financial instability, it is particularly encouraging that so many countries have chosen to move forward rather than backwards," Mr. Clinton said in a statement.

American companies were conspicuous at the negotiations. Citicorp, Goldman, Sachs, Merrill Lynch and numerous insurance companies established command posts at a hotel near the W.T.O. headquarters. As the organization's self-imposed midnight deadline for an agreement approached, many executives conferred with American negotiators.

American representatives quit the trade talks two years ago, complaining that countries were not going far enough on opening markets. Talks began again in earnest this week. As it happened, the deadline was extended by several hours as the United States kept seeking concessions.

"It is all because of les Americains!" one tired trade official said. The European Union had been ready to sign a treaty long before.

The biggest disagreements, according to officials and executives, were with Japan, Malaysia and South Korea. The South Koreans, for example, refused to commit themselves to letting foreigners own controlling stakes in banks, even with the threat of defaults looming over many Korean financial institutions.

The country is already locked in arguments with the International Monetary Fund about opening its system, barely a week after signing a $57 billion bailout with the I.M.F.

In one of the United States' toughest victories, not reached until nearly 2 A.M., Japan agreed to a sweeping array of market-opening measures. Japan had already reached a bilateral agreement with the United States that would give American companies broad access to Japan's insurance market. But Japan had refused to broaden that commitment to all countries in the organization, or to bind those pledges to the legal enforcement mechanisms of the international body.

Under the agreement, each country put forward its own best offers for opening up its local financial markets to foreign companies. The offers differ greatly, but countries become legally bound to stick by those commitments. If they do not, and the World Trade Organization rules that a country has backed away from its word, other countries get the right to seek compensation or impose retaliatory restrictions.

* * *

September 20, 1998

EXPERTS QUESTION ROVING FLOW OF GLOBAL CAPITAL

By NICHOLAS D. KRISTOF

TOKYO, Sept. 19—They were the world's richest and shrewdest investors, and they rode a wave of globalization to buy bonds in a promising developing country. When the country defaulted, they were livid.

"There should be lunatic asylums for nations as well as individuals," one investor wrote in The Morning Post of London, denouncing the defaulting country as "a nation with whom no contracts can be made."

It all sounds a bit familiar, but the year was 1842 and the developing country was the United States. After defaults by Maryland, Pennsylvania, Mississippi and Louisiana, the entire United States was blacklisted and scorned on global markets, with Americans barred from the best London clubs and the Rothschilds warning bitterly that America would be unable to "borrow a dollar, not a dollar."

Globalization, in other words, may not be quite as fresh as it sometimes seems. Since at least the 13th century, when Florentine merchants lent money to the English to pay for King Edward I's wars, international capital has roamed the world in search of high returns. (The start was inauspicious: England defaulted, causing the collapse of two Florentine banks.)

What has changed, economists say, is the scale of the capital flows and their ability to capsize small nations—or even large ones. Many experts say that one factor behind the economic crisis that has devastated Asia and Russia, wobbled South America, and now come knocking on America's own door is the fantastic increase in the pool of capital that sloshes from one country to the next in search of safety and profit.

The sums are so gargantuan—far greater than the amounts that governments can wield—that a growing number of economists are calling for new steps to control these capital flows or at least soften their impact. Some say that the Bretton Woods economic system, which has governed the global economy for half a century, has been eclipsed by these vast pools of capital, and there are calls to design a new "architecture" for the global economic order.

The topic is expected to be widely discussed at next month's special meeting of finance ministers and central bankers from the Group of Seven industrialized countries, summoned by President Clinton to discuss the global crisis. Japan's Finance Minister, Kiichi Miyazawa, has already discussed measures to ease the volatility of capital flows with Treasury Secretary Robert E. Rubin and with his British counterpart, Gordon Brown.

The Federal Reserve chairman, Alan Greenspan, weighed in this week with a denunciation of rigid capital controls but a call to confront the problem by tightening supervision over banks that engage in international finance. All of a sudden, a vigorous debate is under way, and it may shape the global economy for decades to come.

"We'll have to rethink the system in a big way," said Jagdish Bhagwati, a prominent scholar of international economics at Columbia University. "The President has called this conference, and it should be the start of that process."

Professor Bhagwati urged that the new architecture should "give up the notion that the optimal world is one characterized by free capital flows, by capital account convertability, where you just press a button and take out a billion."

The Clinton Administration has led a global push to free the flow of capital around the world, and any new impediments to capital flows would be an abrupt step back for its campaign. As recently as last March, the International Monetary Fund newsletter carried a front-page headline cheerily declaring capital liberalization to be "an irreversible trend."

These days, it looks more reversible. Some economists believe that despite a wealth of scholarly research showing the need for caution, the United States pushed too hard for capital liberalization. The result, they say, was that tides of investment flooded into ill-prepared developing countries and created speculative bubbles, and then surged out, leaving behind shattered nations and a global financial crisis.

"I actually think the I.M.F. was too pushy in going around the accepted wisdom and encouraging countries to liberalize their capital accounts too soon," said Ronald I. McKinnon, an economist at Stanford University and author of a book on capital liberalization. "And not the least of the reasons behind this was arm-twisting by the United States Treasury, which always wants American banks and Wall Street people to be in there, competing freely."

Still, there is no question that freer capital flows have brought tremendous benefits to the global economy, as well as perils. Some places, like Hong Kong, have opened themselves to capital flows without restriction and are examples of the prosperity that free movements of capital can reap. Lawrence H. Summers, the Deputy Treasury Secretary, likens the flows to jet planes, observing that jets bring enormous efficiencies and benefits to the world—but that the crashes are more spectacular than ever.

What are these capital flows?

They are not some sinister force, but simply the result of ordinary people's cash roaming in search of a good return. When an American deposits money at the corner bank, some of that may end up being lent to a Brazilian company, and the same person's pension fund may dabble in the Hong Kong stock market.

In the United States, trading in foreign securities amounted to 2 percent of gross national product in 1975 and 213 percent last year, according to data from the Bank for International Settlements.

Paradoxically, historians sometimes attribute the modern boom in international capital, beyond the easy reach of any regulator, to the Communists. In the 1950's, China and Russia kept their dollars out of the United States, for fear Washington would freeze their accounts, and instead deposited the dollars in Europe.

One result was the "Eurodollar" market and a growing investment pool that flitted from country to country and currency to currency in pursuit of higher interest rates. The amount of foreign currency bank deposits around the world reached $1 billion only in 1961 and now is almost $1.5 trillion.

One problem, though, is that a lot of this is "hot money," or short-term flows that are particularly volatile.

Even in the 19th century, sailing ships used to carry gold to distant countries in pursuit of higher interest rates. In 1849, England raised its interest rate by 2 percentage points, prompting an early demonstration of the volatility of capital flows: ships that were already at sea, headed for America with their gold, turned around and sailed to England to get the higher rate.

Most governments imposed capital controls early in this century and then lifted them in the 1970's and 80's, and limitations on changing money came to be seen as quaint. Paradoxically, it is the holdouts with capital controls, like China and India, that have weathered the financial crisis much better than others, because they were not vulnerable to a sudden exodus of capital.

"I've been told, 'China seems to be coming out of the crisis well because it has capital controls, so what's wrong with reimposing controls?'" said Linda Tsao Yang, the American envoy to the Asian Development Bank.

Ms. Yang and other American officials are wary of capital controls, however, particularly the rigid kind imposed by Malaysia that ban most investments from being taken out of the country within the first year. Scholars say that such capital controls offer short-term benefits but tend to discourage investment in the long run and often get mired in corruption and inefficiency.

"There is a significant risk that over the next three or four quarters short-term results from Malaysia will be seen as beneficial," said William R. Cline, the chief economist of the Institute of International Finance in Washington. "An illusory temporary success could tempt other countries to follow suit."

The United Nations Conference on Trade and Development this week backed the right of countries to adopt emergency capital controls like Malaysia's. Even the Far Eastern Economic Review, a conservative Hong Kong-based magazine owned by Dow Jones & Company, declared its sympathy for capital controls in a recent editorial.

"As we look to Malaysia's unorthodoxy," it said, "we hold our nose and cross our fingers."

While Western economists are mostly unimpressed by Malaysia's controls, many speak highly of a quasi tax that Chile has imposed on short-term borrowings from abroad. With that measure, which the country is in the process of dismantling, Chile has been able to attract foreign capital, but has been less vulnerable to a sudden exodus.

The specific proposals that G-7 finance ministers might discuss to deal with capital flows are unclear. But there is vague talk of increasing supervision over borrowing banks and of establishing funds that could be used to insure depositors or counteract speculative attacks.

"Outright controls on the flow of funds are virtually impossible in this modern, integrated world," said Yuji Tsushima, a finance expert in Japan's Parliament. "But we should have some device through which if the volatility of the market gets too disturbing, it could be mitigated."

* * *

May 2, 1999

OUT OF ASIA:
THE MOVE TOWARD GLOBAL REGULATION

By LOUIS UCHITELLE

WASHINGTON—The Asian crisis is subsiding. Even Russia is reviving a bit. But for all the relief that brings, the global financial meltdown remains a haunting memory—not as searing as the Depression for a generation of Americans, but scary enough. And just as the Depression brought regulation to America's financial markets, the Asian and Russian crises are forcing rules on the global market.

That is a striking shift in course. The thousands of lenders and borrowers who move money among themselves in what is called the global financial market had counted on markets to heal themselves without much oversight. Many economists encouraged that view, until Asia took a dive. And now public officials with the power to regulate global markets are speaking more explicitly than ever about actually doing so.

They are not thumping pulpits about it. But in interviews, speeches and forum discussions at the spring meeting of the International Monetary Fund and the World Bank, held here last week, some officials offered views they would not have dared to put on the record six months ago.

"There is a growing acceptance in the official international community that you tremendously increase the risk of triggering volatility and crisis if rules are not made for the proper structuring of debt," Jack Boorman, the I.M.F.'s director of policy development, said in an interview. Volatility is a euphemism for the panicky rush of foreign lenders out of Asia, then Russia, and then Brazil. Credit even dried up in the

United States last fall, until a worried Federal Reserve abruptly cut rates.

While the World Bank had spoken out for global rule-making, the I.M.F. had held back, and so had the Clinton Administration. But it was clear at last week's meeting that they, too, have now come on board.

The Asian crisis has imposed on all of them a common frame of reference. It goes like this: The global capital market, like national markets, is neither self-regulating nor self-curing. Left alone, lenders and borrowers tend to operate with too much exuberance, on the one extreme, and then pull back too far in panic, on the other.

"Crises are, in a sense, accidents," said Lawrence H. Summers, the Deputy Treasury Secretary, in a speech last Sunday. "As with accidents, crises will never be eliminated, and are not amenable to silver-bullet solutions. Think of auto accidents: If one looks back at any auto accident, there are always many things that could have combined to produce greater safety."

Given that recognition, the new rule-making—or accident prevention, as Mr. Summers put it—is under way. It is now openly recognized that lenders must be regulated, and negotiations have begun over what strictures to impose on them. (Hapless borrowers have been lectured from all sides since the global crisis started in 1997 on how they should have behaved and must now behave.)

"There is more belief now in the necessity of controls on both the lending and the borrowing side," said Stanley Fischer, the I.M.F.'s first deputy managing director.

The lenders, after all, are part of a system that can swing too easily from optimism to pessimism. These swings are facilitated by short-term loans, which lenders prefer to long-term lending. Loans of less than a year are less expensive for lenders because banks need not keep as large a percentage of the loans' value in reserve. And short-term loans can be withdrawn quickly in a crisis, which makes the lenders whole but tends to deepen the crisis.

Borrowers are also tempted by short-term loans. They can often borrow abroad for the short term at relatively low interest rates and re-lend the borrowed money long term at home at higher rates. They gamble that the short-term loans will be renewed indefinitely, not suddenly withdrawn in panic.

One goal of the new rule-making is to discourage short-term lending in favor of long-term loans, which are less likely to finance speculation and more likely to finance factories and similar investments. Not surprisingly, this shift is turning out to be the hardest part of the new rule-making process.

Lenders, naturally, are opposed. "Presumably the market, on its own, will find the right balance between short-and long-term credit," said James Chessen, chief economist of the American Bankers Association.

Public officials are sensitive to this resistance. Still, there is much talk of raising reserve requirements on short-term loans, and of requiring bondholders to postpone repayment in the event of a crisis.

Tougher proposals come more slowly to the table. One is the so-called Chile approach: When short-term foreign loans enter in great quantity, Chile requires the foreign lenders to deposit a percentage of each loan in a noninterest-bearing account—a tax, in effect, that raises a loan's cost. Such a strong deterrent never entered Treasury Secretary Robert E. Rubin's speeches, until April 21, the eve of the meeting here.

"Some countries," he said, "may deem more comprehensive measures—such as Chilean-style taxes on short-term capital inflows—to be appropriate." Caveats filled the next three sentences, but no rejection. The rule makers, mindful of Asia, are clearly moving forward.

A WORLD WIDE WEB

April 15, 1983

THREATS TO U.S. IN TECHNOLOGY

By LEONARD SILK

The United States, powerhouse of the industrial revolution in the 20th century, has been suffering from acute anxiety that it is losing its industrial and technological leadership to other countries, and losing ground in key world markets to countries that have forged ahead through close cooperation between business and government.

To study the problem, the National Academy of Sciences 14 months ago assembled a distinguished panel of economists, businessmen, engineers and scientists, headed by Howard A. Johnson, chairman of the corporation of the Massachusetts Institute of Technology.

Frank Press, president of the academy, said the most remarkable thing about the report was that strong-minded and independent people, who started far apart, came to the unanimous conclusion that United States technological leadership is vulnerable both from domestic weaknesses and from damaging practices of other countries.

The panel reached a double-edged recommendation. The first part was that the United States Government should take a stronger hand in helping to maintain the nation's capacity for technological innovation, to benefit its domestic economy, its national security and its competition for global markets. The second was that the Government should pursue policies to reduce trade frictions troubling economic and political relations among the United States and its principal industrialized allies, and, if necessary, get tough if other countries refuse to cooperate in opening up their markets.

The panel called for "the most immediate hard bargaining" against such unfair trade practices as predatory pricing, the targeting of specific United States advanced technology markets through governmentally orchestrated industrial strategies, government intervention to force the purchase of products from domestic suppliers, and restrictions on foreign direct investment, particularly those that deny distribution outlets for United States advanced technology products.

To deal with such cases, the panel proposed a series of escalating actions, ranging from bilateral discussions to formal dispute proceedings. If all else failed, it called on the United States to take "unilateral action to protect the national interest as a step of last resort."

The panel recommended one major organizational change: a biennial Cabinet-level review of the nation's inno-

vative capacity and trade competitiveness. The review would cover not only research and development but also manufacture and distribution. It would also assess the broad elements that affect innovation, including the macroeconomic environment, regulatory policy, patent policy and the antitrust laws.

Its report calls for greater governmental aid to education, both higher and lower. The American primary and secondary system for teaching science and mathematics is in trouble, the report says, noting that the higher productivity growth of the Japanese economy has been attributed partly to the high quality of that country's precollege educational system.

Thus the American spotlight is back on the factors affecting economic growth. Basically, there are two forces behind growth. One is a set of cultural factors, including science, technology and the skills, education and drive of a nation's people. The other is a set of economic factors, especially the accumulation of capital and its investment in plant and equipment or in research and development.

On the cultural side, the United States still looks very strong. American scientists still lead the world in winning Nobel Prizes. There is a zest in science and engineering that carries over into many high-technology industries—the kind of zest described in Tracy Kidder's book, "The Soul of a New Machine."

But there are deep concerns about the nation's social, economic and educational disparities, with a fissure developing between "upper class" and "underclass." The large number of unskilled and undereducated workers hampers the nation's technical and industrial progress.

On the economic side, persistently high interest rates and low rates of savings and investment are slowing the growth of productivity. While many small companies are showing remarkable dynamism and have ready access to venture capital, America's basic industries are having trouble raising long-term funds at costs below anticipated rates of return.

High interest rates, resulting from the clash between loose fiscal and tight money policies, have made the United States dollar so overpriced as to undermine American exports and overstimulate imports. And high interest rates have helped slow the growth of the United States and the world economy.

The academy report should help mobilize Government support for the nation's slipping technological and international trade position. It could also help improve the macroeconomic and social environment for growth, if the nation's policy makers will read it and take it seriously.

* * *

September 20, 1986

THE NEW TRADING GAME

Financial Innovation and Global Linkage Have Made Markets Complex and Volatile

By KAREN W. ARENSON

It has been more than 300 years since a craze sent prices of tulip bulbs soaring in the normally staid Netherlands. And half a century since a comparable craze sent stock prices soaring, and then crashing, in America, a harbinger of the Great Depression.

Markets—particularly the financial markets—have grown considerably in complexity since those historic episodes. New forms of securities and trading instruments have been devised. New technologies have been brought to bear. The world's markets are now linked so that trading goes on around the clock. Volume has rocketed, and so have the dollars involved.

What have not changed are the crescendos and crashes that periodically grip these markets—such as the stunning 7 percent Wall Street stock plunge a week ago. Nor have the elements that drive the markets changed: a combination of economic sentiment, avarice, psychology and technical trading patterns, all played out in an uncertain environment where no mechanical answers exist.

Sometimes one factor dominates, sometimes another. The shifting mix is part of what makes the markets so unpredictable—and so difficult to explain, even in hindsight. Yesterday, with Wall Street battened down for a hurricane, trading closed with scarcely more turbulence than a summer breeze.

For all their unpredictability, markets are nevertheless considered among the truest gauges of the economy. The market is no more—and no less—than the sum of what thousands and thousands of people decide about it at any one time. The market is where all knowledge about the economy or individual enterprises—the surmises as well as the certainties—is brought to bear, almost instantly.

If Iraq's bombings knock out key oil fields in Iran, or auto sales prove stronger than expected, within minutes the prices of oil contracts, Treasury bonds, stock and options prices—an entire spectrum of financial instruments—begin to move. As soon as news is known, legions of traders are dissecting it for its possible impact on every corner of the economy and for how they can extract a profit.

From the outside, the action often seems puzzling. For what seems to make stocks rise one day may send them tumbling another.

On Monday, for instance, investors may view new strength in the economy as auspicious, a signal that corporations will thrive and earnings rise. So stock prices move up. By Thursday, further signs of economic growth may be regarded as bad; they might rekindle inflation. Fearing that the Federal Reserve might therefore throttle the money supply and choke off growth, traders suddenly pull back. So stock prices fall.

Shifts in "sentiment" such as these have a powerful effect on the market. This is not to say that Wall Street takes lightly the task of assessing the economic value of companies in the stock market. Most brokerage firms employ cadres of highly paid securities analysts to follow company fortunes and to spin out earnings forecasts as the basis for buy and sell recommendations on stocks.

The tension between economic logic and market psychology is not new. The noted British economist John Maynard Keynes, himself an eminently successful investor, once commented: "It is not sensible to pay 25 for an investment of which you believe the prospective yield to justify a price of 30, if you also believe the market will value it at 20 three months hence."

Or, putting it another way, Keynes once likened the market process to a newspaper contest where contestants had to pick the six prettiest faces from hundreds of beautiful faces. A contestant's own preference was not telling. Instead, the winner was to be the person whose six choices most closely matched those chosen by all the voters. Thus the true task was to anticipate which beauties most readers would favor, while their choice, in turn, was also shaped by trying to outguess everyone else.

"We have reached the third degree, where we devote our intelligences to anticipating what average opinion expects the average opinion to be," Keynes remarked. "And there are some, I believe, who practice the fourth, the fifth and higher degrees."

But while Keynes and others understood the forces operating on the markets, they did not reckon with the power that some of these forces unleash today, forces that can pound prices down 4 percent in a day or 7 percent in a week, as they did last week.

The elements include money managers with billions of dollars at their disposal, computers that can perform millions of calculations a second, an array of financial investments so varied and so complex that most traders stick to only one or two rather than trying to understand the intricacies of many. Perhaps more remarkable than the striking volatility is the fact that stability prevails so much of the time.

It is hard to say that any single change has been most important in transforming today's frenetic markets. There have been many.

First, the pools of investment funds slosh from market to market as never before—money with no particular loyalty, either to a country or to a specific investment. A decade ago it was the OPEC nations, as they accumulated huge stores of wealth as oil prices soared. Today it is Japan, with its savings and export proceeds, that has generous pools to invest.

The United States, on the other hand, no longer the largely isolated economy it once was, now has an immense trade deficit to finance. What foreign investors think suddenly becomes critical not only for the Federal Reserve, but also for other players in the marketplace.

Changes in America's pension laws, roughly a decade ago, have contributed to the buildup in large blocks of private funds in the United States.

If the pools of investing funds changed, so too did the behavior of investors. The inflation of the 1970's burned many professional investors who had built portfolios of bonds paying 2 and 3 percent. After that lesson, investors and money managers who had been content to sit on long-term bonds for 30 years now may turn over their portfolios several times a year, contributing to the bond market's greater ups and downs. Stock portfolios, always managed more actively than bonds, are pushed even harder.

Another material change is the proliferation of new financial instruments. Little more than a decade ago, Chicago's commodity markets introduced investment vehicles that have become central to today's financial markets.

First, they initiated options on individual stocks, which give investors the right to buy or sell those stocks at a specific price at a specific date in the future, with limited risk. The idea was not new; buyers have long used options to stake claims on real estate. And stock options had long traded in the over-the-counter market.

But an exchange for listing and trading options on blue chips, and their marketing by major brokerage houses, helped promote widespread use by portfolio managers, both as a means of making bigger profits and as a way of protecting against large declines in stock prices, a practice known as hedging.

Then, they introduced options on groups of stocks, such as the Standard & Poor's index, adding more tricks for portfolio managers to play. So did the advent of futures contracts on stock indexes. These new instruments not only opened new opportunities for speculators, they also opened the way for arbitragers, who seek to profit by exploiting disparities among markets, thereby bringing the multiplicity of markets in line.

Such changes also called for a new tribe of players, more quantitatively oriented than before. Where firms previously hired macroeconomists to forecast the course of the economy, now they seek microeconomists who understand relative values among the myriad financial instruments in the markets and can devise complex arbitrage formulas.

Sophisticated Computers

Sophisticated computers are another requirement in the new trading order. Only a computer can assess, in an instant, the ever-changing value of the 500 stocks in the Standard and Poor's index—and whether their total exceeds or lags the value of the option on the S.&P. 500 or the futures contract on the same index. The 500 stocks could be totaled manually, or with a calculator, but, by then, their values might already have moved significantly.

Traders have portable machines so small that they can be carried home or to a restaurant or to the beach. Market data are fed by satellite; the trader is never out of touch. And if there is an important move in Tokyo or London, after the American markets have closed or before they reopen, the trader can quickly call up market data and make decisions.

Even the average small investor, who traditionally called a broker for information and advice, today can use a personal computer for access to much the same information, and same types of programs, used by the big money managers.

What changes such as these can mean to the functioning of markets is best understood by looking at the market. Last week's plunge offers a prime example.

The markets' big moves—Treasury bonds fell roughly 2 percent on Sept. 11, while the Dow Jones industrial average was off a record 86 points that day—were touched off by a new sense of unease over the economy and some jitters over inflation.

What might well have been a moderate market move, however, appears to have been exacerbated by the swift flow of information to money managers around the globe, and by program trading, by large financial institutions using computers to detect differences in the value of the stock indexes, and the options and futures on stock indexes.

Many on Wall Street believe that even without program trading or the sloshing of other big pools of money, the market probably would have fallen similar amounts but more gradually, perhaps over two or three weeks rather than a day.

Psychology still plays a big role, as it did in the Netherlands in the 1700's, and as it did in New York in 1929. But when the psychology changes now, the market adjustments tend to be a lot quicker—and a lot steeper. Whether last week's episode was an extreme, or whether even steeper moves lie ahead, remains to be seen. What seems certain, however, is that day-to-day volatility is here to stay.

* * *

July 3, 1988

THE NEW HIGH-TECH BATTLEGROUND

By ANDREW POLLACK

SAN FRANCISCO—High-technology battles used to be won or lost in the research laboratory, on the factory floor or in the marketplace. Now it seems they are being won or lost in the courtroom.

American industry in general, and high-technology companies in particular, are increasingly resorting to patent and copyright litigation as a source of new revenue and as a competitive weapon. Companies are viewing such intellectual property rights as key corporate assets to be exploited to the fullest in an increasingly competitive environment.

The effect is similar to what occurred when companies recognized that the real estate they owned, far from being merely shelter for employees, was sometimes more valuable than the company's business operations. Companies large and small are doing the equivalent of combing through their dusty attics, looking for old patents and licensing arrangements that can be turned into new revenue or leverage.

"You're seeing the aggressive use of intellectual property rights as a sword," said S. Leslie Misrock, an authority on biotechnology patent law with Pennie & Edmonds in New York. Ronald Laurie, a San Francisco computer attorney, agreed: "If you have good patents, litigation is a better way of making money than selling products."

In perhaps the best example, Texas Instruments Inc. decided it wasn't receiving enough money from Japanese and Korean chip companies that were using some of its early patents for the production of computer memory chips. After a lengthy legal battle, the Dallas-based chip maker got nine of the foreign companies to pay higher royalties, which last year amounted to $191 million, almost as much as the company's profits from operations. Another $100 million or so might be paid through 1990. "We have had an asset that we have been underutilizing," said Richard J. Agnich, the company's senior vice president and general counsel.

The International Business Machines Corporation is also becoming more aggressive. After losing much of the personal computer market to low-priced clones, I.B.M. is being more vigilant in protecting its next generation, the PS/2. It has raised the royalty rate it is charging for use of its intellectual property to 5 percent of sales from 1 percent, an action that could put the squeeze on the clone makers with the lowest margins. Two weeks ago, I.B.M. struck again. It began approaching companies that use a popular new technology known as reduced instruction set computing, or RISC, informing them that they may be in violation of I.B.M. patents.

The Federal District Court in San Jose, Calif., which serves Silicon Valley, is awash with lawsuits, often over questions for which laws written years before provide no clear answers.

In a case that could have a big effect on future advances in personal computing, Apple Computer Inc. has sued the Microsoft Corporation and the Hewlett-Packard Company for copyright infringement of the screen display used in Apple's Macintosh. The Intel Corporation is locked in a battle with Japan's NEC Corporation over the copyrightability of microcode used in microprocessors.

And the biotechnology industry is rife with patent litigation that will determine who profits from the new technology. Genentech Inc. alone is either attacking or being attacked in 10 intellectual property lawsuits. Last month, it received patent protection for its blockbuster new heart attack drug TPA. The same day, it filed a patent infringement suit against its closest competitors.

Lawsuits are only one manifestation of the intellectual property mania. Another is that companies are being far more selective in licensing their technology to others.

Intel, which licensed early versions of its microprocessors to numerous companies, has kept its latest product, the 80386, to itself, creating a mini-monopoly that has caused its profits and revenues to soar. Rival chip maker Advanced Micro Devices says that under a previous technology exchange agreement it is entitled to a license and it is locked in bitter arbitration with Intel. Not that Advanced Micro itself believes in unrestricted licensing. It has refused to grant a license for another type of chip technology to Samsung, the Korean conglomerate. Last month, Samsung went to court seeking to have Advanced Micro's patents declared invalid.

Even universities and the Federal Government are jumping on the bandwagon, turning to patent licensing either to raise money or to spur commercialization of their discoveries. Membership in the Society of University Patent Administrators has grown to 500 from about 70 15 years ago, according to the society's president, Katharine Ku.

Intellectual property is also increasingly important in international competition and is at the heart of several trade disputes. Efforts are being stepped up to put a stop to illegal copying of products abroad. Such copying, ranging from counterfeit Levi's jeans to thousand-dollar software programs sold in back alleys of Hong Kong for a few bucks, cost American companies more than $43 billion in 1986, according to the International Trade Commission, a Federal agency.

Meanwhile, some experts point out with alarm that foreigners are now getting close to 50 percent of the patents issued in the United States, with the Japanese being particularly aggressive. Some fear that the Japanese will soon do to Texas Instruments as Texas Instruments did to them.

There is a darker side to this as well, a number of experts say. There is a danger that the intellectual property system, which is designed to spur innovation by allowing a creator to reap the rewards of his creation, could instead be used as a tool to stifle innovation and limit competition.

Certainly, those hit with infringement suits often claim that the suer is using litigation as a marketing tool.

But even some people not directly involved are raising questions. Apple in particular has attracted harsh criticism for its lawsuit against Microsoft and Hewlett-Packard. Critics say that having borrowed many of the ideas used in its Macintosh computer from the Xerox Corporation, Apple is now trying to keep others from using those same ideas. Software, some executives say, has always progressed in a pattern in which one person builds upon another's work.

"The way we used to do innovation has been called into question," said Daniel Bricklin, the creator of the original personal computer spreadsheet program, Visicalc, which was eventually surpassed by a more sophisticated product, Lotus 1-2-3. When Visicalc came out in the late 1970's, Mr. Bricklin and his partners were told it could not be patented. By today's legal standards, some lawyers think Visicalc could be patented, which would have kept 1-2-3 and other spreadsheets off the market. "The world's better off that we didn't patent it," Mr. Bricklin said.

Part of the dismay stems from a vague feeling among high-tech executives that the industry has matured into just another bloated, bureaucratic business that must rely on lawyers and political lobbying, rather than on technological wits, to survive.

By this view, Texas Instruments, no longer the dominant player in the memory chip business, can rely on patents it received when it was in its prime to help keep up with the Japanese for a time, at least. Apple, which had long preached that personal computers would spread technology to everyone, is now seen as just another company bent on locking up technology for its own profit.

"They're the evil empire instead of the new frontier," said James H. A. Pooley, a Palo Alto, Calif., intellectual property lawyer who has criticized the Apple suit.

Others contend, however, that having to design around someone else's patent is a bigger spur to innovation than merely copying another's work and building upon it. And Apple argues that other companies can use the same advanced ideas without having the final product look exactly like Apple's.

All this is in contrast to the far greater technology sharing that the industry experienced in years past. The American Telephone and Telegraph Company received only about $20 million in license fees for its invention of the transistor in 1947, the device that set off the electronics boom, according to an estimate by Judith K. Larsen, a researcher at Dataquest Inc., a market research firm in San Jose.

One reason for the change now is that American companies are facing competition from abroad from companies with lower-cost manufacturing. But the Americans still lead in innovation.

"The U.S. companies are trying to exploit their advantage," said Gary L. Reback, head of the technology practice at Fenwick, Davis & West, a Palo Alto law firm that represents Apple and many other high-technology companies.

Higher licensing fees are viewed as a way of getting a better return on increasingly expensive research and development. Another reason, notes Mr. Reback, is that many of the tiny Silicon Valley companies have grown up and now have staffs of lawyers that can afford to deal with these matters.

But the biggest reason seems to be the change in the law's treatment of intellectual property, particularly patents. Some 15 years ago, only 40 percent of patents were upheld in litigation, said John Barton, a professor at Stanford University Law School. Many companies didn't bother to file for patents or protect them.

But that has changed. In 1982, Congress created the Court of Appeals for the Federal Circuit, to which all patent cases are funneled on appeal. The consolidation has resulted in more consistent rulings that often favor patent holders. Not only have patents been upheld, but courts have not been hesitant to levy stiff penalties against infringers.

Eastman Kodak was forced out of the instant photography business by a patent suit filed by the Polaroid Corporation. Now Polaroid is asking for damages of $5.7 billion. Last year, Monoclonal Antibodies, a Mountain View, Calif., biotechnology company, was forced to stop selling products that accounted for 80 percent of its revenues, a development that almost drove it out of business.

"The pendulum has swung rather mightily in the direction of patent enforcement," said Mr. Pooley, who is with the Palo Alto firm of Mosher, Pooley & Sullivan. "The kind of bet-your-company situation that now exists just really didn't obtain before 1982."

As technology races ahead, the law is straining to keep up. New questions arise that are not clearly addressed by existing law. And matters are not helped much by the extraordinarily complicated nature of some of the technology.

Before beginning the trial of the Intel-NEC copyright suit, Federal Judge William P. Gray in San Jose received a two-day tutorial, courtesy of the two companies, on microprocessors and microcode, the tiny instructions that are built into chips. Yet when the trial began last month, Judge Gray was still asking, "What is a microcode?" Some executives and lawyers say that arbitration, which is being used by I.B.M. and Fujitsu in a dispute over I.B.M. software technology, might be a better route than the courts.

There are three main types of intellectual property protection. A patent provides a monopoly on an invention for 17 years. To qualify, an invention must meet three tests: It must be novel, meaning original, it must be non-obvious and it must be useful. Moreover, a patent holder has to fully disclose the invention, which contributes to the advancement of knowledge.

Copyright protection is far more limited, though it can last for the author's life plus 50 years or, in the case of work done for hire, for 75 years. While patents protect an idea, copyright protects only the expression of an idea. Many people can write books about space, songs about love or computer programs for word-processing. But the words, melody or computer code cannot be the same.

The third kind is trade secret protection under state law, in which some advance is simply kept secret, such as the formula for Coca-Cola.

But deciding what qualifies for protection can be difficult. In software, the big issue in both the Apple and Lotus lawsuits is how much of a program's "look and feel"—the manner in which a user interacts with a program—can be protected by copyright.

The real issue is trying to draw the line between the program's function, which cannot be protected, and its expression, which can be. If one program copies the computer code of another, it is clearly infringement. But what if one uses a different code to produce essentially the same result?

Apple's Macintosh makes use of what Apple calls a graphical screen display. Users point to little symbols, called icons, to perform specific tasks, such as a trash can icon to erase a file. Windows open and close on a screen with different tasks inside. Menus pop down on the screen offering choices. Can the use of windows, pop-down menus and icons be copyrighted? Or just the specific way this is done?

The Lotus case might boil down to questions such as whether a choice of particular keys to perform certain functions can be copyrighted.

Some lawyers have argued that in such cases the expression is closely tied to the function. Two dictionaries, for instance, are bound to have the same words and similar-sounding definitions. Some question whether Apple should be able to copyright something as obvious as a trash can icon for disposing of a file.

These questions come up with software because companies often try to make one product compatible with another, to increase sales and make it easier for users to shift from one program or machine to another without having to change all their data.

Compatibility has generally been allowed, so long as actual computer code is not copied. But some recent court decisions, if carried to extreme, would threaten the ability of companies to make compatible computers and programs, according to Mr. Reback, the attorney with Fenwick, Davis & West.

Others have suggested that the desire for compatibility is not necessarily a justifiable one anyway. For instance, a movie producer could conceivably argue that he needs to use R2D2 and C3PO in his space adventure movie, because those characters are familiar to the public and would make the movie more successful. But courts might look askance at the need to make such a "Star Wars"-compatible movie.

Biotechnology is also raising novel questions, mainly with regard to patents. The first question is what can be patented. Courts and the Patent Office have seen fit to allow patenting of natural substances and of genetically altered animals. The next question might arise over the technology of protein engineering, in which natural proteins can be changed. How much of a change, however, will be needed to make the altered substance significantly different from the natural substance to escape its patents?

Many patent disputes in biotechnology center on whether a certain development is obvious, which would disqualify it from a patent.

For years medical scientists had been using a technique called sandwich immuno-assays for diagnosing diseases or conditions like pregnancy. The sandwich consists of two antibodies. When biotechnology developed monoclonal antibodies, a more specific type of antibody, some people thought it was obvious to substitute these newer improved antibodies in the sandwich assay.

Yet Hybritech Inc., a subsidiary of Eli Lilly, was able to obtain a patent covering the use of monoclonal antibodies in such tests. It forced Monoclonal Antibodies to stop marketing its pregnancy and ovulation tests until it agreed to pay a high royalty. Monoclonal plunged into the red, had to lay off 30 percent of its work force and had to cancel a planned merger because of its difficulties. Last month an appeals court upheld an injunction stopping Abbott Laboratories from selling similar products.

In the future, some say, the battle will increasingly be drawn on international lines as the United States struggles to remain industrially competitive.

Intellectual property is becoming a trade issue as well. Some American companies are appealing to the International Trade Commission to stop imports to the United States of products that infringe on American patents. Amgen, a biotechnology company, is now seeking to block imports of erythropoietin, a potentially important drug to treat anemia, claiming infringement by Chugai Pharmaceuticals of Japan.

To some companies, however, the biggest battle is not with Japan, which has relatively strong intellectual property protection, but with nations like South Korea, Taiwan, Hong Kong and Brazil, which have virtually no intellectual property protection. American companies complain that copying of American technology is rampant in these countries, which merely have to read the American patents to learn the technology.

To combat that, Congress passed legislation in 1984 giving the President power to retaliate against countries that do not protect intellectual property adequately. By threatening to close off part of the United States market, the United States has been able to win some increased protection in Korea, Brazil and some other countries, but the progress is slow and spotty.

The new trade bill, recently vetoed by President Reagan for other reasons, contained provisions aimed at providing even better protection for American intellectual property. Meanwhile, companies in the United States, Europe and Japan are pushing their Governments to get provisions for minimum levels of protection into the General Agreement on Tariffs and Trade.

There is also legislation in Congress, which has already passed the House, to make the United States a party to the Bern Convention, an international agreement on copyright protections. For all the preaching the United States does to other nations about improving these protections, its laws are not as strict as the rules adopted by the convention, other countries have pointed out.

*   *   *

November 27, 1990

THAILAND IS THE CAPITAL OF PIRATED TAPES

By STEVEN ERLANGER
Special to The New York Times

BANGKOK, Thailand, Nov. 26—A stroll in any direction from any Bangkok hotel brings one face to face with the souk-like world of commercial piracy: cheap copies of Benetton, Lacoste and Polo shirts, of Rolex and Cartier watches, of Lee and Levi's blue jeans, computer software, prescription drugs and, most especially, thousands upon thousands of videotapes and pop, rock and jazz cassettes.

Businesses worldwide want people to be shocked, of course, because this piracy costs them enormous amounts in royalties and fees. With the help of their embassies, they are pressing Thailand to enforce its laws on intellectual property rights, including copyrights, patents and trademarks.

But a relatively current tape for the Walkman or the car, to get through Bangkok's horrific traffic jams, can be hard to resist at only 80 cents.

That's especially true when the sound quality of the pirated tape is often superior to that on tapes costing $3 to $4 in legitimate shops. Made under copyright in Malaysia, Indonesia or the Philippines, these official products are recorded at blinding speed, sometimes on cheaper, less sturdy cassettes, and are often warped.

Peter Charlesworth/JB Pictures

A shopper looking at pirated cassettes in Bangkok, Thailand, where current tapes cost as little as 80 cents.

The Size of the Loss

Thai labels like Michael: Direct to Disk Master Sound and Sky: Original Master are 2 of at least 15 pirate brands here. And while they are clearly not master tapes, they are sometimes produced at the same factories and use the same distribution network as legitimate labels. The pirate versions have cheap copies of the original album covers, and the cassettes are unlabeled except for a code number. But unlike some pirate videocassettes, the music tapes have the music they claim to, and most vendors will let you try them if you're in doubt.

Of course, this is big business, and big business in Thailand means political influence, petty and not-so-petty corruption and sometimes threats of violence. The United States Government estimates that American concerns lost $61 million last year in Thailand through theft of intellectual property, up from $34 million in 1984.

A Bangkok representative of the International Federation of Phonogram and Videogram Producers, an industry group that tries to track down pirates and have Thailand prosecute them, says royalty losses last year from record and tape piracy alone were at least $6.5 million, and they are expected to increase 15 percent this year.

Since Singapore cracked down on its own pirates in 1985, and Indonesia, Malaysia and the Philippines have agreed to do so more recently, Thailand has become "the piracy capital of Southeast Asia," says Douglas Sheldon, chairman of the intellectual property rights committee of the American Chamber of Commerce in Thailand and vice chairmen of the Asia-Pacific Council of the 16 regional Chambers of Commerce.

A Special Case

"Virtually all the other countries have tightened their laws and improved their enforcement," Mr. Sheldon said. "Thailand stands out. There is a lot of talk, and some nice draft laws sitting around in Parliament waiting for votes, but if someone says, 'Where are the results?' all you really have is talk."

Still, the 1989 figures show Thailand toward the bottom of the regional list for American losses through piracy, surpassing only Singapore and Malaysia. Larger losses are attributed to China, Taiwan, South Korea, India, the Philippines and Indonesia. The Philippines figure, at $117 million, is twice Thailand's.

But Thailand stands out on music and videotapes.

The International Federation of Phonogram and Video-gram Producers says 27 million pirate cassettes are sold here each year and lists their value at $32.6 million. In Bangkok alone, 2,500 shops sell pirated tapes, and 95.5 percent of all tapes sold in Bangkok are pirated, according to federation figures. Outside Bangkok, legitimate tapes represent less than 1 percent of sales.

The only nonpirated cassettes in all of Thailand, the federation says, are collections of jazz songs written or performed by the King of Thailand, Bhumibol Adulyadej. Given that it remains a crime in this country to joke about the King or to step on a rolling coin if your foot happens to land on his head, such caution is understandable.

Bullets Are Warnings

But the federation representative has reason to be cautious, too. Having already received four bullets in the mail from pirate businessmen, he said, he insisted that his name not be used in print.

Working with 10 investigators, the federation identifies shops selling pirated tapes and brings them to the attention of the police. Unfortunately, enforcement varies with the part of town and the susceptibility of the officers to outside inducements. To be fair, Western diplomats say, the police can also be sued for wrongful prosecution. But the federation has started 3,000 cases in the last two years, and nearly 1,000 violators have been sentenced.

Penalties tend to be fines of $800 to $4,000, and sometimes a brief jail sentence, usually commuted to probation. If convicted again within a year, probation is revoked. But the shop owners, who hide behind front companies, are almost never caught. Instead, they nominate a staff member to pay the fine and take the sentence. If the shop is raided again, they nominate a different staff member, so few offenders ever spend time in prison.

Western diplomats and business representatives say Thai pirate companies are waging a concerted campaign against enforcement, including threats of violence. Thailand's public prosecutors are increasingly reluctant to push these cases and insist on overwhelming documentation. In one instance, a diplomat said, the prosecutor wanted the original signed contract between CBS Records and a well-known artist.

Senior Western diplomats give reasonably high marks to the Government, which has committed itself to new and stronger laws on patents and trademarks, which affect pharmaceuticals and fashions respectively.

The Real Issue

But the copyright issue, everyone agrees, is not about legality but enforcement. Saying it was exasperated by Thailand's refusal to act against its pirates, an American industry group, the International Intellectual Property Alliance, filed a petition in Washington on Nov. 16 under Section 301 of the Trade Act, which could result in sanctions against Thai trade with the United States. The group, which includes the Motion Picture Export Association of America and the Recording Industry Association of America, accused the Thai Government of wholesale failure to enforce copyright protections and punish pirates.

The office of the United States Trade Representative has 45 days to decide whether to accept the petition, but industry representatives say they expect the Bush Administration to support them.

A senior Western diplomat who has been dealing with this issue for three years said, however, that the Thais were making an effort. And he noted that demand was as much of a problem as supply.

"I find it amusing," he said, "that those people who come to Thailand to complain about piracy usually go home with cheap tapes in their suitcases."

*   *   *

January 1, 1992

A NETWORK OF NETWORKS THAT KEEPS SCIENTISTS PLUGGED IN

By JOHN MARKOFF

From his laboratory in the hills above Los Angeles, Harvey Newman, a California Institute of Technology physicist, can control and monitor experiments taking place in a giant atom-smashing particle accelerator half a world away in Switzerland.

Dr. Newman is one of a group of international researchers using the atom smasher in their hunt for the Higgs Boson, an elusive subatomic particle whose existence would help confirm the basic theories of modern particle physics.

High-energy physics, along with virtually every other scientific discipline, is in the midst of a remarkable transformation, thanks to an expanding international network of computer links.

Known as the Internet, this network of networks was created in the late 1960's by the Pentagon's Advanced Projects Research Agency. Since then it has expanded into a web containing more than 90 countries, and it is still growing at an astounding rate in response to the declining costs of computer work stations and communications services. In 1991 alone, the data traffic doubled on the NSFnet, the National Science Foundation-operated system that serves as a primary backbone for the thousands of interconnected networks that make up the Internet.

The system has even extended its reach across what was once the Iron Curtain: Dozens of electronic-mail links now tie the former Soviet Union and other former Eastern bloc countries to Western Europe and the United States.

Besides carrying electronic mail, these modern networks let researchers remotely control computers as if they were sitting in front of them, and enable scientists and engineers to instantly disseminate research data to their professional peers.

Although physicists were among the first researchers to use global networks, other scientists are quickly catching up.

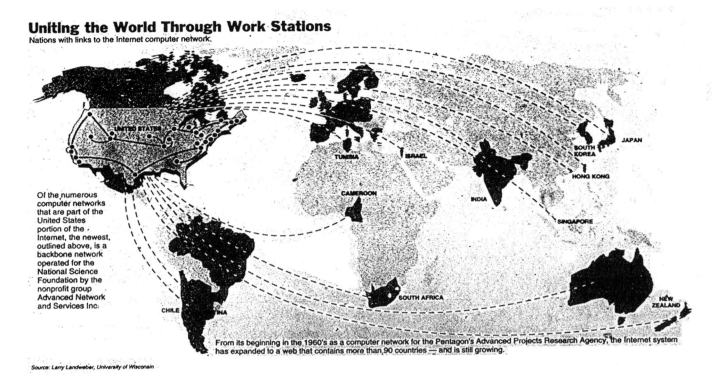

Uniting the World Through Work Stations
Nations with links to the Internet computer network.

Of the numerous computer networks that are part of the United States portion of the Internet, the newest, outlined above, is a backbone network operated for the National Science Foundation by the nonprofit group Advanced Network and Services Inc.

From its beginning in the 1960's as a computer network for the Pentagon's Advanced Projects Research Agency, the Internet system has expanded to a web that contains more than 90 countries — and is still growing.

Source: Larry Landweber, University of Wisconsin

Geneticists at Johns Hopkins University who are collecting data on the human genome are sharing information with researchers in England and Germany through a computer network that uses Internet links.

Just as significant as such multimillion-dollar experiments is the new wave of less formal scientific cooperation that has been fostered by international computer networks.

"Most of the interaction is not the flashy kind," said Larry Landweber, a professor of computer science at the University of Wisconsin. "It's not the kind where people are dialing up a Cray supercomputer or transferring hundreds of gigabytes."

Meantime, large industrial corporations are using private computer networks, connected to the Internet, to create truly global development laboratories.

A striking example is the National Semiconductor Corporation, which operates integrated-circuit design laboratories at its headquarters in Santa Clara, Calif., as well as in Tel Aviv and Tokyo. National Semiconductor has used its global network to solve one of the biggest challenges for chip designers: simulating the remarkably complex circuits.

The simulations, in the form of computer programs, are performed on powerful computer work stations, which can be tied up for weeks or months by such tasks.

But National's chip designers use their network to transfer the simulations from work station to work station, around the world and around the clock.

After the chip designers at one laboratory have gone home each evening, their work stations are used for running the simulation. When they return the next morning, they reclaim their machines and pass the simulation partway around the

globe, where their colleagues are just leaving for the day. And so it goes: Tel Aviv hands off the research to Santa Clara and, when it is time for workers in Santa Clara to begin their day, the torch is passed to Tokyo.

And at just about this same time each day, down in Los Angeles, Dr. Newman may be sitting down to a morning update from the atom smasher in Zurich.

* * *

November 20, 1995

HOW THE EARLIER MEDIA ACHIEVED CRITICAL MASS: WORLD WIDE WEB

If Medium Is The Message, The Message Is The Web

By JOHN MARKOFF

SAN FRANCISCO, Nov. 19—The Associated Press was formed in the mid-19th century when a group of newspapers decided to invest jointly in a newfangled medium—the telegraph—to speed the collection and dissemination of information.

Last week, A.P. announced that it would adopt a newer-fangled medium—the World Wide Web—to begin distributing its articles and photographs over the global Internet. It was simply the latest, but perhaps most historically significant, move yet by an old-line media organization into the World Wide Web, the Internet multimedia information-retrieval system that appears on the verge of becoming a mass medium itself.

If the medium is the message, then the message these days is the World Wide Web.

In short order the Web, which three years ago was little more than a research tool for physicists and computer hobbyists, has flourished. It is being embraced by media concerns, consumer-product companies and businesses of various stripes that are creating thousands of so-called Web sites each month, with the number of computers playing host to one or more of these sites already exceeding 100,000.

Conservative estimates place the number of people who have used the Web in the millions, and it is not hard to find more breathless estimates in the tens of millions.

Capable of letting people use computers to send and receive text, sound, still images and video clips, the Web incorporates elements of the various print and electronic media that have preceded it. And yet, the Web is poised not to replace its predecessors but to take a place alongside them as a social, cultural and economic force in its own right.

Its complementary role is already evident: many radio stations and all the major television networks have Web sites promoting their programs and stars. Newspapers, including The New York Times, are devising cyberspace editions.

And few movies anymore are released without a promotional Web site, including "Goldeneye" the James Bond film that opened this weekend at theaters everywhere and on the Web at the address http:// www.mgmua.com/bond. The site offers the movie's theme song performed by Tina Turner, more than a dozen video clips from the film and illustrated biographies of the cast members.

Prime-time television commercials by Toyota and other advertisers now routinely include a Web address. And Procter & Gamble, whose advertising has long helped underwrite the mass media, has even staked out prime Web real estate by reserving addresses that include flu.com and toiletpaper.com.

"We are poised on the edge of a new medium," Clay Felker, director of the magazine program at the University of California at Berkeley's graduate journalism school, said. "And it's going to change the nature of how we acquire information."

As with each mass medium that has arrived before it, the Web has reached this threshold through a confluence of a key technology, a ready audience and a stream of corporate backers willing to bet that profitable businesses can be built on it. But few experts are willing to declare that the Web has taken its place in the mass media pantheon because the profitable business formulas have yet to be found.

Newspapers and magazines make money by selling individual copies, subscriptions and advertising space. Radio and television stations sell air time to those with money and a message. Movie theaters sell tickets. But on the Web so far, despite seed-money by adventurous advertisers and some tentative efforts to charge for access to sites or services, there is no certainty that this medium will achieve the critical mass that capitalism demands of its mass media.

"How do you make a business out of the World Wide Web?" asked Norman Pearlstine, editor in chief of Time Inc., which has an experimental Web site called Pathfinder that offers selected contents from the company's magazines (http:// www.pathfinder.com). But because ad revenue alone is not carrying the freight, Time Inc. will begin testing ways to charge visitors to its site.

And yet, the technological prerequisites are firmly in place. The Web is an outgrowth of the Internet, which began as an academic research experiment in the late 1960's. For more than two decades the Internet remained largely inaccessible, used mainly by computer scientists and Pentagon researchers, university scholars and students.

Then came the World Wide Web.

Like the Internet, the Web began as a tool to let scientists easily and quickly share information. Conceived in the late 1980's by Tim Berners-Lee, who was then a software designer at CERN, the Swiss physics research center, the basic Web technology was first put to use in 1990.

The big breakthrough came in 1992, when student researchers at the National Center for Supercomputing Applications in Illinois created Mosaic, a simple software tool called a Web browser. Mosaic permitted access to information anywhere on the World Wide Web by letting the user point and click a computer mouse on highlighted words or images on the screen. The browser, which became available in commercial versions like Netscape Communications' Navigator, not only made Web sites easily accessible, it prompted businesses, organizations and even individuals to create new Web sites by the thousands.

Thus did the Web quickly become a standard and accepted way for the growing millions of the computer-literate to communicate and to entertain and inform themselves. And unlike each previous mass medium, the Web does not require its audience to be merely passive recipients of information.

For very little money, and with a modicum of computer skills, virtually anyone can create his or her own Web site. Anyone with a modem is potentially a global pamphleteer.

One consequence of this democratization is that the Web can be a remarkably anarchic forum compared with the old-style mass media. "Think of this as television colliding with the telephone party line," said Paul Saffo, a computer industry consultant at the Institute for the Future, a Menlo Park, Calif., research firm. "In terms of social consequences, the Web is a great experiment. It's going to deliver us community with a vengeance—and we may find we don't want it."

* * *

January 15, 1996

LIMITING A MEDIUM WITHOUT BOUNDARIES

How Do You Let the Good Fish Through the Net While Blocking the Bad?

By PETER H. LEWIS

All over the world, a growing number of governments, schools, special interest groups and families are struggling to find acceptable ways of tapping into the riches of the Internet without also hitting the darker veins of the global computer network.

But with its ability to carry all kinds of information across borders and oceans in a flash, the Internet has evolved faster than the laws and technical structures of the countries it touches. Although communities have struggled for centuries to preserve local laws and standards when they come into conflict with the outside world, the Internet and on-line information networks are presenting them with new problems that defy old solutions.

For example, German officials last month persuaded Ohio-based Compuserve to cut off access to some 200 sex-related news forums worldwide. Chinese officials said last week that they wanted to stop "detrimental information" from entering the country via the Internet. And the United States Congress, in legislation still stalled by disagreement over other issues, has voted to halt the flow of "indecent" computer files through this country, even if the offensive material is created and maintained on computers halfway around the world.

Even as pressure is intensifying to restrict the flow of pornography, hate speech and other offensive material in electronic form, Internet technologists say that ultimately there is no completely effective way to block the relatively small number of "bad bits" out of the torrents of data available to tens of millions of people in more than 150 countries.

But there are some partial solutions. A growing industry has emerged in the last two years to offer individuals, schools and businesses a variety of tools, ranging from complex computer barriers known as firewalls to simple software programs, to screen certain bits while allowing others to pass. Most of these tools are effective in stopping some unwanted data traffic, but none guarantees 100 percent effectiveness.

"Nothing we can do will be a perfect solution, for two important reasons," said Brian R. Ek, spokesman for an industry group trying to create the equivalent of a motion picture ratings system on the Internet. "First, no matter what technologies we come up with, somewhere, somehow, someone is going to figure out a way to circumvent them. That's the nature of programming."

"Second," Mr. Ek continued, "there is an ocean of Web pages and news groups already out there, and being able to rate them all, with several hundred new ones coming on line every day, is an impossibility."

Even so, Mr. Ek and others say, new software and hardware tools hold the promise—or the threat, depending on one's point of view—of allowing people to filter out certain kinds of information while allowing other kinds to be viewed on a personal computer screen. "Yes, with the right software tools you can selectively block access for some people," said Paul Resnick, an AT&T Bell Labs researcher who is co-chairman of the technical committee for PICS, the Platform for Internet Content Selection, the group trying to develop a ratings technology. "The key is to have selective rules rather than blanket rules."

There is disagreement over whether it is technically possible to impose blanket control over incoming information, as Germany is seeking in the Compuserve case, without resorting to Draconian measures that most democratic countries find distasteful, like limiting access to telephone lines or employing vast squads of censors to monitor all data traffic.

The biggest obstacle seems to be the basic design of the Internet itself, which was created during the cold war to allow uninterrupted routing of data traffic even in the event of a nuclear war. At that time, the Internet comprised only a handful of computers, and if one computer failed, the data packets would automatically detour around it.

Today the Internet is composed of millions of "host" computers, all but a few of them privately maintained. Tens of millions of personal computer users tap into this vast ocean of data on any given day. It is as easy to retrieve data files from halfway around the world as it is to get a file from the computer on the next desk, and the data path may snake through dozens of cities and countries along the way.

Trying to keep certain types of information from entering a jurisdiction is as difficult as keeping certain kinds of molecules from entering a country's air space, or certain kinds of fish from swimming in its waters.

"The nature of the Internet, if not contemporary telecommunication and transportation technologies in general, make this intrinsically impossible to achieve," said Anthony M. Rutkowski, an engineer and lawyer who until recently was head of the Internet Society, an international association of Internet access companies.

"One can regard the Internet in some of the same ways as radio waves with respect to the abilities of the medium to transparently flow across national boundaries," Mr. Rutkowski said.

For decades, some countries, like the Soviet Union and what were once its East European satellites, did try jamming radio and television signals, with limited success.

"This century has seen numerous energetic efforts to control information that comes via the airwaves, as well as to stop publications from being smuggled across borders," said Mitchell Stephens, a fellow at the Freedom Forum Media Studies Center and a journalism professor at New York University.

"Some countries have never quite accepted the idea that information goes wherever it damn well pleases, and they try to extend their walls to reach up into the air. It is not surprising that such efforts would be made with computer technology now, especially in light of the incredible potential power inherent in the Internet."

"I suspect we're just seeing the start of this," Professor Stephens said, "because the major authoritarian countries that remain are typically poorer countries, where most of the population does not have access to computers or televisions or other information sources. When that changes, it will be a huge issue."

If access to information on a computer is blocked by one route, a moderately skilled computer user can simply tap into another computer by an alternative route. Or one can easily disguise a flurry of bad bits, either by data encryption, which renders them unreadable except by the intended recipient, or simply by changing the file name to something that will pass through most filtering mechanisms.

An Internet axiom credited to John Gilmore, an engineer at a Silicon Valley networking company, puts it succinctly. "The Internet interprets censorship as damage and routes around it," he said.

Disputes over international broadcasting have been common since 1928, when international delegates gathered in Vienna to discuss cross-border transmissions.

In 1948, at the dawn of television, the United Nations General Assembly adopted Article 19 of the Universal Declaration of Human Rights, which said: "Everyone has the right to freedom of opinion and expression; this right includes freedom to hold opinions without interference and to seek, receive and impart information and ideas through any media and regardless of frontiers." But some governments' efforts to control information have often meant those words constituted little more than an unfulfilled hope. And with each new and more powerful communications medium, attempts to restrict the flow of information across borders increase.

Recent technical advances suggest that it is easier to block the sending of certain forms of information to a specific country or a specific computer than to keep people in that country from reaching across the border to get the information.

"From a technical-feasibility point of view, we could segment content country by country," said George Meng, a manager for the Microsoft Network, which offers Internet connections in 50 countries. "The question is whether that is something we want to do."

But a more intractable problem, he said, arises when an MSN subscriber goes through the system to gain access to the Internet and the World Wide Web. "If they know the URL of a site," he said, "they can enter the Web directly via our Internet Explorer. If we don't maintain the server, my guess is that we could not control the content."

If Internet companies cannot control millions of servers, at least the individual user can control his or her own machine. A small industry has grown up in the United States to produce filtering software, which a parent, teacher or boss can install to keep other users from straying into forbidden areas of the network.

Programs like Surf Watch and Net Nanny typically work by comparing a user's request for information against a list of prohibited sites. Each program's list is compiled from well-known sources of sex-related discussions or pictures, and is updated periodically, either by computer programs that scan the data stream for key words, or by teams of people employed to find objectionable material on the Net.

There are many drawbacks to the filtering approach. First, new data sites are created every day, so even with frequent upgrades the software is always at least partly out of date. Also, content within a site can change at any time, compromising the reliability of any rating system, and a skilled and determined teen-age programmer can generally find his or her way to any filtered site.

But the programs can be effective in stopping casual users from gaining access to the better-known sources of pornography or sex-related discussions.

One promising attempt to filter information is the PICS proposal, which is defining voluntary technical standards to enable individuals, groups, or even government agencies to establish ratings for Internet, Usenet and World Wide Web files.

A ratings tool would be encoded into the browser software used to gain access to Internet data sites, for example. Parents could choose a browser endorsed by the Christian Coalition, for example, or by the local school board or the on-line service provider itself. "We want individual families to set their own selection rules," Mr. Resnick said. "You could have different rules for different countries, too. Of course, we don't get to set the rules for China."

*   *   *

January 18, 1998

VIRTUAL MIGRANTS

Need Programmers? Surf Abroad

By ALLEN R. MYERSON

The nation has a shortage of techies, as last week's Government plan to help train more programmers made clear. But corporate America has already hit on a response. It's global telecommuting, through which this nation's technology companies have created a whole new realm of international trade by exporting their work and hiring programmers overseas to do it.

Having already scooped up any American programmers they could by offering them the chance to ride the Internet to work from their homes in Jackson Hole, Wyo., or Boulder, Colo., the corporations are now reaching out to places like South Africa and the Philippines.

So increasingly, the world's commerce involves not just tankers filled with Brent crude or container ships laden with VCR's, but cables buzzing with computer programming code, product designs and engineering diagrams and formulas. Not to mention overhauls of American software gone too soft. If computer systems squeak into the year 2000 without acting like they're back in 1900, foreign programmers will deserve much of the thanks.

Some companies bring the workers to the work, searching the world for computer specialists willing to come to the United States. But virtual immigration, where the workers stay put, has become far more common, and remains much cheaper. The software unit of a single company, Tata Sons Ltd. of India, has 5,000 developers, a maquiladora of the mind that can immediately deploy 100 techies on an American corporation's mission. India's software exports have grown from $225 million in 1992 to $1.15 billion in 1996, with a year 2000 goal of $3.6 billion.

On the Cheap

Technical advances have made this kind of rapid growth possible. Although banks, among other global institutions, have been electronically advantaged for years, the expense has fallen dramatically. Instead of high-capacity leased lines that can cost hundreds or thousands of dollars a month, a plain old phone connection and an Internet service provider will often do.

"It's no longer an international phone call. Now, it's an Internet file exchange," said Esther Dyson, author of "Release 2.0: A Design for Living in the Digital Age." A cyberdiplomat known for striving to make Eastern Europe at least as wired as its Western neighbors, Ms. Dyson also serves on the board of the PRT Group in Barbados, a software and computer systems design firm, and Softstep, a company doing Year 2000 fixes from Kyrgyzstan in Central Asia.

While some global telecommuters, like many Americans, work at home, most are clustered in the foreign quarters of American companies or in the offices of foreign contractors like Tata. Projects can receive round-the-clock attention as they are handed from continent to continent. I.B.M. teams in Europe, India and the West Coast have kept the development of Java software for the Internet going at all hours, with handoffs over the Internet itself.

Even as the giants like Tata prosper, the Internet is also allowing pipsqueaks to be heard and seen, offering electronic sales pitches and work samples. Corporations like I.B.M. find themselves hiring tiny foreign firms that could never have found their way through these companies' front doors.

Those specialists who do migrate to the United States have an advantage in spotting talent back home. Under Sanjiv Sidhu, a native of Hyderabad, India, and Sandy Tungare, an executive from Bombay, I2 Technologies of Dallas runs software development centers in Bombay and Bangalore, where the neighbors include Motorola, Intel and Hewlett-Packard. Software developers who would earn at least $50,000 in the United States can be had for about a third as much in India, Mr. Tungare says.

The rise of global telecommuting has already begun shaping trade policies and international relations. India, once utterly protectionist, has allowed American computer companies to import equipment by the tax-free boatload, and extends all manner of other tax breaks and real estate subsidies. Although some villages there are still waiting to join the telephone era, India has given industrial parks digital communications links. Many countries have lowered barriers to foreign (especially American) investment. The payoffs include hard currency from exports and a diminished brain drain.

Bane Becomes Boon

Should America's nerds be worried enough to cool their celebrations of their current lordly status?

Edward Yourdon, a software consultant in New York, wrote a book, "The Decline and Fall of the American Programmer," in 1992 to warn that foreign technicians were threatening American jobs. Some professional groups even sought to limit the export of technological tasks. But Mr. Yourdon and others hardly expected there to be so much more work, and in 1996, he wrote "The Rise and Resurrection of the American Programmer." As he says these days, "While this offshore situation still exists, now we are looking at it as a boon rather than a bane."

Already, a new international division of labor is emerging. Americans create programs to make the Internet sing and dance, or computer games to blow out teen-age minds and eardrums, and parental patience. Foreigners are often more like software second-stringers, stamping out bugs, updating the products and programming clunky mainframes.

"That's work that people in the United States don't really want to do," said Paul J. Kostek, president-elect of the Institute of Electrical and Electronic Engineers-U.S.A. and a systems engineer himself. "They want to move on to the next challenge." Foreign software firms also usually buy American computers and American software for assembling and testing their own products.

America's challenge is to keep booming even as Asian markets for American goods shrivel. In an expansion based on technology, though, Asian and other foreign labor sources are providing much of the stamina.

* * *

January 3, 2000

AN UNREGULATED INTERNET MAY BE EXAGGERATING THE MOVEMENTS ON GLOBALIZED, FLUID FINANCIAL MARKETS

By DENISE CARUSO

After a year of big gambles, the biggest of all may be the wager that our exalted Internet, held together with baling wire and chewing gum in every conceivable way—legally, structurally, economically—is going to be able to withstand the coming heavy weather of a truly global, unregulated economy.

Or perhaps the question is whether we will be able to withstand a global, unregulated Internet.

In either case, here at ground zero—in the United States, capital of global capitalism—stock market experts are beginning to acknowledge what some of us have suspected for a long time: technology stocks, in particular, are being kept aloft on their own hot air.

People buy them because they are performing better than regular stocks; they are performing better than regular stocks because people keep buying them.

And the mystery surrounding Internet stock valuations—what are the criteria?—may have been solved last week by Michael Mauboussin, the chief investment strategist at Credit Suisse First Boston.

The more popular the World Wide Web site, he declared, the higher its "ranking," the more the company is worth.

Just like in high school: Web sites with the highest valuations are like football captains or cheerleaders, whose top-of-the-chart popularity ratings give them far greater currency in the social order than, for example, the shy, geeky nerds who may excel in art or science.

Upon these things our new economy is built.

Now take this relatively microcosmic situation—that the Internet stock market in the United States is a popularity contest, based on consumer moods and filled with millions of networked investors bluffing the financial markets like a poker game—and consider what the ripple effect might be on an expanding global economy.

In so doing, some big thinkers—most notably, Manuel Castells, author in 1998 of "The Information Age: Economy, Society and Culture"—start to get a little skittish about our big Internet gamble. In an essay titled, "Information Technology and Global Capitalism," Mr. Castells presents a chilling argument:

As a result of the globalization of largely unregulated and increasingly fluid financial markets, he says, "we may have created an automaton." By that, he means "an electronic-based system of financial transactions which overwhelms controls and regulations by governments, international institutions and private financial firms, as well as individual investors, consumer and citizens."

Mr. Castells' essay is included in a book to be published in London early this year called "On the Edge: Essays on a Runaway World," edited by Anthony Giddens, the director of the London School of Economics, and Will Hutton, the editor of The Observer in London.

Mr. Castells does not mean the term "automaton" literally. There are as yet few instances of financial transactions fully automated beyond the bounds of human intervention—particularly after computer programs helped induce the stock market crash of October 1987 and the Securities and Exchange Commission began setting some limits on program trading.

But he cites a trend toward the computerization of trading systems: Nasdaq in the United States; Eurex in the German bond market; M, the French futures exchange; the London International Financial Futures Exchange, and private trading networks like Instinet, owned by Reuters.

Mr. Castells argues that these increasingly interconnected electronic networks, combined with domestic deregulation, the liberal flow of financial transactions across national borders and a constant, international flow of market-related news and information over the Internet make a "nightmare" of watching machines take control seem "on the edge of becoming reality."

The idea of networked computers with minds of their own is not new. But the computers envisioned in science fiction may belong to Mensa, the social network for those with the highest I.Q.'s; the network of Mr. Castells' nightmare is a dumb brute, knee-jerking to information turbulences that are amplified by inputs from millions of individual investors, creating ever-greater complexity and volatility.

The automaton is only the first problem that Mr. Castells cites for the future of today's go-go Internet economy.

Although American industry has managed to gut its labor movement, he says, Europe and Japan are less thrilled about the potential for "productivity" technology that first takes away jobs, then dismantles government supports.

Whether we like it or not, he continues, if they believe that network technology will do either of these things, "there will be a backlash of social struggles, and political reactions, that will simply block reform and innovation."

And because the United States is now interdependent on global economic performance, such a backlash "will ultimately exhaust the growth capacity of the U.S. economy," he warns.

Mr. Castells' belief, which is bound to be deeply unpopular in the United States, is that healthy global capitalism requires global financial regulations. Further, he argues that those regulations must take into account not only technological productivity and growth spurred by capital investment but also "socio-institutional engineering" that respects, values and includes people and cultures.

Virtually no one in the United States government, and certainly no one who is rolling in Internet clover, wants to touch this issue. Why would they? The United States is far and away the world leader in the information industries. And access to more and more global markets—in part by dismantling regulations and government controls—has been one of the hallmarks of the Clinton administration.

We ignore such issues at our own peril, Mr. Castells says. The fragility of global capitalism is such that a new round of instability, "perhaps induced by the collapse of Internet stocks, or by a sudden panic around electronic trading networks," he writes, could trigger a stampede toward the exits.

But this time, "there could be governments or significant segments of society opting out of global capitalism," he suggests—"not necessarily to build an alternative system, but just to recover some degree of control over their lives and values."

* * *

May 19, 2000

COMPUTER WHIZZES AT PHILIPPINE PAY

---

*Technologically Literate People Service and Supply
U.S. Business*

By WAYNE ARNOLD

MANILA, May 18—Maybe it was a couple of 20-something Filipinos who created the rogue e-mail program that disabled computer systems on May 4. Maybe it wasn't. But there is no doubt that a couple of other young Filipinos played a big part in rubbing the bug out.

The two—Richard Cheng, 24, and Maricel Soriano, 23—were on duty at the Manila office of an antivirus software company, Trend Micro Inc., when the company was first notified of the problem shortly after lunch that day. As the scourge spread across time zones from Australia to Europe, Mr. Cheng was already writing an antidote, and by the end of the day, Ms. Soriano was disseminating instructions to afflicted Trend Micro customers around the world on how to apply it.

"My parents told me I was a hero," said Ms. Soriano, who joined Trend Micro after earning her computer engineering degree from a local college.

Granted, the Philippines' image has not been helped much by its failure to charge any suspects for the destruction or, indeed, to pass a law against what they did. But the "Love Bug" episode may have a positive side. "This virus, if anything, brings a necessary spotlight to the tech scene in the Philippines," said Pindar Wong, chairman of the Asia Pacific Internet Association in Hong Kong.

Mr. Cheng and Ms. Soriano are part of a growing pool of high-technology Philippine talent that is attractive to employers in Europe and the United States, and is increasingly drawing multinationals like Trend Micro, America Online and Motorola to move some of their operations here.

That same computer-literate population is now feeding a surprisingly lively Internet start-up scene, in a country where many annual incomes are typically around $1,000 and less than 1 percent of the population uses the Internet.

"The Philippines may be a poor country, but part of it is English-speaking and educated," said Fernando D. Contreras, vice president-elect of the Philippine Internet Service Organization. "That's what we're trying to emphasize for the Internet."

Nearly 50 years of United States rule, from the end of the Spanish-American War in 1898 until World War II, gave the Philippines an American-style educational system in which English is taught to almost all of the country's 76 million people—95 percent of whom are literate. Its government and judiciary are modeled on those of the United States. And the Philippines retains a distinctly American feel. People here don't follow soccer, they follow the N.B.A.

"Filipinos have two cultures," said Max Cheng, Trend Micro's vice president for global support in Taipei, Taiwan. "One is Western, the other is Oriental."

That is a big part of why Trend Micro decided to open an office here two years ago. Founded on Taiwan but based in Japan, the company now has 124 employees in Manila, all of them Filipinos. Some, like Richard Cheng (no relation to Max Cheng) and Ms. Soriano, are engineers who dissect new computer viruses—most of which originate in the United States—and write solutions. Others field questions by e-mail from customers worldwide.

By October, the company plans to make the Philippines its global call center. Trend Micro customers in the United States who phone the company's toll-free help line may find themselves talking not to a technician in America, but to one here in Manila.

The Philippines long ago attracted its fair share of high-technology hardware makers: Intel, Acer, Texas Instruments, NEC and Toshiba have all established production here. But as new networking technologies made it possible to create corporate telephone networks around the world, more and more companies began moving their software development and behind-the-scenes processes like accounting, data entry and payrolls to nations like the Philippines and India, whose own English heritage makes it a leading competitor for business and investment.

The battle of these two has been going on since the late 1980's, but the Internet is turning up the tempo and the Philippines appears to be keeping pace.

Andersen Consulting, which first set up a data center in the Philippines in 1986, now has 450 employees in the country developing software and offering 24-hour customer support. Fujitsu develops software here. Citibank does its Southeast Asian accounting here.

And on the former United States air base north of Manila, America Online operates a nondescript installation where 830 employees field questions from the company's American clients. Even Motorola plans to begin routing some inquiries from the United States to the Philippines later this year.

Of course, cheap labor is a big part of this country's attractiveness to corporations abroad. But in high-technology industries, labor is only part of the cost of doing business. The Philippines' real advantage, Mr. Cheng of Trend Micro says, is in the quality and dedication of its people.

"In the beginning, I thought it would be hard to find good engineers in the Philippines," Mr. Cheng said. With training, though, he says his engineers are as qualified as those in Taiwan. He even sends them sometimes to train their counterparts in the United States. Trend Micro plans to double its staff of Philippine engineers over the next year.

Despite a seemingly ample supply—there are more than 200,000 students enrolled in computer-related courses at Philippine universities—Mr. Cheng said that finding engineers is getting tougher as more and more companies move in.

The allure of living in the affluent West is another source of competition—and a persistent drain of Philippine talent. President Clinton's recent moves to raise immigration limits on skilled foreign workers, for instance, could make talent here even scarcer. This country already provides some 3,200 such employees to the United States each year.

The brain drain notwithstanding, does the Philippines have what it takes to make the jump from subcontracting for multinationals to creating innovative Internet ventures? Absolutely, said Rey A. Buzon, a Filipino-American who left the San Francisco Bay area this year to become the president of a local venture capital firm, AJOnet Holdings.

"I've discovered that Filipinos are a lot more creative than what I'm used to in Silicon Valley," Mr. Buzon said. His firm now receives as many as 15 inquiries a day from Philippine Internet-related start-ups looking for financing, he said.

One that impressed Mr. Buzon with its youthful initiative was Mp3Manila, a start-up that allows its Web site visitors to download songs by more than 70 Philippine performers. Unlike many ventures that come knocking with nothing more than a business concept, Mp3Manila's five founders had their site up and running on $1,000 of their own savings—all while juggling classes at their university.

Mark K. Escueta, who is 22, got the idea for Mp3Manila two years ago while surfing in vain for digital recordings of his favorite Philippine hip-hop groups. Last October, he and four classmates established a site where local acts with no recording label could get their music out to Filipinos around the world, with advertisers paying the costs.

The friends opened the Web site at a popular downtown bar in January and within a month were getting up to 600 visitors a day. But by March, the pressures of final exams and of financial realities were setting in. The ad model was a failure. "We told ourselves we had to come up with a new model," said Rufino H. Felipe, Mp3Manila's 22-year-old chief executive.

They resolved to become an online record label, using their site to sell Philippine artists' compact discs, downloadable music files and the equipment to play them. To do that, they are now receiving four million pesos in financing—about $96,000—from AJOnet.

The five founders have agreed that anyone who drops out of school before graduating next March forfeits his stake in the venture.

Mp3Manila is counting on the appeal of home-grown music to the roughly more than two million Philippine citizens living in the United States, 80 percent of whom AJONet estimates use the Internet, to overcome the reality that the Philippines remains a minuscule market for online business. Although there are nearly 200 Internet services, there are less than a million Internet subscribers.

Most Filipinos do not have a phone and cannot afford a personal computer. High prices for Internet access, moreover, make downloading large amounts of data, as in music, prohibitively expensive for many people.

The Philippines becomes exciting as an Internet market, industry executives say, when new wireless technologies put the Net into the palms of people's hands.

The Philippines already has more mobile phone users than personal computers. Filipinos are such avid users of digital mobile phone short-messaging that they have turned this "texting" into a telecommunications subculture, sending more messages a day than all of Europe combined.

Cellular phone executives hope that new services using the Wireless Application Protocol, which shrinks Web pages onto mobile phone screens, will find a fast following and help bring e-commerce to more and more people.

But skeptics say that politics, not technology, may be the biggest factor in determining whether the Philippines can bridge the digital divide.

"Sure, we're a very literate country, but there's graft and corruption," said Josefina Trinidad Lichauco, who resigned as under secretary for transportation and communications in January. "Our democracy is not working. The most valuable resource of the Philippines is its people. But they haven't been harnessed in the right direction."

CRITICAL MOMENT: THE OPEC OIL EMBARGO

February 15, 1961

WORLD OIL GROUP LISTS ITS GOALS

***Exporting Countries Will Work Out Proposals on
Prices and Profits***

SEAT TO BE IN GENEVA

***Decisions Made at Caracas Parley Are Reported—
'Understanding' Asked***

CARACAS, Venezuela, Feb. 14—The organization of Petroleum Exporting Countries has decided to ask each member nation to state its position "in the matter of determination of oil prices" and will then decide on measures to

adopt. It has also heard "from most of the members" that oil companies' profits are "in excess of what may be regarded as fair" and will prepare recommendations for the next meeting "in order to correct the position."

However, no specific measures have yet been decided upon.

These were some of the conclusions reached at the recent January conference in Caracas of O. P. E. C. They are being released simultaneously by all of the member countries. The organization said it would refer statements of member countries on prices to its legal advisers and then decide on recommendations "with the object of restoring prices to levels which members consider justified."

The conference also resolved to ask "friendly countries" that had policies of restrictions and quotas—presumably such countries as the United States—for a discussion of these quotas in order to arrive at "satisfactory solutions."

Proposals for Venezuela

Concerning Venezuela, O. P. E. C. said it had been informed "of the curtailment of activities in the development of the Venezuelan petroleum industry" and would examine the situation and propose remedies.

The statement also asked for "a spirit of understanding" in discussions now going on between some of the members and the companies.

The permanent seat of O. P. E. C. will be in Geneva, it was announced.

The organization will consist of a "conference," which will be held twice a year; and a board of governors—each member with one governor—which will meet at least four times a year. The chairman of the board will also be secretary general. The first chairman is Fuad Rouhani of Iran. The secretariat in Geneva will contain the departments of technology, including geology, marketing, production and finance; administration; public relations, and an enforcement section.

Budget Set

The initial budget for the organization will be £150,000.

It is not supposed that the statement on profits applies to Venezuela, which has said it has a satisfactory share, but rather to Middle Eastern countries.

No comment was as yet available concerning the statements made.

It was noted that most of the text had to do with the establishment of the organization and that specific measures on such questions as prices and prorationing were referred to special groups for study and later decisions.

The organization was founded last September in Baghdad with the object of raising oil prices and protecting the interests of member countries. Its members are Venezuela, Kuwait, Iran, Saudi Arabia, Iraq and Qatar—presumably representing more than 90 per cent of the international oil business.

* * *

January 8, 1968

FOR THE OIL INDUSTRY, FUTURE IS WRITTEN IN ARABIC

The oil industry moved into the new year with pride in its 1967 performance, high hopes for its opportunities in 1968—and a premonition that the events of last summer may have signaled the beginning of a new era in petroleum history.

The catalyst was the Arab-Israeli conflict.

It provided the industry with some of its finest hours yet contained the seeds of future troubles.

In the face of war, the closing of the Suez Canal, embargoes and diplomatic embroilment, the industry was able to maintain free-world petroleum supplies without rationing or even a major shortage at the consumer level.

This was no small feat when it is considered that the Arab nations produce one-third of the world's total supply of oil and the Suez Canal is the chief artery for petroleum transport.

When the Arabs turned off the oil taps, Iran (a Moslem but non-Arab nation), Venezuela, Canada and the United States opened their valves wider.

U.S. Production Soars

United States production soared 48 million barrels above normal levels during the summer and early fall to help maintain free-world supplies. During seven of the crisis weeks American refineries broke all records by processing more than 10 million barrels of crude oil a day, compared with an average of 8.3 million barrels a day prior to the conflict.

Of the extra production from June through September, about 22 million barrels went to Europe and 21 million barrels to the east coast of the United States to replace interrupted imports. Exports of crude oil from the United States averaged nearly 8.4 million barrels a month during July and August, a 70-fold increase over the level of exports for the comparable period in the preceding year.

While the United States and other countries were straining to produce more oil the international petroleum companies were busy chartering anything afloat to keep supplies moving. Tanker charter prices soared as the oil vessels were forced to sail around the tip of Africa, a trip 17 days longer than passage through the Suez.

The outcome for the Arabs was a defeat in their economic war against the West just as in their shooting war against Israel. Their embargo of Britain and the United States folded before it even began. Little damage was done to any major oil installation and Arab production was back to normal by the end of the summer.

So for all outward appearances, the international petroleum situation has returned to its prewar status, except for the Suez Canal, which is still closed.

But that is just a surface view. "The war and its aftermath have forced both the producing and consuming nations to examine their basic policies," according to John Lichtblau of the Petroleum Research Institute. Few serious analysts of the industry would disagree.

For the consuming nations it means an attempt to become less dependent on Middle Eastern oil by diversifying their sources of energy.

The search for oil and gas has already intensified in Africa, Indonesia, Australia, Canada, South America, the United States and Europe. Much of the action is offshore, where the play is getting deeper and more expensive.

According to Walter Levy, a noted oil consultant, the complete loss of Arab oil could not be made up by any combination of other sources within a decade, if at all.

The Arabs fully realize the strength of their basic position.

The present courtship between France and Iraq is possibly indicative of an emerging new era in petroleum politics and policy. France is trying to create a "third world" force in petroleum while Iraq is anxious to pay back Britain and the United States for their supposed support of Israel.

Russian Control Seen

A more ominous spector is put forward by a small group of analysts who suggest that Middle East oil will come under Russian control because of the Arab belief that the United States and Britain supported Israel.

On the domestic scene the production push to meet Europe's needs during the crisis moved United States output of crude oil to a record 3.2 billion barrels from the 3,027,700,000 barrels in 1966. In 1968 production is expected to inch forward about 0.5 per cent.

Demand for petroleum in this country is expected to rise 3.4 per cent this year. World petroleum demand is expected to experience an even sharper gain with a 9 per cent increase being the general estimate.

Most companies in the industry reported higher profits last year with the average gain for the major concerns being around 8 per cent. Analysts anticipate a somewhat smaller earnings advance this year.

A few hangover problems from 1967 are expected to enliven the domestic picture this year.

The unused import tickets from the time of the crisis cast a slight shadow over the price situation since many oil men remember the price-depressing glut caused by the flood of imports after the 1956 Suez crisis. Government officials, however, have promised that the timing on the filling of unused tickets will be judiciously decided.

*   *   *

June 6, 1972

OIL-PRODUCING LANDS WEIGH NATIONALIZATION

11 OPEC Members Ask Concerns for Equity Share

By CLYDE H. FARNSWORTH
Special to The New York Times

VIENNA, June 5—The head of an organization representing 11 oil-producing countries warned today that if the countries' demands for 20 per cent equity ownership in Western-owned facilities were not met, they might well nationalize the properties, as Iraq did last week. Their eventual aim is for 51 per cent "participation," he said.

Dr. Nadim Pachachi, Secretary General of the Organization of Petroleum Exporting Countries, warned in an interview that the gap is big—too big" between the countries and the producing companies over participation. He said that a crisis could be avoided only if companies "come down from their high horse and negotiate seriously."

Sheik Ahmed Zaki al Yamani, the Oil Minister of Saudi Arabia, is negotiating with major Western companies on behalf of the Gulf states.

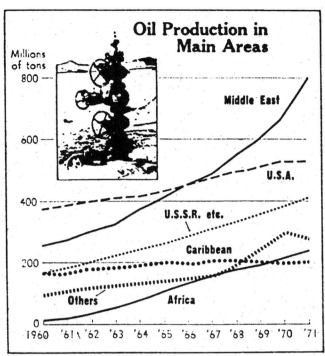

The New York Times/June 6, 1972

Compensation Differences

Essentially the differences are over compensation. Companies are demanding the market value of their assets plus payment for loss of profits until their concessions expire, in some cases at the end of this century. The countries are willing to pay the considerably lower book value, representing what the assets originally cost.

"We are the owners and, therefore, will not compensate for loss of profits," Dr. Pachachi said.

"Participation is the issue of the day," he said. "It overwhelms all other Government-company problems. Failure [by companies] to recognize the force of new trends in public thinking and to take home the lesson of changing circumstances could eventually oblige member countries to take a second look at nationalization.

"Our governments have, so far, acted as 'sleeping partners' and tax collectors," he said. "We wish to have a say on substantial matters and policy decisions."

While 51 per cent is the eventual demand, Dr. Pachachi said, it can be met over "a period" and is "negotiable" with the companies.

He said that had there been participation by Government in the Western-owned Iraq Petroleum Company, "I.P.C. nationalization need never have occurred."

Dr. Pachachi, a dapper, slim Iraqi with slightly stooped shoulders, was interviewed at OPEC's Vienna headquarters in a building shared, by chance, with Texaco, Inc., across the street from Vienna University.

The 12-year-old OPEC is made up of Iran, Iraq, Kuwait, Saudi Arabia, Qatar, Libya, Abu Dhabi, Algeria, Nigeria, Indonesia and Venezuela.

It was not over the controversial participation issue that Iraq nationalized, but over the I.P.C. Consortium's decision to cut crude-oil production in Iraq's northern fields by nearly 50 per cent.

The consortium wanted Iraq to reduce prices by 35 per cent. Iraqi authorities reacted by taking over properties owned for half a century by the consortium, which is owned by British Petroleum, Compagnie Française des Pétroles, the Royal Dutch-Shell Group, the Standard Oil Company (New Jersey), the Mobil Oil Company and the C. S. Gulbenkian Estate.

Dr. Pachachi said, "It was dangerous for the companies to play around with the [Teheran] Agreement," which set a new schedule of oil prices in the Persian Gulf and Mediterranean areas where most of the world's oil is still found.

OPEC issued a formal statement last Tuesday just before the nationalization, applauding the Iraqi authorities for being "right and wise" in rejecting the companies' approach, which, it said, would lead to "disruption of the structure of oil prices."

The Iraq situation will be discussed by OPEC ministers at a special meeting June 9 in Beirut.

Sometime before the next OPEC Congress, which is scheduled for Vienna June 26, Sheik Ahmad Zaki for the Gulf states will resume negotiations with the major oil companies over the deadlocked participation question. That meeting is expected to take place in Riyadh, Saudi Arabia.

"We are headed for a major crisis if the companies persist in their attitudes," Dr. Pachachi said.

Until recently, he said, the companies refused even to consider participation, citing the "sanctity of contracts."

"The basis of a valid contract is the free will of the two parties," he said. "Most of the oil concessions granted in the Middle East before and after World War II were concluded by states under the mandate or influence of a colonial power. The I.P.C. agreement was concluded in 1925."

Dr. Pachachi said that since 1957 all new agreements in the Middle East—with Italian, American, independent and Japanese producers—had included the right of the national oil company to participate in a local venture by up to 50 per cent.

Investment Returns

Discussing the compensation for the 20 per cent equity that the producer governments now demand in the older contracts, Dr. Pachachi said the major oil companies had recovered their investments many times over.

He cited these figures as estimated annual returns on investment: I.P.C., 56.6 per cent between 1952 and 1963, the Arabian-American Oil Company, 61 per cent from 1956 to 1960; the Iran Consortium, 69 per cent from 1959 to 1964 with the average for the Middle East, being 67 per cent from 1948 to 1960.

Dr. Pachachi cited other figures published by the American Commerce Department on direct American investment in 1970. They showed the net assets of the American petroleum industry in the Middle East at $1.47-billion, which yielded $7.16 billion in 1970 in profits. The net assets are book figures, which are substantially undervalued.

This was an annual rate of return of 79.2 per cent.

The rate of return of United States investments in the mining and smelting industries in developing countries, by contrast, was 13.5 per cent in 1970. In manufacturing industries in the developing countries it was 10.2 per cent in the same year.

* * *

October 6, 1972

OIL CONCERNS SET ACCORD WITH FIVE ARAB COUNTRIES

Details of the Agreement for Eventual Control of Western-Held Concessions by Nations Are Not Disclosed

By WILLIAM D. SMITH

Representatives of five Persian Gulf oil-producing countries and the major Western oil companies reached agreement here yesterday on terms for the five countries eventually to take over control of the companies' concessions in the area.

Details of the historic agreement, reached after nine months of sometimes acerbic negotiations, were not made public, pending final approval by the governments of Saudi Arabia, Qatar, Kuwait, Iraq and Abu Dhabi, a member of the Union of Arab Emirates.

Approval seems almost certain in every case except that of Iraq, whose radical Government may disagree with the extent of the provisions for payment to the companies by the countries for equity in the concessions.

Participation Sought

The producing countries originally demanded an initial 20 per cent participation, growing to a 51 per cent controlling interest, in the concessions on their soil.

The companies accepted the principle of participation in March, and seven negotiating sessions since then have been devoted chiefly to setting the price the countries would pay for their equity interests, the timing of the transfer of control to the producing countries and the price to be paid by the companies for the oil they buy back from the countries.

1980 Date Expected

One of the principal provisions of the agreement meets the demands for eventual rise to a maximum participation level of 51 per cent.

Most informed sources believed that the majority control would be reached by 1980. One usually reliable source contended that the agreement called for control by the countries by the end of five years.

As to payment for participation, sources close to the Arab negotiators contended that it would be considerably higher than book value of existing investments. The producing nations originally offered to make payment on book value only. Book value has traditionally been understated by the companies for tax purposes; more importantly it does not take into consideration the multibillion-dollar value of the oil reserves still under the ground.

Sources say that payments by the Gulf states will be 40 to 100 per cent above book value. On a concession with a book value of $800-million, payment at book value for 20 per cent of the concession would be $160-million. The value of the oil in the ground could be many billions of dollars.

The companies are believed likely to try to pass along the costs of participation to the consumers, and prices could go up in Europe and Asia. The United States, where domestic crude oil prices are considerably higher than world prices, should not be directly or immediately affected.

In the future, however, the United States will become increasingly dependent on foreign oil's moving from the present level of about 23 per cent of consumption to 40 to 60 per cent by 1980. The world oil price then will directly affect the cost of driving a car, heating a house or running a factory in this country.

The agreement was a personal triumph for Sheik Ahmed Zaki Yamani, Saudi Arabia's 42-year-old Minister of Oil and Minerals, who beginning four years ago, developed and championed the concept of participation as an alternative to nationalization.

With this agreement—and the likely prospect that other oil countries will demand and get similar arrangements—there will be a basic transformation in the giant international oil industry. Majority control over production of the reserves, which were developed during the last half century by private American and European companies, will pass to the governments of the oil-producing countries, mostly Arab.

Participation, is an attempt to tie together the interests of the producing nations, the consuming nations and the oil companies in a mutually beneficial arrangement while also allowing the countries to have majority control over their own natural resources.

Nationalization on the other hand would be a unilateral expulsion of Western interests.

A spokesman for the companies said:

"We feel that we have now reached a milestone in the relations between the oil-producing countries and the private oil companies. In this new era we hope we can move forward together to discharge our continuing responsibilities to the producing and consuming countries alike."

Sheik Yamani said in his room in the Delmonico Hotel after the final session:

"I believe that participation will be proven to be the only instrument available in the oil trade that will provide prosperity and stability for posterity."

A statement issued by the industry negotiating team, which was headed by George Piercy of the Standard Oil Company (New Jersey), said that the agreement was comprehensive. It calls for each Gulf country or emirate to negotiate separate agreements with the oil companies operating within its territory to implement the over-all arrangements, it said.

The companies affected by the agreement are Jersey Standard; the Standard Oil Company of California; Texaco, Inc.; the Mobil Oil Corporation; the Royal Dutch-Shell Group; the British Petroleum Company, Ltd., and Company, Ltd., and Compagnie Française des Pétroles.

From the very beginning of the negotiations it was obvious that the countries would get what they wanted.

Since the 1967 Arab-Israeli war the balance of power in the oil industry has swung away from the Western companies to the producing countries.

A big question is whether the producing nations will hold to the agreement. In recent years the producers have gathered for themselves a larger and larger share of the revenues from their oil—the split now runs about 79 per cent for the countries and 21 per cent for the companies. On several occasions in the recent past the producers have demanded changes in terms after signing long-range agreements.

Walter J. Levy, one of the world's most respected oil economists, commented: "Considering my natural skepticism with regards to any long-term agreements in the oil business, I am optimistic. I am convinced, however, of the honorable intentions of all parties."

*   *   *

June 10, 1973

THAT ARAB OIL WEALTH

By EDWIN L. DALE Jr.

WASHINGTON—Will the inevitable pile-up of large sums of money in a handful of small oil-producing Arab countries mean "continuous monetary crises" or "a highly advantageous mutual bargain" with the industrial countries?

The first phrase, descriptive of a widespread fear in financial circles here and abroad, comes from a booklet of briefing material prepared for the recent hearings of the subcommittee on international finance and resources of the Senate Finance Committee.

The second phrase comes from a speech in Paris last week by Secretary of the Treasury George P. Shultz on the monetary aspects of the energy problem, which was somewhat overlooked in the flood of other events.

Mr. Shultz spelled out in detail for the first time the Government's case for its view that the "Arab oil money" problem is probably being exaggerated.

The case was also presented, with somewhat less detail, at the Senate subcommittee hearings, by Jack L. Bennett, Deputy Under Secretary of the Treasury for monetary affairs.

Although Mr. Shultz did not put the matter in precisely these terms, a key aspect of the case, surprisingly, is that $100-billion is not really all that much money.

The figure, derived from a recent foreign affairs article by James E. Akins, the State Department's leading expert on

Arab oil, is an estimate of the possible maximum of monetary reserves by 1980 of the four Arab oil-producing states whose populations are so small that they cannot possibly spend all their oil earnings on imports: Saudi Arabia, Kuwait, Abu Dhabi and Qatar. It is a figure that has frightened the financial world.

But Mr. Shultz pointed out that by 1980 the "annual capital formation of industrialized countries will probably approximate $700-billion" and, even more startlingly, the annual issue of new stocks and bonds "will probably be on the order of $250-billion." New issues in the United States alone last year exceeded $100-billion.

And finally, according to Mr. Shultz, "it takes no stretch of the imagination—if one looks beyond the last few months in Wall Street—to suggest that the total market value of outstanding stocks and bonds in the world could exceed $3-trillion by 1980."

What all this means, of course, is that, even if the Arabs have $100-billion, their capacity to "buy up" any significant portion of the assets of the industrial countries would not be large but that, if they invest the money in the industrial countries, they will make a useful contribution in a situation of probable shortage of capital.

But will they invest it? Mr. Bennett suggests that they have no real alternative. He says:

"They will be seeking secure and productive, investments to replace their assets from the ground. They know that their reserves of oil will not last forever and that an important part of their income must be invested wisely in order that it may provide income for the time when their production is declining and newly developed alternative sources of energy have reduced the dependence of the industrialized world on their supplies."

In answer to fears that the Arab money could be "sloshing about" and causing violent monetary instability, Mr. Shultz argues that in their own interest they will have to seek "stable, secure and profitable investment opportunities—not for a year or two, but for long periods." Long-term investments do not slosh about. Mr. Shultz continues:

"As they turn to world financial markets, there is no inherent reason to believe their asset preferences will not be subject to the same profit instincts that lead most investors to place a substantial portion of their funds in longer-term form, provided the climate is favorable."

Mr. Bennett told the Senate hearing that information from "a number" of the Arab oil countries showed that they did not speculate against the dollar in the monetary turmoil in February and March, at least not with government reserves.

But what about the United States in particular, and the impact of the oil picture on the exchange rate of the dollar? Here two points are made.

First, Europe and Japan together will actually increase their total oil imports from the Arab countries by more than the United States will increase them, despite the big projected jump in United States imports. Thus there is no inherent reason why the exchange rate that matters—the

dollar against the European currencies and the yen—should change.

The issue becomes simply one of whether the United States will get its appropriate share of both exports to some oil countries and investments from others. Mr. Shultz was confident on both counts. He said, without too much fear of contradiction, "I am unabashed in feeling we can compete with any nation in investment opportunities."

All in all, Mr. Shultz argued, "the United States could well be the gainer" in its over-all balance of payments vis-à-vis those of Europe and Japan.

None of this is certain, of course, any more than it is certain that the four Arab countries will pile up as much as $100-billion. Also, the Arabs may be of several minds about long-term investments in the industrial countries, despite what seems to be their self-interest. Such a respected Arab official as Abdel-Rahman Salem al-Atiqi, Kuwait's Minister of Finance and Oil, spoke in April of putting an end to "these unsatisfactory relationships which make us a mere source of finance for economies stronger than ours."

But even if the Arab oil countries "invest" their money in the form of aid to the less-developed countries, including other Arab countries, the money will ultimately be spent on imports from the industrial countries.

In any event, all the rich countries are in roughly the same boat as far as oil, the balance of payments and exchange rates are concerned. There is no a priori reason why the United States should come out worse than the others.

* * *

October 18, 1973

ARABS CUT OIL EXPORTS 5% A MONTH

U.S. CHIEF TARGET

Reduction Is Smaller Than Expected—Effect Uncertain

By RICHARD EDER
Special to The New York Times

BEIRUT, Lebanon, Oct. 17—The Arab oil-producing nations proclaimed tonight a monthly cut in exports of oil, with the burden to fall on the United States and other nations considered to be unfriendly to the Arab cause.

The long-awaited formal decision to use oil as a weapon in the Middle East conflict was announced at the end of an eight-hour meeting in Kuwait of ministers from 11 countries.

The monthly export reduction was set at 5 per cent off each previous month's sale, starting with the level of sales in September. The measure was at once more modest, more flexible and vaguer than had generally been predicted.

A Significant Shift

"It was about as mild a step as they could have taken," said one oil expert who had talked to the participants. At the same time, to have finally come to the use of oil as a weapon, as had been threatened for years, marks a significant evolution in Middle Eastern affairs.

The cuts would continue, month by month until Israel evacuated the territories occupied in the 1967 war, and made provision to respect Arab rights. This deliberately imprecise formulation alludes to the claims of the Palestinian refugees.

France May be Exempt

There was no specific mention of any country on the "unfriendly" list other than the United States. This was one of many flexible aspects of the decision. It allows the Arab states to grade customers in order of their support of the Arab cause. The participants promised to insure that the 5 per cent monthly export cut would not reduce sales to "friendly" countries, but again they did not say which countries these were.

Observers at the meeting assumed that France, for example, would not be subject to reductions. West Germany, presumably, might be. Japan, whose position was described by one participant as that of "odious neutrality," might experience some difficulties. It was hard to say what treatment would be given to Britain, which has also tried to be neutral.

The 5 per cent cutback would be computed against the previous month's exports. The cut is less than it would be if this 5 per cent were computed from some single point. Thus, after six months the actual reduction would be 23 per cent instead of 30, and at the end of a year, 43 per cent instead of 60.

The 11 countries involved in the decision, not all of which are oil-producing countries, were Abu Dhabi, Algeria, Bahrain, Dubai, Egypt, Kuwait, Iraq, Libya, Qatar, Saudi Arabia and Syria.

Egypt and Saudi Arabia, opposing more militant proposals, are reported to have insisted on avoiding measures that would put relations with the United States beyond "the point of no return," a phrase used by the Egyptian President, Anwar el-Sadat, in his speech yesterday.

Reduction Is Modest

Tonight's decision appears to take account of this view. The dimensions of the cut were considerably more modest than the kind of all-out action called for by countries such as Syria and Iraq.

The United States uses some 17 million barrels of crude oil and refined products each day, and some 6.4 million barrels of this are imported. From the Arab countries the United States takes a total of crude and heating oil estimated variously at 1.5 million to 1.9 million barrels a day.

This week the United States released figures purporting to show that Americans would not be seriously affected even by major cuts in Arab oil production.

William E. Simon, chairman of President Nixon's oil policy committee, said that the United States could decrease its consumption of oil by as much as three million barrels a day if it made the necessary effort.

* * *

October 30, 1973

OIL-CURB SPREAD WORRIES EUROPE

Extension of Arab Embargo to Dutch a Threat to Major Transport System

RATIONING IS PREDICTED

U.S. Suppliers in Caribbean Will Also Be Affected by Saudi Arabian Cut

By CLYDE H. FARNSWORTH
Special to The New York Times

PARIS, Oct. 29—The Arab boycott of oil shipments to the Netherlands, which would curb supplies sharply in the continent's northern area, has intensified Europe's anxiety over the availability of petroleum products this winter.

One industry analyst, Dr. Paul Frankel, a London-based consultant, said in a telephone interview: "European governments are whistling in the dark if they feel they can postpone a petroleum allocation system, or even rationing, for long."

The embargo on shipments to the Dutch will also affect the United States, to which the Arabs also have cut off shipments. The Netherlands, through her giant port facilities at Rotterdam, is a transit point for oil throughout Northern Europe. In addition, Dutch colonies in the Caribbean make refined products chiefly for the American market from Middle East crude.

Saudi Action

The embargo question became critical over the weekend when Saudi Arabia, the largest oil exporting nation, joined other Arab states in their boycott of the Netherlands because of that nation's alleged pro-Israeli policies.

For the Netherlands herself, the impact will be cushioned by the fact that 40 per cent of her energy requirements are satisfied with natural gas from the neighboring North Sea. The wider worry is the threat to the small nation's role as a major transport and refining center for Europe and elsewhere.

Caribbean Shortages

In the Caribbean, the Shell refinery at Curaçao and the Exxon refinery at Aruba face a supply shortage now that Saudi Arabia has followed Algeria, Iraq, Kuwait, Qatar, the United Arab Emirates and the Sultanate of Oman in banning shipments to Dutch interests.

The Dutch, including their colonies, import approximately 2.5 million barrels daily, two-thirds of which is supplied by the Arab states. Saudi Arabia, alone, supplies one-third.

The United States also gets refined products from another major center in the Caribbean, Trinidad. The effects of the cutbacks on Texaco's refinery there are not yet known.

European countries have been warned by the oil industry that a quota basis will have to be established for them on supplies. Last weekend, Japanese refiners were told by British Petroleum, Shell and Exxon to expect cuts of 10 per cent.

Europe and Japan are far more dependent on Middle East oil than is the United States. The Arabs say their boycotts are meant to strike at the United States for its support of Israel. But the supply cuts ultimately chiefly affect the biggest customers. Apparently, Arab strategy is to get American allies to put pressure on Washington.

Divisions have already begun to appear in the Atlantic alliance against the background of the Middle East conflict, and oil has probably played a major role in the dissension. West Germany has protested against being used as a staging point for American arms shipments to Israel. The United States in turn has criticized the Europeans for not being, in President Nixon's words, "as cooperative as they might have been in attempting to help us work out the Middle East settlement."

Substantial quantities of crude oil landed in Rotterdam are piped directly to West Germany and Belgium; more is transhipped to Scandinavia. In addition, Dutch refineries sell petroleum products to many European countries.

If Saudi Arabia interprets her embargo as covering even transhipments, Europe will face the loss of another 500,000 to 1 million barrels daily on top of an existing shortfall of some 4.5 million barrels daily, according to industry figures.

Action Postponed

Members of the Organization for Economic Cooperation and Development met last week to assess the oil situation. Shelved for the time being was activation by Europeans of an oil-sharing plan. The Europeans were afraid that any concerted action would give Arabs the impression that the industrial states were "ganging up" against them and would lead to even further cutbacks.

Despite the shaky cease-fire in the Middle East, the prospects for an improvement in the supply picture are not considered good.

The Dutch are considering a ban on Sunday driving. The Times of London reported that some British ministers believed gasoline rationing or restriction of supplies to distributors would be necessary within six weeks.

Like the United States, most European governments have so far simply urged their citizens to husband energy resources more prudently.

The Europeans are counting on their plentiful stocks—two to three months' supplies—to see them through. But if the cutbacks continue the situation could easily become critical.

* * *

December 26, 1973

ARAB BRINKMANSHIP

Output Pledge May Signal Recognition of Potential Risk

By LEONARD SILK

The announcement by the Arab oil nations that they will increase production by 10 per cent in January and supply

Britain, France, Japan, Spain and other "friendly countries" with their "full oil needs" suggests that the Arabs have grown wary of causing an economic disaster in the industrial world that could backfire upon them. Speaking in Kuwait, the Saudi Arabian oil minister, Sheikh Ahmed Zaki al-Yamani said, "We do not wish the nations of the world to suffer."

The move suggests that the Arabs see scant immediate prospect that the Europeans or Japanese could bring sufficient pressure on Israel and its principal ally, the United States, to force the Israelis to return to their 1967 borders or yield to other Arab demands. "We only intended to attract world attention to the injustice that befell the Arabs," said Sheikh Yamani.

Nevertheless, the Arabs are keeping the heat on the United States and other countries, including the Netherlands, Portugal, Rhodesia and South Africa, that it accuses of sympathy or support for the Israelis.

The Arabs' announcement of a 10 per cent increase in output—which by somewhat murky arithmetic is described as reducing the cutback from 30 per cent to 25 per cent—will still leave the world short of normal oil requirements, though it is impossible to know precisely how much, since there have been, apparently, surreptitious deliveries to countries above the quotas. The move suggests the familiar tactics of a cartel threatened with "chiseling"—to ease up somewhat on restrictions.

The timing of the announcement also looks like a shrewd way to follow up—and nail down—the 128 per cent increase in the posted price of crude oil announced Sunday in Tehran, Iran.

Alarm has been growing in the West over what looks like economic warfare, or blackmail, even against countries that have "tilted" against Israel.

The aggressive price actions by the Persian Gulf states appeared to be directed, without too much discrimination, against the rich industrial powers that have long dominated the Middle East and North Africa. A British official, hearing the news from Teheran, said, "The last chicken of colonialism is coming home to roost."

Indeed, it seemed clear that the strongest economic monopoly in history—the Organization of Petroleum Exporting Countries, established in 1960—has moved to challenge the rich industrial powers to hand over an almost inconceivable sum of money in exchange for the oil on which 20th-century industrial economies have come to depend.

Shah Mohammed Riza Pahlevi of Iran declared, in announcing the price rise, "The industrial world will have to realize that the era of their terrific progress and even more terrific income and wealth based on cheap oil is finished."

Rules of Game

The Shah in effect told the West it had been living high on the hog long enough—and that the oil-producing countries were moving in to take a major share of the loot.

The Persian Gulf oil ministers, OPEC leaders, deliberately warned the Western countries against increasing prices on their exports, on penalty of a continuing soaring in the price of oil.

The OPEC countries have already demonstrated their recognition of the strength of their hand. Last January OPEC raised the posted price of oil from $2.48 to $2.59. On Oct. 1, just before Egypt and Syria attacked Israel, it raised the posted price of oil to $3.01 a barrel. On Oct. 16, in the midst of the war, and three days before the announcement of the Arab oil embargo, OPEC boosted the posted price to $5.11.

This week's rise to $11.65, effective Jan. 1 and expected to become OPEC-wide represented a 470 per cent price increase in just one year. And even the latest increase, described by the Persian Gulf oil ministers as "moderate," may hold only through the first quarter of 1974, according to Abdul-Rahman Salem al-Atiqi the Kuwaiti minister of oil.

Dollar Flows

The implications for the flow of dollars to the oil-producing states is almost inconceivable. Earlier estimates that the Persian Gulf and North African oil producers would reap revenues of over $80-billion annually by 1980, with cumulative revenues from 1973 through 1980 of about $350-billion, were postulated on an average price of only $5 per barrel of oil.

It is possible to write various horror stories based on that flood of wealth to the oil-producing states—the devastation of the balance of payments of the industrial economies, the collapse of the dollar as an international currency, the unleashing of global inflation or the breakup of the Western alliance, with the European countries and Japan so heavily dependent on Arab oil, splitting off from the United States. There are fears of a major interruption in world production and trade.

To continue: with their untold billions of dollars to spend, Saudi Arabia, Iran and other oil-producing giants could not only acquire a huge stake in Western industries but could also greatly increase their military power—for instance, by purchasing a nuclear capability and the personnel to develop and operate it.

Some Complications

To be sure, such scenarios may be exaggerated and far too simple. The money the oil producers earn in the capitalist world must be spent somewhere or it is nothing but printed paper. Indeed, even gold is basically worthless unless it can be used to acquire goods and services.

Too rapid an escalation of oil prices would inevitably bring an escalation of the prices of Western goods and technology.

The oil exporting countries could find themselves in the position of those classic traders who wound up exchanging million-dollar cats for million-dollar dogs.

Nevertheless, the power of the oil producers to extract monopoly prices and payments can still cause enormous transfers of income and wealth to themselves from the industrial countries, set off shock waves of inflation and recession in the West and Japan, and induce political disorder.

In every Western capital, the question is being asked: How can the power of the oil cartel be curbed?

The history of other international cartels as well as domestic industrial conspiracies may be instructive. All have had a history of instability and ultimately have broken down.

Cartels form and hold together during times of prosperity, when their customers are eager for their goods and prepared to pay higher and higher prices to get them.

But they tend to fall apart when hard times come and the capacity of the cartel members exceeds market demand. Prices then start to drop, chiseling multiplies, and price wars may develop.

If the oil-producing cartel succeeds in causing a serious recession in the West, it would almost certainly create the conditions for its own undoing. This may be the basic explanation of why Sheik Yamani and the other Arab oil ministers are starting to back off from too tough an embargo.

Ununited Front

Even today the oil cartel is anything but rock solid. While Saudi Arabia and most other Arab states have imposed their embargo, Iraq—extremely hostile to Israel—has stayed out, as have such other major OPEC countries as Iran, Nigeria, Indonesia and Venezuela.

Reports from several sources have cast doubt on the actual depth of the cuts in oil shipments. It is conceivable that, with relatively minor cuts in actual deliveries, the Arab states succeeded in panicking the oil importers and users into massive buying and hoarding, in advance of anticipated price increases. This self-fulfilling behavior bred both price hikes and shortages.

The chaotic world oil market was then exploited not only by the Arab states but by all members of the OPEC cartel.

Cartel Weaknesses

Feeding on its triumphs, the cartel now looks stronger than ever. But it is actually a large and diverse assemblage of countries, jealous of one another and with no single producer able to control more than a fraction of total output and exports and thereby enforce discipline, should trouble come in the form of falling sales. As of 1970, the principal oil producers in OPEC, according to the United Nations, were

Country	Production (millions of metric tons)	Exports
Venezuela	194.4	127.6
Iran	191.7	165.4
Saudi Arabia	176.9	148.8
Libya	161.7	160.2
Kuwait	137.4	121.0
Iraq	76.4	73.3
Nigeria	54.2	51.7
Algeria	48.3	46.0
Indonesia	42.2	30.8

Saudi Arabia is currently regarded as the leader of the assault with the oil weapon. King Faisal has threatened to withhold his country's oil if the West does not cause Israel to withdraw to behind its 1967 borders.

Yet Saudi Arabian oil exports constitute only about 15 per cent of the OPEC total—and only 13 per cent of all world oil exports. And not all oil producers would be willing to see their oil exports slump.

Monopoly-Busting

The best way to break the cartel would be for the United States and other oil importers to cut their oil consumption and convert to other technologies.

But cutbacks in oil usage would meet strong resistance from producers, consumers and workers in all countries. Converting to other energy uses would involve massive new investments, research and development outlays and construction that will take years.

However, the enormous increases in the price of oil are giving great impetus to the search for new energy sources and ultimately should lead to the conversion of Western economies to technologies far less dependent on oil.

This is a necessity that would have come within the next half century, even without the squeeze of the OPEC cartel.

Meanwhile, however, the oil cartel is gambling with an economic disaster to the industrial world—which could produce a political explosion that would wreak havoc in the oil-producing countries as well. It remains to be seen whether the Arab oil producers and the other oil states have decided to back off before it is too late.

*   *   *

March 13, 1974

THE PETRODOLLAR FLOW

If the Panglossian Economic Theory Is Right—and It's Not—All Is Well

By LEONARD SILK

There is a school of economics whose fundamental tenet is that everything happens for the best. Among the historic claims for this principle are the following:

- If the taxes of the rich are cut, the benefits will trickle down to the poor. Similarly, if the rich or the middle class build more new houses, this will benefit the poor, because the standing stock of existing houses will trickle down to the poor. (The trickle-down theory is one of the major contributions of this school of Panglossian economics.)

- A fall in output, income and employment is good because it will restore the economy to a sound basis.

- For every seller of stock, there is a buyer. Strong hands will take over the assets once held by the weak.

- Equilibrium is the law of economic life. If people spend more money for food, they will have less to spend for other things, so inflation will not result. If one nation loses monetary reserves, another nation will gain them, so the

world monetary system will not suffer from either inflation or deflation.

- To those principles of symmetry, balance and divine automaticity, the contemporary followers of Dr. Pangloss (Voltaire named him "Professor of Metaphysico-Theologo Cosmolonigology") have added the following doctrines:

- It doesn't matter how much money the oil-consuming countries pay out to the oil-producing countries, because the money will flow back to the oil-consuming countries as investments or to pay for goods.

- It doesn't matter if the outflow of money to pay for oil causes a temporary cut in consumption in the oil-consuming countries, because this will constitute a form of saving, and the "petrodollars" will then increase the world's stock of capital, furthering growth and damping down inflation.

Volume to Be Great

However, the volume of petrodollars may be too great for the world monetary system to handle. The whole system could break down.

J. Carlin Englert of New York University has made fresh estimates of the money flows from 11 major industrialized nations to defray the costs of higher-priced petroleum and petroleum products this year. He found that the United States, Canada, Japan, West Germany, France, Britain and five other European countries would see their oil bills increase from $42.6-billion in 1973 to $108.7-billion in 1974.

What will the Arab oil states do with their money? Much of it will indeed flow west.

Ibrahim M. Oweiss, a native of Egypt who is an associate professor at Georgetown University in Washington, notes that the Arabs have already set up four major financial consortia in collaboration with American and European interests.

One is the Union des Banques Arabes et Française (U.B.A.F.), established in Paris in 1970 with more than $700-million in assets. This is 40 per cent owned by Crédit Lyonnais the big French bank, but it is controlled by 14 Arab banks. U.B.A.F. has subsidiaries in London, Rome, Frankfurt, Luxembourg and Tokyo; partners of these subsidiaries include several big European banks and the Bank of Tokyo.

The three other consortia are:

- The Banque Franc-Arabe d'Investissement Internationaux (E.R.A.B.), chartered in Paris in 1969 by the Kuwait Investment Company in partnership with the French Société Générale and the Société de Banque Suisse;

- The European Arab Bank, started in 1972, with headquarters in Luxembourg, which is made up of 16 Arab financial institutions (including E.R.A.B.) and seven European banks;

- And la Compagnie Arabe et Internationale d'Investissement, incorporated in Luxembourg in January, 1973, which is owned by 24 Arab and other banks, including the Bank of America, West German, Italian, Japanese and French institutions.

Arab Business Sought

In addition to these major Arab combines, many Western banks and brokers are competing for Arab business, led by the First National City Bank of New York, with branches in Beirut, Saudi Arabia, Bahrain and Dubai, and the Chase Manhattan Bank, with branches in Beirut and Bahrain. Chase Manhattan and the Morgan Guaranty Trust Company of New York are the largest holders of Saudi Arabian Government deposits.

But the flow of capital from the oil-consuming to the oil-producing countries is so huge as to threaten hyperinflation in the Western economies.

The more moderate Arab countries, such as Saudi Arabia, Kuwait and Abu Dhabi, appear to recognize this.

Professor Oweiss noted that Saudi Arabia has proposed to reduce the current price of Persian Gulf oil "once justifiable political and economic demands of Arab countries are met and once rich oil-consuming countries pursue a policy of genuine cooperation with the developing countries."

He added that "it is not in the economic interest of oil-exporting countries to push the price of oil beyond the interval in which demand is inelastic."

The sharp increases in oil prices will mean a huge transfer of real income and wealth from the West—a real lowering of living standards.

As economists of the First National City Bank put it, "The discomfort of facing up to this harsh truth has engendered illusions—notably that, for consuming countries, the adjustment can be eased by more rapid inflation or by government intervention in the marketplace."

But the real transfers of income and the potential disruption of the world economy threaten to exacerbate both global inflation and recession.

Hopes for Price Cuts

It is the belated recognition of the gravity of these dangers—not only to the industrialized nations but to the oil-producing states as well—that has given rise to hopes that the Arab states meeting in Tripoli today may be ready to lift the oil embargo and expand production. The Western nations and Japan are also hoping for some price cuts.

The United States has pressed hard for such concessions to the Western nations, while France has been following a go-it-alone line, seeking to make her own deals with the Arabs.

Even if the Arabs end the embargo, however, the threat to the world economy will not evaporate over night. Inflation is raging, and the Western political and economic alliance is severely strained—possibly shattered.

The disciples of Dr. Pangloss should remember that their master barely missed losing his head in the Inquisition and wound up living humbly on the farm of Candide.

* * *

March 31, 1974

WHAT ARABS TAUGHT THE INDUSTRIAL GIANTS

By LEONARD SILK

Like a small bomb triggering a larger one, the October war in the Middle East triggered a larger war: the economic attack by the Arab oil-producing states against the industrialized nations. The oil embargo has largely been lifted, but the consequences of that display of economic power are likely to be long-lasting for the world's economy. Western statesmen and money managers are struggling to find the technical answers to questions raised by the "oil war."

What is the key to the problem?

It is the price of oil. Before October, the price of crude in the Persian Gulf was about $2. Today it's about $8.

That sounds prosaic enough: What will it do to the world economy?

First of all, it will mean a vast transfer of resources from oil-importing nations to the Saudis, Kuwaitis, Iranians and the other oil producers. By the end of this year they will have piled up about $100-billion in investible funds. Of course, oil prices could decline, but if the present price holds—and the oil nations are likely to restrict supply to keep it up—the members of the Organization of Petroleum Exporting Countries could have, according to one estimate, investible funds of half a trillion dollars by 1980.

Will that be inflationary, or will it cause a contraction in the world economy?

It could be both.

First, for contraction. King Faisal, the Shah of Iran and others have transferred money earned in the West to their own accounts. This money has been taken, in the final analysis, from Western consumers paying more for gasoline, electricity, heating oil, food grown on petrochemical fertilizers, synthetic clothing and so on. The more of their real resources Westerners commit to paying for imported oil, the less they will have to spend on other goods. That means a real drain on Western living standards.

The inflationary effect is more obvious. Given current technology, oil is the premier raw material and higher-priced oil raises the production costs of many other goods. That raises the cost of living. But individuals will struggle to maintain their incomes and nations to maintain full employment in the face of those higher oil bills. Governments and central banks will seek to spur employment by putting enough money into the system to offset the contractionary effect of the oil debts paid to foreigners. This will be inflationary and it will only disguise but not reverse the real loss of income.

But will the oil producers not put the bulk of the money they get back into the industrial countries?

Yes. Literally speaking, most of it will never leave the West. Deposits at Western banks will be shifted from American, European and Japanese ownership to Arab and Iranian accounts. Some minor fraction will buy goods or real

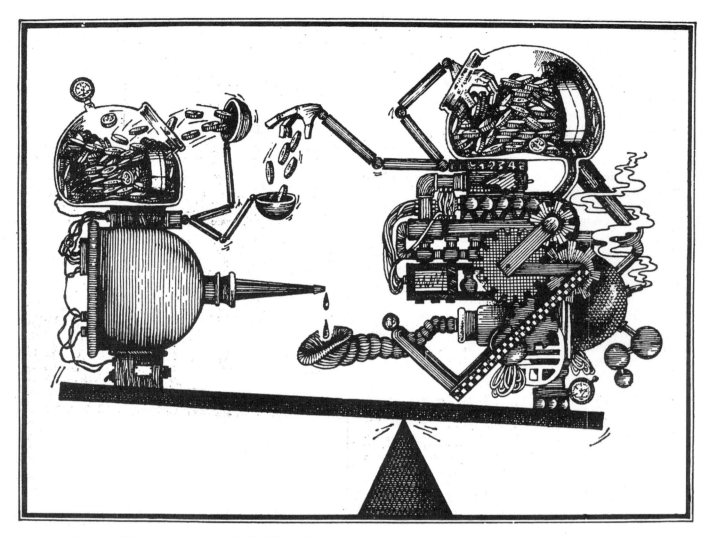

estate—an island off South Carolina, gold, Cadillacs (if they are still being made) and so on. But most of it will be invested in securities of one kind or another.

Much of it now seems to be going into short-term loans in the Eurodollar market. The Arabs, wary of the possibility that their funds could be blocked or investments nationalized, prefer high liquidity and anonymity to long-term direct industrial investment. Some of the money will be invested in the poor lands of Africa and Asia. Arab money, for example, is expected to finance reopening of the Suez Canal and the Arab League last week was told that a development bank for Africa has now reached $231-million in capitalization. But, compared to the billions the Arabs will gain, these funds are small.

If all the petrodollars are used in the world economic system one way or another, what is the danger?

One is that the big shift of funds from buying goods and services to the purchase of highly liquid investments could imbalance the industrialized economies. Money used to buy financial instruments has a different effect from money used to buy plants, machinery, housing or consumer goods.

Another danger is that the recycling of petrodollars may feed money back to big capital markets, such as the United States, West Germany or Switzerland, but leave other countries in heavy over-all balance-of-payments deficit. This could lead them to try to protect themselves by blocking imports. Even without protectionism, their import demand could fall and cause world trade to contract.

A third danger, and in some ways the most serious one, is to the Third World, which literally faces starvation and can be thrown into political upheaval. Poor nations will try to raise the price of their exports—bauxite, copper or whatever—in imitation of the oil cartel. The bauxite producers, for example, met recently in Guinea to try exactly that. Although the effort was less than successful, Jamaica, the second largest bauxite producer, in the past few days has told the United States and Canadian Governments the taxes and royalties on bauxite are going up. Moreover, Jamaica wants a share in ownership of the mines.

Finally, there is the threat to the entire monetary system. Floating exchange rates have taken the shock reasonably well so far, but the highly liquid funds are building up. Chase Manhattan, First National City and Morgan Guaranty are large holders of Arab deposits and the Arabs have also joined four major international banking consortia with billions in assets.

Without intending harm, nervous holders of those billions could shift them from country to country, in a highly destabilizing way. A liquidity crisis in one country could run through the world like wildfire. No present international agency could cope. And no single nation, including the United States, could either.

Is there no alternative to oil?

Prof. William D. Nordhaus, a Yale economist, expects the United States virtually to exhaust domestic petroleum resources by 1980. From then on, until 2000, the nation will have to rely on imported oil and gas. But as this runs out, too, the price will rise and coal and shale will become more economically attractive. For the United States, with enormous reserves of both coal and shale, this will be a buoyant period. Then about 2120, the fossil fuels will be exhausted and the nuclear age, in the form of the breeder reactor, will take over.

But the immediate threat to the world economy is pressing and the need for international cooperation on energy and raw material sources has grown correspondingly. At the Third World's insistence, the United Nations will begin a special session on the subject next week but its effect is not expected, to be great. Producing a workable solution is the key challenge facing the world economy in the seventies. A failure to do so would be devastating.

* * *

September 20, 1974

OIL NATIONS SPUR U.S. INVESTMENTS

Treasury Estimates Figure for the Producing Lands at $7-Billion This Year

WASHINGTON, Sept. 19 (Reuters)—The Treasury Department estimated today that oil-producing nations invested about $7-billion in the United States and about $3-billion in Britain in the first eight months of 1974.

In a report to the Senate permanent Subcommittee on Investigations, the Treasury said that it estimated the member nations of the Organization of Petroleum Exporting Countries may have had a surplus "of somewhere between 25 billion and 28 billion dollars" in the first eight months of this year.

In the report, however, the Treasury stressed it could not be certain of its figures. It said:

"We have pieced together information derived from many different sources. What we have is fragmentary. Many of the reports cannot be confirmed. We can do no more than offer a very rough guess as to where funds may have been invested thus far in 1974."

Of the estimated $7-billion invested in the United States, the Treasury said that some $4-billion was invested in various types of marketable United States Government securities with most of the remainder being placed with commercial banks and a few hundred million dollars invested in corporate securities and real estate.

"At least 3 billion dollars may have been invested in the United Kingdom in sterling, some of which no doubt involved purchases of British Government securities and some sterling deposits in British banks," the treasury said.

The report continued that the Treasury "suspects" that $2-billion or more was invested in Europe through direct placement loans to official or quasi-official agencies as well as through direct purchases of private securities and real estate.

It said the Treasury had received commitments by the OPEC countries to developing nations and international lending institutions.

Receipts Estimated

The Treasury report estimates that the oil producing nations would have receipts of about $80-billion in calendar 1974, of which they would have to invest outside their own countries some $55-billion.

The report notes that some of the OPEC countries have apparently placed "a high value on anonymity" in making their investments in such a way that the owner cannot be traced for fear that the host countries might freeze those assets "to induce modification of governmental policy."

United States imports of petroleum for the first half of the year were estimated at $11.8-billion and this is expected to rise to $14-billion during the second half.

United States exports to producers have more than doubled to $2.4-billion in the first half from $1.1-billion a year ago.

* * *

October 2, 1974

AN EXPLOSIVE MIXTURE

World's Monetary Institutions May Be Incapable of Defusing Oil-Money Bomb

By LEONARD SILK
Special to The New York Times

WASHINGTON, Oct. 1—Damon Runyon, the great sports writer once said that where the human race is concerned, the odds are 9 to 5 against. An observer at the current annual meeting of the World Bank and International Monetary Fund would see no reason to quarrel with that conclusion.

In private conversations here, finance ministers and central bankers, normally given to the softest of euphemisms and the most Pollyannish of prognoses, are expressing grave concern about the dangers facing the world monetary system. Many officials agree that never in the history of these two institutions has anxiety run so high.

The explosive mixture of oil and money is what they are worrying about.

Although inflation, in part aggravated by soaring oil prices, is rampant, many officials are concerned that efforts to stop it by clamping down on monetary growth would result in deflation and bring mass unemployment.

Individual nations facing mounting balance-of-payments deficits are being driven to try to increase exports and cut other imports, to conserve disappearing foreign-exchange reserves. But the battle to increase exports could lead to international price wars, with falling rather than rising prices. And the drive to curb imports could lead to breakdowns in trade and further damage to national economies.

In these alarming circumstances, the most hopeful thing to be said about the present conference is that the finance ministers and central bankers are facing up to reality and refusing to panic. Constructive programs are receiving the most intensive consideration, although action appears unlikely before the meetings adjourn the end of this week.

Prophecies that once would have been dismissed as lunatic or vulturish are now perceived to be a real part of the problem overhanging financial markets and banking institutions.

The most extreme of the black prophecies heard here was offered by Franz Pick, the international currency expert and champion of gold, whose reputation, like that of other gold bugs, has been greatly enhanced by soaring bullion prices in recent years.

Asked for his current prediction, Dr. Pick replied: "Banking holiday. Moratorium on all debts except mortgage debts. Closing Wall street for good including the bond market. Exchanging dollar bank notes for new dollars at a rate of 10 for 1 or 20 for 1."

In the face of such forecasts, and the near panic they have excited in stock and money markets, what can Government officials say that will not sound flatulent or like soft soap?

William E. Simon, Secretary of the Treasury, in his statement to the monetary conference today said he did not believe the world was in imminent danger of a drift into cumulative recession or depression. But, he added, "We must be alert and ready to act quickly" should the situation change unexpectedly.

Borrowings to Mount

Mr. Simon said he did not believe the international financial market was about to collapse, although he did believe individual countries might face serious problems in borrowing to cover oil and other costs. Food is a particular problem, especially as it is being added to the already explosive mix of oil and money.

The question is no longer recognition of the depth and gravity of the danger, but the adequacy of governmental response. Thus far this conference has provided only moderate reassurance on that ground. Mr. Simon, for instance, is still urging nations to give highest priority to the attack on "devastating inflation."

On measures to bring down the price levels set by the Organization of Petroleum Exporting Countries, Mr. Simon was vague. The United States is being accused by others here of, in effect, doing the opposite of what President Theodore Roosevelt prescribed for the conduct of foreign policy: talking loudly and carrying a small stick.

Focus on Recycling

In the general mood of pessimism on prices, the conference is focusing on the issue of how to "recycle" oil dollars—transfer them to nations with the deepest deficits and little or no ability to attract money directly from the oil exporters.

H. Johannes Witteveen, managing director of the monetary fund, has proposed increasing the existing oil facility—christened by the British as the Witteveen Mark I—of $3.4-billion by a few hundred million dollars to get through the current year. Presumably a larger sum will be sought for the future.

Denis Healey, Chancellor of the Exchequer in Britain, wants to build a Witteveen Mark II with a much bigger supply of funds.

The American response to such proposals, as voiced by Mr. Simon, is thus far low key almost to the point of being lackadaisical. Thus far, he suggested, the recycling problem had been handled "quite adequately" in private financial markets.

However, private bankers here—especially those representing British and European institutions—are far less sanguine. Several talk about reaching the limits of their ability to take and recycle petrodollars in the near future.

Quota Alternative

The International Monetary Fund could also provide more money to help governments in trouble by increasing the $34-billion of quotas loaned to the Fund by member governments. Mr. Simon said in an interview that the United States might be willing to see a 25 per cent rise to about $42-billion total.

But he insists the United States should keep its present share of the total—about 23 per cent—although he realizes oil producers want a bigger share, with which would go greater voting power in the fund.

At present Iran's share of the quota total is two-thirds of 1 per cent; Saudi Arabia's is one-half of 1 per cent; Venezuela's is a little more than 1 per cent and Kuait's is two-tenths of 1 per cent. The cumulative total share for all OPEC members is less than 3 per cent.

Speaking Softly

The leaders of the fund and the World Bank are themselves speaking softly to and about the oil producers. Few Arabs are actually in evidence here, this being the period of the religious holiday of Ramadan.

But the address of Robert S. McNamara, president of the World Bank, was printed in Arabic this year; his plans for keeping the World Bank going and growing depend heavily on a continuing inflow of petrodollars.

Likewise, Dr. Witteveen of the I.M.F. refused to comment on the price of oil in response to press questions, saying in effect that it was none of the fund's business.

The bank and fund, with the political cross tugs of oil-producing and oil-consuming, industrial and developing countries may be simply incapable of coming to grips with the grim problems besetting the world economy.

Search for Action

It may be necessary for real action to come from some other grouping.

The so-called Big Five non-Communist financial powers—the United States, France, West Germany, Britain and France—have been exploring new approaches. But, as one West German put it, their discussions thus far have been more in the nature of brain-storming than decision-making.

Some American observers believe that the old Group of Ten—which includes all the Western European democracies, and Canada as well as the United States and Japan—is a better theater for action. However, the Canadians, on all issues, seemed to be behaving like OPEC fellow travelers these days.

No Neat Solution

There appears to be general agreement that there is no neat solution to the problem of how to conduct national economic policy in the midst of this world crisis. Each nation is bound to pursue some unique mixture of unilateral, bilateral and multilateral strategies.

The French, for example, have already announced a $10-billion limit on the amount of oil she will import—unilateral. At the same time they appear determined to continue to pursue bilateral arms and other economic deals with the Iranians and other oil producers.

Yet they appear to be moving closer to multilateral approaches with the United States and other Western nations to problems that might get out of hand.

For balance-of-payments deficits this year will generally be huge. The Italians are apparently headed for a deficit of close to $9-billion. France is expected to run one of about $7-billion. Japan is likely to be in the hole by $7-billion to $8-billion. And Britain's red ink may run to $10-billion.

The cumulative deficit of the oil importers is likely to grow to perhaps $650-billion by 1980, according to estimates of the World Bank itself.

The clock, then, is ticking. A realistic appraisal of the current conference is that nations have begun to respond in a serious and constructive way, and that the situation is not yet hopeless. But too timid or belated a response might make it so.

*   *   *

April 16, 1975

FRUSTRATIONS OF OIL CONFERENCE

By LEONARD SILK

The first conference in Paris of oil-exporting and oil-importing countries, which was supposed to have set the agenda and improved the atmosphere for a world energy conference next summer, has got nowhere. Instead, by over running its intended time limits—it was well into its second week when it adjourned yesterday—and by polarizing the differences among participants, it has served to dramatize the radical conflicts that exist within the non-Communist world over two critical issues:

- Whether the world economy will be run essentially according to liberal principles of trade and payments, which have existed through most of the period since World War II, or whether an open economy will give way to one of bloc trading and price fixing.
- And, closely tied to that issue, how to divide the world's product and its wealth among industrial countries, oil-producing countries and oil-poor developing countries.

The Paris talks have demonstrated how far from resolution these issues remain.

The United States—whose energy and foreign economic policies are now dominated by Secretary of State Kissinger—remains the chief proponent of a tough line of resistance to the oil-exporting countries. Although there are ambiguities in the American position, it still is pointed at reducing the dependency of the West on insecure Middle Eastern oil and, if possible, at breaking the oil cartel, the Organization of Petroleum Exporting Countries.

Algeria, led by President Houari Boumediene, has emerged as the outstanding champion of both the oil-exporting countries and their third-world allies. Algeria—herself oil-rich, per-capita income poor, anti-colonialist in its revolutionary origins and leftist leaning—is a natural bridge between the rich OPEC states and the poor third world.

Seeking to play the role of mediator between the antagonistic views of the United States and Algeria is President Valéry Giscard d'Estaing of France. He pushed hardest to get discussions going between the oil producers and oil consumers; he is still striving to prevent the conference from failing.

Mr. Giscard d'Estaing is well cast in the role of mediator: He has much to offer not only his European partners but also the United States, which is not eager to be cut off from its traditional Western allies over the oil issue. And he has much to offer the oil-producing countries and nonoil-producing third-world countries, especially in Africa, by way of trade and markets.

Nor is the French President isolated from other European leaders in their desire to maintain close economic relations with both the oil-rich and oil-poor third world, even if this involves giving some ground to their demand for "a new economic order."

The OPEC nations issued that demand last month in President Boumediene's capital, Algiers, at a meeting called by "the President of the Revolutionary Council and of the Council of Ministers of the Democratic People's Republic of Algeria."

At the Algiers meeting, the OPEC nations denounced the "short-sighted" economic policies of the industrialized world and rejected "any allegation attributing to the price of petroleum the responsibility for the present instability of the world economy."

They denounced "any grouping of consumer nations with the aim of confrontation," and they condemned any plan or strategy "designed for aggression—economic or military."

They declared their solidarity with nonoil developing countries and declared their support for "exporters of raw materials and other basic commodities in their efforts to obtain an equitable and remunerative price level for their exports."

As a modest olive branch, the OPEC nations said they were prepared to negotiate the conditions for stabilizing oil prices that would "enable the consuming countries to make necessary adjustments to their economies."

But, in exchange, the developed countries would have to support "measures taken by developing countries" directed toward price stabilization of their exports of raw materials and other basic commodities.

What OPEC Wants

The developed countries, OPEC said in the Algiers "solemn declaration," would also have to give financial aid and food to the developing countries, accelerate the transfer of modern technology to them, build "a major portion" of planned or new petrochemical complexes, oil refineries and fertilizer plants in OPEC nations and provide protection against the depreciation of the value of OPEC nations' external financial holdings as well as "assurance of the security of their investments in the developed countries."

The Paris meeting has made plain that OPEC members and third-world countries mean to continue and broaden an attack on the system of liberal international trade, which they believe worked in the past only to the benefit of the rich industrialized countries.

While they recognize that too brutal an attack would backfire, the resource-exporting countries have demonstrated that they are capable of inflicting severe economic damage on the West and the entire world economy.

European leaders recognize only too clearly that the massive increase in oil prices by OPEC has shaken to its foundations the present world economic system. However, they are moving to the position that, if they can only come to satisfactory terms with the oil producers, they can turn the crisis to their advantage by tapping capital flows from the oil states and expanding their markets in those countries.

At the same time they see the diversion of vast flows of funds to the oil-producing states as providing a means of funneling more money to the poor, developing countries and solving one of the most vexatious and dangerous of global problems.

There is recognition in Europe that foreign aid from the industrial states has been inadequate to the task—and is likely to remain inadequate, given the domestic political constraints on aid. Those constraints have been intensified now by huge oil bills and the consequent weakened balance-of-payments positions of virtually all the industrialized countries except West Germany.

But the United States is unwilling to go along with the implied validation of the power of OPEC—and the possibility that it could lead to similar monopolistic extortion from other groups of raw-material producers.

Secretary of State Kissinger's energy policy, emphasizing a high floor price that would cut domestic oil consumption and stimulate production, is designed to break the cartel.

But Mr. Kissinger has been unable to gain support for a high floor price either from the other industrial countries or even from the United States Congress.

Congress wants to make a more direct assault on both OPEC and any OPEC imitators. Congress inserted into the Trade Act of 1974 a clause denying trade preferences to any country that is a member of OPEC or "a party to any other arrangement of foreign countries . . . the effect of which is to withhold supplies of vital commodity resources from international trade or to raise the price of such commodities to an unreasonable level and cause serious disruption of the world economy."

Request From Ford

In his foreign policy address last week, President Ford asked Congress to reconsider this clause. He said it punished two South American "friends" of the United States, Ecuador and Venezuela, as well as other OPEC nations, such as Nigeria and Indonesia, which had not participated in the oil embargo against this country.

Such exclusions, said the President, "seriously complicated our new dialogue with our friends."

However, many European economists feel that both the United States Administration and Congress are barking up the wrong tree if they think that the solution to the threat to world economic stability is a break-up of OPEC and a sharp decline in the external price of oil.

They think the strain on the price now is due almost entirely to the widespread economic slump in Western Europe, the United States and Japan and that recovery—and perhaps a coming boom—will force oil prices higher, unless some progress can be made on price-stabilization agreements.

Many American economists, however, question whether such price-stabilization deals would hold and would prefer the United States and its allies to act now to put maximum pressure on OPEC. Some would do this by fixing quotas against foreign oil, requiring would-be suppliers to compete for "tickets" to sell here. Others, who think they will not work, favor high, discriminatory tariffs that would encourage those nations willing to supply oil on a fair and stable basis.

As the West wrangles indecisively, the OPEC nations bide their time—waiting and hoping for economic recovery that will strengthen the market for oil and their bargaining position.

And the poor, developing countries—despite the damage to their own economies of high-priced oil and shrunken markets in the West, partly due to the impact of the oil crisis—continue to back OPEC.

Ideology may play a part in the poor countries' position, but it also seems to represent a judgment about where power now resides and can be used to fulfill their hopes for extracting more money and resources from the rich, industrial nations.

PART IV

THE HUMAN FACES OF GLOBALIZATION

The expansion of global markets has many consequences that go beyond the dollars-and-cents world of business. Markets connect individuals by exposing them to foreign people, goods, images, inventions, religions, cultures, foods, norms and ideas. These connections both attract us and repel us. They attract precisely because they are new and different, and they repel because they are foreign and appear to challenge what we think we know and what we have been taught to believe. The human face of globalization is therefore both happy *and* sad or fearful, like the ancient Greek masks that symbolize the theatre.

Does globalization mean cultural homogenization? In particular, does globalization mean Americanization? "One World, One Market, One Culture" examines what happens when the globalization blender whirls cultural influences together. These articles show both of the human faces of globalization clearly and also force the reader to confront the ambiguity of their simultaneous display.

An important aspect of the global economy is its relationship to the local. In some respects, globalization makes local identities disappear. Business travelers can be excused for forgetting where they are at times, so much alike have airports, cabs, hotels and conference rooms grown. But the local still exists and even thrives, resisting globalization and even using globalizing forces to strengthen local identity. The articles in "Thinking Global, Acting Local" examine the complex interaction of local and global, implicitly testing the power of each.

We end with a collection of articles that examines the debate over Nike-branded goods and sweatshop labor, a debate that illustrates many important tensions that characterize globalization. On one hand, the global division of labor tends to distance the producers of a good from the final consumer—to "commodify" both consumption and labor. It is easier to be a bargain hunter if you never confront the human beings who make the goods and whose wages and working conditions stand in the balance. In this respect, globalization makes it easier for us to exploit people. On the other hand, globalization creates opportunities to tell the story of these workers through global media and telecommunications networks, exposing us to the consequences of our actions—both bad *and* good—more intensely than we could ever imagine. Paradoxically, globalization simultaneously hides the face of the woman who sewed your shirt and broadcasts it to a hundred million computer screens.

These articles suggest that globalization strands us in an ambiguous moral geography. The wages and conditions of a shoe-worker in Vietnam are much worse than those of workers in the United States, but they may be the typical conditions in the third world. Is sweatshop labor exploitation or opportunity? Which set of norms applies when North trades with South?

ONE WORLD, ONE MARKET, ONE CULTURE?

September 2, 1973

A NEW FORM OF 'IMPERIALISM'

Should Companies Export Ethics?

By JACK N. BEHRMAN

Many countries have felt their independence threatened by political and economic imperialism, and more recently by the spread of the multinational enterprise.

Added to this is a new penetration—ethical imperialism—a direct descendant of manifest destiny, for it avows that nations with power and the demonstrable success of higher living standards also know what is right.

Now as special interests in the United States—representing both stockholders and consumers—demand social, ethical, even religious, changes in companies operating overseas, it is likely that more host countries will be antagonized.

Whether we're tampering with the family structure of French Canadians, the racial laws of South Africa or the leisurely lunch-at-home tradition in Italy, the influence of the company is being extended into new, controversial spheres.

Competitively, the subject is crucial. For the multinational companies based in such countries as West Germany, Japan and Italy, tend not to get into these areas. It's the Americans who tend to try to change things, with their concentration on the almighty dollar gilded with wide-eyed idealism.

Richard C. Gerstenberg, chairman of General Motors, under pressure from some stockholders and black groups, says he wants to see for himself in South Africa "that General Motors is doing everything it can to hasten the day of equality."

The First National City Bank has declared that the social responsibility of a company will be "a new criterion for investment."

And the emphasis in annual reports on socially responsible activities has increased. Given the international activities of these companies, can social responsibility stop at the water's edge?

Several recent cases have demonstrated that United States shareholders and interest-groups consider that these corporations have a responsibility to apply United States ethical standards wherever they may be operating in the world. Polaroid, International Business Machines, Ford and others have been charged with perpetuating apartheid in South Africa by simply following the country's laws.

They have been urged either to break those patterns by not discriminating or to close their facilities. After some soul-searching and on-the-spot investigation, several of the companies have moved quietly to improve the opportunities and pay scales for blacks, concluding that to pull out would be harmful to the workers.

An overt breaking of the customs and laws would likely result in the companies' expulsion, but covert changes have not yet brought down the wrath of the Government or of white citizens.

Yet, the ethical pressures proliferate from other sources. This year the World Council of Churches sold stock worth $1.5-million, representing holdings in 650 companies in the United States, Britain, the Netherlands and Switzerland that have investments in South Africa.

The racial problem is one among the sensitive ethical issues faced by multinational enterprises.

Typically, pressure has arisen in Canada for American-owned affiliates to contribute to educational institutions and community programs in the same way that the parent concern does in the United States. But often the final decisions are made by the parent company, and it is frequently reluctant to establish a pattern of corporate giving that is not accepted by Canadian-owned companies.

Increasing domestic concern over consumer protection has brought pressure for higher ethical standards in product quality and tightened regulations, such as the disclosure on cigarette packs of potential dangers of use. Concerns range from safety in toys and children's clothes to use of radio-active materials in medicine.

American companies, however, seldom give the same warnings or take the same precautions in other countries, where it is not required by local laws or regulations. Many proponents of greater "corporate responsibility in the United States inveigh against this use of situational ethics, and individuals in other countries join in questioning the ethics of a company's selling items that the Food and Drug Administration of the United States has not yet approved.

Attempts to implement the simple prescription "equal pay for equal work" embroils international companies, international unions, host communities and governments in multi-faceted negotiations.

For example, the request by Canadian unions in the auto industry, which is predominantly owned by Detroit companies, for equal pay with American workers was resolved by adopting a cost-of-living differential, which permitted a lower rate of pay in Canada.

Application of the principle would have raised costs to differentially high levels in Canada and hurt sales. Salaries and fringe benefits for engineers and scientists in foreign countries commensurate with those received by engineers and scientists in the United States would break the pattern of wages and in the foreign countries and raise tensions with competing companies. But not to make them equal would raise tensions within the international company.

In the same field of employe treatment, is it ethical for an American international company to impede the formation of labor unions in a foreign country, although such action is consistent with the behavior of locally owned concerns?

Alternatively, should it promote the formation of unions oriented toward collective bargaining, where the traditional objectives of unions are political?

Environmental pollution is another thorny issue. Ford, for example, has been permitted to export to Canada some 1973 autos that have not met environmental specifications domestically.

As Ambassador Charles Malik of Lebanon wrote in 1966:

"The question then becomes: Is the developing country morally prepared to pay the social and cultural price for the coveted development? Is it prepared to transform the family, free women, revolutionize its concept of the child, do away with class distinctions, liberate serfs, promote a free middle class, reform its religion, dignify labor as the noblest thing in the world?

"Confronted with such a price, especially if the full implications are clear, it may balk and say: To hell with all development? It will then begin talking about the value of its culture, about its not wanting to barter away its soul and its distinctive national imprint. But what if imprint, culture and soul are incompatible with development?"

Finally, there is a much larger problem involving the ethics of consumption patterns. There are, for example, considerable ethical connotations in an automobile-oriented economy. The connotations involve concepts of individual freedom implications of personal power, dispersion of the community, isolation from the crowd and the form of pleasure to be enjoyed.

Similarly, decisions to produce goods for upper or middle classes rather than for the poor are ethical judgments. Does development mean a rise in average incomes, despite the distribution of incomes, or does it mean an increase in the standards of living of the poor?

Such issues cannot be avoided. They must be pondered now by a socially responsible business community.

For it is unlikely that Americans would be successful in exporting their ethics piecemeal to different countries in specific situations. Any such attempt would be seen as a new form of imperialism.

Americans can and should demonstrate to others their belief in ethical concepts of freedom with responsibility, opportunity for all to be creative and useful and of the opportunity to belong to and be a useful part of a group—that is, "liberty, equality and fraternity."

But it is difficult to export what we do not have ourselves. Our first task, then, is to give proof of how an ethically based economic system works. Having done so, it is likely that others will import and adapt it as suitable, thereby removing completely the stigma of imperialism.

Professor Behrman teaches international business at the Graduate School of Business Administration of the University of North Carolina, Chapel Hill, and is a former assistant secretary of commerce for domestic and international business.

* * *

September 27, 1987

TOKYO TACOS: THE JAPANESE LOOK TO WEST

By NICHOLAS D. KRISTOF
Special to the New York Times

TOKYO, Sept. 22—Japan's knowledge of the West has come a long way since one of its first visitors to the United States reported in 1860 that all single American women were called Joan, "while married ladies are distinguished by the suffix 'sons,' such as 'Joansons.' "

These days the Japanese are more enthusiastic than ever about learning about the West, and the quality of the information is improving. Partly because of Tokyo's rise as an international financial center, partly because of the emergence of Japanese companies as multinational corporations, Japan is self-consciously trying to become cosmopolitan.

The buzzword in Tokyo is "kokusaika," or internationalization. In pursuit of that goal, students, secretaries and executives more than ever are studying English, traveling abroad, listening to Michael Jackson, dating foreigners and eating pasta.

"English is the international language," said Akira Nambara, research director of the Bank of Japan, in explaining the enthusiasm for learning the language. "Or, I should say, broken English is the international language."

More Foreign Companies

Of course, Japanese have studied foreigners and foreign languages since Commodore Matthew C. Perry opened Japan with his gunboats in 1853. Golf, baseball and rock music have been popular for decades.

But kokusaika has surged in the last few years, partly because of the expansion of Japanese corporations overseas and the arrival of more and more foreign corporations in Tokyo.

"It's kind of a prerequisite for Japanese to go abroad, to learn foreign languages, culture, customs," said Hiromitsu Takemi, deputy manager of the Japan Development Bank.

C. Itoh & Company attracted attention this summer when it became the first large Japanese corporation to appoint a foreigner—in its case, a Korean-American—to its board of directors.

Call for U.S. College Graduates

Japan Air Lines announced this month that it would hire 120 foreign flight attendants. The Sumitomo Life Insurance Company has a young Japanese-speaking American working with its Japanese university graduates.

And Japanese who were spurned even a few years ago because they attended American universities now find employers clamoring for them.

Yet kokusaika is not all work and no play. Ethnic restaurants are the latest rage in Tokyo; Mexican, Indonesian, Indian and Italian restaurants are flowering around the city. So are pool halls and pizza parlors.

It is also becoming more common for Japanese to date foreigners, although families still do not always approve. An

American banker living in Tokyo, a single man, says he knows of only two ways for an American man to end a romance with a Japanese woman.

The first, he says, is for the man to explain coldly that the relationship is finished and that he is flying home for good the next day. The second is to ask to meet the woman's family.

Japanese Marrying Non-Japanese

That might not work these days when there are more mixed marriages. The proportion of Japanese men marrying non-Japanese women has soared nearly fourfold over the last decade, so that today a bit more than one percent of Japanese men marry non-Japanese women. Among Japanese women, six-tenths of one percent marry non-Japanese, double the figure a decade ago.

The figures, particularly for men, are bloated by the practice of importing Filipino wives for Japanese men, and by marriages to ethnic Koreans who have lived in Japan all their lives but are still regarded as aliens.

More Japanese are also living and traveling abroad. The strength of the yen makes it increasingly expensive for foreigners to come here, but the number of foreigners visiting Japan nevertheless rose 4.5 percent in the first half of 1987, to 1.02 million.

Foreign travel, on the other hand, is cheaper for the Japanese. A record 3.08 million Japanese traveled abroad in the first half of 1987, up 22 percent from the same period last year.

Majority Honeymoon Abroad

Eighty-four percent of Japanese couples now take their honeymoons abroad, according to a study this summer by Sanwa Bank. The most popular destination is Hawaii.

English has been widely studied in Japan for decades, but the last few years have seen a special burst of enthusiasm. Large concerns like Nissho Iwai Corporation offer English lessons to employees each morning before work begins.

Some 1,300 English language schools operate in Tokyo alone, and the number is rising by at least 100 a year. It is estimated that 10 percent of the population now studies English.

While the Japanese have picked up foreign words for more than a century, more are now coming from the business world. After returning home from the offisu (office), a salari-man (salary earner) may hang his sutsu (suit) on a hanga (hanger), and read a besto-sera (best-seller) or perhaps a reporto (report) by an economisto (economist).

Japanese Still Sheltered

Yet for all the foreign words and pasta and vacations, many people say that kokusaika is as shallow as it is broad. More Japanese may travel abroad, but often they are sheltered in group tours. Parents may let their daughter listen to Michael Jackson, but they would be aghast if she dated him.

Ki-seang Cheang, an ethnic Korean who grew up in Japan and teaches German at a local university, said that kokusaika has not fostered more hospitality in Japan toward its Korean minority, or interest in neighboring Asian countries.

The economy, he said, is becoming international far more quickly than the society.

* * *

April 16, 1988

AMERICAN 'COCA-COLONIZATION' OF ASIA

VIDEO NIGHT IN KATHMANDU: And Other Reports from the Not-So-Far East
By Pico Iyer
376 pages. Alfred A. Knopf. $19.95.

By MICHIKO KAKUTANI

Once upon a time, travel writers packed their bags and turned their backs on civilization, journeying like Evelyn Waugh "to the Tropics and the Arctic, with the belief that barbarism was a dodo to be stalked with a pinch of salt." Far and wide they traveled, looking for sights that might jar them not with the shock of recognition but with the shock of the unknown, and less than half a century ago they were still able to discover what Waugh called "the moon landscape"—countries and peoples so foreign that they confirmed the traveler's own anomalous identity, places that attested to the prodigal variety of the world.

Today, of course, the world seems a much smaller place, its nations linked not only by a network of political and economic alliances but also by a shared nervous system of cultural axioms and phenomena, most of them American in origin. Just how has "America's pop-cultural imperialism spread through the world's most ancient civilizations"? That was the question the journalist Pico Iyer asked himself as he set off in search of signs of American influence abroad. "I wanted to see," he writes in "Video Night in Kathmandu," "what kind of resistance had been put up against the Coca-Colonizing forces and what kind of counter-strategies were planned. And I hoped to discover which Americas got through to the other side of the world, and which got lost in translation."

As an American resident, a British subject and an Indian citizen, Mr. Iyer was already familiar with what he calls "cross-cultural anomalies and the mixed feelings of exile," and in 1985 he headed for Asia, convinced that it represented "the fiercest and most complex" front in the cultural battle between East and West. He spent seven months crisscrossing that continent, searching for "the brand-new kinds of exotica thrown up by our synthetic age," and his travels have yielded a meticulously observed and reported book—a magical mystery tour through the brave new world of Asia. He takes us to Burma, "the dotty eccentric of Asia, the queer maiden aunt who lives alone and whom the maid has forgotten to visit," and to Hong Kong, "the last treasure left in the oyster that was the Old Boys' world." He shows us the bars of Bangkok, where call girls wear numbers for their customers' convenience, and movie lots in Bombay, where the emphasis is on making everything "bigger, broader, louder."

In the course of his travels, Mr. Iyer repeatedly stumbles across the sort of cultural dislocations usually associated with world fairs. There are Mexican cafes and fern bars in Bali, health-food joints dispensing "Reality Soup" in Nepal. The theme song from "Bonanza" blares from speakers at a club in Manila, while "Augie Doggie and Doggie Daddy" plays on the television in Rangoon. Other American imports seem even more incongruous. Within 10 days of its Beijing opening, he reports, the Rambo movie "First Blood" sold a million tickets. In India, five remakes of the movie have been put into production. In Thailand, 15-foot cutouts of the American vigilante tower over local theaters.

In some cases, the rush to imitate the West has comical results: a shiny new hotel in China, for instance, rises on a windy, isolated site, three hours from the nearest town; tourists are instructed to catch a bus at 5:30 in the afternoon to catch a plane the next morning. In other cases, the consequences are more sobering. In Bali, Mr. Iyer finds, tourists have turned the quiet fishing village of Kuta into a huge, gaudy singles' bar; and in Tibet, "countercultural imperialists" have built facsimile Greenwich Village pads, 1960's style.

As Mr. Iyer sees it, there's a distinct difference between the British legacy in the Far East and the American: "If the American Empire had to do with currency, immediacy, annihilation of the past, its British counterpart had been founded on continuity, tradition, a reverence, and remembrance, of things past." "India seemed to have gained, as a colony," he writes, "a sense of ritual solemnity, a feeling for the language of Shakespeare, a polished civil service, a belief in democracy and a sonorous faith in upstanding legal or educational institutions." In contrast, he adds, "the most conspicuous institutions that America had bequeathed to the Philippines seemed to be the disco, the variety show and the beauty pageant. Perhaps the ideas and ideals of America had proved too weighty to be shipped across the seas, or perhaps they were just too fragile."

Some of Mr. Iyer's observations—unavoidably, perhaps—have a ring of familiarity: the disjunction between the Marcoses' lavish life style and the desperate poverty of the Philippines; or the love of conformity and order that exists in Japan. For the most part, however, "Video Night in Kathmandu" surprises as it informs. Pushing aside such easy formulations as "the First World is corrupting the Third" or the third world "is hustling the First," Mr. Iyer shrewdly observes that "often what we call corruption" other countries are "inclined to call progress or profit."

"The Westerner is drawn to the tradition of the Easterner, and almost covets his knowledge of suffering," he writes, "but what attracts the Easterner to the West is exactly the opposite—his future, and his freedom from all hardship. After a while, each starts to become more like the other, and somewhat less like the person the other seeks. The New Yorker disappoints the locals by turning into a barefoot ascetic dressed in bangles and beads, while the Nepali peasant frustrates his foreign supplicants by turning out to be a traveling salesman in Levi's and Madonna T-shirt. Soon, neither is quite the person he was, or the one the other wanted. The upshot is confusion."

* * *

July 31, 1988

KENYAN ARTISTS STRUGGLE TO MAINTAIN ARTISTIC INTEGRITY AGAINST THE LURE OF TOURIST MONEY

By SHEILA RULE

NAIROBI, Kenya—Beyond the competitive rush of the crowded city center, creativity flourishes in a place of quiet, tree-shaded harmony.

Sculptures, paintings and other art works seem to be in close rapport with the wooded surroundings. The place is the Paa ya Paa art gallery and workshop, the inspiration of Elimo Njau. Mr. Njau is a Kenyan artist who for more than 20 years has been struggling to help other East African artists retain their creative souls amid the economic pressures to design for Western markets and a Western esthetic.

Paa ya Paa is a Swahili phrase that, roughly translated, means "the antelope rises." It is a reference to the ubiquitous animal carvings that look as if they were produced on an assembly line. African craftsmen chisel them out by the dozens and sell them for a few dollars to tourist shops, which sell them for five or ten times that.

In the name of the gallery, Paa ya Paa, Mr. Njau is saying that artistic creativity can transcend the commercialism of that antelope art, that it should rise above the race for profit.

"Many of us move lock, stock and barrel to the Western style," said Mr. Njau. "We uproot ourselves and our creativity becomes just a few spices on the white man's plate. But art should be a way of life, enriching us, nourishing us in body and spirit, and growing from the African soil of which we are a part."

Mr. Njau's battle against the forces of compromise highlights the dilemma that many serious artists here face. Do they forsake their identity, bow to Western tastes and pocket the money? Or do they resist the temptation and, as in the case of Mr. Njau, struggle to survive?

Traditional African art of the kind that influenced Picasso was rarely art for art's or money's sake but, instead, served social functions. Ornately decorated shields were carried by warriors into battle. Finely sculptured walking sticks denoted power and position. Statues were often repositories for ancestors' spirits. Masks and fetishes were tributes to the gods, who were considered the forces of life.

In today's Africa, art critics, apparently reluctant to relinquish a social role for art, have suggested that artists can also contribute to the development of Kenya—relay a message about the history, needs and aspirations of their people, touch the conscience, question the status quo or inspire change. Art might depict the plight of Nairobi's so-called parking boys, children who forage for food in the city's garbage bins. It could celebrate the crucial role of women in Kenya's past and present. For example, in the forest bordering Mr. Njau's gallery, a sculpture carved from trees does address the widespread problem of corruption. The piece depicts a security guard looking at a woman who is dragging cloth that she stole from a market. The question posed is whether the guard will arrest her or ask for a bribe.

But the delicate political and economic environment, overseen by authorities who brook no criticism, has tended to mute or alienate many artists. And the local market, dominated by tourists and expatriates, often mitigates against this type of social expression—not to mention any sort of personal vision.

Added to this is the legacy of the colonial period, which in many ways attempted to dismantle indigenous culture. The result is that some Africans, believing that whatever is foreign or "white" is intrinsically superior, reject the richness and beauty of their heritage.

"The British really did a cultural whitewash in Kenya," said Margaretta wa Gacheru, a writer and art critic. "Today most of the art displayed in Kenya is by Westerners who know how to market. There are two kinds of African artist here. There are those who create beautiful pictures and decorative art and figure out what the market wants. They become professional artists and are able to eat. People who want to use art to say something more about the pressing issues at hand, who want to be the conscience of the nation and decolonize the mind, are quiet with empty tummies, or they have left art, or they have died."

Yet many artists have struggled to find a way of reconciling the goals of survival and soulful expression. The lucky ones, some of whom go on to win international recognition, find local galleries that will market their work and still allow them to express themselves freely. Others lead dual lives. They paint murals of landscapes and giraffes for money and then produce what they want for a much smaller market, sometimes only for their own personal collections. Others sell insurance, teach school or work in different fields by day but, as night settles, sketch or mold their artistic interpretations of life.

"Real reconciliation will only come when the African powers that be acknowledge and encourage the role of the African artist in development," Mrs. wa Gacheru said. "They have to give the space, the sponsorship that patrons give to Western artists.

"Elimo Njau is the best illustration of how painful it is when you are committed to your soul and expressing what you feel about life. He has so much strength, but financially he is not making ends meet very well."

But Mr. Njau's spirit endures. He prefers to call Paa ya Paa a "temple of culture" rather than a gallery, viewing it as a setting where artists can reflect on their craft and "find inspiration in their meditation." He believes that he is succeeding in providing an environment for artistic development in Kenya, and that his difficulties help "stimulate the creative energies necessary to rise above them."

"You can be reduced to the lowest in terms of having no money or having nothing," said Mr. Njau. "But you are still alive and have limbs of creativity. Through these limbs of creativity, you can be born anew."

* * *

November 18, 1988

BUILDING A GLOBAL SUPERMARKET

By STEVEN GREENHOUSE
Special to the New York Times

PARIS, Nov. 17—When Hamish Maxwell, the chairman of Philip Morris, was orchestrating his company's takeover of Kraft Inc., he said one of the rationales for the huge merger was to create a colossus that could sell Cheez Whiz and Jell-O around the globe.

The $13 billion takeover is the latest and most ambitious move in the food industry's drive to build the global supermarket—to sell the same products in grocery stores, bodegas, marches and supermercados.

Coca-Cola—widely considered the most popular product in the world—Kellogg's Corn Flakes and Nescafe are already sold from Alabama to Zambia, and companies like Quaker Oats and Pillsbury and Philip Morris's Kraft and General Foods units hope to do the same with their own products.

A Matter of Taste

But food is a matter of taste and tradition, which makes the marketing of brands across national borders an unpredictable business.

Many marketing executives say the trend toward the global supermarket has been fostered by—and is in turn fostering—a growing similarity in consumer tastes around the world. Such a convergence, business theorists say, is an inevitable result of the cross-fertilization of cultures, with people traveling more than ever and seeing many of the same movies and television serials.

Yet food marketers are discovering that even with some convergence in consumer tastes, the differences, at least in food, continue to outweigh the similarities. Moussaka lovers in Greece might not run to buy Kraft's Philadelphia Cream Cheese while American grits lovers might shun microwaveable chicken tikka dinners from India.

"The globalization of consumer goods markets has become quite trendy," said Ian Davis, a marketing expert in the London office of McKinsey & Company, the management consulting firm. "Still, it is difficult to take a product that is successful in one country and transpose it into another."

Economies Sought

Industry analysts say food companies are starting to copy car, computer and consumer electronics manufacturers in developing a global strategy because they recognize that larger sales mean economies of scale in output and distribution. In addition, food companies see that operating globally can enable them to spend more on research and development to stay ahead of the competition.

And like others before them, food companies find that the lessons they learn in marketing products in one country can help them in others. "There are marketing advantages and manufacturing advantages in taking proven concepts, adapting them here and there and then repeating that success in several countries," said Kamran Kashani, a marketing professor at the Imede business school in Lausanne, Switzerland.

Even so, it is remarkably difficult to discern any general rules for success in foreign markets. Industry executives are often puzzled why some products, like Coke, delight foreign consumers while others fail. Why, they ask, did Perrier, the French mineral water, become a sensation in the United States, while McVitie's Digestive Biscuits, Britain's most popular cookie, has not won the taste buds of Americans?

New Product Ideas

"On the whole, the reason that companies have been successful in going global—these would include Coca-Cola, Marlboro cigarettes, McDonald's hamburgers, Sony Walkmans—is that they have tended to take a new product idea rather than an old idea," said Mr. Davis of McKinsey.

"Launching a soup or a biscuit or a cheese globally is not a new product idea and runs into established competition," Mr. Davis continued. "McDonald's was a new way of retailing food. Coke had a new concept in soft drinks."

But sometimes foreign markets do not embrace "new" ideas either. Campbell's Soup stumbled in Brazil because canned soup—new to Brazil—was found distasteful. When some American companies introduced soft cookies in Britain, they failed to catch on because the British much prefer hard cookies.

Even highly successful global marketers often fall before local competition. Nestle S.A., the Swiss giant, failed to grab a large chunk of Japan's chocolate market because of entrenched domestic competitors. Similarly, France's Chambourcy yogurt, popular in several foreign markets, encountered so much competition in test-marketing in the United States that it withdrew.

Catering to Local Tastes

The companies that are most sensitive to local tastes seem to do best around the globe. Nestle, for instance, produces more than 200 blends of Nescafe to cater to the preferences of different markets. The blends result from extensive taste testing. To please the French, the special sauce on McDonald's Big Macs served in Paris is less sugary and has more of a mustard taste than the special sauce served in the United States.

Sometimes, success is more a matter of image than taste. Heineken has decided that the best way to sell its beer in the United States is as a premium brand, cashing in on the cachet of imported beer. To crack the British market, however, it decided that the most effective approach was to sell itself as a proletarian beer, and it has been successful.

"The great global marketers are really more talented at local marketing than global marketing," said James Schroer, a consumer goods expert with Booz Allen & Hamilton, the management consulting firm.

Europeans Found Ahead

Notwithstanding the success of Coca-Cola and McDonald's, industry analysts say that European consumer goods companies, like Unilever and Nestle, are generally ahead of American companies in going global. French and German food concerns have long sold their products in Spain and Italy—and European companies are pushing harder than ever to expand across borders to take advantage of the economies that a barrier-free Europe will bring at the end of 1992.

The Europeans' experience in global marketing could give Philip Morris problems as it seeks to expand its Kraft and General Food lines abroad. Nevertheless, industry analysts say that the combined might of the two units might give them not only more economies of scale, but also more power to gain entrance into supermarkets from Spain to Singapore.

"Many non-American firms were forced to break out of their small home markets, and many thought it was essential to get into the large American market," said Kenneth Simmonds, a marketing professor at the London Business School. "American companies have often just stayed in the large American market and have not learned how to go into other markets."

Industry analysts say it is not surprising that many American marketers, accustomed to selling a uniform product to the nation's 240 million people, might not see the importance of tailoring their marketing strategies and products to the tastes of other lands.

"The attitude of U.S. companies would be to act in Senegal or Chile as if those countries were an extension of their home market, whereas Nestle, with its small home base in Switzerland, recognizes it has to adapt the product to the tastes of other countries," said James Biggar, president of Nestle Enterprises, one of the Swiss company's two main American operating units.

The Addition of an Egg

Betty Crocker cake mixes offer an example of adapting to local tastes. They flopped in Britain because the English balked at baking a cake without having to even add eggs— they were dismayed that their contribution was so minimal. But when the cake mixes were reformulated to require the addition of an egg, Britain embraced Betty Crocker.

Food executives and business school professors say there is a conflict between the impulse to adapt products to local markets as a way of expanding sales and the desire to standardize products as much as possible to achieve longer production runs and greater economies of scale.

Ted Levitt, editor of the Harvard Business Review and a leading spokesman for the importance of global marketing, sees what he calls a "pluralization of consumption," in which people's tastes are moving closer together in some areas at the same time that regional preferences remain strong.

David Weinstein, a marketing professor at the Insead Business School in Fontainebleau, outside Paris, predicts that tastes around the world will ultimately converge even more, which will allow manufacturers to further standardize their products. This development, he said, would result in part from consumer goods companies marketing their products more and more on an international basis and from increased travel and improved telecommunications.

"If the world continues to converge, eventually you might even get tastes that are similar," Professor Weinstein said. "People used to say that the French would never eat McDonald's hamburgers. Now they appreciate them in the same way as Americans do. So tastes do change across cultures."

* * *

May 3, 1992

WORLD LEADERS: MICKEY, ET AL

By TODD GITLIN

A few years ago, an amazed Japanese girl asked an American visitor, "Is there really a Disneyland in America?"

That should be music to the mouse ears of Euro Disneyland's management, beleaguered by charges that they are defiling the Frenchness of France. Ah, to convince the French that Mickey and Donald belong to Marne-la-Vallee as they do to Anaheim, Orlando and Tokyo. Sensitive to the charge that Euro Disneyland amounts to what the theater director Ariane Mnouchkine, in a widely quoted assessment, called a "cultural Chernobyl," the company tried for months to persuade Europeans that, in the words of a Disney spokesman, "It's not America, it's Disney."

On opening day last month, Disney's chairman Michael Eisner stressed, like a guest too eager to please, that the company had repackaged original European characters: the French Cinderella, the Italian Pinocchio, the German Snow White. More truculently, a Euro Disneyland spokeswoman said: "Who are these Frenchmen, anyway? We offer them the dream of a lifetime and lots of jobs. They treat us like invaders."

Beyond the cultural battle of the moment, both sides can agree on one thing: American popular culture is the closest approximation there is today to a global lingua franca, drawing urban classes in most nations into a federated culture zone. In one month, "Terminator 2" sold five million tickets in France. It is possible to see a Donald Duck decal on a wall in a village in the middle of a Greek island, hear country-western music on the radio in Ireland, buy a Woody Guthrie tribute tape at a gas station in Norway. Charles Bronson, Clint Eastwood, Arnold Schwarzenegger and Coke are, thanks to the multinational corporation, the icons of a global semiculture, helping to integrate at least the plugged-in classes of most nations into a single cultural zone. Entertainment is America's largest export—after weaponry. The question is what this means.

Protectionists, such as the French Minister of Culture, Jack Lang, fear that America's marketing clout will succeed in paving over the profuse variety of global cultures. Once it is overstated, the fear is easy to sweep aside. Obviously, American popular culture does not erase all the vernacular alternatives. The new semiculture coexists with local cultures more than it replaces them.

As the Norwegian media researcher Helge Ronning suggests, it is plausible to suppose that global, largely American popular culture is becoming everyone's second culture. It doesn't necessarily supplant local traditions, but it does activate a certain cultural bilingualism. People from Australia to Zimbabwe acquire a second cultural membership, switching with ease from local news to the American Oscar ceremonies, and back again.

As his Americophile enemies love to point out, even Jack Lang recently conferred France's highest honor in the arts on Sylvester Stallone.

Why were "Dallas" and "Dynasty," at their peaks, on television in 100 countries—popular in all but Japan and Brazil? Indisputably, economies of scale are one reason. The United States can simply undersell other suppliers. A programmer in Copenhagen can lease an hourlong episode of "Dallas" or "Miami Vice" for under $5,000, less than the cost of producing one original minute of Danish drama. American formulas have also helped establish the conventions—the slickness, the melodrama, the cuteness, the glibness, the uplift—that imitators around the world aim to match.

There is evidence that if Europeans had a choice, they would prefer programs produced in their own countries. But in the end, no one is forcing the Danes to watch American shows. In "Dallas" and its ilk they must be attracted by a range of pleasures comparable to those Americans find.

Scholars have demonstrated that when people watch the same program they see the program they are disposed to see. For instance, studies of "All in the Family" in Canada and Holland showed that the audience was divided between those who thought Edith, Gloria and Meathead won the arguments and those who believed that Archie regularly gave them their comeuppance.

Likewise, Tamar Liebes and Elihu Katz, sociologists at the Hebrew University in Jerusalem, have shown that Israeli families of Russian, American and Moroccan provenance interpret the same "Dallas" episode in different ways and like it for different reasons. Indeed, the commercial strength of many American television programs in particular lies in their capacity to speak out of several sides of their mouths at once, enabling, to cite an example, teen-age girls to watch "Beverly Hills 90210" for both its good-looking guys and its "relevance."

Another explanation for the success of American culture is that it has been driven by a single overriding purpose: to entertain. For this reason, it is easy to see why American series have outdone British programs developed in large part for cultural elevation and erstwhile Soviet programs developed for didactic purposes. As a Euro Disneyland official protested last fall, "We're not trying to sell anything but fun, entertainment."

Moreover, as the British sociologist Jeremy Tunstall has observed, by the time it leaves our shores, much American popular culture has been pre-tested in a large internal market that incorporates elements of foreign tastes. America's music derives from the rhythms and songs of African slaves and their descendants. Its comic sense comes principally from English settlers, East European Jews and, again, blacks. By the time commercial work comes out of Hollywood or New York or Nashville, it has already been certified as widely marketable to a diverse population. No competitor from the monocultures of Europe and Asia can make this claim.

In popular music, where production costs are low, multinationals, ever thirsting for novelty, frequently import and reprocess styles from abroad, replenishing the stock of American music and giving something back to the global mix.

First the Bad News: Cultural Fast Food Goes Global

Frequently in movies and television, global semi-Americanization has the effect of withering much of the foreign competition. Hollywood's principal style has narrowed the cultural repertory of film makers and audiences alike. America's so-called high production values, often mechanistic and mindless, have become the fast food of global culture.

The pressure to make films exportable further degrades them into entertainment machines. Many of today's major films are made to open in Paris and Peoria simultaneously and to sell on videocassette everywhere else a few weeks later. "Terminator 2," with its Austrian-born star, its French co-financing and its Spanish-language gags, might as well come from the moon or the Cayman Islands.

The English language, with its vast ready-made market on every continent, boosts the export prospects of these hybrids. Monosyllables help, too, because they are easily grasped and dubbed. To appeal to crowds from Copenhagen to Calcutta, "Terminator 2" and other mainstream Hollywood movies today use words as captions for pictures, which in turn are stripped to their most banal common denominators. Not only is American politics dragged down to the level of "Make my day," "Read my lips" and "Hasta la vista, baby," but many literate young screenwriters in America and elsewhere aspire to write at the primitive level of Steven Spielberg and George Lucas.

Melodrama and comics have long been American specialties, of course, and one could argue that crude cartoon style is America's most potent export. Euro Disneyland may not be all-American—there are European grace notes—but it is Disney, with its squeaky-clean appeal to innocence. Last summer, the author and illustrator Maurice Sendak protested that Disney's cartoon version of Hans Christian Andersen's "Little Mermaid" was "a total contradiction of the original . . . the tale is about sacrifice. The little mermaid doesn't even get what she wants . . . that's a hard lesson. This movie is about getting married, having cupcakes for bras and going to live in White Plains somewhere."

The flip side of Disney cuteness is Hollywood brutishness. In the name of improving the balance of payments, Hollywood sends its most primitive goods abroad. The "Diehard" and "Lethal Weapon" movies reportedly brought in $1 billion worldwide. The glitzier the technology, the more American movies acquire a reputation for speed, savagery, ethical emptiness and smug surface. Fueled partly by the promise of global markets, the industry is in the grip of inner forces whose cynicism is so deep as to defy parody. Driven by economic incentives and a perverse pride in what they consider craft, movie makers concentrate on new ways to savage and kill. Once hooked, viewers everywhere require steadily increasing doses.

The predilections of financiers, directors, writers, makeup artists and teen-age audiences come together to ratchet up the frequency and magnitude of violence. Directors draw pride from their ability to surpass the previous round of abominations. Studio bosses, bankers and distributors see no reason to temper the cycle as long as it pays off. Everyone takes the loop of least resistance, doing more of what they already know how to do.

The secret of the global box-office success of these films is that they evoke a forbidden pleasure in the victim's pain and paranoia. The viewer is not drawn to identify with the victim, who is barely on the screen long enough to warrant a second thought. Instead, there is a delirium of delight in the perpetrator's ability to get away with murder. Freedom becomes another word for no one left to kill.

In the movies, Gresham's law, that most relentless of free-market principles, comes into play. Primitive entertainment drives out the local and complicated, which don't travel well. Local film industries usually cannot compete with Hollywood, much as they may try. Producers in central Europe are in a state of collapse. Small countries like Norway and Switzerland, which make a handful of films a year, drown in American movies, and young film makers in Europe and the third world find it hard to make careers amid the pressure of American imports.

Indeed, the ascendancy of Hollywood exports, along with most Americans' dislike of foreign films and television shows (Americans are allergic to subtitles, and barely 1 percent of American prime-time television comes from abroad), helps explain why the great European film-making generation of Bergman, Fellini, Antonioni, Godard, Truffaut, Rohmer and Resnais seems largely barren of successors.

As for Hollywood importing foreigners to make its movies, this does not represent so much an openness to foreign styles as the capacity to buy film makers into submission. The usual American mode is to take promising film makers from around the world and process them into banality. The Hollywood-financed work of the Australian Fred Schepisi ("A Cry in the Dark") and the Indian Mira Nair ("Mississippi Masala") is the exception. Closer to the rule, unfortunately, is the more-Hollywood-than-Hollywood Americanization of film makers like the Dutch director Paul Verhoeven ("Total Recall," "Basic Instinct") and directors with excellent credits abroad, like the New Zealander Roger Donaldson ("White Sands"), the Englishman Roland Joffe ("City of Joy") and the Australian Peter Weir ("Green Card").

Now the Good News: We're Not So Bad After All

Fortunately, American entertainment has another side. About 10 years ago, a Hungarian media researcher, asked what were the most popular shows on Hungarian television, answered "Kojak" and "The Streets of San Francisco," because Hungarians had good reason to appreciate, even love, the casual, approachable American cops.

Five years ago, with much fanfare, a galaxy of rock stars including Michael Jackson and Bruce Springsteen recorded "We Are the World." Hip critics said it was arrogant and sentimental. Then a multicolored group of South African protesters marched into an all-white neighborhood singing "We Are the World."

Two years ago, the American historian Paul Buhle, visiting East Berlin just after the wall came down, was told by a student: "Last night I dreamed of Route 66." The route she dreamed of, of course, was the one immortalized on the television series of the early 60's.

A year ago, according to an account in The Observer of London, several Serbian students arrested by the Belgrade riot police after an opposition rally were beaten with truncheons, fists and walkie-talkies, "then forced to stand with their hands up against a wall for the next four hours. When anyone dropped their hands, they were kicked in the knees. Then the policemen forced them to stand on tiptoe. Students who disobeyed were beaten. The tiptoe torture was followed by a mockery of a trial. When one student asked for a defense lawyer, he was told: 'You have been watching too many American films!' "

It's all American pop culture: the coupling of irreverence and brutality; intimations of freedom alongside the worship of power; the exaltation of the proverbial little guy alongside technological elephantiasis; the love of the road alongside the degradation of dialogue; the lyrical spunk of R.E.M. alongside the racket of Megadeth. This curious compound will continue to flow into the world for worse, and for better. It will invite immigration, emulation, amusement and revulsion.

Meanwhile, outside our vision, Mexican and Brazilian tele-novelas, Hong Kong kung fu, Finnish-English comedy, Senegalese drama, Polish-French existentialism and the world's other currents swirl into the leftover niches. No other super culture has the capital, organization and ambition to break the world into interchangeable parts. Americans may not feel the need to know what the rest of the world is imagining, but we would do well to open our eyes and see what's happening outside our theme park.

Todd Gitlin, a professor of sociology at the University of California in Berkeley, is author of "Inside Prime Time" and the forthcoming novel "The Murder of Albert Einstein." This article is adapted from an essay written for an American Enterprise Institute conference in March.

*   *   *

January 3, 1994

GILLETTE'S WORLD VIEW: ONE BLADE FITS ALL

By LOUIS UCHITELLE

BOSTON—Some people join the Navy to see the world; Alfred M. Zeien joined the Gillette Company. He spent nine years as an executive in Germany. Some of those years gave him the adventure that he had sought, and others were pure hardship. But out of the experience came a point of view, a way of thinking about the marketplace that shapes Gillette's operations today.

Mainly, he realized that shoppers in Caracas or Bangkok want the same merchandise as those in Chicago or Boston. Acting on this insight, Mr. Zeien (pronounced Zane), now Gillette's chairman, set about transforming the company from a multinational corporation into a global one. The difference: While multinationals spend millions to alter products to suit the tastes of different countries, global companies try to sell the same razor or coffee maker to everyone.

"The most important decision that I made was to globalize," Mr. Zeien said of his years in Frankfurt, as head of Gillette's then newly acquired Braun division. "We decided not to tailor products to any marketplace, but to treat all marketplaces the same. And it worked in most countries."

Mr. Zeien is not alone in this strategy. Gurus of corporate management like Michael E. Porter, a professor at Harvard Business School, say global marketing, when it works, is by definition less costly and more profitable than the old multinational approach. And global marketing works often enough these days to have come of age, changing the criteria for top executives.

An M.B.A. degree, so important in the 1980's, loses some of its priority in the global company. Mr. Zeien, who is 62, does not possess one. Having earned a degree as a naval architect, he dropped out of Harvard Business School several weeks short of graduation, to accept a take-it-or-leave-it offer from Adm. Hyman G. Rickover to build submarines, a job that exempted him from being drafted. The M.B.A. was expendable, but the experience that he accumulated in working and living abroad was indispensable job training, Mr. Zeien said. And his top vice presidents, contenders to succeed him, have all worked overseas.

By 1968, Mr. Zeien had concluded "that shipbuilding in the United States was doomed."

Gillette had just acquired Braun and hired Mr. Zeien to help run the new subsidiary. As the son of European-born parents, he wanted the experience of living there, too, with his wife and three children. Braun then made hi-fi equipment, electric shavers and coffee makers, among other items. Ninety percent of revenues came from Germany.

Traveling out of Frankfurt and exploring markets on every continent, Mr. Zeien discovered he could sell Braun merchandise outside Germany on the strength of the brand name, without redesigning the products. And by 1978, when he returned to Boston for good, 65 percent of Braun's revenues came from non-German sales. Although he had come home in 1973, he was hastily reassigned to Frankfurt the following year to solve a crisis at the subsidiary, and commuted to Boston every two weeks to see his family.

"Of course, by that time, Braun was operating pretty much worldwide; sometimes I would go on to Japan from Boston rather than return to Frankfurt," he said.

What, exactly, did Mr. Zeien discover in his travels, which continue, to this day, at the rate of one overseas trip a month?

"I did not find foreign countries foreign," he said. "They have distinctive characteristics, but they are not foreign. When people shop, they do not think very differently than Americans."

That simple insight is easier to apply to razor blades, Gillette's principal product, than to cars or even hammers (the French, for example, do not buy claw hammers). However easy or difficult the application, Mr. Zeien gambles today that shoppers in Malaysia and Singapore, for example, will buy the same Parker fountain pens (a Gillette product) as Americans shopping at Neiman Marcus—and for the same price or more. "We are not going to come out with a special product for Malaysia," he said.

*   *   *

August 7, 1995

A CYBERSPACE FRONT IN A MULTICULTURAL WAR

By ANDREW POLLACK

TOKYO, Aug. 6—Kozue Yamamoto's job for a Japanese on-line service provider is to demonstrate the wonders of the Internet to potential customers. Miss Yamamoto easily goes through a well-rehearsed presentation, but when it comes to plumbing the wealth of information on the global computer network, she is at a loss. Most of the messages and stored data are in English, which she does not understand.

"I tell the customers, 'You can find anything you want from all over the world,'" she said. "Then I don't even know how to type in a word to retrieve the information."

With the explosion of worldwide interest in the Internet, the dominance of English, stemming from the network's beginnings in the United States, has become a sensitive matter.

One concern is that the vast majority of the world's people, who do not speak English, will be at a disadvantage, unable to avail themselves of the resources of the information age. The issue is likely to become more acute as the use of the network outside the United States spreads from the business and technical elite, who tend to speak English, to the masses.

Another fear is that English, already the international language of business and science, is becoming the lingua franca of the computer world as well, further casting other languages in the shade.

And some countries, already unhappy with the encroachment of American culture—from blue jeans and Mickey Mouse to movies and TV programs—are worried that their cultures will be further eroded by an American dominance in cyberspace.

Yet some foresee an end to this electronic hegemony. "The widespread use of English will eventually be contested and Internet itself will become multicultural," George Yeo, Singapore's Minister for Information and the Arts, predicted at a multimedia conference here in May.

This is starting to happen. A consortium of American computer companies has developed a universal digital code known as Unicode to allow computers to represent the letters and characters of virtually all the world's languages. Software with fonts for everything from Chinese ideographs and Russian Cyrillic to Sanskrit characters are also becoming more readily available.

In many non-English-speaking countries, people are adding data bases and World Wide Web home pages in their own languages. And to allow this information to be exchanged with Internet users in other countries, efforts are under way to develop software that can provide automatic translations.

No one knows the number of Internet users worldwide; estimates vary from 20 million to 40 million. What is clear is that the Net, born in 1969 as a Pentagon research and development network, has become an electronic global village.

According to Matrix Information and Directory Services of Austin, Tex., the tiny island of Macao now has an Internet site. China went from only two sites early in 1994 to 593 early this year; Argentina, from one to 1,415; Japan, from 38,267 to 99,034. In fact, figures for Internet sites worldwide showed a jump to about five million in January, from about two million a year earlier.

Today, half the Internet sites are outside the United States, according to Tony Rutkowski, executive director of the Internet Society, a group that oversees the network's development. And that does not include people outside the United States who use a slower, less popular computer web known as Bitnet.

But now that millions of people are linked up to form a global community, how will they communicate? Many people believe that the need for a common language will inevitably increase the use of English.

But for people like Chung Kyung Chul, an official at I-Net Technologies Inc., an Internet access provider in South Korea, the American-dominated Internet is off-putting. "It's not only English you have to understand," he said, "but American culture, even slang. There are many people who just give up."

Europe, already worried about an invasion of American movies, is now concerned about the American influence from cyberspace. At the multimedia conference here in May, Edith Cresson, a European Commissioner and a former French Prime Minister, said: "For us in Europe, it will no longer be just a question of protecting the broadcasting of films on television, but above all of insuring that there is a minimum of 'European' content on CD-ROM's and other data bases."

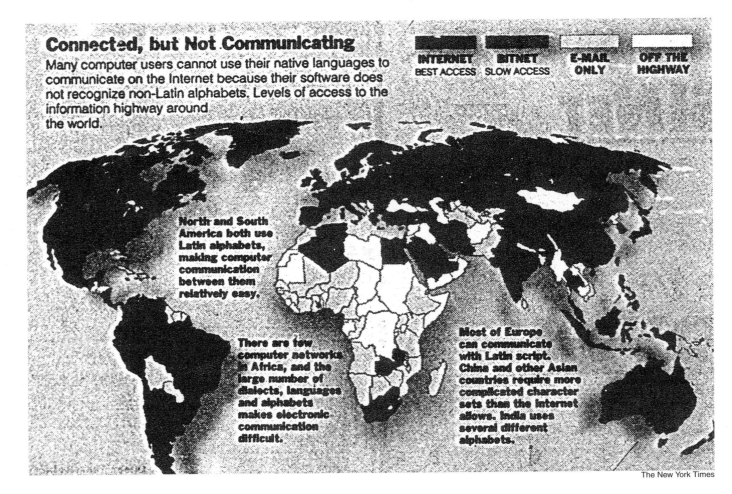

Connected, but Not Communicating

Many computer users cannot use their native languages to communicate on the Internet because their software does not recognize non-Latin alphabets. Levels of access to the information highway around the world.

| INTERNET | BITNET | E-MAIL | OFF THE |
| BEST ACCESS | SLOW ACCESS | ONLY | HIGHWAY |

North and South America both use Latin alphabets, making computer communication between them relatively easy.

There are few computer networks in Africa, and the large number of dialects, languages and alphabets makes electronic communication difficult.

Most of Europe can communicate with Latin script. China and other Asian countries require more complicated character sets than the Internet allows. India uses several different alphabets.

The New York Times

Among the Japanese, who trail the United States in advanced telecommunications, there is fear that if the language of computers remains English, it will be more difficult for them to compete in the information industries of the future.

Nikkei Business, a Japanese business magazine, highlighted those fears in a recent cover story headlined "The Problem Is the Japanese Language." The article noted that English-speaking India has a thriving software industry while Japanese companies have not been able to develop programs that sell outside their home market.

With its use of complex Chinese characters, Japanese has always been more difficult to type than Latin-based alphabets, making personal computers less of a convenience here than in Western countries.

But PC technology has largely overcome those barriers. People can now type in either English letters or simplified Japanese characters, and the computer will instantly convert them into Chinese ideographs.

Still, for most contacts with the rest of the world, English must be used. Even the Ministry of Posts and Telecommunications, which promotes the development of Japan's telecommunications industry, has a home page on the Web in English, not Japanese.

To correct problems like this, some companies are developing the technology to make the Net multilingual. A program by Netscape Communications Corporation, which is used to browse the World Wide Web, will display home pages in Japanese, Chinese and many other languages if the user's computer is equipped with the proper computerized fonts.

Some experts say the computer code named Unicode may hold the most promise for making the Internet multilingual.

Computers represent information as a series of zeros and ones, or digital bits. Computers now often transfer data using the American Standard Code for Information Exchange, or Ascii, which represents each character by a sequence of seven zeros or ones. Because there are only 128 such sequences, Ascii cannot handle many characters other than those in English.

Unicode, on the other hand, represents letters and symbols by a sequence of 16 zeros and ones, allowing for 65,536 different combinations. Within one code, all the characters of all the world's languages can be given their own unique sequence.

Translation software, which once ran only on mainframe computers, is now also available for personal computers. In a few years, predicts Seth Thomas Schneider, editor of Multilingual Computing, a magazine published in Sandpoint, Idaho, such technology will be available as modules for a word-processing program, the way spell-checkers are today.

Efforts are also being made to provide translation to messages in transit so that an E-mail message sent in English, for example, could arrive at the other end in French.

Compuserve, the H.& R. Block unit that is one of the biggest American on-line service providers, uses automatic translation to allow English, French, German and Spanish speakers to participate in forums on international affairs. When a writer posts a message in English, computers translate it into the other three languages in as little as three minutes.

Given such developments, optimists say that far from ending diversity, the Internet will promote it by letting even small groups of people spread their messages worldwide.

"It allows much more effective and wide diffusion of cultures and languages than would otherwise be possible," said Mr. Rutkowski of the Internet Society.

The Internet Multicasting Service, a nonprofit organization in Washington, is even planning an electronic world's fair. If all goes as planned, dozens of countries will showcase their cultures in electronic pavilions on the Internet next year.

* * *

February 12, 1997

THE HOT ZONES

By THOMAS L. FRIEDMAN

ROME—There is a concern that as globalization knits countries and markets together it will flatten cultural differences, as we're all forced to drink Coke, eat Big Macs and compute on Windows 95. In some ways, this is happening. But in other ways a country's distinct political and economic culture actually becomes more important in this brave new world.

For one thing, as globalization shrinks governments and lowers national boundaries, cultures and societies now interact much more directly. And as globalization gives everyone access to the same information, resources, technology and markets, a society's particular ability to put these pieces together in the fastest and most innovative manner increasingly separates winners from losers in the global economy.

Consider Italy. Italy, in some ways, is the ultimate post-industrial society: it has no government!

Well, just kidding, but the fact is that some of Italy's vices during the cold war—its weak governments, its epidemic of tax evasion, the penchant of Italians to work around the state rather than through it—have become virtues in this era of globalization, when, as they say, it's no longer the big who eat the small, but the fast who eat the slow.

Italy today is nothing if not fast. In fact, the fastest-growing and single richest region in Europe today is northeastern Italy (the districts of Lombardy and Veneto). There thousands of small and medium-size Italian entrepreneurs, who are used to operating without state help and often don't pay taxes, have created a beehive of trading companies and small manufacturing operations that have become hugely successful from Slovenia to Singapore.

"Italy is not a computer with a central brain," Prime Minister Romano Prodi explained to me. "It is like the Internet—

everyone gives his contribution. If you give some basic rules and infrastructure for this system, its performance will be unbelievable. You have 6,000 Italian entrepreneurs in Romania today. You wouldn't know the name of a single one of their companies, but they are all over and very active."

Specializing in everything from eyeglass frames to high fashion, these small Italian entrepreneurs have quietly made Italy the fifth-largest industrial power in the world. Because these Italian companies are small and flexible they can convert their industries from pasta to shoes very quickly, according to market demands. Says one U.S. official in Rome: "You come to a Frenchman and say, 'I would like some purple cheese.' He will tell you, 'Cheese is never purple.' You come to a German and ask for purple cheese, he will tell you, 'Purple cheese is not in the catalogue, sorry.' You come to an Italian and ask for purple cheese and he will ask you: 'What shade of purple would you like? Magenta?' "

This fast economic culture, which combines a flair for technological and design innovation, a disdain for government, a trading network linked with a diaspora (overseas Italians), individualism and entrepreneurship, is hardly unique to northern Italy. You see similar hot zones in Hong Kong, Taiwan, Singapore and regions of China (plus the overseas Chinese), Israel (plus the overseas Jews) and parts of India (plus the overseas Indians), as well as Korea, Brazil, Argentina and Chile, to name but a few.

So will these hot zones rule the world? Not yet. Northern Italy may look beyond Italy for its markets, but it's still part of Italy. And the Italian state, no matter how weak, was a typical bloated Western European welfare state, which now has enormous debts that someone has to pay off. So it still matters where you live, and what your national economy is doing. Northern Italy can go a long way, but unless the Italian state can downsize, improve its roads and telecommunications and spur research and development, the north will never achieve its full potential.

So culture matters a lot in this new world, but so still do states, and the trick is getting the right balance. For instance, Germany is too much Alan Greenspan and not enough Benetton. Italy is too much Benetton and not enough Greenspan. France is not enough of either. As Luccio Carocciolo, editor of the Italian foreign policy journal Limes, remarked to me: "If we had German infrastructure and Italian flexibility, we would be a superpower."

* * *

May 11, 1997

CULTURAL INTRUSION IS A BLOCKBUSTER BEST SELLER

By ALAN COWELL

BONN—Goethe and Schiller are probably spinning in their graves: last week only two books on Germany's fiction best-seller lists were actually written by Germans. Legal potboilers by John Grisham, by contrast, appeared four times—

twice among the top 15 hard-covers, twice on the separate list of 15 paperbacks.

Elsewhere, Shakespeare, Moliere and Dante can't rest easy either: translations of foreign fiction (not all of it American) consistently rank high on best-seller lists across Europe, in varying degrees and for various reasons. Mr. Grisham is popular in Britain, too, while the British thriller-writer Ken Follett and Michael Ondaatje of Canada ("The English Patient") have been selling well lately in France; John le Carre of Britain and Wilbur Smith, the South African adventure novelist, are cleaning up in Italy.

The proliferation of foreign titles begs the question: Is the Bildungsroman being Baywatched? That is, is popular fiction becoming globalized in the manner of film and television, with markets dominated by slick American offerings of mass appeal?

"Absolutely, totally yes," said one literary agent in New York who specializes in selling foreign publication rights for American authors.

A German publishing executive demurred, but only slightly. "Perhaps globalization is not the right word," said the executive, Raimund Herder of Kiepenheuer and Witsch, whose foreign titles include the works of Gabriel García Márquez and Mr. le Carre. "It is more a domination of European markets by British and American authors."

In fact, the salability of such authors extends far beyond Europe, as the accompanying best-seller lists suggest. And not surprisingly, such global reach has touched off concerns about national cultural identity, along with no small amount of literary self-criticism. Publishing executives in Germany—by far the most lucrative European market for sales of foreign publishing rights—see the reliance on imported pulp as an indictment of the popular appeal of German fiction.

"Most German authors, the best-known German authors, are very intellectual," said Kristine Gerhardt of the Bertelsmann Foundation, the research arm of one of Germany's publishing giants. "That does not correspond to the tastes of many people. Germans prefer American writers because they are more accessible."

In England, too, despite the international popularity of some British writers, critics fault the narrow appeal of native authors. Lisa Jardine, chairwoman of the judging panel for this year's Orange Prize, an award for woman authors, complained bitterly last week that British fiction was "absorbed with the petty foibles of our insular way of life" and "content endlessly to recapitulate that peculiarly British kind of self-deprecating, parochial sentiment immortalized in the poetry of Philip Larkin."

German publishers in particular have gone on "an enormous binge" in bidding up the prices of foreign publishing rights, said Ion Trewin, an executive with the publisher Weidenfeld and Nicolson in London.

"People perceive that British or American fiction is more entertaining and so German publishers go to buy the rights for enormous sums," Mr. Herder said in Bonn. "And once

International Fiction Best Sellers			
BRITAIN	GERMANY	AUSTRALIA	INDIA
1 The Partner by John Grisham (Century)	1 The Partner by John Grisham (Hoffman & Campe)	1 Silent Witness by Richard North Patterson (Hutchinson)	1 The English Patient by Michael Ondaatje (Picador)
2 Birds of Prey by Wilbur Smith (Macmillan) South Africa	2 The Dark Room by Minette Walters (Goldman)	2 The Echo by Minette Walters (Allen & Unwin)	2 The Tailor of Panama by John le Carré (Coronet)
3 3001: The Final Odyssey by Arthur C. Clarke (Voyager)	3 Hannas Töchter by Marianne Fredriksson (W. Kröger) Sweden	3 Hornet's Nest by Patricia D. Cornwell (Little, Brown)	3 Invasion by Robin Cook (Pan)
4 Rage of a Demon King by Raymond E. Feist (Voyager)	4 Vendetta by Donna Leon (Diogenes)	4 The Partner by John Grisham (Century)	4 The Third Twin by Ken Follett (Macmillan)
5 Hornet's Nest by Patricia D. Cornwell (Little, Brown)	5 Airframe by Michael Crichton (Karl Blessing Verlag)	5 The Deep End of the Ocean by Jacquelyn Mitchard (HarperCollins)	5 The Last Don by Mario Puzo (Mandarin)

Source: Market Partners International. Rankings of hard-cover fiction sales from The London Times (April 20); Der Spiegel (April 19); Australian Bookseller and Publisher (May); Indian Review of Books (May)

The New York Times

you have bought a Grisham for millions you have to sell the book, so the publishers invest large sums in marketing."

But is the cultural intrusion primarily American? That depends.

In Germany, more than in other European countries, the answer is yes, while in France resistance to outside influences is greater. "The Germans are more open," said Friederike Harmgarth of the Bertelsmann Foundation. "We are not like the French. We don't have this feeling that we have to protect our language and promote German to the detriment of others."

Even here, though, that applies largely to fiction. The German nonfiction market traditionally has been dominated by German-produced works—notable exceptions being the self-help books of Dale Carnegie (perennial favorites) and, more recently, "Hitler's Willing Executioners" by Daniel J. Goldhagen of Harvard.

Across Europe, there is a vogue for Scandinavian authors: "Sophie's World" by Jostein Gaarder has lately done for Norwegian writing in Europe what "Smilla's Sense of Snow" by Peter Höeg did for Danish authors. But the trend is toward the American way. "It's the quality of the story-telling that counts," Mr. Trewin said. "And America has always seemed to produce a good crop of high-quality fiction—commercial and literary."

* * *

May 11, 1997

THE UNREAL THING

Un-American Ugly Americans

By BARBARA CROSSETTE

MANDALAY, Myanmar—On the outskirts of Mandalay, the heart of Burmese religious and cultural life, a kind of California suburb is taking shape, with expensive detached houses in landscaped gardens walled off from the city's less prosperous reality. A shopping mall can't be far behind.

Another sign of the Americanization of Asia? Not so, say the neighbors. The big white mansions of concrete and glass are neo-Thai in their inspiration, built with Burmese and Chinese money, at least some of it garnered from narcotics and

Jeffrey Aaronson/Network Aspen

In Beijing: not made in America

the smuggling of Burmese gems and timber. Everything about this phenomenon is Asian. So are the construction companies clawing up virgin rain forests to build golf courses in Malaysia and the studios in Hong Kong and Bombay that make films violent enough to startle Hollywood—and to provoke a burgeoning Asian backlash against perceived threats to family values and decency.

Source of Evil

It used to be that when things started to unravel in almost any Asian country it was easy to finger the culprit: Americanization. Are families falling apart? Dig out the American divorce rates. Kids joining gangs? Talk about Los Angeles and American movies. Rock groups replacing the gamelan? Must be the imported TV programs. The environment in ruins? Blame New York's air conditioners. AIDS? That's a Western disease, the Thais once said confidently as more and more warehouse-sized "massage parlors" opened.

Now in cities, towns and satellite-dished villages across Asia—and in other parts of the world where rising incomes and greater access to goods and information are breeding consumerism and speeding modernization—it is getting much harder to hold the West, particularly the United States, responsible for assaults on local cultures

Worldwide communications—especially satellite television, the fax machine and the Internet—hasten the narrowing of cultural differences. Not everything novel comes from the West, even if most of these now-universal fashions were first popularized in richer Western countries. If trends are set by Japan, this is because the Japanese were the first to break into the top ranks of technology and trade, not only in the region but also worldwide. Others will follow in other regions.

An American diplomat said he was struck by this trend when a Korean radical wearing jeans and smoking an American cigarette lectured him on the perverse effects of American influence. Many Southeast Asians have abandoned traditional costumes for business suits not because Western

Radhika Chalasani/Network Aspen

Cambodia, too, has a growing consumer society that is supplied more or less locally; a monk drinks cola of uncertain origin.

business people dress that way but because the Japanese and Taiwanese do.

And Karaoke, Too

Take a walk in Phnom Penh almost any time of day, and there will be children sitting on the high stools of video-game parlors where the bloodthirsty fare is Japanese-produced. Express boats on Borneo's rivers show Asian-made films in which heroes kick around the faces of bad guys without even smudging their Italian shoes. In the remote Himalayan kingdom of Bhutan, where television receivers are not allowed, the police blamed videotapes from Hong Kong, with their very slick and sociopathic violence, when a Buddhist abbot was murdered a few years ago by local criminals who planned to steal an unlocked temple's treasures.

All over South Asia, middle-class parents worry about the hugely prolific Indian popular film industry with its debased or caricatured women and those silk-shirted toughs living glamorous lives. As for karaoke and what it has done to traditional forms of local entertainment, the less said the better.

"I do believe that mindless imitation of Western patterns of development is an exceedingly serious problem, but you have to accept the responsibility for the fact that this can't happen unless the elite wants it," said Palagummi Sainath, author of "Everybody Loves a Good Drought," a sharp critique of government and the establishment in India, based on his reporting from some of the poorest villages in the country.

"It's a simplification to reduce everything to the word 'Westernization,' and a bit foolish to make the argument that anything and everything that comes from the West is bad," said Mr. Sainath, who added that his most influential and respected teachers in Madras were European Jesuits. "Millions of things have moved both ways over the centuries which we all live with and are comfortable with.

"What I see is something different," said Mr. Sainath. "The super-rich are seceding from their nations. So what you have is not a Western or East Asian or Southeast Asian or Chinese model. We are building enclaves of super-privilege. What you're having is not a global village but a series of global ghettoes. The Western elite is not the sole villain."

But the myth of "Americanization" dies hard, says Francis Seow, a former Solicitor General of Singapore who has been at the Harvard Law School ever since he had a falling out with the country's leader, Lee Kuan Yew, and with his conservative "Asian values." Mr. Seow went to jail for his outspokenness. Politicians, and a range of activists struggling to keep alive old third-world causes, continue to demonize the West. The Burmese military junta, now under an investment embargo by the Clinton Administration, is waging a strong anti-Western campaign in the Government-controlled media.

"Singapore leaders tend to speak smugly of family values as if they are an exclusive preserve of Asian countries," Mr. Seow said. "I have personally seen American children who love and are respectful of their parents and elders, and I am told that in the heartland of America—the real America—these values are the norm rather than the exception."

Many Asian-Americans resent Asian leaders talking about Asian values as much as they object to Americans stereotyping Asians as invulnerable overachievers. "The Lee Kuan Yews talk as if there were an Asia that is homogeneous," said Sumit Ganguly, a political scientist at Hunter College of the City University of New York. "As if the steppes of Central Asia were the same as the plains of Bengal and the plains of Bengal the same as the forests of Sarawak."

In the culturally diverse United States, a politician, however attuned to anti-immigration or even anti-Asian sentiment, would not be likely to reach for the words "Easternization" or "Asianization" when immigrant Thais (some of them in the country illegally) are found running a slave-labor operation in southern California or Chinese and Vietnamese gang executions take place in lower Manhattan.

There is a new catchword in the developing world, however, to cover cultural wounds not believed to be strictly Western, Eastern or self-inflicted; the word is globalization.

It wraps up all the fears of somehow losing control to foreigners, felt as much by Americans who hate the United Nations and immigrants as it is by Indians or Filipinos who feel threatened by the International Monetary Fund, Kentucky Fried Chicken, Joe Camel or Time Warner. That shrinking world everyone was so proud of a decade or so ago has become a cultural strangler.

India's Elite

Francine Frankel, director of the Center for the Advanced Study of India at the University of Pennsylvania, thinks that fears of globalization are setting the stage for a new anti-Americanism among some elite groups in India, which will be the world's most populous nation sometime early in the next century, because satellite television connects the poor not only to the advertising of goods and life styles (for better or worse) but also to ideas (realistic or not) of self-advancement.

"This is at the center of India's political conflict, this challenge of the disadvantaged classes," Ms. Frankel said. "Unrestricted globalization and the penetration of American culture exacerbates this kind of change. Consumerism is really an expression of egalitarianism. The upper castes see that as an imported alien value."

* * *

October 19, 1997

STATESIDE LINGO GIVES JAPAN ITS OWN VALLEY GIRLS

By NICHOLAS D. KRISTOF

TOKYO, Oct. 18—With the forces of globalization gaining ground every day, perhaps it is not surprising that 15-year-old Japanese girls like Kaori Hasegawa use English expressions like "chekaraccho."

English?

Well, a version of English spoken by Japanese teen-agers. Chekaraccho is a corruption of "Check it out, Joe," and is a casual greeting, a bit like "Hi, there."

Japan has always been quick to absorb foreign words along with foreign technology, and in the 19th century there was even serious discussion about whether the country should switch to English. This month, The Japan Times—one of Tokyo's four daily English-language general-interest papers—noted the pressures of globalization and suggested that it might once again be time to consider a switch to English.

Already Japanese is a mishmash of Chinese, English, Dutch and German influences. But what is new this time is the way young people are seizing English words and manipulating them to create their own hip dialect, known as "ko-gyaru-go."

The "gyaru" derives from the English word gal, and ko-gyaru-go roughly translates as "high school gal-talk." It is used mostly among teen-agers, as a secret code by which they can bond and evade surveillance by hostile forces, like parents.

"If I phone a friend, then I can't say openly that I haven't studied for a test, because then my parents will get upset," explained Rie Nishimura, a 17-year-old girl with the trademark "roozu sokusu" (loose socks) of any cool Japanese teen-ager. "So I say the test will be very 'denjarasu' "—or dangerous.

The popularity of ko-gyaru-go underscores the magnetic attraction of American pop culture around the globe and its ability to define what is hot even in breathtakingly different contexts. Some young people here seem to use English in the way a peacock spreads his tail feathers, to demonstrate their own magnificence and lure the opposite sex.

In this vein, two popular words are "wonchu" (I want you) and "gechu" (I get you).

"If a guy came up and used some English words, we'd think, 'Wow, what a cool guy,' " mused Yoko Tago, 18, on a street in the fashionable neighborhood of Shibuya. "I'd want to learn his English words."

One result is that ko-gyaru-go is not always a means of communication, and English words are thrown in simply as ornaments, without any attention to their meaning.

"What does 'rai-a' mean in English?" asked 16-year-old Rie Naoi, giggly and willowy in a school uniform. Told what a liar was, she gasped.

"Oh, no!" she moaned. "I called my English teacher a 'rai-a' the other day. I said, 'Rai-a, rai-a.' "

Japanese grown-ups are almost completely lost when they encounter ko-gyaru-go. When a leading television commentator, Tetsuya Chikushi, described the phenomenon on his program, he began by knitting his brows and displaying a panel with the word "cho beri ba."

"You're probably wondering which country the word I've written on the panel comes from," he said.

In fact, as Mr. Chikushi noted, it is a ko-gyaru-go expression. The "beri" is very, while "ba" is short for bad. Since "cho" is a Japanese word meaning super, cho beri ba means ultrabad.

There are variations, such as "cho beri gu" (ultragood) and "cho beri bu," which can mean ultrablue, or depressing, or ultra-ugly.

Japanese grammar is particularly well suited to adopting foreign words and making them into verbs. For example, in ko-gyaru-go, "deniru" means to go to a Denny's restaurant, and "hageru" means to go to a Haagen-Dazs ice cream outlet.

Some of the new words are conjugated with remarkable sophistication. Ko-gyaru-go has adopted the expression "disu," to diss, or show disrespect, which has a form, disareru, meaning "to be dissed," and even a form meaning "should be dissed," namely disarerubeki.

The enthusiasm for the new words seems partly based on the dominance of English in popular music and partly on the notion that it is more mellifluous than other languages.

"Japanese seems very rigid," scoffed Sato Yu, 16, who was strolling with her friend at dusk. "We don't have much vocabulary in Japanese, so it's just neater to use English."

Jimmy, a 20-something television personality who says his Japanese name is a secret, is about as cool as anybody in Japan, and he says that an essential element of this is his repertory of English. He throws lots of English words into his Japanese conversation, even though he cannot actually speak English.

"Japanese and Korean are not fashionable in their sounds," he explained in Japanese as he wore sunglasses the other night on a street, surrounded by adoring young women. "English is cool, it's fashionable. I like the sound of it."

Just then Jimmy spotted a teenybopper friend, somehow visible through his sunglasses. "Chekeraccho!" he shouted, and she melted.

"Jimmy!" she gushed. "He's so cool in every way!"

Some middle-aged Japanese are bothered by the profusion of English entering their language, but they seem less upset by ko-gyaru-go expressions than by those used in the workplace. Workers learning how to use computers, for example, are overwhelmed when told that to open the "ai-kon" (icon) they must "daburu-kurikku" (double-click) the "mausu" (mouse).

The Health and Welfare Ministry has just banned excessive use of English in its documents, but Japanese newspapers noted that it is unclear whether there will be much "foro-uppu" (follow-up).

The fascination with English is a bit odd in that Japan is probably the worst major country at picking up foreign languages—after the United States. Japanese students study English for about six years, and English is an important component of Japanese college entrance exams, but almost no young Japanese speak it.

Still, they do acquire nifty vocabulary to add to their ko-gyaru-go.

"Now that I'm studying for my college entrance exams, I collect some words from the lists that I'm studying," said Yuki Yutsudo, a high school girl who speaks fluent ko-gyaru-go. "Then I memorize them for use later when I'm chatting with my friends."

*   *   *

March 22, 1998

BIG MACS TO GO

GOLDEN ARCHES EAST: McDonald's in East Asia
Edited by James L. Watson
256 pp. Stanford, Calif.: Stanford University Press. Cloth, $45.
Paper, $16.95.

By NICHOLAS D. KRISTOF

I once asked my 5-year-old son, who has grown up largely in Tokyo, about his favorite Japanese foods. Gregory thought for a moment and decided on rice balls and McDonald's.

It makes perfect sense to think of Big Macs as Japanese food, since McDonald's is a much more important part of his life in Japan than it is when we are on vacation in America. In particular, given the cramped homes in which most Japanese live, when his Japanese friends have birthdays the most common place to hold parties is McDonald's.

"Golden Arches East" is a fascinating study that explores issues of globalization by focusing on the role of McDonald's in five Asian economies, and it comes to conclusions that Gregory would approve of: that in many countries McDonald's has been absorbed by local communities and become assimilated, so that it is no longer thought of as a foreign restaurant and in some ways no longer functions as one.

At a time when academics regularly write impenetrably about abstruse irrelevancies, this book is engaging and arises from straightforward questions: how do countries react to McDonald's, and what does the interaction say about those nations? This book, edited by James L. Watson, a distinguished China scholar and professor of anthropology at Harvard University, was a terrific idea, and the authors pull it off very well. Separate scholars look at McDonald's in Hong Kong, China, Taiwan, South Korea and Japan.

The inquiry is not trivial. McDonald's has had an enormous impact in Asia, affecting manners and mores and the way people live. Ten percent of the beef sold in Japan is in McDonald's hamburgers, and the daily lives of most Japanese people have been shaped more by McDonald's than the State Department.

The most fascinating aspect of this study is its exploration of how McDonald's changed Asia. While America may envision itself as a global beacon for democracy and free markets, this book suggests that the most powerful American influences in East Asia are more mundane.

Take toilets. Bathrooms in Hong Kong restaurants used to range from the merely dirty to the wrenchingly disgusting. And then McDonald's rode into town, in 1975, with bathrooms that offered a novelty—cleanliness. Perhaps the impact is exaggerated, but this book credits McDonald's for helping to raise standards of cleanliness in public rest rooms in Hong Kong.

Likewise, the concept of waiting in line was an alien one in Hong Kong in the old days, and the battle to get on a bus or to get to a cash register was usually like a rugby scrum. Then McDonald's, aghast at the chaos, rigorously imposed lines at its restaurants. The result, many Hong Kong natives think, was that McDonald's helped spread the concept of waiting in line throughout the territory.

Japan's mores have been changing for decades, as an extremely formal country has become steadily more casual, and McDonald's may be a catalyst in that process. Japan has an ancient taboo against tachigui, or standing while eating, but this is breaking down, and this book suggests that part of the reason is the spread of McDonald's—whose first outlet in Japan did not have any seats at all.

In China, restaurants traditionally have been maelstroms of loud conversations and bones strewn on the floor. But according to this book, customers at McDonald's outlets in China spoke in lower tones than in other restaurants and were careful not to spit or throw rubbish on the ground: "People in McDonald's were, on the whole, more self-restrained and polite toward one another. One possible explanation for this difference is that the symbolic meaning . . . of the new food, along with customers' willingness to accept the exotic culture associated with fast food, has affected people's table manners in particular and social behavior in general."

All this may amount to American cultural imperialism. But it is hard to imagine even the most passionate nationalist in Asia denouncing American exports like courtesy or clean toilets.

Nicholas D. Kristof is the Tokyo bureau chief of The Times.

*   *   *

July 19, 1998

ACHTUNG! ENGLISH SPOKEN HERE

In Europe, Steps Toward a Common Language

By JOHN TAGLIABUE

ROME—Uncertain whose side financial history was on, Britain declined earlier this year to abandon its venerable currency, the pound sterling, for the euro, the new currency of the European Union. But while the pound and its keepers at the Bank of England are not represented at the shiny new European Central Bank in Frankfurt, in the heart of Deutsche mark territory, Britain is a presence nonetheless. When the new bank's board holds its regular meetings, the language its 11 members use is English.

"If a Finnish banker wants to address his German colleague," said a bank spokeswoman, "instead of using an interpreter, he simply speaks English." But, she added, English may not be called the bank's "official language," only its "communication language" because the 15-nation European Union has 15 official languages.

Studying Jim Morrison

What this really reflects is that while Europe has at least 15 languages, Europeans are increasingly using one: English.

Of course, Europeans are not about to give up their native tongues. But the trend toward using English runs deep, and not just among globetrotting executives. Europe is uniting rapidly, as the adoption of the euro shows, and Europeans recognize that in a world of collapsing distances and borders, and pervasive American cultural influence, English is the language that the Old Continent must use to communicate.

English seeps into the lives of Europeans at many levels. To liven up a German class, a teacher in Bonn had her students translate a song by Jim Morrison. She assumed, correctly, that they were proficient in English and idolized Morrison, so she sought to hone their German skills by having them put his images into their native tongue.

Thanks to the movies, rural Italians know what the expression "The Full Monty" means. In ads, the inclusion of a few English words has long conferred international flair. In maga-

Increasingly, Europe is adopting English. Its magazines reflect the trend.

zines across the Continent, Bally shoes from Switzerland are advertised with the word "breathtaking." Nokia telephones from Finland are for "connecting the people," whatever their language. In the Netherlands, Philips peddles coffee makers with the slogan, "Let's make things better." In Italy, a company called Clarion sells car radios with the words, "Looking for the top, you'd better look down."

In recent years, English got a big boost as phone deregulation unleashed a wave of ads for competing systems whose slogans are, more often than not, in English. Indeed, Germans were startled earlier this year when their phone company, Deutsche Telekom, changed its bills to read "City-Calls" and "German-Calls," in place of the cumbersome German expressions for local and long distance calls—Ortsgesprache and Ferngesprache. The Institute for the German Language, which defines the rules for the use of German, protested, to no avail. Telekom focus groups reported that the catchy English expressions "reflected the Zeitgeist," wrote the weekly magazine Der Spiegel, "and it speaks English."

The latest and perhaps most forceful boost to English is coming from globalization. As European banks and corporations extend their reach, they are increasingly making English their official language. In Switzerland, where guttural Swiss German is the language of choice among bankers and businessmen, the three biggest banks regularly conduct meetings of senior managers in English. In Italy, the head of Merloni S.p.A., Europe's fourth biggest appliance maker, acknowledged recently that the growing presence in the company of managers from France, Britain, the Netherlands and Portugal forced him to declare English the company language. A young American executive at LVMH, the French conglomerate that makes luxury goods like Louis Vuitton bags, was relieved to learn on his first trip to headquarters in Paris that his inability to speak French would not be a problem. The official language of the company is English.

A Universal Language

Pushing the trend toward English is a young generation of Europeans who have traveled widely, studied and often worked abroad, are at home with English and unabashed about using it. In the past, people from small European countries like Finland or Denmark, with unfamiliar languages, often used English, but now the trend is shifting to the large countries with strong language traditions, like France, Germany and Italy.

Typical of the trend is Francesco Caio, the 40-year old chief executive of Merloni. Mr. Caio had worked in London as a management consultant; his masters degree in business administration is from Insead, the prestigious business school outside Paris where the official language for teaching and research is—mon dieu!—English.

So strong is the tug of English in Europe that some have suggested it may one day emerge as the Continent's universal language, relegating Europe's other languages to the role of regional dialects, in much the same way that languages like Italian, German and even English itself triumphed during the industrialization of the 19th century over local dialects.

The motives for speaking English can vary, at times reflecting a desire to snub a bigger cultural neighbor. In Zurich, Swiss bankers and journalists speak their guttural version of Swiss German among themselves, but prefer to speak English with Germans, even though they are invariably fluent in the language of their big neighbor to the north. Not long ago the Swiss Parliament ordered that all Swiss children above the age of 6 learn English. In a heated parliamentary debate, one legislator argued that children who knew only the three official languages of Switzerland—German, French and Italian—were the equivalent of illiterates.

Inevitably, the triumphal march of English provokes a backlash, though often with mixed results. In Germany, the government's policy of cutting public financing for the Goethe Institute, the organization entrusted with promoting the German language abroad, sparked a bitter protest from the playwright Rolf Hochhuth, who accused Bonn of selling out to the proponents of what he called "one-Reich, one-language raving." In a recent essay in Der Spiegel titled "Deutsch? Bye-Bye!" he lamented the decline of German as a global language of poetry, philosophy and science, which he said was accelerated by German government neglect. Since 1994, he said, government austerity forced the closing of 23 Goethe Institutes around the world, while only four new ones were opened: in Almaty, Tbilisi, Johannesburg and Hanoi. By failing to teach German, he warned, Germany was surrendering influence on world affairs. "It would be foolish to dispute," he wrote. "Language is politics."

In France, the culture minister had sought in 1994 to promote a law requiring that 3,000 English words widely used in France be replaced by French equivalents. But France's Constitutional Council ruled that the government was violating the freedom of expression enshrined in the 1789 Declaration of the Rights of Man. Thus, while government officials had to follow the new rules, they had no right to tell the ordinary Frenchman what words to use. One member of the Council gave an example. "The Sports Minister, commenting on the achievements of the French soccer team," he wrote, "will have to use the expression 'jet de coin,' but the sports commentators will be free to use the word 'corner.'"

But the Government in Paris may have gotten some satisfaction last week after France's victory over Brazil in soccer's World Cup. A banner headline on London's Daily Mail blared out, for all the world to see, "Vive la France!"

*   *   *

February 20, 1999

OUT FROM UNDER THE NATION'S SHADOW

The Hot Subject Today Is the Culture of Regions (Regions? What Regions?)

By PETER APPLEBOME

Academic centers are popping up everywhere to bore into the soul of the Southwest and the Great Plains, the South and New England. As if they were cataloguing newly discovered planets, scholars are busily cobbling together vast compendiums, modeled after "The Encyclopedia of Southern Culture," on the nation's regions and cities.

The study of regional culture and politics, folkways and eccentricities, long dismissed as the minor leagues of academic scholarship, is fashionable at American universities as it has not been since at least the 1930's.

Still, amid the celebration of regional distinctiveness, a nagging question persists: are there still distinctive regions to celebrate?

Many scholars, certainly those involved in regional studies, argue that regional differences persist—may even be accelerating—despite a commercial landscape of McDonalds, Starbucks, Walmart and the Gap that can look the same whether in Boston, Baltimore, Boise or Birmingham.

But the focus on regions is also part of a larger discussion about the nature of culture and how regional differences persist in the face of all the broader forces increasingly pushing toward a homogeneous national culture.

"My colleague George Tindall says it's the cultural equivalent of your life passing before you as you drown in the mainstream," said John Shelton Reed, a sociologist and expert on the South at the University of North Carolina, referring to the eminent Southern historian. "But it's not that simple. I don't think massification and globalization and all those other 'izations' are necessarily hostile to regionalism."

In fact, American history began as regional history told by Virginians or Bostonians, but it was soon supplanted by a national narrative, if one dominated by a New England perspective. In the 1930's, as the age of mass society dawned, sociologists and geographers began to focus again on regional differences—in literature, politics, folkways and art. But that interest soon faded, as national issues again became pre-eminent, and since the 1950's the study of specific regions has had about the same cachet in academia as a small-town mayor does compared with a United States Senator.

"Provincial, antiquarian backwaters. Unanalytical. Unreflective. Nostalgic. That's pretty much what you heard," said Patricia Limerick Nelson, a historian and chairwoman of the board of the Center of the American West at the University of Colorado at Boulder. "It was very uncool."

But just as the dominant cultural cliché came to be that regional differences were disappearing into the great national strip mall, the study of regions suddenly became hot. Most regional programs are aggressively interdisciplinary, as likely to study desert cactus as Navajo poetry or New England immigration patterns or Revolutionary War history.

One of the first regional study institutions was the Center for Great Plains Studies at the University of Nebraska, which opened in 1976. Since then there has been a proliferation: there is the Appalachian Regional Studies Center at Radford University in Virginia and the Center for Appalachian Studies and Services at East Tennessee State University. There is the Center for the Study of the Southwest at Southwest Texas State University and the Southwest Center at the University of Arizona.

There is the Center for the Study of Southern Culture at the University of Mississippi and the Institute for Southern Studies at the University of South Carolina. And there is the Center of the American West at the University of Colorado at Boulder and the New England studies program at the University of Southern Maine.

In 1989, the Center for the Study of Southern Culture made a big splash with its "Encyclopedia of Southern Culture" (University of North Carolina Press). Since then similar volumes have been begun or completed for the West, the Midwest, New England, Appalachia and the Great Plains as well as various cities. In New York alone, the last few years have seen the publication of "The Encyclopedia of New York City" (Yale University Press, 1995) and "Gotham" (Oxford University Press, 1998), a history of New York that in 1,383 pages gets only to the year 1898.

A further push has come from William R. Ferris, who for 18 years presided over the Center for the Study of Southern Culture and was the co-editor of the Southern encyclopedia. Considered a godfather of regional studies, he is now the chairman of the National Endowment for the Humanities. Not surprisingly, his most cherished proposal calls for establishing 10 regional centers around the country to support projects in fields as diverse as folklore, law, medicine, historic preservation, the environment and education.

"Yes, we have interstates and national television programming, and we all watch the same 'Seinfeld' and see the same evening news," said Mr. Ferris. "But when we sit at the dinner table, we hear a very different voice that's rooted in the home and the community in which we live. It's the most powerful anchor of who we are as Americans, and ironically that's the world we have failed to study and understand."

Mr. Ferris also cites the economic importance of cultural tourism as one reason to study and celebrate the music of the South or the cowboy culture of the West.

Still, for some scholars this is an odd time to adopt regionalism as a primary lens for viewing American life.

"There are still important regional differences in this country," said Mark Crispin Miller, who teaches media studies at New York University, "but it's also true that those dif-
ferences have been eroded greatly by the media and the consumer culture. So this study can be valuable as long as it addresses the actual plight of regional distinctiveness. If it just concentrates on these cultural differences it can become a kind of nostalgia, a bookish exercise in looking back at what is now disappearing."

But many scholars like Mr. Ferris say that the rise of a mass culture, rather than diluting regionalism, has made people much more anxious to acknowledge and preserve the alternatives to carbon-copy franchise culture.

Lawrence Levine, who teaches history at George Mason University, does not argue that regionalism is as vital a factor in American life as it once was. But he says it remains a compelling force and an important counterweight to the popular notion that the country is more divided than it used to be. "There are all these people today screaming about fragmentation as if the country was once a unified place and now there are all these competing ethnic groups," he said. "America was never a unified place. It was always divided by ethnicity, by region, by geography, by economics."

Skeptics say regional studies programs can become mere conservators of fading cultural eccentricities, the blues in the South, the whaling industry in New England, the Indian culture of the Southwest.

But Joseph Wilder, director of the Southwest Center at the University of Arizona and editor of the Journal of the Southwest, said it was precisely the urge to turn regional culture into a comfortable commodity that makes serious study and analysis so important now.

"The nouveau riche can move to Santa Fe, but no matter how many Southwestern trinkets they bestow upon themselves or how they decorate their fake adobe with other people's religious artifacts, they're not really touching the indigenous reality," he said. "We're not here to celebrate quaint indigenous customs. Our job, in part, is to make sense of the dynamic of change and to make sure that important knowledge, other narratives and stories which are threatened by mass culture, aren't lost forever."

In the end, it may be that one's image of a region's culture is as important as the substance. Thus, said Burt Feintuch, a professor of folklore and English at the University of New Hampshire and the editor of the Encyclopedia of New England Culture, due out later this year, the landscape of New England has over time been made to look more like an imagined New England than it ever was in the past.

"We take the approach that regionalism is a state of mind and that regional identity remains every bit as strong as it ever has been," he said.

Of course, not everyone is willing to go that far. Instead, they say, the way to view regionalism is as a counterweight to the prevailing pull of mass culture, producing a blend of distinctive regional cultures and homogenous mass ones.

"There's something unsatisfying about the formulation that regionalism is as powerful as it ever was," said Jackson Lears, a history professor at Rutgers University. "It denies the real power of corporations to reshape culture.

"You can't say there's now a force that steamrollers everything in its way. But you can't say nothing has changed, either. That ignores and trivializes the impact of this enormously concentrated power of big corporations and the corporate media to disseminate ideas."

* * *

March 5, 1999

RETHINKING THE WAR ON AMERICAN CULTURE

By SALMAN RUSHDIE

LONDON—A couple of years ago a British literary festival staged a public debate on the motion that "it is the duty of every European to resist American culture." Along with two American journalists (one of whom was Sidney Blumenthal, now more famous as a Clinton aide and impeachment witness), I opposed the motion. I'm happy to report that we won, capturing roughly 60 percent of the audience's vote.

But it was an odd sort of victory. My American co-panelists were surprised by the strength of the audience's anti-Americanism—after all, 40 percent of the crowd had voted for the motion. Sidney, noting that "American culture" as represented by American armed forces had liberated Europe from Nazism not all that many years ago, was puzzled by the audience's apparent lack of gratitude. And there was a residual feeling that the case for "resistance" was actually pretty strong.

Since that day, the debate about cultural globalization and its military-political sidekick, intervention, has continued to intensify, and anti-American sentiment is, if anything, on the increase. In most people's heads, globalization has come to mean the worldwide triumph of Nike, the Gap and MTV. Confusingly, we want these goods and services when we behave as consumers, but with our cultural hats on we have begun to deplore their omnipresence.

On the merits of intervention, even greater confusion reigns. We don't seem to know if we want a world policeman or not. If the "international community," which these days is little more than a euphemism for the United States, fails to intervene promptly in Rwanda, Bosnia, Kosovo, it is excoriated for that failure. Elsewhere, it is criticized just as vehemently when it does intervene: when American bombs fall on Iraq, or when American agents assist in the capture of the Kurdish leader Abdullah Ocalan.

Clearly, those of us who shelter under the pax Americana are deeply ambiguous about it, and the United States will no doubt continue to be surprised by the level of the world's ingratitude. The globalizing power of American culture is opposed by an improbable alliance that includes everyone from cultural-relativist liberals to hard-line fundamentalists, with all manner of pluralists and individualists, to say nothing of flag-waving nationalists and splintering sectarians, in between.

Much ecological concern is presently being expressed about the crisis in biodiversity, the possibility that a fifth or more of the earth's species of living forms may soon become extinct. To some, globalization is an equivalent social catastrophe, with equally alarming implications for the survival of true cultural diversity, of the world's precious localness: the Indianness of India, the Frenchness of France.

Amid this din of global defensiveness, little thought is given to some of the most important questions raised by a phenomenon that, like it or not, isn't going away any time soon.

For instance: do cultures actually exist as separate, pure, defensible entities? Is not melange, adulteration, impurity, pick'n'mix at the heart of the idea of the modern, and hasn't it been that way for most of this all-shook-up century? Doesn't the idea of pure cultures, in urgent need of being kept free from alien contamination, lead us inexorably toward apartheid, toward ethnic cleansing, toward the gas chamber?

Or, to put it another way: are there other universals besides international conglomerates and the interests of superpowers? And if by chance there were a universal value that might, for the sake of argument, be called "freedom," whose enemies—tyranny, bigotry, intolerance, fanaticism—were the enemies of us all; and if this "freedom" were discovered to exist in greater quantity in the countries of the West than anywhere else on earth; and if, in the world as it actually exists, rather than in some unattainable Utopia, the authority of the United States were the best current guarantor of that "freedom," then might it not follow that to oppose the spread of American culture would be to take up arms against the wrong foe?

By agreeing on what we are against, we discover what we are for. Andre Malraux believed that the third millennium must be the age of religion. I would say rather that it must be the age in which we finally grow out of our need for religion. But to cease to believe in our gods is not the same thing as commencing to believe in nothing.

There are fundamental freedoms to fight for, and it will not do to doom the terrorized women of Afghanistan or of the circumcision-happy lands of Africa by calling their oppression their "culture."

And of course it is America's duty not to abuse its pre-eminence, and it is our right to criticize such abuses when they happen—when, for example, innocent factories in Sudan are bombed, or Iraqi civilians pointlessly killed.

But perhaps we, too, need to rethink our easy condemnations. Sneakers, burgers, blue jeans and music videos aren't the enemy. If the young people of Iran now insist on rock concerts, who are we to criticize their cultural contamination? Out there are real tyrants to defeat. Let's keep our eyes on the prize.

Salman Rushdie is the author of "The Satanic Verses," "The Moor's Last Sigh" and the forthcoming "The Ground Beneath Her Feet."

* * *

December 11, 1999

WHEN ALL THE RELIGIONS OF THE WORLD ARE TRULY GLOBAL, SOME OLD ISSUES ASSUME NEW FORMS

By PETER STEINFELS

Globalization: it's a curious contraption of a word, a noun built on a verb, globalize, built on an adjective, global, built on a noun, globe. By now, however, the word not only rolls around rather easily in the mouth; it has also become irreplaceable for discussing the kind of issues that brought demonstrators to the streets in Seattle a week ago. It is also a notion applicable to religion.

The Parliament of the World's Religions, which drew thousands of religious leaders to Cape Town between Dec. 1 and Dec. 8, was a colorful reminder of religious globalization. The original such parliament was held in 1893 in Chicago, in connection with the World's Columbian Exposition. A hundred years later it was repeated, and now its organizers, based in Chicago, plan to make it a perennial event.

When the 6,000 participants were not hearing speakers like Nelson Mandela and the Dalai Lama, they were enjoying something like a global religious fair, rushing back and forth to hundreds of workshops and discussions. As in Seattle, there were even a few demonstrators, in this case denouncing the whole affair as satanic and, of all unlikely things, ridden with Zionists. But like the World Trade Organization's meeting, the parliament was only one manifestation of a process that is irreversibly under way.

The world's great faiths have always interacted, of course. They sent missionaries, they borrowed ideas, they adopted rituals. They even absorbed and transformed deities. And they fought wars. Sometimes they imitated one another, sometimes they defined themselves in contrast to one another.

But this usually happened when religions were neighbors geographically, or when a religion expanded through migration or conquest, or when one faith had emerged from another, like Christianity from Judaism or Buddhism from the Brahmanism of Northern India, or simply when a few mobile and spiritually inquiring individuals cross-pollinated beliefs.

Just as economic globalization is of a completely different order than traditional overseas commerce, today's religious globalization barely resembles these earlier interactions among faiths.

Today, world religions are truly world religions. Every major faith is everywhere, represented by migrant populations or native converts, its beliefs and sacred texts available, at least in introductory form, to virtually any curious seeker. Pope John Paul II, the Rev. Billy Graham and the Dalai Lama are world figures with followings far beyond their own religious groups.

The very fact that marking the millennium has become a global event is suggestive. Even the most secular celebration cannot entirely erase the religious origins of a calendar that is now implanted in the daily life of historically non-Christian cultures.

But this free flow of religions, like free trade in cotton, computers and currencies, has created its own issues and added new twists to older ones. Many of the issues can be grouped under three headings: turf, tolerance and truth. But in fact they are all interrelated.

Turf is the most ancient of these concerns, the one that endures despite the fact—and maybe because of the fact—that barriers to religious alternatives are increasingly harder to maintain. Russian Orthodox leaders protest that Russia is their turf and everyone else is a religious intruder. Roman Catholic leaders often sound much the same way about Latin America. Hindus protest Christian conversions; Islam does the same. Orthodox Judaism claims prior rights in Israel.

Of course, there are opinions within each group challenging this religious equivalent of protectionism. There are vitally important distinctions, moreover, among religious bodies and leaders regarding the lengths to which they will go to protect their turf. There is a growing international lobby against religious persecution. There are advocates of an unrestricted religious marketplace who argue that rigorous competition makes faith stronger, not weaker. And there are also cautionary voices, in the religious sphere as in the economic one, warning that American standards, in this case of church-state separation, cannot be universalized.

Obviously the question of turf is linked to the question of tolerance. In principle, almost everyone favors tolerance. In practice, it can be more difficult to uphold and, sometimes, even to define.

Certainly one of the premises of the Parliament of the World's Religions was that tolerance, if it is to be more than a prolonged truce in religious warfare, requires real respect for one another's traditions, reflected in a willingness to engage in dialogue and cooperate in serving humanity and the environment.

That raises the issue of truth. To some people, genuine respect and tolerance are incompatible with claims that "I have the truth and you don't." To others, the demand that "I abandon my claims to the truth in the name of tolerance" is the very essence of intolerance.

In reality, religious globalization has already dramatically modified the way claims of religious truth are commonly made. Believers today are far less likely than before to deny all the truth in other faiths. The question becomes not true versus false religion, but which faith has the fuller truth, the more adequate grasp on a dimension of reality that will always remain mysterious.

That, of course, still conflicts with the conviction that every religion must be viewed as equally true, and that nothing less can be the basis of genuine respect and tolerance. But to propose that principle as the basis of religious globalization would probably arouse more opposition and outrage than anything the World Trade Organization ever dreamed of.

* * *

April 24, 2000

TO GET TO THE DISCO, JUST FOLLOW THE LLAMA TRACKS

By CLIFFORD KRAUSS

CUZCO, Peru—The stone wall on the western corner of Cuzco's central plaza is all that is left of the grand palace that once housed Wayna Capac, the last great Incan ruler before the Spanish conquest, and later Francisco Pizarro after he seized the Incan capital in 1533.

Today the wall is part of a travel agency that arranges helicopter rides to the ancient Incan city of Machu Picchu.

Above the wall on the second floor, there is the Mama Africa Cybercafe, which offers visitors coca tea, a bank of personal computers with Internet access and a colorful mural featuring Bob Marley, Elvis Presley, Marilyn Monroe and a happy-go-lucky bartender who says, "We love tourists."

Tourists seem to love Cuzco in return. In the last seven years, since the terrorist Shining Path insurrection began to wind down, Cuzco has rapidly become South America's prime tourist destination, aside from such large cities as Rio de Janeiro and Buenos Aires. This city of 300,000 inhabitants welcomed 283,000 tourists in 1999, more than double the number who came in 1995, and hotel managers say the boom is only accelerating this year.

Quechua-speaking Indians, who pose for tourist cameras with llamas decorated with pink ribbons tied to their ears, have begun to ask for tips in smatterings of Italian, French and English. Visa and American Express signs hang ubiquitously over Incan stonework. Diesel exhaust belched from tourist buses now mixes with the traditional Cuzco fragrance of burning eucalyptus, used to make fires here.

"People forget they are in Peru when they come to Cuzco," Stephen Light, editor of The New World News, an English-language newspaper that began publishing last year, said only half jokingly. A restaurant review in a March issue of his semiweekly newspaper complained, "These days, in Cuzco, 'older' means 'established 1990.'"

Globalization has gone on a tear in the old Incan center known by an earlier generation of backpacking tourists for its sublimely exotic spiritual setting. A new five-star hotel that occupies a colonial monastery has hired a French chief, who prepares grilled alpaca in wine sauce and fills croquets with quinua, a traditional Incan cereal. The hotel is refitting a

Ana Cecilia Gonzales-Vigil for The New York Times

Residents of Cuzco do not mind the invasion of tourists, and are happy to re-create Andean culture in exchange for the economic benefits. An Indian woman, posing in traditional dress, asks tourists for tips.

colonial chapel to become its new entranceway, while renovating a second monastery to become Cuzco's first spa.

At last count, Cuzco had 15 discotheques, which go by names like Kamikase and Delirium. European and American tourists dance with young Peruvians, who wear Indian jewelry and headbands to give them a touch of exotic eroticism. Such Peruvians who seek out tourists, sometimes to marry in order to acquire visas to live abroad, have become so plentiful they have been given a name: "bricheros"—a Spanish play on the word "bridge."

One of two Irish pubs that have opened in recent years has even invented a new cocktail called the brichero, an atomic, eye-popping concoction of pisco and other local liquors guaranteed to make any tourist see Incan goddesses in the wee hours of the morning.

For the more conventional crowd, McDonald's is scheduled to open its first restaurant here by the end of the year, not far from a narrow street that has become known as "Gringo Alley" for its popularity among young Americans looking for Mexican food and pizza.

Travelers have been coming to Cuzco for more than 600 years, and abrupt change and odd cultural mixtures are nothing new. Through the 17th and 18th centuries, the Spanish built grand colonial churches over the finely crafted stone foundations of Incan temples, palaces and bathhouses. After Spanish artists taught the Indians how to paint, one Baroque masterpiece of the Cuzco School portrayed a Last Supper in which Jesus and his disciples can be seen eating guinea pig—an ancient Incan delicacy.

A few decades ago, the descendants of 19th-century Chinese railroad workers filled the central square, known as the Plaza de Armas, with Chinese restaurants. But with the tourist boom and the resulting rise in rents, the Chinese restaurants have been replaced by discotheques and bars flashing neon lights advertising American cigarettes, Peruvian beer and Internet services.

"What bothers me is the re-creation of Andean culture for tourists, like people putting on native costumes to have their pictures taken," said Lorena Tord Velasco, an anthropologist who works in Cuzco. "But the thing that I do like is that tourism has made many Peruvians realize the wonders of their culture, to take care of it and take pride in it."

She noted that some Indian villages near Cuzco began to fully appreciate the Incan agricultural mountain terracing only after tourists came to see it.

But the modernization sometimes seems to have no bounds. Three years ago, with the central square becoming crowded by aggressive market hawkers selling alpaca sweaters and other handicrafts, the local government forced the Indians to move their stalls elsewhere in the city. The authorities also uprooted more than a dozen shade trees, saying they spoiled the tourists' view of The Cathedral and La Compania, a pair of 17th-century churches.

Local residents appear to take all the change in stride, and many argue that like Florence and Toledo, Cuzco can change without losing its charm. With unemployment and chronic poverty the alternative, even the market women who lost their stalls in the plaza have mostly good things to say about the invasion of tourists.

"Cuzco is better now," said Julia Cuella Mamani, a 48-year-old Indian vendor of alpaca sweaters on the Plaza Regocijo. "The more tourists the better because the more tourists come, the more commerce we have."

But she quickly added, "The problem is our children are learning to drink and to smoke. And I don't want to talk about the sex."

* * *

November 25, 2000

GLOBALIZATION PUTS A STARBUCKS INTO THE FORBIDDEN CITY IN BEIJING

By CRAIG S. SMITH

BEIJING, Nov. 24—Five million Chinese a year visit the ancient Forbidden City, walking across the acres of gray cobblestone, through the stately vermilion pavilions and beneath the orange glazed roof tiles of the capital's centuries-old palace complex.

But just before they enter the Palace of Heavenly Purity, once the residence of China's emperors and still the symbolic center of the Chinese universe, they now see another color: the forest green logo of Starbucks Coffee.

If ever there was an emblem of the extremes to which globalization has reached, this is it: mass-market American coffee culture in China's most hallowed historic place. Even a McDonald's in the Kremlin would not come as close. Starbucks opened its Forbidden City shop a month ago with a signature menu board advertising the usual Americano and decaf latte coffee and a glass display case filled with fresh glazed donuts, cinnamon rings and banana walnut muffins.

"Chinese people don't like it too much, but we're working hard to change their minds," said Richard Chen, wearing a black shirt and green apron behind the counter of the small, two-table cafe.

As China prepares to join the World Trade Organization and bids to be the host of the 2008 Olympic Games, once-sacred barriers to its fabled consumer market are crumbling like stale biscotti. China is expected to maintain stiff barriers around many leading industries, but the market for most consumer goods and services is already remarkably open—so much so that profits are often disappointing because of rabid competition.

More than ever, educated young Chinese are watching, wearing, eating and drinking products marketed by the world's multinationals, aspiring to be, not necessarily Westernized, but modern.

"These things are the trend, and I just accept them subconsciously," said Huang Hongye, a 26-year-old event organizer waiting for his girlfriend at Shanghai's biggest Starbucks. Mr. Huang wears Lee jeans, made by the VF Corporation, and tan Reebok boots; smokes State Express 555 brand cigarettes by

As Western brands and businesses make deepening inroads into China, a Starbucks coffee shop has opened in the heart of the Forbidden City in Beijing, the country's most hallowed historic place.

British American Tobacco P.L.C. and calls his girlfriend with a Siemens mobile phone. He even reads e-mail on a Nino palm-sized computer by Royal Philips Electronics, which, along with all of the computers at his office, is loaded with Microsoft software.

Zoom out and the smattering of foreign brands looks insignificant in the sea of China's vast population, most of which still dresses in drab colors and makes do with shoddy goods manufactured by state-run industries. And the shallow impact that Western culture has had on broader Chinese life so far could evaporate almost as quickly as the international effervescence that existed in China's cities before the Communist Party came to power 51 years ago.

Simmering nationalism, for example, could turn Western brands into badges of treason overnight. Many McDonald's restaurants across the country were ransacked after the NATO bombing of the Chinese Embassy in Belgrade, Serbia, last year.

But the direction, for now, is unmistakable. Coca-Cola; Head & Shoulders and Tide, both made by Procter & Gamble; Dove, made by Unilever; Wrigley's and Marlboro, made by Philip Morris, are brands already ensconced in the country's first-, second- and third-tier cities. JanSport backpacks and Nike shoes are also becoming ubiquitous.

And though coffee remains a novelty in this tea-drinking land, Starbucks is the latest company to lead the charge here.

The company has opened about 25 stores in China in the last year, 18 in Beijing and 7 in Shanghai, including one opposite Shanghai's teahouse, the city's signature landmark in its oldest district. Starbucks plans to open 5 more shops in China before year's end and 10 more next year.

The company is not only counting on rising incomes to lead to more cosmopolitan tastes, it also is banking on changing lifestyles as urban Chinese embrace new ways. It is betting that its laid-back, smoke-free coffee shops will appeal to people in a land of cramped living quarters and loud, crowded restaurants.

Already, the popular upholstered chairs and roomy seating of Starbucks have inspired copycats in Beijing and Shanghai.

"If we had expected to rely on foreigners to sustain our market, we would never have come," said David Sun, who heads the Beijing licensee. He added that most Starbucks' customers in China are Chinese.

Mr. Sun approached officials of the Forbidden City to rent the space outside the Palace of Heavenly Purity, which was being used to serve cold drinks and the occasional Nescafe. To his surprise, they gave him a one-year lease, though it is not clear whether he will be allowed to renew it.

Foreign companies are periodically forced to retreat from their boldest inroads. The KFC Corporation has been told that when the lease on its fried-chicken restaurant is up in 2002, it will have to move out of a prime location in Beihai Park, the imperial playground in Beijing originally built by Kublai Kahn.

The Forbidden City Starbucks is already causing controversy.

"The reaction has been very intense," said Chen Junqi, the Forbidden City's spokesman. "Some people say this is a gem of Chinese culture and that foreign brands should not be allowed in."

But Mr. Chen dismissed the criticism the coffee shop has drawn so far. "We can't give up eating for fear of choking," he said.

THINKING GLOBAL, ACTING LOCAL

June 23, 1983

LOCAL CONTENT: GLOBAL PRACTICE

By KENNETH N. GILPIN

Data General, the big computer manufacturer, had exported its products to Mexico for years. In 1980 the company had a 5 percent share of a $400 million market that was expanding by roughly 30 percent a year. The country's financial difficulties cut into the growth of the computer market, but Data General continued to ship its products.

Last year, however, the roof fell in. The Mexicans, seeking to develop their own computer industry, imposed investment criteria requiring foreign companies with sales in Mexico to establish plants that would produce some components of their products locally—known as local content.

"If you agreed to those conditions," said John F. Cadwallader, Data General's manager of government affairs, "then the Government would consider your investment application. Since then, a lot of companies have put in proposals for integrating into Mexico. We haven't, because it doesn't make good economic sense, and haven't done much business there since."

The choices are not unique to Mexico, Data General or the computer industry. For a decade or more, as successive rounds of multilateral trade negotiations have led to reductions in tariff barriers, an increasingly large number of countries—many of them developing nations—have weaved an increasingly complex web of nontariff barriers intended to promote employment and develop infant industries.

U.S. Legislation

The concept has reached the United States in the form of the so-called local content bill, which is currently working its way through the House of Representatives and would require that up to 90 percent of an automobile's components be made in the United States as a precondition for sale in this country. A similar measure was approved by the House last year, although no action was taken by the Senate and passage in that body this year is viewed as unlikely.

Nevertheless, domestic content requirements have achieved widespread use worldwide. Spain, for example, is using such an approach to develop its airline industry. Brazil has guidelines governing investment in steel, computers and other industries. Canada's Foreign Investment Review

Agency approves investments that adhere to certain criteria in a wide range of industries.

The requirements are only one of a host of so-called performance criteria that are placed on companies by governments as a quid pro quo for direct investment or market access.

"If you take a broad view, and include employment requirements, foreign exchange balancing schemes or an incentive system which gives cash grants if large amounts of local content are used, then almost every developing country" uses the criteria, said Stephen Guisinger, a professor at the University of Texas at Dallas and a former director of a World Bank group that last year examined investment incentives and performance requirements in 10 countries.

The Office of the United States Trade Representative says of the 50 countries it monitors, 40 have performance requirements. Only 8—Australia, Austria, Canada, France, Ireland, Norway, Portugal and Spain—are considered developed nations.

In most developing countries, local content and other performance requirements are adopted to insure the development of an industry, like auto making, that previously did not exist. Such programs can be beneficial. But there are unpleasant side effects.

Price Rise a Problem

As a trade-off for job creation and industrial development, countries with such laws have seen prices for the locally produced products soar. Since a high percentage of local ownership is required in areas like computers, countries are finding themselves cut off from advances in technology, making the particular industry uncompetitive in world markets.

A recent study by the Commerce Department on the impact of local content regulations in the auto industry in 27 countries found that local content and other performance criteria led to much higher production costs, and higher sticker prices.

In Mexico, for example, where at least 50 percent of all autos must be made from locally produced components, the production cost and price was 50 percent greater than it would have been in the United States, the study said. (The study made its comparisons from an average 1982 sticker price of $9,587 for an American-made automobile).

"The unanimous opinion among economists is probably that local content regulations are an inefficient way to provide an auto industry to a country," said William A. Noellert, an international economist at Verner, Liipfert, Bernhard &

McPherson, a Washington law firm. "But the question governments have to answer is if they want to provide automotive transportation, or build up an industry."

Technology Curbs

The absence of a free flow of technology, which in many cases is caused by import barriers and local ownership requirements, presents a problem for both company and country alike, Data General's Mr. Cadwallader said.

"Even if a country is reasonably successful in attracting investors, the technology they receive at the time will be obsolete in two or three years," he added. "Then they are confronted with two problems: how to shore up an uncompetitive industry, and how to get companies to reinvest. These guidelines are a real pandora's box."

Although companies that go along with performance criteria are guaranteed protection from imports and in most cases exclusive access to a large and growing market, a number of them are less than enthusiastic.

"Local content and other performance regulations decrease our flexibility as a corporation, and force us to do things we otherwise might not be doing," said Thomas R. Atkinson, director of international economic policy at General Motors. "We wish these laws had never been invented, and would not like to see them increased or created in countries where they don't exist now."

Indeed, just as the United States is considering its own performance criteria, a combination of factors—the impact of recession on investment flows and the spread of labor-saving technology to name two—is forcing a number of countries to reconsider their investment guidelines.

Because of those factors, "countries are aware they will have to do more in the way of imposing fewer performance requirements and giving more incentives to invest," Mr. Guisinger of the University of Texas said. "In the future, there will be greater flexibility on domestic content requirements," he added.

"A few years ago Chrysler received a large fine for not complying with domestic content requirements in Mexico," he said. "I doubt that the same thing would happen today."

A Sampling of Domestic Content Regulations Around the World

SPAIN

Under an arrangement negotiated last month with the McDonnell Douglas Corporation, the company can sell F-18A fighters to the country if there is Spanish participation in the manufacture of nine components of the aircraft, the transfer of technology to aid Spain in building a domestic industry and compensatory trade arrangements in the United States.

BRAZIL

In addition to strict domestic content requirements on cars and steel, Brazil requires companies to purchase domestically produced computers—except in extraordinary cases—and to maintain computer data bases inside the country, rather than hooking up to existing data bases outside the country.

INDIA

While India has no formal domestic content law, the nation's trade policies achieve the same effect by discouraging imports of automobile products and encouraging local production. About 98 percent of every automobile sold in India is produced domestically.

MEXICO

Domestic content regulations are tied to export requirements, meaning that local automobile manufacturers must offset imports of components with exports of domestically produced vehicles and parts. There are also requirements governing the manufacture of computers.

CANADA

The United States filed formal complaints last year about the existence of the Foreign Investment Review Board, which it says discriminates against American corporations investing in Canada by requiring them to purchase Canadian-made goods. The Canadians are considering domestic content regulations on automobiles, similar to those under consideration in the United States.

ARGENTINA

In a reversal of policies in place since the 1940's, Argentina relaxed domestic content requirements on cars in 1979. Auto imports rose quickly, and General Motors and Chrysler closed assembly operations in the country. However, because the local content requirements are still stiff, domestic producers have found greater difficulty competing with cheaper imports.

* * *

January 20, 1985

U.S. CITIES SEEKING FOREIGN INVESTING

By MARTIN TOLCHIN

WASHINGTON, Jan. 19—Mayors of the nation's larger cities have opened ambitious campaigns to lure foreign investors in an effort to offset their domestic economic woes.

The mayors are increasingly traveling to Europe and Asia to bring foreign capital to their cities, often hard pressed by a loss of jobs and governmental aid, and are promising would-be investors economic, cultural and social advantages.

This pattern of looking for foreign investors emerged in interviews with more than two dozen mayors at the midwinter conference of the United States Conference of Mayors, which ended today.

Boston recently attracted a Swiss corporation to develop a new hotel, and Newark persuaded Japanese and British manufacturers to build plants that make final preparations on automobiles before delivery. New Orleans successfully wooed British and French investors. A Canadian developer built a shopping mall in Minneapolis, and a West German company built a tire chain factory in Cedar Rapids, Iowa.

Trend Toward Investing

They are among scores of foreign investors that have spent billions of dollars in the nation's cities, in a trend that has gained momentum in recent years.

"It's a realization on the part of the mayors that we live in a global society with a global economy, and there is money to be invested," said Mayor Ernest N. Dutch Morial of New Orleans, president of the conference.

The organization has initiated an "Invest in America's Cities" program, and sponsors an annual visit by mayors to Zurich and Hong Kong, where they try to sell their cities' virtues to European and Asian business executives.

By embarking on this nontraditional role, some widely traveled mayors have been criticized at home as ignoring the nuts and bolts of local government, such as repairing potholes, but the mayors say the effort is important.

Many cities seek foreign investors on their own. Kenneth Lipper, New York's Deputy Mayor for Finance and Economic Development, visited China and Hong Kong in July and said that, as a result, the National Bank of China planned to open a branch in the city. In addition, the Hong Kong and Shanghai Bank recently opened a skyscraper at Fifth Avenue and 59th Street in Manhattan, and several Hong Kong textile companies want to open a joint facility in Brooklyn, to avoid limits on textile imports, Mr. Lipper said.

The mayors have found that foreign investors are interested in more than merely economic factors.

"We talk to them about the quality of life in New Orleans," Mayor Morial said. "We are an international city. We have an abundance of energy, a port, access to the heartland of America by way of the Mississippi River and its tributaries. We have a good supply of manpower, and a city government that's enthusiastic about their coming, and will help package their financing."

"The foreign investor also recognizes the importance of the political climate," the Mayor added.

Schools Seen as a Factor

The quality of a city's schools is also important to some foreign investors. "The Japanese told us right off the bat that in science and math, if their kids stayed in American high schools and returned to Japan for college, they'd be two or three years behind," said Mayor Roger O. Parent of South Bend, Ind.

Mayor Marion S. Barry Jr. of Washington said one of his goals was to persuade foreign investors that the nation's capital was more than a one-industry town. He said the city recently approved legislation that made it easier for foreign bankers to work in Washington.

"We're very aggressive in trying to attract international investors," said the Mayor, who recently visited Peking, Seoul and Bangkok.

Mayor Raymond L. Flynn of Boston said that when a new development, Lafayette Place, was being planned, "we put out the word that we were looking for a reputable foreign company to build a hotel."

"Swissair came over here from Zurich," Mr. Flynn continued. "They put up $30 million, and became the developer of the hotel. They were given a lot of attention, a lot of encouragement, a very businesslike approach."

Mayor Kenneth A. Gibson of Newark has journeyed to Hong Kong and Zurich. "We're trying to reach out to the international financial market, to see what kind of interest we can stimulate," he said.

Some Concerns Are Raised

Newark's major economic attractions are its airport and seaport, Mr. Gibson said, and two automobile manufacturers, Jaguar of Britain and Nissan of Japan, were persuaded to build facilities in the city. In addition, the Maersk shipping company, a European conglomerate, built a major terminal in Newark.

Some foreign investment is less welcome than others. "There has been some concern about foreign investment in Illinois farmland," said Mayor C. Richard Neumiller of Peoria. "People are afraid of losing the land."

But Mr. Neumiller has been aggressive in seeking foreign investors to offset layoffs at the Caterpillar Tractor Company and the closing of the Pabst brewery and Hiram Walker distillery in his city.

He said that the Asia Motors Company of South Korea had agreed to build automobile parts in Peoria, and that Noel Penny, a British company, would build a large plant there to manufacture turbine engines.

* * *

January 4, 1987

CAMBODIAN TO CAJUN, MUSIC FINDS A NEW YORK HOME

By STEVEN SWARTZ

The year was 1974, and Robert Browning and Geno Rodriguez had just opened the Alternative Center for International Arts (later to become the Alternative Museum) as a venue for music from around the world played mostly by New York-based performers. But, as Mr. Browning recalls it, "We were sitting there on summer afternoons wondering why nobody was coming in."

One day, a man from Argentina showed up and proposed holding a concert there with his Andean-music group, Tahuantinsuyo. Mr. Browning and Mr. Rodriguez agreed, and thus was a musical institution born.

That concert became part of a series organized by Mr. Browning. At first it was just a handful of musical events attracting a handful of listeners. Along the way, jazz and experimental music were added, the space moved from East Fourth Street to White Street in TriBeCa, and, by 1985, an average of 40 events a season was drawing near-capacity or overflow crowds in a space holding more than 100 people.

Early appearances by artists such as the saxophonist David Murray, the South Indian violinist L. Subramaniam and the Brazilian capoeira dancer Loremil Machado established the

Alternative Museum's reputation for presenting little-known artists who would soon become prominent. So successful was the series that by 1985 it had outgrown the Alternative Museum's physical and administrative resources, and Mr. Browning split (amicably) with the museum to found the World Music Institute, an autonomous organization presenting world music, experimental music and jazz in spaces as small as Greenwich House and as large as Carnegie Hall. Now in its second season, the institute is offering a rich selection of music from Cambodian to Cajun.

Coming up Saturday at 8 P.M. at the Ethnic Folk Arts Center at 179 Varick Street is the Pericles Halkias Orchestra, playing folk music of the Epirus region of Greece, which borders Albania. On Jan. 16 at 8 P.M. the veteran jazz bassist Reggie Workman performs in collaboration with the Yugoslav choreographer/dancer Maya Milenovic. The synthesizer/reed-flute player Richard Horowitz also performs in this event, at Greenwich House, 27 Barrow Street.

Other events coming up in the next weeks include Laura Simms, a major figure in the storytelling renaissance in America, who will present a concert of stories and music on Jan. 17 at Greenwich House, and the folk music and dance of Lebanon on Jan. 24 at the Ethnic Folk Arts Center performed by Mansour Ajami and Simon Shaheen.

Mr. Browning says it was "a strange mixture of things" that led him to his present area of expertise. "I was born in Singapore and spent my early childhood in Shanghai" [his father was a British banker with the Hong Kong and Shanghai Bank]. "Then I went to boarding school in England and I used to go and visit my father who was working in Singapore, Brunei and various countries in the Far East. I heard Eastern music in the villages and on the radio."

He started out to be an engineer, but in the early 1960's he went to art school in London, coincidentally with a cultural explosion that included a surge of interest in Indian and Far Eastern music. A pivotal event was a concert in 1962 by the North Indian musician Bismillah Khan, who had been brought to England by Yehudi Menuhin.

Soon Mr. Browning began to explore the traditional music of the Middle East as well. At the same time he was involved in multimedia events incorporating visual artists, musicians and dancers. Marriage to an American (Helene Browning, who handles publicity for the institute) brought him to New York, where he was reunited with a former art-school friend, Geno Rodriguez, a New Yorker who had been studying in London on the G.I. Bill. The Alternative Center soon followed, operating at first on a financial shoestring, with eventual help from grants and other contributions.

Early concerts relied largely on musicians who were living in the New York area, and the city has remained an important source of performers. Appearing this season are artists based in the New York area who come from such places as Lebanon, Afghanistan, the Central Asian Soviet Socialist Republic, South Africa and Greece. In addition, the series quickly became well-established, and foreign artists coming to the United States often seek to include an institute appearance on their tours. Now and then, however, Mr. Browning and his staff decide to bring an artist over directly. He frequently learns of significant foreign artists through recordings made abroad.

While traditional music forms the major part of institute programming, Mr. Browning sees jazz and experimental music as equally significant. For both jazz and non-jazz artists, the series provides an intermediate-size space and a level of exposure between small downtown lofts and major festivals such as Horizons or Next Wave.

Programming world music and contemporary music side by side is an explicit acknowledgment of the former's vital influence on the latter. As Mr. Browning observes, "So much of contemporary American and European music has drawn on aspects of our own indigenous cultures and those from elsewhere. American music is part of the world—why should it be separate?"

In effect, the series functions as a resource for musicians who have an ear for the music of other cultures and the traditional music of our own. Ralph Samuelson, president of the Society for Asian Music and a shakuhachi (Japanese bamboo flute) player who has participated in institute concerts, remarks, "The interest of composers and improvising and performing musicians has been growing in world music largely due to what Robert has been doing. The impact is hard to evaluate in quantitative terms; it goes way beyond the number of people who might hear a given event. W.M.I. has been instrumental in stimulating a lot of cross-fertilization between Western and non-Western music."

A more obvious constituency for an ethnic-music concert is, of course, people who have that music in their own cultural background. The institute tries to target its publicity accordingly, but sometimes, as in the case of Afghan music, the local community is rather small, and an audience has to be built for the music. Generally, however, the nature of the audience varies with the type of music. Often the audience for one type of music will shun other offerings, but most listeners appear open-minded, Mr. Browning feels.

As for the Alternative Museum, it continues to be host to new music; its flourishing series is under the direction of the composer William Hellerman. At the same time, other organizations in New York are active in presenting world music, including the Society for Asian Music, the Asian Society and the Ethnic Folk Arts Center.

Eventually Mr. Browning would like to find a permanent home for institute events. Ideally, this would include both an auditorium for formal events and a cafe where listeners could have a drink and dance to a live band playing an Irish reel, a Hungarian csardas or a Cajun two-step—a setting to do justice to dance music. How close is the World Music Institute to meeting this goal? Replies Mr. Browning, "We're one billionaire away."

* * *

June 27, 1988

NEW YORK CITY IS CHALLENGED AS GIANT OF GLOBAL ECONOMY

By THOMAS J. LUECK

At a time when the global economy is being tied together as never before in a network of financial markets and professional services, New York City is facing new challenges to its position as the world's leading center of business.

Executives in Europe, the Far East and the United States said the city remains the leading hub for business and finance, maintaining the primacy that it has held since World War II.

"New York is still the center of it all," said Yoshio Terasawa, executive vice president of the Nomura Securities Company of Tokyo, which has 750 workers on Wall Street.

Strength May Become Weak Point

But what is now the city's outstanding strength may become its most vulnerable point. Other cities around the world have been gaining international business faster than New York, and executives said they expect global enterprise to continue to decentralize, which would mean a shift from Manhattan of businesses now centered here.

"New York is no longer the single, dominant international center it was in times past," said Renato Ruggieo, Italy's Minister of Foreign Trade. He said several cities in Europe and the Far East are gaining importance.

How well it fares in the global competition will be crucial to New York City, where 10 years of robust expansion have been fueled by foreign investment in its financial markets and its real estate, and a huge international market has developed for services emanating in Manhattan.

The global links have brought many benefits. Recent studies show that legal services, accounting and other industries that provide professional services—and export them around the globe—are the fastest-growing industries in the city.

The international business has compensated the city in part for its severe losses in manufacturing. It has also helped diversify the Wall Street investment houses, making them more resilient in economic downturns.

But almost inevitably, executives said, more of that business will in the future be shared with other cities.

"Will New York be the dominant financial center in 1992?" asked John G. Heimann, the vice chairman of Merrill Lynch and Company. Unequivocally, he said, "the answer is no."

"New York won't dominate, nor will London or Paris or Tokyo," he added. Because of advancing technology that allows around-the-clock trading on foreign financial markets, "the dominating factor will be when people work, not where they work."

Measuring precisely how much foreign business is done by investment houses, law firms and other service companies, unlike measuring exports of manufactured goods, is impossible, economists say.

The Forces Shifting Business Abroad

Many economic forces are shifting business from New York. One is the growing concentration of wealth in the Far East, which has created huge new markets for business and professional services in Tokyo, Hong Kong and other cities there.

Rosemary Scanlon, the chief economist of the Port Authority, said that, while Tokyo and Hong Kong have so far captured the bulk of Asia's business, diminishing New York's role in the region, other cities, including Singapore and Los Angeles would become more important in the future.

The United States' huge international debt is creating lucrative business for foreign lenders.

Computers and advanced telecommunications have enabled many New York-based industries, including law, advertising, engineering and accounting, to disperse their operations around the world. At the same time, the deregulation of financial markets in London and other capitals is attracting a surge of foreign investment.

While international business is nothing new to New York—it has been a magnet for multinational corporations throughout the 20th century—experts say the globalization of financial markets and the rapid growth of international markets for the city's professional services have been unique to the last decade.

The city is "emerging as a central brain for the global system," said the Regional Plan Association, a research organization, in a report on the city's role in the international economy.

"So many important decisions affecting world production, trade, investment and finance are made here that decisions themselves might be considered one of the region's most important exports," the group said.

OPEC, Foreign Banks Helped in the 1970's

New York strengthened its international position in banking and finance during the late 1970's, when the oil-rich nations of the Organization of Petroleum Exporting Countries deposited vast amounts of money in banks here.

By the 1980's, foreign banks had rapidly migrated to the city. According to the Port Authority of New York and New Jersey, the number of foreign banks with branches in Manhattan, 244 in 1979, had jumped to 356 by 1986.

Only London, with the branches of 400 foreign banks, has more.

Foreign real-estate investors, who started acquiring Manhattan office buildings when the city was in its fiscal crisis during the mid-1970's, have invested heavily during most of the last decade. Led by the Canadians, who invested early, and the Japanese, who have come in force in recent years, paying top dollar for prime office buildings, foreigners now own 59 million square feet of offices in Manhattan, a fifth of the total.

Perhaps the most important changes during the 1980's have come on Wall Street, which has been selling an array of new financial products and services around the world.

Investment houses that once dealt almost entirely with American customers are scanning the globe for business, selling mergers and acquisition expertise in France, commercial paper in Australia and government bonds in Argentina.

The diverse global business has made many Wall Street concerns less vulnerable to sharp market downturns.

"New York City is so much the vortex of world capital markets, and the processing of those markets, that it will continue to do well," said James Robinson, the chairman of the American Express Company.

"All the new markets are unlikely to contract at once," said Thierry Noyelle, an economist at Columbia University. He added that "Wall has emerged as Main Street, not simply as a place for speculative stock market transactions."

But many executives say foreign competitors are not far behind, creating their own markets and professional services, and several other major cities are gaining ground on New York.

Another powerful force, executives said, is technology, which is making it possible for the business of highly paid professionals in finance, law, accounting and other fields to be dispersed around the world.

"The whole notion of dominant financial centers became antiquated with the telecommunications satellite," said Mr. Heimann of Merrill Lynch.

He added that global communications would enable securities concerns to spread their operations around the world, seeking the least restrictive government regulations and lowest business costs. Singapore and the Netherlands Antilles, for example, have fewer regulations than the United States, On Wall Street, the globalization of stock investing, corporate borrowing, mergers and other financial services is reflected in recent moves by Merrill Lynch, the country's largest securities concern, and Nomura, the world's largest.

Both have been dispatching investment bankers, stock market analysts and other pinstriped professionals into each others' capitals in droves.

Nomura, Merrill Lynch Move In on Each Other

Nomura, based in Tokyo, has offices on Maiden Lane, just off Wall Street. It said it increased its New York work force 78 percent last year, with most of the growth in its United States investment banking operation, which has been in the city for over 50 years.

The Nomura Research Institute, a global financial research organization; the Japan Associated Finance Company, Nomura's venture capital subsidiary; and a Nomura mutual fund unit have all opened offices on Maiden Lane over the last two years.

In an interview in Tokyo, Mr. Terawawa said one reason for Nomura's expanding presence in New York City was the proximity it provided to key executives from around the world.

"The human touch is important," he said. "It's better to meet people, to have personal relations and to be able to have lunch together," he said.

But, while Nomura's strategy reflects the continuing appeal of New York City, its expansion here is capturing a greater share of business that might otherwise go to American securities companies.

Meanwhile, a short walk from Nomura's Manhattan command post, at Merrill Lynch's headquarters in Battery Park City, executives have been casting covetous eyes on the Far East.

Merrill, which has made sharp cuts in many of its United States operations since the October stock market drop, has nonetheless expanded in Japan. The company said it added 110 workers to its Japanese offices over the last 12 months, a 33 percent increase.

The biggest driving force behind Merrill's expansion is the desire to have its representatives in countries that are investing the most money in world markets, said Nassos Michas, chief operating officer of Merrill Lynch International. "Japan is the biggest source," he said.

The globalization taking place at Merrill and Nomura is not confined to the securities industry. Indeed, New York City's commercial banks, law firms, advertising agencies, accounting firms and other service businesses have been swiftly expanding their reach into international markets, while their counterparts abroad have been moving into Manhattan.

The Globalization Of Advertising and Law

In advertising, many New York agencies have been taken over by foreign firms, particularly British ones.

New York "is a key outpost for any company with international ambitions," said Martin Sorrell, the chairman of WPP Group P.L.C., a British concern that last year paid $566 million for the JWT Group Inc., whose J. Walter Thompson subsidiary is the nation's fourth-largest advertising agency.

In the law, major New York firms have been sending large staffs abroad to serve multinational clients, and foreign law firms been moving here.

"There is no place equal to New York in terms of financial transactions," said Giuseppe Bisconti, an Italian attorney with offices in Rome and New York. "Things happen there before anywhere else."

Economists said the growth of advanced services that are exported from New York, although impossible to measure precisely, had clearly become the city's fastest-growing business.

In one study, the United States Bureau of Labor Statistics analyzed employment changes in what it called "major export-oriented industries" in New York City, and found that these industries accounted for most of the city's economic expansion since 1979.

Dozens of industries were counted in the study, ranging from banking to book publishing, all of them serving a market at least in part international. The study concluded that these industries added 203,700 jobs in the city between 1979 and 1987.

* * *

April 9, 1989

AS THE WORLD LEARNS

Global Imperative

By EDWARD B. FISKE

Every weekday afternoon, the New York Life Insurance Company gathers the claims that have come in that day and sticks them in a sack to be put on an Aer Lingus jet to Ireland, where there is a surplus of well-educated white-collar workers to process them.

New York Life's willingness to leap national boundaries in the name of efficiency and economy is a sure sign that the "global office" is now a reality. For Americans, however, there is another, more sobering message: With this nation's labor force vying with workers overseas, schools in the United States are now competing head-on with schools overseas. And the competition does not end in Ireland. . . .

"This country is involved in a global brain race," said David Kearns, chairman of the Xerox Corporation, which in recent years began requiring all managers to judge themselves against the performance of their most effective worldwide competitors. "American schools must also measure themselves on the new global standard."

By that yardstick, American schools don't measure up, routinely scoring near the bottom on international comparisons of mathematics, science and other forms of academic achievement. "We have three kinds of deficits in this country—a trade deficit, a budget deficit and an education deficit," said Lauro B. Cavazos, the United States Secretary of Education. "The last may be the most serious of all."

From elementary schools to colleges, educators are beginning to get the message—that the nation must turn out students who not only have the skills to compete with their counterparts in other countries but who also understand other cultures sufficiently to deal with them.

"Today's students will be working in institutions where the distinction between international and domestic is collapsing," said Thomas C. Heller, director of overseas study programs at Stanford University. "People who will be doing good banking or engineering will be living in institutions that are essentially global in their organization." In such an environment, "know thy competitor" is a law of survival.

Global events have always had an effect on educational institutions at all levels, whether they knew where it came from or not. But school administrators, whose widest frame of reference has been a desk in a state education department, are now being sensitized to the disparate forces from around the world that act on them.

- Refugees from Central America pour into Miami, forcing the Dade County education system to build at least 49 new schools and expanding 180 others, using a $980 million bond issue passed last year.

- The shift of automobile assembly-line jobs from Detroit to South Korea erodes the tax base of public schools in Michigan.

- Racial turmoil in South Africa forces Chicago teachers to change social-studies curriculums.

  Globalization is equally apparent at the college level:

- With the number of 18-year-olds declining, American admissions directors recruit as eagerly in Hong Kong and Kuala Lumpur as they do in Atlanta or Dallas.

- Prime Minister Margaret Thatcher slashes British university budgets, and scores of prominent British professors join American teaching staffs.

Of course, this "small world" syndrome is by no means unique to education. In a recent report titled "America in Transition: The International Frontier," members of the National Governors' Association discussed the consequences of globalization for their state economies and work forces. "Fiber-optic networks span the continents," the report noted. "Billions of dollars move in seconds from Milan to Tokyo to New York. Goods move around the world in a single day. An individual product may contain parts manufactured in five different countries and be assembled in a sixth."

Subjected to these transnational currents, and faced with new and pressing demands, the nation's education system must now respond, preparing students to live and work in a highly competitive global village. According to Ernest L. Boyer, president of the Carnegie Foundation for the Advancement of Teaching, this means that schools must possess an "intellectual understanding of the new global agenda" and then develop new ways to communicate it. Or as Claire Gaudiani, president of Connecticut College, said, schools must start "meeting the needs of people who will operate in an increasingly internationalized environment even if they never leave Duluth."

Until now, schools have relied on a formula of patching on a few requirements. "The usual approach is to stuff a few courses on international affairs into an already overstuffed curriculum and then throw in a little area studies or a foreign language," said Harlan Cleveland, former dean of University of Minnesota's Hubert H. Humphrey Institute of Public Policy.

These solutions, however, have not done the job. Take geography, for instance, which, according to the Governors' Association, "has nearly disappeared as a separate subject" in primary and secondary schools. The report cites evidence that one in seven American adults cannot locate the United States on a world map, and that one out of four high school seniors in Dallas cannot name the country bordering the United States on the south.

Then there is the matter of foreign languages. According to the Education Department, only one elementary school in six offers instruction in a foreign language and only one student in five emerges from high school having studied another language for more than two years.

There are understandable reasons for America's linguistic parochialism. In the United States one can travel 3,000 miles from ocean to ocean and get along with a single language—

in a nation bounded by only two countries, of which the one with the vastly longer border also uses mostly English. Moreover, as some academicians note, most of the rest of the world speaks English.

Other scholars argue that to know a language is to know a culture and a country, and that relying on other people's linguistic abilities is risky. "You can buy in any language," said Robert L. Carothers, chancellor of the Minnesota State University System. "You sell in the language of the customer."

Studying abroad—something that 50,000 American college students do every year—is another longstanding response to the call for globalized education. To this day, however, it has not progressed much beyond what Leon Botstein, president of Bard College, labels "an academic version of the Grand Tour." The Council on International Educational Exchange, a nonprofit group based in New York City that coordinates overseas study and travel, the typical American student abroad is still a "white middle-class female from a highly educated, professional family studying humanities in Western Europe."

Because of an emerging global economy and other pressures, the situation is improving. Andrew Smith of the American Forum for Global Education, a nonprofit organization that promotes a more world-based education, recalls years spent watching the eyes of school administrators glaze over at the mention of those two words. Now, he says, he has "more requests for help than we can handle."

The Modern Language Association reports that foreign languages, including previously unfashionable ones like Japanese, are gaining favor among high school and college students. Last fall, Congress established grants for model foreign-language programs along with awards to elementary- and secondary-school teachers for excellence in foreign-language instruction. The new Omnibus Trade and Competitiveness Act makes money available to colleges and universities to establish international business centers—postgraduate faculties sponsored by a university's business school, area-studies center and foreign-language department. They are designed to train M.B.A.'s who can speak a foreign language and understand a foreign culture.

States are also getting into the act. Arkansas requires every high school to offer a yearlong course on global studies focusing on transnational issues, such as the environment. New York's social-studies curriculum includes a two-year global-studies course required for all high school freshmen and sophomores. Virginia has set up summer language schools for high school students.

Virtually every major American college and university is pursuing foreign interests. Boston University, for instance, has operations in 14 countries, from a traditional junior-year-abroad program in Grenoble, France, to a graduate management program in Kobe, Japan, for Japanese middle managers interested in American management styles. One of every five Boston University education students serves as a student teacher in England, Israel or Nigeria.

In the opinion of an increasing number of educators, however, what is needed is not an expansion of existing approaches but a fundamental change in approach. Global education must be seen not as a topic unto itself, they say, but as an orientation that should infuse every subject.

"Global education is no longer a question of having a fiesta or two to celebrate another culture," Mr. Smith said. "There should be international references in everything we do."

In keeping with such a philosophy, New York City recently established at Washington Irving High School in Manhattan a magnet school for international studies and foreign languages; there, every subject has an international dimension. For example, when ninth-graders study Japan in social studies, they read short stories by Japanese writers in their English class.

Elementary-school teachers in Weston, Conn., assign children's stories that are popular in other countries like Mexico or Japan, while mathematics teachers at Weston's middle school use world population data to teach ratios and percentages. In Redwood Falls, Minn., elementary-school science teachers discuss the basics of energy by examining worldwide patterns of energy production and usage.

At the college level, St. Olaf in Minnesota, Kalamazoo in Michigan and other institutions have already begun reorganizing curriculums on the assumption that students will spend at least part of their four years abroad. According to Glen Gersmehl, coordinator of global studies at Clark University in Massachusetts, the proportion of American institutions offering full programs in international studies has jumped in a decade from 12 percent in 1979 to more than 50 percent today.

In fields where international contacts are increasingly important, notably business and engineering, schools are forging new global links. Georgia Institute of Technology has established China/Tech, a privately held venture with offices in both Atlanta and Beijing, to help American companies enter the Chinese market and familiarize Chinese managers with American technology and skills. Earlham College in Indiana is working to introduce Japanese language and culture into 15 Indiana school districts; Earlham students fluent in Japanese serve as interpreters for American companies involved in joint ventures.

The University of Illinois allows engineering students to add an international flair to their transcripts. Jim Fanning, for example, studied at the University of Dundee in Scotland, then spent a summer in Nanjing studying Chinese and trying out his skills in a foundry. "It will make me a better engineer," he said. "You understand cultural differences. You open up your mind to listen to other people's ideas and point of view."

The faculty of Connecticut College voted in February to establish an optional program called International Studies and the Liberal Arts. Students who enter the program, which begins this fall, can choose any major. They must take a set of courses on global issues, like international economics, study a particular area of the world and learn the language. They then pursue an internship in that area—working in a law firm in Japan, for example—and, returning to the United States, join a seminar where everyone presents a paper based on his particular part of the world.

"The goal is to teach students how to operate as effective adults in a foreign culture," said Ms. Gaudiani, the president. "The Dutch invented the telescope because they were sailors and wanted to see where they were going. We're trying to build in preparedness to deal in an international environment."

In September, Stanford University will open the Stanford Center in Kyoto, Japan. The center will function much like a traditional university campus, offering undergraduate and graduate teaching, research, internships, consulting and more. Like the Connecticut College program, its purpose is to train students so that they are comfortable in the global village.

"Major banks today have to have a physical presence in financial centers around the world," said Mr. Heller, Stanford's director of overseas study. "The same can be said of the manufacturing world. Ford has a home base in Detroit, but it operates through joint ventures all around the world. A great university today must have the same kind of dispersed presence around the world."

*   *   *

August 8, 1989

GROWTH OF TOURISM IS BENEFITING FRAGILE ENVIRONMENT

MANAUS, Brazil—Dotted with monuments from a 19th century rubber boom, this Amazonian river capital eagerly looks forward to a new boom: ecological tourism.

Worldwide concern over the Amazon rain forest is reaching this remote city, bringing waves of American and European tourists and fueling $150 million of new hotel construction.

"In the 1990's, tourism will emerge as the largest single source of income in Amazonas state," Romulo Jose de Paula Nunes, president of the state tourism agency, predicted in a recent interview here.

Gaining popularity among Americans and Europeans, "ecotourism" gives third-world countries economic returns for preserving nature.

Birding, Hiking, Sightseeing

"Ecotourism is protecting the natural resources by stressing the tourism value of those resources over their exploitation or other development," said John Kusler, American coordinator of the Ecotourism and Resource Conservation Project.

Ecological tourism includes birding, hiking, sightseeing and visits to cultural sights. Several examples from third-world countries were cited at a workshop held by the Ecotourism Project last April in Mexico.

In Belize, Central America concern for tourism prompted the government to create aquatic parks along coral reefs and to set aside a forest park to protect black panthers. New hotels in the interior are often of rustic design, resembling native villages.

In Africa, Kenya recently proposed a complete halt to world trade in ivory. Some Kenyans have profited from ivory sales, but officials evidently calculated that elephants are worth more alive than dead. In the last two years, tourism jumped ahead of coffee and tea to become the largest source of foreign exchange for the East African nation.

Business Is Booming

"Many of these countries considered environmental considerations a luxury of rich nations," said Arthur Heyman, of the development office of the Organization of American States. "Now they can't afford not to be conscientious about protecting their environment. If that goes, then tourism follows."

It is not known how many "ecotourists" travel every year. But tour operators say business is booming.

"Trips that used to sell out at the last minute now sell out months in the advance," said Victor Emanuel of Victor Emanuel Tours of Austin, Texas. "More often than not, we have to organize a second group."

In Brazil, tourism is creating a local economic lobby in favor of protecting the Amazon, the world's largest rain forest.

On a recent morning, a Manaus tour boat, the Uruna, nosed through the silt-laden waters of an Amazonian tributary. Watching the lush riverbank foliage slip by, Dionisio Borghi, the boat owner, spoke of the growing economic argument in favor of greenery.

'You Hear Chainsaws'

"You take tourists up a new part of the river, and all of a sudden you hear two chainsaws around the bend," he said "The tourists see the trees cut down and then they turn to me and say, 'Why are you taking me here?' Eventually, there is going to be a conflict. Both the tour operator and the lumberman have to survive."

In June, the governor of Amazonas state announced that he would resume a controversial policy of distributing free chainsaws to jungle settlers. The state accounts for one third of the 1.9-million-square-mile area that Brazilians call "legal Amazonia."

Although still small, Amazonian tourism runs counter to chainsaw development.

Indeed, the growing worldwide interest in ecological tourism may be most visible in Manaus, a state capital of one million people reachable by a five-hour airplane flight from Miami.

The number of foreign tourists arriving in Manaus increased to 70,000 in 1988, from 12,000 in 1983. In a decade, the number should hit 200,000, Mr. Nunes of the state tourism agency, said.

Jungle Tours

A recent edition of the city's bilingual Portuguese-English tourist guide listed 13 companies offering tours of the surrounding jungle, including Amazon Odyssey Tours, Amazon Safari Camp, Amazon Village and Jungle Trips.

Fears about global warming seem to be prompting some tourists to visit the Amazon.

"It's almost paradoxical," Senator Dale Bumpers, an Arkansas Democrat, said after a recent two-day Congressional fact-finding visit here. "The more the greenhouse effect makes the front page, the more tourism increases." Deforestation of the Amazon, among other things, is thought to increase carbon dioxide in the atmosphere and accelerate global warming.

"In Amazonas state, hotels are now getting the tax incentives that 10 years ago went to cattle ranches," said Thomas Lovejoy, an American ecologist with more than 20 years' experience in the Amazon.

Long the preserve of jungle lodges slung with hammocks and of rustic riverboats in the style of the African Queen, Amazonian tourism is expanding into large-scale luxury operations run by multinational corporations.

During the 1988–1989 winter season, 21 Caribbean cruise ships anchored here, up from one in the 1982–1983 season. Eying the projected tripling of luxury hotel rooms here, Eastern Airlines, a subsidiary of the Texas Air Corporation, recently acquired rights to serve Manaus from the United States.

A 330-Room Hotel

The Sheraton Corporation, a subsidiary of the I.T.T. Corporation, in conjunction with a local Brazilian partner, is building a 330-room hotel here. Hilton Hotels Corporation has also shown interest in building here, Mr. Nunes said.

Henry Maksoud, the owner of one of São Paulo's most opulent hotels, the Maksoud Plaza, explained in a recent interview why he decided to build his second hotel in Manaus.

"The idea is to show the world that there is nothing in the world like the Amazon," he said of the 350-room Maksoud Manaus which is to open in 1992. "There is nothing like the size of those rivers, those forests. This is the last frontier of tourism."

'It May Get Out of Hand'

Advocates of ecological tourism caution that too much tourist development can be counterproductive. In Manaus, two large hotels with inadequate sewage treatment have fouled a swimming beach on the Rio Negro.

"If you begin to open up areas based on the ecotourism argument, it may get out of hand and you might end up destroying what you are trying to preserve," said Mr. Kusler of the Ecotourism Project. "You may end up killing the goose that lays the golden egg."

Training for Guides

Furthermore, the successful melding of tourism and environmental protection depends on enlisting the support of local populations. Priority for employment should be given to local inhabitants, especially for training as guides.

In Manaus, the National Institute for Amazonian Research, a government study center here, has agreed to train guides for ecological tours. The guides will learn how to bring tourists to an area without disturbing it.

"Most of the time areas are ruined by people who don't know any better," said William Wendt of the United States National Park Service who often works with foreign park officials. "Destruction is rarely malicious or intentional."

"Ideally, tourists leave footprints and money and only take photographs out," Mr. Wendt said.

* * *

January 20, 1990

SMALL TOWN, U.S.A., IS GOING GLOBAL

By H. BRANDT AYERS

ANNISTON, ALA.—Strange accents will be heard in the local chamber of commerce offices, and there will be new activity out at the industrial park (plant openings, expansions and some closings) because the political plates of Eastern Europe have slipped and thrust that region closer to us.

American industry is interested in the Polish man who will work for $1 an hour for the same reason that the large Hungarian bus manufacturer, Ikarus, assembles frames of buses in Hungary to be completed by workers here in Calhoun County: productivity.

This small county seat town is not unique. It is a metaphor for what is happening in hometowns nationwide, because more than 70 percent of all American products face foreign competition.

Already, 10 percent of this county's workforce is employed by foreign-owned firms; 300 jobs out at Magic Chef are threatened by South Korea's entry into the microwave oven market; nearly a third of the local Monsanto plant's output was shut down because hard currency dried up in China after the Tiananmen Square tragedy.

With an eye to attracting investment, we take a new interest in meeting the needs of foreign businesses. The local university, Jacksonville State, is ready to launch a Saturday school for Japanese children, if we can land a Japanese industry.

Business is out in the global marketplace, and tourists are, too. There has been an increase of nearly 100 percent in foreign travel during this decade—22 million trips abroad in 1980 compared with a projected 42 million this year.

The world has shrunk to the size of everybody's hometown. Which raises a question: How well is one American leadership institution—the press—responding to this phenomenon? The question is pertinent to the 23 newspapers that have overseas bureaus and the 1,627 daily papers that do not.

How well? "The news is dismal," as Fortinbras observed in the final scene of "Hamlet." A 1988 study of the nation's 10 largest newspapers shows that they gave only 2.6 percent of their news space to foreign affairs. A 1971 study of all dailies showed 10.2 percent of the "news hole" devoted to international stories.

Other recent studies show the public is smarter than the editors. In one, 41 percent of the public said it was "very interested" in foreign news but the editors thought only 5 percent of their readers were interested in foreign coverage.

The press evidently doesn't know how to provide that vital link between the world market and workers at places like the local Magic Chef and Monsanto plants. Both academically and professionally that field is a moonscape. There is only one book on how to make foreign affairs a local story, and a survey of nine top journalism schools revealed no course on the topic.

Why has the press missed the story? Editors have been conditioned by the culture of a nation formed by deliberate rejection of older European cultures. That bias was given a language very early, on Sept. 17, 1796, when George Washington said in his Farewell Address: "Against the insidious wiles of foreign influence (I conjure you to believe me, fellow-citizens) the jealousy of a free people ought to be constantly awake, since history and experience prove that foreign influence is one of the most baneful foes of republican government."

Distracted by populating and developing a vast continent, cushioned by two oceans, distant from foreign languages and cultures, lacking much of a colonial experience, America's world role didn't really begin until the end of the Second World War in 1945.

Since then, American business and the American public have ventured forth. The culture is changing. It wants more foreign coverage at a time when the press has decided to give it less.

My guess, though, is that the press will catch up. Editors and reporters on the local paper had fun doing a six-part series on how Calhoun County is tied to the global economy. What the reporters found surprised everybody (including the publisher).

Another reason for confidence that the press will catch up is that committees of the American Society of Newspaper Editors, the New England Newspaper Association and the Alabama Press Association are exploring the subject.

Besides, the press loves surprises. No reporter worth his salt is going to ignore that delegation of foreigners at the chamber or the new factory going up out at the industrial park.

H. Brandt Ayers is editor and publisher of The Anniston Star.

*   *   *

January 1, 1992

TECHNOLOGY WITHOUT BORDERS RAISES BIG QUESTIONS FOR U.S.

By ANDREW POLLACK

Just as they once moved manufacturing plants overseas, American companies are now spreading their research and product development around the world, helping to turn the creation of technology into an activity that transcends national borders.

The trend raises tough new issues for policy makers intent on preserving jobs for Americans and keeping the nation competitive in high-technology industries like aerospace, pharmaceuticals and information processing. But many business leaders say the march toward technology with no

national allegiances—the march toward the borderless lab— is as inevitable as it is irrevocable. Government policies that do not adapt to this fundamental industrial shift, many executives contend, are bound to fail.

"Policy has to deal with these global realities," said John A. Armstrong, vice president for science and technology at the International Business Machines Corporation.

But not all policy makers and strategists agree how to proceed. Some would seek to stem the international flow to safeguard America's braintrust. Others insist that the best Government response is to accept the inevitable, while insuring that the United States offers a supportive economic environment for research and development work by foreign and domestic companies alike.

Most executives tend to be pragmatists who say that innovation recognizes no borders. "We want to be able to tap into technology wherever it is developed," said Geoffrey C. Nicholson, staff vice president for international technical operations at the Minnesota Mining and Manufacturing Company. "It would be naive to think the U.S. is Mecca for all technologies." The St. Paul company, which makes everything from Post-it notes to optical data disks, now has 2,500 technical people stationed abroad, three times as many as in 1980.

Overseas laboratories are not the only mechanism for the globalization of technology development. In the last month alone, other examples have included the acquisition of a majority stake in a promising American pharmaceutical biotechnology start-up, Systemix Inc., by a leading Swiss drug maker, Sandoz Ltd. From across the Atlantic came word that I.B.M. and Siemens A.G. of Germany had jointly developed the prototype for a new generation of computer memory chip. A few days later, across the Pacific, I.B.M. said it would produce a Japanese-English notebook computer for one of its computer rivals, Tokyo-based Hitachi Ltd.

Since the mid-1980's, there have been more than 900 transnational alliances by United States businesses or investments by foreign companies in American technology start-ups, and those deals do not include countless other joint marketing agreements or outright acquisitions.

With more and more products assembled from components made around the world, notions like "made in the U.S.A." and "American know-how" may be destined to take their place alongside such relics as the "space race" and war bonds in the history of American industrial policy. Apple Computer Inc., which a decade ago was considered the epitome of renegade American entrepreneurial verve, is now working to combine its software expertise with the Sony Corporation's ability in miniaturization to develop consumer electronics devices that neither company could produce as well on its own.

Big Risks for U.S. Companies

The advent of the borderless lab raises big risks for American companies and for the United States economy. Since, as is widely acknowledged, American industry often lags behind foreign companies in manufacturing, the nation's competitive edge now depends on being able to create new technologies faster than overseas rivals. But the rapid spread of technological expertise around the globe could dull this edge in the future.

Globalization also makes it more difficult for policy makers to determine how best to serve the nation's interests, or even to define what those interests are. The conundrum is likely to color the industrial policy debate that is starting to revive in this Presidential election year—and cannot help but provide a subtext next week when President Bush visits Japan with 21 American executives in tow.

Among the policy issues is whether the Government should try to stem the overseas migration of American technology by such measures as blocking acquisitions of key American technology companies by foreign corporations.

Other questions: Does it makes sense for Washington to spend money on research and development, or on competitiveness programs like the Sematech semiconductor consortium, if the technological fruits are going to be immediately enjoyed overseas? If the Government does finance such programs, should they include only American-owned companies, or also foreign companies operating in the United States?

Technology at Fire-Sale Prices?

"You don't want a situation in which very significant technology is being bought at fire-sale prices in the United States and commercialized overseas," said Clyde Prestowitz, president of the Economic Strategy Institute in Washington.

Mr. Prestowitz is in the camp of strategists and policy makers who argue that the globalization of technology can still be, and should be, held in check. Access to technology, like access to markets, they say, is not equal around the world. It is far more difficult, for instance, for an American company to buy a Japanese one than vice versa, they note, arguing that the United States would be naive not to look out for its own interests.

"We're the only country in the world that thinks nationality doesn't matter," said Pat Choate, an economist who is a leading critic of foreign investment in the United States.

But another school of thought—whose adherents include many business people—contends that globalization is inevitable and that the best policy is to make sure the United States reaps its share of benefits from the trend.

'A Very Hazardous Exercise'

"The policies that won't work are those that assume the technology base is national," said Proctor P. Reid, who is a senior program officer at the National Academy of Engineering, which advises the Government on technical matters, and is co-editor of "National Interests in an Age of Global Technology," a book recently published by the academy.

"These global networks are already well developed," he said. "To try to tear the fabric to advantage your companies, or companies resident in the U.S., seems to me a very hazardous exercise."

Just how hazardous was shown in the recent controversy over display screens for notebook computers. To help American manufacturers of these flat panel displays, the Government levied tariffs on screens imported from Japan. But American computer companies, led by Apple and I.B.M., said the tariffs hurt them as well as the Japanese because they needed the screens to stay competitive. To avoid the tariffs, Apple and some other companies have already begun moving production of their portable machines outside the United States.

Those who share Mr. Reid's outlook say that as companies become even more globalized, the companies' nationalities will matter less and less. If I.B.M. and Fujitsu Ltd., the Japanese computer giant, were to spread their jobs, profits and expertise equally around the world, the United States might have little interest in which company triumphed in computer sales.

But, according to this line of thought, the United States would have a vital interest in securing the best jobs for its citizens by making this nation an attractive place for both Fujitsu and I.B.M. to conduct their research, development and manufacturing.

Seeking Improvements

Therefore, those who see globalization as inevitable are calling for Washington to improve domestic education, modernize American factories and create advanced telecommunications networks within the United States. Such improvements, they say, cannot migrate across borders as easily as research discoveries.

"The goal is to have a flourishing climate in the United States for the creation of wealth and added value," Dr. Armstrong of I.B.M. said.

Those who think the nation should go with the technology flow also say that rather than worrying about the nation's best ideas being smuggled away, American companies and the Government should concentrate on acquiring more foreign technology and putting it to use in this country—an effort that the United States did not have to make during the decades of American technological hegemony.

Nowadays, parties on both side of the issue acknowledge, the United States no longer holds a near monopoly on technical advances. Indeed, while the earlier movement of American manufacturing abroad was aimed largely at taking advantage of low-cost foreign labor, the movement of research and development is intended to tap foreign knowledge.

Isolation Can Hurt

"If you isolate yourself to the United States you can hurt yourself and your ability to be competitive," said Alexander MacLachlan, senior vice president of research and development at E. I. du Pont de Nemours & Company, the American chemicals giant.

Only 10 percent of Du Pont's current research and development is conducted overseas, Dr. MacLachlan said, and "we recognize that it is not a satisfactory situation." The company is gradually increasing its level of overseas research, he said.

At Motorola Inc., the Schaumburg, Ill., maker of semiconductors and communications equipment, researchers are quick to point out that the Europeans have pioneered many developments in telecommunications, including alternatives to cellular telephones. "We ignore that at our peril," said Dick Heimlich, corporate vice president for international strategy at Motorola, which established a telecommunications research laboratory in England in 1991.

Another motive in conducting research and product development abroad is to increase overseas sales, which already account for more than half the revenues of many technology companies. Companies are also trying to achieve closer cooperation between their research-and-development activities and manufacturing, to speed the introduction of new products.

Products From Singapore

That sometimes means putting research and development near manufacturing plants that moved abroad years ago. The Hewlett-Packard Company, for example, began a few years ago to move some product development activities to a plant in Singapore that in the past simply manufactured products designed in the United States. Recently, an engineer in Singapore developed a key component that will become the basis of an entirely new line of Hewlett-Packard printers.

Sometimes, of course, political factors play a role. Hewlett-Packard's president and chief executive, John A. Young, said some foreign governments let it be known, however subtly, that they considered it good corporate citizenship to place research, development and manufacturing activities within their borders, rather than merely selling products there. The United States has also encouraged foreign companies, particularly Japanese auto makers, to set up plants and design centers in this country.

Despite the various transnational forces, technology development by American companies remains far less internationalized than manufacturing and sales. On the whole, only 10 percent of American corporate research and development funds is spent abroad. Basic research is even more likely than product development to be kept close to headquarters—in large part because the creation of wholly new technology is so close to the heart of a company's business.

Motorola, for instance, gets half its revenues from international sales, and 40 percent of its work force is stationed abroad. But officials estimate that only 20 to 25 percent of product development is conducted overseas and only about 5 percent of pure research. Even I.B.M, whose European researchers have won two Nobel prizes, conducts less than 25 percent of its research and development outside the United States, Dr. Armstrong said.

Where the Benefits Go

Armed with such evidence, some policy analysts argue that globalization is still relatively limited. There is an enduring national component to technology development, the argue, that continues to justify policies favoring American companies. "The primary benefits will always go to the host country," said Dr. Choate, the economist.

Dr. Choate and some other analysts fear that the transfer of high-paying research and development jobs could hurt the American economy by exporting prime cuts of personal income. But on this point, as in the other issues emanating from the borderless lab, corporate executives say that if they fail to direct their energies offshore when appropriate, their companies would be less competitive—and the American economy would suffer even more.

At Hewlett-Packard, one of the nation's largest exporters, Mr. Young said the company had no choice but to continue expanding its overseas research and development. Otherwise, he said, "we wouldn't have a thriving business and we wouldn't be able to do these exports."

* * *

June 28, 1992

THE ROCKY ROAD TO A GLOBAL MARKET

By JONATHAN FUERBRINGER

"Our market will be the market where the action will take place," said Jean-Francois Theodore, the chief executive officer of the Bourse de Paris. It is the kind of comment expected of a man in his job, especially when he is visiting the United States to drum up business for the French stock market.

This is the message he brought to the pension funds, brokerage firms and investment banks that he met with: France is a market poised for explosive growth, especially as the Government moves to sell to the public many state-owned or controlled blue-chip companies, like Rhone-Poulenc, Air France, Banque Nationale de Paris and Credit Lyonnais. It is a market that has been modernized, with a computer trading system driven totally by orders.

"The market is not going to be lively in Germany," Mr. Theodore said. "It is a cultural thing. There is no privatization." And in Britain, he added, "everything has already taken place."

What he did not explain on his tour, but did detail in an interview last week in New York, are his views on the broader future of the French Bourse, which is up 8.5 percent this year, and European stock markets as the political and economic unification of Europe approaches at the end of the century.

On this issue, he embodies all the parochial and national desires that will make this transition difficult, especially in the market for retail investors. He is caught between the market forces that are pushing change and the desire to protect his own turf. His comments on the future should be as much a warning to those who have chosen not to worry about the obstacles ahead as was the Danes' surprising rejection of the outline for political and monetary union in a referendum at the beginning of June.

In a new book, "The End of Geography," Richard O'Brien, chief economist at American Express Bank in London, also issues a warning. He sees market forces, like technological advances and the free flow of capital, pushing financial markets toward a global state in which the location of a company's headquarters or where financial business is conducted will no longer be important.

But the transition to that "seamless" market, he warns, will be grim. "A more sober look at the crystal ball," he writes, "suggests a rather bumpy road toward seamlessness: intense competition among financial firms, with major bankruptcies, forced mergers followed by massive shakeouts, crises for customers and producers alike, repeated losses from overambitious investment in new technologies, financial crises leading to the socialization of losses (a la S&Ls) and seemingly intractable problems in reconciling the fundamental differences between contrasting financial systems."

Mr. Theodore acknowledges that the hegemony of local stock markets in Europe will be challenged, likely by outside trading networks that will try to establish their own pan-European market for big blue-chip stocks. It is the kind of challenge that the London stock market has already offered with its concentration on the trading of foreign stocks. (Mr. Theodore dismisses claims by the London market and others that a major share of French stock trading takes place in London, arguing that the London market "is always counting trades two, three or four times.")

He says there should be more cooperation among Europe's stock exchanges on trading as a defense against the success of some outside network. He lamented the fact that a trading system called Euroquote, which would allow the trading of blue-chip stocks among exchanges, has been stalled because of opposition in Germany and Britain.

But, he still concludes, "I don't believe in a pan-European stock exchange. At the end of the 90's, there will be four or five or six stock exchanges, each having the lead in its own domestic stocks." He argues that despite the internationalization of many companies, like Nestle in Switzerland and Peugeot and Alcatel Alstholm in France, the country where the company is based will still determine where most of its stock is traded and where the stock will be most liquid.

"The internationalization of a company does not mean the internationalization of the stock," he said. "The home country will always mean something."

One reason he thinks a broader market will be difficult to achieve is that the merging of company and takeover laws throughout a unified Europe will be very difficult because of the desire to protect the home base. "It is more difficult to converge on company law," he said, than on inflation.

Despite the problems ahead, Mr. Theodore seems to be resisting the change that is coming. It may not be pan-European, but it seems more likely that there could be a two-tier system, with major blue-chip stocks trading as much outside their own countries as in them, while smaller stocks stay home.

Mr. O'Brien, like Mr. Theodore, thinks it will be much harder to move to a truly global equities market than it has been to create an international foreign exchange market. But he also doubts whether any stock market will be able to maintain a national base in a world where location is losing its importance.

The Bourse approach, Mr. O'Brien writes, "presupposes that in the future it will be easy to identify French versus Italian versus British stocks, when companies themselves are becoming more European and/or global in an end-of-geography world."

He also asks if it will be feasible for French companies to "confine trades in French stocks to one market if those companies could enjoy better conditions elsewhere, as a result of tapping a wider marketplace."

* * *

July 27, 1995

GLOBAL GRASS-ROOTS BANKING

The World Bank, the Agency for International Development and eight other donors have joined to finance small loans to the poorest of the world's poor—loans as little as $100, at low interest rates and with no collateral except the borrower's word. These will be loans to underwrite the aspirations of ordinary people, from funds provided by international agencies accustomed to dealing in tens and hundreds of millions, with a level of caring not routinely shown by even a generous local banker.

"Like slavery in the 19th century, the fact that 700 million human beings are hungry in the 20th century is unconscionable," says Ismail Serageldin, a vice president of the World Bank and chairman of the new aid group. "We are the new abolitionists."

The program builds on the successful model of the Grameen Bank in Bangladesh. Founded in the 1970's and still directed by Muhammad Yunus, Grameen has made some two million small loans, mostly to women. There are similar banks—some run by governments, some not—in Indonesia, Kenya, the Dominican Republic and Colombia.

Contributors to the new program have formed the Consultative Group to Aid the Poor, an independent agency. The agency, in turn, will grant or lend funds to the existing small-loan banks and others yet to be established, and will create a global network to spread the movement's scope. At a pledge meeting last month, prospective donors made a tentative commitment to put up at least $200 million. In addition to the World Bank and A.I.D., they included Canada, France, the Netherlands and several multinational agencies.

As an example of what they hope to accomplish, the Grameen Bank's record is illuminating and inspiring. More than 92 percent of its borrowers are women, commonly heads of families. Half have used the money to start raising livestock and poultry. The other half go into handiwork, manufacturing and the trades.

They maintain an admirable rate of repayment—97 percent, usually within a year. That is better than the rate for poor men in the same program, and much better than the rate for wealthier Bangladeshis with regular bank loans. This is an aid program that works.

*   *   *

February 3, 1996

WHERE SMALL IS BEAUTIFUL

For Italy's Family-Owned Weavers, Life Is Good

By JOHN TAGLIABUE

BIELLA, Italy—Because the weavers on the other side of the valley specialize in cashmere, and the nearby Loro Piana company has a two-year monopoly on the supply of vicuna wool, Paolo Ferla is betting his company's future on the highly prized fleece of the baby alpaca.

Mr. Ferla's company, Lanificio Egidio Ferla S.p.A., is just one of 1,800 family-owned textile producers nestled in the hills around this northern Italian town. Together, they employ 28,000 people—an average of just 16 each. In the era of the global marketplace, where even giant corporations must fight to protect their turf against low-cost third-world competitors, such small-scale operators might seem quaint anachronisms, doomed to extinction.

They are anything but. Not only has Biella beaten back the onslaught of cheap textiles from the Far East, it has also inundated Japan, Korea and China with its own top-of-the-line fabrics. When Europe emerged from recession last year, Biella was at the forefront of the Continent's export push, helping Italy rack up a $15.8 billion trade surplus in textiles ($20.5 billion when leather goods and other apparel are included). Demand for Biella's cloths is so strong that the regional unemployment rate has sunk to 5 percent, less than half Western Europe's overall jobless rate of 12 percent, and local business owners complain of a shortage of skilled labor.

Few Americans may realize it, but in Europe, as in the United States, small businesses are assuming an increasingly crucial role as engines of economic growth. While the problems of huge industrial conglomerates like Germany's Daimler-Benz A. G. or Italy's Olivetti S.p.A. grab the headlines, thousands of family enterprises are quietly innovating, increasing sales and exports, and creating jobs.

Pockets of small-business dynamism are scattered across the Continent, from machine-building companies around Bologna, Italy, or in the Germany state of Baden-Wurttemberg, to the shoe makers and tile producers of the Catalonia region of Spain, to the perfume manufacturers of Grasse, France. Collectively they are a bright spot in a Europe otherwise mired in slow growth, high unemployment and out-of-control budget deficits that threaten outbursts of social unrest like the strikes that recently swept France.

The family-owned textile companies of Biella sometimes seem almost relentless in their smallness, with even companies of a dozen workers or fewer setting up employees as suppliers. Yet they show remarkable agility at solving problems, in part because their size makes them more nimble, but also because of an unusual willingness to share technology, marketing and manufacturing experience, and sometimes even production capacity with their home-town competitors.

And rather than having to fight off Government antitrust regulators, they actually get encouragement from the 15-nation European Union, so long as their collaboration at home does not translate into monopolistic practices abroad.

"The advantage is that at any time you can easily talk to your bank, your competitors, your suppliers," said Mr. Ferla, 38, whose $12-million-a-year company employs 65 people who produce 400,000 yards of fabric a year. "Biella is perfect for business."

Biella's textile-weaving community is the product of centuries of growth. Riccardo Piacenza still lives in the house his forebears used in 1733 to start a textile business. Over a lunch of boiled beef and vegetables, he described how the industry grew rapidly in the 19th century after textile machines were imported from Belgium and Britain. In time, Biella boasted all layers of textile work, from spinning to weaving to finishing. To supply the textile makers, local textile machine companies sprang up.

The town's peculiar mix of cooperation and competition dates back at least to those days, when textile mills routinely let competitors inspect their latest equipment.

In the 1960's, the local industrialists banded together to finance a training school for textile workers. In the 1970's, they started a joint trade fair to promote Biella's textiles. And in the 1980's, local textile-machinery manufacturers formed a consortium to sell their products in China's newly liberalized market.

Today, the textile companies have gotten so chummy that some economists liken them to the divisions of a large corporation. When floods of orders exceed one manufacturer's capacity, competitors are often called in to help assure deliveries—and keep customers happy.

At Ing. Loro Piana & C. S.p.A., Sergio Loro Piana leads a visitor through a new $31 million plant, where computer-controlled machines spin cashmere yarns at dizzying speeds. The equipment is so advanced that only a handful of workers are needed to operate it. Yet far from hiding it from other local textile barons, Mr. Piana, who with his brother Pier Luigi runs the $162 million-a-year company that a forebear founded in 1924, said he would invite them all to inspect the new machinery when the plant is formally inaugurated later this year.

Gestures like that make Biella's companies fiercely loyal to one another. Mr. Ferla said his company paid local suppliers up to 10 percent more than the same goods might cost elsewhere just to maintain a longstanding relationship. "We seldom try to struggle with subcontractors," he said. "We don't want to kill anyone. We learned this from our grandfathers. It's very wise in the long run."

Mr. Ferla's company found itself on the receiving end of its neighbors' largess when it made its move into baby alpaca, a rare and extremely delicate wool. Spinning and finishing the fibers was supposed to be all but technically impossible.

But, working with nearby spinning-machine companies and finishing specialists, Mr. Ferla's company found a way. Now, it supplies the lightweight fabric, half the price of cashmere, to American apparel makers like Hickey Freeman and Oxxford Clothing.

The collaboration in Biella has not touched off any inquiries from Italian or European Union antitrust authorities, perhaps because the weavers seem to have a keen sense of where cooperation ends and competition begins. Rival factory owners will sit over a lunch of polenta and chicken at the local tennis-club restaurant discussing the difficulties of spinning some tricky new fiber or procuring wool supplies. But when they go abroad hawking their wares to apparel manufacturers in Japan or the United States, it is usually other Biella manufacturers they are competing against.

The European Union generally encourages cooperative efforts by regional clusters of small businesses, and the idea has stirred international interest. In the United States, banding together to survive outside competitive threats has become more common for localized industries, but there the small-business partnerships tend to get more of a helping hand from state governments. Richard M. Locke, a specialist on industrial districts at the Massachusetts Institute of Technology's Sloan School of Management, cited programs in both Massachusetts and Pennsylvania to help their garment and machine-tool industries in the 1980's.

European small businesses are beginning to show signs of wanting the same sort of government attention. Biella's industrialists recently joined 13 other Italian districts to form a lobbying organization that seeks links with similar industrial regions elsewhere in Europe. The goal, according to Enrico Botto Poala, a textile maker who is its first president, is to pressure the European Union to shift industrial policy from a focus on helping backward regions to doing more for regional small-business groups.

One reason for Biella's backscratching is an awareness of its vulnerability. Memories of the 1970's, when a sputtering economy and a flood of cheap Asian imports wiped out half of the region's textile companies, remain vivid.

To respond to that crisis, the Biellese brought out innovative new products, including Loro Piana's light Tasmanian wools. To increase efficiency, many companies spun off some of their operations or helped finance start-ups that specialized in various steps of the textile process like spinning, dyeing or finishing. Biella's weavers also invested heavily in research and technology.

To be sure, many locals fear that the region, which is one-fourth the size of Rhode Island and has a population of 190,000, remains overdependent on a single industry. While it has developed other manufacturing, like valves and bathroom fixtures, it still relies on textiles for one-third of employment. Meantime, the growth of Italian textile exports is slowing, and raw-material prices are rising.

But Biella textile makers are responding to the challenges. Many, for example, have shifted some of their production abroad. Piacenza now spins cashmere yarns in China, the world's principal supplier of cashmere wool. Loro Piana does likewise, and last year formed a joint venture in Outer Mongolia, another cashmere region, and signed an agreement to obtain vicuna after helping Peru rescue the endangered species. Earlier, Loro Piana acquired Warren of Stafford, a textile mill in Stafford Springs, Conn.

Arnaldo Bagnasco, an economist at Turin University, said he believed Biella's textile industry would undoubtedly get more efficient if it could win tax concessions from the Italian Government and economic assistance—including money for better roads and telecommunications—from the European Union authorities in Brussels.

Moreover, the textile-mill owners remain confident that the same skills that enabled them to surmount previous crises will steer them through any new troubles. Riccardo Piacenza, a representative of the 13th generation running his family's business, likens Biella's products to Swiss watches that cannot be easily duplicated by would-be competitors.

Mr. Loro Piana is equally upbeat. "There are some very good manufacturers all over the world," he said. "But we don't see, systematically, any other region, any bunch of companies, capable of casting a serious shadow on our district."

*   *   *

February 4, 1996

GLOBAL VILLAGE, LOCAL ANGLE, YOUNG FACES

By RICHARD WEIZEL

When Jim Ziolkowski backpacked through India, Thailand and Nepal in 1990 after graduating from college, he came upon a Nepalese village in the midst of a two-day celebration.

The people of Kari Khola were rejoicing because a British mountain-climbing group had donated $5,000 to build a small school, and that school was ready to open.

The sight of people rejoicing over something that Americans take so much for granted changed Mr. Ziolkowski's life.

Several years later, having landed a job at GE Capital in Stamford, Mr. Ziolkowski still could not get the image of the villagers' school dedication out of his mind.

"Here were people without running water or electricity and living in houses made out of mud getting so excited over the opening of a small schoolhouse," he said. "It was something I knew I would never forget."

And he also never forgot that something so crucial to an entire village for generations to come could be accomplished for just $5,000.

That's when he decided to put together an organization in the United States that would recreate the Nepal experience on an on-going basis. With his brother David and their friend Marc Friedman, Mr. Ziolkowski secured about $20,000 in seed money and office space from GE Capital to create a nonprofit program called Building With Books.

The idea was to build schoolhouses in villages around the world with the help of American high school students, who could raise money for the effort as well as working to help people in their own communities.

"Our vision was to mobilize American students at the grass roots level to take an active role in their own communities in places like homeless shelters, soup kitchens and battered women's shelters, but at the same time get them fired up to do work on a more global level, too," said Mr. Ziolkowski. "Our mission is to include as many American students as we can to build as many schools in poor villages as possible."

And this weekend Mr. Ziolkowski is continuing that mission in the Nepalese village of Rajipur, which borders India, helping inaugurate the community's first real school building—a one-story concrete-and-brick structure with six classrooms—made possible by his group's $10,000 contribution.

Because the village's 180 families are considered untouchables in the Indian caste system, Mr. Ziolkowski said, without help there would have been little hope the children there would ever have had the opportunity for an education.

"Providing education for people enslaved by the caste system is one of the best ways to help them to rise above it," he said. "And it's a very powerful feeling to know that when these schools open, I can stand there representing every one of the American students who donated their time to make it all possible."

Hundreds of American students are now taking part in Building With Books clubs in five American high schools including Stamford High and Morris High in the South Bronx. The others are a private school in Stamford as well as schools in upstate New York and the Middle West.

The students have helped to raise money for five sister school projects on three continents—Asia, Africa and South America.

Mr. Friedman, now the organization's managing director, said that plans are being drawn up to add more schools to the program over the next few years.

"A lot of people thought it was a pretty wild idea at the beginning," said Mr. Ziolkowski, who travels to all the villages the program reaches and uses what he calls video postcards to record conditions in the villages, then share them with American students.

Mr. Ziolkowski said that students in the five schools have helped raise about a quarter of the nearly $38,000 to build schoolhouses in Brazil, Nepal and Malawi. The rest of the money comes from corporate and private donations and fund-raising events.

Students in Connecticut and the South Bronx say they are drawn to the program because of the combination of local and global themes.

"Right from the beginning I was intrigued by the idea that we could help people locally and globally," said 16-year-old Anne Tsai, a senior who is co-president of the Building With Books club at Stamford High School. "It gives you a good feeling to see the people you are helping in places like the Salvation Army and the soup kitchens. But it's also inspiring to know that when we conduct some-

thing like a car wash fund-raiser, that's going to help build a school somewhere, too."

Ms. Tsai is hoping to take the Building With Books program with her to Harvard, where she begins school in the fall. "It's had such a profound impact on my life, and I really think it can be successful at the college level, too," she said.

Jeff Lieberman, a 17-year-old senior at Stamford High School who has been in the program for four years, said it has helped to educate him about how tough the conditions actually are for people elsewhere.

"I don't think global issues are stressed enough in our schools, but being involved in this program has taught me a great deal," said Mr. Lieberman. "Watching the videos and seeing what is really going on is very powerful."

Some students said that watching poor and homeless people respond to their kindness was also powerful.

"It's very rewarding to see it happening right in front of your eyes, to see people in your own community who need your help benefiting from your efforts," said 17-year-old Alison Ballbach, a senior at Stamford High School who has been part of the program from three years.

Students in the South Bronx agreed.

"It's a great feeling to give something to people who have less than you have," said 15-year-old Olga Torres, a sophomore at Morris High School in the Bronx, who helped to raise money for a Thanksgiving dinner that the Building With Books club organized for homeless people.

That's the kind of community spirit that has educators backing the program.

"All of our students are poor themselves, but Building With Books has given them a real opportunity to give to others who are in even more unfortunate circumstances than they are," said the principal of Morris High School, Lourdes Garciá. "It's very empowering for our students to see that they can make a difference in the world . . . both here in the Bronx and in a small African village that they never even knew existed."

Julie Bienvenu, an English teacher at Stamford High School who also serves as the school's Building With Books adviser, added that "The students are so self-motivated that I don't have to do very much except to provide a little structure for them."

"It's really a pleasure to see how dedicated the students are to this program," she said. "There aren't many days when I'm not approached by new students who want to join up and be part of it. It's really something I think can grow around the country."

* * *

December 11, 1996

BIG MAC II

By THOMAS L. FRIEDMAN

OAK BROOK, Ill.—The folks at McDonald's like to tell the story about the young Japanese girl who arrived in Los Angeles, looked around and said to her mother: "Look, mom, they have McDonald's here too."

You could excuse her for being surprised that McDonald's was an American company. With 2,000 restaurants in Japan, McDonald's Japan, a.k.a. "Makadonaldo," is the biggest McDonald's franchise outside the U.S. The McDonald's folks even renamed Ronald McDonald in Japan "Donald McDonald" because there's no "R" sound in Japanese.

"You don't have 2,000 stores in Japan by being seen as an American company," said James Cantalupo, head of McDonald's International. "Look, McDonald's serves meat, bread and potatoes. They eat meat, bread and potatoes in most of the world. It's how you package it and the experience you offer that counts."

The way McDonald's has packaged itself is to be a "multi-local" company. That is, by insisting on a high degree of local ownership, and by tailoring its products just enough for local cultures, McDonald's has avoided the worst cultural backlashes that some other U.S. companies have encountered. Not only do localities now feel a stake in McDonald's success, but more important, countries do. Poland for instance has emerged as one of the largest regional suppliers of meat, potatoes and bread for McDonald's in Central Europe. That is real power. Because McDonald's is gradually moving from local sourcing of its raw materials to regional sourcing to global sourcing. One day soon, all McDonald's meat in Asia might come from Australia, all its potatoes from China. Already, every sesame seed on every McDonald's bun in the world comes from Mexico. That's as good as a country discovering oil.

This balance between local and global that McDonald's has found is worth reflecting upon. Because this phenomenon we call "globalization"—the integration of markets, trade, finance, information and corporate ownership around the globe—is actually a very American phenomenon: it wears Mickey Mouse ears, eats Big Mac's, drinks Coke, speaks on a Motorola phone and tracks its investments with Merrill Lynch using Windows 95. In other words, countries that plug into globalization are really plugging into a high degree of Americanization.

People will only take so much of that. Therefore, to the extent that U.S.-origin companies are able to become multi-local, able to integrate around the globe economically without people feeling that they are being culturally assaulted, they will be successful. To the extent they don't, they will trigger a real backlash that will slam not only them but all symbols of U.S. power. Iran now calls the U.S. "the capital of global arrogance."

People in other cultures cannot always distinguish between American power, American exports, American cultural assaults and globalization. That's why you already see terrorists lashing out at U.S. targets not for any instrumental reason, but simply to reject this steamroller of globalization/Americanization, which has become so inescapable. (The McDonald's people have a saying: Sooner or later McDonald's is in every story. Where did O. J. eat just before the murder of Nicole? McDonald's. What did Commerce Secretary Ron Brown serve U.S. troops just before he died? McDonald's . . .)

"You try to shut the door and it comes in through the window," says the historian Ronald Steel about globalization.

"You try to shut the window and it comes in on the cable. You cut the cable, it comes in on the Internet. And it's not only in the room with you. You eat it. It gets inside you."

The only answer is multi-localism—democratizing globalization so that people everywhere feel some stake in how it impacts their lives. "McDonald's stands for a lot more than just hamburgers and American fast food," argued Mr. Cantalupo. "Cultural sensitivity is part of it too. There is no 'Euroburger.' . . . We have a different chicken sandwich in England than we do in Germany. We are trying not to think as a cookie cutter."

* * *

September 19, 1997

THE CRIES OF WELFARE STATES UNDER THE KNIFE

By ROGER COHEN

BENEVENTO, Italy—At the end of a dim corridor full of yellowing files spilling their forgotten contents onto dusty shelves sits Dr. Mario Maddaloni, the Italian state's inquisitor in this depressed southern town.

His mission is to cut the waste in Italian welfare, saving the state money by rooting out phony invalids. The disabled of Benevento account for an astonishing 21 percent of the population. The culture of dependency is deep-rooted. But if Italy is to balance its budget and qualify for the euro, that culture has to change.

Dr. Maddaloni has already interviewed about 800 local invalids. Of these, more than half were found to be making false claims and lost their benefits. It was wrenching work, the doctor said, because many of the people coming to the office needed the disability pensions to get by.

"But we have to do this," he said. "As long as we waste public money, we will pay more taxes. And Italy will get left behind—a car with a beautiful wheels, a nice paint job and a lousy engine."

Throughout Europe, the euro, like globalization, has proved unforgiving of the inefficiencies of what Germans call the Vaterstaat—the consoling Father-State, always there when needed. It is forcing a radical reconsideration of the model of European society—one that is treacherous politically because it has been decreed by central bankers rather than demanded by voters.

The euro requires countries to cut their budget deficits to 3 percent of total output this year if they are to qualify for the new European money on Jan. 1, 1999. That can only be achieved through cutbacks in the Continent's welfare state. Italy's budget deficit stood at 12 percent as recently as 1992. The euro is shaking Europe like a massive electric shock.

Even in countries whose public finances were less messy than Italy's, the euro is posing a basic question: how much of the welfare state should be sacrificed for it? If European nations give radically different answers, tensions will jolt the single-currency zone.

In Germany and France—with respective unemployment rates at a record 11.6 percent and 12.6 percent—the debate on how to shift from the expensive subsidizing of inactivity to stimulating jobs is already politically explosive. If welfare reform is pushed too hard, there could be social upheaval, as there was in France in December 1995, when strikers virtually shut down Paris to protest proposed changes to social security.

The debate is particularly volatile because it is envenomed by a sense that Europe's social model is under assault from a more vigorous United States.

As Jacques Chirac, the French President, made clear by declining to don cowboy boots at the meeting of leading industrialized nations in Denver in July, he does not want to be an extra in Bill Clinton's global theme park. "We have our model," Mr. Chirac said, "and we plan to stick to it."

But is that model compatible with the euro? France has advanced social protection but also record unemployment, high taxes, labor-market rigidity, low growth and a rapidly aging population. It, and countries like it, will almost certainly find the small budget deficit demanded by the euro's fiscal discipline hard to sustain. It is also likely to need different monetary policies from states that have chosen to sacrifice some social security for jobs and faster growth.

"If countries give radically different answers to the challenge of reforming the welfare state," said Hans Tietmeyer, president of the German Bundesbank, "we are going to have problems in the euro zone."

In Britain, for example, social security spending accounts for about 13 percent of total output, compared with 20 percent in Italy and 23 percent in France. Britain seems set on a radically different course from its Continental neighbors. It is a course that borrows much from the American conviction that reduced taxation, deregulation, labor-market flexibility and a dwindling safety net are the route to success in the jungle of the global economy.

"People look across the Channel and they do not like what they see," said Kenneth Clarke, former Chancellor of the Exchequer. "Confronted with the euro, they ask, why should we be locked into failure? Continental Europe is overregulated and sclerotic, and the key to recovery there is structural change."

British growth was double the French rate last year and, at about 3 percent, will be well above French rates again this year. Unemployment has plunged to 5.8 percent, from 10.4 percent in 1993, as the economy has benefited from lower taxes and the birth of a shareholding culture.

In the Netherlands, consensus has achieved what the Thatcherite revolution did in Britain, bringing unemployment down to 6.5 percent from more than 10 percent a decade ago, without accentuating inequalities as much as in Britain. Growth, as in Britain, has surged. But in both countries, to varying degrees, job security and welfare protection have been sacrificed.

Europe thus offers various economic models, whose differences will be laid bare by the euro. The currency will test the sustainability of different systems even as it exposes them.

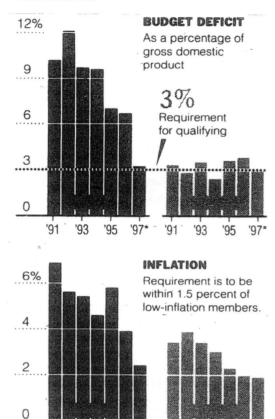

Economic Discipline

Germany will have no trouble qualifying for the euro; it sets the standard for economic stability in Europe. Italy must meet that standard and has been trying hard—as its efforts to cut budget deficits and inflation make clear.

BUDGET DEFICIT
As a percentage of gross domestic product

3% Requirement for qualifying

INFLATION
Requirement is to be within 1.5 percent of low-inflation members.

*Projection.

Sources: European Commission; Organization for Economic Cooperation and Development

The New York Times

A common currency will reveal, for example, that the same brand of Scotch whisky can vary in price by 50 percent, depending on whether it is bought in Spain or Germany. It will also reveal the relative attractiveness of different European economic environments in terms of tax levels, costs of labor, onerousness of welfare, and incentives to business.

"If we get the euro," said Bruce Kasman, a vice president of J.P. Morgan in London, "inefficient policies will be much less sustainable. You are going to see the same kinds of competition as between states in America. There are going to be huge pressures on countries to provide policies conducive to investment."

Italy Fights Its History: A System Corrupted By Cold War Politics

In Italy that pressure is particularly intense. More than 10 percent of Italians—six million people—are officially disabled. They will cost Italy more than $33 billion this year in disability pensions.

Many do have physical handicaps. But many are the healthy beneficiaries of a bygone system. Before the cold war ended, $33 billion was considered a reasonable annual investment in Italian political stability.

For decades Italy produced "invalids" at a remarkable clip. The politician, usually Christian Democrat, who arranged for the payment of a disability pension won votes. Particularly in southern Italy, where jobs were scarce, to be disabled was to gain a passport to money or a job.

It was a costly setup. Budget deficits and national debt spiraled. But the system helped keep the Christian Democrats in office and the Communists out. Italy did not go the way of neighboring Yugoslavia or Albania. Social security meant geopolitical security.

Now, however, a political age has given way to an economic one. Over Germany's border with Poland it is no longer the Warsaw Pact that threatens; it is workers making one-tenth of German salaries. Yesterday's esteemed political client in Italy is today's resented financial burden. It is the euro, not the politburo, that obsesses Europe.

"The euro is my frontier," said Enrico Michele, Undersecretary of State for the center-left Government of Prime Minister Romano Prodi. "Either we make it or this Government falls. And to get there, we have to negotiate reform of a distorted pension system. The welfare state is part of the European idea and cannot be completely dismantled. It must, however, be changed."

Michelangelo Bergamini is leading the campaign for change. As a senior Treasury official, he has been asked to lead a sweeping inquiry to unearth the fraudulent recipients of disability pensions.

Such is the labyrinth of Italy's state-run pension system—costing more than $190 billion a year, or about 15 percent of total national output—that there are three separate categories of invalid, each paid by a different state entity.

Mr. Bergamini was asked to start by investigating the 1.4 million cases handled by the Ministry of the Interior. The number of people receiving these pensions has doubled since 1985; pensions cost the Interior Ministry about $8.8 billion in 1996. Over an 18-month period that is to end on March 31, 1998, Mr. Bergamini's inquisitors, operating throughout the country, are interviewing 150,000 of the 1.4 million "invalids" to examine whether their claims are real.

"We are well into the program," Mr. Bergamini said, "and up to now we have found that one in four of those inspected was a false invalid. We have found blind people who were not blind and people miraculously cured of rheumatoid arthritis. In the most extreme cases—say a blind man working as a bus driver—we are bringing criminal cases."

Mr. Bergamini's agent in Benevento is Dr. Maddaloni. He works in a crumbling palace. There are typewriters but no computers. Just outside town, there are still people living in the mobile housing they were given after the 1980 Naples earthquake.

The bureaucracy of Italian welfare had assumed fantastic proportions before the current attempt at reform began. Under a 1980 law, for example, a person with a peptic ulcer causing "grave digestive disturbance" could claim a disability level of 51 percent to 60 percent. Diabetes of "medium gravity" would confer 31 percent to 40 percent disability. Different ailments could be added—like roulette chips piled one on the next—to increase one's degree of disability.

The degree was critical. Until 1992, a 35 percent disability level was enough to qualify a person for one of the numerous jobs in the public administration and state companies reserved for invalids. In the south, the postal service was a preferred haven.

A politician would send somebody to a friendly doctor who would certify a disability. And the reward would be a flood of votes. "Whoever governed from 1960 to 1990 had to have clients," Dr. Maddaloni said. "Welfare was the means."

The level of disability needed to qualify for a monthly pension is now 74 percent. The pension is quite small—about $250 a month—but a very useful cushion for poor families in places like Benevento.

At 100 percent disability, the situation changes. Authorities may approve a further $450 a month, supposedly to pay for a full-time nurse. There is no verification of the employment of such a nurse. Remarkably, more than 60 percent of the 1.4 million people now under investigation by Mr. Bergamini enjoy this additional benefit.

Italy Eyes the Prize: So Much to Change, So Little Time

Mariano de Luca, president of a Benevento invalids' association, is furious about Mr. Bergamini's campaign. He pointed to the man sprawled on the sofa and urged him to speak. "Say something, Pasquale, say something!" he hollered. No response. "Something, Pasquale, you must say something!"

From Pasquale di Fiori there emerged a groan. The sound slipped from lips contorted into a grimace. His hands writhed with the effort; his body was clearly a vessel he did not control. The sound, a crescendo, was a call from a distant place.

Satisfied, Mr. de Luca turned away. "You see what the Government is doing," he said. "Pasquale can't walk. He can't talk. But the Government calls him a false invalid! So they won't give him the disability pension he deserves. The euro is being used to justify an Italian witch hunt."

Mr. di Fiori has twice requested the extra $450 payment for 100 percent disability and been refused. The authorities argue that his parents can look after him. But to Mr. de Luca, the case suggests that the excess of abuse has been replaced by an excess of reforming zeal.

But Mr. Bergamini remains tranquil in his mission, convinced that Italy should break with its former culture and become a truly modern state with the euro as its currency.

Already this year, his investigation has saved about $150 million, an amount expected to double by the end of the first phase of his inquiry next year. Moreover, the number of invalids—which had been growing more than 10 percent a year in the 1980's—stopped rising last year.

Eventually, it is clear, Italy's entire pension system will have to be reviewed. The three categories of invalid will have to be grouped into one and a rigorous inspection of claims carried out, officials said. Resistance from labor unions is certain to be intense.

All this bodes ill. It is the sheer extent of these needed reforms that causes Arrigo Sadun, an Italian economist, to think that Italy is misguided in its haste to adopt the euro at its planned outset on Jan. 1, 1999.

"There is no question the Germans are right," he said. "Government spending is not yet under control. We Italians are going through a one-shot, unsustainable adjustment. Italy is not ready for the euro."

Still, the strides Italy has made so far are staggering. Nowhere is it more obvious that the euro is fueling profound economic adjustment in Europe.

Inflation has come down to a projected 2 percent this year, from 5 percent two years ago, and is now below the German level. The critical budget deficit figure may be as low as 3.2 percent this year. The national debt—more than 120 percent of total gross domestic product—remains way above the 60 percent target set for the euro, but it is also coming down.

"The euro has been the means to modernize our country," said Giuseppe Zadra, president of the Association of Italian Banks. "Without that external constraint we would have been too lazy to do it ourselves. If we do not make it now, it would be a disaster."

But Hans Zehetmair, culture minister of the German state of Bavaria, is among those unimpressed by Italy's efforts. "When you see how creative the Italians are with bookkeeping," he said, "then I say no, we will not allow this to make the German people suffer. Italy cannot come into the first wave of the euro."

Britain Keeps Its Distance: An Ex-Basket Case, And Proud of It

While the euro has been the agent of change in Italy, Britain transformed itself several years ago and as a result has profound doubts about a common currency. Britain's economic culture is now so profoundly divergent from that of Continental Europe that it is not easy to imagine Britain operating with the same money as its European Union partners.

Britain is an important economy. More than 60 percent of its trade is with other European Union countries. The City of London has by far the Continent's largest securities and capital market. A euro without that market will obviously be incomplete, and a Britain without the euro may face exclusion from a powerful club.

Yet, to travel around Britain today is to be plunged into a world to which Germany and France seemingly have scant relation. The attractiveness of soccer-club shares or building-society shares is the stuff of casual pub conversations. Shareholding has become a kind of national sport.

This radical change struck Walter Hasselkus when he moved from Germany to Britain two years ago to take over management of Rover, which had been acquired by BMW.

Old images of conflict—the miners' strike, auto strikes—inevitably lingered in this German executive's mind from the days when Britain was Europe's basket case. But what he found, he said, was "an acceptance that competitiveness is an absolute must."

"It is amazing, absolutely amazing," Mr. Hasselkus continued, "to see the brutal change of ideological direction here. Britain is very, very far from the social-market model that has served Germany well, and I think we in Germany have to be very careful not to knit the social safety net closer than we can afford."

Olivier Cadic, a French businessman, recently moved part of his electronics business, Info Elec, from France to Britain precisely to escape charges and constraints that he could not afford.

In Britain, he can hire and dismiss easily, and social security taxes add only 10 percent to his wage bill, compared with 50 percent in France. "We can employ people here," Mr. Cadic said, "but in France it has become prohibitive to hire. The French system seems to be conceived so that unemployment can go up."

For Mr. Cadic, Britain has realized, as France has not, that the world has changed. For a long time, the developed world enjoyed a virtual monopoly—of knowledge, of capital, of the most important goods, of military strength. That domination has now been seriously eroded. The knowledge and means exist for things to be made anywhere. This is the challenge that globalization poses.

Eddie George, governor of the British Central Bank, thinks Britain can comfortably live alongside the euro zone for an indefinite period, preserving sterling as its currency, just as Canada preserves its currency alongside the United States. And he sees grave dangers in joining the euro before France and Germany have undergone reform.

"If some European areas are ready to lower minimum wages and achieve a flexible labor market, and others are not," he said, "how can the euro work?"

France Sits in Concrete: Anglo-Saxon Model As Gallic Bugbear

Yet in France, the very word "flexibility"—also favored by Mr. Tietmeyer of the Bundesbank—is taboo. It is seen as a code word for replacing Gallic solidarity with marauding American capitalism. France wants the euro, but unlike Italy it seems unprepared to change to accommodate it.

"An extreme free-market approach may work," said a senior official at the French Finance Ministry. "But it is not for us."

Ed Balls, an aide to the British Chancellor of the Exchequer, worries about what he sees as an effort in Paris to caricature the Anglo-Saxon model as an excuse not to change. "Look," he said, "America has created 30 million jobs since 1979. Surely we can borrow something from this. I say to the French, 'Our model is not perfect but nor is yours. Let's try for dynamism without cruelty.' "

To look at a pay slip from Eric de Cardonnay's BDM decorating company in the Normandy town of Bray-et-Lu is to understand something of France's absence of dynamism. In its way, it is as alarming as the number of invalids in Benevento —and as rich in ominous implications for the economy of the euro zone.

When Mr. de Cardonnay started his company in 1977, there were five lines to a salary slip. Now, after various taxes and charges have been listed, there are 29 lines stretching over two full pages.

At the end of this labyrinth, the cost to Mr. de Cardonnay of employing a worker at a gross monthly salary of 10,111 francs ($1,699) ends up at 15,306 francs ($2,572), or an additional 51 percent. The worker ends up with net pay of 7,882 francs ($1,324).

The charges to Mr. de Cardonnay amount to a grand tour of France's welfare state, one that cossets but also appears to stifle.

There are taxes for family allowances, for a fund offering low-cost housing loans, for unemployment insurance, for work accident compensation, for pensions, for the improvement of security on building sites, for professional training, and even for reducing the social security deficit—an estimated $7.2 billion this year.

Indeed, the charges are so numerous and diverse that this entrepreneur has given up trying to remember what all the acronyms stand for. All he is sure of is this: "These charges are simply uncontrollable. They go up all the time."

That, in turn, creates difficulties. Having expanded steadily through the 1980's, BDM faced a crisis at the beginning of this decade caused by a combination of rising labor costs and falling revenue. Mr. Cardonnay decided he had to lay off six of his 21 workers.

For 18 months after the layoffs, he had to continue paying an amount equivalent to most of the six workers' salaries, so they could be retrained for other jobs. This so-called conversion training has in practice proved largely ineffectual.

"Anyone who has gone through that will never hire again," Mr. de Cardonnay said.

BDM's experience is anything but uncommon. Increasing costs and constraints on dismissals keep entrepreneurs from hiring and expanding. Unemployment rises.

With it, the pressure builds on the welfare state funded by the charges. Taxes must rise further to compensate. The pay slip must grow longer still. The circle is vicious.

"If costs for employers in America were the same as in France," said a leading French banker, "perhaps 25 percent of Americans would be unemployed."

The dangers to the euro in this French situation are clear enough. Unemployment brings anger, and it can take nationalist forms. Already the extreme-right National Front has become the third-largest party in France, with 15 percent of the vote. It constantly attacks the euro as a German plot to take over Europe.

If unemployment continues to rise and change continues to be resisted, the euro may simply prove a catalyst to disaster. It will be the symbol—weak and untrusted—of a stagnant Continent. The state budgets behind the money will be overstretched. Germans will want their mark back. The inquisition at Benevento will have been in vain.

* * *

May 20, 1998

SUHARTO'S STEALTHY FOE: GLOBALIZING CAPITALISM

By NICHOLAS D. KRISTOF

JAKARTA, Indonesia, May 19—For decades President Suharto and other Asian leaders spent billions of dollars hunting down guerrillas in the jungle or building up internal security networks to trap leftists and send them to prison.

But when Mr. Suharto pledged in a sober television address to the nation today that he would step down from office, the force that brought him to this point after 32 years was not a Communist insurgency but a conspiracy of far more potent subversives: capitalism, markets and globalization.

Instead of hiding in the jungle, they established a fifth column in the glass-and-steel towers in the major cities, and Mr. Suharto's security forces never figured out how to handcuff them or torture them into submission.

These forces set off the Asian financial crisis, and Mr. Suharto's armaments were suddenly useless. His sophisticated military equipment can detect a guerrilla in the jungle of East Timor at night, but it was unable to discern bad bank loans or prop up a tumbling currency.

So Mr. Suharto appears to be on his way out, although the timing is uncertain. His vaguely worded pledge to step down was too vague for most people, and the historic confrontation between Indonesia's people and President seems likely to continue.

The tumult here underscores the way that the financial crisis is reshaping Asian politics and society as well as business. The crisis has already helped usher new governments into place in Thailand and South Korea as well as helped assure the rise of China's new Prime Minister, Zhu Rongji, a technocrat who knows much more about markets than Marx.

Asian leaders are being forced to open up their economies and political systems, to break the collusive links that in Asia have made twins of the words "crony" and "capitalism." Some scholars and diplomats believe the result is a historic shift now under way, signifying a landmark in the decline of the old order in Asia, in the way that the popular uprisings of 1848 marked the eclipse of the old social and political order in Europe.

"Economically and politically, what we're seeing today is a watershed," said Linda Tsao Yang, the American envoy to the Asian Development Bank. "You look at country after country, from Thailand to South Korea, and you find governments that are more accountable to the people, with more rule of law, with less rule by man or connections."

"If the region can survive the major, major changes and have a peaceful transition period," Ms. Yang added, "then the Asia that emerges will be much stronger for the exercise."

It is difficult to exaggerate how stunning some of the changes are. A year ago it would have been almost inconceivable that thousands of Indonesian university students would take over the Parliament building and shout "Hang Suharto!" as they did today, or that the resident of South Korea's presidential mansion would be Kim Dae Jung, the longtime dissident whom the mansion's previous residents repeatedly jailed and tried to kill.

Both Mr. Suharto's fall from grace and Mr. Kim's rise to it would have been extremely unlikely if the financial crisis had not created broad dissatisfaction with the existing order.

The changes will take many years, perhaps decades, and they are happening at a different pace in each country. But the process seems under way in much of the region, and it involves opening up society and business as well as politics.

It used to be that each country tended to be governed in part by a quasi-aristocracy of elites who married their children off to one another and controlled key positions in government, business, academia and the news media. This aristocracy, its entitlement deriving from education rather than bloodlines, relied on exchanging favors—politicians gave preferences to their banking buddies, who reciprocated by providing cheap loans—but now that web of favors is in disgrace.

Most political analysts say the old system has been so shattered that like Humpty Dumpty, it can never be reassembled. Socialism has been discredited as an economic system, yet the main alternative—capitalism—nurtures an emerging middle class and creates pressures for change that eventually become irresistible.

"If you want to practice capitalism, you need a pluralist system to make it sustainable," said Dewi Fortuna Anwar, a prominent political analyst in Jakarta. In the end, she argues, it was globalization of markets and information that brought demands for an end to Mr. Suharto's rule.

To be sure, America and Europe also used to be run by tiny elites that functioned as ruling classes. But even if the pressures for pluralism that triumphed in the West have been around for a long time, the forces of globalization seem to be speeding up the process.

"Corrupt, authoritarian governments cannot adjust to the demands of the new globalized world, where you have to have a more transparent, competitive and rational economic structure," said Han Sung Joo, a South Korean political scientist and former Foreign Minister.

"Since capital can go in and out more freely now, any economy that looks opaque will suffer now in a way different from the 1970's and 80's," Professor Han added. "These countries used to be able to get away with it. Now they can't."

The problem for the governments like Indonesia's was that they operated under an implicit social contract: Leaders promised to improve the standard of living, and in exchange citizens allowed the leaders to rule largely without check and to enrich their families and acquaintances. But the financial crisis meant that the governments had failed to deliver the goods, and this failure shattered the social contract and thus the basis for the rule of people like Mr. Suharto.

To be sure, this does not mean that revolutions are going to sweep across Asia. But even in countries like Malaysia, where the Government remains firmly in control, the links between Government and business are eroding.

"The whole basis of cronyism—the awarding of contracts without bidding, the amassing of huge wealth—all this will be affected by the economic crisis," said Muthiah Alagappa, a Malaysian scholar at the East-West Center in Honolulu.

More broadly, the Asian crisis has changed the intellectual basis for the discussion of national policies. It used to be widely accepted in China and other Asian countries that authoritarian systems created stability and thus promoted economic growth. But now few people accept that tradeoff and nobody talks much about "Asian values" that supposedly emphasized a preference for order over freedom.

"The crisis has dealt a blow to what was fashionably presented as the 'Asian model'—an autocratic, highly concentrated, command model," Ms. Yang said. "At a minimum, most people now will want to have their voices heard and taken seriously, and have some degree of participation in decision-making."

*   *   *

February 6, 2000

LEARNING TO THINK SMALLER AT COKE

By CONSTANCE L. HAYS

At Coca-Cola, Roberto C. Goizueta remains a legend, the chief executive whose vision and drive transformed the giant company into a global power. For his successor, M. Douglas Ivester, mastery of the inner workings of the Coke system could not make up for an uninterrupted streak of falling profits and personal faux pas.

Now the corner office at Coke is to be occupied by Douglas N. Daft, a cheerful, unassuming Australian who spent 30 years rising through the ranks. Practically a stranger in Atlanta, because of his overseas postings and constant travel, in just a few weeks he has turned the world of Coca-Cola upside down.

He announced a plan to push worldwide decision-making at the company down to the local level—a plan requiring the layoff of 6,000 workers, including nearly half of those at Coke headquarters in Atlanta. He said the company would embrace local brands and flavors more than it had in the past. He conceded that Coke could not meet long-term targets for earnings growth and that profits had been eroded by bad investments and bad management.

The stock—for most of the last decade as iconic as Coke's brand—has been in a tailspin since, closing on Friday at $56.25, down $6.8125 since the layoffs were announced on Jan. 26.

Whether Mr. Daft, 56, is executing his own plan or one he merely helped to create is not clear. Coke's board is known to have grown more frustrated and demanding over the last year; for his part, Mr. Daft radiates a kind of shock that it is his turn to run the world's best-known soft-drink company.

But the changes he is putting in place surely reflect his view of the way a global company ought to operate—a view developed through a series of assignments in Asia, where he learned the hard way what sold Coca-Cola, and what didn't.

"To me it was so natural and logical," Mr. Daft said in an interview in New York last week, reflecting on the way his restructured Coca-Cola will let local managers make decisions about products, advertising and other functions that previously were controlled from Atlanta. "It's something I've always lived by."

Mr. Daft—now Coke's president, and scheduled to succeed Mr. Ivester as chairman and chief executive on April 19—takes over as the company is discovering the flawed underpinnings of the global expansion model that enshrined the late Mr. Goizueta in the business pantheon.

Mr. Goizueta, Coke's chief executive for 16 years until his death in 1997, long maintained that the company could instill a craving for products like Coca-Cola and Sprite all over the world, from the foothill shantytowns of Venezuela to the boulevards of Paris and Berlin. Mr. Goizueta's early successes in emerging markets, in particular, fueled strong growth at Coke and made it one of Wall Street's best-loved stocks.

But lately, Coke has had to come to terms with a conflicting reality. In many parts of the world, consumers have become pickier, more penny-wise, or a little more nationalistic, and they are spending more of their money on local drinks whose flavors or brand names are not part of the Coca-Cola lineup. The company took an $813 million charge for the costs of carrying poorly performing assets in Russia and the Baltics last year, and more charges are expected for similar investments in India.

"They had the world's greatest brand, and they believed that by the mere fact that Coke was Coke, they could sell it," said Michael Bellas, chief executive of Beverage Marketing, a consulting company. "It worked in the good times."

Moreover, the company's worldwide bottler system—Mr. Goizueta's brainchild, Mr. Ivester's handiwork and the envy of competitors like PepsiCo—faltered as regional economies fell apart, and many bottlers fumed that Coke was greedily profiting at their expense by raising concentrate prices. Along with its dismal earnings news last month, the company disclosed that bottlers in some key markets had too much soft-drink concentrate on hand, suggesting to some analysts that Coke had stuffed the pipeline to meet its own volume targets.

The bleak performance left Coca-Cola looking more vulnerable as its once impeccable public image was stained by crises—from the biggest product recall in company history to a racial discrimination lawsuit filed by a group of its black employees. The company has run afoul of regulators in Europe, Mexico and Australia over its plan to acquire the Cadbury Schweppes brands and over marketing practices like giving incentives to retailers to sell Coke instead of competing products. Then there was the vending machine that Mr. Ivester admired for its ability to raise prices automatically in hot weather.

From an investor's point of view, Coke was broken. But now there is a New Coke—no, not that New Coke, but the restructuring plan devised over the last six months by Mr. Daft and others. The huge layoffs are meant to clear the way for Coke to become a quicker company, a marketer better attuned to customers and other constituents. The central bureaucracy that reacted so clumsily when children in Belgium said they felt sick after drinking Coke products last spring has been pruned to its bare essentials; Coke says it expects to be more responsive to political and social concerns.

And Coke will sell more kinds of soft drinks, catering to local tastes for a change. "They were ignoring the local flavors for years," said Bill Pecoriello, a beverage analyst for Sanford C. Bernstein. "The opportunities were always there. Now they've put a structure in place to go after them."

While trying not to criticize his predecessor, Mr. Daft conveys his belief that Coca-Cola dropped the ball more than a few times. Asked what happened in Belgium, where Coke was perceived as arrogant and uncaring because of its slow response, he said: "Maybe there was no one there who understood the environment. Or, if we had people who understood the environment, we didn't listen to them."

Late last year, the demonstrations during the World Trade Organization meeting in Seattle drove home the point that global companies like Coke are viewed with growing hostility by some groups. The critics are especially irritated by what they regard as the multinationals' belief that the world should play by their rules.

"Consumer democracy is becoming more and more of an issue," said Carl Ware, Coke's executive vice president for communications and corporate affairs. "We have to address it on a local basis."

Call it the next wave of globalization, or the natural byproduct of the consumer culture that Coke helped build up around the world. "They finally see the light," said Jerry Wind, a marketing specialist at the Wharton School of the University of Pennsylvania, adding that other companies, including Procter & Gamble, have been quicker to respond to local markets. "The world is heterogeneous. You have local preferences and tastes. It makes a lot of sense for them to acknowledge the regional or local differences and try to manage their franchise as a portfolio of products that try to cater to different segments."

The light first came on for Mr. Daft when he was assigned to Indonesia in the early 1970's. His job was to sell Coca-Cola, lots of it. "I launched Coke and I pushed Coke for three years," he recalled. "Then I launched Fanta," an orange soda, "and the business just tripled and quadrupled." The lesson? "Brand Coke is the core of our company, then you add on to that the volume that you generate by competing in a wider market."

Subsequent stints in Hong Kong and Japan, and a lot of time spent building Coke's business in China, taught him the value of relationships, of quick decision-making, and of that thing called face time that he says is still key in business. When he was made group president for Asia but posted to

Atlanta in 1991, "that just meant I had to travel all the time," Mr. Daft said.

"You have to be in a place in order to understand it," he explained. "You've got to give attention to people. You've got to be able to see the people within the organization and outside the organization."

Nothing so revolutionary there, but it was not the Coke way. "We had backups in Atlanta in case people failed," he said, "monitoring them, constantly checking on information and receiving information." That was not so helpful to new product development—or to morale. A local manager who wanted to shift advertising dollars among brands, for example, had to wait for clearance from Atlanta before doing so.

And the global "mind-set," to borrow a term from Mr. Ivester's lexicon that Mr. Daft rarely utters, had its drawbacks. Bottled water was a recent example.

"Looking for a worldwide strategy for water slowed us down," Mr. Daft says now. Most Americans consider bottled water an occasional luxury; Europeans cannot live without it. "You can't apply a global standard of measurement to consumers," Mr. Daft says, "because it reduces everything to the lowest common denominator." Coke settled on a plan that required bottlers to buy packages of mineral additives for its Dasani brand water, which is being marketed across the United States; another Coke water, Bonaqua, continues to be sold abroad.

Mr. Daft has also pledged to help improve returns for Coke bottlers. "I think it's very positive," said Morris Strickland, area manager for Coca-Cola Enterprises in Jackson, Miss. "The focus is right. I was at a meeting in Atlanta and I felt more unified with the Coca-Cola Company than I have in a long, long time."

If Mr. Daft's ideas are different, so is his personality. Mr. Goizueta was charming until crossed. Mr. Ivester was great with numbers but not necessarily with people. Mr. Daft is universally described as even-tempered and comfortable with stressful situations. A healer, perhaps.

"The fellow is the right man at the right time at the right place," said Donald R. Keough, the former president of Coke who is now chairman of Allen & Company, the New York investment bank whose president and chief executive, Herbert A. Allen, is a member of Coke's board. Mr. Daft, he said, "can be surgical" in his decision-making, but is also easygoing, a combination Mr. Keough said he valued in a leader.

"He's going to have a lot of fun with it, when all is said and done," Mr. Keough said. "To be a dour, uptight person selling Coca-Cola is a contradiction in terms."

Mr. Daft's conciliatory side was in evidence in one of his first acts upon becoming president on Dec. 6: retaining Mr. Ware, the company's highest-ranking black executive, who to the consternation of civil rights leaders in Atlanta had announced his resignation after a management shuffle left him outside the chief executive's circle.

Mr. Ware changed his mind, he said, after talking with Mr. Daft about his plans for the company. "We had an agreement that much of what we had done in Africa and in Asia could be replicated in other parts of the world," Mr. Ware said.

"He's open to ideas from a whole lot of sources. He has encouraged dialogue, encouraged debate, encouraged everyone to have an opinion, no matter what the issue is." Mr. Daft also moved swiftly to name a second in command, Jack L. Stahl, a concept Mr. Ivester had resisted.

Other colleagues who have worked closely with Mr. Daft say he is quick to decide what needs to be done, but steps back to allow subordinates to make up their minds about how to do it.

"He's very careful about delineating his point of view, but at the end of the day it's: You live here, you're accountable, you make the decision," said Stephen C. Jones, who was the No. 2 executive in Japan and was recently appointed by Mr. Daft as chief marketing officer for Coke.

On trips they took around Japan, Mr. Daft embraced the local culture more deeply than Mr. Jones did, particularly in restaurants. "I avoided the sea urchin," Mr. Jones said, "but he orders it."

Japan has turned out to be Coke's most lucrative market, accounting for 20 percent of the company's profits—about $1 billion last year, on just 5 percent of its overall volume. It is also the place where, under Mr. Daft's direction, Coca-Cola has gone farthest in encouraging local brands that suit local tastes. In Japan, Coke's most popular product is a canned coffee, closely followed by canned teas.

Keeping that market profitable will be a chore. Coke has the largest share of the Japanese cola market, but sales have been hurt lately because Japanese consumers consider other drinks healthier. And the Japanese market is also going through a major shift; increasingly, sales are centered on retail and discount stores rather than on vending machines, where the profit margins are much higher.

Mr. Keough, for one, thinks Mr. Daft can handle the issues he will face. "Wherever there was a place where there was a problem, there he went, and guess what, there was no problem," he said of Mr. Daft's record in Asia. "And you didn't get any six-page report about it."

The child of a shoe-store owner in Cessnock, New South Wales, Mr. Daft joined Coke's planning department in Sydney in 1970, after brief stints as a high school teacher and a computer analyst for an oil company. He was soon sent to Indonesia for a year, which turned into five. In 1975, he left Coke to start a chain of liquor stores in Australia with a friend.

A year later he was back at Coke, assigned to Hong Kong as a marketing manager. He moved to Singapore in 1981, and returned to Hong Kong in 1984 to oversee Coke's business in China for four years.

"In China, I really learned the value of relationships and understanding political agendas, and there was a real need to understand that you sold and marketed to consumers on a local basis," Mr. Daft said. "In a country that large, with that many people, you would really miss a lot if you tried to generalize."

China was one of Coke's fastest-growing markets in the 1990's. But last spring, after American warplanes bombed the Chinese Embassy in Belgrade—an act the United States calls an accident—sales fell off as anti-American sentiment focused on Coke, McDonald's and other American companies in China. Mr. Daft quietly arranged to spend an evening at the theater in New York with China's deputy ambassador to the United States, hoping to smooth some of the anger.

Mr. Daft is said to closely follow changing tastes, not only in soft drinks but also in pop culture, something that he may owe to his 26-year-old daughter, Alexandra, who lives in Portland, Ore., and 22-year-old son, Nicholas, a senior at Williams College. For five years, he held an annual conference for his Asian managers in Park City, Utah. The days were spent in business discussions, the nights spent viewing films like "Big Night" and "When We Were Kings" ahead of the rest of the country, since Mr. Daft timed the conference to coincide with the Sundance Film Festival.

"He said, 'Let's meet for eight hours a day, and then go out at night to see how independent people are telling stories these days,' " Mr. Jones recalled.

Mr. Daft's biggest challenge may be persuading Wall Street the company has righted itself and is positioned to grow. One concern is that there may be more bad news to come.

"I think you're looking at not only this year as a year of recovery, but also part of next year," said Marc Cohen, a beverage stocks analyst at Goldman Sachs. "It could take 12 to 24 months before they hit their stride."

Among the problems yet to be fully aired is India, where costly write-downs are expected to be detailed before long. And the plans to sell more soft-drink brands tailored to local tastes will not be so easy to put into place, Mr. Cohen said; new brands take time to develop, and few are likely to be as profitable as Coke itself.

The circumstances give Mr. Daft at least a chance to come out a corporate hero. If Mr. Ivester succeeded a legend, taking control when Coke was riding high, Mr. Daft has been handed a Coca-Cola at half-staff, with Mr. Goizueta's shadow fading. The market, and his board, will demand results, but the expectations may be easier to manage.

"Unless there is a remarkable recovery in economic growth beyond what people foresee at the moment, this will be a case where they gradually build momentum," Mr. Cohen said. "As they iron out the significant challenges the company has come to face in the last few years, we should expect them to produce better performances. What remains to be spelled out is, how much better?"

* * *

February 29, 2000

RETURN PASSAGE TO INDIA: EMIGRES PAY BACK

By CELIA W. DUGGER

BOMBAY—During the past generation, tens of thousands of Indian engineers left home for America and many got rich—some fabulously rich—in the technology boom. Along the way, they became symbols of a brain drain that scholars believed was sucking the best and brightest minds out of third-world countries.

But an increasing though still modest number of India's biggest American success stories, whose lives are now firmly rooted in the United States, are beginning to come home to India, too, and not just to visit relatives, but also to start companies, invest their capital and indulge in philanthropy. Some of them say they should no longer be seen as proof of the brain drain, but as signs of a brain trust—a view economists say is still overly optimistic.

Even so, in an era when airplanes, telephones, e-mail and fax machines have transformed the lives of prosperous emigrants, economists say that the linear idea of a one-way brain drain is giving way to a different paradigm of brains that circulate between native and adopted countries.

That pattern is now emerging in India, which watched as perhaps 25,000 of its top graduates left for the United States since the late 1960's. In the years when the technology explosion hit America, these Indians emerged as major players and now run more than 750 technology companies in California's Silicon Valley alone.

One of those who got away was Kanwal S. Rekhi, 54, who now periodically comes back for what he calls his "missionary work in India."

He said he went to America so his brain wouldn't go down the drain in socialist India, made $300 million as an entrepreneur, executive and private investor in Silicon Valley, and retired five years ago.

Now, at the request of the prime minister's office in an India that is more market-driven, he is among those trying to raise $1 billion for the six Indian Institutes of Technology, elite public universities that produced the thousands of graduates who left for the United States.

Some of those who left say they are getting involved in India now because they have succeeded as entrepreneurs and have money to spare, because there are economic opportunities in India and because the Hindu nationalist-led government is more open to their participation in the country's affairs.

The government has, for example, challenged them to raise the billion dollars for the institutes that educated them at India's expense before they went to the United States, where they enriched the American economy.

"We're credible, successful people," Mr. Rekhi said. "Many of us are worth hundreds of millions of dollars. We're available to the Indian government and we provide a bridge to the United States. I do fund-raisers at my house for congressmen all the time."

Examples of these to-and-fro millionaires abound.

There's Desh Deshpande, 49, philanthropist. His telecommunications company, Sycamore Networks, was listed on the Nasdaq in October. His net worth has since skyrocketed to between $4 billion and $6 billion—depending, he said, on the stock market and which day the money gets counted. He and his wife plan to give $100 million over 20 years to their alma mater, the Indian Institute of Technology in Madras.

"There is that emotional tie," he said.

Pradeep Singh, 42, a graduate of the New Delhi institute, said his "lottery ticket came through" during eight years as a manager earning stock options at Microsoft.

He quit in the mid-1990's to start his own company, Aditi, which provides customer service via e-mail from India for corporations abroad. He now has two companies, lives four months a year in Bangalore and eight in Seattle, and employs 600 people—350 of them in India.

"My Dad died recently," he said. "He was proud of what I did overseas, but that was nothing like what he felt about what I've done here. He clipped all the stories."

And there's Rakesh Mathur, 43, a graduate of the Bombay technology institute. He and three other Indians founded a Silicon Valley company, Junglee.com—an early comparison-shopping engine on the Web. It was sold in 1998 to Amazon.com in a stock deal that has made Mr. Mathur $90 million richer.

He still has homes in Mountain View, Calif., and Seattle, but last year he also bought one in Pune. He has given $1 million to his alma mater and started a new company, Purpleyogi.com, with offices in Bangalore and Mountain View.

On a recent visit to Bombay, he ventured back to the technology institute's 500-acre campus, driving down a grand main road lined by towering bottle palms and past the new Kanwal Rekhi School of Information Technology now under construction, named for the American-made Indian philanthropist.

For Mr. Mathur, who has the casual style of a Californian, it was a double homecoming. He went to college here and grew up on the campus because his father was a professor. He was back to visit a troika of ambitious students who are determined to get rich off the Internet—and who had succeeded in making him their mentor.

Over 10-cent cups of coffee at a little outdoor cafe on campus, these young men had hatched their ideas, then pursued Mr. Mathur whenever he visited the campus and skipped a week of classes once to meet with him when he was in Delhi.

"We're different than our classmates because we realized there's opportunity here in India," said Kashyap Deorah, 20.

Graduates of the institutes—which are harder to get into than Harvard—have formed a transcontinental good-old-boy network (most of the students are still male) that connects Bombay, Bangalore and Hyderabad to Silicon Valley, Seattle and Boston.

The institutes themselves are among the few entities in India that are still seen as meritocracies, unsullied by political influence. Admission is based solely on a grueling national entrance exam. Last year, of the 98,000 students who took it, only 3,000 won admission.

And the United States continues to exert a magnetic pull on Indian students and other Indian professionals. Last year, a third of the 115,000 visas the United States issued to skilled workers went to Indians.

"Can I be frank?" asked Suman Kar, a 20-year-old senior at the Bombay institute, as he explained why he has accepted a job in Silicon Valley. "It's the money."

He said his new job will pay about $60,000 a year, seven times what he would have earned here.

Graduates of the institutes have been the most sought-after Indians in Silicon Valley—and Indians there have done very well, indeed. AnnaLee Saxenian, an economist at Berkeley, documented in an analysis of a Dun & Bradstreet database that 750 companies there are run by Indians.

Those companies produce more than $3.5 billion in sales and employ more than 16,000 people.

And as Indians have risen to positions of influence in corporate suites throughout the American economy, they have played a crucial role in giving credibility to business people based in India who are selling software services to American companies.

"When the Indian guy comes knocking at your door, selling something, the first thought on your mind isn't snakes and elephants," said Mr. Singh, formerly of Microsoft.

Software exports from India grew by more than 50 percent a year in the 1990's as businesses here found a niche in employing high-skilled, low-wage computer engineers in India to write computer code for businesses abroad. The industry now employs 280,000 people and is expected to have $4 billion in revenues this year, a majority from sales to American companies, according to the New Delhi-based National Association of Software and Service Companies.

Professor Saxenian had once thought that few of them would take their money or themselves back to India, but a recent visit to Bangalore changed her view.

She ran into an Indian entrepreneur from the valley, Sanjay Anandaram, and learned that he had returned to help start a new company that will develop and finance Indian technology ventures—and he was not exceptional.

"Change is happening fast," she said. "At every level, you see personal and business connections to India that were not there even two years ago."

The declining financial situation of the institutes is one of the factors drawing them back. In 1993, the government cut its funding of the institutes and for the first time allowed individuals to donate money directly to them. The alumni in the United States have given most of the millions raised so far for the Bombay institute. The Indus Entrepreneurs, a group founded by Indians in Silicon Valley, has been instrumental in raising the money.

Economists who had once seen the brain drain as harmful, now see the diaspora it has spawned as a source of strength to developing countries.

"The emigres often work as a Trojan horse, lobbying on your behalf," said the Columbia University economics professor Jagdish Bhagwati, himself a native of India. "They use external opportunities to succeed prodigiously in different occupations. And they can bring their skills and funds home to assist the country in its economic takeoff."

Mr. Mathur, the Web entrepreneur, is such a person.

The three students he advises came up with an idea that caught his imagination. On his recent visit, they formally presented their proposal for a Web site called iportia.com—

the site is up and running, but their company's exact product is still undisclosed—in a conference room in a downtown Bombay hotel.

Mr. Mathur and another prominent graduate, Nandan M. Nilekani, chief operating officer of Infosys Technologies, and Deepak B. Phatak, head of the computer science department at the institute in Bombay, listened attentively.

When the students finished, the older men asked them to leave the room, then considered whether to make this the university's first attempt to incubate a student business that it would partly own.

The students stood outside waiting nervously. Would Mr. Mathur put up the $250,000 on the university's behalf that would let them make their dream real?

After a half hour, the students were summoned back. The grownups had decided that the young men had a great idea.

The grinning students took turns shaking hands with Mr. Mathur, who turned to the professor, and exclaimed, "Phatak, Sahib, they have to make at least $100 million for you!"

*   *   *

April 23, 2000

WHEN VILLAGES GO GLOBAL

How a Byte of Knowledge Can Be Dangerous, Too

By SIMON ROMERO

SAO PAULO, Brazil—The prospects seemed bright when the Internet was recently introduced in a remote part of the mountainous Cotopoxi region in Ecuador. Under the guidance of aid workers, Quichua-speaking peasants planned to gather crop information and sell their crafts over the Web.

Soon, though, it was discovered that some of the men were using the computer to visit pornographic sites.

Dismayed, the women began to question how the men were treating them, and a debate ensued over the common practice of beating women. Although use of the Internet was later curtailed, its introduction unexpectedly generated discussion on a once taboo topic.

The changes created by the Internet in rich industrialized nations are well known, affecting everything from how people date to how they work. But less is known about the impact on societies with limited contact with the rest of the world. As such experiments multiply, at least one outcome seems certain: the way people in these communities relate to each other and with the world is likely to be altered forever.

The Ecuadorean peasants were a case in point. "The impact was huge, but as it almost always is when the Internet makes it to such a community, quite surprising," said Amalia Souza, a Brazilian technology expert familiar with the project who has been an adviser on programs that bring the Internet to poor communities in more than 40 countries.

A year and a half ago the women of the impoverished Wapishana and Macushi tribes of Guyana were introduced to the Internet in a project sponsored by Bill Humphries, who headed Guyana Telephone and Telegraph—at the time and was optimistic about technology's money-making potential. The tribal power structures were shaken.

The women began making money by marketing their intricate hand-woven hammocks over the Web at $1,000 each. Feeling threatened, the traditional regional leadership took control of the organization, alienating and finally driving out the young woman who ran the Web site. The weaving group fell into disarray.

"The events should be a case study for students of economics and social work," wrote Indera Ramlall, who is Guyanese, in a letter to a newspaper in the capital city of Georgetown. "Economic advancement is not just about technology and markets; more fundamentally, it is about human relationships."

The Alliance for Progress was the great hope of the Kennedy administration in the early 1960's. Its aim was to thwart communism with American aid to Central America, bridging the gap between poor and rich societies by building roads, factories and bridges. But aid to El Salvador tore the social fabric, contributed to the oppression of the poor, increased the holdings of the land-owning classes and helped fuel civil war.

For many people in developing countries these days, inspiration is increasingly drawn from William H. Gates. Some of the outwardly successful development projects, like the Grameen Bank in Bangladesh, are trying to deal with the unforeseen impact on the people they are trying to help. The Grameen Bank provides small amounts of credit to more than two million poor people, mainly women, enabling them to invest in raising livestock or entrepreneurial ventures like buying rickshaws. But critics say the focus on women, who are considered more reliable borrowers than men, has caused considerable tension between the sexes.

"Redistributing income from men to women, sharing out the misery of a shrinking cake, is not going to solve the people's problems," said Para Teare, a London-based social scientist who has studied such micro-lending programs, in a critique of the Grameen Bank.

Now, as technology starts to blur the distinction between industrialized countries and developing ones, social transition, if not transformation, has become an issue in some of the world's most remote regions. A recent issue of Cultural Survival, a magazine that covers indigenous people and ethnic minorities, described projects to bring the Web to communities as varied as the reindeer-herding Sami of Scandinavia and northern Russia, the aboriginal peoples of the Northwest Territories in Canada, the ethnic minorities of Burma and native Hawaiians.

These efforts represent a departure from the idea that introducing new technologies to indigenous peoples will bring about negative results. Such thinking, which dates back to Jean-Jacques Rousseau, the 18th-century French philosopher who lured Europe into idealizing the simple lifestyle of the noble savage, appears to be coming undone in the digital age.

"It is not realistic to think that as the world gets smaller there should be enclaves untouched by Western technology,"

Reuters

A woman selling calls on a cell phone purchased through a loan program at the Grameen Bank of Banglesh.

said Robert Whelan, a writer on indigenous affairs at the Institute of Economic Affairs in London. "But it is realistic to realize that traditional cultures can be very oppressive, especially for women and wildlife, and that technology can help change this."

Some people think the double-edged nature of technology's impact is beneficial. For the Grameen Bank, credit is considered a weapon for alleviating poverty and oppressive policies affecting women. Yet some societies are better equipped than others to deal with an onslaught of technological change. The American Amish, who are known for their rigid views about technology, have banned the car and computer but not the pocket calculator. A few Amish also use the Internet, albeit quietly.

Others, though, are not so sure about placing too much value on technology's liberating potential.

"When you introduce the Internet to people whose most urgent need is to get enough food to eat each day," said Karin Delgadillo, a coordinator at ChasquiNet, which provides technology assistance to remote communities in Quito, Ecuador, "you see there are other priorities that need to be taken care of first."

CRITICAL MOMENT: THE NIKE SWEATSHOP DEBATE

February 13, 1994

JUST UNDO IT:
NIKE'S EXPLOITED WORKERS

By RICHARD J. BARNET and JOHN CAVANAGH

When confronted about their role in global labor exploitation, many American companies offer a ready excuse. We call it the Ostrich Defense—and we think it's indefensible.

Consider Nike, one of the many big footwear, clothing and retail companies that has its head in the sand on this issue. Nike's sports-shoe revenues alone are $2 billion a year, for which the Beaverton, Ore., company has more than 8,000 people in management, sales, promotion and advertising—plus about 75,000, mostly Asian, employees who actually make the shoes.

Like Reebok and other sports-shoe distributors, Nike uses many contractors in Indonesia. A pair of Nikes made there costs $5.60 to produce, though they sell for many times that—typically between $45 and $80, the company says.

These low costs are no mystery: The Indonesian girls and young women who sew the shoes start at an entry-level rate of $1.35 a day. (Michael Jordan's reported $20 million fee for promoting Nikes in 1992 exceeded the entire annual payroll of the Indonesian factories that make the shoes.) Overtime is often mandatory, and union protections are nearly nonexistent. If there is a strike, the military often will break it up.

Nike and its contractors are in the business of chasing such cheap labor. In the last five years, as wages have risen, they have closed down 20 production sites in South Korea and Taiwan and opened up new ones in China, Indonesia and Thailand, where wages are rock-bottom.

Why is Indonesia the bargain basement of world labor? The reserve army of the unemployed is vast; 2.5 million people enter the job market each year. And foreign investors eager to employ what Government brochures call "nimble fingers" can often set their own terms, with the Government winking at violations of the nation's not-exactly-strict labor laws. For many workers—perhaps the majority—exploitation is not a concept easily comprehended because the alternative prospects for earning a living are so bleak. But some Indonesian workers know they are being exploited, as do some Indonesian officials and union activists.

What does Nike say about these conditions? First, the company's organizational structure insulates it from those conditions. Nike's Asian contractors are responsible for the actual making of the shoes; the company itself runs few factories. "We don't know the first thing about manufacturing," said Neal Lauridsen, vice president for Asia. "We are marketers and designers."

This division of tasks may be highly profitable, but ethical questions are raised when Nike disclaims responsibility for conditions in the very manufacturing operations on which its profits depend. John Woodman, Nike's general manager in

Indonesia, resorted to this disclaimer—the Ostrich Defense—when asked about problems at the company's plants:

Yes, he knew of labor disturbances in the factories, he said, but he did not know what the problems were about and he had not asked. "I don't know that I need to know," he explained. "It's not within our scope to investigate."

We heartily disagree with this approach. We do not deny that these ethical issues are complex. But if Nike, which profits from these shoes, has no responsibility for the people who make them, then who does? This question can only become more urgent as large companies become more dependent on foreign contract labor.

Two other American companies, Levi Strauss and Sears Roebuck, have taken a small step toward greater accountability by agreeing not to contract production to firms that use prison labor or deny basic health and safety standards. But they and other companies should embrace the right to form unions, to strike and they must honor other basic rights spelled out in International Labor Organization conventions.

Such rights, after all, will be meaningful only if enforced. New global rules, grounded in international trade agreements, must guarantee that firms that violate these rights are fined or subject to trade sanctions. This idea was raised during the debate over the North American Free Trade Agreement, but never came to fruition. Unless it is incorporated in future agreements, foreign workers will continue to be vulnerable to exploitation.

Richard J. Barnet and John Cavanagh are fellows at the Institute for Policy Studies in Washington. This article is adapted from their new book, "Global Dreams: Imperial Corporations and the New World Order" (Simon & Schuster).

*   *   *

March 16, 1996

AN INDONESIAN ASSET IS ALSO A LIABILITY

*Low Wages Woo Foreign Business,
But the Price Is Worker Poverty*

By EDWARD A. GARGAN

SERANG, Indonesia—Many days Tongris Situmorang, in his blue baseball hat with a large X on the front, hangs around the gates of the enormous Nike sport shoe factory here, talking to friends leaving the assembly lines at the end of the work day.

The gangly 22-year-old used to work inside the well-guarded gates, but five months ago he was dismissed for organizing workers to demand more than the 4,600 rupiah they are paid each day, about $2.10, the Government-dictated

Indonesian workers leaving a Nike manufacturing plant in Serang earlier this week. The sign above the gate says, "By minding the safety and health of our workers, our work will become more productive." Not all workers think the company, much less the Government, is following that philosophy.

minimum wage. Then, after being dismissed, he was locked in a room at the plant and interrogated for seven days by the military, which demanded to know more about his labor activities.

"We went on strike to ask for better wages and an improvement in the food," Mr. Situmorang explained. "Twenty-two of us went on strike. They told us not to demand anything. They said we wouldn't get any money. But I have sued to get my job back."

Low wages are a big attraction for foreign companies doing business in Asia as high labor costs in the industrialized nations make the manufacturing of many consumer goods uneconomical. Like a wave washing over Asia, labor-intensive factories have swept south and west as incomes and living standards have risen from Hong Kong, Taiwan and South Korea, across Asia to China, Vietnam and Indonesia.

And across the region, businesses in developing economies are feeling pressure from workers like Mr. Situmorang to lift wages. Clashes erupt between workers who want more and businesses and governments that fear that rising wages will drive away jobs to even-lower-wage countries. As strikes and worker-organizing attempts have increased here, the Government has taken a harsher line by cracking down on workers with police and military force.

For some companies, like Levi Strauss, worker complaints were enough to prompt it to leave Indonesia two years ago. But others, like Nike, whose shoes are made in 35 plants across Asia, have expanded in the region to take advantage of cheap labor.

For the Indonesian Government, the long-term solution may be to find manufacturers of products that can support higher wages. "Our strategy is to improve our products so we are not producing products that are made in China, Vietnam, India or Bangladesh," said Tungki Ariwibowo, the powerful Minister of Industries and Trade. "We cannot compete on wages with them."

More than 5,000 workers churn out Nike shoes here, shoes that often sell in stores in Asia, Europe and North America for perhaps $100 a pair. Nike and thousands of other manufacturers have been lured to set up business in Indonesia by the low wages—and the assurance that the Government will tolerate no strikes or independent unions.

Edward A. Gargan/The New York Times

Workers' housing in Tangerang, a town in Western Java where many foreign-owned garment factories operate. The Government says the minimum wage provides only 93 percent of the earnings required for subsistence for one person.

Yet even at a little more than $2 a day, there is a widespread sense in Government circles that even that is too high for Indonesia to stay competitive.

As the Government tries to hold down wages—wages the Government admits provide only 93 percent of the earnings required for subsistence for one person—strikes and worker organizing have increased. And with the increase in labor agitation have come harsher crackdowns by the Government.

A spokeswoman for Nike in the United States, Donna Gibbs, said she was not aware of Mr. Situmorang's case or of the detention and interrogation of workers for a week. However, when pressed, she said, "Our information is that workers were not held for a week."

All the plants that manufacture Nike shoes in Asia, Ms. Gibbs said, are owned by subcontractors, mostly Koreans. Each subcontractor is required to adhere to a code of conduct drawn up by Nike, she said, and managers from Nike are involved in the daily oversight of subcontractors' operations, including not simply quality control matters, but the treatment and working conditions of the labor force.

Nike's code of conduct, Ms. Gibbs said, requires compliance with all local laws, the prevention of forced labor, compliance with local regulations on health and safety and provisions of worker insurance. She said she was unaware of 13- and 14-year-old girls working at the Nike plant here.

"Certainly we have heard and witnessed abuses over time," she said, "and typically what happens is that we ask the contractor to rectify the situation and if it is not resolved we can terminate the business."

Ms. Gibbs said Nike has four to six subcontractors in Indonesia, a number that varies according to production needs. She said the minimum monthly wage was 115,000 rupiah, about $52.50, although the average was 240,000 rupiah, about $110. For a pair of shoes costing $80 in the United States, she said, labor accounts for $2.60 of the total cost.

"The problem is that the minimum wage does not provide for minimum subsistence," an Asian diplomat here said. "And beyond that, the companies don't always pay what is required by law. The level of unrest is not reported, but there are lots of reports from around the country of strikes."

"The philosophy of the minimum wage is to make sure the minimum calorie need per day is fulfilled," said Marzuki Usman, who heads the finance and monetary analysis body for the Finance Ministry and was the first chairman of the Jakarta Stock Exchange. "That is the formula."

On April 1, the minimum wage is to rise in many places to 5,200 rupiah, about $2.37.

"There are so many labor strikes," said Apong Herlima, a lawyer for the Indonesian Legal Aid Foundation who specializes in labor cases in Jakarta. "Employers always call the police and they come and interrogate the workers. Then the workers are fired."

Because Indonesia's press treads carefully around sensitive issues—and social unrest is among the tenderest of subjects—it is difficult to gauge precisely the level of labor unrest. The Government reported that there were 297 strikes last year, although it did not provide the number of workers involved. Independent labor organizers insist the actual number is far higher.

"The number of strikes is increasing," said Leily Sianipar, a labor organizer in nearby Tangerang. "Most factories don't actually pay the minimum wage. Garment factories should pay 4,600 rupiah each day, but there is usually underpayment. So there are strikes. We try to organize workers. The factory owners use the police and the military to crack down. They try to intimidate the workers."

The Indonesian Government recognizes only one Government-sponsored union, the Federation of All Indonesian Workers Union. But most workers and independent activists maintain that the Government union does nothing to represent Indonesia's 40 million workers.

"Since they don't come from the bottom, and they aren't elected by the workers, there is no hope for the Government union," said Indera Nababan, the director of the Social Communication Foundation, a labor education group sponsored by the Communion of Churches of Indonesia. "I don't think over 10 years there has been any considerable change. The workers have no rights here to argue for their rights."

Not far from the Nike factory here, Usep, a lean man of 25, leaned against the cement wall of the tiny room he shares with his 19-year-old wife, Nursimi. Together, said Mr. Usep, who like most Javanese has only one name, the couple earn about $4.10 a day—or $82 a month. Of that, they must pay about $23 for the 6-foot-by-6-foot cement room they live in, with the remainder for their food and other needs.

A single bare bulb dangles from the ceiling, its dim glare revealing a plain bed, a single gas burner, and a small plastic cabinet. Their room, one of a dozen in a long cement building, is provided with one container of water daily. If they want more water, each jug costs 100 rupiah, about 5 cents.

"Of course we're not satisfied with this," Mr. Usep said, his words coming quietly. "We tried to talk to friends about this, but there is no response. Probably they are worried they will lose their jobs."

It is workers like these whom Ms. Sianipar has been trying to organize for the last seven years, a task that entails the constant risk of arrest.

"If we have a meeting, the police take us to the station and want to know if we want to make a revolution," she said, a laugh breaking over her words. "We had a meeting here last week and the police came. So we changed the topic of the meeting, but they took me to the station anyway. The police got angry and banged the table. But they let me go at 4 in the morning. They had the idea that we were doing underground organization."

Still, she admitted, the attitude of the police has moderated somewhat over the years. "Five years ago," she said, "we would have had much more trouble."

Not all foreign investors who use cheap Indonesian labor have ignored workers' complaints. In 1994, the American clothing company Levi Strauss withdrew its orders from a local garment contractor after reports that the management had strip-searched women to check if they were menstruating.

But many factories that manufacture clothing, shoes or electronic goods for American companies are owned by Taiwan or Korean companies, and labor organizers contend that conditions in these factories are much worse than in factories directly owned by Americans.

"American companies are here because they have to pay very little," said an American who works for a private aid organization, but who did not want his name used. "But American companies are not the worst violators of basic working conditions. The Koreans really stand out for poor conditions in their factories."

Outside the Nike factory, Mr. Situmorang continues his vigil, waiting for a court decision on whether he can get his job back. "I've gone to the labor department and the court," he said. He paused and sighed. "I really don't think in the end I will get my job back. This is Indonesia."

* * *

June 14, 1996

NIKE'S BAD NEIGHBORHOOD

By BOB HERBERT

The State Department, in its latest human rights survey, said of Indonesia:

"The Government continued to commit serious human rights abuses. . . . Reports of extrajudicial killings, disappearances and torture of those in custody by security forces increased. Reports of arbitrary arrests and detentions and the use of excessive violence (including deadly force) in dealing with suspected criminals or perceived troublemakers continued. Prison conditions remained harsh and security forces regularly violated citizens' right to privacy."

Welcome to Nike country. Of all the places on the planet, the world's largest sneaker company chose the human rights sinkhole of Indonesia as the spot where most of its footwear would be made. Atrocities, including the Government-sponsored murder of thousands of innocent civilians, can easily be overlooked if there is a large enough labor force willing to work for next to nothing.

There is no need to dwell on this. That is why God made advertising campaigns. We can avoid the bitter reality of Indonesia and concentrate on the magnificent image of Michael Jordan soaring, twisting, driving, flying . . . or Andre Agassi hitting a tennis ball with such authority and power it leaves the racquet like a rocket . . .

Nike can thrill us, amuse us, fill us with good feelings. We don't have to succumb to downers like the following excerpt from a 1994 Amnesty International report about killings in Aceh, a province in which the Indonesian Government has been fighting armed rebels:

"Some 2,000 civilians, including children and the very elderly, were killed by Indonesian soldiers in or near the province of Aceh between 1989 and 1993. Some died in public executions; others were killed secretly and their often mutilated bodies were left in public places. Scores of the dead were dumped in mass graves."

No need to dwell on that. Nothing to do with Nike, after all. Or with Reebok, Adidas, Converse or any other sneaker outfits doing business in Indonesia.

Except that it does.

Nike and the other companies would like to distance themselves from the grotesque activities of the Suharto regime. But they cannot. They benefit both directly and indirectly from the systematic oppression of the Indonesian people. The Government cites the need for stability and security (in the interest of economic development) as a justification for its murderous policies, and then turns a welcoming face to the multinationals.

The response of the multinationals? We don't want to know about the rough stuff, but we're with you.

According to the State Department survey, "The Government continued to impose severe limitations on freedom of speech, press, assembly and association." And, in a policy critical to Nike and the other corporations that are drawn to Indonesia like flies to garbage, the Government continued to suppress the development of "a truly free trade union movement."

Nike is the most vulnerable to criticism of the athletic footwear corporations because it is the biggest, the most visible and by far the most hypocritical. No amount of charitable contributions or of idealized commercial images can hide the fact that Indonesia is Nike's kind of place. The exploitation of cheap Asian labor has been a focus of its top executive, Philip Knight, for more than three decades.

While working toward his M.B.A. at Stanford in the early 1960's, Mr. Knight wrote a paper on the profit potential of manufacturing athletic shoes in Asia. By the mid-80's Nike (co-founded by Mr. Knight) was no longer making shoes in the United States. It was dealing with independent contractors in countries like South Korea. And when workers there began organizing and winning wage hikes, Nike was taking off for places like Indonesia and China, where the crackdowns on labor are swift and effective and the pay is suitably pathetic.

Nike executives know exactly what is going on in Indonesia. They are not bothered by the cries of the oppressed. It suits them. Each cry is a signal that their investment is paying off.

*   *   *

December 25, 1996

AMID NEW WEALTH OF TRADE, A HUMANIZING MOVEMENT

By PAUL LEWIS

Freeing international trade has been the flavor of the closing months of 1996. President Clinton successfully pressed his campaign for zero tariffs on Information Age technology, first at the meeting of Asian and Pacific leaders in Manila late last month, and then at the meeting of the World Trade Organization in Singapore two weeks ago.

But another vision of international trade was also taking shape—the kind that brings the most economic and social benefits to poor people and to developing nations.

This vision of fair trade has scored some modest advances recently:

In London last month, the World Federation of Sporting Goods Industries—which includes household names like Nike, Reebok and Adidas—bowed to pressure from development-oriented charities like Oxfam, Christian Aid and Unicef by setting a Feb. 14 deadline for agreeing to a code of conduct to end the abuse of child labor in low-wage Asian factories. This breakthrough came after the International Labor Organization, a United Nations specialized agency, estimated that 250 million children under the age of 14 were working in developing countries.

The Ford Foundation is providing two modest grants totaling about $75,000 to help the American Fair Trade Association publish a directory of North American fair-trade organizations and stores—entitled "Sweatshops or Fair Trade? Now You Have a Choice!"—and to offer a new brand of fair-traded coffee next year.

In Singapore, the World Trade Organization's 128 members affirmed their support for humane working conditions in factories and agreed to uphold "internationally recognized core labor standards," including the right to form unions. They also agreed not to exploit child labor.

But under pressure from the developing countries, the international trade forum also said that industrial nations must not close their markets to exports from the third world.

Advocates of fair trade, sometimes known as alternative trade, seek to help developing countries sell their goods abroad for as much as they can, while also promoting acceptable working conditions.

In Western Europe, Australia and New Zealand, fair trade is now quite big business, with total sales estimated at $400 million to $500 million a year. Europeans consume 12,000 tons of fair-traded coffee annually; Britain, Switzerland and the Netherlands all have small fair-trading supermarket chains. In London, Christian Aid and Oxfam are trying to persuade Britain's leading supermarket and clothing chains to carry fair-traded food and clothes.

In the United States and Canada, however, fair trade is still in its infancy, with annual sales no more than $40 million.

"American consumers are far less sophisticated than Europeans," said Mimi Stephens, executive director of the Fair

Trade Federation, which includes 95 American organizations. "Most of them don't know where goods come from or what is going on in the rest of the world.

At first glance, fair trade looks like an attempt to interfere with the free play of market forces.

But most economists dispute this, arguing that the essence of a free market is a free choice for consumers and that fair trading actually offers them greater freedom by providing more information about merchandise for sale.

"Some people are prepared to pay a bit more for products produced in a socially responsible way," said Gary Hufbauer of the Institute for International Economics in Washington.

Jagdish Bhagwati, a trade theorist at Columbia University, agrees, saying: "Goods have an array of characteristics, which include how they were made. It is perfectly proper to give consumers this information."

Fair trade organizations operate in three broad ways. Some buy crafts, artifacts and clothing from cooperatives and factories in developing nations that follow acceptable labor practices. They sell these goods in industrial nations, returning any profit to the producers as bonuses, better tools, and services that help design new and better products.

Two American organizations that operate this way are Serrv International and Ten Thousand Villages, based respectively in New Windsor, Md., and Akron, Pa. The two groups, which are affiliated with Mennonite churches, import crafts, furniture and clothes from about 50 developing nations, selling them by catalogue and church-related shops.

"We insist on reasonable working conditions," said Paul Meyers, Ten Thousand Villages' director, "but while we don't buy products made through the exploitation of children, we don't object to children learning a trade in a family workshop or village cooperative—provided they also go to school."

With total sales of around $17.5 million last year, these two groups account for almost half of American fair trade products.

Other organizations include Market Place: Handwork of India, based in Evanston, Ill., which uses a catalogue to sell clothing and housewares made by poor Indian women, and Pueblo to People of Houston, which sells clothes and household items produced in Latin America.

Another approach to fair trade, favored for tropical agricultural goods like coffee and pineapple, is to buy direct from the grower, cutting out middlemen, and then sell the produce under a label certifying that it has been harvested and packed by adults, paid a fair wage and working under reasonable conditions.

The largest American fair-trade coffee importer is Equal Exchange, based in Canton, Mass. which buys coffee from farmers' cooperatives in Latin America and Tanzania. And while it will sell only $3.5 million worth of coffee this year in a $7 billion market, it says that its sales have doubled in two years.

The greatest success for fair trade labeling was scored not by a development organization but by a San Francisco-based conservation group, the Earth Island Institute. Earth Island sued over the slaughter of dolphins by tuna fishermen, and in the process helped sensitize North American and European

consumers to the point that more than 90 percent of the canned tuna sold in these countries now carry certifications that the fish was caught in nets that spare the dolphins.

A third approach, popular with groups like Oxfam or Christian Aid, is to shame industries with extensive factories in the third world, like big sporting-goods makers, into setting minimum standards—banning the use of child or convict labor, for instance.

The planned code of conduct for sporting-goods makers is clearly an example of this, as is another recent agreement banning child labor in the production of soccer balls.

But many developing countries remain intensely suspicious of such agreements, fearing that the West may try to find a pretext for closing off their import markets.

At their insistence, the final World Trade Organization statement adopted in Singapore calls on all countries to enforce humane working standards but says that such standards must be set not by the world body but by the International Labor Organization, and that failure to observe them does not justify protectionist measures.

* * *

February 14, 1997

SPORTING GOODS CONCERNS AGREE TO COMBAT SALE OF SOCCER BALLS MADE BY CHILDREN

By STEVEN GREENHOUSE

In a plan intended to fight child labor, a coalition of major sporting goods manufacturers and child-advocacy groups has pledged to combat the sale of soccer balls stitched by thousands of children in Pakistan, which produces 75 percent of the world's hand-stitched soccer balls.

Close to 10,000 Pakistani children under the age of 14 work up to 10 hours a day stitching the leather balls, often for the equivalent of $1.20 a day.

The goal of the program is to wipe out child labor in the industry in Pakistan within 18 months. The effort sets up a $1 million fund that will pay for independent monitors to inspect ball-making sites and for efforts to educate children, some as young as 6, whose impoverished parents push them into stitching balls rather than going to school.

The program represents the first time that all the major manufacturers in an industry have joined with local contractors and children's groups, including Save the Children and Unicef, to eliminate child labor. The coordinated plan is to be formally announced in Atlanta today.

But some children's rights advocates wonder how far $1 million will go in helping the thousands of children who might lose their jobs.

The sports equipment manufacturers pledged not to sell balls made by children after being embarrassed by news reports and pressed by thousands of soccer-playing children and their parents in North America and Europe who wrote letters and signed petitions voicing concern that they were playing with such equipment. Last September FIFA, the international soccer federation, said it would not endorse soccer balls unless manufacturers certified they were not made by children.

The soccer-ball industry is concentrated in the Sialkot region of Punjab province, where children learn from an early age the art of stitching hexagonal pieces of leather into balls. Jeff Ballinger, director of Press for Change, a labor rights group, said, "The soccer-ball industry is so concentrated in the Sialkot region and child labor is such a hot-button issue that they should be pretty successful in policing it there. But it's possible it could spread to other places in Pakistan, or even other countries."

To prevent Pakistani contractors from using children in the future, the agreement calls for soccer-ball companies to register the names of all contractors, individual workers and work locations to make it easier for monitors to ferret out child labor.

The Human Rights Commission of Pakistan estimates that children make 10 to 20 percent of all soccer balls produced in Pakistan, which produces three-fourths of the 30 million to 40 million hand-sewn soccer balls sold each year worldwide.

According to industry officials, children are paid 60 cents on average for each soccer ball they stitch, usually at the rate of about two balls a day, while adults earn a little more per ball.

Companies taking part in the plan include Adidas, Reebok, Nike, Umbro, Mitre, Brine and 50 others. Corporate officials said the plan might push up the price of soccer balls slightly because of the cost of monitoring labor and the higher salaries for adults.

Dan McCurry, director of Foulball, a group that campaigns against the use of child labor to produce soccer balls, welcomed the companies' pledge, but said, "It would be obscene to raise the price of the balls, which now retail for $30 to $50, because this program means they might pay stitchers 70 cents a ball instead of 60 cents."

Because all major soccer-ball companies are involved, children's advocates say the agreement is more forceful than one in which hundreds of rug merchants, representing a small minority of the industry, pledge not to sell rugs unless factories first certify that they do not use child labor.

In addition to the sporting goods and rug industries, child labor is prevalent in the making of apparel and surgical instruments in third-world nations.

The partners in the effort say they not only will steer children into education, but will seek to offset the income that families lose from having their children stop working. In addition, they pledge to help place parents or older siblings in jobs or provide them with small loans to start their own businesses.

In this way, the plan is intended to avoid an unforeseen result that arose a few years ago when apparel makers in Bangladesh threw hundreds of children out of work when the companies grew alarmed that the United States would ban imports made with child labor. With the sudden loss of employment, many children turned to even worse jobs, like making bricks or even prostitution.

Reebok and Nike had already pledged to sell only balls made in their own factories, and not ones made by subcontractors. This is expected to make it easier to insure that no child labor is used.

Paul Fireman, Reebok's chairman, said, "We'd like to see everyone join with us, and although this will sound bizarre in the world of business, we'd rather see the world operate at a better level. And maybe this will spread to other industries."

The fund to run the monitoring and education program includes $500,000 from the International Labor Organization, $360,000 from Pakistani manufacturers, $200,000 from Unicef and $100,000 from the Soccer Industry Council of America, a trade association.

"The manufacturers aren't reacting to a concern that people aren't buying soccer balls," said John Riddle, president of the United States Sporting Goods Manufacturers Association. "What they're reacting to is a potential degradation of the value of their brand. They think their brands are important, that their corporate good name is important, and they don't want to see that impaired."

American consumers may call a toll free number, 888-NO-1-CHILD (888-661-2445) to learn which brands have pledged not to sell balls made with child labor.

* * *

March 25, 1997

PEERING INTO THE SHADOWS OF CORPORATE DEALINGS

Nike Appoints Andrew Young to Review Its Labor Practices

By DANA CANEDY

As an outspoken civil rights leader, crusading United Nations representative and mayor of Atlanta whose oratorical skills were honed in the pulpit, Andrew Young has rarely been short on words. Yet in his private business dealings, Mr. Young says he can be more effective out of the limelight.

Even so, Nike Inc., masterful at putting its spin on a sweet public relations opportunity, eagerly fired off a news release last month announcing that Mr. Young and his newly created consulting firm, Goodworks International, would review the company's recently updated international labor code of conduct.

Nike—which has sought to shake off claims that its products are manufactured in Asian sweatshops—says that Mr. Young's involvement adds a level of oversight to its commitment to being a leader in international workplace standards. The company's critics take a more cynical view, contending that just as Nike pays Michael Jordan to sell its basketball shoes, Mr. Young has been hired to promote Nike's image.

And while Mr. Young insists on his independence—"I don't see myself as a spokesman for Nike at all," he said in a brief, reluctant interview—the mixed reception underscores the obstacles to the venture's success.

A growing number of corporations have hired high-profile lawyers or former government officials to conduct what the companies say are independent investigations into their affairs; besides Nike, the list includes Mattel, Bausch & Lomb and Mitsubishi Motor Manufacturing of America. But the appointments often just become one more source of skepticism, doing little to appease the critics they are intended to answer.

"Your first inclination from a public relations standpoint is to hire somebody whose credibility will convince the public that in and of itself the conclusion they reach is the right conclusion," said Edwin H. Stier, a lawyer with offices in Bridgewater, N.J., and Washington, who specializes in independent investigations.

But appointing a fact-finder is never enough, he added. "The public has got to be reassured that the process you went through is one that is effective at getting the bottom-line information you need," Mr. Stier said. "If you take the position that 'we'll let you know what the results are but we're not going to tell you how we got there,' then you run into a serious risk that the whole effort will backfire."

When, for instance, Mattel Inc. was in the market last year for a consultant to look into accusations that it had overstated its earnings, the toy maker hired Gary G. Lynch, the former director of enforcement for the Securities and Exchange Commission.

In public life, Mr. Lynch was the scourge of Wall Street, bringing cases against prominent traders like Michael R. Milken and Ivan F. Boesky. But Mattel's accusers objected that among other things the toy maker declined to release Mr. Lynch's report, saying only that he had uncovered no wrongdoing on the part of company executives.

Last May, a month after the Equal Employment Opportunity Commission sued Mitsubishi Motors contending that women at its plant in Normal, Ill., had been subjected to widespread sexual harassment, the company hired Lynn Martin, who served as Labor Secretary in the Bush Administration, to address workplace issues there.

Last month, though, at the end of the nine-month review, a lawyer for 28 women suing Mitsubishi in a private lawsuit questioned the company's commitment to enacting the sweeping changes called for in Ms. Martin's report, though the company insisted that it would.

Mitsubishi, Nike and other companies say that inviting outsiders to look into their affairs signals their commitment to improving their operations or resolving claims of wrongdoing. The corporations note that such inquiries hold them accountable to experts with reputations as staunch opponents of impropriety and say that the reviews give them fresh insights into their businesses.

Yet the companies' critics contend that all too often the corporations are simply looking to cash in on well-known and highly respected names.

In Nike's case, human rights organizations charge that by hiring Mr. Young, the company is mainly trying to deflect criticism that its foreign subcontractors—particularly in Southeast Asia—use child labor, pay abysmally low wages and subject workers to sweatshop conditions.

"Nike all too often looks for superficial solutions," said Medea Benjamin, executive director of Global Exchange, a human rights group in San Francisco that has been critical of the company. "It seems again like Nike looked for someone that would give them some good public-relations play rather than hiring an organization that has a track record."

Nike considers such criticism off point. For one, the company said that by regularly updating its code of conduct for contractors, it demonstrates its continuing commitment to the fair treatment of workers. And few people, Nike said, can match Mr. Young's tenure as an advocate for working people. Coupled with his experience as a diplomat and big-city mayor, that qualifies him as a labor authority who brings a great deal to the table, Nike argued.

"I think he is just without a doubt the foremost leader in this area," said McClain Ramsey, a spokeswoman for the company, which is based in Beaverton, Ore. "I would say that Andrew Young is far more than a name: he is a man with a reputation that goes along with his well-deserved stature."

Mr. Young said that his motivation for working with Nike was the potential to bring about change in working conditions at factories in developing countries. The outcome of his investigation, he said, would depend on information from both Nike's most vocal critics and the company's top executives, as well as from his own assessment of conditions after he tours the plants and talks to workers.

His hope? That his involvement will prompt Nike to set even higher standards that other international corporations will endorse. "I don't know whether that will satisfy Nike or the human rights agencies, but if it creates a lively discussion that keeps the issue alive, I think it will help," Mr. Young said.

Neither Mr. Young nor Nike would say how much the company was paying Goodworks, which was set up in January and is billed in Nike's release as "dedicated to promoting positive business involvement and investment in developing countries and America's inner cities."

Mr. Young, who would not say if Nike was his only client, said it would be up to the company to decide what to do with his report. But, he added, "if I found glaring violations and problems that they are unwilling to correct or address, then I would certainly have to say something about those."

For its part, Nike stopped short of guaranteeing full disclosure of Mr. Young's findings. "We haven't yet determined how his findings will take shape," Ms. Ramsey said, though she added that she did not see a reason why Mr. Young's conclusions would not be made public.

Even so, said Mr. Stier, the lawyer who specializes in such investigations, companies that announce the results of investigations often do so only after sanitizing the findings to present management's version of the facts. Companies "try to rig the outcome," he said, though he was not specifically referring to Nike.

Some observers who question Nike's intentions say that in hiring Mr. Young, the company has opened itself to a potentially harsh review. "Nike is trying to put its best foot forward, but they have chosen a man whose whole life has been directed at helping people," said Richard Ray, secretary-treasurer of the Georgia A.F.L.-C.I.O. "He will give them an honest opinion."

More skeptical critics say that Mr. Young should have done more to preserve his independence. "I would think he sees this as a critical, new and growing area that needs diplomatic expertise," Ms. Benjamin of Global Exchange said of Mr. Young's interest in international labor standards. "In that case, he should not be hired by Nike. He should be a mediator that is being paid by some foundation, so he would not be beholden to the company. When he is under the pay of the company, how is he ever going to be able to respond openly to the critics?"

Such issues have been raised repeatedly about inquiries of this type.

Mr. Lynch, for example, was said to have acted as both umpire and advocate when Kidder, Peabody & Company hired him to look into whether the bond trader Joseph Jett had acted alone to create $350 million in bogus profits even as Mr. Lynch was representing Kidder in a case against Mr. Jett. Kidder said at the time that the investigation was fair and objective—but never billed it as independent.

Critics also complained that no report of Mr. Lynch's findings was ever made public in his reviews at Bausch & Lomb and Mattel. Still, there was no evidence that Mr. Lynch failed to uncover the truth in any of those cases. Mr. Lynch did not return a telephone call to his office seeking comment.

But even companies that announce the results of investigations and commit publicly to making changes do not gain immunity from criticism.

Though Mitsubishi has enacted six of Ms. Martin's initial recommendations for its Illinois plant—and has announced a timetable for adopting 34 more that she offered last month— the lawyer representing women who are suing the company argues that the Martin review was little more than window-dressing.

"There is no question that they went to her for her name and prestige and the fact that she was female," Patricia Benassi, a lawyer in Peoria, Ill., said. Ms. Benassi contended that beyond a new, mandatory training course on sexual harassment, Ms. Martin's work has had "a limited impact on the day-to-day life of the people in that plant."

The company said, however, that it had hired Ms. Martin, in part, for her expertise on labor issues.

"I think what is fundamental is the commitment to operate in good faith to move forward to address the recommendations we have received," Gael O'Brien, a company spokeswoman for Mitsubishi, said.

Ms. Martin, now a consultant in the Chicago area and a professor at Northwestern University's Kellogg Graduate School of Management, said that Mitsubishi's public declaration of a time frame for adopting her proposals spoke to the company's sincerity. "A consultant's report, in general, com-panies can sort of take and throw away," Ms. Martin said. "Mine is different in that not only is it public, but the time frame for accomplishing all of the things suggested is also public. That is the only way I would have done this."

While companies may receive a public relations lift from hiring consultants, there is a downside, too, Ms. Martin said: "They may get some good will, but they sure are going to get public scrutiny."

The arrangement poses risks to consultants, too, Ms. Benassi said. "One of the difficulties someone in Lynn Martin's or Andrew Young's position faces is whether or not when they come to him or her, they really are sincere, or whether this is just wrapping paper on an ugly package," she said. "I don't know if the consultant always knows that."

* * *

April 9, 1997

APPAREL INDUSTRY GROUP MOVES TO END SWEATSHOPS

By STEVEN GREENHOUSE

A Presidential task force that includes human rights groups, labor unions and apparel industry giants like Nike Inc., Reebok International Ltd. and L.L. Bean has reached a groundbreaking agreement that seeks to end sweatshops by creating a code of conduct on wages and working conditions, including a maximum 60-hour workweek, for apparel factories that American companies use around the world.

The task force has also agreed to set up an association to oversee monitors who would inspect apparel factories worldwide and give a seal of approval to companies that comply with the code of conduct.

Task force members vowed to follow the code in the factories they use in the United States and abroad. Participants said they hoped that dozens of other American companies would commit themselves to meeting the standards, and that the effort would eventually lead to a work standards for the clothing industry worldwide.

The members reached agreement at a seven-hour meeting on Monday, attended by Gene Sperling, chairman of the President's National Economic Council. Task force participants said President Clinton hoped to announce the agreement next Monday at a White House ceremony where he will be flanked by industry, labor and human rights officials. Mr. Sperling, who refused to confirm details of the agreement, said, "The progress that's been made represents a unique and historic step to eradicate sweatshops here and around the world."

He said the diverse group of members "were willing to sacrifice each of their sense of what was perfect to achieve something for the common good."

Companies that comply with the code will be able to put a label or tag on their clothing assuring consumers that it was not made in a sweatshop.

Linda Golodner, the co-chairwoman of the task force and president of the National Consumers League, said, "The benefit for everyone is what the whole task force was about: that's to make sure consumers can purchase goods that have not been made in a sweatshop and make sure that there's a process in place to check that factories are not sweatshops."

The agreement came after weeks of meetings in which the apparel companies clashed with labor and human rights representatives about minimum wages and maximum hours in factories and who should monitor the factories. Task force members said they are still debating some wording in the proposed guidelines.

Roberta Karp, the task force co-chairwoman who is general counsel at Liz Claiborne Inc., said, "Industry, human rights, labor and the Clinton Administration shared a commitment and our collective work will result in improved working conditions around the world."

Underlining the difficulty of reaching an accord, the task force agreed on an ambiguous standard for wages, saying that while factories that American companies own or contract with should pay the minimum wage in the countries where they are located, there should be a link between wages and the basic needs of workers. Several labor and human rights representatives on the task force contended that in countries like Haiti, the minimum wage is too low to support a family.

At Monday's meeting in Washington, the most hotly debated issue was working hours. The corporate members, which included Nicole Miller, Patagonia and the Phillips-Van Heusen Corporation, agreed to a maximum 60-hour workweek with several wrinkles: that the maximum standard workweek would be 48 hours in countries that do not already have a standard of fewer hours, while the maximum number of overtime hours required of apparel employees would be 12.

The two labor unions represented were the Union of Needletrades, Industrial and Textile Employees and the Retail, Wholesale and Department Store Union. Jeff Ballinger, president of Press for Change, a labor rights group that has often deplored the working conditions of shoe factories that American companies use abroad, said the 60-hour maximum was an important step forward.

"If orders are backlogged or if there's a rush, many times workers will have to work 65 to 70 hours a week for weeks on end," he said.

The agreement on maximum hours will even affect factories in the United States, where there is a standard 40-hour workweek, but no limit on how many overtime hours can be worked. Under the new code, participants would agree not to force employees in their American factories to work more than 12 overtime hours beyond the 40-hour workweek.

The task force, which was set up last summer, reached an agreement early on child labor. Factories should not use workers under 15, although in some countries they would be allowed to employ 14-year-olds.

In addition, in an industry where workers often say they are hit, fondled or shouted at, the task force agree on anti-harassment provisions that human rights representatives praised. The code states that all workers be treated with respect and "no employee shall be subject to any physical, sexual, psychological or verbal harassment or abuse."

In one of the major sticking points, labor and human rights members said they wanted human rights groups or church groups to monitor factories, while corporate members said the monitors should generally be accounting firms with international offices, because such firms can easily operate anywhere.

Under the deal, companies could choose accounting firms to serve as monitors but those firms would be asked to work with human rights groups.

Task force members said that they needed to work out many details over the next such months, including how the governing association will be structured, who will serve on it, who will finance the association and the monitoring, and what labels would be put on clothing to show they were not been made in sweatshops.

Stanley Levy, a Los Angeles lawyer on the task force who represents apparel companies, said, "It's a difficult task to get all the parties to reach an agreement that sets worldwide standards."

* * *

June 22, 1997

IN PRINCIPLE, A CASE FOR MORE 'SWEATSHOPS'

By ALLEN R. MYERSON

CAMBRIDGE, Mass.—For more than a century, accounts of sweatshops have provoked outrage. From the works of Charles Dickens and Lincoln Steffens to today's television reports, the image of workers hunched over their machines for meager rewards has been a banner of reform.

Last year, companies like Nike and Wal-Mart and celebrities like Kathie Lee Gifford struggled to defend themselves after reports of the torturous hours and low pay of the workers who produce their upscale footwear or downmarket fashions. Anxious corporate spokesmen sought to explain the plants as a step up for workers in poor countries. A weeping Mrs. Gifford denied knowing about the conditions.

Now some of the nation's leading economists, with solid liberal and academic credentials, are offering a much broader, more principled rationale. Economists like Jeffrey D. Sachs of Harvard and Paul Krugman of the Massachusetts Institute of Technology say that low-wage plants making clothing and shoes for foreign markets are an essential first step toward modern prosperity in developing countries.

Mr. Sachs, a leading adviser and shock therapist to nations like Bolivia, Russia and Poland, is now working on the toughest cases of all, the economies of sub-Saharan Africa. He is just back from Malawi, where malaria afflicts almost all its 13 million people and AIDS affects 1 in 10; the lake that provided much of the country's nourishment is fished out.

When asked during a recent Harvard panel discussion whether there were too many sweatshops in such places, Mr.

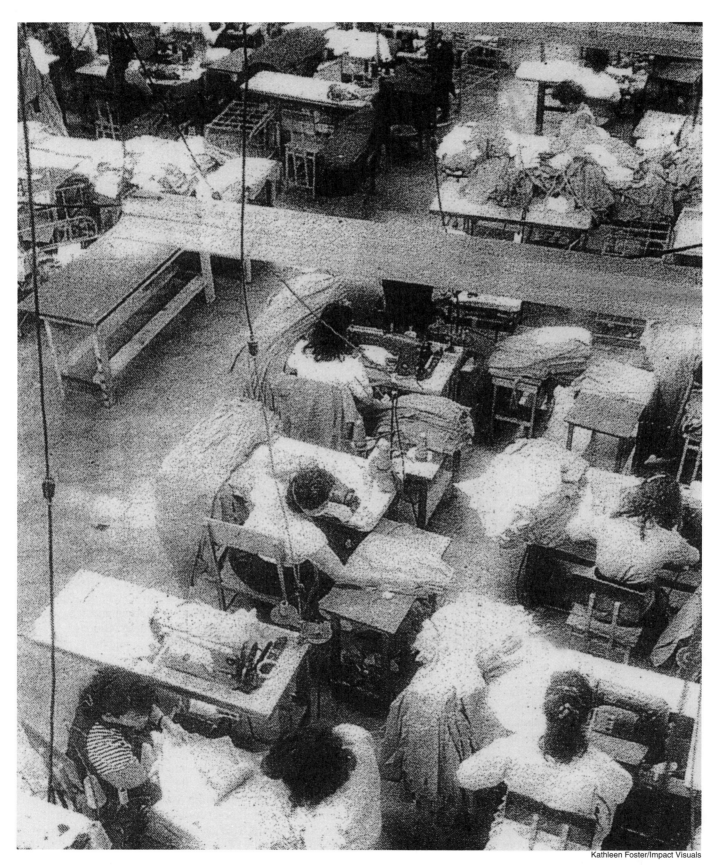

Salvadorans at work. Some economists think low wage factory labor can help poor countries advance.

Sachs answered facetiously. "My concern is not that there are too many sweatshops but that there are too few," he said.

Mr. Sachs, who has visited low-wage factories around the world, is opposed to child or prisoner labor and other outright abuses. But many nations, he says, have no better hope than plants paying mere subsistence wages. "Those are precisely the jobs that were the steppingstone for Singapore and Hong Kong," he said, "and those are the jobs that have to come to Africa to get them out of their backbreaking rural poverty."

Rising Stakes

The stakes in the battle over sweatshops are high and rising. Clinton Administration officials say commerce with the major developing nations like China, Indonesia and Mexico is crucial for America's own continued prosperity. Corporate America's manufacturing investments in developing nations more than tripled in 15 years to $56 billion in 1995—not including the vast numbers of plants there that contract with American companies.

In matters of trade and commerce, economists like Mr. Sachs, who has also worked with several Government agencies, are influential. A consensus among economists helped persuade President Clinton, who had campaigned against President Bush's plan of lowered restrictions, to ram global and North American trade pacts through Congress.

Paradoxically, economists' support of sweatshops represents a sort of optimism. Until the mid-1980's, few thought that third-world nations could graduate to first-world status in a lifetime, if ever. "When I went to graduate school in the early to mid-1970's," Mr. Krugman said, "it looked like being a developed country was really a closed club." Only Japan had made a convincing jump within the past century.

Those economists who believed that developing nations could advance often prescribed self-reliance and socialism, warning against foreign investment as a form of imperialism. Advanced nations invested in the developing world largely to extract oil, coffee, bananas and other resources but created few new jobs or industries. Developing nations, trying to lessen their reliance on manufactured imports, tried to bolster domestic industries for the home market. But these protected businesses were often inefficient and the local markets too small to sustain them.

From Wigs to Cars

Then the Four Tigers—Hong Kong, Singapore, South Korea and Taiwan—began to roar. They made apparel, toys, shoes and, at least in South Korea's case, wigs and false teeth, mostly for export. Within a generation, their national incomes climbed from about 10 percent to 40 percent of American incomes. Singapore welcomed foreign plant owners while South Korea shunned them, building industrial conglomerates of its own. But the first stage of development had one constant. "It's always sweatshops," Mr. Krugman said.

These same nations now export cars and computers, and the economists have revised their views of sweatshops. "The overwhelming mainstream view among economists is that

the growth of this kind of employment is tremendous good news for the world's poor," Mr. Krugman said.

Unlike the corporate apologists, economists make no attempt to prettify the sweatshop picture. Mr. Krugman, who writes a column for Slate magazine called "The Dismal Scientist," describes sweatshop owners as "soulless multinationals and rapacious local entrepreneurs, whose only concern was to take advantage of the profit opportunities offered by cheap labor." But even in a nation as corrupt as Indonesia, he says, industrialization has reduced the portion of malnourished children from more than half in 1975 to a third today.

In judging the issue of child labor also, Mr. Krugman is a pragmatist, asking what else is available. It often isn't education. In India, for example, destitute parents sometimes sell their children to Persian Gulf begging syndicates whose bosses mutilate them for a higher take, he says. "If that is the alternative, it is not so easy to say that children should not be working in factories," Mr. Krugman said.

Not that most economists argue for sweatshops at home. The United States, they say, can afford to set much higher labor standards than poor countries—though Europe's are so high, some say, that high unemployment results.

Labor leaders and politicians who challenge sweatshops abroad say that they harm American workers as well, stealing jobs and lowering wages—a point that some economists dispute. "It is especially galling when American workers lose jobs to places where workers are really being exploited," said Mark Levinson, chief economist at the Union of Needletrades, Industrial and Textile Employees, who argues for trade sanctions to enforce global labor rules.

Yet when corporations voluntarily cut their ties to sweatshops, the victims can be the very same people sweatshop opponents say they want to help. In Honduras, where the legal working age is 14, girls toiled 75 hours a week for the 31-cent hourly minimum to make the Kathie Lee Gifford clothing line for Wal-Mart. When Wal-Mart canceled its contract, the girls lost their jobs and blamed Mrs. Gifford.

No Jobs in Practice

Mr. Krugman blames American self-righteousness, or guilt over Indonesian women and children sewing sneakers at 60 cents an hour. "A policy of good jobs in principle, but no jobs in practice, might assuage our consciences," he said, "but it is no favor to its alleged beneficiaries."

* * *

June 25, 1997

NIKE'S ASIAN FACTORIES PASS YOUNG'S MUSTER

By DANA CANEDY

Andrew Young, the civil rights leader called upon by Nike Inc. to look into its overseas labor practices, said yesterday that a months-long investigation had turned up no evidence of widespread or systematic mistreatment of workers.

Still, the sporting equipment company should do more to insure that its foreign subcontractors comply with its code of conduct, Mr. Young said at a news conference.

"We found Nike to be in the forefront of a global economy," Mr. Young, the former mayor of Atlanta and United Nations representative, said. "Factories we visited that produce Nike goods were clean, organized, adequately ventilated and well lit."

In fact, he said he had anticipated finding much worse conditions in factories in Asia where Nike shoes and apparel are produced.

Nike critics said they were disappointed by Mr. Young's report, adding that his remarks contained surprisingly few criticisms of the company and failed to address at all the issue of low wages paid to workers in many of the factories.

The company, which is based in Beaverton, Ore., hired Mr. Young's newly created consulting firm, Goodworks International of Atlanta, to review its recently updated international labor code. Since March, Mr. Young has toured Nike plants in China, Vietnam and Indonesia and has held several meetings with company executives and representatives of human rights organizations that have been critical of the company.

In remarks yesterday summarizing his findings, Mr. Young advised Nike to continue to "play a leadership role" in the White House Apparel Industry Partnership, which has produced a voluntary, global standard for international labor practices. Nike should also take more aggressive steps to explain and enforce its code of conduct, and it needs to promote the development of worker representation in factories, he said.

In addition, he said, Nike should support third-party monitoring of worker conditions and should endorse an independent grievance system for workers. And it should expand talks with human rights and labor groups in the countries where its products are produced, he said.

Mr. Young came closest to criticizing his client when he said that the factories he visited were "controlled by absentee owners, managed by expatriates who, in Vietnam in particular, do not speak the local language fluently and are overseen by a relatively small number of Nike technical supervisors focused largely on quality control."

The findings seemed to produce few surprises for the company but angered some of its critics.

"I think it was an extremely shallow report," said Medea Benjamin, director of Global Exchange, a human rights group in San Francisco. "I was just amazed that he even admitted that he spent three hours in factories using Nike interpreters and then could come out and say he did not find systematic abuse."

Several human rights groups have said that by hiring Mr. Young, Nike was simply trying to deflect accusations that its foreign subcontractors use child labor, pay abysmally low wages and subject workers to sweatshop conditions.

Nike has repeatedly denied that its goods are made in sweatshops or that factory owners subject workers to inadequate conditions or pay them low wages. The company says that Mr. Young's review provided a level of oversight to its

commitment to setting the standard for global workplace standards, and it said that it intended to carry out all of Mr. Young's recommendations.

Philip H. Knight, Nike's founder and chief executive, said: "We will take action to improve in areas where he suggests we need to improve. For although his overall assessment is that we are doing a good job, good is not the standard Nike seeks in anything we do."

Throughout the investigation, Mr. Young maintained that he was working independently and was not a spokesman for the company. Yet Nike officials accompanied him on all his factory tours, and he presented his findings to the company's board and senior management a week before making them public.

* * *

November 8, 1997

NIKE SHOE PLANT IN VIETNAM IS CALLED UNSAFE FOR WORKERS

By STEVEN GREENHOUSE

Undermining Nike's boast that it maintains model working conditions at its factories throughout the world, a prominent accounting firm has found many unsafe conditions at one of the shoe manufacturer's plants in Vietnam.

In an inspection report that was prepared in January for the company's internal use only, Ernst & Young wrote that workers at the factory near Ho Chi Minh City were exposed to carcinogens that exceeded local legal standards by 177 times in parts of the plant and that 77 percent of the employees suffered from respiratory problems.

The report also said that employees at the site, which is owned and operated by a Korean subcontractor, were forced to work 65 hours a week, far more than Vietnamese law allows, for $10 a week.

The inspection report offers an unusually detailed look into conditions at one of Nike's plants at a time when the world's largest athletic shoe company is facing criticism from human rights and labor groups that it treats workers poorly even as it lavishes millions of dollars on star athletes to endorse its products.

Though other American manufacturers also have problems in overseas plants, Nike has become a lightning rod in the debate because it is seen as able to do more since it earned about $800 million last year on sales of $9.2 billion.

Critics of Nike's working conditions, who had been given a copy of the internal report by a disgruntled employee, made it available to The New York Times and several other reporters, prompting the company to call a news conference yesterday to address the allegations.

"We believe that we look after the interests of our workers," said Vada Manager, a Nike spokesman. "There's a growing body of documentation that indicates that Nike workers earn superior wages and manufacture product under superior conditions."

Dara O'Rourke

Workers at a Nike factory in Vietnam. An accounting firm says that employees are being exposed to carcinogens that exceed local legal standards by 177 times and that respiratory problems are common.

He and other Nike officials said the company had carried out "an action plan" to improve working conditions since the report was issued last January, 17 months after the factory opened. The company said it had sharply cut overtime, improved safety and ventilation and reduced the use of toxic chemicals.

The company also asserted that the report showed that its internal monitoring system had performed exactly as it should have.

"This shows our system of monitoring works," Mr. Manager said. "We have uncovered these issues clearly before anyone else, and we have moved fairly expeditiously to correct them."

While Nike has often been attacked over low pay and long hours, the Ernst & Young report pushed hard on a relatively new front for Nike's critics: air quality in its factories. Ernst & Young found that toluene, a carcinogen, was in the air at different sites in the factory studied at 6 to 177 times the amount allowed by Vietnamese regulations, which itself is about four times as strict as American toluene standards. Extended exposure to toluene is known to cause damage to the liver, kidneys and central nervous system.

The fact that such conditions existed in one of Nike's newer plants and were given a withering assessment by Nike's own consultants made for yet another embarrassing episode in a continuing saga.

Only five months ago, the company had taken out full-page newspaper ads excerpting Andrew Young, the civil rights advocate and former United Nations representative, who had inspected 15 factories last spring at Nike's behest. After completing his two-week tour covering three countries, he informed Nike it was doing a "good job" in treating its workers, though he allowed it "should do better." Mr. Young was widely criticized by human rights groups and labor groups for not taking his own translators and for doing slipshod inspections, an assertion he repeatedly denied.

Like many American apparel makers, Nike uses many subcontractors in Asia, with some 150 factories employing more than 450,000 workers. And like many, that tricky relationship is often offered as a reason for the difficulty in imposing American-style business practices on factories in that part of the world.

The Tae Kwang Vina factory, which was inspected by Ernst & Young, is one of Nike's larger plants. It has 9,200 workers and makes 400,000 pairs of athletic shoes each month at Bien Hoa City, some 25 miles northeast of Ho Chi Minh City, formerly Saigon.

The Ernst & Young report painted a dismal picture of thousands of young women, most under age 25, laboring 10½ hours a day, six days a week, in excessive heat and noise and in foul air, for slightly more than $10 a week. The report also found that workers with skin or breathing problems had not been transferred to departments free of chemicals and that more than half the workers who dealt with dangerous chemicals did not wear protective masks or gloves.

In plain, unemotional language, the report detailed problem after problem.

"Dust in mixing room exceeded the standard 11 times," the report said. And, it added, "There's a high rate of labor accidents caused by carelessness of employees."

Later, the report pointed to two other problems: "workers' inadequate understanding of the harmful effect of chemicals" and "increasing number of employees" with health problems continue to work with chemicals.

The report also stated that "more than half of employees" in several departments who use chemicals "do not wear protective equipment (mask and gloves)—even in highly hazardous places where the concentration of chemical dust, fumes exceeded the standard frequently."

The Transnational Resource and Action Center, a nonprofit group based in San Francisco that often criticizes conditions at American factories overseas, made the report available. The center obtained the report from Dara O'Rourke, an environmental consultant for the United Nations Industrial Development Organization whose job involves inspecting factories in Vietnam and who was given a copy of the report by a disgruntled Nike employee.

Mr. O'Rourke, who is also a research associate at the Transnational Center, said he was making the report public because he wanted to pressure Nike to treat its workers better and because he was convinced that Ernst & Young's inspection report let Nike off easy. Mr. O'Rourke said wages at the plant were the lowest of any of the 50 factories he visited in Vietnam, and that working conditions were well below average.

Tien Nguyen, Nike's labor practices manager in Vietnam, said at a news conference yesterday that as soon as Ernst & Young made its confidential report 10 months ago, the company took numerous steps to improve working conditions.

Mr. Nguyen said that the number of hours worked a week had been reduced to 45, from 65, and that many more fans had been installed. But he acknowledged that the company had done no measurements to determine whether chemical levels were now low enough to meet legal standards.

With the improvements, "it's markedly better than shoe factories in the United States," said Dusty Kidd, Nike's director of labor relations. "The shoe factories in Vietnam are among the most modern in the world. The factories there are excellent factories, but there are a lot of things they could get better."

But Mr. O'Rourke, who has visited the Nike factory three times as part of his United Nations duties, said that when he visited Vietnam last month, several workers said the plant was hardly better than in January. He said many workers still failed to wear protective gear, that pay remained low and that managers still yelled at or otherwise harassed workers.

Mr. Young, who made his visits in June, did not inspect this particular plant. And his report, which pronounced the plants to be "clean, organized, adequately ventilated and well lit" had few findings in common with the Ernst & Young report.

Was he aware of the Ernst & Young study prior to the trip? Doug Gatlin, who toured the Nike factories with Mr. Young, said they were. "We didn't see or read all of the reports they did prior to our going," said Mr. Gatlin, who nonetheless defended the job they did. Mr. Young could not be reached for comment because he was traveling.

As far as the Ernst & Young report went in shedding light on Nike's practices, some found fault with it, too. Mr. Rourke, for instance, criticized its conclusion that most employees were happy with the wages and working conditions. Mr. O'Rourke said the workers whom Ernst & Young interviewed were scared to speak candidly. Mr. O'Rourke said his interviews found much discontent.

He said the audit also let Ernst & Young off the hook over accidents because it concluded that "employee carelessness" caused many injuries. He said a serious health and safety study would have analyzed the underlying causes of accidents, like a lack of training, "rather than simply blaming the victim."

Mr. O'Rourke said the Ernst & Young report had so many inadequacies that it showed the benefits of using noncommercial monitors, like human rights groups, to inspect factories.

* * *

May 13, 1998

NIKE PLEDGES TO END CHILD LABOR AND APPLY U.S. RULES ABROAD

By JOHN H. CUSHMAN Jr.

WASHINGTON, May 12—Bowing to pressure from critics who have tried to turn its famous shoe brand into a synonym for exploitation, Nike Inc. promised today to root out underage workers and require overseas manufacturers of its wares to meet strict United States health and safety standards.

Philip H. Knight, Nike's chairman and chief executive, also agreed to a demand that the company has long resisted, pledging to allow outsiders from labor and human rights groups to join the independent auditors who inspect the factories in Asia, interviewing workers and assessing working conditions.

"We believe that these are practices which the conscientious, good companies will follow in the 21st century," he said in a speech here at the National Press Club. "These moves do more than just set industry standards. They reflect who we are as a company."

Nike said it would raise the minimum age for hiring new workers at shoe factories to 18 and the minimum for new workers at other plants to 16, in countries where it is common for 14-year-olds to hold such jobs. It will not require the dismissal of underage workers already in place.

Footwear factories have heavier machinery and use more dangerous raw material, including solvents that cause toxic air pollution. At overseas factories that produce Nike shoes, the company said, it would tighten air-quality controls to insure that the air breathed by workers meets the same standards enforced by the United States Occupational Safety and Health Administration at home.

Mr. Knight's pledges did not include increased wage, a major complaint of critics who say that Nike and other American companies pay workers in China and Vietnam less than $2 a day and workers in Indonesia less than $1 a day. (A 1996 World Bank report concluded that more than one-fifth of the world's population lives on less than $1 a day.) Still, even with much lower prices in these countries, critics say workers need to make at least $3 a day to achieve adequate living standards.

Nike, in a statement today, cited a report it commissioned in 1997, which said that its factories in Indonesia and Vietnam pay legal minimum wages and more.

In his speech today, Mr. Knight defended Nike's record of creating jobs and improving factory conditions abroad, but seemed to acknowledge that it was time for drastic action. "The Nike product has become synonymous with slave wages, forced overtime and arbitrary abuse," he said. "I truly believe that the American consumer does not want to buy products made in abusive conditions."

The initiatives announced today address the types of issues, like air quality, that were raised by an inspection report prepared for the company by Ernst & Young, the accounting and consulting firm. The report, which found many unsafe conditions at a plant in Vietnam, gained force when it was made public by the Transnational Resource and Action Center, a nonprofit group that often criticizes conditions at American factories overseas.

Critics of Nike responded favorably to many elements of the plan released today, while noting that Mr. Knight had not promised to increase pay. They cautioned that he had not detailed which groups would be allowed to take part in the monitoring of factories or provided other details on that part of his commitment.

"Independent monitoring is a critical element of an overall system of improving labor practices," Mr. Knight said. "Nike's goal is to reach a point where labor practices can be tested and verified in much the same manner that financial audits determine a company's compliance with generally accepted accounting principles."

Monitoring labor standards abroad has divided industry members of a committee established by the White House to consider such standards of American corporations, preventing it for the past year from coming up with recommendations.

Jeffrey D. Ballinger, director of Press for Change, a group that has been critical of Nike, called the company's plan a major retreat and a sign of the critics' growing strength.

Associated Press

Nike's chief, Philip H. Knight, discussing company labor practices yesterday.

"I think on the health and safety question, it is a very significant statement," he said. "There is not a lot of wiggle room. They either fix it or they don't. I really, really believe they are going to get after that problem."

The company has been hurt by falling stock prices and weak sales even as it has been pummeled in the public relations arena, including ridicule in the comic strip Doonesbury and an encounter between Mr. Knight and the gadfly film maker Michael Moore in his new documentary, "The Big One."

Mr. Knight said the main causes of the company's falling sales were the financial crisis in Asia, where the company had been expanding sales aggressively, and its failure to recognize a shifting consumer preference for hiking shoes.

"I truthfully don't think that there has been a material impact on Nike sales by the human rights attacks," he said, citing the company's marketing studies.

But for months, the company, which spends huge sums for advertising and endorsements by big-name athletes, has responded increasingly forcefully to complaints about its employment practices, as student groups have demanded that universities doing business with Nike hold it to higher standards. In January, it hired a former Microsoft executive to be vice president for corporate and social responsibility.

Other critics, such as Thuyen Nguyen, director of Vietnam Labor Watch, were critical when the civil rights figure Andrew Young reported favorably last year on the company's efforts to improve conditions in its Asian factories, saying that he had glossed over problems.

Mr. Knight emphasized today that using objective observers to monitor working conditions would serve not just Nike, but eventually American industry in general, by "giving the American consumer an assurance that those products are made under good conditions."

Some critics, though, stressed that the company could not reassure consumers without improving wages in its factories.

"We see one big gap," said Medea Benjamin, director of the San Francisco-based human rights group Global Exchange. "A sweatshop is a sweatshop is a sweatshop unless you start paying a living wage. That would be $3 a day."

* * *

June 15, 1998

ASIA'S CRISIS UPSETS RISING EFFORT TO CONFRONT BLIGHT OF SWEATSHOPS

By NICHOLAS D. KRISTOF

JAKARTA, Indonesia—Just as pressure is growing in the West against the use of sweatshops in developing countries, the Asian financial crisis is spawning such desperation that more people than ever seem willing to take grim or dangerous jobs in such factories.

While economic misery and differing labor standards have long made sweatshops more prevalent in the third world than in the West, the trend had been toward improved working conditions. But now scholars and labor organizers say that in Asia the trend has sharply reversed, with the financial crisis forcing many workers to compete for jobs that a year ago they would have scorned.

A result is that increasing numbers of desperate workers are lining up to take up precisely the kinds of jobs that are being roundly condemned in the West. In the slums in Indonesia and in Thailand, many workers even speak of sweatshop jobs as their greatest aspiration.

Here in the Indonesian capital, Mrs. Tratiwoon stood barefoot recently in the vast garbage dump where she makes a living scavenging through the rubbish and described her dreams for her 3-year-old son: She wants him to grow up to work in a sweatshop.

Indeed, for Mrs. Tratiwoon, an uneducated woman who cheerfully gave her age as "20 or 30," the sweatshops in the area around the garbage dump look so exalted now—in the aftermath of the financial crisis—that she worries that a job in one for her son might be too high an aspiration.

"He's not going to get an education," said Mrs. Tratiwoon, who like many Indonesians has just one name, "so I don't know whether he can ever get a job like that."

Nicholas D. Kristof/The New York Times

Mrs. Tratiwoon, left, makes a living scavenging through the rubbish of a garbage dump in Jakarta. She hopes her 3-year-old son will have a better life working in one of Indonesia's factories, even though, by American standards, conditions in such sweatshops are often dangerous, dirty and grim.

The campaign against sweatshops has gained momentum in the West in the last few years. Last month, for example, Nike Inc. bowed to pressure and agreed to far-reaching changes in labor practices at factories that churn out its shoes. Nike said it would raise the minimum age for new workers to 16, admit outsiders to inspect the factories, and improve air filtration to meet United States factory standards.

But market forces in Asia are pushing in precisely the opposite direction. In recent years, the rising prosperity of countries like Indonesia and Thailand encouraged workers to demand better conditions and more safety, while businesses were doing well enough that they could afford to improve conditions as a way of attracting laborers. Now companies are trying to reduce costs to survive, and surging unemployment means employees have lost their leverage.

"As a result of the Asian economic crisis, there are lots more people working in sweatshop conditions," said Lee Ji Soon, an economics professor at Seoul National University in South Korea. "We can get over this problem only if Asia recovers from the crisis."

Mr. Lee said governments can help by promoting free education to reduce child labor and work to combat income disparities. But the only way to eliminate dangerous conditions and child labor, he emphasized, is to generate economic growth.

There is no agreed-upon definition of a sweatshop, and so there is no way of calculating how many people work in such places. But scholars and social workers say that the financial crisis that began nearly a year ago in Thailand has clearly extended the longevity of factories that might have emerged from the pages of Dickens.

Mongkol Latlakorn, a 36-year-old laborer doing odd jobs in northeast Thailand, said he worried about his youngest child, Darin. She is working in a tiny sweatshop in Bangkok, the Thai capital, making clothing.

"It's dangerous work," Mr. Mongkol said. "There's lots of machinery, and sometimes it catches her hands. Twice the needles in the machines went right through her hands. But the managers bandaged up her hands, and both times she got better again and went back to work."

Mr. Mongkol said that Darin, who is 15, works nine hours a day, six days a week, and earns $2 a day. That is a considerable sum in the slums, where a meal of street food can be had for about 25 cents, and it is more than he earns from his odd jobs. So he worries not so much about the possibility that Darin might get hurt as about the risk that she might lose the job. "There's all this talk about factories closing now, and she said there are rumors that her factory might close," Mr. Mongkol said. "I hope that doesn't happen. I don't know what she would do then."

Some economists say the campaigns in the West against sweatshops do have an impact on the workers lucky enough to be making branded American merchandise. But for a great majority of Asia's labor force the dominant reality is not the success of the campaigns against sweatshops but the scarcity of jobs. Unemployment in the nine countries most affected by the Asian crisis is expected to reach 21 million this year, including 10 million in Indonesia alone.

"On issues such as safety standards and health standards, the governments may wink at violations now," said a long-time Western analyst in Thailand. "It's better to have an unsafe job than no job at all."

The main problems, most experts say, are with locally owned companies, particularly those that do not produce well-known American brands. There is no evidence that well-known Western companies are taking advantage of the crisis to take short cuts on safety standards.

Robert Broadfoot, managing director of Political & Economic Risk Consultancy in Hong Kong, said the pain of the crisis and the rise of nationalistic sensitivities has made foreign companies very careful to avoid criticism. "If you're a foreign company navigating the environment today, you don't want to be perceived as a sweatshop," he said.

The most troublesome labor conditions often arise in small, locally owned businesses far from a capital. They are places like the sawmill where Mr. Sariman, a muscular man who says his age is "maybe 40," worked in the city of Gresik, 400 miles east of Jakarta.

Mr. Sariman moved from his village to Gresik a few years ago and took a job as a day laborer. Because he was paid by how much he did, he chose to work long hours, often from 8 A.M. to 9 P.M., earning the equivalent of about $3 a day. Then last year, he was lifting beams when one slipped and shattered his left leg.

The factory paid Mr. Sariman $50 in compensation, but since he was not a regular employee it refused to pay his medical bills. Friends carried him to the hospital, but the doctor said treatment would cost almost $200. "I couldn't afford that, so I went home," Mr. Sariman recalled. He went to a traditional healer, but ended up paying more than $150 in medical expenses.

Now Mr. Sariman is better, but he walks with a limp and will never be able to do hard physical work again. So he sells fruit from a pushcart and earns less than $1 a day.

"I'm not mad at the factory," he said, as he sat on a bench outside his home. "It was an accident, and nobody wants an accident to happen. It wouldn't be good to get mad at them unless they didn't try to help at all."

Indeed, Mr. Sariman said he still thinks it was worthwhile to work in the factory. "There's no work in the village, and you only get a harvest once a year," he said. "What if your harvest is bad?"

Mr. Sariman's standard of comparison is a common one. Indeed, the term "sweatshop" is a bit of a misnomer, for the work often involves much less perspiration than hoeing the fields or wading in the paddies.

Likewise, from the perspective of garbage scavengers like Mrs. Tratiwoon, who live day by day surrounded by the filth of the dump, even a dangerous job in a dismal factory would mark one rung up the ladder for her son.

Employees often complain about the dreariness of their work or the harshness of their supervisors. But these days the talk usually turns not to the wretchedness of the work but the difficulty in finding it.

Some labor organizers say that accidents and resentment may eventually create more momentum for labor unions. "The workers here may become so indignant that they become more active," said one Indonesian labor activist.

Because many economists say that the key to improving conditions lies in boosting economic growth, some say that the best thing that the United States could do would be to insure that its markets remain open—or open further—to products made in poor countries.

"If you in America are really concerned with working conditions in poor countries, maybe the best way to help would be to import their products more freely," said Mr. Lee, the South Korean professor.

American unions have resisted this, arguing in part that it is difficult for American laborers to compete with the cheap wages abroad. Indeed, the economics of factory work in Asia is dizzying.

In Gresik, a middle-aged peasant woman named Mrs. Misri makes sarongs six days a week on a heavy hand loom, earning about 42 cents a day for hard work on something that looks like a fiendishly efficient exercise machine. Mrs. Misri sleeps free on the factory floor, but she pays 20 cents a day for street food and 90 cents for a weekly round-trip bus ride to her village to spend Sunday with her husband and children.

A result is that when she does not buy clothing or have medical expenses, she can take home 42 cents to help the children go to school and buy food. It does not sound like much for a week's hard work, but if she were home in the village she would probably earn nothing at all.

In fact, Mrs. Misri's wages are on the high side, because her work takes skill and is physically exhausting.

Mrs. Hanifa, 48, runs a nearby factory in her home and employs 10 women to make red plaid dresses for little girls. She said she pays her best employees about 35 cents a day, but she declined to say how much she paid her worst employees.

"These are tough times," Mrs. Hanifa lamented. "It's hard for anyone to make money. And I'm paying good wages, at least for around here."

*   *   *

November 5, 1998

GROUPS REACH AGREEMENT FOR CURTAILING SWEATSHOPS

By STEVEN GREENHOUSE

After more than two years of debate, a group of human rights organizations and apparel manufacturers, including Nike, Reebok and Liz Claiborne, has reached an agreement intended to curtail sweatshops by setting up a code of conduct and monitoring system for overseas factories used by American companies.

The group that reached the agreement hopes it will reassure American consumers that the clothing they buy is not made in sweatshops, but the nation's leading apparel union rejected the agreement yesterday as not going far enough.

Members of the group said they would seek to carry out the agreement even though the apparel union rejected it. But several members said they feared that American consumers would feel little reassurance that apparel produced under the agreement's guidelines was not made in sweatshops.

The Union of Needletrades, Industrial and Textile Employees criticized the accord for not requiring overseas factories to pay workers enough to meet their basic needs and for allowing American companies to use clothing factories in countries, including China, that repress unions.

"This agreement's not very good," said Mark Levinson, director of research at the needletrades union. "How can you talk about eliminating sweatshops without making a commitment to pay a living wage? And the agreement allows companies to produce in countries that systematically deny worker rights, and it allows them to do that without requiring them to say anything to protect rights in those countries."

Despite the union's rejection, members of the group insisted that its agreement was a giant step forward in combating sweatshops. The four companies and five nonprofit groups that reached the agreement say they hope dozens more companies will sign on and comply with the agreement's requirements to insure that apparel is made under satisfactory working conditions.

"The Administration is convinced this agreement lays the foundation to eliminate sweatshop labor, here and abroad," Labor Secretary Alexis Herman said. "It is workable for business and creates a credible system that will let consumers know the garments they buy are not produced by exploited workers. We remain committed to working with all interested parties to insure its future success."

The agreement grows out of a Presidential task force, the White House Apparel Industry Partnership, that was set up in 1996 after revelations that apparel produced under the Kathie Lee Gifford name was being made in sweatshops in New York and Central America.

After the task force's 18 members remained stalemated for months, 9 of the group's more centrist members began negotiating among themselves before reaching an agreement on Monday. This group presented the agreement to the other members Monday night in the hope that they would accept it.

"It's incredibly important," said Roberta Karp, general counsel of Liz Claiborne and co-chairwoman of the task force. "It's the foundation to move forward to make a real difference in working conditions around the world. It requires monitoring by independent monitors as well as public reporting for the first time ever. It's simply unparalleled."

In interviews yesterday, officials with the apparel union said they would no longer take part in the Presidential task force if other members moved forward with the new agreement.

"We cannot continue to participate in this effort on the basis of this agreement," said Alan Howard, assistant to the president of the needletrades union. "This has been offered to us on a take it or leave it basis and we can't take it."

Companies that participate say they hope that by complying with the code of conduct and monitoring system they will be able to boast—perhaps through advertisements or by tags on their apparel—that their products are sweatshop-free.

The nine task force members that reached the new agreement are Liz Claiborne, Nike, Reebok, Phillips-Van Heusen, Business for Social Responsibility, the Lawyers Committee for Human Rights, the National Consumers League, the International Labor Rights Fund and the Robert F. Kennedy Memorial Center for Human Rights.

Four other corporate task force members, L. L. Bean, Patagonia, Nicole Miller and Kathie Lee Gifford, have accepted the new agreement.

"This agreement is only the beginning," President Clinton said. "We know that sweatshop labor will not vanish overnight. While this agreement is an historic step, we must measure our progress by how we change and improve the lives and livelihoods of apparel workers here in the United States and around the world. That is why I urge more companies to join this effort."

Several corporate members said that if the task force accepted the stricter requirements sought by union leaders, that would make it harder to persuade more companies to join the effort.

Under the agreement, factories used by American companies could not use forced labor and could not require employees to work more than 60 hours each week. In addition, the agreement prohibits factories from employing children younger than 15, although employment of 14-year-olds would be allowed when the country of manufacture allows employment at that age.

The agreement also requires employers to pay the minimum wage required by local law or the prevailing industry wage, whichever is higher. Labor unions have repeatedly complained that in countries like Indonesia and Vietnam, both the minimum wage and prevailing wage are too low to support a family.

Under the accord, a new entity, the Fair Labor Association, would be set up to oversee compliance. The new association would certify which monitors could examine factories, and it could expel companies that do not comply with the code. Many of the monitors would be accounting firms, but the accord urges all monitors to work with nongovernmental groups, like human rights groups, to get an accurate picture of conditions.

The agreement calls for companies to monitor all their factories themselves but in addition requires outside monitors to examine 30 percent of a company's factories in the three years after a company agrees to comply with the code of conduct. In subsequent years, about 10 percent of a company's factories would be inspected annually.

Officials with the needletrades union said it was insufficient for only one-tenth of a company's factories to be monitored each year.

"The monitoring is badly flawed," Mr. Howard said. "We don't think it's very independent monitoring and the compa-nies pick their monitors and the factories to be monitored so there won't be surprise inspections."

The union's biggest criticism is the accord's failure to require that companies pay a living wage.

Human rights groups that backed the agreement said they persuaded the companies to agree to a Department of Labor study on the minimum and prevailing wages in relevant countries and how those wages compare with the amount needed to meet workers' basic needs.

"Those of us on the nongovernment organization side are continuing to fight for higher wages in this industry," said Michael Posner, executive director of the Lawyers Committee for Human Rights. "This issue is central to our thinking going forward. Remember, this a first step and we have a lot of work to do to make this work."

*   *   *

January 26, 2000

ANTI-SWEATSHOP MOVEMENT IS ACHIEVING GAINS OVERSEAS

By STEVEN GREENHOUSE

Apparel and footwear factories overseas have slowly improved working conditions in response to a highly vocal anti-sweatshop movement, labor rights advocates say.

Pressure from college students and other opponents of sweatshops has led some factories that make goods for industry giants like Nike and the Gap to cut back on child labor, to use less dangerous chemicals and to require fewer employees to work 80-hour weeks, according to groups that monitor such factories.

These changes, labor advocates say, could signal the beginning of a broad improvement in conditions for low-paid apparel workers in Asian and Latin American factories after four decades in which the trend has been for American companies to transfer production overseas in search of ever-cheaper labor.

The advocates stress that the improvements have been spotty, and that serious problems remain at factories from Honduras to Hong Kong. Wages are often too low to feed a family, factory air is often filled with chemicals and many managers refuse to let sick employees leave work to get medical attention.

"There has been some improvement on the ground, but nowhere near significant enough," said Charles Kernaghan, executive director of the National Labor Committee, a leading anti-sweatshop group.

At many factories, labor rights advocates say, managers have stopped hitting workers, have improved ventilation and have stopped requiring workers to obtain permission before going to the toilet.

Sweatshop opponents praise some companies, like Liz Claiborne, for improving conditions, while accusing others, like Wal-Mart, of being slow to ensure changes at the overseas factories that produce their apparel.

"Some steps have been taken, but I don't think one can say that conditions have improved in any wholesale way," said Pharis Harvey, executive director of the International Labor Rights Fund, a watchdog group in Washington." A number of companies that produce globally are watching much more carefully to deal with problems before they become embarrassing public problems."

The anti-sweatshop movement has put many apparel makers, like the Gap and Kathie Lee Gifford, on the defensive by picketing in front of stores, holding sit-ins at colleges and bombarding companies with letters.

The movement, one of the nation's largest to push for changes since the 1960's, includes church and consumer groups, labor unions, human rights organizations and college, high school and even middle-school students. The movement's leaders often note that sweatshops are not just found overseas; many remain in New York, Los Angeles and other American cities.

At last month's protests in Seattle, conditions in such factories were a major focus, with many demonstrators demanding that trade treaties punish countries that permit violations of minimum labor standards.

Apparel industry executives say that with shoppers hunting for bargains, they face intense pressure to produce goods as cheaply as possible, encouraging many to turn to substandard factories.

Many corporate executives acknowledge that the anti-sweatshop movement's efforts are paying off.

Phil Knight, chairman of Nike, the world's largest footwear maker, said the movement had gotten his company to accelerate efforts to improve conditions. "It probably speeded up some things that we might have done anyway," said Mr. Knight, whose company uses 565 footwear and apparel factories employing 500,000 workers in 46 countries. "Basically, the workers in footwear factories, not just our factories, are better off today than two years ago."

In one significant move, Nike and its rival Reebok are requiring the many Asian factories that produce for them to stop using petroleum-based adhesives that cause damage to the liver, kidney and central nervous system in favor of safer water-based adhesives.

Labor rights experts point to many improvements. Five years ago, monitoring groups say, apparel factories in Honduras often employed children under 14, but now it is rare to find workers under 16. In Indonesia, managers no longer systematically squash unionization efforts.

Liz Claiborne, the Gap and Reebok have all hired respected human rights groups to monitor a handful of their factories.

"The anti-sweatshop movement has improved working conditions," said Apo Leong, executive director of the Asia Monitor Research Center, a labor rights group based in Hong Kong. "We're seeing the multinationals putting pressure on their contractors, and subsequently conditions have improved."

Mr. Leong noted that factories in China were using less child labor and prison labor. But he said grave problems remained throughout Asia. He said that China often imprisoned union organizers, that many Nike and Reebok plants still lacked adequate ventilation and that many factories in Cambodia had deplorable health and safety conditions.

Sweatshop opponents point to other problems. Jeffrey Ballinger, executive director of Press for Change, a labor rights group, said wages paid by Nike's Indonesian factories had fallen in recent years, after accounting for inflation, an assertion the company denies. " Wages are behind where they were," Mr. Ballinger said. "They're below what is considered necessary to meet the minimum needs of a single adult."

Mr. Kernaghan of the National Labor Committee said, "There are two places where progress seems to grind to a halt: the effort to form unions and the effort to have wage increases."

One recent development is the formation of the Fair Labor Association, a White House-backed group of human rights organizations and companies, including L. L. Bean, Nike and Reebok. This group is setting up a monitoring system to inspect overseas factories to get them to meet minimum labor standards, like not requiring employees to work more than 60 hours a week.

Many campus groups call the association pro-corporate, and criticize it for not requiring factories to pay a living wage. But the association's members defend it as the first serious corporate-backed effort to inspect apparel factories and to put teeth behind basic labor standards.

* * *

September 24, 2000

TWO CHEERS FOR SWEATSHOPS

By NICHOLAS D. KRISTOF and SHERYL WUDUNN

It was breakfast time, and the food stand in the village in northeastern Thailand was crowded. Maesubin Sisoipha, the middle-aged woman cooking the food, was friendly, her portions large and the price right. For the equivalent of about 5 cents, she offered a huge green mango leaf filled with rice, fish paste and fried beetles. It was a hearty breakfast, if one didn't mind the odd antenna left sticking in one's teeth.

One of the half-dozen men and women sitting on a bench eating was a sinewy, bare-chested laborer in his late 30's named Mongkol Latlakorn. It was a hot, lazy day, and so we started chatting idly about the food and, eventually, our families. Mongkol mentioned that his daughter, Darin, was 15, and his voice softened as he spoke of her. She was beautiful and smart, and her father's hopes rested on her.

"Is she in school?" we asked.

"Oh, no," Mongkol said, his eyes sparkling with amusement. "She's working in a factory in Bangkok. She's making clothing for export to America." He explained that she was paid $2 a day for a nine-hour shift, six days a week.

"It's dangerous work," Mongkol added. "Twice the needles went right through her hands. But the managers bandaged up her hands, and both times she got better again and went back to work."

"How terrible," we murmured sympathetically.

Mongkol looked up, puzzled. "It's good pay," he said. "I hope she can keep that job. There's all this talk about factories closing now, and she said there are rumors that her factory might close. I hope that doesn't happen. I don't know what she would do then."

He was not, of course, indifferent to his daughter's suffering; he simply had a different perspective from ours—not only when it came to food but also when it came to what constituted desirable work.

Nothing captures the difference in mind-set between East and West more than attitudes toward sweatshops. Nike and other American companies have been hammered in the Western press over the last decade for producing shoes, toys and other products in grim little factories with dismal conditions. Protests against sweatshops and the dark forces of globalization that they seem to represent have become common at meetings of the World Bank and the World Trade Organization and, this month, at a World Economic Forum in Australia, livening up the scene for Olympic athletes arriving for the competition. Yet sweatshops that seem brutal from the vantage point of an American sitting in his living room can appear tantalizing to a Thai laborer getting by on beetles.

Fourteen years ago, we moved to Asia and began reporting there. Like most Westerners, we arrived in the region outraged at sweatshops. In time, though, we came to accept the view supported by most Asians: that the campaign against sweatshops risks harming the very people it is intended to help. For beneath their grime, sweatshops are a clear sign of the industrial revolution that is beginning to reshape Asia.

This is not to praise sweatshops. Some managers are brutal in the way they house workers in firetraps, expose children to dangerous chemicals, deny bathroom breaks, demand sexual favors, force people to work double shifts or dismiss anyone who tries to organize a union. Agitation for improved safety conditions can be helpful, just as it was in 19th-century Europe. But Asian workers would be aghast at the idea of American consumers boycotting certain toys or clothing in protest. The simplest way to help the poorest Asians would be to buy more from sweatshops, not less.

On our first extended trip to China, in 1987, we traveled to the Pearl River delta in the south of the country. There we visited several factories, including one in the boomtown of Dongguan, where about 100 female workers sat at workbenches stitching together bits of leather to make purses for a Hong Kong company. We chatted with several women as their fingers flew over their work and asked about their hours.

"I start at about 6:30, after breakfast, and go until about 7 p.m.," explained one shy teenage girl. "We break for lunch, and I take half an hour off then."

"You do this six days a week?"

"Oh, no. Every day."

"Seven days a week?"

"Yes." She laughed at our surprise. "But then I take a week or two off at Chinese New Year to go back to my village."

The others we talked to all seemed to regard it as a plus that the factory allowed them to work long hours. Indeed, some had sought out this factory precisely because it offered them the chance to earn more.

"It's actually pretty annoying how hard they want to work," said the factory manager, a Hong Kong man. "It means we have to worry about security and have a supervisor around almost constantly."

It sounded pretty dreadful, and it was. We and other journalists wrote about the problems of child labor and oppressive conditions in both China and South Korea. But, looking back, our worries were excessive. Those sweatshops tended to generate the wealth to solve the problems they created. If Americans had reacted to the horror stories in the 1980's by curbing imports of those sweatshop products, then neither southern China nor South Korea would have registered as much progress as they have today.

The truth is, those grim factories in Dongguan and the rest of southern China contributed to a remarkable explosion of wealth. In the years since our first conversations there, we've returned many times to Dongguan and the surrounding towns and seen the transformation. Wages have risen from about $50 a month to $250 a month or more today. Factory conditions have improved as businesses have scrambled to attract and keep the best laborers. A private housing market has emerged, and video arcades and computer schools have opened to cater to workers with rising incomes. A hint of a middle class has appeared—as has China's closest thing to a Western-style independent newspaper, Southern Weekend.

Partly because of these tens of thousands of sweatshops, China's economy has become one of the hottest in the world. Indeed, if China's 30 provinces were counted as individual countries, then the 20 fastest-growing countries in the world between 1978 and 1995 would all have been Chinese. When Britain launched the Industrial Revolution in the late 18th century, it took 58 years for per capita output to double. In China, per capita output has been doubling every 10 years.

In fact, the most vibrant parts of Asia are nearly all in what might be called the Sweatshop Belt, from China and South Korea to Malaysia, Indonesia and even Bangladesh and India. Today these sweatshop countries control about one-quarter of the global economy. As the industrial revolution spreads through China and India, there are good reasons to think that Asia will continue to pick up speed. Some World Bank forecasts show Asia's share of global gross domestic product rising to 55 to 60 percent by about 2025—roughly the West's share at its peak half a century ago. The sweatshops have helped lay the groundwork for a historic economic realignment that is putting Asia back on its feet. Countries are rebounding from the economic crisis of 1997-98 and the sweatshops—seen by Westerners as evidence of moribund economies—actually reflect an industrial revolution that is raising living standards in the East.

Of course, it may sound silly to say that sweatshops offer a route to prosperity, when wages in the poorest countries are sometimes less than $1 a day. Still, for an impoverished Indonesian or Bangladeshi woman with a handful of kids who would otherwise drop out of school and risk dying of mundane diseases like diarrhea, $1 or $2 a day can be a life-transforming wage.

This was made abundantly clear in Cambodia, when we met a 40-year-old woman named Nhem Yen, who told us why she moved to an area with particularly lethal malaria. "We needed to eat," she said. "And here there is wood, so we thought we could cut it and sell it."

But then Nhem Yen's daughter and son-in-law both died of malaria, leaving her with two grandchildren and five children of her own. With just one mosquito net, she had to choose which children would sleep protected and which would sleep exposed.

In Cambodia, a large mosquito net costs $5. If there had been a sweatshop in the area, however harsh or dangerous, Nhem Yen would have leapt at the chance to work in it, to earn enough to buy a net big enough to cover all her children.

For all the misery they can engender, sweatshops at least offer a precarious escape from the poverty that is the developing world's greatest problem. Over the past 50 years, countries like India resisted foreign exploitation, while countries that started at a similar economic level—like Taiwan and South Korea—accepted sweatshops as the price of development. Today there can be no doubt about which approach worked better. Taiwan and South Korea are modern countries with low rates of infant mortality and high levels of education; in contrast, every year 3.1 million Indian children die before the age of 5, mostly from diseases of poverty like diarrhea.

The effect of American pressure on sweatshops is complicated. While it clearly improves conditions at factories that produce branded merchandise for companies like Nike, it also raises labor costs across the board. That encourages less well established companies to mechanize and to reduce the number of employees needed. The upshot is to help people who currently have jobs in Nike plants but to risk jobs for others. The only thing a country like Cambodia has to offer is terribly cheap wages; if companies are scolded for paying those wages, they will shift their manufacturing to marginally richer areas like Malaysia or Mexico.

Sweatshop monitors do have a useful role. They can compel factories to improve safety. They can also call attention to the impact of sweatshops on the environment. The greatest downside of industrialization is not exploitation of workers but toxic air and water. In Asia each year, three million people die from the effects of pollution. The factories springing up throughout the region are far more likely to kill people through the chemicals they expel than through terrible working conditions.

By focusing on these issues, by working closely with organizations and news media in foreign countries, sweatshops can be improved. But refusing to buy sweatshop products risks making Americans feel good while harming those we are trying to help. As a Chinese proverb goes, "First comes the bitterness, then there is sweetness and wealth and honor for 10,000 years."

Nicholas D. Kristof and Sheryl WuDunn, who received a Pulitzer Prize for their coverage of China, are the authors of "Thunder From the East: Portrait of a Rising Asia" (Knopf), from which this article is adapted.

PART V

THE FINANCIAL CRISES

Think of globalization as one of those Russian nesting dolls, or Matryoshkas. Each doll contains another, smaller doll, which holds within itself a yet-smaller doll, and so on. In some respects, globalization is like that. On the outside are the most obvious aspects of globalization—globally branded goods, huge global companies, and the media and transportation networks that increasingly tie the world together. This colorful facade gets most of the attention, but the real interest lies on the inside.

Inside the first doll is a second doll that represents the global division of labor that helps produce these goods and services. This is the doll of forgotten factories, anonymous labs, and nameless workshops. Hidden within this is another doll that represents transportation, distribution, and telecommunications services—the interlocking layers of networks that connect the millions of people who make globalization happen. Inside *this* doll you will find the doll of global finance. Globalization is, at its core, financial globalization. Financial markets are the most global markets in the world, and without financial globalization, it is argued, the rest of the global economy would be impossible.

And what's inside the global finance doll? Many disturbing answers have been suggested to this question, but the articles collected here suggest the most frightening answer of all: Inside the global finance doll lies chaos.

Financial crises do not occur *only* during periods of globalization, but when finance is global, financial crises are global, too, and so have more serious and widespread effects. Contagion occurs as problems in one country's financial market spread to others.

Part V collects articles about four important financial crises of the post-war ear. Each of these case studies is important from the perspective of economic history and the history of global finance. Together, they show that financial crises happen in poor countries (Mexico, Thailand) but also in rich countries (Britain and the United States, the center of the Bretton Woods crisis). The crises themselves may be economic and at times somewhat technical, but dealing with financial instability is, everywhere and alway, a political process.

One recurring and revealing theme in this collection of articles is optimism. As each crisis winds down, scholars and policy-makers propose reforms and "new architecture" to prevent a repepition of financial catastrophe. The optimism lasts until the next crisis appears on the horizon.

In covering the Bretton Wood crisis of the 1970s, *The Times* mobilized a standard division of labor—political reporters covered the politics, and economics correspondents covered their beat. By the time of the European monetary crisis of 1992–93, however, politics and economics were so intertwined that it was difficult to separate them, and *The Times* looked at the story from top (heads of state) to bottom (pocketbook issues). This technique of clustering many articles together, each taking a different angle on a critical issue, is even more apparent in the articles collected here on the Peso crisis of 1994–95. This crisis was close to home and *Times* readers were treated to broad and deep analysis of its causes and effects.

The Asian financial crisis of 1997 continues this trend. *The Times* was able to mobilize its staff to undertake a remarkably thorough analysis of a complicated and multi-layered problem. A four-part series authored by Nicholas Kristof and three members of *The Times* staff that examines the human consequences of the crisis illustrates how far economics reporting has evolved.

Financial crises are difficult to report and to explain meaningfully, but the articles collected here represent some of the best economics reporting in the history of *The Times*.

THE COLLAPSE OF THE BRETTON WOODS SYSTEM

October 3, 1963

10 NATIONS AGREE ON A WORLD STUDY OF MONEY SYSTEM

Seek Better Payment Plan in First Major Negotiations Since Bretton Woods

By EDWIN L. DALE Jr.
Special to The New York Times

WASHINGTON, Oct. 2—The non-Communist world's 10 most powerful industrial nations announced today that they would start the first major negotiation and study of the world's financial system since the Bretton Woods Conference in New Hampshire 20 years ago.

The Bretton Woods Conference led to the establishment of the present system by which international transactions are conducted. The system has worked well to date, but it has recently shown strains.

The purpose of the new study and negotiation is to see whether the system can be improved and reinforced, with the aim of assuring that world prosperity will not be disrupted by a purely international financial factor as it was in the nineteen-thirties.

The 10 nations announced their decision in a communiqué during the annual meeting here of the International Monetary Fund and the International Bank for Reconstruction and Development. The Monetary Fund will conduct an independent study of the problem, but the results of the 10-nation talks will determine the outcome.

Paris Talks Planned

The talks will be conducted in Paris by high-level officials from the 10 governments, under the chairmanship of Robert V. Roosa, United States Under Secretary of the Treasury. The vice chairman will be Emil van Lennep, director general of the Netherlands Finance Ministry.

All ideas for improvement of the present international monetary system and for elimination of its flaws except two will be considered. Those ruled out are any change in the present gold price of $35 an ounce and freely fluctuating exchange rates among currencies.

Douglas Dillon, the Secretary of the Treasury, issued today's communiqué in his capacity as temporary chairman of the "Group of Ten." The chairmanship at the ministerial level will rotate according to rules still to be established, but the United States will have the chairmanship of the actual study.

Spring Report Is Target

The first Paris meeting of the study group will be in early November. Mr. Dillon said the target was a preliminary report by next spring and decisions, if possible, in time for next year's World Fund Meeting in Tokyo in late September.

The 10 nations hold about 80 per cent of the world's reserves of gold and foreign exchange.

Mr. Dillon explained today that their studies would not be limited to changes or improvements in the International Monetary Fund itself, which has 102 members. He said that "sovereign decisions" by governments would also be considered. These would include such matters as how much gold to hold and how to grant credit to nations suffering deficits in their balance of international payments.

The Monetary Fund, one keystone of the present system, was established at the Bretton Woods Conference. The 10 nations in the study group are the United States, Britain, France, West Germany, Italy, Belgium, the Netherlands, Sweden, Canada and Japan. The main exception among the leading financial nations was Switzerland, but Mr. Dillon indicated that the Swiss would be brought into the study in one way or another.

Switzerland is not a member from the outset only because she does not belong to the International Monetary Fund.

Underlying Aim

The underlying aim of all the members of the study is to prevent the kind of financial chaos that prolonged and deepened the depression of the nineteen-thirties.

At that time nations withdrew credits from each other rather than granting them, and nation after nation, virtually devoid of gold, had to impose restrictions on foreign transactions and trade, as well as imposing domestic restraints on economic growth.

No member of the group foresees such a crisis in the near future. But the purpose of the study is to make sure that one could not arise. The members are also agreed, however, that international credit should not be so easy that individual nations could freely pursue inflationary policies at home and disregard their international payments.

Authoritative sources from the various countries involved were unanimous in private conversation in saying that the results of the negotiation were impossible to predict. However, there was also unanimity that any results would be evolutionary rather than revolutionary.

There could be such results as changes in the means of granting international credit and possibly an enlargement of the sources of such credit. There could be more precise rules on the holding of foreign currencies—chiefly the dollar—as part of nations' reserves.

No Basic Change Seen

But the basic international system—by which nations have fixed exchange rates, hold their reserves in gold and foreign exchange and borrow reserves from the International Monetary Fund or from each other if they need to—will not be changed.

The chances of significant results from the negotiations were difficult to predict today. It was clear that the 10 nations would start with views that differ both on problems and on the solutions to be proposed.

For example, the Continental European countries are interested in a more orderly system of granting credit to deficit countries, such as the United States. Britain is urgently concerned with the problem of "international liquidity"—the total of countries' reserves and their access to credit—particularly when the United States deficit ceases.

All are agreed, however, that the first priority of business is for the United States to reduce and then eliminate its deficit, meanwhile to assure that the deficit does not disrupt the international system.

Today's formal proceedings at the meeting here were devoted to the affairs of the World Bank, which is not directly involved in the international monetary system. It makes loans for the economic development of poorer countries.

The speeches today generally welcomed the bank's new policy, announced Monday by its president, George D. Woods, of slightly liberalizing lending terms.

*   *   *

November 19, 1967

BRITAIN DEVALUES POUND TO $2.40 TO AVERT A NEW ECONOMIC CRISIS; SEVERE RESTRAINTS ARE IMPOSED

REDUCTION IS 14.3%

Curbs Include a Basic Interest Rate of 8% and Spending Cuts

By ANTHONY LEWIS
Special to The New York Times

LONDON, Nov. 18—Britain devalued the pound tonight.

The official value was lowered 14.3 per cent, from $2.80 to $2.40. The announcement was made at 9:30 P.M. (4:30 P.M., New York time) and the new rate was effective immediately.

The devaluation meant that a long struggle to maintain a chronically weak currency at the rate set in 1949 had ended in defeat for the Labor party Government. The consequences for the British people and for the world monetary system just began to be sensed tonight.

The move was made in an attempt to lower the cost of British goods in foreign countries in the hope that exports would rise, and to increase the price of imports in the hope that they would be reduced. The result would be a better balance between exports and imports.

Rumors a Factor

A secondary consideration in the decision to devalue the pound was the hope that the move would end the uncertainty and talk of devaluation that have been common in financial circles recently.

The politics as well as the economics of Britain will be shaken by the decision. It represents a devastating blow to the

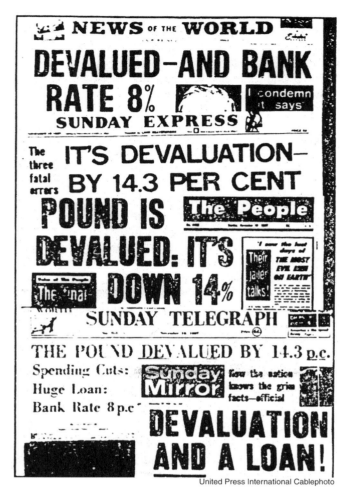

United Press International Cablephoto

TODAY'S HEADLINES: London papers report the news.

Government, and especially to Prime Minister Wilson and his Chancellor of the Exchequer, James Callaghan.

Along with the devaluation the Government, ordered all banks and stock exchanges to remain closed Monday. It also outlined stringent measures designed to slow the economy: higher interest rates and taxes and reductions in Government spending.

At the same time Britain sought huge new international credits totaling $3-billion. The money will be used to replenish her depleted reserves of gold and dollars and to give strength to sterling in the days of readjustment ahead.

Of the total borrowing, $1.6-billion has been pledged by some of the world's leading central banks. The United States is in the pool, but it was not known tonight whether France had agreed to join.

The remaining $1.4-billion has been requested from the International Monetary Fund. A statement from the fund tonight said that Britain had been assured of "prompt and sympathetic consideration" and that a "favorable decision" was expected in a few days.

The lending arrangement was worked out with central bankers in the Group of Ten—the leading countries in world monetary affairs—who were meeting in Paris this week.

The urgent effort was to stop the deterioration of confidence in a major world trading currency. The pound is second only to the dollar in its use for international transactions and its place in many national reserves.

The pound was weak, basically, because Britain continued to import more than she exported.

Drain Turns to Panic

In the last week, events turned the chronic drain into panic. A record trade gap of $300-million was reported for October. As rumors of loans and devaluation circulated without official action, large amounts of Britain's reserves of gold and foreign currencies were poured out in an effort to keep the pound up to the official rate despite selling pressure.

The United States and Britain's friends in Europe were informed a few hours before the devaluation announcement. Their reactions quickly began to indicate what would happen in the world monetary system.

Ireland announced that she would devalue as Britain had, and Israel said she would make an announcement tomorrow. Denmark and Finland said they would devalue to some extent, and Norway may follow suit.

The countries in the sterling area, those that use the pound for trading, will differ in their reactions. In the old days they would have devalued almost automatically with Britain. Now such countries as South Africa and the rich Arab states are economically stronger than Britain.

No Market Devaluation

The Common Market's six members—France, West Germany, Italy, Belgium, the Netherlands and Luxembourg—will not devalue, demonstrating the very strength that makes Britain want to join the market.

The devaluation announcement was a sudden and dramatic turn after days of official silence in the midst of chaos in the financial markets.

Although the experts knew that devaluation was a real possibility after years of abstract discussion, the actual news came as a surprise. The British Broadcasting Corporation continued for an hour with a Doris Day movie on television. Early editions of Sunday newspapers had such headlines as "Why Are We Waiting?"

For three years, since the Labor party took over the Government, it has asked the British people for sacrifice to maintain the value of the pound. In a moment tonight, all the sacrifice—unemployment, lagging wages and a stagnant economy—seemed a wasted effort.

Devaluation Rejected

Moreover, Mr. Wilson and Mr. Callaghan had repeatedly rejected the prospect of devaluation.

On July 24 the Prime Minister said that those who started rumors about devaluation were "wasting their time." The same day the Chancellor said that to devalue would be to "break faith" with governments abroad and "bring down the standard of life of our own people."

The possibility that the Labor party itself would turn against the authors of the old policy could not be excluded. Under the parliamentary system Mr. Wilson could be forced from office by losing the support of his own party.

Edward Heath, the Conservative leader, was quick to denounce the Government tonight. He pointed out that the last devaluation of the pound, from $4.03 to $2.80 in 1949, also took place under a Labor government.

Move Is Condemned

"I utterly condemn the Government for devaluating the pound," Mr. Heath said. "Twice in 20 years disastrous Socialist policies and incompetent Labor ministers have brought about devaluation, created hardship at home and discredited Britain abroad."

A Liberal member of Parliament, Richard Wainwright, called for a new Chancellor of the Exchequer. He said devaluation had come about "in the worst possible way—in a great scramble, surrounded by something close to panic."

The Sunday Express, a Conservative newspaper, said in an editorial: "What should Mr. Wilson do next? Just one thing. Quit."

The pro-Labor Sunday Mirror said devaluation stood for "disaster and disillusion."

The other measures announced by the Government tonight made it clear that the public would have to suffer as part of the price of economic readjustment. These were the major directives:

- The country's basic interest rate, the bank rate, will rise to an extraordinary 8 per cent from 6½ per cent in an effort to slow down economic activity. In addition, banks will have to limit their loans except for such urgent needs as exports.
- The Government will cut defense spending next year by more than £100-million, or $240-million at the new rate. Domestic public expenditure will be slashed by the same amount.
- A large rebate now given to all manufacturing industry on the Selective Employment Tax, a flat tax on every worker employed, will be canceled except in distressed regions. A special export rebate will also be dropped.
- The corporation tax, the Government warned, will be increased in April from 40 to 42.5 per cent. It said a "strict watch" would be maintained to prevent undue increases in dividends.

Freeze Omitted

The one glaring omission from the list of measures was a freeze on wages. Experts have long warned that any devaluation would produce great pressures for higher wages to match the inevitably rising cost of living. But wage increases would kill the aim of keeping exports less expensive in foreign currencies.

The Treasury statement tonight said only that it was "essential" to avoid large wage claims and settlements lest "industrial costs go up once more and the competitive benefits of devaluation be frittered away." It said talks on this matter with labor and industry would begin at once.

At present there is no legal freeze on wages. The Trades Union Congress, parent body of British unions, is supposed to keep some control on increases, though its ability to do so seems doubtful. The Government's Prices and Incomes Board can delay rises briefly while investigating them.

Some thought the Government would inevitably move toward a wage freeze like the one it imposed for six months after the crisis in July, 1966. The theory was that it was merely trying tonight to avoid too much bad news for its union supporters at once.

One of the agonizing questions for the Government was what effect the debilitating drama of the last week, ending in the humiliation of tonight, would have on its already tattered hopes of entering the Common Market.

A Foreign Office spokesman said tonight that devaluation would "not affect our determination to join" and would "put beyond doubt our ability to accept the obligations of membership."

French Opposition

To say that France will not agree with that appraisal is to understate the situation. The French, who have been using all possible means to block the British application, can be expected to say that the devaluation shows that Britain is in much too weak an economic position to be considered.

Others in the community will argue, however, that Britain has taken the painful step urged on her by the market's economists.

The Council of Foreign Ministers of the market is meeting on Monday to consider the British application. From London's point of view the timing could hardly be worse.

Mr. Callaghan will appear in the House of Commons Monday to discuss the devaluation. On Tuesday Mr. Wilson is expected to appear at a long-scheduled meeting of Labor Parliamentary members of economic policy.

* * *

April 23, 1968

THE FINANCIAL CRISIS

The Nation's Money Is in Trouble,
But Government Action Is Curbed

By RICHARD E. MOONEY

The American economy has never produced more than it is producing right now. The rate of unemployment has been below 4 per cent for more than two years. Business profits are higher than ever before.

Yet the chairman of the Federal Reserve Board, William McChesney Martin Jr., says that "we are in the midst of the worst financial crisis we have had since 1931." This is not a contradiction. Mr. Martin himself pointed out that this is not the depression all over again—it is "not a business crisis, but a financial crisis."

In other words, the nation's business is obviously not in trouble at the present time. The nation's money is.

The nation's business is in the eighth year of its longest uptrend in history. For a time last year some economic authorities thought it was ending, but it only slowed down a little and has speeded up since then.

Whole World Involved

How long it will last is impossible to predict. It has already astounded the experts by lasting as long as it has.

Properly managed it could keep on going. Improperly managed it could develop into too strong a boom, followed inevitably by a painful retrenchment—painful for the United States and for the whole world, because no country's economy is as powerful as this one's and every corner of the world is influenced by it.

The possibility of a retrenchment as disastrous as the great Depression of the 1930's is essentially zero. The whole economic community—government, the banks, business, labor, and the academic economists—learned from that experience. The country knows how to keep the economy within bounds now, which it did not know then.

What worries Mr. Martin, and President Johnson and many others here and abroad, is whether the country will do what it knows how to do.

The immediate threat is inflation. In the first half of the 1960's, the economy grew fast and prices held relatively stable. But in the last two years the price trend has been steadily upward, 3 to 4 per cent a year.

Payments Deficit Worse

Related to this is the balance-of-payments deficit. It has been a problem for 10 years, but until recently it appeared to be manageable, and it appeared to be shrinking. Six months ago it started to become sharply worse.

Inflation and payments deficits go hand in hand. When a country is booming and its prices are rising, imports rise and exports slacken.

The boom means greater demand for all goods, domestic and foreign. Thus, there is less reason for American producers to export and more attraction for foreigners to sell here. The higher prices mean that lower-priced foreign goods sell better here, and higher-priced American goods sell less well abroad.

The result: less money flows in from sales of exports, more money flows out to purchase imports, and the payments deficit grows. This is only a very partial explanation of the causes and effects of inflation and unbalanced payments, but it is a critical part.

The classic remedy for both aspects of the problem is to curb the boom. If economic expansion slows down, the pressures of inflation are lessened, imports are weaker, and exports are stronger.

Two Government Tools

The Government has two principal tools for accomplishing this. One is budget policy—taxes and spending. The other is monetary policy—interest rates and other restrictions on the availability of credit through the banking system.

There are, at times, reasons for using one tool rather than the other. Monetary policy can be used more quickly, for instance. A tax cut, or a tax increase, can be aimed more precisely or more broadly—at a specific sector of the economy or at everyone—but it takes longer.

However, when there is a general problem of inflation or recession, the economic consensus says to use both. To use only one is the same as if a man uses only one hand to lift a heavy load. The one has to work harder to accomplish the job.

This is the dilemma of United States economic policy right now. The Government is relying on monetary policy alone to curb economic activity. The Federal Reserve System has tightened up on the availability of bank credit, and interest rates have risen to extraordinary levels.

President Johnson proposed a whole year ago that Congress bring budget policy into play, too, with a tax increase. After a long standoff he agreed to do part of the job himself, with cuts in proposed spending cuts. But Congress has still not budged and shows no sign that it will, so the outlook is for still tighter monetary restrictions.

The psychological effect of this is as important as the practical effect. The policy-making machinery of the greatest economic power that the world has ever known is observed to be operating on only one cylinder, and the problems of inflation and the payments are not being solved.

* * *

November 21, 1968

THE DOLLAR ESCAPES EUROPE'S CURRENCY CRISIS

By GERD WILCKE

Was it a franc crisis?

Or was it a mark crisis?

Answers to these questions depended largely on whether they were posed in Bonn or Paris.

The most that could be said about the hectic developments that moved toward devaluation of the franc was that they were a triumph of nationalism. And the real question was whether Europe could afford this type of nationalism any longer.

The Germans, of course, dealt from a position of strength. The strength was documented in their balance of trade, in their international accounts.

The Germans could insist that right was on their side because no one in Bonn last week held a card big enough to beat them.

But wrong or right, the Germans knew they had the backing of financial markets, as attested by the tremendous flow of foreign funds to their country.

Somewhat surprisingly, Frenchmen saw no direct link between the recent crisis and the political turmoil in their country in May and June that led to the crisis. Unanimously, these Frenchmen pointed out that economic data for October indicated that France had overcome its internal difficulties deriving from the early summer events.

A common theory advanced by bankers and industrialists in New York was that the May-June events may have triggered the crisis, but that its basic root was the lack of a unified currency in the European Common Market.

Common Currency Needed

As one banker put it: "When you remove barriers to let Europeans trade freely, it's absolutely impossible to maintain an equilibrium in balances of payments without a common currency."

For the moment at least, the dollar seemed immune from attack. This was in sharp contrast to the two previous crises, the first following devaluation of the British pound almost exactly one year earlier, the second the run on the dollar last March.

There were reasons. Inflation in the United States had led to higher stock prices and a flood of investment money into the United States from Europe. The booming American economy had caused banks to pull dollars from their branches abroad and from dollars on deposit in European banks. Finally, the restrictions on American capital exports had produced a record volume of dollar borrowing by American and international companies in the so-called European bond market.

All of these things, plus the unwillingness of European central banks to acquire new gold, had led to a shortage of dollars and, for the moment at least, to a fairly comfortable position for the United States currency.

The French banker who criticized the lack of a common currency in Europe cited the analogy of the United States. The United States functioned as a common market, he said, only because it had a common currency, the dollar. Massachusetts or Connecticut, thus, might experience a trade deficit but the free movement of goods, capital and people offset the effect.

Europe, he continued, also was trying to have its own version of free interstate trade. This could not be done painlessly without the benefit of a common currency.

"This time the crisis is in France, the next time it may be Belgium, Italy or even Germany," he said.

The banker continued that the biggest lesson to be drawn from the current crisis would be for the six members of the European Common Market to sit down and work out a common currency.

He acknowledged, however, that the prevalence of nationalistic attitudes in Europe did not make it likely that there could be an early agreement. "In order to create a unified currency you will have to give up a certain amount of national sovereignty," he said.

The banker and a prominent industrialist agreed that aside from the lack of a common currency, another reason for the recent crisis was the lack of confidence in France itself.

The political upheavals of last May were only the beginning. Once they were settled, the Government introduced exchange controls that did not work because there was no machinery to administer them.

The eventual removal of the controls, itself a daring gesture, did little to restore confidence because the Government introduced an internal measure that created a kind of panic.

The measure, a significant increase in inheritance taxes, was coupled with discussions about a possible return of capital taxes.

To the French, who had been subjected to capital taxes after World War II, this was a signal to start moving funds out of the country to the safer grounds of Switzerland, Germany and the United States.

"When money starts running out of your country, it's always a reflection of a lack of confidence, and Frenchmen feared there might be a recurrence of the May upheavals," the banker said.

For most of the week France—joined somewhat incongruously by its ancient allies, the United States and Britain—sought to demonstrate that it was not a franc crisis at all but a mark crisis.

The Germans, supported by Italy, Sweden, Switzerland and the Netherlands, resisted pressure to increase the value of their currency.

By the end of the poker game, the Germans had agreed to change their tax structure. This was aimed at making imports cheaper and exports dearer.

Flow of Funds Stemmed

They also agreed to stem the flow of foreign funds by forcing their banks to freeze all foreign deposits of a speculative and noncommercial nature and turn them over to the German central bank. The regulation, applicable to deposits of nonresidents made after Nov. 15, provided that the deposits would earn no interest for the banks.

This and a promise to make foreign deposits subject to licensing, the Germans hoped would discourage foreign speculators and take the pressure off the mark. During three recent days the Germans accumulated $1.77-billion in foreign funds.

Could all this happen to the dollar?

The French banker said international speculation was always focused on a currency that was most vulnerable at a given time. The crisis was mostly between the French franc and the German mark.

"All the funds that can be concentrated on this speculation game are currently tied up. However, once over, the speculation might turn to any other currency," the banker said.

The factors favoring the dollar at the moment were ephemeral at best. A decline in the stock market, for instance, could arrest the inflow of investment funds from Europe. A slowing of the economy could reduce the demand for Eurodollars.

The warning was clear. The dollar easily could be next.

* * *

September 19, 1970

4,390 ECONOMISTS URGE NIXON TO VETO TRADE BILL

Petition Assails Import-Restricting Plan Now Before House— Move Parallels Smoot-Hawley Protest of 1930

By EDWIN L. DALE Jr.
Special to The New York Times

WASHINGTON, Sept. 18—A group of 4,390 economists urged President Nixon today to veto the import-limiting trade bill if it reaches him in the version now pending before the House.

The statement supported by the economists had a parallel 40 years ago—a petition by more than 1,000 economists to Herbert Hoover to veto the Smoot-Hawley tariff bill, which sharply raised tariffs. President Hoover signed the bill and, partly because of the resulting higher tariffs, United States and world trade declined sharply during the nineteen-thirties.

Although an exact check has not been made, about 15 of the 1930 signers also signed today's statement, including former Senator Paul H. Douglas, Democrat of Illinois. Most of the original signers are dead.

At a news conference this morning, Mr. Douglas said the bill now in the House was worse than the Smoot-Hawley measure. The present legislation calls for quotas that definitely limit imports; the earlier legislation set high tariffs that allowed imports at a steep price.

A spokesman for the National Commission on Trade Policy, which sponsored the news conference, said the bill would probably pass the House if it goes to the floor under a rule that forbids amendments. It is expected to be voted out of the Rules Committee Tuesday.

In the Senate today, Senator Ernest F. Hollings, Democrat of South Carolina, introduced the trade bill as an amendment to the Administration's family assistance plan and the Social Security bill. But its fate in the Senate is up in the air since that body has few rules about amendments.

Also listed as sponsors of today's statement were four former chairmen of the President's Council of Economic Advisers, under both Republican and Democratic Administrations. One original sponsor, Jacob Viner, of Princeton University, was. like Senator Douglas, a signer in 1930, but he died last week before the new statement was published.

The present trade bill is not the same as the Smoot-Hawley measure, though both have import-limiting provisions. The Smoot-Hawley tariff, following the tradition of more than a century, actually fixed the tariff on thousands of products, mainly at a higher level than before.

The bill approved this year by the House Ways and Means Committee directly affects only five items. Chief among them are shoes, textiles and oil. But the bill contains provisions under which it would become easier for other industries to obtain relief from imports through a process of petition to the Tariff Commission, though the President would have the ultimate power of decision.

Caution Expressed

The bill does not, in the main, return to the practice, finally abandoned in 1934, of Congressional tariff-setting. But it is still opposed vigorously by the free-trade forces, though it has strong support from a number of industries and partial support from organized labor.

Today's statement was organized by the Committee for a National Trade Policy, the oldest of the organizations supporting freer trade. Its chairman is Charles P. Taft.

The statement said, "We now seem on the threshold of another massive mistake, which would seriously damage the trade agreements system that, since 1934, has replaced the anarchy of the nineteen-twenties and early thirties."

It continued: "Import controls would be an unproductive and irresponsible answer to the problems and needs of industries and workers seeking Government help against foreign competition. There are serious adjustment problems at home and considerable cause for irritation at the treatment accorded to our exports abroad. But the right answer does not lie in triggering a trade war. That would only make a bad situation worse.

"We therefore urge Congress to reject import controls—direct or indirect, explicit or implicit. The bill reported out by the House Ways and Means Committee provides for and encourages such controls. If such a bill is passed by Congress, we urge the President to veto it."

The former chairmen of the Council of Economic Advisers who sponsored the statement were Gardner Ackley, Walter W. Heller, Leon H. Keyserling and Raymond J. Saulnier.

John W. Hight, executive director of the Committee for a National Trade Policy, said "fewer than 10" of the 10,000 economists to whom the statement was sent specifically opposed it. More than 4,000 have endorsed it. The rest did not reply.

*   *   *

April 5, 1971

MONEY AILMENT IS HARD TO CURE

Lands With Surplus Dollars Avoid a Run on Fort Knox

By CLYDE H. FARNSWORTH
Special to The New York Times

PARIS, April 4—After a movement of billions of dollars into the strong currency nations of Europe last week, Western monetary authorities faced the unenviable task of trying to head off a new financial crisis without being able to tackle the basic cause of the disturbances.

For 20 years the United States has run balance-of-payments deficits, mainly through overseas military and aid spending, which have fed the world with a supply of dollars well beyond basic liquidity needs.

Private forecasts by some of the world's major financial institutions see little improvement at least through the first half of the nineteen-seventies.

Theoretically, the foreign governments should be able to turn in the surplus dollars for American gold.

A Limited Supply

Although the United States is a trillion-dollar economy with nearly $150-billion of overseas investments, it does not have enough gold in Fort Knox to meet the foreign claims.

If the foreigners demanded payment for their chips, they could precipitate a major crisis in international trade and payments. They don't want this any more than the United States does.

The situation has been compared by William F. Butler, vice president and chief economist of the Chase Manhattan Bank, to the man who had his head so firmly wedged in the lion's jaw that the lion could not bite down.

Efforts are concentrated on keeping the system hobbling along by attacking symptoms, and not the cause, of the disease.

One of these symptoms is the interest rate differential between the United States, where expansionary policies are being pursued to get the economy moving again and reduce unemployment, and Europe, where the chief goal of economic policy is still to curb inflations.

These differentials have caused a massive shift of funds from the vast and still little understood Eurodollar market to the European centers—particularly to Frankfurt, but also to Zurich, Amsterdam, Brussels and, before last week's bank rate cut by the Bank of England, London as well.

The Eurodollar market, where foreign-owned dollars are lent at rates influenced by domestic American money rates, is a phenomenon of the surplus dollar situation, and has grown in stride with the American deficits.

As the dollars flow from the Eurodollar pool in to the foreign centers where they are converted into foreign currencies, the conversions have the effect of swelling the foreign countries' money supply, aggravating its problems in curbing inflation.

It is an external force ("A hydra-headed monster" is the label of France's Finance Minister Valéry Giscard d'Estaing), which European central bankers complain reduces their monetary sovereignty.

"Even in its anemic state," read a front-page headline in the liberal Roman Catholic Paris newspaper La Croix, "the dollar makes the law in Europe."

European monetary authorities, two weeks ago at important meetings in Paris, told their Washington counterparts that the United States had gone too far with its easy money policies. They wanted to see somewhat higher short-term interest rates in the United States and more reliance on fiscal measures to spur the economy.

For their part, the Americans thought the Europeans were keeping their interest rates too high.

As part of an international understanding, a sign of the close monetary cooperation that still exists despite the American deficits, the Europeans pledged to reduce their rates, while the Americans said they would continue crying to limit the downward pressures on short-term rates ("Operation Twist" as it is dubbed in the United States).

The American authorities also said they would try to mop up more of the surplus dollars in the Eurodollar market to nudge the foreign dollar rates upward.

* * *

May 16, 1971

EUROPEANS BEAR BRUNT IN CRISIS OF DOLLAR

By EDWIN L. DALE Jr.

WASHINGTON—Last weekend, when the latest international monetary flare-up was wearing its climax, John B. Connally Jr., Arthur M. Burns, Paul W. McCracken, George Shultz and Richard M. Nixon, as far as is known, got some sleep.

Karl Schiller, Karl Klasen, Jeile Zylstra, Nello Celio, Valery Giscard d'Estaing and Guido Carli—to name a few European financial authorities—did not.

Therein lies what is "wrong" with the international monetary system, if anything is. The system has asymmetries. It imposes more burdens on some than on others.

This is a viewpoint that is gaining adherents here and abroad, although no one seems to know quite what to do to make things more even.

The problem of the system, in this view, is not some imminent and ill-defined "collapse." It is not a "weak" dollar, whatever that may mean—the dollar, as a result of the crisis, lost slightly in value against only four of the world's 120-odd currencies and is still accepted everywhere.

It is not a failure of the system to accomplish its purpose, which is to permit one currency to be exchanged for another. After a few days' interruption, exchanges continued normally.

From Lima to Bonn, from Cairo to Berne, from Buenos Aires to Tokyo, from Belgrade to London, foreign governments have to cope from time to time with a decision that is as difficult, even grave, as any government can face short of going to war: whether to change the exchange rate of the currency. It is a decision, as we have just seen, that causes sleepless nights.

Only Washington is immune from this, because of the way the present world monetary system was built.

Economists can argue until they are blue in the face that a government that raises the international value of its currency is actually doing a good turn for its citizens. They may be right, but most of the millions who gain do not realize it, or understand it, and the sizable minority who lose, chiefly the vast exporting industries, are loud in their anger.

Economists may argue, too, that devaluations too long put off—as in the case of Britain from 1964 to 1967—cost the citizens dearly. Again, they are probably right. But none of

France-Soir

"Vous n'auriez pas autre chose que du dollar?"
"Don't you have anything else than a dollar?"

this makes the decision to devalue easy for the government in power. Again, people do not understand. Everything from prestige to the cost of imported food is at stake.

The agonies in Europe this past weekend were very real. The calm in Washington was equally very real, despite headlines about a "crisis of the dollar." The difference is that the Europeans had to make decisions about exchange rates and the Americans did not.

In a complex world, it is as simple as that.

The exchange rate decisions were forced upon the Europeans through no real fault of their own. They had the unpleasant options of exchange controls (which many of them, to American applause, do not like because controls interfere with the free market); swallowing more dollars, with a consequent increase in their own money supply and hence a worsening of their inflation problem; or an upward change in the exchange rate. Four chose the route of the exchange rate, with great reluctance, two by the route of floating.

The situation was particularly unfair for the three small countries—Austria, Switzerland and the Netherlands. They had to make their decision, in effect, because West Germany, their largest trading partner, did, and West Germany had to make its decision because of an uncontrollable flood of dollars.

Most of the mature and intelligent Europeans involved do not charge this injustice—and that is what it is—to some kind of intentional American power-grab, or American evil, or, for most of the recent period, to poor American monetary and fiscal policy.

But they still feel the injustice. And they feel frustrated.

For they know that, in the end, there is one dominant set of facts: the American economy is huge enough to be of great importance to them, but international transactions are so small a part of the American economy that nothing they could do would really cause wide-spread difficulty here, even if they wanted to cause difficulty.

Taking American gold would do them no good. And there would be a great cost in terms of inconvenience and uncertainty in trying—even if it could be done—to remove the dollar's central role as a world-transactions currency. Yet as long as it has that role, the asymmetry on the key matter of exchange rates will remain.

So far as is known here, nobody has a real answer to this injustice—certainly no answer that has won any kind of general acceptance. France has suggested the United States ought to raise the official $35-an-ounce price of gold, but her Common Market partners have opposed making any such demand.

Perhaps the most promising is the idea of "wider bands" around a currency's par value, to let market forces, rather than politicians, make small changes in exchange rates and perhaps to minimize vast flows of funds based on interest-rate considerations. But this is still not accepted by some important countries and many small ones.

Meanwhile, those—mainly Americans—who talk about the tolerability and workability of a dollar-based system, with its implied need for occasional revaluations and devaluations by others, tend to ignore the political problem for the Government's changing the exchange rate.

The chances are that the system will continue, and with it the implied injustice. At least the system works.

* * *

May 29, 1971

CONNALLY TELLS BANKERS U.S. WILL DEFEND DOLLAR

Burns, Also at Munich Meeting, Calls for a U.S. Incomes Policy

By CLYDE H. FARNSWORTH
Special to The New York Times

MUNICH, West Germany, May 28—Treasury Secretary John B. Connally Jr. voiced today the United States Government's determination to defend the dollar and said that other industrialized nations must respond by assuming greater world responsibilities.

In a tough speech to international bankers gathered in this capital city of Bavaria, the silver-haired Texan demanded that Western Europe, Canada and Japan "share more fully in the cost of defending the free world."

He also called on these nations to undertake more liberal trading arrangements to permit American exports to expand.

"No longer does the United States economy dominate the free world," Mr. Connally said. "No longer can considerations of friendship or need or capacity justify the United States carrying so heavy a share of the common burdens."

Mr. Connally spoke to the international monetary conference of the American Bankers Association. The heads of

most of the world's major banks were present as well as leading monetary officials.

Also addressing the forum was Arthur F. Burns, chairman of the Federal Reserve Board, who once again stressed the need for an effective incomes policy in the United States to check wage and price increases.

The first reaction of West German officials at the meeting was that Mr. Connally was making a political speech for home consumption. They did not take his remarks very seriously.

There was an element of friction between American and German officials at the week-long conference. This arose because of the West German Government's decision earlier this month to stop supporting the dollar in the exchange markets.

One of the signs of the tensions was the absence at the gathering of West Germany's Economics and Finance Minister, Karl Schiller.

By detaching the mark from its fixed dollar peg and permitting it to float upward, Mr. Schiller, in effect, devalued the dollar in terms of marks.

German Inflation Curbs

The Germans acted to curb domestic inflation. They are also pressing for some fundamental changes in the monetary system—moves toward acceptance of greater currency flexibility.

Mr. Connally pointedly referred to the floating-mark experiment in his speech. "To revert to the use of exchange rates as a supplementary tool of domestic policy is fraught with danger to the essential stability and sustainability of the system as a whole," he said.

But he did indicate that the United States would support moves toward limited flexibility that are being studied now by the International Monetary Fund, the quarter-century-old monetary institution of the West.

"The question of codifying a degree of additional flexibility with regard to exchange-rate practices is clearly relevant," Mr. Connally said. "De facto events have brought some elements of flexibility. But I doubt that any of us could be satisfied with the variety of responses to the imperatives of speculative pressures."

Monetary Flexibility

Flexibility essentially is the provision for permitting currencies to fluctuate across wider bands, for installing a system of more frequent parity changes and for legalizing temporary floats such as are now being carried out by Canada, Germany and the Netherlands.

Under the rules, currencies fluctuate within 1 per cent above and 1 per cent below their fixed parity against the dollar. There is no provision for a temporary float.

Both Mr. Burns and Mr. Connally also went on record for the first time in support for some form of institutionalized controls over short-term international dollar flows.

Differences in Germany

It was the massive movement of dollars into Germany that set off the Bonn Government's decision to float the mark.

The powerful German Economics and Finance Ministry remains opposed to exchange controls of any sort. The Bundesbank, the central bank, with its coffers overflowing with dollars, is more favorable.

There has been a good deal of talk about controlling the dollar flows, but no one is quite sure yet what form, if any, international action along these lines will take.

The Bundesbank president, Karl Klasen, spoke at the meeting today about Germany's inflation problem, pointing out that the public had to be convinced that higher wages or profits did not automatically mean more purchasing power.

Alluding to remarks by the First Secretary of the Soviet Communist party, Leonid I. Brezhnev, at a recent party congress in Moscow, Mr. Klasen said this was a problem that was faced both by Communist and capitalist countries. Mr. Brezhnev had said: "One can only distribute and consume what has been produced, this is an elementary truth."

* * *

August 16, 1971

NIXON ORDERS 90-DAY WAGE-PRICE FREEZE, ASKS TAX CUTS, NEW JOBS IN BROAD PLAN

SPEAKS TO NATION

Urges Business Aid to Bolster Economy—Budget Slashed

By JAMES M. NAUGHTON
Special to The New York Times

WASHINGTON, Aug. 15—President Nixon charted a new economic course tonight by ordering a 90-day freeze on wages and prices, requesting Federal tax cuts and making a broad range of domestic and international moves designed to strengthen the dollar.

In a 20-minute address, telecast and broadcast nationally, the President appealed to Americans to join him in creating new jobs, curtailing inflation and restoring confidence in the economy through "the most comprehensive new economic policy to be undertaken in this nation in four decades."

Some of the measures Mr. Nixon can impose temporarily himself and he asked for tolerance as he does. Others require Congressional approval and—although he proposed some policies that his critics on Capitol Hill have been urging upon him—will doubtless face long scrutiny before they take effect.

2 Tax Reductions

Mr. Nixon imposed a ceiling on all prices, rents, wages and salaries—and asked corporations to do the same voluntarily on stockholder dividends—under authority granted to him last year by Congress but ignored by the White House until tonight.

The President asked Congress to speed up by one year the additional $50 personal income tax exemption scheduled to

go into effect on Jan. 1, 1973, and to repeal, retroactive to today, the 7 per cent excise tax on automobile purchases.

He also asked for legislative authority to grant corporations a 10 per cent tax credit for investing in new American-made machinery and equipment and pledged to introduce in Congress next January other tax proposals that would stimulate the economy.

Combined with new cuts in Federal spending, the measures announced by Mr. Nixon tonight represented a major shift in his Administration's policy on the economy.

Cuts Ruled Out Earlier

Only seven weeks ago, after an intensive Cabinet-level study of economic policy, the President announced that he would not seek any tax cuts this year and would hew to his existing economic "game plan," confident of success.

Eleven days ago, Mr. Nixon reasserted his opposition to a wage and price review board—a less stringent method of holding down prices and wages than the freeze he ordered—and said only that he was more receptive to considering some new approach to curtailing inflation.

The program issued tonight at the White House thus came with an unaccustomed suddenness, reflecting both domestic political pressures on the President to improve the economy before the 1972 elections and growing international concern over the stability of the dollar.

The changes represented an internal policy victory for Paul W. McCracken, chairman of the Council of Economic Advisers, and Arthur F. Burns, chairman of the Federal Reserve Board, both of whom had pushed over a number of months for a wage-price curtailment. It marked the first major defeat for George P. Shultz, Mr. Nixon's director of management and budget, who has vigorously opposed such an incomes policy.

The President adopted the new tactics following a weekend of meetings at the Presidential retreat at Camp David, Md. With him there were Dr. Burns, Mr. McCracken, Mr. Shultz and John B. Connally, the Secretary of the Treasury.

'Action on 3 Fronts'

"Prosperity without war requires action on three fronts," Mr. Nixon declared in explaining his new policies. "We must create more and better jobs; we must stop the rise in the cost of living; we must protect the dollar from the attacks of international money speculators.

"We are going to take that action—not timidly, not half-heartedly and not in piecemeal fashion," he said.

As a corollary to his tax cut proposals, the President announced that he would slash $4.7-billion from the current Federal budget to produce stability as well as stimulation. The budget cutback would come from a 5 per cent reduction in the number of Federal employes, a 10 per cent cut in the level of foreign aid and through postponement of the effective dates of two costly domestic programs—Federal revenue sharing with states and localities and reform of the Federal welfare system.

President Nixon after delivering televised address.

Mr. Nixon's sudden adoption of a wage and price freeze represented his most drastic reversal of form. He established an eight-member Cost of Living Council to monitor a program under which management and labor must keep wages and prices at the same levels that existed in the 30 days prior to tonight.

Wage or price increases that had been scheduled to go into effect during the next 90 days, such as a 5 per cent raise for the nation's rail workers due to take effect on Oct. 1, must be postponed at least until the 90 days expire. But wage improvements that took effect before tonight, including the 50-cent-an-hour increase won by the steelworkers on Aug. 2, will not be affected.

The White House did not include interest rates in the freeze on the theory that they cannot properly be kept under a fixed ceiling. Although describing the freeze as "voluntary," officials noted there was a provision for court injunctions and fines as high as $5,000 for failure to adhere to the ceiling.

The freeze could be extended after 90 days if Mr. Nixon should decide it still is needed. This authority to impose a ceiling will expire on April 30.

Political pressures for some form of an incomes policy have been building for weeks. Public opinion polls have certified concern over unemployment and prices as the No. 1 domestic issue. Democratic Presidential hopefuls have singled out the economy as the primary area for criticizing Mr. Nixon.

At a White House briefing just before the President's address. Secretary Connally said that the changes had been "long in the making." But he conceded in response to questions that he had left last week on vacation without any expectation that Mr. Nixon would put the program into effect tonight.

Why Strategy Changed

In explaining why the White House had shifted its economic strategy since he expressed confidence on June 30 that "we're on the right path," Mr. Connally cited tonight an "unacceptable" level of unemployment—currently running at an annual rate of 5.8 per cent—as well as continued inflation, a deteriorating balance of trade and an "unsatisfactory" balance of payments in dealings abroad.

Congress, which is in recess until after the Labor Day weekend, must approve the President's request for new consumer tax breaks and investment credits.

The individual income tax exemption, currently $650 for each member of a family, is scheduled to rise to $700 next Jan. 1, and $750 a year later. Mr. Nixon asked that it go to $750 in one step next January.

"Every action I have taken tonight is designed to nurture and stimulate [the] competitive spirit, to help snap us out of the self-doubt, the self-disparagement that saps our energy and erodes our confidence in ourselves," the President said.

In calling for repeal of the tax on automobiles, the President said it would represent an average drop of about $200 in the price of a new car. "I shall insist that the American auto industry pass this tax reduction on to the nearly eight million customers who are buying automobiles this year," he emphasized, but did not say how he would keep that pledge.

The tax would continue to be collected until Congress acts to repeal it, with the provision for rebates later to customers who do not wait to purchase a car.

Mr. Nixon's political advisers have been hoping to cast him as the President of peace and prosperity in a bid for re-election next year.

With every speech in recent weeks emphasizing his initiatives toward global peace—his forthcoming journey to Peking, disengagement from Vietnam and negotiations on arms, the Middle East and Berlin with the Soviet Union—Mr. Nixon has faced a proliferation in Democratic statements criticizing him for permitting continued unemployment and inflation.

Possible 1972 Theme

Mr. Nixon's address tonight contained the kernels of what could become, if his policies have the desired impact, the prosperity rhetoric of 1972.

"Today we hear the echoes of those voices preaching a gospel of gloom and defeat," he said.

"As we move into a generation of peace, as we blaze the trail toward the new prosperity," he added, "I say to every American—let us raise our spirits, let us raise our sights, let all of us contribute all we can to this great and good country that has contributed so much to the progress of mankind."

The Cost of Living Council, which will recommend to Mr. Nixon some form of "second-stage" of wage and price stabilization to follow the 90-day freeze, will be chaired by Mr. Connally and will also have Mr. McCracken and Mr. Shultz on it.

The other members are:

Clifford M. Hardin, Secretary of Agriculture.

Maurice H. Stans, Secretary of Commerce.

James D. Hodgson, Secretary of Labor.

George A. Lincoln, director of the Office of Emergency Preparedness.

Virginia H. Knauer, assistant to the President for consumer affairs.

Dr. Burns will serve as an adviser to the council.

* * *

August 17, 1971

NIXON SEVERS LINK BETWEEN DOLLAR AND GOLD

A WORLD EFFECT

Unilateral U.S. Move Means Others Face Parity Decisions

By EDWIN L. DALE Jr.
Special to The New York Times

WASHINGTON, Aug. 15—President Nixon announced tonight that henceforth the United States would cease to convert foreign-held dollars into gold—unilaterally changing the 25-year-old international monetary system.

How many pounds, marks, yen and francs the dollar will buy tomorrow will depend on decisions of other countries. In some countries, the value of the dollar may "float," moving up and down in day-to-day exchanges. A period of turmoil in the foreign-exchange markets is all but certain, which means uncertainty for American tourists, exporters and importers.

The President said he was taking the action to stop "the attacks of international money speculators" against the dollar. He did not raise the official price of gold, which has been $35 an ounce since 1934.

Devaluation Denied

Mr. Nixon said he was not devaluing the dollar. But, he said, "If you want to buy a foreign car, or take a trip abroad, market conditions may cause your dollar to buy slightly less."

In addition to severing the link between the dollar and gold, the President announced a 10 per cent extra tax on all dutiable imports, except those that are subject to quotas, or quantitative limits.

The tax will thus apply to cars but not to coffee, to radios but not to sugar, to shoes but not to oil. Coffee and other items, such as bananas, grown in tropical countries are exempt because no duty is charged on them. Oil and sugar are exempt because they are under quota. The President said he had legal authority for the new surcharge.

Foreign Action Favored

The change in the world monetary system brought about by the President's decision to cease converting foreign-held dollars into gold is entirely uncertain. That was the word used by Secretary of the Treasury John B. Connally. What matters most is exchange rates among currencies and Mr. Connally said he did not know what would happen.

The purpose of Mr. Nixon's move was clear. The President said, "The time has come for exchange rates to be set straight and for the major nations to compete as equals." This means a desire for other countries to raise their currencies' value in terms of the dollar. In effect, therefore, the dollar would be devalued.

Mr. Connally said, "We anticipate and we hope there would be some changes in exchange rates of other currencies."

But this will depend on other countries. For 25 years non-Communist nations have maintained the international exchange value of their currencies by "pegging" them to the dollar. Their central banks would buy or sell their own currencies in daily trading in the foreign-exchange market to keep the value within one per cent either side of "par," expressed in a precise dollar amount for each unit of the other currency.

After Mr. Nixon's action tonight, they can still do so, if they so wish. But they are no longer obligated to do so under the rules of the International Monetary Fund. Their obligation to peg their currencies to the dollar was a counterpart of the United States's obligation to exchange dollars for gold. The United States has now renounced that obligation.

Referring to the 1944 conference in New Hampshire that established the I.M.F. and the present rules for monetary exchange, Arthur M. Okun, Chairman of the Council of Economic Advisers under President Johnson, said tonight, "We just ended the Bretton Woods system forever."

Mr. Okun said he could not say by what degree other currencies would rise in value relative to the dollar, but he was certain that they would rise.

Apparently more than 100 countries are going to have to make decisions within the next 48 hours as to what to do. In Europe, as it happens, most foreign-exchange markets will be closed tomorrow because of the Feast of Assumption, giving Governments and central banks a little more time to decide.

Although the President's unilateral action may cause difficulties in the nation's foreign relations, particularly with industrialized countries, he held out an olive branch. He said his action "will not win us any friends among the international money traders," but he added:

"In full cooperation with the International Monetary Fund and those who trade with us, we will press for the necessary reforms to set up an urgently needed new international monetary system. Stability and equal treatment is in everybody's best interest."

A Treasury statement said, "United States officials will promptly be meeting with their colleagues from other countries to explain the background and details of the President's program. They will develop United States proposals for both dealing constructively with the immediate repercussions of today's decision and employing . . . the opportunity opened by today's action for speeding the evolution in the international monetary system in directions that serve the common needs of trading nations."

The background of the President's action was a long series of deficits in the nation's balance of international payments. Recently, the picture darkened as one key element in the balance of payments, the trade balance of exports and imports, swung into deficit in the second quarter for the first time

since an abnormal period in 1946 immediately following World War II.

Last week, the dollar was under heavy selling pressure in European foreign-exchange markets. Where it could weaken, it did—as in West Germany, which has a temporary "floating" exchange rate, following pressure last spring for an upward revaluation.

The President emphasized that, although imports might cost more as a result of his action, "if you are among the overwhelming majority who buy American-made products in America, your dollar will be worth just as much tomorrow as it is today."

Technically, the Treasury announced these steps:

- The United States "notified the International Monetary Fund that, effective today, the United States no longer freely buys and sells gold for the settlement of international transactions." This withdraws a commitment made in 1947.

- Use of monetary reserve assets, including gold and other assets such as drawing rights or "paper gold" on the International Monetary Fund, will be "strictly limited" to "settlement of outstanding obligations and, in cooperation with the I.M.F., to other situations that may arise in which such use can contribute to international monetary stability and the interests of the United States."

- The President "requested" the independent Federal Reserve Board to cease the automatic operation of its system of "swaps" with other countries, which is a means of converting dollars into other currencies and temporarily averting conversion of foreign-held dollars into gold.

The statement said no "new decision" had been made regarding the present controls over the outflow of United States capital, such as investments by United States companies abroad and purchase by Americans of foreign securities, now subject to an "interest equalization tax." These restraints remain in effect, the statement said.

* * *

September 13, 1971

TRADING PARTNERS OF U.S. HURT BY IMPORT SURCHARGE

Survey Finds Nixon Economic Program, Including Decision to Float Dollar, Stirring Resentment Abroad

By BRENDAN JONES

Most of the United States' main trading partners have been hurt in some degree by the international measures—primarily the 10 per cent surcharge on imports—included in President Nixon's economic program.

The surcharge, combined with the decision to let the dollar float downward in exchange markets while other currencies are pressured upward, has also caused considerable resentment abroad at what is regarded as a one-sided American action.

Although in some countries, notably West Germany, there is a feeling that the surcharge may not be as damaging as first feared, in many there is worry that its effects could severely check business and perhaps contribute to recession.

Trade War Feared

There is fear, too, that the American surcharge and general currency-value uncertainties could be the spark that might set off cut-throat competition among nations grimly determined to maintain trade in any and all markets, especially the United States.

These are some of the highlights of a 15-country survey just completed by New York Times correspondents on the effects of the American economic policies on international trade. The countries covered accounted for more than 75 per cent of the $40-billion of United States imports in 1970.

The survey showed that, slightly less than a month after the Administration's surcharge and monetary actions, most countries have not yet been able to calculate the full effects of the measures on their trade.

It was evident in the survey, however, that the surcharge particularly—as designed and expected—is having upsetting worldwide repercussions.

Surcharge Assessed

In a number of countries—Canada, Mexico, Italy, Japan and West Germany—it was found that the main adverse effects of the surcharge are being felt by small and medium-sized industries.

These are mainly concerns producing sundry goods—footwear and light manufactures—or specialized products such as optical or surgical instruments.

One West German executive of a small surgical instrument manufacturer said that the American surcharge, together with the higher floating value of the mark, "will strangle us to death."

A Brazilian official remarked that "it is now a case of push or be pushed" for countries scrambling for trade as a consequence of the surcharge-monetary turmoil. A British manufacturer termed the surcharge "a bloody nuisance."

So far, the reports indicated there has not yet been any widespread wave of unemployment caused by the surcharge. But there have been some layoffs in Japan and cutbacks in working hours in West Germany that might be the start of a trend.

Swiss Affected

In Switzerland, watch imports have been hard hit by the surcharge and there is unemployment in the industry for the first time in years.

In Britain and other West European countries—and Canada—the proposed American 10 per cent investment tax credit on new industrial equipment is regarded—in addition to the surcharge—as the most disturbing new trade barrier.

The credit would not apply to imported equipment and would thus be a discriminatory measure against which other countries might retaliate.

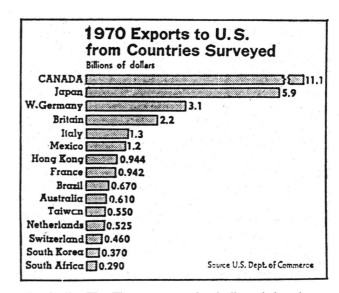

1970 Exports to U.S. from Countries Surveyed
Billions of dollars

Country	Billions of dollars
CANADA	11.1
Japan	5.9
W. Germany	3.1
Britain	2.2
Italy	1.3
Mexico	1.2
Hong Kong	0.944
France	0.942
Brazil	0.670
Australia	0.610
Taiwan	0.550
Netherlands	0.525
Switzerland	0.460
South Korea	0.370
South Africa	0.290

Source U.S. Dept. of Commerce

Ironically, The Times survey also indicated that the surcharge seems to be having more adverse effect on imports from Western Europe, where the United States enjoys a trade surplus, than on Far Eastern countries whose competitive exports the levy was largely designed to check.

There is evidence also that the surcharge is having a kind of chain reaction on trade between other countries.

Australia, for example, is a major supplier of raw materials to Japan. But Australians, although not directly feeling the surcharge too much, see Japan's loss of exports as a loss for them, notably in such exports as wool.

Importers Protest

The United States surcharge—a full 10 per cent addition on top of regular ad valorem duties for most dutiable imports—became effective Aug. 16. The sudden impact, especially on goods tied up by the West Coast dock strike or already in bonded warehouses, brought vigorous protests from importers.

As a result of these, a measure of relief was granted on Sept. 1, which exempted goods in transit before Aug. 15 as well as those strikebound or in bond if they are cleared by Customs before Oct. 1.

The surcharge does not apply to duty-free imports such as green coffee, iron ore or newsprint, nor to those under import quotas such a crude oil, cotton textiles and beef.

However, roughly 60 per cent, or $24-billion to $25-billion, of American imports are subject to the surcharge. This amount represents about 8 per cent of total world exports by other than Communist countries.

In many of the countries surveyed there is appreciation that the American trade measures are designed to spur needed realignment of major world currencies.

But in developing countries, especially, it is asked why solution of this problem, primarily one for the developed countries, should entail harm to their exports.

Resentment against the American action in many cases is combined with a determination "to beat the surcharge," to compete more vigorously.

But there is sentiment also that the sooner the surcharge is ended and monetary stability attained, the better off all countries will be.

Following are some of the main points in the survey reports:

CANADA

OTTAWA—Precisely how much the American surcharge will hurt Canadian exports is unclear, but there are unmistakable grounds for concern, particularly for the effects on comparatively new manufacturing industries and on employment.

Although Canada is the United States' chief trading partner and source of a fourth of American imports, there might seem to be little cause for Canadian worry about the surcharge.

The import levy does not apply to three-fourths of Canadian exports to the United States. The bulk of these enter duty-free or under quotas.

Autos Also Exempt

Also exempt are autos, which cross the border duty free under the 1965 Canadian-American auto trade pact. And if repeal of the American 7 per cent auto excise does switch buyers to North American makes, Canada's auto plants are likely to share in the increased production.

Some $2.5-billion of Canadian exports, however, are subject to the surcharge. A good part of these are the products of industrial plants concentrated in Ontario and Quebec. Development of this so-called secondary industry has been a major Canadian policy aim.

These industries have borne the brunt of the 1970 business recession and also the adverse trade effects of an upward floating Canadian dollar. They will be hurt most by the new American import levy. Thus, there is an added worrisome aspect for Canadians in that 85 per cent of their finished manufactures go to the United States.

Some Ottawa economists have advised "adjustment," letting barely profitable manufacturers go under. The Government, however, a year or less away from an election, has just announced an $80-million employment support fund—in effect, a subsidy—for exporters hit hard by the surcharge.

As for employment effects, Ottawa fears that the surcharge will nip in the bud the long-awaited decline in the national employment rate, which in July was 6.3 per cent.

Particularly worrisome is that unemployment will be aggravated in Quebec, where it has been chronically higher (8.6 per cent in July) and where it contributes to the social unrest that fuels the separatist movement.

JAPAN

TOKYO—The heaviest blow of the surcharge will be sustained by Japan's small and medium-sized enterprises that turn out sundry goods. The surcharge also has raised a formidable barrier to textile exports.

Larger, highly-efficient industries—autos, steel and cameras—are optimistic, however, that their competitive power will make it possible for them to absorb the impact of the surcharge in a short time.

But the immediate prospect is that the combination of the surcharge and the higher exchange rate of the yen will sharply reduce total Japanese exports by about 12 per cent of last year's $19.4-billion total.

The Ministry of International Trade and Industry estimates that exports to the United States will decrease on an annual basis by $1.67-billion. A decline of $710-million in exports to other countries is expected to result from the side-effects of the surcharge and currency revaluations.

For sundry-goods producers, which have shipped about half of their annual $2-billion of exports to the United States, the surcharge and yen revaluation are expected to cut sales by as much as 50 per cent.

Japan's auto industry, however, is hopeful that it will be able to attain about 90 per cent of the 600,000-unit export set for this year.

The steel industry is confident that it can absorb the surcharge on its own exports, but it is worried about the indirect impact of the levy on the domestic industries which are important steel users.

So far, the major action move affecting employment has been the announcement by Mitsubishi Metal Mining, Japan's largest copper refiner, of a 10 per cent reduction in its 1,000-worker force. The Labor Minister said that 50 enterprises have suspended their plans for hiring fresh graduates of high schools next spring.

WEST GERMANY

BONN—West German business men still show restraint in making precise statements about the repercussions of the American surcharge. There appears to be growing sentiment that they will be less harsh than originally feared, that sales will dip but not slump.

Over-all, the prospect is that the expected sales dip will tend to accentuate the present domestic trend toward shrinking business, if not a recession.

After two years of hectic business boom, with swiftly rising prices and wages, domestic demand has been falling off noticeably in the past few months.

Thus, the most-heard forecast here is that dwindling sales in the United States will cause lay-offs and short-hour work in at least some major industries.

According to the Federation of German Industries in Cologne, about 90 per cent of West Germany's sales in the United States will be affected by the surcharge.

Autos, the most important item, however, are expected to escape some of the brunt of the import levy with prospective repeal of the American auto excise tax.

By far the hardest hit German industry are the makers of surgical instrument, mostly small family enterprises in Baden-Wurttemberg.

Of 280 such small and medium-sized companies, more than 200 sell at least 80 per cent of output to the United States and some produce only for American customers.

BRITAIN

LONDON—No exact estimates have yet been made on the impact of the American surcharge on British exports, but it is widely assumed that it will cut profits if nothing else.

The United States is Britain's main export market, accounting for $2.2-billion of sales last year, or about 12 per cent of total exports.

About 40 per cent of the exports to the United States are machinery and transportation equipment, chiefly autos, while 25 per cent is manufactured goods.

The greatest impact of the surcharge thus is seen in the machinery and auto industries. In addition to the surcharge, the proposed American 10 per cent investment tax credit that will apply only to domestically-produced capital goods will result in a marked competitive disadvantage for foreign-made equipment.

While some auto makers are hopeful about holding markets for sports cars, others expect to feel some pinch in sales because of the surcharge.

British complaints about the American import levy have been inhibited by the fact that Britain itself resorted to a surcharge in 1964–66 as a means of correcting a payments deficit.

"More monetary sense was less trade nonsense" has become an official slogan among members of the Confederation of British Industry, which is roughly equivalent to the American National Association of Manufacturers.

The comment reflects the bitterness of many manufacturers here that the American surcharge is being used as a lever to bring about monetary and currency realignments.

"It's all just intended to make Japan see some sense, isn't it?" a chemical producer asserted. "In the meantime, we all have to suffer."

In contrast to the announced plant closings, layoffs and predictions of falling business in Italy, West Germany and Japan, British manufacturers have been quiet. Detailed studies await the resumption of full-scale business activity this month after the vacation period.

ITALY

ROME—No reliable estimate is available on how the surcharge and other factors will affect Italian imports.

The American market, however, is Italy's third largest export outlet, after West Germany and France, and there is general worry over the effects on the major items of this trade—footwear, textiles and autos.

Although Italian Government officials recently have exhorted industry to look for alternative markets, there is considerable fear that there will be cutthroat competition with other nations equally affected by the American protectionist moves, such as West Germany and Japan.

From Piedmont to Florence, entire plants, sometimes entire towns, depend on the American market. This is particularly true of the footwear industry, which is based on hundreds of small and medium-sized factories in and near such centers as Varese, Bologna and Florence.

Last year, Italy exported 80-million pairs of shoes (including sandals) to the United States, two-fifths of its entire footwear sales abroad.

Elio Camagna, president of the Italian Footwear Manufacturers Association, said, "The United States measures make it almost impossible to hold the positions that our industry has conquered. The consequences will be very grave."

MEXICO

MEXICO CITY—Because of this country's close economic ties with the United States, Mexico is bound to be badly hit by the American import surcharge.

The United States is overwhelmingly Mexico's largest trading partner, buying more than 70 per cent of Mexico's exports and supplying 63 per cent of its imports.

The American trade restrictions have dealt a blow particularly to Mexico's efforts to balance, which has been deteriorating in recent years to a minus last year of $865-million.

Mexico's trade balance with the United States—$833-million of exports, $1.565-billion of American imports—further intensifies Mexican complaints against the surcharge measures.

According to Finance Minister Hugo Margain, more than 50 per cent of Mexican exports to the United States—some $480-million worth—are affected by the surcharge, although it is not clear how much can be passed on to American importers and consumers.

The maximum loss for the balance of this year—roughly three months—is estimated at $48-million. Newly-developed border industries, as well as Mexico's young industrial sector, have been badly hit by the surcharge on semi-manufactured goods.

Among the products most affected are processed foods. Some unemployment is expected to result from the drop in exports of these products and of manufactured goods.

With the peso floating in close relations to the American dollar, Mexico, however, hopes to gain in tourism as a result of an upward revaluation of European currencies. More Americans, it is thought, visit Mexico because of the higher costs of European vacations.

Tourism is an essential part of the Mexican economy and, as the largest dollar earner last year, brought in $575-million.

A typical view of the surcharge action by one Government official was:

"There was no reason why developing countries should suffer from a measure directed at developed nations."

HONG KONG

HONG KONG—Washington's new trade barriers are regarded here generally with equanimity as not presenting any insurmountable obstacle to Hong Kong's export to the United States, its biggest single market.

As long as the colony's main competitors face the same conditions in entering the American market, Hong Kong business men and leaders express confidence that the extra costs can be absorbed and competitiveness maintained.

The main Hong Kong exports to the United States are finished and unfinished textile manufactures and half of these are made of cotton. As such, they come under the cotton import quota and are exempt from the surcharge.

One Hong Kong exporter said, "We will only have to watch out for American products being able to sell better under the protection of the surtax, but I don't really think we will be beat out on this."

He added that the surtax costs "could be absorbed at various places along the line and the price to the consumer will rise very little, if any."

FRANCE

PARIS—Only 6 per cent of French exports go to the United States, so the surcharge is regarded as "annoying, but certainly not catastrophic."

The American market, however, has been the biggest growth market for French exports this year. The French therefore find the American surcharge an irritation when they are in the midst of a campaign to redress a substantial trade deficit with the United States—roughly a two-to-one imbalance.

French business leaders expect the surcharge to have a marginal effect on their exports. But they are more worried about the indirect effects, which they feel will deflect more Japanese and West German products into domestic markets and increase competition for French products in foreign markets.

Steel is expected to be the main French product affected by the surcharge. For other leading items such as wines and perfumes, the import levy is either negligible or not considered a threat to French quality and distinction.

BRAZIL

RIO DE JANEIRO—Although all of Brazil's major exports to the United States—coffee, iron ore, cotton, sugar and cocoa—are not touched by the surcharge, the import levy nonetheless has aroused complaints.

The reason is that Brazil has just recently begun to increase production and export of a wide range of manufactured products. These include shoes, ready-made clothes, office equipment, tools and canned corned beef.

The surcharge, therefore, is a blow to Brazilian aspiration for diversifying trade. Ministry of Finance officials estimate that the surcharge will affect some $160-million of Brazilian exports, or about 6 per cent of the total.

One main alternative cited by business men is to find more markets in Europe, where currency revaluations have made Brazilian products more attractive in price.

The Brazilian cruzeiro is tied to the dollar, and has depreciated in terms particularly of the German mark and Japanese yen.

AUSTRALIA

SYDNEY—As far as Australian exports to the United States are concerned, most of them are exempt under duty-free or quota status given raw materials such as mineral ores.

However, as Japan is Australia's leading customer—taking 25 per cent of all exports—there is definite anxiety here that losses of Japanese export markets because of the surcharge and revaluation of the yen will soon be felt in reduced trade by Australia.

Because long-term agreements for export of Australian minerals to Japan are covered by contracts written in terms of dollars, it is estimated that the losses from currency value changes could add up to as much as $100-million.

Most of the contracts do not have renegotiation clauses, but some Japanese buyers have indicated willingness to make price adjustments.

Australian press comment on the American economic policies has been generally unsympathetic, with one nationally-circulated newspaper calling it "blackmail."

TAIWAN

TAIPEI—Officials here have been more concerned with the effects on trade of the United States West Coast dock strike than with the new surcharge. Most exporters, however, express optimism about being able to adjust to what may be tougher competitive conditions.

The Government has shunned criticism of the Nixon policies and concentrated in urging exporters to increase productivity, lower costs and diversify markets. It has offered to provide loans to tide over companies hurt by the dock strike and the surcharge.

So far, most economic indicators are holding up, among them production of synthetic fibre and plastics. Factories are running full blast on full order books.

Revaluation of the Japanese yen is seen as likely to make Taiwan more attractive to Japanese investors seeking a lower-cost production environment. The higher yen costs may also make American raw materials more competitive with those from Japan, presently Taiwan's main supplier.

THE NETHERLANDS

THE HAGUE—Dutch brewers who have successfully gained markets in the United States appear to be the most likely to suffer losses because of the American surcharge.

But apart from some worry over exports of flower bulbs and canned hams, the Dutch feel that much of their goods such as chocolates and liquors are "status" products that will not suffer from some rise in prices.

Combined with the surcharge, however, the rise in value of the Dutch guilder has given exporters cause for concern about surviving against competitors.

While hoping that the surcharge will not last too long, they are looking to cost-sharing arrangements with importers and also profit-trimming.

SWITZERLAND

GENEVA—According to Government sources here, 93 per cent of Swiss exports to the United States—machinery, watches, chemicals, textiles, shoes and cheese—are subject to the surcharge.

Watch exports have been hardest hit by the surcharge while machinery exports are expected to be hurt by the United States investment tax credit. In addition, the rise in the Swiss franc has added to competitive problems for exporters.

Switzerland's economy has been booming and with the import of some 500,000 foreign workers, there has been negligible unemployment. No one anticipates any real unemployment problem, but the Nixon program is expected to take a lot of zip out of the boom.

SOUTH KOREA

SEOUL—The surcharge already has resulted in a drop of about $30-million in South Korea's exports during August as compared with the previous month.

According to revised estimates by the Korean Traders Association, the surcharge-caused loss this year will amount to at least $50-million, or 7.5 per cent of the $670-million goal set for exports to the United States in 1971.

Some 95 per cent of Korea's exports to the United States—plywood, noncotton textiles, wigs and electronic products—are affected by the surcharge.

So far, there have been no repercussions on employment and export industries are taking a wait-and-see attitude in the hope that the world trade situation may be settled soon.

Because of yen revaluation, the Government is planning to diversify import sources to decrease dependence on Japan, which accounts for 40 per cent of Korean imports.

SOUTH AFRICA

JOHANNESBURG—In face of the confused world currency situation and the American surcharge, South Africa finds herself in the position of having to meekly wait while other countries determine the value of its chief product—gold.

Uncertainties about the future role of gold—as well as its price—in monetary terms has brought a fall in gold mining shares and official pleas for a direct devaluation of the dollar.

But meanwhile, the South African currency, the rand, has been floating with the dollar and, without its old tie to sterling, has depreciated about 2 per cent.

The American surcharge is expected to affect some $70-million of South African exports on an annual basis.

*   *   *

October 6, 1971

FOREWARNING ON DOLLAR

Prophecy by Triffin Recalled as a New Money Is Backed

By LEONARD SILK

Twelve years ago a group of the world's leading economists gathered at Elsinore, Denmark—the scene of Hamlet's tragic story—to enjoy the autumn weather by the sea and condemn inflation. But on the first day of their meeting, Prof. Robert Triffin of Yale arose like Hamlet's father's ghost to warn the economists of a greater danger than inflation. The international monetary system, he said, could not go on expanding indefinitely, based as it was on gold and national currencies, especially the dollar.

A day would come, Professor Triffin predicted, when the monetary system would fall apart as it had done in 1931, dragging the world into deep depression, unless a new international money were created to supplant dollars and gold.

Last week at the International Monetary Fund's meetings in Washington, Professor Triffin had the pleasure, granted to very few Cassandras, of hearing the finance ministers of the major nations repeating his grim prophecy and calling for his own remedy as though they were listening to a voice in the air.

However, the more sophisticated ministers knew that the voice they heard was that of Mr. Triffin.

He had foreseen back in 1959 two evolving threats to the international monetary system.

The first derived from the difficulty of providing enough gold for an expanding world economy. Gold production and Russian gold sales were not keeping pace with the increase of world trade—and with the need of nations to increase their monetary reserves to cover their balance-of-payments deficits.

The second threat resulted from the first. To palliate the gold shortage, the capitalist nations were rebuilding the old gold-exchange system.

Increasingly, they were using United States dollars as monetary reserves, acquired through the deficits in the American balance of payments. But Professor Triffin warned that chronic United States deficits would inevitably undermine confidence in the dollar.

A dollar crisis would come when nations had acquired more dollars than they were willing to hold.

During the 1960's, the crisis was forestalled when the United States induced other nations to convert dollars into other forms of debt.

The master of this Fabian defense of the dollar was Undersecretary of the Treasury Robert V. Roosa.

But that defense could not last indefinitely. The first massive attack on the dollar standard came in March, 1968. It was staved off by the creation of the two-tier gold system, which prevented private holders of dollars from claiming official gold.

The second blow to the dollar came last May. It was brought on by the rush of hot money out of dollars and into German marks and other European currencies, partly as a result of interest rate differentials between the United States and Europe, partly because of rumors of an impending German upvaluation, but most fundamentally because of the widespread belief that the dollar had been weakened by a long series of American deficits in the balance of payments.

American Government officials went on insisting that the dollar was as strong as ever. Indeed, they had taken this line throughout the preceding decade.

American administrations have always been convinced that when they really wanted to, they could eliminate the deficit in the balance of payments.

Eisenhower Proposals

At the end of the 1950's, the Eisenhower Administration urged European nations to pick up more of the west's defense burdens, step up their own foreign aid and capital exports, and drop discrimination against dollar goods.

Nevertheless, the payments gap was not closed. Vietnam and a stepup in United States inflation widened the gap after the mid-1960's.

However, Professor Triffin had foreseen that the real trouble would begin not while the balance-of-payments deficits of the United States continued but when they were ended.

The reason was that "a successful readjustment of the United States balance-of-payments is bound to bring to the fore the latent crisis of international liquidity."

As the liquidity squeeze developed, the high pace of expansion in the world economy maintained since the end of World War II would slow down.

Nations would feel increasing pressure to clamp on trade and exchange restrictions or to engage in competitive devaluations.

These pressures would spread from country to country and might be aggravated by speculative capital movements "culminating in a financial panic a la 1931," said Professor Triffin.

The decision of President Nixon on Aug. 15 to suspend gold convertibility and float the dollar, together with his imposition of the 10 per cent imports surcharge, are intended to close the United States balance-of-payments gap and swing it into surplus.

The world now faces the necessity of finding a new source of liquidity other than dollars or gold. Special Drawing Rights, created as a supplement to gold and dollars as monetary reserves only last year, may ultimately replace them.

Some economists would prefer a system of floating exchange rates that would keep nations' payments in continuous balance, thereby obviating the need for monetary reserves to cover deficits.

But most proposals for international monetary reform being offered these days are a blend of these two key elements—new international monetary reserves and more flexible exchange rates.

Which route or combination of routes the world takes toward reform is a matter of politics more than economics.

Nations highly sensitive to the pressures of industrial interest groups at home will not let the international markets freely determine exchange rates. Similarly, nations anxious to bind their economies closer together—such as the European Common Market countries—want highly stable exchange rates but realize this means they must closely coordinate their monetary and fiscal policies.

The major monetary powers—the United States, West Germany, France, Britain and Japan—are not yet ready to

choose either the course of closer integration or floating exchange rates.

"These two roads are very different and it is extremely difficult to determine in which direction the international monetary system will evolve," says Lawrence B. Krause of the Brookings Institution, in a new tract, "Sequel to Bretton Woods: a Proposal to Reform the World Monetary System."

Straddle of Routes

"At this juncture, however, the world can keep one foot on its path without much discomfort," says Mr. Krause.

Whether the world can actually straddle the two routes of greater flexibility of exchange rates and closer economic integration or whether it must choose one group or the other is the crucial issue for world monetary reform.

However, to reject both of those routes would mean the fracturing of the international monetary system and a growing trend toward protectionism, capital controls, and economic self-sufficiency for individual nations and regional blocks.

*   *   *

December 19, 1971

10-NATION MONETARY AGREEMENT REACHED; DOLLAR IS DEVALUED 8.57%; SURCHARGE OFF

NIXON HAILS PACT

He Makes a Surprise Appearance—Gold Goes to $38

By EDWIN L. DALE Jr.
Special to The New York Times

WASHINGTON, Dec. 18—The world's 10 leading non-Communist industrial nations reached agreement tonight on a new pattern of currency exchange rates, including a devaluation of the United States dollar by 8.57 per cent.

Speaking to reporters as the negotiations ended, President Nixon said, "It is my great privilege to announce, on behalf of the finance ministers and the other representatives of the 10 countries involved, the conclusion of the most significant monetary agreement in the history of the world."

The new United States 10 per cent import surcharge will be removed next week. The surcharge was imposed, and the entire recent monetary turmoil began, with President Nixon's dramatic domestic and international economic measures of August 15.

Yen to Go Up

Several other currencies, led by the Japanese yen, will be revalued upward.

Treasury Secretary John B. Connally said that the over-all effect would be an effective devaluation of the dollar by 12 per cent. This figure is arrived at by allowing for United States trade with each of the countries. The Canadian dollar, which will continue to float in daily trading, was left out of the calculation.

A communiqué issued by the Group of 10, said that most foreign exchange markets would be closed on Monday, but Mr. Connally said the United States market would be open.

The dollar devaluation figure of 8.57 per cent used by Mr. Connally results from a proposed increase in the official price of gold from $35 to $38 an ounce. Congress, however, will not be asked to approve the necessary legislation to increase the gold price until the United States wins concessions from Japan, the European Common Market and Canada on trade matters.

However, foreign exchange trading—that is, the actual exchange rate of the dollar against the other currencies—will be conducted at levels as if the new gold price were already in effect.

As in all cases of changes in a currency's exchange rate, the percentage of dollar devaluation can be calculated in two ways. The figure used by Mr. Connally of 8.57 per cent will be the increase in the cost of a currency—such as the British pound, which did not change in value—to an American buyer. For a foreigner buying dollars, the devaluation will be 7.89 per cent.

The latter figure is the technically more correct of the two.

The Group of 10 communiqué left to each country to announce its new exchange rate. However, most of the rates quickly became known here.

For example, the Japanese yen will rise in value against the dollar by just 16.88 per cent with a new yen rate reported at 308 to the dollar. The 17 per cent upward revaluation of the yen comes in part through the devaluation of the dollar and in part through a revaluation of the yen.

The British pound and French franc will remain unchanged in terms of gold, meaning they will rise by 7.89 per cent against the dollar. The West German mark will be set at 3.22 marks to the dollar for an upward revaluation of about 12 per cent.

Lira and Kronor Revalue

The Italian lira and Swedish kronor will both be devalued slightly—1 or 2 per cent against gold. This will still leave them significantly higher in relation to the dollar than before.

The Canadian dollar will continue to float. The Canadian Government pledged not to manipulate the rate through intervention by its central bank in foreign exchange trading. Mr. Connally said he expected the Canadian dollar to rise somewhat from its present value of almost exactly one United States dollar.

Besides the currency realignment, the agreement included another significant change. For the indefinite future, currencies will be allowed to fluctuate above and below their par values by 2.25 per cent, compared with only 1 per cent under the former monetary rules. It is hoped that this change will both ease the transition to the new exchange rates and reduce heavy flows of speculative funds.

Convertibility Unsettled

Under the agreement, dollars held by foreign central banks will continue to be inconvertible into gold or any other United States monetary reserve asset. That is, President Nixon's suspension of buying and selling of gold remains in effect.

The delicate question of ultimate convertibility of the dollar will be negotiated as part of a sweeping reform of the world monetary system. But meanwhile, ordinary trading, travel, and investment can proceed at reasonably known and fixed exchange rates.

The agreement—the first in history involving a multinational negotiation of exchange rates—was reached after two days of secret talks among finance ministers and central bank governors of the 10 nations in the 116-year-old red castle building of the Smithsonian Institution. Just before the final communiqué was issued, President Nixon appeared dramatically before nearly 400 representatives of the world press in the Art and Industries Building next door, accompanied by many of the ministers of the 10 nations.

Besides the United States, the countries in the Group of 10 are Britain, Canada, Japan, Sweden, Belgium, France, West Germany, Italy and the Netherlands.

Asking himself the hypothetical question of "who won and who lost," the President said "the whole free world has won."

Simultaneously with the removal next week of the 10 per cent import surcharge, the President will also end the "Buy American" aspect of the new business investment tax credit just enacted by Congress to help stimulate the domestic economy. As enacted, the bill provided that this special tax benefit would not apply to purchases of imported machinery and equipment as long as the import surcharge lasted.

The communiqué recognized that scores of nations, including such important trading nations as Australia, were not represented here. It said:

"The ministers and governors recognized that all members of the International Monetary Fund not attending the present discussions will need urgently to reach decisions with respect to their own exchange rates. It was the view of the ministers and governors that it is particularly important at this time that no country seek improper competitive advantage through its exchange rate policies. Changes in parities can only be justified by an objective appraisal which establishes a position of disequalibrium."

Despite this admonition, many countries including most of Latin America, are expected to devalue along with the dollar. There would presumably be no international objection to such a move.

* * *

February 13, 1972

U.S. ORDERS DOLLAR DEVALUED 10 PER CENT; JAPANESE YEN WILL BE ALLOWED TO FLOAT; NIXON TO SUBMIT TRADE PLAN TO CONGRESS

GOLD TO BE $42.22

Controls on Lending Abroad Also Will Be Phased Out

By EDWIN L. DALE Jr.
Special to The New York Times

WASHINGTON, Feb. 12—The United States announced tonight a devaluation of the dollar by 10 per cent against nearly all of the world's major currencies.

The action was taken in an effort to halt the latest currency crisis, in which there has been a flight from the dollar in international monetary markets.

The devaluation will be greater than 10 per cent against the Japanese yen, which will float upward in foreign-exchange trading for an indefinite period.

This is the second devaluation of the dollar in 14 months.

Tonight's announcement by Secretary of the Treasury George P. Shultz contained two other elements:

- The President has decided to submit to Congress comprehensive trade legislation with the aim of lowering trade barriers but with unspecified provisions for "safeguards" against disruption of domestic industries as a result of imports.
- The United States will phase out three controls on investment and lending abroad that go back to 1963. They will be ended by the end of 1974 or earlier. They cover buying of foreign stocks and bonds, bank lending to foreigners and direct investments abroad by United States corporations.

The announcement by Mr. Shultz came shortly before 11 P.M. at an unusual late evening news conference. As he was completing the news conference, Prsident Nixon returned to the White House. Mr. Nixon had cut short his stay in San Clemente, Calif., and flew back to the capital tonight.

Change 'Acceptable'

Mr. Shultz's announcement said that "the proposed change in the par value of the dollar is acceptable" to "our leading trading partners in Europe." He told the news conference that he did not anticipate any changes in exchange rates by other leading countries apart from the float of the Japanese yen.

While emphasizing that each foreign government would speak for itself, Mr. Shultz said he expected that the three currencies that are now floating—the Canadian dollar, the British pound and the Swiss franc—would continue to float. Floating currencies are allowed to find their own levels in international trading.

The devaluation of the dollar requires the formal approval of Congress. However, as with the devaluation of December, 1971, it will go into effect in currency trading immediately.

Under the rules of the International Monetary Fund, the dollar will be devalued by changing the official price of gold to $42.22 an ounce, compared with $38 an ounce now and $35 up to the end of 1971.

The effect of the devaluation will be some increase to American consumers and businessmen of imported products. But the amount of the increase is uncertain and will depend on pricing decisions by foreign exporters.

The purpose of the dollar devaluation is to improve the nation's international accounts—the trading account, which showed a record deficit last year of $6.4-billion, and the over-all balance of international payments. By the most common definition, the deficit in the balance of payments last year was about $10-billion, though the official figures have not yet been published.

The devaluation of the dollar of 8.57 per cent in December, 1971, which worked out to about 11 per cent after counting upward revaluations of several currencies such as the Japanese yen and the West German mark, has so far not produced the desired results in improving the nation's international accounts.

At the news conference at the Treasury Department, Secretary Shultz issued a formal statement and answered questions briefly.

Seated near Mr. Shultz, though not making any comments, were William P. Rogers, Secretary of State; Peter M. Flanigan, Assistant to the President for International Economic Affairs; Arthur F. Burns, chairman of the Federal Reserve Board, and Herbert Stein, chairman of the Council of Economic Advisers.

Mr. Shultz said that the latest devaluation was designed to "speed improvement of our trade and payments position in a manner that will support our effort to achieve a constructive reform of the monetary system."

Nixon's Decision

Mr. Shultz said the "basic fact" about the dollar was that the United States economy is "healthy" and is showing a slower rate of inflation than nearly all other countries. But he said that the devaluation announced tonight "dramatized" the importance of "getting on with the task" of world monetary reform, in which the United States has made major proposals.

President Nixon, Mr. Schultz said, made his "basic decisions"—presumably meaning the devaluation—last Tuesday and had made his final decision this morning.

Although the United States has always been theoretically able to devalue the dollar by simply notifying the International Monetary Fund, in practice it is not possible without international agreement.

Other countries could nullify the devaluation by changing their own exchange rates by the same amount.

International agreement was achieved in the present case during a hurried trip by Paul A. Volcker, Under Secretary of the Treasury for Monetary Affairs, who visited Tokyo and the main European capitals starting last Wednesday.

The essence of the agreement was that key countries such as Germany and France would not change their exchange rates and that Japan would allow the yen to float.

Mr. Shultz said that he expected the floating of the yen would be upward, meaning a "larger" change than the 10 per cent devaluation of the dollar against the major European currencies.

Mr. Shultz's statement said that the United States has "undertaken no obligations to intervene in foreign exchange markets." This means that the new set of exchange rates will be defended by foreign central banks, not by the Federal Reserve.

This was the case both before and after the Smithsonian agreement of December 1971. Only in a reformed world monetary system might the United States, like other countries, use central-bank intervention in foreign-exchange markets to keep the dollar's exchange rate within its internationally agreed limits.

Mr. Shultz, conceding the "serious deficit" in United States foreign trade, said: "Other nations have been slow in eliminating their excessive surpluses, thereby contributing to uncertainty and instability. In recent days currency disturbances have rocked world exchange markets. Under the pressure of events, some countries have responded with added restrictions, dangerously moving away from the basic objectives we seek."

Tonight's announcment was vague on the contents of the forthcoming trade legislation to be sent to Congress, other than the disclosure that the President had "decided" to propose a bill.

Mr. Shultz said there would be "intensive consultations" with business, labor and other groups, including members of Congress, before the legislation was submitted. He said the legislation would provide for reducing tariffs and other barriers to trade but would also "provide for raising tariffs when such action would contribute to arrangements assuring that American exports have fair access to foreign markets."

The action in Washington followed intensive meetings in European capitals over the last few days. They involved Paul A. Volcker, Under Secretary of the Treasury, the finance ministers of four European nations—Helmut Schmidt of West Germany, Valéry Giscard d 'Estaing of France, Anthony Barber of Britain and Giovanni Malagodi of Italy—and Takashi Hosomi, a special representative of the Japanese Finance Ministry.

* * *

August 2, 1972

REFORMING MONETARY POLICIES

Group of 20 Faces a Need to Revive Keynes's Trigger

By LEONARD SILK

The job of reforming the world monetary system is about to begin. The board of governors of the International Mone-

tary Fund has formally approved a new "Group of 20" to negotiate a new monetary system for the 120-nation body that includes the whole of the non-Communist world. The most difficult and important issue the top financial brains of G-20 will face, when they meet for first time in Washington in late September during the annual World Bank and monetary fund meetings, will be how to devise an orderly procedure for preventing nations from getting into deep deficits or heavy surpluses in their balances of payments.

Failure to solve that problem has bred crisis after monetary crisis in recent years, culminating in President Nixon's new economic policy of last Aug. 15. One of the critical elements of that program was ending the convertibility of the dollar into gold.

Cutting the golden knot set the United States dollar free to float in the world exchange markets—until it and other currencies were again fastened to new moorings at the Smithsonian Institution in Washington on Dec. 18.

The world has not increased its faith in paper currencies in the meantime. The price of gold has been driven upward; yesterday it exceeded $70 an ounce in London and Paris. This was the highest gold prices ever.

Some monetary experts—such as Miroslav Kriz, a vice president of the First National City Bank of New York—think the official gold price might be raised to $70 by the monetary agreement that the members of G-20 will soon be negotiating.

Significant to Gold Holders

That is not an insignificant issue to gold holders, whether they are private speculators or national Governments—including the gold-producing states, primarily South Africa and the Soviet Union.

As weighty as the gold issue may be, however, it is less significant—and certainly less complicated—than achieving equilibrium in the nations' balance of payments.

The fatal flaw in the monetary system negotiated at the Mount Washington Hotel in Bretton Woods, N. H., 28 years ago during World War II, was the rigidity of exchange rates. Economists generally regard exchange rates as the primary mechanism for restoring balance to a nation's external payments: devaluation makes its exports cheaper and imports dearer, and shrinks a payments deficit; an upward revaluation does the reverse and shrinks a surplus.

It was no accident that the world monetary system acquired extremely rigid exchange rates at Bretton Woods. The United States—by far the dominant power at that conference—wanted it that way.

The American delegation knew that the dollar would be strong in the postwar years, as the products of its undamaged and expanded economy flowed out to a war-shattered world. The United States preferred to supply foreign aid to cover the payments deficits of other countries than to have continuous devaluations against the dollar.

Thus America's White Plan for international monetary reform of 1944—named for Harry Dexter White, Assistant

Secretary of the Treasury and chief United States negotiator—sought to discourage rate flexibility by proposing that "changes in the exchange value of the currency of a member country shall be considered only when essential to the correction of fundamental disequilibrium in its balance of payments, and shall be made only with approval of three-fourths of the member votes. . . ."

The chief British negotiator at Bretton Woods, the eminent economist John Maynard Keynes—by then Lord Keynes—foresaw the problems to international monetary system that an overly rigid exchange rate system would cause.

He was not only concerned about international balance of payments troubles that might result but also about the possibility of jeopardizing a nation's ability to preserve domestic full employment. The crucial background of Lord Keynes's thinking was undoubtedly Britain's long struggle in the nineteen-twenties to defend an overvalued pound, which had caused mass unemployment, necessitated welfare and weakened the nation in the years preceding the Great Depression and World War II.

Inflation Was a Problem

Lord Keynes did not foresee that the principal long-term postwar problem would be inflation rather than depression, in large part as a result of his own influence. But that post-war economic difficulties resulted more from inflation than depression did not affect Lord Keynes's central point: That nations would have their hands tied in dealing with domestic problems, if exchange rates were rigid.

The Keynes Plan for the new monetary system, therefore, included a proposal for a "trigger" an objective criterion that would touch off action by the governing board of the monetary fund to get a nation's balance of payments back into equilibrium—when the nation was in excess deficit or surplus.

The equal responsibility of nations in surplus to take remedial action with those in deficit has been heavily stressed lately by American monetary officials, most recently by Arthur F. Burns, chairman of the Federal Reserve Board, in his Montreal speech of May 12.

Lord Keynes's trigger would have been kicked off by changes in a country's debit or credit balance with the I.M.F. When a country was running deficits and its debit balance reached half its quota with the fund, the governing board could require it to take one or more of the following actions: 1) devalue its currency by a suitable amount; 2) impose tighter controls on outward capital flows; or 3) pay up a suitable proportion of its gold or other liquid reserves to reduce its debit balance. Step 3 was a form of discipline that might force some domestic deflation, if required.

But when the Keynesian trigger was touched off by a country's mounting surplus, it required that country to restore equilibrium by taking one or more of the following steps: 1) expand domestic credit and demand—to help pull in more imports and reduce its exports; 2) revalue upward its currency in terms of what Lord Keynes called "bancor," a rough equivalent of what we now know as special drawing rights; 3) lower its tariffs or other trade barriers against imports; or 4) increase international development loans.

But the Keynes Plan was largely abandoned in favor of the White Plan.

During the earlier postwar years, the Keynesian trigger was neglected in the archives, as the world economy flourished and expanded within a fixed-rate monetary system made possible by continuous deficits in the United States balance of payments—and by occasional devaluations against the dollar.

The heavy loss of American reserves and the growing weakness of the dollar—and of the United States trade position—finally wrecked that system and has caused monetary reformers to search for a way to correct national deficits or surpluses before they breed more monetary crises.

Some economists—such as Prof. Milton Friedman of the University of Chicago—think the whole adjustment problem can be solved simply by letting all currencies float. The adaptation of exchange rates to the market forces of supply and demand for money would, according to this view, keep nations continuously in equilibrium—and thereby virtually obviate the need for monetary reserves to cover actual or potential deficits.

But other economists—such as Dr. Walter S. Salant of the Brookings Institution—contend that market-induced changes in exchange rates cannot be relied upon alone to handle the entire adjustment problem, especially after the much closer integration of the world economy in the postwar years, the rise of multinational corporations, the growth of the huge Eurodollar market, the speed of electronic communications, and the enormous pool of highly liquid capital—amounting to tens of billions of dollars—that can anticipate and swamp a currency devaluation or upward revaluation, or even force one to happen, whether warranted by market conditions and underlying price and wage trends or not.

Dr. Salant says: "Speculation can be massive even when there is no fundamental disequilibrium. . . . The idea that if there's massive speculation there must be fundamental disequilibrium appears to me groundless superstition of market-worshippers. The growth of internationally mobile capital has been all out of proportion to the growth of reserves plus borrowing facilities, and I think too little attention has been devoted to the implications of that fact."

One implication is that a massive increase in world monetary reserves, together with facilities for financing countries in deficit, is needed, in order to defend currencies—such as the dollar—from speculative raids.

A second implication is that exchange-rate changes must be relatively small, frequent, controllable and objectively justifiable, in order to keep the system in relative balance and remove opportunities for huge speculative gains.

Hence the search is on, among the world's monetary reformers, for new mechanisms for bringing about international exchange adjustments. The effort will be to update and, if possible, improve upon the old Keynesian trigger.

* * *

June 6, 1973

MARKET MOOD: ANXIETY BUT NO PANIC

By LEONARD SILK

Gold keeps climbing: It closed at $126 an ounce in London yesterday, almost double the price at which it started the year. The dollar keeps sinking: It has now lost about one-fifth of its value in relation to the West German mark since December, 1971. The United States has been suffering from its worst inflation in half a century—and its most intense Presidential crisis in a century. Is panic nigh? The answer seems to be no.

The stock market staged a lusty rally yesterday, suggesting that courage and cool have not deserted the professionals of Wall Street.

Secretary of the Treasury George P. Shultz says he is puzzled by the weakness of the dollar and the stock market, and confidently declares that there are "bargains galore" and he would be buying good common stocks if the funds he manages did not belong to the United States Treasury.

Chairman Arthur F. Burns of the Federal Reserve Board journeys to Kirkaldy, Scotland, to celebrate the 250th anniversary of the christening of Adam Smith, worldly philosopher, and announces that there will be no new credit crunch.

On both the Smithian and no-crunch counts, Dr. Burns establishes his credentials as a non-forgetter of history. The only major historic instance when monetary policy was used drastically to support a weakening dollar was in 1931, after the devaluation of the British pound.

On that occasion, the Fed's shift to tighter money in the face of heavy gold losses drove down the price of bonds and caused the collapse of many banks already weakened by the Depression. It was probably the worst blunder in the Fed's history.

Today the banking system is not in weakened condition, although some stockbrokers are. But Dr. Burns does not intend to take any chances of repeating the Fed's 1931 boo-boo.

He has been trying to bring monetary policy around to restraint more cautiously—and to be ready to switch policy on an instant's notice if the brakes show signs of grabbing.

He is back to his old pitch of urging the Administration to adopt a tougher wage-price policy—a pitch that got him in trouble at the White House in the period just before the President switched to Phase 1 in August, 1971.

Dr. Burns is leaning on commercial bankers to keep interest rates from rising too much. And he is trying to "encourage the others"—such as Mr. Shultz and the Cost of Living Council's director, John Dunlop—to toughen the price and wage restraints for which they are responsible.

The Senate Democratic caucus has called unanimously for a mandatory 90-day wage-price freeze. And Senator Hugh Scott of Pennsylvania, the Republican leader, has indicated the President is thinking about tighter anti-inflation moves.

As Wall Street grows desperate over prospects of ever tighter money and higher interest rates, its spirits rise on hopes of stiffer price and wage restraints.

Private economic forecasters these days are widely dispersed on when the next recession will start and how sharp it will be—with the opening dates staggered from late 1973 to mid-1974 and with the degree of severity ranging from about as sharp as 1957–58 to the mildest sort of "growth recession" in which gross national product will not decline at all but simply slow down for a while.

Some Wall Streeters contend that the best news imaginable would be clear signs that the slowdown has actually begun, since this would mean easier money and credit conditions. They are ready to plunge for stocks on the first downward movement of the prime rate of interest.

Watergate appears to be worrying domestic investors as much as foreign holders of dollars. Fear of protracted crisis, immobilizing national economic policy, is the biggest current cloud hanging over Wall Street.

Investors' second biggest worry is the dollar—and the durability of the present international monetary system. Rumors are flying that gold will be officially revalued upward by about threefold—roughly to the current market price of $126.

Gold Futures Up

Gold futures run still higher. At the Winnepeg Commodity Exchange this week, gold contracts for delivery in July, 1974, went up to $139.40 an ounce.

Some economists begin to suspect that in so chaotic a world monetary situation, with the dollar seemingly floating out to sea, gold may indeed regain its position as the premier world money.

As Prof. Henry C. Wallich of Yale said in his Per Jacobsson Lecture at the International Monetary Fund in Washington last September, "If efforts to negotiate a new international monetary system should fail, if in some crisis national or international credit instruments should cease to be universally acceptable, worldwide belief in the 'intrinsic value' of gold, now buttressed by mounting industrial demand, might again restore gold as the basic world money."

Meanwhile, the Committee of 20 of the I.M.F. limps along, with the major nations still badly divided on how to reform the world monetary system.

The European Parliament in Strasbourg has urged the Common Market to reject Secretary Shultz's plan for world monetary reform and to submit a plan of its own.

Yet, with so many reasons for alarm, the mood of markets at home and abroad is more anxious and uncertain than desperate or panicky.

Reasons for Hope

What one needs to explain are the reasons for persistent hope rather than the causes of immediate gloom.

The hopeful reasons appear to be these:

• All major countries are enjoying prosperity—or excess demand—and have not been weakened by a severe world slump. Modern fiscal and monetary policies seem capable of warding off or checking such a slump, if it should start.

- The resort to floating exchange rates has staved off the kind of massive speculation that marked earlier monetary crises.
- The danger that the Western world would split into hostile, competing trade blocs has been held in check by the rise of multinational corporations—with their significant power and their will to hold world trading and investment opportunities open.

- There is recognition that beggar-my-neighbor policies could beggar oneself—and this realization brings in its train a considerable degree of patience and a determination to avoid drastic or sudden steps (including an official lurch back to gold) to cure the uncertainties of the moment. The present may be awful, but one can imagine much worse.

THE EUROPEAN MONETARY CRISIS

September 11, 1992

CURRENCIES TEACHING EUROPE THAT UNITY CAN BE PAINFUL

By RICHARD W. STEVENSON
Special to The New York Times

LONDON, Sept. 10—Europe's plans for further unification may be up in the air, but people from Helsinki to Rome have been learning an often painful lesson in recent weeks about how entwined their economies have already become.

The agent of their discomfort has been the effort by most European nations to link the value of their currencies by maintaining relatively stable exchange rates. In doing so amid a worldwide recession, nations have increasingly been torn between their short-term domestic economic needs and their long-range goal of creating a single European market with stable prices and steady growth.

In more cases than not, the domestic needs are losing out, bringing more insistent calls from recession-racked consumers and businesses for governments to rethink their policies.

As a result, exchange rates, once of concern only to international travelers and multinational companies, have emerged as a dominant factor in the economic policies of most European nations. And they are developing into a political issue that seems certain to endure no matter what the outcome of the French referendum later this month on whether to approve the next stage of European monetary and political unification.

The issue has become more visible because of the turmoil that has gripped the foreign currency markets in the last month. To a degree, the turmoil is a result of uncertainty about the French vote on Sept. 20 and what it would mean for closer economic cooperation in the region. But the upheaval has been driven primarily by the surge in the value of the German mark against the dollar and most European currencies.

The United States has paid little attention to the weakness of the dollar against the mark, choosing instead to maintain its policy of lower domestic interest rates in the hopes of spurring an economic recovery. But throughout much of Europe, nations are making exactly the opposite decision.

Despite being mired in a severe slump, Italy has raised interest rates sharply this month to defend the value of the lira. Britain has said repeatedly that it will do whatever is necessary to defend the pound, even if it means raising interest rates, a prospect that has horrified many homeowners and business executives who are calling for lower rates.

Sweden this week pushed a key interest rate up to 75 percent—a level unheard of among industrialized nations—to defend its currency, forcing up mortgage rates and the costs of business loans and bringing turmoil to its financial markets.

The hope of those nations is that the discipline of maintaining stable currency values through the European exchange rate mechanism will bring wage and price stability throughout the region and help create a vibrant trading market. Their strategy has been to keep the value of their currencies pegged to the mark. Backed by the Bundesbank, Germany's tight-fisted central bank, the mark has long been the world's standard for anti-inflationary credibility.

"These nations believe that a stable exchange rate system is the best way to reduce inflation and that low inflation is the best basis for growth," said David Roche, an economist with Morgan Stanley International in London. "The worst solution is to allow currencies to devalue and inflation to creep up."

Inflation rates have in fact come down throughout Europe. In Britain, for example, inflation stood at 9.5 percent when the nation joined the exchange rate mechanism just under two years ago. Today it stands at about 4 percent.

But lower inflation has not yet brought the advertised resumption of steady economic growth across Europe. And the theoretical long-term benefits of stable prices seem increasingly lost on homeowners who fear rising mortgage payments, on shop owners who see their business drying up and on the unemployed who want to see interest rates drop, even at the cost of a devalued currency, to stimulate the economy.

Pressure to Devalue the Pound

"They must devalue the pound," said Belinda Handman, a real estate investor and entrepreneur in London. "If they raise interest rates, businesses will be on the floor."

On Britain's Isle of Wight, Derek Pullen, a 50-year-old home builder, has seen his business fall 20 percent in the last year, and he is paying 13.5 percent for business loans. He gives the Government high marks for bringing inflation down, but he sees little gain in further unification with Europe and no reason for the Government to defend the pound at all costs.

"If the Government raises interest rates, it will affect me something wicked," Mr. Pullen said.

Not all nations have chosen to stick to their exchange rates. Finland sent shock waves through the currency markets this week when it decided to let the markka float in value against other currencies, a move tantamount to substantial devaluation.

Officials in Helsinki said they could not afford to defend the currency in the markets, and the nation's economy, battered by a sharp drop in trade with the republics of the former Soviet Union, would have suffered additional damage if the Government had raised interest rates.

Finland is not a member of the European Community or its exchange rate agreement, but had been voluntarily linking its currency to other European currencies in preparation for joining. Analysts said Sweden, which has applied for membership in the community, was sending a signal with its decision to raise rates that it could be counted on by Europe as a partner in a stable monetary system.

"You've got a stark contrast at the moment between weak domestic economies demanding lower interest rates and weakness in the currency forcing upward pressure on interest rates," said Peter Fellner, an economist with NatWest Capital Markets in London.

Much of the tension stems from Germany's policy of keeping its interest rates high to ward off inflation as it absorbs the costs of unification with the former East Germany. Some economists are predicting that Germany will lower rates within the next six months to give a boost to its weak economy. But outside Germany there is a growing backlash against the notion that domestic economic decisions are captive to the Bundesbank.

"France is now paying the economic price of German reunification," said Jean Francois Braunstein, a philosophy professor at the University of Amiens in France.

But Mr. Fellner said that unless members of the European exchange rate mechanism decided that they wanted to devalue their currencies against the mark, they had little choice but to wait until the Germans decided that they could safely lower rates, a step that would decrease the value of the mark.

"The argument that this is a German problem and shouldn't be inflicted on the rest of the E.R.M. countries is a valid one," Mr. Fellner said. "The problem is, how do you get out of it without undermining the credibility of the other nations that are making an effort to stick to their exchange rate commitment."

Although political support for remaining within the exchange rate mechanism remains strong in most countries, a growing number of politicians are breaking ranks with their leadership and calling for devaluation to spur growth and reassert control over domestic economic policy-making.

* * *

September 17, 1992

EUROPEANS' CURRENCY SYSTEM SHAKEN AS BRITAIN CUTS FREE

By RICHARD W. STEVENSON
Special to The New York Times

LONDON, Thursday, Sept. 17—After a futile day of trying to defend the value of the pound, Britain dropped out of the European Monetary System on Wednesday, at least temporarily. Its departure from the monetary system, a cornerstone of greater European unity, left the program of economic coordination in tatters.

Before taking that unexpected step, which effectively allowed the pound to drop sharply in value, Britain desperately tried to pump up the currency. First it raised one of its key interest rates to 12 percent from 10 percent. Only hours later—after the pound had sunk still further—it announced another increase, to 15 percent. By raising rates so sharply, Britain hoped to make the pound more attractive to investors and stop concerted selling by speculators that was pushing it down.

Early this morning in Brussels, finance officials from the 12 European Community nations attempted to restore some order to the chaotic currency markets by devaluing the Spanish peseta by 5 percent and allowing the Italian lira to fall freely. The lira had been devalued 7 percent on Sunday.

Currency Restrictions

Like the other European members of the monetary system, Britain has been obliged to keep its currency within certain bounds relative to other currencies—and particularly the German mark, the strongest of the group. It was the pound's decline below that limit on Wednesday that forced Britain's costly measures: first to bolster the pound, then to pull out of the system altogether.

The situation prompted only mild concern outside Europe. United States officials said the turbulence could actually benefit European and American economies, leading to lower interest rates that would spur growth in Europe and eventually give the United States a lift.

While Britain's decision to depart, at least temporarily, from the monetary system raised problems for Britain's allies, it also created a political crisis for Prime Minister John Major. While Margaret Thatcher had only reluctantly agreed to greater integration with the rest of Europe, Mr. Major embraced the prospect. He has staked the credibility of his Government on maintaining the pound's value at almost any cost, as a willing participant in the monetary system.

New Questions for Europe

And with France set to vote on Sunday on whether to approve the treaty outlining the next stages of European unification, the shift by Britain raised new questions about whether Europe can or should continue its push for monetary union.

The British move came at the end of a day in which speculators sold huge amounts of Europe's weaker currencies,

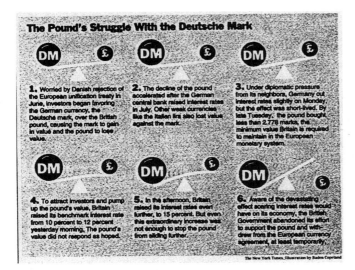

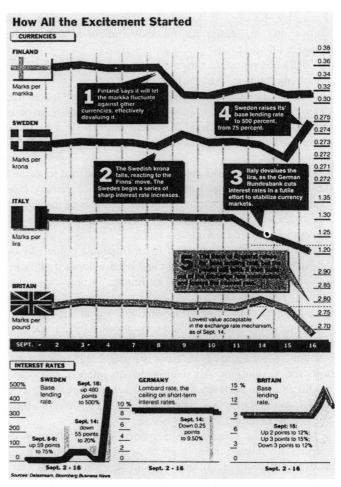

including the pound, the lira and the peseta, and plowed funds into the German mark, traditionally the strongest and most stable currencies. The shifts threw out of whack Europe's strategy for closer economic ties.

As Britain raced to defend the pound on Wednesday, Italy and Sweden were also struggling to maintain their own weak currencies.

Italy spent large sums selling marks and other currencies in return for lira in an attempt to bid up the lira's value. Sweden, which is not yet a member of the European Community but is trying to get its finances in order in preparation for joining, pushed the rate for its most expensive loans to banks to an almost unheard of 500 percent.

But in the face of the overwhelming movement of funds out of the weak currencies, even those strategies accomplished little. As the pound slipped, so did the lira, despite having already been devalued by 7 percent. And from London to New York, the markets degenerated into something akin to a feeding frenzy, with speculators convinced they could profit by pushing the mark higher.

"The markets have become a monster, and the reason is the disastrous mistake of devaluing the lira," said William Ledward, an economist at Nomura Securities International in London. "In agreeing to a 7 percent devaluation, you gave the speculators a big profit, and these people are like vampires. Once they taste blood, they have to have it again."

In Brussels, the European Community's monetary committee convened shortly before midnight Wednesday in an emergency session called by the British.

Six hours later, representatives of the central banks and finance ministries of the European Community nations issued a communiqué noting the British decision to pull out of the European Monetary System and a subsequent move by the Italian authorities to allowing the lira to fall freely rather than be supported by government intervention. They then disclosed the 5 percent devaluation of the Spanish peseta within the exchange rate system.

The actions mean that the German mark and its closely associated currencies, like the Belgian franc and the Dutch

guilder, will be stronger within what remains of the exchange-rate system while the weaker currencies, which had been under heavy speculative pressure, would lose weight.

In their communiqué, the finance officials tried to put the best face on the proceedings by saying that Britain and Italy had stressed "their unanimous commitment to the European Monetary System as a key factor of economic stability and prosperity in Europe."

They urged a return of the pound and the lira to the exchange rate system "as soon as possible."

Little Choice for Major

While detaching the pound from the other European currencies and letting it drift lower was an outright reversal of his stance—as well as an unpopular step that would increase the cost of Britain's imports—Mr. Major had little choice. Politically and economically, he was unable to raise interest rates any higher. Higher rates will be poison for Britain, already in the grip of recession. And the country was running out of foreign currency reserves to defend the pound. This evening, he gave in to the markets.

The reversal came in the form of a decision to withdraw from the agreement among 11 of the 12 European Community nations to keep currency values within a relatively narrow range. Instead, the Government said, it would allow the pound to float freely, its value set by market forces.

The decision was tantamount to a large devaluation, a step that both Mr. Major and Norman Lamont, the Chancellor of the Exchequer, had repeatedly ruled out. Soon after the announcement tonight, the pound was trading at 2.70 German marks, far below its lower limit under the European exchange rate mechanism of 2.778 marks.

"What was supposed to be the centerpiece of the Government's economic policy has been removed at a stroke and Britain, having wanted to be at the heart of the new Europe, is now thrown off again to the periphery," said Nigel Gault, the chief European economist in London for DRI/McGraw Hill, an economic consulting firm.

Theo Waigel, the German Finance Minister, said he thought Britain would soon rejoin the monetary system and that there would not be a devaluation of any other currencies.

But there were clearly strains within the European Community over Britain's decision. British officials openly criticized Helmut Schlesinger, the head of the powerful German central bank, the Bundesbank, for reportedly suggesting in an interview on Tuesday that he favored further revaluations with the exchange rate agreement. Although Mr. Schlesinger said he never made the remarks, currency traders took the reports as a signal that the Bundesbank would not act to halt a slide in the pound or the lira by cutting interest rates. The Bundesbank cut rates slightly on Monday in a failed attempt to stabilize the currency markets.

Sir Norman Fowler, the chairman of Britain's governing Conservative Party, said, "The fact is that the turmoil on the foreign exchanges has been caused by the uncertainty over the French referendum result and unnecessarily by the Bundesbank president's remarks."

The Spanish and Portuguese currencies are expected to come under severe pressure today, as will the currencies of nations like Sweden that are likely to become European Community members within a few years. Analysts said that if there were wholesale readjustments in the values of currencies to each other beyond the bounds now called for, the credibility of the exchange rate system would be seriously wounded.

At best, they said, it would be a long time before the currency markets took the commitment to stable exchange rates seriously even if France approves the unification treaty on Sunday.

"The very existence of the European Monetary System is in doubt," Mr. Ledward of Nomura Securities said.

Two-Tiered System?

Some analysts, however, predicted that the process of unification might now proceed on a two-tiered basis, with Germany, France and a handful of other nations moving toward a single currency and monetary policy, while others, including Britain, watch from the sidelines.

Devaluation makes one nation's currency worth less in relation to that of another nation. The process has certain advantages, including making a nation's exports less expen-

sive, and therefore more desirable. But it tends to cause inflation because it makes imports more expensive and because it leads investors, wary of further devaluations, to demand higher interest rates.

The devaluation of the pound does not eliminate the basic pressures that set off the currency speculation. Interest rates in Germany remain at very high levels, making the mark attractive. Rates in Germany are high because the Bundesbank is fearful that the higher-than-expected costs of reuniting East and West Germany will ignite inflation, and because higher rates attract the capital that Germany needs to fund the reunification.

At the same time, the world's other major currency, the dollar, remains relatively weak because interest rates in the United States are at their lowest point in decades, making investments in dollars relatively unappealing. The United States is more insulated from other currency moves because it imports considerably less than the nations of Europe, and because oil, a critical import, is priced in dollars.

The uncertainty over the outcome of Sunday's vote in France on the Maastricht treaty outlining the course of further European unification has only hurt the situation. Investors are fearful that French rejection of the treaty would end efforts at monetary union.

Without the goal of monetary union to motivate them, some nations might choose to abandon the exchange-rate ties and the need to maintain fiscal and monetary discipline that goes along with them. Without that discipline, the investors fear, nations like Britain might once again pursue inflationary policies, making their currencies less valuable.

*   *   *

September 17, 1992

WHY THE CURRENCY CRISIS ERUPTED: A PRIMER

By PETER PASSELL

A currency crisis is something that is not supposed to happen these days. The very idea evokes images from old newsreels, with grave statesmen in top hats emerging from limousines to urge calm in gravelly voices. But suddenly Europe is up to its eyebrows in one. And while the immediate impact on most people's daily lives will be slight, it could derail the drive to European unity that only a few months ago seemed as inevitable as tomorrow's sunrise.

How could something so important have happened with so little warning? And why are elected officials who have staked their careers on the currency arrangement known as the European Monetary System seemingly powerless to prevent its meltdown? The answers lie in the basic economics of international finance—and the even more basic conflicts between domestic and regional political priorities.

Trading Francs for Pounds

Francs are the coin of the realm in France. But when a French company wants to import machinery from a producer in Manchester, England, it must pay the bills in British pounds. And to obtain the pounds, the company must find someone willing to exchange British currency for francs.

The exchange rate is thus the price of pounds in francs, or francs in pounds. And it must roughly reflect the relative purchasing power of the two currencies in their home markets. If, for example, a drill press costs 1,000 francs in Paris and £200 in London, the exchange rate had better be more or less 5 francs to the pound. Otherwise, both the British and the French will buy all their drills presses on one side of the Channel.

But like life, economics rarely works out so neatly. In the short run, currency exchange rates are influenced by many factors, including the behavior of governments. And since the rates have enormous impact on where goods that can be traded are made and how much they cost, exchange rates are a matter of great interest to the people in charge of national economies.

Most countries (including the United States) allow their currencies to "float" against others. Voluntary transactions between private buyers and sellers determine a currency's value. That suits many politicians, since setting a fixed exchange rate would force them to balance the interests of domestic producers against those of consumers buying goods from abroad.

But European leaders are immensely taken by the idea of maintaining very stable exchange rates within the greater European economy, and for two reasons. First the system eliminates uncertainty, greasing the wheels of commerce within Europe. A German truck maker can set a price for its trucks in Italian lira, for delivery in six months, because it knows what the exchange rate between marks and lira will be.

More important, a fixed exchange system imposes a collective discipline on all the national economies linked to the system. If, for example, Italy allows inflation at home to drive up production costs at its factories, a fixed exchange rate with the mark (and pound and franc) will make Italian products from those factories too expensive to sell abroad.

Indeed, from this perspective, the only other thing better than maintaining fixed exchange rates among European currencies is the adoption of a single currency for the whole European economy. And that is just what European Community leaders proposed to do in the Maastricht agreement on European political and economic union, which they signed last December.

The signatories at Maastricht, visionaries who generally speak of the agreement in political terms, appeared to comprehend that a successful currency union—or for that matter, a stable fixed exchange rate system—demanded coordination of virtually all aspects of national economic policy. But they were unable to accomplish that before the currency crisis erupted.

Price of Unification

Two years ago, West Germany took on the burden of paying for German unification. But the price of bringing eastern Germany up to snuff and subsidizing the easterners' living standards in the meantime has been far higher than anyone guessed. And the Government of Chancellor Helmut Kohl has balked at raising taxes sufficiently to keep Germany's budget in balance.

Germany's inflation-wary (and very independent) central bank reacted by jacking up interest rates. Foreigners responded by purchasing tens of billions of dollars' worth of German marks and investing the proceeds in German bank deposits paying as much as 9 percent interest—a far higher interest rate than they could get by depositing their money in New York.

Not surprisingly, the price of the mark soared with respect to the dollar as traders found it evermore difficult to find people to sell them the German currency. What should not have surprised anyone, but somehow did, was the reaction in currency markets in the rest of Europe.

Since, by government agreement, all the leading European currencies were tied to the mark, they, too, rose sharply in value relative to the dollar. But in the last month, the banks and corporations that control much of the worlds' currency in private hands wondered whether these agreements would stick. And with good reason.

Last Thing They Wanted

To maintain fixed exchange rates with Germany, other European countries were forced to raise their interest rates to make it as attractive for investors to hold these nations' currencies as it was to hold German marks. But with Britain deep in recession and other European economies heading there, the last thing that European leaders wanted to do was to discourage domestic spending by raising interest rates.

Check that: the very last thing they wanted to do was to allow their currencies to remain high against the dollar for very long. Much of their trade, after all, is with the United States. And a strong pound or franc or lira makes their goods more expensive and harder to sell in the country that pays its bills in greenbacks.

The more traders thought about it, the less they wanted to take the chance of being caught holding currencies other than German marks on the day that European governments were unable to defend fixed exchange rates. Britain tried to bluff, effectively arguing that it would do anything to hold the line. But in the end, the traders' prophecy proved to be self-fulfilling.

The economic damage is likely to be modest. Indeed, the currency realignment forced by the German policy of tight money and high interest rates could do a lot of good in the short run.

The longer-term impact is harder to assess. In the best of worlds, it will teach Europeans a relatively painless lesson about the importance of coordinating their economic policies.

* * *

September 17, 1992

HOW EUROPE'S MONETARY SYSTEM WORKS

The European Monetary System, begun in 1979, was designed to foster currency stability and promote economic policies to reduce inflation throughout Europe.

The currencies of the 11 members (before Britain's decision to suspend participation yesterday) are linked in trading bands. For Belgium, Luxemburg, Denmark, France, Germany, Ireland, Italy and the Netherlands, their currencies are allowed to trade 2.25 percent above or below and central rate. In Britain, Spain and Portugal, the allowed range is 6 percent.

When a currency hits the bottom or the top of its range, the country's central bank must act to keep it within the trading band. This can be done by intervening in the foreign exchange market to buy or sell the currency or by moving interest rates up or down. In the current crisis, the pound and the lira have fallen through the bottom of their trading rage against the German mark.

If action by a central bank does not prevent a breach, a revaluation of the currency is required. The Italians agreed to such a revaluation on Sunday, in effect devaluing the lira 7 percent.

The British tried to defend the pound yesterday by raising interest rates. When that failed, they in effect unilaterally devalued the pound by suspending their participation in the European Monetary System.

Since the beginning of the monetary system there have been 10 realignments or revaluations of members' currencies. But the Italian move was the first since 1987.

The European Monetary System was seen as sort of the training ground for the move to a single European currency by the end of 1999. The next steps are outlined in the Maastricht Treaty, which was signed in the Dutch town of the same name in December. The treaty sets out the procedure for establishing a European central bank and the levels inflation must fall to before countries can become part of a single currency plan.

The rejection of the Maastricht Treaty by the Danes in June and the threat that it will be rejected by the French on Sunday is one of the causes of the turmoil in foreign exchange markets.

*   *   *

September 17, 1992

FED ACTION ON EUROPE NOT EXPECTED

By STEVEN GREENHOUSE
Special to The New York Times

WASHINGTON, Sept. 16—The turmoil in European's financial markets is primarily a European affair and the United States will not get involved in trying to help steady Europe's jitters, officials of the Bush Administration and the Federal Reserve said today.

In fact, the turbulence could actually help both the American and the European economies, the officials said, because it could lead to lower interest rates and thus spur growth in Europe that would ultimately give the United States a boost as well.

Beyond that, Europe's foreign exchange trauma has given the Federal Reserve more flexibility to lower interest rates, because the trauma has strengthened the dollar, they said. The dollar's extreme weakness early this month prevented the Federal Reserve from cutting rates by more than the one-quarter point cut it announced on Sept. 4.

Fed Under Pressure

In a speech today in Los Angeles, David W. Mullins Jr., the vice chairman of the Federal Reserve, said the present European turmoil was essentially a European phenomenon.

"We're staying on the sidelines," said one Fed official.

But clearly the United States is not unaffected. Since the election season began, the Fed has been under intense pressure from both Congress and the White House to lower interest rates even further than they have. The rates are now the lowest they have been in three decades.

Fed officials acknowledged that if they had wanted to lower rates this week, they probably could not have done so. The step would have been akin to throwing a great rock into an already unsettled pond.

An American rate cut would probably strengthen the German mark, and increase tensions in Europe, pressuring other nations to raise their interest rates and protect their currencies against the mark.

More Flexibility for Fed

"What's happening in Europe gives the Fed a little more flexibility," said Geoffrey Dennis, an international economist with James Capel Inc. in New York. "They certainly won't cut rates this week, but they might do it in early October when the September employment report is released. I expect unemployment to be higher in that report."

One senior Administration official praised the idea of devaluations in Europe, saying that they would spur growth there. Faster growth in Italy or Britain should ultimately mean that those countries would import more American goods.

That official also said that such devaluations would lessen the need for these devaluing countries to jack up interest rates to defend their currency from falling against the German mark. Under the European Monetary System, member nations are required, barring a formal devaluation, to keep their currencies from falling against the mark.

Lower interest would spur growth in the devaluing nations and help spur their growth—and growth throughout Europe.

Rooting for German Cuts

European Community finance ministers are expected to announce more devaluations along the lines of the devaluation of the Italian lira.

[In Brussels early Thursday, the European Community finance ministers agreed to devalue the Spanish peseta and suspend the lira from the exchange rate system.]

"We want more of the same," said John Williamson, an economist with the Institute for International Economics. He said he feared that the Europeans might decide to keep some currencies at unrealistically high levels against the mark and that this could hinder growth by forcing some countries to raise rates. He was also rooting for further rate cuts by Germany's central bank.

American officials said the devaluations in Europe were not unalloyed good news because they could strengthen the dollar vis-a-vis the pound and lira, and thus make American goods less competitive versus British and Italian goods. But these officials said the devaluations might help strengthen the mark against the dollar, and that could help America's competitive position.

Market Plunge Feared

The big fear that American officials expressed was that the commotion in Europe could cause American stock and bond markets to plunge. One official said the fact that the New York Stock Exchange slid today while the dollar strengthened showed that the European situation was undermining investor confidence.

American officials said Europe's exchange rate markets will be at or near the top of the agenda when the Group of Seven's finance ministers meet Saturday in Washington. Originally, the weak dollar was scheduled to be topic No. 1.

Some economists suggested that the United States might push the Europeans to structure their monetary system in a way that countries other than Germany do not repeatedly have to jack up their interest rates to defend their currencies, thus slowing their economic growth.

* * *

September 17, 1992

IN POLITICS AND FINANCE, A DEVALUATION IS COSTLY

By WILLIAM E. SCHMIDT
Special to The New York Times

LONDON, Sept. 16—Prime Minister John Major faces a crisis that imperils not only his Government's economic and European policies, but possibly his own political future.

In a day of extraordinary financial initiatives and embarrassing reversals, Mr. Major staked his credibility on a bold effort to rescue the pound from devaluation by raising interest rates once, then twice, by a total of five percentage points.

In the end, he retreated in defeat, forced to cut the sagging pound loose from other European currencies, and it sank even further.

As a measure of the depth of the crisis, Downing Street bowed to demands late tonight that the Prime Minister recall Parliament from its summer recess next week to figure out what Britain should do next to address its financial problems.

Looking pale and drawn, the Chancellor of the Exchequer, Norman Lamont, the Government's economic architect,

appeared briefly outside the Prime Minister's residence at 10 Downing Street tonight to talk of what he described as "an extremely difficult and turbulent day." Mr. Major did not appear.

Chaos and Criticism

The turbulence was the latest and most extreme indication of the chaos that has seized European financial markets in the days leading up to the French referendum Sunday on the treaty of European union.

Throughout the day, Mr. Major's Government found itself under increasingly sharp attack from rival politicians, business people, consumers and union leaders, who argued that the five-point rise in benchmark interest rates, to 15 percent, only aggravated the ills of Britain's faltering economy, which is already saddled with high unemployment and slow growth.

The Government had said it would increase interest rates only to 12 percent.

Gordon Brown, the opposition Labor Party's economic spokesman, said tonight that the Conservative Government had "lost the confidence of the people and of Britain."

"In one day," he said, "we have been forced to leave the European currency mechanism, watched interest rates go up, saw the devaluation of the pound and seen millions of people confronted with further financial hardship."

Mr. Major's allies warned that he is almost certain to face a much sharper challenge in the coming months over his support for a stronger European union, including the treaty on European cooperation.

Keeping a Key Man

Late tonight, Downing Street rejected calls from some union leaders and rival politicians, including some members of Mr. Major's own party, for Mr. Lamont's resignation.

Sir Norman Fowler, chairman of the Conservative Party, said the party fully supported the Chancellor. "Frankly, if anyone should resign it should be the president of the Bundesbank," he said, referring to Germany's central bank. The British argue that the Germans aggravated the collapse of the pound by hinting that sterling would be devalued.

Over the last year, Mr. Major's insistent support for closer European political and economic cooperation had appeared to overcome the opposition of skeptics within his own party.

But even if French voters ratify the treaty on union, which was signed in December by Mr. Major and other European Community leaders in the Dutch city of Maastricht, critics here say that the accord is all but certain to face determined political opposition from those who argue that the events of the last few weeks illustrate the folly of European integration.

"We are now sacrificing people's lives and mortgages and businesses for the sake of a European economic dogma," said William Cash, chairman of the European affairs committee in Parliament and a longtime skeptic on European union.

Until tonight, the Government has consistently defended the European currency system, arguing that it was only uncertainty over the French referendum that stirred currency speculation. Earlier today, when he announced the first set of interest-rate increases to prop up the pound, Mr. Lamont described the currency system, the European Rate Mechanism, as a means for insuring price stability.

The Prime Minister's heady gamble reflected both his commitment to Europe and a determination to do whatever was necessary to keep the pound aligned with other currencies within the European system. Part of a long-term political commitment to the process of monetary integration, the strategy is regarded by Mr. Major as the Government's surest weapon against inflation.

His opposition to currency devaluation—in a speech last week he described it as "a betrayal of our future"—reflects, in part, an understanding of the political costs.

Downing Street had become increasingly apprehensive about the pound after it continued to falter despite a small cut in German interest rates on Sunday.

There are also signs that British public support for the Maastricht treaty is weak and uncertain. In a poll released today by The European, a Paris-based newspaper, more than half those polled in Britain said they did not know how they would vote if given the opportunity. The Major Government plans to exercise its option to submit the treaty to Parliament, not to the public, for approval.

Twenty-four percent of those surveyed said they favored the treaty and 22 percent said they were opposed.

Only three months ago, in a similar sampling by Market and Opinion Research International in London, 35 percent favored the treaty, 30 percent were opposed and 35 percent did not know how they would vote.

The last time the British devalued sterling was in November 1967, when Harold Wilson, a Labor Prime Minister, ordered a 14.3 percent reduction after a long struggle to support the pound's value.

The Chancellor of the Exchequer at the time, James Callaghan, resigned, conceding that devaluation represented a repudiation of his economic policies. Two and a half years later, amid growing economic problems, Mr. Wilson's Government was also defeated.

*　　*　　*

September 17, 1992

THE HIGH COST OF UNITY

By ALAN RIDING
Special to The New York Times

PARIS, Sept. 16—The currency systems of Western Europe were thrown into disarray today when speculators took hold of exchange markets. They sold weaker currencies like the British pound, the Italian lira and the Spanish peseta, and bought the strongest currency in Europe, the German mark.

But more fundamentally, the chaos occurred because of an underlying crisis afflicting the economies of Europe. The crisis is rooted in the high cost of German unification, which is driving up German interest rates at a time when other European countries need lower rates to help them out of their economic slowdown.

The immediate spur of the buying and selling by currency speculators over the last 10 days was a growing fear that France will vote on Sunday to reject the Maastricht treaty on European union—in the process sinking the European Community's plan to create a single currency by the end of the decade.

Many currency traders believe that a French "no" in the referendum would put on hold plans for a single European currency and disrupt the community's system of linked exchange rates.

Winners and Losers

Their concern was that in this disruption, Britain and other countries with weak currencies would be forced to devalue, letting the worth of their money drop even further in relation to the German mark. By rushing to buy marks, the speculators thus engaged in self-fulfilling prophecy.

The Italian lira was the first to give way when the lira was devalued by 7 percent on Sunday. Today, Britain was forced to cut loose the pound from the fixed values of other European currencies, allowing it to "float" and effectively devaluing it. And the peseta also came under market pressure.

Currency devaluations are anything but an academic exercise in Europe. The value of money is a much greater political issue than, for example, in the United States because European consumers depend so heavily on imports. A devaluation raises the price of foreign goods, bringing higher living costs and inflation.

Currency gyrations may slow in coming days once the French referendum on the European treaty is decided and some of the current uncertainty is eliminated. But the underlying forces in the current crisis, the high cost of German unification and the European-wide economic slowdown, will not disappear even if French voters approve the treaty.

This slide into recession follows a burst of rapid growth in the late 1980's. Through much of Europe, unemployment is on the rise, investment is down and business confidence has evaporated.

French approval of the European union treaty would therefore give the community a much-needed psychological lift by preserving the principal blueprint for the future, including the goal of a single currency by 1999. But it would not mean that the 12 nations in the community had turned the corner economically or were secure from new currency crises.

[The European Community's monetary committee decided in Brussels early Thursday that further steps were necessary. It voted to let Italy set the lira free from the exchange-rate system and to allow Spain to devalue the peseta by 5 percent.]

In recent months, most European economies have become hostage to the unexpectedly high cost of German unification. Germany has long had the region's strongest economy and currency and, in the 1980's at least, its monetary discipline proved to be a stabilizing influence.

But it has become clear that the financial burden of trying to develop the former East Germany is much greater than many Germans and other Europeans had expected. By some accounts, the cost could be $100 billion in the next few years.

Enforcing Frugality

This burden has spawned new inflation in Germany. To fight this, the German central bank, the Bundesbank, has raised domestic interest rates as a way of persuading people to save rather than spend—the theory being that, with less money circulating, inflation will come down.

The Germans have also had to raise interest rates to attract the large amounts of money needed to carry out the reconstruction of the east without raising taxes.

Adopted for purely German reasons, this policy was bound to have an impact on Western Europe's interdependent economies. And as German interest rates went up, foreign investors abandoned currencies that offered less attractive returns and rushed to buy marks to take advantage of these higher rates.

Under free-market conditions, the mark's value would normally increase until investors considered it too expensive to buy. And this is what has hurt the dollar: Its value against the mark has tumbled in recent weeks, not least because interest rates are so much lower in the United States than in Germany.

Within Europe, the situation is more complicated since the major currencies are linked. Under this system, they can fluctuate only within narrow margins of their basic value, as expressed in European Currency Units, or ECU's. The value of the ECU against, say, the dollar reflects the weighted values of all the European currencies.

As a result, as German interest rates began drawing investors and pushing up the mark's value, other community governments had to bolster their own currencies to keep them within the permitted margins of the so-called exchange rate mechanism. And they had to do this by raising their own interest rates to make them competitive.

In other words, community members found themselves importing Germany's economic problems. For example, although French inflation is low, high interest rates began driving the French economy into a slump. And Britain, which had succeeded in lowering inflation, found that its high interest rates stood in the way of a resumption of economic growth. Italy was particularly vulnerable because of a huge budget deficit.

Part of the deal was that Germany would take the pressure off the other currencies by lowering its rates. But when the Bundesbank reduced key rates by only 0.25 percent on Monday, foreign-exchange markets concluded that it was not sufficient, and the attack on the pound stepped up.

Today, announcing Britain's temporary withdrawal from the community's linked currency system, the Chancellor of the Exchequer, Norman Lamont, pointed his finger at the culprits. "As a result of uncertainties caused by the French referendum," he said, "massive speculative flow have continued to disrupt the functioning of the exchange-rate mechanism."

After the Bank of England had raised interest rates by five percentage points in two stages earlier in the day to sustain the pound, speculators no longer believed that the British currency could avoid devaluation.

With the shadow of the French referendum hanging over the community, exchange markets are certain to remain unstable.

It is not clear whether today's sterling crisis will have any effect on the result of the French vote. After German interest rates were slightly lowered on Monday, Finance Minister Michel Sapin held out the carrot of lower French interest rates—if voters say yes on Sunday.

Supporters of the European union treaty have insisted that the current crisis is itself proof of the need for a single currency, arguing that without competing currencies, community governments would not have to engage in interest-rate wars.

France also sees a single currency managed by a regional central bank as the best way of breaking the Germans' grip on its monetary policy. In other words, as only one of several countries represented in a regional central bank, Germany would presumably be unable to impose its will on the community.

For this very reason, many senior Bundesbank officials are less than enthusiastic about a single currency. And if France approves the union treaty, German concern about "losing" the mark seems certain to surface when the treaty comes up for ratification in Parliament this fall.

If France rejects the treaty, however, most financial experts anticipate a new wave of currency speculation, perhaps against the French franc, as well. And in that case, the only way of restoring market stability could be to carry out a broader realignment of currencies within the exchange-rate mechanism—something European governments are eager to avoid.

* * *

September 18, 1992

CRISIS HITS EUROPEANS IN THEIR POCKETBOOKS

By ALAN COWELL
Special to The New York Times

ROME, Sept. 17—After the week's high drama and big talk, millions of Europeans faced the icy realization today that the mystifying crisis on their money markets had come down to something alarmingly simple: cancel the dinner reservation, forget the theater tickets, postpone the vacation and don't even begin to think about the new compact sedan in the dealership.

With some obvious exceptions—Germans shielded by their invincible marks and tour operators and exporters praying for a slice of them—many sense that this week's devaluation of the British pound, the Italian lira and the Spanish peseta will push up their inflation rates, make imports and foreign travel more expensive and bring them up short against tough options.

And, for all the politicians' talk of Europe's very destiny being molded in a crucible of big money and gung-ho speculation, the concerns, particularly of middle-class Europeans, seemed far more to reflect the worry that life's little extras—the very stuff of comfort and status—risked becoming life's burdens.

Fewer Dinners in Restaurants

"I'll stop going out for dinner and learn how to cook and stay home more," said Luigi Antonelli, a 35-year-old engineer in Rome. "And I'll have to avoid superfluous things like the cinema and the theater."

José Paniagua, a 52-year-old Spaniard dealing in imported French cars, said: "This is the biggest crisis in my entire business career. My business has been doing badly for two years, but this is the coup de grace. Customers will not want to buy now, because they are worried about the economy. People will rather wait and see before buying a new car or even a good used one. This is a disaster."

Referring to the complexities of the European Exchange Rate Mechanism, Dominic Gray, a 32-year-old camera store manager in London, said: "The E.R.M.? I haven't the faintest idea how it works. I haven't a clue. But I know bad news when I see it."

Interviews with people in Rome, Paris, London, Madrid and Bonn suggested that like Mr. Gray many found the inner workings of the fickle currency markets incomprehensible but understood only too well the impact on their pocketbooks.

On Wednesday, for instance, the British authorities raised interest rates twice before reducing them again today to their old level of 10 percent. The alarm was instantaneous, because British mortgages for home purchases, unlike those in the United States, are instantly adjustable to prevailing interest rates.

Effect on Mortgages

"My daughter was on the phone yesterday asking me: 'What are we going to do? How are we going to pay the mortgage?' " Wendy Kehoe said at a leather goods store in London. The British, she said, understand the effect of increases in interest rates "much better than exchange mechanisms or parity or whatever."

Nick Nicolaides, a tax accountant in London, said: "I couldn't believe my ears when I heard what had happened with interest rates. I thought they had gotten caught up in some sort of Monopoly game. Let's raise rates by 2 percent, 5 percent. Who cares?"

While people in Britain seemed relieved at the subsequent reduction in interest rates, many still felt that the current economic slide, long predating the turmoil on the exchange markets, was far from over.

"The economy has been going steadily down," said Mark Galvin, a 25-year-old British bicycle messenger. "You'd think it would get better. But then things like yesterday happen."

If he seemed resigned, some veered closer to the apocalyptic. "It's going to make me re-evaluate all my plans, my decision to start a family," said Gianpiero Mazzoni, a 33-year-old engineer in Rome. "I've just married, and I couldn't have chosen a worse time, a more negative climate, and that's a drama.

"My daily life will be hardest hit. I won't be able to change cars. I'll go less to the theater, to the movies, out for dinner. I've even decided to stop smoking."

The Eye of the Monetary Storm

The crisis on the money markets was touched off by uncertainty over the outcome of Sunday's referendum in France on European unity. Yet, in Paris, at the epicenter of the crisis, currency markets have not moved significantly, and attention is far more focused on Sunday's vote than on the turmoil it has unleashed.

"All these things are above me," said Pierre Levi, a drugstore owner near the Paris Opera. "I don't understand anything of these matters. There are no changes so far. And it's hard to predict."

If Europe's cloud has a kind of silver lining, it is denominated in dollars and German marks. "Americans make up a large portion of my clientele and they will now have larger purchasing power, so for my business it's good news, but for the country in general it's bad," said Miguel Bajo at his souvenir store in Madrid opposite the Prado museum.

At an American Express office in Madrid, Maria Angeles Juan said, "It's been a madhouse this morning with all the tourists cashing in dollars at a higher rate."

Spanish exporters of luxury goods like marble and sparkling champagne seemed overjoyed at the devaluation of their currency, because it meant that their goods would be cheaper for foreign buyers. "We are delighted with the news," said José Ferrer Sala, the chairman of Spain's largest sparkling wine producer.

In Germany, Glee and Caution

The glee extended to Germany, too.

"The German tourist and consumer has the last laugh," said Helmut Wienholt, a German business spokesman in Cologne. "The stronger the mark, the more favorable it is for us to buy abroad."

The mark's strength against the dollar, while it hurts German exporters by making their products more expensive, could well bring some windfalls to Americans. "It may be that people will take an autumn holiday in the Dolomites in Italy," a travel specialist in Munich said. "But Los Angeles, San Francisco and Miami are the real hot destinations for winter holidays."

Reflecting their country's familiarity with their buying power in other European lands, several Germans in random interviews on the streets of Bonn said the devaluations would not really make much difference to them, and some worried that they might be seen as exploiters if they vaunted their wealth.

"I wouldn't make use of the difference in currency rates for something like a shopping trip, because I see Europe as a unity," said Helga Payerle, a 40-year-old bank teller in Bonn. "It would not be correct to milk the system."

But there seemed little doubt from interviews in other European countries that the mark's strength and the German central bank's effort to keep it strong had fueled old resentments of Bonn's economic power—or at least had inspired some dark humor about it.

"Do you know how to speak German?" one man was overheard asking the conductor on a London bus today. "No," replied the conductor.

"Well, you'd better learn, because they'll be running the country soon," the other man said.

*   *   *

September 18, 1992

I.M.F. CHIEF DEFENDS CENTRAL BANKERS

By STEVEN GREENHOUSE
Special to The New York Times

WASHINGTON, Sept. 17—The head of the International Monetary Fund went to bat today for central bankers humiliated by this week's crisis in European currency markets, asserting that the underlying reason for the chaos was less-than-stellar policy making by elected officials.

In a news conference, Michel Camdessus, the fund's managing director, singled out Germany's Government, saying its failure to rein in its huge budget deficit had virtually forced its central bank to raise interest rates.

And in an interview with a French newspaper, he urged the United States to play a more active role in calming Europe's market turbulence. Recognizing the powerful role the United States plays in the world economy, he said, "You cannot stabilize international markets without the cooperation of the United States."

'Not Enough on the Budget Side'

The high German rates had forced other European countries, many of them in or near recession, to raise their rates to keep their currencies from falling against the mark. This week, despite large-scale central-bank intervention, the British pound, Italian lira and Spanish peseta, under the attack of currency speculators, had to be devalued.

"If we went through these tensions, it's probably because not enough was done on the budgetary side," Mr. Camdessus said.

He spoke two days before the world's central bankers and finance ministers gather here for the annual meeting of the International Monetary Fund and World Bank. He also spoke two days before a meeting of Group of Seven finance ministers in Washington.

Asked whether Germany's central bank, the Bundesbank, has been too tough in raising its key rates above 9 percent to cut inflation, Mr. Camdessus responded: "I wouldn't say that. I would say that too much burden has been put on them."

Mr. Camdessus insisted that the European currency crisis could end up strengthening Europe's system of fixed exchange rates rather than weakening it.

"In spite of the formidable turmoil of the last few days, the system has once again demonstrated its remarkable resilience," he said.

In the interview with the French newspaper Les Echos, Mr. Camdessus asserted that the crisis in Europe stemmed in large part from the huge gap between America's low interest rates and Germany's stratospheric rates.

This gap pushed the mark so high that it became difficult for other European countries to keep their rates linked to the German currency. He criticized America's huge budget deficit, saying that because the deficit made it difficult for Washington to use fiscal policy to stimulate the economy, the burden fell on the Federal Reserve to keep cutting rates.

U.S. Emphasizes Growth

With the United States economy anemic for the last three years, the Bush Administration has been pressing other industrial nations to put more emphasis on growth. In a news briefing today, David C. Mulford, Under Secretary of the Treasury, said he welcomed this week's currency devaluations as well as Monday's interest rate cut by the German central bank, saying they would help spur economic expansion worldwide.

Mr. Mulford said this week's actions showed the Europeans were finally backing the American approach.

The week's decisions in Europe "were very, very important," he said.

"They reflect a recognition of the consensus that has been building—the United States has been promoting these views for about a year and a half now—of the importance of strengthening world growth."

He said he was optimistic that Germany's central bank would cut rates again. "As you look forward, I think you can say that in due course in Germany, we will look forward to lower interest rates," he said. "That's clearly the signal that they've sent." He added that the timing of that was "a complex matter."

Mr. Mulford said the United States had been "relatively unaffected" by Europe's currency crisis, although he expressed concern that turmoil in currency markets could spill over into other financial markets. But he said Europe again was stabilizing, so there was "a minimum of risk" for such financial market turmoil.

He said that at Saturday's Group of Seven meeting, the finance ministers would discuss developments in currency markets, as well as ways to spur world growth, help the developing world, and aid the former Soviet bloc as it adopted a market economy.

The seven ministers will meet with Russia's Deputy Prime Minister, Alexandr Shokhin, to discuss that nation's economic reforms, and they will also debate a plan to grant large-scale debt relief to Russia.

As Mr. Camdessus described it, the agenda for next week's I.M.F.-World Bank meeting will largely overlap that of the

Group of Seven meeting. At the I.M.F. session, ministers will discuss how to end the economic doldrums in the industrialized world, how to help the former Communist world stabilize and grow, and, in his words, how to "consolidate and generalize the progress we observe in many developing countries."

Mr. Camdessus complained that many industrial countries had not pursued their commitments to get their economic houses in order. The I.M.F.'s World Economic Outlook, a semiannual report that was issued Wednesday, criticized the United States, Germany, Britain and Italy for not doing nearly enough to reduce their deficits. He said the large deficits were placing too much weight on central banks to run economic policy.

I.M.F. officials say the large deficits are slowing growth worldwide by pushing up long-term interest rates and by diverting money for consumption that could be used for private investment to build for the future.

*   *   *

September 18, 1992

MONETARY ACCORD SOUGHT IN EUROPE BUT CRISIS REMAINS

By RICHARD W. STEVENSON
Special to The New York Times

LONDON, Sept. 17—A day after the near-collapse of Europe's system of economic coordination, the currency markets stabilized today and European officials reiterated their pledges to seek closer monetary cooperation.

But as these officials wait uneasily for France's vote on the European unification treaty on Sunday, few ideas have emerged to solve the problem that pushed the system into crisis in the first place: By keeping its interest rates high to hold down inflation as it borrows huge sums to pay for its own unification, Germany has made it increasingly difficult for other nations to stimulate their economies out of prolonged slumps.

Limits to Coordination

Speculators who spotted these stresses pushed the system beyond its capabilities, demonstrating the limits to economic coordination.

Germany's central bank failed to ease the pressure on its neighbors by declining to cut interest rates further today, after its minimal reduction on Monday. Few had expected Germany to provide any easy solutions, even after Britain suspended its participation in the monetary system on Wednesday. That decision effectively led to a sharp drop in the pound's value.

Nonetheless, Germany's continued adherence to tight money policies seemed certain to bring additional pressures on it at the annual financial summit meeting of industrial nations in Washington this weekend.

Markets Calm Down

The currency markets stabilized this afternoon after they strained the limits of European cooperation this week by pushing the British pound, the Italian lira and the Spanish peseta below their agreed-upon values in the European Monetary System. But traders today then turned toward other vulnerable currencies.

Italy joined Britain today in withdrawing from the European Monetary System, following an emergency meeting of European Community officials in Brussels early this morning. And Spain said it would reduce the value of its currency. Under the monetary system, European nations had pledged to keep the values of their currencies stable relative to each other.

Italy said it hoped to rejoin the system on Tuesday. Britain also said it planned to rejoin the system, although it was vague about the timing.

But doubts persisted about whether Europe can or should bring the 11 members of its exchange-rate agreement back together again. That program is the first big step toward the creation of a unified market with a single currency and a single monetary policy. Greece is the only one of the 12 members of the European Community not to participate in the exchange-rate agreement.

Added Flexibility

Economists said Britain would have to consider remaining outside of the monetary system for an indefinite period, despite its rhetoric about rejoining as soon as the time is right. They said that by not rejoining immediately, Britain would gain the added flexibility of not having to keep interest rates high to defend the pound against the mark. Lower rates could help Britain break out its longest recession since World War II.

This morning, Britain rescinded the two-point interest rate increase that it imposed on Wednesday, bringing its benchmark lending rate back to 10 percent. Hours later, it announced that unemployment had reached 9.9 percent, its highest level in five years.

"If Britain goes back into the exchange-rate mechanism, the cost will be high interest rates for some time," said David Currie, director of the Center for Economic Forecasting at the London Business School. "The Government has to wonder if that's the right policy. They might instead stand aside, let the pound float and cut interest rates to get a recovery."

Attention throughout Europe seemed increasingly focused on the extent to which nations are willing to set aside domestic needs to adhere to the long-term goal of creating a Europe with price stability and burgeoning trade. The immediate answer seemed to be: not much.

German and British officials spent much of the day sniping at each other about the causes of Wednesday's tumult in the currency markets, with Britain complaining that German officials had set off a run on the pound by suggesting it was overvalued.

Analysts said it was increasingly likely that the monetary system could be split into two camps. One, consisting of Germany, the Netherlands and Belgium, might move rapidly toward a single currency and united monetary policy, perhaps along with France. The second group, including Britain,

Italy, Spain and others, might choose or be forced to watch from the sidelines for an indefinite period, participating in the common European market but without the advantage of currency stability.

"The exchange-rate mechanism will probably survive because there's such a huge amount of political capital invested in it," said David Morrison, a foreign exchange analyst at the brokerage firm of Goldman, Sachs & Company. "But the cracks are fairly wide between the core group around Germany and those with currencies like the pound that cannot be expected to come in anytime soon."

There were indications today that the currency turmoil was not over, and that the strains among nations could worsen again.

Like machine gunners who have finished off one set of targets, currency speculators and other investors swiveled today and put a number of other currencies in their sights, including the Irish pound, the Portuguese escudo and the Danish krone. All of them were sold heavily in foreign exchange markets as traders bet that they would be devalued.

The Spanish peseta also dropped under heavy selling pressure, suggesting that it might have to be devalued again.

And economists said that if France rejects the unification treaty on Sunday, the franc would immediately face pressure for devaluation.

Following a sharp drop in the morning, the British pound stabilized in value just below 2.65 marks this afternoon in London, or nearly 5 percent below the minimum value it was supposed to maintain as a member of the exchange-rate system.

The lira also leveled off and even gained back some of its value late in the day after the Italian Government announced a plan to slash its huge budget deficit. The lira ended in Europe at about 833 to the mark, down from 826 to the mark on Wednesday.

"It looks as if sterling and the lira have gotten through the worst of what could have been expected," said George Magnus, an economist at S. G. Warburg & Company. "It now behooves the markets to wait and see what happens in the French vote."

*   *   *

September 19, 1992

SOME UNEXPECTED SUSPECTS IN CURRENCY TURMOIL

By JONATHAN FUERBRINGER

Currency traders who have been placing high-risk bets have had a lot to do with the crisis that is rolling through Europe. The word speculator, an accusation in itself, has rolled easily off the lips of finance ministers, like Norman Lamont of Britain, who are looking for scapegoats.

But there is growing evidence that it is the much more conservative institutional investors—the mutual funds, corporations and pension funds—that have humbled the British pound, the Italian lira and the Spanish peseta and helped to

threaten the future of the European Monetary System and economic unity.

These institutions have invested hundreds of billions of dollars in Britain, Italy and Spain, where interest rates are high, on the assumption that the European Monetary System was providing them inexpensive protection against adverse currency fluctuations. The underlying weakness of these currencies, which normally would threaten to wipe out gains from the investments, could be ignored.

But as the European Monetary System crumbled this week the safety of those investments and corporate strategies has been undermined. And the sudden rush of many institutions to protect their investments by buying strong German marks and selling the weaker currencies in Europe—the pound, the lira, and the peseta—may well have provided the weight needed to break the system's back.

"If you add up the funds, it is billions and billions of dollars that trickled in slowly, but they all wanted to get out at once," said Richard Jaycobs, the managing director of Finex, a financial exchange in New York that offers instruments for protecting against currency fluctuations.

Other financial executives offer similar views.

"I think the market is driven by the big investors: the mutual funds, the pension funds, the endowments," said David W. Rossmiller, vice president of international fixed-income management at the Travelers Investment Management Company in Hartford. He said he had contributed to the currency turmoil himself by shifting his strategy earlier this month in a way that forced the selling of the weaker European currencies.

"It is portfolios like these that are really driving the market, and it is the speculators that come in and chase the trend," he added.

Safety Was Attractive

In fact, it appears that it was the very credibility of the European Monetary System, which attracted so much investment money, that helped bring the system down so quickly, market participants said. The system provided a safety net that allowed money managers to take risks that they would not ordinarily consider.

It was taking such risks that allowed mutual funds investing in high-yield short-term investments around the world to pay attractive returns. Such funds were run by big firms like Merrill Lynch in the United States and Lombard Odier in Europe. Corporate treasurers also used the security of the monetary system to reduce their costs. And funds protecting themselves against money-losing currency swings—a practice known as hedging—also depended on the European Monetary System.

"They would never have dreamed of taking these risks," Matthew Daniel, manager of financial markets at Union Carbide, said. "Why did they? They had the safety net of the European Monetary System under them. Now that has been blown out of the water."

Indeed, the breakdown has changed all these equations. "It was the strength of the system that had sucked in so much money," said David Smart of Fiduciary Trust in London. "And now it had brought about the potential demise of the system."

At the heart of this currency crisis is a practice in the arcane world of currency risk management called proxy hedging.

For example, a rise in the dollar cuts the gain from foreign bonds when the foreign currency earnings are translated back into dollars. To protect those gains, an investor who put $50 million in British bonds might try to offset the risk of a falling pound by selling an equivalent amount of pounds for dollars when the investment was made.

But because of the stability of the European Monetary System, a trader did not have to hedge in the same currency as the investment, but could use a stronger currency, like the mark; that is the practice of proxy hedging. The attraction was that short-term interest rates in Germany were lower than in Italy or Britain, which made the cost of hedging in marks cheaper than in pounds. Theoretically there was little risk because the monetary system made the mark and other currencies move within set trading ranges of each other, and that limited the potential losses.

Arthur Zeikel, the president of Merrill Lynch Asset Management, said this opportunity made the global income funds possible. In discussing the rupture of the system this week—and the losses for his fund and others—he sounded like a man whose faith had been betrayed. Without the insurance of the monetary system, his costs of operating will rise sharply.

"By doing cross-hedging and capturing the disparity in interest rates, you create a fund with less volatility and higher return," he said, adding, "In my lexicon, risk and volatility are synonymous."

Corporate treasurers and other fund managers who had also used such techniques were forced to unwind their positions last week, adding to the downward pressure on Europe's weak currencies.

Mr. Rossmiller of Travelers and Thomas J. Berger, a director of Lombard Odier International Portfolio Management Ltd. in London, both made such shifts recently. Mr. Berger, who manages the $1 billion Blanchard Short-Term Global Income Fund, got out of his proxy hedges in early September, as the pressure began to build.

"The speculators may be driving the train but we had to get on to be prudent," he said.

* * *

September 20, 1992

INDUSTRIAL NATIONS STRIVE TO RESOLVE CRISIS ON CURRENCY

By STEVEN GREENHOUSE
Special to The New York Times

WASHINGTON, Sept. 19—Finance ministers and central bankers of the leading industrial countries met here for more than seven hours today, searching for a way out of Europe's currency crisis and forging contingency plans in case the financial markets erupt again on Monday.

A Global Agenda

Saturday (Washington)
Finance ministers of the U.S. and its major allies – the Group of Seven – opened talks in Georgetown, focusing on recent turmoil in Europe.

The Group of 24 developing nations met, and asked developed nations to buy more of their goods.

Today (France)
The French vote on the Maastricht treaty, a major step toward a single European currency.

Monday (New York)
The foreign ministers of the Group of Seven meet at the United Nations. The French vote and how to restore unity in Europe are on the agenda.

Markets in Japan, Europe and the United States are expected to react to the French vote.

Tuesday and Wednesday (Washington)
The International Monetary Fund opens meetings. Topics include Europe, the developing world, aid to Russia and other ex-Soviet republics.

In a brief communiqué after the meeting, the officials gave no clear indication of whether Germany had agreed to lower its interest rates further, as many countries have pressed it to do.

But eyes were on France as much as Germany as the ministers sequestered themselves at Dunbarton House, a 200-year-old mansion in Georgetown surrounded by a high brick wall that is the headquarters of the National Society of the Colonial Dames of America.

Narrow Vote Seen in France

French citizens will vote on Sunday on a single European currency and other bold steps toward European unity, and the vote is expected to be close. Foreign exchange traders predict that a rejection of the Maastricht Treaty will bring the franc and other European currencies under heavy fire, just as the Italian lira and British pound were driven down in value this week.

In contrast to the harsh words exchanged on Friday by British and German leaders, Norman Lamont, Britain's Chancellor of the Exchequer, took pains after today's meeting not to criticize Germany.

"Everybody is of the view that we would like, including the Germans, that we would like in time to see lower interest rates," he told reporters.

Germans Vow to Hold Firm

German officials continued to insist this evening that they and the nation's central bank, the Bundesbank, would not be swayed by outside pressures. "These decisions have to be taken on the basis of sound economic policy," said Horst Kohler, Under Secretary of Germany's Finance Ministry.

The communiqué included a clear signal of a preference for lower rates. The group noted that several countries had recently lowered interest rates and said, "These measures will strengthen the global economic recovery and foster greater stability of exchange markets."

By all accounts, this meeting of the Group of Seven, scheduled months before the European currency system exploded this week, was a calm one. American officials said they firmly made their views known about why they favored lower interest rates; German officials said they firmly responded why they did not think that was appropriate.

This afternoon, President Bush invited the ministers and bankers from two dozen industrial and developing countries to a Sunday meeting at the White House, making the most of an opportunity to demonstrate global leadership during his re-election campaign. Administration officials have made clear that they think the United States has much more to fear from European fragmentation than from European consolidation.

Problems With the System

At the center of the talks here was the 11-nation European Monetary System, created in 1979 to link exchange rates in order to eliminate fluctuations and to provide a stability that would encourage trade, investment and growth.

Germany's high interest rates have forced other nations to keep their rates high to prevent their currencies from sliding in value against the mark. But these higher rates hurt investment and growth in Europe. On Monday, the Bundesbank cut its main interest rate by a quarter point, the first such reduction in five years. But the move left intact the large spread between German and American interest rates, and Britain decided on Wednesday to suspend its participation in the monetary system and let the value of its pound be determined by market forces. A day later, Italy dropped out.

For all the criticism of Germany's interest rates, few nations came to the table with clean hands. The United States, for example, faced renewed pressure to cut its $320 billion annual Federal budget deficit, which other nations complain pushes up long-term interest rates around the world.

After the meeting today, Finance Minister Michel Sapin of France said, "The American problem is its budget deficit." He said American officials had said "nothing very precise" about their plans.

As for the United States, Treasury Secretary Nicholas F. Brady said, "There was broad recognition that measures to strengthen recovery would also further greater exchange-market stability."

Among the contingency plans being discussed here are further devaluations of some currencies, buying of currencies by central banks to bolster weak currencies, changes in fiscal policies and even a wholesale change in the structure of Europe's system of fixed exchange rates.

American officials said they wanted today's meeting to give new impetus to international economic cooperation. That was the buzzword of the late 1980's as nations agreed to coordinate interest rates and exchange rates, helping to fuel a period of unusual growth and stability. The golden moment of economic cooperation came in the Plaza Accord of 1985, when James A. Baker 3d, then the Treasury Secretary, now the head of President Bush's re-election campaign, orchestrated an international effort to bring down the dollar from its stratospheric heights.

For the last two years, however, cooperation has largely broken down, with the Group of Seven—the United States, Britain, Canada, France, Germany, Italy and Japan—adopting vastly different and often conflicting economic policies.

While the Americans and British say Germany's high rates are hurting growth, Helmut Schlesinger, the president of Germany's central bank, has repeatedly argued that high rates are needed to reduce German inflation to 2 percent from its current 3.5 percent rate. Germany's large budget deficit, which has fueled inflation there, is mostly a result of the high costs of German unification. The Government is spending $122 billion this year to help rebuild eastern Germany.

Up in Germany, Down in U.S.

To counter inflationary pressures, the Bundesbank has pushed its most important interest rate to 9.5 percent. At the same time, in Washington, the Federal Reserve Board has adhered to easy-money policies, pushing rates down to 3 percent in the hope of stimulating borrowing and investing and reviving the American economy.

"The Group of Seven has been in total disarray for at least a couple of years," said C. Fred Bergsten, director of the Institute for International Economics, a Washington research group.

One concession Germany could be seeking is for the United States to ease its tough stance in the world trade talks in Geneva. The United States has been combatively demanding that the Europeans drastically reduce their subsidies to farmers, an issue that has produced a deadlock in the talks.

The Bundesbank might gain some leeway to cut rates because further devaluations by other nations could be in the offing. When Germany's trading partners devalue their currencies, that helps hold down inflation in Germany because it makes imports cheaper.

A factor behind Germany's large budget deficit is its substantial aid to Eastern Europe and the former Soviet Union, so Bonn might press its allies to carry more of the load. It might also demand reciprocal deficit-reduction pledges from other big-deficit countries—the United States, Britain and Italy.

Thatcher Backs British Pullout

Margaret Thatcher, John Major's predecessor as Prime Minister, said at a conference in Washington today that Britain should not re-enter the European Monetary System, and she praised Mr. Major for withdrawing. She argued that the system had a "perverse alchemy" that was strangling growth and was "a grave obstacle to economic progress."

Whatever the results of Sunday's vote in France, several officials predicted that the European Monetary System could be substantially changed.

Finance ministers from the 12 countries of the European Community are scheduled to meet here late Sunday to discuss their next steps.

Some say the Group of Seven might push for a slimmer system that would include just five nations, probably Germany, France, Belgium, Luxembourg and the Netherlands.

Countries with high inflation, like Spain and Italy, would not be included, freeing them from the need to raise their rates to keep their currencies from plunging against the mark.

*   *   *

September 27, 1992

THE U.S. ISN'T IMMUNE TO GLOBAL CHAOS

By MADIS SENNER

When European financial markets plunged into chaos two weeks ago, the world glimpsed firsthand the awesome power investors and speculators can wield across borders. The United States should take note.

Within hours, speculators forced Italy to devalue the lira by 8 percent while Britain was forced to raise its prime lending rate by five percentage points in a three-day period and to sell 25 percent of its dollar reserves to save its currency from free fall. Sweden was forced to raise its overnight lending rate to 500 percent to prevent foreign and domestic capital outflows. Last week Spain slapped restrictions on trading in the peseta.

Fear that European monetary coordination would not survive triggered the activity in the currency markets. But regardless of what started the activity, the more ominous aspect is that it was an unpredictable chain reaction fueled by a mob mentality among global capital traders. At the slightest loss of confidence in their capital placements, investors fled and speculators sold short.

The United States has so far been a beneficiary of the chaos because investors fled to the traditional safe haven of the dollar. Interestingly, however, the American bond market has benefited only slightly, a marked departure from the past. This is a strong indicator of future capital-market trends.

In the 1980's, foreign investors began a process of global diversification by investing in financial markets around the world. By the end of the decade the United States was the big winner as foreigners poured more than $750 billion into American investments, allowing Washington to run huge deficits.

Since then, the supply-demand relationship for global capital has changed drastically. Japan is no longer the exporter of capital that it once was, and Germany has become a leading capital importer, running deficits as it absorbs its eastern half. Not only has the supply-demand equation changed, but the process of globalization—which initially benefited the United States—is maturing, with emerging markets competing for funds.

The world's currency speculators are watching the American Presidential campaign as closely as they watched the French referendum on European unity. If the traders, with their mob mentality, perceive the policies of President Bush and Gov. Bill Clinton as quick fixes that will lead to still higher deficits, the fiscal integrity of the United States could be brought into question. In light of the fickle nature of these global investors, there could be a move to dump the dollar as quickly as there was a move to buy it just before the French

vote. A sell-off of dollars could trigger a sell-off of stocks and bonds, which could lead American investors to move their money overseas. If that happened, the Federal Reserve, following Sweden's example, would be forced to raise interest rates to stop huge capital outflows, which would plunge the economy back into recession.

The chaos in Europe should teach Mr. Bush and Mr. Clinton that the global nature of the world's financial markets no longer allows politicians the luxury of quick fixes. Monetary and fiscal policy must be set in a global context and foreign investors' interests must be kept in mind. Quick-fix stimulus will only provoke fear among traders and lead to massive capital outflows. The world's currency speculators want government policies that are prudent. They will hold dollars as long as inflation is low and there is progress in bringing down the Federal deficit.

Madis Senner is a global bond manager at Chase Manhattan Private Bank in New York.

*   *   *

September 28, 1992

HIGH NOON IN EUROPE'S CURRENCY STANDOFF

By PETER PASSELL

"I will fight, we will fight, France and Germany will fight," vowed Michel Sapin, France's Finance Minister, as he declared war last week on speculators who were betting that a French franc would soon buy fewer German marks.

If Mr. Sapin seemed overwrought, it was understandable. The stability of the exchange rate between the franc and the mark had, for better or worse, come to symbolize the stability of the French-German alliance. And those who expected the franc to crack under pressure as easily as the British pound or the Italian lira did were clearly mistaken.

But for all the resolute words, there is still some reason to doubt the lock will hold. Defending a fixed exchange rate, even one that by all accounts reflects the relative values of the two currencies, can be very costly. And while France and Germany apparently have had the financial muscle to fend off the speculators so far, it is not clear even they would have the will to sacrifice jobs and output to manage the feat for any prolonged period.

Most countries, most of the time, allow the "price" of their currencies in terms of others to be set much the way supply and demand determine the price of bananas. And in the long run, exchange rates between currencies roughly track the relative value.

But the emphasis is on "long" and "rough." Businesses that depend on imports or sell much of what they make abroad crave certain knowledge of what exchange rates will be next week, next month and next year.

Governments have their own reason for preferring a currency lock: an obligation to sustain a fixed exchange rate justifies the sacrifices needed to hold down domestic inflation. That largely explains why Europe, led by France and Germany, has invested so much political capital in the European Monetary System.

But the work of a decade went up in smoke just days earlier as holders of Italian lire and British pounds rushed to profit—or to avoid losses—by exchanging tens of billions of dollars' worth of the two currencies for German marks. France and Germany have the means to resist a similar run on the franc, if it resumes. The issue, in the end, is whether they have the stomach.

Limit to Reserves

France's first line of defense is to buy francs with foreign currency it holds in reserve, much the way Washington supports the price of wheat by purchasing the commodity from growers. France did indeed buy francs this week. But there is a limit to its reserves, and after a week of heavy outlays the cupboard is nearly bare.

The Bundesbank, keeper of the German currency, is under no such constraint. It can create as many marks as it wishes and use them to buy francs. Can—and has: the Bundesbank reportedly purchased more than $10 billion worth of francs in three days.

There is, however, a cost to this defense. Marks sold for francs end up as private deposits in German banks, swelling the amount of money circulating in Germany.

Germany has methods for offsetting this undesired—and potentially inflationary—growth in the money supply. But Richard Cooper, an economist at Harvard, points out that its methods are crude compared with those routinely used in the United States by the Federal Reserve. The Fed, unlike the Bundesbank, owns enormous quantities of Government securities that it can buy and sell and in the process increase or decrease the quantity of money held in private bank accounts.

And there is thus a real risk that the inflation-phobic Bundesbank will be unable to "sterilize" the inflow of cash, generating self-fulfilling expectations that the cost of living will rise.

Raising Interest Rates

An alternative to direct intervention on behalf of the franc is to raise the price of speculation. Higher interest rates make it more attractive to keep cash in France. More important, higher rates increase the cost of borrowing francs in order to exchange them for marks.

Sweden used this approach two weeks ago, with great success.

The catch is that it takes very, very high rates to change incentives very much. A speculator who borrowed francs at a 12 percent rate would be paying just 1 percent of his money to gamble that the franc would fall in value within a month. That is why Sweden briefly raised its rate to 500 percent—no misprint—in order to deter speculation.

The interest rate weapon is thus the bluntest weapon of all, a doomsday machine. It can deter only if speculators believe the French Government will, in the end, be willing to shut down all businesses dependent on borrowed money.

Germany might give speculators reason to think twice by lowering its interest rate by a more modest amount—say a percentage point. That would not change the arithmetic of gain and loss to speculation very much, but might well convince speculators that the Bundesbank was serious about defending the franc.

The catch is that the symbol cuts two ways. While it would show the Bundesbank's resolve to back France, it would undermine the bank's take-no-prisoners stance against inflation in Germany. It was, after all, the Bundesbank's stubborn resistance to a cut in German interest rates that set off the European currency crisis in the first place.

The last weapon against speculators is currency controls. This week Spain imposed one form, a requirement that banks lending pesetas to foreigners deposit an equal sum with the Government in an account that pays no interest. This raised the cost of speculating against the peseta without raising the cost of borrowing for other purposes.

Would something similar work for France? Perhaps, though not nearly as well. Virtually all pesetas are in Spanish banks. But tens of billions of dollars' worth of francs are held outside France, and thus not subject to French currency rules. And in any case, currency controls would amount to a defeat nearly equal to the loss of the fixed exchange rate.

Countries joining the European fixed exchange rate system pledged not to resort to controls because they were viewed as barriers to Europe's economic integration. Indeed, under the Maastricht accord, approved by French voters on Sept. 20, France is legally obliged to eschew currency controls of any sort by the end of 1992.

France and Germany plainly have the weapons at hand to defeat speculators. And if speculators were sure the weapons would be used, the speculation would end. But they can never know that until they have tested the franc to its limits. Neither, presumably, can the French and German Governments, whose resolve must ultimately turn on the fortitude of the electorate.

*   *   *

October 9, 1992

PAPER GAMES AND MONETARY CHAOS

By JOHN RALSTON SAUL

TORONTO—Determined naiveté is the best way to describe the reaction of financial experts to the continuing global monetary crisis. Government bankers, currency traders and economists have generally put forward two childlike scenarios: either there is a battle going on between nations and speculators or the international markets are merely seeking realistic values for local currencies. In both of these scenarios, the billions of dollars spent driving down or propping up money are presented as the natural costs of survival in an uncontrollable global market.

This is a false picture of the currency markets. For a start, there is a profound and passive complicity among the state bankers, ministers of finance, currency traders and speculators. They're almost all middle- to upper-middle-class taxpaying citizens of the Group of Seven, Europe and the Organization for Economic Cooperation and Development. Even offshore speculators could not function without the cooperation of the developed world.

The idea that none of this can be regulated begins with a continuing acceptance of the financial deregulation of the 1980's. Yet that deregulation has produced turmoil and bankruptcy in everything from local banking to world markets. The explosion in new communication technologies is presented as a decisive factor that makes regulation no longer possible. But technology is merely that. Machinery. Inanimate.

It is our technocratic elites who believe that systems and structures are a religion in which technology determines the creed. In the absence of policy and direction, they argue for passivity and the worship of methodology. They are intellectually unable to imagine controlling technology and therefore managing markets.

In the middle of the British pound crisis last month, Milton Friedman wrote in The Wall Street Journal that it was yet another example of why currencies cannot be managed. "How many more fiascos will it take before responsible people . . . are finally convinced that a system of pegged exchange rates is not a satisfactory financial arrangement . . . ."

Mr. Friedman's litany of past fiascos is a comic parody of anarchism. In place of his list of monetary crises you could put military crises and then argue that there is no point in working for peace, because perpetual war and disorder is the natural way to regulate human relationships.

What most of our financial elites turn their backs on is their own failure to deal effectively with an artificial battle between graduates of the same schools and residents of the same cities whose careers are spent throwing large amounts of the citizens' money at one another.

Some economists intentionally misrepresent what it means to peg currencies. The European Monetary System, for example, does not try to freeze currencies at unrealistic levels. Each currency is given a high-low range measured against those of other member countries. The idea is to allow values to rise and fall slowly so as to preserve the confidence needed for society to function without crises.

In truth we are still suffering from President Nixon's destruction in the early 70's of the Bretton Woods system of pegged exchange rates. Created in 1944, it grew to include most currencies outside the Soviet bloc and, although increasingly old-fashioned, survived three decades of global change.

Mr. Nixon could have devoted himself to modernizing and reforming Bretton Woods in the interests of international stability. Instead he chose to solve some of his short-term international debt problems by scrapping it altogether, leaving currencies no choice but to "float" against one another in a market where the initiative lay with speculators and others

seeking short-term profits. In what was perhaps the single most destructive act of the postwar period, the West was returned to the monetary barbarism and instability of the 19th century.

Attempts at reform such as the European Monetary System are hampered because they regulate only part of the West. This facilitates speculative runs from other Western countries, which in turn encourage speculation from within Europe itself. The question therefore is not whether the European Monetary System can work but whether a looser version of its principles could be applied to the O.E.C.D. as a whole.

As for deregulation, it has merely encouraged the inflation of financial markets to as much as a trillion dollars a day. These sums bear no relationship to real economic activity. They represent an artificial paper game. Those players who are involved but are also attached to the real world—corporate treasurers and fund managers—must follow the lead of the speculators for fear of losing their organizations' money.

It is a curious contemporary paradox that management, in its modern, self-directing but directionless incarnation, is far too important to be left to managers. Our governments cannot hope to create and maintain systems to stabilize currencies unless they concentrate on how to manage both modern technology and our own technocratic elites.

The crisis in Europe last month was in fact an attack against the very idea of Europe. Without the European Monetary System, the Maastricht treaty is meaningless. In that sense, the recent financial speculation could be interpreted as a political act to protect and prolong not global markets but global monetary disorder.

To deal with this internal undermining of the West, we must first recognize that it is indeed internal, that is national and not global. To pretend that the money markets are the prisoners of technology and cannot be managed is a form of willful ignorance which amounts to masochism.

John Ralston Saul is author, most recently, of "Voltaire's Bastards—The Dictatorship of Reason in the West."

* * *

July 31, 1993

EUROPEAN SYSTEM TYING CURRENCIES FACES A RUPTURE

By ROGER COHEN
Special to The New York Times

PARIS, July 30—The European Monetary System, the cornerstone of exchange-rate stability within the European Community since 1979, was threatened with extinction today after speculators decided that France could no longer defend its currency and mounted an all-out attack on the franc.

The battle, pitting currency traders against both the French and German central banks, is especially bitter because it is about a lot more than money. The steady exchange rate in recent years between the German mark and French franc has come to symbolize the strength of the French-German alliance and Europe's aspirations toward greater monetary and political union.

But today the parity between the two currencies appeared on the verge of collapse—a development that would destroy the vestigial credibility of the European Monetary System and make a mockery of Europe's plans for further integration.

Franc Falls to Its Limit

Despite the Bundesbank's huge outlays to support the franc by buying it—currency dealers in London said the German central bank spent about $8.6 billion today—the French currency plunged to its floor of 3.4305 francs to the mark before rising very slightly by the end of trading in Europe. In New York late today, the franc-mark rate was right at the 3.4305 floor, or the equivalent of 0.2915 franc to the mark.

Under the monetary system's rules, a currency's floor is the lowest limit at which the currency is permitted to trade. The system sets broadly stable rates, and currencies are allowed to fluctuate only within a narrow band.

Stocks Drop in U.S.

Investors pushed up stock prices in Paris, Madrid and London on the assumption that interest rates will fall outside Germany, inducing an economic recovery. But stocks fell in Frankfurt as disappointed investors digested the Bundesbank's action. The flow of money into European markets also hurt share prices in the United States. The Dow Jones industrial average fell 27.95 points, to 3,539.47.

And panicked investors seeking a safe place for cash amid turmoil in the currency market rushed to buy gold, pushing prices to levels not seen in nearly three years.

By the close of trading in New York, gold for current delivery closed at $407 an ounce, up $9.20.

Money also moved to the Japanese yen, which is seen as a safe haven amid the turmoil. The yen strengthened to about 104 yen to the dollar—a postwar high—before settling late in the day at 104.70.

The attack on the franc came after a decision on Thursday by the Bundesbank to fight German inflation by refraining from a cut in its discount rate. That rate sets a floor on short-term interest rates in Germany and in countries like France whose currencies are closely tied to the mark. Instead, the bank trimmed the Lombard rate, which serves as a ceiling for money market rates.

Those moves signaled to traders that the French Government would not be able to cut interest rates quickly to jump-start its economy and ease pressure on the franc. As a result, currency traders sold francs heavily.

The speculators calculated that France could not long battle a deepening recession and rising unemployment as long as it had to maintain the high interest rates necessary to keep its currency attractive to investors, and so insure the franc's parity with the German mark.

The franc was not the only currency under attack today. The Belgian franc, the Danish krone, the Spanish peseta and

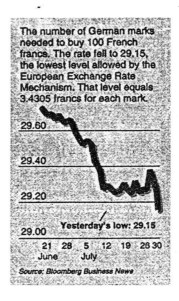

The number of German marks needed to buy 100 French francs. The rate fell to 29.15, the lowest level allowed by the European Exchange Rate Mechanism. That level equals 3.4305 francs for each mark.

Source: Bloomberg Business News

the Portuguese escudo were all pegged at or close to their floors in trading today. Over all, traders estimated that the central banks of Germany, France, Belgium, Denmark, the Netherlands, Spain and Portugal spent about 30 billion marks, or $17.25 billion, supporting the weak currencies.

Traders were virtually unanimous in saying that France would have to seek a devaluation or, more likely, abandon the monetary system as Britain and Italy did almost a year ago. "It's hard to see how the franc can hang on," said J. Paul Horne, the chief economist in Paris for Smith Barney, Harris Upham, the American brokerage firm. "There'll probably be a generalized floating of the European currencies."

Defending 'Le Franc Fort'

There were widespread suggestions from traders that the European Community's monetary committee would meet this weekend to decide on a franc devaluation or on its flotation outside the system. But a spokesman for the German Finance Ministry, Karlheinz von den Driesch, insisted that such talk was "pure speculation" and said the French economy remained fundamentally strong.

The French Government—which has made a defense of "le franc fort," or a strong franc, the cornerstone of its economic policy—vowed to resist. Prime Minister Edouard Balladur said the monetary system continued to function and vowed, "France will not allow anything to be imposed on it." A spokesman for the French central bank, who insisted on anonymity, said, "Franco-German solidarity cannot be abandoned."

But although France and Germany battled shoulder-to-shoulder today, their alliance looked frayed after the Bundesbank precipitated the crisis. But the Bundesbank—an institution that has become, for many European countries, synonymous with stubborn rigidity over the last year—continues to insist that rates cannot fall too quickly as long as inflationary pressures stemming from German reunification have not been tamed.

Indeed, George Soros, the New York financier who made close to $1 billion last year by speculating against the pound before Britain withdrew from the monetary system and allowed the pound to float, said the Bundesbank's decision meant the end of the system.

In a statement released in New York, he said, "It is futile to attempt to protect the European Monetary System by abstaining from trading in currencies when the anchor of the system, the Bundesbank, acts without regard to the interests of other members."

He added, "I think that the system is now going to be broken."

Earlier in the week, before the Bundesbank's decision, Mr. Soros had told Le Figaro, the French daily, that he was not speculating against the franc because he did not want to be accused of destroying the system. That commitment, he made clear today, is now void. For France and Mr. Balladur, the options look bleak: either devalue, which would amount to a political humiliation after vows of resistance, or try to hang on, at potentially devastating further cost to the economy.

The woes of the franc today coincided with an announcement that France's unemployment rose by 44,600 people in June to a record 3.2 million, or 11.6 percent of the work force. The economy continues to slow, and it is now expected to contract by seven-tenths of a percent this year.

In these circumstances, just as in the last American recession, economists believe French interest rates must come down sharply. European rates remain several points higher than those in the United States.

But if the pressure remains on the franc, and France decides once more to stay in the monetary system and try to avoid devaluation, a raising of French rates may well be necessary to make the franc more attractive. Already last week, the Bank of France was obliged to raise overnight rates to 10 percent from 7.75 percent.

A growing number of politicians, including members of the governing centrist and conservative Gaullist parties, argue that this policy amounts to political suicide for Mr. Balladur, the Prime Minister. They say the time has come to break free of the monetary system, devalue, slash interest rates and seek growth that creates jobs.

Britain has followed this sort of course since leaving the monetary system last year and is the one European Community country showing glimmerings of economic growth after a bruising recession.

So far, Mr. Balladur has resisted. Indeed, he has said he would rather resign than devalue. His determination, shared by the Socialist President, Francois Mitterrand, is rooted in a political conviction that France's future lies in an integrated Europe.

Both men therefore see the assault on the franc as, in some ways, an attack by American and British speculators on Europe's plans for union.

The Bank of France's reserves, at the end of last week, stood at $21 billion—higher than economists had expected. So the country may have the means to defend the franc by buying it for a while.

If not, the alternative is either a realignment of the system—which would probably involve a devaluation of the Danish, Belgian, Spanish and Portuguese currencies, as well as the franc—or a French decision to leave the system. Economists say the latter course is more likely because it would give France greater economic freedom and avoid the risk of a renewed assault on the franc at a lower level.

A franc devaluation, however, accompanied by devaluations of other currencies, would at least have the merit of conserving the monetary system, albeit in tenuous form. For if the franc is withdrawn, there will effectively be nothing left, at least for now, of a system that is supposed to lead Europe to a single currency by 1999.

* * *

August 2, 1993

FINANCIER DENIES ROLE IN THE CURRENCY CRISIS

By LOUIS UCHITELLE

While European ministers struggled in Brussels to save the European Monetary System, George Soros lounged by the pool at his Southampton, L.I., home yesterday, portraying himself as an elder statesman among foreign exchange traders and not a speculator out to make another huge profit from a currency crisis.

"Exactly because I don't want to drive the markets crazy, I am not going to say what I am doing," Mr. Soros said in a telephone interview.

For years he has been a hugely successful money manager and investor, but the $1 billion that he reportedly made in just a few days in September by betting against the British pound has turned him into a guru—and his investments are mimicked across the world.

Mr. Soros insisted that whatever he had been doing—if anything—during the latest crisis for the European Monetary System, he did not start doing it until last Friday at noon, New York time. So he had not made any money speculating that the French franc, the victim currency this time, would continue to fall in value. Since Friday noon, he noted, the value of the franc has hardly moved up or down against other currencies.

"I am a great believer in Europe and in having the system, and participants ought to care about preserving the system and not just making a profit for themselves," said Mr. Soros, who grew up in Hungary.

Planning to Stay on L.I.

The 62-year-old financier had told Le Figaro, the French daily, early last week that he had refrained from speculating against the franc because he did not want to destroy the European Monetary System. And with currency traders driving down the value of the franc on Thursday, Mr. Soros went that evening to his Long Island home. He plans to remain there into this week, trying, he said, to be an elder statesman rather than a trader.

The huge sum that he made in a few days last September during an earlier currency crisis has turned George Soros, the Wall Street financier, into a guru—and his investments are mimicked worldwide.

"There has to be a modification of the European Monetary System," Mr. Soros said, referring to the system that ties the value of nine European currencies to one another, with the German mark as the dominant one. "Either there has to be a floating of the currencies or a readjustment of the exchange rates or a broadening of the band" in which each currency can rise or fall.

After hours of deliberation, European finance ministers and central bankers, meeting in Brussels, announced last night that they had agreed to broaden the band. Mr. Soros said he was not impressed.

"The wider band will help the French to lower interest rates, but if they don't lower interest rates now, they will have the worst of all possible worlds, which means currency instability and continued recession," Mr. Soros said.

The British, in fact, lowered rates and devalued the pound last September, after currency traders began to sell pounds in huge amounts, betting that the British currency could not keep pace with the mark, mainly because the Germansresisted lowering interest rates to make their own currency less attractive vis-a-vis the pound. Speculating with huge sums in that selloff, Mr. Soros came away a huge winner.

Further Abstention Unneeded

Until noon last Friday, Mr. Soros and the operations he directs, the Soros Fund Management and the Quantum Fund, had carefully refrained from trying to duplicate the feat. But in a statement issued then in New York, he said that further abstention would be futile because the European Monetary System had been broken by the German failure to concern itself with the needs of its European partners.

Did that answer mean that Mr. Soros had traded since Friday noon or had not? "No comment," he said yesterday.

Did he think that being so influential a trader, he should withdraw from currency markets during crises that threatened the European Community?

"It is my business to trade, it is my role, it is my professional activity," Mr. Soros replied. "I could not carry on managing a fund if I did not take positions in stocks, bonds and currencies. So I took a position in Newmont mines and look what happened."

The Newmont episode, coming in April—seven months after his success with the British pound—made Mr. Soros very acquainted with his new influence. He bought a stake in Newmont Mining, mainly a gold-mining company, and that produced a rally in the price of gold and gold-mining stocks. Also in April he became involved in a British real estate venture, and that set off a rally in British real estate stocks.

Then in June, a Soros letter in The Times of London said the German mark was bound to fall, and it did just that for a while.

Although the Europeans came up with a different solution last night, Mr. Soros said he would prefer for the mark to float, thus helping the Germans through their own economic difficulties as they try to unify the economy of the former East Germany with that of the West.

"I think it is the German mark that should float and not the other currencies," Mr. Soros said, adding that if the mark floated it would probably go up and then come down, "very much as the dollar did during the Reagan Administration."

*   *   *

August 3, 1993

CENTRAL BANKS MAKE IT EASY TO BET BIG ON A SURE THING

By FLOYD NORRIS

Once again, European central banks have given away hundreds of millions, if not billions, of dollars. The recipients were currency traders, speculators and all the others who thought it profitable, or just prudent, to sell overvalued currencies to the central banks.

The latest failure of Europe's attempt to sort-of-fix exchange rates in the face of hostile markets emphasized the profits that can be made, at minimal risk, from currency crises. And it again raised the question of why European governments, which end up paying the losses of their central banks, have been so willing to put up with a system that makes such losses a periodic inevitability.

The swiftness of last week's collapse of the French franc, and to a lesser extent some other European currencies, emphasized just how fast the markets can move. The Bundesbank, the Bank of France and other central banks were reported to have spent up to $40 billion defending the currencies. But that was not enough.

That money was largely spent buying French francs at or near the previous floor rate of 3.4305 francs to the mark. Now all those central banks own francs that late yesterday were trading at about 3.5 francs to the mark. If they sold the francs at that price, the loss to the central banks would be more than $800 million.

The sheer size of the financial markets was shown by the fact that all that intervention could not stem the tide. By late Friday, there was a piling-on as speculators who had not bet against the franc decided it was foolish to stay on the sideline.

And much of the selling of francs came from people who thought they were not speculating, merely hedging. Investors who owned French stocks and bonds wanted to avoid the losses they would suffer from a devaluation of the franc. So they sold francs. So, some think, did some non-European central banks that had held francs as part of their foreign currency reserves.

"The problem was that the risks and rewards were not symmetric," William Dudley, a senior economist at Goldman, Sachs, said. "The possibility of a sizable devaluation had to be weighted against the risk of rather small upward appreciation if the French currency managed to remain within" the limits set in the Exchange Rate Mechanism that the central banks were trying to maintain.

George Soros, the New York money manager who is said to have made $1 billion last year when a similar crisis forced the devaluation of the British pound—thereby becoming a celebrity in much of Europe—began last week by offering the opinion that the franc was fairly valued. But on Friday, he declared that he now felt free to speculate.

Mr. Soros said over the weekend that he had not done any selling of francs before noon Friday, New York time. He would not say what he did after that. But it is clear that there was a lot of selling late Friday, as many speculators sought to exploit the asymmetry noted by Mr. Dudley: when a currency is under siege, there is a "heads-I-win-tails-we-break-even" aspect to the game of currency trading for those selling to the central banks. And the more people who play the game, the less likely it is that tails will come up.

Just how much the central bank intervention cost the governments may never be known. It depends on how much intervention there was, and at what price the central banks unwind their positions. Even now, some think the French currency may strengthen soon because of France's good inflation numbers and trade surplus. But for now, at least, a lot of money has been made by traders at the expense of the central banks.

The crisis erupted after Germany's central bank, the Bundesbank, declined to cut the country's discount rate on Thursday, despite numerous indications that it would do so. The move appeared to have surprised other European central banks as much as it did traders. With France needing lower interest rates to try to get out of recession, the belief quickly spread that a lower franc was inevitable. And that belief became a self-fulfilling prophecy.

In the aftermath, there has been criticism that if the Bundesbank was going to take that step, it might have found a way to warn other central banks and perhaps precipitate the steps that ended up being taken anyway. The result would have been the same, but without the windfall profits for speculators.

"They might have broken out of this before the weekend," said Neal M. Soss, the chief economist at First Boston and a former Federal Reserve official. But he noted that defending a currency can be like a war. "You're so caught up in the transactions of the moment that you don't see where you are being taken."

For now, Europe's Exchange Rate Mechanism is operating with such wide bands of permissible trading—30 percent of value, up from 5 percent before yesterday—that a new crisis is unlikely soon. But if the Europeans hope to revive their system and narrow the bands to move eventually to a single currency, they may want to look for a way to make people believe that the game of speculating in a crisis is not such a sure thing.

In the aftermath, one such tactic suggests itself. Had the Bundesbank turned around over the weekend and cut its discount rate, it would have been criticized for inconsistency and for knuckling under to the markets. But it might also have saved a lot of money for the central banks and persuaded speculators that betting against these banks had some risks.

THE PESO CRISIS

December 23, 1994

BOOM SHOWS ITS DARK SIDE

By TIM GOLDEN
Special to The New York Times

MEXICO CITY, Dec. 22—In the financial capitals of the developed world, a favorite story of Latin American success in recent years was about a closed economy thrown open by bold technocrats trained in the Ivy League. It told of investments pouring in, inflation being vanquished, democracy taking root.

By today, however, the tale that investors called "the Mexico story" had suddenly turned darker.

After the Government announced Wednesday night that it would abandon its defense of the peso and let the currency trade freely against the dollar, Mexicans awoke to a country that most thought had been consigned to their turbulent economic past. It is a place of threatening inflation, recession and myriad uncertainties.

The sudden collapse of the peso was in fact neither so sudden nor so complete. In the long run, some investors said, the economy will have a more solid foundation if the peso can be wrestled down to a more stable, if weaker, level. The three-week-old Government of President Ernesto Zedillo Ponce de León gave just that explanation for its move.

Yet by the awkward handling of an adjustment in the currency that both some Government officials and many of their political opponents have long thought necessary, Mr. Zedillo was seen today as having lost control of the Mexican economy.

The peso's fall has impoverished Mexicans by at least 30 percent in terms of the dollar, jeopardizing the new President's already uncertain mandate. Perhaps worse, Mr. Zedillo appears to have shattered foreign investors' confidence, which was crucial to the country's economic boom.

To many, the amended Mexico story is a cautionary tale. It is about what can go wrong when hopeful foreigners with money get together with the innovative but unsteady managers of what has always been a complex, unwieldy developing country first and an "emerging market" second.

It may also be about former President Carlos Salinas de Gortari's strategy of postponing a democratic opening of the political system until often-unpopular economic reforms are concluded. After a year that has seen a peasant revolt, two political assassinations and a tumultuous election campaign, many Mexicans say economic stability might have been better preserved by more aggressive democratic change.

"They put things off and put things off and put things off," Juan Molinar Horcasitas, a senior official of the federal elections board, said of former President Salinas's determination to postpone many political changes until after the economy had largely been overhauled. "And so they explode."

The notion that Mexico's peso was overvalued against the dollar is hardly new. Economists who warmly praised the restructuring carried out by Mr. Salinas had warned for at least three years that Mexico's trade deficit would force a peso devaluation. As the economy grew, sucking in goods from abroad, it required continuing injections of foreign money to support the spending spree. To preserve the flow of capital, Mexico faced a choice between raising interest rates to levels that might choke off growth and allowing the peso's value to drop.

Two officials said that during the course of this year, some Government economists argued strenuously for a devaluation, only to be blocked by other, more senior officials. The latter were said first to have feared a backlash against the governing party by impoverished voters in the Aug. 21 presidential election, then a stain on the image of Mr. Salinas, 46, a candidate to lead the new World Trade Organization next year.

The peso had a central place in the economic strategy in Mr. Salinas's economic strategy. For the six years of his administration, a stable currency fixed the confidence of foreigners who poured tens of billions of dollars into Mexico.

Most of it the money went into relatively liquid assets like stocks and bonds. But at a time when exports and domestic savings could not sustain the country's growth, the foreign money financed most of the gaping deficit that the Government ran to service its huge international debt and pay for imports.

While interest rates were falling abroad, particularly in the United States, Mexican risks brought extraordinary rewards: in 1991, values on the stock exchange rose an average of 118 percent in dollar terms; two years later, they rose almost 49 percent.

With the ratification of the North American Free Trade Agreement last year, investors cast Mexico in an even more glowing light. Mr. Salinas spoke of a country surging decisively toward the first world; outside of Mexico, particularly, many people believed him. But as the boom faded and stock yields declined, high interest rates became a more crucial lure for foreign capital to cover the current-account deficit. At the same time the high rates became a greater burden for Mexican companies needing credit to grow.

The devaluation of the last few days was intended to resolve the current-account shortfall in part by making Mexican exports cheaper. But by raising the cost of imports in an increasingly open economy, it will also bring immediate inflation.

It also shocked an investment community that had grown trusting in the economic team formed by Mr. Salinas and largely ratified by his hand-picked successor, Mr. Zedillo.

When investors began to cry betrayal after a first effective devaluation of 15 percent on Tuesday, it was not coincidental that many focused their anger on a Mexican official who became well known abroad as an advocate for the trade agreement, former Commerce Secretary Jaime Serra Puche.

In his new job as finance minister, Mr. Serra proved less smooth a salesman. Though devaluations are never announced in advance, many investors appeared to take him at his word when he flatly ruled out the possibility late last week.

After the first adjustment was announced, investors complained that Mr. Serra and other senior officials had misled them when they did not ignore them. And at a moment when the Government was clearly shifting its strategy, many considered it at least farfetched that he would attribute the devaluation to the flight of capital caused by peasant rebels' relatively inconsequential movements in a southern state, Chiapas.

At another level, however, the Zapatista rebels were very much at the source of the devaluation.

At the end of 1993, Mexico boasted more than $25 billion of hard-currency reserves. But that total fell steadily as the Government sought to defend the peso against the pressure of nervous Mexicans and foreigners who took their money out of the country in the face of the political instability stirred by the insurgents and their demand for wider democratic change.

By the time the rebels threatened new fighting last week, Mexico's reserves may have been less than $10 billion, people close to the Government said.

*   *   *

December 23, 1994

WITH PESO FREED, MEXICAN CURRENCY DROPS 20% MORE

By ANTHONY DePALMA
Special to The New York Times

MEXICO CITY, Dec. 22—Mexico's economic crisis deepened, sending the peso plummeting nearly 20 percent further today, after the Government adopted an emergency plan late Wednesday night to allow the currency to trade freely against the American dollar.

The decision to float the peso was made under extreme pressure by the Government of President Ernesto Zedillo Ponce de León, who took office only three weeks ago, to calm financial markets after several days of intense speculation and plunging indexes.

The peso was previously controlled by a trading band that let it fall not much lower than 3.46 pesos to the dollar before the Government intervened.

This floor was dropped on Tuesday to just over 4 pesos to the dollar. But the resulting confusion, which battered Mexican stocks, led the Government Wednesday night to give up and allow the peso to trade freely. Today, the peso closed at 4.80 to the dollar—down almost 30 percent for the week.

The casualties of the devaluation included United States banks, mutual funds and private investors who hold high-interest Mexican treasury notes that are now worth substantially less as a result of the cheaper peso.

Companies that have invested heavily in Mexico reacted with alarm to the peso's plunge. Manufacturers that export to Mexico face losses because those goods became more expensive on paper this week.

Several companies said the sudden devaluation had sorely tested their confidence in the Mexican Government, which had long pledged to defend the currency. Now, some fear that the economy is headed for a period of wage and price inflation, and even the risk of new recession.

Critics of the North American Free Trade Agreement said the peso's steep drop, by making Mexican exports to the United States much more competitive with American goods, would make the United States regret its agreement to freer trade.

Stockholders of Mexican companies were also hurt when values of their shares plunged on the Mexican stock exchange. The depreciation fell hardest on companies that are loaded down with debt that must be paid back in dollars.

The faltering of what had been considered Mexico's textbook economic restructuring, a model copied by other Latin American countries, amplified investor disillusion concerning the resolve and abilities of Mr. Zedillo's economic team and its economic policies.

The Mexican stock market today had one of the year's most erratic trading days, yet made up some of the heavy losses of the last few days with an increase of 4.7 percent at the close. But in New York, Mexican issues traded on the New York Stock Exchange plunged nearly 20 percent.

Many American investors said that they felt misled by President Zedillo's administration, which had tied its currency problems to reports of a renewed offensive by Indian rebels in Chiapas—especially after it became known that the rebels had not made any substantial gains.

The abrupt devaluation also angered investors because the Finance Minister Jaime Serra Puche and other officials had said only last week that the Government saw no need to devalue the peso.

The currency changes will have a profound effect, at least temporarily, on trade between Mexico and the United States. American exports overnight became more expensive, although the Government has ordered that domestic prices be frozen for at least 60 days. But Mexican exports to the United States are expected to enjoy a big boost because the sudden decline in the peso makes them cheaper.

There is usually an export advantage to a currency devaluation, but financial experts believe that Mexico's gains will be threatened as pressure builds to increase wages and the rate of inflation creeps back up.

To help Mexico defend its currency, the United States Treasury and the Federal Reserve today gave it permission to exchange up to $6 billion worth of pesos for an equal sum in dollars, and the Canadian Government authorized an exchange up to $1 billion (Canadian).

Mexico can use the dollars to buy pesos in foreign-currency markets, bidding up the peso's value or at least restraining its fall.

Much of the criticism about the week's events has been directed at Mr. Serra, a Yale-educated economist familiar to many investors as Mexico's chief negotiator for the North American trade pact.

Mr. Serra flew to New York today and met with about 100 investment bankers and analysts to explain his actions and to try to rebuild confidence that was shattered when he announced on Mexican television early Tuesday morning that the peso-to-dollar exchange rate would be increased, still insisting that this was not a devaluation.

"I did not find it convincing," said John F. H. Purcell, managing director of emerging markets research at Salomon Brothers, who attended the meeting today. "I think it's going to take them a very long time, probably the whole of this administration, to regain the confidence of investors."

Mr. Purcell said the audience had expressed "a tremendous amount of hostility and a sense of betrayal."

The peso has been devalued so often over the past three decades that many Mexicans have come to expect it. Several devaluations have come before Christmas or Easter, prompting measured annual runs on the peso at these times. The devaluation in 1982 set off Mexico's debt crisis, which later spread to many Latin American countries.

The trading band for the peso was instituted in 1987 and maintained until it was abandoned yesterday. The band was intended to rebuff deeply rooted public fears by letting the peso slide by a minute daily amount in order to avoid the kind of shock that occurred today.

Some economic experts had insisted that Mexico's peso was overvalued. The peso stunted Mexican exports and added to a crushing trade deficit that could approach $30 billion next year.

Protecting the peso's value also forced the Mexican central bank to push up rates on treasury bonds, sometimes above 18 percent, which some economists believed stunted Mexican economic growth.

Over the last six weeks, such analysts expected the Government to accept the need for devaluation. But former President Carlos Salinas de Gortari and his Finance Minister, Pedro Aspe, refused to do so, leaving the problem for Mr. Zedillo.

When rebels of the Zapatista National Liberation Army threatened to resume hostilities in Chiapas beginning early this month, stock investors, uncertain of Mr. Zedillo's ability to handle the problem, began retreating and dumping their pesos for dollars. Mexican officials estimate that no less than $4 billion left the country over the last month.

On Monday, the Zapatista leader, known as Subcomandante Marcos, announced that rebels had occupied 38 municipalities in Chiapas—a report that later was found to be untrue. The peso plummeted and the stock market had one of its worst trading days of the year.

After meeting late Monday night with Mexican business and labor leaders, the new finance minister Mr. Serra announced Tuesday morning on Mexican television that the peso would be technically devalued by 53 centavos. That only encouraged speculators.

"It was like defending a castle without bullets," said Eduardo Cepeda, managing director of J. P. Morgan in Mexico. "If you declare that you do not have the reserves to defend the peso, and then you declare a new trading floor, well basically you know that the enemy will storm the castle."

By last night, when Mr. Serra called other Cabinet ministers together for a damage-control meeting, the reserves of the Mexican central bank were reported to have dropped to as low as $6.5 billion, and the stand-by swap agreements with the United States and Canada for $7 billion were activated. About 11:15 P.M. the national television news program reported that the traditional trading band had been jettisoned in favor of a free-floating peso.

Kristin Lindow, a senior analyst with Moody's Investors Service in New York, said Mexican banks would be hard-pressed to handle a free-floating peso and that some would probably need help from the Government to withstand a run on the banks. She also said that some Mexican companies without export business might need to be bailed out, especially if they had taken on foreign debt.

Ms. Lindow said that any chance of Mexico's receiving an investment-grade rating on its Government debt in the near future had grown more distant. It now has a Moody's rating of Ba2, two notches below the lowest investment grade.

Mexican banks, already hit hard by lower profit and large portfolios of bad loans, tried to play down the latest disruptions.

Manuel Somoza, director general of Banco Mexicano, said the devaluation had not caused a panic because the Mexico of today is different from the Mexico that existed in 1982. Then, oil was practically the country's only export and its productive capacity was weak and business, uncompetitive.

"I'm quite calm," Mr. Somoza said. "I plan to have a great game of golf on Saturday and then a magnificent Christmas dinner with my family on Sunday."

But some commercial banks in Mexico City were selling dollars today for 5.50 pesos, compared with just over 4 pesos on Wednesday. And one exchange facility in the border town of Nuevo Laredo, where trading is usually volatile, offered as many as 6.50 pesos to the dollar.

Brokerage houses in the capital had a roller-coaster day. "I didn't sleep at all last night," said Daniel Somuano Spears, a trader with Valores Finamex. "It's as if we're in a different country and everything has changed in the last two days."

* * *

December 23, 1994

POLITICAL PERILS SHOWING IN FREE TRADE ACCORD

By KEITH BRADSHER
Special to The New York Times

WASHINGTON, Dec. 22—Ross Perot is not quite saying "I told you so," but he and other critics of the North American Free Trade Agreement are coming pretty close.

To the discomfiture of the White House, which has counted the passage of the North American Free Trade Agreement as one of President Clinton's clearest triumphs, this week's financial turmoil in Mexico has revived the political perils involved in the agreement. And the peso's steep drop in currency markets, by making Mexico's exports to the United States much more competitive with American goods, can only make the President's job more difficult.

If more goods from Mexico start pouring into United States markets, how will the White House persuade the public that free trade enriches the country and does not destroy jobs, particularly manufacturing jobs?

Several Administration officials were quick to point out privately today that the peso's plunge might not have much effect on trade. Decisions to buy and sell goods across international boundaries are typically made many months in advance, and nobody knows how long the peso will stay at its current value, said the officials, who insisted on anonymity.

Economists typically estimate that it takes at least six months for a shift in exchange rates to show up in trade patterns, and then the changes generally are slow to happen. Still, none of that prevented Mr. Perot from enjoying the moment.

It is not clear who will benefit politically from the troubles in Mexico, other than Mr. Perot and perhaps any liberal Democratic challengers to Mr. Clinton's renomination for President. A broad coalition of moderate Democrats and Republicans were involved in the passage of the agreement and, earlier this month, a global free trade pact.

During his campaign against the North American agreement last year, Mr. Perot had warned that the Mexican Government would devalue the peso by 25 to 30 percent in 1994 and unleash a flood of low-priced goods on the American market once trade barriers were removed.

"I do not want to be vindicated, and I would like to be wrong," Mr. Perot said in a telephone interview today.

While most professional economists may disagree with what Mr. Perot says, other critics of the agreement, like Ralph Nader, were quick to join him today in denouncing the Administration's decision to make available a $6 billion line of credit to Mexico. "Nafta was supposed to be about two-way trade, not U.S. taxpayer welfare to prop up the Mexican peso and the Mexican oligarchs," said Mr. Nader, the consumer activist and critic of free trade.

The agreement took effect on Jan. 1 of this year, immediately eliminating three-fifths of the tariffs on trade among Canada, Mexico and the United States and gradually eliminating the rest over 15 years. The House and Senate approved it in November of last year after vigorous lobbying by the Clinton Administration.

Administration officials refused to discuss the free trade pact publicly today, as part of a general reluctance to offend Mexico or frighten financial markets already agitated by the peso's 28.1 percent fall.

Some Administration officials, though, pointed out today that by conventional economic theories, the total volume of trade matters much more than surpluses or deficits with one nation. Trade allows each country to specialize in producing whatever goods it can make most efficiently, while importing the rest. This specialization increases economic output around the globe.

That argument may score with economists, but politically, trade balances between nations take on great importance, notably in the case of Japan.

Through October, the United States surplus with Mexico rose to $1.71 billion from $1.32 billion in the first 10 months of last year, although in October the United States ran a rare deficit of $89 million. This, and the fact that relatively few jobs have been lost to low-wage Mexican competition, has helped the Administration to silence the critics from organized labor, environmental and consumer groups who fought the agreement last year.

The main reasons cited for the Mexican action this week— two political assassinations, a guerrilla insurgency in southern Mexico and a change of government—are not what Mr. Perot specifically mentioned. But the effects could be the same: the shrinkage or elimination of the United States' trade surplus with Mexico, as the falling peso makes American goods more expensive in Mexico and Mexican goods cheaper here.

At a hearing before a House panel on March 24, 1993, Mr. Perot warned that, "These guys are just playing poker with us, and they are going to have to devalue the peso."

* * *

December 23, 1994

U.S. BUSINESS GETS MEXICAN SHOCK

By JAMES BENNET

To protect its investment in plants in Mexico, the Chrysler Corporation has periodically considered hedging against fluctuations in the peso. But it has always decided that hedging was not worth it.

Then the peso dived 28.1 percent this week, falling from 29 American cents on Friday, to 20.83 cents yesterday. "I was shocked," said Bob Lippens, Chrysler's senior international economist. "The new Government had sworn up and down that the peso was essentially untouchable."

The effect of the change on the Chrysler is obvious, he said. "It reduces our profits; that's pretty clear, straight up," Mr. Lippens said.

Companies that have invested heavily in Mexico reacted with alarm yesterday to the peso's plunge. Several said the devaluation had sorely tested their confidence in the Mexican Government, eroding some of the good faith built up by the signing last year of the North American Free Trade Agreement.

"They're just going to have to work hard in regaining investment confidence from the U.S.," Mr. Lippens said of the Mexican Government. "That doesn't come back overnight."

The devaluation underscored how intertwined the economies of Mexico and the United States already are. Executives at several companies said that, because they sell products with parts from both countries in both countries, the effect of the devaluation on their bottom lines and their business plans was unclear.

In general, American companies importing goods from Mexico that are made with Mexican components should benefit from the devaluation, since the goods will seem cheap to people paying in dollars.

But those selling products in Mexico whose components are mostly from the United States could see overall profits suffer, since the drop in the peso's value makes dollar-based goods more expensive there.

For example, the devaluation appeared to be a setback for America's Big Three auto makers who have been shipping more vehicles to Mexico as tariff barriers have declined. The Ford Motor Company says it will export about 25,000 cars and light trucks to Mexico this year, up from zero in 1992.

The companies selling goods in Mexico that are made in the United States cannot immediately pass their higher costs along to consumers there, they said, because the Mexican Government has asked them not to raise prices for 60 days.

No one, however, was talking about abandoning a market that all said holds great promise.

"We look at it as a cost of doing business internationally," said Jay J. Fitzsimmons, vice president of finance for Wal-Mart Stores. "We're in Mexico for the long term."

Mr. Fitzsimmons said that Wal-Mart's greatest concern was the impact of the devaluation on the Mexican economy. If inflation rises and the economy slips into recession, Wal-Mart might slow its expansion there. "The real impact

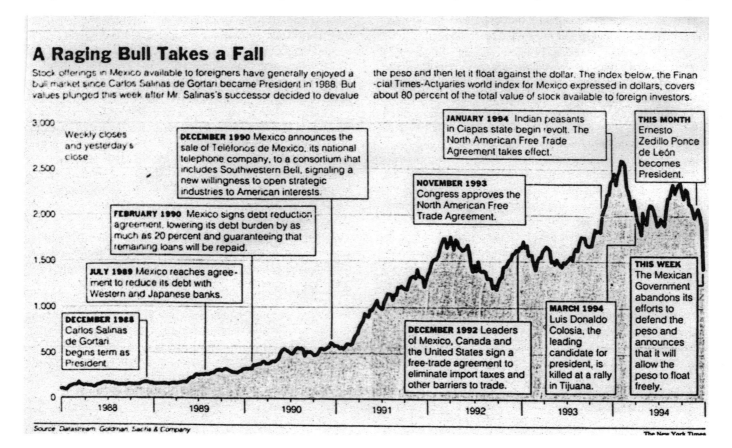

A Raging Bull Takes a Fall

Stock offerings in Mexico available to foreigners have generally enjoyed a bull market since Carlos Salinas de Gortari became President in 1988. But values plunged this week after Mr. Salinas's successor decided to devalue the peso and then let it float against the dollar. The index below, the Financial Times-Actuaries world index for Mexico expressed in dollars, covers about 80 percent of the total value of stock available to foreign investors.

DECEMBER 1988 Carlos Salinas de Gortari begins term as President.

JULY 1989 Mexico reaches agreement to reduce its debt with Western and Japanese banks.

FEBRUARY 1990 Mexico signs debt reduction agreement, lowering its debt burden by as much as 20 percent and guaranteeing that remaining loans will be repaid.

DECEMBER 1990 Mexico announces the sale of Telefonos de Mexico, its national telephone company, to a consortium that includes Southwestern Bell, signaling a new willingness to open strategic industries to American interests.

DECEMBER 1992 Leaders of Mexico, Canada and the United States sign a free-trade agreement to eliminate import taxes and other barriers to trade.

NOVEMBER 1993 Congress approves the North American Free Trade Agreement.

JANUARY 1994 Indian peasants in Chiapas state begin revolt. The North American Free Trade Agreement takes effect.

MARCH 1994 Luis Donaldo Colosia, the leading candidate for president, is killed at a rally in Tijuana.

THIS MONTH Ernesto Zedillo Ponce de León becomes President.

THIS WEEK The Mexican Government abandons its efforts to defend the peso and announces that it will allow the peso to float freely.

Weekly closes and yesterday's close

Source: Datastream, Goldman, Sachs & Company

The New York Times

A Floating Peso, Trade and American Business

Mexico's decision to allow the peso to find its own level in world currency markets will directly affect the $100 billion in annual trade between Mexico and the United States and the hundreds of American companies doing business in Mexico. But not all the effects will be simple shifts in prices and costs, because much cross-border business is wholly or partly insulated from currency shifts.

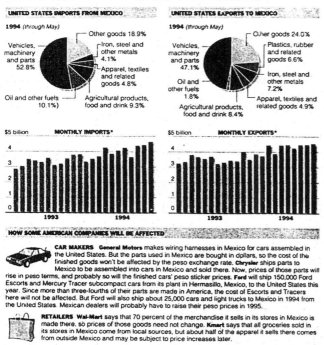

UNITED STATES IMPORTS FROM MEXICO

1994 (through May)
- Vehicles, machinery and parts 52.8%
- Other goods 18.9%
- Iron, steel and other metals 4.1%
- Apparel, textiles and related goods 4.8%
- Agricultural products, food and drink 9.3%
- Oil and other fuels 10.1%)

UNITED STATES EXPORTS TO MEXICO

1994 (through May)
- Vehicles, machinery and parts 47.1%
- Other goods 24.0%
- Plastics, rubber and related goods 6.6%
- Iron, steel and other metals 7.2%
- Apparel, textiles and related goods 4.9%
- Agricultural products, food and drink 8.4%
- Oil and other fuels 1.8%

MONTHLY IMPORTS* ($5 billion) — 1993, 1994

MONTHLY EXPORTS* ($5 billion) — 1993, 1994

HOW SOME AMERICAN COMPANIES WILL BE AFFECTED

CAR MAKERS **General Motors** makes wiring harnesses in Mexico for cars assembled in the United States. But the parts used in Mexico are bought in dollars, so the cost of the finished goods won't be affected by the peso exchange rate. **Chrysler** ships parts to Mexico to be assembled into cars in Mexico and sold there. Now, prices of those parts will rise in peso terms, and probably so will the finished cars' peso sticker prices. **Ford** will ship 150,000 Ford Escorts and Mercury Tracer subcompact cars from its plant in Hermosillo, Mexico, to the United States this year. Since more than three-fourths of their parts are made in America, the cost of Escorts and Tracers here will not be affected. But Ford will also ship about 25,000 cars and light trucks to Mexico in 1994 from the United States. Mexican dealers will probably have to raise their peso prices in 1995.

RETAILERS **Wal-Mart** says that 70 percent of the merchandise it sells in its stores in Mexico is made there, so prices of those goods need not change. **Kmart** says that all groceries sold in its stores in Mexico come from local sources, but about half of the apparel it sells there comes from outside Mexico and may be subject to price increases later.

*For exports, C.I.F. basis, for imports, F.A.S. basis.   Data sources: National Trade Data Base; Datastream; listed companies

Continuing to Fall

Exchange rate of Mexican new pesos to the dollar. The scale is inverted to reflect the peso's decline.

2 pesos

Old trading range allowed by the Mexican Government ▼

Yesterday: 4.80

9 13 14 15 16 19 20 21 22
Dec.

Source: Bloomberg Financial Services

going forward depends on how the Mexican consumer responds," he said.

Wal-Mart has moved aggressively into Mexico, opening 22 Sam's Clubs and 11 supercenters there in the last two and a half years; in the coming year, it had planned to open 13 more Sam's Clubs and 12 more supercenters. While Wal-Mart has bought almost all the land it needs for the stores, it may delay some construction, Mr. Fitzsimmons said.

Big Losers

The five biggest declines on the New York Stock Exchange yesterday were Mexican depository receipts, which represent a different number of shares in each company. Two Mexican companies were also among the most heavily traded on the exchange.

	Yesterday's close	Change from Wednesday	Percent change
Grupo Mexicano de Desarrollo/B American depository receipt. Construction company.	$9.875	−$2.375	−19.39%
Grupo Financiero Serfin American depository receipt. Financial services company.	8.875	− 2.00	−18.39
Grupo Embotellador de Mexico Global depository receipt. Bottler for Pepsico Inc.	14.875	− 3.00	−16.78
Empresas La Moderna American depository receipt. Tobacco company.	17.00	− 2.875	−14.47
Consorcio G Grupo Dina American depository receipt. Truck manufacturer.	7.75	− 1.25	−13.89

	Yesterday's close	Change from Wednesday	Yesterday's volume
Teléfonos de Mexico American depository receipt. Telephone company.	$40.625	−$4.375	20.5 million
Grupo Televisa Global depository receipt. Television company.	32.375	− 3.625	3.2 million

Other companies, including Chrysler, said the peso's devaluation could actually accelerate their expansion in Mexico, by forcing them to switch more of their suppliers to Mexico from the United States. The weakness of the dollar against the Japanese yen has had exactly that effect on Japanese auto makers in the United States.

"We've been down this road before," said Fred Standish, a spokesman for Nissan Motor Company. On Monday, Nissan said that in the spring of 1995 it would begin exporting United States-made vehicles to Mexico for the first time. The devaluation should make those vehicles more expensive, but Mr. Standish said Nissan had no plans to change its strategy.

Some companies with large Mexican investments will suffer almost no impact from the peso's drop.

The General Motors Corporation's $25 billion parts-making operation, for example, has some 40 plants, employing about 40,000 people, just south of the United States border. But almost all the equipment in the plants, and all the materials used to produce wiring harnesses, steering wheels and other parts there, were bought in dollars in the United States to be sold in dollars.

"We really don't have much exposure down there," said Fred J. Bellar 3d, assistant finance director for G.M.'s Automotive Components Group Worldwide.

Similarly, the Ford Motor Company imports about 150,000 small cars—Ford Escorts and Mercury Tracers—from a plant in Hermosillo, Mexico. But to comply with certain United

States regulations, more than 75 percent of the parts in those vehicles are from the United States. As a result, on those vehicles, Ford should gain little from the peso's drop. Ford has also begun producing Ford Contour and Mercury Mystique compact sedans at another plant in Cuautitlan, but it was not clear what their Mexican content was.

In the short term, operations like G.M.'s and Ford's Hermosillo plant may have lower labor costs because of the cheaper peso. But Mr. Bellar, like other executives, said wages would undoubtedly rise in Mexico to match prices, erasing reduction in labor costs.

Indeed, without some increase in wages, one effect of the devaluation could be to further aggravate Mexican wage earners. "The immediate short-term effect of this is obviously going to be to cut purchasing power, which was already at perilous levels," said David M. Johnson, an international representative from the United Electrical, Radio and Machine Workers union who helps organize workers in Mexico.

The 60-day waiting period sought by the Mexican Government may sound Draconian, but it could actually have little effect on corporate books. For example, Mr. Fitzsimmons said Wal-Mart already stocked about 60 days' worth of dollar-denominated goods in Mexico. The cost of those goods has already been converted to pesos.

* * *

December 23, 1994

INVESTORS WEIGH A MARKET'S SAFETY

By KENNETH N. GILPIN

In large measure, Mexico's financial future rests with American investment firms. But the events of the last two days, the latest in a string of shocking surprises this year, have led some to wonder if Mexico is truly on its way to becoming a relatively safe place to invest.

"The assumption was that in 1995 Mexico would become investment grade," said Joyce Chang, a director of emerging markets research at Salomon Brothers in New York. "In the short term, that is not now likely to happen."

The stunning decision by Mexico to devalue the peso, and then allow its currency to float against the dollar, has shaken but not completely shattered Wall Street's confidence in Mexico's continued transition from a debt-ridden third-world nation to a prosperous, free-market-oriented economy.

The damage suffered by Mexico's credibility can be measured in the way financial markets have treated the country's assets: In the space of two days, the value of peso-denominated assets like stocks and bonds have fallen by nearly 30 percent.

"We feel Mexico will recover," said Ed Cabrera, manager of Latin American strategy for Merrill Lynch & Company. "The question is how long that will take."

Yet even before the current crisis, money managers were starting to move substantial amounts of money out of Mexico. After heavy inflows from 1991 to 1993, it was a development that the members of the international financial community had anticipated.

"It is important that investors in these markets recognize the uncertainties, and it is probably most practical to take a medium-term perspective," said Charles Dallara, managing director of the Institute for International Finance in Washington, which represents commercial banks around the world.

Since the start of the year, most of the money that has flowed out of Mexico has come from its bond market, according to statistical estimates from the institute.

From a peak in February to Dec. 8, offshore holdings of peso-denominated bonds shrank by nearly two-thirds, to slightly more than $5 billion. That number is almost certainly smaller now.

The drop in equity holdings has not been nearly as severe.

At the end of November, the institute estimated, foreign holdings on the Mexican stock exchange and in Mexican stocks that traded in American depository receipts in the United States amounted to slightly more than $50 billion, down from a peak of more than $60 billion in January.

Those changes, along with the decision that many Mexicans have apparently made recently to get some of their own money out of the country, have driven down Mexico's foreign reserves to an estimated $8 billion, from about $30 billion at the start of the year.

"Two weeks ago," Ms. Chang of Salomon Brothers said, "people didn't think that Mexico would have lower foreign exchange reserves than Venezuela."

What had once been seen as only a slow seepage turned into a rapid outflow of funds this week.

On Monday, the day before the devaluation, the value of J. P. Morgan's emerging market bond index, a basket of 25 bonds, closed at 189.35. The index fell sharply on Wednesday, and was down by almost 3 percent yesterday, closing at 175.27. Since its peak in early January, the index has lost nearly 20 percent of its value.

There have been worse one-day declines. The biggest was on April 4, when the J. P. Morgan index fell by 4.2 percent. And on March 23, two days after the Mexican presidential candidate Luís Donaldo Colosio was assassinated, the index lost 3.7 percent of its value.

Despite the carnage, some investors now see a chance to pick up bargains. "Investors are very angry about what has gone on, but a lot of people think it is too late to sell," said Geoffrey E. J. Dennis, head of Latin American equity research at Bear, Stearns & Company. "We have talked to a lot of clients who are looking for opportunities to buy."

* * *

December 25, 1994

WITH PESO'S DEVALUATION, POLITICAL PROBLEMS LOOM

By TIM GOLDEN
Special to The New York Times

MEXICO CITY, Dec. 24—When Ernesto Zedillo Ponce de León first stood before the nation as President less than a month ago, the plans he unveiled were a measure of Mexico's recovery from its foreign-debt crisis of the 1980's.

With the economy apparently restored to health, Mr. Zedillo proposed finally to risk the power of his long-governing party with "definitive" steps toward democracy. With investment rising, he could afford to promise more public spending to help the millions of poor Mexicans left behind by the country's progress.

But as Finance Ministry technocrats scrambled this weekend to redraw their entire economic strategy in light of an uncontrolled devaluation of the peso, Government leaders also found themselves facing political challenges more daunting than any Mr. Zedillo had foreseen.

As spending is cut back, inflation surges and real wages fall, he must now sell heavy new sacrifice to a labor movement that has grown steadily more independent of the Government in recent years. In the southern state of Chiapas, where a peasant insurgency has helped unsettle the financial markets with threats of renewed fighting, the need for peace is becoming more urgent.

Opposition parties that have been in disarray since Mr. Zedillo's sweeping victory in elections in August have begun showing new signs of life. Perhaps the most telling indication of the President's straits is that his promise to reform an authoritarian political system—a central problem of his administration until last week—may now be one of the more straightforward tasks ahead.

"We are really, as you say, back to the drawing board," a senior official said.

Government officials and their supporters are quick to argue that the economic crisis that Mexico now confronts is not comparable to those that came with its big devaluations of the currency in 1982, when the debt crisis began, and in 1987.

Mr. Zedillo's decisions this week to allow a 15 percent devaluation of the peso, and then to let it trade freely against the dollar, incensed foreign investors, who saw their assets fall by about one-third of the value they had last week.

But after several years in which the Government depended on vast, steady flows of capital from abroad to cover a day-to-day shortfall in its accounts, the volatility of that equation has been reduced. Although the country's debt payments in dollars will be more costly, the other main source of its deficit, a huge demand for imported goods, is certain to fall as the costs of those products rise.

Officials said they expected the deficit in Mexico's current account, the sum of its trade imbalance and debt-service pay-

Associated Press

The peasant revolt in the Mexican state of Chiapas has contributed to jitters in financial markets. One year after the rebellion began, soldiers yesterday guarded the town plaza in San Cristóbal de las Casas as the Government of Ernesto Zedillo Ponce de León sought a settlement.

ments, to drop to about $20 billion next year from the more than $30 billion they projected before the devaluations.

While foreign investments in Mexican stocks and bonds will drop, the partnership of Mexico with the United States and Canada in the North American Free Trade Agreement will also help it to capitalize on the fact that direct investments like automobile plants and real estate will now be cheaper for foreigners. Though a more open economy will mean a greater jump in inflation as imports become more expensive, the Government's budget has been balanced, its tax collection has greatly improved and Mexican workers have grown more productive.

When Mexico's economy collapsed in 1982 and 1987, however, much of what set the country apart from others in the Latin American debt morass was the Government's overwhelming political control, particularly of organized labor.

A principal mechanism of that control was a national wage-price accord that has been periodically renewed since 1987. Under the accords, big labor confederations belonging to the governing Institutional Revolutionary Party joined with business chambers largely beholden to the Government in agreeing to fight inflation by holding down salaries and consumer prices to certain levels. Serious labor strife became routine elsewhere in the region; in Mexico, it remained the exception.

The Government's power over labor has been eroding slowly over the last decade as the informal economy has grown, independent unions have proliferated and those that were once pillars of the PRI, as the governing party is called, have established some distance. But the face that labor showed Mr. Zedillo's aides this week looked angrier than it has been before.

"We were confident that all of the sacrifices we have made were bringing us in to safe port," the leader of the telephone workers' union, Francisco Hernandez Juarez, said in an interview on Friday. "And now we find ourselves once again in the middle of a turbulent sea with no way back."

Mr. Hernandez Juarez, who has been a supporter of both Mr. Zedillo and his predecessor, Carlos Salinas de Gortari, continued: "If we have to row, we will row, but we cannot make gratuitous concessions. If they say we have to start over, it is not going to be the same. If I tell the telephone workers that we have to hold down salaries like we did in 1987, I am afraid they will not accept it."

To win labor's agreement to preserve the 10 percent ceiling on salary increases that was negotiated in September, officials quickly accepted the insistence that prices be frozen for 60 days, officials on both sides of the talks said.

But when the Finance Secretary, Jaime Serra Puche, proposed on Thursday that labor and business leaders sign a statement saying they "shared" the Government's decision to float the peso, Mr. Hernandez Juarez and other more independent unionists rejected the language out of hand.

Officials acknowledged that labor support for the 60-day pact was strictly conditioned on business leaders' success in holding down consumer prices. By Friday, however, such prices were already shooting up by as much as 40 percent, and were coming on items like rice, beans, chicken and cigarettes that are produced in Mexico and should therefore be less affected by the higher cost of imports with a weaker peso.

Despite a wave of criticism of the Zedillo Government for mishandling the devaluation, a few opposition politicians appeared to sympathize with officials who ascribe the crisis largely to Mr. Salinas, his Finance Minister, Pedro Aspe Armella, and the president of the Central Bank, Miguel Mancera Aguayo.

Officials said one of Mr. Aspe's former deputies, Guillermo Ortiz, now Mr. Zedillo's Secretary of Communications and Transportation, and a senior economic adviser to Mr. Salinas, Fernando Clavijo, argued forcefully this year that the Central Bank's hard-currency reserves were insufficient to sustain the current account deficit. Mr. Aspe was so opposed to a devaluation, one official said, that it was thought he would resign if one was ordered. But Mr. Zedillo was also said to have supported the policy at the time.

What marginal political distance might be established between Mr. Salinas and Mr. Zedillo, his hand-picked successor and his Minister of both Planning and Budget and of Education, does not necessarily work in Mr. Zedillo's favor.

"Salinas knew how to control the country," Arturo González, a 31-year-old cabdriver, said as he stared at the rates in an exchange house along Mexico City's main boulevard, the Paseo de la Reforma. "Look at all the things that he handled this year. Now, in three weeks, look at what has happened."

One crisis to which Mr. González referred, the uprising in Chiapas on Jan. 1, has plagued Mr. Zedillo since before his inauguration and now seems to be growing only more problematic.

Though he moved quickly to try to restart talks with the insurgents, Mr. Zedillo has yet to produce any concrete proposal for a settlement. He also managed to diffuse responsibility for the problem by persuading opposition parties to join a new negotiating commission, but had no choice but to reverse himself on Friday after the rebels rejected its authority.

Glossing over the economic miscalculations that his aides have increasingly acknowledged, Mr. Zedillo has publicly continued to attribute the devaluation to capital flight resulting from the threat of new fighting in Chiapas. In so doing, several Mexican political analysts said, he may have contributed to the rebels' growing political isolation, but he has also helped them rise again to the top of the country's agenda.

In Chiapas, as elsewhere in the country, Mr. Zedillo's basic problem now is that he must face demands for greater democracy without the political cushion of a stable and growing economy.

"The political situation has clearly changed," said a political adviser to the President, Federico Estevez. "The political constraints on the Government are much greater than they were at any time under Salinas."

* * *

December 26, 1994

U.S. LOSSES IN MEXICO ASSESSED

By LOUIS UCHITELLE

The steep decline in the value of the Mexican peso has resulted in a potential loss of roughly $8 to $10 billion for American investors in Mexican stocks and bonds, according to estimates by Wall Street investment experts.

American owners of Mexican stocks took the biggest hit, suffering not only from the peso's devaluation but also from falling stock prices. Their holdings were worth roughly $20 billion on Dec. 1 and $13.5 billion on Friday, the experts estimated. In addition, the $12 billion to $15 billion in peso notes and bonds held by Americans shed $3 billion or so as a result of last week's devaluation.

"These losses are spread out over a lot of people and institutions in the United States," said Lawrence Brainard, head of research for Chase Securities Emerging Markets Group, a subsidiary of Chase Manhattan Bank. "And now these investors are trying to figure out whether to stay in Mexico or sell their securities, take their losses and leave."

Mr. Brainard, Nariman Behravesh, international economist at DRI/McGraw-Hill, and Brian Barish, head of emerging market research at Lazard Freres, said Americans represent $45 billion to $50 billion of the $73 billion in foreign investment in Mexico. Roughly $15 billion is in direct investment in factories, machinery and buildings—investments that are largely immune to devaluation, particularly if their goal is to make goods for export from Mexico. The remaining $30 billion to $35 billion is in stocks, Government bonds and other forms of interest-bearing peso securities.

The $8 billion to $10 billion in losses, if they are realized, are a significant sum, and Mexico's economic future might hinge on whether American investors will decamp, at least for a while, as they did after financial crises, in the 1970's and 1980's. Already, Mexican Government officials and some American bankers and financiers are arguing that nothing has really changed; that the Mexican peso, having lost nearly 27 percent of its worth in American dollars in a single week, is now at its proper level, and Americans can once again invest safely and profitably in Mexico.

That was the message from Mexico's Finance Minister, Jaime Serra Puche, when he met with American executives at the Federal Reserve Bank in New York on Friday. He said that Mexico would hold to policies that restrict domestic credit, balance the budget and maintain the peso's value, now that the pressure on the peso had been relieved. While some Americans at the meeting raised doubts about the future, others backed Mr. Serra's effort to get investment back on track.

"If the Mexican Government implements the program as outlined by Minister Serra, this should give additional opportunities for accelerated Mexican export growth and therefore make Mexico attractive for investment," said William R. Rhodes, vice chairman of Citibank, a major holder of Mexican debt.

Mutual funds and pension funds, the biggest holders of Mexican debt, apparently suffered the biggest losses from last week's fall in the peso, and some brokerage houses that trade in Mexican securities also may have lost money. No one has announced actual losses from the sale of securities as prices dropped last week, but there were broad indications of paper losses.

Fidelity Investments, the big Boston-based mutual fund company and one of the biggest investors in Mexican stocks and bonds, said that eight of its funds had held about $800 million in Mexican securities on Dec. 19, the day before the Mexican Government announced a 14 percent devaluation in the peso, beginning a process that accelerated when the Government decided to float the peso, which finished the week down nearly 27 percent.

For Fidelity, that would be roughly a $215 million loss just from devaluation if all of the securities were held. A Fidelity spokeswoman did not say what might have been sold in the heavy trading last week.

Clients of Bear, Stearns & Company held more than $1 billion in Mexican securities, according to Alan Greenberg,

chairman of the Wall Street house. That would mean a paper loss of about $265 million or more as a result of the fall in the peso, if the securities were held all last week.

Bear, Stearns is one of the most active American investment houses in the Mexican market, trading not only for clients but investing tens of millions of dollars of its own money. Mr. Greenberg and Warren Spector, the firm's executive vice president, declined to say if Bear, Stearns itself had lost money as a result of the falling peso, but in a telephone interview on Friday they suggested that the firm had not.

"We are very pleased with our performance," Mr. Spector said, "and we are not reducing our commitment to Latin America."

Mr. Spector and Mr. Greenberg in effect lined up with Mr. Rhodes in arguing that Mexico remains a good investment, because its economy is slowly gaining in efficiency and industrial production. "People will get their confidence back and once again they'll be buying Mexican securities," Mr. Greenberg said.

The Mexicans certainly hope so. American investors have provided the dollars to pay for much of their estimated $29 billion deficit in trade and other transactions this year. American investors are also big purchasers of the bonds floated for spending on roads, harbors, airports, power stations and the like.

But others on Wall Street are less sanguine than Mr. Greenberg and Mr. Rhodes. "The Mexican Government still needs to spell out a coherent set of economic policies given that the peso has been devalued," Mr. Brainard said.

Taking a similar view, Moody's Investors Service reaffirmed on Friday its ratings of Mexican securities as less than investment grade.

"Our ratings reflected and still reflect a structural dilemma in Mexico," said David Levey, managing director for sovereign risk at Moody's. "The dilemma was the overvalued peso which drew money and imports into Mexico and brought about the huge deficit in international transactions. Correcting this current account deficit is likely to require a recession or a number of years of slower growth than many people would like."

*   *   *

December 28, 1994

MEXICAN CURRENCY RESUMES ITS FALL, OFFICIALS SILENT

By TIM GOLDEN
Special to The New York Times

MEXICO CITY, Dec. 27—Mexico's economic crisis took a new turn for the worse today as investors dumped more of their holdings in pesos, driving the value of the Mexican currency down by nearly 10 percent more against the dollar.

Despite a brief rally late in the trading day, the peso closed at 5.70 to the dollar, or about 40 percent less than it was worth when the crisis broke out a week ago.

Mexican stock prices also fell, bringing demands from both Mexican executives and foreign investors that the Government explain how it would try to stabilize the economy.

Instead, for the fourth straight day, Government officials gave virtually no public indication of their plans. Spokesmen for President Ernesto Zedillo Ponce de León denied reports that he would speak to the nation tonight, apparently contributing to the confusion and concern.

"People this morning were hoping to see some demonstration of leadership from the Zedillo administration or from Zedillo himself, but it didn't come," said Marla Marron, a Latin American equities analyst at Salomon Brothers in New York.

The peso's continuing fall added to the huge losses—on paper and in some cases, real—of Americans who invested tens of billions of dollars in Mexican stocks and bonds.

It also heightened concern that at a time of considerable political tension in Mexico, the Government will have to cut spending deeply, hold down wages and raise interest rates sharply to avoid a return of runaway inflation.

The cheaper peso did make Mexico more attractive as a destination for foreign tourists.

Rumors persisted about what the Government might do. With the peso already well below the levels where many economists expected it to settle after the Government floated the currency last Thursday, speculators played on fears that Mexico might not be able to cover some of its short-term debts or might impose exchange-rate controls.

Despite a commitment from the United States last week to provide $6 billion in emergency credits to help Mexico cope with the depletion of its hard-currency reserves, pressure appeared to be increasing on the Clinton Administration to come to the rescue with more substantial aid.

Such a move could put the Government in the uncomfortable position of bailing out United States investors who had made considerable profits on stocks they knew to be risky. Yet a further deterioration of the Mexican economy could increase the flows to the United States of cheap Mexican exports and of undocumented migrants seeking jobs.

In Washington today, Under Secretary of the Treasury Lawrence H. Summers, said the peso had depreciated far more than was justified by the Mexican economy's condition.

"Excessive depreciation is in no one's interest," said Mr. Summers, who is the senior official involved in talks with Mexican officials.

Still, there was little sign this afternoon that his remarks had buoyed investors' confidence. Some analysts of Mexican securities predicted that even an economic-stabilization program that included deep cuts in public spending would only be persuasive if it were endorsed by the International Monetary Fund or some other pillar of international finance.

Mexican officials who spoke on condition of anonymity said the day's turmoil reinforced their conviction that they should not present a stabilization plan until they were certain they had a plan that would work. Two senior officials said this would not be before next Monday, although another said it might be finished Thursday or Friday.

"If we come out with any document that is not 100 percent sure and 100 percent credible, it is going to be counterproductive," a senior economic official here said. "We cannot take the risk of putting out something that is not perfect."

Such caution may reflect one of the more painful lessons learned by the economic team that took office with Mr. Zedillo at the start of the month. The Government found itself low on the dollar reserves used to support the peso when its value fell to the bottom of a range within which it was allowed to trade, so last Tuesday the Zedillo administration widened the so-called trading band, effectively letting the currency be devalued about 15 percent.

But many economic analysts said Mr. Zedillo erred in not devaluing the peso further and absorb all the pressure for an adjustment. When the currency's value quickly fell to the bottom of the new trading band, the Government was forced on Wednesday night to announce that it would eliminate the band altogether and let the peso float freely.

Part of the reason that both the peso and the Mexican stock exchange were whipsawed today, analysts said, was that the New York markets had been closed Monday. Thus, there were relatively few buyers even for what might seem like bargains next week. American mutual funds that held sizable positions in Mexican securities were also said to have begun selling shares.

"Even in this crisis, Mexicans are on vacation," said David L. Roberts, a vice president at Duff & Phelps Credit Ratings, which continued this week to rate some Mexican debt issues as investment grade. "It is the people in California and New York who are working this week who had to sell positions. All the decisions are being made by sellers."

Today, stocks fell 65.89 points on the Mexican stock exchange, to close at 2,276.90, a drop of 2.81 percent. In a sign that foreigners were instrumental in driving down the market, one of the stocks most widely held in the United States, Teléfonos de Mexico, plummeted more than 6 percent.

The analysts said investors also worried that the Government might have trouble paying off more than $5 billion worth of short-term debt, which falls due over the next six weeks and is pegged to the prevailing exchange rate. Yet because the debt is due in pesos, it is doubtful that the Government would be caught short even if the bonds were not rolled over.

The challenge that Mr. Zedillo and his advisers now face is how severe an adjustment to make. If it is too sharp, it could strangle the economy, said Nora Lustig, an economist at the Brookings Institution in Washington. But if inflation is allowed to rise quickly, it will frighten away investors, bring demands for higher wages and erode the effect of a cheaper peso in making exports more competitive.

"Until we see what they are going to do in the short run, what they are going to do in the middle run, we are in a no man's land," she said. "The irrationality in the markets is going to continue."

* * *

January 4, 1995

A DARKER SIDE FOR U.S. IN THE MEXICAN SOLUTION

By DAVID E. SANGER

Special to The New York Times

WASHINGTON, Jan. 3—Just before the peso crisis began two weeks ago, Clinton Administration officials celebrated the anniversary of the approval of the North American Free Trade Agreement by proudly announcing the first fruits of victory: Mexico had overtaken Japan as the No. 2 consumer of American exports.

Now the Administration is facing the darker side of the broad economic alliance it pressed so hard to bring to pass. To restore confidence in the Mexican economy, it has supported—and helped shape—a plan that is almost certain to cut back the pace at which American goods flow across the border. Moreover, it is a plan that seems certain to increase the inducements for Mexican workers to come to the United States illegally.

For one thing, the decision announced today by President Ernesto Zedillo Ponce de León to let the peso float freely at its devalued levels will mean that American wages are now about 30 percent more valuable to Mexican workers than they were just a few weeks ago.

The result, Administration officials conceded today, will likely be visible within weeks along the 2,000-mile-long border. In the name of stabilizing the Mexican economy over the next year or two, Mr. Clinton's aides have decided to run the risk of another wave of illegal immigration into regions of the United States that are growing increasingly intolerant of the cost it imposes on American workers and taxpayers.

"In the end there is no choice," one Administration official who has been involved in the growing trade with Mexico said today. "Mexico has become an integral part of the North American market. That started way before Nafta. The two economies are intertwined in trade, in commerce, in the movement of people. And in the end, the bigger need is to have a stable country on our border."

Throughout the currency crisis, the White House has been acutely aware that while the political stakes are enormous for Mr. Zedillo; they may also loom large for Mr. Clinton.

After a contentious debate in the fall of 1993 before approval, the North American trade agreement faded as an issue, costing Mr. Clinton little. But that calculation may now change, especially in Texas and California, two states that are critical to his re-election hopes. Many residents there are among those most suspicious that they are paying the price for helping Mexico overcome its economic problems. Opponents of the trade accord, who said American workers would be hurt more than they were helped, may look more prescient in coming months if the flow of both low-priced goods and low-wage immigrants from Mexico to the United States sharply increases.

"The Clinton Administration has fallen into the same trap as the Reagan and Bush Administrations," said Jeffrey J. Schott, a senior fellow at the Institute for International Economics, who has written extensively about the benefits of the trade accord. "It has been forced to oversell the effects of a trade deal on American economic growth. And sometimes, it comes back to haunt you."

Certainly there is good news as well for Washington in the economic recovery package announced today by Mr. Zedillo, who has been in office for less than a month. Mr. Zedillo's insistence that unions agree to wage increases of no more than 7 percent, and that corporations keep their profits minimal in an effort to keep prices down, seem likely to cut off the momentum of devaluation and inflation that many feared could cause the economy to spin out of control.

More important, Mr. Zedillo has chosen to speed changes in the economy that the North American Free Trade Accord set in motion. He is allowing private investment in railroads and satellite operations, promising to further liberalize foreign investment rules and promoting more competition in domestic telephone services.

All those steps are likely to eventually benefit American companies racing for a firmer foothold in the Mexican economy. In some areas, Mr. Zedillo is handing Washington openings it sought—and was denied—when the trade agreement was negotiated under the Bush Administration.

The Mexican President is also hoping to wean his country from its dependence on short-term investments to finance its current-account deficit—the difference between what it takes in from exports and what it pays for imports and to meet its foreign-debt obligations. Those investments make the economy more vulnerable to market speculators, who helped send the peso on its fall.

Instead, Mr. Zedillo hopes to pay for Mexico's deficit with more direct investment from foreign companies, getting them to build factories and businesses in the country. That may be more attractive than ever, because the cost of investing in Mexico has declined by a third.

But American companies will have to be convinced that Mr. Zedillo has the unions and the country's elite behind him. They also have to be persuaded that they will not suffer a similar fate to that of investors of recent months and years, who have been hit with millions of dollars in losses in the last two weeks.

And they must learn to live with slower growth—much slower than the 4 to 6 percent growth that Mr. Zedillo was confidently predicting in Washington a few weeks ago, before his inauguration.

Such problems, of course, are not inherent to investors in Mexico. China, the largest potential investment market of all for American companies, already has a surging inflation rate of 24 percent and seems ripe for a Mexico-style market correction. Throughout much of Eastern Europe, the kinds of tough economic choices that Mexico deferred during its presidential election last year have also been avoided.

But as President Clinton learned during the national debate in 1993 over the North American trade deal, there is something special about Mexico. The specter of more illegal immigration and of political trouble on the United States' border gives a vivid immediacy to the country's economic troubles that outweigh Mexico's size or influence on the American economy.

What the Clinton White House still has not learned, some experts contend, is that its much touted foreign economic policy must be approached like arms control: The focus has to be on prevention, not response.

"What we need now is a new method for consultation and support between the two countries to reduce the likelihood that problems like this become crises," said Robert A. Pastor, the director of the Latin American and Caribbean program at the Carter Center at Emory University in Atlanta. "That will be the most important long-term change."

*   *   *

January 15, 1995

IN MEXICO, HUNGER FOR POOR AND MIDDLE-CLASS HARDSHIP

By ANTHONY DePALMA
Special to The New York Times

MEXICO CITY, Jan. 14—The three weeks since the peso was abruptly devalued have not been kind to the people of Mexico. The worst economic crisis in a decade has splashed icy water on many who thought they had worked themselves up the ladder, and on many who remain at the bottom.

Prices have risen far more than the 10 percent wage increase the Government allowed in a recent pact with labor and business. For Mexicans who are poor—more than 45 percent of the 90 million people—that means staples like cooking oil, eggs and milk have become distressingly like luxuries.

José Socorro Palomares, a 64-year-old street sweeper who earns Mexico's official minimum wage of what now translates to about $3 a day, says he has no idea how he will make ends meet now. His wife, Aurora, is also a street sweeper, and together they barely made enough before the crisis to pay the rent and feed their seven children.

But many of the most disillusioned are among the more than 40 million in the rapidly expanding middle class—defined here as everyone who earns enough to keep from being hungry, but not enough to be considered among the richest 10 percent. The steep rise in interest rates that has accompanied the devaluation has hurt them. Monthly payments on adjustable-rate mortgages suddenly eat up an entire salary; credit cards are charging interest rates as high as 80 percent; payments on car loans have ballooned.

Carlos García Frutes, a 38-year-old sales manager and father of two, thinks back to the dozen years in which he cinched his belt because the Government asked Mexicans to sacrifice now for benefits later. Just last October he was finally confident enough to take out a 21 percent adjustable-rate mortgage for 250,000 pesos, the equivalent at the time of about $75,000. The coffee-colored dream house in a Mexico City suburb was finally his.

Now he finds that since the devaluation his monthly mortgage payment could double and the value of what he has saved in the 14 years he has worked at Ingersoll-Rand of Mexico has dropped sharply. His only hope is a grace period from the bank.

Intoxicated by an overvalued peso before the current crisis, many Mexicans binged on imported stereos, videocassette recorders and other goodies. New cars, new coats, California vacations—all could be paid for on credit, because things would only get better. But now those goods seem unaffordable to many people.

The wealthiest Mexicans worry also about their profit margins and the survival of their businesses. But many have dollars saved and will tap them during the crisis to get along.

Many Mexicans are disgusted about their situation.

"I really thought we were growing and that our economy had reached new stability," said José Romero, a 40-year-old carpenter. Framing the roof of a concrete hut at the edge of this huge city, and wearing a Zedillo for President cap, he called the Government's promises of a better future "pure lies."

"They've just been trying to trick us," he said.

Many in the middle class now worry about keeping their jobs. And they are skeptical of the Government's emergency stabilization plan, which asks them to accept cuts in purchasing power to help keep inflation under control.

Lydia Barbosa, an executive assistant in Mexico City for Detroit Diesel-Allison de México, is one of many Mexicans interviewed who think their sacrifice has become perpetual. "They're asking us to sacrifice and we'll do it, not because we're in a mood to do so but because there's no other choice," she said. "But we want to know if the sacrifices are going to result in anything positive for us this time."

The linchpin of the Government's rescue plan is the ability to control inflation. Analysts say that while big stores like Kmart, Wal-Mart and the Mexican chain Aurrera will probably get special scrutiny to make sure they abide by the plan, there is no guarantee that owners of small stores will not panic and raise prices.

The Federal Office of the Attorney General for Consumer Affairs is charged with the nearly impossible task of enforcing Mexico's pricing guidelines. To cover the entire country, the agency has 550 investigators, about half of them here in Mexico City, where there is also a consumer complaint hot line.

"This morning I received a call from someone wanting to buy a Mercedes-Benz," said Lucía Cabrera, one of 15 operators taking call after call from angry consumers. "Before the devaluation, the car was priced at 196,000 pesos and now the price is 370,000."

In a nearby cubicle, Guillermina Velázquez used a stern, grandmotherly voice to lecture some shopkeepers who had been caught trying to evade the price guidelines.

"We've been getting a lot of calls from people telling us that the prices of the basics—beans, sugar, eggs—are going up," she said. "Imagine, these products have nothing to do with the dollar—they are pure Mexican goods. There's absolutely no reason to raise their prices."

Since prices were frozen in the week before Christmas, the consumer agency has temporarily closed hundreds of stores for exceeding the price guidelines. And most Mexicans say they have seen widespread price gouging and even some hoarding by shopkeepers who remove items from the shelves until there is a shortage and demand allows them to charge whatever they want.

"I'm angry—everybody is angry—but what am I going to do with that anger?" said Mr. Socorro Palomares, the street sweeper.

Mr. Socorro Palomares said it was the small stores that had blatantly violated the price guidelines for everything from cooking oil to cigarettes, but he does not go to the big stores because they charge too much to begin with.

So he shops in the markets of the Tepito District of Mexico City, a chaotic haven for illegally imported products to which Mexicans have been going for generations. Vendors there say they have their own troubles.

"My father and my grandfather were also street vendors here, so we have all experienced devaluations before," said Claudia Ramirez, an enterprising 25-year-old who six days a week tries to sell handheld imported video games, X-Men dolls and a few Mexican toys. Business, she said, has dropped 70 percent since the peso collapsed. In mid-December the exchange rate was 3.4 pesos to the dollar. Now it is generally exceeding 5.5 to the dollar.

"Somehow this one seems harder," she said, referring to the devaluation. "There is more competition and it's taking longer for the exchange rate to stabilize."

The Trade and Commerce Ministry has been holding meetings with the nation's largest manufacturing companies to fix the allowable price increases for a group of basic products. The increases range from 10 percent to 30 percent; only tortillas and sugar remain unchanged.

Ricarda Martínez de Suárez has already determined what she must do to survive on the pension she and her 83-year-old husband, Martín, receive. "Chicken," she said, referring to the heads and feet that were all she used to buy. "We've cut it out completely."

President Ernesto Zedillo Ponce de León has told the Mexican people that if the country really unifies and works together, the period of sacrifice will last only until the economy begins to recover. But many Mexicans find it hard to trust such promises.

"We don't have much confidence that the program will have any positive impact in the short term," said Rocio Olivera, 24, the director of human resources at Detroit Diesel.

Ms. Olivera lives with her mother and helps with house expenses. Her mother's monthly car payment has jumped 22 percent, and the family, like many Mexicans, is dreading the determination of January's mortgage payment.

"Look," she said, "we fortunately don't have to live day to day worrying about what to eat." But she has had to scrap her plan to buy a new car this year and perhaps move into her own apartment. She doubts she will be able to take a vacation in the United States.

Mr. García Frutes said he had put off buying the new car he wanted, and he is hoping his children's school does not increase tuition before next September.

Mrs. Martínez is now raising half a dozen chickens to replace what she can't afford to buy at the market.

Ms. Barbosa and her husband, Igor, have decided to wait before starting the family they had planned. "We have had to put it off a little bit more to see how the future is," she said. "All we know now is that the future will be more difficult."

* * *

January 20, 1995

FLOOD OF DOLLARS, SUNKEN PESOS

By RONALD I. McKINNON

STANFORD, Calif.—The spectacular fall of the Mexican peso more than 35 percent since Dec. 20—can't be attributed to the two-month old administration of President Ernesto Zedillo Ponce de León, who spent last week calmly trying to appease international creditors while reforming the country's electoral system.

Nor can it be attributed to the previous President, Carlos Salinas de Gortari, and his American-trained technicians who over the last six years did most things right: privatizing and deregulating most industry and agriculture; dismantling long-standing restrictions on imports and some exports, and opening Mexico's repressed economy into a market-based system. These steps laid the basis for robust economic growth.

What caused the crisis? In large part, the major institutions of international finance—banks in New York, Tokyo and London as well as stock and bond mutual funds (mainly on Wall Street)—which have a lemming-like bent to overlend in emerging markets.

Once a long-repressed economy, as Mexico's was before 1989, appears to be liberalizing successfully, it suddenly appears on every banker's list as newly credit-worthy and also becomes a target for mutual funds. A flood of foreign capital can destroy a developing economy by creating a crippling current-account deficit—the difference between what is taken in from exports and what is paid for imports and interest on foreign debt. Foreign investors are also likely to pull their money out in a crisis, further destabilizing the economy. (Corporate investment in plants and equipment is not a problem because it produces goods and cannot be quickly withdrawn.)

Although Mexico is the most dramatic example of this trend, the International Monetary Fund has identified five similar cases: Chile after 1989, Colombia after 1991, Egypt after 1990, Spain after 1986 and Thailand after 1987. (Today, Argentina and India could be added to the list.)

It can happen in more developed countries as well. In the early 1980's, Margaret Thatcher's successful deregulation of the British economy attracted foreign investment, which caused stock and property market booms from 1986 to 1988. The inevitable bust came in 1990 and led to the pound falling out of the European Monetary System in September 1992.

In 1994, the net total of foreign capital streaming into Mexico rose to $30 billion, more than 8 percent of Mexico's gross domestic product. Yes, the Government bears some of the blame for overborrowing, but the international banks are also at fault for being so eager to overlend.

Along with the buildup of foreign debt, the flood of money has had two further unfortunate consequences. It has led to a general relaxation of credit constraints on domestic borrowing, which caused Mexicans to consume more and save less—the rate of personal savings fell from about 15 percent of the G.D.P. in 1988 to about 7.5 percent in 1994. Foreign investment also spurred domestic prices to rise. This overvalued the peso, which hurt Mexican competitiveness in international trade and put a squeeze on exports.

Although the economy may appear to be a shambles, part of the problem will take care of itself. The peso is now so undervalued in relation to the dollar that exports will rise, creating new jobs. As Finance Minister Guillermo Ortiz has said, the immediate problem is to prevent Mexico's financial arteries from failing as jittery foreign banks and mutual funds try to pull their money out of the country.

President Clinton is right to propose setting up an emergency credit line to stabilize the peso in international markets, both because Mexico is a friend in need whose economy is linked to our own and also to atone for the destabilizing behavior of U.S. banks and mutual funds.

But emergency credit will not be enough. Mexico has about $28 billion dollars in debt to U.S. banks that will come due this year. This is mostly in so-called tesobono bonds, which must be paid back in pesos but are pegged to dollars, so that the Government's obligations have soared since the devaluation.

Mr. Ortiz should not have to go hat in hand back to New York to refinance Government debt at exorbitant interest rates—as American financiers seem to be demanding. Tuesday's "successful" Wall Street sale of $400 million worth of tesobono bonds at 19.75 percent interest will leave Mexico with a crippling future burden. Instead, the U.S. Government should offer to help Mexico refinance at a rate only slightly above that on Treasury bonds—something like 8.5 percent.

The U.S. should also see that Mexico is able to refinance its internal debt (money owed to Mexican bondholders and banks) at reasonable interest rates, possibly through the I.M.F. This would calm jitters in Mexico's domestic financial markets. None of this should be contingent on Mexico selling off its state-owned petroleum monopoly or enacting new labor reforms, as U.S. critics of helping Mexico have argued.

What should the Mexican authorities pledge in return? They must agree to limit the future use of foreign capital—possibly through setting limits on the amount that foreign banks can invest or by taxing all large foreign investments. If international financiers knew today that the Government was committed to limiting foreign capital in the future, they would feel more secure about their current investments and might stop pulling money out.

Putting such limits on foreign money could, of course, put the brakes on economic growth. The Government could rectify this by limiting all forms of consumer credit until equilibrium is restored; Mr. Ortiz should go ahead with his plans to make credit cards and home loans far more difficult to obtain. In the longer run, the Government could require Mexicans to put some fraction—say 10 percent—of their income into a privatized social security fund that is used for investment, as Chile and Singapore do.

If Mexico is ever to become truly stable, it needs a long-term policy of reducing dependence on foreign capital. The Zedillo administration must take the lead, but the I.M.F. and American regulatory agencies should keep an eye on the amount of money flowing into Mexico and sound the alarm when they think the country is overextending itself.

This crisis is not just about Mexico. As the Treasury and Commerce Departments continue their gung-ho efforts to help American banks get unrestricted access to emerging economies in Asia, Latin America and Eastern Europe, they should look at Mexico and realize that a little restraint is in order.

Ronald I. McKinnon is professor of economics at Stanford University.

* * *

February 1, 1995

SLOW-BUILDING DESPAIR LED TO DECISION ON AID

By DOUGLAS JEHL
Special to The New York Times
WASHINGTON, Jan. 31—The decision by President Clinton to assert executive authority on Mexico's behalf came at a late-night meeting on Monday in the Oval Office, when his top advisers told him that two weeks of trying and failing to persuade Congress to act had left him with no other course.

It was a path that the White House had previously rejected, partly because the advisers believed it essential that the President and the Congress present a common front to the markets and a wary public. But by Saturday, with the peso still plunging and the plan for action on Capitol Hill fading, Treasury Secretary Robert E. Rubin and other top officials concluded that it was time to review their options.

With the President's approval, they set Monday as the deadline by which Congress would at least have to settle on a bill. But by Monday night, at the end of a long White House day that began in hope and ended in despair, Mr. Rubin and the rest of the team had only bad news for Mr. Clinton when he returned to the White House from a political dinner.

Senior White House officials who provided an account of the decision-making today said that Leon E. Panetta, the chief of staff, and other top advisers told Mr. Clinton that they believed it would be at least two weeks—if ever—before the Congress would approve the $40 billion loan guarantee package to which the President and Republican leaders had pledged their support.

That was too long to wait, the advisers said, and the President agreed.

"We could not allow the situation to continue in which we were just waiting for Congress to take action and watching Mexico collapse," said a White House official who took part in the session, which began about 11 P.M.

A crucial final detail of the package did not fall in place until after dawn today, when Lawrence Summers, the Under Secretary of the Treasury, received word that the International Monetary Fund would put up the additional $10 billion in loan guarantees that the White House thought necessary. And the go-it-alone plan did not become official policy until Mr. Clinton met with Congressional leaders early this morning to hear first-hand of their pessimism.

But even Speaker Newt Gingrich, who had become increasingly candid about the opposition the package faced, knew when Mr. Panetta called him late Monday night that the die had been cast. If Mr. Clinton went ahead and took sole responsibility for the rescue plan, the Speaker told Mr. Panetta, he would hear from the Congress "a huge sigh of relief."

The story of how the President finally decided to devote $20 billion from an obscure Treasury Department fund to prop up Mexico's economy is in part the story of a White House reluctant to use its authority for an unpopular purpose. But it is also the story of a new era in which a Democratic President and the Republican leaders of Congress could not—despite 18 days of joint effort—rally their followers behind a $40 billion loan guarantee that they declared fundamental to American interests.

Asked tonight whether the White House was blaming recalcitrant Republicans or Democrats, a senior official replied: "I think this is one you probably have to lay on both sides. You really do."

Since Mr. Clinton first met with his advisers on Jan. 12 for a formal discussion of the Mexican crisis, the White House had recognized that it had the power to step in and provide the loan guarantees the President's advisers believed necessary to avert a collapse.

But the emergency stabilization fund on which Mr. Clinton finally relied had never been used for that purpose, and it contained only about $20 billion, a sum the White House feared would be inadequate.

Still, the more central reason for the reluctance was related to politics. With Republicans holding sway in Congress, Mr. Clinton's advisers worried that action by the President alone would be laughed off by the markets and scorned by the public.

Yet even after winning agreement from Mr. Gingrich and Senator Bob Dole of Kansas, the Republican leader, to push for a full-scale $40 billion plan, the White House remained apprehensive. As a member of Congress, Mr. Panetta had watched how controversial rescue plans for New York City and the Chrysler Corporation had generated opposition in the 1970's, and top officials said they were on his mind as he

worked the telephones trying to line up Democratic support for a plan that opinion polls and Congressional reaction was quickly showing to be almost as unappealing.

Mr. Rubin, who was sworn in as Treasury Secretary just as the battle began, also made the quest for passage of the plan a personal cause, spending nearly every day on Capitol Hill.

The Administration also got an unusually public declaration of help from the chairman of the Federal Reserve, Alan Greenspan, who went before Congress several times to express support for the package.

But by last Wednesday, mounting pessimism within the Administration—fed by evidence from Capitol Hill and around the country that sentiment against the $40 billion plan was hardening—led the department to begin to give the go-it-alone option another look.

Still, the White House was far from giving up hope. The meeting on Saturday at which Mr. Panetta, Mr. Rubin and others, including Samuel R. Berger, the deputy national security adviser, agreed to set a deadline, was filled with hope that it could be met. And on Sunday, when Mr. Clinton placed after-church telephone calls to Senator Dole; Speaker Gingrich; Senator Tom Daschle of South Dakota, the Senate minority leader, and Representative Richard A. Gephardt of Missouri, the House minority leader, he was assured by each that they would do their part.

On Monday, the White House set its sights on the House as the pressure point. But while Mr. Gingrich expressed enthusiasm in a noontime telephone conversation with Mr. Panetta, that soon gave way to silence as the Speaker met with Republican governors and then with Mr. Dole to try to find a package that they, too, could support.

Mr. Panetta and Mr. Rubin had expected to go to the Capitol by late afternoon to work with Mr. Gingrich on a final proposal. But as they waited anxiously, Mr. Panetta heard first from his Mexican counterpart, who said that the situation there was worsening. And when he finally heard back from the Speaker, more than two hours after he left an urgent message with an aide, the news was just as bad: Mr. Gingrich said he now believed that it would be mid-February at the earliest before the Senate would be ready to vote.

As Mr. Panetta and his colleagues saw it then, that left them no choice but to act alone.

As they worked late into the night in his office to draft a fallback plan for the President, a senior official said today, their consensus was that, for Mexico, any alternative would have meant "chaos—a total unraveling."

* * *

February 5, 1995

A STRONG LEASH FOR CURRENCIES ON A RAMPAGE

By NATHANIEL C. NASH

Hong Kong did it in 1984. Argentina in 1991. Estonia in 1992 and Lithuania last year. Soon, El Salvador and Jamaica might do it. Brazil is studying it. And even Mexico—grappling with a wobbly peso and its attendant woes—sees it as a possible path to financial stability.

"It" is the adoption of the currency board, an idea making the rounds in countries struggling with the addictive quick fix (print more money), investor nervousness, flight capital and chronic inflation.

Basically, a currency board has four tenets. A government must cut its spending or increase its taxes to eliminate all but the smallest budget deficit—thus removing its need to print money, which is inflationary. It prohibits its central bank from printing money that is not fully backed by foreign exchange reserves. It fixes the value of its local currency to that of its dominant trading partner. And it makes its local currency fully convertible, upon demand, into the reserve currency.

The new board essentially replaces the central bank, and its members may or may not include members of the old central bank. Unlike the central bank, which could be pressured by politicians to printing money to cover budget deficits, the board is free of political interference. Its sole responsibility is to defend the value of the local currency at the fixed exchange rate, which can only be changed by Congressional action.

Besides putting the brakes on inflation, such a set-up bolsters investor confidence. Investors know that whenever they want to get out of the local currency, there will be the dollar or mark or yen available.

"You are giving investors a total guarantee that their investments will not lose value from a deflated currency," says Domingo Cavallo, Argentina's Economy Minister and architect of the country's highly successful "convertibility plan," which is patterned after a currency board.

Thus far, in the places that have embraced the idea, the tactic has done the near-impossible: stabilize gyrating economies. "No currency board ever set up has failed," says Steve H. Hanke, professor of applied economics at Johns Hopkins University and author of two books on the subject.

But what isn't clear at the moment is whether a currency board will have the same success in large countries like Mexico, Brazil and Russia.

The currency board, which could well be a 21st century answer for restoring confidence to developing countries, has 19th-century origins.

When the Bank of England in its 1844 charter made it part of its mandate to insure that the pound was fully convertible into gold, it had to set up a system where all its paper money was backed by gold reserves and convertible upon demand.

The first country to adopt a currency board was Mauritius (1849), followed by New Zealand (1850). And the idea spread. During the Bolshevik revolution, the British economist John Maynard Keynes set up a currency board in northern Russia that lasted two years until capitalism was outlawed. The present-day currency board, however, has certain advantages over the gold standard. With a dollar or mark peg, you are dealing in a much more liquid and negotiable instrument. You also earn more interest on exchange reserves than you would on gold deposits. In addition, foreign exchange is not as

prone to huge price swings as gold is, thus affording more price stability.

Over the years, Milton Friedman and Sir Alan Walters, chief economic adviser to Margaret Thatcher, have been two of the staunch advocates of this idea. It was Sir Alan who set up the currency board in Hong Kong in 1984. With the territory increasingly unsettled by the prospect of returning to Chinese domination in 1997, the Hong Kong dollar was gyrating because investors were fleeing with their money. After the Hong Kong dollar was pegged to the United States currency calm was restored and capital flight arrested.

The change in Argentina was even more dramatic. There, the inflation rate in 1989 rose to more than 2,000 percent. In 1991, Mr. Cavallo introduced his convertibility plan, pegging its austral, and later the peso, to the dollar. Argentina saw its inflation drop to single-digits in a little more than a year as foreign investment flowed into the country. During the Mexican peso devaluation crisis last December, there was speculation that the Argentine currency would be devalued. Mr. Cavallo, however, pledged he would sell all the dollars in the Argentine treasury before he would devalue. "Once the market realized we had no reason to devalue," says Mr. Cavallo, "everything quieted down, and there was no loss of reserves."

Similarly, Estonia and Lithuania have found a financial haven in currency boards. After the collapse of the Soviet Union, Estonia and Lithuania were plagued by high inflation because of their close ties to the Russian ruble. In 1992, Estonia pegged its kroon to the German mark and watched as foreign investment poured in. Last year, Lithuania pegged its lita to the United States dollar and has seen its foreign exchange reserves increase by 10 times.

"There was a very strong lobby against the law," recalls Adolfas Slezevicius, Prime Minister of Lithuania. "Commercial banks and some financial groups did not like it because they were using our very unstable situation to make a lot of money. Now they can't take advantage in big fluctuations in the value of our currency." Mr. Slezevicius says he and Nursultan A. Nazarbayev, President of Kazakhstan, have been talking about establishing a currency board in that former Soviet republic.

Opinion is divided as to whether a currency board should be set up in Mexico.

"A currency board is a straitjacket on a central bank, an extreme discipline on extremely bad behavior," says Jeffrey Sachs, a professor of economics at Harvard. "A general view among monetary experts is that for large economies it gives up too much, taking away flexibility." He adds: "The question for Mexico is, is monetary policy so politicized that you simply can't trust a central bank to use discretion? I would say that despite mistakes, especially last year, the answer is no. I would rather Mexico faced up to its mistakes, have a sensible, transparent monetary policy, but leave itself some flexibility."

Some economists point out that although Mexico created excessive debt levels over the past year, its management of the economy since the mid-1980's until last year (low levels of inflation, strong economic growth) has shown that its monetary institutions are reliable. These economists say that with the International Monetary Fund loan package in place and Mexico's promise to adhere to strict financial discipline, investor confidence should return.

Others disagree. They argue that a currency board is the kind of financial discipline Mexico needs, as distasteful as the idea is politically. The peso's fall of nearly 50 percent wiped out more than $100 billion of stock market assets, and unless a monetary straightjacket is imposed, investors will not return there in the same numbers.

"The idea of a country as large as Mexico introducing a currency board would have been unthinkable three months ago," noted David Hale, chief economist for the Kemper Financial Companies in Chicago, at a session of the World Economic Forum in Davos, Switzerland, last month. "But as a result of the severity of the recent crisis, it now deserves serious consideration."

According to Mr. Hanke, the idea of setting up a currency board in Mexico "is actively being studied at the highest levels." Mexican officials confirm that that is an option. Setting the proper exchange rate would be key, economists say. They argue that in order for Mexico's exports to be competitive, a rate that is slightly under the perceived market value is critical, somewhere between five to six pesos to the dollar.

A currency board has to begin with enough reserves to support the local currency in circulation. Since Mexico's monetary base was 51 billion pesos at the end of January, reserves of no more than $10 billion would be needed. Mexico currently has some $3.5 billion in reserves. Therefore, economists say, only around $10 billion in international support would be needed— far less than the $50 billion package announced by the Clinton Administration. Proponents also say that a currency board makes sense for Mexico because of its economic integration with the United States through the North American Free Trade Agreement.

Mr. Hanke, perhaps the economist most aggressively promoting the idea of currency boards, became interested in them when he and Sir Alan, were colleague at Johns Hopkins University in the late 1980's. Mr. Hanke and his team of assistants have helped the governments of Argentina, Estonia and Lithuania set up currency boards, and they are working with the governments of Jamaica and El Salvador to have similar boards established.

Economists, however, doubt that a currency board would work in Russia. In theory, they say, it would work. But economic and political chaos there, coupled with pervasive corruption, would make it extremely difficult for a Russian currency board to adhere to the rules of the game.

"I question whether they could implement anything that was not subject to larceny," says Mr. Hanke. "You could only do it if you had a five-man board—with two Russians, an American, a German and a Brit, and kept the reserves in a carefully controlled Swiss bank account."

* * *

February 19, 1995

PREVENTING THE NEXT PESO-STYLE CRISIS

By PAUL LEWIS

Was the world's currency cop napping on the beat when Mexico's peso got mugged, costing investors millions and pushing the country toward recession?

That is not quite how C. Fred Bergsten put it last week at a meeting of the Institute for International Economics, which he directs. But it is what he implied when he asked Michael Mussa, the International Monetary Fund's chief economist, why the body set up to maintain good monetary order had issued no warning on Mexico.

Mr. Mussa replied that it was "outside the bounds of acceptable behavior" for an international financial institution "to create an international financial crisis" by telling investors to shy away from Mexico.

And even if it started issuing warnings, Mr. Mussa said symmetry would require the fund to do so for the rich as well as the poor and that would quickly get it into political hot water. Surely, he argued, all those well-paid economists at banks and mutual funds ought to be the whistle-blowers.

Yet in practice few did so, probably because the firms they work for were already too deeply committed to the Mexican market to welcome inconvenient news.

As Henry Kaufman, who runs his own investment firm after serving as Salomon Brothers' legendary Wall Street guru, puts it: "The objectivity of many analysts and economists has been compromised. Even those with the best intentions get caught up in the swirl of a deal."

So the hunt is on for a new early warning system to alert investors about trouble in emerging market economies, as well as a safety net to protect them against sudden speculative outflows in today's new world of volatile capital movements.

In a new study of the global debt problem, published by Mr. Bergsten's institute last week, William R. Cline suggests creating an International Bondholders Insurance Corporation within the World Bank to insure up to 80 percent of government loans in emerging markets.

Not only would this make it easier for such countries to attract foreign capital, but the proportion of a loan the I.B.I.C agreed to insure would serve as an index of a government's credit rating.

But, as Mr. Bergsten pointed out in Congressional testimony this month, the challenge of any early warning system is that it risks "triggering the very crisis one wants to avoid." He suggests tighter monitoring of vulnerable countries by a small, secret subcommittee of the I.M.F.'s executive board. This group would send its findings both to the country concerned and to the Group of Seven Finance Ministers.

The ministers could then offer financial aid to countries that cooperate but threaten to publish the subcommittee's unfavorable findings if they did not.

Mr. Bergsten suggested that such an early warning system should also be accompanied by a new $100 billion I.M.F. lending facility to help emerging market countries that suffer a sudden capital outflow restore confidence in their economies.

Robert Solomon, a former chief international economist at the Federal Reserve now with Washington's Brookings Institution, also favored closer monitoring of the International Monetary Fund and the creation of a new lending facility. At last week's meeting he called those steps "preferable to a return to capital controls or a slowdown in economic reform."

Today's huge capital flows were never foreseen by the fund's creators, he said, adding that given the present level of capital mobility, "crises like that experienced by Mexico can be expected to re-occur."

The I.M.F. should lift its self-imposed ban on financing large capital outflows, Mr. Solomon said, although it could still probably lend to countries suffering a reversal of capital inflows if they had a current account deficit, "which is more than likely."

Michel Camdessus, the I.M.F.'s managing director, is known to favor tighter surveillance, a new emerging economy safety net, as well as a $35 billion increase in world reserves through a new Special Drawing Right issue that would lift the financial strength of emerging economies, especially in the former Soviet empire.

All three reforms would also increase the power and prestige of the fund which, like the World Bank, is in danger of becoming marginalized by the growth of the private capital markets that last year supplied developing economies with $174 billion—compared with $49 billion in 1989.

But the Group of Seven Finance Ministers strongly oppose a big Special Drawing Right issue as inflationary. Mr. Camdessus should offer to reduce his request if the ministers will give serious consideration to tighter surveillance and a new safety net for emerging economies at the April meeting of the I.M.F.'s governing interim committee in Washington.

* * *

February 20, 1995

MEXICAN CRISIS DEPRESSING BRAZIL AND ARGENTINA STOCKS

By JAMES BROOKE
Special to The New York Times

RIO DE JANEIRO, Feb. 19—Two months after the start of Mexico's financial crisis, the shock waves are rippling south, depressing stock markets in Latin America's two other major economies—Brazil and Argentina.

Despite rallies Friday, the markets in São Paulo and Buenos Aires fell almost every trading day in February. Since Dec. 20, the day the Mexican crisis broke, São Paulo's Bovespa index has dropped 34 percent and Buenos Aires's Merval index has dropped 37 percent.

"There is a lot of potential supply, but virtually no demand," said Alden Brewster, New York partner for Banco Icatu, a Brazilian investment bank. "Speculators and bottom fishers don't want to go into what is perceived as a crisis situation."

While traders joke nervously about "submerging" markets, the steady outflow of capital from South America's largest stock markets is provoked by a variety of factors: rising interest rates in the United States, disappointment over a cautious privatization program in Brazil, and anxiety over a possible devaluation of the peso in Argentina.

Oddly, the sharp downturn in the Bovespa index in São Paulo coincides with a surge in long-term factory investment by foreign companies in Brazil. While hundreds of millions of dollars are flowing out of foreign-held stock portfolios in Brazil, foreign companies are pursuing 1995 investment plans in Brazil that total $5 billion, double the $2.5 billion invested last year.

Brazil investments by Ford Motor, Volkswagen and General Motors will total $2 billion through the end of 1996. With Brazil expected to repeat last year's growth of 5 percent, this year's overall investment rate is expected to hit 21 percent, a level not seen here since the "miracle" growth years of the 1970's.

While Brazil's production of color televisions, videocassette recorders and refrigerators is running at double the levels of two years ago, São Paulo's stock market, now Latin America's largest, is at its lowest level in 10 months.

Many foreign investors were heavy buyers of stocks in Brazil's state oil, electricity and telephone companies, gambling that President Fernando Henrique Cardoso would privatize these companies. But as a presidential candidate last fall, Mr. Cardoso said only that he would open these state monopolies to joint ventures with private partners. Last Thursday, he submitted to Brazil's Congress constitutional amendments to allow joint ventures.

"In the case of telephones, I cannot open to exploitation by private capital only the filet mignon, leaving the state with only the bones," Mr. Cardoso said when asked about disappointed stock market investors.

Today, stocks in the three state utility companies—Petrobras, Eletrobras, and Telebras—are worth roughly half of what they were in late September, a few days before Mr. Cardoso's election. Previously, foreign investment in Brazil's stock markets had soared.

"There is disappointment in the market over Brazil's definition of privatization," said Laurie W. Higgitt, director of Stephen Rose & Partners, a London brokerage firm specializing in Brazil and Argentina.

After Mexico's debacle with the overvalued peso, there also is concern that Brazil's new currency, the real, is overvalued by at least 25 percent. Used as a price anchor, the strong real contributes to Brazil's new low inflation rate— about 1 percent a month.

Coinciding with an opening to imports, the strong currency has pushed Brazil from enjoying a fat trade surplus into watching a trade deficit run for three consecutive months. In November and December, the United States maintained trade surpluses with only two of its major trading partners—Hong Kong and Brazil.

"The crisis in Mexico has not created any diversion for us; we are focusing on Brazil as one of the top three emerging export markets in coming years," Jeffrey E. Garten, United States Under Secretary of Commerce for International Trade, said in an interview today in Río, a stop in a 10-day tour of Argentina and Brazil.

Charles Dusseau, Florida's Secretary of Commerce, said after visiting São Paulo last week, "With everything that has happened to the Mexican peso, Brazil will be Florida's largest trading partner in 1995."

But Brazilians are afraid that their 1994 trade surplus of $10 billion will erode to a few billion dollars this year. Liquid reserves are already dipping, hitting $37 billion today, from a high of $41 billion last September.

"We can't keep losing reserves and we can't keep showing foreign trade deficits," said Carlos Langoni, a former Central Bank president.

Fears about an overvalued currency are undermining South America's second-largest stock market—Buenos Aires.

Although Argentina's peso can be devalued only through an act of Congress, nervous Argentines have withdrawn an estimated $2 billion from banks since the Mexican crisis. That is severely straining the banking system and forcing Argentina into an economic slowdown. In recent weeks, 1995 growth forecasts have been reduced to zero to 2 percent from the 5 or 6 percent level.

"Banks are delaying payments, there is no liquidity," said a Brazilian banker who asked not to be identified. "You have a country that is very much dependent on foreign money, and that spigot is off."

* * *

February 22, 1995

WITH DEEPER PAIN AHEAD, MANY MEXICANS ACCUSE PRESIDENT OF YIELDING SOVEREIGNTY

By ANTHONY DePALMA
Special to The New York Times

MEXICO CITY, Feb. 21—Almost before the ink dried on today's agreement to provide Mexico with $20 billion in emergency help from the United States, President Ernesto Zedillo has found himself accused in Mexico of trading his nation's sovereignty for a sack full of American dollars.

The severe economic restrictions that United States officials placed on the $20 billion in loans and loan guarantees mean that Mexico has surrendered an almost unprecedented degree of control over the management of its economy to its big neighbor at a critical time. Mr. Zedillo's presidency is already weakened less than three months into his six-year term, and social unrest is simmering through this country.

"As a Mexican, I'm really angry that these decisions are being made in Washington, not here," said Benjamin Miranda, a middle-class manager who was getting his shoes shined in front of the stock exchange here this afternoon. "People here are tired of so many drastic measures. It's like we're all in a pressure cooker that is about to explode."

While the agreement signed in Washington today may help ease the economic crisis set in motion by the peso's devaluation two months ago, it will force this nation and its embattled President to pay dearly in political as well as economic terms.

But it could also tarnish the United States in Mexican eyes by portraying it as an economic bully.

Most postwar economic rescue plans have been carried out by a number of countries and administered by the International Monetary Fund, which is also providing $17.8 billion to Mexico.

The fund's bureaucrats were blamed for the pain caused by the economic rigor those rescue packages demanded. But their professional anonymity diluted any political backlash against their prescriptions.

With the United States firmly in command of this Mexican rescue operation, the blame for the economic medicine to be swallowed by Mexico has become more focused.

"We had to pawn our oil to get this help, and I don't think it's really in our best interest," said Raul Cruz, a 24-year-old messenger at a downtown Mexico City office. "I'm worried that the Government is going to just use up all the money, like you'd use a Christmas bonus."

While the United States did not force Mexico to accept political concessions like breaking diplomatic relations with Cuba, as some members of the American Congress had demanded in Washington, Mexico did agree to raise interest rates and to allow the United States to review its handling of the economy.

There were some Mexicans, though, who agreed with Clinton Administration officials' insistence on strict guarantees from the Mexican Government.

"I think the United States has all the reason in the world to ask for guarantees," said Genaro Velázquez, a 56-year-old bank clerk. "They're giving us money and they want to protect themselves, to make sure we pay it back. Yes, we're losing a little of our sovereignty, but what does that matter if you don't have enough to eat?"

Yet, Mexico has agreed to cut its spending so severely that a deep recession seems inevitable. If that leads to deeper unemployment and poverty, as expected, this country's uneasy social order could erupt.

With the Mexican economy already teetering on the edge of recession and the peso still wobbly, President Zedillo may have had no choice but to accept the tough conditions placed on the money by Americans, who were not convinced that Mexico was ready to change the way it managed its economy.

If Mexican officials were hoping that the signing of the accord would buoy the peso or the stock market, they were disappointed. Stocks continued their slide today, losing a further 86.95 points, or 4.92 percent, to close at 1,679.19. Analysts said higher interest rates made investors switch from stocks to Government bonds and certificates.

And the peso closed at 5.605 to the dollar, down slightly from Monday's close of 5.565. A peso was worth almost 29 cents on Dec. 19. Now it is worth just under 18 cents.

In an interview with Mexican radio from Washington, Finance Minister Guillermo Ortiz tried to anticipate criticism that Mexico had surrendered too much authority to the United States. "There is absolutely no kind of political condition in this agreement," he said. "And the economic conditions that are included are ones that we ourselves have selected and that have been supported by international financial organizations."

Whether in fact the United States officials dictated policy or prescribed tough but necessary fiscal and monetary steps for Mexico, the impression that Mexico is bowing to Washington is widely held here.

Reaction was particularly negative to the requirement that receipts from export sales by Pemex, the state oil monopoly, be placed in an account at the Federal Reserve Bank of New York, where the United States will have a first claim on them in case Mexico defaults on its repayments of the $20 billion package.

"Part of the reserves of Mexico will be controlled not by a Mexican plan to protect our money supply but by the demands of the United States," the left-leaning daily La Jornada declared.

President Zedillo has spent much of his two and a half months in office struggling to get the Mexican economy back on the track that until recently made it one of the most attractive emerging markets in the world. But a series of missteps and seeming policy flip-flops have left him open to charges of being a weak leader—anathema in a Mexico that still expects a President to wield unquestionable authority.

Mexican officials said they will use the money from the $20 billion package to help reduce the Government's over-reliance on short-term debt denominated in dollars. Investors will be encouraged to trade one-year bonds for 5- and 10-year obligations. Other bonds will be paid off and retired. Mexican finance officials say that since the beginning of the year, the Government has reduced the value of outstanding bonds paid in dollars from $30 billion to just under $21 billion.

The details of the package announced today also make it possible for Mexico to use the money to help support some of Mexico's 18 largest commercial banks that have been forced to the brink of failure by the devaluation.

The rigid fiscal and monetary restraints that United States Treasury officials have forced upon Mexico will reduce consumption and restrict the outflows of money.

But what concerns most analysts and economists is that higher interest rates will choke off what little strength the Mexican economy has left and submerge Mexico in a deep recession. Since the financial crisis began in December, more than $10 billion has left the country. Automobile sales dropped by 50 percent in January, while sales of buses and trucks fell 84 percent. And unemployment has jumped substantially.

Rogelio Ramírez de la O, an economist here who often criticizes Government policies, said that instead of an economic-stabilization plan, the Government had put together "a bunch of gimmicks." And lacking a strong president who can lead the country through difficult times, Mr. Ramírez de la O said that Mexico's prospects for recovery, even with the $20 billion from the United States and billions more from other international sources, were dim.

After two months of crisis, many Mexicans seem to have lost some of their faith that the Government can turn the situation around.

"Supposedly, this package is going to save us," Humberto Hernández, a 42-year-old salesman, said of the foreign bailout. "It sounds so good what they say. But I have my doubts."

* * *

February 23, 1995

A STRUGGLE TO DEAL WITH A $20 BILLION PRECEDENT

By DAVID E. SANGER
Special to The New York Times

WASHINGTON, Feb. 22—As the United States and Mexico argued about the last details of a $20 billion rescue plan last week, one of the Clinton Administration's top economic officials fielded the same question time and again in his travels through Brazil and Argentina: If Mexico's ills spread, is the United States prepared to bail out its other big trading partners?

Much like other Administration officials, from Treasury Secretary Robert E. Rubin to Secretary of State Warren Christopher, Jeffrey E. Garten, the traveling Under Secretary of Commerce for international trade, hemmed and hawed a bit in response to the question.

"Of course, I told them Mexico was a very special case for us," Mr. Garten recalled replying, "because much more was at stake here than just trade. But honestly, no one can answer this question. And if we could you could never signal the answer in advance."

It is an uncomfortable question because it cuts to the heart of the emerging American post-cold-war role in the world. American troops have been stationed in Europe and Asia for decades as the guarantors of territorial security and protectors of United States interests abroad. But in Mexico, the United States has just stationed billions of dollars of capital and an elite unit of financial police, declaring that otherwise hundreds of thousands of American jobs might be lost and a financial panic could spread through emerging markets around the world.

It is compelling if unpopular logic. But it has left many in Washington wondering where to draw the line: What countries are now so vital to the new American economy that they cannot be allowed to fail?

Moreover, doesn't the Mexican bailout send an unwanted message to countries and those who invest in them around the world? Overborrow, overspend and fear not, because in the new international economy, everyone is so interdependent that there is always a bailout around the corner.

Not surprisingly, the message that the Administration is trying to send to the markets these days is a simple one: Don't count on it.

"Mexico was unique," Mr. Rubin said. The reason, of course, is the porous border with the United States. The financial turmoil in Mexico City, the White House kept reminding Congress, would be measured by the number of illegal aliens flowing into California and Texas. And then there are the 700,000 jobs the Administration contends are dependent on exports to Mexico, including 130,000 created in the last year.

Indeed, Mexico has virtually matched Japan as the second-largest market for American exports behind Canada. Through the third quarter of last year, Mexicans bought more than $51 billion in goods from the United States, compared with $51.7 billion by Japanese and $112 billion by Canadians.

Mexico had other special characteristics. More than most other big emerging-market countries like Argentina and China, it has been heavily dependent on short-term financing from abroad. That is the kind of investment that mutual fund managers can redirect with a few clicks on their computer keyboards, calling their money back to the United States or sending it elsewhere.

One lesson of the crisis is that it is safer to follow the example of countries like China and Indonesia, which have depended more heavily on foreign direct investment to build roads, factories and other necessary supports for economic growth. It takes a lot longer to move a car factory out of the country than it takes to get a short-term bond out.

And finally, as Mr. Rubin has said many times, Mexico has been the prototype economy, an exemplar of the way to privatize big industries, open markets and create a growing middle class eager to buy imports. If the prototype failed, he argued, it would discourage countries like Russia or even South Korea from following the same path.

But in one respect, Mexico was hardly special. It was one of the many emerging markets outside the United States, Europe and Japan in which Americans had dived headlong in recent years through mutual funds, lured by projections of huge profits and apparently unconcerned that they had only a vague idea of what made those economies tick.

Mr. Rubin feared that if investors decided to bail out of Mexico, they would bail out of everything that vaguely resembled Mexico in what he termed a "catalytic effect." There are suggestions that he was right. When Mexico's stock market declined, it took much of Latin America with it many days, and it was blamed, rightly or wrongly, for plunges as far away as Poland and Hong Kong.

That could have happened 20 years ago as well, of course. But as the chairman of the Federal Reserve, Alan Greenspan, pointed out in recent testimony, now it can happen so much more quickly. "In today's world," he said, "Mexico became the first casualty, if I may put it that way, of the new international financial system."

Mr. Greenspan is among those warning that the bailout, which he heartily supported, could create what economists call a "moral hazard." That is, investors looking at emerging markets could factor in the prospects of a bailout if everything goes bad. That, in turn, could keep the markets from accurately assessing the risk of investing in, say, Argentina or Indonesia.

As a result, Mr. Greenspan urged that any bailouts must emulate the Mexican rescue and carry such high costs and rigorous terms that investors worry that they would pay a price, as well.

Now the bailout theory has a new wrinkle. Because this one cost the United States so much, there is a new drive to overhaul the International Monetary Fund and other international organizations so that the United States Treasury does not become the World Market-Emergency Fund. Here, too, the fear is that such an overhaul might encourage more countries to live at the edge, knowing that there are bigger institutions around to save their necks.

The issue will be among the key topics at the Group of Seven meeting of leading industrial nations in Halifax, Nova Scotia, this summer. But in the meantime, the United States is saying anew that no one should expect to be treated the way the Mexicans were.

"It would be very foolish if we didn't learn from this," Mr. Christopher said last week to the Senate Foreign Relations Committee. "It was fortunate that the President had available $20 billion in a stabilization fund that he could bring to bear on this particular crisis."

But $20 billion does not grow on trees, he noted, and "the United States probably could not handle a second crisis like that."

*   *   *

February 26, 1995

ECONOMY REELING, MEXICANS PREPARE TOUGH NEW STEPS

By ANTHONY DePALMA
Special to The New York Times

MEXICO CITY, Feb. 25—Clear signs that Mexico's economic crisis is worsening have forced the Government to concede that its original economic stabilization plan has failed and that a tougher new plan of budget cuts and tax increases will have to be enacted soon.

President Ernesto Zedillo announced his original damage-control plan on Jan. 3, but Mexican officials say it failed to arrest stampeding inflation and an impending recession largely because the United States took too long to deliver the vital financial assistance that President Clinton offered to help Mexico.

Ever since the $20 billion American rescue package was finally signed on Tuesday, President Zedillo has been busy telling Mexicans the crisis is under control. Meanwhile, his top financial advisers have been drafting a darkly realistic new rescue plan that shows Mexico is slipping further into the inflationary whirlpool of rapidly rising wages and prices that it had vowed to avoid.

Government officials who have worked on early drafts of the new plan, which Mr. Zedillo said would be announced "very soon," say it slashes predictions of economic growth for 1995 from 1.5 percent to zero or even negative growth, which would mean that the Government is finally acknowledging the inevitability of a recession. Many economists say one has already begun. Inflation, which was projected at 19 percent in the original plan, is now expected to soar to almost double that figure.

The projected exchange rate of 4.5 pesos to the dollar, on which the economic projections of the plan were based, is replaced with an imposing new rate of 5 to 5.5 pesos to the dollar. This means that the peso would be worth no more than 18 to 20 cents, rather than 22 cents.

The new plan anticipates that taxes will be increased sharply, prices for gasoline and electricity produced by the state will rise, and the federal budget will be cut severely to produce the surplus of five-tenths of 1 percent that United States officials demanded as one condition for signing a $20 billion rescue package. The American assistance will go a long way toward resolving Mexico's most immediate problem—paying off billions of dollars in short-term debt—but it will do little to solve the economy's fundamental problems.

"Since Jan. 3, we've been fighting not to adjust the economy but simply to control a situation of economic panic," President Zedillo said during an informal talk over tequila and chimichangas after several optimistic speeches on Thursday in the central state of Zacatecas, where he had gone to raise the spirits of Mexicans. He said the original plan might have been successful in controlling Mexico's out-of-balance current account deficit, the broadest measure of a nation's goods and services, "but now we know the problems go far deeper than that."

Mexican officials working on the new economic stabilization plan also say it will differ from the original because it abandons the social pact between Government, labor and business that has long characterized the preferred method of controlling the economy.

Instead of sitting down with labor and business leaders to negotiate the kind of wage and price controls that so far this year have failed to hold the line, officials say the Government will act on its own powers. That will entail sharply cutting the federal budget and maintaining interest rates at historically high levels to restrain inflation and stabilize the exchange rate.

Minimum wages might be raised by 5 percent, but the increase will not be used as a guideline for union contract wages, which will be negotiated separately, officials said.

The Government is also preparing an emergency employment program to relieve the pressure of the budget cuts from areas where social and political tensions have been high, like the southern states of Chiapas and Tabasco.

Mexican officials say their initial plan of Jan. 3 was intended to work in tandem with a quick infusion of money from the United States. One important member of Mr. Zedillo's economic team, who spoke on the condition of anonymity, said the assistance was expected to come a few days after President Clinton and Congressional leaders in Washington announced on Jan. 12 that the United States would provide $40 billion in loan guarantees.

Despite the strong initial backing of President Clinton and Congressional leaders, that offer of help met stiff opposition in Washington and was eventually abandoned. Mr. Clinton used his executive powers to put together a $20 billion package that did not need Congressional approval.

"In the end it really took quite a long time for the money to come," the Mexican official said. "In the meantime there was a lot of nervousness in the market. People were getting worried. Investors wanted to see a signed agreement. As time passed, the uncertainty affected interest rates and the exchange rate."

The official said it was clear that as inflation and unemployment worsened and prices headed for the heavens, the economic targets of the Jan. 3 stabilization plan had become impossible to reach. "But," he said, "it wouldn't have made any sense for the Government to put out new figures until the American package was signed."

Even the signing of the agreement with the United States on Tuesday has failed to calm Mexico's financial markets. Since Tuesday morning, the Mexican stock exchange has fallen 212 points, including a drop of 57.8 points, or 3.6 percent, on Friday. In all, the exchange's index dropped 15 percent this week.

The conclusion of the American assistance package on Tuesday also did not help the peso much. On Friday, its value fell another 3 percent to close at 5.875 to the dollar. Since its devaluation in December, the peso, once worth almost 29 cents, has lost 41 percent of its value and is now worth just over 17 cents.

There are several other signs that Mexico's economic crisis is deepening. The Bank of Mexico reported on Thursday that inflation for the first half of February was 2.2 percent, which would amount to 67 percent on an annual basis, another indication that the initial stabilization plan failed to control prices.

Interest rates also have soared to historic levels in Mexico, causing further havoc with the economy. Just this week, rates on Government treasury certificates reached 59 percent, while an important interbank interest rate soared to 74 percent. That bank rate is used to determine interest for mortgages, car loans and credit cards, which now charge 97 percent annual interest.

Those interest rates have forced many debtors to fall behind on bank loans. The Government this week required banks to increase their reserves to cover uncollectable loans.

Mexico's businesses have also been hammered by the interest rate increases and other effects of the peso's devaluation. The president of one of Mexico's most important business councils, Luis German Carcoba, estimated this week that 250,000 jobs had been lost since January.

Mexican officials say they think the new plan being worked on at Los Pinos, the Mexican White House, will not put the economy back on track before the end of the year. They call it an adjustment of the original, which they say was at least successful in reducing the trade imbalance that contributed to Mexico's economic woes.

Figures released on Thursday show that Mexican exports shot up 35 percent in January, largely because the devaluation has made the country's products cheaper. But imports increased 7.9 percent, indicating that Mexicans' craving for foreign products has not gone away.

Mr. Zedillo told cheering supporters in Zacatecas on Thursday that Mexico "will not be conquered by a temporary crisis," but members of his administration say there have been serious setbacks and the future remains uncertain.

"We have had to recognize that the financial markets haven't evolved as we thought they should," said a presidential adviser familiar with the new recovery plan. "The shocks to the market have been longer and deeper than we originally thought. How much longer or deeper will they go? I couldn't say."

* * *

March 1, 1995

THE GLOBAL CASINO

By THOMAS L. FRIEDMAN

WASHINGTON—So I decided to put a little money into global markets last year. I brushed up on Spanish and invested in Argentina. Took a Berlitz course in Japanese and bought a few Tokyo bonds. Lavishly tipped the waiters at the House of Hunan Chinese restaurant and picked up some stock tips in Shanghai. I even learned the difference between G.N.P., G.D.P., DDT and AT&T and invested in equities from Paris to Istanbul. For old times' sake my broker suggested I buy some Lebanese bonds, but I told him our house already had wallpaper.

At the end of the year, I looked over my dismal balance sheet and realized that with all my multilingual, multicultural, multinational research there were two little words I forgot to learn: "Alan Greenspan."

Like me, so many mutual fund holders who sailed off into international waters pretended that they really understood the economic reforms under way in Mexico or Thailand or China and found them worthy investments. In reality, though, they were simply going offshore because interest rates in the U.S. had fallen so low that when presented with the chance to earn 10 percent they jumped at the opportunity without comprehending the risks.

But as soon as Mr. Greenspan started hiking interest rates a year ago, a lot of that hot money that had been flowing mindlessly into emerging markets like Mexico hiked right back home into safe, well-paying U.S. T-bills. As that happened, the emerging markets became sagging markets and investors got ravaged.

Lesson 1: If you are investing in international markets you are much better served by studying the words of Chairman Greenspan than the words of Chairman Mao (or Zedillo, or Menem or Rao). In a world where money flows back and forth across borders, no one has more influence over the direction and rate of that flow than Mr. Greenspan. So skip the Chinese takeout and throw away the Japanese language tapes. The best language to be fluent in on the global investment highway is "Greenspanese." Understanding what he is doing with interest rates at home is the first step to investing abroad.

But 1994 was rich in other lessons about the global economy as well.

Lesson 2: Daddy always said, "Diversify, diversify, diversify." So a lot of global investors diversified. They bought bonds in Japan, bonds in China, bonds in Mexico and bonds in Germany. And guess what happened? They got killed all across the board. They thought they were diversified, but in fact they just owned bonds in what is now a single, unified global marketplace. The linkages between global markets today are so tight that you cannot diversify by simply investing in a smorgasbord of different countries. The only way to really diversify is not by country, but by investment instrument and level of risk. You have to spread out among low-medium- and high-risk stocks, bonds, currencies and commodities. If you just buy bonds in different countries you will quickly discover that you never left home.

Lesson 3: Governments may have lost a lot of power to markets, but they still matter. It is government policies that first shape the quality of the bonds and currencies trading around the globe. Mexico initially got into trouble because its Government tried to buy an election by printing money without devaluing the fixed-rate peso. All the money managers did was tell Mexico this was unsustainable. That is why the global investor George Soros likes to say, "I am the most highly paid theater critic in the world." The leaders put on the show, the money managers write the reviews and the countries suffer (or enjoy) the consequences.

Lesson 4: With markets opening up in China, Eastern Europe and the former Soviet Union, never have more people been making more investments in more places they cannot find on a map with more people whose names they cannot pronounce in more financial instruments they do not understand. Robert Baldoni, head of the Emcor derivative consulting firm, has a golden rule for navigating the new world. It applies to individual investors, treasurers of Orange County and 28-year-old traders at Barings. Says Mr. Baldoni: "I invest money for my mother, who is now retired. I will invest in a variety of instruments, but I won't make any investment for my mother the logic of which she can't repeat back to me."

THE ASIAN FINANCIAL CRISIS

June 26, 1997

THE ECONOMY AND MARKETS FRAIL, THAIS BREED SKEPTICS

By SETH MYDANS

Thailand's new finance minister has moved to repair the country's troubled financial system, but analysts see little evidence so far that the Government has found the resolve to rejuvenate the faltering economy.

The Thai stock market reacted with initial relief to assurances by the new minister, Thanong Bidya, a 49-year-old economist and banker appointed last Thursday, that he would stick to his predecessor's economic recovery plan.

The main stock index surged 8.6 percent in a two-day rally on Friday and Monday before retreating 2.3 percent Tuesday on profit taking and continued concern about the country's trade deficit and weakening currency. Yesterday, it rose modestly despite new doubts raised about the Government's recovery program and new fears of a currency devaluation.

Mr. Thanong won Cabinet approval on Tuesday for two measures aimed at reviving the financial system—one that would allow property loans to be repackaged and sold as securities and the other that would promote mergers among ailing finance companies.

But yesterday, analysts expressed skepticism about the initiatives, saying they were unlikely to have much impact. "They're something of a fudge," said Richard Henderson, research chief at Krungthai Thanakit P.L.C. "The real alternative is to let genuine bankruptcies happen."

The analysts said the Government had yet to overcome the political infighting that has held up meaningful economic change. Indeed, they said, the resignation last week of the previous Finance Minister, Amnuay Viravan, star of the Government's onetime economic "dream team," in a dispute over excise taxes underscored a paralysis in the country's political leadership.

Prime Minister Chavalit Yongchaiyuth, taking a break from economic and political crisis, flew to Phnom Penh, Cambodia, over the weekend for an official visit. But when he returned to Bangkok, there was increasing disillusionment with his handling of the economy and doubt about the durability of his seven-month coalition Government.

"Party politics has prevailed and the economy is again the biggest loser," the English-language Bangkok Post said in an editorial.

The appointment in December of Mr. Amnuay as Finance Minister had aroused resentment from other members of the governing coalition because the new minister had not earned his spurs by running for Parliament. From the start, his policies faced challenges from political opponents in the six-party coalition.

When Moody's Investors Service lowered Thailand's long-term credit rating in April, it said that although eco-

nomic fundamentals were sound, the nation's unstable, personality-based coalition governments were prone to exactly the sort of pressures and infighting that in time brought down Mr. Amnuay.

Although Thailand's economy is humming along nicely by American standards, this country has been one of Asia's "tigers," where growth that would be considered extraordinary in much of the rest of the world is almost expectable here.

Last year, the Thai growth rate fell to 6.7 percent from an average of more than 8 percent in previous years, and last week the central bank lowered its projection for 1997 growth to 5.9 percent from 6.8 percent. If the economy continues on its present course, analysts say, Thailand could end the year with both an unaccustomed trade deficit and its first budget deficit in 10 years.

Yesterday, there was more bad news as economists estimated that Thailand had spent $5 billion in May shoring up its currency, the baht, and analysts questioned how long the Government could head off a devaluation. And the political climate heated up, with opposition members of Parliament demanding during a budget debate that Prime Minister Chavalit account for $2.1 billion they said was missing from the treasury.

The country's economic woes and political tensions have been painfully reflected in the Thai stock market, East Asia's weakest in the last year and a half. In 1996, what had been a booming market lost nearly 39 percent of its value, and so far this year, the main stock index is down nearly 40 percent beyond that.

The financial system is increasingly vulnerable. Thailand's rapid economic growth had been fueled in part by a construction boom that produced a glut in office and apartment buildings, golf courses, shopping centers and entertainment complexes. And the banks and other lenders that financed the expansion are left holding a lot of bad loans, dragging down the broad economy.

Thailand's slowdown has raised fears among some of its fast-developing neighbors that they might be heading toward the same sorts of financial strains. The Philippines, in particular, has experienced a construction boom that has some people fretting it might become the "next Thailand."

Mr. Amnuay's recovery package included a multibillion-dollar government cost-cutting program, tighter controls on lending, forced mergers of troubled finance companies and a $2 billion property rescue.

But as the economy continued to falter, he became the target of growing criticism. The last straw was the decision by the Cabinet, under pressure from affected industries, to overturn an excise tax increase levied weeks before on motorcycles, batteries and granite. When that happened, he quit in protest.

Almost from the moment that Mr. Thanong was appointed as Mr. Amnuay's successor, he came under criticism as too inexperienced and politically weak to deal as finance minister with the country's economic problems.

But Prime Minister Chavalit said that he already had plenty of economic policies and that what he needed was "someone to do the job." He said he would take charge of economic policy himself, although he has said in the past that he knows little about the field.

"The basic problem," a Western financial analyst remarked, "is that Thailand has no central leadership—an unstable, inefficient leadership. The country as a whole is stable, but its coalition governments are tremendously unstable. People who have bet their fortunes on continued growth are suffering."

Still, he said, "it's hard to cry too much over economic growth rates that are still 5 or 6 percent."

* * *

July 3, 1997

THE THAI GAMBLE: DEVALUING CURRENCY TO REVIVE ECONOMY

By SETH MYDANS

The central bank of Thailand's decision yesterday to devalue the currency, which caused it to tumble as much as 20 percent against the dollar, represents a gamble by Thai policy makers to shore up the country's faltering economy.

By instituting what it called a "managed float," in which the baht will be allowed to fluctuate more widely against other currencies—in effect, a devaluation—the bank took pressure off the Government's foreign-exchange reserves, which had been drained of billions of dollars as officials sought to prop up the currency against assaults by speculators. A weaker baht also lowers the cost in other currencies of Thai exports and stocks, making them attractive.

And the devaluation may eventually lead to an easing of monetary policy; by keeping interest rates high, the central bank tried to support the beleaguered currency.

On the other hand, while interest rates might eventually fall—helping the economy regain the kind of growth that had turned Thailand into one of Asia's "tigers"—the central bank's immediate move on rates was quite different. Accompanying the currency devaluation, the bank raised a key lending rate by two percentage points to guard against a surge in inflation—now a sharper threat. By requiring more baht to buy a dollar, a weaker currency could raise the cost of imports.

The devaluation will also hurt the many Thai companies that have heavy debts denominated in foreign money.

"It was a very risky move, courageous and risky," said a Western economist, who insisted that he not be further identified. "The consequences are totally unknown. It's an extremely fluid situation."

The move came after repeated Government assurances that the baht would not be devalued. Three days ago, Prime Minister Chavalit Yongchaiyudh repeated the assurances in a

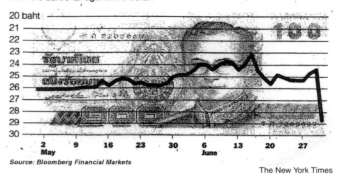

Letting the Baht Float

The number of Thai baht to the dollar, plotted daily. The chart has been inverted to show the baht's fall against the dollar.

Source: Bloomberg Financial Markets

The New York Times

televised speech, saying that if the currency were devalued, "we will all become poor."

What, then, pushed the central bank to take this gamble? After all, with a fast-growing economy in a fast-growing region, Thailand has been a free-market success story.

Bangkok, where most of the growth has been concentrated, has been awash in more money than it sometimes seems to know what to do with. Above the proliferating wine bars and auto showrooms, an overpowering new skyline has emerged—hundreds of imposing modern buildings filled with enough unsold space to satisfy residential and commercial needs for the next five years, according to some estimates. And the building boom continues.

But over the last year, the economy has slowed, with growth falling to 6.7 percent last year from 8.5 percent in 1995, and people have become worried. Exports are down sharply and the nation is facing a budget deficit for the first time in a decade. Until a rebound yesterday, the stock market had dipped to eight-year lows, the trade deficit had risen and bad property loans had brought crisis to financial institutions.

Aggravating the crisis, foreign speculators, expecting the baht to fall sharply, began selling the currency, forcing the central bank to try to prop it up.

A hedge fund operated by George Soros, the billionaire investor, was known to be among the bigger speculators involved in selling the currency short, hoping to profit from an anticipated decline in its value.

Reports in a Thai publication said Mr. Soros's hedge fund was involved in a $4 billion bet that the currency would fall sharply, a strategy he employed to great profit in the early 1990's shorting the British pound.

But Stanley Druckenmiller, the chief fund manager at Soros Fund Management L.L.C., said that reports of a $4 billion bet were "greatly exaggerated." He said that although the fund expected to profit from the devaluation, it had previously suffered some losses because of the central bank's strategy of thwarting speculators by delaying a devaluation and restricting borrowing the currency to sell at a profit.

"I think they won the battle against the speculators," Mr. Druckenmiller said yesterday. "A lot of speculators lost money. And the central bank was successful in getting us to reduce our position, but we've made some profits."

In response to the currency attacks, the devaluation was an unexpectedly decisive step by a Government that has been criticized for vacillation in the face of growing economic problems. Its success or failure could determine the future of the shaky seven-month coalition Government led by Mr. Chavalit.

"You have to admire Chavalit" for endorsing the devaluation, the Western economist said. "Either he's crazy or he's very brave."

Still, the decision, coming after the new Thai Finance Minister had promised investors there would be no sharp changes in economic policy, could be seen as a measure of the unreliability of the country's economic managers, the Western economist said. "Their credibility is not strong," he added. "They've broken their word several times."

One skeptic was Barton M. Biggs, global strategist at Morgan Stanley, who contended that the Thai central bank had shown little ability in managing a precarious situation. "Investing in Thailand has become a lot riskier than it was three months ago," he said. Yet stocks are more than 30 percent cheaper than they were at the start of the year, he said, "so you have to weigh the trade-off."

After the central bank said yesterday that it would let the currency float, the exchange value dropped as much as 20 percent, to 29.50 baht to the dollar offshore. In New York yesterday, it settled at 28.7 to the dollar.

The main Thai stock index rose 7.9 percent on the news, its biggest rally in more than five years, and the index of the 50 largest stocks was up 9.27 percent.

But with many Thai companies carrying such heavy foreign-currency debt, the long-range consequences of the devaluation were still in question.

Thai companies and individuals hold more than $70 billion in foreign debt, equivalent to about half the country's economic output last year. A de facto currency devaluation of 20 percent, therefore, would mean that the debt jumps by the equivalent of $14 billion, an increase that could be fatal to many banks and property companies.

Some economists argued against a devaluation, saying that it would create additional difficulty for companies that relied on foreign-currency dealings and for manufacturers that imported components from abroad. Economists also warned that devaluation could bring inflation and even risk recession.

After Mexico devalued the peso more than two years ago, it was forced to raise interest rates. They soared eightfold before falling, and are still double what they were before devaluation. And Mexico has yet to fully recover from the economic crisis its devaluation unleashed.

There is also concern in Asia that the ripple effects of the baht's devaluation might be felt outside Thailand. In rapidly growing countries like the Philippines, Malaysia and Indonesia, banks have extended large loans to their fast-growing property markets, risking similar problems that helped precipitate the Thai crisis.

This lending has been more restrained in those countries, amid alarm about the "Thai model" of overbuilding and over-extended property investments.

Still, the Philippines and Malaysia moved yesterday to protect their own currencies—the Philippine central bank raising the overnight borrowing rate twice, to 24 percent, and Malaysia's central bank intervening to buy its currency, the ringgit, for dollars.

*   *   *

July 24, 1997

FOR A NEW GENERATION OF ASIAN TIGERS, A HARSH CURRENCY LESSON

By PETER PASSELL

The first to fall was Thailand, which was forced to devalue its currency earlier this month to prevent a horde of speculators from draining its Government reserves dry. Then, in quick succession, the currencies of Malaysia, the Philippines and Indonesia were battered by secondary shocks.

To some conservative analysts, the lesson here is that these emerging markets erred by abandoning fixed exchange rates and will now suffer the consequences. But that criticism appears to be putting the cart before the horse. Given the policy mistakes of the recent past, if this generation of Asian tigers had tried even harder to prevent devaluation, it would probably have made a bad situation even worse.

What the currency shock has done is remind Asia's fast-growing economies that the old rules—high savings rates, a strong work ethic and a welcome mat to foreign investors—are not quite sufficient to insure their prosperity indefinitely. More is needed to complete their transformation to the full-scale industrial status of their predecessors in the development race like South Korea and Taiwan. To cope with mobile global capital, they also need well-regulated banking systems and, most likely, probably, exchange policies that force outside investors to bear more of the risk of rate fluctuations.

When the Mexican peso toppled in 1993, it seemed only natural that the currencies of most other Latin American economies would come under pressure. "There was a history of linkage dating from the debt crisis," noted Peter Kenen, an economist at Princeton University.

More than a few experts were embarrassed, though, after the devaluation of the Thai baht caused the flight of capital from a group of Southeast Asian economies long viewed as models of development. "Nobody expected this level of contagion," Mr. Kenen said.

The simplest explanation is that all of these partly developed economies were weaker than generally recognized— and vulnerable to competition from below. China, which has considerably lower wages, is challenging them in a variety of export markets, while Vietnam and India are waiting in the wings.

Yet all of them, noted Jeffrey Sachs, director of the Harvard Institute for International Development, inadvertently handicapped their exporters by linking their currencies to the high-flying United States dollar.

One way or another, Mr. Sachs said, capital imports must be paid for out of revenues from sales abroad. So by allowing their exports to become expensive in terms of both the Japanese yen and European currencies, they shot themselves in the foot. "Emerging-market countries need to tie their currencies to broader trade-weighted baskets," Mr. Sachs concluded.

There is more to the story, though, than a technical error, argues David Hale, an economist at Kemper/Zurich in Chicago. Open global capital markets made it possible for Thai banks to borrow tens of billions of dollars from their foreign counterparts. In turn, these dollars fueled domestic consumption and a speculative boom in real estate. This put the Thai Government in a bind.

On the one hand, allowing the baht to appreciate against the yen and European currencies as the dollar rose put Thai exports, and exporters, at a serious disadvantage.

On the other, devaluing the baht at a time when Thai banks—and their customers—were saddled with more than $60 billion in dollar-denominated debt would drive the banking system underwater.

The baht did fall, of course, after it became obvious that betting against the Thai currency was a no-lose proposition. Now Thailand faces the unenviable problem of coping with insolvent financial institutions as it tries to jump-start the economy. "Open capital markets demand well-regulated banks," Mr. Hale concluded.

By the same token, the crisis calls into question the wisdom of fixing exchange values. A fixed rate is seductive, reducing the need for traders to hedge against currency risks and serving as a buffer against import-fueled inflation.

Indeed, a handful of economies—most notably Hong Kong, Estonia and Argentina—have taken fixed rates to the logical extreme, effectively adopting strong foreign currencies as their own.

But in Thailand, a fixed exchange rate camouflaged the economy's increasingly precarious position and forced the Government into a corner. And in Malaysia, where Prime Minister Mahathir Mohamad railed against the speculation of a "certain American financier," namely George Soros, the central bank spent $3 billion in a matter of days simply to contain the fall of the Malaysian ringgit to 4 percent.

In Indonesia, by contrast, the official policy of allowing the rupiah to fluctuate across a wide band reduced the need for Government intervention and probably saved Indonesia tens of billions of dollars in currency reserves. "The case here for exchange rate flexibility is compelling," Mr. Kenen argued.

In a perfect world, private capital markets, international and domestic, would police themselves: both the risk of exchange rate depreciation and lender default would be fully factored into investment decisions. In the real world, capital flows are subject to fad, speculation and distorted incentives. "One wishes the markets were less fickle," said Derek Hargreaves, an economist at J. P. Morgan. But fickle they are.

And as Southeast Asia's (presumably temporary) fall from economic grace suggests, in the absence of effective self-discipline there is no substitute for prudent regulation.

*   *   *

August 12, 1997

I.M.F., WITH THE HELP OF ASIANS, OFFERS THAIS $16 BILLION BAILOUT

By ANDREW POLLACK

TOKYO, Aug. 11—The International Monetary Fund and a group of Asian nations led by Japan agreed today to a $16 billion rescue of Thailand's troubled financial system, which has been jolted by a currency crisis that has spread through South and Southeast Asia, threatening the region's rapid growth.

The package of loans, announced after a meeting here, is the second-largest international bailout, though significantly smaller than the $50 billion rescue of Mexico from the peso collapse of 1994–95.

The money will be used by Thailand to help shore up its foreign reserves, which were depleted by a futile attempt to save its currency, the baht, from being devalued last month. The reserves are needed to pay for imports and to meet some foreign-debt obligations.

Officials announcing the package called it a precedent-setting example of regional cooperation, as Asian nations acted to keep Thailand's problems from spreading. "What is impressive about the financial package this time is we have substantial contributions from the countries of the Asia-Pacific region," Eisuke Sakakibara, Japan's vice finance minister for international affairs, said at a news conference.

The United States attended today's meeting, as did Germany, Britain, France and Canada, but those nations are not taking part in the rescue directly. This appears to result in part from a feeling that the Asians, with the most at stake, can and should handle the problem.

Among the countries taking part, Japan—Asia's dominant economy and with huge investments in Thailand—is playing the leading role, contributing $4 billion. That matches the amount to be contributed by the International Monetary Fund. Australia, Hong Kong, Malaysia and Singapore will each contribute $1 billion, while Indonesia and South Korea will chip in $500 million apiece. The remaining $3 billion or so is expected to come from the Asian Development Bank, the World Bank and possibly from China. The loans will come due in three to five years, and will generally be in line with market rates.

In addition to the government and international lending agency help, Thailand is expected to receive billions of dollars in new financing from commercial banks, led by those in Japan. The Thai Finance Minister, Thanong Bidaya, is scheduled to meet with major Japanese banks on Tuesday. And Mr. Sakakibara of the Japanese Finance Ministry remarked, "I think the discussion between the Thai authorities and Japanese banks will proceed smoothly."

Once the paragon of a fast-growing Asian economy, Thailand has suffered a slowdown in exports because of new competition from China and other nations with lower wages, and also because the baht had been tied to a strengthening dollar. Even more damaging has been a huge-scale bad debt problem caused by overinvestment in real estate and factories.

After long denying the severity of its problems, the Thai Government was forced last week to agree to emergency measures to restructure its economy in return for the loans announced today.

Other Asian countries have an incentive to help Thailand because many of them are affected, though perhaps to a smaller degree, by the same economic problems and pressures on their currencies. However, previous agreements among Asian central banks to cooperate on currency stabilization were ineffective in preventing the recent turmoil.

Since Thai officials gave up trying to defend the baht—allowing it on July 2 to float at market rates—the currency has fallen about 20 percent against the dollar. The Philippine peso, Malaysian ringgit and Indonesian rupiah have fallen roughly 6 or 7 percent. Three and a half weeks ago, the International Monetary Fund approved a $1 billion loan to the Philippines to help it cope with the currency crisis.

But the problems in Thailand have wider effects, and pose a particular threat to Japan. Its auto makers control virtually all of the Thai car market; its electronics companies have made Thailand a big manufacturing and export base, and Japanese banks hold about half of the country's $89 billion in foreign debt. Already, some Japanese-owned auto plants in Thailand have had to slow operations because of the financial crisis.

Yet Tokyo, which since the end of World War II has been reticent about taking the lead in world affairs, has not played as strong a role as Washington did in rescuing Mexico. Although the Japanese are exercising influence, they have allowed the International Monetary Fund to be out in front. The rescue generated little controversy here, unlike in the United States when the Mexican bailout was proposed. There was perhaps some worry that Japan would set a precedent, that it might have to rescue other Asian nations in financial trouble. But by enlisting the help of other countries in the region, it mitigated such concerns.

Officials at today's meeting here said that Thailand required $14 billion for 1997 and 1998, so the $16 billion agreed upon should be more than enough for current needs.

While the rescue package is expected to shore up international confidence in Thailand, the hard work of changing some aspects of the Thai economy lies ahead. Dissatisfaction in Thailand, both with the Government's perceived mishandling of the crisis and with the bitter economic medicine to follow, has caused speculation on a coup attempt, though the Prime Minister, Chavalit Yongchaiyudh, has insisted that he has full control of the often-assertive Thai military.

To qualify for the international bailout, Thailand agreed last week to reduce public spending, raise the value-added tax to 10 percent from 7 percent, and suspend the operations of 42 debt-ridden financial companies.

The nation's currency losses mean that interest payments on the Thai foreign debt have swelled 20 percent, as measured in baht. Prices on imports will climb, contributing to inflation. The slowdown in construction, factory production and consolidation of the financial industry is expected to increase unemployment.

"We realized the devaluation of the baht will create some inflationary pressure in Thailand," Mr. Thanong, the Finance Minister, said at the news conference today. "But somehow we feel it's a necessary step to make Thai exports more competitive."

He predicted that Thailand will grow 3 percent this year and 4 percent next year, well down from growth of more than 6 percent in 1996 and the 9 percent spurts that were once considered normal. Mr. Thanong said he expected Thailand to resume rapid growth in 1999. Some economists find these projections optimistic.

*　*　*

September 22, 1997

PREMIER OF MALAYSIA SPARS WITH CURRENCY DEALER

By EDWARD A. GARGAN

HONG KONG, Sept. 21—It was high noon in Hong Kong this weekend.

Like gunfighters on a dust-blown street, one of Asia's most outspoken leaders, Prime Minister Mahathir Mohamad of Malaysia, faced off against one of the world's most formidable currency speculators, George Soros. In their holsters were weapons of oratory, currency and clout.

At stake was nothing less than Malaysia's national prestige, the future of Southeast Asian economies and, by some accounts, the very shape of the global financial system.

Even more, the standoff pitted two worlds against one another, an Asia of growing economic might and a West convinced that free-wheeling trade—in ideas, capital and goods—is the best recipe for development.

The forum was the usually somber gathering of finance ministers, bankers and economists at the annual meeting of the World Bank and International Monetary Fund. On successive evenings, Mr. Mahathir and Mr. Soros squared off, denouncing each other in vitriolic language seldom heard in such settings.

Yet Malaysia's economy is in crisis, its currency has collapsed and blame had to be fixed.

Lashing out at currency traders like Mr. Soros as "morons," Mr. Mahathir castigated them on Saturday as "a group of ultra-rich people."

"For them wealth must come from impoverishing others," Mr. Mahathir said, "from taking what others have in order to enrich themselves. Their weapon is their wealth against the poverty of others."

While not mentioning Mr. Soros by name—although in previous comments to newspapers in Malaysia, Mr. Mahathir specifically blamed Mr. Soros for orchestrating Malaysia's economic crisis—he told the assembled bankers and economists that Mr. Soros's ilk had to be stopped.

"I am saying that currency trading is unnecessary, unproductive and totally immoral," Mr. Mahathir declared. "It should be stopped. It should be made illegal. We don't need currency trading."

Then tonight, before a standing-room-only crowd, Mr. Soros fired back at the Malaysian leader.

"Dr. Mahathir's suggestion yesterday to ban currency trading is so inappropriate that it does not deserve serious consideration," Mr. Soros said.

"Interfering with the convertibility of capital at a moment like this is a recipe for disaster. Dr. Mahathir is a menace to his own country."

Since July, in the churning wake of the collapse of Thailand's currency and banking system, Malaysia has foundered. Its currency, the ringgit, has plunged 20 percent against the dollar. On the heels of the tumbling ringgit, the Malaysian stock market crashed and the country's banking system began to creak. Foreign investors fled.

For Mr. Mahathir, who has seen his country's annual per-capita output soar from $350 to $5,000 in four decades, the assault on the ringgit smacked of a conspiracy wrought by international currency traders.

For a man who has built the world's tallest buildings and Southeast Asia's largest airport and who harbors visions of a glittering new capital, a high-tech corridor intended to rival Silicon Valley and immense hydroelectric dams, the economic train wreck has been an affront, to him personally and to Asia.

"We like to think big," Mr. Mahathir said. "But we are not going to be allowed to do this, because you don't like us to have big ideas. It is not proper. It is impudent for us to try, or even to say we are going to do it. If we even say that when we have the money we will carry on with our big projects, you will make sure we won't have the money by forcing the devaluation of the currency.

"If the countries of Europe and of North America can be almost uniformly prosperous, we don't see why we cannot be allowed to be a little prosperous."

Then tonight, 24 hours after Mr. Mahathir's broadside against Mr. Soros, currency traders and the international financial system, Mr. Soros stood behind the same lectern and declared that the problem with Malaysia was not the world, but Mr. Mahathir himself.

"He is using me as a scapegoat to cover up his own failure," Mr. Soros said. "He is playing to a domestic audience, and he couldn't get away with it if he and his ideas were subject to the discipline of an independent media inside Malaysia."

Later, at a news conference, Mr. Soros elaborated on his comments. "I want to express my sympathy for poor Malaysians who were hurt" by the collapse of the country's currency and stock market, "but not for Dr. Mahathir, because he's responsible."

The war of words reverberated through the cavernous conference halls, startling government officials and private bankers used to more measured language.

An Indonesian Government economist, who spoke on condition of anonymity, was angered by Mr. Mahathir's pronouncements.

"It's very unfortunate that we are neighbors," the economist said. "I know we shouldn't interfere in other countries' policies. But all I can say is that it was very interesting. As an economist there are things that I disagree with. But because of our good neighbor policy, I can't really comment on his speech."

A Malaysian banker, who also insisted that he not be quoted by name, suggested that the Prime Minister was out of touch with reality.

"There are not two ways of doing these things," the banker said. "We have to get our own house in order. He really hasn't thought these things out. He's just spouting off."

* * *

September 22, 1997

ASIA'S ECONOMIC TIGERS GROWL AT WORLD MONETARY CONFERENCE

By DAVID E. SANGER

HONG KONG, Sept. 21—After a decade of persuading nations to open their financial markets, American officials at a tense conclave here have run into a wall of resistance as angry Asian leaders charge that foreign investors and Wall Street-style trading exacerbated Southeast Asia's financial crisis.

The most extreme of the accusations came from Prime Minister Mahathir Mohamad of Malaysia. In a fiery speech on Saturday evening, he accused the "great powers"—a clear reference to the United States—of pressing Asian countries to open their markets and then manipulating their currencies to knock them off as competitors.

Few Asians at the meeting of world financial leaders here have fully endorsed Mr. Mahathir's conspiracy theories or his contention that most forms of currency trading are "unnecessary, unproductive and immoral" and "should be made illegal."

Nonetheless, several have made clear that they are planning to slow—and may reverse—the liberalizations that have opened their economies to global forces.

In short, what has broken out at this usually plodding annual meeting of the World Bank and the International Monetary Fund, with its endless seminars bearing titles like "Pension Reform and the Creation of Efficient Capital Markets," is a nasty skirmish in the escalating war between nations and global markets.

The search to assign blame comes as Asian officials are still struggling to contain the damage from a brutal cycle of currency devaluations, stock market sell-offs and, in the case of Thailand, political upheaval that has swept through the region.

Treasury Secretary Robert E. Rubin is caught in the middle of these arguments, at once making the case for further opening of Asia's markets and fencing with Asian leaders over whether the fault for the current crisis lies in the markets or in themselves.

Mr. Rubin is a veteran of Wall Street who brings an international investor's eye to every policy debate.

He has spent the weekend arguing in private meetings that the markets are imposing badly needed discipline on countries that failed to regulate their banks, pursued huge national projects that they could not afford and let cronyism win out over good judgment.

It is not exactly a welcome message.

At some moments the conflict here has mirrored the arguments in Congress over whether free trade accords undercut American workers. At other times it has been tinged with anti-American oratory, with particularly resentful comments about Washington's failure to take part in a bailout of Thailand this summer led by the monetary fund.

"It's really been quite remarkable," Mr. Rubin reflected tonight after a long dinner with his delegation, which is headed to China this week to assess many of the same issues addressed here. "For years, when I was at Goldman, Sachs and then when I first came to Washington, a number of us wondered when countries would fully engage in the debate about the effects of linking global markets."

Now, he said, as a result of an unexpected economic crisis, "people are beginning to put all the pieces together."

The crisis began in Thailand, one of the most successful of the "tiger" economies, which attracted billions of dollars in foreign investment—more, it turns out, than it could wisely invest.

It quickly spread to Indonesia and Malaysia, where Mr. Mahathir quickly ordered restrictions on short sales—trades that bet on a decline in prices—and moved to prop up stock prices for Malaysians, but not for foreign investors.

That led investors to flee, and Mr. Mahathir was soon forced to make a sharp U-turn. But the damage to his country's financial credibility was done.

It would be easy to dismiss Mr. Mahathir's speech on Saturday as the angry ruminations of a prickly leader who enjoyed a string of economic successes only to see his grand plans to build airports, dams and a Southeast Asian Silicon Valley evaporate like numbers blipping off a trader's screen. Even in Southeast Asia, Mr. Mahathir's views are considered extremist.

But the fundamental emotion that he expressed clearly carries an extra resonance now, far beyond his country of 21 million.

This morning, for example, Finance Minister Thanong Bidaya Sunmday of Thailand agreed that Southeast Asia needed to create a "good system" to prevent speculators from driving down currencies. But when asked whether he endorsed the Mahathir idea that currency trading should be illegal, Mr. Thanong said, "I have no opinion."

Indonesia has sent mixed signals. In late August a newspaper close to the Government ran a public service advertisement with a picture of a currency trader wearing a terrorist mask made of American $100 bills. "Defend the Rupiah," it urged. "Defend Indonesia." But the country has largely kept its markets open and even relaxed rules on foreign ownership of some companies.

Leaders of 24 developing countries meeting here warned that proposals within the monetary fund to require further relaxation of investment rules around the world would "put additional stress on the economies that are already straining to adjust to globalization."

"The smell of things is definitely in the direction of slowing down, of reassessing," the president of the World Bank, James Wolfensohn, said in an interview today.

Sitting on the stage with Mr. Mahathir on Saturday, he said that "you could just feel the rapt attention" as Mr. Mahathir deftly wove his theories of Western desires to suppress Asian competitors with the economic events of the last two months.

But Mr. Wolfensohn warned, "Of course you have to be careful that when you stop the flow of capital, you have the greater danger of stopping the flow of technology with it."

While there have been financial crises before—Mexico in 1995, Latin America in the early 1980's—the feel of what has happened in Southeast Asia is in some ways quite different. Asia's emerging markets came to view the private foreign investors as a virtually unlimited source of funds.

It is easy to understand why. Only seven years ago, private investment in developing nations around the world was a mere $30 billion, compared with official development aid of nearly $65 billion. Now the proportions are starkly different. Official aid has declined to $45 billion last year, and private investment ballooned to roughly $245 billion.

When that money was flowing in, Asian leaders had no complaints. They were being rewarded, they said, for hard work, rising productivity and the emergence of an educated middle-class that saved at rates that put Americans to shame.

Now that the money has begun to flow the other way, leaving many countries with huge debts denominated in dollars that must be paid back with devalued local currencies, their attitudes have begun to change. Quickly the argument has become part of the debate over "Asian values" versus "Western values," labels that overlook a diversity of views in both camps.

Mr. Rubin has become the standard-bearer of the Western view that markets impose discipline on nations, economies and, most of all, politicians. His 26 years in investment banking at Goldman, Sachs & Company steeped him in the belief that markets go to extremes but that in the long run, they reward countries that keep their houses in order and punish those that do not.

He is sometimes so cautious, though, about the market's potential response to his every utterance that he often uses terminology that obscures his message. This weekend he indirectly answered Mr. Mahathir by saying currency speculation is "part of the total activity in secondary markets" that "increases liquidity and lowers costs."

The Rubin prescription for avoiding crises like those in Mexico and Southeast Asia is to get countries to disclose financial information that many treat as state secrets. This weekend he pressed a plan to get central banks to publicize their own maneuvering in currency markets so that investors could better assess a country's financial reserves.

If countries know that alert investors are watching, the theory goes, they will hesitate before engaging in financial maneuvering that will prompt investors to hit the "sell" button.

Of course, national leaders do not like to hear that they must abide by the dictates of currency and bond traders. Like many American politicians, they argue that global market forces should be channeled to serve their national goals rather than dictate those goals.

"The Asian message is that they are not going to adopt the wholesale, free-market capitalism that America is pushing," said Robert Hormats, the vice chairman of Goldman, Sachs and one of the thousands of investment bankers here to take the temperature. "There is resentment of the American pressure, and countries are pushing back."

It may be only temporary. After all, once Mexico got through the worst of its crisis, it again embraced the global financial markets. Asian countries have emerged from downturns before and concluded that they had no choice but to introduce more competition to their markets.

*   *   *

October 24, 1997

THE RISKS TO AMERICA IN ASIA'S PLUMMETING MARKETS

By DAVID E. SANGER

WASHINGTON, Oct. 23—Since he came to office President Clinton has repeated, time and again, that America's economic fortunes are tied to the spectacular growth of the powerhouses of the Pacific Rim. And the business world was far ahead of him, already building ventures from Kuala Lumpur to Hong Kong to New York.

But shared prosperity brings with it shared risk. And the question now is whether the financial earthquake that started somewhere under Thailand early this summer, and spread to Indonesia, Malaysia and Hong Kong, will end up here.

Some of the many possibilities being discussed on Wall Street and at the Treasury Department today were that the United States could become a safe haven for investors who now believe there is no place in Asia to hide—not even Hong Kong, which today saw the biggest one-day market drop since the killings at Tiananmen Square in 1989.

But there is little question that the United States is at risk. Consider that in 1995, when Mexico plunged into a similar crisis after a currency devaluation late the previous year, America did about $100 billion in business across its southern border. That was a big figure—big enough to spur President Clinton to bail out the Mexican economy. But it is dwarfed by United States trade with Asia, which last year was just shy of $300 billion, even without Japan.

Yet in Washington, there is no talk of a Mexico-pattern rescue for Southeast Asia, because the problems there vary greatly from country to country—and in some places are barely understood at all.

"Mexico was relatively clean, one country with a diagnosable set of problems," a senior Administration official said recently.

But in Asia there is no such simplicity. Thailand suffers from a banking system built on a house of cards and a property market gone wild; Malaysia from trade and investment deficits; Indonesia from corruption and dubious accounting. But none of the quick fixes and austerity measures attempted over a long, hot summer of currency runs has succeeded in re-establishing confidence.

And now the crisis has hit Hong Kong—the well-regulated, British-designed center of commerce that the rest of Asia was told to emulate.

It is Hong Kong's crisis that has alarmed the Clinton Administration as it finds itself struggling to douse the few flames that jumped the Pacific today, sending Wall Street stocks down more than 2 percent and many markets in Europe, 3 percent-plus. But American officials seemed to decide that anything they might say would only make a bad situation worse.

In his one public appearance today, Secretary of the Treasury Robert E. Rubin sidestepped a question about the markets by pointing to Secretary of State Madeleine K. Albright, who was sharing a platform, a joint appearance to press Congress into giving President Clinton new negotiating authority for trade accords.

"I will pass that question to the Secretary of State," Mr. Rubin said. "She is highly trained in the art of diplomacy—talking a lot and not saying too much."

Nonetheless, American officials today were trying to think through a range of short- and long-term implications of the Asian markets' plunge.

The most obvious is the effect on exports. The first casualty of the Asian crisis is the cancellation or delay of scores of major public works projects, from dams and bridges in Indonesia, to a desperately needed light-rail project in Bangkok, to many elements of Prime Minister Mahathir Mohamad's ambitious plan to turn Malaysia into the Silicon Valley of Southeast Asia.

American technology underlies many of those projects, and over the next few months major companies could be scaling back their profit estimates as big-ticket sales evaporate. That alone would not be so worrisome. But with Japan still in recession, and Europeans crawling their way out of double-digit unemployment, those projects were among the hottest tickets in the world.

Perhaps the bigger political risk in Washington is that the trade deficit with Asian nations is almost certain to rise, and rise sharply. Not only are their consumers becoming more frugal, but the wave after wave of currency devaluations are making Asian goods a lot cheaper. For the Clinton Administration, that is bound to cause a revival of political tensions, especially if the widening trade gap is combined with a slowing United States economy.

Harder to predict is the effect on the American stock and bond markets. While stocks were hurt today, bonds gained and the dollar rose against Asian currencies, suggesting that investors around the world were desperately seeking safety—and found it here.

So the biggest impact indeed seems the political one. Underlying the Clinton Administration's drive to increase economic engagement with Asia was a sense that American influence through the region had been in decline. Washington's reaction so far has done nothing to reverse that view.

"There were a lot of Asians wondering why the Americans sat out during the emergency package for Thailand," said C. Fred Bergsten, president of the Institute for International Economics here, and a central figure in the first meetings that brought together heads of state from the nations that make up the Asia Pacific Economic Cooperation forum, or APEC. "In their view, it is another test of Washington's commitment."

Today, the American representative to APEC, John S. Wolf, seemingly took note of Asians' ambivalent feelings when he told reporters: "Some are saying the United States and developed countries actually welcome the financial crisis now happening. Nothing could be more wrong."

But whether they are suspicious of the American reaction or not, the Asians are bound to be more cautious about opening their markets.

Many leaders in the region blame their moves toward openness, and the pressures to allow in even more foreign competition, for increasing the volatility of their currencies. While few subscribe to Prime Minister Mahathir's accusation that Southeast Asia was made a target for devaluation by a Jewish conspiracy, or at least by evil currency speculators, many say they share his suspicion that the West is perfectly happy to see the Asians, tigers and others, declawed.

* * *

October 24, 1997

A PLUNGE IN HONG KONG SHAKES MARKETS

By JONATHAN FUERBRINGER

A plunge in the Hong Kong stock market, touched off by an attack on the local currency, shook financial markets around the world yesterday.

Stocks lost 10.4 percent of their value in Hong Kong, causing a frantic selloff first in Japan and then on Europe's stock exchanges when they opened for business. Hours later, Wall Street was engulfed as well.

Nerves played a part, as did renewed concerns that stocks in the United States and other markets have risen too far too fast.

Tokyo's Nikkei index dropped 3 percent, London's leading stock index plunged 3.1 percent and Germany's DAX index dropped 3.6 percent. In New York, the Dow Jones industrial average finished the day down 2.3 percent, or 186.88 points, at 7,847.77, with other market gauges showing similar losses. Some smaller stock markets, including those in Brazil and

Mexico, came under even more pressure, falling 5 percent or more, as confidence was shaken in many emerging markets.

The selloff spread as investors woke up to learn that what appeared in July as an isolated currency problem in Thailand has become a full-blown crisis in Southeast Asia, encompassing Malaysia, Indonesia, the Philippines, Taiwan and now Hong Kong, the region's premier economy.

Thailand was forced to devalue its currency in early July because it had borrowed heavily from abroad to finance its own growth and had allowed very low interest rates to fuel an overheated property market. One by one, other countries in the region have watched their currencies fall in value and then their stock markets succumb. When Hong Kong fell, the tremors were felt keenly in Washington.

Hong Kong sought to buck the trend yesterday by vowing to support its currency, which is pegged to the United States dollar, and by sharply raising overnight interest rates, to 300 percent. Investors responded by selling off Hong Kong stocks on fears that higher rates would mean shriveling profits for the financial and property companies that are the market's backbone.

Early today, there were signs that Asian markets were stabilizing. In Hong Kong, the benchmark Hang Seng index rose as much as 2.8 percent in the morning before relinquishing most of those gains, then climbed 4.49 percent later in the session. In afternoon trading in Tokyo, the Nikkei index was up 1.15 percent. Markets in Australia, New Zealand, Singapore and South Korea, though, were still trading sharply lower.

If the crisis continues, it could lead to a broad regional economic slowdown that would dampen the sales and earnings not just of local companies, but of major corporations from the United States to Europe that operate there.

Some market analysts said that the selloff was not the start of a larger and longer decline and pointed to some stabilizing influences. One was an immediate drop in interest rates in the United States and Europe, which could in turn make stocks more attractive.

Indeed, as investors looked for havens yesterday, they bought bonds. Prices for the benchmark 30-year United States Treasury bond rose sharply; the yield, which moves in the opposite direction of the price, dropped to 6.31 percent, from 6.41 percent on Wednesday.

"The end of the bull market or something like the crash of 1987 is unlikely," said Robert Farrell, a senior market analyst at Merrill Lynch & Company. "I've been a market technician for a long time, and when you have a market that has set all kinds of records—record highs on very heavy volume—there's much more room to go."

Other factors work in favor of United States investors, said Edward Kerschner, the chief investment strategist for Paine Webber. "We have pretty solid growth; the U.S. currency is strong; inflation is low," he said in an interview from Tokyo.

But there were signs yesterday that the crisis could continue for some time. For one, the Government of Thailand remains in turmoil following the resignation of its finance minister and the submission of undated resignations from the rest of the Cabinet; the Government is thus unable to put into effect a $17 billion rescue program backed by the International Monetary Fund. Protests against the current Government fueled discussion yesterday of new elections as well.

In Washington, there was no talk of a rescue like the one engineered for Mexico a few years ago—largely because the problems in Southeast Asia vary greatly from country to country, thwarting a single solution. Firm leadership by the United States in organizing a bailout of $50 billion for Mexico limited the impact of its currency crisis, which began at the end of 1994 with the sudden devaluation of the peso.

Investors in the United States and Europe have reason to fear a major slowdown in Asia's economic growth. In addition to cutting into sales by American and European companies in the region, a slowdown would hurt those companies in their home markets, since sharp declines in Asian currencies against the dollar make Asian products cheaper and more competitive when sold abroad.

And investors are nervous about anything that would dampen corporate earnings. The American and European stock markets are considered expensive by many traditional measures and fell yesterday only after setting record highs earlier this month. The Mexican and Brazilian markets had also been near peaks.

"It is a warning sign to investors globally that maybe equities are overvalued," said Bob McKee, the chief economist at Independent Strategies in London, a financial consulting firm.

But many market analysts believe that American investors will continue to regard lower stock prices that result from such selloffs as a good opportunity to buy, something that has helped pull the stock market out of every big decline of the last two years. This willingness to hunt for bargains, and a decline in interest rates, could bring some stability to the American stock market.

Analysts also suggested that Federal Reserve policy makers would now be less likely to raise short-term interest rates at their November meeting. One reason is that a move by the Fed could add to the worldwide turmoil. Another, according to Kermit Schoenholtz, the London-based chief economist for Salomon Brothers, is that the same slowdown in Asia and stronger American dollar that make Asian products cheaper also reduce inflationary pressures.

The decline in the Hong Kong stock market was touched off by an assault on the Hong Kong dollar, which has been pegged at 7.75 to the United States dollar. Since the Southeast Asian financial crisis began with the devaluation of Thailand's currency, the baht, currency traders and big global investment vehicles known as hedge funds have looked for the next currency to bet against—finding them in Malaysia, the Philippines, Indonesia and Taiwan. Now, they are testing the resolve of Hong Kong.

Until Hong Kong, the markets under fire were quite small. But Hong Kong's stock market is twice the size of Indonesia, Malaysia, the Philippines, Thailand and Singapore combined. The attack on Hong Kong—which is also more economically sound than its neighbors and serves as the gateway to China—has raised doubts about the containment.

"Everybody thought Hong Kong was different because of China," said Byron R. Wien, the United States investment strategist at Morgan Stanley, Dean Witter, Discover & Company. "The fear now is that the Hong Kong peg to the dollar goes, then all of Asia is a less satisfactory consumer of American and European products."

For Hong Kong, the battle to protect the value of its currency—which went into full swing on Wednesday when the benchmark Hang Seng stock index dropped 6.2 percent—means raising interest rates. Higher rates pull capital into Hong Kong and spur buying of Hong Kong dollars. Speculators who have borrowed Hong Kong dollars also wind up paying much more for their loans, which could cause them to abandon their position.

The higher interest rates, though, spell trouble for the property and finance companies that are at the heart of the Hong Kong economy. Higher rates make it more expensive for them to do business.

And even if Hong Kong can defend its currency, higher rates could slow growth significantly if the battle lasts a long time. "There will come a point where the underlying economic situation will make it difficult to keep interest rates high," said David Webb, head of Asian equities in Hong Kong for Chase Asset Management.

A devaluation of the currency could be even worse for Hong Kong, though, damaging its credibility as an international financial center.

In the United States yesterday, the worries about slowing growth in Asia undermining the sales and earnings of American companies could be seen in the sharp fall of stocks that are sensitive to economic growth.

The Aluminum Company of America, which fell 3½ a share, to 77¼, helped pull the Dow down. An index of major companies with extensive business overseas, the Morgan Stanley multinational index of 50 corporations, also dropped sharply, falling 2.1 percent.

And technology stocks took a beating. I.B.M. led the Dow down with a decline of 4¾, to 100 ³/₈. The Nasdaq composite index, which is heavy with technology issues, fell 36.83 points, or 2.16 percent, to 1,671.25.

Correction:

A front-page article misstated the German DAX 30 index. It closed on Thursday at 3,977.26 points, not 3,976.38. It was down 4.66 percent for the day, not 3.60 percent.

* * *

October 24, 1997

DEFENDING FIXED EXCHANGE RATE AT FURTHER COST TO STOCKS

By EDWARD A. GARGAN

BANGKOK, Thailand, Friday, Oct. 24—How much longer can the bloodletting in stock markets go on?

The damage worsened on the Hong Kong stock exchange Thursday, with the benchmark Hang Seng index plunging 1,211 points, or 10.4 percent, after a 6.17 percent fall the day before. It was the steepest one-day drop there since Chinese forces snuffed out pro-democracy demonstrations at Tiananmen Square in Beijing in June 1989.

The Government pledged to defend the Hong Kong dollar against currency speculators—a policy that has accelerated the exodus from stocks. Whether the authorities can do so indefinitely is the $80 billion question everyone is asking, from small investors to monetary authorities in Japan and the United States.

"The key issue is really the currency—the battle between the Hong Kong Monetary Authority and the speculator in the Hong Kong dollar," said John M. Mulcahy, a vice president of W. I. Carr, a brokerage firm in Hong Kong. "And what we have seen in the market today is a very significant increase in money market rates."

Hong Kong authorities said they had not yet touched an $80 billion foreign-exchange war chest to defend their currency. Instead, they jacked up interest rates as high as 300 percent for overnight deposits. But the consequence of preserving the Hong Kong dollar's peg to the American dollar at a rate around 7.75 to 1, most analysts and fund managers agree, will be further losses in stocks.

"If the peg remains, you'll see a sharp deflation in assets, particularly property assets," said Diahann L. Brown, a vice president at Thornton Management Asia Ltd. "And property makes up a significant component of the market index."

Already with some of the most expensive real estate anywhere—this summer, an old colonial home tucked onto the top of a wooded ridge on Hong Kong island sold for $100 million—there has been rumbling about the prospect of Hong Kong's pricing itself out of competition. In the last two months, the number of tourists has plummeted, particularly from Japan, where Hong Kong was long regarded as a shopper's paradise. Now, Japanese tourists say, Hong Kong is simply too expensive.

Moreover, because of its link to United States currency, the Hong Kong dollar has appreciated 20 to 40 percent against free-falling regional currencies like the Thai baht and the Malaysian ringgit. This further erodes Hong Kong's competitive position by making its exports more expensive.

Since Aug. 7, when the Hang Seng stock index hit an all-time high of 16,673.27, nearly 40 percent of its value has been erased. The damage has now spread through Asia and started to take a toll in Europe, driving markets and currencies lower.

For much of this week, Hong Kong has been swept by repeated rumors that its dollar, tightly linked to the American dollar for 14 years, would be devalued. "It seems that people are trying to create a level playing field," said Miron Mushkat, chief Asian economist for Lehman Brothers there. "They've brought down the other markets in Southeast Asia, and now they're focusing on Hong Kong."

On Thursday, that seemed only to harden the authorities' line against speculators. "The first priority is to defend the exchange rate," said Hong Kong's financial secretary, Donald Tsang, at a news conference after the market closed. "We believe it is right to do so."

The Monetary Authority's chairman, Joseph Yam, told the news conference that his agency would charge high penalties to traders who needed to borrow Hong Kong dollars to cover their short positions today. It "should be a very interesting day," he added.

Ms. Brown of Thornton Management said the authority was certain to do all it could to squeeze speculators. She predicted that interest rates would remain "very, very high" for the next several days. While ordinary lending rates were nowhere near the triple-digit levels of overnight funds, three big Hong Kong banks on Thursday raised the rates they charge their best customers by three-quarters of a percentage point, to 9.5 percent.

Higher rates are bad for Hong Kong because they deter borrowing, slow the sale of property, a key sector of the economy, and drive money out of stocks and into bonds.

Some analysts saw glimmers of hope. Mr. Mushkat predicted victory for the Government over speculators. And Carlton Poon, a director at Worldsec International Ltd, said many Hong Kong stocks were looking cheap.

"There's a 50 percent sale in Hong Kong—the Christmas sale has started early," Mr. Poon said. "I see this as a buying opportunity."

Mostly, though, the mood seemed gloomy. Throughout the day, small shareholders huddled around trading screens set up in banks. One investor was shown on Hong Kong television staring helplessly at a monitor. "There's nothing we can do," he said.

The newspaper Sing Pao reported Thursday morning that a senior British executive at a major financial institution had committed suicide over the market's collapse. The executive, who was not named in the report, was found dead in his luxury apartment on the high-rent south side of Hong Kong island.

Throughout the day, there was a mixture of anxiety, nervousness and bravado as people sought to plumb the meaning of the market crash and the prospects in coming days. Yet the prevailing attitude was to flee the market until assaults on the Hong Kong dollar eased and interest rates stabilized.

"People have cut quite a bit of Hong Kong from their portfolios," Ms. Brown said. "I'm holding more cash than I ever held. The next three days to a week will be critical."

The turmoil spilled over into world markets on Thursday, from India and Japan, to the financial capitals of Europe, to

Wall Street. And China—which re-established control of Hong Kong, as a special administrative region, less than four months ago—was not spared.

The so-called red chips, the stocks of Chinese mainland companies that are traded in Hong Kong, have been hammered all week. Once seen as the go-go stocks of the market, in large part out of a sense they had strong backing from Beijing, they have been swept aside in the rush to sell. The newest and brightest issue, China Telecom, traded at 18 percent below its issue price. On the New York Stock Exchange, the company's American depository receipts declined 37.5 cents on Thursday, to $27.625.

Still, a Chinese spokesman, Shen Guofan, said in Beijing that the Government would not intervene in Hong Kong's financial crisis. "The central Government is responsible only on foreign and defense affairs of Hong Kong," Mr. Shen said. "Hong Kong has the strength to deal with it."

*   *   *

November 3, 1997

THE WRONG MEDICINE FOR ASIA

By JEFFREY D. SACHS

CAMBRIDGE, Mass.—In a matter of just a few months, the Asian economies went from being the darlings of the investment community to being virtual pariahs. There was a touch of the absurd in the unfolding drama, as international money managers harshly castigated the very same Asian governments they were praising just months before.

The International Monetary Fund has just announced a second bailout package for the region, about $20 billion for Indonesia. That should, in principal, boost confidence. But if it is tied to orthodox financial conditions, including budget cuts and sharply higher interest rates, the package could do more harm than good, transforming a currency crisis into a rip-roaring economic downturn.

In the Great Depression, panicked investors fled from weak banks in the United States and abroad. Since banks borrow short term in order to lend long term, they can be thrown into crisis when a large number of depositors suddenly line up to withdraw money. In the days before deposit insurance, individual depositors would all try to be first in line for withdrawals.

In 1933, the Federal Reserve played it disastrously wrong. Rather than lending money to the banks to calm the panic and to show the depositors that they could indeed still get their money out, the Fed tightened credit, as financial orthodoxy prescribed. Confidence sank, and the banking system crumbled.

The Asian crisis is akin to a bank run. Investors are lining up to be the first out of the region. Much of the panic is a self-feeding frenzy: even if the economies were fundamentally healthy at the start of the panic, nobody wants to be the last one out when currencies are weakening and banks are tottering because of the rapid drain of foreign loans.

It is somehow comforting, as in a good morality tale, to blame corruption and mismanagement in Asia for the crisis. Yes, these exist, and they weaken economic life. But the crisis itself is more pedestrian: no economy can easily weather a panicked withdrawal of confidence, especially if the money was flooding in just months before.

The I.M.F. has arrived quickly on the scene, but the East Asian financial crisis is very different from the set of problems that the I.M.F. typically aims to solve.

The I.M.F.'s usual target is a government living beyond its means, financing budget deficits by printing money at the central bank. The result is inflation, together with a weakening currency and a drain of foreign exchange reserves. In these circumstances, financial orthodoxy makes sense: cut the budget deficit and restrict central bank credits to the government. The result will be to cut inflation and end the weakening of the currency and loss of foreign exchange reserves.

In Southeast Asia, this story simply doesn't apply. Indonesia, Malaysia, the Philippines and Thailand have all been running budget surpluses, not deficits. Inflation has been low in all of the countries. Foreign exchange reserves, until this past year, were stable or rising, not falling.

The problems emerged in the private sector. In all of the countries, international money market managers and investment banks went on a lending binge from 1993 to 1996. To a varying extent in all of the countries, the short-term borrowing from abroad was used, unwisely, to support long-term investments in real estate and other non-exporting sectors.

This year, the bubble burst. Investors woke up to the weakening in Asia's export growth. A combination of rising wage costs, competition from China and lower demand for Asia's exports (especially electronics) caused exports to stagnate in 1996 and the first part of 1997. It became clear that if the Asians were going to compete, their currencies would need to fall against the dollar so their costs of production would be lower. It also became clear that with foreign lending diverted into real estate ventures, there was some risk that the borrowers, especially banks and finance companies, would be unable to service the debts if the exchange rates weakened. After all, rentals on real estate developments would be earned in local currency, while the debts would have to be repaid in dollars.

The weaknesses in the Asian economies were real, but far from fatal. The deeper strengths—high savings, budget surpluses, flexible labor markets, low taxation—remain in place, and long-term growth prospects are solid. But, as often happens in financial markets, euphoria turned to panic without missing a beat. Suddenly, Asia's leaders could do no right. The money fled.

In this maelstrom, the I.M.F. is now reportedly pressing the Asian countries to raise existing budget surpluses still higher and to tighten domestic bank credit. In the Philippines recently, short-term interest rates were briefly pushed above 100 percent a year to meet I.M.F. credit targets.

And, in a move that is supposed to engender confidence but almost surely does the opposite, the I.M.F. has reportedly called on Thailand and Indonesia to close down several weak banks that have been caught up in the boom-bust cycle of foreign lending. Since the treatment of depositors in such cases is open to doubt (as deposit insurance is implicit rather than explicit), these calls for bank closings also worsen the investor flight from the region. Of course, one can't be absolutely sure what the I.M.F. is advising, since I.M.F. programs and supporting documents are hidden from public view. This secrecy itself gravely undermines confidence.

The Asian region needs more creative policies than these. The first step would be for the international investment community to tell the truth: the currency crisis is not the result of Asian government profligacy. This is a crisis made mainly in the private, albeit under-regulated, financial markets.

The next step would be to let the Asian currencies float downward, so that these countries' exports will be cheaper and therefore more competitive. Once export growth starts to pick up, then panicked money market managers will begin to remember why they were until recently singing the praises of the region. This is what happened in the aftermath of the 1994 Mexican crisis, when money managers who swore they had left Mexico for good quickly reconsidered in the wake of an export boom.

Floating the exchange rate would have two more advantages: foreign reserves would not be squandered in a failed attempt to defend the currency, and interest rates would not need to be raised in an illusory quest to keep the currency strong.

The third step would be to moderate the strong forces pushing Asia into a recession, rather than adding to them. The region does not need wanton budget cutting, credit tightening and emergency bank closures. It needs stable or even slightly expansionary monetary and fiscal policies to counterbalance the decline in foreign loans. Interest rates will drift higher as foreign investors withdraw their money, but those rates do not need to be artificially jacked up by a squeeze on domestic credit. The regulation of the banking sector should be strengthened not by hasty bank closures, but by pushing weak banks to merge with stronger ones and by pushing the banks to raise their capital bases.

Southeast Asia surely needed a correction to restore its competitiveness. A moderate cut in foreign lending was needed; the panic was not. If the currency crisis is well managed, Asia will be able to resume its rapid economic growth. If it is managed with unthinking orthodoxy, the costs could be very high, for Asia and the rest of the world.

Jeffrey D. Sachs is director of the Harvard Institute for International Development and an economic adviser to governments in Asia and other parts of the world.

*   *   *

November 26, 1997

COULD JAPAN BE NEXT?

By DAVID E. SANGER

WASHINGTON, Nov. 25—Could Japan be next?

For months, as the contagion in the Asian markets spread from Thailand to Indonesia to South Korea, that question has lurked in the background at the White House, next door at the Treasury, behind the sealed doors of the Federal Reserve and on Wall Street. Few officials in the Clinton Administration will discuss the subject publicly, except to recite the reasons why Japan is different and will not succumb. The reasons are compelling: the Japanese have prodigious national savings, a war chest of $230 billion in United States Treasury bonds and industrial strength that is rivaled only by the United States.

So far, though, none of that has compensated for a series of huge miscalculations that has mired Tokyo in economic trouble since 1991. A sudden collapse of the kind that afflicted the smaller Asian economies seems highly unlikely. Nonetheless, with every bit of economic evidence suggesting that things in Japan could worsen before they improve, Washington and the markets are awash in gloomy visions in which a panic in Japan—or even Japanese efforts to quell one—could leap the Pacific.

It seems even less probable that the United States will catch Asia's flu—indeed today Wall Street shrugged off a 5.1 percent drop in the Japanese stock market.

To a large extent, Asian markets are responding to the collapse of a huge speculative bubble that began in Japan and spread through Southeast Asia, fueled by cronyism and, it turns out, a good deal of old-fashioned fraud. But markets feed off one another in unpredictable ways, as Americans were reminded last month after a run in Hong Kong resounded here. As one senior Administration official put it the other day, "It's hard to imagine the world's second-largest economy going into a convulsion without affecting us."

That may explain why a series of letters from Treasury Secretary Robert E. Rubin to his Japanese counterpart, Hiroshi Mitsuzuka, have taken on a more urgent tone in recent months, as American officials insisted the Japanese were deceiving themselves into thinking the worst was over. It also explains President Clinton's apparently toughly worded caution to Prime Minister Ryutaro Hashimoto on Monday in Vancouver, British Columbia, that the time had come to "move decisively" before Japan's financial problems become the world's. Mr. Hashimoto reportedly conceded that Japan had "miscalculated" when it dismissed the warnings earlier this year.

Details of that conversation were conveyed to reporters not by Mr. Clinton's aides but by Mr. Hashimoto's in a clear attempt to create the impression at home that the Prime Minister was under excruciating pressure to take unpopular actions—starting with the use of public money to bail out the same Japanese institutions that a decade ago seemed ready to bury their American rivals.

"What's happened now is that every scenario for the next few months in Japan is filled with bad news," said Edward

Lincoln, a senior fellow at the Brookings Institution who served as chief economic adviser to Walter F. Mondale, the American Ambassador in Tokyo until the end of 1996. "But that said, the theories about what will happen next—and what their effect could be here—are diametrically opposed."

The future that Japanese Government officials are peddling is that a new age has dawned—one in which they will not let problems linger by propping up failing companies.

Finally, Japanese companies will sink or swim, this line of reasoning goes. The weakest—even giant, venerable institutions like Yamaichi Securities, the century-old trading house that announced on Monday that it was liquidating—will go out of business. Depositors will be protected, the Japanese say, but banned forever is the instinct to interfere with market forces whenever they threaten the established order.

It is an appealing pitch, a signal to the world that Japan is finally going to let market forces rule its economy, rather than insist that the country's bureaucrats bend the market forces. But it also seems to contradict the Government's gradual move toward injecting huge sums into the financial system to stabilize it.

Letting a large number of companies die would also lead to a time of extraordinary pain, one in which workers who thought they had jobs for life could be out on the street, investors in loss-plagued businesses could lose their money and the economy's growth could dwindle to zero.

"This is a reality that has been discussed more realistically in the United States than in Japan," a leading Japanese lawmaker said on a visit to the United States last week. "I think Japan is only now waking up to what this means."

Believe it or not, that's the optimistic outlook. It involves a lot of short-term agony, but, in the minds of American officials, it sets the Japanese economy on the path to growth.

No doubt American companies with heavy exports to Japan will suffer. Japan may also sell some of its huge holdings of Treasury securities to smooth over a rough patch, and depending on the magnitude of the sale, that could roil the American bond market, weaken the value of the dollar and in the worst case, lead to higher interest rates in this country. There is always the possibility, however, that Japan's Finance Ministry is telling something short of the full truth when it insists Japan is changing so quickly.

There is plenty of reason to be skeptical. Mr. Hashimoto has promised before that Japan's financial sector was cleaning up its act—in 1991, when he served as Finance Minister. It was on his watch that the country faced the first of a series of financial scandals, in which the four biggest securities houses admitted they had compensated big customers for losses when the Japanese market began to turn down. They apologized and said it would never happen again. Mr. Hashimoto resigned. And the practices went on, leading to Yamaichi's admission on Monday that it hid more than $2 billion in off-the-books losses for years.

The fear in Washington is that Mr. Hashimoto will bend to pressure to funnel aid to companies that deserve to fail—perhaps acting overtly or perhaps in the more cloaked, traditional manner of Japan.

"This would be the worst outcome because the banks and the securities houses would only weaken and the pain would go on much longer," Mr. Lincoln said. Japanese industry, despairing of selling more at home, would seek to let the yen weaken so that Japan's cars and computer chips remain competitive with goods made by South Korea, Taiwan and the Southeast Asian nations. That would be good for American consumers—who would pay less for Japanese goods—but the trade deficit with Japan would surge.

Eventually, a growing deficit could threaten American jobs, particularly in industries that compete directly with Japanese products. The stock prices of companies facing more intense price competition would undoubtedly drop. Mr. Clinton told Mr. Hashimoto quite explicitly on Monday that any effort by Japan to export its way out of trouble would lead the two countries into "political problems," Japanese officials say.

But Japan has been through plenty of political problems in Washington before, and may decide it is worth the risk—and better than wallowing in whatever disease has swept through some of the world's most promising economies.

* * *

December 4, 1997

PACKAGE OF LOANS WORTH $55 BILLION IS SET FOR KOREA

By ANDREW POLLACK

SEOUL, South Korea, Dec. 3—South Korea formally agreed today to terms for the largest international economic rescue ever—a $55 billion loan package that will revamp the country's financial system, likely creating substantial hardship for the nation's citizens in the process and slowing the pace of one of the world's fastest-growing economies.

Government officials and private analysts predicted that the severe cuts in public spending and other austerity moves would cause unemployment to double or even triple in a land where lifetime employment has long been taken for granted. Bankruptcies, already running at a high rate, are expected to skyrocket. Some economists said it would be two years or more before the economy recovered.

"I have come here to beg the forgiveness of the Korean people," Lim Chang Yuel, the Minister of Finance and Economy, said in a nationally televised speech tonight. "Please understand the necessity of the economic pain we must bear and overcome."

The battered South Korean stock market surged 6 percent by midday Thursday in reaction to the bailout package, signaling investor optimism that it would succeed.

The agreement came about after several days of tense negotiations in which the reluctance of the Korean Government to swallow both its pride and some distasteful economic medicine seemed to draw out the discussions. Under the terms of the deal, the International Monetary Fund, the leader of the bailout, will provide South Korea with $21 billion in credits. The World Bank promised to provide $10 billion and the Asian Development Bank $4 billion.

The United States and several other nations agreed to provide $20 billion more as a "second line of defense" if the initial money from the international organizations proves insufficient. Some $5 billion will come from the United States, $10 billion from Japan and the rest from Australia, Britain, Canada, France, Germany and possibly other nations.

The money will initially be used to help shore up South Korea's nearly depleted foreign currency reserves. That should help stanch the rapid devaluation of the Korean won and allow the nation to pay off foreign debt. Some $66 billion is due within a year, and about $20 billion of that is due by the end of this year.

The money will also be used to help restore the health of the financial system, which has been weakened by haphazard lending to the country's supercorporations, huge industrial conglomerates that were nurtured by the Government as the engine for the country's remarkable growth.

In return for the money, Seoul must cut public spending, open its market more to foreign goods and investors and curb the ability of the conglomerates to expand.

For a nation that grew from an impoverished backwater to the world's 11th-largest economy, it marked the humbling end of the economic miracle and the beginning of a period of what President Kim Young Sam has described as "bone-carving pain." It was only last year that South Korea proudly joined the Organization for Economic Cooperation and Development, the club of advanced nations.

Michel Camdessus (pronounced Cam-da-SOO), the managing director of the I.M.F., who arrived here this morning to complete the deal, called it "a strong economic program that provides for a decisive and welcome response to the country's present financial difficulties."

South Korea is the latest and largest "Asian tiger" to fall victim this year to sharp devaluations of its currency and soaring debts. The amount of money available to Korea is larger than the $17 billion offered to Thailand, the nearly $40 billion promised to Indonesia in recent months and the $48 billion offered to Mexico three years ago. Mr. Camdessus said he hoped the loans to South Korea would help stabilize the region.

The Clinton Administration applauded the plan for one of its key Asian allies. "We have a vital national economic and security interest in helping Korea to restore market stability as soon as possible," Treasury Secretary Robert E. Rubin said in a statement. The United States, the largest shareholder in the I.M.F., played a big role in pushing Seoul to adopt stern reforms.

Under terms of the bailout, the South Korean Government agreed to stop pressuring banks to make loans to troubled or politically connected companies.

South Korea also agreed to take steps to attract more foreign investment, including allowing companies to raise money abroad through debt issues. American officials also said they were hopeful that United States and other foreign banks would acquire South Korean banks.

Among the other elements of the proposal is a requirement that South Korea drop some of its trade barriers and that the Government press for legislation making the central bank independent of Government control.

"The program's policy commitments will bring about very substantial changes in the Korean financial sector, which in turn has the potential to open up the Korean economy," another Treasury official said.

The $5 billion United States contribution will come from the Exchange Stabilization Fund, a pool of money that the President can use at his discretion to maintain stability in currency markets. Use of the fund does not require approval by Congress, where there is some resistance to international bailouts.

The package still needs formal approval by the I.M.F. executive board, which is expected as early as Thursday. Until then, full terms of the agreement were not being released.

Because South Korea will hold elections on Dec. 18 and Mr. Kim is constitutionally barred from running again, Mr. Camdessus took the unusual step of seeking pledges from South Korea's three presidential candidates that they would honor the agreement. The candidates gave their promises, some reluctantly.

The Korean stock market, after plunging early in the day, rallied at the end of trading to close up 0.65 percent, ending nine days of consecutive decline.

The rally was fueled by reports that the I.M.F. agreement would raise the percentage of a Korean company's stock that could be owned by foreigners to 50 percent from 26 percent immediately and to 55 percent next year. That portends an influx of foreign money into the stock market.

With the new austerity program, many economists predict unemployment, now at 2.5 percent, will double or even triple as huge layoffs mark a nation in which lifetime employment is considered a right.

Lee Jeong Ja, head of research for the Seoul branch of HSBC James Capel, a securities firm, said she would not be surprised to see as many as one-fourth of the more than 700 companies listed on Korea's stock exchange go bankrupt. She said the economic downturn would last two years, but other analysts said it would be longer.

"I would say we're not going to see any return to growth over 5 percent for the next few years," said Eugene Ha, head of research at J. Henry Schroder in Seoul. South Korea is expected to grow about 6 percent this year, but the target for next year under the plan is about half that.

In addition to bemoaning the pain, there was also some anger here that the nation had surrendered control of its economy.

"With the complete opening of Korea's financial market, foreign capital will virtually be in control of the profits and management of Korean companies," an announcer on the state-owned Korean Broadcasting System said tonight. He also warned, "U.S. automobiles and Japanese products are expected to pour into Korea."

But any long-term gains for the United States and other nations from market openings in the package will be at least partly offset by South Korea's economic slowdown, which will cut its imports. Many civic groups are starting frugality campaigns, urging consumers to help save the economy by not buying foreign products because they contribute to the nation's trade deficit.

In some cases, the I.M.F. package will give the South Korean Government the cover to make reforms that special interests in the country had prevented thus far.

President Kim, for instance, came into office pledging to pare down the industrial conglomerates but has been unsuccessful.

The huge conglomerates, known as chaebols, have enjoyed ready access to bank loans because they were favored by the Government. With ready credit, they expanded haphazardly into numerous industries and developing markets worldwide. The result was a buildup of huge debts.

Now, many of those diversification attempts are failing, and chaebols are falling like dominoes. Seven of the top 40 have become insolvent this year. The Halla Group today barely avoided becoming the eighth when creditors agreed to postpone a deadline for debt repayment.

The I.M.F. agreement would limit the ability of one unit of a chaebol to guarantee the debts of another subsidiary, according to Korean media reports. This should help slow their expansion.

South Korea had announced several times this week that it had an agreement with the I.M.F., only to retract the statement later.

Officials said that the I.M.F., in part prodded by Washington, added more demands for market-opening measures and structural reforms. A big sticking point was over whether failing banks should be liquidated or allowed to reorganize. Korean officials say liquidation of commercial banks will not be required.

* * *

December 4, 1997

A BAD SIDE OF BAILOUTS: SOME GO UNPENALIZED

By LOUIS UCHITELLE

Much of the $55 billion that has been pledged by the international community to South Korea—like the $40 billion for Indonesia and the $17 billion for Thailand before it—will ultimately go to lenders who dished out huge sums for risky projects that failed to pay off.

The rescue plan centers on shaky Korean banks. The nation's industrialists, who borrowed billions of dollars from them for new factories and such, have not made enough profit to repay their debts.

The banks, of course, got their money in part from Korean depositors. Other money came from foreigners—big European, American and Japanese banks, for example—that lent enthusiastically to the Korean banks, in hopes of sharing in the profits.

The bailout money, from the International Monetary Fund, the World Bank and individual countries, will be channeled through the Korean Government and its central bank in great measure to the private banking system. In some cases, foreign creditors may be paid off directly. Mostly, the money will go to salvage some institutions and to close others while paying off creditors. The bailout will, in effect, repay the depositors and the foreign lenders. At the end of last year, South Korean banks owed nearly $60 billion to foreign banks, according to the Bank for International Settlement.

"We keep blaming this crisis on corruption and bad banking practices," said Jeffrey Sachs, a Harvard economist. "But this all happened in the private marketplace. It was so often a case of big foreign lenders pushing their money on the Koreans and the Korean banks enthusiastically taking it in."

Of course, some of the bailout money is earmarked for specific projects, like public works. That is particularly true of the World Bank's $10 billion contribution. But money that the Korean Government is now spending on such projects will simply be freed up for the financial rescue.

All of the Asian aid packages, already totaling more than $100 billion, are prompting many economists and investment bankers to argue anew that bailouts, even when they accomplish their immediate goals, set a bad precedent. By making the lenders whole, they encourage more careless lending and fresh crises.

"If we practice bailing out countries whenever they get into trouble," said Richard Cooper, a Harvard economist, "then lenders everywhere will come to count on that and they will continue to make loans they should not make."

That view, widely held, is producing numerous proposals for change. Mr. Cooper suggests that new regulations should be adopted by all countries that would cause the owners of banks—the shareholders—to lose their investments in such situations. That would make lenders more cautious, reducing bank failures and the need for bailouts. Robert Hormats, a vice president of Goldman, Sachs, argues that developing countries should adopt capital controls, dictating how loans can be dispersed, particularly those from abroad. That, too, could force lenders to be more cautious.

Henry Kaufman, an economist and money manager, says a new layer of international supervision and lending standards is needed. "There is simply no effort today to manage global liquidity," he said.

A national bailout is the only tool readily available today to reverse financial crises that a government cannot handle on its own. These crises are almost always rooted in the unrealistic view of lenders and borrowers that they will profit. When those profit hopes were dashed in Asia in recent months, devaluations, bankruptcies and bank failures followed.

The I.M.F. will feed the $55 billion to South Korea in stages. The money will go to the Ministry of Finance or the central bank, where it will augment Korean Government funds. The additional funds may help restore confidence in the country and stabilize the slide in its currency.

Or it may be used to directly solve the banking crisis.

A Korean bank, for example, may have made a five-year, $100 million loan to an auto company, which has defaulted. The bank may have received its funds from $100 million in six-month loans from American and Japanese banks.

As long as the Korean economy seemed sound, even booming, the foreign banks were willing to roll over these short-term loans. Indeed, they were eager to do so because they were lending to Korean banks at much higher rates than they would charge domestic customers. But in the current crisis the American and Japanese banks, fearful of losing money, want quick repayment. And new lending from abroad dries up.

With the I.M.F. bailout, the foreign banks may choose to roll over their loans, expecting that in time, they will be repaid in full. That happened in Mexico. The $48 billion that was made available to the country, $20 billion of it from the United States, reassured most foreign investors and they left their money in place. But the big Mexican debtor was the Government, while in Asia's crisis, the private sector owes the money.

If the foreign banks—American and Japanese in this example—insist on quick repayment, the Korean Government can do this as well, with its newfound money. Or the process can be less direct. The Ministry of Finance can buy the bad loans from the Seoul bank. The Seoul bank, in turn, buys foreign currency with the proceeds and repays the American and Japanese banks.

A similar reimbursement process functions for Korean depositors whose money has gone to bad loans. The Korean Government can replenish the deposits, in whole or in part, by buying up the bad loans, using general funds to do so. In this case, the I.M.F. bailout adds to the Government's available funds.

But for Joseph E. Stiglitz, chief economist at the World Bank, the bailout solution is unlikely to deter the unrealistic lending practices that inject money from all parts of the world into a Korea or a Thailand.

"To the extent that private investors who made bad decisions are bailed out," he said in a speech on Monday, "their incentives will be distorted, exacerbating the problems governments face in trying to stabilize capital flows."

*   *   *

February 15, 1999

WHO WENT UNDER IN THE WORLD'S SEA OF CASH

By NICHOLAS D. KRISTOF with EDWARD WYATT

Mary Jo Paoni stood contentedly in her front yard, as firmly planted in Middle America as any of the cornstalks out back.

"I wouldn't invest in Asia," she said, shaking her head decisively. A 59-year-old secretary with big, sparkling eyes, a plaid shirt and no pretensions, she added, "Investing in Asia frightens me."

Her husband, George, a retired meat cutter, was standing beside her as the sun set over Cantrall, Ill., a farm town about 130 miles southwest of Chicago. He was equally adamant. "If I'm going to gamble," he said, "I want to sit down with my friends."

Yet Mrs. Paoni, who has never traveled outside the United States, is in fact invested in Asia and all over the world, although she does not know it. After retiring in April from her job as a secretary with the state government, she will rely on a pension fund that has large investments abroad, giving her indirect ownership of stocks in Indonesia and Russia and Brazil. And the cash she tucked away in an A. G. Edwards money market account was funneled to big banks, which helped build elegant hotels and office towers from Argentina to Vietnam.

Millions of Americans have become, like the Paonis, the unknowing financiers of developing countries, for money swishes around the world today from Cantrall to Russia to Brazil to China, connecting the most unlikely people. Among them are Mrs. Paoni and an Indonesian rickshaw driver named Salamet, a 27-year-old with a drooping mustache, an angry wife and three hungry children.

For Mrs. Paoni and most Americans, these are still good times economically. But elsewhere in the world, hundreds of millions of people like Mr. Salamet are still caught in a severe crisis, one that has recast lives and will haunt a generation in the East just as the Great Depression shaped a generation in the West.

It is still not clear that the financial upheavals, which began in Thailand in July 1997, will ever damage the United States. But the collapse of Brazil's currency in January and the jolt that brought to markets worldwide underscored the continuing risks of "the most serious financial crisis in a half a century," as President Clinton called it in his State of the Union address.

This series of articles is a narrative of the worldwide financial crisis that over the last 20 months has toppled some governments and hobbled others. The crisis has turned Mr. Salamet's life upside down without affecting Mrs. Paoni at all—but it illustrates how globalization increasingly stitches lives all over the world into a single economic quilt.

In the new economic landscape that has emerged in recent years, the pool of international investments has grown to dwarf the sums that governments can muster, and money zips around the globe far faster than ever before. One result is a world more prosperous but also, perhaps, more wobbly.

"More and more people are asking whether the international financial system as it has operated for most of the 1990's is basically unstable," Ian McFarlane, governor of Australia's central bank, said at a recent conference in Singapore. "And I think by now the majority of observers have come to the conclusion that it is."

Salamet, the Rickshaw Man

Mr. Salamet, a burly man with an expression as hard as his biceps, knows nothing of finance, but he understands that his world is falling apart.

Money on the Move: How the World Financial Landscape Has Changed

Finance has been international for hundreds of years, and globalization is not new. But several forces have conspired in recent years to create a fundamentally new financial landscape that has fostered a world crisis. Here are five examples:

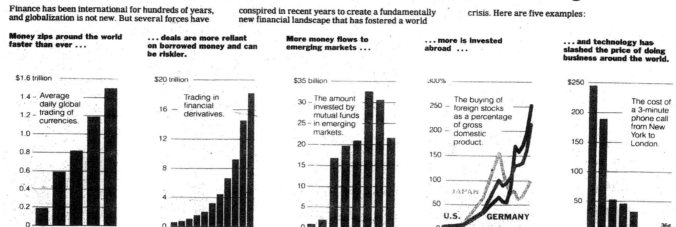

Money zips around the world faster than ever ...

Average daily global trading of currencies. (in $trillion: scale 0 to $1.6 trillion, years '86 '89 '92 '95 '98)

... deals are more reliant on borrowed money and can be riskier.

Trading in financial derivatives. (scale 0 to $20 trillion, years '87 '89 '91 '93 '95 '97)

More money flows to emerging markets ...

The amount invested by mutual funds in emerging markets. (scale 0 to $35 billion, years '91 '92 '93 '94 '95 '96 '97 '98)

... more is invested abroad ...

The buying of foreign stocks as a percentage of gross domestic product. (scale 0 to 300%, decades 70's 80's 90's) U.S., GERMANY, JAPAN

... and technology has slashed the price of doing business around the world.

The cost of a 3-minute phone call from New York to London. (scale 0 to $250, years '30 '50 '70 '90 '98, 36¢)

Sources: ATT; Bank for International Settlements; Financial Regulation in the Global Economy; International Monetary Fund; Gary Hufbauer, Institute for International Economics; Morningstar Inc.

As he sat on the porch of his little white house in a remote corner of Indonesia, his thoughts were on his mother. He sat brooding, his stomach tying itself in knots, as his mother's gasps filtered through the curtain from the next room.

She was lying on the floor, dying of cancer, a huge tumor growing inside her breast. What gnawed at Mr. Salamet each waking moment was not just her gasps, but also his guilt at the knowledge that he could help her but had decided not to.

The doctor had prescribed a painkiller costing $2 a month, a sum that Mr. Salamet earns in two days and could afford. But as his wife, Yuti, reminded him sharply, if he were to buy the painkiller, then he would get further behind in making payments on his rickshaw, meaning that it might be seized and he would lose his livelihood. Or he would have to stop paying school fees, meaning that his son Dwi might be forced to leave the second grade and never get an education.

Although Mr. Salamet has always been poor, the financial crisis has deepened the desperation in his home and countless others. Indeed, if Dwi drops out, he will have plenty of company: The Asian Development Bank estimates that 6.1 million children have left school in Indonesia in recent months because of the economic crisis.

Mr. Salamet contemplated his options as he sat, stony-faced, beneath the mango trees of Mojokerto, a mid-sized town 400 miles east of the Indonesian capital of Jakarta. He is quiet by nature, and when his wife scolds him for not earning enough money he does not shout at her or hit her, as other men in the neighborhood might.

"Instead, he just sulks," said Mrs. Yuti, a slim woman with high cheekbones, and an embarrassed grin spread across her face and then was mimicked by the baby she was carrying in her arms.

Mr. Salamet, who like his wife and many other Indonesians uses only one name, pondered the bleak options in a flat voice, weighing what flexibility he might have. Would the school really expel Dwi if he got further behind on the school fees? How long could he delay payments before the rickshaw would be seized? How little pain reliever could he get away with giving his mother to ease the worst of her agony?

Tired of this calculus, he shook his head.

"If it were like before and I had money," he growled, "of course I would buy her more painkillers. But now I can't spare the cash for her."

From Speculation to Crisis

The initial impulse in America as the crisis erupted was to see the problems as an outgrowth of Asian corruption and cronyism. These probably made the situation worse, but a growing body of evidence suggests that there was nothing uniquely Asian about these countries' problems, and that the catastrophe was worsened by folly and hubris in the United States and Europe.

It was bankers and investors in Moscow and the Thai capital, Bangkok, who speculated wildly on stocks and real estate and thus built up catastrophic bubble economies. But it was American officials who pushed for the financial liberalization that nurtured the speculation (even if developing nations themselves welcomed it). And it was American bankers and money managers who poured billions of dollars into those emerging markets. Then, when the crisis hit, American officials insisted on tough measures like budget cuts and high interest rates, which many economists argue made things worse.

The failure in January of the $41.5 billion bailout of Brazil demonstrates that the West still has not found a reliable formula for dealing with these crises. Experts continue to worry about the danger of a global recession or worse, and about the risk that economic woes may tear apart countries like Indonesia and even China.

Resentment at American policies—and, perhaps, at America's economic success—has also led to a sense in many countries that the global economy is at an ideological turning point. In particular, there is a growing backlash against what some nations regard as an American model of laissez-faire capitalism, which rescues Connecticut hedge funds but sacrifices Indonesian children.

Particularly in Tokyo and Paris, where markets have always been regarded as something like ornery oxen—best when firmly yoked and even then prone to leave messes—there is talk of sturdier harnesses to guide capital flows, speculators and markets themselves.

What does all this portend? And how can it be that, as David Hale, chief economist of the Zurich Group, describes the financial upheaval of the last year and a half, "a real estate crisis in Bangkok set in motion something that has no parallel in human history?"

Early Gains for Salamet

The saga begins in places like Mr. Salamet's riverside neighborhood in Indonesia, then a poor country that had not yet taken on the glitter of an emerging market.

For countless generations, Mr. Salamet's ancestors have been agricultural laborers, owning little or no land, struggling to survive and often not even managing that. When Mr. Salamet was 10, his father fell to his death from a palm tree he was pruning.

Mr. Salamet's mother remarried, and the boy and his new stepfather labored side by side each day, lugging sacks of sand from riverbanks to sell to cement factories. It was backbreaking work, but it was accompanied by breathtaking progress.

As foreign investments poured into Indonesia, the town of Mojokerto thrived in the general prosperity. Mr. Salamet and his stepfather, Pirso, rented rickshaws and began driving them—a business that boomed as people made a bit more, and as mud paths were paved to make rickshaw travel feasible.

Indonesian families are usually close-knit, and Mr. Pirso sent some of the money to help his own mother, Mariyam, in the town of Kediri several hours' drive to the south.

Mrs. Mariyam, a thin and energetic gray-haired woman, was sitting one day recently in her store-bought wooden chair, beside her nicely finished bureau, on which rested a black Deluxe All Transistor Radio that in English pledged INSTANT SUPERB SOUND. The floor was concrete, the roof was tile, the walls were covered with tattered wallpaper and a curtain covered the bedroom next door. It had become a genuine house, no longer a hut, and outside was a pump and outhouse-cum-bath built five years ago by Mr. Pirso.

"It's a big improvement," she said, "because the river was far away. And it's nice, because I can bathe without everybody seeing. It's supposed to be that if you're bathing in the river, people stay away. But some of the men are naughty."

These gains over the years have been enormous, and so far they have proved reasonably durable. The deprivation and hunger are serious, but as yet there is little evidence that the financial crisis has sent Asia 20 or 30 years backward or that it has destroyed the middle class.

Third World Is Renamed

Traditionally, Mrs. Paoni's savings would have stayed far from any place where people have to bathe in rivers. Her money would have remained where she still thinks it is, entirely in nice and safe American communities like hers. Mrs. Paoni and her husband have invested in stocks, but they say they have stuck to blue chips like Coca Cola and Disney.

She wants security above all. Risk is acceptable when confined to her Mary Higgins Clark mysteries and Stephen King horror novels, but she is counting on safe investments and her pension income when she and her husband pull up stakes this year and move, perhaps to Florida.

Income in retirement will come from the Illinois state pension fund, which like most pension funds has the same deeply conservative instincts as Mrs. Paoni.

But even that is slowly changing, as fund managers seek higher returns. In 1980 fewer than 1 percent of pension fund assets in the United States were invested abroad, but by 1997 that figure had risen to 17 percent. And so, as part of the process bandied about as "globalization," Mrs. Paoni has tiny financial stakes in dozens of countries around the world.

One reason Americans like her and her pension fund managers used to be unwilling to invest in places like Indonesia was the description "third-world markets," which had an ominous ring. In the mid-1980's, the International Finance Corporation of the World Bank was trying to drum up support for a third-world investment fund, when one listener complained about the terminology.

"No one wants to put money into the third-world investment fund," the man protested. "You'd better come up with something better."

So in just a few days officials dreamed up an alternative— "emerging markets"—and it proved a winner. The first emerging-markets fund came out in 1986, and the craze was born.

Emerging markets quickly produced emerging gurus. One of the most prominent is J. Mark Mobius, 62, who is instantly recognizable at investment conferences with his shaven head and stern, lean look.

Templeton Funds recruited Mr. Mobius in 1987 to figure out the small markets of the world, and under him the Templeton Emerging Markets Fund was a success almost immediately. In 1988 the fund gained 37 percent, and then it soared 98 percent in 1989. After a small dip in 1990, it rocketed 112 percent in 1991 and after another dip soared 100 percent in 1993.

"The 1987 crash was very bad for emerging markets," Mr. Mobius said. "But in 1988–89 the recovery came, and the ball started rolling as people started waking up to the tremendous returns that were possible."

The bullishness was, in part, self-fulfilling. The stock markets in small countries were tiny, and modest investments by Westerners tended to bid up prices, thus attracting more investors.

A result was that hubris increased more rapidly than the caliber of most investment research. Bright young men and women who could barely read a spreadsheet moved to Asia and ended up getting hired as research analysts by investment banks. They sometimes made hundreds of thousands of dollars a year picking stocks in countries whose languages they could barely speak.

The Capital Starts to Flow

Even more than pension funds and mutual funds and other stock purchasers, banks were piling into emerging markets—particularly banks from Europe and Japan. Investors bought $50 billion worth of stocks and bonds in emerging markets in 1996, but that year international banks poured $76 billion into those countries.

From Mrs. Paoni's money market account at A. G. Edwards, the American brokerage company, cash then flows to major American banks, like J. P. Morgan and Chase Manhattan. There is no risk to Mrs. Paoni, but from the big banks some portion of her savings journeys abroad.

All this capital made a spectacular difference to emerging-market countries.

"When history books are written 200 years from now about the last two decades of the 20th century," Deputy Treasury Secretary Lawrence H. Summers said recently, "I am convinced that the end of the cold war will be the second story. The first story will be about the appearance of emerging markets—about the fact that developing countries where more than three billion people live have moved toward the market and seen rapid growth in incomes."

Countries like Chile and Egypt and Russia and Vietnam became enmeshed in the international economy. In Moscow, tycoons dripping with gold and diamonds began to drop hundreds of dollars at trendy new restaurants, and in the early 1990's more Mercedes 600 SEL sedans were selling in Moscow, at $130,000 apiece, than in New York City. In the Russian city of Volgograd, one wealthy citizen plunked down $300,000 to buy two stretch limousines.

In Brazil's biggest city, São Paulo, homeless children slept under billboard advertisements for mutual funds, and farther south, in Argentina, cash machines spat out American dollars and televisions offered 50 cable channels.

And in the ancient Chinese lakeside city of Hangzhou, two "dakuan," or fat cats, got into a contest to see who was wealthier. They began burning real currency to show off, and in a blink they had each burned $400.

In one sense, today's crisis fits neatly into a long history of financial manias and panics. Emerging markets have been risky ever since the 1320's, when England, then a developing country, defaulted on loans to banks in the Italian city-state of Genoa. In the 19th century, states like Mississippi defaulted on debts just as Russia did last year.

Yet for all the parallels with the past, new elements are at work to make the global economy very different from the one of a century ago, or even a decade ago. Most fundamentally, finance and technology have exploded in importance and now dominate the economic horizon.

In a typical day, the total amount of money changing hands in the world's foreign exchange markets alone is $1.5 trillion—an eightfold increase since 1986 and an almost incomprehensible sum, equivalent to total world trade for four months.

"It's no longer the real economy driving the financial markets," said Marc Faber, a prominent fund manager in Hong Kong, "but the financial markets driving the real economy."

Already, a 15 percent increase in American stock prices bolsters American wealth by $1.7 trillion, which is considerably more than the value of all the manufacturing that takes place in a year in the entire United States. This capacity for wealth creation has delighted Americans, but there is also a converse: a 15 percent drop in the market erases wealth equivalent to the entire annual output of all American factories.

Economists are still charting this new global economic landscape, but they point out some of its features:

- The amount of investment capital has exploded. By 1995, mutual funds, pension funds and other institutional investors controlled $20 trillion, 10 times the figure of 1980. The global economy is no longer dominated by trade in cars and steel and wheat, but rather by trade in stocks and bonds and currencies.

- Far more wealth than ever before is stateless, circulating wherever in the world the owner can find the highest return. Thus spending by investors in industrialized countries on overseas stocks increased 197-fold between 1970 and 1997, and each nation's capital market is beginning to merge into a global capital market.

- New technologies have vastly reduced the importance of physical distance. In 1930 a three-minute telephone call from New York to London cost $245. Now it runs 36 cents. In cyberspace, every market is next door.

- Investments are increasingly leveraged, using borrowed money so that a $1 million bet becomes a $5 million bet, or they are channeled through complex financial instruments known as derivatives to multiply the potential profits. Derivatives have grown exponentially, with those traded in 1997 valued at $360 trillion, a figure equivalent to a dozen times the size of the entire global economy, and they bring important benefits but also new risks of turbulence.

- Public funds are increasingly used to bail out losers, like banks. The latest crisis has forced an international rescue on a scale like nothing before, with roughly $175 billion in public money raised so far for the various international bailouts. At least some of that public money has gone to rescue bankers and politicians from their own mistakes.

For all the dazzling size and complexity of the global financial markets, it is not clear that the markets are operating with an intelligence that matches their scale. There may be computer equipment analyzing blips in exchange rates, but investors are fundamentally prey to emotions and panics and tend to overshoot.

Paul Samuelson, the Nobel laureate in economics, argues that sophisticated analysis has done a marvelous job in achieving "microefficiency" in financial markets. The result is that share prices adjust almost perfectly to specific news like currency movements or changes in dividends.

"But I also believe the evidence is overwhelming that there is no macro-efficiency of speculative markets," Professor Samuelson added. "They experience self-fulfilling swings, and they can swing far above and below any kind of sensible fundamental value. There does not exist an efficiency which is self-correcting, except in the case that every bubble will someday burst."

How do these speculative swings come about?

Part of the answer is changes in market sentiment because of pronouncements by people like Barton M. Biggs. One of the gray-haired elders of Wall Street, Mr. Biggs, 65, the chief global investment strategist for Morgan Stanley Dean Witter & Company, commands the attention of pension fund managers in Illinois and around the world. In an industry that has drifted toward computer models and number crunchers, Mr. Biggs is a generalist who is famous for his brilliantly written investment reports, which are often funny and always influential.

In 1993, in typical seat-of-the-pants style, he made a weeklong trip to China and came out starry-eyed. He urged investors to increase their holdings of Hong Kong stocks six-fold, to 7 percent of a global stock portfolio.

"We were all stunned by the enormous size of China," he declared. "Sometimes you have to spend time in a country to get really focused on the investment case. After eight days in China, I'm tuned in, overfed and maximum bullish."

Hong Kong stocks soared at those words, and gained 28 percent over the next seven weeks. Then, in August 1994, Mr. Biggs declared that the smaller Asian markets—Thailand, Indonesia and Hong Kong—would be "the best place in the world to be for the next five years."

Mr. Biggs's comments were representative of Wall Street's euphoria about Asia. When executives of an obscure Indonesian polyester company called Polysindo visited New York in 1996 to discuss issuing bonds, they were squired around and accorded meetings with top executives at Merrill Lynch and Morgan Stanley. No comparable Chicago company could ever have got such a welcome.

American investment banks were so eager to arrange stock offerings for the likes of Polysindo that they often charged Asian companies about 3 percent of the value of the deal, compared with 6 percent that they would charge companies in the United States. This reflected the ease with which some foreign companies could raise money, and the head of an American corporation plaintively queried a New York investment bank, "Why do I have to pay 6 percent when you charge an Indonesian company only 3 percent?"

At Templeton, Mr. Mobius was more careful in his pronouncements than many other analysts, emphasizing that emerging markets can go down as well as up. But his moderation was taken as simply a token of his modesty, and he was rapidly becoming a celebrity. An investment of $10,000 in the fund at the beginning of 1988 would have turned into $100,000 by the end of 1993, and Templeton began to use his picture in its advertisements. His shaven head smiled out at investors, and he came to symbolize the truly global fund manager.

Mr. Mobius speaks at least a bit of six foreign languages—Chinese, Korean, Japanese, German, Spanish and Thai—and he comes across as a citizen of the world. In 1992 he dropped his American nationality for German citizenship, for tax reasons, and he spends most of his time in hotels.

Nominally a resident of Singapore, with a second home in the Philippines, he travels 250 days a year, roaming Asia, Latin America and Eastern Europe. In a typical week he might visit 4 cities and 20 companies.

"My job is to go out and find bargains," he said at an investment conference in Chicago. "You can't find bargains sitting at a desk reading annual reports."

On March 8, 1996, the first shot was fired at the emerging markets. A New York hedge fund sold $400 million worth of the Thai currency, the baht, betting that it would fall.

Hedge funds, famous for secrecy, are large pools of speculative funds that make investments for banks, pension funds or other large investors. The first hedge fund was founded in 1949, but they came into their own only in the 1990's, with their assets soaring twelvefold between 1990 and 1997. Now there are 3,500 hedge funds, managing $200 billion. And they are able to leverage that, through borrowing, into a much greater sum.

The baht was pegged to the dollar so that they rose and fell together, and the peg was frequently praised as a source of stability for the Thai economy. But the hedge fund managers were shrewd enough to see that Thailand's economy was faltering, its exports slowing, its property sector sagging and its banks sinking under bad loans.

The baht should have weakened along with Thailand's economy, but instead the peg kept it as strong as the dollar. The hedge fund managers sensed that the baht was too strong considering Thailand's weaknesses, and they knew that if Thailand's slowing economy forced the Government to float the currency they could make a quick killing.

In this case, though, that first hedge fund's bet against the baht fizzled, and a few days later the fund gave up.

Most analysts continued to rave about Asia. At Morgan Stanley, Mr. Biggs had been wrong when he predicted that stock markets in Thailand would soar in 1996 (instead, Thai stocks fell 36 percent), and so in January 1997 he went on what he called a fact-finding mission so as "to clarify my thinking on the Thai stock market."

The facts that Mr. Biggs found were, on the whole, positive ones. He said at a Morgan Stanley investment seminar in Tokyo on Jan. 14, 1997, as recorded by Bloomberg News Service: "We tend to think there are a lot of opportunities in Asian emerging markets," and he specifically referred to Thailand, South Korea, India and Singapore.

"When you have a market that is down 50 percent," Mr. Biggs told the investors, "you have to be looking for values. We can find values for Thailand."

Others could not. From that date through the end of 1997, Thai stock prices fell 75.3 percent in dollar terms.

Tracking Capital Flight

In judging countries like Thailand, bankers and investors rely partly on expert assessments from credit rating institutions like Standard & Poors and Moody's Investors Services. So what was S & P saying?

"Standard & Poors does not expect that the likely scale of financial-sector losses will seriously impair the kingdom's credit standing," S & P said about Thailand on March 18, 1997. It added that any crisis in Thailand was "most unlikely" to approach the levels of the problems in Mexico in 1995 or Indonesia or Finland in the early 1990's.

If S & P's prediction was off base, that might not have been so unusual. Scholarly analyses find that the rating agencies usually offer warnings only after it is too late. For example, a study by two American economists, Carmen M. Reinhart and Morris Goldstein, looked at 72 financial crises around the world since 1979 and concluded that rating agencies tended to react after crises instead of anticipating them.

S & P sees things differently. John Chambers, one of its managing directors, said that his company's analysis had been thorough and had identified potential risks.

For all the scorn heaped on Asians for their cronyism and other foolishness, local people in Thailand, Malaysia, Russia and South Korea were showing the most savvy. They were selling—usually to the kind of enthusiastic, well-trained foreigners who were making many times their salaries.

Capital flight is hard to track precisely, but it is the main reason for the "errors and omissions" line in the International Monetary Fund data. These data show that there was no significant capital flight from emerging markets between 1990 and 1995.

Capital flight soared to $16 billion in 1996, a full year before the crisis began, and reached $45 billion in 1997. This money then ended up in major banks based in Switzerland, London and New York.

Drenched in a 'Blood Baht'

Japan, the dominant economy in Asia and the one that might have been the locomotive to pull countries like Thailand out of their difficulties, instead administered the coup de grace. On April 1, 1997, against the strenuous protests of Mr. Summers, who flew to Tokyo to deliver a testy complaint from Washington, Japan raised its sales tax to 5 percent from 3 percent.

Mr. Summers had insisted that the tax increase would harm Japan's incipient economic recovery by dampening consumer spending, but Japanese officials scoffed at that argument. Eisuke Sakakibara, Japan's Deputy Minister of Finance for International Affairs, was particularly emphatic that Japan was doing just fine. He told reporters that those who denied Japan's being on a recovery course were irrational.

"I am an optimist on the Japanese economy," he said in May 1997, adding a month later, "Real growth in Japan's gross domestic product will exceed the Government's projection."

But it was Mr. Summers who was proved right. In the second quarter of 1997, Japanese economic output was actually plunging at an annual rate of 11 percent. Japan became mired in its worst recession in six decades, and instead of dealing decisively with its troubles it steadily sank deeper. Japan's imports from Asian countries like Thailand slumped.

With Thai exporters now struggling, along with property developers and hotel companies, the entire country became edgy. The overvalued currency resulted in alarming trade deficits, and speculation grew that the peg would be broken and the baht devalued.

Thailand's own investors and companies began buying dollars, attracting the attention of foreign speculators. In May, Tiger Management, based in New York and one of the biggest hedge funds of all, began to bet heavily against the baht, and other banks and hedge funds piled on as well.

It looked as if the speculators would win. Normally baht-dollar trades totaled $200 million a day, but the amounts now soared. On May 13, 1997, the Thai central bank sold $6.3 billion to buy baht that everyone else was selling. A central banker wrote that day in a sober memo to his bosses, "The market was not afraid."

The next day, officials met in the central bank to try to figure out what to do. There was fury at hedge funds, but most of all there was utter desperation.

"Everyone panicked, and some even cried," Rerngchai Marakanond, the head of the central bank, recalled later before a Government commission.

If Thailand had decided on that day to give up and devalue the baht, while it still had reserves left, the world might have been able to avoid the worst of the financial crisis. Thailand would have faced a severe domestic banking crisis and property glut, and other countries would also have faced slumps. But the country would have saved its reserves and perhaps avoided a severe panic, and the fury of the crisis and the impact on nations as far away as Brazil and Russia might have been minimized.

The meeting went the other way, with the central bank now determined to risk everything in a battle against speculators. That day the central bank intervened again, selling more than $10 billion. It was one of the biggest interventions any central bank had ever made, but it had little impact.

The Thai central bankers had one more trick up their sleeves. On May 15, 1997, they sold dollars and simultaneously ordered banks not to lend to foreign speculators. The speculators were unable to unwind their bets as their losses mounted, and they screamed into their phones, threw chairs across the room and watched their computer screens in horror. In one day, the hedge funds lost around $450 million, according to Callum Henderson, a currency analyst who wrote a book about the crisis. That day became known among traders as the "blood baht."

The Thai Prime Minister telephoned the central bank to congratulate officials and promise a celebration party, but it was a Pyrrhic victory. The central bank had supported the baht by selling dollars in forward contracts, committing itself to using its dollars to buy baht in the future. In practical terms, this meant that its official reserves of $30 billion were mostly already pledged and no longer usable to defend the baht. And speculators continued the attack, carefully but constantly keeping up the pressure.

Who were these speculators? They were mostly American, and the hedge funds were prominent among them. But they also included major American banks, trading for themselves to make a profit. Mrs. Paoni could not have known it, but a tiny fraction of her savings might have been thrown, by a circuitous route, into the attack on the baht.

Some of the funds in Mrs. Paoni's money market account, for example, went to J. P. Morgan, and J. P. Morgan said in a court document that it had traded $1 billion worth of baht in the fall of 1996. The bank did not disclose its trades in the spring of 1997, and bank officials refused to comment.

Thai officials were furious that American hedge funds and banks were investing billions of dollars in a bid to destabilize their country, and they worried about the consequences of such speculative battles on all of Asia. In May 1997 Mr. Rerngchai, the central bank chief, sent a secret letter of complaint to Alan Greenspan, the chairman of the Federal Reserve, urging him to rein in American hedge funds and other financial institutions.

Mr. Rerngchai warned that the attack on Thailand "could have far-reaching implications on the economy both of Thailand and the Asian region" and "threatens to jeopardize the stability of international financial markets."

A similar letter was sent to Hans Tietmeyer, the president of the central bank in Germany, noting that one German bank had joined in the attack on the baht. Mr. Tietmeyer quickly responded himself, a Thai official recalled, with a question of his own: which of our banks? That warmed hearts at the Thai central bank, but the response from Washington annoyed them.

The correspondence, made available by a Thai central bank official and confirmed by another Government official, shows that the Fed's response came not from Mr. Greenspan but an from aide, Edwin M. Truman, He blandly acknowledged that "large financial firms" can disrupt markets of countries like Thailand but added that these matters were best left to the markets.

Mr. Greenspan declined to comment. "All communications with other central banks are private," said Lynn S. Fox, spokeswoman for the Federal Reserve in Washington.

There was another opportunity for the leading countries to confront the problems before the crisis erupted. In late June, the seven leading industrialized nations held their summit meeting in Denver, and aides say that in the confidential discussion among leaders, the Japanese Prime Minister at the time, Ryutaro Hashimoto, called for the industrial countries to discuss the financial instability in Thailand.

Japanese officials were expectant, waiting for President Clinton and other leaders to take up the matter. But according to one American official who was there, Mr. Hashimoto was typically understated, tentative and vague (as is considered polite in Japan), and did not call for any specific action.

So President Clinton and the other world leaders paid no attention.

The View From Ground Zero

Thanong Bidaya, one of Thailand's most respected bankers, is an imposing man with a round face, a gentle manner and a passion for collecting antique watches. A fluent speaker of both English and Japanese, he flew to Hong Kong for a weekend in June 1997 with his wife, planning to scour the shops for old watches. He settled into a hotel in the Tsim Sha Tsui district, and the phone rang. It was the Thai Prime Minister, asking him to take over as Finance Minister.

"If you've found no one, I'll do it for you," Mr. Thanong agreed.

Later, he recalled thinking, "The situation can't be that serious." So the next day Mr. Thanong flew back to Bangkok. And then, on the evening of June 27, 1997, he climbed into a navy blue Mercedes-Benz limousine and zigzagged through throngs of traffic to the central bank headquarters. He wanted to meet Mr. Rerngchai, an old friend from the time they had both studied in Japan.

As Mr. Thanong's car approached the stately gates to the majestic eight-story central bank building, a guard waved it through. It was about 7 P.M. when they entered a conference room, and Mr. Rerngchai gave his friend the shock of his life.

Thailand was out of cash, Mr. Rerngchai explained. After subtracting the dollars that had been committed in forward transactions, Thailand had just $2.8 billion in usable foreign exchange reserves.

Even though he was Finance Minister and one of his country's most experienced bankers, Mr. Thanong was stunned. Mr. Rerngchai had brought reams of studies examining the options, but he and Mr. Thanong both knew that it was all over.

The foreign banks and hedge funds had won, and Thailand had lost. The two men agreed that since Thailand had run out of money, it would have to drop the peg with the dollar and let the baht float at whatever rate the market set. It was a foreshadowing of what would happen in Brazil 18 months later.

"I said I didn't see any choice in dealing with the situation," Mr. Thanong recalled.

A few days later, on July 1, the Thai Prime Minister, Chavalit Yongchaiyudh, declared that the baht would never be devalued. But that night, if anybody had noticed, the lights burned brightly at the central bank. Officials stayed up all night, first calling major central banks abroad. Then, at 4:30 A.M., central bankers called the homes of the heads of all Thai banks and major foreign banks in Bangkok, summoning them to an emergency meeting that would begin at 6 A.M.

When the bleary-eyed bank executives had taken their seats, an official grimly announced that Thailand could no longer stand behind the baht. Instead of being pegged to the dollar, it would float freely.

The global crisis had just detonated.

* * *

February 16, 1999

HOW U.S. WOOED ASIA TO LET CASH FLOW IN GLOBAL CONTAGION

By NICHOLAS D. KRISTOF with DAVID E. SANGER

They were serious men, prosperous and pinstriped, and they derided "the politics of class warfare" as they conducted a job interview with the young Governor from Arkansas.

It was steak dinner in a private room of the "21" Club in June 1991, and the top Democratic executives on Wall Street were gathered at a round table to hold one of a series of meetings with Presidential aspirants in what an organizer called "an elegant cattle show." They were questioning a man with a meager salary but a silver tongue, and this was another show in which Gov. Bill Clinton charmed his way to a blue ribbon by impressing the executives with his willingness to embrace free trade and free markets.

"What was discussed was the need for the Democratic Party to have a new and much more forward-looking economic policy," Roger Altman, a leading investment banker and an organizer of the evening, recalled recently. "The Democratic Party needed to move into a new economic world."

Aides describe that evening as an important step in the business education of Mr. Clinton, who came to repeat and amplify the themes—especially the need to move away from protectionism and push for more open markets in Asia and all over the world.

It was also the time that Mr. Clinton first met Robert E. Rubin, then the head of Goldman Sachs & Company, and although the initial encounter was cool, the two men eventually forged a close partnership that has left an enormous imprint on the global economy.

Mr. Clinton and Mr. Rubin, who became his Treasury Secretary in 1995, took the American passion for free trade and carried it further to press for freer movement of capital. Along the way they pushed harder to win opportunities for American banks, brokerages and insurance companies.

This drive for free movement of capital as well as goods was one factor in the long American-led boom in financial markets around the globe. Yet, in retrospect, Washington's policies also fostered vulnerabilities that are an underlying cause of the economic crisis that began in Thailand in July 1997, rippled through Asia and Russia, and is now shaking Brazil and Latin America.

Countries like Thailand and Russia and Brazil are in trouble today largely for internal reasons, including poor banking practices and speculation that soared out of control. But some economists also say that if those countries had weak foundations, it is partly because Washington helped supply the blueprints.

They argue that the Clinton Administration pushed too hard for financial liberalization and freer capital flows, allowing foreign money to stream into these countries and local money to move out. In many cases, foreign countries were happy to open up in this way because they thought it was the best road to economic development, but a wealth of evidence has shown that overhasty liberalization can lead to banking chaos and financial crises.

Even some former Administration officials acknowledge that they went too far. Mickey Kantor, the former trade representative and Commerce Secretary, now says that the United States was insufficiently aware of the kind of chaos that financial liberalization could provoke.

"It would be a legitimate criticism to say that we should have been more nuanced, more foresighted that this could happen," he said. Speaking of the risks of financial liberalization without modern banking and legal systems, he compared them to "building a skyscraper with no foundation."

Although the Clinton Administration always talked about financial liberalization as the best thing for other countries, it is also clear that it pushed for free capital flows in part because this was what its supporters in the banking industry wanted.

"Our financial services industry wanted into these markets," said Laura D'Andrea Tyson, the former chairwoman of President Clinton's Council of Economic Advisers and later head of the National Economic Council.

Ms. Tyson says she disagreed to some extent with the push and was concerned about "a tendency to do this as a blanket approach, regardless of the size of a country or the development of a country." Free capital flows, she worried, could overwhelm small countries or those with weak banking and legal systems, leading to a "run on a country."

This is not to say that American officials are primarily to blame for the crisis. Responsibility can be assigned all around: not only to Washington policy makers, but also to the officials and bankers in emerging-market countries who created the mess; to Western bankers and investors who blindly handed them money; to Western officials who hailed free capital flows and neglected to make them safer; to Western scholars and journalists who wrote paeans to emerging markets and the "Asian Century"—and to the people who planned an empty city named Muang Thong Thani.

High-Rise Ghost Town

Muang Thong Thani rises up above barren fields on the edge of Bangkok, Thailand. It is a dazzling complex of two dozen huge gray-white buildings soaring nearly 30 stories high, and surrounded by streets lined with shops, town houses and detached homes. Walk closer and it feels eerie, for it is a ghost city.

Along one street of 100 houses, the windows are mere holes in the walls, and yards have weeds that grow as high as a person.

Muang Thong Thani was built during Thailand's boom as a product of free capital flows and financial liberalization. It was the great dream of Anant Kanjanapas.

One of 11 children born to an ethnic Chinese business tycoon in Thailand, Mr. Anant grew up with the wealth that his family had acquired through developing property and selling watches in Asia.

The family's Bangkok Land company began acquiring parcels of property near the airport, and they broke ground in

1990 on a megaproject to build a privately owned satellite city for Bangkok. Muang Thong Thani was to have a population of 700,000, bigger than Boston's.

"We have all intentions to develop Muang Thong Thani as a city, a complete city run by private-sector people," Mr. Anant said. "It was not a stroke of genius. It was logic."

The project was greeted enthusiastically, as all proposals were in the early 1990's, and Bangkok Land issued shares on the Thai Stock Exchange in 1992 to raise money. Its shares were hot, picked up by J. Mark Mobius, the emerging-markets guru, and by funds like the Thai International Fund and the Thai Euro Fund, which between them bought more than one million shares of Bangkok Land.

In Illinois, the state pension fund bought shares in both the Thai International Fund and the Thai Euro Fund, and that made Mary Jo Paoni, a secretary in Cantrall, Ill., a roundabout owner of a tiny part of Bangkok Land and Muang Thong Thani. Mrs. Paoni knew nothing of this, of course, and disapproves of the giddy investment sprees in Asia.

"When things are tough," she said, "you don't start spending like a drunken sailor. There are some people who take risks, but not us."

Bangkok Land also borrowed $2.4 billion from banks domestic and foreign. In that sense, some minute fraction of Mrs. Paoni's money might also have been channeled to the company as loans. Her money market account at A. G. Edwards went to buy commercial paper of major banks, and her pension fund also held stock in Bangkok Bank, which lent to Bangkok Land—an illustration of the way in which globalization now gives just about everybody some tiny financial stake in everybody else.

Cash Controls Eased

Free movement of capital is nothing new, for it was the norm during most of Western history. At the beginning of this century, anyone could move money across borders without difficulty.

The Great Depression changed all that. Governments moved to control capital so as to avoid what they saw as the chaos of capital rushing out of countries and setting off financial crises.

A result was that most countries of the world (including the United States in the 1960's) limited the right of companies and citizens to buy foreign securities or invest overseas. People were often allowed to buy only small amounts of foreign currency.

Then, as memories of the Depression faded, the tide shifted again in the 1970's and '80's. Starting in the United States and Europe, it became fashionable to let money move freely, and the Reagan Administration began to push for free capital flows in other countries.

"Our task is to knock down barriers to trade and foreign investment and the free movement of capital," Ronald Reagan declared in 1985. George Bush described his Latin America program, the Enterprise for Americas Initiative, as a

commitment to "free markets and to the free flow of capital, central to achieving economic growth and lasting prosperity."

The Clinton Administration inherited that agenda and amplified it. Previous administrations had pushed for financial liberalization principally in Japan, but under President Clinton it became a worldwide effort directed at all kinds of countries, even smaller ones much less able to absorb it than Japan.

"We pushed full steam ahead on all areas of liberalization, including financial," recalled Jeffrey E. Garten, a former senior Commerce Department official who is now dean of the Yale School of Management. "I never went on a trip when my brief didn't include either advice or congratulations on liberalization."

This push for financial liberalization reflected President Clinton's growing enthusiasm for markets and his desire to make the economy a centerpiece of his foreign policy. He created the National Economic Council as a counterpart to the National Security Council, and asked Mr. Rubin to be its first head. More broadly, this push was part of a global ideological shift in favor of free markets, as well as an increasing enthusiasm among developing countries themselves for lifting restrictions on the flow of money.

"We were convinced we were moving with the stream," Mr. Garten said, "and that our job was to make the stream move faster."

"Wall Street was delighted that the broad trade agenda now included financial services," he added.

Mr. Garten said he could not recall hearing any doubts expressed about the policy, either within the Administration or among officials overseas. Referring to Mr. Rubin, Mr. Kantor and the late Commerce Secretary Ron Brown, Mr. Garten said, "There wasn't a fiber in those three bodies—or in mine—that didn't want to press as a matter of policy for more open markets wherever you could make it happen."

"It's easy to see in retrospect that we probably pushed too far, too fast," he said, adding, "In retrospect, we overshot, and in retrospect there was a certain degree of arrogance."

The push for financial liberalization was directed at Asia in particular, largely because it was seen as a potential gold mine for American banks and brokerages. Neither Mr. Clinton nor Mr. Rubin had much experience in Asia—Mr. Clinton as Governor had led trade delegations to promote Arkansas chickens and rice, and Mr. Rubin had done business in Japan for Goldman, Sachs. But Mr. Clinton as President has worked hard to strengthen American ties with Asia, as well as his own.

The idea was to press Asia to ease its barriers to American goods and financial services, helping Fidelity sell mutual funds, Citibank sell checking accounts and American International Group sell insurance. Mr. Clinton's links to Asia caused embarrassment after they led to the campaign finance scandals of 1996, but fundamentally they reflected an appetite for business opportunities in Asian countries that had changed, as Mr. Clinton once put it, "from dominoes to dynamos."

His Cabinet approved a "big emerging markets" plan to identify 10 rising economic powers and push relentlessly to win business for American companies there. Under Mr. Brown, the Commerce Department even built what it called a war room, where computers tracked big contracts, and everyone from the C.I.A. to ambassadors to the President himself was called upon to help land deals.

The stakes could be huge. Japan had been the first target of pressure for financial liberalization, even under the Reagan Administration, and these days it is finally engaged in what it calls a "big bang" opening of its capital markets. The upshot is that American institutions are swarming into Tokyo and finally have a chance to manage a portion of the $10 trillion in Japanese personal savings. And when a big Japanese brokerage, Yamaichi Securities, collapsed 15 months ago, Merrill Lynch took over many of the branches—an acquisition that would have been unthinkable just a few years earlier.

Real Estate Visionary

Freer flow of money pumped up the Thai economy, and with the help of foreign cash Mr. Anant began to realize his dream. Muang Thong Thani gradually emerged from the surrounding fields, with its skyscrapers focused on a business district called Bond Street.

Mr. Anant, who is expert at playing official connections, was able to coax the Government into approving a convenient expressway exit, which made the area very accessible. He also managed to persuade the Thai Defense Department to move its headquarters and staff residences to Muang Thong Thani.

Critics cried foul, but Mr. Anant denies wrongdoing. During a 90-minute interview he was edgy, and at one point he seemed about to stalk out of the room. But then he calmed down and continued his spin.

"It makes sense to do this," he said. "But you need a lot of determination."

A result is that since the crash, Muang Thong Thani has everything but inhabitants. Bond Street is a mile-and-a-quarter strip of modern, window-lined buildings, but aside from a handful of colorful storefronts—a bank, a restaurant, a pharmacy and a few others—they are empty.

In the pharmacy at 11 Bond Street, Pornsawan Rakthanyakarn is fighting the ghostliness. A big Thai woman with a bouffant hair style, a brown flowered print dress and a diamond ring as large as her knuckle, she sits by the cash register, waiting for customers to come in and buy her Vaseline Intensive Care Lotion and Pond's Cold Cream.

Mrs. Pornsawan, a jeweler who hit it rich during Thailand's boom, heard about Muang Thong Thani on the grapevine. She inquired from the official sales agent and was told demand was so strong that she would have to pay a $27,000 surcharge per parcel of land.

That convinced her, and she ended up paying nearly $500,000 for a house and for the building that includes her shop.

"I'm upset with the salespeople here who cheated me," she said morosely. And she is trying to adjust. Originally she had planned to open a jewelry store, but when the economy crashed her son suggested that a pharmacy might bring more business. And she tries to raise money in other ways.

"Would you like to buy my diamond ring?" she asked hopefully. She held it out and suggested, "Five million baht?" That is about $137,000, more than a typical visitor might be expected to have on hand, but Mrs. Pornsawan pressed her case.

"That's a very good price!" she exclaimed.

The command center for free markets is the third floor of the United States Treasury, where Mr. Rubin and his deputy, Lawrence H. Summers, share a suite facing the Washington Monument. Mr. Rubin presides in a spacious office decorated with modern art and family photos—just about all he sees of his family on weekdays, since his wife works in New York and he joins her each weekend.

At the other end of the suite is Mr. Summers's office, covered with photos of his son and twin daughters, and equipped with a small refrigerator stuffed with Diet Cokes. The two men are the closest of partners, and when Mr. Rubin is puzzled about something, he sometimes wanders over in his stocking feet to consult with Mr. Summers.

Historically Treasury has tended to stake out free-market positions, but Mr. Rubin stepped up the pace even further, for he showed an intuitive tilt toward the market based on his three decades as an investment banker.

"Bob comes from this very Wall Street view," said a senior Administration official. "He reflects that experience."

The 2 at Treasury

Within the Clinton Administration, Mr. Rubin and Mr. Summers won increasing influence because of their skill at marrying international finance and foreign policy. Mr. Summers had been a prominent economics professor at Harvard, and Mr. Rubin had made a fortune on Wall Street, enabling him to take off on vacations with a fly-fishing rod that, as an aide joked, "probably costs more than your house."

For the most part, Mr. Rubin and Mr. Summers were not forcing financial liberalization down unwilling throats. Rather, Washington was leading more than pushing. The United States pressed for capital liberalization, recalled a former top Thai official, but he added that it was like pushing on an open door.

Within the Administration, there were occasional arguments about the virtues of free capital flows. Academic economists like Ms. Tyson and Joseph Stiglitz, former chairman of the Council of Economic Advisers, sometimes argued that Treasury was too dogmatic in insisting upon free flows.

One day in 1995, the National Economic Council called an interagency meeting in the ornate, high-ceilinged rooms of the Old Executive Office Building, next to the White House. Negotiations were under way with Chile over a free-trade agreement, and the topic of the meeting was whether as a condition of the deal the United States should force Chile to drop an innovative system that amounts to a tax on short-term capital inflows.

"The Treasury came in and said that Chile's controls had to go," recalled one participant, saying others had argued that "a sensible set of capital controls" was reasonable for small nations that could be devastated by a sudden outflow of money.

The issue never ultimately came to a head—and Mr. Rubin and Mr. Summers say it never rose to their level—because Congress did not pass the legislation needed to conclude a trade agreement with Chile. Still, there is considerable evidence that top Clinton Administration officials were involved in some efforts to seek freer capital flows, as when they pressed South Korea to liberalize its financial system.

After interagency discussions, the Administration dangled an attractive bait: if Korea gave in, it would be allowed to join the Organization for Economic Cooperation and Development, the club of industrialized nations.

"To enter the O.E.C.D.," recalled a senior official of the organization, "the Koreans agreed to liberalize faster than they had originally planned. They were concerned that if they went too fast, a number of their financial institutions would be unable to adapt."

The pressure on them is reflected in an internal three-page Treasury Department memorandum dated June 20, 1996. The memo lays out Treasury's negotiating position, listing "priority areas where Treasury is seeking further liberalization."

These included letting foreigners buy domestic Korean bonds; letting Korean companies borrow abroad both short term and long term, and letting foreigners buy Korean stocks more easily. Such steps would help Korean companies gain more access to foreign loans and investment, but they would also make Korea more vulnerable to precisely the kind of panicky outflow of capital that unfolded at the end of 1997.

Moreover, for all Washington's insistence that it emphasized building financial oversight, nowhere in the memo's three pages is there a hint that South Korea should improve its bank regulation or legal institutions, or take similar steps. Rather, the goal is clearly to use the O.E.C.D. as a way of prying open Korean markets—in part to win business for American banks and brokerages.

"These areas are all of interest to the U.S. financial services community," the memo reads.

In the end, Korea opened up the wrong way: it kept restrictions on long-term investments like buying Korean companies, but it dropped those on short-term money like bank loans, which could be pulled out quickly.

Then, in April 1997, Mr. Rubin headed a meeting in which finance ministers of the seven leading industrialized countries issued a statement "promoting freedom of capital flows" and urging that the International Monetary Fund charter be amended so that it could lead the charge for capital account liberalization.

Some Treasury officials now portray the effort to amend the charter as a fund initiative that they were not directly involved in, and indeed Britain was an early public backer of the idea. But a senior Treasury official acknowledges that the idea originated with American officials based in the fund who report to Treasury, and who consulted on the idea with members of the Administration. Indeed, in a speech delivered in March 1998, eight months after the crisis began, Mr. Sum-

mers reaffirmed his support of capital liberalization, although he cautioned that it could be phased in.

The records of the monetary fund—which was in many ways an instrument of American policy—also show that it was urging some countries in this direction already. In July 1996, the fund's executive board praised Indonesia's "open capital account" and, a few months later, "welcomed the recent acceleration of capital account liberalization" in South Korea.

Mr. Rubin argues now that it is wrong to suggest that the Clinton Administration was pushing for free capital flows while neglecting efforts to build modern financial and legal systems. As for pressing capital account liberalization, Mr. Rubin said his far greater concern was to strengthen banks, regulatory oversight and legal systems in other countries.

"Reducing capital controls was undoubtedly an objective of some of the things the Administration did," Mr. Rubin said. "But I never would have recollected it as a priority."

Still, he said the attempt to revise the monetary fund charter to promote capital liberalization was no longer a priority, and he hinted that this reflected changing views.

"As you go along," he said, "you adjust your position to reflect your experience."

Money Floods Asia

A flood of capital poured into emerging markets in the early and mid-1990's, including $93 billion in 1996 alone into just five countries: Indonesia, Malaysia, the Philippines, South Korea and Thailand. Then there was a net outflow of $12 billion from those five countries in 1997.

This turnabout, which was most evident in short-term loans, amounted to a financial hurricane, one that would harm any country in the world.

So while economists welcome free capital flows in principle, extensive scholarly work had clearly established the importance of "sequencing"—meaning that countries should liberalize capital flows only after building up bank supervision and a legal infrastructure. A French scholar, Charles Wyplosz, of the Graduate Institute of International Studies in Geneva, concludes in an academic paper that "financial market liberalization is the best predictor of currency crisis."

Mr. Summers himself had emphasized the need for caution in financial deregulation in 1993, when he was still chief economist at the World Bank. He noted in a paper then that poor countries usually have "only quite limited bank supervision," adding, "As is true for nuclear power plants, free entry is not sensible in banking."

That scholarly emphasis on caution was drowned out in the rush to open financial markets. And one intrinsic problem was that while developing countries had a strong vested interest in opening up to foreign capital, to let money come in, they saw little benefit in building modern banking and legal institutions. Indeed, in some cases, top officials and their friends had a major stake in maintaining financial systems in which what counted above all was political connections.

"Financial liberalization was undertaken in countries that didn't have the infrastructure to support it," reflected Ricki R.

Helfer, a leading international bank regulator and former chairwoman of the Federal Deposit Insurance Corporation. "That was one of the principal causes of the Asian crisis."

Given their backgrounds, Mr. Rubin and Mr. Summers were more aware of the risks than most others, and they did urge better regulation of international banking. For instance, at the 1995 meeting of the seven leading industrialized nations in Halifax, Nova Scotia, an American-led initiative called for improved financial regulation and data reporting for industrialized nations and eventually others as well.

Still, these steps to improve banking oversight were modest and proceeded slowly, while liberalization hurtled along. American officials pressed for oversight, but they continued to press harder, and certainly more effectively, for liberalization.

A former senior Treasury official ruefully recalls arguments with Mr. Stiglitz, then in the White House as an adviser. Mr. Stiglitz was warning about the need for slower pacing of financial liberalization abroad, but nobody listened.

"I viewed 'pace' as an excuse by countries to keep their markets closed," the Treasury official said.

W. Bowman Cutter, who served as Mr. Rubin's deputy at the National Economic Council, said that all of the policy makers understood the risks and that in speeches "every one of them gave the qualifications—that before you opened your markets to free flows of capital, you need to have the institutional strength to deal with it."

"Having said that," he added, "I think that we all missed the true importance and the difficulties created by the enormous growth of the amount of free cash floating around the world. In the speeches, we said the right things. But it was a question of where was the emphasis and where was the force."

In practice, liberalization frequently takes place without any improvement in bank supervision, and it is often accompanied by a rise in shady dealings. In 1996 Thailand's Justice Minister accused his fellow Cabinet members of taking $90 million in bribes in exchange for handing out banking licenses. And when the Bangkok Bank of Commerce, Thailand's ninth-largest bank, collapsed in 1996 it turned out that 47 percent of its assets were bad loans, many of them to associates of the bank's president.

Still, cronyism and corruption, while aggravating factors, were not necessary to touch off a crisis.

"The simple fact," said James Wolfensohn, president of the World Bank, "is that very sophisticated banks loaned to Indonesian companies, without any real knowledge of their financial condition, based on name, based on competition. So you have to say to yourself, would it have made any difference if they had known? Well, maybe, but they did go nuts."

Turning Point in '95

In 1995 governments did two things that would set up the emerging markets for trouble. What appeared to be a brilliant bailout of Mexico, led by Mr. Rubin and Mr. Summers, convinced investors that some countries were too strategically important to be allowed to fail. And then, when finance ministers from the Group of Seven industrialized countries gath-

ered in Washington on April 24, 1995, they agreed to try to push up the value of the dollar against the Japanese yen.

The accord worked. The dollar rose smartly against the yen, easing the risk of a global crisis at that time.

But the pact also caused the rise of currencies like the Thai baht and the South Korean won, which were informally pegged to the dollar. Thailand and South Korea had already lost some competitiveness when China devalued its currency in 1994, and now they were tugged upward along with the dollar so that their exports became more expensive and even less competitive.

The upshot was that goods made there had more trouble competing abroad. Thai exports were stagnant in 1996 after having soared 23 percent in 1995, and the Thai current account deficit (a broad measure of the balance of trade) rose to 8 percent of gross national product in 1996, up from 2 percent in the late 1980's. Foreign currency reserves began to drain away to pay for the deficits, and the seeds of the crisis were sown.

* * *

February 17, 1999

OF WORLD MARKETS, NONE AN ISLAND

By NICHOLAS D. KRISTOF with SHERYL WuDUNN

In Red Square, just across from the mausoleum where Lenin lies in state like some old biological curiosity preserved in formaldehyde, there is a grand three-story stone building that these days is in about the same shape.

The rococo facade of the GUM department store resembles that of a cathedral, but its gaudy interior is an emporium with mink coats on hangers and on customers. GUM seemed a symbol of Russia's hope, for the spiffily dressed chairman of the board, Yuri B. Solomatin, 44, came across as a Russian capitalist with a difference.

Mr. Solomatin eschewed the mob, limousines and bodyguards; he did not wear fat diamonds on his fingers or endless-legged women on his elbow, and he boasted of running the most open, market-oriented, Western-style company in all Russia—proving this by granting himself and other managers stock options that soared fifteenfold. He sold more than half GUM's stock to foreigners, mostly Americans and Europeans, an unheard-of feat in nationalistic Russia.

Then came the Russian devaluation and market meltdown in August, and suddenly GUM crumbled. Its stock has fallen to 25 cents a share, from a peak of $5.40, and its shops today are a sea of signs that scream skidka—discount.

"Overnight," Mr. Solomatin said heavily, sitting in a third-floor conference room, "we were made paupers."

How did GUM get hit by what started as a run on the Thai currency in July 1997?

Why did the crisis ripple from country to country and end up leaving Russia facing hunger and economic chaos, with 30 percent of Russians living below the poverty line, up from 18 percent at the end of 1996?

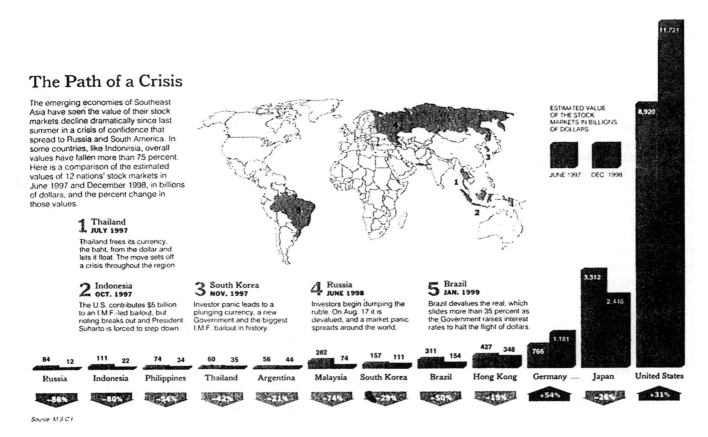

The Path of a Crisis

The emerging economies of Southeast Asia have seen the value of their stock markets decline dramatically since last summer in a crisis of confidence that spread to Russia and South America. In some countries, like Indonesia, overall values have fallen more than 75 percent. Here is a comparison of the estimated values of 12 nations' stock markets in June 1997 and December 1998, in billions of dollars, and the percent change in those values.

ESTIMATED VALUE OF THE STOCK MARKETS IN BILLIONS OF DOLLARS

1 Thailand
JULY 1997

Thailand frees its currency, the baht, from the dollar and lets it float. The move sets off a crisis throughout the region

2 Indonesia
OCT. 1997

The U.S. contributes $5 billion to an I.M.F.-led bailout, but rioting breaks out and President Suharto is forced to step down.

3 South Korea
NOV. 1997

Investor panic leads to a plunging currency, a new Government and the biggest I.M.F. bailout in history.

4 Russia
JUNE 1998

Investors begin dumping the ruble. On Aug. 17 it is devalued, and a market panic spreads around the world.

5 Brazil
JAN. 1999

Brazil devalues the real, which slides more than 35 percent as the Government raises interest rates to halt the flight of dollars.

Source: M.S.C.I.

And why has it now hit Brazil and shaken financial markets in Argentina, Colombia and Mexico?

The answers will be hotly debated for years, but some tentative explanations are emerging for what is known as the contagion effect: the tendency of a financial crisis to spread and "infect" other nations.

The growing interdependence through the fabric of the world economy connected GUM even to Mary Jo Paoni, a secretary in Cantrall, Ill. Mrs. Paoni patronizes a Bergners department store, and her husband frequents Kmart, but through her Illinois state pension fund she was in a sense a tiny part owner of GUM.

The pension fund owned $7.2 million worth of the Brinson Emerging Markets Fund, and records show that Brinson in turn bought $138,000 in GUM stock.

Mrs. Paoni was linked to GUM in another way, for her pension fund has $1 million worth of shares in Germany's Dresdner Bank. And Dresdner, excited by GUM's prospects, lent it $10 million.

In the Soviet days, GUM was the best department store in the country, with lines of people waiting each morning to enter, and it set aside a special area on the third floor, Section 100, where ordinary shoppers were banned and top Communist Party officials could pick up fine clothing unavailable anywhere else in Russia.

Partly because of its fame, GUM was among the first Russian companies to be privatized after the fall of the Soviet Union. It became an upscale shopping mall, and every day 200,000 shoppers trooped down its aisles.

More than 40 international retailers occupied space, paying what analysts said were higher rents than anywhere else in Europe. Samsonite reported that it sold more per square foot in its luggage store in GUM than in any of its other outlets around the world.

Over all in GUM, sales soared to an average of $926 per square foot, one of the highest such figures in the world. In contrast, Bloomingdale's in New York says that its sales are $267 per square foot.

Fund managers were impressed by all this and by GUM's declared commitment to international standards. It even put out annual reports in English as well as Russian.

"GUM has a strong balance sheet, no long-term debt and high liquidity," wrote Sector Capital, a Moscow investment bank, in 1996. "The company is very profitable, with a 40 percent return on assets. Together with the company's financial stability, this makes GUM a very attractive investment."

In retrospect, GUM and its American owners made the same kind of mistake as the Thai real estate developers who started the whole mess. They became so accustomed to the long summer days that they came to disbelieve in winter.

When Thailand floated its currency on July 2, 1997, the date that is now regarded as the beginning of the global financial crisis, the only shudder passing through GUM was one of delight—at its rising stock price. Over the next three months the stock rose 37 percent, to a new peak.

Thai Problems Spread

Nobody else was initially very worried that Thailand's problems would radiate around the world. While some of Thailand's underlying problems were well known, on the day of the devaluation the Thai stock market rose 7.9 percent, its biggest gain in more than five years.

In hindsight, absolutely everyone seems to have made a catastrophic misdiagnosis of the problem, one that resulted in Thailand's getting insufficient treatment and in exposing other countries to the contagion. The misdiagnosis was two-fold: first, that Thailand probably faced a typical temporary downturn, rather than a staggering depression that would last for years; second, that the problem was largely confined to Thailand rather than the beginnings of a serious global crisis.

The Clinton Administration initially saw the crisis as a replay of what had happened in Mexico in 1995, and prescribed the same mix of austerity and aid. So in the late summer of 1997, Treasury Secretary Robert E. Rubin and his deputy, Lawrence H. Summers, signed on to a standard International Monetary Fund plan: spending cuts, high interest rates and a repair job on the Thai banking system. But over the protests of the fund, the United States declined to contribute to a bailout.

Mr. Rubin and Mr. Summers were adamant that they could not contribute because of Congressionally imposed restrictions. The State and Defense Departments were unhappy with Treasury's tightfistedness, but Treasury officials suggested sarcastically if any other department had a spare billion or two in its budget and wanted to help the Thais, it should feel free to do so.

Mr. Rubin still insists that he made the right economic decision, but he seems less sure that he got the diplomacy right.

"I don't think it would have made a difference economically," he said of a contribution to Thailand. "Diplomatically, I don't know."

A senior State Department official said flatly, "In hindsight it was a mistake."

Thailand appealed to Japan for financial help that summer of 1997, and officials in Tokyo say they thought seriously about arranging a big package of loans. But in the end they did not, partly because Washington insisted that a rescue be made only through the monetary fund and only after imposing tough conditions on Thailand.

With the firm backing of Treasury, the fund initially forced Thailand to accept austerity, including budget cuts and high interest rates. The idea was that sky-high interest rates would attract capital back to Thailand and stabilize exchange rates, but they also ended up devastating otherwise viable businesses. Many economists, including those at the World Bank, have criticized the fund's approach as initially worsening Asia's problems, and even the fund has admitted that its budget cuts were too harsh.

By early 1998, recognizing that the slump was unexpectedly serious and that the initial conditions had been too tough, the fund and Treasury reversed course. They steadily allowed Thailand to reverse planned budget cuts and to ease the austerity, but the damage had been done.

Tumbling Prices

The Commodity Research Bureau Index of all commodity prices.

Source: Bloomberg Financial Markets

Mr. Rubin stands his ground, saying that the higher rates were needed to stabilize currencies in Thailand and South Korea, laying the groundwork for eventual recovery.

The alternative is "likely very chaotic conditions, far greater inflation and a risk that confidence will not come back for a recovery," he said. Countries like Indonesia that resisted the fund's medicine ended up even worse off, he notes.

After initially bowing to Washington's desires and declining to rescue Thailand directly, Japan became more assertive as it saw the crisis worsen. In September 1997, Japanese officials proposed a $100 billion bailout plan called the Asian Monetary Fund, to be paid for half by Japan and half by other Asian countries.

This would not have cost the United States a penny, but Mr. Rubin was furious about it, partly because the Japanese had not consulted him. He fumed as he strolled about the Air Force jet carrying him to the annual meetings of the fund and World Bank in Hong Kong.

Mr. Rubin, who has often shown a deep distrust and distaste for Japanese officials, gathered with Mr. Summers and other aides in the forward compartment of the plane to plot strategy. As the group nibbled on nachos, Mr. Rubin complained that the proposal would undercut American interests and influence in Asia, and that Japan would lend the money without insisting on tough economic reforms.

Mr. Rubin and Mr. Summers succeeded in killing the plan, with the help of Europe and China. Many in Asia now regard that as a crucial missed chance, and there is real bitterness that the United States should have muscled in to prevent Japan's attempted rescue of its neighbors.

Treasury officials stand by their opposition to the Asian Monetary Fund, saying that the plan would not have changed anything, for it would have taken time to implement and, as Japanese officials later acknowledged, Japan was itself hard up for cash.

"The Japanese plan was vapor," a Rubin associate said recently. "It wasn't going to happen. It was ill thought out."

Yet some other American officials now say, a bit sheepishly, that if they had realized the seriousness of the crisis, they might have been more accepting of the proposal. In November 1998, a year after Washington killed the plan,

Japan came back with another one, on a smaller scale. Instead of trying to subvert it, Mr. Rubin now called the idea constructive. President Clinton hailed it as one of Japan's "important contributions to regional stabilization."

An Economy Self-Destructs

Treasury opposed the first Japanese fund in part because it—along with everybody else, including investors, scholars and journalists—thought that the storm over Asia would probably pass. Yet something fundamental had changed. Perceptions of risk had altered, and people began to get nervous about holding any Asian currency.

The anxieties became self-fulfilling, particularly as Thailand's economy began to self-destruct. Speculators, stock investors and local business people alike wanted the safety of dollars, and during the fall of 1997 currencies fell in the Philippines, Malaysia, Indonesia, Taiwan and South Korea.

Since many Asian countries had problems with heavily indebted corporations, inflated stock and property prices, overvalued currencies, and bad loans, it was easy to find similarities to Thailand once people began to look. Just as Western capital had flooded into emerging markets as a group in the early and mid-1990's, now it began to ebb.

Take Barton M. Biggs, the strategist at Morgan Stanley who a few years earlier had helped ignite the Asian investment boom. As Thailand began to fall apart in the fall of 1997, he made another trip to Bangkok, and this time his advice was grim.

"I really went with the idea that Asia was sold out and bombed out and that there must be some attractive values," he said in a teleconference with investors on Oct. 27, 1997, recorded by Bloomberg. "And I've got to say that I was disappointed."

Mr. Biggs told investors to sell all their holdings in markets like Hong Kong, Singapore and Malaysia, and to cut by one-third their investments in emerging markets like Thailand and Indonesia.

U.S. Banks Casualty-Free

The dominoes began to fall. In late October 1997, right after Mr. Biggs's announcement and partly because of it, the Hong Kong stock market plunged 23 percent over four days. The debacle in Hong Kong suddenly caught Wall Street's attention, and in New York on Oct. 27, the Dow Jones Industrial Average tumbled 554 points, its biggest one-day point loss in history.

"That changed everyone's calculations," recalled Stanley Fischer, the fund's deputy chief. Suddenly contagion was the buzzword, and there were regular meetings on the crisis in the Situation Room at the White House. Yet while White House officials pondered what to do, investors were busy selling. Anything that seemed to hint of emerging markets was dumped, and stock markets in Brazil, Argentina and Mexico also suffered their worst one-day losses ever.

Mrs. Paoni's money in the Illinois pension fund joined the rush to the exits. Records show that the fund managers sold Indonesian stocks that had cost them $3.3 million, Malaysian

stocks that had cost $1.9 million, Philippine stocks that had cost $1.5 million, South Korean stocks that had cost $1.1 million, and Thai stocks that had cost $2.2 million. Across the world, everybody was doing the same.

Soon Indonesia was forced to accept a $17 billion bailout, later raised to $23 billion, to which the United States agreed to contribute—an implicit admission that it had made the wrong call with Thailand. Pressure grew on South Korea, Taiwan, Malaysia, Brazil, Russia and other countries. Everybody seemed alarmed except President Clinton, who in November 1997 tried to sound reassuring.

"We have a few little glitches in the road here," he said. "We're working through them."

Mr. Clinton was perhaps listening too closely to the State Department, for American diplomats in Bangkok were sending out rosy cables, and their counterparts in South Korea were similarly oblivious to the Korean economy's disintegration, which was then well under way. In Washington, Mr. Rubin and Mr. Summers had a far clearer sense of what was happening in South Korea, and were openly disparaging of the diplomatic reports from the field.

The State Department missed its cues because historically it had focused on the threats from Communists who carry grenades, not on the threats from business executives who wear neckties and trade currencies. The same was true of the Central Intelligence Agency, which proved itself, in the words of one of its top officials, "completely unprepared to deal with questions of an economic nature."

Yet by Thanksgiving Day 1997, it was clear to all top officials in Washington that South Korea was on the brink of an economic catastrophe. After five hours of conference calls among top American officials, President Clinton telephoned President Kim Young Sam of South Korea and told him he had no choice but to accept an international bailout.

Mr. Kim bowed to the inevitable and accepted a bailout that swelled to $57 billion, the biggest ever. But with that money now flowing into South Korea, Western banks saw a chance to take it and run. The banks called in their loans, hoping to flee while they could.

Mr. Rubin quietly called the heads of major banks and urged them to reschedule their loans, and in the end they did.

But the bailout still ended up bolstering Western banks. South Koreans lost their businesses and in some cases were even driven to suicide. But foreign banks—among them Citibank, J. P. Morgan, Chase Manhattan, BankAmerica and Bankers Trust—were rewarded with sharply higher interest rates (two to three percentage points higher than the London interbank rate) and a government guarantee that passed the risk of default from their shareholders to Korean taxpayers. The banks say that this was only fair, because they were extending their loans up to three years and thus assuming an extra burden.

Yet in contrast to previous financial crises, which were resolved by banks' effectively paying a good share of the bill, this was a huge bailout with public funds, and the banks did not chip in major new money.

Mr. Rubin defends the bailouts, saying that he "wouldn't spend a nickel" to bail out banks or investors, but that helping the country often means ensuring that it can pay off its creditors.

But critics note that the some of the biggest beneficiaries are the banks. "The effort is hurting the countries they are lending to, and benefiting the foreigners who lent to them," argued Milton Friedman, the Stanford University economist and Nobel Prize winner. Mr. Friedman argues that the monetary fund does more harm than good and is bitterly critical of these bailouts.

"The United States does give foreign aid," he said. "But this is a different kind of foreign aid. It only goes through countries like Thailand to Bankers Trust."

Investors Run From Risk

With the collapse of South Korea, investors rushed from any sign of risk. At Morgan Stanley, Mr. Biggs had bought emerging markets early in 1997 for his own portfolio, but now he sold frantically. Records at the Securities and Exchange Commission show that in December 1997 he sold $56,000 worth of his own company's Malaysian Fund, $650,000 worth of Emerging Markets Fund, $80,000 worth of India Investment Fund, $137,000 in the Pakistan Investment Fund and almost $1.6 million worth of Asia Pacific Fund.

Tens of thousands of other investors were doing likewise, liquidating their holdings in emerging-markets funds. This created another kind of contagion. Sales of emerging-markets mutual funds forced fund managers to pare down their portfolios to pay back shareholders. This meant that fund managers had to trim holdings even in distant countries, even in stocks that they regarded as still valuable.

In this way the electronic herd rushing away from Korea ended up trampling stocks in Argentina and Mexico. The world seemed to be coming apart, and so was the United States Government's consensus on what to do. Indonesia was particularly nettlesome because of the question of how to treat President Suharto, the aging dictator, whom President Clinton had supported.

While on a trip to Texas on Jan. 8, 1998, President Clinton telephoned President Suharto from Air Force One to urge compliance with the monetary fund program. But Mr. Suharto stuck to some of his ideas about how to run the economy, like a "currency board" to back Indonesian money with dollars.

A White House aide recalls Mr. Suharto's growling, "Look, I understand that this doesn't cure anything, but the I.M.F. isn't curing anything either."

American officials were puzzled about what to do, and they had no intuitive feel for what might happen next.

"The nature of the crisis was not understood," recalls a senior official who weathered the thick of the crisis. "We didn't really grasp everything that was going on."

Nation's Drive-By Shooting

Indonesia has been hit hardest, but what remains unclear is whether it had to suffer at all. Some economists argue that Indonesia was simply the victim of the international equivalent of a drive-by shooting.

Its trade balance was in relatively healthy shape. It had a respectable $20 billion in foreign exchange reserves and did not squander them trying to defend its currency. Credit had grown more slowly than in other countries, and there was less indication of a bubble. The Government initially reacted with foresight, going to the fund before any severe problems developed.

Yet in the end the Indonesian currency lost 85 percent of its value, riots cost more than 1,000 lives and hunger became widespread. Today there are doubts about whether Indonesia can survive as a nation; some fear that it will fragment like Yugoslavia.

"These horrendous things did not have to happen," argues Jeffrey Sachs, a Harvard economist, who blames the United States and the monetary fund for deepening a financial panic. "The crisis was pushed to an extreme that it never had to take."

Indonesia was particularly vulnerable to panic because most of its private wealth is in the hands of ethnic Chinese who are unusually likely to seek safe havens for themselves and their money. Public confidence was therefore Indonesia's most precious commodity, but it dissipated as officials from Washington tangled repeatedly with the Indonesian Government over how to deal with the crisis.

Mr. Suharto's handling of it was disastrous. He backtracked on closing banks, adding to confusion, and resisted many reforms that would have threatened his family empire. The fund forced Indonesia to close 16 banks, but then in an internal document acknowledged that it had gravely erred and that the closures had triggered bank runs around the country.

Both Treasury and the fund ridiculed Mr. Suharto's budget proposal, which because of exchange-rate movements showed a 32 percent spending increase in local currency terms. But three weeks later, having already irreparably harmed Indonesia's image, the fund quietly approved a budget with a 46 percent spending increase.

Anatomy of Derivatives

As currencies and countries tumbled, another form of contagion began to take a toll on world economies: financial derivatives.

Originally called synthetic securities, derivatives are so named because they are derived from something else—an underlying stock or bond. They can be as simple as an option to buy a stock, or they can be complex products involving multiple currencies, loans and bonds. In effect they are repackaged securities, stuck together like a complex work of financial Lego.

There is nothing inherently harmful about derivatives, and they can be very useful to protect against risks. But they can also be used to speculate. Their tremendous variety is reflected in the nicknames given to various kinds: the jellyroll; the iron butterfly; the condor; the knockout option; the total return swap; the Asian option.

These are jellyrolls that really sell. Western sales teams were active in Asia, and they often peddled complex financial products to customers who sometimes did not understand what they were getting into.

No one believes that derivatives actually caused the crisis. But although the point is bitterly contested by some investment bankers, a number of economists believe that once the crisis started, derivatives helped deepen it and infect other countries. They cite several mechanisms.

First, derivatives made it easier to make high-risk bets on Asia, but these were not publicly reported. As a result, no one had any idea how much betting was going on.

"Derivatives enabled a lot of hot money to flow into Asia below the radar," said Frank Partnoy, a former derivatives salesman and now an assistant professor of law and finance at the University of San Diego.

Second, the riskiness creates a rush to cover bets when the market goes the wrong way, and this scramble sometimes causes wild market swings.

As Mr. Partnoy explained the scramble: "It's as if you're in a theater, and say there are 100 people and you have the rush-to-the-exit problem. With derivatives, it's as if without your knowing it, there are another 500 people in the theater, and you can't see them at first. But then when the rush to the exit starts, suddenly they drop from the ceiling. This makes the panic greater."

Third, derivatives increased the linkages from one country to the next. South Korea, in particular, invested in derivatives and other high-risk securities that were tied to Thailand, Russia, Indonesia and Latin America. South Koreans bought 40 percent of one Russian bond issue and almost all of a Colombian bond issue.

So when those countries soured, South Korean financial institutions were badly hit as well. Derivatives had allowed them high yields but also meant that they stood to lose far more than their principal.

"I think it is quite clear that derivatives are vectors of contagion," said Martin Mayer, a senior fellow at the Brookings Institution in Washington.

Why did derivatives flourish in Asia? One reason was that until the crisis, they were enormously profitable for everyone. Some Asian financial institutions now grumble about them, but until a couple of years ago Korean mutual funds managed to earn exceptionally high returns in part because of their derivative investments.

Moreover, American banks often made huge sums selling these products in Asia. Jan A. Kregel, who has researched the issue as a senior fellow at the Jerome Levy Economics Institute in Annandale-on-Hudson, N.Y., concludes that in the boom years of both Thailand and Indonesia, Western banks made incomparably more money selling derivatives than making loans, and that in any case much of the lending was linked to derivatives as well. Most of the major American banks—Bankers Trust and Chase and J. P. Morgan and others—were actively selling derivatives in Asia.

The problem was not that Westerners were fleecing Asians, for in Asia one of the biggest derivatives players was a Hong Kong investment bank, Peregrine Investments, run by a British former race-car driver named Philip Tose. Founded only in 1988, Peregrine came from nowhere to register an astonishing $25 billion in revenues in 1996.

Then, early last year, Peregrine returned to nowhere. It collapsed in a sea of debts in Indonesia and elsewhere, and the shock then rippled through Asia and around the world.

"It was a major local player," said Christopher Barlow, a finance expert at PricewaterhouseCoopers who is presiding over the liquidation of Peregrine. "A collapse like this causes shock waves in the system and damages confidence." Mr. Barlow said Peregrine had more than 2,000 creditors, with claims of more than $4 billion.

One of the losers was the Illinois state pension fund, which manages Mrs. Paoni's retirement money. The fund had bought $358,000 of Peregrine stock, all of it now worthless, although this had only an infinitesimal effect on Mrs. Paoni's holdings.

"Derivatives are like power tools," said Brian C. Lippey, managing director of Tokai Asia Ltd., an investment company in Hong Kong. "If you know how to use them, they're great. But if you don't know how to use them, you'll drill a hole in your head."

Salamet Loses Fares

In the Indonesian town of Mojokerto, high finance began to close in on Salamet, a rickshaw driver.

Mr. Salamet (who like many Indonesians uses only one name) cannot read, so he had not learned from the newspaper that the Thai baht had plummeted and the Hong Kong market had plunged. But he was shocked when Agus Santoso came home.

Mr. Santoso, a slight 40-year-old neighbor, too frail a man to make a decent ditch-digger, had been the talk of the town. He had managed to learn how to drive a car and had got a job driving new cars to dealerships all over Indonesia.

The job paid $400 a month, a colossal sum that had tongues wagging all over the neighborhood. Mr. Salamet had dreamed that he, too, might learn to drive a car and follow in Mr. Santoso's lead.

But cars and car parts are imported, so they began to soar in price as the Indonesian rupiah lost value. Indonesians stopped buying new cars, and Mr. Santoso was dismissed and moved back home.

Meat and rice soared in price, and people in Mojokerto began to cut back to two meals a day. The poor began to walk instead of taking rickshaw rides, and Mr. Salamet's earnings fell by half, to less than $1 a day.

It is still unclear how severe the impact has been across the region, and the last few months have seen a statistical battle, as international organizations and aid agencies have issued a flood of reports offering widely divergent portraits of Asia in crisis. Invariably, the bleakest assessments have tended to get the most attention.

In Indonesia, for example, estimates by the Government and some aid agencies have suggested that the proportion of people living in poverty has risen to 40 percent or even 50 percent. But three carefully prepared World Bank reports released in January suggest that the increase has been much more modest, to 13.8 percent in 1998 from 11 percent in 1997.

As the World Bank sees it, "Rather than the universal devastation in poverty, employment, education and health so widely predicted and repeated in the media," the reality is increased poverty and a rising number of school dropouts, but not on the scale that aid agencies had suggested.

Still, although the scale is uncertain, everyone agrees that the crisis has left millions of people in great distress. And in Mr. Salamet's extended family, there is no doubt that life has taken a turn for the worse, even if it is difficult to measure.

Mr. Salamet took his wife, Yuti, and their baby daughter to visit his in-laws in a village near Mojokerto, and there they sat down beside a hut to chat. No food was served, for there was none.

The matriarch, Sambirah, who does not know her age but appears to be in her 80's, cradled her great-granddaughter in gnarled arms so frail that they seemed to rattle in the breeze, and for a moment her rheumy eyes glowed with pride. Mrs. Sambirah's pale mouth turned up at the corners, revealing two yellowed teeth, tusks emerging from an expanse of gum.

Then the tusks disappeared, and Mrs. Sambirah's eyes clouded. She sighed and described how she now pawns her sarongs so that the children do not starve.

"I can put up with it if I don't eat," she said. "But the children aren't used to it. They cry and cry."

A Pulp Tycoon's Woes

Across the globe, on the 22d story of a skyscraper in Rio de Janeiro, Carlos Aguiar began to feel Indonesia's pain.

Mr. Aguiar, 53, president and chief executive of a pulp and paper company called Aracruz Cellulose S. A., is solid and plain-speaking. His hair is neatly parted on the side; his manner suggests a waltz rather than a samba. He worked his way up through the business, and his heart is not in Rio but 375 miles north in the company town of Aracruz, where most company timber plantations and pulp mills are.

Mrs. Paoni is among those with a stake in Aracruz. Her state pension fund bought into the Brinson Emerging Markets Fund, which in turn owned 102,000 shares of Aracruz preferred stock.

Many investors picked up Aracruz, for the paper industry was doing well in the mid-1990's and investment analysts were recommending the stock. But a problem was developing behind the scenes: Asian companies were building a quantity of enormous paper mills in Indonesia and other countries, dramatically increasing worldwide output. Global pulp capacity has soared to 35 million tons, from 25 million tons in 1990.

"Everybody saw Asia as being this great market," Mr. Aguiar said morosely. "China, India, they have enormous populations, and everybody was betting on them. That was why the Indonesians built these giant factories, because they were expecting that paper use in China would go from 17 kilos a person now, to 30, then to 100. It didn't happen."

On top of the glut, the devaluations in Asia meant that Indonesian companies lowered their prices. So the price of Aracruz pulp dropped to $420 a ton today from $850 a ton at its peak in 1995.

Pulp offered simply one example of a global slump in commodity prices. The world abruptly found itself bedeviled by excess capacity just as demand slumped, and so markets were awash with Russian steel, Chilean copper, American grain, Colombian coffee and Saudi oil.

Astonishingly, after one of the great booms in economic history, commodity prices on average are still 12 percent lower than the average in 1990. Metals on average now cost just two-thirds as much as eight years ago. After adjusting for inflation, oil costs less than it has for 25 years, since before the 1973 oil shock.

On Russia in Debt

Falling commodity prices were making ripples around the world. They were especially brutal to Russia, whose main export is oil and gas, with the upshot that Russia's economy was falling apart.

Nobody much noticed at first. As with Asia a year earlier, it was too easy to be dazzled by the black Mercedes-Benzes, the diamond rings and the crowded discos. In 1997 Russia's stock market performed the best in the world, rising 149 percent in dollar terms, according to the calculations of the International Finance Corporation.

At GUM department store, Mr. Solomatin, the chairman, had been equally optimistic. He had sunk GUM's entire nest egg of liquid assets—then worth $33 million—into the stock and bond markets. It had seemed a good deal, for the bonds were paying interest rates of 100 percent or more.

But behind the scenes Russia's economy was showing severe strains, and many of them were unrelated to the Asian crisis. Tax collection was abysmal, Government budget deficits were growing, short-term debt was rising and President Boris N. Yeltsin's health seemed to be fading.

Asian countries had had problems with private debts, but Russia's problems were a bit different: the Government itself was addicted to debt. And with one-third of Government revenues coming from taxes on oil and gas that were steadily falling in price, it was difficult to foresee an improvement.

"I think the main reason for our crisis was not the Asian crisis," said Sergei V. Kiriyenko, who at 37 became Russian Prime Minister last spring. "It was that for years we had expenses higher than revenues."

More broadly, in contrast with Asia and Latin America, where markets were deeply rooted, Russia had only the flimsiest attachment to market principles and was being savaged by corruption and organized crime. Russia's top prosecutor, Yuri Skuratov, estimates that half of all Russia's commercial banks are mob-controlled and that criminals control about half of the gross national product.

Even as Russia's economy was quietly disintegrating, public support from the United States, Germany and other countries bolstered the impression that, as one economist put it, Russia was "too nuclear to go bust."

In July 1998, the Clinton Administration pushed the monetary fund for a major bailout, even though officials worried privately about whether it would work. In the end the fund worked out a $17.1 billion deal.

Perhaps Americans did not fully notice the crisis developing, but Russians did—and their behavior undermines the notion that around the world it was only Western investment bankers who took poor locals to the cleaners. In Russia it was more the other way around. Russian capital flight steadily averaged $1 billion per month for the last three years, moving to places like Britain and Switzerland, which Russians felt they could trust. The first $4.8 billion installment of the fund bailout quickly disappeared as Russian oligarchs cashed out their rubles and took their money out of Russia.

As Charles H. Dallara of the Institute of International Finance in Washington described it, "So in a broad sense, you had the West, the I.M.F., Western banks and Western governments pouring money in the front door, and a select group of Russian citizens taking it out the back door."

Meanwhile the Russian legislature balked at many of the required reforms. Investors panicked, and on Aug. 17, computer screens flashed the bad news: the bailout had collapsed, and Russia stopped propping up the ruble and defaulted on domestic bonds. Overnight the bonds were virtually worthless, and stocks fell from dollars to pennies.

Still, Mr. Rubin says he has no regrets about the July bailout. "I'd do the same thing again," he said. "Given the stake we had in an economically viable Russia, it was a risk worth taking. It had a realistic chance."

GUM, which had been seeking listings on overseas stock exchanges, sent despondent faxes that day to its investment banker friends, postponing those plans indefinitely. The crisis sent the ruble tumbling to more than 18 to the dollar from 6, and so in effect all the imports in GUM (and most of the inventory is imported) tripled in price just as Russian consumers were losing their jobs.

The shock waves from the Russian default were felt around the world, partly because they shattered the assumption of an international safety net. The United States and the monetary fund had wanted to save Russia, and their failure sobered investors, sending them scurrying once more away from risk.

After the Russian crisis, the upheavals in international markets nearly destroyed Long-Term Capital Management, the most glamorous of America's hedge funds. More than a year earlier, the hedge funds had helped to trigger the financial crisis in Thailand, setting in motion a chain reaction that ultimately came back to take Long-Term Capital to the brink of collapse.

Long-Term Capital tumbled for the same reasons that Thailand did. American financiers may like to think of themselves as a world apart from Thai bankers, but there was a certain symmetry in what went wrong.

Thailand and Long-Term Capital were both victims of their own successes, which bred hubris and carelessness toward risks. They also both borrowed more money than they should have, and got into trouble when their bets went wrong. And, to be fair, both had a certain amount of bad luck.

On When to Bail Out

The Russian default sideswiped Brazil, which for a time lost money from foreign reserves at the rate of $1 billion a day. So when Brazil wobbled, the United States braced itself. In November 1998 the Brazilian Government agreed to a $41.3 billion bailout package from the fund, which President Clinton arranged early, while Brazil was still solvent.

For the United States it was a remarkable turnaround. A bit more than a year earlier, the Clinton Administration had refused to contribute money to the Thai bailout and had prevented Japan from distributing aid. This time President Clinton himself led the intervention and the United States came up with $5 billion of the package.

Yet it was a bad bet. Despite widespread recognition that the Brazilian currency, the real, was overvalued, Washington made essentially the same mistake as it had in Russia: it trusted the legislators to quickly pass reforms that would reassure investors. Again the markets won, and in January Brazil was forced to float the real.

The collapse of the currency in turn forced Brazil to raise interest rates to try to attract foreign money—the pattern that had occurred a year earlier in Indonesia or South Korea. And the high interest rates, in turn, are depressing Brazil's economy and casting a shadow over Argentina, Mexico and all of Latin America.

At Aracruz, Mr. Aguiar has solemnly watched the stock price fall, from $22 a share in the summer of 1997 to $11.81 yesterday. Over the years, he has taken desperate measures to compete globally, trimming Aracruz's work force by nearly two-thirds, cutting back on health and dental benefits, and turning to a cheaper contractor to run the company cafeteria. Just since the crisis hit in the fall, he has pared staffing another 10 percent, and he prays it will be enough.

On the other end of the globe, in the third floor boardroom of GUM, Mr. Solomatin has a grand view of Red Square—and a terrible view of his company's future.

All the company's plans are on hold; the money in defaulted bonds is locked up; all the stock is now worth only $36 million, about the cost of the inventory.

That makes GUM a candidate for a takeover by a foreign company, and two European companies are said to have been eyeing it. But Mr. Solomatin sounds skeptical.

"Who would take us over?" he asked. "Investor fear of Russia is so great that nobody would consider buying us."

*　*　*

February 18, 1999

WORLD ILLS ARE OBVIOUS, THE CURES MUCH LESS SO

By NICHOLAS D. KRISTOF

Pigs to the left, pigs to the right, pigs all around him, Charles E. Burrus stood in the cacophonous center of his barn, gesturing at the indignant squealers. He felt like squealing, too.

"I don't know what we're going to do in the next three months," said Mr. Burrus, oblivious to the stench of the 7,000 animals around him. "We're losing $10,000 to $15,000 a semi load."

Mr. Burrus, a 65-year-old whose gray hair peeks through his farm cap, has seen some tough times in a life of hog farming, including a fire that ripped through his barns in 1978 and roasted 1,200 pigs alive. But nothing, he said, has ever been nearly so devastating as today's prices. These days he is bleeding money so badly that he worries about losing his 600-acre farm here among the cornfields near Cantrall, Ill., 130 miles southwest of Chicago.

"This is something we've never seen in the livestock business," Mr. Burrus said dolefully. "We've never seen this heavy a loss in the pork industry, not even in the Depression."

The problems on the Burrus farm, a sprawling collection of 14 hog buildings with temperature controls and automatic curtains on the windows, underscore how the economic crisis that began 19 months ago in Thailand is knocking on the gates of the American heartland.

The only real chance of a rescue for Mr. Burrus would come through an economic revival on the other side of the globe, in Asia, where his hogs usually end up between chopsticks.

So far, the United States as a whole has been remarkably impervious to the crisis, and much of American industry has benefited from the cheaper oil and imports resulting from the downturn elsewhere.

Still, it is not clear whether the United States can remain unaffected, and the crisis presents the country—and the rest of the world—with far-reaching political and economic challenges.

If the Cuban missile standoff was a quintessential cold-war crisis, then today's global economic upheaval may be a landmark crisis of the post-cold-war era.

The simplest challenge is for the United States to sustain its strong growth rates. But the broader task will be to prevent nationalistic cataclysms in the worst-off countries, like Russia and Indonesia, and to contain the political and security risks of explosive frustration if the crisis bites further into places like China and Latin America.

The American economy has demonstrated tremendous flexibility and resilience, but uncertainties arise because the American stock market is 64 percent higher than on Dec. 5, 1996, when Alan Greenspan, the Federal Reserve chairman, warned about "irrational exuberance."

Moreover the Brazilian crisis—marking the failure of the November bailout—underscores that the storm has not necessarily passed.

"To some extent Brazil's problem is a reflection of slowing economic activity," said Henry Kaufman, a Wall Street economist who now runs his own consulting company. "We have to consider whether there is more to come. Developing countries are still coming to grips with a slowdown in the global economy. If the economic revival in Europe is subdued and the American economy slows down, that is bound to put some pressure on other parts of the world."

The message from Washington during these upheavals strikes some foreigners as hypocritical. When Thailand and Brazil were hit, the Clinton Administration's message was firm: raise interest rates, cut government spending, put up with a recession if necessary, allow banks to fail, be stoical.

Yet in September when the crisis seemed as if it might strike the United States, the Administration had a change of heart. President Clinton went into overdrive in September, welcoming three interest rate cuts by the Federal Reserve, pressing Europe and others to cut rates as well, and finally getting money out of Congress for the International Monetary Fund. The Federal Reserve even coordinated the rescue of Long-Term Capital Management, a hedge fund backed by wealthy investors.

The rate cuts were precisely the opposite of the prescription that the United States had handed out to everyone else. And these days, there is a lurking fear in Washington that these countermeasures may have worked too well—creating a false sense of security.

At Treasury and the Federal Reserve, officials were concerned to see that their actions seemed to have moved millions of investors from an excess of fear to a new spasm of exuberance, sending the market to a new high. Officials say they worry that the eventual fall, if there is one, may be that much farther.

For all the condemnation of cronyism and mismanagement abroad, there are signs in America and Europe of some of the vulnerabilities that brought down Asia.

The crisis abroad was partly a consequence of success: soaring growth rates led to excess confidence, excess borrowing, excess investment and excess capacity. Not everyone agrees, but some economists see similar patterns in corporate giants like U.S. Steel and even on farms like the one Mr. Burrus runs.

When pig prices were 80 cents a pound of live weight, Mr. Burrus borrowed from the banks to build new barns. In fact, he just completed his latest barn a few months ago. But the high prices were also driving every other hog farmer in the world to increase production as well, and in hindsight it was a pig bubble that popped.

So now Mr. Burrus is getting 17 cents a pound for his pigs, even though his costs are running 38 cents a pound. Bankers in Cantrall are nervously eyeing hog farms the way bankers in Rio de Janeiro are anxiously examining coffee plantations.

Just a couple of hours' drive from Mr. Burrus's farm is steel country, the huge chimneys and fiery vats of molten steel that represent the traditional sinews of American industry. These days steel companies are crying foul and laying off workers, saying they are facing a deluge of imports from Japan, Russia, Indonesia and other countries.

These nations worry about a new round of protectionism, and on Friday the United States announced penalties against Japan and Brazil for selling hot-rolled steel in the United States below cost.

In a broader sense, however, the steel companies' problem reflects the pattern of excess capacity that one sees in hogs, cars or Indonesian rickshaws. During the boom years, steel companies all over the world invested huge sums in production, in anticipation of the Asian market—which then shriveled.

So far U.S. Steel and Mr. Burrus are both exceptions, and the American economy is still growing strongly. Yet apprehensions arise because the global economy is a three-engine jet, with one engine dead (Japan's) and another losing speed (Europe's). It all comes down to how much fuel is left for the final, American engine. The gauges are broken, the pilots are arguing and the journey has already set a distance record—the United States' longest peacetime expansion, now almost eight years.

Slender Gains for Salamet

In the remote Indonesian town of Mojokerto, Salamet is in mourning. Mr. Salamet, a rickshaw driver, was outside trying to get rides one afternoon recently when his mother finally died in her sleep on the floor of his little house.

It was a relief, for she had groaned piteously from the pain of breast cancer, and he had been unable to afford painkillers. Yet Mr. Salamet now found himself faced with another bill he could not pay: the $28 for the coffin and burial.

In the end neighbors stepped in to lend him the money. But custom dictates that a bereaved son not leave the neighborhood for 40 days. This made it more difficult than ever to find the rickshaw rides that would buy food for his three hungry children and pay the fees to keep his eldest son, Dwi, in the second grade.

Yet to keep it all in perspective, Mr. Salamet is in the worst-off group—the urban poor—in the worst-off country of all, Indonesia, and even he is managing to get by.

In Mr. Salamet's neighborhood, no one thinks that the quality of life has retreated even to the level of 1990.

Asked about how much the depression had pushed his life backward, Mr. Salamet (who like many Indonesians uses only one name) described the positive changes over the last decade, and emphasized that these have been enduring.

"The biggest change was electricity, which came about six years ago," he reflected. "It cheers us all up, and at night there's light. And then there's also television now as well.

"The second-biggest change is that the roads here got paved. It used to be that in the rainy season, everything got so muddy you couldn't go anywhere. But now we can get around in all seasons, and I can drive the rickshaw and earn a living even after it's rained."

"The third change is the toilets," he concluded. "They were built four years ago. Until then everybody just used the river, but that was a problem at night. It was far away, and there were snakes that used to bite people."

These kinds of gains are still fragile, particularly in places like Indonesia, China and Russia, where there are serious risks of political instability. But for now at least, they have not come close to being undone.

More broadly, the striking thing about the economic news from Asia these days is that so much of it is good. A year and a half after the Asian crisis began, countries like Thailand and South Korea are showing signs of bottoming out. Asia's currencies have recovered sharply, with the Indonesian rupiah now standing at about 9,000 to the dollar, compared with 16,650 in June (or 2,500 before the crisis).

Interest rates have fallen as well, and this has bolstered the stock markets. They remain far, far below their precrisis levels, but Asian stock markets were some of the best performing in the world last year. South Korea's rose 121 percent in dollar terms in 1998, and Thailand's was up 34 percent—both from abysmal lows.

If countries like South Korea and Thailand really restructure their economies in fundamental ways—which so far has not happened, despite a lot of promising talk—then it is possible that they will emerge that much stronger from the crisis, with better banking systems, more open economies, stronger legal systems and more democratic political structures. President Kim Dae Jung of South Korea argues that the crisis will be remembered as a blessing, because it is forcing essential economic changes.

"I believe that having to restructure our economy under the agreement of the I.M.F. is ultimately a big help for our economy," Mr. Kim said.

Whether the recovery is slow or rapid, the emerging markets eventually are expected to regain their pulse. Although they make up just 7 percent of the global value of stocks around the world, emerging markets account for 70 percent of the world's land, 85 percent of the world's population, and 99 percent of the anticipated growth in the world's labor force.

The Sandwich Man

Sirivat Voravetvuthikun offers a hopeful image of Asia's future, one in which Asians manage to rebuild their lives in new ways and thus achieve greater prosperity.

Mr. Sirivat, 50, a Chinese Thai businessman who went to high school and college in Texas, was a successful investment manager and property developer in Bangkok. With his brother, he built 28 lavish homes in the middle of a vast golf resort, with no luxury spared, from the swimming pools to the landscaping beneath mango trees and coconut palms.

The development cost $12 million, $10 million of it borrowed from banks and much of the rest from Mr. Sirivat's savings. It is in a lovely spot, nestled among the hills 115 miles northeast of Bangkok, but just as it was being completed the property market collapsed. Now the homes are empty and the main pool is green with algae.

The homes did not sell, and interest costs soared. Banks pressed him for payment, and Mr. Sirivat could not meet the payroll for his staff. He and his brother began quarreling.

That was when Mr. Sirivat, like thousands of other businessmen around Asia, decided to start again.

Drawing on his years in the United States, he decided to become a sandwich peddler. Sandwiches are not a customary food in Thailand, so Mr. Sirivat decided it would be a good market niche in a country whose young people are increasingly experimental about foreign foods.

"My wife started by making 20 sandwiches," Mr. Sirivat remembered. "I told my staff we had to sell them on the street. I remembered people in the States selling popcorn, carrying bags of it, and I thought, we'll try this. It's illegal to have pushcarts or to set up a table on the sidewalk, but I thought it would be O.K. if we just carried the sandwiches in a box."

Mr. Sirivat's business—now known as Sirivat Sandwiches—is thriving, and he is turning a nice profit on it. The first 20 sandwiches took six hours to sell, but now daily sales have reached 550 sandwiches.

Mr. Sirivat has rented another building in Bangkok to make sandwiches and to experiment with new varieties. He aims to emerge as the sandwich king of Thailand.

"This is going to be big," he boasted, adding that he was trying to build a strong brand name and ultimately hoped to list Sirivat Sandwiches on the Thai stock exchange.

Rocky Roads, Resentments

In assaying what comes next, some of the most fundamental concerns are not economic but social and political.

A growing backlash is evident against Western capitalism, and especially against the Americans who exemplify it. This is most apparent in countries like Russia, which has already defaulted on its debts, but it is found even in Japan, where politicians heap abuse on what they call Anglo-Saxon capitalism, deriding its ferocity and lack of civility.

In a rebellion against the American-led drive for free markets, the Finance Ministers of the second- and third-largest industrial countries, Japan and Germany, have both spoken about the need for tighter controls on currency movements. And late last year, a three-year-old international effort to achieve a Multilateral Agreement on Investments—which would have promoted globalization and cross-border investments—collapsed after France, applauded by Australia and Canada, backed out of the talks. They all worried about surrendering power to foreign companies and open markets.

Malaysia, once a darling of international investors, went the furthest in thumbing its nose at the markets. Prime Minister Mahathir Mohamad has denounced Jews and the West for conspiring against him, and has warned that people in the developing world will stage "a kind of guerrilla war" against Western corporations that buy overseas companies at depressed prices.

Despite warnings from the West, Malaysia adopted capital controls on Sept. 1. The controls, which are now being relaxed to lure foreign investors back, seemed to help: the currency was stable, the stock market more than doubled and foreign exchange reserves rose sharply. Moreover, with interest rates of just 7 percent (compared with 38 percent in Indonesia), Malaysia is expected to eke out a bit of economic growth this year—even as a continued dip is anticipated in Indonesia. Western officials worry that other countries may adopt Malaysia's methods.

Less dramatic capital controls, like Chile's system to encourage long-term inflows rather than short-term ones, now are also widely praised. Chile dismantled them late last year—because at the moment there is no problem with excess capital inflows—but those controls may become a model for other developing countries.

One of the greatest worries in the West is about the future of Russia. The stock market there plunged 84 percent last year in dollar terms. President Boris N. Yeltsin, once seen as President Clinton's ally and the man who would tug Russia toward the West, has now faded into the backdrop along with reforms.

Oleg N. Sysuyev, a top aide to Mr. Yeltsin, sat in his immense office in the old Central Committee Headquarters one day recently and said that reforms very likely were dead for the next five years in Russia. He added that unless the monetary fund gave in and offered Russia major support, there were only two scenarios for the country.

The first, Mr. Sysuyev said as he chain-smoked Marlboro Lights, is ruthless budget-cutting, which might lead voters to choose old-style, totalitarian candidates in the parliamentary elections in 1999 and the presidential elections in 2000. The second, he went on, is hyperinflation. "This scenario—not as fast—may lead to the same consequences," he said.

As for China, it has evaded the crisis, and what saved it from catastrophe may in part have been its unwillingness to listen to Western economists.

Urged to make its currency freely tradable with the dollar, it resisted. If the Chinese yuan had been convertible, then Chinese would have sent their money fleeing as Thais and Indonesians did, and China might also be mired in a major financial crisis.

China claims economic growth last year of almost 8 percent—a tribute to the Government's $1.2 trillion stimulus plan and probably to the audacity of the statisticians.

Yet one troublesome parallel with the hardest-hit countries of Asia is found in a vast hole in the ground in the Pudong district of Shanghai.

The hole, swarming with construction workers, is scheduled to become the Shanghai World Financial Center, the tallest building in the world. At 1,509 feet tall, it will be 27 feet taller than the Petronas Towers of Malaysia, which in 1997 surpassed the Sears Tower to become the tallest.

Someday it may pay off. But for now it is scheduled to cost $625 million and provide 3.6 million square feet of floor space (twice as much as the Empire State Building) just as the Pudong business district finds itself with dozens of new buildings and an overall occupancy rate of only 30 percent.

This real estate bubble is linked to Japan, for the World Financial Center is backed in part by Japanese banks and is the brainchild of Minoru Mori, chief executive of the Mori Building Company.

Mr. Mori is a visionary in Japanese business circles, a man who reveres the French architect and planner Le Corbusier and who also aspires not just to put up roofs but to shape society.

Mr. Mori is unabashed. He argues that while Shanghai property may look like it is heading for a bust, in the long run there will be another boom as well.

"I think the abacus will show a profit for us," he said, but he acknowledged that completion of the World Financial Center might now be delayed a couple of years after the original target date of 2001.

On the wall of his boardroom, on the 37th floor of his Ark-Mori building in Tokyo, is a painting from Mr. Mori's outstanding collection of Le Corbusiers, bearing a large inscription by the artist: "Je revais," or "I was dreaming."

Precariousness Defined

The real estate glut in China is at the heart of a banking mess perhaps more serious than anywhere else in the world.

Chinese banks have lent heavily to construct buildings that are now largely vacant and worth little. Three of the four major banks are effectively insolvent by a huge margin, even though these are boom times.

So long as depositors keep their money in the accounts, the banks can keep functioning indefinitely. But the moment depositors start asking for their money back, the banking system in China will face the possibility of collapse.

China's bad bank debts are staggeringly large, totaling about 40 percent of gross national product, compared with 3 percent in the United States during the savings and loan crisis. Nonperforming loans (those that are not being paid back) are about 25 percent of the total at the big banks, significantly higher than in other countries when they were hit by the crisis.

Paradoxically, there seems little prospect that China will face an international currency crisis of the kind that hit Thailand and Indonesia. Beijing has $145 billion in foreign exchange reserves, exceeding the country's entire $131 billion foreign debt.

That leaves the risks of political upheaval in China coming from two directions, both economic.

One danger for the Government is a banking crisis, driving furious depositors to the streets to demand their money back.

The second risk comes from workers who lose their jobs at state-owned companies. The Communist Party has reiterated its plans to close down money-losing companies, but those workers may represent the sternest challenge to the Communist Party since the democracy movement in 1989.

Officially, 11.5 million people are unemployed in China, but that figure is not very meaningful because it excludes people who have been laid off as well as rural workers and peasant migrants to the cities. Estimates of total unemployment range up to 260 million, which is also not very meaningful, because many of these people manage to get odd jobs or make money on their land.

Still, no one doubts that there are tens of millions of Chinese workers and peasants who are unemployed or under-employed and who are a potentially dangerous element in the social mix. Outside the southern city of Changsha, near where Mao grew up, thousands of people clashed with the police early in January, and one man was killed when he was hit with an exploding tear-gas canister and bled to death.

Earlier, some 500 laid-off workers from a defunct wire-cable factory marched through Changsha and were joined by several thousand sympathetic onlookers who brought traffic in the downtown area to a standstill for most of the day.

Wang Weilin, 45, one of the onlookers, acknowledged that these protests might not lead anywhere, for workers are very careful not to push too far or to come across as protest leaders, for that might mean arrest.

Still, the frustrations were evident in the placards that workers carried, declaring, "We have no food," and "We don't want fish or meat, just a bowl of rice."

"These people," Mr. Wang said, "have nothing to eat."

Panic Spawns the Ninja

Indonesia offers frightening images of how economic distress can tear a society apart. Optimists sometimes used to say there was a possibility that China could turn out as well as Indonesia, but now Indonesia seems less a model than a nightmare.

Indonesian Muslims have been burning down churches, and Christians have been attacking mosques. In the capital, Muslim mobs have chased down and hacked Christian men to death as police officers and soldiers stood by. And when there is no other target around, rioters attack ethnic Chinese.

In the East Java region of Indonesia's main island, mysterious groups of men dressed in black have been killing Muslim religious leaders, chopping up the bodies and throwing the pieces into mosques. This has created a panic, leading to a witch hunt—literally—for the killers.

Called ninja by local people, these killers are believed to be sorcerers, and panicked mobs sometimes beat to death those whom they think might be ninja. More than 200 people have been killed so far, either by real ninja or by mobs looking for ninja, and crowds have sometimes paraded the heads of their victims on pikes.

Such brutality seems particularly incongruous because Java was civilized before England and has an ancient culture emphasizing harmony and restraint. The killings and mutilations have been a gruesome reminder of how rapidly economic crises can cause societies to mutate in horrific ways.

In Mojokerto, even Mr. Salamet, the rickshaw driver, has joined a posse to guard against ninja. He goes out each evening with a group of men, armed with clubs and sickles. Mr. Salamet is the most reasonable of the group, but some of the men spend their days sharpening their sickles and talking proudly of hacking to death any intruders they find.

Down the street from Mr. Salamet, a Muslim activist named Ahmed Banu claims to have beaten two ninja to death, and he shows off a pair of boots that he says belonged to one of the dead men. In fact, the entire episode seems to have been fictional, but Mr. Banu is a charismatic man with a growing following.

After prayers on a recent evening, he held an open meeting of local Muslims to deal with the supposed ninja menace. Mr. Salamet stayed away, but 24 men attended, listening intently as Mr. Banu warned passionately that the ninja were ready to destroy the neighborhood and vanquish all Muslims.

"If we Muslims are being treated like animals," he said, his voice rising, "will we stand for it?"

"No!" his followers yelled back.

"If we catch the ninja, what should we do? Give them to the police or kill them?"

"Kill them!"

White House Brainstorms

On Labor Day last year, as financial markets worldwide were tumbling in the aftermath of Russia's financial turmoil, an impatient and annoyed Bill Clinton summoned his top advisers to the Yellow Oval Room on the third floor of the White House. Mr. Clinton, in cowboy boots, settled in his favorite chair by the fireplace, and Treasury Secretary Robert E. Rubin sat directly opposite, as he likes to do, so that he could look the President in the eye.

Mr. Clinton said he wanted to attack the crisis more directly and more openly. He also wanted his Administration to lead the way in remaking the global financial system, so as to reduce the risk of another crisis down the road. He had been speaking on the telephone with Prime Minister Tony Blair of Britain, and they had agreed that world leaders should step out and convey a sense of urgency about altering the international economic order—and so he was frustrated with Mr. Rubin's caution.

"Clinton was leaning on Treasury for some action," recalled one participant. "He was leaning hard. And of course the Treasury wanted to be cautious. It was telling the political types in the White House that this is sensitive stuff—you say one wrong thing and you can mess things up."

The underlying problem is that today's Bretton Woods economic structure—based on fixed exchange rates and the World Bank and International Monetary Fund—is widely regarded as outdated and insufficient to steady today's markets.

"We need to establish a new system for the 21st century," said Eisuke Sakakibara, Japan's Vice Minister of Finance. "You could call it a new Bretton Woods. It's difficult, but it's got to be done."

But what precisely is to be done?

While almost everyone agrees that the present system is inadequate, there is no consensus on what would be better. Ideas range from radical proposals for a global central bank and semifixed exchange rates among major currencies to more modest suggestions for tougher bank standards and curbs on hedge funds.

At the annual World Economic Conference in Davos, Switzerland, recently, some European officials urged the creation of an "early warning system," roughly equivalent to a weather satellite alerting the world to approaching economic tornadoes. But the technology simply does not exist.

Others argue for an "exit tax," which would require investors to pay a fee for removing their money from a country quickly—an experiment that Malaysia is now trying. But Mr. Rubin fears the tax could scare off investors.

Just as Mr. Clinton's enthusiasm for doing something seems to have ebbed as the sense of crisis faded, there seems little chance that the present debate will lead to any major changes soon in the international economic system.

One reason is that for all the tragedies now unfolding in places like Indonesia, supporters of the current economic system say that over all, it has done an excellent job of promoting economic growth. By some economic measures, Indonesians are better off materially today, in the bust stage of their boom-bust cycle, than if they had bought stability at the price of sacrificing growth in the boom years.

"All countries have benefited from the free market system," said Jurgen Stark, vice president of the Bundesbank, Germany's central bank. "I am a little worried about all the talk about a 'new financial architecture.' What's new? What would it accomplish?"

The upshot is that although the metaphor is always "new financial architecture," the proposals for the financial system are usually fairly small-bore.

"I think architecture is a bad word," said John Heimann, who recently stepped down as chairman of Merrill Lynch Global Capital Markets to head a new bank supervisor training institute. "What you need is more attention to the plumbing and electricity. That's not as dramatic, but it's the plumbing and electricity that make the house work."

A number of these kinds of changes are under discussion. At the global level, the 22 leading industrialized countries proposed 44 initiatives, ranging from an international accounting code to better supervision of banks, insurance firms and brokerages.

Some countries are trying to take dull but important steps to reduce the risks of crises: improving their legal systems; creating a modern bankruptcy structure; fighting corruption, and hiring bank supervisors. But these steps often run into entrenched local interests, and the progress is slow.

"Have the lessons been tough enough so that people in individual countries are moving to actually fix their financial market infrastructure?" asked William McDonough, president of the New York Federal Reserve Bank and chairman of the Basel Committee on Banking Supervision. "Probably not. Should the effort be made? Yes. Definitely.

"Is there a simple or common solution to these types of problems? I don't think so."

The Danger of Hubris

So what are the lessons of Asia and Russia as they apply to the American economy?

There is not much agreement on that. The lessons on which a consensus has emerged seem surprisingly obvious and modest for an economic catastrophe that has destroyed so much wealth and transformed the prospects of nations from Indonesia to Russia to Brazil. Historians may eventually elicit more subtle conclusions, but for now the lessons are almost embarrassingly straightforward.

One is the danger of hubris. The crisis arose in part because emerging-market countries built up too confidently, because Western investors and bankers were too optimistic in their assessments of risk and because Western Governments were too convinced that they had the right solutions. Throughout the crisis, expert predictions have invariably been wrong and even miracle economies have crashed.

A second lesson is the importance of prudence in the banking system, the pillar of any modern economy. Financial institutions have generally been better supervised in America than in many other countries, but the near-failure of Long-Term Capital Management underscored the risks even in the most sophisticated and best-supervised market in the West.

And a third lesson is the danger of stock and property manias. Many Asians say glumly that they have learned the hard way the importance of scrutinizing the foundations of any economy, however dazzling it seems. And as they say that, they look—jealously, resentfully and nervously—at the American economy and especially at the United States stock market.

Still, there is a dispute about whether that lesson applies to the United States. America has far less corruption and cronyism than Russia or Indonesia, and no one thinks that America has built a bubble on the scale of Japan's in 1990, so some analysts argue that any parallel with Asia is ridiculous.

"I do not accept the comparison between Asia and the United States," said Abby Joseph Cohen, co-chairwoman of the investment policy committee at Goldman Sachs & Company and so far one of the most bullish and accurate of Wall Street strategists. Ms. Cohen emphasized that while Asia's boom was fueled by cheap credit—artificially low interest rates—this has not been true of the United States. In addition, she noted that American accounting and banking standards are more rigorous than those abroad.

"The Asian economy has been having difficulty recovering because banks have large portfolios of underperforming loans," she said. "But here the level of bank regulation has been much higher. Regulators are really paying attention, and shareholders are paying attention."

Economists and policy makers in Asia, with a biting skepticism that comes from seeing their own economies swell and pop, are often contemptuous of the American explanations. They point to the banking crisis in Texas in the late 1980's as an example of the foolishness that even highly regulated banks can engage in.

"If you look at it objectively," said Mr. Sakakibara, "the United States now has a bubble."

Skeptics like him say that the United States has followed the Asian pattern of an upward spiral whereby higher stock prices lead to rising investment and consumer spending, which leads to higher stock prices and pushes the spiral even higher. Moreover, the United States is financing its growth the Thai and Indonesian way—by borrowing from abroad, although it has the advantage of being able to borrow in its own currency.

The American stock market has also soared to its highest ratio of market capitalization to gross national product (140 percent) ever recorded in history, a ratio that compares with a previous peak of 81 percent in 1929. The American ratio is more than twice as high as Indonesia's or Brazil's at the time their crises hit.

In the broadest sense, one of the central problems in Asia and Russia was that investors were so used to success that they did not contemplate catastrophe. In the same way, the long bull market in the West since 1982 means that most stock market investors cannot conceive of how devastating a bear market can be, even if the market turbulence in the fall did shake them up.

Charles P. Kindleberger, an economic historian and author of the book "Manias, Panics and Crashes," said he was "troubled by the volatility" of the American stock market today. "I've been thinking for two or three years that the market was too high," he added. "When it collapsed in August, I thought it might be becoming sensible again. But it turned out that the Fed reduced interest rates three times, and the market returned to its previous level."

Mr. Kindleberger also expressed concern over the parallel with Japan in the late 1980's. In the face of a global slowdown, Japan cut interest rates to stimulate its economy, and the result was even more frenzied speculation, which eventually collapsed and proved catastrophic to Japan and the world economy.

So, looking at the financial crisis, John Kenneth Galbraith, the nonagenarian Harvard economist, concludes that "the overwhelming lesson is to be aware of the history" of speculative mania, and to be "further aware that the United States is also part of the history."

"The speculative mood," he added, "can pervade Wall Street as much as Tokyo or Malaysia."

Explaining a Crisis

Economists and government officials have offered an abundance of neat explanations for the crisis. Some attribute it to crony capitalism and fundamental weaknesses in overseas countries. Others point to the fickleness of international capital flows and the entire global economic system. Still others say that the culprit was the United States and the monetary fund, or alternatively the venality and incompetence of governments in Russia, or Indonesia, or other countries.

Economists will dispute for years which factors leading to the crisis were necessary, and which sufficient, and which tangential. But the causes seem so many and so intertwined that it is difficult to fit them together in any neat equation.

Moreover, for all the talk in recent months about grand solutions to crises, there is a growing sense that no good answer may be out there, and that one price of economic development has perhaps been a loss of control over the markets that nurtured the development.

Rising prosperity in general has led to what seems an unstoppable trend toward steadily greater oceans of capital sloshing around the globe, and all that cash in turn creates new instability. For all the post-cold war sense of triumphalism, for all of the high-speed computer networks that in an instant can graph the trend in the yen-dollar rate, fundamentally the world's economies come across as corks bobbing in the sea. And, unless the United States economy was badly hit, it would be difficult to imagine world leaders galvanized to devise a new approach to international finance.

Some of the key causes of this crisis may lie not in economic ratios but human nature. In explaining the way that international economic crises have rippled around the globe, historians have often concluded that the most important factor was psychology. The same may be true today.

Computers and "rocket scientists" and first-rate research have yet to overcome the instinctive tendency of markets to overshoot up and down. The herds went from mania to panic in an instant, and this process trampled Asia and Russia. It is also what some economists worry about when they look at the United States.

"The old human emotions of fear and euphoria still prevail," said Laura D'Andrea Tyson, the former head of President Clinton's Council of Economic Advisers. Ms. Tyson said that Alan Greenspan, the Federal Reserve chairman, had once made the same point to her, noting that if one looked at a graph of jumps and dips in stock prices, it would be impossible to tell whether one was looking at the 1890's or the 1990's.

The crisis suggests that the old high-tech tools are still in frail human hands.

Mr. Galbraith, musing on the crisis, said: "I wouldn't be as severe on the regulators as on those being regulated. When you are dealing with insanity, one looks first at the insane and then at those supervising them."

Back on the Home Front

In Cantrall, not far from Mr. Burrus's hog farm, Mary Jo Paoni is planning to retire in April from her job as a secretary. Whatever the uncertainties, and despite her pension fund's loss of $2.7 million on Indonesian stocks, it has still ridden the boom in American stocks and is in strong shape. Mrs. Paoni and her generation of Americans will be able to retire without difficulty.

Yet she is also embedded in her community, and these days it is showing signs of vulnerability. The corn that surrounds her home sold for $5 a bushel two years ago; now the global economic difficulties have sent corn plunging to $2.12.

"We're worried," she said, exclaiming: "Good God, look what's on TV now! How about the layoffs!"

The restructuring and downsizing strike a particular nerve in the Paoni household because the supermarket chain where Mrs. Paoni's husband, George, worked for 32 years was bought out by a distant company just nine months before his retirement. He did not lose his job as a meat cutter, but he lost his holiday pay and five weeks' vacation.

Mrs. Paoni is apprehensive about stock market levels and also about local signs of disquiet: With farmers in trouble, tractor sales have slumped, and the nearby John Deere plant has announced layoffs. Banks are nervously checking their exposure to the agricultural sector. And Mrs. Paoni, after some reflection and several hours of interviews, has decided that she is linked to the global crisis.

"I sit here in this kitchen and say I don't have anything do with Asia, but I do," she said. "There's always some tentacles out there. Asia will definitely have an effect on Iowa and Illinois."

PART VI

RESISTANCE TO GLOBALIZATION

The economist Joseph Schumpeter famously characterized economic change as a powerful wind of creative destruction, and his term aptly describes the process of globalization.

When the winds of creative destruction blow, as they did forcefully at the end of the 20th century, social and political systems will inevitably react. Part VI examines one form of reaction—protesting and resisting the destructive element of economic change. Resistance is news by its very nature; protesters seek to create events that will draw media attention and help them publicize their message. Resistance to globalization was a primary focus of The New York Times's economic coverage at the end of the century, a focus shaped and sharpened by the protests and debates surrounding the Seattle meetings of the World Trade Organization in November and December 1999.

Resistance is an important response to creative destruction, but it is not the only response. While one side of human nature seeks to preserve and protect that which is threatened by seemingly uncontrollable forces, another side yearns for the opportunities that may be created by globalization. This second reaction to creative destruction seeks to ride the winds of economic change and use them to navigate the treacherous path to prosperity. This approach is less newsworthy, but it exists and is an important force nonetheless.

Part II of this book covered this double reaction to economic change as a factor in the formation of the political foundations of the post-war economy. As the global economy slowly opened in the early post-war years it unleashed two forces: economic nationalism, which sought to hold back the wind, and economic regionalism, which determined to shape the forces of economic change to benefit regional alliances of nations.

The articles collected here in Part VI capture this double response to globalization at the end of the 20th century. "Backlash" collects articles that report on radical responses to globalization, such as the burning of McDonald's restaurants in France, and also on the backlash against the backlash. The articles in "North-South Tensions" illustrate the conflicting fears that less developed countries have of forging stronger links with the global economy and of being left out of its creative sphere.

We conclude with the final critical moment in globalization's 20th century history, "The Battle in Seattle." The Seattle meetings of the World Trade Organization were supposed to produce a political consensus in favor of further deepening of global economic integration, building upon the cracked political foundation of the Uruguay Round of GATT meetings. Instead, the Seattle meetings brought together all the forces of globalization, both those who sought its creative potential (from multinational corporations such as Boeing and Microsoft to trade ministers of third-world countries) and the many forces of resistance (labor unions, environmentalists, and even anarchists).

The Times articles collected here provided readers with a remarkably balanced and thorough view of the many reactions to the creative and destructive forces of globalization.

BACKLASH

August 28, 1988

BUSINESS FORUM: THE 'SELLING OF AMERICA'

The Dark Side of Globalization

By ROBERT L. DILENSCHNEIDER

Money talks. Koreans own The Washington Times. From the G. Heileman Company Inc.—the brewer—to Bonwit Teller—the department store—Australians have come up from down-under to buy companies throughout the United States. And you can drive all over this nation on General Tires—made by a company now owned by the Germans—or on tires made by Firestone—which was recently bought by the Japanese.

Money talks, but are we listening? Globalization is the rage in business today but it has a dark side. We overlook that businesses are globalizing more quickly than they can adjust to the new international economic environment. We overlook the disruption to the historical and traditional ways in which business is conducted. And we have ignored serious public policy questions that are urgently in need of debate.

American companies, though vulnerable, are not the only international takeover targets. Earlier this year, Italian financier Carlo de Benedetti mounted a bold move to buy Belgium's largest company, Societé Generale de Belgique. This bid is viewed by many as a precursor to what will happen throughout Europe if international takeovers continue. French and Spanish companies are especially vulnerable to increased globalization. In fact, any mature economy that fails to motivate its workers sufficiently to keep pace with the Japanese and the Koreans may soon see large shares of its national assets sold abroad.

Economic internationalism is a wonderful thing, but it also suggests that the world is one seamless plane, which it is not. Once investment passes through borders it becomes enmeshed in a host of long-standing, traditional and often conflicting laws and practices—many of which could not have anticipated today's global climate.

There also are a host of questions with which we must now wrestle. For example, what should be our policy on buying from national cartels? How and where will mega-multinationals bankroll their research and development and which division in what countries will benefit? Should accounting practices be standardized worldwide? And what special obligations—if any—do foreign employers have to their American workers?

Isn't it time to take a serious look at the ramifications of globalization? But if we listen to the candidates on the campaign trail, one hears the old songs, or no songs at all, about these important international economic and financial problems. When a foreign interest can come in and buy a domestic company with only the most minimal of restrictions, to

focus the debate on protectionism versus free trade—as the candidates are doing—is akin to arguing about the value of cavalry versus foot soldiers in the midst of a nuclear war.

It seems only fair that if a foreign takeover occurs, the new employer must treat its American management and workers in a manner at least equal to the way the employees were treated by the American company. And foreign workers employed in American-owned companies abroad should demand no less of their American employers.

Companies working in the United States need to commit themselves to the communities in which they operate, especially with respect to worker retraining and charitable giving. Additionally, unless the managements of offshore companies enter into a frank and open dialogue about their problems and opportunities with the American media, their operations in this nation will suffer.

Should we bar foreign companies from the United States at least until some of these issues are addressed? Do we need to nationalize certain vital industries to protect them until a policy is formulated? Should we use foreign exchange controls as a weapon to prevent foreign takeovers?

These are complex questions. Each should be debated and considered but, in the final analysis, dismissed. And 50 different solutions to these puzzles, by 50 different states, can only compound the problem. We need a national forum and it is up to the business leadership of this country to advance that dialogue from the executive suite to Capital Hill, to the general election and beyond.

Our response to globalization is deserving of discussion and debate by our Presidential candidates. We should know how they plan to handle tax issues affecting offshore interests and what incentives they favor for American corporations that compete globally. Don't we have a right to know how each candidate will treat globalization at the next round of the General Agreement on Tariffs and Trade, and what he plans for the future of the United States Trade Representative position?

If we do not put the global economy under the nation's center spotlight, we may make ourselves stage hands and not actors in the rapidly unfolding tale of our economic future.

Robert L. Dilenschneider is president and chief executive of Hill & Knowlton Inc.

* * *

October 7, 1996

TRADE VS. CULTURAL IDENTITY IN CANADA

By ANTHONY DePALMA

TORONTO—Canada knows that by charging excise taxes of 80 percent on Canadian editions of Sports Illustrated and other American magazines, it can keep those publications off the nation's newsstands and out of its advertising market.

Canada contends that it is only trying to protect the country's national identity and help support its own modest magazine industry.

But the United States contends that Canada's real goal is to stifle competition. After years of complaining to the Canadians without satisfactorily resolving the issue, the United States has finally taken its grievance to the World Trade Organization in Switzerland, where it filed a formal complaint in September.

The United States is asking the international organization, which represents the trading interests of nations that have signed the General Agreement on Tariffs and Trade, to determine whether Canada is using cultural identity to conceal unfair trading practices.

The United States also objects to postal rates in Canada that are much lower for Canadian magazines than those imported from the United States and to a 30-year-old ban on Canadian editions printed in the United States.

Canada's response, citing what it believes are GATT provisions allowing countries to protect cultural resources, was filed Sept. 26. A hearing will be held this Friday at the World Trade Organization in Geneva and a ruling is due by Feb. 21.

Whatever the organization decides, the issue has already raised hackles in a Canada increasingly apprehensive about the encroaching American culture.

"There is a very strong dominance in the cultural industries of the Canadian marketplace by the United States," Arthur C. Eggleton, Canada's Minister for International Trade, said. "We come at this from the point of preserving culture and identity, while the U.S. comes at it from the standpoint of wanting to do business in our country."

Mr. Eggleton said that 70 percent of the magazines sold in Canada already come from the United States, and that allowing Canadian editions—cheap to produce and full of local advertising—would further shrink the small pool of advertising open to Canadian publications.

Canadian magazine publishers insist that existing trade agreements do not guarantee the United States free access to Canadian advertising. They say that opening the market to Canadian editions of United States magazines would threaten the survival of Canadian magazines.

"American publishers have virtually unlimited access to Canadian readers," said Catherine Allman, acting president of the Canadian Magazine Publishers Association. "The question is, will Canadian readers have unlimited access to Canadian magazines" if the magazines cannot survive competition that the Canadians regard as unfair?

Canada's cultural concerns go far beyond magazines. The Government has not allowed the United States bookstore chain Borders to establish a Canadian branch because the company and its Canadian partners did not satisfy standards for substantial Canadian control of the enterprise. And Government action in 1994 effectively threw out the Country Music Television cable channel to make way for a Canadian competitor. Eventually, the two companies involved negotiated a joint venture.

A United States trade official, who spoke on condition he not be identified, said that the two nations had been jousting over the real meaning of cultural exemptions in trade for a long time, usually without filing any formal complaints.

"But when certain actions are taken like chasing a business out of the market, we have to weigh in and say, 'You've gone too far,' " the official said.

The issue of cultural influences is one of the most sensitive in the modern global economy, and an especially important part of the trading strategy pursued by the United States. With the decline of traditional manufacturing, intellectual properties like movies, magazines and books are now considered to be among the most attractive exports of the United States.

Canada is not alone in restricting intellectual imports from the United States. Some European countries have limited the showing of movies and television programs from the United States.

Before Canada signed the North American Free Trade Agreement with the United States and Mexico in 1993, it fought hard to exempt sectors of the economy essential to its cultural identity. Because of the difference in language, Mexico did not fight as hard for such cultural safeguards, although representatives of Mexican media groups warned that there was no way Mexico could compete with Hollywood.

Canada's cultural exemptions in the North American accord meant that the United States complaint on magazines would have a better chance in front of the World Trade Organization, United States trade officials said.

Canada's protectionism goes back at least to the 1960's, when Canadian editions of United States magazines were not allowed across the border. Technological advances later made it possible to print these editions in Canada.

In 1993, Time Warner Inc. introduced a Canadian edition of Sports Illustrated. It included a small amount of material on Canadian sports but most of the magazine was identical to issues sold in the United States. It then sold advertising in the regional, or "split run" editions, to Canadian companies.

A Canadian Government task force estimated that 53 other United States magazines and 70 trade journals might also try to publish split-run editions. As a result, Canada last year imposed an excise tax of 80 percent on the total dollar value of the advertising in almost every split-run magazine sold in Canada, except for Reader's Digest and Time, which had longtime Canadian editions.

For example, an issue of Sports Illustrated that carried $100,000 in ads would be charged $80,000 in excise taxes.

On top of that, a 1976 law prohibited Canadian companies that advertise in the regional editions from deducting those costs from their taxes, as they would if the ads ran in a Canadian magazine. And postage rates were higher for Sports Illustrated.

* * *

October 12, 1999

FRENCH SEE A HERO IN WAR ON 'McDOMINATION'

By SUZANNE DALEY

MONTREDON, France—At home here in his 500-year-old stone farmhouse, Jose Bove seems pretty relaxed for someone out on $17,000 bail.

He moves around in his slippers and turns off his cell phone so he can answer questions without being interrupted. His antique dining-room table is covered with stacks of paper, mostly faxes and printouts from Internet sites. Outside his windows, tucked among the trees, are the other five houses of this village and, beyond them, hundreds of Mr. Bove's sheep leisurely picking over the grass.

Since he was arrested in August on charges of vandalizing a nearby McDonald's restaurant under construction—though his principal complaint is about American tariffs on luxury food—this wiry, 46-year-old union leader and sheep farmer has become something of a national hero.

Hardly a day goes by that French newspapers fail to mention Mr. Bove, lauding him for his refusal to bow to globalization, publishing photographs of him with his hands clenched above his head and his wrists cuffed, and suggesting that he may be the only man left in France willing to go to jail for the republic.

He has been praised by France's highest officials, including President Jacques Chirac, who has declared that he, too, detests McDonald's food. Prime Minister Lionel Jospin has also weighed in, comparing Mr. Bove with other noted leaders who have emerged from grass-roots movements in recent years.

Mr. Bove, who lives in Larzac, an area of southwest France that is one of the country's best-known gastronomic regions, organized the destruction of the McDonald's in nearby Millau—using tractors to tear down half the roof—to

Agence France-Presse

The arrest of José Bové, a French farmer accused of vandalizing a McDonald's restaurant in Millau, above, has aroused Gallic gastronomic pride and led to other protests, like one at the McDonald's in Toulouse, next page.

highlight what he sees as the unfairness of the United States's decision to levy high tariffs on Roquefort cheese, pate de foie gras and other luxury imported food. Washington acted in retaliation for the European Union's decision to ban America's hormone-treated beef. He attacked McDonald's because it was a symbol of industrialized agriculture, "where quality doesn't matter anymore," he said.

"There have been three totalitarian forces in our lifetime," said Mr. Bove, who supplies sheep's milk to makers of Roquefort cheese. "The totalitarianism of fascism, of communism and now of capitalism. How can people try and tell us that we must import hormone-enhanced beef? What is that?"

Mr. Bove hardly looks militant. His eyes twinkle over his handlebar mustache when he is asked about all the attention he is getting. "There was some luck in it," he confides. "The judge threw me into jail. People didn't like that."

But some say Mr. Bove's crusade—only the most conspicuous of a rash of protests against McDonald's—has tapped into far larger issues gnawing at the French lately, including a general annoyance with the power of the American economy and a nostalgia for a way of life, including long lunches, that is disappearing yet still held in high regard. Every year, new McDonald's franchises open and flourish in France.

However, few people admit to indulging in those quarter-pounders. Spotted under the Golden Arches, the French "often behave as if they just got caught leaving an X-rated movie," said Jean-Pierre Poulain, a sociologist at the University of Toulouse recently quoted in the newspaper Le Monde.

Having recovered from Mr. Bove's attack, the Millau McDonald's was doing brisk business the other day. "I come here only once in a great while," said one customer, Laurent Jeniez, who was getting into his car alone. "I do it only with my children," he added, though none could be seen.

Yet Millau is awash in pro-Bove graffiti. "End McDomination" and "Free Bove" are scrawled on roadside signs, bus shelters and walls.

Mr. Bove himself favors a rhyming slogan that uses the French nickname for McDonald's: "McDo Dehors, Gardons le Roquefort!" (McDonald's Get Out, Let's Keep the Roquefort!). That is what he painted on the McDonald's construction site on Aug. 12. He considers his actions that day to be rather ordinary. This is, after all, a country where protesting is a national pastime. The development that really shocked Mr. Bove, who heads a farmers' union called the Confederation Paysanne, was being put in jail five days later.

"They never do that," he said. "But there was a young judge and they are independent and they just saw property damage."

Mr. Bove clinched his moment of fame when he initially refused to be freed on bail, even though his supporters had come up with the cash. It was a stand that lasted only three weeks. He smiles when asked about his change of heart. "The conditions in there were really bad," he said. "And the food was inedible. And I said to myself, 'If all these people are

trying to help me by raising the money, why should I refuse to come out?'"

Mr. Bove said his actions had been announced in the local paper the day before. "There was nothing menacing about it," he said. "The children were there. There was singing. It had a festival atmosphere."

The owner of the McDonald's, Marc Dehani, sees it a bit differently. He says $120,000 worth of damage was done. But even though Mr. Bove awaits trial on state criminal charges, McDonald's has decided not to take any civil action against him, out of fear of turning him into a martyr. The restaurant chain has lately tried to calm protests by issuing statements pointing out that the franchises in France are owned by the French, employ French workers and almost exclusively sell food grown in France.

In the press, Mr. Bove is often described as the last holdout against creeping American imperialism. But he is eager to say that he likes Americans. His parents were researchers who spent years at the University of California at Berkeley studying diseases that attacked citrus trees. Mr. Bove lived there until he was 7 and still speaks English.

But his contempt for American eating habits is obvious. He offers statistics on the rate of obesity in America—about three times that of the French—and disdains Americans for eating all day long. He says America has no right to force its hormone-enhanced food down French throats.

Mr. Bove said he intended to travel to Seattle in November, when the World Trade Organization is expected to meet and consider the tariff issue again. The United States' decision to impose the tax was authorized by the W.T.O.

With four other farmers, Mr. Bove owns about 500 sheep. About half are raised to produce milk for Roquefort cheese. The rest are sold as meat.

Mr. Bove says he has never eaten at McDonald's, not even once. No, he insists, he is not curious. He does, however, like grilled hamburgers with sliced tomatoes and onions. "And mayonnaise," he added. "But only the homemade kind."

* * *

February 6, 2000

GLOBALIZATION:
IF YOU CAN'T BEAT IT, RESHAPE IT

By JOSEPH KAHN

With security agents toting submachine guns, army helicopters buzzing overhead and protesters breaking windows in yet another McDonald's, Davos man, the elite agent of global capitalism, is under siege.

It's not hard to reach that conclusion after attending this year's session of the World Economic Forum in Davos, Switzerland, where government officials, chief executives and leading economists gathered to schmooze and ponder globalization under heavy guard. The road to the Alpine resort was icy, and the confidence of the power brokers there seemed to be slipping. Since the disastrous global trade talks in Seattle not long ago, many of those who have long favored closer integration between nations are on the defensive.

But it's probably a mistake to think that globalization itself is threatened. On the contrary, the unions and environmental groups that assail the World Trade Organization seem on the whole to prefer that nations become more like one another faster—and in a greater variety of ways. They are not so much trying to block globalization as to hitch a ride.

Thousands of groups are seeking to influence the Davos crowd in the service of causes from protection of sea turtles to elimination of child labor. They do not speak with a single voice. But their pleas no longer fall on deaf ears.

The human rights group Amnesty International, the environmental action organization Greenpeace and the A.F.L.-C.I.O. were all invited to Davos this year, and they pushed similar agendas. Globalization cannot really be resisted, they said, but neither should it be limited to commerce.

"Globalization is happening one way or another and it can't be stopped," said John J. Sweeney, president of the A.F.L.-C.I.O., "but it must be made to work for workers." Beyond going slow with new trade agreements to protect union jobs in the developed world, that means compelling poor countries to rewrite their labor laws to conform more closely with those of rich countries—in effect, globalizing labor standards.

Groups like Greenpeace and the World Wildlife Fund are taking a similar tack. They want the W.T.O. to inject some environmental horse-trading into trade talks—say, freer imports of third-world textiles in exchange for stricter limits on logging in rain forests.

That some protest groups accept globalization—albeit on their own terms—helps explain why President Clinton, whose free-trade credentials are well established, extended an olive branch to those who led the Seattle demonstrations. In Davos, Mr. Clinton embraced the "new forces" that demand a say in how nations relate to one another, effectively offering them a seat at the negotiating table. And he agreed with them that defining globalization merely in trade terms is no longer enough; instead, the world should start talking about the globalization of society.

"We cannot isolate economics as distinct from the environment and labor," said Charlene Barshefsky, the United States trade representative. "That's a distinction that's artificial."

The idea struck a responsive chord with the executives at Davos. In fact, this year's conference may be remembered as the time businesses and advocacy groups stopped fighting each other and started talking.

Business leaders proposed a flurry of ways they could become more socially conscious. Louis Schweitzer of Renault, for example, suggested restricting political contributions by multinationals, to restore faith that public policy is not beholden to corporate interests.

Monsanto was another company welcoming a "new dialogue" with its adversaries. "Companies need to understand what society's expectations are and be ready to change a strategy if it does not meet this test," said Nick E. Rosa, senior vice president. The company has overhauled the way it uses genetics to modify crops, largely in response to pressure from Greenpeace and other environmental groups, Mr. Rosa said.

The big problem with all this coziness is that poorer countries like Mexico, South Africa, India and China—the ones that would have to do all the changing and harmonizing to suit rich-country standards—are balking at this expanded view of globalization.

"Most developing countries have a knee-jerk reaction to this—they are not ready to discuss it," said Supachai Panitchpakdi, a deputy premier of Thailand, who is due to take over the leadership of the World Trade Organization in 2002. "I'm afraid we won't see much progress on trade right away."

That prediction remains to be tested. The Clinton administration is still hoping to kick-start a new round of global trade talks before its term expires. And if Davos was any indication, globalization in the broadest sense is just getting started.

* * *

April 15, 2000

STOPPING THE WORLD

In Washington this weekend, a disparate gathering of protesters will be rallying against what they view as the malign forces of economic globalization. The dissidents' message is sometimes confused and misplaced, especially in wanting to dismantle essential institutions like the World Bank, the International Monetary Fund and the World Trade Organization. But the protesters, who call themselves the Mobilization for Global Justice, also represent a popular response—misguided but heartfelt—to a worldwide economic transformation that is not fully comprehended even by the experts. To be sure, some interest groups are trying to manipulate public concern for their own advantage. But it would be dangerous to ignore a growing popular unease over these trends and the need for broader educational efforts.

Despite the dramatic stock market decline yesterday, the fact remains that the United States has on balance benefited from the unbridled flow of capital, goods, people and information that is called globalization. The dislocations felt by American workers have been far outweighed by the benefits of cheap imports, low inflation and expanding opportunities for American businesses overseas. Abroad, the poor countries benefiting from expanded markets outnumber those hurt by them.

Nevertheless, the new world order has created hardship in declining or newly uncompetitive industries. Some nations see globalization as a code word for American domination. Many fear that the World Bank, I.M.F. and W.T.O. are pursuing the interests of an American-led elite, to the detriment of the poor and the environment. Critics on both the left and right have begun to question whether the world would be better off without these institutions.

Certainly the institutions that manage the world economy must be more sensitive and transparent. But their real challenge is to help everyone understand that there is no realistic—or beneficial—way to reverse or even slow the forces that are driving the world economy. Just as American businesses have begun to discover that in the world of an Internet-driven economy the old rules have to be scrapped or adjusted, so countries around the world will have to learn to adjust to the new market forces if they want to harness them to their advantage. Underdeveloped countries have to learn that capital is voluntary, and does not flow to countries that do not obey its rules.

Since the end of the cold war, there have been at least four major currency crises that threatened to destabilize regional economies: in Europe in 1992–93, Mexico in 1994–95, East Asia in 1997 and Russia and Brazil in 1998. Each had the potential for spiraling out of control. The critics descending on Washington argue that the I.M.F. and the World Bank sometimes made these crises worse, while their defenders assert that without the difficulties inflicted, the crises would have grown worse. One thing is certain. There will be more crises to come in the years ahead. The institutions that handle them need to be reformed, not weakened.

The anti-globalization protesters invoke the tactics and styles of the 1960's. But a closer analogy may be early struggles over the burgeoning of capitalism in the 19th century. It was then that disputes between owners and workers and about public costs and private gain led to an age of ideological conflict.

Today's struggle has the added element of changing definitions of national sovereignty. Indeed, poor countries are not the only worriers. Europeans are also increasingly wary of American demands to open their economies to American products. As boundaries become more economically irrelevant, one question is whether people will seek refuge in their national identities or in the familiar if transitory comforts of placards, chants and street theater in places like Washington.

Yet today's global economic drama is deeply familiar to students of American history—how to reconcile the demands of economic growth and opportunity with the need to preserve fairness, stability and the health and welfare of each country's citizens. It is today a challenge without borders. Meeting it calls for more sophisticated international institutions, not a retreat into nostalgia and economic nationalism.

* * *

July 1, 2000

FRENCH TURN VANDAL INTO HERO AGAINST U.S.

By SUZANNE DALEY

MILLAU, France, June 30—Fearing that the trial of Jose Bove would turn their quiet little town into an actual battleground for the forces of anti-globalization, most store owners kept their iron gates closed today. The McDonald's restaurant, which Mr. Bove is charged with ransacking last year, was blockaded by two dozen police vehicles.

But as the trial opened, the atmosphere seemed more like a French Woodstock than a Seattle. Thousands of teenagers with green hair gathered along with middle-aged men with pigtails and retirees wearing T-shirts that said, "The world is not merchandise and I'm not either."

Others set up tents and strummed guitars in the streets in support of Mr. Bove, the sheep farmer who has become something of a national hero with his fight against multinational corporations and what he calls the industrialization of agriculture.

Since the McDonald's attack, Mr. Bove has become a national celebrity. He now has a busy speaking schedule, a more prominent job with his union and dinner invitations from high-level government officials, including Prime Minister Lionel Jospin.

Some of those who set up their tents in the fields around this town and then boarded shuttle buses to the courthouse said they had come to pay homage to a hero, a man who was willing to stand up to the forces of globalization and the American government.

Mr. Bove, who has an amiable grin under his handlebar mustache, added to the carnival air by riding into Millau's main square with his nine co-defendants on a cart pulled by a tractor—a not-so-veiled reference to the way the condemned once went to the guillotine.

And when he finally climbed the courthouse stairs, he stood at the door with his fist raised long enough for the pack of news photographers to get good shots.

Inside the courtroom, the defendants, dressed in sports shirts, laughed and joked as the charges were read and they were asked to respond to them. One, accused of spraying the McDonald's with orange paint, said he was only sorry he had not used green paint. Another, accused of using a screwdriver to commit vandalism, acknowledged that he had, but said it was a small screwdriver.

Mr. Bove, was a bit more serious. At one point he compared himself to Gandhi, saying that Gandhi, too, had been accused of violence in his day. "The dismantling of McDonald's was a strong action, symbolic and nonviolent," Mr. Bove told the court, adding that the fast-food giant's arrival in Millau was a "provocation."

The trial is expected to last two days.

Mr. Bove was a little-known farmer and union official until last August, when he and the nine other men took a tractor, pick axes and power saws to the local McDonald's. Mr. Bove said at the time that he was incensed by what he saw as the unfairness of the United States to tax French delicacies like Roquefort cheese and pate de foie gras in retaliation for Europe's decision not to import hormone-treated American beef.

"That tax decision was outrageous," said Arianne Gurreau, a schoolteacher who was camping with her boyfriend. "I think the judge needs to see that there are all these people who think what he did was correct. We are fighting for values here, for the right to care about what we eat."

Many came with their own fights inspired by Mr. Bove. "What prompted us to come is the problem of water," said Giselle Joffre, a retired government worker. "In our town it is terribly expensive because we are working with a big company. It is the same with all these multinationals doing what they want."

This was clearly not what many Millau residents had braced for. Most had seen pictures of protesters, including Mr. Bove, at the World Trade Organization meeting in Seattle and feared that this demonstration would be just as disruptive.

"People were so scared," said Christianne Chazal-Martin, the owner of a gift shop near the courthouse who decided to stay open. "First one got talking and then another, and they went on and on about how bad it was going to be."

Mr. Bove's attack on the McDonald's here last August was only one of a number of assaults on the fast food chain, which is often a target of anti-American protesters. But Mr. Bove became instantly famous when he was thrown in jail for it, and then refused to pay bail for three weeks in protest. Eventually, he did pay the bail with money supplied by a group of supporters, many of them American.

Mr. Bove faces charges that could result in a fine of as much as $70,000 and up to five years in jail. But it is considered unlikely that he or any of his co-defendants will serve any jail time for the vandalism, which resulted in $110,000 worth of damage.

Mr. Bove's lawyers, including a former president of a prominent human rights organization, have lined up more than a dozen witnesses, most of whom are also farming advocates from other countries. Much of the first day was spent arguing about pictures of the McDonald's after the ransacking.

Mr. Bove's lawyers pointed out that some of the windows remained unbroken.

Organizers of the demonstration had hoped to gather 30,000 people for the opening of the trial, though police officials said they believed the number was closer to half that. With speakers, a farmers' market and a free rock concert in the evening, however, there was plenty to do. Many said they came as much to have fun as to make a political statement.

"We came first for the party," said Michael Phelippeau, 16, who came with his friend Dennis Roulleau and was wandering from booth to booth with his sleeping bag under his arm. "But my father is a farmer, and I am here representing my family, too. We believe in what Mr. Bove believes in. We don't want the multinationals to tell us what to eat."

* * *

July 18, 2000

FRENCH CHEFS CAST AN EYE ON LE BIG MAC

By JOHN TIERNEY

American fast food has become the despised symbol of globalization in France, where the men on trial for wrecking a McDonald's have become national heroes. But there are other gastronomic imperialists with a far more insidious record of globalization: French chefs.

Shouldn't proud New Yorkers be rising up against the foreigners imposing their tastes on us? How can indigenous cuisine survive when culturally oppressed diners keep giving so much of their money to ruthless French capitalists? Alain Ducasse's new restaurant here (he has 10 others around the globe) has a three-month waiting list of natives desperate to pay $50 for an appetizer.

Some chauvinists might feel an urge to retaliate for the McDonald's attack by spray-painting the rosewood walls and silk upholstery at Ducasse, but violence is not the answer. What we need is a Franco-American dialogue on culinary globalization.

Seeking to ease international tensions (and perhaps subconsciously hoping to avenge personal humiliations at French restaurants), I asked several of the city's greatest French chefs to contemplate McDonald's cuisine. They were surprisingly kind, even about ketchup.

"Ketchup is not that bad," said Christian Delouvrier, the executive chef at Lespinasse. Mr. Delouvrier, who once had a signature dish of a foie gras "burger," said he had no objection to the ground beef variety.

"When you eat a good hamburger that's cooked properly, it's delicious," he said. When pressed, Mr. Delouvrier couldn't quite bring himself to put the Big Mac in that category, but he was diplomatic nonetheless. "I'm not interested in a well-done hamburger, but I'm pretty sure some French people like it." He also called the French fries "pretty good."

Eric Ripert, the executive chef at Le Bernadin, cheerfully confessed to the occasional Big Mac attack himself. "I guess I'm becoming a local," he said. "To stop at McDonald's is amusing to me. About twice a year I go. I get the fries and the Coke, and I take a ton of ketchup and mayonnaise with the hamburger. My favorite was the Arch Deluxe hamburger. It was very simple, with a mustardy sauce. I don't know why they stopped making it."

Daniel Boulud, the chef responsible for Daniel and Cafe Boulud, recalled a furtive McDonald's meal at Dulles Airport. "There was no other choice," he said. "I took my hamburger and French fries, went to an empty gate and ate in a corner with no paparazzi around."

How was the food? Mr. Boulud was tactful. "There is no shame in going to McDonald's," he said. "The food is predictable. You go there 20 years later, and it tastes the same. It's very hard for any restaurant to do that. McDonald's is helping a lot of people. If you ask a French kid today what he wants, he will say McDonald's."

Then why are the McDonald's bashers so popular in France? "The French are jealous," Mr. Boulud said. "The hamburger may be the most successful snack in the world. The French wish they could have invented McDonald's."

Then Mr. Boulud made an extraordinary gesture to bring Americans and French together at the peace table. The revered chef from Lyon offered to create a burger.

I rushed to his restaurant on East 65th Street to witness the grande premiere. Mr. Boulud let me sit in what he called his sky box, a glass-walled room overlooking the kitchen of Daniel, as he deftly assembled the ingredients.

The bun was a petit pain rond, in texture a cross between a baguette and focaccia. Instead of ketchup, Mr. Boulud used a tomato confit with olive oil, herbs and garlic, plus a horseradish mayonnaise and curly chicory.

The burger consisted of two patties of Wyoming beef sandwiching a daring central layer: Black Angus short ribs from Colorado that had been braised in red wine sauce, shredded and mixed with black truffles.

"The braised beef gives it a different dimension," Mr. Boulud said. "It's an adult burger." He said he might add it to the lunch menu, perhaps for $26 or $28, although he was also beginning to get into the spirit of McDonald's.

"I'll call it the DB Burger," he said, smiling. "Maybe we'll open a drive-in window and sell it in a bag."

I had intended to head straight from Mr. Boulud's restaurant for a comparative taste test at McDonald's, where, I hoped, the culinary patriot in me would find the Big Mac

superior. But I gave up that plan as soon as I bit into the DB Burger. Call me a traitor, but globalization suddenly seemed sublime.

* * *

August 5, 2000

ANARCHISM, THE CREED THAT WON'T STAY DEAD

The Spread of World Capitalism Resurrects a Long-Dormant Movement

By JOSEPH KAHN

Since Karl Marx bested the anarchist leader Mikhail Bakunin in a struggle to shape world revolution a century and a half ago, anarchism has undergone a half-dozen resurrections and almost as many deaths.

It was crushed with the Paris Commune in 1871, suppressed in the United States after an anarchist shot President William McKinley in 1901, destroyed by Franco in the Spanish Civil War of the late 1930's and left to wither away with the 1960's student radicalism. Ideologically opposed to power and ambivalent about organization, anarchists perpetually live on the fringe of great movements—and on the verge of defeat.

Yet the very qualities that consign anarchism to obscurity also endow it with many lives, if only as a prefix: anarcho-collectivism, anarcho-syndicalism, anarcho-mutualism, anarcho-individualism, anarcho-ecologism. And at the turn of this century, it is undergoing a fresh resurgence.

Black-masked anarchists stoned chain stores in Seattle during global trade talks last year. Protesters with giant A's pasted on their shirts blocked intersections in Washington during demonstrations against international lending agencies last spring. They were in the streets of Philadelphia during the Republican National Convention this week and have promised to stalk the Democratic National Convention in Los Angeles this month.

Self-described anarchists are small in number. But anarchism, broadly construed, is becoming fashionable. There are hints of it in the way protesters of diverse loyalties—labor, environmental and consumer groups among them—have sought to become a mass but leaderless movement, a collection of affinity groups that operate by consensus. Many of those who oppose the institutions that enforce rules of international capitalism call for a return to local decision-making, echoing longtime anarchist objections to the way nation-states usurped the power of cities and towns.

The protests have often been condemned in the mainstream news media as imbecilic and chaotic, all action and no theory. But that is also an anarchist trait. Its adherents have long been dismissed as uneducated and unwashed. Anarchism's most memorable slogan, coined by Enrico Malatesta of Italy, is "propaganda by deed."

ANARCHY, THEN AND NOW Mikhail Bakunin, inset, defined and popularized it in the 19th century. Above, anarchists meet in Seattle during global trade talks last year.

"With the decline of socialism, you have seen anarchism go through a revival as an easy way to oppose global capitalism," said Paul Avrich, a leading historian of anarchism who teaches at Queens College in New York. Mr. Avrich, who has written extensively on early-20th-century American anarchists, said anarchist cells all but disappeared by the 1970's as the last of the European immigrants who brought the creed to the United States died. But anarchist groups are reappearing in every major city, he says. Today they have their own bookstores, like Blackout Books on the Lower East Side and Social Anarchism in Baltimore. They read The Match, a popular magazine published in Tuscon, Ariz., or Fifth Estate, a Detroit newspaper.

Pierre-Joseph Proudhon was probably the first person to call himself an anarchist when he wrote "What Is Property?" in 1840. (His answer: theft.) Proudhon advocated free bank credit and rejected parliamentary politics as hopelessly dominated by the elite. But anarchism was defined and popularized by Bakunin, a heavily bearded Russian insurrectionist who helped foment uprisings across Europe in 1848.

Bakunin's motto was, "The urge to destroy is a creative urge." Unlike Marx, Bakunin did not justify his theory as science. He described anarchists as people who know what they are fighting against more than what they are fighting for.

Anarchism reached critical mass as a revolutionary movement only once, during the Spanish Civil War of 1936–39. But it has long touched a political and cultural chord in the United States.

Henry David Thoreau was an exemplary anarchist, though he never called himself one. Emma Goldman, a Russian immigrant who advocated free love, women's rights and armed insurrection, was the best known of the immigrant anarchists who helped prompt a red scare around World War I. (She appears in E. L. Doctorow's novel "Ragtime" and in Warren Beatty's movie "Reds.") In 1927 the Italian immigrants Nicola Sacco and Bartolomeo Vanzetti, both avowed anarchists, were executed after being convicted of killing a paymaster and his guard at a shoe factory near Boston.

Anarchists consider themselves of the left, not the right. But antigovernment ideas that sound anarchist themes are common across the political spectrum. John Wayne, in many of his Westerns, and Mel Gibson, in "The Patriot," play reluctant but violent American heroes called on to smash evil so they can return to a life of bucolic isolation. The quest for pure rebellion in some punk rock lyrics reflects the spread of anarchism, or perhaps nihilism—anarchism without the utopian impulses—among teenagers.

But nothing has revived anarchism like globalization. Anarchists are now battling what they see as a concentration of power in multinational corporations. Many oppose the spread of corporate investment across national boundaries, which, they say, lets companies like Nike and General Electric evade local labor and environmental laws. They have also attacked the World Bank, the World Trade Organization and the International Monetary Fund because these are seen as superseding national governments.

"For the first time since the 1960's we are actually putting thought into action," said John Zerzan, a leading anarchist thinker who lives in Eugene, Ore. He distinguishes anarchists from traditional labor and environmental groups that oppose many of the same aspects of globalization, though he's not opposed to sharing the stage with them.

"We are succeeding because the liberals failed," he said. "We are less polite."

Mr. Zerzan, 56, is a leading proponent of anarcho-primitivism, which combines radical environmentalism with an extreme antitechnology bent. His essays and his book "Future Primitive" espouse a theory that time and technology are not neutral scientific realities but carefully constructed ways to enslave people. For example, he said, the computer and the Internet atomize society, create new divisions of labor, demand ever more efficiency and consume ever more leisure time. To cope with the increasing strains of our technology-driven society, alienated people by the millions are resorting to drugs like Ritalin and Prozac.

"What we have learned is that our problem is not just control of capital," he said. "It is also science and technology."

Mr. Zerzan says that society should return to the Stone Age. He says that more than 12,000 years ago, before agriculture allowed a class of people to leave food production to others, hunter-gatherers were as intelligent and as healthy as people today. And he argues that an old anthropological conundrum— why it took man so long to develop agriculture—should now be posed in reverse. "The question now is why we ever developed agriculture," he said.

Mr. Zerzan writes long hand. He does not use the Internet and owns no car. He lives in cooperative housing in Eugene, which he has helped turn into a beehive of anarchist activity. Like Bakunin and earlier American anarchists, he argues that property damage is a legitimate tactic, an effective way to attract attention.

"We are not library theorists," he said. "We are activists." But he added that while he approved of the antitechnology principles of Theodore J. Kaczynski, the Unabomber, he condemned the taking of human life.

Many other anarchists call anarcho-primitivism a disturbing trend, and, perhaps not surprisingly, sectarian strife among the anarchists is rampant. An old guard supports ethical anarchism, a type of modified socialism that calls for eliminating the nation-state while embracing nonauthoritarian local government. Ethical anarchists reject violence, and some view technology like the Internet as tools to achieve freedom. Many also say that anarcho-primitivists tend to be antiwork and antiworker, which forecloses the possibility of a lasting alliance with labor unions

The anarcho-primitives "carry a black flag in one hand and a welfare check in the other," an anarchist named Janet Biehl wrote in a recent Internet essay. Others have called Mr. Zerzan a "McAnarchist" who dumbs down anarchism and corrupts" "young gullibles" with mystical visions of life before civilization.

Murray Bookchin, an 80-year-old Vermont-based social theorist who calls himself a communalist, has sharply criticized recent trends in anarchism, though he claims his own writings have contributed to the rise of Direct Action Network and other antiglobalization protest groups.

Mr. Bookchin wrote "Post-Scarcity Anarchism" in the 1960's. In that book, he merged environmentalism and anarchism into a broader theory of how the state and capitalism are at war with nature. But he says some anarchist groups have taken the ecological message too far, becoming misanthropic nihilists who ignore anarchism's core humanitarian message.

"Just when there is rising interest among young people," Mr. Bookchin said, "we are shooting ourselves in the foot"

*   *   *

September 27, 2000

PROTESTS DISTRACT GLOBAL FINANCE MEETING

By JOSEPH KAHN

PRAGUE, Sept. 26—Black-masked protesters hurled cobblestones ripped from Prague's medieval streets and attacked the police with homemade gasoline bombs today, trying desperately—but unsuccessfully—to shut down the global finance meeting here.

The riot police had to escort government ministers attending the annual conference of the International Monetary Fund and the World Bank into special subway cars to whisk them away from their meeting at the end of the session, though by evening, normal access had been fully restored.

The violence, which both the police and many protesters said was provoked by squadrons of European anarchists and communists, did not stop the meetings.

But it did steal the media spotlight, giving it to protesters who had vowed to re-create the blockade of the trade talks last year in Seattle.

Inside the halls, financial leaders who are here to discuss aid policies tried to show that they are at least as passionate about the poor as the protesters are. Many pledged to rededicate themselves to fighting poverty, even to inspiring a new spirituality.

At the Conference Center in Prague, World Bank and International Monetary Fund delegates were briefly bottled up yesterday by the demonstrations.

Everyone seemed to cite the statistic that 3 billion people live on $2 or less a day.

"Something is wrong when the richest 20 percent of the global population receive more than 80 percent of the global income," James D. Wolfensohn, the president of the World Bank, said in his keynote address. "Our challenge is to make globalization an instrument of opportunity and inclusion—not fear."

The leaders of the World Bank and the I.M.F., and finance ministers from some rich nations that back them, said they would speed up debt relief, allow poor countries to have more say in planning loan programs and consider replacing some loans with grants.

But by afternoon, protesters had stolen the show, at least as far as the television cameras were concerned. The demonstrators included Czech anarchists, Italian Communists, British schoolteachers and German truck drivers, many of whom contended that the lending agencies are the problem, not the solution.

The Prague police had prepared for a siege, with 11,000 officers around the city. In the end, the police estimated that there were 6,000 demonstrators. The protesters, who once expected 20,000, claimed that they actually had 10,000. Even if they were right, they still failed to match the police one for one, and they fell short of the tally in Seattle and at other recent protests.

Early in the day, in what has become the signature vandalism, several people smashed the windows and tore up the interior of a McDonald's in Wenceslas Square, the site of the peaceful protests during Czechoslovakia's Velvet Revolution in 1989.

Near the hilltop Congress Center, where the meetings were held, a small group of demonstrators provoked the police by hurling fist-sized stones that later littered the street behind police lines. Some protesters wore black masks and carried the red-and-black flag of anarchists. Several threw Molotov cocktails, igniting the uniforms of officers stretched in a line across the street.

The police responded with repeated shots of tear gas. They sprayed water from cannons to disperse the crowd, while armored personnel carriers raced into position to close off the streets.

The police said as many as 65 people were taken to hospitals with injuries, most of them officers involved in the melee. There were dozens of arrests. A few demonstrators were hurt by the police who seized them, with one man bleeding from the face after four officers threw him to the ground.

The skirmishes spread to the valley below the meeting hall, where demonstrators burned barricades of wood and tires to keep the police back, then smashed windows and destroyed a car. An American flag was burned, while protesters yelled, "No new world order."

Italian protesters used inner tubes to shove the police.

Tomas, a 19-year-old from the Moravia region of the Czech Republic with orange hair and a rooster cut, was there throwing plastic bottles at the police. "I hate the police and they hate me," he said. "I would like some real fighting to happen."

A 23-year-old man from Berlin who refused to give his name carried several cobblestones as he prepared to rush police lines. He removed his black mask to reveal his face, seared red from pepper gas.

"To fight them for me is symbolic of fighting the I.M.F., which will never change on its own," he said.

Today's protests did succeed in blocking access to the conference center for several hours in the afternoon. But by that time meeting participants had already arrived, and their sessions continued uninterrupted, though delegates surrounded television monitors to get the latest news from the barricades.

By late afternoon, some people at the meeting were complaining to guards that they had planes to catch and had to leave the center immediately, prompting authorities to open a subway station to officials only.

Protesters had been gathering in Prague for a week, with many of them vowing to turn this session into a repeat of Seattle, when demonstrators briefly kept delegates away from their meetings.

Many protesters decried the violence.

"We're really disappointed," said Chelsea Mosen, an organizer. "We were really hoping for a nonviolent protest on the basic issues of the I.M.F. and the World Bank, but instead now the focus has shifted to the streets of Prague."

Catherine Devon, 38, a teacher who traveled from Birmingham, England, by train for 24 hours to reach Prague this morning, said, "This is not what I came for." She said she decided to join the demonstrations because her son often woke up in the middle of the night, frightened about global warming.

"I want to tell him I am doing something about it," she said. "We must show up every time these people meet. Someday, they will get the message."

Though they attracted less attention, delegates at the meetings from developing countries also challenged the lending agencies and wealthier governments to improve their policies.

Trevor A. Manuel, South Africa's finance minister and the honorary chairman of this year's meetings, scolded the representatives of wealthy nations for pressing poor nations to embrace free markets while often protecting their own markets from the goods that developing countries produce.

"The robust state of the global economy is due in no small measure to the success of the fundamental reforms undertaken by developing countries," Mr. Manuel said. "Their boldness needs to be matched by the richer countries."

The United States treasury secretary, Lawrence H. Summers, who addressed the opening ceremonies early in the day, prodded the World Bank to spend more on human development projects, including education. Such proposals have met some resistance on the bank's board.

Mr. Summers also called on the bank to provide some grants as well as its traditional loans, echoing a recommendation first made by a Congressional review panel that was highly critical of the bank's practices.

Mr. Summers said the grants would go to programs like those that help prevent the spread of AIDS, whose benefits cannot be measured in money.

It was left to Vaclav Havel, the Czech president and former dissident, to try to reconcile the demands of protesters with the money controlled by the ministers. He asked whether all the proposals to increase material well-being had obscured the task of improving spiritual health.

"We often hear about the need to restructure the economies of the poorer countries and about the wealthier nations being duty bound to help them accomplish this," Mr. Havel said. "But I deem it even more important that we should begin also to think about another restructuring—a restructuring of the entire system of values that forms the basis of our civilization today."

*   *   *

December 18, 2000

ADVOCATES GAIN GROUND IN A GLOBALIZED ERA

By ALAN COWELL

LONDON—De Beers, the global diamond giant, has a payroll of more than 20,000 people in about 20 countries. It operates from imposing offices in Johannesburg and London and, in the first half of this year, sold diamonds that totaled $3.4 billion in value.

Global Witness, a seven-year-old not-for-profit advocacy group, employs 14 people in two countries. It operates from offices cluttered with computers and the odd bicycle in what used to be a spectacles factory on a nondescript residential street in North London. It runs on a budget of about $800,000 a year.

On the surface, the two organizations might seem unequal foes. Yet, in the last two years, Global Witness, a member of a fast-growing network of bodies known as nongovernmental organizations, has been at the forefront of a largely successful campaign to turn De Beers' corporate strategy around, pressing the multinational colossus into a reversal of its attitude toward so-called conflict diamonds to cast itself these days as the champion of a cleaned-up world diamond trade.

Indeed, for the first time this year, De Beers began certifying the provenance of its diamonds, offering a written guarantee that they do not come from areas where they fuel insurrection.

The campaign and its fruits, though, go beyond diamonds, because they reinforce one of the most striking effects of the globalization that has been under way since the end of the cold war. Increasingly, with multinational corporations gathering unparalleled power as the standard-bearers of free-wheeling capitalism—in many countries, more powerful than

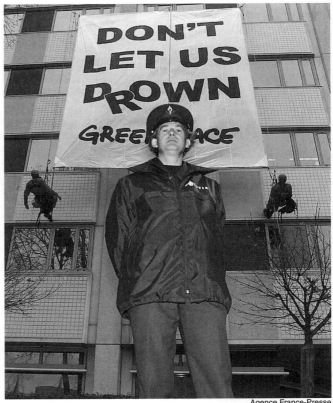

Agence France-Presse

Greenpeace activists hung a banner on the Congress Center in The Hague as a protest to the World Climate Conference. Greenpeace also boards vessels at sea to advertise its causes.

the governments themselves—they are being held to account by shoestring advocacy groups like Global Witness that have filled the vacuum created by the end of the ideological contest between East and West, between capitalism and socialism.

De Beers is not alone in acknowledging the power of the nongovernmental organizations. This year, both the United Nations and the World Economic Forum in Davos, Switzerland, recognized the organizations' role, conferring a new legitimacy as many corporations move from confrontation to at least the appearance of cooperation with them.

De Beers, for instance, has given one board-level executive, Andrew Coxon, responsibility for dealing with the organizations. And significantly, the World Economic Forum has increased the number of nongovernmental organizations—known as NGO's—that are invited to next year's glittery gathering in Davos. There, a central theme will be "bridging the global divide," a debate that acknowledges the role of the NGO's as champions of the world's have-nots as they press their case onto the global corporate agenda.

The issues they are championing vary from the environment to food safety, from the oil business to mining to financial services. But for many companies, the clamor of nongovernmental organizations' pressing businesses to assume social and other responsibilities as part of their corporate mission can seem almost deafening. "They are part of

Friends of the Earth demonstrated at the World Climate Conference in The Hague earlier this year.

the 21st-century economic landscape," said Andrew Lamont, a spokesman for De Beers.

Indeed, businesses like BP Amoco, the world's third-largest oil company, have taken those demands a step further, weaving them into the corporate image of an environmental pioneer.

Of course, for many casual observers, nongovernmental organizations are associated with the rowdy protests at the gatherings of such international institutions as the World Bank, the International Monetary Fund and the World Trade Organization over the last year in Seattle and Prague.

Far from projecting an image of noble intentions, the protesters have seemed to some to be more intent on wrecking McDonald's or Starbucks outlets, venting their rage at the perceived emblems of globalized business and subordinating private property rights to the dictates of direct action. One group, Friends of the Earth, routinely tears up fields of experimental genetically modified crops. Another, Greenpeace, developed the hallmark tactic of boarding vessels at sea to advertise its protests.

But beyond that, linked by the Internet and a sense of shared objectives, nongovernmental organizations are building networks of influence as the representatives of what they term the "civil society," acting essentially as self-appointed watchdogs on dubious corporate behavior.

"We look for the white underbelly of the dragon," said Patrick Alley, the director of Global Witness.

Once that "underbelly" has been identified—be it to establish the role of diamonds in fueling African conflict or the status of oil companies in the same conflicts—"we use the media as a tool to illuminate the target so that the company, decision makers and the public know that there's an issue," he said.

Similar tactics have been used to protest the labor practices involved in the manufacture of Nike shoes and the environmental impact of Royal/Dutch Shell's oil operations in Nigeria, forcing both companies into reappraisals of their public posture on labor rights and the environment.

Indeed, as corporations consolidate in quest of economies of scale, there is some evidence that advocacy groups are seeking the same sort of power through the politics of scale.

Just last month, 263 consumer advocacy groups, grouped as Consumers International, gathered in Durban, South Africa, to press for changes in the World Trade Organization, the World Bank and other international financial groups and to advocate "social justice and consumer protection in the global market."

The sectors and issues selected as targets, according to a statement, included e-commerce, food safety, corporate responsibility, pharmaceuticals, tobacco, financial markets and health care.

And while corporations are generally able to deploy vastly greater resources in public relations, litigation, lobbying and advertising and are often skilled at co-opting adversaries, "it's not such an unequal power relationship," an executive from a London-based international mining corporation said.

"You can be an $8 billion company or whatever," he continued. "But in the court of public opinion, the nongovernmental organizations start with more credibility than businesses."

Not only that, the push for corporate responsibility has received the imprimatur of the United Nations—the biggest nongovernmental organization of them all. Almost two years ago, Kofi Annan, the United Nations secretary general, warned that suspicion of the globalized economy made it "fragile and vulnerable to backlash from all the -isms of our post-cold-war world: protectionism, populism, ethnic chauvinism, fanaticism and terrorism."

And in July, more than 50 corporations—very few of them American—joined with nongovernmental organizations to sign a United Nations global compact to promote high standards on human rights, the environment and labor practices among transnational corporations.

"Business has to accept that it has to demonstrate that it can deliver responsibly," Mark Moody-Stuart, the head of Royal Dutch/Shell, a signer of the compact, said in remarks published at the end of the meeting.

Yet the relationship between these organizations and business is less evident.

In using the term "civil society" to denote their purported following, nongovernmental organizations, as some see it, are assuming a mandate that has not been granted by any democratic or representative process of accountability.

In parts of Africa, nongovernmental organizations involved in relief work have been accused of prolonging rather than ending wars and of acting as surrogates for their governments back home.

The question of legitimacy is important because, as not-for-profit organizations, many of these groups need to promote their own credentials in seeking financing from foundations and charitable trusts.

"If people think you are a charlatan," said Mr. Alley at Global Witness, "then your life expectancy is short, and rightly so."

But the question arises: who watches the watchdogs?

That question has not been adequately answered. Activists like Mr. Alley, for instance, say that NGO's themselves should be as accountable to the public as corporations are to their shareholders.

But such is the breadth and complexity of the NGO's—ranging from local, village-level groups in the developing world to well-financed groups like Oxfam, one of the best-endowed charities—that there are no general standards of transparency.

Even tactically, the NGO umbrella covers movements from politically active advocacy groups to the looser and sometimes violence-prone organizations that staged the protests in Seattle and Prague—groups that might lose most of their impact and support by accepting restraints.

Similarly, though, the NGO's themselves face a quandary: their strength lies, essentially, in their freedom to act outside formal strictures. And, as soon as they are drawn into formal alliances with more strait-laced, formal bodies, they risk being enfeebled.

And corporations can be adept at manipulating what some of them depict as a new partnership—using advocacy groups to shield themselves from the protests against globalization. When the United Nations global compact was signed, some nonparticipating advocacy groups accused the United Nations of providing organizations with a kind of political cover without being able to force them to change corporate practices.

Some nongovernmental organizations remain wary of the corporations they deal with, sensing that their interlocutors may be only too ready to use private dialogue as a means of stifling public debate, or of co-opting their adversaries.

Yet, whether the assessment is cynical or not, the publicly offered wisdom among some executives these days is that in a globalized era, the range of stakeholders in any corporate venture has broadened far beyond just the stockholders to encompass advocates for a range of human rights and environmental and labor issues.

Profit, therefore, these executives argue, must be coupled to corporate responsibility to avoid protests that would do far more damage to business.

That may be no more than lip service, but it also acknowledges a shift in the way that labor unions, advocacy groups and grass-roots organizations are able to articulate demands and grievances.

"Businesses do not do this sort of thing out of a lack of self-interest, but perhaps out of philanthropic self-interest," a mining company executive said. And sometimes, corporate interests overlap with those of their challengers.

By publicly supporting the campaign against conflict diamonds, for instance, De Beers strengthened its position in the far more valuable market for clean diamonds. "They used the campaign to their advantage," Mr. Alley at Global Witness said. "If business can operate more responsibly, and make more money, that's ideal."

NORTH-SOUTH TENSIONS

October 1, 1980

McNAMARA CALLS ON WORLD BANK TO INTENSIFY FIGHT AGAINST POVERTY

By CLYDE H. FARNSWORTH

WASHINGTON, Sept. 30—Robert S. McNamara, in his valedictory address as president of the World Bank, said today that the agency had "barely begun to develop its full potential" as an institution of assistance to the poorest countries.

In an impassioned speech to representatives of 141 governments attending the 35th joint annual meeting of the bank and the International Monetary Fund, he warned that, despite advances of the last quarter-century, 600 million people were likely to be living in absolute poverty by the year 2000.

Mr. McNamara, 64 years old, will retire next June after 13 years as head of the bank, which is known formally as the International Bank for Reconstruction and Development; his successor has not been named.

Speaking shortly before President Carter delivered an official welcoming address, Mr. McNamara said global needs would require a tripling of the bank's annual lending rate by the mid-1980's. He called for considerably more support from its biggest shareholder, the United States.

Referring to Cyrus R. Vance, Mr. McNamara said: "The former Secretary of State called the United States' performance 'disgraceful,' and I agree with him."

He also singled out the Soviet Union, which is not a member of the bank, and Britain and Japan for criticism as shirkers of their aid responsibilities.

'Strong and Bold Vision'

In an emotional conclusion that drew a thunderous ovation in the ballroom of the Sheraton Park Hotel, the former Defense Secretary said a "clear, strong and bold vision" was needed to face the uncertain future.

Quoting George Bernard Shaw, he said: "You see things, and say why. But I dream things that never were, and I say why not." President Carter called for greater cooperation between oil producing and consuming countries in an address that seemed pale by comparison and drew only polite applause.

Mr. Carter devoted a substantial portion of his remarks to the world oil situation and implications of the Iran-Iraq war. "The world's oil stocks are at an all-time high, and these reserves will help to offset the effect of temporary reductions in supply such as that caused by the president conflict between Iran and Iraq," the President said.

"However, we are keenly aware that some nations are seriously threatened by even a temporary interruption. Thus we are working to end this conflict as quickly as possible."

The President pledged to urge Congress to release more funds to the World Bank, and, in an allusion to a conflict over representation of the Palestine Liberation Organization, said that neither the bank nor the fund should be "diverted by extraneous political disputes."

Persian Gulf oil states had sought observer status at this meeting for the Palestinian guerrilla group. The United States managed to defeat the effort, and negotiators are now hopeful that procedural compromises will be worked out to avoid a disruptive floor fight.

The World Bank lends about $12 billion a year to help countries strengthen their economies through construction of irrigation works, power stations, port facilities and other such projects.

Under Mr. McNamara, it has also been lending increasingly to improve housing, education, water and food resources to meet human needs.

Although Mr. McNamara has had great difficulty getting his own government to put up money for the World Bank, he has been given generally high marks by most in the third world for his zeal as a development technician and strategist.

Fund's Austerity Clauses

The Monetary Fund provides shorter-term loans to countries that are in balance-of-payments difficulties. Today these include just about all countries of the third world, expected as a group to record a deficit in trade and services this year of more than $70 billion.

The fund, because it applies conditions of belt-tightening for the loans it grants, is far less popular in the third world than the bank. The austerity-reduced consumption that can often be socially explosive—is intended to help countries "put their house in order"—the phrase used by economists to signify efforts to become self-supporting again.

"What kind of sense is it when the thatched roof of that house is catching fire, and the floods or blizzards are deluging in at the same time?" asked Amir H. Jamal, Tanzania's finance minister and chairman of the conference.

Mr. Jamal and other third world representatives argued that the burden of adjustment falls too heavily on the poor countries. They want greater third world control over both the bank and the fund, and two weeks ago at a special session of the United Nations conference called for oversight by that body, where they are dominant.

The United States and other developed countries are strongly resisting the pressure, fearful that financial integrity of the institutions would be threatened.

Jacques de Larosiere, managing director of the fund, spoke with some pessimism of the current economic climate. "I see no course of policy that could make the economic situation truly satisfactory over the next several years," said Mr. De Larosiere, formerly a ranking French Treasury official and a close friend of President Valery Giscard d'Estaing.

Mr. De Larosiere warned that the No.1 priority had to remain fighting inflation, even though many representatives of the third world openly fear the deflationary and recessionary consequences of further consumption cuts.

Mr. McNamara provided some World Bank numbers to demonstrate what is likely to lie ahead. Over the next five years, these show the average annual growth of developing countries at 1.8 percent, compared with 2.7 percent over the last decade and 3.1 percent in the 1960's.

"More depressing still," according to McNamara, is the outlook for the 1.1 billion people who live in the poorest countries. Their already-low per capita income of less than $220 a year is likely to grow by no more than 1 percent a year—an average of only $2 or $3 for each individual.

* * *

October 8, 1980

CARDINAL SAYS MULTINATIONALS BRING FAMINE TO AFRICA

By UPI

ROME, Oct. 7—A Roman Catholic Cardinal from Africa said today that the practices of multinational corporations bring "famine and destitution" to the people of his continent and the rest of the third world.

Paul Cardinal Zoungrana, Archbishop of Ouagadougou, Upper Volta, made his accusations at a Vatican news conference discussing the progress of the Fifth World Synod of Bishops that began Sept. 26.

"The bishops of Africa have stressed this exploitation of the poor," Cardinal Zoungrana said. "Poverty and dejection are imposed as a condition on the family. This pressure and oppression comes from the outside."

"This is direct oppression, he said, adding that the practice of multinationals "brings famine and destitution to families."

* * *

October 26, 1981

WITHOUT GUILT OR SHAME

By FLORA LEWIS

MIAMI, Oct. 25—For delegates who wanted rosy headlines, the Cancun summit conference on development was a great success because the U.S. accepted a distant pledge of "global negotiations." For others, it was a disappointment because no specific approach and no deadline was set.

Either way, the nebulous idea of some kind of universal free-for-all, where everyone would be asked to settle everything between industrial and developing countries, was offered as a test of progress.

"Global negotiations" is the code for all kinds of concessions from richer to poorer societies. The phrase has become a yardstick simply because there isn't any concrete measure for so vast a notion as a "new world economic order" supposed to result from some gigantic bazaar. So yes or no to "global negotiations" is supposed to identify the white hats from the black hats.

Of course, it doesn't mean much, as Britain's Margaret Thatcher said with her powdered smile. In fact, it wouldn't cost the U.S. a penny or feed a single child if everyone agreed on attempting the clear impossibility of settling anything that way.

Refusal to indulge in that particular kind of empty rhetoric merits no Brownie points, however. President Reagan offered his own Horatio Alger formula for poor countries to pull themselves up by their bootstraps through the "magic of the marketplace," and India's Indira Gandhi noted dryly that hundreds of millions have no boots to pull.

In fact, the U.S. shies away from "global negotiations" because they have come to imply windy debates in the United Nations where we are made the scapegoat for the world's ills, as well as more U.N.-type votes proclaiming the virtues of the needy. You can't vote wellbeing into existence, though you can toast to health and prosperity for all.

That makes politicians look better for a little while, and it even makes people feel a bit better because it seems to recognize they have as much right as anyone to a decent life and are not preordained to misery by some immutable natural hierarchy.

The main achievement of Cancun, however, was what didn't happen. Leaders of 22 countries managed to identify tangible global problems without just exchanging insults.

That is a key first step. The essential aim of the meeting was to shift the focus of North-South argument from slogans to realities. Slogans have gotten in the way of dealing with harsh facts.

The facts are that the world is producing people faster than it is producing goods to meet their basic needs; the political system of sovereign states and modern communications are producing demands for a better distribution of what there is; and knowledge that more could be done is producing an angry rejection of age-old assumptions that the pestilence of poverty can only be endured.

But if more and better is possible, why isn't it forthcoming? The temptation too easily accepted is to say that's because the rich are too selfish to share. President Reagan is right in answering that distributing shortages doesn't increase wealth—producing does. The leaders of the third world are right in saying good intentions fill no bellies—that takes substance.

The time has really come to move to the substance of the North-South problem, not only because it's immoral and unjust for people to suffer more than is avoidable, but also because world peace will depend on demonstrating that the possible is being done.

Tackling substance and doing the possible in the complex but feasible world of production and trade is harder than slogans make it sound. For countries that have developed the possible, it may only be a matter of will to provide aid, finance, investment, new techniques—in short, the money and brains that exist, but are never in sufficient supply.

For countries that only glimpse possibility from afar, however, the problem goes much deeper. It is a matter of identity and culture. They are really facing the question—though seldom admitted—of whether the same levels of material satisfaction are possible for them. Are modernization and well-being synonymous with Westernization? If so, these countries are doomed to be losers because they will never be as Western as the West.

Nobody has put the dilemma more honestly and more poignantly than V.S. Naipaul, the Anglo-Indian writer who has shown that talent, brilliance and inspiration are not the monopoly of any culture.

When painful candor replaces resentment and the sloth of frustration, today's world also shows that there is no monopoly on the capacity for management, organization and production. Have the Japanese become honorary Westerners or have they modernized within their own culture?

After Cancun, the West needs to move on and do what it knows it can do, without guilt. But the rest of the world needs even more to get on and be practical, without shame.

* * *

August 12, 1984

BRAZIL'S HARD LIFE WITH AUSTERITY

By ALAN RIDING

RIO DE JANEIRO—During one of their twice-yearly visits to Brasilia, economists from the International Monetary Fund this month will wade through reams of weighty documents in order to gauge the Brazilian Government's compliance with an austerity program worked out by the two parties late in 1982.

But a cursory glance at the country itself would provide them with ample evidence of the program's effectiveness: The economy as a whole is in its fourth year of recession, with much of industry struggling to stay afloat, while the living standards of all but a tiny elite are being eroded daily by inflation above 200 percent annually.

Signs of austerity are everywhere, from the street vendors competing for sidewalk space with derelicts in downtown Rio de Janeiro to the 300,000 construction workers who have lost their jobs in São Paulo. And no sector has escaped. Wage cuts have prompted hundreds of the Government's best-trained employees to leave for jobs with multinational corporations. University budgets have fallen by 60 percent in real terms since 1981, prompting many professors to strike. Small companies that export oranges or shoes are flourishing, while auto makers, appliance manufacturers and food processors trying to sell their products to Brazilians are in crisis.

Every morning, the flights to Brasilia from São Paulo and Rio de Janeiro are still full of businessmen. But a few years ago, they were arriving to compete for lucrative Government contracts; today, they fly to the capital to plead for long overdue payment on those contracts, which were completed months ago.

For most Brazilians, then, "austerity"—the standard medicine prescribed by the I.M.F. for ailing third-world economies—requires no proving. For them, the evidence that Brazil is being "governed" from abroad is overwhelming. Even in the two areas of special interest to the I.M.F.—Government spending and exports—the country is behaving well, pushing up exports at the expense of domestic consumption and spending less on a variety of Government programs. But what Brazilians have yet to see are the rewards—the economic recovery—promised by the I.M.F. in exchange for the sacrifice that is permitting the country to keep up with its foreign debt payments.

Brazil is a good case study of how an austerity program works, not only because of the country's size and complexity and its disciplined and successful response to the I.M.F. of late, but also because the impact of austerity on its economy and society is dramatically visible. Brazil is also a fair case to study because, at the time the fund entered the picture, Latin America's largest nation had already experienced two years of recession accompanied by tumbling per-capita income.

That raised and still raises the question whether the Government would have been forced anyway to impose unpopular austerity measures to revive the economy—even without the prodding of the I.M.F. The passions stirred in Latin America by the mere mention of the I.M.F. complicate the search for answers to this question.

The clouds began to gather over Brazil's economic "miracle"—its years of rapid economic growth and industrialization—as early as 1973 with the first sharp rise in world oil prices. But, despite its overwhelming dependence on imported oil, it chose to keep growing, depending increasingly on foreign borrowing to pay the oil bill. After the second oil price shock of 1979, however, a growing current account payments deficit forced the Government to retrench by cutting back Government expenditure and imports.

Like many developing countries, Brazil had required a high level of imports—and a permanent trade deficit—in order to sustain its rapid economic expansion during the 1960's and early 1970's. With the oil crisis, it was forced to accept a slower growth rate to keep the trade deficit under control. It achieved this partly by slashing imports needed for growth, including machinery and raw materials for its new factories, and partly by stimulating exports through a currency devaluation. The devaluation had the additional effect of feeding inflation and eroding local purchasing power.

The 1979 oil price rise had one salutary effect in that Brazil was at last prompted to invest heavily in developing alcohol as a gasoline substitute and in increasing domestic oil output. As a result, five years later, Brazil's oil import bill has fallen by half, to an estimated $5 billion this year. But new "external" shocks awaited the country, principally when Mexico's financial collapse in August 1982 led nervous foreign banks to cut back on new loans here.

Brazil still did everything possible to avoid turning to the I.M.F. It argued that it was voluntarily taking all the necessary austerity measures, but merely needed "new money" to deal with "cash flow" problems aggravated by high interest rates. Only when foreign banks linked disbursement of this money to an agreement with the fund did Brazil's long-time economic czar, Planning Minister Antonio Delfim Netto, swallow his pride and call in the I.M.F.

The fund arrived with the same prescription it has applied in developing countries for the past three decades—to reduce the public-sector deficit and to record a trade surplus large enough to finance foreign interest payments without excessive new borrowing. But to achieve these goals implied pushing the economy into a still deeper recession.

With no available alternative, the Government went about squeezing the economy into a different shape. Eighteen difficult months later, on the eve of the I.M.F.'s visit this month, Finance Minister Ernane Galveas was able to proclaim, "We're fabulous, aren't we?" because Government spending was down from $19 billion last year to an estimated $12 billion in 1984 and a $6.1 billion trade surplus in 1983 should be followed by an $11 billion surplus this year. Brazil was also up to date on its foreign debt interest payments—$12 billion is due this year—despite rising interest rates, while the Government was confident of negotiating new postponements for payment of the principal on its $93 billion debt maturing in 1985.

But Mr. Galveas's euphoria was shared by few Brazilians. In order to smother demand for imports and create the trade surplus, a "maxi-devaluation" of the cruzeiro early in 1983 and regular devaluations since then have pushed up the price of foreign goods. Cutbacks of public spending in a country where federal, state and municipal governments account for 50 percent of the gross domestic product have further reduced demand, and, with the elimination of many subsidies, fed inflation.

Last October, overriding strong protests from Congress, the Government also directly attacked wages, permitting twice-yearly increases equivalent to only 80 percent of inflation during the previous six months. With real wages falling ever farther behind an inflation rate that exceeded 200 percent in 1983 and will do so again this year, the cycle was repeated: Falling demand and production created new unemployment, which in turn affected demand and production and so on.

Only businesses involved in exporting and substitution of essential imports flourished. For example, farmers producing oranges for export to the United States and sugar cane for use in the alcohol fuel program did better than ever, while shoe manufacturers were encouraged to find new markets abroad to replace those that had collapsed at home. But their impact on the economy was limited.

The automotive industry—as in the United States, a sector that is highly sensitive to economic cycles—has suffered badly, with sales of new cars down 18 percent during the first six months of this year compared with the same period last year. But more than just General Motors and Ford, with big factories here, were affected: Hundreds of smaller suppliers of parts and services were also forced to lay off workers and shut down assembly lines.

Similarly, tumbling demand for domestically made appliances and other electrical goods and processed food—down 15 and 11 percent, respectively, between January and June this year—had a multiplier effect that was felt sharply in commerce. Rather than close their gates permanently, however, many manufacturing companies have declared themselves technically bankrupt and have suspended payments on their cruzeiro debts. Nationwide, industrial production has dropped by 22 percent since 1980.

One unexpected consequence of the slump is that the national confederations of industry and commerce have recently begun campaigning against the Government's wage law, which has put the legal minimum wage at the equivalent of $47 a month, about half its dollar value two years ago. The confederations argue that the law has deepened the recession without slowing inflation. "With wages losing 7 percent of their real value each month, how can we think about a recovery?" one businessman said.

The Government itself has not escaped the bite of "a crise," as the slump is known here. The budgets of such huge state enterprises as the Vale do Rio Doce mining company have been reduced by 15 percent, resulting in a slowdown of investment. In dollar terms, even the salaries of senior officials have fallen drastically, provoking a "brain drain" to better-paying jobs in multinational corporations. "The central bank must be working with its third team," one foreign bank representative complained. "You go in there and it's chaos, with papers piled high on desks. Many of the best people have deserted the ship." Reductions of federal and state budgets have in turn affected myriad other areas. Federal universities have been on strike for the past two months because the Education Ministry cannot meet the wage demands of professors who already "moonlight" to make ends meet. Three months ago, doctors in several states struck for the same reason, while police in Rio de Janeiro have threatened to stop work if their wages are not soon increased.

Brazil's social fabric has been particularly strained in congested urban areas. In São Paulo and Rio de Janeiro, unemployment—one million youths reach working age each year, but few can find job—has spawned an unprecedented crime wave which, more than anything, has brought home the reality of the crisis to the middle classes. They, too, have been forced to cut their spending—from trips abroad to visits to the movies—but the fear and reality of assaults and robberies have created a siege mentality and added to class tensions.

One recent morning, three men dressed in the uniforms of municipal bus drivers climbed on a bus in Rio de Janeiro and announced they were unemployed. The passengers immediately feared they were victims of a "routine" bus assault. "Look, we have children to feed," one said. "We don't want to rob or assault, but we need money. Whatever you can give will help us." Another man then passed around a shopping bag and most passengers dropped in the equivalent of a nickel or a dime.

In the absence of welfare payments for the unemployed, others who have lost their jobs—including not a few white-collar workers and professionals—improvise an income by selling everything from kites to candies on the streets, swelling an "underground" economy that includes many wives making clothes or shoes at home for sale to friends and relatives. The Government puts the unemployment rate at about 13 percent, but this does not attempt to count the under-employed.

The reduced real wage—the $47-a-month minimum is about one-third of what is considered necessary to support a family of four—have brought increased malnutrition and related ailments to a country that suffered from these problems even in the boom years. "The population has less access to food and medicines," Eduardo Costa, Secretary of Health for Rio de Janeiro state, said. "In the past, it was rare for our clinics to receive cases of extreme malnutrition, but we're getting more and more. At the same time as our budgets are being cut, there is a growing demand for medical attention.

One emergency clinic we studied is handling twice as many patients as a year ago."

At all levels, then, since Brazil turned to the I.M.F., its social crisis has worsened, but is this an unavoidable consequence of a "stabilization" program? In a recent article, the I.M.F.'s Managing Director, Jacques de Larosiere, implicitly denied responsibility by noting that "the fund cannot take upon itself the role of dictating social and political objectives to sovereign governments."

The institution would support financially squeezed governments willing to limit domestic consumption, increase domestic savings and expand exports, he said. "It is up to you, within the framework of macroeconomic parameters negotiated by mutual agreement, to arrange your own social and political priorities."

Clearly, the I.M.F. cannot be blamed for the economic troubles that force governments to appeal for its help. But once it becomes involved, many Latin economists believe it is unrealistic for the fund not to participate in setting the "social and political priorities" required to preserve stability during a period of austerity. This feeling is particularly strong in countries like Argentina where new civilian administrations are trying to consolidate democracy in the midst of economic disorder and meeting stiff public resistance to austerity measures. Brazil, too, is moving toward a change of Government, with a civilian administration to take over early next year from the military for the first time since 1964.

But with all the social and economic pressure, Brazil continues to play the game by the written rules, and this requires the regular approval of visiting I.M.F. missions for the nation's austerity program. In Brazil's case, the plaudits it expects from the I.M.F. this month may even be worth a cut in the interest rate on the foreign debt of half a percentage point in the country's next round of debt rescheduling.

* * *

December 5, 1984

GAS DEATHS IN INDIA EXCEED 1,000, WITH THOUSANDS HURT; GANDHI SEEKS COMPENSATION

By Reuters

BHOPAL, India, Dec. 4—At least 1,000 people were reported to have been killed by poison gas that leaked from an American-owned insecticide plant here Monday. Prime Minister Rajiv Gandhi broke off an election campaign tour to visit the city and said he would seek compensation.

A spokesman for the state government of Madhya Pradesh said the official death toll from the accident, one of the largest industrial accidents in history, had reached 546. But the United News of India said its reporters put the figure at 1,200.

Hundreds of Burials

The agency said that 345 victims had been buried at Bhopal's central Sirdaus Manzil graveyard and that 445 had

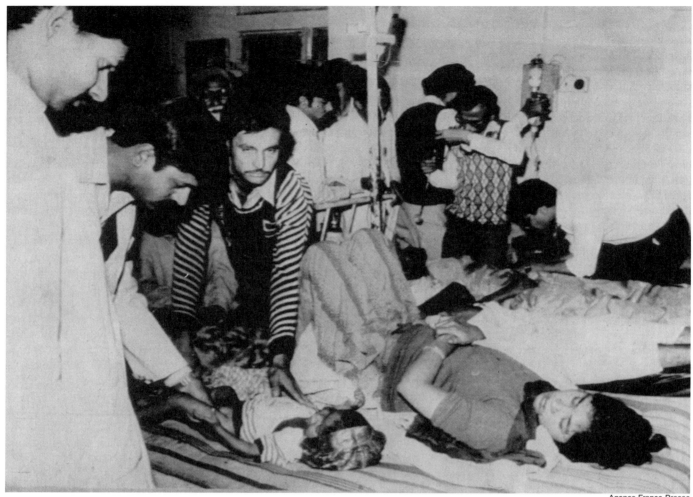

Agence France-Presse

Hospital personnel and relatives attending to people felled by toxic gas on Monday in Bhopal, India.

been cremated in an area of the city called Chola Vishram Ghar.

(The Associated Press quoted two doctors as saying that at least 1,000 people had been killed. They were quoted as saying that they counted 500 corpses at the city's major hospitals and had reports of at least 500 more dead at hospitals on the outskirts of Bhopal. Doctors said as many as 200,000 people were affected, the AP reported, and one doctor estimated that 20,000 might suffer serious aftereffects. Some women may be sterile, he said, and some victims may be blinded.)

Staff at city hospitals said 4,000 people had been badly gassed and some died in neighboring towns after fleeing Bhopal, 300 miles south of New Delhi, when the gas cloud spread over the city.

Gandhi Breaks Off Campaign

Mr. Gandhi, who toured the area and visited victims in various hospitals, said emergency steps had been taken to stop the spread of toxic effects of the gas on animals and crops. He gave no details.

Mr. Gandhi told a news conference that the disaster was "a result of planning in an uncontrolled manner." He added, "We are concerned not only about this plant but about similar places as well."

He told reporters his Government would review its policy on where to allow potentially hazardous factories to locate. Stringent safeguards would be introduced before such installations were allowed to operate, he said.

Mr. Gandhi also said compensation would be sought from the factory's owners, saying, "We will also ask Union Carbide to pay compensation."

Throughout the city, flags were flown at half-staff on offices. Stores, except for pharmacies, were shut. An acrid odor hung in the streets. The gas, identified as methyl isocyanate, escaped early Monday from one of three underground storage tanks at the Union Carbide Company plant, according to the chief minister of Madhya Pradesh, where Bhopal is located. The managing director of Union Carbide in India, Y. P. Gokhale, was quoted as saying Monday that a tank valve apparently malfunctioned after an increase in pressure, causing the gas to leak into the air for 40 minutes early Monday.

(A plant official, S. Mitra, said the gas had escaped from a 15-ton tank that had not been tapped since October, the AP reported. It quoted him as saying that so much pressure had built up within the tank that it had "overpassed" a safety filter. He said steps had been taken to prevent further leakage.)

The chairman of Union Carbide Limited, Keshub Mahindra, today expressed deep grief over the accident and said every effort would be made to help the families of those who died and were injured.

Meanwhile, leaders of a union at the plant accused plant management and the state government of "total apathy and negligence." The leaders, Madanlal Ganji and R. K. Yadav, said they had warned the management many times that working conditions at the plant must be improved.

Hundreds Are Blinded

Hundreds of people blinded by poisonous fumes groped their way through the streets in search of medical treatment.

Squatting on a hospital floor, a woman who identified herself only as Manorama said the fumes hit her around 1 A.M. while she was in bed with her two children.

"It was as if someone threw red chilies at my face," she said.

Manorama, her husband and the children ran out of their house, in a slum beside the factory, and collapsed on the road.

The police brought her to the hospital at about 7 A.M., a nurse said.

"Her husband was dead by then and the two children were missing," the nurse added.

Babu Khan, 45 years old, a laborer who lived near the factory, sat on the floor of a hospital corridor vomiting. His eyes were bloodshot, puffed and watering, and his voice was hoarse as he gasped for breath.

"My wife and children have been vomiting since yesterday," he said. "Now I don't even have the strength to sit up."

His 2-year-old son, who was blinded, asked for water but could not drink because of a sore throat.

500 on the Hospital Floor

Nearly 500 other victims lay moaning on the hospital floor, shivering in the morning cold.

Rahis Bano, 20, wept for a young son she left behind when escaping the fumes. "I could carry only one child," she said, "and now I don't know how to find my other son.

"I awoke when I found it difficult to breathe," she continued. "All around me my neighbors were shouting, and then a wave of the gas hit me."

She said she fell down vomiting. Her two sons rolled in agony beside her. She took the nearest child and ran outside before collapsing on the road, where she lay until volunteer rescue workers found her in the morning.

Inside the emergency ward, two patients shared each bed and young interns stood by to remove the dead.

Soldiers, policemen and students stood outside hospitals to help patients able to leave.

At the mortuary, bodies were draped with cloth and laid in a long row on the floor.

'Remove the Bodies Quickly'

A reporter visiting one hospital heard a senior pathologist telling doctors, "Remove the bodies quickly before they start to decompose."

Trucks waited outside the mortuary to load the bodies and take them to relatives, cremation grounds and cemeteries.

The city crematory ran out of wood for the traditional Hindu rites Monday. New supplies have arrived and there were rows and rows of burning pyres. Seventy fires could be seen burning at one time.

* * *

December 16, 1984

DISASTER IN INDIA SHARPENS DEBATE ON DOING BUSINESS IN THIRD WORLD; CORPORATION FORCED TO REASSESS RISKS AND TO REVIEW SAFETY RULES

By STUART DIAMOND

The escape of poison gas from a chemical plant in India on Dec. 3 has raised broad ethical, legal, social and technical questions for multinational corporations.

The questions concern not just chemical companies like the Union Carbide Corporation, which owns a majority interest in the plant at Bhopal, where at least 2,000 people died, but all companies that do business in developing nations, those that produce toxic materials anywhere and the governments that permit such production.

A Widening Debate

These issues, often confined to disputes among ecologists, politicians and corporate officials, are suddenly being debated throughout the world.

Demands are being made for basic changes in the way hazardous substances are produced, stored, shipped, regulated and explained to the public.

There is growing sentiment that some materials should not be produced in certain countries and that all multinational corporations should give greater emphasis to cultural differences that might increase the risks associated with products assumed to be safe.

A Lesson Is Seen

"This accident will be a lesson to all transnational corporations," said Noel J. Brown, a leading official of the United Nations Environment Program, which has studied hazardous materials for five years.

"This accident has brought into focus a wide range of questions that would otherwise have remained dormant," he added. "Local regulations, inspections, monitoring, maintenance, training, education, siting, cultural differences, corporate responsibility and the transfer of technology must be reviewed directly and quickly. And it must be done with broad cooperation between governments and industry."

Interviews of international experts since the Dec. 3 leak reveal a belief that responsibility for the accident is shared between the company and the Indian Government.

The Bhopal plant did not meet American standards, according to Union Carbide's own inspector, and had not been inspected by headquarters auditors in two and a half years. The Indian Government permitted thousands of people to live near the plant fence, and there were virtually no effective evacuation procedures, Indians familiar with the Bhopal plant say.

Role of Government

"Union Carbide plants in Germany, the United States and other countries are safer than Bhopal because the governments require it; why should it be different in India?" said Rashmi Mayur, a founder of the Urban Development Institute, a Bombay environmental research organization financed by the Government and private groups. "The Indian Government should have protected its citizens."

Among the issues raised by the Bhopal disaster, experts said, are these:

- The extent to which multinational companies should maintain identical standards at home and abroad, regardless of how lax the local laws may be.
- The advisability of locating a complex and dangerous plant in an area where virtually the entire work force is unskilled and the populace ignorant of the risks posed by such plants.
- The wisdom of laws that require the staffing of plants entirely by local workers.
- The responsibility of corporations and governments in allowing the use of otherwise safe products that become dangerous because of local conditions.
- The extent to which safer chemicals, drugs, equipment and methods are available.
- Whether, after reviewing the problems, companies should not locate a plant in a developing nation.

Union Carbide officials declined to be interviewed last week on these issues.

Issue Arose in 1970's

The issue of differing standards in different parts of the world arose in the 1970's, when American companies continued to export pesticides and drugs that were restricted in the United States after the rise of the environmental movement. The pesticides DDT, aldrin, dieldrin and others linked to cancer were used in developing countries, often by illiterate farmers who did not understand the needed precautions.

Poisonings occurred. In 1972 between 400 and 5,000 Iraqis died after consuming mercury-treated grain imported from the United States. In 1975 the Velsicol Chemical Corporation exported the unapproved pesticide leptophos, sold as Phosvel, which subsequently killed some Egyptian farmers and made many others ill.

Some companies built asbestos and pesticide plants overseas that would have violated American standards that entailed greater expense.

The companies usually violated no foreign laws, but after the Bhopal disaster a growing number of experts insist that corporations have a moral responsibility to enforce high standards, especially in countries unready or unable to regulate their operations.

'An Ethical Obligation'

"For the most part, the law in developing countries is not yet equipped to handle the high technology of multinational companies," said Frank J. Barros, a specialist in third-world issues at Developing Systems Ltd., a Washington economic consulting firm. "There is a lag between new technology and regulation. Companies have an ethical obligation to recognize this and to do everything in their power to follow the same safety standards they follow at home."

Efforts in the United States to pass laws that would force American companies to meet the same standards in domestic and foreign operations have been opposed by multinational interests. In 1981 Jack D. Early, president of the National Agricultural Chemicals Association, called such efforts "regulatory imperialism." Some argue that American companies are at a disadvantage against foreign multinationals that meet only the lower standards of the host country.

Mr. Barros said that issue "is a good question to argue before you have a catastrophe, which is very definitely an economic disadvantage." He suggested that the Bhopal disaster will dramatically change the cost-benefit analyses that companies typically perform, increasing the emphasis placed on longer-term business risks.

Principle and Practice

American chemical companies insist that in principle they treat all overseas operations the same. But in practice, they acknowledge, it does not always work that way, particularly when local interests control a plant's operation, as many governments in developing countries require.

The Pennwalt Corporation of Philadelphia, for example, owned 40 percent of a Nicaraguan chlorine and caustic soda factory that in the 1970's was the source of a major outbreak of mercury poisoning among workers and contaminated a lake that provided fish for Managua.

In 1978, after that incident, the board of directors of the Nicaraguan company approved a $3 million dividend while declining to install a $650,000 pollution control system. Peter J. McCarthy, Pennwalt's director of advertising and public relations, saying that his company's two board members had voted for the cleanup, added last week, "This puts American corporations in an extremely difficult position.

"If we had insisted that the Nicaraguans make the changes," he said, "we would be accused of being ugly Americans, the gringo who knows best. Instead, we were criticized in America for not doing enough." Pennwalt has ended its interest in the plant.

Union Carbide owns 50.9 percent of the Indian subsidiary that runs the Bhopal plant. A Union Carbide spokesman said the frequency of headquarters audits was determined by the corporation in India.

Perhaps the most significant issue raised by the disaster in India, most experts agree, is that people of developing countries often are not aware of the dangers of new technology.

"Three-quarters of the population of India doesn't know what ecology means and has no understanding of the concept of hazardous chemicals," Mr. Mayur declared. "There is no continuum of intelligence, as in the United States. There are only two layers: a thin veneer of highly skilled people at the top and hundreds of millions of people who don't have a basic understanding of industrialization at the bottom."

Without an "industrial culture," as Mr. Brown of the United Nations Environment Program put it, workers may master certain steps or techniques but cannot solve crises. "They have not internalized the technological culture," he said.

Minimal Training Cited

Union Carbide's 1982 audit of the Bhopal plant underscored that point.

Training, the inspectors' report said, comprised "rote memorization" without "a basic understanding of the reasoning behind procedures." The safety valve testing program, it said, "does not seem to be well understood." Maintenance people signed work permits they could not read, the inspectors said, and critical pressure gauges for toxic chemicals were broken.

There was a high turnover rate, they added, and "personnel were being released for independent operation without having gained sufficient understanding of safe operating procedures."

Many experts say that preventive maintenance is a concept alien to much of the developing world.

In the face of this unfamiliarity with technology, many governments in developing countries enforce policies designed to reduce automation and create more jobs. Some key safety systems at Bhopal relied on manual operation, according to C. S. Tyson, a Union Carbide inspector, because that approach requires more workers than the automated systems used here.

"Industries operating in the third world simply have not developed adequate training and education programs," contends A. Karim Ahmed, a Pakistani biochemist who is research director for the Natural Resources Defense Council in New York. Cultural differences raise significantly the risks inherent in some technologies, he said.

"Many people think of pesticides as beneficial medicine because they kill worms and bugs and help subsistence," he said. In Latin America, he added, "workers come home with their woolen parkas soaked with pesticides and sleep in them."

A similar problem faced Nestle S.A., a Swiss corporation, when mothers in developing countries, to hold down costs, began diluting its instant baby formula with unsanitary water.

After years of disputes, Nestle last year changed its marketing practices.

Thousands of Substances

Governments in developing countries often lack the staffs and the knowledge to study the thousands of substances that might be made or sold there by multinational corporations, and the United States has repeatedly balked at providing information.

In 1981 President Reagan canceled an executive order recently issued by President Carter requiring notification of a foreign government when a restricted substance was being exported. Twice since 1982, the United States has been the only United Nations member to vote against authorizing the publication of a list of products banned or restricted by 60 countries.

But even without technological sophistication, many governments insist upon a degree of control that multinational corporations increasingly find unacceptable, for business reasons as well as for reasons of safety and health. Both the International Business Machines Corporation and the Coca-Cola Company, for example, have declined to do business in India because they would not give up sufficient control to satisfy the Indian Government.

"We are now generally only interested in building plants where we can maintain not only majority ownership, but control over the operation," said Robert A. Smith, director of corporate safety for the Dow Chemical Company. He said the company had declined to expand and change plants in Brazil because of that country's restrictions.

Calls for Cooperation

There have been many calls for international cooperation. But the major motivating factor for companies to change their practices, many experts say, is financial, and that impetus will now increase. Union Carbide faces at least $35 billion in damage claims, and its stock has lost nearly $1 billion in aggregate value since Dec. 3.

"The operating assumption in many cases has been that a company in the third world has less regulation and less liability if things go wrong, so it can afford to have double standards," said Barry I. Castleman, a Baltimore consultant to Federal agencies and the United Nations. "If this accident shows that a company can't afford double standards, there won't be any."

*   *   *

November 10, 1985

U.S. SHOULD HEED THIRD WORLD DEMANDS

By JAGDISH N. BHAGWATI

The General Agreement on Tariffs and Trade has provided a mechanism that has facilitated the phenomenal postwar growth of world commerce. But it oversees only trade in goods.

Services, now estimated at up to a quarter of world trade, have no corresponding international pact that defines rules and procedures that govern their trade. For half a decade now, the United States has led efforts to fill this vacuum. But, at the November 1982 GATT interministerial meeting and again last month at an ad hoc senior ministers' meeting in Geneva, important developing countries led by Brazil and India adamantly opposed these initiatives.

Now, with the GATT annual meeting scheduled for Nov. 25, it can only be hoped that a conciliatory atmosphere can be created. For the confrontation is unfortunate, souring relations just at a time when compromise seems possible.

In recent years, the developing countries have abandoned impassioned rhetoric and confrontational tactics in favor of pragmatism. And the United States, as evidenced in the policy moves of the Treasury Secretary, James A. Baker 3d, at the I.M.F. and World Bank meeting in Seoul, South Korea, last month, has also taken a pragmatic, interventionist turn after years of ideologically inspired rigor mortis. But the atmosphere of confrontation threatens to push America, through ire and impatience, into opting yet again for bilateral and regional moves.

Developing countries must therefore be brought on board in the negotiations on international transactions in services. How can this be done?

The key lies in recognizing that our negotiating positions have unwittingly tended to press our advantages in services of interest to ourselves instead of seeking mutuality of interests within the broader service sector. To see how this has occurred, we need only to examine why the United States pressed the issue in the first place.

One factor, with which few would quibble, is the economic philosophy of free trade, and the obvious logic that it should apply to transactions in services as well as goods. However, the major thrust has been supplied by interest groups lobbying for particular service sectors, first multinational banks and corporations in the new "telematics" sector (satellite data transmission), and later, companies providing insurance, accounting and other business services.

These lobbies have buttressed their claims with arguments about the national interest, claiming that the nation's export advantages have shifted decisively to the service sector and away from manufacturing. They argue that it is unfair to open our markets to foreign goods while foreign markets are closed to our services. This is simply another instance of the increased demands for aggressive reciprocity.

The legitimacy of these claims, while certainly debatable, is not the issue here. The concern is that, by attending to the squeakiest wheels, the Administration has focused its energies mainly on those service sectors where we have the exporting edge. Conveniently omitted are those areas, such as construction, where our service businesses might face stiff competition from foreign businesses.

We have therefore encouraged the notion that service trade is for our export benefit, and trade in goods is for that of the developing countries. Thus, our concessions on trade in manufactured goods with developing countries have become a quid pro quo for their concessions on trade in services. Many developing countries find these aspects of our position unfair. If service negotiations are going to reflect the export interest of the developed countries, what do they get? We have suggested offering "rollbacks" on VER's (voluntary export restrictions) and "standstills" on new protection on goods of interest to developing countries.

But the developing countries correctly see all recent and threatened trade barriers on goods as de facto violations of GATT obligations anyway. Rollbacks and standstills are seen, therefore, not as concessions, but as compliance with existing GATT obligations. In short, since services are a new area not contemplated in the original GATT protocol, the developing countries think they are being offered a raw deal: an unrequited concession on services masquerading as a quid pro quo agreement!

We must recognize the legitimacy of this view and look for service sectors where the developing countries have the export edge. The quid pro quo must be sought within the service sector itself. Among the most obvious services in which many developing countries have recently acquired a trading advantage is construction.

South Korea, India, the Philippines, Egypt, Pakistan and a growing number of developing countries are already waiting to do in the developed countries what they have been doing in the Middle East: building highways, hospitals, schools and playgrounds, using skilled and unskilled labor from home.

Conceptually these are indeed services, and international transactions in them cannot legitimately be excluded from a services compact. Willingness to include them, and related transactions, in the negotiations that we seek would help convince the developing countries that the emerging discussion of the rules will be even-handed.

Since we would face obvious difficulties in moving to a free market in services such as construction, this role reversal would also make us more sensitive to the serious difficulties that the developing countries have in opening their markets, fast and fully, to services in which we have the export advantage. These also require special handling.

Other service sectors require special handling. Banking raises issues of fiduciary and monetary control. Several countries, therefore, have extensive, often excessive, regulation, extending, as in France and India, to substantial nationalization. In telematics, there is widespread fear of losing political control over a highly strategic sector of technology that promises increasingly to define economic and social evolution and thus to shape national destiny. These are sectors that independent-minded countries will not leave to the marketplace. The analogy has to be partly with armaments negotiations: We would not expect nation states to let market forces determine the location of defense production.

We cannot realistically expect that such service sectors can be brought altogether under a GATT-type "rule of law" trade regime. "Who gets what," not just "What rules do we play by," becomes a critical question.

A significant reduction of our demands here, as we simultaneously extend the proposed pact to services like construction, is necessary.

Jagdish N. Bhagwati is professor of economics at Columbia University.

*   *   *

February 21, 1988

BUSINESS FORUM: MULTINATIONALS AND THE THIRD WORLD

Sell Solutions, Not Just Products

By KLAUS M. LEISINGER

Some say multinational corporations threaten the economic and political independence of developing countries and represent one of the greatest obstacles to development. Others find progress in the third world inconceivable without companies operating on an international scale. Multinationals, they say, transfer technologies, as well as exemplary standards for production safety, the environment and social responsibility.

In truth, neither extreme paints the complete picture. Multinationals today are as heterogeneous as developing nations. Some export high technology to the third world to promote development. Others refuse to do so, transferring intermediate technologies instead. Some restrict their activities purely to business. Others also get involved in charitable projects. Generalizations will not do.

The special responsibilities that corporations take on in dealing with developing nations do bring trouble and expense in the short and medium term. At Ciba-Geigy, we find that sometimes it takes years for the company to see the benefits from its third-world activities.

Since markets in industrialized nations are usually more attractive, why get involved in the third world at all? Because the problems of underdevelopment constitute the most pressing social issue of the 20th century. All who can contribute to solutions must do so, not only out of humanitarian motives but also in the interest of insuring long-term peace.

What's more, in recognizing their special responsibilities and working sensitively in developing countries, multinationals can expect a smoother and more sustained market development in the long run. In other words, good ethics is good business.

The ethical challenges of doing business in the third world can be met in two mutually reinforcing ways. Corporations should develop policies—a kind of internal code of conduct—for sensitive areas like marketing, product quality and environmental protection. Not everything that is legal locally is ethical. And they should nurture managers who can act on what Pope John Paul II called a "unity of knowledge and conscience."

The challenge often also requires extra effort. Ciba-Geigy, for example, was recently approached by the agricultural ministry of a rice-growing sub-Saharan African country. The ministry was interested in one of our pesticide products.

So, together with the country's government, we undertook a scientific investigation to determine the specific pest problem. We created an organizational infrastructure—including reporting lines and job descriptions—so that all of those involved, within and without Ciba-Geigy, knew exactly what part they played in the project.

We also trained local farm workers to use our product, oversaw the pesticide's safe application and began an educational project that eventually reached 40,000 farmers. The monetary return on investment in this project has been far below the average profit for Ciba-Geigy's agricultural operations. But our corporate policy allows for extending profit expectations over the longer term in third-world projects.

Other rules in our own code of conduct include having no differences between industrial and developing nations regarding quality of products and services, product safety, instructions for use and production safety. We also call for pursuing the same goals in the third world as anywhere else when it comes to environmental protection. This mostly means far exceeding local standards.

Of course, international development cooperation—private and public—can only facilitate or at best accelerate approaches already in place on the local level. It cannot be a substitute for them. Responsible leaders in third world countries must design specific development processes themselves and keep them going by working with all sectors of the population.

But an adherence to certain principles can improve the corporate contribution to development policy—a policy of avoiding aggressive marketing in traditional societies, for example, or a commitment to selling solutions rather than products.

It would be unrealistic not to take seriously the conflicts that always arise between the pressures to increase sales in the short term and the need to preserve sound business in the long term. But such basic conflicts can be made less serious.

At Ciba-Geigy, we put salesmen in developing areas on minimal commission so that there is no pressure to cash in and disappear. We do not want to tempt our customers to buy something they can't use correctly. The aim is to warn, explain and develop long-term understanding.

In 1977, in response to an initiative by the World Health Organization, we founded a subsidiary, Servipharm Ltd., to offer a wide range of high-quality pharmaceutical products and services at low cost to people in developing countries.

Servipharm has supplied products to about 900 million patients in 60 countries. We hoped to get a return on our investment in five years; 10 years later, we still haven't made a profit. Nevertheless, we continue to operate the company and have not given up the hope of seeing a return.

We have also set up a charitable unit, the Ciba-Geigy Foundation for Cooperation with Developing Countries, that supports agricultural research and works with a host of international agencies.

Corporate policies conceived with realism, as well as enlightened self-interest, are thus one precondition for a successful approach to business ethics in the third world.

An emphasis on picking the right managers is also of overriding importance. Initiatives to develop appropriate policies and make them part of the corporate reward-and-punishment system must come from the top. But any institutional ethic, code of conduct or corporate policy is only as good as the executives handling it.

Companies must help these managers go beyond entrepreneurial skills to develop virtues such as humility, sensitivity and social responsibility. Ethical corporate conduct needs individuals who find themselves forced to account for their motivations and who are able to gauge the likely consequences of their activities.

There is growing international sensitivity to the non-economic consequences of economic activity. The actions of major institutions are being questioned more than ever. In the long run, real or perceived unethical conduct is likely to put the social acceptability of the activities of multinationals and the credibility of the free market system at stake.

Only if entrepreneurs offer constructive solutions to important societal problems in an ethically acceptable way will they enjoy freedom of action. Ethical conduct in third world business—and in business everywhere—is vital to the long-term existence of any corporation.

Klaus M. Leisinger is director of third world relations at Ciba-Geigy Ltd.

*   *   *

March 29, 1992

A REVOLUTION TRANSFORMS INDIA: SOCIALISM'S OUT, FREE MARKET IN

By EDWARD A. GARGAN
Special to The New York Times

NEW DELHI, March 28—George Fernandes, a Socialist member of Parliament and a former Minister of Industry, spoke nostalgically about the time he threw Coca-Cola out of India.

"When I chucked out Coca-Cola in 1977, I made the point that 90 percent of India's villages did not have safe drinking water, whereas Coke had reached every village," he recalled. "Do we really need Coke? Do we need Pepsi?"

Now, to his great dismay, not only is Coke coming to India; but Pepsi is already back. So are I.B.M., General Motors, Corning Glass and Kellogg. But the influx of foreign investment is just the edge of an economic revolution that is sweeping across this land where 850 million people average just $350 in income annually.

Over the last eight months, India has begun the tortuous process of transforming its sclerotic, largely state-controlled economy while abandoning the insularity that has left it lagging economically far behind virtually every other Asian country.

The socialist principles on which India was founded in 1947 by its first Prime Minister, Jawaharlal Nehru, have been jettisoned. Gone is the belief that the state should determine the nature and pace of economic growth. Gone is the attitude that consumerism is evil. Gone is the notion that links with the outside world imply the destruction of Indian sovereignty.

In rapid succession, India's Finance Minister, Manmohan Singh, a Sikh technocrat with a cherubic smile, ordered a sharp devaluation of the overvalued rupee, a slashing of the Government's budget deficit, and the abolition of a wide range of restrictive licenses on industry, including crippling import licenses.

Mr. Singh cut subsidies to the country's farmers, none of whom pay taxes, began the process of closing bankrupt public-sector industries, offered the first tentative proposals for sweeping tax reform, and began energetically wooing foreign investment.

In no small measure, the collapse of the Soviet Union, India's main economic, military and ideological benefactor since independence, shed the harshest of lights on the country's economic inadequacies.

"There have been in the last 20 years studies on the need for this kind of reform," said Surendra L. Rao, the director general of the National Council of Applied Economic Research, a private research institute. He said both Prime Minister Indira Gandhi and Rajiv Gandhi, her son and successor, had initiated economic reforms but failed to sustain them.

"If we had continued those trends, much of what we would have seen would have been gradual reform over the last 10 years," Mr. Rao said. "But we didn't."

As a result, India's economy, sagging under an increasingly onerous burden of state spending and borrowing, has been a major underlying factor in the nation's recent political turbulence, including three Prime Ministers in the course of 18 months. After the assassination last year of Rajiv Gandhi during the national election campaign, the victorious Congress Party turned to a dour, longtime party official, P. V. Narasimha Rao, as a compromise Prime Minister, the least likely to offend or harm any of the party's powerful factions. Mr. Rao, 70 years old and thought to be in poor health, was almost universally viewed as a transitional figure.

But, to the surprise of both his party and the opposition, Mr. Rao seemed electrified by his sudden ascent to power. He quickly reached out to a group of economic technocrats to salvage the country's economy and ordered the sweeping transformation of India's economic and financial structure.

"It had become clear that India was definitely out of control," Mr. Rao said of the economic council. "The Indian Government was borrowing heavily on the foreign and domestic markets. People began to see that we had this huge expense on government, defense, on the public sector. The balance of payments situation was the immediate trigger. We were about to default."

Indian security forces holding back opposition-party demonstrators protesting the budget at a rally last week in New Delhi.

With the help of more than $3 billion in loans from the International Monetary Fund and the World Bank, India staved off default, but with the loans came obligations to both international agencies to restructure the nation's economy radically. Unlike his predecessors, the Prime Minister agreed.

Ramesh Vangal, the managing director of Pepsi Foods Ltd., recalled the struggle to enter the Indian market. "We made our first application in 1985," he said. "At that stage a project like soft drinks was not allowed. It was rejected in two months fairly peremptorily."

Undeterred, Pepsi pushed forward over the next year, broadening its proposal to include food processing and snack foods.

But some of India's soft-drink makers cried foul and attributed all sorts of crimes to Pepsi, ranging from the threat to the nation's foreign exchange reserves to murky ties with the Central Intelligence Agency. That the charges were groundless was irrelevant. What mattered was the political clamor they stirred, a clamor that effectively prevented Pepsi from being sold to India's consumers.

An Unacceptable Name

"The bogies that had been raised on Pepsi made the Government wary to do anything," Mr. Vangal said. "To operate here

you need about 100 operating licenses. At the top they may make the macro decision, but it still has to percolate down. At that time, general foreign investments were not welcomed."

In July 1990, Pepsi finally began operations. But India's bureaucrats were not through. The Government vetoed Pepsi's plan to label its bottles sold in India "Pepsi Era." "They said, 'It's not Indianizing the foreign brand name,' " Mr. Vangal said. "So they chose the name 'Lehar Pepsi.' "

In a reflection of the xenophobia that hampered access to India's markets, foreign products sold here were required to have Indianized brand names, like Modi Olivetti, Hero Honda and Maruti Suzuki.

Now all that has changed, and products will be allowed to be sold under their own brand names. Coca-Cola, the company evicted from India by Mr. Fernandes, will be one of the first investors to benefit. Rajan Pillai, an Singapore-based Indian industrialist, announced recently that he would bring Coke back to India. "We're moving in the right direction in India," he said. "Under this arrangement, Coke will maintain its secret formula," a guarantee that would have been inconceivable only months ago.

Other investors, many of them American, are also testing the waters with small projects in India. I.B.M. has teamed up with Tata Industries Ltd., a large industrial company, to man-ufacture computers, and Corning Glass has just won permis-sion to produce the shells for television picture tubes.

Distrust Still Runs Deep

Limits remain, to be sure, including the Indian insistence that no more than 51 percent of an enterprise can be owned by a foreign company, a condition that places India at a distinct disadvantage with the rest of Asia, including its adversary and neighbor, Pakistan.

Moreover, distrust of foreign investment still runs deep here, fed by experiences like the gas leak at the Union Car-bide plant at Bhopal in 1984, which left 4,000 people dead and tens of thousands permanently injured, a catastrophe that soured much of the political establishment on an increased foreign presence.

Despite the flurry of high-profile investments, there is still a widespread acknowledgement that in comparison with the rest of the region India has a long way to go. "It's peanuts," said a senior Western diplomat concerned with commercial issues. "The reforms haven't filtered down through the bureaucracy. The regulations are gone, but the regulators are still in place."

This week, as Finance Minister Singh addressed a gather-ing of foreign and Indian bankers and industrialists in the ballroom of one of this city's sumptuous hotels, a goat herder outside, dressed in a long-tailed, soiled kurta, scurried around his flock as he maneuvered its wayward members past the hotel's soaring, guarded entryway. Inside, Mr. Singh spoke dispassionately about the boldness of India's economic poli-cies. For his part, the goat herder moved off toward the pas-tures of Buddha Jayanti Park, following the rhythms of pastoralism, seemingly indifferent to the hum of urban life around him.

Labor Fights Dismissals

This contrast illustrates India's daunting problem of trying to modernize to ease entrenched poverty and escape the bur-dens of its past.

The Finance Minister has observed that it is still not clear how the Government will close the 90 of India's 244 enor-mous state-owned industries that are completely bankrupt; these "patently unviable" enterprises, to use Mr. Singh's phrase, employ some 800,000 people and taxed state coffers $750 million in 1990. Although Mr. Singh has said they must shut down, India's socialist traditions have made industrial layoffs all but impossible.

To that end, the World Bank has agreed to provide $500 million to create a National Renewal Fund, which would be used to retrain laid-off workers. But India's powerful trade unions, many organized over the years by the country's left-wing parties, have taken to the streets frequently in the last few months to protest any dismissals. On Friday, workers in the country's state-owned banks went on a one-day strike to protest Government plans to make the banks more effi-cient, in part by introducing computers, and to allow greater freedom for foreign banks to operate in India.

But as in the economic restructurings in Eastern Europe and Latin America, the pain of adjustment is inevitable. In India's tumultuous political environment, if the pain of aus-terity becomes too severe, Mr. Rao's Government could be forced from power.

"In India's case, there has to be a general measure of pop-ular approval," said Lal Kishan Advani, the leader of the parliamentary opposition and president of the Bharatiya Jan-ata Party, a Hindu revivalist political party.

Mr. Advani's own party, while publicly committed to the virtues of free enterprise and the demise of socialism, has been torn in recent weeks by a bitter battle over foreign investment.

Some party members, particularly those vehement in their espousal of Hindu religious and cultural supremacy, see for-eign investment as eroding Indian culture and values and have called for a ban on all foreign products. Others in the party, including Mr. Advani, while not endorsing the ban, have urged some restrictions.

"Multinationals," he said, using a word that evokes enor-mous emotional antipathy among Indians, "should be con-fined to high-tech areas. We need not bring in multinational corporations in consumer durables and low-tech areas."

But the central problem now confronting Mr. Singh and his technocrats in the Finance Ministry is the threat posed by inflation. Many prices in India have been suppressed by stat-ute or custom for years. In Calcutta, rents have not been raised on most apartments since the 1930's. As the Govern-ment tries to let the market regulate the supply of goods and services, many politicians and economic analysts are worried that the entire reform process could easily become derailed.

From the perspective of India's leftists, the standard-bear-ers of India's past, the sudden economic changes are threat-ening everything they have worked for. "The state has been hijacked by the elite," Mr. Fernandes said, "by the Indian upper caste, the Western-educated elite. I believe in the model of Mahatma Gandhi, who spoke of a wholly decentral-ized state and a plan which puts emphasis on human resources. There'll be a tremendous fight back. This whole concept of privatization will be fought by the workers. The fear of losing jobs is there."

Yet, as the Prime Minister deftly shepherds his latest bud-get, a document that further cements the economic transfor-mation of his country, through Parliament, there is a growing confidence that the past is being left behind. As Business World, a leading business magazine, put it in its latest issue: "The Indian economy is savoring the spirit of freedom for the first time in its post-independence history. The funeral rites of the command economy mark the end of a sorry chapter which witnessed the grounding of an entire generation's hopes and aspirations for prosperity."

*   *   *

September 7, 1994

A BOOM, FOR THE FEW

Latin Economic Speedup Leaves Poor in the Dust

By NATHANIEL C. NASH
Special to The New York Times

PENALOLEN, Chile—The much-hailed economic recovery in almost all of Latin America has politicians and Government economists preaching the benefits of open markets, privatization, fiscal discipline and deregulation.

It would seem they have good reason. Having put aside the politics of protected markets and nationalism, and welcomed vast new foreign investment, the region's economies are expected to grow an estimated 3 percent this year. That would be the fourth consecutive year of such growth, the most robust economic expansion in Latin America in decades.

But if things are so rosy, why did peasants rise up this year in southern Mexico? Why has Venezuela had two coup attempts and continued unrest? Why have Bolivian workers staged national strikes? And why, in Argentina, considered a stellar example of economic transformation, did workers burn a provincial government building last December and march on the capital this summer?

Bernardo Ruz, a 22-year-old electrician living in this Chilean shantytown outside Santiago, the capital, has one explanation.

"The rich are making a lot of money, but we're not," he said. "There are a lot of fancy buildings that have been built, making the big businessman richer. The humble people like us got jobs for a while, but that is over. I haven't had work in months and everything is now more expensive. We've forgotten what meat tastes like."

The tiny, drafty wooden shack in which he lives with his 17-year-old wife, Ibe, and their 18-month-old son, Hua-yasqui, has no heat, and it is unlikely to for years to come. The Ruzes, along with several hundred other families, claimed this piece of land two years ago by invoking squatters' rights. They cannot afford the investment of building secure homes until they get title to the land. They steal water from a nearby pipeline.

Indeed, for all the benefits of Latin America's new economics—the revamping of industry, the new jobs, the controlling of inflation, the stabilization of currencies and the relatively stable process of democracy—millions of people have been left out.

Some politicians at the national level invoke the need to fight poverty and to help those living on the margins of society. But they are generally far more inclined to point to economic successes like the rise in foreign investment, their latest privatization deals or the renegotiation of debt with international lending organizations.

The neo-liberal economic model came to be adopted as governments realized that closed economies, with their high barriers to imports, left them isolated and woefully outmoded in their industrial base.

In many countries, the last four years of growth will statistically almost make up for the vast loss of spending power in the 1980's, often called the "lost decade" because of the region's debt crisis, a deep recession and a loss of investor confidence.

Rich in natural resources, Latin America is now a favored investment site for world-class corporations. And with Mexico, likely to be followed by other Latin countries, entering into the North American Free Trade Agreement, economists are predicting continued good times through the end of the century.

New Wealth Flows, But Not for All

But economic growth has been highly uneven. The new wealth has flown mostly to the rich, as wealthy families that

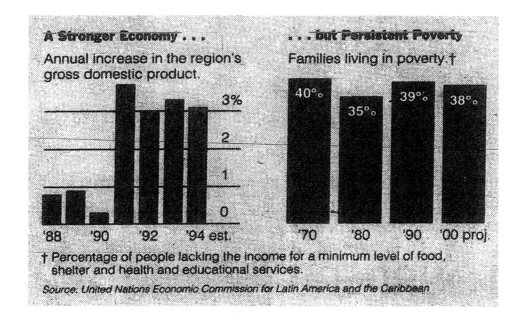

A Stronger Economy . . .
Annual increase in the region's gross domestic product.
'88   '90   '92   '94 est.

. . . but Persistent Poverty
Families living in poverty †
40%   35%   39%   38%
'70   '80   '90   '00 proj.

† Percentage of people lacking the income for a minimum level of food, shelter and health and educational services.

Source: United Nations Economic Commission for Latin America and the Caribbean

made money doing work for the Government made even more money buying up Government assets. New jobs tend to be either short-term, low-paying construction jobs or highly paid managerial jobs. Many in the middle class lost work when state payrolls were cut or when managers at newly privatized companies slashed work forces.

Others say investment has been focused on the capitals, leaving more remote areas struggling, with little hope in the near-term that new foreign investment will reach them.

Nor is there much optimism among the tens of millions of people living in vast shantytowns throughout the continent.

"The resumption of economic growth has been bought at a very high social price, which includes poverty, increased unemployment and income inequality, and this is leading to social problems," said Louis Emmerij, an economist and specialist on social reform at the Inter-American Development Bank, in Washington.

United Nations economists say that despite projected economic growth through the end of the century, no progress will be made in reducing poverty, creating the potential for more social unrest. Poverty is even likely to increase slightly. As of 1986, 37 percent of the region's families were living in poverty; by 2000, the economists say, the figure will be 38 percent, or 192 million people.

"The coming years will be quite difficult for these countries," said Peter Jensen, regional coordinator for human settlements at the United Nation's Economic Commission on Latin America and the Caribbean, in Santiago. "Growth has been really on only one end of the spectrum, the wealthy. The rich are getting richer and the poor are getting poorer. And this will generate social conflict."

A $110 Billion Bill For Decent Housing

For the purpose of statistics, the United Nations defines Latin America as stretching from the Rio Grande to Tierra del Fuego, embracing the Caribbean islands and Central and South America.

Mr. Jensen estimates that 10 million families, or 46 million people, are without homes in the region. Another 18.4 million families, or 85 million people, live in homes in such poor condition that they should be demolished. Still another 23 million homes, housing more than 100 million people, many of whom consider themselves part of the middle class, lack water, electricity or proper construction. The population for the region in 1990 was 441 million.

The bill for providing proper housing would exceed $110 billion, Mr. Jensen said.

All this is not to say that the economic experiment over the past five years was misguided, or that the flood of new investment has not been critical to the region's recovery, or that new investment and economic growth in the long term are not the answer to reducing poverty, most economists say. But long-term means several decades, and misery and unrest are growing.

Though no one is predicting that over the next few years Latin American voters will reject leaders who have espoused open markets, there are signs that patience with being told to wait for trickle-down benefits is wearing thin.

The uprising in January of peasant Indians in the Mexican state of Chiapas, which sent shock waves through many capitals, was viewed as a result of Mexico's inattention to rural poverty and of delays in land reform.

Official corruption has also stirred unrest. The army officers who made two coup attempts in Venezuela last year cited corruption as their justification.

Economic discontent is palpable in a number of big cities. In Buenos Aires, the number of homeless people is increasing, as is the number of poor who pick over trash on the street.

"When people ask me about the Menem-Cavallo plan and all of its greatness, I tell them about my conversations with taxi drivers in Buenos Aires," said Ernesto Sabato, a noted Argentine writer, referring to President Carlos Saul Menem and Economy Minister Domingo F. Cavallo. "I always ask a taxi driver what he used to do. They are former engineers, businessmen, teachers, almost anything. And you say this is not explosive?"

Even With Progress, Unrest Continues

To be sure, not all Latin American countries are experiencing the same income gaps. According to the United Nations, Brazil continues to have the widest gap between rich and poor and is the one dominant country on the continent that has yet to tame inflation and open its economy to international competition and investment.

Countries like Chile, Colombia, Costa Rica and Argentina have shown the most economic growth since the 1980's, but that does not exempt them from social unrest.

Chile has made the greatest inroads against poverty, bringing almost a million people out of poverty over the past four years, but it has been unable to improve living conditions much in the shantytowns.

Hyperinflation in Argentina pushed the poverty rate to 20 percent of the population in 1989. Reining in inflation brought the figure down to 10 percent by last year. But since then poverty rates have increased again, as unemployment has doubled, to almost 12 percent.

In Bolivia, inflation has been tamed since the mid-1980's, but economic growth has barely exceeded that of its population, so little progress has been made against poverty.

In Peru, where a severe economic adjustment under President Alberto K. Fujimori has brought down inflation, the restrictions on Government wages, the shrinking of the economy and the dislocation of workers have been staggering. Just last year, the economy began to grow again after years of decline, and the Government hopes the billions of dollars from the sale of its state industries will help. But economists fear that the Government is too optimistic.

It is not clear how politicians will react to the growing unrest among voters about how slowly economic change reaches them, nor how long voters will support leaders oriented to the free market.

In Bolivia, anti-privatization sentiment is so great that President Gonzalo Sanchez de Lozada has had to promise to place in the hands of all Bolivians a large portion of the stock in privatized companies.

The Pudding's Proof, Public and Private

What most economists say is that the "obvious" policy changes—privatization and opening doors to investment—have been made and that the hard part now begins: restructuring provincial governments, creating competent bureaucracies and getting the private sector to accept slightly higher taxes.

The return could be a better-trained work force and surer prospect of political stability.

"Governments also need to get serious about social spending programs," said Sebastian Edwards, chief economist at the World Bank for Latin America.

Finally, social programs remain to be developed, economists say, without returning to deficit spending.

"The great debate for Latin America over the next 20 years is, how do you spend the money generated by these huge inflows of capital?" said Miguel Angel Broda, a Buenos Aires economist. "There are two ways to go, the European rout of the big social-welfare state, or the American model."

"The U.S. has created 41 million new jobs over the past 22 years, with five out of six in the private sector. In Europe, during the same period, eight million new jobs have been created with 6 out of 10 in the public sector. Given our history, if Latin America goes the European way, we don't have a chance."

Indeed, what the poor in Latin America want may not be to sit on the boards of major corporations. Mr. Ruz, for his part, said he had no desire even to ascend into the ranks of the middle class—he does not covet an office job, for example, or a house in a bourgeois neighborhood, or an array of consumer appliances.

"We are a humble family and we want to stay that way," he said. "But we want enough food to eat."

* * *

September 2, 1997

TRADE ACCORDS THAT SPREAD THE WEALTH

By ROBERT B. REICH

CAMBRIDGE, Mass.—The contest at United Parcel Service may be over, but a much larger labor battle begins in just a few weeks when the Clinton Administration introduces a "fast track" bill to make it easier for the President to negotiate trade deals.

The White House needs such legislation in order to extend the North American Free Trade Agreement to Chile and the rest of Latin America, and to expand trade with Southeast Asia. Organized labor and (if you believe opinion polls) a large percentage of Americans on the bottom half of the income ladder don't want more trade with developing nations.

And here is the crux of the problem: more trade is good for the American economy over all, yet not necessarily for all Americans. Trade hasn't been the main cause of the widening gap between rich and poor during the past decade and a half, but surely it has played a role—accounting for perhaps a quarter to a fifth of the nearly 20 percent increase in wage disparities between skilled and unskilled worker.

Trade on a far greater scale with poorer countries presumably will widen the gap still further. The only way to prevent such downward competitive pressure, say some opponents of fast track, is to condition such trade on a developing nation's willingness to raise its wages and working conditions to a level approximately as high as our own minimum standards.

Yet any such requirement would be protectionism in another guise. Most nations of Latin America and Southeast Asia cannot afford to meet our labor standards. Their economies aren't rich or productive enough. If global companies had to meet minimum United States standards in Latin America or Southeast Asia, they simply wouldn't build factories there.

What level of wages and working conditions should we expect developing nations to achieve? Is it any business of ours to begin with? These are moral as well as economic questions. It's unrealistic to expect that workers in poorer nations will receive American-style wages and working standards. But we can and should insist that as these nations become steadily wealthier, their bottom-rung workers do better. The benefits of trade and growth should be widely shared.

Our national interest does not lie in protecting American jobs from cheaper goods produced by lower-wage workers in developing nations. Yet the United States has a legitimate interest in spurring the creation of broad middle classes in these nations—large enough to buy our export goods, strong enough to stabilize democratic institutions, confident enough to affirm our values about how human beings should be treated at work. To the extent that the benefits of economic growth in these countries are concentrated in narrow economic elites, while the ranks of the poor stay the same or even increase, these aims are thwarted.

In many developing nations, the record to date has not been encouraging. The widespread adoption of market reforms, including deregulation and more open trade, has boosted growth rates: Latin America as a whole is now growing at a rate of over 3 percent a year, up from 1.5 percent in 1988. In Southeast Asia, growth has soared during the past decade.

But too often, the gaps between rich and poor have widened, and middle classes have shrunk. The United Nations Conference on Trade and Development reported last month that in almost all developing nations that have rapidly liberalized trade, inequality has increased as the wages of unskilled workers have dropped—by 20 to 30 percent in some Latin-American countries.

Fast-track legislation should commit the United States to negotiate trade accords requiring developing nations to spread the benefits of economic growth. At the very least, we should insist that as their economies grow, their minimum wages should rise in tandem, workplace health and safety standards should become stricter, and the minimum age for child labor should increase.

These nations should establish credible means of independently monitoring and enforcing these rising standards, and their workers should be able to organize unions so that they have the bargaining leverage they need to press for continuing gains.

Such a principle of steadily increasing wages and working standards in proportion to a nation's capacity to afford them is consistent with new initiatives by global lending institutions.

Until very recently the International Monetary Fund focused almost exclusively on getting developing nations to deregulate and open their markets. But several weeks ago the fund extended a line of credit to Argentina on the condition that it give priority in public spending to improving health and education and reducing poverty. I.M.F. officials are now saying that long-term growth depends on more than open markets; it requires political stability and broad middle-class prosperity.

American manufacturers in developing nations should be guided by the same principle. Clothing and sneaker manufacturers with factories in Latin America and Southeast Asia face growing criticism for running "sweatshops." The companies claim they're just paying the going wages, even at pennies an hour, and doing what every other employer does there, like employing young teen-agers for long stretches at a time.

"The minimum standards have to be put in place by the governments involved," says Andrew Young, the former United Nations Ambassador, who was recently hired by Nike to inspect and report on its overseas plants.

While we cannot expect American companies to give their third-world employees United States levels of wages and working conditions, we should expect something more from them than merely following accepted practices or meeting minimum legal requirements in these nations. American companies should exert leadership by being among the first to raise their workers' pay and to improve working conditions in line with productivity gains.

Third-party monitors should assure American consumers that our companies are setting the rising trend.

Ultimately, if America is to make a convincing case for sharing the fruits of growing prosperity within developing nations, it must dedicate itself to the same principle at home. The most advanced of all advanced nations is now enjoying its most buoyant economy in decades, but median incomes are scarcely rising, and a large fraction of the American work force has been losing ground. A backlash against trade is but one consequence of the top-heavy gains of economic growth here at home. Surely in this era of extraordinary prosperity, we, too, can afford to do better for all our people.

Robert B. Reich, former Secretary of Labor, teaches social and economic policy at Brandeis. His most recent book is "Locked in the Cabinet."

*   *   *

June 17, 1998

G.M.'S PLANT IN BRAZIL RAISES FEARS CLOSER TO HOME

By KEITH BRADSHER

DETROIT, June 16—The strikes now crippling General Motors, while partly about short-term job security and workplace safety disputes, reflect a larger struggle over how far G.M. will go in adopting at home the manufacturing techniques it is introducing abroad.

G.M.'s operations in Brazil have copied Japanese manufacturing practices and have become the company's most profitable, efficient and flexible. When G.M. introduced new midsize sedans in the United States and Brazil two years ago, a Kansas factory took seven months to make the switch while the Brazilian factory reached full production in three months.

The last two presidents of G.M.'s Brazilian operations, G. Richard Wagoner Jr. and Mark T. Hogan, now run G.M.'s North American operations and are trying to apply Brazil's lessons here. "We can take what we've learned in the manufacturing and technology in Brazil and apply that in the United States, and that's every bit my intention," said Mr. Hogan, G.M.'s vice president for small cars, in an interview last year in São Paulo.

Outside suppliers in Brazil are assembling many parts for G.M. cars before delivering them to the assembly plants—sending partly assembled dashboards, for example, instead of speedometers, gas gauges, radios and glove boxes. Auto makers used to bolt these parts together inside an assembly plant, and G.M. still does in the United States, even though this occupies costly space and increases labor costs.

G.M.'s efforts to vastly increase efficiency with pre-assembled parts is part of a trend sweeping the entire auto industry. But where G.M. sees efficiency, the United Automobile Workers union sees a threat. Many of G.M.'s moves in Brazil have reduced the people needed for each vehicle produced, particularly during final assembly. Brazilian unions have accepted this because G.M. has been hiring as it builds more factories in Brazil's expanding market.

In the United States, G.M.'s share of the American car market has shrunk from 40.7 percent in 1985 to 31 percent last year. The company has been steadily closing factories as a result. So proposals to reduce employment more quickly at the remaining factories have alarmed an already angry U.A.W. and its workers. Particularly galling for the union is that G.M. is cutting back in the United States—and buying more parts from nonunion suppliers—even as it builds new assembly plants in Poland, China, Thailand and Argentina along Brazilian lines.

G.M. is "ignoring their social contract with America, by transferring jobs, technology and capital from the U.S.," said Richard Shoemaker, the U.A.W.'s vice president for G.M. issues.

Strikes at two parts factories in Flint, Mich., have forced G.M. to close 17 of its 28 North American assembly plants so far for lack of parts. G.M. has temporarily laid off 71,700 workers, including 2,300 today at an assembly plant in Shreveport, La., that makes small pickup trucks.

In the course of expanding overseas, G.M. has discovered that it can operate far more efficiently than in the United States. That has been particularly true in Brazil.

The differences in G.M. operations start with the shape of the factories: They are L-shaped or T-shaped in Brazil, while G.M.'s factories in the United States still tend to be gigantic squares, with each side as long as several football fields. The advantage of the Brazilian design is that it offers more exterior walls for loading docks, which allows outside suppliers to produce more of a vehicle.

Toyota Motor has been asking its suppliers for years to deliver partly assembled sections of cars, and it dramatically reduces the number of assembly plant workers that are needed. G.M.'s operations in the United States have been slow to learn from the company's 15-year-old joint venture to built cars with Toyota in Fremont, Calif. But many of the G.M. managers from that joint venture have gone on to Brazil.

G.M. has begun reviewing whether to build a Brazilian-style factory with lots of loading docks in the United States. The company is also trying to expand the role that outside suppliers play even at existing American factories with few loading docks. Other auto makers are undertaking similar experiments—Volkswagen at one of its Brazilian factories and Mercedes-Benz at factories in France and at a non-union factory in Alabama. Ford Motor and Chrysler are moving to buy more partly assembled car systems.

But while American auto makers' assembly plants in the United States are entirely unionized, most suppliers are not, and that upsets the U.A.W. The suppliers' employees do not pay union dues and commonly earn a third less than the $20 an hour paid to U.A.W. members. According to Mr. Shoemaker, one of the many thorny issues in the Flint strike has been G.M.'s desire to have metal stamping equipment there maintained by outside contractors instead of U.A.W. workers.

G.M.'s labor contracts effectively bar it from dismissing U.A.W. workers. But the company has tried for years to avoid replacing workers who retire, and will have even less incentive to hire new workers as it copies the Brazilian model here. That alarms U.A.W. members who want jobs for their children.

To be sure, auto makers all over the world have tried to emulate elements of Toyota's lean manufacturing strategy, which seeks to minimize waste of labor, investment and materials. But G.M.'s Brazilian operations have gone further than many manufacturers. Even G.M.'s Saturn factory in Spring Hill, Tenn., seems out of date to many manufacturing experts because it cannot easily accommodate the delivery of partly assembled pieces of cars.

G.M.'s factories in Brazil have also embraced Japanese labor practices, with workers and managers eating together and with G.M. providing extensive information to the workers about how each segment of an assembly line is doing in terms of productivity and safety. A few G.M. factory managers have taken the same approach in the United States, but many factories retain a strong caste system in which white-collar and blue-collar workers stay apart while managers provide little information to assembly line workers.

G.M.'s high profits in Brazil have suffered this year as the country's economy has slowed. But G.M. continues to invest heavily there, contending that the market is growing and the Brazilian operation's efficiency should be rewarded.

By contrast, G.M. has delayed investments in some American factories, including those struck in Flint, while demanding that the workers put in longer hours or make other changes to improve productivity. The U.A.W. contends that inadequate investment and poor management are to blame for lagging productivity, not the workers.

Although the current negotiations in Flint focus on narrow issues of work rules and investment at G.M. auto parts factories in Flint, the workers see the strike in international terms. "G.M. is done with America," said Glenn Reynolds, a 57-year-old metal stamping worker on strike in Flint, as he left his local union hall today.

G.M. insists that none of the foreign assembly plants being built will be used to ship cars back to the United States.

For now, G.M.'s international expansion has mostly hurt American workers by limiting exports from the United States. G.M. has been shipping Chevrolet Blazer sport utility vehicles from São Jose dos Campos, Brazil, to Russia, for example, even though G.M.'s Blazer factory in Moraine, Ohio, is much closer.

* * *

December 2, 1999

CARRYING THE FLAG FOR FREE TRADE

Brazil Still Embraces Globalization

By SIMON ROMERO

SÃO PAULO, Brazil, Dec. 1—Acquiring a telephone was a distant dream for Rene Vieira da Conceicao Muniz, a maid in a small town in southeast Brazil. The government's inefficient telecommunications monopoly made telephone lines a luxury of the upper classes, far from the reach of Ms. Muniz, a mother of three whose monthly salary is the equivalent of $57.

But the privatization last year of Brazil's phone system, part of a much wider opening of the nation's economy to foreign investment, trade and competition from abroad, has changed the situation. Two months ago, Telefonica, the Spanish telecommunications company that bought the local telephone operation in Ms. Muniz's region, began an installment plan for low-income clients to buy cellular phones over several months.

"Before, I would have had to save for many years to get a phone," Ms. Muniz, 31, said, "and then it would have cost 2,000 reais," or about $1,036, compared with the $150 she will spend for her cell phone. Recently, the local priest called her to see if she was available to clean twice a month for about $10. "My life is hard, but it is better," she said. "My dream now is to buy a computer for my son."

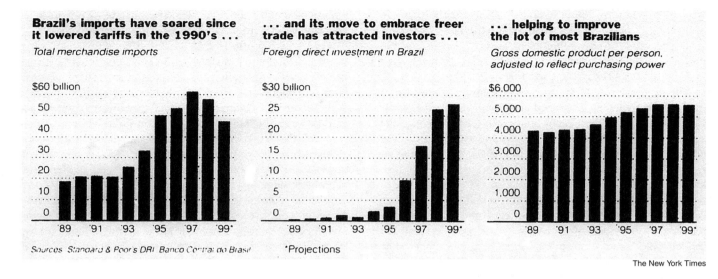

Brazil's imports have soared since it lowered tariffs in the 1990's . . .

Total merchandise imports

$60 billion
50
40
30
20
10
0

'89 '91 '93 '95 '97 '99*

Sources: Standard & Poor's DRI; Banco Central do Brasil

. . . and its move to embrace freer trade has attracted investors . . .

Foreign direct investment in Brazil

$30 billion
25
20
15
10
5
0

'89 '91 '93 '95 '97 '99*

*Projections

. . . helping to improve the lot of most Brazilians

Gross domestic product per person, adjusted to reflect purchasing power

$6,000
5,000
4,000
3,000
2,000
1,000
0

'89 '91 '93 '95 '97 '99*

The New York Times

Brazil, one of the biggest emerging-market members of the World Trade Organization, points to itself as an example of the positive economic change that can come from policies advocated by the 135-nation group. And despite the financial turmoil that struck this nation earlier this year, Brazil remains committed to freer trade and globalization as the best way to improve the standard of living of ordinary people.

The anti-trade protests this week at the W.T.O.'s meeting in Seattle have focused attention on what critics call the evils caused by free trade—economic disruptions, environmental degradation, exploitation of cheap labor by rich multinational corporations. But advocates of open markets argue that most developing countries that have joined the W.T.O. are better off than before and note that the largest emerging-market country, China, is about to join the organization in a move aimed at lifting itself up the next rung of the economic ladder.

Before the opening of Brazil's economy, the availability of basic technological services to people beyond an urban elite was virtually unthinkable. The government in Brasila was unable to invest in such things as it scrambled to deal with the more pressing priority of hyperinflation. And officials were wary that the entry of foreign investment threatened national sovereignty.

Then, in a policy shift at the start of the 1990's, Brazil took the first steps toward embracing the global economy. It began by auctioning several state companies and lowering many of its steep import tariffs. Barriers to the entry of goods ranging from Compaq personal computers to artificial flowers to Harley-Davidson motorcycles were reduced. With the onset of a more competitive marketplace, the first Brazilian multinational corporations were groomed and began to prosper.

Nowhere are the changes more apparent than in the country's consumer and business cultures.

As large swathes of Brazil's population of 165 million benefited from advances like the expansion of telephone service or were provided with an opportunity to buy imported goods, Brazilian business underwent a metamorphosis. Since

1996, Brazil has received $81 billion in direct investment from abroad, as foreign concerns took notice of the potential of the world's ninth-largest economy.

WEG, a company based in the southern Brazilian state of Santa Catarina, is a product of this new environment. Founded nearly 40 years ago in an enclave of descendants of German immigrants—Weg is German for road—the company, a producer of electric motors, embarked on a dizzying expansion spree in the 1990's. WEG is now the fifth-largest producer of electric motors, selling in markets from New Zealand to Mexico.

"We knew early on that to survive we had to become competitive abroad," said Decio da Silva, WEG's president. "That's why we were prepared when Brazil's own form of protectionism was eased."

Another example of a new generation's flexing its muscle abroad is Empresa Brasileira de Aeronautica, or Embraer, a privatized producer of small passenger jets. Strong sales in Europe and the United States transformed Embraer from a money-hemorrhaging state enterprise into Brazil's largest exporter.

In fact, Embraer's success has led to one of the W.T.O.'s most high-profile mediations of a trade dispute this year, as Bombardier, a Canadian competitor, accused the plane maker of benefiting from overly generous government subsidies. Embraer has tried to politicize the dispute by promoting itself as a symbol of Brazil's new industrial might.

Or there is Gerdau, a steel producer that has aggressively expanded through acquisitions in Latin America and North America. Thanks to companies like Gerdau, Brazil surpassed Canada last month as the largest supplier of foreign steel to the United States.

Of course, there is a flip side to this transformation, as free-trade opponents are quick to point out. In this city, for instance, not too far from the glimmering postmodern skyscrapers housing the local headquarters of large multinationals, there are neighborhoods like Barra Funda, a sprawling district of low-slung warehouses and old, abandoned brick factories. This is where Lorenzo Bertini has his office.

Three years ago, Mr. Bertini was the owner of Seda Flor Industria e Comercio, a company producing artificial flowers made with silk. He had a factory that employed 120 people. Then the government started to lower the tariffs on imported artificial flowers—from 73 percent to 16 percent.

"You know how a wave wipes out a castle made of sand?," Mr. Bertini said. "That's what happened to us."

In an illustration of how Brazil's opening has added to unemployment problems, especially in cities like São Paulo, Mr. Bertini's company has only 10 employees. He closed his factory and now runs a wholesale operation from a converted warehouse, selling flowers imported from countries like Thailand and South Korea.

Like Mr. Bertini's company, some Brazilian companies that have come under strain are struggling to reinvent themselves. And many have failed in the current economic downturn, helping to push unemployment close to a 14-year high.

Nonetheless, public support for freer trade appears to be growing. For instance, in a recent poll conducted by a São Paulo newspaper, most respondents were in favor of opening the airline industry to foreign competition if that would bring ticket prices down.

"Brazilians at large are very friendly to the opening efforts," said Gustavo Franco, a former president of the central bank and one of Brazil's leading economic thinkers. "A constituency supporting liberalization has been created, and it is not averse to voicing its concerns."

Still, Brazil has a long way to go before thoroughly reaping the rewards of free trade. Brazil's share of world trade is still relatively tiny, accounting for only nine-tenths of a percent of the world's exports. Mexico, with an economy about half the size of Brazil's, accounts for 2 percent of the world's exports. While exports of goods and services account for 6 percent of Brazil's gross domestic product, they represent 26 percent of G.D.P. in nearby Chile.

To increase exports, Brazil, with the backing of the United States, is pressing Europe and Japan to ease restrictions on the entry of agricultural goods. That would help Brazil, as the world's largest coffee producer and the second-largest producer of soybeans, to expand its share of the foreign market for such basics. Marcus Vinicius Pratini de Moraes, Brazil's agriculture minister, said this was the least the rich industrialized countries can do after Brazil opened its economy to so much foreign investment.

For the time being, though, it seems Brazilians are content to continue linking with a global consumer culture. This year, for instance, McDonald's became Brazil's largest private-sector employer. Or there is the Brazilian experience of Harley-Davidson, another icon of globalization.

Four years ago, Brazil unilaterally increased tariffs on imported motorcycles above 70 percent. After United States trade representatives pressed their Brazilian counterparts, the government agreed to reduce the tariff to less than 20 percent. Subsequently strong sales led Harley to build its first

assembly plant outside of the United States, in the Amazonian city of Manaus.

* * *

October 1, 2000

THE WORLD'S BANKERS TRY GIVING MONEY, NOT LESSONS

By JOSEPH KAHN

PRAGUE—A snapshot from Prague: One cool, hazy night, a day after black-masked anarchists attacked police lines and rattled delegates to the meeting of the World Bank and the International Monetary Fund, Horst Kohler and James D. Wolfensohn, respectively the new managing director of the I.M.F. and the World Bank president, stood at an outdoor ceremony with fixed smiles on their faces.

Jubilee 2000, a leading pressure group for third-world debt relief, presented them with a petition, and gave them a dressing down.

"Your declarations have proven to be empty promises once again," one speaker scolded. The two officials vowed to do better and left shaking hands.

Just a decade ago leading economists in the United States and Europe settled on a new strategy for fighting poverty. In return for long-term loans, poor nations got mandatory lessons in capitalism, what might be called the teach-a-man-to-trade theory of aid.

It seemed like a great solution at the time. After the fall of Communism, poor nations hungered for unbridled capitalism. And the industrial countries had more energy for lecturing than they did money for traditional aid, which plummeted in the 1990's.

But as Prague sweeps up the shattered shop window glass left over from the violence-plagued meeting of global aid agencies last week, one thing has become clear: The old way of thinking is now economically debatable and politically untouchable.

In its place is emerging a new consensus about helping the poor that shifts some of the burden to the rich. It has the

Associated Press
An elderly woman begging in La Paz, Bolivia

A rickshaw driver in Calcutta takes cover under a plastic sheet.

potential to raise living standards, but will cost a great deal more money.

The new consensus has three main elements. First, loans are fine, but grants are better, especially for humanitarian projects like fighting AIDS and malaria. The World Bank and other development agencies keep even their low-interest loans on their books as assets. Grants, however, are write-offs, and will require more cash infusions from donor countries if the aid agencies want to preserve their capital.

Second, debt relief must come faster and be more generous. There are 41 nations eligible for debt relief, whose average debt load is 125 percent of their gross domestic product. Rich nations have begun a slow process of relieving this crushing burden, but the drumbeat to forgive much more of the third world's debt is deafening for government ministers, who seem to up their pledges with every anti-globalization riot.

Third, trade is a two-way street. There is broad agreement that poor nations have done more than their fair share to free up trade, and the pressure is on rich nations to open their markets wider to the things poor countries make.

For Europe and Japan, that means lowering the wall protecting their farmers. For the United States, it means a showdown with the influential textile and sugar lobbies.

The betting is that these kinds of changes will throw a lifeline to the world's poorest people, defined as those earning $2 or less a day. They number a staggering 3 billion, roughly half the world's population.

The World Bank acknowledges that the poor in Africa, Latin America and the former Soviet Union did not benefit much from the roaring prosperity of the 1990's. They may eventually benefit from the almost universal shift toward market economics, but that has not happened yet.

The new thinking aims for more immediate results. Easing debt loads, handing out grants directly to villages, clinics and

A 1-year-old girl suffering from malnutrition in a Turkish shantytown.

schools, and providing more export opportunities for the crops grown and the shirts stitched by the poorest workers could help. But there will be a price to pay.

"We have to tackle the selfishness of wealthy countries," says Mr. Kohler. "This is a question of morals."

And of expediency. The I.M.F. and the World Bank, its fellow Washington-based global lender, have been front-line targets of the anti-globalization movement that has spread from Seattle to Washington and Prague.

But Mr. Kohler and Mr. Wolfensohn are edging closer to their critics, even pandering a little. Though they still espouse free market capitalism, they argue for a humane approach to poverty relief that puts developing nations in charge and cuts some strings attached to aid.

When the aid experts talked about economic overhauls in Prague, they were as often calling for changes in wealthy nations as for the 90's-formula medicine prescribed to the poor.

Their message is: We want to fight poverty more effectively, but it will only work if industrial countries dip into their pockets and challenge their entrenched domestic interests on trade and, by extension, on employment.

"The globalization battle is really about the parsimony of the G-7," said Trevor A. Manuel, South Africa's finance minister, who chaired the Prague sessions. He was referring to the United States, Japan, Britain, France, Germany, Italy and Canada, members of the Group of 7 developed countries.

Financial leaders from rich nations are beginning to feel the heat, and they are touting their own anti-poverty strategies.

Treasury Secretary Lawrence H. Summers, who said in Prague that the poverty battle has become "the overarching economic and humanitarian challenge of our time," proposed last week that the World Bank replace some loans with outright grants, a first. The proposal echoed a key demand made by a Congressional commission that recently criticized the bank as a feckless anachronism.

Trouble is, Congress is still practicing tough love. American foreign aid declined an average of 8 percent annually in the 1990's. The average American had $42 of his taxes devoted to foreign aid in 1993, and $32 in 1998, according to

World Bank figures. The United States is the stingiest rich nation, but aid declined in many European countries as they tightened their budgets for monetary union.

With the backlash against globalization mounting, the next president will probably have to figure out a way to persuade lawmakers to provide more aid and debt relief, even while making politically tricky compromises on trade. It will be a hard sell, but Mr. Kohler of the I.M.F. says he has the solution.

"It will be very helpful," he says with a smile, "when these groups that have been attacking us turn their attention to the Congress."

CRITICAL MOMENT: THE BATTLE IN SEATTLE

November 20, 1999

TRADE PACTS MUST SAFEGUARD WORKERS, UNION CHIEF SAYS

By STEVEN GREENHOUSE

WASHINGTON, Nov. 19—Raising the stakes in labor's dispute with President Clinton over trade, the A.F.L.-C.I.O.'s president, John J. Sweeney, called on the administration today to scuttle a worldwide round of trade-liberalization talks unless negotiators first take steps toward protecting workers' rights.

Mr. Sweeney, already angry about last week's trade agreement with China, said American labor unions want Mr. Clinton to persuade trade ministers gathering in Seattle on Nov. 30 to allow trade sanctions against countries that violate basic labor standards, like the ban on child labor.

The labor movements in the United States and in other industrialized countries are taking a much more aggressive approach toward the Seattle trade talks than toward previous rounds of negotiations, insisting that workers' rights be included in any new trade agreements. In past rounds of trade talks, corporations and developing nations prevailed with their arguments that worker rights have no place in trade accords.

In what was billed as a major address to the National Press Club here, Mr. Sweeney rejected accusations that labor's attacks on the World Trade Organization and the China deal stemmed from protectionism and isolationism.

"The debate isn't about free trade or protection, engagement or isolation," he said. "The real debate is not over whether to be part of the global economy, but over what are the rules for that economy and who makes them—not whether to engage China, but what are the terms of that engagement, and whose values are to be represented."

Union leaders view the Seattle trade meeting as a landmark opportunity to establish for the first time a worldwide system of enforceable labor rights. Labor officials say these rights would enable workers, and not just corporations, to enjoy the fruits of expanded trade.

Mr. Sweeney said it was time to ensure that any future trade agreements take into account not just corporate concerns, but also the concerns of workers, environmentalists and human rights advocates.

Mr. Sweeney said he was pleased that President Clinton had backed labor's call to have the trade organization minis-

ters set up a committee that would draft rules on core labor standards. But with developing countries vowing to block such a move, union leaders fear that Mr. Clinton will drop his commitment to labor rights, rather than block the planned round of worldwide trade talks from moving forward.

"Until the W.T.O. addresses these important issues, there will be no support for a major new round of trade negotiations," Mr. Sweeney said.

Some labor leaders are warning that if President Clinton leaves the Seattle talks without winning an international pledge to create a system of worker rights, he will further antagonize union members who are already fuming about his deal to let China join the W.T.O. Union leaders are angry that the administration agreed to China's membership in the trade organization without having gotten China to agree to allow independent trade unions and to free imprisoned labor leaders.

Gene Sperling, the president's economic adviser, said: "There's no question that Bill Clinton is the single head of state fighting hardest for and leading the effort for a working group on labor. We will continue to make an all-out effort to achieve that goal."

The anger at the administration, union leaders say, might not only soften labor's support for Vice President Al Gore in his campaign for the presidency but cause a diversion of union money and manpower from Mr. Gore's race to a fight against the China trade accord and the W.T.O.

The A.F.L.-C.I.O. is working with environmental, consumer and human rights groups to sponsor a large rally in Seattle to protest what they see as the trade organization's pro-corporate tilt and its frequent overruling of countries' environmental and consumer protection laws.

The trade organization's meeting, scheduled to run from Nov. 30 to Dec. 2 and bring together ministers from 135 countries, aims to set ground rules for a multiyear round of trade talks that would liberalize trade in agriculture, financial services, Internet services and other areas.

As an example of how labor values might be included in trade rules, Mr. Sweeney argued that W.T.O. rules should allow China's trading partners to seek sanctions against China for using forced labor and barring trade unions.

"This is a country where anyone attempting to organize a union is immediately arrested and imprisoned—no exceptions," Mr. Sweeney said of China.

Developing countries are seeking to block the trade organization from creating enforceable core labor standards and even from taking the preliminary step of setting up a working group on labor rights. Such core labor standards, union officials say, would include a ban on child labor and on forced labor, and a right to form trade unions and engage in collective bargaining.

Third-world countries fear that allowing their trading partners to seek sanctions for violations of such labor standards would pave the way to banning their exports.

"These countries say that we'll just slap restrictions on their exports and make them poorer," said Jeffrey Schott, senior fellow at the Institute for International Economics.

Thomas Donohue, the president of the United States Chamber of Commerce, expressed alarm at Mr. Sweeney's call on Mr. Clinton to block the new trade round unless worker protections are included. Mr. Donohue has backed creating a working group on labor.

Insisting that the new trade agreements will increase American exports and jobs, Mr. Donohue said, "I think John Sweeney and other labor leaders are smart enough to recognize that to scuttle this trade round and the China-W.T.O. deal would not be in the interests of this country, its workers, its economy or its national security. This is a watershed opportunity to bring China into the international trading system and to get it to adhere to the international law."

Mr. Sweeney's speech made clear that he would rely on an alliance with environmental, consumer and human rights groups to pressure the W.T.O. "We will continue to organize in the Congress against any trade accords that do not include workers' rights and environmental protections," he said.

* * *

November 28, 1999

A TURBULENT TRADE MEETING

Officials from the 135 member countries of the World Trade Organization will meet in Seattle starting Tuesday, not to solve the world's trade disputes but merely to set an agenda for the next round of negotiations. Even that will not be easy. Rich countries are squabbling with poor countries. Thousands of street demonstrators are expected to denounce the organization for trampling on the rights of third-world workers, the sovereignty of individual countries and the environment.

In such a turbulent setting, a productive agenda will almost certainly elude the assembled ministers unless they focus tightly on a few achievable measures aimed at expanding trade. The most important of these will benefit the world's poorest countries.

Third-world farmers want access to closed agriculture markets in Europe and Japan. This demand deserves to be met. Developing countries also want the United States to limit the use of "anti-dumping" laws. The rules governing the use of these laws deserve tightening. Unfortunately, the United States almost surely will not go along. Another proposal from third-world countries is to rewrite rules that force

them to pay prohibitively high prices for pharmaceutical drugs. Here the patent rights of Western drug manufacturers must yield to common sense and decency.

Trickier than any of these issues is a proposal by the developed countries that they be allowed to impose tariffs on imports from countries that exploit unskilled workers. Poor countries believe this proposal masks a protectionist purpose. It is true that working conditions in third-world countries can be horrific, but the tariffs could eliminate the jobs of millions of workers in these countries. Rich and poor countries are nowhere near a consensus on fair labor practices, and the Clinton administration wants to set up a working group to study the issue. That makes sense.

The advanced countries also want to incorporate—over the objections of developing countries—environmental concerns into trade agreements. Environmental groups point with alarm to rulings by W.T.O. judicial panels that, they say, tampered with the United States' right to enforce high environmental standards. But these criticisms distort the record. W.T.O. panels did, for example, rule against specific sanctions that the United States imposed on foreign fishermen for practices that threatened dolphins and other endangered species. But the panels did not dispute America's right to set its own standards. They only insisted that American laws not discriminate against foreign suppliers.

The Clinton administration has offered some proposals that environmentalists can like. For example, it proposes to cut subsidies that governments provide for farmers and fishermen. Cutting subsidies not only improves trade patterns, but it also reduces incentives to overuse fragile land and fisheries. Environmental advocates object to an administration proposal to reduce tariffs on wood products. That, they say, would increase the demand for wood and, thereby, logging in Indonesia, Malaysia, Finland and the United States. This criticism deserves careful consideration, but on balance, the administration's general strategy—to tackle key environmental issues case by case—appears sound.

Lost among the disputes is the fact that open trade promotes prosperity. Economists are hard pressed to identify a single economy that prospers without a vigorous export-oriented policy. And for every exporter there needs to be a willing importer. The goal of trade talks is to guarantee that countries that want to export can find countries willing to import—a goal that can start to be met if the trade ministers drop proposals that cannot yet be resolved by consensus and focus on the few that can.

* * *

November 28, 1999

MEET YOUR GOVERNMENT, INC.

By DAVID E. SANGER

WASHINGTON—They are pouring into Seattle this weekend in vans and on buses, by air and on foot—the college students and the church groups, the environmental campaigners, the Teamsters, Ralph Nader, Chinese dissidents and the man who became a hero in France for defacing a McDonald's.

All of them say they are outraged at the growing power of a group few even heard about five years ago, the World Trade Organization. And so, with tens of thousands massing, they are planning to turn what initially sounded like the yawner of all international meetings—a gathering of trade ministers from 135 countries to start the "Millennium Round" of trade liberalization talks—into the Woodstock of the era of globalization.

But of course the W.T.O. itself, with its paltry annual budget of $80 million, not even enough to buy a fleet of black helicopters, isn't the real target of the protesters. It's merely a symbol, a bureaucratic metaphor for the idea that the markets have become the real governing force of the '90's—frequently with the willing participation of governments and politicians.

The real target is the blurring of the role of the private sector and the role of the public sector, which is supposed to rein in of market forces. For a ready example, think of those so-called non-commercials on public TV that, with each passing year, seem to turn into longer and longer plugs for corporate sponsors.

It is not simply that governments have shrunk and the private sector has risen. In fact, the public sector has increasingly become the champion of private enterprise. That reflects a sea change in traditional political constituencies. The parties that used to get elected by arguing that government must tame capitalism's excesses and stand up for those left behind—big-government Democrats, Europe's battered Socialists—have mostly retooled themselves and changed the priorities of governments, aligning them more closely than ever with those of corporations and their swelling class of worker-investors.

Not surprisingly, the shift has created a lot of political confusion about whose interests are being protected. Consider the union members in Seattle. True, the forces of global trade are threatening to move their jobs to China. But like many workers across America, the union members have huge pension funds and 401-K's spiking upward precisely because they are invested in companies and countries that have benefited greatly from ever-freer trade.

"It used to be that trade only affected major corporations," Mickey Kantor, the former Trade Representative and long-time Democratic political strategist, said last week. "Now it affects people's jobs, their education and of course their portfolios. And it creates some pretty wacky politics."

The degree to which left and right have unified to become the champion of corporate priorities was on full display in the Congressional session that just ended. Democrats and Republicans may be in a death-battle for control of the White House and Congress, but they managed to find common ground on repealing Depression-era laws preventing banks, securities firms and insurance concerns from merging those businesses (while doing nothing about those $1.50 ATM fees that drive most banking customers crazy) and passing a law limiting lawsuits arising out of Y2K disasters.

And look at the legislation that business got killed: There was no increase in the minimum wage, no new limits on "soft money" in political campaigns, no ban on agricultural mergers.

Or look abroad: The generals who staged the coup in Pakistan made their first priority a crackdown on corruption. The country's terrible reputation among foreign investors, they warned, was as big a threat to the nation as India's nukes.

This is not to say governments have entirely given up on reining in market forces. Japan is focusing its attentions at Seattle on retaining protections for farmers, steelmakers and industrial dinosaurs. France is forever battling the spread of American-dominated industry and culture. Here at home, even the market-friendly new Democrats of the Clinton administration have breathed new life into anti-trust laws.

Drive a few miles north of the W.T.O. meeting in Seattle, and Microsoft employees will offer up an earful about how the Justice Department is mired in old economic thinking, and is threatening the economic engine that has driven one of the greatest expansions in American history.

But even those protests are muted by the not-so-secret belief among Microsoft's investors that a breakup of the company might turn into a bonanza for their shareholdings—exactly what happened after the government went after A.T.&T.

So is the public good suffering as the role of government and the role of business blur? It depends on what you think governments ought to be doing for a living.

Those promotional spots for sponsors on public television have expanded precisely because there is increasing opposition to using taxpayer money to fund TV or the arts. So now the P in PBS now stands for something more like "public-private partnership," and it seems likely that public financing will play an ever smaller role.

And of course the most sacrosanct of public functions—education—is a constant battleground in the public-private wars. School vouchers, charter schools and for-profit educational companies that run schools all blur the line between what governments can achieve and what the private sector can.

In each of these cases, good civic and economic arguments can be made for more private financing. But with the loss of public money inevitably comes a loss of public control, and less of a voice for public debate over priorities.

And that, at the heart of it, is the argument that will be shouted on the streets in Seattle. People who don't usually have much in common—the Rainforest Action Network and the United Steelworkers, for example—are convinced that the W.T.O.'s rise represents the ultimate victory for corporate interests that want the rules of the global economy written on their terms.

"There are enough examples on the table now, from the arguments over whether countries can ban genetically modified foods, or the argument that we can't ban products made by child labor because it violates some trade agreement," said Mr. Nader, the longtime consumer advocate who years ago moved beyond auto safety to make the case that a global economic rule-setter like the W.T.O. is unsafe at any speed. "People aren't buying the idea anymore that globalization is inevitable and their governments have to go with the flow of the market. That's what is unifying the protesters you are going to see."

The fight over genetically modified food is a prime example of the alliance of governments and corporations—and the growing frictions over national standards. While American companies and regulators argue that these foods are safe, Europeans have banned many of them as threats to consumer safety and the environment. Washington responds that health is a phony argument to justify trade barriers. So far, it's winning its W.T.O. case and losing European consumers.

Or consider the explosive issue of how to handle the concerns of labor. Unions will be in Seattle to argue that global trade agreements should protect the rights of workers, just as they have long protected intellectual property and investments abroad. They want the new trade agreement to include provisions that set minimum labor standards in factories around the world. They oppose imports from countries that ban unions, China included. In an election year in which Vice President Al Gore is desperate for deeper union support, they have more than a little political leverage.

But developing nations like India and China say that such restrictions are simply a form of American protectionism. They insist that labor issues are a domestic concern unrelated to trade, and want any rulemaking relegated to the toothless International Labor Organization. The Clinton administration supported that position a few years ago, but now wants a study group within the W.T.O. to take up the issue.

To the protesters on the street, a study doesn't go far enough. To the developing nations, it's far too much. All of this has opened up the new divide of globalization, the argument over who will make the rules, and on whose behalf. "It's not going to be the W.T.O. with its closed-door, big-business policies," vows Mr. Nader. He could be right: The very fact that a W.T.O. negotiation is triggering screaming in the streets could mean that the pendulum is beginning to swing back, and that global politics may rear its head and attempt to trump the imperatives of global economics.

*　*　*

November 28, 1999

GLOBAL TRADE FORUM REFLECTS A BURST OF CONFLICT AND HOPE

By JOSEPH KAHN

For the last half-century, government officials from around the world have gathered every few years to talk about trade. Delegates, who could often fit in a single hotel, debated arcana of tariff tables and export subsidies and were largely ignored by the world press.

When trade ministers assemble in Seattle this week to attend the meeting of the World Trade Organization, the scene will be almost unrecognizable. Negotiating teams from 134 countries have booked almost every hotel room in the city. Tariff reductions are still on the agenda, but they will be fighting for attention with health care, food safety, clear air, endangered species, child labor and cultural imperialism.

And that's only inside the closed-door sessions. Outside, tens of thousands of demonstrators plan to use the Seattle meeting to campaign against what they see as the trade organization's role in worsening air pollution, killing animals and undermining national sovereignty—in short, letting globalization run amok.

The trade forum hopes that the meeting will start up a new round of global trade talks, tentatively named the "Millennium Round," that would flatten trade barriers to their lowest levels in modern history and gain greater access to world markets for service providers like telecommunications companies.

But the talks will also test support for freer trade in both rich and poor countries, especially since delegates will face a giant, 1960's-style protest campaign meant to mobilize worldwide opposition to new trade efforts.

Trade forum members and observers of the talks say there is a reasonable chance that the Seattle meeting will result in only token progress, disappointing agriculture, entertainment and electronic commerce industries hoping for new liberalization, but cheering critics who would like to see the group hobbled.

Despite weeks of meetings to work out a formal agenda for the meeting, negotiators broke off last week without agreeing on what to talk about. Further complicating the picture, the United States and the Europeans want the trade group to help resolve global disputes on labor and the environment that even a few years ago were considered beyond the purview of its small, specialized bureaucracy. The push for expanding the Geneva-based trade group's mandate has divided the developed and less-developed countries.

"There's a real worry that the W.T.O. could become a victim of its own success," says Daniel K. Tarullo, a former Clinton administration economics official who is now a professor at Georgetown University. "It was effective in freeing up trade, but it's straining under the weight of issues that go well beyond conventional trade."

The Clinton administration is determined to make the best of the Seattle talks. Charlene Barshefsky, the trade representative, says the United States hopes to make progress on reducing tariffs on farm goods and promoting trade in services. "Failure is not an option," she said late last week.

But Washington has an uphill battle. Japan and the European Union, determined to protect their heavily subsidized farmers, have fought broad cuts on agricultural tariffs.

The Clinton administration's effort to make labor and environmental issues a central part of negotiations has brought a backlash from poorer countries and only tepid support from rich ones.

Economic analysts are more optimistic about prospects for extending the tax-free treatment of electronic commerce around the world, a high priority for the United States and Internet companies.

Other rounds of trade talks have begun amid heavy politicking but have ended up producing broad accords that free up trade. Just four years ago, the trade organization was born of a much weaker negotiating group, the General Agreements on Tariffs and Trade. By many measures it has been a success. Borders are now more open, and trade is more important to the international economy than at any time since before the Great Depression.

Yet the issues this time are especially tricky, in large part because the definition of trade keeps getting broader. When the talks were mostly about tariffs, they involved the way countries treated imports at their borders. But with tariff levels lower, the emphasis has shifted to services like banking, telecommunications and even education and culture. Thus trade issues are cutting deeper into local policy and politics.

"Trade has become a more intrusive issue in domestic politics," said Peter S. Watson, a Washington trade expert and former head of the International Trade Commission, "and that has, unfortunately, made it a vehicle for discontent."

Seemingly overnight, the trade group has become the target of those opposed to what they consider the excesses of globalization.

The protesters now descending on Seattle represent groups pushing environmental, labor and third-world development causes, and they do not speak with once voice. Among the divisions is whether the trade group should be abolished or reformed. But common refrains include accusations that the forum tramples social standards in the name of trade and that it acts in secrecy and without democratic oversight.

"This is about democracy—about letting an unelected bureaucracy in Geneva undermine our laws," said Jerry Mander, director of the California-based International Forum on Globalization. "We need to stop it in its tracks, before it starts controlling agriculture and bioengineering and many other things."

In Seattle, which finds itself gearing up for large street protests, the celebratory mood that accompanied the city's selection as host site is clearly tempered by nervousness.

Protesters say they expect 50,000 people, possibly many more. Publicly at least, city leaders insist that the groups are welcome and that Seattle, site of the nation's first general strike in 1919, will be a model host for ministers and dissenters alike.

Some union members plan a Seattle Steel Party, modeled on the Boston Tea Party, in which they will dump Chinese steel into the city harbor here. (In deference to the environment, the steel will be retrieved.)

Free trade has many supporters, of course, and Seattle is also the home of Boeing and Microsoft, two of America's largest exporters. At least one group, Working Families for Free Trade, which is being organized by Christian conservative leaders, plans a rally on Monday.

The trade group has become such a target of ire in part because it has proved one of the most powerful world bodies of any kind. Unlike the trade and tariffs group, its predeces-

sor, this trade group has the power to decide disputes on its own and impose penalties on countries that do not abide by its conclusions. To avoid pressure from lobby groups and possible adverse effects on international financial markets, three-judge panels decide cases in closed chambers without having to reveal much about the process. Most of the appointee judges are trade lawyers.

The group has heard almost 200 trade disputes in four years. Most are garden variety protectionist issues, such as whether Japan can tax domestic saki at different rates from imported whiskey, and whether Canadian scallops sold in France can be called coquilles Saint-James.

But several cases brought before the forum have linked trade to the environment and health. In one, for example, a trade group panel ruled against the United States, which had banned imports of shrimp from Asian countries that do not use fishing nets intended to protect endangered turtles.

The case that got the most attention was brought by the United States and Canada against the European Union, which banned the import of hormone-treated beef raised in North America. Two trade panels—the first ruling was appealed— decided that the European Union did not have an adequate scientific basis for excluding such beef.

Critics have argued that the ruling limits the rights of governments to set basic food-safety standards. But supporters of the trade forum dismiss the criticism as hyperbole. The group has not tried to legislate environmental or food safety standards, they say, but simply to ensure that a country does not use such standards as a pretext for discriminating against imported goods.

But even the Clinton administration, a strong proponent of the group, has called for changes. President Clinton, who will attend the Seattle talks for two days this week, plans to push for reforms. Among his proposals: introduce more transparency into the trade group's decision-making, and let observers attend some sessions.

One reason that the group has become more prominent— and contested—is that Mr. Clinton and leaders of the European Union keep trying to expand its role. Mr. Clinton has been seeking to persuade trade forum members that the group should set and enforce international labor standards and outlaw at least some kinds of child labor. This could give the group sweeping powers to police treatment of workers. The proposal seems designed to satisfy unions, many of which argue that recent free-trade agreements have given American jobs to countries with lower wages and less rigorous labor laws.

Developing countries have strenuously opposed the labor initiative as protectionism. The European Union has offered only tepid support, and experts do not expect major progress on the issue at this meeting.

There is stronger Western backing for another Clinton initiative: giving environmentalists more power to review trade agreements. Ms. Barshefsky, the trade representative, has called for the forum to monitor trade issues "proactively" to weigh environmental impact. Having had several environmental laws challenged by developing countries, the Clinton administration wants the group to respect its right to exclude imports that do not meet United States environmental standards.

"Many third world countries think environment and labor are a Trojan horse for turning the W.T.O. into a forum that enforces Western rights," said Mr. Watson, the Washington analyst. "To the extent that the W.T.O. is not about trade—and reducing trade barriers—it is on shaky ground."

*   *   *

November 29, 1999

SHAPING THE FUTURE IN SEATTLE

By BILL GATES

SEATTLE—This week, representatives from more than 130 countries will gather here for a meeting that will help set the global economic agenda for years to come. The greater the success of this meeting at establishing fair and predictable conditions for expanded world trade, the better the future prospects not only for our own economy but for global prosperity.

The World Trade Organization is the principal organization dedicated to developing international trade rules, maintaining nations' access to one another's markets, resolving trade disputes and encouraging trade liberalization. This round of meetings will provide an important opportunity to explore ways that government, industry, interest groups and the public can work together to ensure the continued expansion of free, open and fair trade.

I became co-chairman of the Seattle host organization for this event because I believe that fair and open international trade is good not only for companies that depend on exports; it is good for the global economy and for opening up lines of communication and progress throughout the world.

Perhaps more than any other city in America, Seattle illustrates the benefits of global commerce. More than $34 billion in exports flow through our region's ports each year, making the Seattle-Tacoma region the nation's No. 1 exporter. One of every three jobs in Washington State is directly tied to international trade—exports, imports or both—and the figure is much higher in the Seattle area itself. Our region is vivid proof that trade creates jobs and bolsters wages, stimulates economic growth, expands consumer choice and ultimately increases productivity and competitiveness.

At Microsoft, overseas sales of our software products totaled $10 billion last year, nearly two-thirds of our revenues. Another company in our region, Boeing, is America's largest exporter, shipping $30 billion in aircraft and other goods and services overseas last year. A third, Weyerhaeuser, shipped more than $1 billion in wood and wood products to 60 nations. And our region's farmers shipped nearly $2 billion in wheat, apples, livestock and other products to literally dozens of countries.

And Seattle's story is increasingly the nation's. The economic health of the United States as a whole is increasingly based on international trade. Thanks in part to lower trade barriers and strong exports, our economy is the strongest it has been in a generation. International trade can continue to drive domestic economic growth and job creation, so long as we have the appropriate global framework in place.

The World Trade Organization provides its member countries with exactly that: a forum for negotiating agreements that remove barriers to the free exchange of goods and services and for resolving trade disputes before nations take unilateral actions that could threaten millions of jobs and global economic progress. If the W.T.O. didn't exist, the nations of the world would have to invent it.

The recent agreement to bring China into the trade group has the potential to open new opportunities for American goods and services, ultimately benefiting the United States as well as China and the rest of the world. Those of us who helped arrange the conference hope significant strides will be made here to help bring this agreement closer to fruition, and we will continue to encourage Congress to ratify the agreement and support permanently improved trade relations with China.

Trade affects virtually every community and every industry, and high technology is no exception. The W.T.O. agenda includes a number of issues critical to the continued growth of the American high-tech industry, which now accounts for more than 8 percent of the American economy and one-third of our economic growth in recent years.

The high-technology industry supports creation of a "tariff-free zone" for economic transactions over the Internet, as well as other free-trade steps to encourage the growth of electronic commerce. We support consistent international rules for the electronic marketplace to give companies the confidence to invest and consumers the benefit of greater choice. And we encourage the trade organization to finish putting in place the international treaty for protection of intellectual property rights, which is fundamental to the continued strength of American technology companies.

In addition to providing a meeting place for the governmental delegations, Seattle expects visits from thousands of citizens and advocacy groups. Their concern emphasizes the effect that international commerce increasingly has on every aspect of our lives, from the environment and public health to education and international labor standards.

The Seattle meetings will provide opportunities for a wide range of viewpoints to be heard, and the W.T.O. needs to continue its efforts to open up the dialogue and provide more opportunity for citizens and advocacy groups to follow its work.

Regardless of one's view on any single issue, one fact cannot be disputed: The world we live in is changing. Borders and barriers are coming down; actions in one corner of the world will affect people around the globe. The World Trade Organization will play a vital role as we learn to adapt to a new world economy.

Bill Gates is the chairman of Microsoft.

*   *   *

November 29, 1999

A CARNIVAL OF DERISION TO GREET THE PRINCES OF GLOBAL TRADE

By STEVEN GREENHOUSE

SEATTLE, Nov. 28—There will be hundreds of protesters in sea-turtle costumes and stilt walkers dressed as monarch butterflies. Thousands of people will tie up the downtown area during a giant demonstration, and protesters will chain themselves to buildings or scale walls to unfurl banners denouncing the target of their ire: the World Trade Organization.

In what is shaping up as one of the biggest protest efforts in years, people from more than 500 organizations have poured into Seattle. They are here to accuse the W.T.O., the 135-nation Geneva-based trade group that is holding its ministerial meeting here this week, of favoring free trade at the expense of the environment, consumer safety and workers' rights.

The protest groups range from the well-known, like Friends of the Earth and the Humane Society, to the obscure, like the Ruckus Society and Raging Grannies.

Several, including the Sierra Club and the United Steelworkers of America, are planning a Seattle Tea Party on Monday with the slogan, "No Globalization Without Representation." Imitating their Boston forebears, the protesters plan to throw steel imported from China into the sea, along with some shrimp, hormone-treated beef and other goods they view as tainted by the trade group's decisions.

"The W.T.O. responds to the needs and interests of the very rich and corporations, but it doesn't respond to the needs of the environment, labor, the poor, women or indigenous people," said Alli Starr, a dancer in the radical group Art and Revolution, who flew in from San Francisco to protest and do street theater.

Borrowing a page from Vietnam War protests, the trade organization's critics have scheduled a weeklong cavalcade of activities, including teach-ins, concerts, mock trials of corporations and appearances by sympathetic members of Congress. Like the 1968 Democratic Party convention in Chicago, the trade meeting has become a magnet for all manner of protest.

On Monday night, hundreds of protesters plan to form a human chain around Seattle's exhibition center to demand that wealthy nations cancel the debt owed by the world's poor nations. The biggest event will be a protest march on Tuesday sponsored by the A.F.L.-C.I.O., which wants the trade group to allow trade sanctions against countries that violate core labor standards, like prohibitions against child labor.

Some of the groups hope to persuade the trade body to change its ways, while others want to disrupt it, with the ultimate goal of destroying it. In 1919, Seattle endured one of the nation's first general strikes, but it has never experienced protests with people from so many different groups—labor unions, farm groups, environmental groups—and so many countries, including Canada, France, Panama and India.

Ten years ago, trade ministers' meetings attracted only a handful of protesters who were largely seen as cranks, but the protests have mushroomed and include many mainstream groups. The protests have been fueled by the Internet, anxiety about globalization and anger with World Trade Organization rulings.

In the most-criticized ruling, the United States was found to have acted illegally in barring imported shrimp caught by fishing fleets whose nets do not contain devices allowing sea turtles to escape. The protesters also attack a ruling that an American requirement for a smog-fighting gasoline additive was an unfair trade barrier and another that concluded that Europe had no scientific basis for barring hormone-treated beef from the United States and Canada.

"So many people are upset with the W.T.O. because of the expansiveness of its limits on government health and safety actions," said Lori Wallach, director of Public Citizen's Global Trade Watch, a Ralph Nader group that has been the main coordinator of the protests. "The W.T.O. has managed to gore everyone's ox. Its track record has been that every single environmental or health policy it has reviewed has been found to be an illegal trade barrier."

The ministers gathered here plan intense, closed-door talks to decide what specific areas of trade should be included in a multiyear round of negotiations aimed at reducing trade barriers. In contrast, many protesters hope to make their protests as visible as possible.

In many ways, the meeting has become ground zero for anyone with a complaint about the world economy. There are protesters against the growing gap between rich and poor, against genetically engineered products, against despoiling rain forests and against America's economic and political dominance.

"We will be using a carnival festival model to oppose the W.T.O.," said Brooke Lehman, a New York-based protester active in a group called No to W.T.O.

Sixty groups in a coalition called the Turning Point Project are spending more than $100,000 on full-page advertisements attacking the trade group, saying that expanded agricultural trade is hurting small farmers in dozens of countries and causing more pollution and energy use.

The Geneva-based trade group's defenders say globalization and expanded trade are vital for helping the economies of poor countries, and some proponents suggest that many protesters want to stop economic progress altogether.

With so many protesters crowding into Seattle, police officials here say they fear some violence. Three protesters were arrested on Saturday. Two had suspended a protest banner from a highway retaining wall. But many protest leaders say they fear that violence would detract from their message.

"I'm scared that if one anarchist throws a brick through a store window downtown, that will become the big story, and our whole critique of the W.T.O. is going to get lost," said Michael Dolan, Public Citizen's main coordinator of the protests.

* * *

December 1, 1999

NATIONAL GUARD IS CALLED TO QUELL TRADE-TALK PROTESTS

Seattle Is Under Curfew After Disruptions

By SAM HOWE VERHOVEK and
STEVEN GREENHOUSE

SEATTLE, Nov. 30—Downtown Seattle was placed under curfew and the National Guard was called in tonight, after the city was engulfed in demonstrations that threw the opening of global trade talks into turmoil.

The protesters surrounded the convention hall, pinned trade dignitaries in their hotels and stopped traffic at several intersections. By late afternoon, clouds of tear gas set off by the police wafted through downtown streets populated by Nordstrom, Nike and Starbucks, and Mayor Paul Schell declared a state of emergency and a curfew that he said would last until sunrise on Wednesday.

The protests forced the postponement of opening ceremonies for a meeting of the World Trade Organization that President Clinton, who is scheduled to arrive here early Wednesday, had hoped would showcase American leadership on free trade.

The global organization is meant to resolve trade disputes and promote free trade, and the Seattle meeting is intended to open a new round of negotiations.

But the protesters have descended on Seattle with an eclectic array of grievances, most centered around the sentiment that the trade organization is a handmaiden of corporate interests whose rulings undermine health, labor and environmental protections around the world.

In Seattle the police used tear gas, pepper spray and rubber pellets at some intersections to break up the groups of demonstrators.

A small group of men, dressed in black clothing and masks and ignoring cries of "Shame on you!" from other protesters, smashed windows and spray-painted graffiti at downtown stores like Nordstrom, Niketown, Starbucks and the Gap. Both were jarring sights in a city that prides itself on its laid-back image.

Secretary of State Madeleine K. Albright and other scheduled speakers for opening ceremonies this morning were unable to get through the crowd, which in many cases blocked intersections by linking hands or lying down in the street.

With thousands of protesters already gathered downtown and about 20,000 additional marchers in a union-backed rally headed that way, the trade body's director general, Mike Moore, a former prime minister of New Zealand, announced early this afternoon that the opening ceremonies would be put off. But he vowed that the trade talks would go on. In fact, he held meetings today with a few trade ministers who managed to leave their hotels.

"Negotiating groups are in full swing," Mr. Moore said. "This conference will be a success."

Outside, protesters chanted: "Whose world? Our world! Whose streets? Our streets!"

Reaction of the trade delegates here seemed to run the gamut, from bewilderment to bemusement to, in some cases, anger. As demonstrators shouted "Go home! Go home!" a German delegate, Arnold Schwez, made his way back inside the Sheraton Hotel after he could not get through the crowd.

"These people don't understand the benefits of free trade to the developing nations," Mr. Schwez said.

Early tonight, as Christmas lights and displays came on in parts of downtown streets, demonstrators continued to hold their positions, and a few fires, most set in trash cans, burned in the street.

The governor of Washington State, Gary Locke, in announcing that he was calling in at least 200 troops from the state National Guard, said the troops were "trained in crowd control" and would be unarmed.

Mr. Moore told reporters: "This is a sad day. To those who argue that we should stop our work, I say: tell that to the poor, to the marginalized around the world who are looking to us to help them."

A spokesman for the Seattle police, Clem Benton, said tonight that he could confirm at least 19 arrests of protesters, several of whom were charged with assault, and that number appeared likely to rise.

The police continued to move through parts of downtown with armored personnel carriers. As white clouds of tear gas passed down the streets, protesters coughed, cried and asked for water. Further back, groups of demonstrators chanted, "The whole world is watching!"

In at least a few instances, uniformed officers fired rubber-coated capsules at protesters who the police believed were charging police lines. The pellets, which the police said contained chemical irritants, hit some of the protesters in the leg or the arm, causing visible welts.

"We are here peacefully; we just want our message to be heard," said Gloria Haselwander, a 21-year-old clerk in a Seattle music store who said she believes that the world trade group's rulings contributed to environmental destruction and ever-greater gaps between the world's richest people and its poorest. "We kept saying, 'No violence, no violence,' " she added, "but there was just this mass of gas. My throat hurts, my lungs still hurt."

Bill Simpich, a lawyer from San Francisco, said most protesters were intent on being nonviolent, but were also intent on continuing their demonstrations until the trade body's procedures were reformed to take account of health and environmental issues.

"We will keep marching until the process is open and until they let the people in the door when the decisions are made," said Mr. Simpich, who started his day in the rainy, pre-dawn darkness by gathering with other protesters in a park near the Pike Place Market and then marching toward the convention hall. Rain continued intermittently through the morning, but then stopped for most of the rest of the day.

Police officers in Seattle used tear gas to disperse protests against the World Trade Organization yesterday.

For Mayor Schell and other city leaders, who had once eagerly sought the meeting to showcase Seattle's role as a major exporter in one of the most trade-dependent regions of the country, the immediate focus tonight was simply on restoring order. But they were bound to face questions in the days ahead about their preparations for protests and, perhaps, to face conflicting criticism that the police moved too harshly on the protesters or did not act aggressively enough to head off the chaos.

Most of the demonstrators were clearly opposed to the window-smashing and other destructive acts by a small knot of protesters, most of whom were young men wearing masks and declining to give their names when asked by reporters.

"Anarchy rules!" said one, carrying a trash can down the street and then using it to smash a window of a Starbucks coffee shop.

At a news conference tonight, both the mayor and the police chief said they respected the right of protesters to gather here, and they blamed a small percentage of them for the violence. "We have demonstrators who are continuing to express their point of view," Chief Stamper said. "Most are doing it nonviolently; some are doing it violently."

The United Nations secretary general, Kofi Annan, was unable to deliver his speech to delegates. In his prepared text, he said: "Unless we convince developing countries that globalization really does benefit them, the backlash against it will become irresistible. That would be a tragedy for the developing world."

This morning, close to 20,000 union members and their allies packed Memorial Stadium, next to the Space Needle, to hear speeches by opponents of the trade organization. The speakers ranged from James P. Hoffa, the Teamsters union president, to Carl Pope, the executive director of the Sierra Club, and Wei Jingsheng, a Chinese dissident.

Speaker after speaker voiced anger that, in their depiction, the trade organization favored corporations and overturned national laws that protected the environment, endangered species and consumers.

Several union leaders also belittled the organization's push for free trade, saying it has encouraged American companies to move operations overseas where workers are paid far less and have few rights.

To thunderous applause, Jay Mazur, president of the Union of Needletrades, Industrial and Textile Employees, said, "The rules of this new global economy have been rigged against workers, and we're not going to play by them anymore."

A few union leaders took a protectionist tone, condemning the flood of imports, which they said had wiped out hundreds of thousands of well-paying American manufacturing jobs. But most union leaders focused on pressing the trade organization to protect workers' rights as a way to lift living standards around the world and to close the growing gap between rich and poor in many developing countries.

John Sweeney, the A.F.L.-C.I.O. president, said, "Until the W.T.O. addresses these issues, we should not and must not permit our country to participate in a new round of trade negotiations."

After the rally, the union members, joined by environmentalists and other protesters, began a two-mile-long march that skirted the area of the sit-ins and the tear gas. Protesters carried signs that included, "Labor Rights Not Trade Wrongs" and "End Corporate Rule."

As the marchers snaked through downtown, most of the best-known department stores, including Nordstrom and Bon Marche, were closed. Even many Starbucks were shut, with a protester painting "We Want Fair Wages" on the door of one.

The protesters marched past the Westin Hotel, where the American delegation is staying. The hotel was ringed by city buses that were purposely parked bumper to bumper to prevent the organization's critics from approaching the hotel.

The sit-ins brought traffic in many parts of the city to a standstill and angered many motorists. A sit-in at the corner of Sixth Avenue and Seneca Street prevented cars from leaving a freeway exit during the morning rush.

Stephanie Derouin, a customer service worker for Amazon.com. who was trapped for half an hour after taking the Seneca exit, said: "I sympathize with them, but I wish they didn't put me out like this. But if I didn't have a job, I'd probably be out there protesting with them."

* * *

December 1, 1999

SENSELESS IN SEATTLE

By THOMAS L. FRIEDMAN

Is there anything more ridiculous in the news today then the protests against the World Trade Organization in Seattle? I doubt it.

These anti-W.T.O. protesters—who are a Noah's ark of flat-earth advocates, protectionist trade unions and yuppies looking for their 1960's fix—are protesting against the wrong target with the wrong tools. Here's why:

What unites the anti-W.T.O. crowd is their realization that we now live in a world without walls. The cold-war system we just emerged from was built around division and walls; the globalization system that we are now in is built around integration and webs. In this new system, jobs, cultures, environmental problems and labor standards can much more easily flow back and forth.

The ridiculous thing about the protesters is that they find fault with this, and blame the W.T.O. The W.T.O. is not the cause of this world without walls, it's the effect. The more countries trade with one another, the more they need an institution to set the basic rules of trade, and that is all the W.T.O. does. "Rules are a substitute for walls—when you don't have walls you need more rules," notes the Council on Foreign Relations expert Michael Mandelbaum.

Because some countries try to use their own rules to erect new walls against trade, the W.T.O. adjudicates such cases. For instance, there was the famous "Flipper vs. GATTzilla" dispute. (The W.T.O. used to be known as GATT.) America has rules against catching tuna in nets that might also snare dolphins; other countries don't, and those other countries took the U.S. before a GATT tribunal and charged that our insistence on Flipper-free tuna was a trade barrier. The anti-W.T.O. protesters extrapolate from such narrow cases that the W.T.O. is going to become a Big Brother and tell us how to live generally. Nonsense.

What's crazy is that the protesters want the W.T.O. to become precisely what they accuse it of already being—a global government. They want it to set more rules—their rules, which would impose our labor and environmental standards on everyone else. I'm for such higher standards, and over time the W.T.O. may be a vehicle to enforce them, but it's not the main vehicle to achieve them. And they are certainly not going to be achieved by putting up new trade walls.

Every country and company that has improved its labor, legal and environmental standards has done so because of more global trade, more integration, more Internet—not less. These are the best tools we have for improving global governance.

Who is one of the top environmental advisers to DuPont today? Paul Gilding, the former head of Greenpeace! How could that be? A DuPont official told me that in the old days, if DuPont wanted to put a chemical factory in a city, it knew it just had to persuade the local neighbors. "Now we have six billion neighbors," said the DuPont official—meaning that DuPont knows that in a world without walls if it wants to put up a chemical plant in a country, every environmentalist is watching. And if that factory makes even a tiny spill those environmentalists will put it on the World Wide Web and soil DuPont's name from one end of the earth to the other.

I recently visited a Victoria's Secret garment factory in Sri Lanka that, in terms of conditions, I would let my own daughters work in. Why does it have such a high standard? Because anti-sweatshop activists have started to mobilize enough consumers to impress Victoria's Secret that if it doesn't get its shop standards up, consumers won't buy its goods. Sri Lanka is about to pass new copyright laws, which Sri Lankan software writers have been seeking for years to protect their own innovations. Why the new law now? Because Microsoft told Sri Lanka it wouldn't sell its products in a country with such weak intellectual property laws.

Hey, I want to save Flipper too. It's a question of how. If the protesters in Seattle stopped yapping, they would realize that they have been duped by knaves like Pat Buchanan—duped into thinking that power lies with the W.T.O. It doesn't. There's never going to be a global government to impose the rules the protesters want. But there can be better global governance—on the environment, intellectual property and labor. You achieve that not by adopting 1960's tactics in a Web-based world—not by blocking trade, choking globalization or getting the W.T.O. to put up more walls. That's a fool's errand.

You make a difference today by using globalization—by mobilizing the power of trade, the power of the Internet and the power of consumers to persuade, or embarrass, global corporations and nations to upgrade their standards. You change the world when you get the big players to do the right things for the wrong reasons. But that takes hard work—coalition-building with companies and consumers, and follow-up. It's not as much fun as a circus in Seattle.

* * *

December 2, 1999

REBELS IN SEARCH OF RULES

By NAOMI KLEIN

TORONTO—It is all too easy to dismiss the protesters at the World Trade Organization meeting in Seattle as radicals with 60's envy. A seemingly more trenchant criticism is that they are simply behind the curve, fighting against a tide of globalization that has already swamped them. Mike Moore, the director of the W.T.O., describes his opponents as nothing more than protectionists launching an assault on internationalism.

The truth, however, is that the protesters in Seattle have been bitten by the globalization bug as surely as the trade lawyers inside the Seattle hotels—though by globalization of a different sort—and they know it. The confusion about the protesters' political goals is understandable: this is the first movement born of the anarchic pathways of the Internet. There is no top-down hierarchy, no universally recognized leaders, and nobody knows what is going to happen next.

This protest movement is really anti-corporate rather than anti-globalist, and its roots are in the anti-sweatshop campaigns taking aim at Nike, the human rights campaign focusing on Royal Dutch/Shell in Nigeria and the backlash against Monsanto's genetically engineered foods in Europe.

At any time, one huge multinational company may be involved in several disputes—on labor, human rights and environmental issues, for example. Activists learn of one another as they aim at the same corporate target. Inadvertently, individual corporations have become symbols of the global economy in miniature, ultimately providing activists with name-brand entry points to the arcane world of the W.T.O.

This is the most internationally minded, globally linked movement the world has ever seen. There are no more faceless Mexicans or Chinese workers stealing our jobs, in part because those workers' representatives are now on the same e-mail lists and at the same conferences as the Western activists. When protesters shout about the evils of globalization, most are not calling for a return to narrow nationalism, but for the borders of globalization to be expanded, for trade to be linked to democratic reform, higher wages, labor rights and environmental protections.

This is what sets the young protesters in Seattle apart from their 60's predecessors. In the age of Woodstock, refusing to play by state and school rules was regarded as a political act in itself. Now, opponents of the W.T.O.—even those who call themselves anarchists—are outraged about a lack of rules and authority. They are demanding that national governments be free to exercise their authority without interference from the W.T.O. and asking for stricter international rules governing labor standards, environmental protection and scientific research.

Everyone, of course, claims to be all for rules, from President Clinton to Microsoft's chairman, Bill Gates. In an odd turn of events, the need for "rules-based trade" has become the mantra of the era of deregulation. But deregulation is by definition about the removal of rules. The W.T.O., charged with defining and enforcing deregulation, is only concerned with rules that regulate the removal of rules.

The W.T.O. has consistently sought to sever trade, quite unnaturally, from everything and everyone affected by it: workers, the environment, culture. This is why President Clinton's suggestion yesterday that the rift between the protesters and the delegates can be smoothed over with small compromises and consultation is so misguided.

The face-off is not between globalizers and protectionists, but between two radically different visions of globalization. One has had a monopoly for the last 10 years. Then other just had its coming-out party.

Naomi Klein is the author of "No Logo: Taking Aim at the Brand Bullies."

* * *

December 2, 1999

PRESIDENT CHIDES WORLD TRADE BODY IN STORMY SEATTLE

By DAVID E. SANGER

SEATTLE, Dec. 1—With Seattle's streets locked down by the police and National Guard, President Clinton delivered two impassioned pleas today for nations of the world to use trade agreements to protect the rights of laborers and the environment, and delivered a pointed attack on the World Trade Organization for the secrecy of its operations.

In several appearances here that took him past the shattered windows and closed shops of a normally vibrant downtown, Mr. Clinton sided with the cause of many of the peaceful demonstrators who jammed Seattle's streets on Tuesday, even as he denounced those who engaged in violence.

"What they are telling us in the streets is that this is an issue we've been silent on," Mr. Clinton told the ministers from 135 members of the World Trade Organization, which sets the rule for trade among their nations. "And we won't be silent anymore."

He said that "the sooner the W.T.O. opens up the process" of rule-making to outside groups, "we'll see less demonstrations and more constructive debate."

Even as Mr. Clinton spoke at Seattle's busy port and then to the group itself, the protests continued, though on a far

Reuters

President Clinton urged safeguards for workers' rights at the World Trade Organization meeting yesterday.

smaller and less destructive scale, and they prompted the city's mayor to extend a curfew to a second night.

Thousands of policemen, backed by 200 National Guard troops carrying clubs and by hundreds more waiting just outside the city, arrested more than 400 people who sat at intersections or who tried to block the delegates from getting to their meetings today.

Tonight, tear gas floated through the streets again around Mr. Clinton's downtown hotel, and the police struggled to break up demonstrations near Seattle's famous waterfront market.

Apparently under the strong suggestion of the federal authorities, the city radically changed its tactics for dealing with the demonstrators today, closing down virtually all streets where protesters had been allowed to roam freely on Tuesday and leaving broad boulevards eerily empty at midday. Even on the fringes of downtown, the officers confiscated cell phones and gas masks from the demonstrators, denying them the·two tools that allowed the protesters to run circles around the police the day before.

The results were immediate: Virtually all the trade group's delegates were able to move through the city easily. These

included trade ministers and foreign ministers, bureaucrats and hundreds of Clinton administration officials. On the top floors of the giant convention center here, with Secret Service agents controlling access, diplomats began hashing out the framework for a trade negotiation that will take three years or more to complete.

But questions about how city officials and the police handled the protests continued, and one American official said Britain's top representative here had told his hosts that "this was the most incompetent police operation I have ever seen."

While refusing to criticize Seattle officials in public, in private several American cabinet members fumed about how the city had handled the protests, saying in interviews that they had spent months warning the Seattle police about the possibilities of violence. "We even sent them a tape of a violent demonstration at the W.T.O.'s headquarters in Geneva," said one. "And when we got here, we looked out the windows and were astounded to discover they hadn't even put up barricades."

In an interview, Seattle's mayor, Paul Schell, defended his decision to allow protesters to gather. "If I had closed the city and denied the protesters' a chance to make their voices heard," he said, "we would have been severely criticized for denying free speech and perhaps for provoking more serious violence."

In another bid to show that he was listening to the protesters who gathered for the meeting, which ends Friday. Mr. Clinton announced two initiatives to help the poorest nations, mostly in Africa, which have complained that the global trading system victimizes their populations. The most important was relaxation of American trade rules that the president said would make it less expensive for African nations to purchase and distribute drugs that fight AIDS, including AZT.

Until recently the United States had backed major drug companies, which have insisted on strict control of the distribution of their drugs, often at high prices. Today the administration said it would allow nations to buy those drugs through "parallel distributors" in other developing countries, where the same drugs are often available more cheaply. But it is unclear how much of a difference the change will make for people with AIDS in Africa, most of whom are desperately poor.

Mr. Clinton, who is staying in Seattle overnight to attend some events on Thursday, said the United States would support an initiative to end tariffs on all goods exported by the poorest nations. But the details were sketchy, and it appeared, for instance, that the administration would bow to pressure in Congress and maintain high tariffs on textiles from Africa, one of the region's main exports.

This evening, trying to demonstrate that the effort to put an agenda together for the trade talks was back on track, the United States trade representative, Charlene Barshefsky, said, "Differences are definitely being narrowed." She and the chief of the trade organization, Mike Moore, canceled a dinner and reception for the ministers tonight, saying it was more important to negotiate than to socialize.

But in an interview this morning, Ms. Barshefsky conceded that most developing countries still oppose the top item on the American agenda: creating a "working group" in the trade organization that would examine issues of child labor, working conditions and the right to unionize. India, Brazil and other developing nations believe that even beginning talks on the topic is a step toward empowering the trade group to impose sanctions against countries that do not enforce a minimum set of labor standards. Indian officials charged again today that the United States and other nations would use such rules for protectionist purposes.

"It will be very, very tough," Ms. Barshefsky said of getting the trade group to look at labor issues, as her staff watched workers board up windows in the streets. "But perhaps these protests left an impression."

In fact, the American negotiators appear to be backing off a bit from their labor initiative. In private, several officials hinted they would probably accept any plan that allowed several international organizations, including the trade group, to examine the relationship between workers' rights and trade. The text of the American proposal calls for the International Labor Organization, the World Bank, the International Mone-

tary Fund and the United Nations to join in examining that relationship.

"What's important is the substance, not where the group is located," an American official said.

Mr. Clinton's strongest comments focused on one of the greatest complaints of environmental and labor groups: that the World Trade Organization is far too secretive, banning spectators and reporters from its court, and conducting almost all of its business behind closed doors.

"I think it's imperative that the W.T.O. become more open and accessible," Mr. Clinton told the ministers at a lunch today. "If the W.T.O. expects to have public support grow for our endeavors, the public must see and hear and, in a very real sense, actually join in the deliberations. That's the only way they can know the process is fair, and know their concerns were at least considered."

"I know there's a lot of controversy about this," he said, alluding to European and Asian nations that have argued that openness would make the trade group more political, and risk embarrassment for some governments as documents about their most politically sensitive industries became public.

Mr. Clinton also argued that developing nations should not be concerned that the United States would use the imposition of labor standards on other countries for economic advantage. He said, "I freely acknowledge that, if we had a certain kind of rule, then protectionists in wealthy countries could use things like wage differentials to keep poorer countries down," by arguing that "you're not paying your people enough."

The answer, he said, "is to write the rules in such a way that people in our position, the wealthier countries, can't do that, can't use this as an instrument of protectionism," adding, "We can find a way to do this."

* * *

December 2, 1999

THE VIOLENCE

Black Masks Lead to Pointed Fingers in Seattle

By TIMOTHY EGAN

SEATTLE, Dec. 1—It took only a few minutes for the people in the monarch butterfly costumes and union jackets to realize that what was planned as the biggest American demonstration yet against global trade here had turned into a burst of window-breaking and looting late Tuesday afternoon.

A surge of violence that ended in a civil emergency began when a knot of people dressed in black broke away from the main demonstration and started overturning trash containers, stoking fires and smashing windows of stores and restaurants. It died out with the image of a grinning young man in a Gap sweatshirt trying to cart off a satellite dish from a Radio Shack store.

How the thin line was crossed from nonviolent protest to urban disorder was being dissected here today as the World Trade Organization got down to business. The conclusion: the anarchists were organized.

One person in black, who refused to identify himself, said anarchists had planned all along to incite the crowd.

Some blamed the police for mounting a show of force with rubber pellets and tear gas against largely nonviolent protesters, and then backing off to leave a lawless zone within the city's most gilded retail corridors. At first, the protesters tried to police themselves—something they said they were incapable of doing once the more militant elements took hold.

Veteran demonstrators, who have logged years of protest against corporate retail chains like Nike and Starbucks, suddenly found themselves trying to defend them.

"We turned at one point to protect Niketown, of all places, from these people who were trying to smash the storefront glass with metal newspaper boxes," said Ken Butigan, a professor of theology from Berkeley, Calif. "They turned on us and called us counterrevolutionaries."

Mr. Butigan teaches protest tactics at Berkeley, he said. He and other demonstrators had expected—and prepared for—the police to make about 1,000 arrests. But they made only a handful of arrests, relying on the stinging vapor of tear gas to disperse people who refused to allow delegates into the trade group's opening session.

Young people in black masks, some of them speaking by two-way radios, used the police reaction as a cue to go on a rampage. They sprayed a symbol for anarchy—a circled A— on store walls, then quickly expanded to window breaking and some looting. Some identified themselves as members of Black Clad Messengers, a self-proclaimed anarchist group.

For merchants in a downtown known as one of the nation's most prosperous and vibrant—as the eyes of the world were looking this way and holiday shoppers were expected to crowd the aisles—it was a pure terror.

"We called 911 from inside our store, asking for help, telling them that people were rampaging in the streets, but they said they were too busy," said Maryann Swissa, who runs a jewelry store with her husband, Monty. "We ended up getting an ex-National Football League player to stand guard at the door."

At the peak of the disorder, even protesters who had planned to be arrested were calling for help.

"Here we are protecting Nike, McDonald's, the Gap and all the while I'm thinking, 'Where are the police? These anarchists should have been arrested,' " said Medea Benjamin, a leader with Global Exchange, a San Francisco-based protest group. Ms. Benjamin was arrested later inside the trade meeting on trespassing charges.

The Seattle police said today that their primary goal was to protect trade delegates and allow them to enter the meeting. When violence began, they did not have enough force to go into the unruly crowds, Police Chief Norm Stamper said. Today, the police made about 400 arrests of mostly nonviolent protesters.

"What we did today was utterly impossible yesterday," Mr. Stamper said. "We would have had to have double and triple the number of officers on hand. And the mayor did not want to send a message that Seattle is a police state."

The major demonstrations—one organized by labor unions, the other by environmentalists—attracted up to 30,000 people, Mayor Paul Schell said. They passed through the city in a festive mood, their banners referring to efforts by Europeans to protect cheese and Americans to protect jobs. One banner read: "Hormone beef—no. Roquefort Cheese—yes."

But minutes after the union and environmental groups passed through downtown, the mood changed. Shouts of "Anarchy!" "Property is theft!" and "Close it down!" went up, as up to 50 people unveiled hammers, spray paint and large firecrackers known as M-80's from backpacks. They smashed windows of branches of virtually every major retail chain, including F. A. O. Schwarz, Old Navy, Planet Hollywood and McDonald's.

A security officer who tried to defend a city bus was attacked. The authorities later said that several bus drivers were assaulted and that two police officers suffered minor injuries. They said there were no major injuries to demonstrators, although hundreds of people complained about stinging tear gas.

The violence's peak lasted about an hour, in late afternoon, with virtually no police response. Some demonstrators shouted at the vandals to stop the violence. At Niketown, three men climbed atop of the store's outside entrance and began twisting away the metal letters spelling out the store name. As this went on, others shouted "Shame, shame, shame" at the vandals.

Prompted by desperate complaints from merchants and television images of a near riot, the Seattle police changed tactics early in the evening, after Mayor Schell asked for the National Guard troops and declared a 7 p.m. curfew and civil emergency. From then until about 10 p.m., the police gradually moved the thinning crowds out of downtown.

The police said today that they had arrested several people who they said were part of the Tuesday violence, though they offered few details on where they were from or the extent of their plan. Mr. Stamper defended the police tactics, though he was criticized for refusing an earlier offer of National Guard help. Today, about 300 National Guard troops helped to patrol the city.

By this morning, the groups that had planned to be arrested all along sent out a call for a "massive cleanup" of the damage done by people they labeled as vandals. Dozens of the protesters took brooms to the fresh scars of the city's retail core.

*　*　*

December 3, 1999

U.S. EFFORT TO ADD LABOR STANDARDS TO AGENDA FAILS

By STEVEN GREENHOUSE and JOSEPH KAHN

SEATTLE, Dec. 2—The Clinton administration failed today to rally broad support among nations to add labor standards to the World Trade Organization agenda, threatening its most important goal at a meeting here that has been plagued by sometimes violent protests.

Caught between clashing demands of poor nations and the American labor movement, the administration struggled to work out a compromise that would have the trade organization set up a study group on labor standards. Such a move is widely seen as a first step toward having the body consider issues like child labor and workers' rights when setting trade rules.

But the negotiations, never easy, stumbled badly after President Clinton stunned the delegates, and even his own negotiators, when he told The Seattle Post-Intelligencer this week that the trade group should at some point use sanctions to enforce core labor rights around the world.

His suggestion went well beyond the official administration line that it was pushing members of the trade organization merely to set up a study group on labor issues—not to punish countries that do not live up to the Western ideas of labor rights.

The president ended his day-and-a-half visit here and left Seattle today. The meeting is scheduled to end on Friday afternoon.

The Egyptian trade minister, Youssef Boutros-Ghali, said the proposal on sanctions derailed any hope of a compromise agreement on the issue. "If you start using trade as a lever to implement nontrade related issues," Mr. Boutros-Ghali said, "that will be the end of the multilateral trading system, maybe not this year, but in 10 to 15 years."

A trade minister from Pakistan, discussing labor issues at a negotiating session today, used blunt language on the matter, according to one Western official who was briefed on the meeting. "We will block consensus on every issue if the United States proposal goes ahead," the official quoted the Pakistani minister as saying. "We will explode the meeting."

Administration officials spent much of the day seeking to calm the storm that Mr. Clinton's comments had produced. Officials said they were looking to assure other countries that his use of the word sanctions did not amount to a mandate for the trade group to dictate labor standards or to punish countries that failed to live up to them.

"There's no question that our effort to have a working group of trade and labor is a tough fight, and one that has required us to do significant amounts of outreach to try to explain what the intent and purpose of this is," said Gene Sperling, the president's economic adviser. "By no means would we ever want something dealing with core labor standards to ever be used as a facade or guise to do anything that would be harmful to developing countries."

The American labor movement's campaign to link trade rules with workers' rights has emerged as a pivotal issue at the ministerial meeting of the trade organization here, where 135 nations are wrangling over a multitude of issues like biotechnology and subsidies for farm exports.

The meeting has been the target of thousands of protesters, who have demanded that the trade group do more to protect the environment and the interests of workers. The protests, which were marred by an outbreak of violence on Tuesday, dwindled today. But opponents of the group marched on the King County Jail this afternoon to demand the release of 500 people who were arrested as the police sought to restore order to downtown.

Mr. Clinton signed a treaty today that bars the most abusive forms of child labor, including the use of children as indentured laborers or in prostitution, mines and armies. Mr. Clinton said the treaty should be a model for enforcing other labor rights.

The European Union trade minister, Pascal Lamy, voiced concern that there was so much friction at the talks that they could fall apart without fulfilling the goal of setting up an agenda for a fresh round of talks, tentatively dubbed the Millennium Round, that would last for three years and aim at further reducing trade barriers.

The United States trade representative, Charlene Barshefsky, was far more upbeat, saying the talks were moving steadily forward. She said that progress had been made on a range of issues and that she remained optimistic that members would agree to a negotiating framework for the future talks.

Angering many developing countries, the American labor movement has pressed the Clinton administration to make the World Trade Organization allow members to impose trade sanctions on other nations that violate basic workers' rights like prohibitions on child labor and the right to form trade unions.

The A.F.L.-C.I.O., already upset at Mr. Clinton over his trade deal with China, pressed him fiercely this week to gain an agreement that could ultimately lead to letting trade sanctions be used against countries that violate basic workers' rights.

The thousands of protesters who paralyzed Seattle this week have also pressed the administration to use the talks to make W.T.O. rules what they consider friendlier to labor, human rights and the environment.

But India, Brazil and Egypt, taking the lead for the developing world, sought to block the creation of a panel that could lead to trade sanctions over labor rights. Many ministers from developing countries said such sanctions could be disguised protectionist measures that would be used to ban imports from developing countries.

Mr. Boutros-Ghali attacked Mr. Clinton's call to link trade with labor rights. "It is nonsensical," he said. "The question is why all of a sudden, when third-world labor has proved to be competitive, why do industrial countries start feeling concerned about our workers? When all of a sudden there is a concern about the welfare of our workers, it is suspicious."

Administration officials suggested gingerly that they might move toward a compromise European Union proposal that would set up a group outside the World Trade Organization to study the link between trade and labor rights.

Opposing such a compromise, the president of the A.F.L.-C.I.O., John Sweeney, insisted at a private meeting with Mr. Clinton that any working group should make its recommendations directly to the World Trade Organization.

Mr. Sweeney's approach, union officials say, would accelerate the timetable for the trade group to adopt enforceable labor rights. "I reiterated to the president how important it was to get these things in our trade agreements," Mr. Sweeney said in an interview. "The president says he's all for it. But he said he's having a tough time with the developing countries."

White House officials fear that if they disappoint American labor, that could badly hurt Vice President Al Gore, who is counting on unions' support in his campaign for the presidency. Mr. Sweeney indicated that if disappointed, the unions would redouble their efforts to press Congress to defeat the president's trade pact with China.

Several trade officials said Mr. Clinton clearly intended to soften developing countries' opposition to an accord on labor rights by granting them two large concessions on Wednesday. He announced that the United States would cut tariffs on developing world exports and would ease patent rules to enable developing countries to buy pharmaceuticals more cheaply.

But the administration was still having trouble having the developing countries agree to a panel that makes recommendations to the Word Trade Organization.

The trade minister of Kenya, Nicholas Biwott, said, "The best forum to deal with such matters is the International Labor Organization." That organization is an international body under the United Nations that researches labor issues and promotes workers' rights, but has minimal enforcement powers.

For years, labor leaders around the world have complained that the I.L.O. is a toothless, underfinanced agency unable to stop child labor and to protect other rights.

The European Union has proposed setting up a forum in which the World Trade Organization, the International Labor Organization, the International Monetary Fund and multilateral groups examine how globalized trade affects workers around the world.

America's organized labor, which is critical to Mr. Gore's political future, wants any such group to be a part of the World Trade Organization. "We don't care what it's called," Mr. Sweeney said. "You can call it anything you want, so long as it is done the way we want and is part of the W.T.O."

* * *

December 3, 1999

DARK PARALLELS WITH ANARCHIST OUTBREAKS IN OREGON

By SAM HOWE VERHOVEK and JOSEPH KAHN

SEATTLE, Dec. 2—They call themselves anarchists, and they go by first names only: Spider, Possum, Nimo, Hawaii, Burdock, Rob. Some come from Eugene, Ore., where the anarchists have had regular clashes with the police, most seriously after a march last June turned into a riot, with smashed windows and 19 people arrested.

And early this week, just before the World Trade Organization meeting was getting under way here, the teenagers and young 20-somethings came to Seattle. They took over a privately owned, vacant warehouse at the edge of downtown here, which they now call "the Squat," and proclaim to be their home. "Rent is Theft," says the sign one posted to a window the other day.

Many are clad head to toe in black, complete with bandannas, and security seems to be a big issue for them these days. "Security guards" communicated to each other via walkie-talkies as they escorted a visitor along the dark passageways of the Squat and up to their communal meeting room today.

"We're not really into having our identities known," said one young man, who gave his name as Black. Another explained that they hoped to avoid the "hassles" of a lawsuit brought by the warehouse owner, Wah Lui, who has been negotiating fruitlessly to get his building back while the police, wary of a violent confrontation, have so far held off from storming the building.

While they accepted the term anarchist, some suggested that "anti-authoritarian" or "humanist" better expressed their basic belief that all governments and corporations are bad and should be drastically curtailed if not abolished. Many are articulate and evidently well read, but few said they wished to discuss much about their upbringing. All in the group of roughly two dozen meeting today were white. The police in Eugene said many of the anarchists there were young men and women from middle-class backgrounds who congregated in the city after fallings-out with their parents.

With the authorities here blaming young anarchists for causing much of the smashed windows and other vandalism that racked the downtown area on Tuesday, it is not at all surprising that most in the group of squatters here were somewhat evasive about where they were that day and what they did.

A few, in fact, said they might have smashed a window or two, but carefully noted that any destruction they might have committed was against stores representing what they said were "multinational corporations" like Starbucks, Nike or the Gap. "We didn't hurt any person or any living thing," said a young bandanna-wearing man who would not give his name.

Just what involvement any particular person in this group had in Tuesday's events remains unclear, and Seattle police conceded today that they have arrested only a fraction of the

Members of a group that occupied a warehouse in Seattle did not mind the label anarchist. Some suggested "anti-authoritarian" or "humanist."

people, many clad in black clothes and masks, who they believe ran wild on Tuesday and caused mayhem even as other protesters shouted "Shame, shame" or even tried to stop the destruction.

Seattle authorities said they could not state that there was a direct connection between the Eugene group and the chaos in the streets, but the police did say they were talking to police investigators in Eugene to learn more about the group there, which is relatively visible in that university town.

Nearly 75 showed up at a Northwest anarchist conference in Eugene in June, and shortly afterwards eight police officers were injured when a march called by the Anarchist Action Collective turned into a riot, in which the anarchists hurled rocks and bricks through bank signs, shop windows, a hotel and motorists' cars.

"The event they staged here was so similar it is almost spooky," Capt. Thad Buchanan of the Eugene police said in an interview today, comparing it to the anarchists' apparent role in the Seattle melee. "We were assured in advance that it would be a peaceful protest, and the next thing we knew they were doing damage all over the place."

The group's intellectual cheerleader is a 56-year-old author of anarchist tracts, John Zerzan, who has attracted some local attention by carrying on a regular correspondence with Theodore J. Kaczynski, the man imprisoned as the Unabomber.

Mr. Zerzan, who was in Seattle on Monday and Tuesday, declined to say whether he knew anyone who damaged property on Tuesday. "I can't be sure," he said in a telephone interview today. "After all, they were all wearing masks." But he did offer a spirited defense of the basic idea of anarchy and of the means that some might choose to achieve it.

"The question is, what does it take to be effective when things are at this stage of crisis?" said Mr. Zerzan, citing teenage alienation and suicide, homelessness, environmental degradation as symptoms of the planet's despair.

Anarchists' protests in Eugene have often focused on environmental issues, including a fervent campaign against plans to remove dozens of old trees in the downtown area to clear room for a parking lot and new residential buildings.

Though the young men and women gathered here at the Squat spoke of their desire to get rid of corporate rule, they did not seem at all bellicose during their communal meeting here. They spent considerable time discussing basic issues like how to make their home more livable—"if anybody here knows something about plumbing, that'd be rad," said one young woman.

Several in the group said they were there to make a stand against homelessness. "Housing is a right, not a privilege, and that's the bottom line," said one man with a green bandanna around his face, who gave his name as Rahnna. Yet, when two homeless men who appeared to be in their 40's came by today looking for space in the warehouse, they were sent away by the young squatters, with the explanation that the collective would need to discuss whether they were welcome.

The Seattle police are taking a decidedly hands-off view of the squatters.

"The situation is being monitored," said Randy Huserik, a detective with the Seattle Police Department. "Once the W.T.O. wraps up, our attention will probably return there. With the number of people in there, there would be a great deal of tactical issues to deal with" in getting them out, he added. "And we have bigger fish to fry right now."

Mr. Buchanan, of the Eugene police force, said he had learned that a "sizable contingent" of Eugene anarchists had made their way to Seattle to participate in the demonstrations. But, as both he and the Seattle police emphasized, they could not say how many from that group had been involved in Tuesday's vandalism.

And Jan Power, a spokeswoman for the Eugene department, said not all anarchists were bent on property destruction. "There's a core group that's into violence," she said. "But there's a broader group that's just more philosophically into the concept of anarchy."

* * *

December 8, 1999

SENSELESS IN SEATTLE II

By THOMAS L. FRIEDMAN

Now that the Seattle World Trade Organization summit meeting is over, we can ask: Was it a turning point, or just an exclamation point? That depends entirely on how the protesters and governments interpret Seattle. Here is my own guide:

What the serious protesters got right: My environmentalist allies say my criticism of the protesters in Seattle was too broad-brush. There were some serious groups there raising serious points, particularly the notion that the W.T.O. has no need or right to be so secretive. If it is deciding that a U.S. law banning tuna caught in nets that also catch dolphins is a trade barrier, the W.T.O. should at least allow environmentalists to file a brief or meet with judges. The W.T.O. can't promote open trade by ruling in the dark. It would enhance its own legitimacy if it opened up.

What the protesters got wrong: The biggest negative fallout from Seattle is the way it smeared free trade. I fear that politicians all over America will look at Seattle and say, "Wow, if that's what you get when you support free trade, I'm hiding."

President Clinton has been a real stand-up guy on free trade—until last week. I know in an election year he has to tip his hat to the A.F.L.-C.I.O. But we can't afford the full-body kowtow. Mr. Clinton effectively kidnapped the

Democratic Party seven years ago, moved it into the Republican economic agenda—including free trade, Nafta and the W.T.O. for China—while holding onto much of the Democrats' social agenda. But his tacit ally in this was Newt Gingrich. As long as the "evil Newt" was out there with his extreme agenda, Mr. Clinton was able to hold the Democrats behind him. But what you saw in Seattle is what the activist base of the Democratic Party looks like—without the fear of Newt. It is a wildly diverse coalition that, without strong leadership from the top of the Democratic Party, could really pull it over a cliff on free trade.

Where we go from here: "It's amazing how caught up some activists are in the old world," says Paul Gilding, the former head of Greenpeace who now advises multinationals on sustainable development. "The old model is you go into the streets, raise the outrage of the community, get the government to pass a law, the companies resist, eventually a compromise is reached and in five years things change."

The groups making the biggest difference today are those working with multinationals and consumers—showing the companies how they can be both green and profitable, while making clear to them that if they don't upgrade their environmental and labor practices, the activist community will mount a campaign against them through the Internet and consumers all over the world. "The smart activists," says Mr. Gilding, "understand that the market, and global integration, is now king, and this can be a great boon to environmentalists and a great threat to big companies."

Sure, the W.T.O. ruled against the U.S. laws banning tuna caught in nets that also catch dolphins. But I just went to my Giant supermarket and checked every can of tuna. They all said: "Dolphin safe." Now how could that be? Because the smart activists ignored the W.T.O. ruling, mobilized consumers to pressure the tuna companies, the tuna companies pressured the fishermen and Flipper got saved. That's how you change the world. If we didn't have free trade with Mexican fishermen, would we have been able to pressure them into using dolphin-safe nets on the tuna they sell us? Not a chance. "Our decision to go dolphin safe was purely based on consumer feedback," Michael Mullen, spokesman for StarKist tuna, told me. "We get about 1,000 calls and 300 consumer e-mails a week."

Laws and regulations protecting workers, water and trees still matter. My argument is simply that the best way to strengthen those laws, and to get developing countries to abide by them, is by activists mobilizing consumers, pressuring companies and using free trade—not choking it.

But too many unions and activists want the quick fix for globalization: just throw up some walls and tell everyone else how to live. There was a country that tried that. It guaranteed everyone's job, maintained a protected market and told everyone else how to live. It was called the Soviet Union. Didn't work out so well. In the end it probably did more damage to its environment and workers than any country in history.

* * *

December 13, 1999

CAUGHT IN A U.S. CIVIL WAR

By NORBERT WALTER

FRANKFURT—In the eyes of most outsiders, the United States, with its dynamic companies and strong lead in high technology, is the prime beneficiary of globalization. And yet, in the wake of the disastrous World Trade Organization meeting in Seattle, it is effectively presenting itself as one of globalization's most aggrieved victims.

No wonder, then, that many abroad see the United States as a nation divided against itself. It dominates the world economy with its strong economic performance, but at the same time feels deeply insecure about participating in the global economic system.

In my view, this confusing attitude is to a large extent due to one phenomenon: Quite a few Americans are currently determined to make globalization the catch-all phrase for issues that primarily warrant debate within the United States: American wage inequality and the accessibility of American workers to benefits.

American labor unions and their allies opposing globalization argue that free trade is costing American workers their well-paying manufacturing jobs with generous benefits, and thus contributes to growing wage inequality. But the entire set of worker issues has much deeper roots than globalization.

To prove this, you just have to look to Europe. While we have our fair share of problems to deal with, sharp income disparities are not among them, despite globalization. Moreover the same corporations often give their employees higher wages and better benefits in Europe than in the United States.

The American political system has chosen great flexibility in the labor market and comparatively little government intervention in the economy. These choices work well for many Americans but leave others behind. And all of the issues they raise have been around since long before globalization dominated the scene.

That is why people outside the United States worry now that, for many Americans, the rest of the world simply provides a convenient stage on which to carry out an internal debate. The W.T.O.—with its power over the entire world economy—is not the right forum for dealing with what essentially are domestic American problems. Wage inequality in the United States will hardly be resolved by imposing labor standards on developing countries and enforcing them with sanctions, as President Clinton has suggested.

Observers who are not part of the internal American debate should be forgiven for their irritation at being dragged into this family quarrel. Viewed from abroad, the rather unexpected American attack on the global trading system appears particularly strange. The current system and its institutions—like the International Monetary Fund, the World Bank and the W.T.O.—were created largely by American design.

Now that most countries around the world are, at least to some degree, embracing the American-inspired free-market

model that drives them, it is bewildering to see significant forces inside the United States trying to distance themselves from it.

Of course, the root of the conflict is in domestic American politics. Some analysts have begun to compare the trade policy of the United States to its conduct of the Kosovo conflict, with losses to be avoided at almost any cost. This leads to a surreal negotiating strategy: unless American politicians can ensure that globalization makes every last American a complete victor and satisfies every American concern, it is an unacceptable proposition for the United States.

This is disconcerting.

Historically, most successful trading regimes have relied on at least one country that is strong enough—and, above all, willing—to enforce the rules and, if needed, make some concessions to keep the process moving. In the 50 years since the end of World War II, the United States has done a tremendous job of filling this role.

Americans will be quick to point out that others, especially the Europeans and the Japanese, must share the burdens of economic leadership. But political realists also have to consider that Europe and Japan are in the midst of the painful transformation that the United States economy underwent in the late 1980's and early 1990's.

The United States economy is strong and continues to grow. The United States has it in its power not to shun its global responsibilities. At a minimum, other countries, facing their own adjustment costs from continued change in the world trading system, will not agree to the American demand that no American be disadvantaged by global trade.

Norbert Walter is chief economist for Deutsche Bank.

* * *

December 17, 1999

WHY INDIA AND OTHERS SEE U.S. AS VILLAIN ON TRADE

By CELIA W. DUGGER

NEW DELHI, Dec. 16—The week after global trade talks collapsed in Seattle, India's commerce and industry minister rose in Parliament here to denounce what he called a pernicious attempt by the richest, most powerful nations—led by President Clinton—to rob developing countries of their great advantage in trade: cheap labor.

And, he said, what had really galvanized the developing countries' rebellion against the creation of a working group on labor in the World Trade Organization was Mr. Clinton's remark, in an interview with a Seattle newspaper, about an eventual use of trade sanctions against nations that failed to comply with international labor standards.

The cabinet minister, Murasoli Maran, who was India's chief representative at the talks, described Mr. Clinton's statements as having electrified envoys from developing countries, made the danger to their economic interests clear, and unified them in opposition to any linkage of trade and labor standards.

"Sir, finally the last straw was cast by President Clinton himself," Mr. Maran declared. "It made all the developing countries and least-developing countries to harden their position. It created such a furor that they all felt the danger ahead."

In large part because of Mr. Clinton's handling of the issue, the American attempt to add labor issues to the international trade agenda widened the gulf between rich and poor nations and contributed to the collapse of the latest efforts to further free up world trade.

In the eyes of India, Egypt and other third world nations, Mr. Clinton's call to link trade accords to labor standards for workers around the world was protectionism in the guise of idealism, motivated by his desire to woo labor union support for the presidential campaign of his vice president, Al Gore.

Some delegates from developing countries even expressed the belief that he had orchestrated the sometimes violent street protests in Seattle to justify the American position.

"The Western world, the industrialized world, wants to take away our comparative advantage," Mr. Maran said. "It is a pernicious way of robbing our comparative advantage. The developing countries consider it as a maneuver by wealthy nations to force our wages up, to undermine our competitiveness. This is the secret."

Opposition to the inclusion of labor standards in trade deals was not limited to government officials. In India, even labor unions that regularly battle employers for higher wages and improved benefits opposed using trade negotiations as leverage for a better deal.

Before the Seattle talks began, while American unions and others were planning street demonstrations to demand that trade accords protect workers' rights, Indian unions were quietly meeting with government officials and agreeing to oppose any linkage between trade and labor standards.

D. L. Sachdev, secretary of the All India Trade Union Congress, which represents 2.5 million workers in industrial and service jobs, said it was peculiar to stand on the same side as employers and the government.

But he and other union leaders here maintained that making trade agreements conditional on meeting labor standards could be used to keep out goods from low-wage countries like India, damaging workers and employment in those industries.

"Unfortunately, trade unions in developed countries feel that because of cheap labor and relocation of industries by multinational corporations, their employment prospects are imperiled," Mr. Sachdev said.

With some trade unions' backing, a group of cabinet ministers headed by Prime Minister Atal Behari Vajpayee agreed before the country's delegation left for Seattle that India would oppose the proposal for a working group on labor and trade.

"This was not an issue on which there could be compromise," said N. K. Singh, a civil servant who is one of Mr. Vajpayee's top advisers.

The developing countries won vigorous backing from a group of African, Latin American and Asian academics, led by the Columbia University economist Jagdish Bhagwati. They, as well as a variety of labor and nongovernmental leaders, signed a statement against including labor and environmental issues in trade deals. Their contention was that the labor issues in particular are selectively used against developing countries for the economic gain of the richer nations. For example, President Clinton had cited child labor, a problem of developing countries like India, but had made no mention of lax enforcement of laws to protect workers in garment sweatshops or migrant farm workers in the United States.

Professor Bhagwati, who began calling for India to open itself to foreign trade and investment 25 years before it began to do so, said that those who signed the statement were strong opponents of child labor and bad working conditions, but thought that trade deals were the wrong place to combat them.

The Indian delegation arrived in Seattle not expecting that the labor issue would be at the top of the American agenda. Just a month earlier, the United States trade representative, Charlene Barshefsky, had met in Lausanne, Switzerland with ministers from more than 20 countries, including India, Brazil, Egypt, South Africa and Argentina, and assured them that the United States wanted a group that would only study labor issues, officials here said. It had no intention, the officials added, of taking the matter any further.

Since the Seattle talks collapsed on Dec. 3, President Clinton has said that India and Pakistan, another outspoken opponent of linking trade and labor standards, had misunderstood his remarks.

The president said he had not meant to suggest that the United States would cut off American markets to India and Pakistan if they did not raise wages to American levels.

But government officials and labor leaders here say they see the United States as calculatingly pursuing its own interests on trade—and they are girding for future battle.

Mr. Maran, speaking in Parliament, said, "If you ask me to tell you in one word what happened in Seattle, my answer will be, 'We have postponed D-Day.' "

GENERAL INDEX

accountability, corporate, 368, 374–76, 518
Acheson, Dean, 99
Adidas, 32, 374
ADMs. *See* anti-dumping measures
Advanced Micro Devices, 285
advertising: Canadian taxes on, 507; English
    language dominance and, 330–31;
    European Common Market and, 180–81;
    globalization of, 344; Internet and, 291
AFL-CIO: and corporate accountability, 376; and
    globalization, 151; and global
    rule-making, 152; NAFTA and, 156, 164,
    165, 168; and protectionism, 147; at
    Seattle meeting of WTO, 544, 550, 553,
    558, 559; at World Economic Forum
    meeting, 510
Africa: AIDS in, 556; art in, 317–18; ecotourism
    in, 347; nongovernmental organizations
    in, 520; poverty in, 522; as Republican
    paradise, 39; sub-Saharan, 271, 377.
    See also specific countries
Agency for International Development, 352
agricultural biotechnology, 232
agricultural subsidies, European Community, 117,
    119, 120–21, 185; U.S. objections to, 122,
    123, 125, 139, 176
agriculture: anarcho-primitivist rejection of, 515;
    industrialized, McDonald's as symbol of,
    509, 511; tariffs on, 125; Uruguay Round
    of GATT on, 114, 115, 116, 125, 129, 130.
    See also farmers
aid, foreign: *vs.* bailouts, 493; within European
    Community, 197, 198; and gender issues,
    366–67; grass-roots, 354–55; Kennedy
    Round of GATT and, 113; loans *vs.* grants
    as, 542, 543; microlending and, 352–53,
    366; OPEC's demand for, 312;
    post–World War II, 96; *vs.* private
    investment, 468; U.S. and, 543–44.
    See also bailouts
Airbus Industrie, 150, 253
airline industry: European, 150; international
    cooperation in, 252–53
Albright, Madeleine K., 39, 469, 551
Algeria, 311
Allende Gossens, Salvador, 214, 218, 220
Alliance for Progress, 366
Allied Signal Inc., 169
Amazon.com, 365
American Express Company, 257
American Fair Trade Association, 372

American Federation of Labor. *See* AFL-CIO
Americanization, 320–22, 356; of Asia, 316–17,
    326–30, 337–39; backlash against, 48,
    334, 508–10, 511–12, 516; Canadian
    apprehensiveness about, 506–7;
    explanations for, 320–21; Internet and,
    323–24; of literary tastes, 325–26; myth
    of, 328; positive impact of, 330
American Motors Corporation, 239
American Selling Price (ASP) system, 113
American Telephone and Telegraph Company
    (AT&T), 286, 546
America Online (AOL), 296
Americas, Free Trade Area of, proposal for, 191.
    See also Western Hemisphere free-trade
    zone
Amish, 367
Amnesty International, 372, 510
anarchism, 513–15, 516, 541, 552, 554, 557,
    559–61
anarcho-primitivism, 515
Andean nations, free trade area of, 182
Andersen Consulting, 47, 296
Angola, 39
Annan, Kofi, 552
Annecy accords (1949), 106
anti-dumping measures (ADMs): developing
    countries' demands on, 545; GATT and,
    121, 131; restraint on use of, 146
AOL (America Online), 296
APEC (Asia Pacific Economic Cooperation),
    268–69, 470
apparel industry: labor standards in, 553;
    pressures on, 388; sweatshops in, 244–45
    (*See also* sweatshops); White House
    partnership with, 376–77, 380, 386–87.
    See also textile industry
Apple Computer Inc., 229, 285–86, 349, 350
Arab-Israeli conflict, oil as weapon in, 298–99,
    302–6, 521
Arafat, Yasser, 7, 23
arbitrage profits, 264, 284
arbitration. *See* dispute-settlement mechanism
Argentina: Asian financial crisis and, 493;
    austerity measures in, 525; currency board
    in, 454; domestic content regulations in,
    340; foreign investment in, 233;
    globalization and, 48; IMF line of credit
    to, 538; international trade of, early
    20th-century, 58–59; and Mercosur, 189;
    Mexican peso crisis and, 456, 457;

poverty in, 536; protectionism in, 126;
    U.S. protectionism and, 81–82
Armco Steel Corporation, 212
ASEAN (Association of Southeast Asian
    Nations), 174
Asia: Americanization of, 316–17, 326–30,
    337–39; cartoon studios in, 249–51;
    construction boom in, 462, 463, 485–86;
    crony capitalism in, 360, 361; financial
    crisis in (*See* Asian financial crisis);
    foreign investment in, 480–81, 482;
    regionalism in, 174, 176; sweatshops in,
    31–32, 368–69, 384–85, 389; trade
    policies in, 126; unemployment in, 385.
    See also specific countries
Asian Development Bank, 476
Asian financial crisis, 462–503; compared to
    bank run, 473; conspiracy theories
    regarding, 466–67, 470; contagion effect
    of, 277, 464, 474, 489–96; factors
    responsible for, 479, 485, 488–89; and
    fear of globalization, 12, 20; and financial
    regulation, 281; and Geneva trade
    agreement (1997), 278, 279; IMF bailout
    package for, 473–74, 481; Japan's
    experience in, 474–75; lessons from,
    468–69, 501–3; management of, steps to,
    474; prevention of, missed opportunities
    for, 483–84, 491; recovery after, 498–99;
    social impact of, 360–61, 494–95, 498;
    and sweatshops, 384–86; and U.S.,
    469–70, 471, 474, 478, 496, 497–98, 503
Asian Indians, 24–25
Asian Monetary Fund, proposal for, 491
Asia Pacific Economic Cooperation (APEC),
    268–69, 470
ASP (American Selling Price system), 113
Aspe Armella, Pedro, 440, 446
assembly plants: in Brazil, 538–39; in Mexico,
    30–31, 157
Associated Press, 290
Association of Southeast Asian Nations
    (ASEAN), 174
athletes, and social issues, 31–32
AT&T, 286, 546
Attac (organization), 48
austerity measures, 522, 523–25, 534
Australia: economic nationalism in, 215; tariffs
    in, 76; and Thai rescue package, 465;
    U.S. tariff surcharge (1971) and, 405,
    408

Austria: Bretton Woods crisis and, 399; and
  European Community, 175
authoritarianism, *vs.* globalization, 34, 361
automobile industry
  Brazilian, 524
  European, 150, 223
  German, 234–36
  global division of labor in, 237–40, 245–47
  global markets and, 222–24, 226–27
  Japanese, 125, 222, 223, 224
  joint ventures in, 245–47
  local content regulations and, 339
  pre-assembled parts in, 538–39
  Uruguay Round of GATT and, 125
  U.S., 222–24; European tariffs on, 79, 83;
    imported parts and, 237–38, 239;
    investment in Mexico, 157–58; Mexican
    peso crisis and, 442, 443–44; NAFTA and,
    166–67, 169; protectionism and, 148;
    recession of 1980s and, 139; tariff
    surcharge and, 406
  See also specific companies
AVX Corporation, 242

baht (Thai), devaluation of, 462, 463–64, 465,
  466, 483, 484
bailouts, financial: in Asian crisis, 473–74, 481; as
  bad precedents, 477–78; banks as
  beneficiaries of, 492–93; of Brazil, 479,
  496; of Indonesia, 23, 50, 474, 477, 492; of
  Mexico, 452–53, 457–59, 460, 471, 489;
  public funds used for, 481, 492; of Russia,
  19, 496; of South Korea, 475–78, 492; and
  sovereignty loss, 476; of Thailand, 465,
  466, 468, 474, 477, 491, 492
Baker, James A., III, 183, 430, 530
Bakunin, Mikhail, 513, 514, 515
balance-of-payments adjustments, multinational
  corporations and, 210
balance-of-payments deficits
  oil crisis and, 302, 305, 308, 310, 311
  U.S., 206, 207, 395, 398, 404, 409–10; dollar
    devaluation and, 412; and economic
    expansion, 414
balance of trade, NAFTA and, 168
Ball, George W., 109
Balladur, Edouard, 129, 434, 435
bancor, 414
Bangladesh, microlending in, 352–53, 366, 367
Bankers Trust Company, 256
bank holiday, U.S. (1933), 91
banking: GATT on, 125, 129, 130, 530; in New
  York City, 256–58; prudence in,
  importance of, 502. *See also* banks; central
  banks; finance
Bank of England, 269, 270, 276, 454
banks: arbitrage profits of, 264; central (*See*
  central banks); emerging markets and,
  481; foreign, in New York City, 343–44;
  information age and, 8; international
  expansion of, 259–61; U.S., Asian

financial crisis and, 492–93, 494. *See also
  specific banks*
Barclays Bank, 262, 263
Barings P.L.C., 269–70
barriers: to capital flows, 259; to foreign
  investment, 127, 133, 144, 208; to trade
  (*See* trade barriers)
Barshefsky, Charlene, 18, 20, 279, 510, 547, 548,
  556, 558, 563
Baucus, Max, 114–15
bauxite producers, 308
beggar-my-neighbor trade policies: Clinton
  Administration and, 124; danger of, 416;
  Hawley-Smoot tariff bill and, 78
Belgium, and GATT, 102
Belize, ecotourism in, 347
Benetton, 325
Bennett, William, 33
Bentsen, Lloyd, 162
Bergsten, C. Fred, 143, 187, 188, 191, 430, 455,
  470
Bermuda, foreign investment in, 233
Bern Convention, 287
Berners-Lee, Tim, 291
Bhagwati, Jagdish: on diasporas, 365; on fair
  trade, 373; on global financial system,
  280; on global trade, 13–14, 184; on labor
  standards and trade, 563; on regionalism,
  122, 182, 187, 188, 191
Bhopal industrial accident, 525–29, 534
Bhutan, controlled tourism in, 38
Biggs, Barton M., 482, 492, 493
bilateral trade agreements, U.S. and, 179, 188
bin Laden, Osama, 40
biotechnology industry: and foreign alliances,
  232; and patent litigation, 284, 285, 286,
  297
Bismarck, Otto von, 276–77
Black, Eugene R., 105
Black Sea free trade area, 182
Blair, Tony, 501
Blumenthal, Sidney, 334
BMW, 234, 235; European Monetary Union and,
  274; and reduced working hours, 36
Boeing Company, 236, 237, 252, 253, 548, 549
Bolivia, 536, 537
bonds, floating-rate, 258
Bonfiglioli Group, 34–35
book industry, globalization and, 325–26
Borah, William E., 73, 74–75
Borg-Warner, 238
Boskin, Michael J., 182
Bove, Jose, 48, 508–10, 511–12
boycotts: against sweatshops, 389, 390; against
  Wisconsin products, 75–76
BP Amoco, 520
brain drain: from India, 364, 365; to multinational
  corporations, 523, 525
Brazil: Asian financial crisis and, 495; austerity
  program for, 523–25; automobile parts
  produced in, 238; coffee trade in, 57–58;

currency crisis in (1997), 277, 478, 497;
  domestic content regulations in, 340;
  economic nationalism in, 140–41;
  economic restructuring in, 539–41;
  ecotourism and, 347–48; financial bailout
  of, 479, 496; foreign investment in, 140,
  456, 540; GATT and, 101, 116, 117; and
  Mercosur, 189; Mexican peso crisis and,
  456; NAFTA and, 189–90; natural
  resources of, 59; rich-poor gap in, 536;
  trade with U.S., 59, 117, 456–57;
  unemployment in, 525, 541; U.S. tariff
  surcharge (1971) and, 405, 408
"breathing factories, " 35
Breeden, Richard C., 267
Bretton Woods system, 279–80, 501; collapse of,
  392–416, 433; creation of, 94–96, 392;
  fatal flaw in, 413; Keynes Plan for, 414;
  lasting role of, 107–8; nationalism and
  crisis in, 396–97; and post-World War II
  reconstruction, 99–101; purpose of, 95;
  ratification ceremonies for, 98–99; U.S.
  adoption of, 96–98; White Plan for,
  413–14. *See also* General Agreement on
  Tariffs and Trade; International Monetary
  Fund; World Bank
Brezhnev, Leonid I., 401
bribes: multinational corporations and, 219–21; in
  Thailand, 489
Britain
  European integration initiatives and, 170, 185;
    Common Market, 109, 110, 113, 173, 185,
    197–98, 206, 394, 395; single currency,
    275, 330, 359; withdrawal from European
    Monetary System, 417–19, 421, 427, 430,
    435
  financial crises in: dollar shortages (1949),
    104, 105; pound devaluation (1967), 393–
    95, 396, 399, 423; pound devaluation
    (1992), 416–19, 421, 422, 423; suspension
    of gold standard (1931), 86–91
  foreign investment by, 89
  foreign investment in, 206, 309, 451
  foreign workers in, 46
  and GATT, 102
  hegemonic power of, 141
  imperial legacy of, 317, 318
  international trade of, late 19th-century, 51
  and Maastricht Treaty, 193–94, 195–96, 201,
    203, 204
  and monetary sovereignty, 192, 193
  money market in, early 20th-century, 55
  multinational corporations in, 215
  social security spending in, 357
  unemployment in, 3, 9
  U.S. tariff surcharge (1971) and, 407
British, as global tribe, 24–25
broadcast industry, European, 180–81
Brown, Ron, 486, 487
Brown, Winthrop G., 101
Buchanan, Patrick J., 33, 147, 151, 164, 553

budget deficits: Russian, 495; Thai, 462, 463; U.S., 115, 426, 430

budget policy, as inflation management tool, 395, 396

building industry. *See* construction

Building With Books, 354–55

Bundesbank: and European monetary crisis, 417, 419, 422, 426, 429, 437, 438; *vs.* Federal Reserve, 432

Burke-Hartke Bill, 214, 215

Burma, 328

Burns, Arthur F., 400, 401, 414, 415

Bush, George: and free trade, 185; Gulf crisis and, 120; Japan visit, 350; monetary policies of, 486; and NAFTA, 191; reelection campaign of, 430; and regionalism-globalism dichotomy, 187; trade policies of, 122, 144, 147, 149, 177, 183; and Uruguay Round of GATT, 119, 120; and U.S.-Mexico free trade agreement, 153, 155, 162

Bush, George W.: foreign policy team of, 23; globalization identity of, 41

buyouts, reasons for, 6

Caess, 243

Cairns Group, 131

Cambodia, 390

Camdessus, Michael, 23, 426–27, 456, 476

Canada
    domestic content regulations in, 340
    economic nationalism in, 215
    foreign investment in, 233
    and GATT, 102
    multinational corporations in, 314
    and OPEC, 311
    protectionism in, 506–7
    U.S. free trade agreement with, 122, 153, 155 (*See also* North American Free Trade Agreement); debate on, 176–78, 254; dispute-resolution mechanism in, 145, 187; and government intervention, 166; impact on global trading system, 178–79
    U.S. trade with: in 1980s, 5; Hawley-Smoot tariff bill and, 80; Kennedy Round of GATT and, 113; tariff surcharge (1971) and, 406; tensions in, 208

Cancun summit conference on development (1981), 522, 523

Canon Inc., 229

capacity: excess, pattern of, 497–98; sources of, 11–12

capital controls, 278; as anti-speculation weapon, 432; Asian financial crisis and, 477; in Chile, 278, 281–82, 487–88, 499; financial crises and, 280–81, 499; Great Depression and, 486; history of, 280; in Malaysia, 280, 281, 499; necessity of, 281; reducing, U.S. objective of, 488

capital flight, 483; from emerging markets, 488, 492, 493; from Russia, 496

capital flows: 19th century *vs.* 20th century, 14; barriers to, 259; free, 486 (*See also* financial liberalization); impact of, 206; increase in, 279; from rich to poor countries, 270; taxes on, 48; tourism and, 65; volatility of, 279–80, 281. *See also* investment

capitalism: casino, 262; *vs.* communism, 29; criticism of, 17, 21, 29, 32; crony, 43, 360, 361, 474; global, 9, 236, 295, 499, 509; laissez-faire, backlash against, 480; and pluralism, 361; U.S., dominance of, 20; victory of, 28

capital markets. *See* financial markets

capital mobility: in 19th century, 13; globalization and, 478, 480, 481, 486, 490, 494; and social changes, 361

Cardenas, Cuauhtemoc, 161–62

Cardoso, Fernando Henrique, 456

cartels, 305; oil (*See* Organization of Petroleum Exporting Countries); steel, 3

Carter, Jimmy, 521, 529

cartoon industry, 249–51

casino capitalism, 262

Castells, Manuel, 295

catastrophe theory, 29

Caterpillar Inc., 150–51, 152, 167

Cavallo, Domingo, 454

CDs (certificates of deposit), 259

censorship, of Internet, 292–93

central banks: currency board and, 454; European (*See* European Central Bank); global, 501; new role of, 263, 264, 266, 268; Thai, 483. *See also specific banks*

certificates of deposit (CDs), 259

chaebols, 477

chaos, financial, 267; efforts to prevent, 392; euro and fear of, 274; liberalization and, 485. *See also* financial crises

chaos theory, 29

Cheney, Dick, 7

Chessen, James, 281

child labor: alternatives to, 42; alternative views on, 379; in Asian factories, 372, 373, 374; banning of, 151, 152, 372, 373–74, 382–83, 385, 558; in garment industry, 244; multinationals' agreement on, 377

Chile: capital controls in, 278, 281–82, 487–88, 499; multinational corporations in, 214, 216, 220; NAFTA and, 189; poverty reduction in, 536; preferential trade area and, 191

China
    and capital controls, 280
    competition from, 237, 464
    construction boom in, 499, 500
    currency crisis in (1930), 71–72
    economic growth in, 499
    financial crisis, resistance to, 499
    forecasts regarding, 236
    foreign investment in, 221–22, 271, 449, 482

    Hong Kong financial crisis and, 473
    multinational corporations and, 236–37, 363–64
    political changes in, globalization and, 34
    silver demand, in 16th–18th centuries, 13
    sweatshops in, 389
    transition to market economy, 19
    travel in, 36–37, 37–38
    U.S. trade with: in early 20th century, 53–54, 59, 60–61; in late 20th century, 25–27, 45–46, 151, 559; during cold war, 135–36
    Western influences in, 337–39
    and World Trade Organization, 19, 45, 130, 236, 540, 544, 549

Chinese, as global tribe, 24–25

Chirac, Jacques, 199, 357, 508

Chrysler Corporation, 222, 237, 239, 539; alliances with Japanese companies, 246, 247; Mexican peso crisis and, 442, 443

Ciba-Geigy Ltd., 531–32

Citibank, 241, 296

Citicorp, 279

citizenship: corporate, 207, 351; global, 48

Cline, William R., 280

Clinton, Bill: Asian financial crisis and, 469, 474, 475, 478, 484, 491, 492, 496, 501; on big government, 33; and China policy, 45, 236; and fast-track authority, 128, 191, 537; and financial liberalization, 486; foreign policy of, 23; and free trade, 185, 485, 561; and Geneva accord (1997), 278, 279; and globalism, 186; globalization identity of, 41; and labor standards, 376, 387, 558, 559, 562, 563; and labor unions, 544; links to Asia, 486–87; Mexican peso crisis and, 449, 450, 452–53, 460; monetary policy of, 497; and NAFTA, 159, 160, 162, 163, 167, 187, 188, 191, 441; problems facing, 185–86; trade policy of, 123–24, 128–29, 147, 379; at World Economic Forum meeting (2000), 510; and WTO, 548, 554, 556; and zero tariff campaign, 372

Coca-Cola Company, 164, 229–31, 319; and cultural imperialism, 316, 318; overseas operations of, 529, 532, 533; restructuring of, 361–64

coffee trade, 57–58, 64; fair, 373

cold war: defense strategies in, 2; disciplinary effect of, 202; *vs.* globalization, 39–40; Internet during, 292; and regionalism, 174; trade barriers during, 139; trade policies during, 109, 110–11

cold war, end of: economic problems associated with, 185; and financial markets, 268; and focus on economics, 123; and regionalism, 182; and trade rivalries, 128; and U.S. role, 458. *See also* communism, collapse of

Colgate-Palmolive Company, 180, 226

Comecon, and European Community, 175, 176

commercialism, and indigenous culture, 317–18

common markets: European (*See* European Economic Community); Latin American, 173–74; North American, 156, 179 (*See also* North American Free Trade Agreement); Southern Cone (*See* Mercosur)

Commonwealth of Independent States, 197

Communications Decency Act, 33

communism
as blueprint for change, failure of, 30
vs. capitalism, 29
collapse of, 17, 18, 28; and European Community, 192, 194–95; and monetary crisis, 203; opportunities opened by, 27; and travel boom, 37
and foreign investment, 280

Communist bloc: U.S. trade policies toward, 109; and World Bank, 108

comparative advantage, rule of, 126

compensation trade, 221

competition: among banks, 259–61; benefits of, 145–46; from China, 237, 464; and cooperation, 145; education and, 345; euro and, 357; European integration and, 180; intellectual property and, 285, 287; multinational corporations and, 27; trade and, 127 (*See also* trade wars); U.S.-Europe, 109, 110, 112–13, 119; U.S.-Japan, 228; U.S. retreat from, 145–47

competitiveness, 369–70; cheap labor and, 369–70, 563; flexible work hours and, 34–35

computer industry: in Brazil, 140–41; in France, 206–7; in India, 365; in Mexico, 339; in U.S., 349, 350. *See also* software industry

computers: countries compared to, 43; and financial markets, 284; global inequalities in, 15, 19; information represented by, 324; in Japan, 324; predictions regarding, 17–18

Conable, Barber B., Jr., 119–20

conglomerates, industrial, in South Korea, 477

Congress of Industrial Organizations. *See* AFL-CIO

Connally, John B., Jr., 400, 401, 402–3, 410, 411

construction: in Asia, 462, 463, 485–86, 499–500; developing countries' advantage in, 530; in U.S., 67

consulting companies, 47

consumerism: in Asia, 327; ethics of, 315; in India, 532; in Indonesia, 231; in Mexico, 163–64

consumer markets: in China, 337; global, 322–23

consumers, influence of, 561

Consumers International, 520

consumption: currency devaluation and, 450; moving production to low-wage economies and, 237; pluralization of, 319

contagion: Asian financial crisis and, 277, 464, 474, 489–96; currency crises and, 277; definition of, 490; derivatives as vectors of, 494; Great Depression and, 85;

liquidity crisis and, 309; Mexican peso crisis and, 456–57, 459

Continental Illinois Corporation, 257

cooperation
and competition, 145
global: in aircraft development, 252–53; in biotechnology, 232; economic, 430; and nationalism, coexistence of, 4, 95; post-World War II development of, 95–96; scientific, Internet and, 289–90; in semiconductor industry, 253–54; U.S. and, 3
principle of, Japanese and, 2
public-private, 215–16, 546, 547
regional, in financial bailouts, 465
small-business, in Italy, 353–54
U.S.-European, 399
U.S.-Japan, 228–29, 245–47

coordination, economic, 3, 427

copyright protection, 286; advances in, 553; international agreement on, 287; lack of (*See* pirated products); litigation for, 284–85

corporate citizenship, 207, 351

corporations, 212. *See also* multinational corporations

corruption: alternative views on, 317; in Asia, 361, 479; capital controls and, 278; global financial system and, 266–67; in Italy, 357–58; in Latin America, 536; multinational corporations and, 219–21; in Russia, 495; in Thailand, 288, 489

credit, international, 392

crime, globalization and, 8

crises. *See* economic crises; financial crises

crony capitalism: in Asia, 360, 361, 474; globalization as enemy of, 43

cruzeiro (Mexican), devaluation of, 524

culture: American, success of, 320–21; Canadian, 506–7; and economic growth, 25, 127, 282; economic *vs.* national, 325; and financial markets, 266–67; foreign, education regarding, 346–47; global, in New York City, 341–42; globalization and, 49, 314–39, 356; homogenization of, 8, 43–45, 316–17, 320, 337–39; indigenous, commercialism and, 317–18; joint ventures and, 245–47; McDonald's and, 356; multinational corporations' impact on, 314–15; pure, problems associated with, 334; regional, 332–34; and technological development, 213; tourism and, 37, 38

currency
common European (*See also* euro; European Monetary Union); debates on, 192–93, 195, 196, 197; European Monetary System as training ground for, 421; lack of, and Bretton Woods crisis, 396; need for, 420, 424; perspectives on, 272–77; purpose of, 9

devaluation of (*See* devaluation)
overvalued, 438, 450, 452, 456, 483, 492, 496
stable, European efforts toward, 416
See also specific currencies

currency boards, 453–55

currency controls. *See* capital controls

currency crises. *See* financial crises

currency trading, ban on, 467, 468

current-account deficit: foreign investment and, 450; Mexico's, 460

customs unions, in Latin America, 189

Czechoslovakia, and GATT, 101

Daewoo Corporation, 31

Daft, Douglas N., 361–64

Daiwa Securities Company, 222

Davos, Switzerland. *See* World Economic Forum

De Beers, 518–20, 521

debt: Chinese, 500; international, financing of, 258, 259; Mexican, 154; South Korean, 477; U.S., 343

debt crisis: in Latin America, 114, 535; in Mexico (1982), 440, 445

debt relief, 271, 516, 542

defense: during cold war, 2; European Community and, 193, 194, 196–97, 202

defense contractors, bribery practiced by, 220

deficits. *See* balance-of-payments deficits; budget deficits; trade deficits

de Gaulle, Charles, 206, 207

de Larosiere, Jacques, 522, 525

Delors, Jacques, 122, 194, 197, 199, 203

democracy: financial markets and, 268, 269; free market economy and, 200; globalization and, 34; *vs.* market economy, 203–4; promise for, in Mexico, 445

Democratic Party (U.S.), 3, 485, 561

Deng Xiaoping, 236

Denmark: and Bretton Woods system, 99; and European integration, 185, 199; and Maastricht Treaty, 200–201, 203, 204, 421

depression: trade blocs and, 122. *See also* Great Depression

deregulation of financial markets: in 1980s, 260, 433; Geneva accord (1997) and, 278–79; WTO and, 554

derivatives, financial, 269, 270, 272, 481, 493–94

Derivatives Policy Group, 272

Deutsche Telekom, 331

devaluation, 419; of baht, 462, 463–64, 465, 466, 483, 484; of cruzeiro, 524; of dollar, 403, 404, 410, 411, 412, 415; economic effects of, 442; and economic growth, 421–22; export advantage to, 440; of franc, 396; and inflation, 416–17, 419, 439, 524; and interest rates, 460; of peso, 438, 440, 447; political effects of, 422–23; of pound (1931), 86–91, 415; of pound (1967), 393–95, 396, 399, 423; of pound (1992), 416–19, 421, 422, 423; risks of, 464;

of ruble, 496; of rupee, 532; and wages, 394–95; of won, 476

developed countries: economic growth in, 12; and financial speculation, 433; multinational corporations in, 215; workforce in, globalization and, 9. *See also specific countries*

developing countries: anti-globalization protesters and, 517; currency crises in, 277–78; defaults by, 279; ecotourism and, 347–48; financial systems in, 278; foreign investment in, 12, 270–71, 339–40, 438; GATT and, 113, 114, 115, 116–17, 119, 120, 130, 530; globalization and, 510; international development agencies and, 522; labor standards and, 537, 544–45, 548, 562–63; multinational corporations and, 16, 209, 213, 215, 225, 531–32; oil embargo and, 308; OPEC and, 311–12; sweatshops in, 377–79; U.S. trade with, 537; workforce in, globalization and, 9; WTO and, 540, 545, 556, 558. *See also* emerging markets; North-South tensions; poorest countries; *specific countries*

diasporas: and economic success, 24–25, 325; and support for developing countries, 364–65

digital divide, 15, 19

Dillon, Douglas, 392

Direct Action Network, 515

discrimination, against U.S. concerns, 207–8

Disneyland, 320, 321

dispute-settlement mechanism: in GATT, 115, 145; in joint ventures, 246; in U.S.-Canada free trade pact, 187; in U.S.-Japan relations, 145

diversification: global, 431, 461; local, foreign investment and, 7

Dole, Bob, 453

dollar (Hong Kong), 472

dollar (U.S.): agreement to stabilize (1987), 263; Bretton Woods crisis and, 399; British suspension of gold standard and, 89; decline in (1980s), 264; deficiency problems with (1940s), 104–5, 170; devaluation of (1970s), 403, 404, 410, 411, 412, 415; euro as rival of, 275; in Eurobond market, 259; European monetary crisis and, 421, 422; exchange rates pegged to, 404; as global transactions currency, 400, 409; movements of, New York banks and, 257; overpriced, 282; surplus of, 398; upward valuation of, 489

domestic content requirements, 339–40

domino theory, 174

Dow Chemical Company, overseas operations of, 212, 529

downsizing: causes of, 9; in U.S., cheap-labor countries and, 30–31, 254–55. *See also* job loss; unemployment

Drucker, Peter F., 20

dumping: multinational corporations and, 218; by Russia, fear of, 86; by U.S., fear of, 83. *See also* anti-dumping measures

Dunkel, Arthur, 120, 122–23

duplication, benefits of, 146

Du Pont, 218–19, 350, 553

Dyson, Esther, 294

Earth Island Institute, 373

Eastern Europe: Coca-Cola Company in, 231; and European Community, 175, 176, 181, 203; and GATT, 101; political changes in, 348; and World Bank membership, 108. *See also specific countries*

Eastman Kodak Company, 278, 286

East-West divide, cultural, 316

EC. *See* European Community

economic crises, 40, 43. *See also* financial crises

economic growth: as antidote to poverty, 22; in China, 499; culture and, 282; in developed world, 12; educational system and, 282; European monetary crisis and, 421–22; multinational corporations and, 209–10; small businesses and, 353; sweatshops and, 389, 390; in Thailand, 462; trade and, 126–27; Uruguay Round of GATT and, 118; in U.S., 11

Economic Security Council (U.S.), 185

ecotourism, 38, 347–48

ecu, 198, 424

education: globalization and, 345–47; in India, 364, 365; information age and, 8; in U.S., shortcomings of, 282, 345–46

EEC. *See* European Economic Community

efficiency, globalization and, 12

EFTA (European Free Trade Association), 182

Eisenhower, Dwight D., 410

El Salvador: aid to, 366; U.S. business in, 241–44

emerging markets: capital flight from, 488, 492, 493; expectations regarding, 498; investment in, 208, 438, 451, 461, 468, 480–81, 488; multinational corporations and, 212; origins of term, 480

employment: in financial services industry, in New York City, 256; multinational corporations and, 217–18, 226, 232, 233, 234; NAFTA and, 162, 164, 166–67, 168, 169; U.S.-Canada free trade agreement and, 179; U.S.-Mexico free trade agreement and, 159, 254–55

energy crisis. *See* oil crisis

energy market: U.S.-Canada free trade agreement and, 178. *See also* petroleum industry

Engels, Friedrich, 16–17, 216

England. *See* Britain

English, as global language, 15, 37; backlash against, 332; entertainment industry and, 321; European Union and, 330–32; Internet and, 323–24; Japanese fascination with, 315, 316, 328–29

entertainment industry, American, 320–22. *See also* Hollywood

environment: Clinton Administration and, 548–49; concerns about, and trade, 151; ecotourism and, 38, 347–48; information age and, 8; multinational corporations and, 218, 315; NAFTA and, 159, 162, 188; trade talks and, 510, 517, 545; Uruguay Round of GATT on, 130; WTO and, 545, 548

environmentalists: and anarchists, 515, 560; at Seattle protests, 517, 551, 553, 557

Equal Exchange, 373

equalizer effect, multinational corporations and, 210

Ernst & Young, 380, 381–82

Estonia, currency board in, 454

ethical anarchism, 515

ethical imperialism, 314–15

ethics: of consumption patterns, 315; of international business, 219–21, 314, 361, 368, 531–32

ethnicity, and economic success, 24–25

euro: perspectives on, 272–77; and welfare system, challenges to, 273, 356–60. *See also* currency, common European

Eurobond market, 258–59

Eurobrands, 179–80

Euro Disneyland, 320, 321

Eurodollar market, 280, 398, 414

Euronotes, 258–59

Europe: American cultural exports and, 323; anti-Americanism in, 334; cereal market in, 27–28; financial crisis in (*See* European monetary crisis); Great Depression in, 85; integration (*See* European integration); international trade in, late 19th-century, 51; and Middle East oil dependence, 304; as superpower, 202; takeovers in, 506; trade barriers within, 85–86; U.S. corporations in, 247–49; U.S. investment in, 206–7. *See also* Eastern Europe; European Community; Western Europe

European Atomic Energy Community, 171, 172

European Central Bank, 330; discussions regarding, 195, 196; euro and, 273, 276; intervention in monetary crisis, 437–38; need for, 424

European Commission, 197

European Common Market. *See* European Economic Community

European Community (EC): and agricultural subsidies, 117, 119, 120–21, 185; and currency issues, 192–93, 195, 196, 197, 201–2; and defense issues, 193, 194, 196–97, 202; divisiveness in, 181, 184–85; dynamics of, 204; economic nationalism in, 150; economy of, 275; English-language dominance in, 330–32; expansion of, 175–76, 181, 197, 199; and harmonization, 198, 267;

and homogenization, 179–81; and Latin
American trade links, 190; NAFTA and,
190; and political integration, 192, 196,
197, 198; "poor four " in, 197, 198, 199;
test of viability of, 203; U.S. exports to,
184; widening *vs.* deepening of, 192. *See
also* European Economic Community
European Currency Unit (ecu), 198, 424
European Defense Community project, 171
European Economic Community (EEC)
    birth of, 171–72, 197
    Britain's entry into, 206
    celebration of creation of, 191
    and GATT, 107
    and government-business collaboration, 215–16
    and monetary reform, 415
    and multinational corporations, attacks on, 16,
        18, 206–7, 225
    opportunities and challenges in, 172–73
    and single currency (*See* currency, common
        European)
    and U.S.: competition between, 109, 110,
        112–13, 119; conflict over gas pipeline
        from Soviet Union, 139; dispute over
        agricultural subsidies, 122, 123, 125, 139,
        176
    See also European Community
European Free Trade Association (EFTA), 182
European integration, 175, 203, 239; currency
    crisis as strain on, 416, 419, 422, 427;
    difficulties associated with, 185; euro and,
    273; initiatives for, 170; *vs.* national
    identity, 204; two-tiered approach to, 419,
    427–28; United States and, 170, 181–82;
    Uruguay Round negotiations and, 123.
    See also European Community; European
    Economic Community; European
    Monetary Union
European monetary crisis, 201–2, 203, 416–38;
    and Britain, 416–19; central bank
    intervention in, 437–38; factors
    responsible for, 419–20, 423–24, 427,
    428–29, 432; and France, 431, 432,
    433–35, 437; Group of Seven's meeting
    on, 426, 429–30; IMF response to,
    426–27; and Italy, 427, 431; lessons from,
    431; political effects of, 422–23, 433;
    socioeconomic effects of, 424–26; Soros
    on, 434–37; stabilization in, 427, 428; and
    U.S., 421–22, 426, 430, 431
European Monetary Institute, 194
European Monetary System, 421, 430; Britain's
    withdrawal from, 417–19, 421, 427, 430,
    435; demise of, 201–2, 428; investment
    attracted by, 428–29; Italy's withdrawal
    from, 427; limitations of, 433; speculative
    attacks on, 433–34, 435
European Monetary Union: discussions of,
    192–93, 194; nervousness about, 33, 195;
    perspectives on, 272–77. *See also*
    Maastricht Treaty

European Parliament, 204; co-decision powers of,
    194, 197
European Union. *See* European Community
European Union Treaty. *See* Maastricht Treaty
Europol, 196
Euroquote, 352
Euroyen market, 259
exchange controls, 399
exchange rates: asymmetries in, 400; basis for,
    420; dollar as peg for, 404; European
    nations and, 416; fixed, 278, 431, 465;
    flexible, case for, 465; floating, 261, 262,
    400, 404, 410, 411, 412, 414, 416, 420,
    474; pegged, destruction of, 433;
    petrodollars and, 302; policies on, 399;
    rigid, 414; semifixed, 501; Smithsonian
    agreement on, 410–11; stable, within
    Europe, 420; volatility of, 263
Exchange Stabilization Fund, 476
expansion periods, genesis of, 51
expatriates, American: in El Salvador, 241–42;
    wages of, 249
Export-Import Bank, 151–52
exports: devaluation and advantage for, 440; *vs.*
    foreign investment, 232; Uruguay Round
    of GATT and, 118; U.S., World War I and,
    79
export subsidies, European Community and, 117,
    119, 120, 121
Exxon Corporation, 219

factories. *See* assembly plants
Fair Labor Association, 387, 388
Faisal, King, 305–6, 307
farmers
    in India, 532
    third-world, demands on, 545
    U.S.: Asian financial crisis and, 497–98;
        GATT and, 104; Hawley-Smoot tariff act
        and, 74, 81; NAFTA and, 166
    See also agriculture
fast-track negotiating authority: Bush
    Administration and, 122; Clinton
    Administration and, 128, 191, 537
fatalism, globalization rhetoric and, 10
federalism, euro and, 275
Federal Reserve: Asian financial crisis and, 471,
    484, 497; *vs.* Bundesbank, 432; economic
    regulation by, in 1970s, 11; European
    monetary crisis and, 421; during Great
    Depression, 473; Mexican peso crisis and,
    440
Federation de Internationale des Bourses de
    Valeurs, 267
films: Asian-made, 327; global market in, 320,
    321; Uruguay Round of GATT on, 126
finance, 256–82; casino image of, 262;
    globalization of, 259–61, 264–66, 295,
    343, 352; innovations in, 258–59;
    international, politics and, 54–56;
    multinational corporations and, 210;

outlook for 1900, 51–52; revolution in,
    261; risks of, 269; in U.S., 256–58,
    259–61. *See also under* currency
financial center: antiquated notion of, 344;
    characteristics of, 256–57; London as,
    67–68, 88, 89, 192, 256, 258, 260, 263,
    343, 359; New York City as, 65–67, 69,
    256–58, 263, 343–44
financial crises: in 20th century, 14; in 1990s, 21,
    511; Asian (*See* Asian financial crisis);
    Bretton Woods, 392–416; and capital
    controls, 280–81; as consequence of
    success, 497; and contagion, 277; currency
    board as remedy for, 453–55; dollar
    shortages (1940s), 104–5, 170; early
    warning system for, 455, 501; European
    (*See* European monetary crisis); foreign
    investment in emerging markets and, 451;
    global, 484, 485, 490–91, 497, 502–3;
    global factors behind, 279–80;
    globalization and, 265, 266, 269; Great
    Depression and, 71–72, 86–91;
    independent economic policies and
    (1980s), 3; lack of global leadership and,
    141; liberalization and, 485, 488–89;
    Mexican (*See* Mexican peso crisis);
    multinational corporations and, 210; profits
    in, 437; rating agencies' reaction to, 483;
    reducing risks for, 501; roots of, 477; Rubin
    prescription for avoiding, 468; social effects
    of, 494–95, 498; technology and spread of,
    284
financial liberalization: Asian financial crisis and,
    467, 470; and crises, 485, 488–89;
    international bailouts and, 477; problems
    associated with, 280; "sequencing " of,
    488; and speculation, 479; U.S. push for,
    486–89
financial markets: deregulation of, 260, 278–79,
    433; discipline imposed by, 271; and
    economic policy, 265, 266; evolution of,
    283–84; forces operating on, 265–66, 283;
    foreign exchange trading in, 262–64;
    global, 258, 281; and governments, balance
    of power between, 266, 268; instability of,
    481; international politics and, 55; investor
    psychology and, 265–66; microefficiency
    in, 481–82; *vs.* nation-states, 268, 461, 467,
    469; petrodollars and, 301–2, 305, 306–11;
    regulation of, 261, 266–67, 268, 271–72,
    278, 281, 295, 433, 489; technology and,
    260, 261, 264, 268, 283, 284, 295, 433, 481;
    volatility of, 264, 283. *See also* stock
    market
financial scandals: in Germany, 266; in Japan, 475
financial services: GATT on, 125, 129, 130, 530;
    in New York City, 256–58; prudence in,
    502
financial speculation. *See* speculation
financial system: asymmetries in, 399–400;
    evolving threats to, 409; instability of, 478;

multinational corporations and, 210; "privatization" of, 262; reform of, need for, 410, 411, 412, 413, 501

Finland, currency devaluation by, 417

First Boston Corporation, 259

Fischer, Stanley, 277, 281, 492

flexibility: Coca-Cola Company and, 230; and competitiveness, 35; *vs.* currency board, 454; Italian entrepreneurs and, 325; monetary, 400

flexible manufacturing, 248

food: genetically engineered, 510, 520, 546, 547; hormone-enhanced, European ban on, 119, 509, 510, 548; Japan's dependence on foreign countries for, 61–62; luxury, U.S. tariffs on, 508, 509, 510, 512

food aid, Kennedy Round of GATT and, 113

food industry: Americanization of, 508–10; globalization and, 318–20, 512–13

Ford, Gerald, 312

Ford, Henry, 237

Ford Motor Company, 539; in Europe, 226–27; Japanese competition and, 222, 223; local content rules and, 184; and Mazda, alliance with, 245, 246, 247; Mexican peso crisis and, 442, 443–44; in Mexico, 157–58, 166, 169, 524; multinational nature of, 239; productivity at, 235

foreign aid. *See* aid

foreign currency reserves: China's, 500; Mexico's, 439, 444

Foreign Earned Income Act of 1978 (U.S.), 240

foreign exchange market, 262–64

foreign investment: in 19th century, 13; attracting, 6, 340–41, 347, 476; barriers to, 127, 133, 144, 208; in Brazil, 140, 456, 540; in Britain, 206, 309, 451; in China, 221–22, 271, 449, 482; communism and, 280; concerns about, 341; in developing countries, 12, 270–71, 438; and diversification, 7; in emerging markets, 208, 438, 451, 461, 468, 480–81, 488; European Monetary System and, 428–29; *vs.* exports, 232; in Hong Kong, 482; in India, 532, 533–34; in Indonesia, 271, 480, 482, 488; in Japan, 19; labor unions' demand for restrictions on, 214; in Latin America, 142, 535, 536; in Malaysia, 271, 488; in Mexico, 30–31, 155, 157–58, 161, 233, 438–39, 444, 445, 447, 449; nationalism as barrier to, 133; oil-producing countries and, 302, 305, 307–8, 309; performance criteria for, 339–40; in Philippines, 488; pros and cons of, 5, 6; rules for, 461; short-term *vs.* direct, 459; in South Korea, 476, 488; taxes on, 452; in Thailand, 271, 482, 488; Uruguay Round of GATT on, 125; by U.S., 66, 206–7, 232–33, 247–49; in U.S., 4–7, 143–44, 206, 208, 224, 309, 340–41, 347, 350

foreign languages, study of, in U.S., 345–46

foreign ownership: pros and cons of, 6; of U.S. firms, 227–28, 506

Forrestier, Viviane, 49

Foulball, 374

franc, devaluation of, 396

France: Bretton Woods crisis and, 396–97; computer industry in, 206–7; cuisine of, globalization and, 43–45, 509–10, 512–13; currency crisis in (1992), 431, 432, 433–35, 437; Disneyland in, 320; economic crisis in (1980s), 3; euro and, 275, 359; European common market and, 172, 185; European integration initiatives and, 170–71, 185; and GATT, 101, 102, 114, 115, 123, 129; and gold standard, 68; insider trading in, 266–67; international trade of, 51, 52; language policies in, 332; Maastricht Treaty and, 195, 198, 199, 201, 203, 432; Maastricht Treaty referendum in, 202, 203, 416, 417, 419, 422, 423, 424, 425, 429; McDonald's in, 508–10, 511–12; money market in, early 20th-century, 55–56; multinational corporations in, 215; oil crisis and, 311; protectionism in, 150; stock market in, 351; taxes in, 359, 360; unemployment in, 9, 357, 359; U.S. investment in, 247–48; U.S. protectionism and, 82, 83; U.S. tariff surcharge (1971) and, 408; World Bank loan to, 100–101

Franco, Itamar, 190

Franklin, Benjamin, 83

free markets, 43; and democracy, 200

free trade: benefits of, 125, 126–27, 540, 545, 549; China and, 45; Clinton and, 185, 485, 561; criticism of, 441, 540–41; decline of, in 1980s, 142; economic philosophy of, 530; and global security, 83; *vs.* managed trade, 124; Nixon on, 135; and North-South tensions, 537–38, 539–41; Seattle protests and, 561; Truman on, 132; U.S. support for, 185, 485. *See also* trade liberalization

free-trade agreements: in Europe (*See* European Economic Community); in Latin America, 173–74, 182; in North America (*See* North American Free Trade Agreement; U.S.-Canada free trade agreement; U.S.-Mexico free trade agreement); proliferation of, 182; purpose of, 153; reservations about, 156

Free Trade Area of the Americas, 191. *See also* Western Hemisphere free-trade zone

Free Trade Association, 110

Friedman, Milton, 414, 433, 454, 493

Friends of the Earth, 520

FSX, 229

Fujimori, Alberto K., 536

fusion cuisine, 43–45

futures contracts, 284

G-7. *See* Group of Seven

Galbraith, John Kenneth, 502, 503

Gandhi, Indira, 522, 532

Gandhi, Mahatma, 534

Gandhi, Rajiv, 525, 526, 532

Gap, 388

garment industry. *See* apparel industry

Garten, Jeffrey E., 458, 486

Gates, Bill, 7

GATT. *See* General Agreement on Tariffs and Trade

gender issues, aid programs and, 366–67

General Agreement on Tariffs and Trade (GATT): aim of, 124; Annecy Round of, 106; benefits of, 103; debate on, 268; decisions by consensus at, 116–17; dispute settlement mechanism of, 115, 145; effectiveness of, 116; enforcement institution for, 125; European Common Market and, 107; and intellectual property protection, 125, 131, 187; Kennedy Round of, 111–13, 118; limitations of, 107; Mexico and, 153; and most-favored-nation treatment, 103, 121; and North-South tensions, 114, 115, 116–17, 119, 120, 529–31; origins of, 118, 132, 133; provisions of, 103–4; *vs.* regional trade agreements, 182, 184, 186–88; signing of, 101–2; strengthening of, 117–18; Tokyo Round of, 114, 118; Uruguay Round of, 114–31, 179, 185, 186; U.S. and, 102–3, 104, 115, 118; violations of, 116, 121, 530

General Electric, 212

General Mills Inc., 27–28

General Motors Corporation: advertising by, 181; alliances with Japanese companies, 246–47, 539; competition of, 222, 223, 224; and corporate accountability, 219; Mexican peso crisis and, 443; NAFTA and, 167, 169; overseas operations of, 212, 238, 239, 314, 524, 538, 539

Genetech Inc., 285

Geneva trade agreement (1997), 278–79

Geneva Trade Conference (1947), 101–2, 104, 132, 133

Genscher, Hans-Dietrich, 194

George, Eddie, 276, 359

Gephardt, Richard A.: globalization identity of, 41; Mexican peso crisis and, 453; on NAFTA, 162; and protectionism, 177; and trade pact with China, 46

Germany: automobile industry in, 234–36; cultural intrusion in, 325–26; English language use in, 331, 332; euro and, 272, 274, 276–77; and European monetary crisis, 417, 419, 422, 423, 425–26, 433–34; and European Monetary Union, 33, 185; financial scandal in, 266; foreign workers in, 46, 47; and gold standard, 68; interest rate policy of, 417, 420, 423, 424, 426, 427, 430; international trade of, early 20th-century, 51, 52–53, 58, 59, 63; and Maastricht Treaty, 192, 195, 198, 199,

201, 202, 204; money market in, early
20th-century, 55; reunification of, 202,
276, 417, 420, 423, 424, 430; and social
security system, 359; South American
trade, 58, 59; trilateralism and, 143;
unemployment rates in, 357; at Uruguay
Round of GATT, 123; working hours in,
35–36. *See also* West Germany

Gifford, Kathie Lee, 377, 379, 386

Gillette Company, 233–34, 322–23

Gingrich, Newt: and Clinton, 561; globalization
identity of, 41; Mexican peso crisis and,
453

Giscard d'Estaing, Valery, 199, 311, 413

glasnost, *vs.* perestroika, 29

Glass-Steagall Act (U.S.), 260

global citizenship, 48

global economy: birth of, 13; collapse of, in
1930s, 69–91; ethnicity as factor in, 24;
everyday life and, 200; features of, 481;
multinational corporations and, 209;
political foundation for, 94–96; rules for,
setting, 151–52; in rural U.S., 4–7, 25–27;.
See also global market

Global Exchange, 375, 376, 380, 384, 557

global financial crisis, 497; beginning of, 484,
490–91 (*See also* Asian financial crisis);
causes of, 485; explanations for, 502–3

global financial market, 258, 281

globalization: 19th-century, 13, 14, 20, 21, 24, 51,
279; and anti-American sentiment, 334;
and capital mobility, 478, 480, 481, 486,
490, 494; challenges of, 12; China and,
236; *vs.* cold-war system, 39–40; and
competition, 146; and culture, 49, 314–39,
356; early stages of, 151; and education,
345–47; father of, 15; fears of, 8, 12, 20,
328; financial, 259–61, 264–66, 295, 343,
352; and financial crises, 265, 266, 269;
fundamental contradiction of, 237;
identities based on, 41; impact of, 22, 40;
inevitability of, 7–8; liberating effect of,
48; and multinational corporations,
225–28, 229; myth about, 13; political
dimensions of, 23–24, 41–42; and reform,
554, 561; religious, 335; reservations
about, 32–34; resistance to, 18, 20, 21, 32,
49–50, 356, 480, 506–21, 552 (*See also*
protest movement); retreat from, in 20th
century, 13; as revolution from beyond, 34;
rhetoric of, 9–10; and rich-poor gap, 15,
17, 22, 48, 49, 328, 481; of society, 510;
stresses of, 18; summit conference on,
proposal for, 12; sustainable, 40, 41–42,
43; of technology, 349–50; term, 22, 328,
335; and terrorism, 8, 24; U.S. as
beneficiary of, 562; and wages, 228

global-local tensions. *See* local-global tensions

global market: and automobile industry, 222–24,
226–27; for books, 325–26; and
governments, 9; and interdependence,

228–29; single, 230; U.S. dependence on,
114

global negotiations, use of term, 522

global networks, 289–90; and software industry,
296. *See also* Internet

global products, *vs.* local products, 248–49

global tribes, 24–25

global warming, 517

Global Witness, 518, 520

Goizueta, Roberto C., 229, 230, 231, 361, 362,
363

gold: demand for, in late 19th century, 52; price of,
411, 415, 434; U.S. embargo on, 91.
See also gold standard

Golden Age (1945–1970), 28; *vs.* 1990s, 10–12;
explanations for, 29

Goldman, Emma, 514

Goldman, Sachs & Company, 260, 279, 468

Goldsmith, Sir James, 33

gold standard, 68; British suspension of (1931),
86–91; *vs.* currency board, 454;
information standard replacing, 261;
return of, prospects for, 415; threats to,
409; U.S. suspension of (1971), 403–4,
410, 411, 413

Goodyear Tire and Rubber Company, 228

Gorbachev, Mikhail S., 29, 176

Gore, Al: and free trade agreements, 33;
globalization identity of, 41; on NAFTA,
163; Seattle WTO meeting and, 544, 547,
559, 563

government intervention: and currency crises
prevention, 277; in Japan, 146; *vs.* market
reform, 19; and productivity, 166

governments: and corporations, 546, 547; *vs.*
global governance, 553; globalization and
pressure on, 12, 34, 265, 325, 360, 361;
inflation management by, 395–96;
information age and, 8; international
markets and, 9; multinational corporations
and, 213, 214, 215–16, 217, 219, 529; and
technological innovation, 282

Grameen Bank, 352–53, 366, 367

Gramm-Rudman-Hollings law, 115

Great Depression, 69–91, 392, 473; *vs.* Bretton
Woods crisis, 395; British currency crisis
and, 86–91; and capital controls, 486;
Chinese currency crisis and, 71–72;
conditions leading to, 237; European
aspects of, 85–86; Hawley-Smoot tariff
bill and, 72–85, 139, 184; lack of world
leadership and, 141; stock market crash of
1929 and, 69–71; tactics contributing to,
96, 115, 132, 144; U.S. bank holiday
during, 91

Greater East Asia Co-Prosperity Sphere, 176

Greenpeace, 510, 520

Greenspan, Alan, 42, 325, 461; on Asian financial
crisis, 484, 497, 503; on capital controls,
280; on Mexican peso crisis, 453, 459

Greider, William, 9

Group of Five, and Plaza Accord of 1985, 263–64,
430

Group of Seven (G-7): Asian financial crisis and,
280; Clinton and, 185; criticism of, 50,
543; European monetary crisis and, 426,
429–30; and globalism, 186; limitations
of, 12; on Special Drawing Rights, 456

Group of 10: British currency crisis and, 393; oil
crisis and, 311; Smithsonian agreement of
(1971), 410–11, 413; study of Bretton
Woods system by, 392–93; at Uruguay
Round of GATT, 115, 117

Group of 20, 413

Group of 77, and multinational corporations, 225

growth. *See* economic growth

Gulf Oil Company, 219

Gutt, Camille, 105

Haig, Alexander M., Jr., 139

Haiti, globalization and, 48

Hamilton, Adrian, 261

Hamilton, Alexander, 206

Hanke, Steve H., 454, 455

Hanna-Barbera studio, 250, 251

Harley-Davidson Inc., 148, 541

Harriman, W. Averell, 208

Hashimoto, Ryutaro, 474, 475, 484

Haskins, Caryl, 213

Havana Conference (1947), 101, 102, 103

Havel, Vaclav, 518

Hawley-Smoot tariff bill, 72–85, 397; domestic
effects of, 76–78, 80–81; foreign reprisals
to, 78–80, 81–85; international
repercussions of, 132, 139, 184; Senate
debates on, 72–76

health: information age and, 8; WTO and, 548.
See also safety standards

hedge funds, 482; and Asian financial crisis, 483,
484; and Russian financial crisis, 496;
U.S. rescue of, 497

hedging, proxy, 429

hegemony
functions in world economy, 141, 142
U.S., 206–7; backlash against, 18, 356, 467,
468, 499; decline in, 174; globalization
and, 15, 511; regional pacts and, 191

Heineken, 319

Herman, Alexis, 386

Hewlett-Packard Company, 140, 226, 285, 351

high-technology industry: globalization and,
349–50; labor shortages in, 46–47, 293;
in Mexico, 157–58; and patent and
copyright litigation, 284–87; in
Philippines, 296–97; in U.S., 349–50;
WTO agenda and, 549

Hills, Carla A., 144, 146, 155, 156, 255

Hitachi Ltd., 253, 349

Hobsbawm, Eric, 28–30

Hochhuth, Rolf, 332

Hoffman, Paul G., 170

Holbrooke, Richard C., 275

Hollywood: cultural impact of, 321; foreign contracting by, 249–52; Uruguay Round of GATT and, 126

Honda, 223, 224

Honduras, multinational corporations in, 219

Hong Kong: American influences in, 330; currency board in, 454; economic growth in, 379; financial crisis in, 469, 470, 471, 472–73, 492; foreign investment in, 482; and Thai rescue package, 465; U.S. tariff surcharge (1971) and, 407–8

Hoover, Herbert, 75, 76, 78, 397

hot market, 280

house building industry. See construction

Hufbauer, Gary, 148, 162

human nature, and economic crises, 503

human rights: international law on, 48; travel as, 38; Universal Declaration of, Article 19 of, 293

human rights abuses: in Indonesia, 371–72; in Pakistan, 373, 374; in Vietnam, 380–82

IBM: cooperation with Japanese firms, 228, 350; foreign operations of, 140, 211, 294, 529, 533–34; and intellectual property rights, 127, 285; joint venture with Siemens, 253; and technological development, 349, 351; before United Nations, 219

Iceland, and European Community, 175

ILO. See International Labor Organization

IMF. See International Monetary Fund

immigrants
in U.S.: Asian, 328; and capital flows, 65; illegal, 244; Mexican, 153, 155, 156, 166, 449; traveling to country of birth, 37
virtual, 294
in Western Europe, 46, 47–48

imperialism: cultural, 316–17, 318; ethical, 314–15; vs. global arrogance, 41

import controls: Japanese automobile industry and, 224; U.S. and, 397–98, 403, 404–9, 410

independence: declarations of, 2, 3; vs. globalization, 12; threats to, 314. See also sovereignty

India: Bhopal industrial accident in, 525–29, 534; and capital controls, 280; economic revolution in, 532–34; emigration from, 364, 365; foreign investment in, 532, 533–34; high-tech talent in, 46, 47, 296, 364–66; and international trade, early 20th-century, 63–64; labor issues in, 562–63; software industry in, 294, 324, 365; trade policies in, 340; travel in, growth of, 38; Uruguay Round of GATT and, 116

Indians, Asian, 24–25

individuals, globalization and, 40

Indonesia: consumer potential of, 231; economic crisis of late 1990s, 23, 43, 464, 465, 478–79, 493, 494–95, 498, 500; economic problems of, 469; foreign investment in, 271, 480, 482, 488; human rights abuses

in, 371–72; IMF bailout in, 23, 50, 474, 477, 492; labor strikes in, 369, 370–71; monetary policies of, 468; multinational corporations in, 236; political crisis in, 360–61; revolution in, globalization and, 34; social upheaval in, 500–501; sweatshops in, 31, 32, 368–72, 379, 384; and Thai rescue package, 465; unemployment in, 385

Industrial Revolution, 17; in Asia, 389; and corporations, 212

inequalities, in wealth distribution. See rich-poor gap

inflation: in 1970s, impact on U.S., 11; currency board and, 454; devaluation and, 416–17, 419, 439, 524; in Europe, 416; in Germany, 401, 424; in India, 534; management of, 395–96; Mexican peso crisis and, 445, 450–51, 459, 460; oil embargo and, 307, 309–10; payment deficits and, 395; post-World War II, 414; and protectionism, 116; in U.S., 396, 401, 415

information: computer representation of, 324; efforts to control, 292, 293

Information Revolution, 8, 20

innovation: globalization and, 349; government support and, 282; intellectual property system and, 285, 286

Institutional Revolutionary Party (Mexico), 153, 154, 160, 445

integration: vs. economic nationalism, 184–85; European (See European integration); global, and domestic economic politics, 4; globalization and, 39–40, 553

Intel Corporation, 285

intellectual property
imports of, restrictions on, 507
protection of: GATT and, 125, 131, 287; importance of, 127; lack of (See pirated products); litigation for, 284–87; types of, 286

interdependence
and contagion effect of financial crises, 490
declaration of, proposal for, 3
European, 84, 424
global, 3, 4, 19; in 19th century, 56; financial, 265, 269, 458; post-World War II, 95
global markets and, 228–29
vs. hegemony, 141
of Japan and U.S., 144
as war deterrent, 144

interest rates: in 19th century, 51; Asian financial crisis and, 463, 498; budget deficits and, 115; German policy on, 417, 420, 423, 424, 426, 427, 430; Mexican peso crisis and, 460; swap arrangements, 258; Swedish policy on, 416, 417, 418, 432; Thai bailout and, 491; U.S., 282, 421, 461, 497; U.S. vs. European, 398–99, 416, 424; as weapon in currency crisis, 432

International Bank for Reconstruction and Development. See World Bank

international banking zone, 257

International Bondholders Insurance Corporation, proposal for, 455

International Business Machines Corporation. See IBM

International Chamber of Commerce, 209–10, 215

International Federation of Human Rights, 48

International Intellectual Property Alliance, 289

International Labor Organization (ILO), 36, 42, 368, 372, 373, 374, 547, 559

International Monetary Fund (IMF): Asian financial crisis and, 277, 466–69, 473–74, 476, 477–78, 493; and austerity measures, 523–25; and Bretton Woods system study, 392; British currency crisis and, 393; and capital controls, 281; and capital liberalization, 280; capital mobility index of, 13; capital resources of, 108; changes in, 50, 538; charter of, efforts to amend, 488; creation of, 98; and development assistance, 271; on dollar deficiency problems, 104, 105; European monetary crisis and, 426–27; and financial crisis prevention, 455–56, 511; functions of, 105, 522; India's economic problems and, 533; Indonesian financial crisis and, 23, 50; Japan's funding for, 142; lasting role of, 108; limitations of, 12; Mexican peso crisis and, 453, 455, 457; and monetary system reform, 413; oil crisis and, 309–11; and poverty relief, 541–44; Prague meeting of (2000), 515–18, 541–44; proposals for, 94; protests against, 45, 48, 49–50, 515–18; reform of, call for, 186, 459; Russian economic crisis and, 19, 496; and South Korean rescue package, 476, 477–78; and Thai rescue package, 491; and Uruguay Round of GATT, 119; U.S. investment in, 97; U.S. suspension of gold standard and, 404

International Organization of Securities Commissions, 267

International Telephone and Telegraph Corporation, 214, 218, 220

International Trade Commission, 285, 287

International Trade Organization (ITO), plans for, 102, 104, 107, 118, 133

Internet, 289–97; access to, 15, 19; anarchists and, 515; development of, 289–90, 291; economic transactions over, 549; and English-language dominance, 323–24; and financial markets, 295; and global division of labor, 293–94, 296–97; impact of, 20, 366; Italy compared to, 325; and media organizations, 290–91; multilingual, attempts at creating, 324–25; and protest movement, 48, 520, 550, 554; regulation of, 292–93, 295; as symbol of

globalization system, 40; and travel, 37; and worker protection, 553
Internet start-ups, 46–47, 296, 297
intervention, governmental. *See* government intervention
investment: cross-border, and trade agreements, 182–83; leveraged, 481; new vehicles of, 284. *See also* foreign investment; private investment
investor confidence, currency board and, 454
Iran, view of U.S., 40–41
Iraq, nationalization of oil companies in, 299, 300
Ireland: cartoon studios in, 251–52; and European Community, 175; and Maastricht Treaty, 199, 201
isolationism: post-World War I, 21; Truman's warning against, 132; U.S., 39
Isuzu Motor Company, 239
Italy: corruption in, 357–58; currency crisis in (1992), 431; entrepreneurs in, 325, 353–54; euro and, 275, 359; and European Monetary System, 427; globalization and, 325; U.S. tariff surcharge (1971) and, 407; welfare system in, 356–60; workweek in, 34–35
ITO. *See* International Trade Organization
Iyer, Pico, 316–17

J. P. Morgan, 484
Jacobsson, Per, 108
Jamaica, 308
Japan: American cultural influences on, 328–29, 330, 363; Asian financial crisis and, 474–75, 483, 491–92; automobile industry in, 125, 222, 223, 224; China as competitor of, 237; and cooperation principle, 2; cooperation with U.S., 228–29, 245–47, 253; economic crisis in (1990s), 18, 277, 278, 483; economic reforms in, 19; economic success of, competition and, 146; English language use in, 315, 316, 328–29; and European Community, 176; financial liberalization in, 487; financial markets in, 264, 265–66; financial scandals in, 266, 267, 475; and food aid program, 113; food supply of, 61–62; foreign investment in, 19; foreign trade of, early 20th-century, 59–60; Geneva accord (1997) and, 279; as global leader, 141–43; internationalization (*kokusaika*) in, 315–16; investment abroad, 223; investment in Latin America, 142; investment in Mexico, 30–31; investment in U.S., 5, 6, 341; labor practices in, 539; McDonald's in, 329–30, 355–56; Middle East oil dependence of, 304; protectionism in, 120, 121, 145; and real estate bubble, 499–500; Socialists of, 32; Thai financial crisis and, 465, 466; trade with Soviet Union, 143; trade with U.S., 54, 59, 60–61, 62–63, 134, 139, 141, 143, 144–45, 148; U.S. tariff surcharge (1971) and, 405, 406
"Japan, Inc.," 214, 215

Japanese, as global tribe, 24–25
Japanese language, foreign influences on, 328
J.C. Penney, 163
Jefferson, Thomas, 2
Jews: as global tribe, 24–25; Soviet, emigration policies for, 138–39
job creation: in Europe, 46–47; globalization and, 12
job insecurity, in 1990s, 10
job loss: China and threat of, 237; Mexican peso crisis and, 460; NAFTA and, 30, 31; restrictions on foreign investment and, 144. *See also* downsizing; unemployment
job mobility, 46–47
Jobs, Steve, 229
Johnson, Howard A., 282
Johnson, Lyndon B., 111, 113, 174, 395, 396
Johnson & Johnson, 212
joint ventures, 209; in automobile industry, 245–47; China and, 221, 222; *vs.* compensation trade, 221; limitations of, 209, 246; in Mexico, 158; multinational corporations and, 227; in semiconductor industry, 253–54; in textile industry, 354; U.S.-Japan, 245–47
Jordan, Michael, 31–32, 368, 371, 374
Jospin, Lionel, 508, 511
Jubilee 2000, 541

Kaczynski, Theodore, 17, 515, 560
Kantor, Mickey, 485, 486, 546
Kaplan, Robert, 37, 38
karaoke, 328
Kaufman, Henry, 455, 477, 497
Kellogg Company, 27–28, 36
Kenen, Peter, 464, 465
Kennan, George F., 174
Kennedy, John F., 109, 113, 134–35
Kennedy, Paul, 141
Kennedy Round of GATT, 111–13, 118
Kenya: art in, 317–18; ecotourism in, 347
Keynes, John Maynard: and currency board in Russia, 454; on market psychology, 283; monetary system plan of, 414; and pound devaluation, 88; on World Bank, 94–95
KFC Corporation, 339
Khashoggi, Adnan M., 220
Khrushchev, Nikita, 111
Kimberly-Clark, 243–44
Kim Dae Jung, 361, 498
Kim Young Sam, 33, 476, 477, 492
Kindleberger, Charles P., 141, 210, 502
Kissinger, Henry, 138, 143, 312
Klein, Julius, 85–86
Klein, Lawrence, 11
Kmart, 163, 450
Knight, Philip H., 372, 380, 382, 383, 384, 388
Kohl, Helmut, 185, 277; and Croatia, recognition of, 181; and euro, 274, 275, 276; financial policies of, 202, 420; and globalism, 186; and Maastricht Treaty, 192, 194, 196, 197,

199, 204; and Uruguay Round of GATT, 123
Kohler, Horst, 49, 50, 543, 544
Korea. *See* South Korea
Kotkin, Joel, 24–25
Kraft Inc., 318, 319
Krugman, Paul, 33, 126, 276; on sweatshops, 377, 379
Kuttner, Robert, 9

labor
cheap, 32; in Asia, 249–51, 368, 372; and competitiveness, 369–70; in Japan, 134; in Mexico, 166, 254, 255; in Philippines, 296
child: alternatives to, 42; alternative views on, 379; in Asian factories, 372, 373, 374; banning of, 151, 152, 372, 373–74, 382–83, 385, 558; in garment industry, 244; multinationals' agreement on, 377
export of (*See* immigrants)
foreign: exploitation of, 368, 372; and U.S. capacity, 11–12, 26
global division of, 237–55; in aircraft industry, 252–53; in auto industry, 237–40, 245–47; in cartoon industry, 249–52; illegal immigrants and, 244–45; Internet and, 293–94, 296–97; joint ventures and, 245–47; multinational corporations and, 238–39, 247–49; sweatshops in, 368–69; tax policies and, 240–41
high-tech, shortages of, 46–47, 293, 296
mobility of, in 19th century, 13
prison, 152
retention measures, 47
labor market, U.S., effect of NAFTA on, 30, 31
labor standards: Clinton on, 376, 387, 558, 559, 562, 563; monitoring of, 374–76, 379–80, 383–84, 538; as protectionism, 537, 547, 548, 563; Seattle WTO meeting and issue of, 544–45, 547, 548, 550, 552, 556, 558–59, 562–63; tools for improving, 553; Uruguay Round of GATT on, 130
labor strikes, in Indonesia, 369, 370–71
labor unions: in automobile industry, 538–39; in Britain, 395; and foreign investment, 214; and globalization, 151, 152, 510; illegal immigrants and, 244; in India, 563; in Indonesia, 371, 372, 386; Mexican peso crisis and, 445–46, 460; and multinational corporations, 217, 225, 235, 314–15; NAFTA and, 162, 164, 165, 167, 168, 169; and protectionism, 147, 562; at Seattle WTO meeting, 544, 547, 551, 552, 557, 558; on shorter workweek, 35, 36; sweatshops and, 386, 387; and U.S.-Mexico free trade agreement, 157, 162, 164, 165, 167
La Follette, Robert, 73–74
laissez-faire capitalism, 480. *See also* free trade
Lamont, Norman, 419, 422, 423, 424, 428, 429
Lang, Jack, 320

language: foreign, study of, in U.S., 345–46; as politics, 332. *See also* English

Latin America: currency crises in, 277; debt crisis in, 114, 535; economic expansion in, 535; economic nationalism in, 133, 140–41, 153; and European Community, 190; free trade areas in, 173–74, 182; growth rates in, 537; Japanese investment in, 142; multinational corporations in, 214; NAFTA and, 188–90, 537; privatization in, 536, 537, 539, 540; protectionism in, 188; rich-poor gap in, 535–37; U.S. objectives in, 133–34; U.S. trade with, 188–89. *See also specific countries*

law: globalization of, 344. *See also* litigation

Lazard Freres & Company, 257

leadership: global 132, 141, 185–86, 262, 562 (*See also* hegemony); technology, U.S. and, 216–17, 282

Leahy, Patrick J., 119

Leeson, Nick, 269

lender-of-last-resort, 262, 265

Levin, Sander M., 45–46

Levi Strauss, 368, 369, 371

Levitt, Arthur, Jr., 268, 272

Levitt, Ted, 229–30, 319

liberalization. *See* financial liberalization; trade liberalization

Liberia, 39

Lie, Trygve, 103

Lipsey, Robert E., 232

liquidity, international, 393

liquidity crisis, 309, 410

Lithuania, currency board in, 454

litigation, patent and copyright, 284–87

living standards: in 1990s, 21; globalization and, 12; oil embargo and, 307

Liz Clairborne, 387, 388

Lloyd George, David, 87

loans: *vs.* grants, as development aid, 542, 543; guarantees of, World Bank and, 96; reconstruction and development, World Bank and, 105–6; short-term, Chile's tax on, 281–82, 487–88; small, to poorest countries, 352–53, 366

lobbying: Japanese corporations and, 224; multinational corporations and, 215

local content regulations, 339–40

local-global tensions, 339–67; aid projects and, 355; Coca-Cola Company and, 361–64; culture and, 320–22; ecotourism and, 347–48; in education, 345; financial centers and, 344; financial markets and, 351–52; foreign investment and, 4, 7, 341; immigration and, 364–66; Internet and, 292–93; McDonald's and, 355–56; newspaper coverage of foreign affairs and, 348–49; performance requirements for investment and, 339–40; small businesses and, 353–54; tastes and, 318–19, 337–39, 361–64; technological development and,

349–50, 366–67; in U.S. academia, 332–34

local products, *vs.* global products, 248–49

London, as financial center, 67–68, 88, 89, 192, 256, 258, 260, 263, 343, 359

Long-Term Capital Management Fund, 496, 497, 502

Luxembourg, and GATT, 102

Lynch, Gary G., 375, 376

Maastricht Treaty (1991), 192–204, 420, 421; accomplishments of, 195–97; British public opinion on, 423; Danish referendum on, 200–201, 203, 204, 421; debates on, 192–94, 198–201; European Monetary System and, 433; French obligations under, 432; French referendum on, 202, 203, 416, 417, 419, 422, 423, 424, 425, 429; importance of, 195; obstacles to, 201–4; political opposition to, 422; purpose of, 9, 193; ratification process for, 203, 204

Mahathir Mohamad, 23, 465, 466–67, 468, 469, 499

MAI (Multilateral Agreement on Investment), 152, 499

Major, John, 185; and globalism, 186; and Maastricht Treaty, 194, 195, 196, 197, 198, 202, 203; monetary policies of, 417, 418, 422, 423, 430

Malaysia: Asian financial crisis and, 23, 361, 464, 465, 466–67, 468; and capital controls, 280, 281, 499; economic problems of, 469; foreign investment in, 271, 488; multinational corporations in, 236; and Thai rescue package, 465

managed trade, *vs.* free trade, 124

management: in Chinese factories, 221; cultural diversity and challenges of, 245; governments and, 213; of multinational corporations, 240–41

Mandela, Nelson, 7, 335

M&Ms, 16, 180

manifest destiny, 314

manufacturing: flexible, 248; U.S. foreign investment in, 232, 233, 247–49

maquiladoras, 30–31, 157, 294

market: free, 43, 200. *See also* financial markets; global market

market economy, *vs.* democracy, 203–4

marketing: European Common Market and, 180–81; global, 230, 231, 318, 319, 322; litigation as tool for, 285

market reformers, *vs.* government interventionists, 19

market socialism, 236

mark (German): and European monetary crisis, 417, 418, 425; as standard for anti-inflationary credibility, 416

Marshall Plan, and European integration, 170, 171

Mars Inc., 180

Martin, William McChesney, Jr., 395

Marx, Karl, 16–17, 29, 36, 216, 513

Mattel Inc., 375

Mayer, Martin, 261, 494

Mazda, 223, 239; alliance with Ford, 245, 246, 247

McCloy, John Jay, 99–100

McCracken, Paul W., 401, 403

McDonald's: in Asia, 329–30, 338; backlash against, 48, 508–10, 511–12, 516; in Brazil, 541; in France, 512–13; global spread of, 41, 337, 355–56; local tastes and, 319, 320; as multi-local company, 356

McDonnell Douglas Corporation, 252, 253, 340

McKinnon, Ronald I., 280

McNamara, Robert S., 310, 521–22

media industry: Canadian, 506–7; and Internet, 290–91; U.S., globalization and, 348–49

Mercedes-Benz, 234, 235, 236

Merconorte, plan for, 190

Mercosur, 189; commercial potential of, 190; countries excluded from, impact on, 191

mergers: European, 150, 195; *vs.* joint ventures, 247

Merrill Lynch & Company, 258, 259, 279, 344, 487

Mexican peso crisis, 191, 271, 438–61; aftermath of, 464, 469, 474; contagion effect of, 456–57, 459; currency board as remedy for, 454–55; domestic impact of, 450–51; factors responsible for, 438–39, 451–52; impact on U.S., 441–44, 446–47, 448; international implications of, 442, 452; lessons from, 459, 461; political effects of, 445–46; U.S. rescue package, 452–53, 457–59, 460, 471, 489; worsening of, 447–48, 459–61; Zedillo's damage-control plan, 449, 450, 451, 459

Mexico: Asian financial crisis and, 493; controlled tourism in, 38; debt burden of, 154; domestic content regulations in, 340; economic crisis in (1980s), 3, 524; economic nationalism in, 153, 160; European Union and, 190; foreign investment in, 30–31, 155, 157–58, 161, 233, 438–39, 444, 445, 447, 449; high-tech industrial zone in, 157–58; joint ventures in, 158; NAFTA and, 31, 160–64, 439; political reform in, 154–55; protectionism in, 179; as prototype economy, 459; second revolution in (1980s), 155; shopping habits in, 163–64; and U.S., mutual industrial reliance of, 155, 156; U.S. tariff surcharge (1971) and, 407; U.S. trade with, 5, 163–64, 440, 441, 459 (*See also* U.S.-Mexico free trade agreement); Zapatistas in, 32, 439, 440, 446, 536

microlending, 352–53, 366

Microsoft Corporation, 20, 21, 47, 285, 546, 548, 549, 553

Microsoft Network (MSN), 293
middle class: Latin American, 536; Mexican, peso crisis and, 450
Middle East: and globalization, resistance to, 23; multinational corporations in, 220; oil as weapon in, 298–99, 302–6;
military power: *vs.* economic power, 137; U.S., 143
Millennium Round, 558
Minnesota Mining and Manufacturing (3M), 211, 349
Mitsubishi Motors Corporation, 223, 239; and Chrysler, alliance with, 246, 247; sexual harassment suit against, 375, 376
Mitterand, Francois, 3, 123, 181, 194, 195, 196, 199, 435
mobility: capital (*See* capital mobility); job, 46–47; labor, in 19th century, 13
Mobilization for Global Justice, 511
Mobius, J. Mark, 480, 482, 486
Model, Leo, 207–8
Modern Language Association, 346
monetary crises. *See* financial crises
monetary policies: coordination of, 3; as inflation management tool, 396
monetary sovereignty, Britain and, 192, 193
monetary system. *See* financial system
money market. *See* financial markets
Monsanto, 232, 510
Montevideo, treaty of (1960), 173–74
Montreal conference (1988), 118–19, 179
Moore, Mike, 551, 554, 556
moral hazard, 459
Morgan, J. P., 90
Morgan Stanley & Company, 232–33, 260
Morgenthau, Henry: on Bretton Woods system, 95–96, 99; on Hawley-Smoot tariff bill, 84–85
most-favored-nation treatment: emigration policies and, 138; GATT and, 103, 121; Hawley-Smoot tariff bill and, 80, 82
motorcycle manufacturers, protectionism and, 147, 148, 541
Motorola, Inc., 226, 253, 296, 351
Mozambique, IMF and, 50
multiculturalism, in Europe, 46–47
Multi-Fiber Arrangement (1974), 131
Multilateral Agreement on Investment (MAI), 152, 499
multilateralism, *vs.* regionalism, 182, 184, 186–88
multi-local companies, 356
multinational corporations, 206–37; accountability of, 368, 374–76, 518; automobile industry and, 222–24, 234–36; brain drain to, 523, 525; Brazilian, 540; characteristics of, 209; and China, 236–37; code of conduct of, 531–32; competition among, 27; and corruption, 219–21; criticism of, 218, 233, 522; cultural impact of, 314–15, 320; and developing countries, 16, 209, 213, 215, 225, 531–32; dominance of, 20, 206–8;

362; and economic growth, 209–10; and economic nationalism, 151, 152, 214–15, 216; and ecotourism, 348; in El Salvador, 241–44; English as official language in, 331; European monetary union and, 274–75; European opposition to, 16, 18, 206–7, 225; evolution of, 214, 247; explosion of, 216, 217; fears regarding, 214–15; German, 234–36; *vs.* global corporations, 322; and global division of labor, 238–39, 247–49; globalization and, 225–28, 229; and global-local tensions, 355–56, 361–64; in India, 532, 533, 534; Japanese, 315; life cycles of, 216; in Mexico, 30; and monetary system, 210, 416; *vs.* nation-states, 212–14, 215, 216; New York City as magnet for, 343; nongovernmental organizations and, 520, 521; and peace, 216; in Philippines, 296; political influence of, 214, 215; protests against, 48, 508–10, 511–12, 515, 518, 554, 561; recession and, 211–12; regulation of, 218–19, 225, 368; responsibility of, 314–15, 372, 538; safety standards of, 525–29; sweatshops and, 387–88; and technology transfer, 212, 213, 214, 225, 226; U.S., 206–8, 225–28, 229, 232–34, 240–41, 247–49; U.S.-Canada free trade agreement and, 179; workforce diversity in, 240–41; working philosophy of, 214–15
multipolar era, 135–37
Munich world economic summit meeting (1992), 123
music, globalization and, 341–42
music recordings: pirate versions, 287–89; Uruguay Round of GATT on, 126
Mussa, Michael, 455
mutual fund market, global equity funds in, 265
Mycogen, 232

Nader, Ralph, 151, 152, 218, 441, 546–47, 550
NAFTA. *See* North American Free Trade Agreement
Narayan, Deepa, 49
National Cash Register Company (NCR), 212
National Center for Supercomputing Applications, 291
National Economic Council (U.S.), 486
national identity: *vs.* European integration, 204; and multinational corporations, 248–49
nationalism, economic, 132–52; as barrier to globalization, 151; and Bretton Woods crisis, 396–97; disruptive effects of, 213; euro and, 276; in Europe, 150, 200–201, 202; *vs.* integration, 184–85; and international cooperation, 4, 95; in Japan, 141–43; in Latin America, 133, 140–41, 153, 160; Maastricht Treaty and revival of, 200–201, 202; in Mexico, 153, 160; multinational corporations and, 151, 152, 214–15, 216; retreat into, 511; U.S.

investment in foreign countries and, 207, 208; in U.S., 143–50, 191, 237, 544. *See also* protectionism
nationalization: of oil companies, 215, 299–300, 301; participation as alternative to, 301; in service sector, 530
national power, elements of, 136–37
National Semiconductor Corporation, 290
nation-states: and cold-war system, 40; erosion of, 29; *vs.* financial markets, 268, 461, 467, 469; *vs.* multinational corporations, 212–14, 215, 216
NATO. *See* North Atlantic Treaty Organization
Nau, Henry R., 114, 119
NCR (National Cash Register Company), 212
NEC Corporation, 285
Nestle S.A., 27–28, 175, 180, 319, 529
Netherlands: Bretton Woods crisis and, 399; foreign investment by, 210; and GATT, 102; multinational corporations in, 215; oil embargo and, 303; U.S. tariff surcharge (1971) and, 408; welfare system in, 357
networks, global, 289–90; and software industry, 296. *See also* Internet
newly industrialized countries (NICs), and technology trade, 140
newspapers, U.S., globalization and, 348–49
New World Order, 522; hardship created by, 511; multinational corporations and, 216; rules for navigating, 461; trade side of, 182
New York City: as financial center, 65–67, 69, 256–58, 263, 343–44; global culture in, 341–42; sweatshops in, 244–45
New York Stock Exchange, 20; crash of 1929 and, 69
NGOs (nongovernmental organizations), 518–21. *See also* protest movement
Nike Inc., 32; efforts to improve working conditions, 382–84, 385, 388; investigation of labor practices of, 374–76, 379–80; protests against, 520, 557; sweatshops associated with, 368–72, 380–82
Nissan Motor Company, 223, 224, 238, 443
Nixon, Richard: and Bretton Woods collapse, 433; and dollar devaluation, 412; economic policies of, 11, 135–36, 138–39, 215; and gold standard suspension, 403–4, 410; and import controls, 397, 403, 404; on new era, 136, 137; oil crisis and, 304; and Smithsonian agreement, 410, 411; and wage-price freeze, 401–3
Nomura Securities Company, 343, 344
nongovernmental organizations (NGOs), 518–21. *See also* protest movement
non-tariff barriers to trade, 116; local content regulations as, 339–40; Uruguay Round of GATT and, 130
North American Common Market, idea for, 156, 179
North American Free Trade Agreement (NAFTA), 153–69; approval of, 160, 162, 188;

benefits for Mexico, 31, 160–64, 439; benefits for U.S., 159–60, 163, 164, 165, 167; countries excluded from, 191; criticism of, 33, 165–66, 441; cultural safeguards in, 507; debates on, 159–60, 167–68, 368; early results of, 168–69; European response to, 190; extending to Latin America, 537; first fruits of, 449; formal announcement of, 182; global precedent in, 188; and job loss in U.S., 30, 31; Latin American response to, 188–90; Mexican peso crisis and, 439, 440, 441, 445, 449; political battle over, 124, 128; potential impact of, 159, 162; and protectionism, concerns about, 184

North Atlantic Treaty Organization (NATO): European integration and, 175, 194, 196, 197; Western European Union and, 198

Northrop Corporation, 219, 220–21

North-South tensions, 521–44; austerity measures and, 522, 523–25; free trade and, 537–38, 539–41; GATT and, 114, 115, 116–17, 119, 120, 529–31; labor standards and, 537, 544–45, 548, 562–63; multinational corporations and, 525–29, 531–32, 538–39; poverty and, 521–23, 535–37, 541–44; Seattle WTO meeting and, 545. *See also* rich-poor gap

Norway, and European Community, 175

O'Brien, Richard, 351–52

Obuchi, Keizo, 19

OECD. *See* Organization for Economic Cooperation and Development

oil companies: multinational, 216; nationalization of, 215, 299–300, 301; nongovernmental organizations and, 520; and OPEC, 301. *See also* petroleum industry

oil crisis: Carter on, 521; and global finance, 256, 301–2, 305, 307–8; impact on Brazil, 524; impact on developing countries, 308; impact on U.S., 11, 303, 311, 312; Paris conference on, 311, 312; politics and, 298–99, 302–6; World Bank/IMF response to, 309–11

oil prices: increases in, OPEC and, 304–5, 307, 524; and protectionism in 1980s, 115

OPEC. *See* Organization of Petroleum Exporting Countries

Opel, 234, 235, 236, 239

Organization for Economic Cooperation and Development (OECD): on free trade, 126; and Multilateral Agreement on Investment, 152; oil embargo and, 304; South Korea and, 476, 488; on Uruguay Round of GATT, 124

Organization for Trade Cooperation (OTC), 107

Organization of Petroleum Exporting Countries (OPEC), 297–312; Algiers meeting of (1975), 311–12; establishment of, 297–98; and financial markets, 301–2, 305, 306–11;

and foreign investments, 302, 305, 307–8, 309; members of, 298, 299, 305; and nationalization of oil companies, 215, 299–300, 301; and New York banking, 343; and oil companies, 301; oil embargo by, 302–4, 305–6, 307; and politics, 298–99, 302–6; and price increases, 304–5, 307, 524; weaknesses of, 305

Oriental Exclusion Act (U.S.), 224

origin, rules of, 184, 189

O'Rourke, Dara, 382

Ortiz, Guillermo, 458

Orwell, George, 176

OTC, (Organization for Trade Cooperation), 107

outlook. *See* predictions

overcapacity in manufacturing, 141

Overseas Development Council, 12

overtime hours: *vs.* flexible hours, 35; limit on, 377

Oye, Kenneth A., 184

Pacific Rim Productions Inc., 250

Pahlevi, Shah Mohammed Riza, 304

Pakistan, child labor in, 373, 374

Palestine Liberation Organization, 521

Palme, Olaf, 225

Panama Canal, 21

Panetta, Leon E., 452, 453

panic, financial: of 1893, 66; of 1898, 56; globalization and, 265; Great Depression and, 69–71; Mexican peso crisis and, 460

Paris Convention of 1883, 225

Parliament of the World's Religions, 335

patent protection, 286; Group of 77's demands regarding, 225; litigation for, 284–85; Paris Convention of 1883 and, 225; of pharmaceuticals, developing countries and, 545; Uruguay Round of GATT and, 119, 125, 127

peace: interdependence and, 144; multinational corporations and, 216

Pennwalt Corporation, 528

pension funds, 480, 486, 490, 494

Pepsi Foods Ltd., 229, 230–31, 532, 533

Peres, Shimon, 23

perestroika, 176; *vs.* glasnost, 29

peril point mechanism, 109, 110

Perot, Ross, 9, 33; globalization identity of, 41; Mexican peso crisis and, 441; on NAFTA, 159, 162, 163, 164, 166, 167

Perry, Matthew C., 315

Persian Gulf crisis: and European Community, 194; repercussions of, 119–20

Peru: economic crisis in, 536; tourism in, 336–37

peso (Mexican), devaluation of, 438, 440, 447. *See also* Mexican peso crisis

petrodollars: and financial markets, 301–2, 305, 306–11; recycling of, 308, 310

petroleum industry
Arab-Israeli conflict and, 298–99, 302–6
Mexican, 458

U.S.: Hawley-Smoot tariff bill and, 76; during oil crisis, 298, 299
See also Organization of Petroleum Exporting Countries

Peugeot, 239

pharmaceutical industry: and developing countries, 545, 556; GATT and, 125, 127, 129

Philip Morris, 318, 319

Philippines: construction boom in, 462; financial crisis in, 464, 466; foreign investment in, 488; high-technology talent in, 296–97; IMF pressure on, 473; U.S. impact on, 317

Phillips Corporation, 228

Pick, Franz, 310

pirated products, 140–41, 285, 287–89

Plaza Accord of 1985, 263–64, 430

pluralism, capitalism and, 361

Poland: and GATT, 101; shift to market economy, 18

Polaroid Corporation, 286

political integration, European Community and, 192, 196, 197, 198

politics: American pop culture and, 322; Asian financial crisis and, 360–61; domestic, trade and, 548; economic distribution and, 29; *vs.* economics, 19; European monetary crisis and, 422–23, 433; floating exchange rates and, 410; global integration and, 4; of globalization, 23–24, 41–42; and international finance, 54–56; language as, 332; Mexican peso crisis and, 445–46, 453; and multinational corporations, 213; NAFTA and, 160–62; petroleum, 298–99, 302–6; and single European currency, 9; trade balances and, 441; and trade negotiations, 123; U.S., and Seattle WTO meeting, 558–59, 562;

pollution, multinational corporations and, 218, 315

poorest countries: Clinton's initiatives to help, 556; microlending in, 352–53; OPEC and, 311–12; outlook for, 522; Uruguay Round of GATT and, 131

pop culture, U.S., spread of, 320–22, 329

population, global trends in, 8

Porter, Michael E., 322

Portugal: euro and, 275; Uruguay Round of GATT and, 130

pound (British), devaluation of: in 1931, 86–91, 415; in 1967, 393–95, 396, 399, 423; in 1992, 416–19, 421, 422, 423

poverty: in Africa, 522; causes of, 213; in India, 534; in Indonesia, 494–95; international development agencies and, 49, 50, 515–16, 521–22, 541–44; in Latin America, 536; and North-South tensions, 521–23, 535–37; reduction of, 22; in Russia, 489; spread of, 48; sweatshops as solution to, 379, 390. *See also* poorest countries; rich-poor gap

Powell, Colin, 23

predictions: for 20th century, 51–52; for computers, 17–18; inaccuracy of, 16, 18; for poorest countries, 522

press, U.S., globalization and, 348–49

Prestowitz, Clyde, 33, 227, 350

Price Club, 164

prices: ceiling on, Nixon Administration and, 401–3; of oil (*See* oil prices); rise in, local content regulations and, 339

prison labor, 152

private investment: in Asia's emerging markets, 468; moratorium on, call for, 207; World Bank and, 100, 105

private-public partnerships, 546, 547

privatization: Brazil and, 456; in Latin America, 536, 537, 539, 540; of monetary system, 262; Russia and, 490

Procter & Gamble, 291, 362

Prodi, Romano, 325

productivity: of Chinese workers, 221; competitive advantage and, 145; globalization and, 12; government intervention and, 166; reduced working hours and, 36; in U.S., post-World War II, 11; U.S. *vs.* Mexico, 165; wages and, 159, 160, 165

products, local *vs.* global, 248–49

prosperity: in early 20th century, 56, 57; in late 20th century, 10–12; in Europe, 180; free trade and, 126, 545; old rules for, 464; rise in, and instability, 502–3. *See also* wealth

protectionism

anti-dumping measures as form of, 121

Argentinian, 126

arguments for, 134

Brazilian, 140–41

Canadian, 506–7

costs of, 147–48

cultural, 320

European, 150, 176

global financial crisis and, 498

globalization rhetoric and, 10

and Great Depression, 144

Japanese, 120, 121, 145

labor standards as form of, 537, 547, 548, 563

labor unions and, 147, 562

in Latin America, 188

local content regulations and, 339–40

managed trade as alternative to, 124

Mexican, 179

mixed effects of, 149

new forms of, 530

petrodollars and, 308

problems associated with, 116

vs. protection, 42

quantitative restrictions and, 107

recession of 1980s and, 3, 115, 139–40

regionalism and, 182, 184

religious, 335

Seattle protests and, 554

success story in, 148

threat of, Truman on, 132–33

Uruguay Round of GATT on, 115–16, 118, 120

U.S.: in early 20th century, 52, 72–85, 114; in late 20th century, 116, 123, 177, 185, 224; Bretton Woods crisis and, 397–98; against Japanese products, 134; local content bill and, 339; Mexican concerns over, 155; results of, 147–49

See also tariffs

protest movement: anarchism and, 513–15, 516, 541, 552, 554, 557, 559–61; anti-globalization, 48–50, 511; in China, 500; criticism of, 553–54, 561; domestic problems and, 562; image of, 520; against multinational corporations, 48, 508–10, 511–12, 515, 554; nongovernmental organizations and, 518–21; against Uruguay Round of GATT, 130; against World Bank and IMF, 23, 45, 48, 49–50, 515–18; against World Trade Organization, 18, 20, 21, 50, 362, 388, 510, 514, 540, 544–63

proxy hedging, 429

psychology: and economic crises, 503; investor, influence on markets, 265–66, 283

Public Citizen, 550

public-private partnerships, 215–16, 546, 547

publishing industry, globalization and, 325–26

quotas, 125; cost of, 147, 148; mixed effects of, 149

railroads, 20, 66, 67

R&D. *See* research and development

Rao, P. V. Narasimha, 532

Reagan, Ronald: and budget deficits, 115; defense budget of, 2; monetary policies of, 486; on poverty relief, 522; *vs.* protectionism, 177; and safety standards, 529; trade policies of, 139; Uruguay Round of GATT and, 114; and U.S.-Canada free trade agreement, 179; on wealth creation, 523

real estate bubble: and Asian financial crisis, 473; Japan and, 499–500

recession: in 1980s, 139; in 1990s, 416, 423; in Brazil, 523, 524; global, 479; management of, 396; Mexican peso crisis and, 457, 458, 460; multinational corporations and, 211–12; nationalism and, 150; trade barriers and, 118, 124; trade blocs and, 122

Reebok, 32, 368, 374, 388

reform: of financial system, 410, 411, 412, 413, 501; of international development agencies, 186, 517–18; market, *vs.* government intervention, 19; mobilizing for, 554, 561

regionalism, 170–92; Asian, 174, 176; benefits of, 174; concerns about, 159, 162, 183–84, 186, 187, 190–92; cultural, 332–34;

European, 170–73, 175–76, 179–82; financial bailouts and, 465; and global liberalization, 191, 199; lack of global leadership and, 141–42; Latin American, 173–74, 182; *vs.* multilateralism, 182, 184, 186–88; multinational corporations and, 227; North American, 176–79; precedent-setting by, 187–88; proliferation of, 182–83; and protectionism, 182, 184; Uruguay Round stalemate and, 122; Western Hemisphere, 188–90. *See also* trade blocs; *specific regional trade agreements*

Regional Trade Agreement Act of 1934 (U.S.), 184

regulations

of financial markets, 261, 266–67, 268, 271–72, 278, 281, 295, 433, 489

global: lack of, 33–34; setting of, 151–52

of Internet, 292–93, 295

of multinational corporations, 218–19, 225, 368

of trade, WTO and, 553, 554, 558

Reich, Robert B., 4, 5, 31, 247, 268

Reischauer, Edwin O., 141

religion, globalization and, 335

religious wars, 2

Renault, 223, 510

Republican Party (U.S.), 39

research and development: globalization and, 349–51; Internet and, 289–90; return on, licensing fees and, 286; spending by multinational corporations, 226

reserves, monetary: China's, 500; dollars and, 409; increase in, need for, 414; Mexico's, 439, 444

responsibility, corporate, 314–15

restaurant industry, globalization and, 43–45, 512–13

revolution, globalization as, 34

Rey, Jean, 112

Ricardo, David, 126

Rice, Condoleezza, 23

Richards, Ann, 160

rich-poor gap: aid programs aimed at closing, 366–67; globalization and, 15, 17, 22, 48, 49, 328, 481; in Latin America, 535–37; in technology access, 15, 19; trade and, 537–38; WTO and, 551. *See also* poverty

Rockefeller, David, 143

Rolfe, Sidney E., 209, 210

Roosevelt, Franklin Delano, 60, 91, 184

Rostow, W. W., 174

Roth, William M., 111, 112

Rousseau, Jean-Jacques, 366

Royal/Dutch Shell, 520

Rubin, Robert E., 468, 487; Asian financial crisis and, 278, 279, 280, 282, 467–69, 474, 476, 489, 491, 492, 501; on bailouts, 493, 496; and capital liberalization, 488; and Clinton, 485, 486; Mexican peso crisis and, 452, 453, 458, 459, 489

ruble (Russian), devaluation of, 496
rules of origin, 184, 189
Rumsfeld, Donald, 23
Runyon, Damon, 309
rupee (Indian), devaluation of, 532
Russia: corruption in, 495; currency board in, 454, 455; economic conditions in, late 19th-century, 51; financial crisis in, 42–43, 489, 495–96, 499; IMF lending to, 19, 496; impact of globalization on, 42; international trade of, early 20th-century, 52; nouveau riche in, 481; privatization in, 490; shift to market economy, 18. *See also* Soviet Union
Russo-Japanese war: and financial markets, 55–56; and international trade, 61
Rwanda, 39

Sacco, Nicola, 514
Sachs, Jeffrey, 277, 278, 377–79, 454, 464–65, 477, 493
Sadat, Anwar el-, 303
safety standards, of multinational corporations, 525–29
Safire, William L., 135
Salant, Walter S., 414
Salinas de Gortari, Carlos, 153–54, 155, 156, 160–61, 164; and Mexican peso crisis, 438, 439, 440, 446, 451
Salomon Brothers, 260
Samsung, 30
Samuelson, Paul, 481–84
Saudi Arabia, and oil embargo, 303, 304, 305–6, 307
Save the Children, 373
scandals, financial: in Germany, 266; in Japan, 266, 267, 475
Schlesinger, Helmut, 419, 430
Schmidt, Helmut, 139, 413
schools: building, aid program assisting with, 354–55. *See also* education
Schröder, Gerhard, 46, 47
science cooperation, Internet and, 289–90
Sears Roebuck, 368
Seattle meeting. *See* World Trade Organization
Securities and Exchange Commission (SEC), 267, 268, 375
securities industry, globalization of, 344
security
  economic, Clinton and, 185
  global: free trade and, 83; regionalism and, 174; Uruguay Round of GATT and, 119
  national: computer industry and, 140; European Community's policies on, 193, 194, 196–97, 202; global division of labor and, 238
self-determination, 2
self-fulfilling prophecy: Asian financial crisis as, 492; European monetary crisis as, 423, 437; speculative markets and, 482
Sematech, 228

semiconductor industry: Internet and, 290; joint ventures in, 253–54; and protectionism, 147; Uruguay Round of GATT and, 129
Serra Puche, Jaime, 439, 440, 446, 447
Serrv International, 373
service sector: GATT and, 114, 116, 117, 120, 125–26, 127, 129–30, 131, 530–31; U.S.-Canada free trade agreement and, 178
Shamrock summit meeting (1985), 179
shipping industry, in early 20th century, 51, 63
Shultz, George P., 138–39, 301, 302, 401, 403; on dollar devaluation, 412, 413, 415
Siemens A.G., 36, 236, 253, 349
Simon, William E., 310
Singapore: economic growth in, 379; financial market in, 269, 270; and Thai rescue package, 465
Singh, Manmohan, 532, 534
small businesses: and economic growth, 353; Italian, 325, 353–54
Smith, Adam, 136, 261, 268, 415
Smith Corona Corporation, 254–55
Smithsonian agreement (1971), 410–11, 413
Smoot-Hawley tariff bill. *See* Hawley-Smoot tariff bill
soccer-ball industry, child labor in, 373–74
socialism: anarchism and, 514, 515; in India, 532, 534; market, 236
software industry: in India, 294, 324, 365; labor shortages in, 293–94; patent litigation in, 285–87; in Philippines, 296–97
Solow, Robert M., 10, 11
Sony Corporation, 228, 229, 349
Soros, George, 9, 32–33, 461; Asian financial crisis and, 463, 465, 466–67; European financial crisis and, 435–37
South Africa: apartheid in, multinational corporations and, 314; U.S. tariff surcharge (1971) and, 409
South America. *See* Latin America
Southern Cone Common Market. *See* Mercosur
South Korea: automobile parts produced in, 238; economic growth in, 379, 390; financial crisis in, 43, 277, 492, 494, 498; financial liberalization in, 488; foreign investment in, 271, 488; Geneva accord (1997) and, 279; globalization and, 33; and OECD, 476, 488; rescue package for, 475–78, 492; and Thai rescue package, 465; U.S. tariff surcharge (1971) and, 409
South-North tensions. *See* North-South tensions
sovereignty
  degrees of, 200
  limitations of, 204
  loss of, concerns about: European economic union and, 192, 193, 195, 198, 199, 203, 273, 275; global markets and, 269; international rescue packages and, 476; Mexican peso crisis and, 457; multinational corporations and, 208, 213

Soviet Union, 561
  and Bretton Woods system, 98
  collapse of: economic problems associated with, 185; impact on European Community, 192, 194–95; impact on India, 532
  emigration policies of, 138–39
  and European Community, 176, 181
  and GATT, 120
  Japanese trade with, 143
  social system in, 29
  U.S. trade policies toward, 109, 110–11; Nixon Administration and, 135, 136, 138–39; Reagan Administration and, 139
Spaak, Paul-Henri, 171, 172
Spain: currency controls in, 432; domestic content regulations in, 340; euro and, 275
Special Drawing Rights, 410, 456; Keynesian equivalent to, 414
special interests, 127
specialization, 126
speculation, financial: and Asian financial crisis, 463–64, 472, 479, 483–84; Barings P.L.C. and, 269–70; and Bretton Woods crisis, 397; derivatives and, 493; developed countries and, 433; and European monetary crisis, 428, 429, 431, 433–34, 435, 437–38; Rubin on, 468; self-fulfilling swings of, 482; weapons against, 432
Spencer, William I., 216
Sri Lanka, 553
stability. *See* security
Standard Oil Company, 211
Standard & Poor's index, 284
Stanley Works, 227, 247–49
Starbucks, 337, 338, 339, 552, 557
start-up companies: biotechnology, 232; Internet, 46–47, 296, 297
state-owned enterprises: in India, 534; *vs.* investor-owned multinationals, 16. *See also* nationalization
states: *vs.* "supermarkets, " 40. *See also* nation-states
steel industry: global financial crisis and, 497–98; Uruguay Round of GATT and, 126; U.S.-Mexico free trade agreement and, 156; in U.S., 3, 139, 149
Stein, Herbert, 11
Stiglitz, Joseph E., 478, 487, 489
stock market
  in France, 351
  in U.S., 502, 511; Asian financial crisis and, 471; crash of 1929, 69–71, 283; crash of 1987, 265, 266, 295, 480
Strange, Susan, 261–62
strikes, in Indonesia, 369, 370–71
"submerging " markets, 456
sub-Saharan Africa, 271, 377
subsidies, agricultural. *See* agricultural subsidies
Suetens, Max, 101, 102
Suez Canal, 298

Suharto, 23, 43, 360, 361, 372, 493

Summers, Lawrence H., 22, 50, 487; Asian financial crisis and, 483, 489, 491, 492; on capital flows, 280; and capital liberalization, 488; on emerging markets, 481; on European monetary union, 275; on financial crises, 281; on interdependence, 19–20; Mexican peso crisis and, 448, 453, 489; on poverty relief, 543; on regionalism, 191–92; on World Bank reform, 517–18

"supermarkets, " vs. states, 40

superpowers: economic, 135; Europe as, 202; sense of mission and, 141

suppliers, importance for foreign investment, 158, 538–39

supply: global chains of, 238; global problem of, 237; shortages in 1970s, 11

sustainable globalization: geo-economics of, 43; politics of, 41–42; U.S. responsibility for, 40

Sutherland, Peter, 124, 128, 131, 186

sweatshops, 368–90; in Asia, 31–32, 368–69, 384–85, 389; Asian financial crisis and, 384–86; East-West divide in perceptions of, 388–89; as first step to prosperity, 377–79, 385, 389, 390; improved working conditions in, 387–88, 553; in Indonesia, 31, 32, 368–72, 379, 384; monitoring of labor practices in, 382–83, 538; in Pakistan, 373–74; in Thailand, 385, 388–89; in U.S., 244–45; White House agreement on, 376–77, 380, 386–87

Sweden: and European Community, 175; financial market in, 267; interest rate policy in, 416, 417, 418, 432; multinational corporations in, 225; welfare system in, 23

Sweeney, John J., 152, 510, 545, 553, 559

Switzerland: Bretton Woods crisis and, 399; capital controls in, 278; English language use in, 332; and European Community, 175; foreign investment by, 210; multinational corporations in, 215; U.S. tariff surcharge (1971) and, 405, 408–9

Taco Bell, 163

Taft, William Howard, 97

Taiwan: automobile parts produced in, 238; economic growth in, 379, 390; U.S. tariff surcharge (1971) and, 408

takeovers, international, 506

tariffs, 125
 Australian, 76
 European Common Market and reductions in, 172–73
 international agreement on (See General Agreement on Tariffs and Trade)
 Internet transactions and, 549
 Latin American, reductions in, 188–89
 vs. quotas, 147

reductions in, impact on multinational corporations, 227
 regionalism and, 184
 as taxes, 164
 U.S.: domestic effects of, 76–78, 80–81; foreign reprisals to, 78–80, 81–85; Hawley-Smoot tariff bill, 72–85; on luxury foods, 508, 509, 510, 512; political economy of, 78–80; reductions of, 106, 109–10; surcharge on (1971), 397–98, 403, 404–9, 410

tastes, globalization and, 318–20, 322, 325–26, 338, 361–64

taxes: on advertising, in Canada, 507; exit, proposal for, 501; on foreign investments, 452; in France, 359, 360; on international capital flows, 48; on short-term loans, Chile and, 281–82; tariffs as, 164; Uruguay Round of GATT on, 125; U.S., on income earned abroad, 240–41

TDMs (trade-distorting measures), 119

tea trade, 64

technology: access to, 350; anarcho-primitivist rejection of, 515; classes of, 213; competition in, U.S.-Japan, 228–29; corporations and, 213; dangers of, in developing countries, 529; and film industry, 321; and financial industry, 260, 261, 264, 268, 283, 284, 295, 433, 481; globalization of, 349–50; impact on indigenous peoples, 366–67; innovation in, foreign investment and, 144; multinational corporations as response to, 209; rich-poor gap in, 15, 19; U.S. leadership in, 216–17, 282. See also computers; high-technology industry; software industry

technology transfer: barriers to, 339, 340; Group of 77's demands for, 225; multinational corporations and, 212, 213, 214, 225, 226; newly industrialized countries and, 140; OPEC's demand for, 312; trade and, 127

telecommunications: European developments in, 351; and finance, 344; U.S. protectionism of, 120–21, 123

telecommuting, global, 293–94

television: high-definition, 228, 229; imports, 320

Ten Thousand Villages, 373

terrorism: in El Salvador, 241, 242, 243; globalization and, 8, 24; against U.S. targets, 356

Texas Instruments Inc., 169, 228; in El Salvador, 242–43; joint venture with Hitachi, 253; and patent protection, 285

textile industry: in Africa, 556; in China, 221–22; in El Salvador, 242; in Italy, 353–54; Japanese exports to U.S., 134; Uruguay Round of GATT and, 126, 129, 130, 131; U.S.-Mexico free trade agreement and, 156. See also apparel industry

Thailand: bailout of, 465, 466, 468, 474, 477, 491, 492; construction boom in, 462, 485–86; corruption in, 288, 489; economic problems of, 469; financial crisis in, 18, 43, 462–63, 465, 466, 470–71, 482–83, 490–91, 496, 498; foreign investment in, 271, 482, 488; pirated goods in, 287–89; sweatshops in, 385, 388–89; tourism in, 38

Thanong Bidaya, 462, 465, 466, 468, 484

Thatcher, Margaret, 197, 200, 345, 417, 430, 451, 454, 522

Theodore, Jean-Francois, 351, 352

third world. See developing countries

Thoreau, Henry David, 514

3M, 211, 349

Tietmeyer, Hans, 484

Tokyo Round of GATT, 114, 118

Toshiba, 253

totalitarianism: of capitalism, 9, 509; globalization and pressure on, 34

tourism: and capital flows, 65; cultural, 333; cultural homogenization and, 316–17; ecological, 38, 347–48; growth in, 37; and indigenous culture, 317–18; Japanese and, 315, 316; Mexican peso crisis and, 448; in Peru, 336–37; Uruguay Round of GATT and, 131. See also travel

Toyo Kogyo. See Mazda

Toyota, 223, 224, 235, 239; and General Motors, joint venture with, 247, 539

trade: in 19th century, 13, 14; in 20th century, early, 51–54, 57–65; Bretton Woods crisis and, 404–9; cold war and, 109, 110–11; compensation, 221; and domestic politics, 548; environmental concerns and, 151; fair, 372–73; free (See free trade; trade liberalization); globalization and, 12; and growth, 126–27; impact on everyday life, 546; managed, 124; New World Order and, 182; and rich-poor gap, 537–38; rules-based, 554; as two-way street, 542

Trade Act of 1974 (U.S.), 114, 312

Trade Act of 1988 (U.S.), 144

Trade Agreements Act, 109

trade balance, NAFTA and, 168

trade barriers: in 19th century, 13; during cold war, 139; within Europe, 85–86; non-tariff, 116, 130, 339–40; reducing, U.S. role in, 132; types of, 125; World War I and, 20. See also protectionism; tariffs

trade blocs: European Community and, 200; lack of global leadership and, 141–42; vs. multinational corporations, 416; proliferation of, 176; Uruguay Round stalemate and, 122; and U.S.-Mexico relations, 155

trade deficits
 Brazil's, 456, 524
 Mexico's, 161, 438, 440, 445, 447, 460–61
 U.S., 115, 116, 283, 393, 404; with Asian nations, 469; with China, 237; dollar

devaluation as attempt to improve, 412, 413; with Japan, 139, 224, 475; multinational corporations and, 226

trade-distorting measures (TDMs), 119

trade liberalization: arguments for, 134; benefits of, 121; regional bargaining and, 188, 191; tradeoffs in, 118–19; U.S. and, 109–10. *See also* free trade

trade secret protection, 286

trade wars: Hawley-Smoot tariff bill and, 78–80, 81–85, 132; lack of global leadership and, 141; U.S.-European, 123–24, 184, 509; U.S. import controls and fear of, 405

Transnational Resource and Action Center, 382, 383–84

travel: cultural homogenization and, 316–17; European monetary crisis and, 425; as human right, 38; increase in, 36, 37–38; Japanese and, 315, 316; mass, impact of, 36–37, 38; U.S. politicians and, 39. *See also* tourism

Treaty of Rome (1957), 171–72, 192

Treaty on European Union. *See* Maastricht Treaty

Trend Micro Inc., 296

tribes, global, 24–25

trickle-down theory, 306

Triffin, Robert, 409, 410

trigger price mechanism, 149

triggers, Keynesian, 414

trilateralism, 143

tropical products, Uruguay Round of GATT on, 119

Truman, Harry S., 97, 104–5, 132–33

Turkey, and European Community, 175–76

Tyson, Laura D'Andrea, 33, 124, 485, 487, 503

UNCTAD (United Nations Conference on Trade and Development), 280–81

Underwood Tariff of 1913, 102

unemployment: in Asia, 385; in Brazil, 525, 541; in China, 500; foreign investment and, 144; GATT and, 121; in South Korea, 476; tariff policy and, 77; U.S. tariff surcharge (1971) and, 406; in Western Europe, 9, 35–36, 46, 85, 273, 353

UNICEF, 373

Union Carbide Company, 211, 526–28, 529, 534

Union of Needletrades, Industrial and Textile Employees, 386, 387, 552

unions. *See* labor unions

United Automobile Workers, 538, 539

United Brands Company, 219

United Fruit Company, 214

United Kingdom. *See* Britain

United Nations, 520; developing countries and, 522; Environmental Program, 527; and GATT, 103; and multinational corporations, 218–19; reform of, call for, 186; on rich-poor gap, 15

United Nations Conference on Trade and Development (UNCTAD), 280–81

United States

Asian financial crisis and, 469–70, 471, 474, 478, 496, 497–98, 503; impact on banks, 492–93, 494; rescue package for, 476, 491, 492; responsibility for, 493

Asian regionalism and, 174

automobile industry in, 222–24; European tariffs on, 79, 83; imported parts and, 237–38, 239; investment in Mexico, 157–58; Mexican peso crisis and, 442, 443–44; NAFTA and, 166–67, 169; protectionism and, 148; recession of 1980s and, 139; tariff surcharge and, 406

bank holiday of 1933, 91

Bretton Woods crisis and, 395, 396, 397–98, 399, 400, 401–4

Bretton Woods system and, 96–98, 108

budget deficits in, 115

and capital liberalization, 280

cultural imperialism of, 316–17, 320–22, 323–24, 326–30

dominance (hegemony) of, 206–7; backlash against, 18, 356, 467, 468, 499; decline of, 174; globalization and, 15, 511

economic nationalism in, 143–50, 191, 237, 544

education in, shortcomings of, 282, 345–46

euro and, 275

and European Common Market: agricultural subsidies dispute, 122, 123, 125, 139, 176; competition between, 109, 110, 112–13, 119; conflict over gas pipeline from Soviet Union, 139

and European integration, 170, 181–82

European monetary crisis and, 421–22, 426, 430, 431

and financial liberalization, 486–89

financial markets in, 56

as financial stabilizer, 262

and food aid program, 113

foreign aid by, 543–44

foreign investment by: in early 20th century, 66; in late 20th century, 232–33; in Europe, 206–7, 247–49

foreign investment in, 206, 208; attracting, 6, 340–41, 348; criticism of, 350; economic nationalism and, 143–44; Japan and, 4–7, 224, 341

foreign ownership in, 227–28, 506

foreign policy of, 39

GATT and, 102–3, 104, 107, 115, 118; Uruguay Round of, 114, 120, 121, 123–24, 130

and Geneva accord (1997), 278–79

and global economic crisis, 485

globalization and, 15, 511, 562

and global market, 4–7, 25–27, 114

golden era in, *vs.* 1990s, 10–12

and gold standard, 68

immigrants in: Asian, 328; and capital flows, 65; illegal, 244; Indian, 364–65; Mexican,

153, 155, 156, 166, 449; traveling to country of birth, 37

intellectual property protection in, 284–87

isolationism of, 39

and Japan, 228–29, 245–47, 253

and labor standards, 376–77, 380, 386–87

and Latin America, objectives in, 133–34

and Latin American common market, 173

leadership of, 132, 141, 185–86, 262, 562

love-hate relationship with, 40–41

Mexican peso crisis and: economic impact of, 441–44, 446–47, 448; rescue package for, 452–53, 457–59, 460, 471, 489

multinational corporations in, 215, 226; backlash against, 206–8; in Europe, 247–49; exodus abroad, 225–28, 229, 232–34; non-American managers in, 240–41; social responsibility of, 314–15, 538

NAFTA, 159–60, 163, 164, 165, 167

oil consumption in, 303

oil crisis and, 11, 303, 311, 312

post-cold war role of, 458

protectionism: in early 20th century, 52, 72–85, 114; in late 20th century, 116, 123, 177, 185; Bretton Woods crisis and, 397–98; against Japanese products, 134; local content bill and, 339; Mexican concerns over, 155

railroad construction in, 66, 67

and regional trade pacts, 183

responsibility of, 40, 132, 262, 562

steel industry in, 3, 139, 149

stock market in, 502, 511; Asian financial crisis and, 471; crash of 1929, 69–71, 283; crash of 1987, 265, 266, 295, 480

sweatshops in, 244–45

tariffs in: Hawley-Smoot tariff bill, 72–85; reductions of, 106, 109–10

technological leadership of, 216–17; vulnerability of, 282

trade of: early 20th-century, 51, 52–54, 56–57, 64–65; with developing nations, 537

trade deficits of, 115, 116, 283, 393, 404; with Asian nations, 469; with China, 237; dollar devaluation as attempt to improve, 412, 413; with Japan, 139, 224, 475; multinational corporations and, 226

trade with Brazil, 59, 117, 456–57

trade with Canada (*See also* U.S.-Canada free trade agreement); in 1980s, 5; Hawley-Smoot tariff bill and, 80; Kennedy Round of GATT and, 113; protectionism in, 506–7; tariff surcharge (1971) and, 406; tensions in, 208

trade with China: in early 20th century, 53–54, 59, 60–61; in late 20th century, 25–27, 45–46, 151; during cold war, 135–36

trade with Japan: in early 20th century, 54, 59, 60–61, 62–63; in late 20th century, 141;

protectionism and, 148; tensions in, 134, 139, 143, 144–45
trade with Latin America, 188–89
trade with Mexico, 5, 163–64, 459 (*See also* U.S.-Mexico free trade agreement); peso crisis and, 440, 441
U.S.-Canada free trade agreement, 122, 153, 155; debate on, 176–78, 254; dispute-resolution mechanism in, 145, 187; global trading system and, 178–79; and government intervention, 166. *See also* North American Free Trade Agreement
U.S.-Mexico free trade agreement, 122, 179; debate over, 254–55; negotiations for, 153, 155–56, 158. *See also* North American Free Trade Agreement
United States of Europe, 193, 204
Universal Declaration of Human Rights, Article 19 of, 293
universal values, 334
Uruguay Round of GATT, 114–31, 179, 185; accomplishments of, 129, 130; call for rescue of, 119–20; completion of, 127–30, 186; developing countries and, 114, 115, 116–17, 119, 120; focus on protectionism at, 115–16; goals of, 124, 125; objective of, 115, 116; optimism about, 122–23; pessimism about, 116, 117; potential benefits of, 118; protests against, 130; signing of agreement, 130–31; stakes at, 124–26; stalemate at, 120–21, 122, 123; unresolved problems at, 130

values: restructuring of system of, 518; universal, 334
Vance, Cyrus R., 521
Vanzetti, Bartolomeo, 514
Venezuela, petroleum industry in, 298
venture capital, 232
Vernon, Raymond, 15–16, 151, 215, 216–17, 228, 233, 234
VERs (voluntary export restrictions), 530
Versailles summit meeting (1982), 3, 139
Vietnam, Nike shoe plant in, 380–82
Vietnam War: and concept of national power, 137; defense of, 174; economic conditions during, 135
Vinson, Fred M., 98, 99
violence: anti-globalization protesters and, 48, 516, 517, 550, 551, 552, 555, 556–57, 559–61; in films, 321, 327; financial crises and, 500–501
Volcker, Paul A., 412, 413
Volkswagen, 150, 157, 223, 234, 235, 239, 539; losses of, 263; model for cutting working hours, 35–36
voluntary export restrictions (VERs), 530
Voluntary Restraint Agreement (VRA), 146, 148, 149
Volvo, 225; operations in China, 236, 237

VRA (Voluntary Restraint Agreement), 146, 148, 149
Vredeling plan, 225

wages: of American expatriates, 249; ceiling on, Nixon Administration and, 401–3; devaluation and, 394–95; of German auto workers, 235; globalization and, 228; in Indonesia, 368, 370; inequality of, in U.S., 562; Mexican peso crisis and, 444, 445; minimum, standards for, 377, 387; NAFTA and, 159, 166; and productivity, 159, 160, 165; rise in, world-wide, 227, 389; sweatshops and, 383, 384, 386, 388
Wallich, Henry C., 415
Wall Street. *See* New York City
Wal-Mart, 163, 232, 233, 379, 387; Mexican peso crisis and, 442–43, 444, 450
Walter, Norbert, 275
Walters, Sir Alan, 454, 455
war: interdependence and prevention of, 144. *See also specific wars*
war loans: post-World War I, 89; post-World War II, 94
Washington, George, 349
Watergate investigation, 219, 220, 415
Watson, James L., 329–30
Watson, Thomas J., Jr., 211
Waugh, Evelyn, 316
wealth: Adam Smith on, 136; globalization and, 481; inequalities in distribution of (*See* rich-poor gap); Ronald Reagan on, 523. *See also* prosperity
Web browser, 291
Weintraub, Sidney, 161
Welch, Jack, 7
welfare systems, European, 8, 23; adoption of euro and challenges to, 273, 356–60
Western Europe: Bretton Woods crisis and, 399–400; fair trade in, 372; fatalism in, 10; immigrants in, 46, 47–48; local stock markets in, 351, 352; protectionism in, 150; small businesses in, 353, 354; unemployment in, 9, 35–36, 46, 85, 273, 353; U.S. protectionism and (Hawley-Smoot tariff bill and), 78–80, 82–85; and U.S. multinational corporations, 16, 18; welfare systems in, 8, 23; adoption of euro and challenges to, 273, 356–60. *See also* Europe; European Community; *specific countries*
Western European Union, 194, 197, 198, 202
Western Hemisphere free-trade zone, 142, 188–90, 191
West Germany: Bretton Woods crisis and, 396, 397, 399, 400–401; economic crisis in (1980s), 3; European Common Market and, 173; financial market in, 265–66; U.S. tariff surcharge (1971) and, 405, 406
White, Henry, 99

White House Apparel Industry Partnership, 376–77, 380, 386–87
White Plan, 413–14
Wilson, Harold, 206, 263, 394, 423
Wilson, Woodrow, 83
Witteveen, H. Johannes, 310
Wolfensohn, James D., 19, 48, 49, 50, 468, 489, 516, 541, 543
won (Korean), devaluation of, 476
workers' rights. *See* labor standards
work ethic: in El Salvador, 242; ethnicity and, 24, 25
workforce, globalization and, 9. *See also* labor, global division of
Workforce Investment Act, 42
working hours: in Germany, 235; reductions in, 34–36; standards for, 377, 387
World Bank: Asian financial crisis and, 466–69; and capital controls, 281; changes in, 49, 50; and controlled tourism, 38; creation of, 98; and development assistance, 271; on dollar deficiency problems, 105; financial crises and, 511; first president of, 99–100; on free trade, 126; on globalization, 22; and India, 533, 534; on Indonesian financial crisis, 495; Japan's funding for, 142; liberalization of lending terms, 393; limitations of, 12; membership in, increase of, 108; microlending by, 352; oil crisis and, 309–11; plan for, 94–95; and post-World War II reconstruction, 99–101; and poverty relief, 49, 50, 521, 541–44; Prague meeting of (2000), 515–18, 541–44; protests against, 23, 45, 48, 49–50, 515–18; purpose of, 96, 105; reconstruction and development loans by, 105–6; reform of, calls for, 186, 517–18; report on capital flows, 270–71; and South Korean rescue package, 476, 477; and Uruguay Round of GATT, 119–20
World Development Report, 50
World Economic Forum: 1997 meeting of, 7–9, 32, 501; 1999 meeting of, 501; 2000 meeting of, 510; and nongovernmental organizations, 518
World Intellectual Property Organization, 225
World Tourism Organization, 37, 38
World Trade Organization (WTO), 131, 151
  achievements of, 548
  authority of, 187
  budget of, 546
  and China, 19, 45, 130, 236, 540, 544, 549
  vs. consumers, influence of, 561
  criticism of, 552, 554, 556
  and environmental concerns, 545, 548
  and Geneva accord (1997), 278–79
  and global rule-making, 152
  and Indonesia, 34
  and labor standards, 372, 373
  leadership of, 438
  origins of, 130

positive impact of, 540

as protest target, 50

role of, 549, 551, 553

Seattle meeting of, 544–63; agenda at, 547–48; labor unions' demands at, 544; protests at, 18, 20, 21, 362, 388, 510, 513, 540, 545–48, 550–61

unpopular decisions by, 550

U.S. complaint against Canada and, 507

World War I: isolationism after, 21; and trade barriers, 20; unemployment after, 85; and U.S. exports, 79

World War II: economic development after, in U.S., 10–11; economic recovery after, 95–96; Great Depression and, 144; inflation after, 414; reconstruction after,

Bretton Woods system and, 99–101; U.S. leadership after, 141; and World Bank, 94

World Wide Web, 290–91. *See also* Internet

WTO. *See* World Trade Organization

Wyndham White, Eric, 111, 112, 113

Xerox Corporation, 243, 285, 345

Yamani, Sheikh Ahmed Zaki al, 299, 300, 301, 304, 305

Yeltsin, Boris N., 197, 495, 499

yen (Japanese): in Eurobond market, 259; upward revaluation of, 411, 412, 434

Yeutter, Clayton K., 114, 115, 116, 176, 179

Young, Andrew, 374–76, 379–80, 381

Yugoslavia: conflict in, and European

Community, 194, 202, 203; World Bank loan to, 106

Zapatistas, 32, 439, 536; and Mexican peso crisis, 439, 440, 446

Zedillo Ponce de León, Ernesto, 438, 439, 440, 445, 446, 447, 458; economic recovery plan of, 449, 450, 451, 459, 460; U.S. rescue package and, 457

Zeien, Alfred M., 322–23

Zenith Electronics Corporation, 228, 254, 256

zero tariff option, 120; Clinton's campaign for, 372

Zerzan, John, 515, 560

Zhu Rongji, 19, 360

Ziolkowski, Jim, 354–55

BYLINE INDEX

Andersen, Kurt, 16
Andrews, Edmund L., 278
Apple, R. W., Jr., 184
Applebome, Peter, 332
Arenson, Karen W., 283
Arnold, Wayne, 296
Ayers, H. Brandt, 348

Barnet, Richard J., 368
Basler, Barbara, 249
Behrman, Jack N., 314
Bejarano, Jose R., 212
Belair, Felix, Jr., 109, 132
Bennet, James, 166, 442
Bennett, Robert A., 256
Berkow, Ira, 31
Bhagwati, Jagdish N., 529
Bleakley, Fred R., 241
Bowermaster, Jon, 4
Bowles, Samuel, 165
Bradsher, Keith, 124, 182, 254, 441, 538
Brooke, James, 188, 456
Burns, John F., 176
Butterfield, Fox, 221

Callender, Harold, 170
Canedy, Dana, 374, 379
Cardenas, Cuauhtemoc, 154
Caruso, Denise, 294
Cavanagh, John, 368
Cloke, H. Walton, 104
Cohen, Roger, 48, 127, 229, 272, 356, 433
Cortesi, Arnaldo, 171
Cowell, Alan, 325, 424, 518
Crider, John H., 96
Crossette, Barbara, 36, 326
Cushman, John H., Jr., 382

Dale, Edwin L., Jr., 217, 301, 392, 397, 403, 410
Daley, Suzanne, 508
DePalma, Anthony, 30, 162, 439, 450, 457, 506
Diamond, Stuart, 527
Dilenschneider, Robert L., 506
Dobrzynski, Judith H., 7
Dugger, Celia W., 364, 562

Eder, Richard, 302
Egan, Timothy, 556
Egol, Morton, 143
Erlanger, Steven, 287

Farnsworth, Clyde H., 111, 118, 139, 178, 210, 299, 303, 398, 521
Feder, Barnaby J., 232
Fiske, Edward B., 345
Friedman, Thomas L., 34, 39, 267, 325, 355, 461, 553, 561
Fuerbringer, Jonathan, 351, 428, 470

Gardin, John, 54
Gargan, Edward A., 25, 368, 466, 472, 532
Gates, Bill, 549
Gilpin, Kenneth N., 339, 444
Gitlin, Todd, 320
Golden, Tim, 160, 438, 445
Greenhouse, Steven, 147, 175, 318, 373, 376, 380, 386, 421, 426, 429, 544, 550, 558
Greider, William, 236
Grimes, William, 43

Hays, Constance L., 361
Heffernan, Paul, 107
Henriques, Diana B., 266
Herbert, Bob, 371
Hills, Carla A., 159
Hoffman, Michael L., 101, 106
Hoffmann, Stanley, 28
Holusha, John, 245, 252
Hufbauer, Gary, 164
Hunter, Marjorie, 138
Hurd, Charles, 100

Ikenberry, G. John, 186

Jehl, Douglas, 452
Jensen, Michael C., 219
Joffe, Josef, 201
Jones, Brendan, 209, 214, 404

Kahn, Joseph, 21, 49, 510, 513, 541, 547, 558
Kakutani, Michiko, 316
Kilborn, Peter T., 115
Klein, Naomi, 554
Krasner, Stephen, 174
Krauss, Clifford, 336
Kristof, Nicholas D., 13, 279, 315, 328, 360, 384, 388, 478
Krugman, Paul, 9, 21

Larudee, Mehrene, 165
Lefkovitz, Herbert, 80
Leisinger, Klaus M., 531

Lewis, Anthony, 393
Lewis, Flora, 176, 181, 199, 203, 522
Lewis, Paul, 117, 225, 372, 455
Lewis, Peter H., 292
Lohr, Steve, 15, 258, 262
Lueck, Thomas J., 127, 343

MacDonald, Carlisle, 78
Markoff, John, 289
McDowell, Edwin, 237
McKinnon, Ronald I., 451
McLaughlin, Kathleen, 208
Miller, Edward, 61
Miller, Judith, 15
Mooney, Richard E., 134, 206, 395
Mydans, Seth, 462
Myerson, Allen R., 168, 293, 377

Nash, Nathaniel C., 190, 234, 453, 535
Naughton, James M., 401
Norris, Floyd, 20, 437
Norton, Henry Kittredge, 78

Okihiro, Gary Y., 24
Onis, Juan de, 173

Paish, George, 65
Passell, Peter, 126, 186, 190, 270, 277, 419, 431, 464
Philip, P. J., 82
Pollack, Andrew, 284, 323, 349, 465, 475
Porter, Michael E., 145
Porter, Russell, 94
Prokesch, Steven, 179

Reich, Robert B., 537
Reston, James, 2
Riding, Alan, 116, 130, 140, 193, 423, 523
Rohter, Larry, 153
Romero, Simon, 366, 539
Rosenbaum, David, 167
Rossant, M. J., 207
Rowland, Benjamin M., 261
Rule, Sheila, 317
Rushdie, Salman, 334
Russo, Thomas A., 271

Sachs, Jeffrey D., 473
Salmans, Sandra, 240
Sanger, David E., 18, 32, 228, 253, 449, 458, 467, 474, 485, 545, 554

Saul, John Ralston, 432
Schmidt, Helmut, 192
Schmidt, William E., 422
Schmitt, Eric, 45
Selden, Charles A., 86
Seligsberg, Louis, 57
Senner, Madis, 431
Sewell, John W., 12
Silk, Leonard, 122, 135, 216, 282, 304, 409, 413
Smith, Craig S., 337
Smith, William D., 300
Steinfels, Peter, 335
Sterngold, James, 259
Stevenson, Richard W., 150, 269, 416, 427

Stokes, Henry Scott, 222
Sutherland, Peter D., 12
Swartz, Steven, 341

Tagliabue, John, 27, 34, 46, 330, 353
Teltsch, Kathleen, 218
Thompson, W. B., 59
Thurow, Lester, 3
Tierney, John, 512
Tolchin, Martin, 340
Tritton, J. Herbert, 67

Uchitelle, Louis, 10, 141, 150, 157, 225, 232, 247, 281, 322, 435, 446, 477

Verhovek, Sam Howe, 551, 559
Vernon, Raymond, 144

Walter, Norbert, 562
Wayne, Leslie, 264
Weintraub, Sidney, 155
Weizel, Richard, 354
Whitney, Craig R., 197, 200, 204
Wilcke, Gerd, 396
Wills, Kendall J., 244
Wilson, A. J., 51
WuDunn, Sheryl, 388, 489
Wyatt, Edward, 478

Zakaria, Fareed, 23